The Bristol Blenheim

A complete history

The Bristol Blenheim

A complete history

Graham Warner

Crécy Publishing

'Ride on, ride on in majesty!
The winged squadrons of the skies
Look down with sad and wondering eyes
To see the approaching sacrifice.'

Written for Psalm Sunday in 1827 by Rev Henry Milman (1791-1868), and heard being sung over the R/T as a section of Blenheims ran in low over the sea to attack an escorted convoy.

The pleasing lines and the agility of the Blenheim are displayed in L4842 by Bristol Test Pilot Bill Pegg on a publicity sortie in 1938. Other photographs taken on the same flight are in Chapter 7 – the aircraft Failed To Return from a reconnaissance sortie with 53 Squadron in France on 17 May 1940.

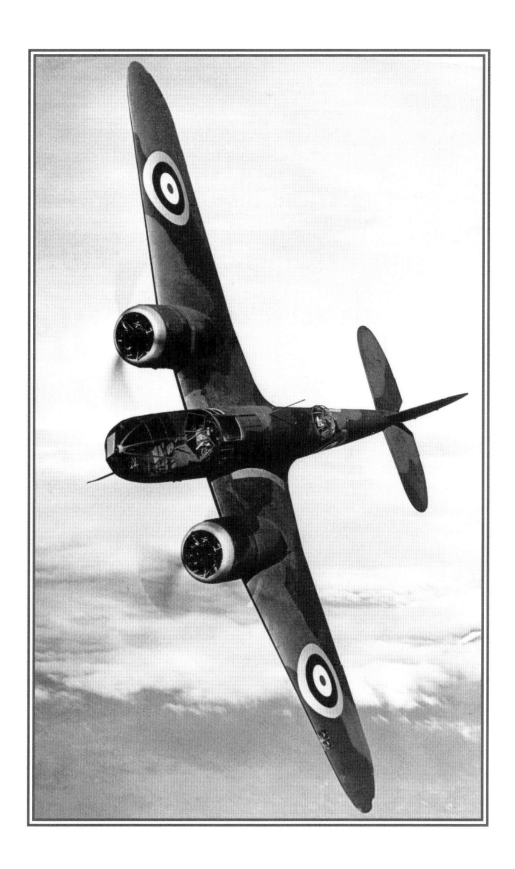

Published in 2002 by Crécy Publishing Limited
Second edition 2005

A CIP record for this book is available from the British Library

ISBN 0 859791 01 7

Cover illustrations courtesy of
John Dibbs
The Bristol Aircraft Company
Imperial War Museum

Printed and bound in the UK
by Cromwell Press

Crécy Publishing Limited
1a Ringway Trading Estate, Shadowmoss Road, Manchester M22 5LH
www.crecy.co.uk

Contents

Foreword

By Marshal of the Royal Air Force Sir Michael Beetham GCB CBE DFC AFC

At the outbreak of World War 2 the Royal Air Force, like the Army and Navy, was ill-equipped to fight a major war against a formidable and ruthless enemy. The nation had not woken up to the threat from Nazi Germany until the late 1930's but re-equipment is not achieved overnight.

Fortunately, in the growing aviation industry there were some far-sighted and enterprising individuals who had seen the danger and developed new aircraft on a private venture basis. Thus was born the Blenheirn, the first of a modem generation of British aircraft which, when war came, formed the core of RAF offensive operations, notably in the Battle of Britain and subsequently in all the major theatres of war.

If you ask the 'man in the street' what were the most famous British aircraft in World War 2 he will probably say the Spitfire and the Lancaster. They were certainly great aircraft and deserve all the accolades awarded them. But the Blenheim had to bear the brunt of the initial German onslaught and the Blenheim contribution to the Battle of Britain was quite outstanding. It was not enough to defeat the Luftwaffe over the skies of Southern England to scupper the planned German invasion, magnificently though the Spitfires and Hurricanes performed. The Blenheim contribution, albeit at heavy cost in crews and aircraft, in bombing enemy barges in the Channel ports, the enemy airfields and many other military targets, was vital in persuading Hitler to call off the invasion. The Blenheim anti-shipping operations were also vital, again at heavy cost, both in the Battle of Britain and in the desperate days of the Battle of the Atlantic.

The individual losses of crews and aircraft as tabulated in detail in this volume makes poignant reading. The same story emerges in the other theatres of war, in all of which Blenheims were engaged.

In spite of the losses, the Blenheim was very popular with its crews for it was a lovely aircraft to fly. It was the timescale and the desperate state of the war when we were fighting, with our backs to the wall against heavy odds that was the main reason for the losses.

This meticulously researched volume describes in very readable fashion how the Blenheim came into being and how it served so extensively and so valiantly in the war. It is a story that needed to be told and is a great tribute to the bravery of the crews operating always in a very hostile environment. The Blenheim must go down as one of the 'greats' in the history of the Royal Air Force and I commend the book to you.

Marshal of the Royal Air Force Sir Michael Beetham GCB, CBE, DFC, AFC FRAeS, Former Chief of the Air Staff, President Royal Air Force Historical Society, President Bomber Command Association, Chairman of Trustees RAF Museum.

To illustrate the human tragedy behind each of the thousands of Blenheim crew casualties listed. 20-year old Sgt Richard Carter was injured when T2078 of 248 Squadron crashed on return from a patrol at 01.10 hours on 5 July 1941 near Massingham, Norfolk, attempting to locate West Raynham flare-path in bad visibility. He died four days later in Ely Hospital and was buried in Ely Cemetery; his grieving parents follow the coffin borne by his comrades.

Acknowledgements

The following, nearly all ex-Blenheim air- and ground-crews (together with their relatives) have supplied anecdotes, copies of flying log-books, personal and official photographs, correspondence, results of their own researches, etc, over many years for use in this history. Many of them, who took part in the actual events or operations described, have checked my account and suggested amendments or improvements, while others kindly allowed recorded or filmed interviews. Their generous contribution, especially in sending several hundred photographs, is invaluable, and I extend my heartfelt gratitude to all of them. All too many, alas, have passed away during the preparation of this volume, so were unable to see the end result of their input – but without it the book would be far less informative, and far less interesting. Most of them felt, some very strongly, that a detailed, accurate and comprehensive account of the major part played by Blenheims in all Commands and all Theatres of War was well overdue. I honour and respect them all, and hope that this volume does not disappoint them.

Denis Ager (18 and 614 Sqns), Geoff Allison (107 Sqn), Don Anderson (29 Sqn), Eric Applebee, (114 Sqn), Len Archer (CO 59 Sqn), Eric Atkins (18, 114, 139 Sqns), Anthony Ayris (59 Sqn), Edgar Baker (13 Sqn), Tom Baker (114 Sqn), Geoff Bennett (110 Sqn), Ian Blair (113 Sqn), Harold Brittain (82 Sqn), Sir Ivor Broom (107, 114 and 105 Sqns), Fred Bunting (614 Sqn), Bill Burberry, (114 and 13 Sqns), Graham Burrell (114 Sqn), Albert Butterworth (18 Sqn), John Caddy (8 and 14 Sqns), Philip Camp (15 Sqn), Tony Carlisle (88 Sqn), John Castle (110 and 226 Sqns), Norman Chapman (139 Sqn), Sir Gareth Clayton (107 and 105 Sqns), Les Clayton (18 Sqn), Ken Collins (82 Sqn), Rupert 'Tiny' Cooling (516 Sqn), Frank Coxhall (107 Sqn), Edward Crew (604 Sqn), John Cunningham (604 Sqn), Fred Deeks (107 and 110 Sqns), Tony Dudgeon (CO 55 Sqn), James Dunnet (11, 57 and 211 Sqns), Ralph Fastnedge (139 Sqn), Len Fearnley (107 Sqn), Les Foster (254 Sqn), Teddy Frayn (105 and 114 Sqns), Bill Furguson (113 Sqn), Bill Gatling (18, 105 and 110 Sqns), Hugh George (XV Sqn), Arthur Gill (84 Sqn), Eric Gill (226 Sqn), Ron Gillman (107 and 114 Sqns), Eric Greenwood (110 Sqn), Wilf Hepworth (139 Sqn), William Huggard (60 Sqn), Len Hunt (59 Sqn), Roy Kendrick (114 Sqn), Jim King (139 Sqn), Aubrey Lancaster (235 Sqn), Dickie Leven (107 Sqn), Stan Lee (101, 18 and 113 Sqns), George Lush (4 B&GS, 7 AOS, Canada), Bill Magrath (64 and 82 Sqns), Dick Maydwell (53, and CO 14 Sqn), Alec McCurdy (59 and 18 Sqns), Don McFarlane (82 Sqn), Don McLeod (53 Sqn), John McMichael (82 Sqn), Tony Mee (82 and 105 Sqns), Frank Metcalfe (82 Sqn), Douglas Moore (106 and 18 Sqns), James Moore (18 Sqn), Basil Mortimer (59 Sqn), Frank Moseley (244 Sqn), Dick Muspratt (53 Sqn), Terrence O'Brien (53 Sqn), Bill O'Connell (226 Sqn), Eric Olliver (84 Sqn), Charles Patterson (114 Sqn), Norman Payne (88 Sqn), James Pelly-Fry (88 Sqn), Roger Peacock (90 and 40 Sqns), Doug Pole (235 Sqn), George Pushman (23 Sqn), Paddy Quirke (107 Sqn), Hal Randall (254 Sqn), David 'Robbie' Roberts (53 Sqn), Dickie Rook (114 and 105 Sqns), Geoffrey Rowlands (105 Sqn), Peter Sarll (21 Sqn), Mrs Vera Sherring, Sid Sills (39 Sqn), Sir Laurence Sinclair (CO 110 Sqn etc), Ted Sismore (105 and 107 Sqns), Tony Smyth (101, 55, 14, CO 11 Sqn), Ian Spencer (82 and 107 Sqns), George Spiers (254 Sqn), Terry Staples (114 Sqn), Pat Stapleton (614 Sqn), Frank Westbrook (13 Sqn), Ken Whittle (139 Sqn), John Wray (53 Sqn), Cliff Wright (Radar Trials), Ken Wyatt (18 Sqn).

With sincere apologies to any whose names have been inadvertently omitted. (For the sake of brevity it is not possible to include ranks, decorations, and service other than with Blenheim Squadrons.)

Apart from the ex-Blenheim people mentioned above, I must thank most especially:

Hugh Wheeler, past archivist of the Blenheim Society, who has been building up a most comprehensive database of Blenheim service and losses for several years, and whose contribution in helping to compile and check the appendices to the chapters has been inestimable; Pelham Temple, who kindly made available his in-depth research into RAF bomber losses in the Middle east; Geoff Dewing, who has been a great help with research on details of Blenheim losses at the PRO, Kew, and the RAF Museum, Hendon; the late Sir Archibald Russell CBE FRAeS; Stephen Payne, Canada Aviation Museum; Betty George, Hon Sec Blenheim Society; Julian Horn, RAF Watton Museum, Kjeld Sasbye (Denmark); and Sir George White Bt, grandson of Sir Stanley G. White Bt, Managing Director, Bristol Aircraft Company; Anthony Edwards, son of Sir Hughie Edwards; James Halley MBE of Air Britain (Historians); David Parry of Imperial War Museum Photographic Archive; RAF Historical Branch; RAF Museum, Hendon; Public Record Office, Kew; and various Squadron Associations.

Glossary

AA	Anti-Aircraft Fire		GP	General Purpose (bomb)
A&AEE	Aeroplane & Armament Experimental Establishment		He.	Heinkel
			Ju.	Junkers
AASF	Advanced Air Striking Force France 1939/40		KIA	Killed in Action
			ME	Middle East Theatre of Operations
ACM	Air Chief Marshal		Me.	Messerschmitt (wartime usage, rather than Bf.)
AFC	Air Force Cross			
AI	Airborne Interception (radar)		MIA	Missing in Action
ALG	Advanced Landing Ground		MU	Maintenance Unit
AM	Air Marshal		OADU	Overseas Aircraft Dispatch/Delivery Unit
AOC	Air Officer Commanding			
AOC-in-C	Air Officer Commanding in Chief		Obs	Observer
AP	Armour Piercing (bomb)		OR	Operational Requirement
ASR	Air-Sea Rescue		OTU	Operational Training Unit
ASV	Air to Surface Vessel (radar)		PAFU	Pilots Advanced Flying Unit
ATA	Air Transport Auxiliary		PoW	Prisoner of War
AVM	Air Vice Marshal		PR (U)	Photographic Reconnaissance (Unit)
BEF	British Expeditionary Force to France 1939/40		RAAF	Royal Australian Air Force
			RAE	Royal Aircraft Establishment (Farnborough)
CAS	Chief of the Air Staff			
CFS	Central Flying School		RAeS	Royal Aeronautical Society
CO	Commanding Officer		RAuxAF	Royal Auxiliary Air Force
DBF	Destroyed by Fire		RAFVR	Royal Air Force Volunteer Reserve
DBR	Damaged Beyond Repair		RCAF	Royal Canadian Air Force
DCAS	Deputy Chief of Air Staff		RFC	Royal Flying Corps
DCO	Duty Carried Out		RNZAF	Royal New Zealand Air Force
DFC	Distinguished Flying Cross		RR	Rolls Royce
DFM	Distinguished Flying Medal		R/T	Radio Telephony
DNCO	Duty Not Carried Out		RTB	Returned to Base
Do.	Dornier		SAAF	South African Air Force
DSO	Distinguished Service Order		SAC	School of Army Co-operation
ETA	Estimated Time of Arrival		SAP	Semi Armour Piercing (bomb)
FAA	Fleet Air Arm		SASO	Senior Air Staff Officer
FE	Far East Theatre of Operations		SOC	Struck Off Charge
Fi.	Fieseler		u/c	Undercarriage
Flak	German Anti-Aircraft		VC	Victoria Cross
FTR	Failed to Return		VGO	Vickers Gas-Operated Machine Gun
Fw.	Focke-Wulf		WOp/Ag	Wireless Operator/Air Gunner
GC	George Cross			

Introduction to first edition

The Bristol Blenheim was engaged extensively and frequently in the fiercest fighting with our enemies throughout the first two and a half frantic years of the Second World War – desperate years when the British nation stood alone and with 'its back against the wall'. Blenheims were involved repeatedly in the thick of this fighting as the most widely-used – indeed often the only – offensive aircraft available to the RAF at that time, especially for highly hazardous low-level daylight attacks. They were the only Royal Air Force aircraft to serve in all the contemporaneous RAF Commands and in every Theatre of War. The first offensive sorties against all three of the Axis Powers – Germany, Italy and Japan – were carried out by Blenheims. The RAF had more Blenheims on charge at the outbreak of the war than any other type of aircraft. They were used in vulnerable pioneering roles such as the use of airborne radar, to initiate and develop many new forms of tactical deployment, and they notched up a most impressive and unequalled list of 'firsts' while in RAF service.

One would therefore expect Blenheims to be as proudly remembered and highly regarded as are Spitfires and Lancasters, but they certainly are not – indeed, they were virtually ignored, practically forgotten and poorly regarded. There are some 50 books to spread the fame of the Spitfire, and more than 30 on the Lancaster legend, but a mere handful about the Blenheim, for it has been singularly ill-served by historians and aviation authors alike. The daring deeds of the Blenheim crews, frequently deployed in the most deadly dangerous actions at very low level, have neither been acknowledged sufficiently nor given anything like the credit that, in my view, they warrant.

It is clear that the very considerable contribution made by the hard-pressed Blenheims to the nation's war effort has been largely disregarded or understated. These embattled aircraft and their courageous crews have been allowed to fade from our collective memory, despite their widespread employment and the horrendous levels of losses they incurred. It is understandable that these losses were subsequently overshadowed completely by the far greater number of casualties suffered by Bomber Command crews during the massive strategic offensive in the later stages of the war; but proportionally the losses to Blenheim crews were far higher and their chances of surviving a tour of operations even less.

These appalling losses led to the blackening of the reputation of the Blenheim itself, so that it became, quite unjustifiably, a much-maligned and derided aeroplane; if it is remembered at all, it is usually recalled in a negative and derogatory way. In fact, it was a well-designed and soundly constructed aircraft, very advanced for its day, completely safe if handled correctly, and a delight to fly. But, alas, in so many of the roles in which it was forced to operate, the Blenheim was not a good machine in which to go to war – especially against a ruthless and efficient enemy. That is why it is necessary to put the record straight and to set the Blenheim in the true context of its time. Then one can see that, in the circumstances then pertaining, the value of its operational service with the RAF was quite outstanding.

Another most valuable – but normally completely overlooked – contribution made by Blenheims to the war effort was their extensive service in the Support and Advanced Training roles across the world and right until the end of the war. Tens of thousands of air-crew improved their skills at the Pilots Advanced Flying Units, the Air Observers Schools, and the Air-Gunners Schools, and learned to fly together as crews at the Operational Training Units. Unfortunately, Blenheims suffered thousands of accidental losses during their continuous and widespread service in this supporting role, which further darkened their name.

This book therefore is a belated attempt to rehabilitate the poor reputation of the aircraft, to redress these unfavourable balances, to provide the historical perspective, and to increase general awareness and appreciation of the nature and extent of the Blenheims' service, together with the unmatched courage of their crews. The term 'unmatched courage' is justified as I have found that the exemplary bravery of the 'Blenheim Boys' was widely acknowledged and admired by their wartime peers – the crews of other RAF Commands and other Groups within Bomber Command. I feel that the narrative unfolded in this volume, supported by facts and figures and the selection of human stories that lay behind such statistics, fully deserves to be placed before a wider readership so that a better understanding and recognition of the heroic contribution made by the Blenheims and their courageous crews can be attained.

I made this plea also in my two earlier books, *The Forgotten Bomber* and *Spirit of Britain First*, and – although they were principally concerned with my own involvement in the restoration to flying condition of two derelict Blenheim airframes – I am pleased to say that this call drew widespread support, especially from surviving ex-Blenheim crews! This support is encouraging, and I draw comfort that these books, together with the flying displays performed before millions by the only airworthy Blenheim in the world – now up in its rightful place alongside the Spitfire, Hurricane and Lancaster – have helped my oft-stated aim of 'putting the Blenheim back on the map'. I trust that by studying this volume you too will be persuaded that this is indeed a worthy aim, and should this volume be accepted as a further contribution to that cause I will rest content.

Thanks are also due to authors Theo Boiten, Chaz Bowyer, Michael Bowyer, Ken Ellis, Martyn Ford-Jones, Mike Henry, 'Jeff' Jefford, Don Neate, Graham Pitchfork, Mark Postlethwaite, 'Hal' Randall, Ole Ronnest (Denmark), Stuart Scott, Andy Thomas, Joe Warne, and Ken Whittle, for their kind help in supplying information and photographs. For further reading, I can recommend their publications concerning Blenheims, details of which can be found in the Bibliography.

Saffron Waldon, 2002   Graham Warner

Introduction to 2nd edition

The excellent reception, in particular from ex-Blenheims crews, and the number of highly favourable reviews, accorded to the First Edition was most gratifying; but even more so was the unexpectedly large volume of letters received from all over the World. Many contained wartime photographs, mostly not published before, so I am delighted to be able to include several in this Edition.

Further in-depth research, with the continued kind assistance of Hugh Wheeler and Pel Temple (as mentioned in the Acknowledgements) has resulted in some 800 extra entries in the Appendices of losses, making them a more complete record than before; the Air Historical Branch (RAF) has been most helpful in supplying fiurther information to this end too.

Please remember that each and every name in the long lists of casualties represents a personal tradgedy for the family, relatives, and friends of the Blenheim crewman concerned. They deserve our honour and respect for the sacrifices they made over 60 years ago to preserve the free and democratic society we now enjoy.

Storrington, West Sussex 2005   Graham Warner

PART 1

GENESIS

The Bristol Type 142, the sire of the entire Blenheim, Beaufort, Beaufighter, Buckingham, Brigand family of Bristol aircraft commissioned by Lord Rothermere and named 'Britain First' by him, on test at Martlesham Heath in June 1935 with RAF markings as K7597.

The Type 142M prototype Blenheim K7033, also at Martlesham Heath for the inspection in 1936 by King Edward VIII and his brother, about to become King George VI as described in Chapter 4.

Chapter 1

The background to the Blenheim

The Bristol Blenheim was born in the most unusual circumstances during the early 1930s. It is difficult to appreciate nowadays, some seven decades later, not only the effect of the political climate of that time, but also the parlous state into which the British armed forces and their vital supporting industrial base – in particular the aircraft industry – had been allowed to decline. I will try to sketch in these interrelating factors and indicate the background to that period, but the brush-strokes will need to be both broad and brief.

The political climate was dominated totally by the aftermath of the 1914-18 war, known then as the Great War, but known now as the First World War. Foremost in the minds of statesmen was horror at the mass slaughter that led to the cream of the manhood of most European nations being decimated in years of gruesome trench warfare. To this was added a deep-seated fear of the dreadful new weapons such as poison gas, tanks, and attacks from beneath the seas and – most significantly of all – the new dimension of attacks from the skies above both sea and land. The mass of ordinary people – virtually all of whom had been affected directly and personally by the Great War – shared the views and the fears of the politicians. They shared too the fervent desire that such a cataclysmic conflict must never be allowed to occur again.

Tragically, the Treaty of Versailles, imposed by the victors in 1919 and intended to ensure that it would be indeed 'the war to end all wars', had the reverse effect and sowed the seeds of the second worldwide conflict that erupted 20 years later. Punitive reparations and sanctions imposed against Germany, mainly at the insistence of the French, led to high unemployment, hyper-inflation and a worthless German Mark, and contributed to the general economic depression of 1929. Resentment at what the Germans felt was unjust treatment – for Germany had accepted the Armistice of 11 November 1918 but had not surrendered – fuelled the rise of extreme German nationalism. This was exploited effectively by Adolf Hitler and his ruthless gang of National Socialists to seize and consolidate power, then to commence re-armament.

But 'disarmament' was the cause pursued fervently for 16 years by the other European nations. Despite clear signs to the contrary, they deluded themselves that no military threat was posed either by Germany governed by the Nazis, or by Italy ruled by Benito Mussolini and his Fascists, who had similarly harnessed strong nationalist feelings. The League of Nations, a forerunner of the United Nations, was set up, but proved an ineffective 'talking shop' and quite unable to restrain the relentless dictators. The armed forces of the peace-loving democracies were run down further and further; in Great Britain in particular, less and less money was provided for the three services. Further, only a thin 11 per cent slice of even this meagre cake was allocated to the Royal Air Force. The Treasury insisted that this parsimony was justified not only because of the very gloomy economic outlook, but also under the notorious 'Ten Year Rule', introduced by the Cabinet in 1919 but regularly and absurdly extended until 1932, which stated that planning of defence expenditure was to be 'based on the assumption that there would be no major war involving Great Britain within the next ten years'.

It was not until mid-1934 that Britain seriously contemplated re-armament – the perceived threat then being Japan rather than Germany – and the first of several major expansion schemes for the RAF was drawn up. The expansion put forward ten years earlier in 1923 to add 34 squadrons to the home air force of 18 squadrons had not been carried through. Of those 52 proposed squadrons, 35 were to be bombers and 17 fighters – a ratio of two to one.

Apart from the general political and economic background, we need to look at the formation and development of the Royal Air Force, its peacetime role and its projected wartime role. Of particular relevance to this survey are the requirements for large numbers of bombers under the various RAF expansion schemes proposed in the mid to late 1930s. These led to no fewer than 11,000 Medium Bombers – the Hawker Hind (and variants), the Fairey Battle and the Bristol Blenheim – being ordered during that period. Also highly relevant to these huge and unprecedented peacetime orders, some half of which were for Blenheims, were the particular circumstances prevailing both at the Bristol Aeroplane Company and at the Bristol Engine Division, for it was the exceptional combination of all these interlinked factors that exerted such a powerful effect upon the birth and subsequent deployment of the Blenheim.

The Royal Air Force

Most people know that the Royal Air Force was founded on 1 April 1918 from an overdue amalgamation of the air arms of the Navy (Royal Naval Air Service) and the Army (Royal Flying Corps). But the background to the launch of a new fighting service at such a difficult stage in a long war is not so well known. The War Cabinet, headed by Prime Minister Lloyd George, had acted on the recommendations of an Air Policy Committee chaired by the South African General Jan Smuts, who had relied heavily on advice from Major General Sir David Henderson, Director General of Military Aeronautics (the initial Commanding Officer of the RFC), Sir William Weir, Controller of Aeronautical Supplies, and Winston Churchill, another strong advocate of the independent use of air power, who was then Minister of Munitions. Lloyd George had progressed from this latter post to Minister for War, then to Prime Minister, succeeding Asquith at the end of 1916. There had been two earlier Air Boards set up under Lord Curzon and Lord Cowdray in 1916 to arbitrate on the conflicting aviation demands of the Navy and the Army, but they had been advisory only and the Asquith Government had not grasped the nettle of amalgamating the air arms. Sir William Weir served most ably on both Boards, and his now little-known name will re-appear several times. Winston Churchill, when First Lord of the Admiralty earlier in the war, had pressed vigorously for the development of naval aircraft, with the result that the RNAS was more advanced and forward-looking in aviation matters than the RFC. It was naval aircraft that carried out bombing raids on Zeppelin sheds; puny though these raids were, their purpose was strategic rather than tactical. A significant new factor had been introduced into the way that wars were waged.

A most far-reaching development of this new factor – the initiation of the bombing of civilian targets in England, including London, by German Zeppelins and Gothas literally over the heads of our Navy and Army – became the catalyst. Although small in scale, the impact of these raids – and our apparent inability to counter them – had a disproportionate effect on the opinions of the Government and led to widespread public anxiety, causing Lloyd George to set up the Air Policy Committee under Smuts in August 1917. The Navy, as traditional defender of the British Isles, had moved RNAS squadrons to the South East Coast; the Army responded by moving RFC squadrons from France to defend London. Lloyd George had to act; his choice of Smuts was shrewd, for included in the Smuts Committee's report was this prophetic – indeed for 1917 quite revolutionary – passage:

> 'Unlike artillery, an air fleet can conduct extensive operations far from, and independent of, both armies and navies. As far as can be foreseen, there is absolutely no limit to the scale of its future use, and the day may not be far off when aerial operations, with their devastation of enemy lands and destruction of industrial and populous centres on a vast scale, may become the principal operations of war, to which the older forms of military and naval operations may become secondary and subordinate...'

The Committee concluded that aerial bombing of the enemy's heartland was neither a naval nor an army matter, and this strategic overview provided the main justification for creating a separate air force, independent of the other services but including formations dedicated to providing direct tactical support for them. However, the Navy, the Army, and their previously ancillary Air Services, all resented the formation of an independent air force and regarded it as a temporary wartime measure only. The Admiralty wished to regain full control of all aircraft and crews operating over the sea or in connection with naval actions, as did the War Office in regard to those aircraft supporting land battles, as they had with the RNAS and the RFC.

Therefore the RAF had a troubled infancy and, for many years after the Armistice, was forced to fight hard for its very existence as a separate force against strongly pressed claims from the two older services. Fortunately the RAF had a doughty champion in Air Marshal Sir Hugh Trenchard, the first and most forthright Chief of the Air Staff. He regarded the Air Force as a 'striking force' for offensive rather than defensive purposes, but his dogmatic dissemination of the doctrine of the overriding importance of the bomber had unfortunate repercussions later as we shall see.

Nicknamed 'Boom' Trenchard, and known colloquially as 'the Father of the RAF', he was a man who expressed his views forcefully. In 1915, as Colonel H. M. Trenchard, he was Officer Commanding the RFC in France, and at the start of 1918, as Major General Sir Hugh Trenchard, he was appointed the First Chief of the Air Staff by the newly created Air Council. Initially he was not in favour of an independent air force, a view encouraged by his friend Field Marshal Sir Douglas Haig, who commanded the British Armies in France, but he was persuaded to

Hugh Trenchard, Chief of the Air Staff until 31 December 1929. His policy of the primacy of the bomber dominated RAF planning between the World Wars.

accept the post of inaugural Chief of the Air Staff by Sir William Weir, now on the newly formed Air Council as Director General of Aircraft Production. Weir saw clearly the need to rationalise the procurement and production of military aircraft, up until then specified and ordered entirely separately by the Admiralty and the War Office to suit their own requirements, with the resultant dissipation of industrial resources and unnecessary competition for scarce materials and skilled labour. Weir had inherited a logistic nightmare – 55 different types of aircraft and 35 different aero-engines were in production – a situation that he was determined to simplify drastically and urgently. So he stopped the state design and production of aircraft and engines for the RFC by the Royal Aircraft Establishment (previously the Royal Aircraft Factory) at Farnborough, channelling orders to the most successful of the private companies who had supplied the RNAS or acted as sub-contractors to the RAE – Sopwith, Bristol, Vickers, Handley-Page, Short Brothers, de Havilland, A. V. Roe, Blackburn, and Fairey. These companies were run by the great pioneering aviation entrepreneurs whose names they largely bore, very powerful and often autocratic individuals who became well known to Weir, and who respected his undoubted ability as much as he respected theirs.

On 3 January 1918 Prime Minister Lloyd George appointed Lord Rothermere (Edward Harmsworth before being created Viscount) as President of this inaugural Air Council, and Great Britain's first Secretary of State for Air, a vital post at a most critical stage of the war. The new Minister was proprietor of the influential *Daily Mail*, a consistent supporter of the development of aviation from its earliest days, and a strong critic of the previous air policy. Lord Rothermere soon realised that Trenchard was not actively following the instructions from the War Cabinet to implement the recommendations of the Smuts Committee, but preferred to rely on established RFC policies and procedures. Like Trenchard, Lord Rothermere was a very forceful character, and it was not long before differences of opinion and a clash of strong personalities led to the resignation of Trenchard, followed ten days later by that of Lord Rothermere and Sir David Henderson, Vice-President of the Air Council. The newly created Air Ministry had lost its three most senior members in just over three months! Another factor that deeply affected Lord Rothermere was his devastation at the loss of his youngest son Vere Harmsworth, followed by his much-loved eldest son, the Hon Vyvyan Harmsworth, in the mud and the blood of the trenches on the Western Front.

The second Secretary of State for Air was Sir William Weir, created Lord Weir, and he appointed Major General Sir Frederick Sykes as Chief of the Air Staff and persuaded Trenchard to accept command of the Independent Bombing Force, established in France, so as not to come under Haig. Weir and Sykes, both staunch supporters of a separate and independent air force, overcame the difficulties caused by the resignations and nurtured the infant RAF skilfully until January 1919, when Weir relinquished his post as Air Minister. He considered his job done as the war was over, and he wished to return to his own engineering business in Scotland. He arranged the re-appointment of Trenchard as Chief of the Air Staff, with the new Secretary of State for War and Air, Winston Churchill, who moved Sykes sideways to be Controller of Civil Aviation, which came under the Air Ministry. In the interim Trenchard's Independent Bombing Force had been upgraded in October 1918 to become the Inter-Allied Independent Air Force by including French and American elements. The war ended before this new force could make any real impact, but the command established Trenchard's personal doctrine of the predominance of bombing, which determined the central role of the fledgling RAF. Post-war, Lord Weir remained extremely influential and chaired several important Government Committees studying the role of the armed forces; later he was appointed principal adviser to Lord Swinton, who became the Secretary of State for Air at a crucial time in 1935. But before then both Weir and Churchill backed Trenchard firmly in defending the independent Air Force, especially against the claims of Lord Beatty, the First Sea Lord. Had the latter succeeded in his demands to resume control of naval aviation – and he, with all the other Lords of the Admiralty, threatened to resign – the Air Force would not have survived as a separate service. It is most unlikely that air forces subordinated to the two older services would have been able to win the Battle of Britain in 1940 – with incalculable results that would have necessitated the re-writing of history.

Despite the financial stringency imposed upon the Air Ministry over the next 15 years, Hugh Trenchard was an inspiring leader who built up the esprit de corps and morale of the young Air Force and provided solid foundations for its future expansion. During his term as the decisive Chief of the Air Staff, he created the RAF Cadet College at Cranwell, the Staff College at Andover, the School for Technical Training at Halton, and the Aeroplane & Armament Experimental Establishment at Martlesham Heath; he also inaugurated the annual Hendon Air Displays and encouraged participation in the Schneider Trophy, together with a series of record-creating flights by RAF aircraft. He established the Short Service Commission Scheme in 1919, and formed the first Auxiliary and University Air Squadrons in 1925 – three means of ensuring a steady flow of young pilots. He seized the opportunity to demonstrate the use of air power by taking over the Army's colonial role of policing troublesome tribes in the Middle East, and in 1928 arranged the evacuation by air of hundreds of Europeans from Kabul in Afghanistan. He made sure that the public was aware of all of these achievements.

Typical of Trenchard was the manner in which he personally informed Richard Fairey, following a demonstration to him of the Private Venture Fairey Fox light bomber prototype, that 'he had decided to order a squadron of Foxes', thus bypassing completely the normal protracted Air Ministry procedures for procuring aircraft. Fairey had imported some American V12 430hp Felix engines in 1925, and designed around them a very clean biplane bomber that was several years ahead of the aircraft being built in this country, and one that could comfortably out-perform all the RAF fighters. No 12 (Bomber) Squadron was duly equipped with Foxes and for four years, until the Bristol Bulldog entered service, they continued to do so. This was the prime attraction to Trenchard, as it reinforced his doctrine of the inviolability of fast bombers, a doctrine to be echoed ten years later with the Blenheim. The whole episode of the Fox, especially as it used a foreign engine, caused red faces at the Air Ministry, and therefore did not endear Fairey to them, and they subsequently passed over several promising designs submitted by the Fairey Aviation Company.

Long after Trenchard relinquished his post of CAS at the beginning of 1930, he continued to be the most revered, the most senior, and the most influential 'father figure' in the Royal Air Force, maintaining close contact with the Air Staff. There were only 30 to 40 Officers of Air Rank in the RAF throughout the period prior to the hasty expansion of the late 1930s – and Trenchard made it his business to know them all and to imbue them with his spirit and his doctrine that the RAF was 'an offensive not a defensive force'. The RAF effectively had only three more Chiefs of the Air Staff from 1930 until 1940, when Charles Portal was appointed: Sir John Salmond (his brother Sir Geoffrey had served but a month before dying), Sir Edward Ellington, and Sir Cyril Newall. Trenchard had taught the first three to fly at the Central Flying School at Uphaven in the very early days, while Salmond succeeded him as OC of the RFC and Newall was his number two in the Independent Air Force. Other pupils of Trenchard at Uphaven were Hugh Dowding, Edgar Ludlow-Hewitt and Arthur Barratt, who later commanded Fighter Command, Bomber Command and RAF France respectively, while his own Instructor was Arthur Longmore, who later commanded Coastal Command, then the Middle East Theatre. Long after retiring, Trenchard used his seat in the House of Lords to offer very public advice – usually neither welcome nor heeded – on how the RAF should be run. He also subjected his successors as Chief of the Air Staff, members of the Air Staff and the Air Council to a series of memos, even sending them to Prime Minister Churchill during the war, when he appointed himself a sort of unofficial Inspector General, visiting many RAF stations. It is difficult to name any single individual since Trenchard who has exerted such an overriding and long-lasting influence on one of Britain's fighting services.

You may be wondering why I have highlighted the roles of Weir, Trenchard and Churchill when sketching the background to the birth of the Blenheim, but these three core personalities were instrumental in shaping the nature and structure of the Royal Air Force throughout those formative years. Later, when Lord Rothermere returns to the scene that particularly concerns us – the genesis of the Bristol Blenheim – we will find that these four assisted the birth of the Blenheim in various ways. Rothermere did so most significantly and publicly, by commissioning and publicising 'Britain First', while Weir and Trenchard worked more behind the scenes, but all pressed for the RAF to be re-equipped with large numbers of fast modern bombers, the Blenheim appearing to them as the ideal candidate. By calling for re-armament – especially the expansion and modernisation of the RAF – Winston Churchill, swimming against the tide in the mid-1930s while in opposition in Parliament, helped to create the conditions for the unprecedented orders for thousands of Blenheims 'straight from the drawing-board'. Later still, in the early 1940s as the wartime Prime Minister, Churchill was directly involved in the operational deployment of those very Blenheims.

The Bristol Aeroplane Company

Having given a brief summary of the creation of the RAF, the bomber-orientated direction of its development, and the urgent need by the mid-1930s for re-equipment after years of penny-pinching neglect, we need to go back a little and look at the British aircraft industry in general, and at the Bristol Aeroplane Company in particular.

The First World War had seen the phenomenally rapid expansion of a handful of small, almost 'one-man-band' enterprises that manufactured a few very rudimentary aeroplanes with elementary engines – a total of only 211 in the whole of 1914 – into an entire aviation industry employing some 350,000 men and women to manufacture huge numbers of far more elaborate machines. This vast expansion, which took place in less than four years, was force-fed by the parallel and equally rapid growth of the air arms of the Allied Services. In the last six months of the war this mushrooming new industry produced 26,685 aircraft and 29,561 aero-engines – astounding totals. At the end of the First World War the RAF was by far the largest air force in the world, with some 300,000 personnel and 22,647 aeroplanes. Unfortunately, the rate of post-war contraction was equally rapid, for by 1926 the remnants of our aviation industry were struggling to survive, and the RAF had shrunk to fewer than 30,000 personnel and only 740 aeroplanes! But around that time, as mentioned above, Trenchard fortuitously proved the effectiveness of the RAF by policing a troublesome Iraq from the air at a cost far less than the alternative methods of a large standing army mounting punitive expeditions. This impressed the Government, pleased the Treasury, and virtually ensured the continued independent existence of the Royal Air Force.

Prominent among the burgeoning new breed of wartime aeroplane manufacturers

Sir George White, far-sighted founder of the British & Colonial Aeroplane Company in February 1910. He died in November 1916, and his brother Samuel was elected Chairman and his son G. Stanley White Managing Director. The Company was reformed as the Bristol Aeroplane Company Ltd in 1920 – Sir G. Stanley White Bt held the helm with a firm hand right until 1955.

Captain Frank Barnwell RFC. He was a brilliant designer, and for more than 20 years was responsible for a string of successful Bristol aircraft, including the Blenheim.

was the British & Colonial Aeroplane Company Ltd, reformed and renamed more appropriately as the Bristol Aeroplane Company on 31 December 1919. Founded in February 1910 in tram sheds near the village of Filton by Sir George White, who had introduced trams and buses to London and Bristol, this pioneering and properly financed aircraft company expanded rapidly. One of the first talented young designers engaged by White was Frank Barnwell, who joined in 1911 to develop naval aircraft. The company had progressed from the crude pre-war Boxkite to producing the Bristol Scout, designed by Barnwell. In 1915, at Bristol's request, Barnwell was recalled from the RFC, where he had served as a Captain, so that his talents could be more usefully employed. This resulted in his first great success, the famed Bristol F2 Fighter, of which more than 5,000 were built. Incidentally, the first ever operational sortie by the newly formed Royal Air Force was carried out by 22 Squadron before dawn on 1 April 1918 in Bristol F2B Fighters. These continued in service until 1929, when another well-known design by Barnwell, the Bristol Bulldog, was put into production. Until then the RAF had to continue operating aircraft that were basically modified versions of First World War machines. Manufacture of the Bulldog continued until 1934, by which time Barnwell and the Bristol company were involved with 'Britain First', and enormous advances in aircraft design, construction methods and performance were taking place – aided greatly by the increased power and reliability of a new generation of aero-engines. This leads us to another link in the chain that led to the Blenheim family of aircraft.

Bristol Aero-Engines

Typical of the manner in which the aircraft industry grew so rapidly from small beginnings is the way that Bristol Aero-Engines came into being, initially as a department of the Bristol Aeroplane Company, then as a major company in its own right – and one that for several years between the wars kept the parent company afloat. Another 'mighty oak' that had grown from 'a little acorn'!

During the First World War a number of motor vehicle manufacturers were contracted to develop and manufacture aero-engines to cater for the drastically increasing demand: Rolls-Royce, Napier, Bentley, Wolseley, Armstrong-Siddeley and Sunbeam, for example. Another was a small company called Brazil Straker, which prior to the war had manufactured 1,000 buses and about 150 excellent Straker Squire cars at Fishponds near Bristol. The company's chief engineer was the highly respected A. H. Roy Fedden, who had joined them in 1906 while still a student. Straker Squire was initially asked by the Admiralty to rectify the shortcomings of the Curtiss OX-5 engine, which Fedden, ably assisted by L. F. 'Bunny' Butler, achieved by virtually redesigning it. Straker worked to sufficiently high standards of engineering that it was contracted to manufacture the Renault V8 aero-engine. It also became – at the suggestion and recommendation of Sir William Weir – the only company licensed by Rolls-Royce to rebuild its Eagle and to produce its Hawk and Falcon aero-engines. Hundreds of Straker-built Falcons were used to power the renowned Bristol F2 Fighters. However, Rolls-Royce recognised that Fedden was a brilliant design engineer and did not wish a possible rival to benefit from such an intimate knowledge of its own products, so the contract stipulated that he should not design or develop any water-cooled or in-line aero-engines. This stipulation had a most far-reaching but totally unforeseen effect on the entire future development of British aero-engines, for it diverted Fedden exclusively towards air-cooling and the radial layout – a diversion of basic design philosophy that continued until gas-turbines supplanted piston aero-engines in the 1950s.

Consequently, when Fedden and Butler were contracted by the Admiralty to design a 300hp engine, they came up with a small diameter (3ft 6in) air-cooled radial engine. The resulting twin-row 14-cylinder Mercury ran in July 1917 and met the specification; 200 were ordered by the Admiralty, but the order was over-ruled by Lord Weir, then the Controller of Aeronautical Supplies. He was influenced by Henry Royce, head of the Admiralty's leading aero-engine supplier, who advised against air-cooled radial engines, and had warned Fedden that 'an attempt to tackle an engine of this layout would lead to failure'. In view of the enormous demand for aero-engines, Weir decided to order both in-line and radial engines, but his decision on the latter type was disastrous, and apparently justified Royce's warning, as the chosen radial engine – the ABC Dragonfly, a promising single-row nine-cylinder engine, and much cheaper than the Mercury – had been inadequately tested and became a complete failure. Nearly 12,000 Dragonflies were ordered for delivery in 1918 from 17 different motor vehicle manufacturers, but only a few were delivered from eight of these contracted companies, and fewer than 10 actually flew! Weir had hoped to standardise on a few engines for the entire Air Force – from Armstrong-Siddeley, Napier and Rolls-Royce – together with the ABC Dragonfly, but the latter vibrated so badly that it suffered crankshaft failures or overheated and cooked itself to destruction on the test-bed. Had the war not ended with the unexpected Armistice that November, the RAF would have had a major mechanical catastrophe on its hands. Weir wrote to Fedden:

> 'I wish to impress upon you that the changed conditions due to the Armistice do not affect the importance of your experimental and development work in connection with engines, and it is most desirable that you should continue with your efforts in this direction.'

In 1918 the Straker Company was taken over by the giant Cosmos Engineering Ltd, so Fedden's early engine became known retrospectively as the Cosmos Mercury to distinguish it from the Bristol Mercury units later to power the Blenheim. Fedden and Butler also designed and built a far simpler nine-cylinder single-row radial engine, named Jupiter. This brilliant engine aimed at 500hp, but with four valves and two spark-plugs per cylinder, was very advanced and potentially even more powerful. The Cosmos Mercury was flight-tested in a modified Bristol Scout in 1919, and the Cosmos Jupiter in a Bristol Badger the same year, and in a Bullet in 1920/21, all with impressive results. Fedden and his team also laid out a twin-row 1,000hp radial, effectively a doubled-up Jupiter, which he called Hercules – he liked mythological names and used this one later for the most widely used engine of the Second World War. But, alas, in February 1920 Cosmos Engineering foundered due to an ill-starred international venture, and the promising Jupiter engine seemed destined to fall with it.

The Air Ministry was anxious that this advanced engine, and the expertise of Fedden, Butler and their talented team, should not be lost, so it assisted Fedden's efforts to find a buyer by promising an order for ten production Jupiter engines. Indeed, Weir wrote to Fedden:

> 'I need not enlarge upon the success of your work nor upon the high hopes this department has regarding the "Jupiter" beyond stating that it is of very great importance to the Nation, as far as aircraft are concerned, that you should press on in all haste to perfect the "Jupiter", which I feel sure has a considerable future in front of it for civil aviation.'

However, Fedden initially received cold indifference from Bristol, a rebuff from Armstrong-Siddeley, and rejection by Vickers, which thought it unwise to produce airframes and engines under one roof. They were the only potential purchasers. So Weir (possibly to redress the Dragonfly fiasco) used his considerable influence with the Bristol Chairman, Sir Stanley White, to recommend the purchase; he was aided by Sir Henry White-Smith, the nephew of the founder, Sir George White, and they persuaded the very diffident Bristol Board to buy the aero-engine side of Cosmos from the Official Receiver. Thus, in what was probably the bargain of the decade, the Bristol Aeroplane Company purchased all the Cosmos patents, designs, jigs, tools and patterns, together with five Jupiter engines (two of which were sold) and 50 engine-sets of raw materials, for 25 per cent of the book value – a

The successful Bristol Jupiter radial engine, the demand for which enabled the Company to survive the Depression.

mere £15,000. The Directors also gained the services of Fedden and his entire team, so in July 1920 formed the Bristol Engines Department and appointed Roy Fedden as its Chief Engineer. They then agreed, most reluctantly, to his requirement for funding over the following two years to develop the Jupiter and to set up aero-engine production facilities. It is just as well that they did, for otherwise the Blenheim and its entire progeny – the range of Bristol aircraft that led right up to Concorde – could not have been created.

Even then it was a very close run thing, because the Board had allocated £200,000 (a huge sum in those days) and – worried lest they had 'let a cuckoo into the nest' – allowed only two years for the 35-strong Engine Department to 'get itself off the ground' and into profit. But £197,000 and 18 months later it had not, so the Directors decided to cut their losses and close the department down at the end of the year. However, due to much hard development work by Fedden's team, the 400hp Jupiter II became in September 1921 the first aero-engine to pass the new and very stringent Air Ministry 100-hour test at full power. Fedden persuaded the Board to exhibit a Jupiter at the Paris Air Show in October 1921, displaying the results of this test alongside, and – to the great relief of all at Filton

– the renowned Gnome et le Rhone Company was so impressed that it paid handsomely for a licence to build the engine in France. This was followed by lucrative licence agreements with aero-engine companies in many other countries, such as Siemens in Germany, Alfa-Romeo in Italy, PZL in Poland, and Nakajima in Japan, and the Jupiter became by far the most successful of the first post-war generation of aircraft engines. The RAF initially ordered 81, and many more later; they were also ordered by the newly created Imperial Airways, KLM, Air France and Sabena. In the next ten years the Jupiter was progressively developed and more than 7,000 were built, frequently being proposed in Air Ministry specifications. The Bristol Engine Department became renowned throughout the world for its engineering excellence, and was soon a thriving and profitable concern. It is worth reiterating that if it had failed to succeed – and as already stated, it was twice 'a very close run thing' indeed – the creation of the Blenheim and its entire family of successors just would not have been possible.

The Bristol Company during the Depression

The original aircraft business of the Bristol Aeroplane Company struggled, as did all of its competitors, throughout the 1920s and the early 1930s. Despite strenuous efforts, the company's attempts to find a market for civil aircraft were far from successful, and the worldwide depression at the end of the decade made these attempts even more difficult. Bristol had been saved from closure in 1920 by a contract to build 215 new Bristol Fighters for Army Co-operation use, some 84 from a pile of surplus airframes that had been awaiting engines at the end of the war, together with further orders up to as late as 1927. The company also converted a few for civilian use, and received orders to recondition and update hundreds of RAF Bristol Fighters. However, together with the other major manufacturers such as Vickers, Handley-Page, Hawker (reformed from Sopwith), Shorts, Avro, Fairey, de Havilland, Blackburn and Armstrong, Bristol urgently sought Government orders for new types of military aircraft at the start of the new decade. But these were the years of disarmament and endless Peace Conferences – the so-called 'years the locusts ate' – and such orders were very hard to obtain. The Air Ministry, anxious to keep the various design teams going, issued a series of specifications and rationed out the contracts for the construction of prototypes to a few invited concerns, and the selected aircraft companies built them in the hope – usually unfulfilled – of obtaining production orders. However, these production contracts were awarded very rarely, and then for relatively small numbers, and had to survive through 22 lengthy stages from the issue of an Air Staff Requirement to a final production order, often including comparative trials with prototypes from rival manufacturers. The 1929 order for the Bulldog helped Bristol to recoup the losses incurred in building a series of prototypes over ten years.

Of some 45 designs submitted by Bristol to meet Air Ministry specifications between 1920 and mid-1935, 20 were awarded contracts for prototypes only, and five of those were Private Venture, only one – the Type 105 (A to D) Bulldog – resulted in production contracts. Bristol also tried designs for the civil market but without success.

Frank Barnwell spent a couple of years in Australia from 1921 to 1923 as technical adviser to the RAAF's experimental department, and visited aircraft manufacturers on the continent of Europe. He was welcomed back to Bristol as Chief Designer and, with Leslie Frise and Archie Russell forming the core, the design team was kept very busy on all the types mentioned above, but prototype orders were unprofitable and only the Bulldog secured a production order – times were hard.

Fortunately, Roy Fedden, Bunny Butler and their now quite large team in the Engines Division had been very busy too. They had developed the Jupiter into a major success for Bristol and had minor successes with smaller versions using Jupiter cylinders – the three-cylinder Lucifer and the five-cylinder Titan – and a baby engine, the flat-twin Cherub. In 1927 they were contracted to produce a special short-stroke version of the Jupiter for a Short Seaplane designed as a competitor in the Schneider Trophy. The 1-inch-shorter stroke

The Bristol Bulldog (Type 105). Fitted with Jupiter, then Mercury, engines, the prototype flew first in May 1927. The Bulldog served in RAF Fighter Squadrons until July 1937, some months after the Blenheim entered service.

reduced the piston speed considerably; it also reduced by 2 inches the overall diameter, and thus the drag, of this large radial engine. This version became the famous Bristol Mercury, and a continuous improvement and development programme over the next decade turned it into another substantial success following that of the Jupiter. Apart from the advanced design features, the renowned reliability of Bristol production engines was ensured by the meticulous attention to detail of Fred Whitehead, in charge of the demanding task of series production of identical engines in the actual metal. Whitehead too was a genius, forever pressing industry for constant improvements in the many alloys and steels used in engine manufacture, and taking full advantage of these better materials as soon as they became available.

Without this growing contribution from the Engines Division it is most unlikely that the Bristol Aeroplane Company would have been able to survive the 1920s. This may be illustrated by the accompanying table of annual purchases (in thousands of 1920s pounds) from Bristol by the Air Ministry during the decade, showing how the Bristol Engines Division overtook the airframe side in 1927, then out-performed the original business:

Year	1923	1924	1925	1926	1927	1928	1929	1930	Total
Airframes	201	371	346	237	151	243	157	276	1,982
Engines	149	174	158	152	234	338	548	743	2,496

(Source: PRO File AIR2/1322)

Fedden had for some years been seeking an alternative to pushrod-operated overhead valves; overhead camshafts were much more efficient but far more difficult to incorporate in radial engines than in engines with their cylinders in line, such as the Rolls-Royce with two banks of six cylinders in V formation. Together with Harry Ricardo, he had long been investigating (and building single-cylinder testing rigs to develop) sleeve-valves – where a metal sleeve is inserted between piston and cylinder and partially rotated with a reciprocating motion so that openings cut into it uncover inlet and exhaust ports in the cylinder walls. The improvement in efficiency demonstrated enabled him finally to persuade the Bristol Board to sanction the building and testing of a prototype of a compact sleeve-valve nine-cylinder radial engine, which he called Aquila; it ran well on the test-bed and produced 500hp. Vickers used it in its Venom, a prototype fighter built for the F5/34 specification, but no orders resulted. As Bristol had no suitable airframe in which to install this new engine, and there were no other orders in prospect, it is understandable that the Board would not sanction production.

Frank Barnwell visited the United States in 1934, where he saw examples of an entirely fresh generation of machines using new materials that finally made practicable the adoption of a radical improvement in the method of aircraft construction that had been pioneered by Dr Adolph Rohrbach in Germany in the later stages of the war and in the 1920s. This method, where the skin covering the airframe and not the frame itself carried most of the loads, had been the subject of lectures given by Rohrbach to the Royal Aeronautical Society and in the United States. Barnwell had studied the published data carefully and the Air Ministry had authorised Bristol to carry out a research programme into these methods in conjunction with the Royal Aircraft Establishment at Farnborough. Thus he was able to commence incorporating some of the principles and the new materials into the partially stressed-skin designs he was working on at the time – the Type 130 Bomber/Transport and the Type 133 Fighter.

Roy Fedden, the pre-eminent designer of the family of famous air-cooled radial aircraft engines produced by the Bristol Aircraft Company.

However, during these early years of the 1930s Barnwell had also been sketching the layout of a light and very neat twin-engined 'commercial monoplane', which, for the first time, he designed to use stressed-skin construction throughout. His 'dream machine' became known in the company as 'the Captain's Gig', and Roy Fedden saw that this project would be ideal for two of his new Aquila engines.

The scene was set – the aircraft that would become the Blenheim had been conceived.

Chapter 2

The birth of the Blenheim

An innovative all-metal design

On 28 July 1933 Frank Barnwell allocated the Bristol Type Number 135 to the design for his proposed light-twin 'commercial monoplane' and prepared more detailed drawings, which included the installation of two of the new Aquila sleeve-valve engines. He compared drag and structure weight estimates for a wing and fuselage of the same shape and dimensions with both high-wing and low-wing layouts, and the latter showed the best results. He therefore laid out the aircraft as a low-wing monoplane built around a straight centre-section with twin spars, carrying at their outer ends the engine and main undercarriage units, the fuel tanks mounted between the spars inboard, and the spars continuing to the tips of the tapering outer wing panels. The undercarriage had 'apron' fairings and retracted rearwards into nacelles behind the engines; retractable split-trailing-edge flaps ran from aileron to aileron. A slim fuselage was mounted above the centre-section, with the pilot in a streamlined nose and six passengers in the cabin, which tapered to a shapely single fin and rudder. The aircraft was to be constructed throughout in light alloy, including the entire stressed-skin covering, except the control surfaces, which were fabric covered; the only steel to be used was in the tubular mounting frames for the engines and undercarriage, and the flanges to the webs of the wing spars. This method of all-alloy construction based on a stressed-skin semi-monocoque was rare in the early 1930s, but such was the accelerated development of aircraft design during this period that it became the norm by the end of that decade, and with but few exceptions is now universal.

It is necessary to explain these terms 'semi-monocoque' and 'stressed-skin', for they are central to the creation of the Bristol Blenheim. In the early days of heavier-than-air flying-machines the airframes were based on a warren-girder triangulated-truss type of structure, still to be seen in crane jibs today. Wood was the material used initially for the main airframe members, and each bay was kept rigid by a diagonal member that acted in tension or compression and removed bending loads from the main members. These triangulated bays were usually rectangular in section and cross-braced with wire, and if it was not possible to fit a diagonal member in any bay it had to be strengthened by a full or partial diaphragm bulkhead or similar stiffening. In some instances sheets of plywood were fixed to the sides of several bays to stiffen the structure. In the earliest days fuselages were left uncovered and only the upper sides of the lifting surfaces were covered in fabric, but the undersides of wings were soon covered too, and it was not long before fuselages were covered as well – usually over lightweight wooden formers and stringers giving the desired drag-reducing shape – to provide some protection for the crew. A few years later advances in metallurgy made it possible for the main structural members to be made of thin-walled tubular steel; originally drawn then usually rolled from steel strip, and often rectangular or oval in section, they were sometimes made in two flanged halves riveted together, mainly with steel bracket fittings at the joints rather than welding, and still frequently wire-braced. This made for very strong and relatively light basic structures, which, although merely refined versions of early First World War construction methods, became common in the period between the wars and remained in use right up to the Second World War. Indeed, many famous aircraft using that type of tubular-frame construction were to give noble service in that conflict, including the Gloster Gladiator, Westland Lysander, Avro Anson, De Havilland Tiger Moth, Fairey Swordfish and – most famously of all – the Hawker Hurricane.

Barnwell was well aware at an early stage of the advantages of using metal for aircraft construction, but the virtually insoluble difficulty lay in making such structures light enough yet strong enough with the materials then available. Back in 1916, as an alternative to the tubular warren-girder frame approach, Barnwell, assisted by Wilfred Reid, had designed the all-metal MR1, a two-seater fighter biplane very similar to his famous F2 Fighter then going into production. The fuselage of this Type 13 was dual-skinned in alloy with channel-section bulkheads supporting an inner-skin that was corrugated lengthways for stiffness and riveted to a smooth duralumin outer skin, varnished to resist corrosion. However, they were unable to make the wings stiff enough using duralumin and first flew the aircraft in 1917 with conventional wooden wings. They sub-contracted the wings to the Steel Wing Company of Gloucester, which had made wings using a rolled-steel strip primary structure that had been tested on an Avro 504 and a BE2. This move delayed completion until the end of 1918, when the Armistice was declared, and further development was abandoned – but the MR1 did gain the distinction of being the first all-metal aircraft ever to fly in Britain. In April 1919 Barnwell ferried it to Farnborough for tests, but managed to fly it into a tree upon arrival!

Also in 1919, and on a more positive note, Barnwell persuaded his directors to erect a wind-tunnel for aerodynamic research and to test design features in a practical way; although other wind-tunnels were added to the Filton factory later, this original one remained in use until it was destroyed by a German bomb in 1942!

During the First World War other designers such as Adolph Rohrbach and Hugo Junkers had adopted a similar approach to metal aircraft construction. In addition they not only pioneered monoplanes but also tried to spread a major part of the loads from the inner frame on to the outer covering. But the corrugated alloy skins plus the deep wing-spars on the Junkers J1 to J10 monoplane fighter designs of 1915-18 made them heavier, more cumbersome, and often slower than contemporary fabric-covered aircraft. At that period small biplanes were generally lighter, stronger and more manoeuvrable than monoplanes, as their inter-wing struts and bracing wires stiffened the whole structure. Nevertheless, in the 1920s more than 300 Junkers F13 single-engined all-metal passenger monoplanes with corrugated skins, developed from the earlier designs, were built, and these led in 1930 to the Ju.52. This aircraft's wings had four spars of narrow box section with corrugated alloy vertical webs, joined by ribs made of triangulated alloy tubing. Then two more engines were added to create the Ju.52/3m Tri-Motor Transport, which was used by the Luftwaffe throughout the Second World War.

A true monocoque has all the loads carried by the outer structure without any support from internal formers or bulkheads – the perfect example being an egg. It was not possible to incorporate this pure form of monocoque into the construction of aeroplanes as they needed openings in the shell, so a light internal structure of formers and stringers was used to locate and support an outer skin, which was riveted to it to form a light but rigid structure. The outer skin itself carried nearly all of the loads imposed upon the aircraft and was stressed to fulfil this function, so was known as a 'stressed skin'. This type of aircraft construction was originally and correctly termed 'semi-monocoque', although the 'semi' dropped from use and nowadays it is usually referred to by the name given to the covering – 'stressed-skin'.

Dipl Ing Adolph Rohrbach, the now-forgotten name mentioned above, had been senior designer at the *Zeppelinwerke* during the First World War, and back in 1919 designed the forerunner of most Second World War bombers and post-war airliners, the all-metal E4250, which had four engines mounted on the leading edge of a cantilever stressed-skin monoplane wing. (A 'cantilever' wing is one that is strong enough to bear all the loads imposed upon it without any external struts, stays or wires in support.) This very advanced machine was broken up on the orders of the Allied Control Commission, but Rohrbach moved to Copenhagen in 1922 to avoid the restrictions. There his company built about 30 high-wing cantilevered all-alloy monoplanes of various designs in the RO series. Incidentally, one of Rohrbach's assistants in Berlin had been Claude Dornier, who set up his own company in Switzerland for the same reason that Rohrbach moved to Copenhagen, where the last of the RO series, the RO IX fighter of 1926, was designed by one Kurt Tank, who left to join the new company of Heinrich Focke and Georg Wulf. Kurt Tank later designed the FW Condor and his masterpiece, the FW 190 – with an air-cooled twin-row BMW radial engine – which first flew in June 1939 and proved to be the most efficient fighter of the Second World War.

The Air Ministry was quite forward-looking in the early 1930s, for by then nearly all of the aircraft specifications it issued stipulated that 'all parts of the aircraft which contribute to its strength in flight shall be of metal'. The Ministry also awarded several other contracts to encourage aircraft companies to investigate the advantages of new forms of construction. These included Specification 1/32, issued to Avro for converting the wooden-wing of its licence-built Fokker VII tri-motor to a metal one – this cannot have been successful for Avro used the same wooden wing on its Anson until 1946, when the company finally substituted a metal wing. Vickers had experimented with a form of all-metal aircraft construction designed by the Frenchman Michel Wibault, but the thin corrugated skins carried only a small part of the loads and were not fully stressed.

Of great importance to Bristol was the contract it was awarded under 21/32 for 'Test specimens for the investigation of the strength of metal-covered structures'. This led to a systematic programme of applied research into semi-monocoque and stressed-skin construction in conjunction with the RAE Structures Department at Farnborough. Archibald Russell, from Bristol's Stress Office, and Dr A. G. (later Professor Sir Alfred) Pugsley at the RAE worked closely together, resulting in the Bristol Design Team acquiring a much greater depth of knowledge of these new structures at the very time that Barnwell was laying out the Type 135 'commercial monoplane' – the aircraft that became the Blenheim. But this was very much a low-priority 'back-burner' project for Barnwell and his outstanding team of designers, as most of their energies were focused firmly upon military projects.

An unexpected change of priority

Among the highly talented men that Barnwell had harnessed in his design team were Cliff Tinson, who had worked with Roy Chadwick at Avro; Harry Pollard, who had specialised in high-tensile steel rolled strip at Boulton & Paul; Leslie Frise, who invented the differential Frise ailerons and did much of the design work on the Bulldog; and Archie Russell, whose brilliant mind transformed the Bristol Stress Office. They were all working hard at that time on the design of three of these high-priority and important military aircraft prototypes, and while each contributed to the design of the Blenheim, one was to have a most profound effect on the entire future of the Bristol Aeroplane Company. The prototypes were the Type 123, the last Bristol biplane, and Types 130 and 133, both advanced all-metal cantilever monoplanes with Bristol engines.

The Type 130 was a large high-winged Bomber/Transport with two Pegasus (long-stroke Mercury) engines built to the 1931 Specification C.26/31; it was based on the projected Type 115, also a high-wing monoplane but with three Jupiter engines, which had been submitted (unsuccessfully) to Specification C.16/28 for a Troop Carrier to replace the ancient Vickers Valentia biplanes. Both these designs benefited significantly from the lessons learned from the complete failure of Bristol's first twin-engined monoplane, the Type 95 Bagshot. This was built to Specification 4/24 for a three-seat 'heavy-gun' (twin 37mm cannon) fighter, and had two Jupiter engines. The fuselage was built as a tubular steel warren-girder with the three main longerons forming an inverted triangle in section; the wing had two steel spars and alloy ribs and was cantilevered outboard of the engines. All was fabric-covered. Unfortunately the wing was not sufficiently rigid in torsion so that when the ailerons were applied at a speed approaching 100mph they twisted the whole wing and the aircraft turned in the opposite direction from that demanded by the pilot! This failure resulted in extensive research by Bristol and the RAE into the torsional stiffness of cantilever wings, and led to cross-braced multi-spars being designed by Harry Pollard for the wings of the abortive Type 115. This trend was further developed in the Type 130, the 96-foot-span wings of which had no fewer than seven spars each. These had deep alloy webs with steel stiffening flanges, joined by pressed alloy ribs to give the required profile, the alloy skins being riveted to both, forming a series of 'boxes' that gave the wing the required strength both in bending and in torsion. Archie Russell recommended that a simpler and lighter twin-spar wing be used, which his calculations showed to be strong enough, but Barnwell supported the 'belt-and-braces' view and the seven spars were retained. A complete wing mounted on a test-rig was demonstrated at full design load to Pugsley and his Structures Team from the RAE at Farnborough; it exceeded their requirements comfortably and they admired the improved torsional stiffness. The Air Ministry had made the contract conditional upon a satisfactory outcome to these tests.

The Type 95 Bagshot with twin Jupiter engines, which suffered from twisting of the cantilever wings, reversing the effect of the ailerons. (Below) Undergoing static tests to determine the torsional stiffness of wings. A contract with the RAE to research this problem led to the strong wings of future Bristol designs, a strength that helped many Blenheims, badly damagerd in action, to return safely to base.

So the contract for the prototype to Specification C.26/31 was awarded in March 1933 and the aircraft first flew in June 1935 – then the largest Bristol aircraft to fly. Despite successful flight trials, the production contract was not issued until July 1937, when the Air Staff realised that it had no equivalent to the Ju.52 troop transport. The aircraft was named Bombay, and as by then the Filton factories were flat out producing Blenheims, the Air Ministry arranged for production at the new 'shadow' factory in Belfast operated by Short and Harland as their first product. The first production Bombay flew in March 1939, and the aircraft gave good service in the Middle East Theatre of War. Incidentally, the wings of the post-war Bristol Type 170 Freighter were based on the wings of the Bombay, having the same aerofoil section, span, thickness and taper ratio, but with two instead of seven spars. Archie Russell was by then Bristol's Chief Designer!

The other important design that affected the creation of the Blenheim, and indeed changed the whole nature and course of the Bristol Aeroplane Company, was the Type 133 Fighter.

It will be recalled that for more than 20 years Bristol's success had been built entirely on single-engined aircraft – the Scout, the F2 Fighter, and the Bulldog. Of more than 130 Bristol designs, only a handful had been for multi-engined aircraft, and even those had resulted in prototype orders only – the production order for the Bombay had not at that stage been awarded. The Air Ministry Specification F.7/30 for a single-seat four-gun fighter, which set, for those days, a very high level of all-round performance, including a top speed of 250mph, was issued to tender in October 1931 at a critical juncture in the development of aircraft design, with 'substantial' orders promised to the winner. Bristol and most of the other leading aircraft companies between them tendered 12 different designs, six for biplanes and six for monoplanes, but four remained paper rather than metal aeroplanes. The Air Ministry ordered prototypes from three manufacturers, Supermarine, Blackburn and Westland, and asked the others to construct Private Venture prototypes at their own expense; these were Bristol (with two PV designs, the Type 123 biplane and the Type 133 monoplane), Hawker, Gloster, Armstrong and Vickers. The Bristol Type 123 Biplane had the Rolls-Royce Goshawk engine, a steam-cooled version of the Kestrel that was the engine preferred by the Air Ministry, though not by many of the designers! The 123 was designed principally by Leslie Frise, and was built on a tubular steel frame, while the wings had metal spars riveted to dural leading-edge sections to form torsion boxes. Construction began in March 1933 and it first flew in June 1934, but proved unstable at high speed due to flexing of the outer sections of the lower wings. The design was abandoned, marking the end of an era as it was the last of the many thousands of Bristol biplanes to be built at Filton. It was also the last aircraft to be built at Filton using an engine that was not manufactured 'in house' by Bristol.

Frank Barnwell's ideas were evolving towards the design that would emerge as the Blenheim, for his Type 133 monoplane was much more advanced and of all-metal construction. It had a tubular-frame front fuselage with an enclosed cockpit, and a semi-monocoque rear fuselage; the twin-spar gull-wing had a then novel rearwards-retracting undercarriage with 'apron' fairings, set at the lowest point of the crank. Split trailing-edge flaps, and (originally) full-span drooping ailerons were fitted to give the required 50mph landing speed. The 133 was the first Bristol aircraft to use the new American Alclad alloy sheet for much of the skin. Supplies of this essential material, a sandwich of duralumin between thin outer coats of aluminium, were assured when the Northern Aluminium Company set up a plant at Banbury. Interestingly, the Supermarine entry for F.7/30 was R. J. Mitchell's Type 224, which first flew in February 1934 – and was only one step away from his immortal Spitfire. This was also an all-metal gull-wing monoplane of similar layout and construction to the Bristol 133, but it had a fixed spatted undercarriage, and chord-wise corrugations in the wing-skins to give them the required stiffness. The mixed construction used by Barnwell, of a tubular forward fuselage mounted on to the wing centre-section and married to a monocoque rear fuselage, was subsequently used by many designers, including Sydney Camm for the Hawker Typhoon and Tempest fighters a decade later.

Bristol chose its own Mercury engine for the Type 133 rather than the Rolls-Royce engine recommended by the Air Ministry. Tests with the sole prototype 133, which first flew on 8 June 1934, showed that it exceeded the requirements of the demanding specification. 'We have a winner here,' said Cyril Uwins, Bristol's Chief Test Pilot. Bristol was so confident of obtaining a substantial order that it enlarged its factory space, took on extra employees, and increased the rate of production of Mercury engines. But, alas, on the eve of delivery to the RAF A&AEE at Martlesham Heath for the comparative trials, the 133 – the company's pride and joy – crashed to the ground, and the high hopes came crashing down too. Uwins, who had successfully completed all the test flying, including high-speed dives and spinning trials, had allowed a friend, Company Pilot F/Lt Thomas Campbell, to fly the 133, and he tried a spin with the undercarriage down – whether inadvertently or not we do not know. The extra keel area of the 'apron' fairings so far forward flattened the spin, the engine cut out as the centrifugal force starved it of fuel, and 'Jock' Campbell had to take to his parachute while the one and only 133 was destroyed. Bristol had placed 'all their eggs in one basket' with but a single prototype, and it makes one wonder what the outcome would have been had either of the sole prototypes for the Spitfire and Hurricane been lost in 1935 or 1936 – could the RAF still have won the Battle of Britain? The comparative trials at Martlesham were won by the far slower Gloster SS.37, a developed version of the company's open-cockpit Gauntlet biplane with a Mercury engine, and in July 1935 a production contract for the Gloster Gladiator was issued. As far as F.7/30 and the Type 133 was concerned, the Bristol company had faith, it certainly had hope, but fate showed charity to Gloster and its Gladiator, which achieved glory in Malta five years later!

The prototype 133 fighter was abandoned in a flat-spin and crashed on 8 March 1935. Bristol was not awarded the expected large-scale contract, so had to bring forward its Type 135 'commercial monoplane' project.

So it is not surprising that Frank Barnwell's pet project, the Type 135, did not receive the 'go ahead' from the Bristol Board to build a prototype, despite the entreaties of Roy Fedden, who saw it as the ideal vehicle for his new Aquila engines. However, they persuaded the Bristol directors to sanction the building of a full-size wooden 'mock-up' of the 135 fuselage for exhibition at the Paris Aero Salon later in 1934. Bristol was going through another very lean patch on the airframe side, as none of a long series of expensive prototypes had gained any production orders. Although the company had been buoyed slightly in March 1933 with the receipt of an order for the prototype Type 130, the resultant Bombay production order was still four years away. Morale was at a low ebb, and Bristol was aware that the RAF was about to undergo rapid expansion, but the only orders that it could see heading in its direction were for the manufacture of other companies' products. This unsatisfactory prospect appeared to be even more likely when, in 1934, Bristol received an order to build 141 Audax biplanes for its rivals Hawker. These were delivered during 1936 and at least kept the increased workforce in employment.

Lord Rothermere to the rescue

At this difficult juncture, Roy Fedden gave a talk on aviation at a Bristol Yacht Club function at the Spa Hotel, Clifton, enthusing about the projected design at Filton of a fast all-alloy six-passenger monoplane with exciting and novel features, built by radical methods, and using two brand-new Bristol radial engines of advanced design that were 'small, smooth and powerful'. Among his audience, and very impressed by what he heard, was Robert T. Lewis, Editor of the *Bristol Evening World*. This Bristol area newspaper was part of the *Daily Mail* and Associated Newspapers Group, owned by Viscount Rothermere, the previous Secretary of State for Air, who kept his eye on aviation matters and had been for many years an advocate of the benefits to be gained from aeroplanes in both war and peace. Rothermere was also an outspoken critic of the Air Ministry, claiming that the outdated front-line aircraft of the RAF were deficient in performance and had not kept pace with the more advanced designs on the continent and in the United States.

In February 1934 Lord Rothermere hosted a working luncheon for his editors on the subject of these developments in modern aviation, and his desire to make his readers more air-minded. The *Daily Mail*, inspired by the personal zeal of its imaginative proprietor, had encouraged aviation since the earliest years of flying by offering a series of large prizes for a string of pioneering initial flights – the first across the Channel, London to Manchester, the first transatlantic flight, and so on. When Robert Lewis (known as 'Blos'), travelling to that fateful meeting with his boss, boarded the early morning London train at Bristol station he quite by chance bumped into Roy Fedden, who was on his way to town on completely unconnected business. They breakfasted together in the dining-car and found that they had a mutual interest in fishing, but naturally the conversation soon turned to the topic of aviation. Lewis mentioned the subject of the editorial meeting later that day. Fedden again enthused about the proposed 'light commercial twin', as he saw that it could have the potential use of delivering passengers from around the country to airports for international flights – nowadays termed a 'feeder' airliner – and thus help to increase the number of those choosing to travel abroad by air. He expanded on the ultra-modern features of the proposed aircraft, the innovative all-alloy construction, the streamlined shape, and the high performance expected. He emphasised the smoothness, reliability and relative economy of the compact but powerful sleeve-valve engines. Fedden in full flight on a subject so close to his heart was very persuasive and utterly convincing. However, he did not tell Lewis that it was most unlikely that this proposed machine would ever be built, as the Bristol Board of Directors had wholly rejected the proposal.

Lord Rothermere addressed his assembled editors and journalist guests that day, recalling proudly the great part played by the *Daily Mail* in encouraging aviation in its infancy, saying that they should bring this role right up-to-date by pointing out to businessmen the many advantages of the rapid means of transport then being offered by civil aviation. He would like to see the *Daily Mail* take the lead and set an example by being able to fly reporters and photographers to cover an important story that was 'breaking' anywhere in Europe within a few hours, whereas their rivals might take days to arrive by train, ferry and road transport. After the meeting Robert Lewis told Lord Rothermere what he had learned about the proposed project at Filton, emphasising the anticipated high levels of performance, as it appeared to him to meet exactly the requirements just announced by his proprietor. He added that the Bristol

Lord Rothermere, first Secretary of State for Air and Proprietor of the Daily Mail, expressed interest in the Type 135 as the fastest possible transport aircraft for his newspaper empire. He commissioned the civil Type 142, which was, in effect, the prototype Blenheim.

Aeroplane Company was 'the largest single unit in the world building planes and engines'. Lord Rothermere expressed an immediate and positive interest and particularly welcomed the opportunity to demonstrate that the British aviation industry could produce the fastest commercial aeroplane in Europe – for that was what he was determined to have. So he instructed Lewis to approach Bristol on his behalf, 'find out all about it', and 'report back with full details in one week's time'!

Lewis telephoned this exciting news to Roy Fedden straight away; they met and consulted Frank Barnwell, Lewis being shown the drawings of the attractive 135 for the first time. There was a major snag, however – the new Aquila engine had not yet even run on the test-bed, and did not in fact do so until September that year. Lewis knew that Lord Rothermere would not countenance such a delay, and Barnwell enquired if the greater priority was high performance or economy of operation; Lewis confirmed that Lord Rothermere had made it clear that he wanted to own 'the fastest commercial aeroplane in Europe' and was looking for 250mph and a 1,000-mile range. On 6 March Barnwell proposed the substitution of supercharged Mercury engines of proven power and reliability for the as yet untried Aquila units. A few days later, after calculations revising the weight/drag/power estimates, he quoted a maximum speed of 240mph at 6,500 feet for an aircraft weighing 9,300lb in this form – giving it the new Type Number of 142. Lewis passed this information to Lord Rothermere, and on 26 March telephoned Fedden to say that his Lordship was delighted, adding that he also wished to show the Air Ministry that a small civil transport could be made that was faster than any of the RAF's fighters and far faster than any of its bombers, and would like an early meeting to discuss a firm order.

The next day Lewis, Barnwell and Fedden attended a specially convened meeting of the Bristol Board of Directors, who had very mixed feelings – indeed, some had grave reservations – about the proposed transaction, however prestigious it may appear to be. They were most anxious not to offend the Air Ministry, which had always been their principal customer, and were particularly wary of Lord Rothermere's declared intention of using the Type 142 to demonstrate the obsolescence of the RAF's front-line equipment. The designers substantiated their performance calculations and emphasised that they were very keen to go ahead, as was the Editor, and they put forward their strongly held view that although the enormous publicity the aeroplane would doubtless attract would make the Air Ministry 'sit up and take notice', this could only be beneficial to the company. The Board were far from convinced, so a few discrete soundings were made by telephone on the 'old boy's network'. Apparently Air Marshal Sir Hugh Dowding, the Director of Supply and Research on the Air Council, had no objection, and indeed approved, Lord Weir encouraged the proposal warmly, and Viscount Trenchard gave it his support and blessing. Sir George Stanley White, the Bristol Company Chairman, agreed to go with Lewis, Barnwell and Fedden to see Lord Rothermere at his London Headquarters on the morning of the 29th, the day before Good Friday.

They duly met at Stratton House, and Lord Rothermere re-stated his requirements exactly, was given the performance estimates and was shown the general layout drawings. He was impressed with what he heard and saw at that fateful meeting. A price of £18,600 was quoted, based on Bristol's standard figure of £2 per pound of weight for a prototype, and he was asked to pay half of this amount upon signing the contract and the other half in 12 month's time. This was agreed, but Lord Rothermere added the proviso that the aircraft had to have flown by then. The terms were settled, the order – then just for a 'one-off', but an order that was to have momentous consequences – was confirmed, the noble Chairmen shook hands, and the party adjourned for luncheon. The two designers, their Chairman and the Editor then returned to Bristol, pleased that the project had been given the green light.

Then an unexpected red light was shown to the project, throwing its future into doubt. For Lord Rothermere's respected principal adviser on aeronautical matters, Brigadier General P. R. C. Groves, formerly Secretary General of the Air League of the British Empire and air adviser to the British Government at the Disarmament

The neat new sleeve-valve Aquila engine intended for the Type 135 and 142.

Conference, possibly upset at not being invited to attend the meeting at which the contract for the Bristol 142 was agreed, declared himself entirely against it. He advised Rothermere strongly not to proceed, saying that he was making a fool of himself, or being made a fool of. Groves submitted a hostile report, which had it been more reasoned would probably have been effective in halting the projected purchase. But he angrily overstated his view by claiming that 'if the aeroplane ever flew it would be the joke of the technical press', and even that 'it would kill any passengers foolish enough to fly in it', so the report became counter-productive. Friends of Lewis at Stratton House quickly advised him that the project was in great danger of being cancelled. With considerable courage he suggested to his proprietor that Groves had not kept himself informed of recent technical developments, and persuaded Lord Rothermere that Fedden should be allowed to justify in person the claims made for the 142. Having heard Fedden extolling the virtues of the aircraft, Lewis was aware that he was a very persuasive advocate, but he still briefed him carefully to explain matters in non-technical language so that his listener was not 'blinded by science', also warning that Lord Rothermere was minded to cancel the proposed contract, which was still being drawn up by the Company Solicitors.

Most fortunately, Fedden was able to meet this formidable challenge, and when he was given the opportunity arranged by Lewis for a personal exposition to an increasingly doubtful Lord Rothermere, he was at his lucid and most convincing best. He explained how the estimated performance figures had been calculated and showed that they were not exaggerated, but if anything were on the conservative side. He painted an attractive and compelling picture of 'how on a long June day we could have toast and coffee at Croydon, land in Paris for breakfast, Nice for aperitifs, Rome for lunch, Vienna for tea, dinner at Brussels, and back to London for coffee and liqueurs.' Lord Rothermere was won over, discarded Groves's critical report, and instructed the Solicitors to proceed with all haste to complete the contract. (Incidentally, this delay proved providential, for the prototype 142 was not finished until April 1935, so the original 12-month provision could not have been met.) This meeting was of crucial importance to the future of the Bristol Aeroplane Company and indeed of this country, for if Roy Fedden had failed to persuade Lord Rothermere to go ahead, there would have been no Blenheim family of aircraft, and the history of the RAF in the critical early years of the Second World War, when Britain stood alone, would have been so different that it may well have been denied the narrow victory.

The Board were very relieved when Fedden confirmed that the 142 could go ahead after all. They were so pleased that they went further and agreed to sanction the building of the prototypes for two very similar 'commercial monoplanes' – the Type 142 'sports car of the air' for Lord Rothermere, and the Type 143, with the accent less on high performance and more on economy of operation. This had a pair of the smaller Aquila engines, reverting to the Type 135 proposal, and a larger fuselage to provide room for eight passengers, both changes intended to make it more attractive to commercial operators. The 143 would be relatively economical to produce for it shared the centre-section and outer wings, tail unit, undercarriage, control systems and surfaces, etc, with the Type 142; indeed, only about 30 per cent of the airframe was different. The drawing office became a hive of activity and it was not long before metal was being cut in the Experimental Shop and the 142 and 143 were being constructed side by side. At that stage there was no thought of adapting either design for military purposes. The Blenheim might be in gestation, but it was not yet born.

The monocoque fuselages of the Types 143 and 142 under construction.

A view of the experimental shop at Filton, showing the 142 and 143 (background). Tthe seven-spar wing (foreground) is for the Type 130 Bombay, as described on page 36.

The older but well-proven Mercury VI-S engine was chosen for the 142, and consequently the 142M Blenheim, while the advanced Aquila was kept for the 143.

The American Lockheed 12 of Lord Beaverbrook, proprietor of the Daily Express and a great business rival of Lord Rothermere, who was determined to show that the British aircraft industry could produce a better design.

THE BRISTOL BLENHEIM

The Type 142 fuselage mounted on the centre-section showing the passenger door and windows, plus the variable-incidence tailplane. The engines are installed and an undercarriage unit lies against trestles in the background, while the tail-wheel fork under the stern-post rests on a hydraulic jack.

The 142 with the undercarriage (in retracted position) and parts of the nacelle installed. The tubular-steel undercarriage mounting frame between the wing spars, and that for the engine ahead of the front spar, are shown clearly.

Chapter 3

'Britain First'

What had been happening in the rest of the world while the design of the aircraft that was to become the Blenheim was progressing from Frank Barnwell's preliminary sketches for the Type 135 'commercial monoplane' early in 1933 to the completion of the prototype of the Type 142 in April 1935? Ominous and ever-lengthening shadows were being cast on the prospects for international peace. Both America and Europe were emerging from an economic depression that had bitten deep into millions of lives. 'Financial stability' became the watchword, nations begrudged even the smallest expenditure on re-armament, and endless but fruitless Peace Conferences engaged the attention of the statesmen.

However, Japan had invaded Manchuria, walked out of the Geneva Disarmament Conference – which for over two years had not produced any results – and left the League of Nations. Of more significance to the probability of another European war, Germany – under her new and strongly nationalistic Chancellor Adolf Hitler – followed suit. That same month, October 1933, Winston Churchill warned the House of Commons that Germany was re-arming covertly. In February 1935 the German Air Force, although prohibited by the Versailles Treaty, was reborn. Hitler announced the formation of the Luftwaffe on 8 March, and six days later he repudiated the Versailles 'Diktat', as the Germans regarded the Peace Treaty, introduced conscription and created an Army of 36 Divisions. Then he really 'put the cat among the pigeons' by announcing to Sir John Simon, the Foreign Secretary, who was on an official visit to Berlin with Anthony Eden at the end of March, that the Luftwaffe had already reached parity with the RAF and would soon equal the French Air Force. Hitler was comparing his Luftwaffe only with the home RAF, for many of Britain's squadrons and their obsolete aircraft were scattered throughout the British Empire and unavailable for a European war. The Führer was demanding *Lebensraum* ('living space') for the Germanic peoples and casting covetous eyes to both East and West.

Mussolini then flexed his military muscles by invading Abyssinia (Ethiopia). The League of Nations imposed sanctions, mainly at the insistence of Eden and the British Foreign Office, but they proved ineffectual. Great Britain thus antagonised the Fascist dictatorship of a previously friendly country that straddled the Mediterranean sea and air routes to India, Australasia, and many other important parts of the then British Empire. This led Mussolini and Hitler to form an uneasy alliance as the Axis Powers. Josef Stalin subjugated the vast USSR and became a dictator in all but name; Russia too began to rebuild its armed forces, and soon claimed to have the largest air force in the world. The strong isolationist lobby in the United States ensured the passage through Congress of a series of Neutrality Acts, presented by President Roosevelt as part of his 'New Deal', thus signalling to the dictators that America would not become involved in any future European war.

American influence on advances in aeronautical engineering

Throughout this portentous period rapid developments in aircraft design, together with improved methods of construction using better materials, were accelerating at an ever-increasing pace. These, together with the more powerful engines, more efficient propellers, and better fuels then becoming available, led to higher levels of all-round performance. The speed section of the Mildenhall to Melbourne Air Race of October 1934 was won by the all-wood de Havilland Comet, the handicap section by a Douglas DC2 airliner, demonstrating the advantages of modern twin-engined low-wing cantilever monoplanes with retractable undercarriages. At the time of commissioning the 142, Lord Rothermere had asked, with an excess of optimism, if his aeroplane could be ready in time for that highly publicised race, only to be told that it was impossible – if the contract had been signed six months sooner or the race held six months later, the 142 could well have won, given a trouble-free run. De Havilland suggested a high-speed unarmed bomber version of the wooden Comet – thus presaging the Mosquito only five years away – but the Air Ministry poured cold water upon the idea.

In the early spring of 1934, before the Bristol Types 142 and 143 were given the 'go ahead', Frank Barnwell made a trip to the United States to bring himself up to date on the latest developments in aeroplane design and construction techniques, which were well in advance of those in Britain. He visited Douglas, where he was shown the DC2 (progenitor of the famous DC3 Dakota); Boeing, where he saw the 247 Airliner (and may have seen the prototype of the B17 Flying Fortress under construction, as it first flew in July of 1935); Glenn Martin, to view the innovative B.10 Bomber; and Lockheed, where he inspected the 10 and 12 passenger models. All of these aircraft were all-metal, low-wing monoplanes, with stressed skins of the new Alclad material, had fully cowled air-cooled radial engines, variable-pitch propellers, landing flaps, and retractable undercarriages. They confirmed his own findings on the high-wing versus low-wing alternatives, and the correctness of the remainder of his chosen layout for the Bristol

The Martin B.10 of 1934 – the forerunner of many types of monoplane twin-engined medium bombers produced throughout the following decade.

Types 142 and 143. By far the most significant of these American types was the 200mph Martin B.10, which, apart from leading directly to the Martin Maryland, Baltimore and Marauder bombers of the Second World War, was the true progenitor of all the twin-engined Medium Bombers that would appear in the air forces of many nations during the next decade. Glenn Martin approached the British Air Attaché in Washington and offered to build a modified version for the RAF, but the proposal was not taken up. The Martin B.10, which flew first early in 1932, was also the first bomber to mount a nose gun turret. This was more than two years before one was mounted on a British bomber when Boulton Paul converted its stately Sidestrand twin-engined biplane to become, with a change from Jupiter to Pegasus engines, the Overstrand, the last of a small production batch being delivered to 101 Squadron RAF in 1936 – four years later!

In the United Kingdom the prototype of the Avro Type 652A Anson, a low-wing monoplane of similar general layout, flew for the first time on 24 March 1935. The 'Annie' had twin Armstrong Cheetah radial engines, and a steel-tube fuselage frame with wooden formers and stringers, which was fabric-covered and mounted on wings made of wood. The undercarriage was retractable, then a novelty for the RAF, but had to be wound up laboriously by hand, so was often left down, especially on circuits and landing! Over

11,000 Ansons were to be built in the next 17 years. The Air Ministry had purchased a Northrop 28D-C – an all-metal stressed-skin low-wing monoplane two-seater light bomber with a Wright Cyclone radial engine – for evaluation; it was delivered to A&AEE on 10 November 1934 as K5053. It then went to the RAE for research into reducing drag. Roy Fedden inspected it and admired the engine installation and cowling arrangements. In Germany the prototypes of the Dornier Do.17 and the Heinkel He.111, both twin-engined stressed-skin monoplanes with retractable undercarriages, had flown in November 1934 and February 1935 respectively. Both were ostensibly passenger/mail aircraft, but they were really built for military use as the Do.17 'Flying Pencil' and the He.111 bombers, which were used extensively by the Luftwaffe five years later.

The RAF prepares to expand

In the RAF Air Marshal Sir Cyril Newall became Air Member for Supply and Organisation, while Air Marshal Sir Hugh Dowding's post of Air Member for Supply and Research – which he had held since 1930 – was changed to Air Member for Research and Development, a rational division of a heavy burden of responsibilities. They both served under Sir Edward Ellington, the Chief of the Air Staff. Hugh Dowding had hopes of succeeding Ellington as CAS but, following the re-organisation of the RAF into functional Commands in 1936, he was given the new Fighter Command and Sir Cyril Newall was appointed CAS shortly afterwards. Viscount Trenchard continued to exert his influence and the Air Staff continued to follow his vision of the overriding importance of the bomber. In July 1934 the British Government made the first tentative proposals to increase the strength of the RAF to 500 bombers and 336 fighters by March 1939 – known as Expansion Scheme A.

Following a meeting of Air Staff Members on 16 October 1934 to discuss 'Experimental Aircraft for 1935', and the specifications they could issue in the budget available, Hugh Dowding met the leaders of the British aviation industry on 23 November and expressed his concern at 'Britain's backwardness in comparison with the very great progress which has been made recently by some other nations', adding that 'the main difficulty was that it took much too long to get an aeroplane through from the design stage to the production stage.' He was aware that this process had taken up to eight years for a new bomber in the recent past.

This meeting was held just before he received a minute from Edgar Ludlow-Hewitt, the DCAS, on 26 November saying, 'We ought to consider a specification of a medium bomber, since I understand that the medium bombers of the old specification will be obsolescent by the time they come into production.'

Dowding replied on the 29th: 'I think there is some misunderstanding. I do not think the medium bombers will be obsolescent when they emerge. Their speeds should range from 225 to 240 [mph], so we ought to be able to choose one with a very respectable performance judged by modern standards.' He added in a further note that he 'wanted to learn what we could from the Northrop'.

The DCAS responded on 5 December: 'The phrase above [re obsolescence] was an exaggeration, even so I suggest the medium bomber specification having been made out when the recent advances in speed were not quite so apparent as they are now, we should do well to make early provision for a medium bomber to a new and more up-to-date specification.'

After these exchanges Specification G.4/31 was re-written as P.22/35 for the Vickers Wellesley, and P.27/32 was revised as 23/35 for the Fairey Battle. Thus the Bristol Type 142, which was about to burst upon this scene, arrived at a most opportune time, and the great impact it made can be appreciated more readily.

A most significant development took place at the end of 1934. A. P. Rowe of the Directorate of Scientific Research at the Air Ministry, alarmed at the poor state of Britain's aerial defences, suggested to Lord Londonderry (the Air Minister) the formation of a committee of eminent scientists to investigate and evaluate any new scientific discoveries that could assist the effectiveness of the RAF. The Chairman of the civilian Aeronautical Research Committee, Professor H. T. Tizzard, also headed this new Committee, and Professor Blacket and Dr A. V. Hill were other prominent members. They consulted Robert Watson-Watt, and his research into the reflection of transmitted radio beams led to the creation of Radio Direction Finding – what we now know as radar. Dowding had supported this from the beginning, and the chain of coastal radar stations in operation by 1940 enabled him to deploy his fighters most effectively in the Battle of Britain, which certainly tipped the scales in favour of the RAF. As we will see later, Blenheims were to play a crucial role in the development of radar. Although the Air Staff did not realise it, this scientific application marked the beginning of the end for 'the supremacy of the bomber' philosophy that had always formed the core of RAF policy. Radar was to strengthen immeasurably the ability of all defending forces to inflict heavy losses on enemy aircraft, eventually turning night into day and removing the protective cover of darkness, as both the Luftwaffe and the RAF were to discover to their great cost.

Back in 1930 Lord Rothermere had forecast in the *Daily Mail* that Adolf Hitler would become the leader of Germany, which three years later he did. This formed the basis of an odd relationship born of mutual respect, and linked by a shared view on the long-term threat posed by the Bolsheviks. He visited Hitler several times, and received many long letters from the Führer; it seems that Hitler hoped to influence British opinion by this means, for he was well aware of the powerful position held by the newspaper magnate. Indeed, Hitler, one of the first experts in news management, gained the maximum impact for his announcement of the formation of the Luftwaffe on 8 March 1935 by making it exclusively via the *Daily Mail*.

However, Rothermere sent regular reports and copies of the copious correspondence to Vansittart, Permanent Head of the Foreign Office. Rothermere had been shocked by the ruthless murder on Hitler's direct order of the Führer's former friend Ernst Rohm and 76 of his 'Brownshirt' SA colleagues at Weissee on 30 June 1934, the 'Night of the Long Knives', saying in a letter to Neville Chamberlain: 'The oligarchs of Germany are the most dangerous, ruthless men who have ever been in charge of the fortunes of a people 67 million in number. They will stop at nothing. Violent as they were on the night of 30 June in internal politics, they will be equally or even more violent in external politics.' He pressed the need for re-armament ever more strongly in the pages of the *Daily Mail*, he expressed most forcefully his deep concern at Britain's lack of preparedness for war, he lambasted Lord Londonderry, the Air Minister, warning especially about the lamentable state into which the RAF had been allowed to fall, and he gave extensive publicity to Winston Churchill's speeches on the same subject in the House of Commons. Their views were unpalatable to politicians and unpopular with the public. Lord Rothermere and Winston Churchill had also joined forces in the early 1930s to support and publicise the Indian Defence League in opposition, together with some 50 back-bench Conservative MPs, to the India Act that set British-controlled India on the road to become a self-governing Dominion. These views were also unpopular with the Government, and it seemed as if Churchill would never again achieve Ministerial Office.

The civil Type 142 takes to the air

By 1935 Cyril Uwins had been Bristol's Chief Test Pilot for some 17 years and was highly respected for his proficiency. He had been seconded to Bristol as a Flight Lieutenant from the fledgling RAF in October 1918 to succeed RFC Captain Hammond, who had been killed testing an American-built Bristol Fighter. (Lord Weir sent Barnwell to the States to sort out the many problems with the Curtiss-built Bristol F2 Fighters in which the Americans had installed their own Liberty engine.) Incidentally, Uwins's first flight in his new post at Filton was in the prototype Bristol Scout F powered by the experimental Cosmos Mercury engine, and in 1919 he tested the Cosmos Jupiter in a Bristol Badger.

Cyril Uwins made the first flight in the Type 142. He was Bristol's Chief Test Pilot from 1918 to 1947 – a truly outstanding career.

Now he opened the throttles of two 650 horsepower Bristol Mercury VI S-2 engines, developed by Fedden and Butler directly from those early designs, and the sleek Type 142 took to the skies for the first time on 12 April 1935. It created an absolute sensation. The attractive lines of the ultra-modern shape were highlighted by the highly polished smooth alloy skins. It looked fast sitting stationary on the ground, and even faster in the air when the bulky undercarriage retracted rearwards and its large 'apron' fairings merged with the streamlined lower nacelles behind the closely cowled engines. These large tear-drop shaped nacelles divided another innovative feature – the trailing-edge flaps that ran right along the wings from aileron to wing-root. Both undercarriage and flaps were hydraulically operated, unheard of in British aircraft at that time. Pneumatic wheel brakes were fitted to the retractable main wheels, the tail-wheel had a neat little spat, and the 142 had a landing-light in the centre of the pointed nose like the eye of Cyclops.

Uwins was ecstatic about the performance, which exceeded the estimates even with the fixed-pitch four-bladed wooden propellers that were installed initially. He was also delighted with the handling qualities, for the 142 had light and well-harmonised flying controls, was free of any aerodynamic vices, could be trimmed to fly 'hands off', possessed an adequate margin of control for safe single-engine flying, and proved remarkably agile in the air.

The aircraft, which had the Constructor's Sequence Number 7838, was allocated the registration letters G-ADCZ by the CAA in February 1935, but it did not carry these civil markings, initially carrying only the experimental mark R-12. Four weeks after the first flight, a pair of American Hamilton-Standard three-bladed variable-pitch metal propellers were fitted. These were specially imported by Lord Rothermere at the suggestion of Roy Fedden and conferred a drastic improvement in take-off and climb performance and enabled the top speed with a light load to exceed 300mph for the first time – this made the 142 'commercial twin' an even greater sensation.

The Type 142 at Filton before her maiden flight in April 1935. Note the fixed-pitch four-blade wooden propellers, and large 'apron' wheel fairings.

The Type 142 with specially imported Hamilton-Standard variable-pitch three-blade metal propellers, which improved performance considerably.

Lord Rothermere was delighted with the great acclaim that surrounded his private aeroplane, and turned the spotlight of newspaper publicity full upon it. Even before its official trials the aviation press was commenting that it was 'way ahead of any aircraft possessed by, or even in prospect for, the RAF', and Trenchard commented that it 'appeared to be far faster than any Interceptor Fighter in service anywhere in the World'. It is hard, at this great remove in time and with the present-day generation regarding high-speed aerial – even space – travel as completely commonplace, to convey the sheer sensation that this small private aeroplane created in those far-off days of 1935. Since then only the Concorde, a parallel example of forward-looking aviation design – also created at Filton – has so captured the imagination of the British public. With patriotic fervour Lord Rothermere named his civil passenger aircraft 'Britain First'. He was justly proud to be able to demonstrate to the world that the British aircraft industry could produce such an advanced machine. He revelled in scoring points over his friend and greatest business rival Lord Beaverbrook, the Canadian proprietor of the *Daily Express*, the main competitor to the *Daily Mail*, who had just ordered a Lockheed 12 Electra, (pictured on page 42) which although more economical to operate, was 100mph slower than 'Britain First'.

'Britain First' becomes a catalyst in RAF expansion schemes

Lord Rothermere and the *Daily Mail* had been particularly scathing in their attacks on Lord Londonderry's performance as Air Minister, claiming that he had been taken by surprise at the size of Hitler's air arm despite their repeated warnings. The worried Government then recalled Lord Weir to the centre of policy-making for the aircraft industry in relation to re-armament. Apart from being Chairman of his own company, President of the then Confederation of British Industry, and a Director of ICI, Shell and Lloyds Bank, Weir had served on the Supply Committee, an offshoot of the Committee of Imperial Defence, and also on the Defence Policy and Requirements Committee. He had therefore been kept well informed on aviation matters at the highest level, and could 'get a grip on things' immediately. His closest friend was Sir Philip Cunliffe-Lister, shortly to become, as Earl Swinton, the Secretary of State for Air, who had chaired yet another committee formed on 30 April to look at the 'air position' following Hitler's claim of 'air parity'. The committee's swift report on 8 May 1935 resulted directly in Expansion Scheme C (Scheme B had not been put forward). Weir met Lord Londonderry with the CAS, Sir Edward Ellington, and Air Marshal Sir Cyril Newall, the Air Member for Supply and Organisation, at Londonderry House on 18 May to agree this Scheme before the Cabinet approved it three days later. Expansion Scheme C aimed to create by March 1937 a home-based air force of 1,500 aircraft to regain parity with the German air force, and resulted directly from the shock that the Government had received when Hitler had made his unexpected claim

Lord Weir, highly influential and referred to as the Architect of Air Power, instigated the 'Shadow Factory' scheme and actively encouraged the contract for the military version of the Type 142.

about the Luftwaffe, mentioned above, during the Berlin talks a couple of months earlier. The Scheme called for 950 bombers and 480 fighters – again in the ratio of two to one – although 492 of the bombers were Light, 216 Medium and 240 Heavy. The 27 Overseas Squadrons and their 292 obsolete aircraft were left untouched.

The Scheme, which would effectively triple the home RAF in less than two years, was announced on 22 May, and Weir contacted B. E. Holloway, Director of Contracts at the Air Ministry, that day and received particulars of all contracts running, both for production and development, and the characteristics of the aircraft concerned. He also asked for any known performance figures for advanced aircraft in America, Germany, Italy and France. Five days later he saw Londonderry and the CAS (Ellington) again, asking the latter for 'a brief outline of the tactical schemes you have in mind for the attack and destruction of enemy machines on their own aerodromes, with particular reference to the types required by us for this purpose.' The Bristol 142 seemed an ideal candidate to be adapted for this use.

Stanley Baldwin formed a new Government, appointing Swinton as Air Minister in place of Londonderry on 7 June 1935, with Weir, working from his own office, as his Principal Adviser, a partnership that was to serve with great effect throughout the rapid expansion of the British aviation industry. In those days the aircraft manufacturers were not run by the faceless corporations of today but by strong-willed entrepreneurs – great individual 'Captains of Industry'. Weir was on first name terms with the heads of all the major aeroplane companies: Sir Frederick Handley Page, Sir George Stanley White, Geoffrey de Havilland, Oswald Short, 'Tom' Sopwith of Hawker, Robert Blackburn, Richard Fairey, Roy Dobson of Avro, and Petter of Westland. He could also talk directly to the Chief Designers, Sydney Camm of Hawker, Frank Barnwell and Archie Russell of Bristol, Rex Pierson and Barnes Wallis (the new Head of Structures) at Vickers, Roy Chadwick of Avro, John Lloyd of Armstrong-Whitworth, Arthur Gouge at Shorts, George Volkert at Handley-Page, and Reginald Mitchell at Supermarine, as well as Ernest Hives of Rolls-Royce, Roy Fedden of Bristol, Sir John Siddeley of Armstrong-Siddeley, and Frank Halford of Napier, the four main aero-engine companies. These personal contacts were to prove extremely useful in the tumultuous years of unprecedented expansion that lay just ahead.

During the following ten days Weir made the rounds of the leading aircraft manufacturers, including discussions with Roy Fedden at Filton, to (in his own words) 'have a quiet talk so that each of them could show me their existing facilities and explain their production situation'. He realised that there was no way that the Expansion Scheme could be implemented within the 21-month time-scale using the Air Ministry's existing time-consuming methods of ordering, where it took several years to advance a new type from prototype to production status so that they were almost obsolete before entering squadron service. Clearly drastic and fundamental improvements were needed, so he made the revolutionary recommendation that the decision to order some urgently needed types into production should be made 'from a careful study of competitive designs and information and not on the test results of a variety of prototypes'. He advised the Minister that 'the technique of aircraft design and the capacity of the technical side of the industry has reached a stage at which the actual performance and qualities of design can be accurately predicted from the design.' This drastic step of ordering large-scale production direct from designs and drawings on paper, and the designer's calculations, without the lengthy wait for physical prototypes to be built and tested, was about to be taken for the first time.

The Type 142 running up its port Mercury at Filton; the drag-producing 'apron' wheel fairings were later reduced in size.

The Type 142 on its final approach to Filton, showing the large area of extended flaps that ran from aileron to fuselage on either side.

As the 142 and 143 were both Private Venture prototypes, and not built under Air Ministry contracts, Bristol was left free to negotiate sales of either civil or military versions of each type to friendly foreign governments. To this end, a fuselage of the 143 had been exhibited at the Paris Aero Salon in November 1934, where it created considerable interest. However, no Operational Requirement for a fast Medium Bomber had been contemplated, yet alone raised, by the Air Staff, and no specification had been issued – not even one remotely similar. Finland was the first country to express interest in a multi-purpose military version of the 143, because its fuselage was roomier than the 142, and Barnwell submitted details of the Type 143F. This would, like the 142, have Mercury rather than Aquila engines, and was adaptable to a variety of transport and military uses – one version had two forward-firing 20mm Madsen cannon, and several had a free-mounting for a Lewis machine-gun in the dorsal position. Negotiations started in February 1935, a couple of months before the 142 flew, and were for a prototype 143F and nine production machines, with a possibility of licensed manufacture later. The 143 was completed by the end of 1935, but was awaiting type approval of its new Aquila engines, which were being endurance-tested in a Bulldog, so was unable to make its first flight until January 1936, by which time it had literally been left standing by the 142.

The 143 running up her Aquilas early in 1936 – note the smaller diameter of the sleeve-valve Aquila compared with the poppet-valve Mercury of the 142. The Finnish Air Force expressed an interest in a military version of the 143.

For by May 1935 RAF interest in a military version of the 142 had been aroused, and any thoughts of producing either type for the civil market were swept away by rapidly unfolding events. The Resident Technical Officer of the Air Ministry at Bristol had witnessed all the euphoria surrounding the 142 and had heard the outstanding performance being talked about excitedly in the Officer's Mess of RAF Filton, on the north side of the company airfield, so he alerted his superiors. Meanwhile, the Air Minister had received and acted on the strong recommendation of Lord Weir in a memo that called for an immediate report on 'the private-venture civil machine designed by Bristol and built for Lord Rothermere'. Weir's memo concluded that 'if the report is satisfactory it might be wise to make two or three sets of jigs and tools for this type'. The CAS, Sir Edward Ellington, responded, '...I agree that the Bristol twin should be considered as a medium bomber if Bristols have a reasonable proposition to put forward for the supply of this type in reasonable numbers. In this connection I suggest that we should offer to test the aircraft made for Lord Rothermere at Martlesham free of charge in order to ascertain its performance and characteristics. This offer should be made to the Company and they should obtain the assent of Lord Rothermere if such is necessary.' The Air Staff reacted rapidly and, as suggested, offered to test the aircraft at the RAF Aeroplane & Armaments Experimental Establishment at Martlesham Heath.

Although strictly a civil aircraft, the Bristol 142 was freely – but very prematurely – referred to as 'The Rothermere Bomber', as in captions to these 1935 pictures in Aeroplane.

["Aeroplane" photogra

HOW THE ROTHERMERE BOMBER REALLY LOOKS.—The Bristol 142 (two 645 h.p. Bristol Mercuries) seen in side and front elevation, with undercarriage up and down.

From executive civil transport to armed military bomber

On 29 May Barnwell submitted proposals for a military conversion of 'Britain First', reverting to supercharged Aquila engines. He estimated a top speed of 262mph at 15,000 feet at an all-up weight of 9,600lb, which included a bomb-load of 1,000lb and a two-man crew, with a range of 1,000 miles. Roy Fedden, ever the visionary, was looking ahead and considered the new sleeve-valve Aquila to be preferable to the pushrod poppet-valve

Mercury – a developed version of the Jupiter that had been designed during the First World War. He argued that the 500hp Aquila was considerably smaller, lighter and more economical than the 650hp Mercury, so the aircraft would need less power for a given performance, and less fuel capacity for a given range. He pointed out that the neat Aquila was at the beginning of its development process, whereas the Mercury was nearing the end. He knew that Lord Rothermere had been unwilling to wait for the new Aquila, but persuaded Frank Barnwell to recommend it to the Air Ministry, as his Engines Department was working flat out to improve it. One major difficulty was that each of the early sleeve-valve engines had been hand-assembled, with their cylinder bores, valve-sleeves and pistons meticulously mated and lapped in together to critical tolerances, a process that simply could not be repeated for mass production with the materials then available. Another serious snag was that there was no variable-pitch propeller available in a size to suit the Aquila.

Barnwell carried out a further series of weight/power/drag calculations and on 20 June submitted a revised proposal, estimating that the military 142 with Mercury VI engines, an all-up weight of 10,400lb for the same range, crew and 1,000lb bomb-load, would have a top speed of 278mph. This was at a time when the front-line RAF Fighter Force comprised eight squadrons of the Bristol Bulldog IIAs with a top speed of 174mph, three squadrons of Hawker Fury Is, which could reach 207mph – both single-seat interceptors – and three squadrons of the 182mph Hawker Demon two-seater fighters.

Lord Rothermere 'blows the trumpet' for 'Britain First' in the Daily Mail.

"BRITAIN FIRST" ASTONISHES AIR OFFICIALS

Original caption reads THE REMARKABLE SPEED of Britain First- generally known as the Rothermere Bomber- has just been demonstrated in a novel and convincing way. This machine, seen above, was built by the Bristol Aeroplane Company to the specifications of Viscount Rothermere and presented by him to the Royal Air Force on behalf of 'The Daily Mail,' so that this country should possess a fast weight-carrying 'plane out-rivalling those of the United States, Germany, France and Italy. Having to meet important officials at an aerodrome 50 miles distant, the pilot of Britain First telephoned to inquire the time of the conference. He was told it was due to begin in 15 minutes- and was severely taken to task for being so far away. Climbing into his machine he completed the journey with two minutes to spare! The machine had developed a speed of over 280 mile an hour.

By then 'Britain First' had been at Martlesham Heath for a couple of weeks for testing under Contract No 419009/35, and now carried RAF roundels and the serial number K7557. The RAF pilots quickly confirmed Uwins's findings on the outstanding performance and the excellent handling qualities. Their enthusiastic endorsement of the 142 may be better understood when it is taken into account that the A&AEE at Martlesham had only just completed flight-testing of the Boulton-Paul Overstrand, a fabric-covered fixed-undercarriage biplane Medium Bomber with twin Pegasus engines and a top speed of 148mph. As mentioned, the Overstrand was the first RAF bomber to have a power-operated gun turret – a pneumatically powered nose turret – and was developed from that company's earlier Sidestrand with Jupiter engines, which could only manage a top speed of 135mph. It was not until June 1938 that 101 Squadron started changing its Overstrands for Blenheims!

The Air Ministry preferred the Mercury-powered version of the 142 – it knew that the engine was an improvement on the Jupiter, which for ten years had been the most successful and reliable aero-engine in the world – and was reluctant to be committed to reliance on the new sleeve-valve engines for such an important programme. The Director of Technical Development of the Air Staff, Air Commodore Verney, acting on Ellington's instructions, called a design conference at the Air Ministry for 9 July 1935, where Barnwell submitted general layout drawings of the Type 142M – for Military – now a mid-wing aircraft with an internal bomb bay below the centre of gravity and a retractable dorsal turret. He accompanied his drawings with the following explanatory note:

> 'This machine is a direct development of the Bristol Type 142 twin-engined high-speed transport monoplane. The major alterations in design are as follows: A Browning gun and bomber's station have been accommodated in the nose of the body. The wings, complete with engine nacelles and undercarriages, have been raised about 16 inches. This allows for internal bomb-storage inside the body and below the wing spars; it also makes the machine practically a "middle-wing" instead of a "low-wing" monoplane, which should if anything be an aerodynamic advantage. An enclosed rear-gunner's turret, of partially retractable type, is fitted into the body aft of the trailing edge of the wing and projects through the top of the body. The tailplane and elevators have been raised by about 8 inches and are of increased span. The tailplane has been altered from "adjustable" to "fixed" type, hence the elevators have been increased somewhat in chord also and have been fitted with tabs (operable in flight by the pilot) to afford pitching trim. As a result the stiffness and strength of the body-with-tail anchorage have been somewhat improved and there are gains in cleanness and mechanical simplicity. The structure has now been increased in strength as requisite to allow for the increased weight and for the higher load factors. All the passengers' fittings, doors and windows have, of course, been deleted. In all other respects, 142M is of the same overall design as 142, and is of the same structural design except where obvious minor improvements are possible as a result of experience in building and testing 142.'

The Air Ministry accepted this proposal without alteration and raised Specification 28/35D for a development aircraft so that detail design and the construction of a prototype could commence. This was a rare specification as it did not follow on from an earlier Operational Requirement, but OR 26 for a 'Medium Bomber conversion of the Bristol Type 142 to Specification 28/35' was issued later to cover it.

Lord Rothermere had rammed home his public and patriotic message and, as soon as he learned that the RAF was interested in a military conversion and wished to keep 'Britain First' at Martlesham for further testing and evaluation as a potential bomber, he made the magnanimous and unprecedented gesture of presenting his private aircraft to the Air Council. His views on the necessity for re-armament and the urgent need to modernise the equipment of the RAF were well known, so he offered it as a 'peace gift to the nation', saying that 'a Britain well armed is the best guarantee of peace'. The 142M was given the green light by Lord Weir to bypass completely the protracted Air Ministry procurement procedures. In this case the Air Ministry was presented with a completed and very advanced prototype aircraft, which had publicly demonstrated its high performance. The saving of these years from the usual sluggish and convoluted methods of ordering new aircraft for the RAF was to prove crucial only five years later.

Ian Blair gives scale to 'Britain First'. He had a remarkable Air Force service on Blenheims: as an airman armourer he qualified first as a WOp/Ag, then as an Observer, winning the DFM when he took over the controls from his pilot, who was killed in action (see the photograph in Chapter 22). He later trained as a Pilot and gained his wings – the only airman qualified to man all three crew positions in a Blenheim!

Even while the tests of 'Britain First' were creating such an impression at Martlesham, and these decisions were being made to provide the future equipment for the RAF, the obsolescence of its present equipment was being paraded before the King at the Jubilee Review. On 7 July 1935 – wearing RAF uniform for the first time – HM King George V, with Queen Mary and their sons David, Prince of Wales, and 'Bertie', Duke of York, both future Kings, inspected serried ranks of 350 biplanes at Mildenhall from an open Rolls-Royce, then watched some of them fly past in serene formation at Duxford: 20 huge Handley-Page Heyford bombers at 98mph, a formation of 54 Hawker Harts at 110mph, and 81 mixed fighters at 115mph. All were fabric-covered fixed-undercarriage biplanes, as was the new Gloster Gauntlet, which had a maximum speed of 230mph but did not take part as it was not yet in squadron service.

In Germany the *Reichs Luftfahrt Ministerium* (RLM) also took notice of all the fuss over 'Britain First', and in August 1935 it issued a requirement for a *Schnellbomber* – a twin-engined all-metal 300mph 'fast bomber' with a crew of three. Junkers engaged two designers who had gained experience in stressed-skin construction in America, Alfred Gassner and Will Evers, to work on the project, and in May 1936 the Junkers EF.59 flew for the first time. This was developed into the prototype of the Ju.88, which first flew in December 1936 and was destined to become the most successful and versatile of all German wartime bombers. The prototype of the Ju.87 single-engined dive-bomber – the infamous *Stuka* – had first flown in 1935 (with a Rolls-Royce Kestrel engine!) but it crashed, and the more familiar version with a Jumo engine flew for the first time later that year and was in full production in 1936. (Incidentally, *Stuka* is a shortened version of *Sturzkampfflugzug*, the German generic term for dive-bombers, but became synonymous with the gull-winged Ju.87.) Of even more ominous portent to future Blenheim crews was the first flight in September 1935 of the all-metal monocoque Messerschmitt Bf.109-A – also with a Rolls-Royce Kestrel engine. By January 1936 the Bf.109-B had the Jumo engine and a licence-built American Hamilton variable-pitch propeller, and the 109-D and -E with the Daimler-Benz V12 engines were soon gaining vital operational experience with the 'Condor Legion' in Spain. The 109 *'Emil'* became the RAF's principal adversary during the Battles of France and Britain.

The tests of the 142, which had exceeded 300mph at Martlesham, were interrupted on 17 July 1935 when the undercarriage failed to lock down and the aircraft was quite badly damaged and had to be returned to Filton for major repairs. The Bristol engineers took the opportunity to improve the 'apron' undercarriage fairings and replace the Palmer wheels with Dunlop wheels and brakes. RAF Martlesham was literally a heath, and a very hard and uneven one too, causing many prototype aircraft being tested there to experience problems with their undercarriages.

However, by the middle of August the Air Ministry was convinced by the favourable reports on the tests of the civil 142, and had received corroboration of the outstanding performance. As the Ministry was no longer required to wait for the customary construction and testing of a military prototype, on 22 August 1935 it was able to take for the first time the revolutionary step of ordering 150 production examples of the 142M conversion 'straight from the drawing-board'. The official A&AEE Report on the Bristol 142, No 677, was submitted to the Air Ministry in September and confirmed its favourable findings.

Whereas the meeting of members of the Air Council held in November 1934 to consider 'The Order of Priority for 1935' made no mention at all of a twin-engined Medium Bomber, the next of these annual meetings for the same purpose held in November 1935 to determine 'The Order of Priority for 1936' had this type right at the top of the list as 'Further development on the lines of Bristol 142'. Their proposed deployment over the following years listed '18 Squadrons of Bristol 28/35 Medium Bombers in service during 1937/38'.

The Bristol Blenheim, although not yet christened as such, had been born.

BRISTOL TYPE 142 ("BRITAIN FIRST")

GENERAL CATEGORY AND TYPE

Twin-engined commercial aeroplane.

This aeroplane was originally designed as a commercial type with "Bristol" sleeve-valve engines, but was modified and fitted with "Bristol" Mercury engines, which made it the fastest aeroplane of its kind in the world.

ENGINES

Two "Bristol" Mercury engines, VI s 645 h.p. each, at 15,000 feet.

ACCOMMODATION

Originally designed as a ten-seater (pilot and navigator and eight passengers). Actually this particular aeroplane is a six-seater, the pilot's compartment being in the nose, with two seats for two pilots with dual controls.

OVERALL DIMENSIONS

Length	39 ft. 10 in.
Span	56 ft.
Height	12 ft. 2 in.

UNDERCARRIAGE

Retractable, hydraulically-operated, fitted with hydraulic brakes.

AILERONS

"Bristol-Frise" ailerons; massed-balanced. Split trailing-edge flaps.

WINGS

Low-wing all-metal stressed-skin monoplane, designed for high-speed transport of passengers, freight or mail.

FUSELAGE, Etc.

Monocoque construction. Body, wings, tail plane and fin are all entirely of metal construction with metal covering.

Two Data Sheets published by Aero Engineering in 1936.

"BRISTOL" BLENHEIM BOMBER

GENERAL CATEGORY AND TYPE

Twin-engined high-performance medium-bomber aeroplane.

The "Bristol" Blenheim Bomber (Type 142M) is a military version of the "Bristol" Type 142 all-metal low-wing monoplane, fitted with two "Bristol" Mercury engines, which was built for Lord Rothermere and presented by him to the nation in 1935 as the fastest aeroplane of its class in the world ("Britain First"). The following is the only information which is available for publication at the present time.

POWER PLANT

Two "Bristol" Mercury VIII air-cooled radial engines.

ACCOMMODATION

Three, as a bomber.

OVERALL DIMENSIONS

Length	39 ft. 9 in.
Span	56 ft. 6 in.
Height	9 ft. 9 in.

WINGS

Mid-wing monoplane, all-metal construction, with hydraulically-operated retractable undercarriage and split trailing-edge flaps.

FUSELAGE

Monocoque, all-metal, stressed-skin construction.

Chapter 4

The pace quickens

Into production

The order for 150 of the Type 142M transformed the Bristol works at Filton into an extraordinary hive of activity, not only for the rest of 1935 but also throughout 1936 and onwards. This order from the Air Ministry, Contract 43506/35, was accompanied by an 'Instruction to Proceed' authorising the ordering and purchase of long-term items and sufficient materials for a further 450 aircraft. The demand for 600 bombers was without precedent in peacetime and marked a complete sea-change for Filton, not only in the advanced nature of the product itself but also because the new type required entirely different methods of production. Indeed, the airframe and engine factories, stores, design offices, development and testing facilities all commenced a period of unrelenting and unprecedented expansion and modernisation that continued without let-up right into the war. The last dozen Bulldog biplanes, a type first flown back in 1927, left the Filton lines and were delivered between March and May 1935, even as the Type 142 'Britain First' was making its sensational appearance. The batch of 85 Audax biplanes built as sub-contractors for Hawker, mentioned earlier, was built between July and November 1936, long after the 142M prototype had flown and while production clearance was awaited on the Blenheim, as the 142M would be named by then. Now it was necessary to introduce a completely new type of construction to supplant the old-fashioned methods that had been used for many years to build these tubular-framed, fabric-covered, fixed-undercarriage, open-cockpit biplanes.

On 1 August 1935 Leslie Frise circulated a memo to the design and drawing office staff giving some details of how this was to be done. The most important feature was breaking the aircraft down into 15 major sections that could be manufactured on separate jigs placed in different parts of the factory, each providing ready access for the operatives, the separate

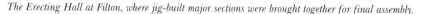

The Erecting Hall at Filton, where jig-built major sections were brought together for final assembly.

sections then being brought together and assembled on production lines into complete aircraft. For example, the fuselage was split into three sections, nose/cockpit, main fuselage and rear fuselage, as was the wing, into centre plane, and port and starboard outer wings. This method, now universal but then innovative, also facilitated easier repair and transport of the jig-built interchangeable major airframe sections when the aircraft was in service. The operatives also had to learn a range of new skills in working with alloy sheets – cutting, pressing, folding, rolling, shaping, welding and riveting.

On the airframe side, new buildings were constructed to cater for the series production of the 142M – the largest aircraft to be built in any numbers at Filton up to that time. The already cavernous Erecting Shop, little altered since 1916, was doubled in size and given direct access to the airfield perimeter road. The tool-rooms and machine-shops were greatly extended and re-equipped with the latest and best machinery, so that they could re-tool the factory for the new airframe. The construction of accurate jigs for all the main airframe sections and components was commenced. A large new shop was built solely for the construction of the wings; extensive anodising, cadmium-plating and nickel-plating plants were added, together with an enormous new metal stores for the many tons of Alclad alloy sheets in different gauges needed for the stressed skins. A massive Press Shop was built and equipped with the latest power-presses and drop-hammers. New buildings for the Experimental, Flight Production and Assembly Departments were built, and another wind-tunnel. An impressive new cellulose paint-spraying shop was constructed in place of the old fabric and doping shops. An extensive department was created to design, develop and manufacture the new hydraulic systems and the engine-driven pumps for the operation of the undercarriage and flaps, as well as the hydraulically operated gun turret – this new department later became a complete Armaments Division.

Pairs of power-plants, on their mounting frames, complete with all ancillaries, are lowered into position on twin hoists; there are some centre-sections in the right background.

Clearly, many more facilities for the production and testing of Mercury engines on an even larger scale were also needed, and the provision of these was soon under way. A new 200,000sq ft engine factory was built across the Gloucester Road at Patchway, with two further extensions of similar size planned. Vast machine-shops were equipped with lines of the latest machine-tools, and the engine experimental and development departments were enlarged, as were the Engine Division's drawing offices, laboratories, and the installation department. The PTR (Physical Testing Research) Lab became larger than the previous Engine Lab. A whole row of new engine-testing buildings was constructed and equipped, including a Heenan & Froude Dynamometer in each bay to measure the output of every engine built. A separate new plant, called the Rodney Works, was built specially to produce engine cowlings and exhaust systems. It is interesting to note that in April 1935 the Bristol Airframes Division employed 1,416 and the Engines Division almost twice as many, at 2,695.

The extra capital required for this massive expansion was raised by changing the company on 15 June 1935 from the private concern of the White family into a public limited liability company with a share capital of £1.2 million (more than £50 million at today's values). New Filton House, an impressive modern headquarters building with a stylised 'Britain First' and a Mercury engine both carved into the stone facade, was built fronting the Gloucester Road and opened in April 1936; it replaced the original 'Old' Filton House, a converted private residence that had been in use by the company since 1910. George White, the son and heir of Sir G. Stanley White, was appointed Works Director, with Harry Pollard as Works Manager. The design offices were moved and enlarged; Archie Russell was put in charge of a new Technical Office group to cover stressing, aerodynamics and weight estimation, together with the development and testing of airframe structures. The related drawing offices were also extended, and many talented graduates engaged to man them. By September 1935 Bristol's drawing office staff (for airframe and engine divisions) had grown to a total of 338 – this compares with 234 at Shorts, 176 at Vickers, 161 at Armstrong-Whitworth, 114 at Avro, and 104 at Handley-Page at the same date (source: Weir Papers 19/23A).

New Filton House, opened in 1936 with white stylised stone reliefs of 'Britain First' and Mercury, which also featured in coloured glass on the main staircase and window.

The shortage of suitably qualified draughtsmen restricted the expansion of several aircraft manufactures, as did the shortage of trained machine-tool operators. During the frantic second half of 1935, the skilled labour force of 4,200 at Filton was doubled to 8,233, having already doubled from a total of only 2,005 in October 1933, and was to double again to an amazing 16,542 by October 1939! These figures demonstrate the scale of the rapid recruitment and intensive training of the large numbers of highly specialist engineers required.

The 142M was not the only type that demanded the attentions of the staff in the design and drawing offices, the experimental assembly shop and the flight sheds during this hectic period. Its sister, the Type 143, was completed by November 1935, but could not be flight-tested until 20 January 1936 when its new Aquila engines were finally granted type approval.

The last two single-engined Bristol monoplanes were built in 1937; both were all-metal monocoques with retractable undercarriages and flaps and powered by Mercury engines.

The Type 146, an eight-gun fighter to specification F5/35, was designed for the Perseus sleeve-valve engine, but this was not ready, so the neat 146, which pioneered the sliding 'bubble' cockpit canopy, was tested with a Mercury; however, it was damaged in an accident and the design was then abandoned as the Hurricane and Spitfire were by then in production. The Type 148 was a two-seater Army Co-operation aircraft to A39/34, although it had a wide speed range of 62 to 255mph; the production contract was awarded to the Westland Lysander and the two prototype 148s were retained by Bristol as engine test-beds for the Perseus and Taurus sleeve-valve units. These engines were needed for the new Bristol Type 152 Beaufort, the design for which was submitted by Frank Barnwell in April 1936 to Specification 10/36 for a General Reconnaissance and Torpedo Bomber, and was first ordered in September 1936 – more than two years before the first prototype flew. This aircraft, a 'beefed-up' and re-engined Blenheim, was involved intimately with the Bristol Type 149 Blenheim IV, and led via the 153A directly to the Type 156 Beaufighter – a relationship to be examined later.

In September 1935 the Air Ministry expressed concern lest the mid-wing of the 142M, by passing through the centre of the monocoque main fuselage, would weaken it in the most highly stressed area compared with the 142, where the fuselage was mounted on top of the wing. The Bristol design team assured the Ministry that calculations showed that the addition of a substantial keel plate in the centre of the bomb bay beneath the wing would result in a fuselage structure even stronger in beam than the low-wing layout of 'Britain First'. The designers resolved the problems caused where other openings such as hatches and the turret aperture compromised the integrity of the monocoque by providing specially strengthened frames and stringers around them. Few other design changes were made to Barnwell's submission of 9 July 1935: the 'Browning machine-gun' was moved from 'the nose of the body' to the port outer-wing and became a Vickers; 'ball-bearing' main wheels with larger brake drums and heavy-duty tyres were adopted; the tail-wheel was made retractable; and crew entry hatches were provided above the cockpit and rear fuselage. Unfortunately a general strengthening of the structure to cater for increased loads also increased the weight of the airframe, with consequent reduction in the expected performance.

After the trials at Martlesham Heath, 'Britain First', now Air Ministry property and still in its polished alloy finish, marked with RAF Roundels and the serial K 7557, went to the RAE at Farnborough in April 1936 for further tests, then (after another spell at Filton) to 24 Squadron in November and 101 Squadron in December 1936 for trials by service pilots. It is not recorded if Lord Rothermere ever flew in his pride and joy – certainly the *Daily Mail* was unable to use it for the purposes for which it had, ostensibly, been purchased. This historically important aircraft returned to the RAE in April 1937 and continued flying, mainly on experimental work with radio and radar equipment, until 1942, when it was damaged by an enemy bomb and became an instructional airframe, being finally scrapped in 1944.

Medium Bombers the core of RAF expansion

In November 1935 the Air Staff submitted Expansion Scheme F (Schemes D and E had not been put forward), which aimed to increase the RAF to a total of 2,204 front-line aircraft by March 1939; no fewer than 1,022 of these would be bombers, while the number of fighters, at 420, remained the same as Scheme C of March 1935. Revealing the pivotal importance of the Blenheim as the core of Scheme F – the only Scheme that was actually completed – was the fact that, whereas the number of fighters stayed constant, as did the number of Heavy Bombers at 240, the number of Medium Bombers, as the Blenheim was then classified, would be more than trebled from 216 to 750. Also, for the first time, Scheme F provided for adequate reserves in excess of double the first-line strength; whereas Scheme C meant producing 3,800 new aircraft in two years, F called for no fewer than 8,000 new aircraft to be built in three years! It also called for rapid increases in aerodrome construction, training facilities, personnel, and the production of munitions – especially guns and bombs for the aircraft, plus anti-aircraft guns and searchlights. Although Scheme C had been largely

A sad end for an historic aircraft – camouflaged K7557 'Britain First' being dismantled in 1944 after years of use for radio trials, communications, and as ground instructional airframe 2211M. She was scrapped by Morris Motors.

political 'window dressing' in response to Hitler's claim that Germany had achieved 'air parity', Scheme F demonstrated that this country was deadly serious about re-arming in general and modernising and re-equipping the Air Force in particular. This complete change of attitude in only seven months was brought about not only by the Air Staff realising that a war with Germany was inevitable, but also by a change of Government, together with the change of Air Minister from Londonderry to Swinton, and also by the down-to-earth practicality of Lord Weir, who convinced the Cabinet that nothing less than this scheme would suffice. Although expenditure on the RAF virtually doubled from £9.9 million in 1935 to £18.6 million in 1936, and more than doubled again to £39.3 million in 1937, it had always lagged well behind expenditure on the Royal Navy, not overtaking this until 1938 and 1939 when UK aircraft production increased under the impetus of impending war from fewer than 3,000 to almost 8,000 annually.

The Air Staff, in full agreement with Swinton and Weir, were aware that the Light Bombers in production in 1935 – variants of the single-engined Hawker Hart and Hind family of open-cockpit biplanes – were already obsolescent, but due to their simple construction, production could be expanded rapidly and inexpensively in 1936 so that they would provide a useful interim type – indeed, they were sometimes referred to as the 'interim bomber' in Air Ministry documents. They were descended directly from the two-seat Light Bombers of the First World War; being only able to carry 500lb of bombs to a target 250 miles away at around 150mph, they could be of very limited tactical use in European warfare. Nevertheless, they helped the industry to expand its capacity and labour force, while also providing an effective aircraft in the training role for the new squadrons and the growing number of pilots, observers and air-gunners, prior to the introduction into service of the new generation of monoplane Light and Medium Bombers.

Their replacement was the first RAF production aircraft to use the new Rolls-Royce V12 Merlin engine – the Fairey Battle. The clean-looking Battle was based on a tubular frame with a semi-monocoque rear fuselage and built to P.27/32, which was a very advanced specification for that time. Bristol had proposed its Type 136, a two-seat day bomber with a Perseus sleeve-valve engine, but it was not adopted. Marcel Lobelle, the Chief Designer at Fairey, refined his original design following a visit to America in 1934, and the prototype Battle first flew in March 1936, four years after the specification was issued. It went to the A&AEE at Martlesham Heath in October, but a further year elapsed before the first production aircraft (to P.23/35) was ready to fly, even though Fairey was given priority on the supply of Merlin engines. This decision delayed the production of the Hawker Hurricane, which we now know to be a far more important aircraft. Large orders for Battles were placed as the Air Staff endorsed Trenchard's vision of 'swarms of light-bombers, fast and almost impossible to intercept'. A further 900 Battles were ordered in 1936, even though it was apparent by then that the gap between fighter and Light Bomber performance had widened to the degree that interception became not only possible but most probable. Battles could carry 1,000lb of bombs for 1,000 miles (that is to a target within 500 miles) at around 200mph, and were all-metal monoplanes with a retractable undercarriage, so they appeared to be a great improvement on the Hind, but their defensive armament had not improved at all from their First World War ancestors. They were still far too slow, cumbersome and vulnerable, thus completely obsolete by the time war broke out – facts well known to the Air Staff. However, aircraft production lines cannot be turned on and off like a tap, so, despite these dangerous shortcomings, Battles continued to be produced in large numbers until well into the war. No fewer than 2,185 of these virtually useless aircraft were built for the RAF – an expensive, even wasteful, use of manufacturing resources and valuable Merlin engines, and, when the real war started, tragically expensive and wasteful of the precious lives of their crews too.

In March 1936 the name 'Blenheim' was chosen for the Bristol Type 142M, the RAF's new Medium Bomber being named after the great palace and estate near Woodstock that was given by a grateful Queen Anne to the First Duke of Marlborough following his famous victory in 1704 over the French at the small Bavarian village of Blindheim near the Danube – anglicised as Blenheim. Marlborough was an ancestor of Winston Churchill, who was born at Blenheim Palace.

Throughout 1936 Churchill was still pressing for re-armament, and without success asked for a defence debate in secret session at Parliament, but he did arrange a most unusual and special meeting with the Prime Minister, and was received by Baldwin, Lord Halifax and Sir Thomas Inskip on 28 July. Churchill's high-powered entourage included Lord Salisbury and MRAF Viscount Trenchard, and they tried to galvanise the Government into action. Churchill's peroration concluded: 'We must increase the development of our air-power in priority over every other consideration... We must accelerate and simplify our aeroplane production and push it to the largest scale... The months slip by rapidly. If we delay too long in repairing our defences we may be forbidden by superior power to complete the process.' Trenchard backed Churchill's message in his usual forceful style, but the delegation received no response until November. This was partly because Inskip, a previous Solicitor-General and Attorney-General, appointed in March to the newly created post of Minister for the Co-ordination of Defence, was casting his cold and critical legal eye over such demands. Churchill became increasingly restive at this delay, Swinton and Weir were disturbed but continued to work hard to expedite the re-equipment of the RAF, while senior Air Staff members, especially Wilfrid Freeman, the new Air Member for Research and Development, were alarmed at the delay and pressed their claims even harder. Meanwhile, outside these 'corridors of power', the Rothermere newspapers continued their vociferous press campaign.

The first Blenheims fly

The initial production batch of Blenheims, with factory sequence numbers 7986 to 8135, were allocated the RAF serials K7033 to K7182. Thus K7033, as the first of these to be built – only 10 months after receipt of the initial order – became in effect the prototype Blenheim. She was wheeled out proudly for photographs early in June 1936, looking sleek yet purposeful, resplendent in polished alloy, and devoid of markings. The absence of the 142's cabin windows and entrance door, together with the raising of the wing to the mid-wing position, made the Blenheim fuselage appear far slimmer than the 142, although they were the same height. The dorsal turret was not ready, so the first Blenheim had a neat cupola set in the fully retracted position, offering less drag than the production turret. No service equipment was fitted at this stage. She flew for the first time on 25 June 1936 in the hands of Cyril Uwins, to the cheers of large numbers of the workforce who had got wind of the imminent maiden flight. The next day a large number '5' was painted on the rear fuselage, as it was intended to show the ultra-modern

K7033 'wheeled out proudly for photographs in June 1936, looking sleek yet purposeful, resplendent in polished alloy, and devoid of markings'.

Blenheim alongside other exciting newcomers in the New Types Park at the imminent RAF Pageant at Hendon – but this was not possible, for reasons soon to be explained, and 'Britain First' was substituted and shown at Hendon with the '5' hastily applied.

It is interesting to note the quite exceptional array of important new prototypes that were displayed statically with the Bristol 142 at the RAF Pageant on 26 June 1936. They were the Vickers Type 271, which became the Wellington, the Handley-Page HP52 Hampden (both to specification B.9/32), the Armstrong-Whitworth AW38 Whitley to B.3/34 – these four types were twin-engined bombers – the Fairey P.27/32 Battle mentioned above, the Vickers Type 281 Wellesley, a long-range Light Bomber with a single Pegasus engine, the Westland Lysander, the Vickers Venom (with Bristol Aquila engine), the Hawker 'Interceptor Monoplane' – named Hurricane that very day – and the pale blue Supermarine Type 300, the very first Spitfire. Six of these new types had Bristol radial engines and three the new Rolls-Royce Merlin. All except the Venom were to be produced in very large numbers during the expansion schemes, and were to prove of great significance to the future of the RAF. It will be noted that these comprised six Bomber types, one Army Co-operation type, and two Fighter types, which confirms the predominant position occupied by the bomber vis-à-vis the fighter in contemporary Air Staff requirements for re-equipping and modernising the RAF. Three days later Cyril Uwins displayed 'Britain First' at the SBAC Show at Hatfield – one report referred to it as 'the RAF's Rothermere'!

Significant developments were also taking place in 1936 regarding new bomber aircraft for the Luftwaffe. Apart from the Ju.88, the German Chief of the Air Staff, General Wever, had authorised construction of two four-engined strategic bombers, the Junkers Ju.89 and the Dornier Do.19. These were known as the 'Ural Bombers', as they had the range to bomb targets beyond the Ural Mountains should Russia evacuate her arms factories there. But Wever was killed in an aircraft accident and was succeeded by Kesselring, who believed that aircraft would be best employed to give direct support to the Wehrmacht; he was supported

Rare picture of K7033, the Blenheim prototype, marked No 5 ready for display at the Hendon Pageant. However, the incident described in the text prevented this, and K7557 'Britain First' was sent instead – seen here wearing No 5 at Hendon.

New Types Park at Hendon in June 1936 – 'the quite exceptional array of important new prototypes'. Out of picture to the left is No 1, the Hawker Hurricane, No 2, the Supermarine Spitfire, No 3, the Vickers Venom, No 4, the Fairey Battle, No 5, the Bristol 142 'Britain First', No 6, the Armstrong Whitworth Whitley, No 7, the Vickers Wellington (lost in a crash), and No 8, the Handley-Page Hampden. Facing the airfield is the Westland Lysander, with the Vickers Wellesley hidden by tents. All were placed into quantity production (bar the Aquila-engined Venom) and formed collectively the equipment with which the RAF went to war.

by *Reichsmarschall* Hermann Goering, head of the Luftwaffe, who preferred the far larger numbers of single or twin-engined tactical warplanes that could be obtained for the same expenditure. So Germany dropped the development of strategic bombers, while the RAF issued Operational Requirements Nos 40 and 41 in 1936 for four-engined Heavy Bombers. The Air Staff had calculated that at least 4,000hp would be required to give the proposed bombers the lifting capacity, cruising speed and range they were looking for, and their foresight resulted in the Short Stirling, the Handley-Page Halifax and the Avro Manchester – sire of the Lancaster. The Luftwaffe was to have no equivalent Heavy Bombers.

Frank Barnwell showed considerable foresight too, for in December 1935 – after the initial order for 150 was received, but before the prototype 142M flew in June 1936 – Bristol submitted a design for a four-engined 'big brother' to the Type 142M. This design incorporated all the lessons learned concerning drag and performance plus structure weight, stiffness and construction methods during the wind-tunnel and flight-tests of 'Britain First'. Barnwell and Archie Russell were able to calculate the weights and strength of the new structure accurately as it was an enlarged version of the 142M. They scaled up the 142M structure, areas and profiles proportionally, but using flush instead of mushroom rivets for the stressed skins to further reduce drag over the greater swept areas. The proposed high-speed bomber had retractable dorsal and ventral turrets, with a crew of four, a 4,000lb bomb-load, and a speed of 275mph with four Mercury engines in 142M nacelles, or 300mph with four Taurus sleeve-valve engines, for a range of 2,000 miles. They considered the design just as great an advance over its contemporaries as 'Britain First' had been, as it comfortably exceeded the demands of the then current specification B.1/35, which called for a 2,000lb bomb-load at a cruising speed of 195mph for a range of 1,500 miles – the specification that produced the Vickers Type 248 Warwick four years later. Airspeed tendered a design with four Bristol Aquila engines, but it was not accepted; neither, however, was the advanced 'super Blenheim' proposal from Filton, although Bristol was requested later to tender for the two 1936 four-engined Heavy Bomber specifications mentioned above.

The factory flight trials of the first Blenheim K7033 continued, and revealed very few problems indeed. There was one notable exception, which took all of Cyril Uwins' great expertise to overcome; this was a major malfunction that in other hands would probably have led to the loss of this important aircraft on only its second flight, which would have been a disaster. For when he selected 'flaps down' to start his approach to land, the port flap extended fully but the starboard flap remained retracted, causing the aircraft to yaw and roll very violently! Uwins regained control – it took almost full deflection of the ailerons just to keep level – but neither the engine-driven nor the hand-operated hydraulic pumps would budge the asymmetrically jammed flaps either up or down, so he was forced to carry out a very difficult side-slipping cross-wind landing in poor weather with no margin of control whatsoever had he not judged, with consummate skill, his approach and landing exactly. If he had abandoned or crashed the aircraft the whole Blenheim programme would have been thrown into chaos at that crucial period with incalculable results.

The aircraft was quickly towed into the flight sheds, behind closed doors, Uwins climbed out – probably to go for a stiff drink – and Harry Pollard with Archie Russell started to investigate the cause of the flap malfunction. Pollard climbed into the cockpit to operate the hydraulic hand-pump while Russell stood under the inner port wing behind the engine nacelle where, with the inspection panels removed, he could observe the operation of the flap mechanism. Pollard started pumping, and immediately there was a loud crash as the starboard undercarriage collapsed and that wing and propeller struck the floor. Russell seized the knuckles of the scissor-hinge at the point of maximum advantage on the folding bracing-rods of the port undercarriage to prevent it too from retracting and held tight until they were secured by a rope – had that side collapsed he would have been crushed beneath several tons of aircraft and almost certainly killed. Sir Stanley White appeared and instructed Pollard and Russell to repeat their actions exactly. Pollard called out once more that he was commencing pumping and did so; Sir Stanley said, 'Pollard, you've selected the undercarriage again. You've been working too hard. Take a fortnight's holiday.' But the pressure of work prevented poor Pollard from taking his holiday; indeed, all the design and drawing office staff in both the airframe and engine divisions, as well as the engineers in the engine and flight-testing departments, were kept far too busy to even think about holidays.

The fault with the flap actuation was soon rectified, but the prototype needed a new starboard outer wing and propeller, and the engine and undercarriage were stripped, inspected and rebuilt as a precaution. This work delayed completion of Bristol's own flight trials and – far worse – caused the Blenheim to miss its place in the queue of the new types shown at Hendon, which were awaiting testing by the A&AEE at Martlesham Heath. The next aircraft, K7034, from a pre-production batch of six, was completed and employed to continue the flight trials through the autumn of 1936. In November it was transported to Paris and displayed at the Grand Salon Aeronautique, creating a striking exhibit mounted in a flight attitude on trestles with the undercarriage, including the tail-wheel, retracted. It was fitted with spinners, devoid of all markings, and shown in a highly polished alloy finish. Although the cockpit was sealed, close attention was paid by the foreign Military and Air Attachés, for external inspection revealed most of the design and construction features of this important new weapon in the nation's armoury.

The flight trials and tests revealed that only a few modifications were necessary. The most important was the addition of a ring of moveable cooling gills at the rear of the engine cowlings; these could be adjusted by the pilot from the cockpit with small hand-cranks through a system of chains and sprockets to control the rate of air flow over the cylinders – and thus their temperatures – as the cooling air exited through the gap between the cowlings and the inner engine nacelles. The efficiency of the carburettor air intakes was enhanced, various propeller-spinners were tried, the exhausts were arranged to discharge

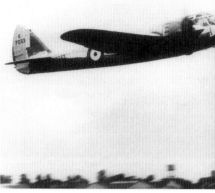

"Flight" photo.

K7033 as it appeared, still unpainted, both airborne and earthbound in a contemporary Bristol advertisement in Flight. The cooling-gill ring, spinners and retractable tail-wheel are shown; both the latter were soon discarded. The turret cupola is fully retracted and no armament is carried.

at an angle outwards, and the cockpit glazing was improved to reduce draughts and water leaks. The spinners improved the appearance, but as they had no measurable effect on performance and would increase maintenance demands, they were not adopted.

The repaired K7033 completed flight trials of only 22 flying hours and was flown to Martlesham on 22 October 1936. Four vital months had been lost. A replacement for the damaged Hamilton-Standard two-position propeller was not available, as the first pair had been specially imported and de Havilland had yet to commence licence production, so K7033 was delivered to the A&AEE with a new starboard propeller 3 inches smaller in diameter than the 10ft 9in of the original port propeller! Ballast replaced the missing operational equipment to give representative weights and centre of gravity positions for the trials. The 'go ahead' for full production could not be given until these trials were completed satisfactorily to make sure that no further modifications were required. Despite the urgency of the order, and the bottleneck of partially completed airframes building up at Filton, the Air Ministry was unable to authorise full-scale production until mid-December 1936. The only major modification decided upon was to fix the retractable tail-wheel in the 'down' position and delete the heavy system of chains, sprockets and links that provided mechanical operation as a 'slave' unit driven from the port main undercarriage. This lengthy actuating system stretched slightly in use, sometimes failing to lock the tail-wheel in either the 'up' or 'down' positions, and caused maintenance problems.

K7033 went on to the RAE at Farnborough for further tests in April 1937, and suffered the collapse of an undercarriage leg during a heavy landing there on 28 May; it had a busy life and was used for a series of trials at Filton and Farnborough right through until November 1940. After the exhibition at Paris, K7034 was fitted with full operational equipment, including a functional Bristol B1 turret with a Lewis Mk III gun, and did not arrive at Martlesham until January 1937. It too had a hard and useful life, alternating between there and Filton for various modifications and trials, mainly concerned with armament, until June 1940. The 39th aircraft of this initial production batch of 250 Mark 1 Blenheims – K7072 – was also retained by the factory for trials and in fact became the prototype for the Mark IV, as will be described later.

Two further orders for large numbers of Blenheim Mark Is to be built by Bristol at Filton were confirmed: 434 were ordered in July 1936 under contract 527111/36, soon followed by Contract 529181 for another 134, making 818 in all. Clearly the Blenheim was to feature at the central core of the urgent re-equipment with more modern aircraft intended to increase the striking power of the RAF.

The need for re-armament became more urgent as the international scene continued to deteriorate. In March 1936, three months before the first Blenheim took off, German armed forces re-occupied the Rhineland. France and Great Britain huffed and puffed but no one called Hitler's bluff. In May Mussolini's forces occupied Addis Ababa, and Italy annexed Abyssinia, as Ethiopia was then known. The *Daily Mail* continued to call for re-armament, and carried many articles by Winston Churchill on the same theme; in May 1936 Associated Newspapers published collections of these articles: 'Arming in the Air: the *Daily Mail* Campaign: Warnings of Three Wasted Years'. In July the Spanish Civil war started, the Russians supported the Republicans, but the Fascists supported Franco's Nationalists, and before long German and Italian aircraft were gaining valuable operational experience. The Berlin/Rome Axis was formed in October; Germany and Japan signed the Anti-Comintern Pact in November; and Japan recommenced her invasion of mainland China in December. While this re-alignment of the most powerful nations into their wartime alliances was taking place – with America strongly isolationist and Russia's intentions unclear – the British were pre-occupied with a constitutional crisis that led to the abdication of King Edward VIII, who gave up his throne for Wallis Simpson, an American divorcee, to be succeeded by his brother, who became King George VI.

On 8 July, before the abdication crisis, King Edward inspected his Air Force flying in his own Airspeed Envoy accompanied by his brother the Duke of York, soon to be King. They were shown round the fighter station at Northolt by ACM Sir Edward Ellington, the CAS, and watched three linked Gauntlets perform close-formation aerobatics; they then flew to Mildenhall, a bomber base, then to Wittering, a Training Station. Finally the Royal party flew to the 'experimental and development' base at Martlesham Heath where they inspected a line-

The application of camouflage makes K7033 look far more warlike.

up of all of the new types, every one of them in those pre-camouflage days immaculate in silver or polished alloy with RAF markings. They were most impressed by a short flying display put on by the two most exciting types, the Spitfire and the Blenheim. The Spitfire was demonstrated by S/Ldr Anderson, CO of the Fighter Test Flight, and the Blenheim by S/Ldr Ted Hilton, CO of the Bomber Test Flight. *Flight* magazine reported: 'The Spitfire roared past the Royal Standard at well over 300mph, followed by the Blenheim, the speed of which was a revelation of what a modern monoplane bomber can do. There seemed little to choose between them. We certainly have a bomber which can out-fly any fighter in service in the world today.' No wonder that the RAF awaited its new Blenheims with such eager enthusiasm.

The RAF re-organises for war

For the RAF, too, 1936 was a seminal year, for apart from the schemes to re-equip the force with modern aircraft, a fundamental reorganisation took place: the service was re-formed into Commands based on operational function rather than area. This new structure had a major impact throughout the service and continued in place not only for the duration of the Second World War, but also continues, in modified form, to the present day. At that stage Bomber Command was the only one of the newly created home Commands to be involved with the Bristol Blenheim, although as we will see it was to be operated later with distinction by Coastal Command, Fighter Command, Army Co-operation Command and Training Command. Indeed, Blenheims went on to become the only RAF aircraft to serve in all of the contemporary RAF Commands both at home and overseas. The RAF Volunteer Reserve was formed, and the Auxiliary Squadrons expanded, to provide the large number of trained new crews that would be needed.

The new Bomber Command, with Headquarters at High Wycombe, was formed initially into three Groups: 1 and 2 Groups, with Headquarters at Abingdon, had 17 squadrons between them – all re-equipped with Hinds except 101, which had Overstrands, and 35 and 207, which had Fairey Gordons – and 3 Group, with an HQ at Andover and equipped with 12 squadrons of ancient 'heavy' bomber biplanes, Handley-Page Heyfords and Vickers Virginias, plus a couple more (114 and 139 Squadrons) that had Hinds and were soon to transfer to 2 Group. It was intended that each Group would be equipped with one of the new bomber types that were due to enter service in 1937 and 1938: 1 Group would have Fairey Battles; 2 Group would have Bristol Blenheims; 3 Group would have Vickers Wellingtons; 4 Group would have Armstrong-Whitworth Whitleys; 5 Group would have Handley-Page Hampdens; and 6 Group would contain the 'pool squadrons', two of each type of aircraft, later becoming the Training Group. The number of squadrons per Group would vary considerably, the Light Bombers of 1 Group and the Medium Bombers of 2 Group being far larger numerically than the Heavy Bombers of the other Groups. Prior to delivery of the eagerly awaited new generation of monoplanes, nearly all the squadrons of 1 and 2 Groups, including many re-formed under the expansion scheme, were re-equipped with Hawker Hinds, which proved to be very useful 'stepping stones' to the more advanced aircraft. This process ultimately affected 30 squadrons and continued from January 1936, when Nos 21 and 34 Squadrons were re-formed, right up to August 1937, when 211 Squadron was re-formed; they did not change their Hinds for Blenheims until May 1939! Full-scale manufacture of the Blenheim commenced right at the end of 1936 and the rate of production built up steadily over the next two years.

There were important changes, too, among the highest ranks of the Royal Air Force. Sir Edward Ellington was an industrious Chief of the Air Staff from 1933 to 1937 and oversaw all the far-reaching changes in the service that took place throughout that period, and continued as Inspector General of the RAF for the following three critical years. In the vital post of Air Member for Research and Development, Hugh Dowding was replaced by the perceptive and dynamic Wilfrid Freeman. The trio of Swinton, Weir and Freeman worked together most effectively and determined the quality and quantity of the aircraft that would equip the RAF in the Second World War, also creating the industrial capacity to produce them. Most fortuitously, Dowding was appointed to head the new Fighter Command and applied his great ability to creating an effective force; he had the seniority (and expectation) to succeed Ellington as CAS, but in 1937 was leap-frogged by the AMSO, Sir Cyril Newall, who led the RAF into the war, now but two years away. Many senior officers who were to achieve distinction in the war came to the forefront during this period: the Director of Training, Air Commodore Arthur Tedder, had pushed for the creation of the RAFVR; the first AOC of 4 Group Bomber Command, then of 5 Group, then in 1942 of the whole Command, was Arthur Travers Harris; AVM Charles Portal was promoted to Director of Organisation and later Air Member for Personnel; Edgar Ludlow-Hewitt became Deputy CAS and was later AOC Bomber Command from September 1937 to April 1940; Air Commodore Sholto Douglas became Director of Staff Duties and later followed Dowding as AOC Fighter Command; and Group Captain John Slessor was appointed first as Deputy Director, then Director of Plans at the Air Ministry. Newall, Portal, Tedder and Slessor were destined to climb to the top of the tree and become Chiefs of the Air Staff; while all of these senior officers were to be involved directly with the operational deployment of Blenheims in the climactic years that followed.

The nation was re-arming belatedly but pragmatically, the aircraft industry was expanding rapidly, the Air Staff was planning for a war with Germany that it now regarded as inevitable, and the RAF was fundamentally re-organised and was being re-equipped with many new types of modern aircraft of advanced design, the bulk of which were bombers. The Bristol Blenheim was at the very heart of all of these developments.

L1515 of the second production batch gets airborne. As a 600 Squadron Mk 1-F it was shot down over Waalhaven on 10th May 1940 and the crew killed.

K7037, the first fitted with full military equipment, at Filton in February 1937 prior to delivery to 114 Squadron.

Chapter 5

Into service

Full-scale production of the Blenheim at Filton commenced in January 1937, manufacturing aircraft at the rate of four a month initially and building up to a peak of 16 a month by January 1938. However, the Air Ministry was far from satisfied at this rate of delivery and constantly pressed for improvement. Of the 330 scheduled during 1937, only 117 were actually delivered. It was an enormous order for peacetime and, despite great efforts at Filton to increase production, Bristol was hampered by a shortage of skilled labour and severe difficulties in obtaining supplies of many of the special steels and alloys it needed. The supply of the dorsal turrets, sub-contracted to the Daimler Motor Company, fell behind the rate of airframe deliveries, and Bristol made hasty arrangements to produce more at Filton.

Rows of nose and fuselage sections, ready to be mated to centre-sections and engines (background) at Filton Assembly Hall.

Completed aircraft awaiting air-test at Filton.

Each airframe contained over 80,000 separate parts, made from materials to more than 3,000 different and rigorously controlled specifications, as detailed on more than 14,000 individual blueprints. The manufacture of each airframe took some 65,000 man-hours from the highly skilled workforce, using over 600,000 rivets in the process – that was 2.5 million rivets to be drilled off and hammered home every week, so the assembly shops must have been exceptionally noisy places in which to work! Each stage of manufacture and assembly was subject to the most searching inspection procedures to ensure consistency and the interchangeability of components. The figures behind the production of each engine are even more daunting, for every Mercury incorporated

The Mercury engine in its frame mounted on front of the undercarriage frame between the wing spars, showing the wheel in its retracted position.

many different types of highly specialised steels and even more types of specialised alloys, every one of which had to be manufactured to the most demanding specifications and required a large number of exceedingly labour-intensive processes and treatments. These involved many complicated casting, forging, boring, milling, machining, treating, polishing and fitting-up procedures, every one of which had to be executed to an extreme degree of accuracy – and every process in the manufacture of each component was inspected rigidly and constantly to make sure that they did. Each completed engine was then run and 'bedded in' for several hours before being checked thoroughly at full power in the rows of testing bays – more very noisy locations!

The shadow factories

A further most important development in the British aircraft industry was taking place at this time, and another in which the Blenheim played a pivotal part. This development was initiated in 1936, grew rapidly, and was to have many major long-term effects. It was brought about mainly by the unprecedented demand in peacetime for the new generation of bombers, mainly Blenheims and Battles, and the engines to power them, in such large numbers that the existing aircraft industry simply could not cope. This lack of capacity existed despite the huge and rapid expansion of production facilities both at Filton (as described at the beginning of the previous chapter) and at a new factory that the Fairey Aviation Company had built at Stockport for Battle production – one that was twice the size of its original factory at Hayes. So a complete 'shadow' aircraft industry to manufacture both aero-engines and airframes was created and pressed into large-scale production in a remarkably short time. It was based originally on several well-established companies in the motor industry who were accustomed to the line-production of vehicles and engines in large volumes. Lord Weir had first put forward the 'shadow industry' scheme to the Chiefs of Staff Committee, under the chairmanship of Sir Maurice Hankey, back in February 1934, and the Defence Policy and Requirements Committee accepted these proposals in full in December 1935 after overcoming objections from the Treasury and the then Chancellor, Neville Chamberlain. The following month, Weir was invited to serve on this, the most powerful of all the Defence Committees – it comprised the Prime Minister, Chancellor, Foreign Secretary, Lord President, the three Service Ministers, and the President of the Board of Trade – so that the shadow industry scheme could be implemented.

It was intended originally that these Government-built shadow factories would be set up, given a short run of 50 engines to produce, then be held in reserve to be re-activated in wartime. But Swinton and Weir calculated that the existing professional aircraft industry, even in its newly enlarged form, would not be capable of meeting the demands of Expansion Scheme F in the time scale set down. Therefore it was necessary to set up the new factories so that they could commence full-scale production at the earliest practicable date.

It was decided that the Bristol Mercury engine would be the first product to be manufactured in these shadow factories. So on 13 March 1936 Lords Swinton and Weir, Air Marshal Sir Cyril Newall (then still the AMSO), together with Sir Christopher Bullock (Permanent Secretary at the Air Ministry) met Sir Stanley White and other members of a somewhat reluctant Bristol Board, who were not too keen on seeing business lost to other companies making large numbers of their engines for a mere fee. However, when the Air Minister Lord Swinton appealed on patriotic grounds, they agreed instantly. Weir confirmed that the Bristol company had been selected because of its long experience of arranging licence production of its engines in many other countries, and reminded the Board that these arrangements had been highly profitable for the company. In all 4,000 extra Mercury engines were required in addition to the greatly increased production under way at Filton (some of which went to foreign aircraft manufacturers), for apart from their use in the new Blenheims, these engines were installed in the Gloster Gladiator and the Westland Lysander, all three types being in quantity production for the RAF. On the other hand, Rolls-Royce had always avoided licensing production to other manufacturers and remained aloof when the new shadow scheme was put to it, even though the need for more Merlin engines was just as pressing. Later a large new factory was built for the company at Crewe, which it managed itself.

Hugh Dowding, still the Air Member for Research and Development at that time, was therefore authorised to set up the scheme in co-operation with Roy Fedden. The dynamic Fedden, with the support and authority of Weir, soon arranged for five car factories to each make different components of the Mercury, with a sixth to assemble and test the complete engines, all under the close supervision of Bristol, and each with resident Air Ministry Surveyors and Inspectors to keep a watching brief and to ensure constant quality control.

Seven car companies were approached: Rootes Ltd (Humber, Hillman and Sunbeam Talbot), the Austin Motor Company, Rover Cars, the Standard/Triumph Motor Company, Singer, Wolseley, and the old-established Daimler Company. Singer dropped out, while Ford and Vauxhall, both American-owned, were not invited to take part at that stage. Morris Motors, the largest UK motor manufacturer, which included Wolseley, MG and Riley, under Lord Nuffield – a powerful but awkward magnate – took part in the initial discussions, but declined to take part in these arrangements. The car companies set up a small committee, with Herbert Austin – Nuffield's principal rival – in the chair, to thrash out the details. A couple of years earlier Nuffield had resurrected the First World War aero-engine department at Wolseley, and built a special factory, but the low-powered Wolseley radials were only used in a few Airspeed Envoys and, much to his annoyance, the Air Ministry did not wish to purchase any. Nuffield offered to manufacture 2,000 complete Mercury engines, but this did not fit in with the wider Air Ministry plans, and neither did his proposal to make Pratt & Whitney radial engines under licence. He could see only that the Air Ministry was seeking urgently extra production capacity for Mercury aero-engines and that he had an almost empty factory, which he thought suitable even if they didn't. Like many magnates he was used to getting his own way, and felt frustrated and slighted when he didn't; but he failed to appreciate the wider picture. This rebuff, and the strange omission of Alvis from the discussions, had unfortunate repercussions for Swinton and Weir. Alvis had established a new facility in 1935 to produce various Gnome-Rhone radial engines, all based on Bristol designs; Fedden must have been aware of this and possibly did not approve.

Blenheims formed the core of the RAF expansion and preparation for war, and Rootes' shadow factory at Speke rapidly increased the rate of production.

The first aircraft manufactured by the British motor industry under the expansion schemes was L8362, built by Rootes in its new shadow factory.

Within months, as re-armament accelerated, additional Government-financed shadow factories were also organised to produce complete airframes, and the Blenheim and Battle were the first aircraft to be produced by this new method. Apart from a free £50,000 factory, the shadow manufacturers were to receive a management fee of £225 per Blenheim airframe and £200 per Battle, with £75 per Mercury (all at 1930s values, of course). Eventually there were 11 such shadow factories supporting the parent aircraft companies. Rootes Securities Ltd, which had been the most enthusiastic initial participant in the shadow scheme, was awarded a contract under Specification 33/36P in October 1936 for 250 complete Blenheims, and the Austin Motor Company another (32/36P) for 500 Fairey Battles, orders later increased to 1,000 of each type. Bristol supplied Rootes with complete sets of all the drawings, jigs, patterns and tools needed for manufacture, as the Air Ministry contracts stipulated that all airframe components should be completely interchangeable irrespective of which factory produced them. The economies of scale were apparent, too, for H. J. Pollard calculated that the cost to produce each Blenheim in a run of 400 aircraft was just half that of the cost per aircraft if only 25 were produced.

Ratio of bombers to fighters escalates

These shadow factory contracts were in addition to the further 450 Blenheims ordered from Bristol at Filton in 1936 (under Contracts 527111/36 and 529181/36), as were a further 500 Battles ordered from Fairey to Specification 14/36. In February 1937 A. V. Roe Ltd was instructed to build 250 Blenheims to Specification 2/37 at its new Chadderton factory under Contract 568371/36, again to drawings, jigs and tools supplied by Bristol. Avro referred to as a 'daughter' firm in the specification, went on to manufacture 1,000 Blenheims before turning to construction of its own Manchester.

If I may digress a little, this Blenheim contract provided Avro with its first experience of all-metal stressed-skin aircraft, and the company's chief designer, Roy Chadwick, appears to have studied the layout and detail design of the Blenheim structure while drawing up the Type 679 Manchester to satisfy the demands of Operational Requirement No 41, which resulted in Specification P.13/36. This called for a 275mph twin-engined Medium Bomber with a maximum bomb-load of 8,000lb, a range of 2,000 miles, and power-operated gun turrets in nose and tail, so the aircraft would clearly be far larger and heavier than the Blenheim and would need much more powerful engines. Chadwick selected the new Rolls-Royce Vulture, a 1,750hp X-24 engine based on two V-12 Kestrel cylinder banks mounted above and below a common crankshaft. However, the Vulture was under-developed due to Rolls concentrating its efforts on the Merlin, and it proved to be the Achilles' heel of the Manchester – although the Vultures gave the designed power, they were unreliable and too

THE BRISTOL BLENHEIM

heavy, which led to their replacement by four Merlins on a wider centre-section resulting in the immortal Avro Lancaster. Apart from the troublesome engines on the Manchester, both it and the Lancaster suffered several aerodynamic and structural problems during early test flights, mainly reflecting Avro's inexperience in the construction of alloy stressed-skin aircraft. Compared with the Blenheim's span of 56ft 4in, the Manchester wings were initially of 72-foot span, later increased to 80 feet, then to 90 and finally to 102 feet on the Lancaster. Both the vertical and horizontal tail surfaces also had to be enlarged considerably. In contrast, Barnwell's Blenheim design was 'right from the start' both structurally, aerodynamically and aesthetically, and needed no major alterations.

L6594, the first Avro-built Blenheim and the first-ever all-metal aircraft to be manufactured by A. V. Roe & Co, influenced the design of the Manchester and Lancaster.

Although few nowadays would recognise any link between the Blenheim and the Lancaster, the influence of the former on the latter is clearly discernible. The fundamental design of the Manchester was exactly the same as the Blenheim: a mid-wing monoplane with stressed alloy skins throughout, with wings of the same twin-main-spar construction and the same straight centre-section passing right through the middle of the fuselage, carrying the bomb-load internally beneath it, and the fuel load between the spars of both the centre and outer wing sections, similar tubular frames for the twin engines and rearwards-retracting undercarriage units mounted at the outer ends of the centre-section. Each type had all the dihedral angle on the detachable outer wings, and split flaps were fitted under the trailing edge of both centre and outer sections. The light-alloy fuselage was made in the same demountable main sections, and the stressed skins were mounted on the same type of transverse formers and longitudinal stringers that later became universal practice. Similar systems on both aircraft operated the undercarriage, flaps and turrets hydraulically, and the wheel brakes pneumatically. Apart from the greater size and weight, and the nose and tail turrets required by the specification, the main difference in layout between the two aircraft was the twin fins and rudders of the Avro designs. Incidentally, the original P.13/36 Specification called for the internal carriage of two 18-foot torpedoes, and this led to the large and unobstructed bomb bay of the Lancaster, which was to prove so useful as 4,000, 8,000 and 12,000lb bombs became available later in the war.

Anyway, back in 1937, Hawker Hind two-seater Light Bomber biplanes were still being ordered as late as 31 May, and continued in production – there were hundreds of orders still outstanding. In addition 100 Vickers Wellesley long-range bombers and 400 Hawker Henley two-seater light day bombers to Specification P.4/34 – both single-engined monoplanes – were ordered into production (although this latter order was transferred to Gloster as Hawker was busy developing and producing Hurricanes, and was later halved as Air Ministry policy changed). Also placed into full production by 1936 were the Vickers Wellington, the twin-engined big brother of the Wellesley, both with the novel geodetic alloy basket-weave framework designed by Barnes Wallis, and earlier orders for the Armstrong-Whitworth

Whitley Heavy Bomber were increased. In addition, 100 Handley-Page Harrow bomber-transports, and 180 Handley-Page Hampdens with Bristol Pegasus engines, plus 100 of the Hereford version with Napier Dagger engines, had been ordered. To this list must be added the orders for two twin-engined bombers built for the combined Specification 10/36 for a General Reconnaissance and Torpedo Bomber: Contract 563935/36 for 486 of the untried Blackburn Botha and Contract 552915/36 for 400 of the Bristol Type 152 Beaufort (a specification that closely involved the Type 149 Blenheim IV, as will be described later).

So, by the time the Blenheim was ready to enter RAF service the Air Ministry had ordered well over 5,000 bombers, but fewer than 1,000 fighters (310 Spitfires and 600 Hurricanes), although 210 undelivered Gladiator biplane fighters were still awaited, 158 of which were not built until 1938. This overwhelming disproportion of bombers to fighters, which had escalated from a ratio of two to one to five to one, was not even partially redressed until after the Munich Crisis over Czechoslovakia in September 1938 – by which time it was almost too late. Not included in these figures are the 1,495 twin-engined coastal-reconnaissance Avro Anson Is ordered by 1938, together with a further 1,500 in 1939, and yet another 4,300 ordered in 1940! Certainly no fighter, 'Faithful Annie' was reliable although slow; while it had the same poor armament as the Blenheim, a single fixed machine-gun plus another in a dorsal cupola, it had a pitifully small bomb-load. More than 8,000 Ansons were built in the UK, which seems an uneconomic use of scarce industrial resources when the priority need was for larger numbers of fighter aircraft and more effective bombers. Most Ansons were later used for training purposes, as indeed were thousands of Blenheims, Battles and Wellingtons as their operational usefulness declined, but these types were all ordered initially for operational use.

Apart from this plethora of single-engined Light Bombers, and twin-engined Medium, Coastal and Heavy Bombers ordered for the RAF, the first steps had been taken towards procuring the second generation of four-engined really heavy bombers that were to serve in Bomber Command from 1942 onwards. The bomber was clearly the very epicentre of the RAF. Even the Editor of *Aeroplane*, the pertinacious C. G. Grey, commented in 1937: 'When we invented the science of boxing, the nobility and gentry who supported it called it "the noble art of self defence". So if our grandfathers regarded pounding one another to jelly as self-defence, we may come to regard bombing other nations as a form of National Defence considering that the Air Ministry programme seems to consist of colossal orders for bombers whilst those for single-seat fighters are very much smaller.'

The reasons for this fundamental imbalance in the equipment and deployment of the RAF at the outbreak of the Second World War, and during the first two to three years of combat, merits both investigation and explanation. It led not only to an ineffective Bomber Command, which suffered unnecessarily heavy losses – especially losses of Blenheims and their precious crews, of particular concern to this narrative – but also to a Fighter Command that was only just strong enough by the narrowest of margins to win the Battle of Britain. The effect can be observed, too, on a Coastal Command that was equipped with ineffectual and obsolescent aircraft, and on both the Army Co-operation Squadrons, later Command, and the Fleet Air Arm being saddled with equipment even less suitable for the onerous tasks they were called upon to perform.

This most unsatisfactory situation stemmed not only from the need to recover from years of parsimony from successive peace-seeking Governments, but also from the ethos instilled during the First World War by Trenchard, augmented by him as CAS throughout the 1920s, and actively continued by successive Air Staffs through the 1930s – that the RAF was first and foremost an offensive force and needed 'interceptor fighters' only in sufficient numbers to defend the home base. This philosophy of a 'striking force' operating independently from the other services was indeed the very raison d'être for the existence of the RAF. The problem of establishing air supremacy over enemy territory so that this 'striking force' of bombers could operate effectively was not addressed. It had not needed to be, and during the many years that the RAF was subduing rebellious tribesmen with two-seater Light Bombers in the

Middle East and the North West Frontier region of the Indian sub-continent, not a single fighter squadron was sent overseas to defend these 'striking forces'. The RAF staff believed that the adoption of power-operated gun turrets – a field in which British aircraft manufacturers led the world by the end of the 1930s – would enable formations of daylight bombers to defend themselves adequately in a major European war, for no long-range fighters would be available. Another problem barely addressed at all was how the bombers in bad weather or at night would be enabled to locate, let alone hit, their targets.

The Air Ministry tended to replace obsolete aircraft with more up-to-date versions of the same basic types, so perpetuating a lineage without sufficient reappraisal of its fundamental role and purpose. Most new types, although taking advantage of the progressively available developments of greatly improved performance, far more aerodynamically efficient modern construction, and much more powerful engines with better propellers, were merely updated versions of their predecessors. Thus we can trace a line of two-seat Light Bombers from the DH4 and DH9A of the First World War through the Fairey Fox, the Hawker Hart and Hind series to the Wellesley and Battle with which the RAF entered the Second World War; a line of two-seat fighters from the Bristol F2 Fighter through the Demon to the Defiant; a line of Bomber/Transports from the Vimy through the Valentia to the Harrow and Bombay; a line of short-range single-seat interceptors from the Pup and Camel through the Bulldog, Fury and Gladiator to the Hurricane and Spitfire; a line of twin-engined medium bombers from the Handley Page 0/100 through the Virginia and Sidestrand, to the Anson, Hampden, and Blenheim; and a line of twin-engined Heavy Bombers from the Handley Page 0/400 through the Heyford and Hendon to the Whitley, Wellington and Warwick. But the whole concept of two-seater single-engined Light Bombers, as well as that of two-seat fighters, was completely outmoded by the time war broke out, and the need for colonial-type Bomber/Transports had passed long before. All the types of twin-engined bombers available to the RAF in 1939 and 1940 proved unsuitable for daylight operations and largely ineffective in night-time operations; the interceptor fighters were far more effective but lacked the range to escort the bombers in daylight, other than to the northern fringes of France.

A further factor that influenced Government and Air Ministry thinking during the 1930s was the fear of a 'knock-out blow' being delivered by massive enemy air attack at the opening of hostilities. This deep-seated worry about the effects of heavy bombing on the civilian population had been increased by the German bombing of Guernica in Spain in April 1937 and by the Japanese bombing of Nanking in China, and exacerbated by alarming estimates of the number of air-raid casualties that could be expected in London by the then unknown effects of large-scale bombing. Prime Minister Stanley Baldwin – an early master of the 'sound bite' – had not allayed public concern by his oft-quoted statement in the House of Commons that 'I think it is well for the man in the street to realise that there is no power on earth that can prevent him from being bombed. Whatever people may tell him, the bomber will always get through.' This view was further reinforced in March 1938 by heavy casualties caused by the bombing of Barcelona.

However, a few months earlier the Minister for Co-ordination of Defence, the lawyer Sir Thomas Inskip, challenged the basic tenet of the RAF that it existed primarily as a 'striking force'. He argued that 'If Germany is to win she must knock us out within a comparatively short time owing to our superior staying power. If we wish our forces to be sufficient to deter Germany from going to war, our forces … must be sufficiently powerful to convince Germany that she cannot deal us a knock-out blow. In other words, we must be able to confront the Germans with the risks of a long war, which is the one thing they cannot face.' He advised the Cabinet that 'the role of the RAF was not an early knock-out blow, but preventing the Germans from knocking us out', and, with a critical eye on the growing costs of expanding the RAF, suggested substituting 'a larger proportion of light and medium bombers for our very expensive heavy bombers' – a view he knew the Cabinet would receive favourably. They did, and further orders for Blenheims were placed.

L8732, the first of many Blenheim Mk IVs built by the Rootes Group of Motor Manufacturers.

Senior members of the Air Staff, whose thought processes were largely determined by their experiences in the First World War, had planned to create a force of bombers strong enough to deter any potential aggressor from attacking Britain or its allies. However, in the event the bombing force they were able to deploy did not deter Hitler and the Wehrmacht in the slightest from their intention of taking what they wanted by force – so as a deterrent the policy pursued by both Inskip and the Air Ministry was a signal failure. Prime Minister Neville Chamberlain, determined to 'draw the line' after his Munich Agreement with Hitler had failed to save Czechoslovakia from occupation by German forces, and without consulting the Cabinet, let alone Parliament, offered a Guarantee to Poland against German aggression, and the Foreign Office persuaded a reluctant France to support it. The die was cast – Hitler ignored the Guarantee and invaded Poland anyway. The British Chiefs of Staff had advised the Prime Minister that British land and naval forces could do nothing to help the Poles to resist this invasion, neither could the RAF offer any military assistance as it, too, was incapable of taking part in the fighting in Eastern Europe. Similarly the Air Force assembled at the outbreak of war was unable to deflect attacks by German bombers on Britain's allies in France and the Low Countries, or on Britain itself, by bombing the German home bases and airfields, as was intended before the war. In the desperate and dramatic events of 1940 that led to the evacuation from Dunkirk, the RAF proved unable, despite the most valiant efforts, to be of much practical help to our own armies on the continent. It was unable, also, to provide more than token assistance to the Royal Navy in the first few years of the war, although it made great and costly efforts to do so. However, one must recognise that the Air Staff and the Government in the mid to late 1930s had to resort to much 'crystal ball gazing', for no one knew at that time just how air power would be employed in a future war. Also military aircraft themselves were changing constantly, with their performance and capabilities improving rapidly, factors that made forward planning particularly difficult.

Nevertheless, at the outbreak of the Second World War the RAF had more Blenheims on charge than any other type of aircraft, so clearly they were heavily and critically involved in these various attempts to put into practice peacetime theories, many of which proved to be untenable if not fallacious when faced with the harsh realities of modern mobile warfare.

The heavy losses incurred by Blenheims in these circumstances gave rise to subsequent critical comments that it was an inadequate aircraft, too vulnerable, obsolete, too lightly built, a 'widow-maker', and so on, earning it a poor reputation. But this reputation is undeserved, for the Blenheim was a fine aircraft, well designed and well built, graceful, stable, beautifully balanced aerodynamically, with responsive flying controls, and – once its idiosyncrasies had been mastered – a joy to fly. The aircraft cannot be blamed for the uses to which it was put. Any aircraft attacking a well-defended target at low level in daylight and faced with concentrated fire from multiple *flak* cannon stood an equally high chance of being shot down. Any formation of bombers flying at medium level by day was just as vulnerable to accurate anti-aircraft fire. Any bomber that was slower and less manoeuvrable than attacking fighters

THE BRISTOL BLENHEIM

The assembly lines of Mk IVs under construction by Rootes at Speke, Liverpool, stretch right into the distance. Rootes built more Blenheims than any other manufacturer, including the Bristol Aircraft Company.

was in the same great danger, especially if the armament of the fighter out-ranged that of the bomber. The Blenheim was no worse in these respects than any of its contemporaries – indeed, it was better than most of them – but it was deployed mainly in daylight against formidable defences and usually at such a low level that if hit by enemy fire it struck the ground or the sea almost immediately, giving the crew virtually no time to bale out. The other RAF bombers were soon restricted to night-time operations, but the Blenheims were required to face continually the far greater dangers of operating by day. They were pressed into service as fighters, too, both by day and by night, a use for which they were adapted but not designed. The Blenheims had to pay a high price, which included the unjustified opprobrium of a bad reputation, while the RAF was being taught many lessons. These lessons were to be learned painfully in the hard school of wartime experience, but they stood the RAF in good stead later in the war – the Blenheim sacrifices were not in vain.

The Blenheim enters RAF service

However, before we describe the cruel and costly awakening that was to be inflicted upon the wartime Blenheim squadrons, we need to look at their much-heralded and eagerly awaited entry into peacetime RAF service. Proudly hailed as 'the fastest bomber in the world', which at that time they certainly were, production Mark I Blenheims finally received clearance for release to squadron service in late February 1937. We have already seen how the first two from the initial production batch of K7033 to K7182 acted as prototypes and were retained at Filton for manufacturers' trials. Those of K7033 lasted from the first flight of a Blenheim on 25 June 1936 – apart from a period for repairs following the mishap on its second flight – until it was delivered to the A&AEE on 27 October 1936, still ballasted to compensate for the lack of military equipment, then to the RAE at Farnborough on 19 April 1937 for further trials. K7034, meanwhile, which was fully equipped, was sent to the A&AEE on 25 January 1937. March 1937 was an historic month as the RAF took delivery of its first ever all-metal monocoque monoplane with retractable undercarriage, wing flaps, variable-pitch propellers, and a power-operated gun turret. K7035 was converted to dual controls and delivered on 1 March to 114 Squadron based at Wyton, the squadron chosen to be the first to change its Hawker Audax biplanes for Blenheims; K7036/37/38 were cleared to 114 on 4 March, with K7039 to K7046 following from 12 March to 7 May. Of these, K7037, the fifth from the Filton line, was the first to be built to the full production standard and to carry all the military equipment specified.

This introduction was far from auspicious, for only six days later, on 10 March 1937, the proud pilot of K7036, the second of the above batch of 12 brand-new Blenheims to arrive at RAF Wyton, carried out a fast and low pass to the delight of the assembled squadron, then lowered the wheels and flaps for his approach and landing. All was well until he applied the wheel brakes for, not being familiar with the power of such newfangled devices, he applied them a mite too harshly. The tail rose high, the propellers dug into the

K7035, the first Blenheim delivered to the RAF at Wyton, on 1 March 1937. Note two of 114's Hawker Hinds in the background.

turf, the Blenheim cart-wheeled instantly on to its back, which was broken just behind the turret, and the aircraft was damaged beyond repair and struck off charge on 8 June, having spent a mere 2 hours of its short life in the air. The CO of 114, Squadron Leader Hugh Hamilton-Brookes (later Air Vice Marshal, CB CBE DFC), was not amused. This incident, which has often been described as involving the first Blenheim to be delivered to 114, should have provided a prophetic warning, for it was a foretaste of the many Blenheim accidents that were to come. K7036 was replaced by K7057 on 18 June, but it too crashed when the pilot became disoriented during a night landing at Wyton on 30 September 1937. It had been taken from the batch K7047 to K7059, which were delivered to 90 Squadron at Bicester between May and June. This squadron was the next to be re-equipped with Blenheims, which replaced its Hinds, and it was followed by 139, like 114 an Audax Squadron, which received the batch K7060 to K7071 and K7074 during July and August, apart from K7067/68, which went to 90 Squadron as replacements.

K7036, the brand-new Mk I for 114 Squadron that overturned on landing at Wyton on 4 March 1937 when the brakes were applied too fiercely. P/O Perry was greatly embarrassed but unhurt; sadly, he was killed with his crew on 10 May 1938 in K7037.

K7040, delivered to 114 in May 1937, coded V on the cockpit sides, and with the Squadron number displayed on the fuselage flanks.

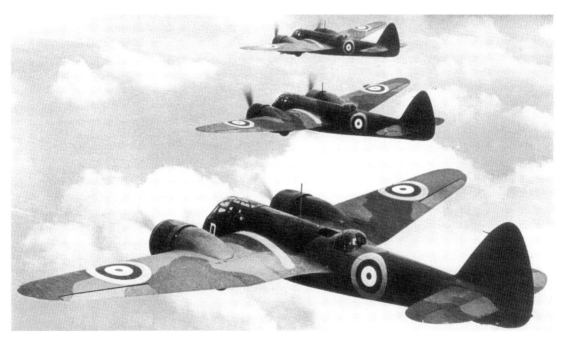

A trio of 114 Squadron Mk Is in echelon-port, photographed in June 1937. The tail-wheels are retracted and the cupolas over the empty turrets lowered; the WOp/Ag's entry hatch (normally closed in flight) is open.

A 'beat-up' of parked 114 Squadron Blenheims at Wyton on 3 June 1937. The original caption states: 'By far the fastest bombers in service anywhere in the World'.

One may wonder why 90 Squadron required replacement aircraft straight away, so let us pause a moment and look at what happened to each of the first 12 brand-new Blenheims delivered to the squadron during May and July 1937, and their seven replacement aircraft, for their fates provide an excellent and illustrative sample of so many Blenheims (see Appendix 1). 90 Squadron re-equipped with Mk IV Blenheims in early 1939, sending its Mk Is, as noted below, to Maintenance Units for overhaul and re-issue to other units, whilst 90 became a Group Pool (or Training) Squadron on the outbreak of war in September. Six of the first seven brand-new replacement Blenheims, all delivered to 90 Squadron during 1937, were also lost later in a variety of accidents (see Appendix 2).

The retractable tail-wheel on early Blenheims proved troublesome and was soon fixed down. In 1940 the aperture was used for a 'lash-up' mounting of a rear-defence gun, but was faired over in later production aircraft.

The very heavy losses sustained by Blenheims as lessons were being learned in wartime operations have been mentioned. But why was it that 16 of these 19 Blenheims were lost in accidents, and none of them through enemy action, with only three of them surviving to what in aircraft terms is a fairly ripe old age? The answer to the first part of this question lay partly in the failure of RAF pilot training before the war to equip many of the standard service pilots with the skills needed to cope with such an enormous advance in performance and increased mechanical complexity that the Blenheim posed compared with the simple biplanes they had flown up to that time, or to provide sufficient training and practice in flying on instruments or at night. The middle part of the question is answered by the fact that 90 Squadron was a Training Squadron, tasked to provide Blenheim crews to other squadrons, so was withdrawn from the front line upon the outbreak of war and did not see operational service with its Blenheims. The latter part, concerning the only three to survive, was due simply to good luck. The pre-war losses of Blenheims were alarming, and of course once war was declared the operational Blenheim squadrons suffered not only this unusually high rate of attrition through accidents but also from the many losses inflicted by the enemy. So, as we will see, the dice were loaded very heavily against operational Blenheims, placing the chances of survival for their crews more firmly than ever into the capricious hands of 'Lady Luck'.

Pre-war RAF modernisation is exemplified in this press cutting at the 1937 Hendon Air Day: a quartet of 114 Squadron's Blenheims with a Hind in the foreground and a Wellesley in the background.

THE BRISTOL BLENHEIM

Appendix I

Fates of the first 12 Blenheim Mk Is delivered to 90 Squadron

K7047 lasted a year in service until belly-landed by mistake at Bicester 20-6-1938.

K7048 did better, passing to 101 Squadron 21-6-1938 and serving in several units until lost an engine and crashed on approach with 17 OTU at Upwood 10-10-1941.

K7049 was lost 17-7-1937 when pilot was thrown out after losing control in cloud. He was court-martialed but exonerated due to lack of instrument flying practice.

K7050 was damaged when undercarriage was retracted on ground on first day with Squadron; repaired on site and passed to other units in June 1940, being finally burned out when attempting to land on 'Q site' decoy airfield at night while serving with No 12 Pilots Advanced Flying Unit 10-8-1943.

K7051 was passed to 1 AACU 4-5-1938, returning to 90 Squadron 1-10-1938, then serving with 61, 222 and 145 Squadrons until 9-1-1940, becoming ground instructional airframe 28-4-1941, and being struck off charge 2-5-1943.

K7052 crashed when stalled attempting forced landing near Weston-on-the-Green, Oxon, while on fuel consumption trials 17-12-1937 (see picture page 104).

K7053 was Squadron's dual-control training aircraft; crashed 30-6-1937 near Stanton Long, Salop, after control lost in cloud during navigation exercise, killing the three crew.

K7054 was damaged beyond repair when it overshot flare-path on night of 6-5-1938; sent to Orfordness and used for research involving armament development.

K7055 was also damaged beyond repair 13-1-1938 when it stalled while landing at Bicester after engine cut; sent to Shoeburyness for similar research.

K7056 suffered hydraulic failure and belly-landed at Wormwell 26-11-1937, becoming ground instructional airframe at Henlow.

K7057 crashed with 114 Squadron 30-9-1937 when pilot became disoriented during night landing at Wyton, as mentioned in text.

K7058 led a hard life with 90 Squadron before going back to Filton for major overhaul 19-11-1938; served with training units, twice suffering collapsed undercarriage, one after swinging on landing, before being delivered to RAE 13-4-1942 and being finally struck off charge 4-12-1943.

K7059 led similar life with 90 before going to an MU for repair 9-5-1939; then with 141 Squadron until 29-2-1940, becoming ground instructional airframe 19-2-1941, and being struck off charge 8-4-1944, six years after entering service.

A 90 Squadron crew dismounting from 'B for Beer', later called 'B for Baker' and 'Bravo' in current terminology.

Appendix 2

Fates of the seven replacement Blenheim Mk Is delivered to 90 Squadron

K7067 lasted a year before being abandoned in air and crashing on Cottonhopehead Moor, Northumberland, 30-8-1938 after control lost in icing conditions.

K7068 served with 90 Squadron before going to 6 MU for major overhaul 24-4-1939. Joined No 5 BGS 25-6-1940 and crash-landed near Drogheda, in neutral Eire, 14-3-1941 after crew became lost in bad visibility; they were interned.

K7091 served with 90 until 24-4-1939, when it went to 6 MU for major overhaul, going to 145 Squadron 21-12-1939. Collided in mid-air with K7114 near Gatwick 10-2-1940, but both aircraft managed to land safely. After repair went to No 1 then No 2 OTU 21-12-1940, serving until 6-5-1942 when it crashed near Sandingholme, Yorks, after control was lost at night.

K7092 also served with 90 until 24-4-1939, when it too went to 6 MU for overhaul, passing through three other MUs until going to 23 Squadron 10-8-1940, where it swung on take-off on night of 29-8-1940 and struck the Watch Office at Wittering; went to the Rootes shadow factory 12-9-1940 for possible rebuild but was struck off charge 2-11-1940.

K7113 was the only one of the seven replacement aircraft to survive; served with 90 Squadron until going to 6 MU 2-5-1939 for major overhaul, then serving with 25, 68 and 153 Squadrons and the PAFU until 20-3-1943 when it had a major rebuild at Airwork and was passed to Admiralty 2-8-1943 to serve with 759 Squadron Fleet Air Arm in air-to-air training exercises with FAA fighters. Neither RN nor RAF records reveal subsequent fate.

K7114 served with 90 until 5-5-1939 when it went to 6 MU, passing to 145 Squadron 25-11-1939; while with them it collided with K7091 (above) 10-2-1940; repaired on site. Passed to No 5 OTU 16-4-1940, then No 54 OTU 16-12-1940, until an engine cut in circuit at Church Fenton 9-3-1941, control was lost and it spun into ground.

K7126 served with 90 Squadron until 24-4-1939 when, like several others, it went to 6 MU for major overhaul, passing to 600 Squadron at Manston 6-6-1940. Only 20 days later undercarriage collapsed while engines were being run up; repaired on site, but then overshot landing at Catterick on night of 19-11-1940 and undercarriage collapsed again. Once more repaired on site, passing to 54 OTU 19-5-1941, going on to Cranwell, then No 3 Radio School, 60 OTU, and to 12 PAFU 2-1-1943, finally being damaged beyond repair in heavy landing at Spittlegate 4-5-1943 and struck off 12-8-1943.

90 Squadron, the second squadron to receive Blenheims in May and June 1937. K7054 'F for Freddie' is shown at rest. The phonetic alphabet was changed in 1943 – the aircraft became 'F for Fox'.

A formation of 90 Squadron Blenheims showing the change to their post-Munich markings of TW – not all aircraft have individual letters yet.

Chapter 6

Trials and tribulations

Problems in service

Within months, hundreds of new Blenheims were rolling out of three factories – and at an ever-increasing rate – as production at Avro and Rootes came on stream to supplement that from Filton. Even so, the factories of these three major constructors were unable to cope with the demand for Blenheim wings, although Bristol had installed further wing jigs, so Dobson & Barlow, a large engineering firm in Bolton, was sub-contracted to manufacture and assemble extra sets of wings for all three plants. Shortages of turrets also caused problems, and nearly 200 aircraft were delivered without them, mainly with just the cupola fixed in the retracted position. The Daimler Car Company had been contracted to produce the complex hydraulic turrets for the Rootes and Avro factories, but found the task far more difficult than expected and deliveries fell way behind, so Bristol had to install another production line for turrets at Filton. Blenheims formed the spear-point of the overdue expansion of the RAF and were pre-eminent in its re-equipment with modern aircraft, but, as we have seen, this rapid re-equipment created a number of serious problems.

When seeking some of the reasons that lay behind the high numbers of pre-war accidents to Blenheims, it is interesting to note the types of aircraft that the various squadron pilots had been flying before converting to their new Blenheims. Bear in mind that these conversions took place before OTUs and OCUs (Operational Training and Conversion Units) were formed, and before Pilot's Notes with the 'Vital Actions' for the new types were introduced. Familiarisation training on new types was carried out by the squadrons themselves, with instruction usually given by the Flight Commanders who were often almost as inexperienced on the new machines as the pilots to whom they were giving advice. Often it was just a short flight, with one engine throttled back for a few moments at a safe height to demonstrate the swing. Some squadrons tied a card to the control column giving rudimentary check-lists, speeds, etc.

The delivery schedule

Deliveries of the first production batch of Mk I Blenheims from Filton continued throughout 1937 and the beginning of 1938. Following on from 114, 90 and 139 Squadrons, the serial numbers of whose aircraft were listed in the previous chapter, they were allocated in the following sequence:

144 Squadron at Hemswell received K7073/75/76/77/79/80-86/90 and 7119-22 between August and October 1937.
44 Squadron at Waddington took delivery of K7127-42 in December 1937.
30 Squadron at Habbaniyah, the first overseas Blenheim squadron, received K7093-7108, via the Packing Depot at Sealand and the Aircraft Depot at Aboukir, in January 1938, with K7177-82 (the last of this first production batch) following by March 1938.
110 Squadron, also at Waddington, received K7143-58 in January 1938.
61 Squadron at Hemswell took delivery of K7159-72 and 7175-76, replacing its nine-month-old Ansons, also in January 1938.
62 Squadron at Cranfield received from February 1938 K7173-74, plus L1101/03-10/13-16 from the second production batch.

The Bristol factories at Filton carried straight on producing this second batch of 450 Mk I Blenheims – three times the size of the original order – under Contract 527111/36, and they were given RAF serials L1097 to L1546, all being delivered between February 1938 and March 1939. At the same time the first 250 were ordered from A. V. Roe Ltd under Contract 568371/36, with RAF serials L6594 to L6843, delivered from August 1938 to March 1940, together with the initial 250 from the Rootes shadow factory under Contract 551920/37, with the serials L8362 to L8731, delivered between November 1938 and August 1939.

Space precludes listing by serial number the units to which they were delivered, or their individual histories and ultimate fates, but commencing in 1937 and continuing throughout 1938 and 1939, the squadrons – impatient 'to get their hands on' these exciting new machines – received them in the sequence shown in the accompanying table, which also lists the aircraft they were flying at the time.

Squadron deliveries of Blenheims and the aircraft they replaced

Squadron	Base	Aircraft type replaced	Commencement date
Bomber squadrons			
114	Wyton	Audax	March 1937
90	Bicester	Hind	May 1937
139	Wyton	Audax	July 1937
144	Hemswell	Audax, Anson	August 1937
44	Waddington	Hind	December 1937
110	Waddington	Hind	January 1938
61	Hemswell	Anson	January 1938
62	Cranfield	Hind	February 1938
82	Cranfield	Hind	March 1938
57	Upper Heyford	Hind	March 1938
104	Bassingbourn	Hind	May 1938
101	Bicester	Overstrand	June 1938
34	Upper Heyford	Hind	July 1938
107	Harwell	Hind	August 1938
21	Lympne	Hind	August 1938
53	Odiham	Hector	January 1939
59	Old Sarum	Hector	May 1939
18	Upper Heyford	Hind	May 1939
Fighter squadrons			
23	Wittering	Demon	December 1938
29	Debden	Demon	December 1938
64	Church Fenton	Demon	December 1938
25	Hawkinge	Gloster Gladiator	December 1938
600 Auxiliary	Hendon	Demon	January 1939
601 Auxiliary	Hendon	Gloster Gauntlet	January 1939
604 Auxiliary	Hendon	Demon	January 1939
Overseas squadrons			
30	Habbaniyah	Hardy	January 1938
84	Shaiba	Wapiti	February 1939
55	Habbaniyah	Vincent	March 1939
211	Helwan	Hind	May 1939
113	Heliopolis	Hind	June 1939
60	Ambala	Wapiti	June 1939
45	Ismailia	Wellesley	June 1939
39	Risalpur	Hart	August 1939

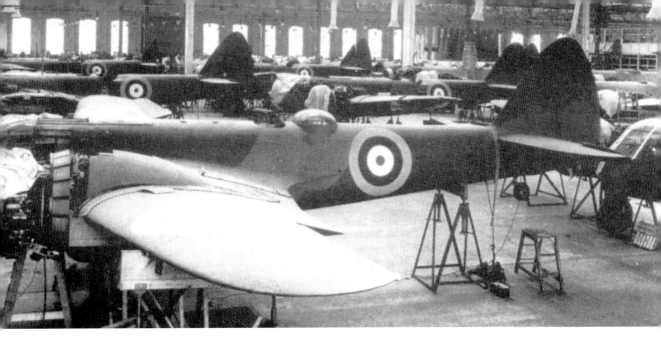

The three main factories were producing hundreds of Blenheims each month.

Most squadrons converted to Blenheims from Hawker Hinds (or from Hind variants such as the Audax, Hector and Demon) – a big step forward indeed.

An 82 Squadron airman proudly examines his new Blenheim at Cranfield in April 1938.

139 Squadron lines up with its new steeds at Wyton, August 1937.

30 Squadron at Heliopolis, Egypt, received K7103 in December 1937; it was lost in Greece in December 1940.

The table reveals that, of the first 32 squadrons to be re-equipped with Blenheims (excluding 61 Squadron, which was fortunate to have had Avro Ansons for a few months), only one had any experience with twin-engined aircraft (101 with its Overstrands), and only one operated aircraft with a retractable undercarriage (45 Squadron with it Wellesleys), while all the other squadrons had been equipped with simple and relatively slow single-engined open-cockpit fixed-undercarriage biplanes. The 650 or so standard service pilots involved had been trained on even simpler and even slower biplanes, and new intakes of fresh and very inexperienced pilots were being posted to the squadrons. It can be seen that most squadrons converted from the Hawker Hart series of two-seater Light Bombers (the Hart, built to a 1926 specification, first flew in June 1928!), which developed into the Hind, the Hardy, the Demon two-seater fighter, and the Audax Army Co-operation variants, with the Hector being the latter with a Napier Dagger engine in place of the Rolls-Royce Kestrel. They were all heavily strutted and wire-braced fabric-covered biplanes, they all had open cockpits, fixed-pitch propellers and non-retractable undercarriages, and they were not fitted with flaps or, apart from the Hind, with wheel brakes. The fastest of the family was the Hind, with a maximum speed of 186mph, but this was still far slower than the Blenheim. Other squadrons changed from the 135mph Westland Wapiti of 1927, or from 140mph Vickers Vincent, modified in 1934 from the 1932 Vildebeest torpedo aircraft.

Further RAF expansion

In March 1938 the Government announced that the 'front line' of the RAF would comprise 68 Bomber Squadrons, 30 Fighter Squadrons, 15 General Reconnaissance Squadrons and 10 Army Co-operation Squadrons – fighters were still less than 30 per cent of the operational aircraft. A few days later Germany annexed Austria, and could therefore out-flank the Czechoslovakian defences. On 12 May, in a debate in the House of Commons on the Air Estimates, there was fierce criticism of the handling by the Air Ministry of the expansion programme and the disappointingly low rate of production of the much-needed new aircraft, and MPs asked why Lord Nuffield's huge Morris Motors concern, and the Alvis Company, had been excluded from the shadow aircraft factory scheme. Unfortunately, the Secretary of State for Air, the very efficient but somewhat abrasive Earl Swinton, and his highly influential guru, Lord Weir, were both in the House of Lords and not able to respond to the attacks in person. They refrained, out of loyalty to the Government, from giving the main reason behind the lower than required production figures – namely that Prime Minister Neville Chamberlain, still hoping for peace, had persistently refused to sanction the creation of the extra industrial capacity the situation demanded.

On 16 May Swinton, Weir and Winterton, the Deputy Air Minister, resigned, leading to a period of greatly lessened effectiveness and diminished decisiveness during a most critical period in the expansion and re-equipment of the RAF. Air Marshal Sir Wilfrid Freeman was appalled at the resignations, but fortunately for the country he was kept in his post on the Air Council as Member for Research and Development, although he was soon also given responsibility for organising production, and in August his appointment was changed to Air Member for Development and Production. Sir Kingsley Wood had become the new Air Minister, assisted by Harold Balfour, but lacked the drive of Swinton,

61 Squadron proudly showing its Blenheims at a RAeS Garden Party at Fairey's Great West Road Aerodrome (now Heathrow Airport) in May 1938. Some squadrons painted individual aircraft letters on the cowlings, as here, others on the side of the nose, or in front of the fuselage roundel.

which, combined with the personal contacts and invaluable advice of Weir, had made possible the unprecedented growth of the RAF and the greatly improved supporting industrial base. To placate Nuffield, Sir Kingsley Wood awarded Morris Motors the contract to manage a huge new shadow factory built at Castle Bromwich to mass-produce Spitfires, but, to look ahead for two years, none had been produced by May 1940 and Lord Beaverbrook put Vickers in charge, as Swinton had wanted to in the first place, and aircraft were coming off the production lines by September. Morris Motors later built 2,000 of the very simple DH Tiger Moth. Bristol was fortunate that the Blenheim shadow contracts had been awarded to the Rootes Group and not to the Nuffield organisation.

Blenheims, although the most numerous, were of course not the only new-generation types being introduced into squadron service at that time of rapid expansion. Nor were they the only new type to suffer from numerous flying accidents before the war, but a closer look reveals that they suffered a greater rate of accidental loss than any of the other types. To help put this aspect into perspective, the accompanying table repays a close look, for it contains many famous names and gives the chronological order of the introduction into squadron service of this rush of new types.

Introduction of new aircraft types

Type	Initial deliveries to	Commencement date
Avro Anson	48 Squadron, Manston	26 March 1936
Handley-Page Harrow	214 Squadron, Feltwell	13 January 1937
Gloster Gladiator	72 Squadron, Tangmere	22 February 1937
Hawker Hector	4 Squadron, Odiham	26 February 1937;
all six Army Co-Operation Squadrons were equipped by December 1937		
Bristol Blenheim Mk I	114 Squadron, Wyton	1 March 1937
Armstrong-Whitworth Whitley Mk I	10 Squadron, Dishforth	10 March 1937
Vickers Wellesley	7 (later 76) Squadron, Finningley	20 March 1937
Fairey Battle	63 Squadron, Upwood	20 May 1937
Airspeed Oxford	Central Flying School	October 1937
Hawker Hurricane	111 Squadron, Northolt	20 December 1937
Westland Lysander	16 Army Co-op Sqn, Old Sarum	May 1938
Supermarine Spitfire Mk I	19 Squadron, Duxford	4 August 1938
Handley-Page Hampden	49 Squadron, Scampton	September 1938
Vickers Wellington	99 Squadron, Mildenhall	October 1938
Bristol Blenheim Mk IV	53 Army Co-Op Sqn, Odiham	January 1939
Lockheed Hudson	224 Squadron, Leuchars	May 1939
Bristol Bombay	216 Squadron, Heliopolis	October 1939

Some causal factors behind Blenheim accidents

It will help to understand why there were so many accidents to Blenheims during this period (see Appendix 1) if we look at some of the factors that contributed to them. Apart from the obvious need to assimilate information quickly, react more rapidly mentally and physically, and to think ahead and anticipate more, all attributes necessary to cope with the increase in performance from their new Blenheims, it was the unfamiliar mechanical complexity that added most to the work-load of the pilots. Dealing with this was not made any easier by the poor location of the controls – other than the primary flying controls – in the Blenheim cockpit, and the particularly awkward method of operation of several of them. The science of ergonomics in the layout of cockpits, instrument panels and controls still lay in the future. These fresh factors were in addition to the normal but ever-present hazards of flying itself – getting lost, encountering bad weather, running out of fuel, airframe icing, striking obstacles by flying too low, becoming disorientated in cloud and losing control, carburettor icing, flying into mountains or high ground in bad visibility, mechanical failure, wheels-up landings, and so on. To remind the pilot to lower the undercarriage before landing, a horn sounded if the throttles were brought more than two-thirds back, as they would be on a landing approach. Additionally there were mechanical and electrical indicators, which showed green lights if the wheels were locked down and red lights if they were unlocked, and pilots were instructed to look out of the cockpit side window to confirm visually that the port wheel was in place, and to ask their observer to do the same for the starboard wheel!

What were these new and troublesome mechanical complexities and why were the secondary controls so tricky to operate – especially in an emergency – until they became familiar through thorough practice? Foremost was the operation of the hydraulic system, which pilots would not have come across before. A hydraulic pump, which Bristol had to design and manufacture itself, was driven by the port engine to circulate and pressurise the fluid throughout the system, which included a reservoir and a pressure-relief valve. When the pilot selected the service required, this pressurised fluid was applied to the applicable hydraulic jack, which

The cockpit of an early Mk I, showing the engine boost and rpm gauges above the turn-and-bank indicator and ASI, with the compass and altimeter below, and throttles and mixture controls on the left; other engine instruments were on the inboard side of the engine nacelles. On the right of the seat are trimming-wheels and the three plunger controls for the hydraulics – the front one, for the undercarriage, is partly obscured by the hydraulic hand-pump handle.

exerted sufficient power to operate the service. Each undercarriage had one of these powerful jacks to retract or extend the main wheels, and a smaller one to operate the 'up' and 'down' locks; the flaps had a large jack connected to the port flaps, which was linked by a heavy cable to the starboard flaps for their simultaneous operation; and the turret had four smaller jacks, two for traversing and two for elevation and depression. When not required to operate a service, the hydraulic fluid was circulated via a 'neutral' loop just sufficiently to maintain pressure in the reservoir, so when a service was required the circuit could be energised and the pressure diverted to the service desired.

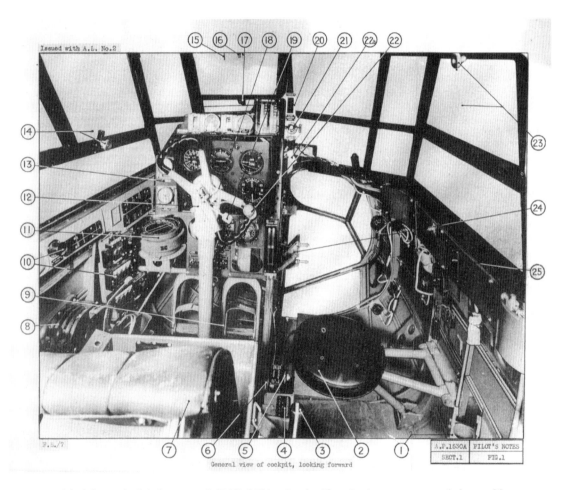

General view of cockpit, looking forward

Later aircraft had the standard six-instrument RAF Blind Flying Panel, with engine instruments mounted above and boost gauges (13) now to the left. The control column contains the brake lever (19) and gun-firing button (22); the bracket (24) to the right of the panel is for the Mk IX bombsight, above the Observer's circular folding seat (2).

The controls comprised three vertical plungers, each with an identical small stirrup-type alloy handle with the function embossed upon it, mounted in a line to the rear of the trimming hand-wheels on the right of the pilot's seat just below his thigh. The rearmost, marked 'selector' and just behind the seat, had three positions: from a central 'neutral' position it was pushed 'down' to release hydraulic power to the circuit for the undercarriage and flaps, and pulled 'up' to divert power to the turret circuit. The foremost plunger controlled the undercarriage: from a central 'neutral' position it was pulled 'up' to retract the wheels, and pushed 'down' to extend them. The three-position control in the middle acted in a similar fashion on the flaps. However, neither of these latter two controls would operate the service required unless the main 'selector' control was set at the 'undercarriage/flaps' position; if it was left in the 'neutral' position (as was normal in the cruise) or set at the 'turret' position, nothing would happen!

To prevent inadvertent retraction while the aircraft was on the ground, each undercarriage had a large red-flagged 'safety link' inserted manually to lock it in the 'down' position. After the pilot had started, warmed up and run up the engines and carried out his other checks, he signalled to the ground staff for these pins to be removed before taxying out – they were shown to the pilot, then handed to the Wireless Operator/Air Gunner, who secured them in a special stowage near his open hatch. The reverse procedure was followed after taxying in from a sortie and before the port engine, which drove the hydraulic pump, was shut down – the WOp/AG often hopped out at the end of the landing run and inserting them even before taxying in. Should the pilot pull the wrong one of the two identical plungers – which was all too easy to do, especially at night – when attempting to raise the flaps after landing and before these pins had been re-inserted, the undercarriage would unlock and retract with embarrassing and expensive results. It was not long before an

The Pilot's seat with the armrest (56) folded up, and the hydraulic hand-pump (50) just behind the trimming-wheels (5 and 6). A spring-loaded flap (48) now protects the undercarriage retraction control (49) – the flap control (51) and the control to divert hydraulic power to the turret (53) are not protected – and (54) is the cowling gills control hand-wheel.

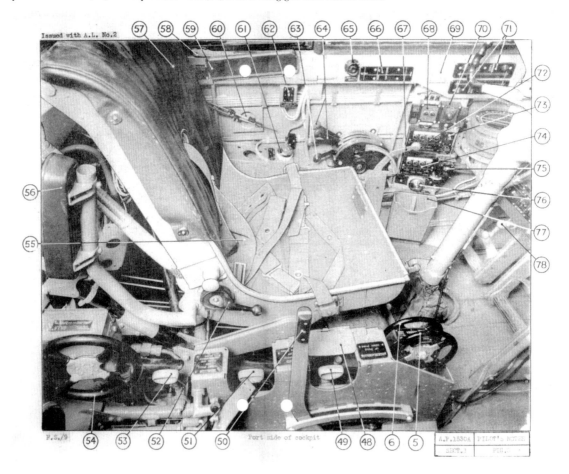

THE BRISTOL BLENHEIM

awkward-to-release spring-loaded metal flap was fixed over the undercarriage control to prevent such mistaken selection, and this vicious device skinned the knuckles of most Blenheim pilots even if they wore gloves. Of course, if the crew took off without removing the pins the undercarriage could not be retracted, which would be dangerous if an engine failed. Much later these removable pins were replaced by weight-sensitive switches that prevented undercarriage retraction while the aircraft was still on the ground.

Another difficulty was that the Blenheim had the throttles mounted to the left of the pilot so that he had to transfer his left hand from them to the control column immediately after take-off in order to use his right hand to operate the hydraulic controls on the right of his seat. If he failed to tighten the 'throttle friction damper' sufficiently, vibration would often cause one or both throttles to close suddenly, an alarming situation, especially when taking off fully laden, and one where a third hand would have been very useful. Conversely, if it was tightened too much it made the throttles too stiff to open smoothly over the 3-second period that was essential with Mercury engines when applying full power for take-off. Blenheim throttles needed treating with care, as hasty or jerky opening could result in a 'rich cut' as the powerful accelerator pumps in the carburettors

The rear of the cockpit, behind the Pilot's right shoulder, showing the main fuel control wheels (103 and 104), the fuel suction balance cock (105), and the fuel delivery balance cock (106), plus engine temperature gauges (102). On the roof behind his left shoulder are the fuel-contents selector switch (107) and fuel-contents gauges (108). The locations of the air-intake controls (99), carburettor cut-outs (100), and propeller pitch controls (101) are shown on the right.

Pilot's cockpit, looking aft

came into action, pumping neat fuel into the twin chokes. Idling the engines for more than a few minutes while waiting to take-off had to be avoided, as the spark-plugs fitted to early Blenheims tended to foul easily and could cause an engine to cut just as full power was needed on taking off – pilots soon learned to 'clear' their engines by giving a burst of power with the brakes applied immediately before starting their take-off run.

The engine-cooling gills had be opened for taxying to provide sufficient air flow to keep the cylinder-head temperatures within limits, but they had to be wound to the 'closed' position immediately before take-off, or so much drag was caused that the take-off run was stretched to dangerous – often fatal – lengths. Cylinder head temperatures were critical and had to be kept within the limits of between 190 and 210 degrees Centigrade – too cool and the engine would not respond properly and was liable to 'spit back'; too hot and dangerous detonation in the cylinders was likely. Similarly the oil temperature had to be kept within strict limits of 70 to 80 degrees to ensure that the correct pressure of 80psi was available to circulate the oil to all the bearings, and that it was not too hot to carry out its lubricating and heat-removing functions properly. The Carburettor Air Intake Control had to be set to 'Cold' or 'Hot' depending on the ambient temperature and relative humidity; the Mixture controls needed setting to 'Normal' ('Automatic Rich') for take-off and not to 'Weak'; and the Propeller controls needed setting to 'Fine Pitch' not 'Coarse Pitch' – failure to set these correctly would result in the aircraft failing to leave the ground, usually with disastrous results. These propeller pitch-change controls were potentially the most dangerous of all the secondary controls and undoubtedly led directly to many accidents.

Situated to the rear of the pilot's seat, just behind his left elbow, was a panel with three pairs of levers. The lower pair controlled the propeller pitch-change mechanism – the knobs (coloured red for the port prop and green for the starboard one) were pushed in for 'fine pitch', the low gear used for take-off, and pulled out for 'coarse pitch', the high gear used for cruising. Immediately above them were two identical knobs, also coloured red and green, which operated the carburettor cut-outs and were used to stop the engines – it was not long before these too were shielded by a spring-loaded flap! Above these were the two levers, with knobs similarly coloured, that operated the 'warm' and 'cold' air intake shutters. In normal circumstances each of these three pairs of controls would be operated together as a pair – the difficulties started when only one of a pair was needed, as it would usually be needed most urgently. Further above this bank of important secondary controls, on later aircraft, was the 'fuel jettison lever',

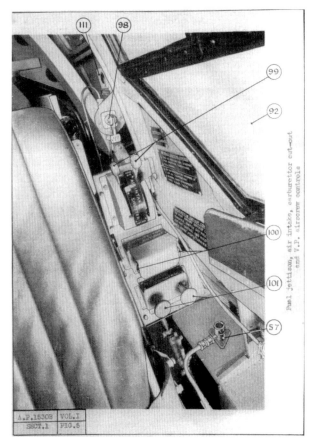

Behind the Pilot's left elbow (from the top): pairs of carburettor air-intake control levers (99), carburettor cut-out controls, protected by a spring-loaded flap (100) to prevent inadvertent operation, and identical propeller pitch-change controls (101).

which opened valves to dump the fuel from the outer tanks to bring the landing weight back within limits if the aircraft had taken off with a full fuel load and needed to land again. Even normal operation of the pitch-change controls was awkward, and entailed another change of hands (although some pilots loosened their harness and twisted round in their seat to use their right hand beneath their left arm), but execution of the rapid actions vitally necessary in an emergency was made far more difficult by the poor positioning of these controls.

The pilot would have to take several of these vital actions instantly and correctly if control was not to be lost should an engine fail soon after take-off – not infrequent on Blenheims, often due to the lack of one or more of the necessarily careful engine-handling procedures mentioned above. The greater the take-off weight, the more power was being applied at the moment of failure, and the less the speed and height that the aircraft had reached, the more dangerous and immediate were the difficulties facing the pilot. The sudden asymmetric forward thrust from the good engine, acting about the vertical axis in the same sense as the rearward drag from the failed one, would cause the aircraft to swing violently towards the failed engine, the outer wing accelerating and rising rapidly. Within seconds the aircraft would become inverted and spiral downwards uncontrollably – and usually fatally – if the proper corrective action was not taken immediately. The pilot had to identify the direction of the swing and counter it with the instant application of opposite rudder and some aileron input too, at the same time lowering the nose to prevent the airspeed from decaying – but the lower the speed the less effective the rudder became. It might also be necessary to reduce power on the good engine to prevent the swing, but prevent it he must.

He would also have to raise the undercarriage immediately to reduce drag – particularly necessary on a Blenheim as the large 'apron' fairings acted as air brakes – and thus help the airspeed to increase so directional control could be maintained. Should his hand fall in error on the rear of the three hydraulic controls, pulling it up would not raise the undercarriage but divert the hydraulic power to the turret; should it fall by mistake on the centre control, pulling that up would raise the flaps. In either event the high-drag undercarriage would remain down, making it much harder to gain vital airspeed. If he had used 15 degrees of flap to assist take-off in a heavily laden condition, raising them would cause the aircraft to sink into whatever lay ahead. To reduce the asymmetric drag he had the urgent need to change the pitch of the failed engine from 'fine' to 'coarse' – clearly it was absolutely essential to identify and pull the correct propeller control from the pair behind the left of his seat. He would also need to wind closed the cooling gills of the failed engine, and adjust those of the hard-working good engine, choosing for each operation the correct hand-wheel from the pair to the right rear of his seat. Then he would have to turn off the fuel supply to the failed engine (not that to the good one!) by turning the correct fuel-cock of the pair of concentrically mounted hand-wheels mounted right over on the starboard cockpit wall well behind his seat (the port fuel-cock hand-wheel was slightly smaller and coloured red, the starboard one slightly larger and coloured green). In addition he would have to turn off the correct pair of magneto switches mounted centrally on the lower part of the instrument panel and hidden by the control column, pull the correct carburettor cut-out control from the pair under the flap behind the left rear of his seat, and re-trim the rudder to relieve the heavy foot load using the small hand-wheel at the front right-hand corner of his seat – remembering that it wound forward for bias to starboard and rearwards for bias to port.

Should the port engine be the one that had failed, hydraulic pressure would be rapidly lost as the single pump was driven by that engine; therefore the stand-by hydraulic hand-pump to the right of the pilot's seat would have to be pumped vigorously, a task normally given to the Observer, but if the pilot was flying solo he had to cope with this too. Throughout all of this feverish activity involving the secondary controls, the aircraft would still have to be flown properly with the primary flying controls.

A few moments' thought about the layout of the secondary controls positioned beside and behind the pilot's seat on both sides as described above will reveal just how difficult it was to carry out these truly vital actions in the few seconds available before disaster struck. At night all of these difficulties were exacerbated to a frightening degree – an inexperienced pilot had little chance of retaining control and preventing a major accident, which often cost his own life and that of any other crew members in the aircraft. Blenheim pilots have said that, when faced with such an emergency, 'Your hands had to dart all around the cockpit like the proverbial one-armed paper-hanger on speed'; 'One needed to have colour-sensitive elbows that could see at night'; and 'If only we had four hands it would have been a great help.' Fortunately the large rudder of the Blenheim was powerful and effective, and the trim-tab also acted as a servo-tab to assist the manual input of the pilot, so correcting the initial swing was not too difficult if it was caught quickly enough, and the aircraft could then be trimmed to remove the high foot loads. The aircraft could also be persuaded to climb straight ahead on one engine, unless it was fully laden, and gentle turns could be made, but only against the good engine.

The steps taken to reduce the large number of accidents centred mainly on intensive training, for nothing could be done to improve the layout of the Blenheim controls without seriously delaying production. At that time there were no Conversion Units to teach the special flying techniques required for twin-engined aircraft, so training was carried out by the squadrons themselves. A few could borrow the odd Avro Anson, but it was not very suitable for this purpose, being a very slow and docile aeroplane that was particularly easy to fly. Ansons were without flaps and used a very shallow approach, 'floating' over the airfield even with the engines throttled right back until settling gently down. Blenheims had the built-in air-brake of the wheel fairings, together with the large and powerful flaps, which, when lowered fully, resulted in a very steep approach with a rapid loss of height if the engines were throttled back, and the need for a strong 'flare' prior to touchdown. Ansons frequently overshot the chosen landing path, Blenheims often undershot it. The Blenheim had a higher wing loading, which led to a more sudden stall at a slightly higher speed – especially dangerous when turning on to the final approach. The Airspeed Oxford was a much better twin-engine trainer, but did not start coming into service until December 1937.

'Careful engine-handling was essential'. The starboard Bristol Mercury of a Blenheim showing the push-rod tube at the centre of each cylinder, the baffles between the cylinders, the two oil-cooler inlets, and (at the foot) the air-intake for the up-draught twin-choke carburettor mounted below the supercharger on the rear of the engine.

The engine with the cowling removed, showing the exposed inlet valves (the equally exposed exhaust valves are obscured by baffles), the exhaust manifolds running forward to the collector-ring (forming the cowling leading-edge), and the ring of controllable cooling-gills.

THE BRISTOL BLENHEIM

The RAF had always taught the 'glide approach' where the throttle was closed completely on the base (cross-wind) leg and no power was applied until after the touchdown (when it was needed to taxi in!), or if the attempt at landing was abandoned and the pilot 'went round again', when full power was employed. The need to apply some power to correct any tendency to undershoot was frowned upon, and squadron pilots were often 'fined' in the Mess if this use of power was heard to have been necessary.

This universal 'glide approach' technique was not suitable for the Blenheim because of the steep approach path mentioned above, and because the large air-cooled engines often dropped below their optimum working temperature during the descent, so if the pilot realised he was undershooting and applied power, one or both engines was liable to cough or 'spit back' and not produce the power that was needed ever more urgently. Also, if the engines had been left idling for several minutes with the throttles closed during the approach, the plugs tended to 'oil up' and prevent clean acceleration of engines that were not firing fully on all of their cylinders. A further difficulty was that, as for take-off, the throttles had to be opened smoothly – a pilot seeing the ground coming up rapidly and needing more power urgently, and who pushed the throttles open too quickly, was liable to get a 'rich cut' with the resultant misfiring, and the opposite effect to the one he required. If one engine failed to respond fully through any of these causes the pilot was faced with asymmetric power at a low height and at a low speed. Any attempt to raise the nose to stretch the approach would result in a stall or, if the aircraft was turning, in a spin from which it would be impossible to recover at such a low height. It was discovered, therefore, that it was far safer to use an engine-assisted approach, which resulted in a flatter approach path and also meant that the engines, being at, say, 1,000rpm, would respond immediately if extra power was needed. This method is used nowadays by all aircraft, and RAF pilots only employ the 'glide approach' when practising forced landings at an early stage of their flying training. In addition to 'motoring the aircraft in', many Blenheim pilots also selected half-flap on the approach and extended them fully only upon crossing the hedge.

The dangers of losing an engine immediately after take-off were minimised by cockpit drills to ensure careful engine handling, and by the use of pre-take-off and pre-landing check-lists of 'Vital Actions'. But a considerable contribution to safety was made by teaching the method of 'holding the aircraft down' parallel to the ground as soon as it became airborne to allow it to accelerate to a 'safety speed' while the wheels were retracting, before commencing to climb. This 'safety speed' was the minimum speed at which directional control could be maintained by the application of rudder alone if an engine failed. The figure rose with the take-off weight and the amount of power available, and varied between 85mph at a light load and +5lb boost, to 115mph with a full load and +9lb boost. Pilot's Notes were introduced giving these cockpit drills and check-lists with mnemonics for the 'Vital Actions', and details of engine-handling, safety speeds, and other emergency procedures. A 'Blind-Flying Panel', with the six basic flight instruments, was standardised on all RAF aircraft in 1938, and flying on instruments was practised in the air and on the ground in the Link Trainer – the first flight simulator. Expensive lessons had been learned, but constant training gradually improved the situation and the RAF accident rate in relation to the increasing numbers of new aircraft coming into service started to decline. However, the RAF still lost through flying accidents over 10 per cent of all the Blenheims that entered service before the war, a higher percentage than any other type (see Appendix 1), and in addition hundreds more were damaged, for example by carrying out a 'wheels-up' landing, but were repaired and returned to service.

Further complications in engine handling arose when Roy Fedden insisted on importing 100 octane fuel in 1938, just as he had pushed for the introduction of 87 octane fuel in 1934, then being instrumental in persuading the Air Ministry to press the oil companies to refine these better aviation fuels in the UK. These improvements in octane rating permitted the use of progressively higher compression ratios, and were an essential element in increasing engine output – yet another example of the rapid technical progress being made at that time. But the introduction of 100 octane fuel caused further problems for Blenheim pilots, inadvertently leading to even more accidents. Because of the severe shortage of 100 octane petrol, and the priority in allocation given to Fighter Command, Blenheims were adapted to carry it only in the outer tanks, with 87 octane in the inner tanks. To take full advantage of 100 octane petrol the supercharger pressure could be increased from the normal 'Plus 5lb/sq in boost' by the operation of an 'Emergency Boost Override' lever on the instrument panel. This overrode the Automatic Boost Control to allow 'Plus 9lb' pressure, and was used for take-off and in emergencies only, for a maximum of 5 minutes. It was normally applied solely at full throttle, and ground-running engines at '+9' was permitted for 2 seconds only!

Quoting from the Blenheim IV Pilot's Notes of 1939: 'After take-off at 85-90mph, raise the undercarriage and hold the aircraft down until the speed reaches 120mph. At 120mph move the high-boost control to "up" and then change pitch to coarse. It is essential that the boost should be reduced from +9lb/sq in to +5lb/sq in before pitch is changed to coarse, otherwise the rpm will drop below the minimum permissible at +9lb boost and serious detonation will result. It is also essential that the high-boost control should be moved "up" to give +5lb boost before throttling back.' So the pilot had to remember not to change propeller pitch, or reduce power from the full-throttle setting, in the busy period just after take-off, unless he had de-selected the 'Plus 9 boost' lever first. He also had to remember to select the fuel supply from the outer tanks, not the inner ones, prior to take-off, before operating the 'Plus 9' lever, because the higher level of supercharger pressure would cause severe detonation in the cylinders, leading rapidly to engine failure, if it were applied while running on 87 octane – and he had to rely on the correct grade of fuel having been loaded into the correct tanks. Thus the extra complications produced by the introduction of 100 octane fuel increased the pilot's work load by imposing additional and critical engine-handling criteria. These in turn caused further potential hazards, especially during take-off, and laid deadly traps for the unwary or careless pilot – in addition to all of those mentioned above – resulting in even more Blenheims being lost in accidents.

An improvement was made to the cockpit transparent panels. In the original production batch they were made of 'cellastoid', a thick celluloid, but in service use it was found that they often cracked in use, shrank in low temperatures and sometime blew out at high speeds or altitude, exposing the crew to a sudden icy blast – believed to have caused several otherwise inexplicable accidents. The 'cellastoid' panels also discoloured in strong sunshine, reducing visibility, and although the ceiling of the Blenheim was 31,000 feet, the panels restricted it to 18,000 feet, or -25 degrees Centigrade. So, following manufacturer's trials, they were replaced with Perspex, then a superior new material, with the individual panels located and sealed more effectively.

144 Squadron based at Helmswell collected their new Blenheims from Filton in August 1937, gun turrets are not fitted – just the cupola. K7080 had an engine cut on take-off on 10 May 1938 and crashed a mile west of the airfield, killing both crewmen.

However, there was hardly any 'gloom and doom' among the squadrons, for once pilots had adapted to the idiosyncrasies of the layout of the ancillary controls and appreciated the need for careful engine handling, they found that their exciting and ultra-modern Blenheims were an absolute delight to fly, possessing effective and well-harmonised primary controls. Most RAF pilots were full of the self-confidence of youth, and thrilled with their super new kit, and even if some other pilots 'bought it' they were convinced that 'it could never happen to them'. The Pilot's Notes, uniquely for a bomber, gave speeds and engine settings for all the standard aerobatic manoeuvres such as loops, barrel-rolls, and 'rolls off the top' – that is the first half of a loop followed by a half-roll from the inverted position back to a level attitude.

The first fighter Blenheims

It may have been surprising to note in the table giving the order in which RAF Squadrons received their Blenheims that in December 1938 four regular Fighter Command Squadrons (23, 25, 29 and 64) converted to them, with the three Auxiliary Squadrons at Hendon (600, 601 and 604) following suit in January 1939, as prior to then all Blenheims had gone to Bomber Squadrons. This was a result of the Munich Crisis of September 1938 when the politicians only averted a war over Czechoslovakia by appeasing the German dictator. They had brought Britain to the brink of war, although our armed services were totally unprepared for such a conflict. The Minister for Co-ordination of Defence, Sir Thomas Inskip, was fully aware of this; he had for some time questioned the still prevailing Trenchard philosophy that the RAF was primarily a bombing force, and now pressed the need to increase the nation's aerial defences. This pressure and the shock of the Munich Crisis brought home to the Air Staff the relative shortage of fighter aircraft in its armoury, and to the lack of any long-range fighters and of any dedicated night-fighters. From that time onwards it moved the provision of more fighters to the head of its list of priorities, and increased fighter orders by 30 per cent, although the Air Staff still planned, in the longer term, to equip its cherished 'striking force' entirely with four-engined Heavy Bombers.

The Air Staff had noted how the Blenheims had outrun and evaded the biplane fighters in the 1937 defence exercises, and were aware that they possessed a greater range than any of the single-seat interceptors, so in the post-Munich alarm a fighter conversion of the Blenheim seemed appropriate. Indeed, it was the only aircraft that was both available and appeared to be suitable, even if only as a 'stop-gap' measure. These remarks were to be applied to the Blenheim on many more occasions in the future as many more 'gaps' appeared that had to be 'stopped' many more times. In the initial discussions, held on 7 November 1938, it was referred to as an 'intermediate fighter' required 'in view of the late delivery of modern fighters' to bridge the gap between the Demon and the much delayed Defiant. The Blenheim was easily adapted to this unexpected new role by fitting an external pack containing four fixed Browning .303 machine-guns beneath the bomb bay, mounted on a sub-frame of mild steel tubing within the bay, which also contained 2,000 rounds of ammunition – 500 rounds for each gun, giving more than 20 seconds of continuous firing. The total weight of this armament was only slightly less than the normal bomb-load. This package was first flight-tested at the A&AEE on L1424, which arrived at Martlesham Heath on 28 November 1938 at the height of the post-Munich 'flap', and improvements to the ammunition feeds were made, together with provision for heating to prevent the gun-oil from freezing at altitude. Manufacture of these gun-packs and their mounting frames was sub-contracted to the Southern Railway workshops at Ashford in Kent, which produced more than 1,300 sets altogether, as the main Blenheim factories were too busy constructing airframes. The single fixed Browning in the port wing was retained, as was the dorsal turret with a single Vickers machine-gun, which gave some protection against attacks from behind. Dowding had wanted the turrets removed, to improve performance by saving drag and 500lb in weight, but the Air Staff wanted to retain a lookout to the rear; Dowding suggested a small streamlined 'observation cupola', and this was agreed on 16 January 1939, but the

Fighter Blenheims of 29 Squadron parked at Debden, and L1440 of 25 Squadron landing at Hawkinge, still with Fighter Command half-black/half-white under-surfaces. Both squadrons were still awaiting their four-gun belly-packs in March 1939. The code letters, applied at the time of the Munich crisis, were changed on the outbreak of war.

thought of an unarmed Rear Observer was anathema to staff accustomed to two-seater fighters with a rear gun, and the ACAS, AVM Sholto Douglas, reversed the decision. This particular argument was to resurface two years later!

Trials of the full 'fighter' conversion were carried out with L1512 and L1525 at the A&AEE from January 1939. Armour-plating to give some protection to the pilot from the front was rejected because of the increased weight penalty. At this stage there was no talk of use of the fighter conversion as a night-fighter, and that possibility was not raised until the spring of 1939.

The 'auxiliary fighter' Blenheims were designated Mark I-F and were a considerable improvement on the Demon biplanes they replaced, but the 1938 exercises had shown that Blenheims could no longer outrun the new Hurricanes that had been entering RAF service throughout the year. Clearly they were no match in a dog-fight with the faster, much smaller, lighter, and far more manoeuvrable eight-gun Hurricanes. Nor would they be with the Spitfire that would enter service a few months later, let alone with the formidable Bf.109-E of Britain's potential adversary.

The fighting efficiency of the Messerschmitt 109 had been proved in action in the Spanish Civil War, not simulated in exercises, and this operational service led to several technical improvements and significant developments in the tactical use of German fighters. The most notable was the employment by the Luftwaffe of the *Staffel*, consisting of three (sometimes four) relatively free-roaming *Schwarme*, each comprising two *Rotte* (pairs of aircraft) where the *Katschmarek* (wing-man) watched and protected the tail of his *Rottefuehrer* (leader). Adopted later in the war by RAF Fighter Command as the 'finger four', this unit was far more effective in combat than the RAF's inflexible system, whereby a squadron flew in four 'vics', each comprising three aircraft in close formation, whose pilots had to give nearly all of their attention to strict station-keeping. During the Battle of France in 1940 both Fighter Command Hurricanes and Bomber Command Blenheims were to suffer severe losses when their traditional 'vic' formations were attacked by Messerschmitts using these more flexible tactics – another lesson that had to be learned in the hardest possible way.

THE BRISTOL BLENHEIM

Appendix 1

Blenheim losses in the UK to 31 August 1938 (Munich Agreement)

All 'K' and 'L' series aircraft up to L8731 are Mk Is, apart from L4823-4906, which are Mk IVs.

10-03-1937 K7036 114 Squadron: overturned after landing on delivery to Wyton; P/O D. Perry uninjured.

30-06-1937 K7053 90 Squadron: dived into ground out of cloud on navigation exercise at Brown Clee Hill, Stanton Long, Salop. Destroyed by Fire (DBF), Sgt E. Moorhouse, AC2 A. Martin and AC1 S. Coomber killed. K7053 was 90 Squadron's dual-control training aircraft.

17-07-1937 K7049 90 Squadron: control lost in cloud, P/O P. Edwards (Pilot) thrown out of aircraft, which crashed at Pitton Hill, near Salisbury, Wilts, he and Cpl T. Robson killed.

30-09-1937 K7057 114 Squadron: Sgt E. Piercy became disorientated turning on approach for night-landing at Wyton and aircraft struck ground; he was only slightly injured.

01-10-1937 K7066 139 Squadron: engine cut after take-off at Wyton. A single-engined circuit was completed but aircraft spun into ground on approach, killing Sgt J. Williams, solo pilot.

26-11-1937 K7056 90 Squadron: hydraulics failed and aircraft belly-landed at Warmswell; became instructional airframe 1027M at Henlow.

03-12-1937 K7110 114 Squadron: control lost in cloud, and pilot baled out. Observer Cpl Tom Barnes belly-landed at Hinckley, Leics, killing a cow, and was awarded AFM. Aircraft Damaged Beyond Repair (DBR).

17-12-1937 K7052 90 Squadron: engine failed during fuel consumption trials, and stalled in forced landing near Weston-on-the-Green, Oxon. DBR.

08-01-1938 K7150 110 Squadron: undercarriage (u/c) collapsed in heavy landing at Waddington. DBR and sent to Shoeburyness.

11-01-1938 K7082 144 Squadron: made forced landing in fog. DBR and sent to Shoeburyness.

13-01-1938 K7055 90 Squadron: engine cut and aircraft stalled attempting single-engined landing at Bicester. DBR and also sent to Shoeburyness for gun-damage trials.

18-01-1938 K7145 110 Squadron: u/c not locked down and collapsed on landing at Waddington. DBR and also sent to Shoeburyness.

27-01-1938 K7078 44 Squadron: control lost during aerobatics near Waddington; aircraft abandoned and destroyed; P/O A. Macfarlane (NZ, solo pilot) baled out but struck tail and was killed.

27-01-1938 K7134 44 Squadron: u/c retracted in error after landing at Waddington. DBR and sent to Shoeburyness.

11-02-1938 K7119 144 Squadron: flew into hailstorm and hit trees during turn at Oulton, Norfolk. Destroyed By Fire, P/O L. Mitchell, Cpl G. Henderson and AC1 C. Smith killed.

07-04-1938 K7168 61 Squadron: u/c retracted in error after landing at Hemswell. DBR.

08-04-1938 K7041 114 Squadron: engine cut and u/c jammed; belly-landed at Wyton, overturned. DBR.

22-04-1938 K7127 44 Squadron: engine cut on take-off, swung and hit ground; P/O T. MacDonald (Pilot) injured, Cpl L. Tidey killed.

22-04-1938 K7146 110 Squadron: control lost in cloud and aircraft dived into ground at Crowland, Lincs; P/O H. Green, Cpl C. Badger and AC2 F. Howard killed.

06-05-1938 K7054 90 Squadron: overshot flare-path in night landing at Bicester and struck obstruction. DBR and sent to Orfordness research depot.

10-05-1938 K7037 114 Squadron: engine cut on take-off at Wyton and control lost; P/O D. Perry, AC1 J. Rice and AC1 F. Crimes killed.

10-05-1938 K7080 144 Squadron: engine cut on take-off and aircraft crashed 1 mile from Hemswell; P/O R. Maxwell and Cpl D. Wissett killed.

12-05-1938 K7128 44 Squadron: u/c retracted in error on landing at Waddington; became instructional airframe 1107M at Manston.

10-06-1938 L1157 110 Squadron: engine cut and aircraft overshot landing at Ronaldsway and hit wall.

13-06-1938 L1150 114 Squadron: belly-landed at Penrhos; became instructional airframe 1116M.

14-06-1938 K7149 110 Squadron: engine cut and aircraft belly-landed 4 miles from Waddington; became instructional airframe 1113M at Cosford.

20-06-1938 K7047 90 Squadron: belly-landed in error at Bicester; reduced to spares.

18-07-1938 L1153 139 Squadron: became lost on exercise with Observer Corps and was abandoned when out of fuel near Stratford-upon-Avon, Warks; Cpl D. Day (Obs) killed, P/O M. McColm (Pilot) and AC1 J. Gordon safe.

20-07-1938 L1143 57 Squadron: engine cut and aircraft belly-landed. DBR and became instructional airframe 1136M.

27-07-1938 K7074 139 Squadron: engine cut on take-off at Wyton, aircraft lost height and hit trees; Sgt J. Parkinson and two crewmen injured.

30-08-1938 K7067 90 Squadron: control lost in icing conditions; aircraft abandoned and crashed on Cottonhopehead Moor, Northumberland. F/O H. Edwards, Sgt Nish and AC1 Theophilus all injured; Hughie Edwards struck aerial and spent nine months in hospital, but recovered and later gained VC, DSO and DFC.

A typical example of the many 'Crashed in attempted forced-landing' entries in these Appendices. As the cockpit of K7052 (90 Squadron) was relatively undamaged on 17 December 1937, the crew escaped uninjured.

On 8 April 1938 K7041 of 114 Squadron at Wyton had an engine cut, the undercarriage jammed, and the aircraft overturned attempting to belly-land.

Even when their flying days were over, Blenheims gave valuable service as ground-instruction airframes: K7060 (ex-139 Squadron) and K7040 (ex-114 Squadron) arrrive on 21 February 1938 at No 1 School of Technical Training at Halton, serving there for many years.

Chapter 7

The last year of peace

Bristol: the world's largest aircraft manufacturer

The last year of peace, from the Munich Crisis of September 1938 to the outbreak of war just one year later, saw not only the massive and unprecedented expansion of the RAF but also – due mainly to this very expansion – the Bristol Aircraft Company at Filton continue to grow until it became the largest aeroplane manufacturer in the world. Its factories at Filton were the largest both in terms of floor area, at 2,688,324 square feet, and the number of employees, at 20,464 – although this would grow to 52,095 in 1942. The company had increased its issued share capital from the £1.2 million in 1935 mentioned in Chapter 4 to £3.9 million in 1939, a vast sum in those days. Its capital investment in airframe production facilities between 1935 and 1938 was the highest of all the bomber manufacturers – at £853,000 it was more than the £779,000 combined total of Vickers (£347,000), Armstrong-Whitworth (£269,000) and Handley-Page (£163,000) (source: PRO Cab 16/227). During this period Vickers had constructed extra factory space and made the tools and jigs for, and were busy producing, the Wellesley and Wellington, Armstrong-Whitworth the Whitley, and Handley-Page the Harrow and Hampden. That Bristol at Filton had reached this pre-eminent position among the world's aircraft manufacturers stemmed directly from the production of the Blenheim and its immediate progeny. And that the company was able to design and manufacture the airframes for the latter – the Beaufort and Beaufighter – in such a short time-span was due to the experience gained in the creation and large-scale production of the Blenheim.

Bristol's investment in its Engine Department was even higher, at the then astronomic sum of £2 million, as Roy Fedden, 'Bunny' Butler, Fred Whitehead and Frank Owner led the team that struggled to develop the new range of sleeve-valve engines and make them suitable for volume production. These difficulties were not resolved until late in 1938

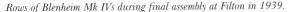

Rows of Blenheim Mk IVs during final assembly at Filton in 1939.

when High Duty Alloys perfected a special light alloy with 12 per cent silicon from which to forge the cylinders, Vickers Firth developed a high-expansion steel from which the sleeves were cast centrifugally, and Whitehead, the production genius at Filton, finally discovered the hitherto elusive method of grinding them into perfectly circular sleeves.

Let us now take a closer look at British aero-engine manufacturers in general, and at Bristol in particular, as the products that they were able to supply had such a profound effect upon the aircraft that the RAF could deploy during the Second World War, an effect that impinged directly upon the deployment of the Blenheim and the development of its descendants.

Military aero-engines

The Bristol Aeroplane Company had maintained its proud independence during the round of mergers involving British aircraft manufacturers that took place just before this period of rapid expansion of the aviation industry. Sopwith's Hawker company merged with Armstrong-Whitworth Aircraft Ltd and Armstrong-Siddeley Motors, and acquired A. V. Roe Ltd, then (as the Hawker Siddeley Group) also took over Gloster and High Duty Alloys. Vickers purchased Supermarine, the old-established maker of flying-boats; this was partly to secure the services of Reginald Mitchell, who had designed the Schneider Trophy seaplanes, then the immortal Spitfire. However, tragically he died of cancer in June 1937, and the Supermarine Type 316, a promising four-engined bomber he had designed, was never completed.

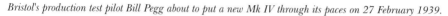

Bristol's production test pilot Bill Pegg about to put a new Mk IV through its paces on 27 February 1939.

Bristol was able to remain independent through the strength of its aero-engine department and the profitability of its numerous licensing agreements with foreign countries. Bristol and Rolls-Royce thus became the only two major UK companies left in the business of producing powerful military aero-engines. Their other two main competitors, Napier and Armstrong-Siddeley, had faded away since the end of the First World War, following the similar decline of Sunbeam and Wolseley aero-engines. To counter this the Air Ministry had awarded contracts to encourage Napier – which had been its foremost supplier, with the Lion, in the 1920s – to develop the Dagger, a 1,000hp engine with an H-24 layout of small cylinders, and to Armstrong, which was only producing single-row radials of modest power such as the Cheetah and the earlier Jaguar, to develop the Tiger, an 850hp twin-row radial, and the Deerhound, a 1,200hp triple-row overhead-camshaft radial. However, the air-cooled Dagger, Tiger and Deerhound were all unsuccessful. Neither Handley-Page, Vickers nor Shorts manufactured aero-engines, Fairey had tried but could not obtain orders from the Air Ministry, and De Havilland had built up a sound business between the wars by concentrating on light civil and basic-training aircraft, together with the simple low-powered engines to suit them. Thus the Bristol Aeroplane Company Ltd became the sole major manufacturer of military aircraft that also produced its own engines.

The troublesome Taurus sleeve-valve engine, which with the Hercules took so long to develop that new aircraft to replace the Blenheims were delayed, so the latter had to remain in front-line service for very much longer than intended.

Fedden had abandoned his earlier double-row Hydra with poppet-valves actuated by overhead camshafts, and set Bristol irrevocably upon the path of the large-capacity sleeve-valve air-cooled radial engine (it will be remembered that his First World War contract with Rolls-Royce precluded him from designing engines with in-line cylinders). The 600hp Perseus radial, with a single-row of nine Mercury-size cylinders, first ran in 1932, the smaller 500hp Aquila in 1934, followed by the large twin-row 14-cylinder 1,300hp Hercules and the compact 1,000hp Taurus, with the same layout of smaller cylinders, both running initially in 1936. Among other troubles, the Taurus suffered from distortion due to uneven cooling, problems proving difficult to overcome and delaying clearance for flight trials. These difficulties were exacerbated by the approach of war, as Bristol was running out of the much-needed development time in which to satisfy the conflicting demands of achieving high power outputs with an acceptable level of reliability in service use – and to overcome the intractable difficulties encountered in making sleeve-valve engines suitable for the volume of mass-production that a war would demand. These delays with the engine programmes had a major effect not only upon the development of the Blenheim itself, and upon Bristol's unsuccessful attempts to produce a Medium Bomber successor to it, but also upon its immediate family, the Beaufort and Beaufighter.

Roy Fedden was a titan among engineers, single-minded, absolutely indefatigable – he worked a constant 80- to 90-hour week – and a very hard taskmaster. He drove his entire department forward relentlessly throughout the 1930s when it was deeply involved in designing and developing the Bristol family of sleeve-valve engines. Small numbers of the Perseus had run successfully in a hand-built production form since October 1935, but it was not ready for full production until 1937, being delivered later in some quantity in a developed 900hp version. The neat Aquila did not enter production at all, and the troublesome Taurus was placed in production prematurely and was still experiencing major difficulties well into the war. But the most expensive project in terms of time, money and sheer effort was the massive task of developing the Hercules, a powerful twin-row radial engine with 14 Mercury-sized sleeve-valve cylinders. This ran for the first time in January 1936 when it developed 1,290hp, was improved to give 1,425hp on 87 octane fuel, then intensive effort improved it further to give a dependable 1,590hp on 100 octane. It became one of the most important British aero-engines and saw extensive use throughout the Second World War, being finally developed to give 2,140hp with complete reliability. By the mid-1930s Fedden had seen the need for an engine in the 2,000 to 3,000hp class and was developing a twin-row 18-cylinder sleeve-valve engine, still with Mercury-size cylinders but with a longer stroke. This was the Centaurus, which first ran in 1938, and was type-tested at 2,000hp in 1939, although the pressures of trying to get the other engines right prevented further development in the early war years. Eventually the Centaurus became the finest piston aero-engine ever built, giving more than 3,220hp in its post-war direct-injection Mk 373 form. At the epicentre of this exciting but demanding activity, the ever-forward-looking Fedden certainly did not expect that the elderly Mercury and Pegasus engines, originating from the First World War Jupiter, with their exposed poppet-valves operated by pushrods, would continue to be produced by the thousand throughout the forthcoming conflict. For he was already dreaming up his Orion – a 4,000hp-plus version of the Centaurus.

There was an exact parallel to Bristol's long struggle to develop the power and reliability of the Taurus and Hercules, and to overcome the difficulties of making them suitable for mass production, which so seriously delayed the Centaurus development programme. For Rolls-Royce had been kept so busy since 1933 developing its Merlin range that it did not have the facilities available to resolve the problems with its X-24 Vulture and V-12 Peregrine engines, to the detriment of the Manchester and Whirlwind programmes. Nor, until late in the war, was the company able to develop its more powerful Griffon, which (unlike the smaller-capacity Merlin) was dimensionally the same as the 1931 R-Type V-12 Schneider Trophy racing engine. For the same reasons Rolls-Royce was unable to devote sufficient resources or management effort to its promising 1,200hp Exe (a small 24-

cylinder sleeve-valve air-cooled X engine) or to its magnificent 3,500hp H-24 Eagle sleeve-valve liquid-cooled engine, which did not run until after the war, although it had been worked on throughout the conflict. Similarly, Napier had given up on its air-cooled Dagger and spent many years and millions of pounds developing its sleeve-valve water-cooled H-24 Sabre. This gave 1,350hp in 1938, but despite intense pressure from the Air Ministry it took Napier until 1944 to persuade the Sabre to produce a not very reliable 2,600hp (using cylinder sleeves from the Bristol Taurus), finally reaching 3,000hp after the war. The cost of developing the Sabre had brought the once omnipotent Napier company to its knees, and it was absorbed by the English Electric Company. The unfortunate result of all this delayed and protracted development work was that the RAF was denied urgently required engines in the 2,000 to 3,000hp range until the final stages of the war.

The Westland Whirlwind, plagued by problems with its Rolls-Royce Peregrine engines, equipped only two Squadrons, while the Gloster F.9/37, which flew with both RR Peregrine and (as shown) Bristol Taurus engines, was not ordered into production. Both these cannon-armed long-range fighters were faster than the contemporary Spitfire. The lack of these aircraft meant that the much slower, poorly armed Blenheim Fighters had to continue operating although obsolescent.

    A further and most unfortunate result of these problems with engine development, which directly affected the Blenheim, was the absence of a long-range fighter in the RAF's armoury in the earlier stages of the war. The Westland Whirlwind and the promising Gloster F.9/37, both twin-engined cannon-armed fighters, were in difficulties following delays in resolving troubles with their Peregrine and Taurus engines, and both programmes were cancelled later. Both aircraft had exceeded 360mph in tests, faster than the contemporary Spitfire. Once more the much slower and far less powerfully armed Blenheim had to fill the gap and was pressed into service in a role for which it was not suited, and made to suffer accordingly, until the Beaufighter – and later the Mosquito – became operational. The Bristol Type 156 'Beaufort-fighter' was proposed by Leslie Frise and Roy Fedden in October 1938 specifically to fill that gap as quickly as possible.

However, the first developed version of the Blenheim itself was concurrent with and linked intimately to the Type 152 Beaufort and came into being through an unlikely and twisting path; I will attempt to set out the stepping-stones in sequence, although several were taken almost simultaneously and virtually in parallel.

The Blenheim Mark IV

In the spring of 1935 Barnwell had sketched a layout for an improved 142M with sleeve-valve engines and a fuselage that was wider and slightly deeper as far aft as the turret, giving this project the type number 149, but it did not conform with any Specification and was not pursued. In June that year the Air Ministry, spurred on by Expansion Scheme C, decided that it should replace the Vickers Vildebeest biplane (which ten years earlier in 1925 had won a competition for a 'torpedo-bomber land-plane' under Specification 24/25), so it issued Operational Requirement No 22 for a 'Shore-based twin-engined Torpedo Bomber'. This led to Specification M.15/35, and Bristol submitted its Type 150, another proposed developed version of the 142M Blenheim via the Type 149 design study. The 150 had a 58-foot wing-span, two Perseus sleeve-valve engines, a fuselage with the increased cross-section of the 149 and also greater length, achieved by moving the pilot's cockpit forwards 4ft 6in, with a profile later to be seen on the initial 'long-nose' Blenheim, and the dorsal turret moved rearwards to maintain the balance. This extra length was to allow the large torpedo to be carried internally under the centre of gravity. Work included making a wooden mock-up of the fuselage in the experimental shop, but there was insufficient room for the Navigator in the nose, and the fuselage was too shallow to accommodate this essential crew member above the extended bomb bay, so the proposal was not accepted. Blackburn submitted its Type 26, also with twin Perseus engines, but this was not accepted either and the specification was abandoned.

The following Operational Requirement, No 23, was for a militarised version of the civil Avro 652 and resulted in Specification 18/35 for a 'Coastal Reconnaissance Aircraft' and the Avro 652A – the Anson, as described in Chapter 6. Shortly afterwards OR No 25 for a 'General Purpose Reconnaissance Land-plane' was issued, and Bristol started design work to modify a 142M Blenheim to suit Specification G.24/35 for this requirement. This had the fuselage from the original 149 project that was wider and slightly deeper from nose to turret, and as Bristol considered this to be a continuation of that earlier design work, it transferred to it the type number 149. But, like the Type 150, the proposal was not taken up when submitted to the Air Ministry in November 1935. Westland, Boulton Paul, Avro and Fairey also submitted designs for G.24/35, but none of them was selected for production, so this Specification, too, was left unfilled. Also, as mentioned earlier, in December 1935 Barnwell had submitted two proposals for a four-engined 'Super Blenheim', scaled up directly from the 142M with either four Mercury or four Taurus engines, both versions giving a performance that far exceeded the demands of Specification B.1/35, but these designs – advanced for their time – were not accepted either. Barnwell also put forward, unsuccessfully, the Type 153A, a single-seat fighter with twin Aquila engines, twin end-plate fins and rudders, and the fuselage nose positioned a third back chord-wise from the continuous leading edge of the low wing that mounted four cannon centrally – a design later copied by Grumman in the USA for the XF5 Skyrocket, a predecessor of that company's Tigercat. So the Bristol design office was a veritable hive of activity.

By early 1936 the Air Ministry was aware of the inadequacies of the Anson, and that the RAF still had no new torpedo-bomber in prospect. So, following prompting from Frank Barnwell, the Ministry issued OR No 38, combining the above fruitless specifications 15/35 and 24/35. This led to Specification 10/36 issued on 30 June 1936 – five days after the first flight of K7033, the prototype Blenheim I – under which Bristol submitted its Type 152, which became the Beaufort, and Blackburn its Type B26, which became the Botha. Both types initially relied on Bristol Perseus sleeve-valve engines, but the Beaufort was upgraded to the more powerful Taurus engines as the weight grew steadily during the design process. Because of the urgency of the requirement, both types were ordered into production in August 1936, long before a prototype of either had flown. This short-cut may have worked well with the Blenheim, which was based directly on the proven 'Britain First', but was to result in many difficulties with the new designs of the Beaufort and Botha. Within months these orders for the untried new types were increased to 426 Beauforts and no fewer than 1,256 Bothas, the far larger number of the latter design being ordered because Blackburn had much less work in hand than Bristol. This turned out to be a big mistake, as the Bothas failed to reach proper operational status and Blenheims had to deployed in their place.

The prototype Beaufort L4441; note the small-diameter Taurus sleeve-valve engines. The Blenheim-type 'apron' wheel fairings were changed to side-hinged doors, and overheating led to controllable cooling-gills, as on the Blenheim's Mercuries. The Blackburn Botha with Perseus engines, also pictured, was a complete flop. This and the long delays in making the Beaufort fit for operations meant that Blenheims became the RAF's principal anti-shipping aircraft.

It was intended that the Beaufort would take the place of the Blenheim on the Filton production lines as soon as Blenheim production had been transferred to the new shadow factories. However, such were the expected delays in getting either of the new 10/36 types into service – expectations fully justified, as it transpired – that in July 1936 the Air Ministry issued OR No 39 for an 'Interim General Reconnaissance Aeroplane', deleting the torpedo-carrying capability, under Specification 11/36. Frank Barnwell once again submitted a revised Bristol Type 149, but now it was a modified and strengthened 142M Blenheim, reverting to the original slimmer fuselage cross-section to avoid the need for fresh jigs and tooling. Also retained were the Mercury engines, but in the slightly more powerful XV version, and it had extra fuel tanks, together with a proper position for a Navigator in an extended nose. Barnwell resisted Fedden's urging that all fresh Bristol types should use one of the new range of sleeve-valve engines rather than the elderly Mercury or Pegasus range, from which all the power possible had been squeezed. Barnwell had decided to minimise the changes so that the modifications could be introduced on the existing Blenheim production lines, for this would reduce considerably the time required to put the aircraft into service in the numbers required. As the Air Ministry regarded the Bristol Type 149 merely as a 'stop-gap' aircraft this submission was accepted and a production order to Specification 34/36 was awarded in October 1936, for which the name Bolingbroke was chosen.

When the Blenheim Mk I entered widespread RAF service, several bomber squadrons voiced concern at the relatively limited range and criticised the very cramped Observer's position. Bomber Command was therefore not happy at the thought of the improved Type 149 Bolingbroke going to Coastal Command while it was expected to continue operating the Type 142M 'short-nose' Blenheim Mk I. Bomber Command did not have much difficulty in persuading the Air Staff to change its outstanding orders to the modified type, especially as the Air Ministry took the opportunity to install much more equipment, such as the bulky T.1083/R.1082 wireless sets, all of which increased the weight so that it needed the more powerful engines to restore the performance. The name Bolingbroke was abandoned for UK production, partly for contractual reasons, but mainly because the aircraft built to the 34/36 'Interim GR' specification was rightly considered to be a modified Blenheim Mk I. So it was decided that the Type 149 would continue with the Blenheim name. As the Mks II and III were only one-off stages in the long development process, and did not enter production, the 149 was called the Mk IV.

This, then, was the winding path that resulted in the famous 'long-nose' Blenheim Mk IV, which instead of being merely an interim replacement for the Anson prior to the Beaufort and Botha entering service, found itself serving as the RAF's main Medium Bomber and principal anti-shipping aircraft for the first two and a half years of the war.

Providing extra range had not been too difficult; an additional 94-gallon tank was fitted between the spars of each outer wing in a similar fashion to the 140-gallon main tanks mounted in each side of the centre-section, giving a fuel capacity of 468 imperial gallons. Although the undercarriage was strengthened, the extra fuel made the landing weight and the landing run excessive, so 'dump' tubes were fitted to enable the fuel in the outer tanks to be jettisoned should a landing be necessary with a full load. These modifications were flight-tested on L1222 in September 1938. Extra power was also needed, and as there were no other Bristol engines in the 1,000 to 1,200hp range available in sufficient quantity at that time, it could only be provided by substituting Mercury XVs of 920hp for the Mercury VIIIs of 840hp in the Blenheim I. The aged Mercury had reached the end of the long development road, and the 10 per cent increase in power was largely gained by the XVs being modified to run on 100 octane fuel. Limited supplies of this petrol were being imported from America, as a direct result of strong lobbying by Roy Fedden – as he had also pressed just as hard four years earlier in 1934 for the introduction of 87 octane fuel, which permitted the use of higher compression ratios resulting in a 15 per cent power increase. That year the Mercury and Pegasus became the first engines to be type-tested and cleared for this fuel, and for Hamilton-Standard variable-pitch propellers. Fedden was a single-minded visionary, constantly striving not only to improve the engines he designed but also to drag the rest of the British aircraft industry forward so that it could face the crucial challenge from Germany that he believed to be imminent.

Two views of K7072 with its initially extended nose at Filton in September 1937.

Providing a satisfactory station for the Observer/Navigator proved almost as difficult; the first solution was to extend the entire nose-section by 3 feet, as had been tried in October 1936 on the mock-up mentioned above. But when this extended nose was built on an actual aircraft in September 1937 – the 40th production aircraft, K7072, was taken from the line for this purpose – the windscreen proved to be too far from the pilot's eyes, and reflections from the many glazing panels proved troublesome. Cyril Uwins was far from happy with this layout, and it took only three and a half hours of flight-tests in November for the A&AEE at Martlesham Heath to reject it. By December the nose was fitted with a stepped windscreen set at the same distance from the pilot as on a Mk I and with a curved glazed canopy over the navigation position – but this restricted the pilot's view for take-off and in particular for approach and landing, so this layout was also rejected after further flight-tests. It took another seven months before the definitive asymmetric nose, with the port side of the Navigator's canopy scalloped down to keep it below the pilot's line of sight, was fitted, tested at Martlesham Heath in July 1938, approved, and cleared for production. This was a lengthy delay at a period when the RAF was crying out for deliveries of the improved aircraft, but probably resulted from Bristol's pre-occupation with the contemporary Beaufort. The Navigator sat on a sideways-facing folding seat in the starboard side of the nose with his table on the port side beneath the scalloped portion of the glazed canopy. Thus came into being the familiar lopsided 'long-nose' that became such a distinctive feature of the Blenheim IV.

These modifications were introduced into the production lines as soon as details were settled, drawings prepared, and the jigs and tooling altered. Only one 'short-nose' Mk I aircraft, L1222 mentioned above, from the second Filton production batch of 450, had the extra fuel tanks and strengthened landing-gear, and was known as the Mk II. Because of a shortage of these additional fuel tanks, 68 airframes were built initially as 'long-nose'

The modified extended nose was lowered in front of the windscreen (which reverted to its previous position), as fitted to K7072 in January 1938, but it still obscured the Pilot's view, especially on landing.

aircraft without the increased fuel capacity and known as the Mk III, but neither Mark was put into production. When the long-range tanks were later fitted to the 'long-nose' aircraft built without them, they were referred to by the unofficial designation of Mk IV-L. Therefore all Blenheims were delivered as either the Mk I or were modified, during production or retrospectively, to full Mk IV standard. For example, the third production batch at Filton built during this change-over period under Contract No 529181/36, all of which started out on the lines as Mk Is, were actually delivered as 34 Mk Is and 84 Mk IVs; and the second batch, built by Rootes under Contract No 551920/37, were delivered as 250 Mk Is and 130 Mk IVs. However, all 220 of the third batch from Rootes, ordered as Mk Is under the earlier Contract No 569202/36, were delivered as Mk IVs, even though the first 80 had been built as Mk Is and had to be modified to Mk IVs. The first Mk IV was not delivered until March 1939.

THE BRISTOL BLENHEIM

The production version of the Type 149 Blenheim Mk IV seen in two fine studies of Bill Pegg in L4842 on a Bristol Aircraft Company publicity sortie in 1938. Another photograph taken on this sortie forms the Frontispiece.

The British aviation industry was shaken when the Air Ministry announced on 9 June 1938 that it was purchasing from the United States 200 Lockheed Hudson coastal patrol bombers and 200 North American Harvard advanced trainers. The Hudson, a militarised Lockheed 14 airliner, joined the Blenheim in taking over from the Coastal Command Anson squadrons due to the delays and troubles with the intended Beaufort and Botha replacements, and some 1,800 were to be delivered eventually. We have seen how the lack of an advanced twin-engine training aircraft caused problems to pilots converting to Blenheims, until the Airspeed Oxford entered service; similarly, future fighter pilots lacked an advanced trainer, as the Miles Master I, with a Rolls-Royce Kestrel engine, was not ordered until June 1938, and only seven were in service at the outbreak of war. The 900 Master Is were followed by 1,750 Master IIs with Bristol Mercury engines. The Harvard filled the gap admirably – 4,763 were to be delivered to the RAF, and they served from December 1938 right until 1954!

Death of Frank Barnwell

The other personality besides Fedden absolutely central to the design and development of the Blenheim up to this point in the story was of course Frank Barnwell, in whose fertile mind the design had been created. However, he had always been a far better designer and draughtsman than he was a pilot, and had wrecked several Bristol machines, being fortunate to escape without serious injury. As he was uninsurable, partly in view of his age (58) but mainly because of his immense value to the company, the Bristol Directors had banned him from flying solo in their aircraft. But he had built with some friends a very small wooden single-seater, for possible use under the Civil Air Guard Scheme, at Whitchurch, Bristol's airport. This was fitted with a 25hp two-stroke engine from the Scott Squirrel motorcycle manufacturers, but disaster struck when it gave trouble soon after his second take-off on 2 August 1938. He attempted to turn back to the airfield but stalled and crashed fatally. This tragedy cost the nation, and particularly the Bristol Aeroplane Company, the services of a very gifted designer with an impressive string of fine machines to his credit. Although Frank Barnwell OBE AFC BSc had built up an excellent design team with Leslie Frise, Archie Russell, Cliff Tinson and Harry Pollard, who were working flat out on the many projects under way at that critical time, his acute overview and central guiding hand were to be sadly missed, and thereafter the design office lacked the unity of purpose that he had instilled.

At the time of his death the first offspring of the Blenheim family, the Type 152 Beaufort prototype L4441, was almost completed and was rolled out on 27 September 1938. This was the last design Barnwell worked on and was a further development of the Type 150 and 149 designs. Structurally it was the same as the Blenheim except that he replaced the steel spar-booms and angles with alloy extrusions in hiduminium to save weight. The Beaufort was a clever design and could carry double the bomb-load of a Blenheim, plus another 100 gallons of fuel, with wings only 2 feet greater in span (7 per cent greater area) and only a 20 per cent increase in engine power. This was due to the 40 per cent higher wing loading, which, in pounds weight per square foot of wing area, had risen to 45 in the Beaufort as against 32 in the Blenheim (for comparison the Bulldog was only 10lb/sq ft). This higher wing loading resulted in a higher stalling speed, and therefore approach speed and landing run, together with a much longer take-off distance. The Beaufort specification permitted the use of 3,000-foot runways, treble that specified for the Blenheim. By raising the pilot's cockpit in a deeper fuselage, which ran straight back over the fourth crewman's position to blend with the dorsal turret, Barnwell enabled the Beaufort pilot to see over the nose glazing without the scalloping needed on the Blenheim IV. He did not live to witness the ground runs that revealed the overheating problems with the aircraft's new Taurus engines, or to observe it take to the air on 15 October 1938. By then Type 149 Blenheim Mk IVs had been introduced to the production lines at Filton, and the lines at Avro and Rootes soon followed suit.

Unfortunately Frank Barnwell was also fated not to see any of the last trio of Bristol Types that he had designed – the 130 Bombay, 149 Blenheim IV, or 152 Beaufort – enter squadron service. Such a close involvement with aviation exacted a very heavy price from the Barnwell family; his brother had been killed in a flying accident while serving as a test pilot with Vickers, and sadly all three of his sons were to be killed in action as RAF pilots during the war – one of them, 19-year-old David, in a Hurricane defending Malta, and the other two in Blenheims, Richard in a bomber and John in a night-fighter.

In October 1938, soon after Barnwell's death, Leslie Frise and Roy Fedden proposed the Bristol Type 156 'Beaufort-fighter' to the Air Ministry specifically to meet the need for a long-range 'heavy' fighter as quickly as possible. Clearly influenced by Barnwell's abortive Type 153A, the 156 was a version of the 152 Beaufort, fitted with more powerful Hercules engines and a slim forward fuselage. The greater diameter of the propellers led not only to the raising of the engines on the wing, but also to the snub nose behind the plane of the propellers, which gave the aircraft such a pugnacious look. Four 20mm cannon were mounted in place of the torpedo, plus six machine-guns in the wings, so it had devastating fire-power. This proposal was readily accepted by the Air Ministry, which quickly realised its potential as a night-fighter too – another gap in RAF equipment that the Blenheim was being pressed into service to fill – so the Beaufighter, the second 'son of Blenheim', was born.

Frank Barnwell OBE AFC BSc, eminent Chief Designer and Chief Engineer of the Bristol Aircraft Company, in a portrait taken shortly before his death on 2 August 1938.

Roy Fedden's relationship with the Bristol Board

As a brilliant engine designer striving constantly to produce more horsepower, Fedden had become ever more frustrated at seeing 'his' engines installed in aircraft with fixed-pitch propellers, comparable to fitting a highly-tuned engine into a racing car with only a single-speed gearbox. The two-position bracket-type propeller as fitted to 'Britain First', then to the Blenheim and many other contemporary aircraft, at least gave the equivalent of a 'low' and a 'high' gear. A variable-pitch propeller also fitted with a constant-speed unit would govern the engine rpm to the level set by the pilot and would be even more efficient. So Fedden argued and cajoled for Bristol to produce its own variable-pitch constant-speed propellers – it had made small numbers of fixed-pitch props in both alloy and compressed laminated wood – but when the Board declined to become further involved, he arranged for supplies to be imported pending the creation of manufacturing facilities in the UK. He had obtained a production licence from Hamilton-Standard in the USA, and, when Bristol did not take it up, he passed it on to De Havilland, which went on to manufacture tens of thousands of DH propellers; they were fitted to most wartime aircraft, including of course the Blenheim, so Bristol missed out on a huge amount of business. Fedden then invited two leading Directors of Bristol's strongest competitor, Rolls-Royce – Arthur (later Sir Arthur) Sidgreaves and E. W. (later Lord) Hives – to lunch at the Royal Thames Yacht Club, and they reached agreement that the Bristol Aeroplane Company and Rolls-Royce Ltd would found a joint company to produce variable-pitch propellers in the UK. Owned and managed on a 50/50 basis, this new company, called 'Rotol' by amalgamating the names, was formed in March 1937. A new factory was built at Staverton between Cheltenham and Gloucester, which soon grew, like De Havilland Propellers Ltd, into a vast business, now part of a group with Dowty and Messier, both companies that started as manufacturers of hydraulic pumps and undercarriages.

It was Roy Fedden's vision, his unmatched drive, and his tenacity in analysing and resolving mechanical problems that had pushed the Bristol Engines Division forward to its pre-eminent position. Yet his relations with Bristol's autocratic Board of Directors were often strained, and he was not appointed to it, although he was responsible for the bulk of their business. For some 20 years they had responded to many appeals for further

Roy Fedden, the outstanding designer of the Bristol range of radial piston aero-engines, including the Jupiter, Mercury, Pegasus, Taurus, Hercules and Centaurus.

finance, but sometimes had to restrain his more expansive enthusiasms. This was difficult, as there was no engineer on the Bristol Board, and Fedden was widely travelled and highly respected in the international aviation industry, while they were patrician and insular, but in general they achieved the right balance between support and restraint.

Hugh Dowding could also see the vital improvements in the performance of RAF aircraft to be gained from both 100 octane fuel and variable-pitch propellers, so he encouraged the aviation industry to adopt these developments as soon as it could. Early Hurricanes and Spitfires had wooden fixed-pitch propellers, then the metal variable-pitch bracket-type, as on the Blenheim – a 'crash' programme to convert the fighters at the squadrons to constant-speed units did not start until 22 June 1940, and was barely completed in time for the Battle of Britain! Surprisingly, priority for production of VP and CS propellers had been given to bombers, not fighters. Spitfire Mk IIs, with Merlins IIIs giving 1,160hp on 100 octane fuel (compared with 1,030hp on 87 octane), did not begin to reach the squadrons until October 1940. Dowding also pushed forward the creation of the coastal radar screen and the command system to take full advantage of the information it provided. In my view, no two single individuals contributed more to preparing the RAF for the epochal struggle that lay just ahead than Fedden and Dowding – yet both men were destined to be sidelined.

K7072, with a scalloped port side of the final nose shape, was shown at the 1938 Paris Salon in flying attitude and fitted with Rotol constant-speed propellers, although these were not fitted to production aircraft until the later Mk V.

Aeroplanes at the Paris Aero Show

BRITISH AND BEST.—The latest version of the Bristol Blenheim which, with two 920 h.p. Bristol Mercury VIII aero-motors and two Rotol constant-speed airscrews, is the best looking bomber at the Paris Aero Show. We have been told by those who know that there are more Bristol Blenheims flying in the World to-day than any other type of bomber.

Blenheim exports

The Bristol company had been active in the export market while all this was going on, and was busy negotiating sales of Blenheims – then advertised as 'the fastest bomber in the world' – to several foreign governments. This might seem a strange state of affairs, but the original 142 had been a Private Venture aircraft, so the Air Ministry did not object, providing that the foreign country was considered 'friendly' and any export orders did not interfere with deliveries to the RAF. Yugoslavia and Lithuania headed the queue, but Finland – following on from its interest expressed early in 1935 for a militarised version of the Type 143 – made the initial purchase, ordering 18 on 6 October 1936, and these were delivered between 29 July 1937 and 27 July 1938 (see Note 1). Yugoslavia, whose purchasing commission had visited Filton on 22 May 1936 – before the first Type 142M Blenheim Mk I had flown – bought 20 (see Note 2). Turkey purchased 12, then a further 18 (see Note 3), and, slightly later, Greece bought 12 Mk IVs (see Note 4). Romania, in a futile diplomatic attempt to persuade her to join the Allied side, was sent 13 followed by a further 26 (see Note 5), all delivered before the outbreak of war. Later several of these countries (plus Portugal) purchased further Blenheims, but these came from RAF orders or stocks. Early in 1938 Finland and Yugoslavia decided to manufacture modest numbers of Blenheims under licence, and the necessary arrangements were concluded as the war clouds darkened, the licence to Yugoslavia being delayed by Government procrastination from both parties. Finland manufactured 45 Mk Is, modified to accept Swedish bombs, and Yugoslavia 16 before the Germans stopped production.

Typical of the hundred-odd Blenheims exported before the war are these Turkish Air Force Mk Is of the 2nd Air Division.

Romanian 'top brass' inspect some of the 39 Blenheims received by the FARR (Fortele Aeriens Regale Romaniel) before the war.

Three of the main self-governing Dominions in the then British Empire wished to follow the example of the RAF and equip their air forces with modern aircraft. South Africa began negotiations in 1937 to buy 'a Squadron of Blenheims', but a sample aircraft (L1431) was not shipped out until early 1939. It greatly impressed during trials at Waterkloof in March 1939, and 'large orders' were discussed, but in view of the rapidly deteriorating position in Europe, these orders could not be implemented. Incidentally, L1431 remained with the SAAF until 29 August 1940, when it was returned to the RAF and issued with the fresh serial AX683, becoming the only Mk I in the double-letter series.

The other two Dominions, Canada and Australia, wished to modernise their own air forces by manufacturing considerable numbers of Blenheims under licence. The Air Ministry supported this plan as it offered effective dispersal of UK production facilities that might be disrupted by heavy air attack. Arrangements with the Canadians went ahead smoothly. The RCAF requirements for longer range and better navigation facilities were met by the Bristol Type 149 intended for use by RAF Coastal Command, and licensed production was placed in the hands of the small Fairchild Aircraft Company at Longueuil, Quebec. The contract was announced on 16 November 1938, and special extensions to the Fairchild factory were built to facilitate production. A full set of jigs, tools, specifications and drawings was dispatched to them and K7072, the guinea-pig 'long-nose' aircraft that was in effect the prototype Mk IV, was sent out as a pattern aircraft, having served the same purpose at the Rootes shadow factory. The RCAF chose to retain the Bolingbroke name for its Canadian licence-built Type 149s, the name originally given by the British Air Ministry to the UK-produced Type 149, which was later designated Blenheim Mk IV – all very confusing!

The Australians had tried to order 40 Blenheims in 1936, while they were creating facilities for licensed production. Specification 10/37 for the manufacture of these Type 149s, headed 'Australian Bolingbrokes', was sent to Bristol on 21 May 1937, and called for

702, the first Type 149 long-nose Blenheim IV built under licence in Canada; the RCAF preferred the name Bolingbroke and the Fairchild Aircraft Company production line at Longueuil, Quebec.

Mercury XI engines, Vickers rather than Browning guns, and no camouflage. However, delivery was so delayed that by 1938 it was realised that a heavier, torpedo-carrying aircraft with a longer range would be more suitable for patrolling the vast oceans surrounding Australia. This led to their decision, announced in March 1939, to build the Beaufort rather than the Blenheim. Production facilities had to be created from scratch with assistance from Filton, for there was no indigenous aircraft industry. The Australians soon overcame the difficulties with the Taurus engines – they fitted American Pratt & Whitney Twin Wasp R1380 1,200hp engines instead!

Final peacetime activities

Bristol Blenheims were the star attraction at the 1937 Hendon RAF Pageant. Mk Is of 114 Squadron took off in close formation right over the huge crowds and climbed over the built-up areas that surround the airfield, a manoeuvre that would not be allowed under today's more safety-conscious regime. Early in 1938 the Air Ministry announced that this very popular event would not be held that year, giving as a reason that 'the airfield at RAF Hendon was too small for modern aircraft', but it was really because the Ministry was busy preparing for the far more serious events it regarded as inevitable. However, the public still had the chance to admire Blenheims, looking very warlike in their green and brown camouflage paint, at the Empire Air Days held at most RAF stations. The serious attrition of Blenheims through flying accidents continued throughout the post-Munich period from September 1938 right up to the last days of peace, as listed in Appendix 1.

Bomber Command conducted some important – but most discouraging – trials over five fine days in September 1938 to 'discover the effect of air attack on dispersed aircraft'. Thirty redundant Bristol Bulldogs with full petrol tanks and containers with incendiary ammunition were tethered out in the open on a 1,000-yard-diameter dummy airfield, two pairs of them in protective pens, then six Blenheims in a shallow dive to 2,000 feet dropped 72 40lb GP (general purpose) bombs. These left craters from 50 to 200 yards from the nearest Bulldogs, but caused no damage to them. Six more Blenheims aimed 24 250lb GP bombs from 2,000 feet at the pens, leaving craters from 30 to 100 yards from them but causing 'negligible' damage to the parked aircraft. A further six came down to 1,000 feet to drop 24 250lb GP bombs with a 12-second delay; these fell 'close to the target aircraft' but caused no damage. Several of the 250lb bombs broke up on impact and failed to explode; if dropped in a salvo 'there were often two in one crater, one shattered by the other'. Then nine Battles dropped 36 250lb GP bombs with instantaneous fuses, straddling the tethered aircraft, destroying three and damaging two more. The very poor results achieved in perfect peacetime conditions against such soft targets did not bode at all well for the future.

In March 1939 the Germans declared Czechoslovakia a Protectorate and, in blatant breach of the Munich Agreement, occupied that unfortunate country – on the 31st of that month Chamberlain announced his Guarantee to Poland in the House of Commons. In April Italy occupied Albania. On 11 July 1939 Blenheims headed a formation of 240 RAF aircraft including Wellingtons and Whitleys on a 'flag-waving' exercise over Paris and Lyons intended to raise the morale of the French. On 12 August two Blenheim squadrons, 34 and 62, were sent with their Mk Is to the Far East to reinforce Britain's weak forces there. The Germans stunned the world by announcing a Non-Aggression Pact with Russia on 23 August, and the British signed the Anglo-Polish Mutual Assistance Pact in London the following day. Neither party could foresee that poor Poland would be dismembered by Germany and Russia just a few weeks later.

Blenheims played a major part in the annual Defence Exercises. We have already seen that in the 1937 exercise the Blenheims had sufficient advantage in performance to evade the Gauntlets, Demons and Furies sent up to intercept them, but in 1938 the Gladiators could catch them occasionally, while the new Hurricanes were able to carry out many more dummy attacks as they caught the Blenheims relatively frequently. By the time of the exercises, held on 8-11 August 1939 over South East England, the bombers were being

Formation take-off over the crowd by section of 601 (Aux.) Squadron Mk 1s at Empire Air day, Hendon, 25 May 1939. Another Mk 1 , plus an Oxford and Spitfire are on static display.

Blenheims were the centre of attraction at RAF Open Days.

The AOC of Bomber Command reported to the Air Staff just before the war that demands upon the Air Gunner were 'almost superhuman', and 'it is utterly fantastic to expect the efficient defence of the aircraft'.

intercepted more readily – the pilots of the 1,300 aircraft talking part did not realise that many of the interceptions were being made possible by the use of the chain of still secret radar stations around that stretch of coast. Clearly a single firing pass from a fighter armed with eight rapid-firing Browning machine-guns would count as a 'kill', and the single pan-fed Vickers gun in the turret of the Blenheim could offer little effective defence.

The head of Bomber Command, Ludlow-Hewitt, had already reported his grave concerns in May 1939, highlighting this particular weakness. 'We have all this valuable equipment and highly trained personnel depending for its safety upon one inadequately trained and inexperienced individual with a single relatively inadequate gun in a very exposed position... Here he has to face the full blast of the eight-gun battery of the modern fighter. The demands which will be made on the coolness, presence of mind, skill and efficiency of this single individual are, in exacting conditions, almost superhuman and ... it is utterly fantastic to expect the efficient defence of the aircraft.' Apart from the 'almost superhuman' demands made on the Air-Gunner, his Vickers K, the 'single relatively inadequate gun' in the Blenheim turret, had a rate of fire of 650 rounds per minute and a useful range of 400 yards – the cannon in a Messerschmitt could deliver over four times the weight of fire from an effective range of 1,000 yards. The Air Staff was no doubt aware of these grave deficiencies, but could not act to remedy them before the ammunition being fired at the Blenheims was all too real.

Germany invaded Poland on 1 September and ignored the ultimatum demanding withdrawal issued by Britain and France, who mobilised their forces. War was declared on 3 September.

Blenheims played a major role in the 1938 and 1939 Defence Exercises and on the latter occasion the national markings were toned down, as on L1426, a 25 Squadron Mk I-F from Hawkinge, seen over Tilbury and three more 'attacking' two British Army mobile Bofors AA guns – the soldiers are wearing anti-gas-masks and overalls.

The crew of a Mk I-F of 29 Squadron are wearing their 'tin hats' for the 1939 Exercises, and the four-gun ventral pack is shown clearly. In the other view ground-crew practice wearing gas-masks while loading four 250lb bombs.

Notes

Note 1: Exports to Finland

18 aircraft, Construction Nos 8137 to 8154 inclusive, were delivered between 29 July 1937 and 27 July 1938, becoming BL104 to BL121. A production licence was granted to *Valtion Lentokonetehdas* (State Aircraft Factory) on 12 April 1938.

Blenheims at Filton marked with Finnish swastikas in blue; 18 aircraft were delivered between July 1937 and July 1938, and a production licence granted.

Note 2: Exports to Yugoslavia

Two pattern aircraft, Construction Nos 8814 and 8815, were flown out as G-AFCE and G-AFCF to Ikarus AD at Zenum in November 1937, given the JKRV serial Nos 160 and 161. A licence to produce 50 aircraft was granted to Ikarus AD in April 1938.

The first of two Blenheims purchased by Yugoslavia as pattern aircraft for their licensed production.

Note 3: Exports to Turkey

Two sample aircraft, Nos 8155 and 8156, were sent by sea in October 1937. Ten aircraft, Nos 8157 to 8166, were flown out between March and June 1938 carrying the UK Civil Registrations G-AFFP and G-AFFR to G-AFFZ inclusive. Eighteen aircraft, Nos 9222 to 9239, were flown out from November 1938 to February 1939 carrying UK Civil Registrations G-AFLA to G-AFLP and G-AFLR/S. A further ten from RAF stocks were sent on 21 September 1939: L1483/5/8/9/93/7 and L4821/4/6/8.

Turkey bought 30, and here are the first batch with Turkish 'Crescent and Star' markings on a red background. They bought ten more, delivered late in September 1939.

Note 4: Exports to Greece

Twelve unarmed Mk IVs, taken from RAF orders with Bristol at Filton, were flown directly out to the Royal Hellenic Air Force from 13 October 1939: P4910, with the UK Civil Registration G-AFXD, P4911 (G-AFXE), P4915 (G-AFXF), P4916 (G-AFXG), P4921 (G-AFXH), P4922 (G-AFXI), P6891 (G-AFXJ), P6892 (G-AXFK), P6897 (G-AXFL), P6898 (G-AXFM), P6903 (G-ADXN, and P6904 (G-AXFO).

Greece also purchased Blenheims, its first 12 Mk IVs being ferried out via Hungary in 1939, carrying British civil markings.

Note 5: Exports to Romania

39 aircraft from RAF orders were sent out from 17 May to 26 June 1939: Avro-built Mk Is L6696 to L6708 and L6713 to L6718, and Rootes-built L8603 to L8608, L8619/20/22/24/30/32, and L8652 to L8654.

Note that, to provide continuity, the above schedules contain some Blenheim exports, delivery of which took place after the declaration of war.

Romania was another recipient of Blenheims in an effort to counter Axis influence, but they ended up fighting alongside Germany against Russia. This example, Red 17, has yellow Theatre Bands and wing-tips and was lost over Odessa in September 1941.

L1108 overshot it's landing at West Freugh in the rain on 14 November 1938, skidded into the Watch Office and was Damaged Beyond Repair.

THE BRISTOL BLENHEIM

Appendix I

**Blenheim losses in the UK, 1 September 1938 to 3 September 1939
(Munich Agreement to the outbreak of war)**

Aircraft are all Mk Is except the seven Mk IVs noted as such.

18-09-1938   K7163 61 Squadron: stalled while turning in rainstorm; P/O A. Newton thrown out and parachuted down safely, aircraft crashed near Beamish, Co Durham; Cpl H. West and AC1 J. Gray killed.

22-09-1938   L1136 57 Squadron: undercarriage (u/c) retracted prematurely on take-off at Upper Heyford; aircraft struck ground and Damaged Beyond Repair (DBR); became 1223M.

26-10-1938   L1252 34 Squadron: control lost in cloud due to icing; aircraft crashed on Wemergill Moor, Yorks, and destroyed by fire; P/O J. Sowerbutts, AC1 W. Ashridge and AC2 H. Redfern (aged 18) killed.

27-10-1938   L1182 104 Squadron: engine cut and aircraft belly-landed at Aston Abbots, Bucks; became instructional airframe 1184M.

03-11-1938   L1144 57 Squadron: u/c jammed up and aircraft belly-landed at Upper Heyford; became 1227M.

07-11-1938   L1160 61 Squadron: engine caught fire and cowling was lost; aircraft dived into sea off Holbeach, Lincs; P/O A. Steele-Perkins injured, Cpl J. Bentley killed, AC1 A. Laurens drowned.

08-11-1938   L1116 62 Squadron: stalled and belly-landed on Luce Bay Ranges, Wigtown, after run over target; DBR.

Becoming lost was a frequent cause of pre-war accidents, as with L1112 of 82 Squadron; an engine cut when it ran low in fuel, it force-landed and ran into a ditch at Chellaston, near Derby, on 11 August 1939, slightly injuring the crew and writing-off the aircraft. Note the ever-present schoolboy!

12-11-1938   L1208 139 Squadron: control lost in cloud; aircraft stalled and dived into ground near Rugeley, Staffs; P/O R. Tate, Cpl H. Kennett and AC1 R. Salter killed.

14-11-1938   L1108 62 Squadron: overshot landing in rain at West Freugh, and skidded into Watch Office; DBR (see the picture on page 128).

24-11-1938   L1346 21 Squadron: u/c retracted prematurely on take-off at Eastchurch; aircraft sank back and hit ground; DBR.

24-11-1938   K7121 144 Squadron: undershot flare-path at Hemswell and u/c collapsed; became instructional airframe 1246M at Cranwell 25-04-1939.

28-11-1938   L1368 21 Squadron: lost power on overshoot at Eastchurch, ran into ditch.

06-12-1938   K7079 144 Squadron: engine cut and aircraft undershot at Hemswell; became instructional airframe 1245M at Cranwell.

12-12-1938   K7111 114 Squadron: belly-landed in error at Wyton (having earlier been hit by Hind K6738 while parked at Waddington 12-05-38, and repaired on site); became instructional airframe 1345M at Cosford.

14-12-1938   L1201 A&AEE: engine cut, stalled in forced landing at Orfordness; DBR.

05-01-1939   L1456 23 Squadron: u/c retracted after landing at Wittering; became 1360M.

10-01-1939   L1114 62 Squadron: engine cut, aircraft overshot forced landing, overturned at Gransmoor, E Yorks.

22-01-1939   K7164 61 Squadron: engine cut, aircraft stalled on approach to Hemswell; P/O J. Guthrie and crew slightly injured, aircraft DBR.

23-01-1939   K7081 144 Squadron: engine cut, aircraft lost height and belly-landed at Kirton Lindsey, Lincs; DBR.

24-01-1939   L1199 44 Squadron: aircraft hit ridge on take-off at Waddington, and landed with u/c jammed partly retracted; became instructional airframe 1342M.

30-01-1939   K7138 44 Squadron: engine cut on approach to Waddington, wing struck ground and aircraft cartwheeled; P/O D. Penman and crew slightly injured, aircraft DBR.

30-01-1939   L4836 53 Squadron: engine cut and aircraft stalled in circuit and hit ground at Odiham; pilot, P/O P. Jameson (flying solo), killed.

30-01-1939   L1476 64 Squadron: aircraft flew into high ground in cloud at Bleaklow Moor, Derby; P/O S. Robinson and P/O J. Thomas killed.

02-02-1939   L1443 34 Squadron: engine cut and aircraft lost height on overshoot and crash-landed at Upper Heyford.

06-02-1939   K7046 114 Squadron: accidentally damaged and became 1329M at 1 EWS.

09-02-1939   L1455 23 Squadron: u/c damaged on take-off from Wittering, aircraft belly landed; DBR; became instructional airframe 1355M.

12-02-1939   L6613 604 Squadron: u/c jammed up, aircraft belly landed at Hendon; DBR.

15-02-1939   L1155 44 Squadron: engine cut on take-off, aircraft stalled and hit ground at North Coates; F/Lt E. Withey and AC2 J. Richardson killed, AC2 A. Lithgow injured, aircraft DBR.

18-02-1939   L1176 601 Squadron: u/c retracted in error while parked at Hendon; DBR.

27-02-1939   L1099 114 Squadron: engine cut on take-off at Wyton, control lost and aircraft spun into ground nearby; F/O W. Lupton, Sgt C. Belsham and AC1 G. Hopley killed.

08-03-1939   L1461 23 Squadron: u/c jammed and aircraft belly-landed at Usworth; became 1483M.

14-03-1939   K7144 110 Squadron: engine cut on approach to Waddington and aircraft belly-landed; DBR.

17-03-1939   L1165 18 Squadron: u/c retracted in error after landing at Ternhill; became 1455M.

17-03-1939   L1364 21 Squadron: bounced during heavy landing at Watton; DBR.

20-03-1939   L1459 23 Squadron: lost power in cloud and spun into ground near Banbury, Oxon; P/O Raven killed.

21-03-1939   L1447 23 Squadron: hit ridge on take-off and crashed on landing at Wittering; became 1352M.

22-03-1939   L1262 62 Squadron: control lost in hailstorm and aircraft hit ground at Cranford, near Kettering, Northants; P/O D. Shine, Sgt J. Wiles and AC2 F. Lewis killed.

28-03-1939   L8388 3 Blenheim Delivery Flight: overshot landing at Thorney Island, ran into ditch and overturned; became a Ground Instruction Airframe.

28-03-1939   L8370 64 Squadron: u/c retracted on ground; went to Orfordness for trials.

30-03-1939   K7042 114 Squadron: transparent panels cracked at high altitude, plus other faults; became instructional airframe 1372M at Cosford.

01-04-1939   L1398 600 Squadron Mk I-F: u/c retracted prematurely on take-off and aircraft crash-landed at Hendon; became 1486M.

18-04-1939   L1314 139 Squadron: aircraft swung on landing at Wyton, u/c collapsed; DBR.

06-05-1939 L1399 600 Squadron: u/c raised in error after landing at Hendon; DBR.

09-05-1939 L4863 59 Squadron Mk IV: u/c raised in error after landing at Old Sarum; crew safe but aircraft DBR.

18-05-1939 L1439 25 Squadron Mk I-F: control lost in cloud at night, and aircraft crashed near Dartford, Kent; pilot Sgt J. Lingard baled out safely but AC2 F. Jones killed.

19-05-1939 L6604 601 Squadron: u/c retracted in error while running-up at Hendon.

20-05-1939 L1477 64 Squadron: u/c retracted in error while taxiing at Church Fenton.

07-06-1939 L1464 29 Squadron Mk I-F: engine cut and aircraft bounced during single-engined landing at night at Church Fenton; DBR.

12-06-1939 N6167 59 Squadron Mk IV: landed with brakes on and overturned at Andover.

12-06-1939 L4886 101 Squadron Mk IV: overshot landing in poor visibility at Debden, skidded and struck boundary; sent to Admiralty Compass Laboratory.

19-06-1939 L1244 57 Squadron: overshot landing in heavy rain and skidded into wood at Marham; DBR.

21-06-1939 L1504 29 Squadron Mk I-F: failed to climb after night take-off at Debden and struck trees; destroyed by fire; solo pilot, P/O S. Lyttle, killed.

26-06-1939 L1411 18 Squadron: overshot night landing and hit boundary at Upper Heyford.

26-06-1939 N6196 110 Squadron Mk IV: brakes failed on landing and aircraft over-ran at Wattisham.

27-06-1939 L1247 62 Squadron: belly-landed at Cranfield after u/c jammed; DBR.

09-07-1939 L1423 25 Squadron Mk I-F: swung on take-off from North Weald; u/c raised to stop, F/Lt C. Bull uninjured, aircraft DBR.

10-07-1939 L6687 Blenheim Delivery Flight: u/c retracted prematurely on take-off from Thorney Island and aircraft sank back into ground; DBR.

10-07-1939 L8547 59 Squadron: caught in slipstream on take-off, struck ground and belly-landed at Andover; DBR.

11-07-1939 L1293 107 Squadron: u/c retracted in error after landing at Boscombe Down; DBR.

13-07-1939 L1510 25 Squadron Mk I-F: u/c collapsed during heavy landing at Hawkinge; became 1637M.

20-07-1939 L8368 23 Squadron: collided with L1448 and crashed; Pilot, Sgt J. Bullard, gave his parachute to an Oundle schoolboy passenger who was saved, but he was killed; L1448 landed and was repaired.

22-07-1939 L8405 Central Flying School: engine cut, aircraft lost height on overshoot and struck ground at Upavon.

24-07-1939 L1156 110 Squadron: engine cut, aircraft overshot landing and ran into wood at Debden.

25-07-1939 L1465 23 Squadron: abandoned in air when lost in bad weather; F/O P. Walker baled out safely but Sgt L. Tarrant killed.

01-08-1939 L1241 25 Squadron: overshot landing and hit bank at Hawkinge; P/O B. Rofe unhurt, airframe became 1635M.

07-08-1939 N6180 107 Squadron Mk IV: became lost in bad weather and crashed into Beachy Head; Sgt H. Farrow, Sgt A. Sargeant, AC2 L. Phillips and Miss M. Savesy, civilian on ground, killed.

08-08-1939 L1282 57 Squadron: hit tree during forced landing in bad visibility at Great Canfield, Essex; DBR.

11-08-1939 L1475 64 Squadron: tyre burst while taxiing at Duxford and aircraft tipped up; DBR.

11-08-1939 L1112 82 Squadron: engine cut and aircraft force-landed, hit ditch and tipped up at Chellaston, near Derby; DBR.

14-08-1939 L1446 18 Squadron: overshot landing at Upper Heyford and hit fuel dump; destroyed by fire; Sgt A. Thomas (Pilot) injured.

16-08-1939 L1436 25 Squadron Mk I-F: landed with u/c unlocked at Sutton Bridge; P/O A. Pattison unhurt, airframe became 1648M.

29-08-1939 N6152 114 Squadron Mk IV: u/c collapsed on landing at Wyton; became 1649M.

30-08-1939 N6187 107 Squadron Mk IV: crashed on landing at night at Wattisham.

01-09-1939 L1352 21 Squadron: engine cut in circuit at Watton, aircraft belly-landed; DBR; crew uninjured.

K7144 of 110 Squadron burst a port tyre landing at Waddington in 1938 and tipped up. It was written off on 14 March 1939 when an engine cut on approach and it belly-landed.

N6196, one of 110 Squadron's first new Mk IVs, was DBR when its brakes failed and it over-ran at Waddington on 26 June 1939.

PART 2

WARTIME SERVICE

Revealing the human tragedy behind each of the thousands of Blenheim crew casualties listed. A typical 'Blenheim Boy' who made the ultimate sacrifice. Sgt Dennis Wilson, the 19-year-old WOp/Ag of 139 Squadron was killed when Z7448 was shot-down near the Knapsack Power Station, Cologne, in the famous daylight raid of 12 August 1941; he is buried in Rheinburg War Cemetery, his Pilot and Observer were injured, captured, and became Prisoners of War.

Chapter 8

War is declared

Dispersal

Under a pre-arranged plan, the ten squadrons of Battles that comprised No 1 Group RAF Bomber Command were sent to France upon mobilisation, and the Blenheim squadrons of 2 Group were dispersed around England. One squadron of each pair was relocated from its normal home base to various dispersal airfields in anticipation of the 'knock-out blow' that the RAF expected the Luftwaffe to attempt to deliver. The Air Staff noted how most of the Polish Air Force had been destroyed on its bases by the Germans in the first few hours as the Panzer columns invaded Poland to start their *Blitzkrieg* (literally 'lightning war') at dawn on 1 September 1939.

Dispersing the Blenheims caused considerable confusion, some delays and difficulties with communications, and further difficulties with the location not only of the wartime stores now needed, but also supplies of spare parts for maintenance work. Further difficulties and complications arose as working parties in the hangars of several squadrons were still involved in a hectic programme of bringing up to specification those aircraft that had not been modified to full Mk IV standard, by installing the new outer fuel tanks for 100 octane petrol, plumbing the jettison systems, changing the engines to Mercury Mk XVs, and fitting the 'emergency override boost' controls. They often found themselves having to complete this urgently required work in the open air alongside the hedge of some strange airfield, and much 'borrowing' and scrounging of parts and equipment took place, but the modifications were all completed by 7 October.

The relocation of the Bomber Command Blenheim squadrons upon the outbreak of war was as follows (No 2 Bomber Group comprised five Wings each of two squadrons):

83 Wing: **107** Squadron stayed at Wattisham; **110** Squadron dispersed to Ipswich.
79 Wing: **21** Squadron stayed at Watton; **82** Squadron dispersed to Horsham St Faith (now Norwich Airport).
81 Wing: **101** Squadron stayed at West Raynham, **90** Squadron dispersed to Weston-on-the-Green. (These two became the Group Pool Squadrons, for training and as a reserve.)
82 Wing: **139** Squadron stayed at Wyton, **114** Squadron was dispersed to Hullavington.
70 Wing: **18** and **57** Squadrons stayed at Upper Heyford, as it was considered to be relatively safe, and they were detached from 2 Group to go to France with the British Expeditionary Force, there to join **53** and **59** Army Co-operation Squadrons from Odiham and Andover respectively.

Further dispersal was ordered at 1415 hours on 3 September:

101 Squadron was sent from West Raynham to Brize Norton
21 Squadron was sent from Watton to Sealand but returned 5 days later
82 Squadron was sent from Horsham St Faith to Netheravon, then Watton

In the following weeks, the squadrons that had remained at their home bases took their aircraft, fully bombed up, each evening to dispersal airfields, returning at daybreak each day. For example, for several weeks 107 flew to Benson each evening, returning to Wattisham first thing each morning, before being dispersed to Ipswich alongside 110 Squadron.

At Bassingbourn 104 and 108 Squadrons were withdrawn from the front line and transferred to 6 Group in the training role, as was 35 Squadron at Cranfield and 90 at Upwood. (Six months later Bomber Command's first Operational Training Units were formed, and in April 1940 104 and 108 merged to become 13 OTU at Bicester, while 35 and 90 became 17 OTU at Upwood.)

Some Fighter Command Blenheim Mk 1-F squadrons were also relocated to their immediate war stations during that hectic first weekend of September 1939:

601 went from Hendon to Biggin Hill

604, also from Hendon, went to North Weald

25 Squadron had only just moved from Hawkinge to Northolt, but moved to Filton later in the month, maintaining a Flight at Martlesham Heath

600 Squadron stayed at Northolt to be near London

23 Squadron remained at Wittering, **64** at Church Fenton, and **29** at Debden

The Blenheims of D Flight A&AEE at Martlesham Heath, the radar development flight controlled from Bawdsey Manor by Robert Watson-Watt and his team of scientists, moved to Perth, but this proved unsuitable and they relocated to St Athan as the Special Duty Flight a few weeks later. The rest of the A&AEE decamped to Boscombe Down to continue its vital air-testing and armament trials activities. They flew off with the Blenheims that they were testing and developing: the Armament Flight took K7044, L1253, L1495, L8662 and L8689; the Performance Testing B Flight took L1348 (which was modified extensively to increase the speed, including fitting Rotol constant-speed propellers) and L4835; while C Flight took L1222 to develop a heating system. In October L4838 went to Boscombe for Gunnery Trials, together with L6594 (for trials with the 37mm Coventry Ordnance Works cannon), joined in December by P6961, the first of several that worked with the Special Duty Flight for the then little-known chemical warfare establishment at Porton Down. Others joining this secret work during 1940 were L9337 and T2354, with L1407 and L1173 added in 1941.

Aircraft available to RAF Commands

To put these Blenheim dispositions into their contemporary context, the accompanying table summarises the numbers of the different types of aircraft that were available to the operational RAF Commands at the outbreak of war, and makes most interesting reading.

Aircraft types available to RAF Commands at the outbreak of war

	AASF	Bomber Command	Fighter Command	Coastal Command	Reserves or Overseas	Total
Blenheim	–	231	111	–	747	1,089
Battle	160	80	–	–	774	1,014
Anson	–	–	–	301	459	760
Hurricane	–	–	347	–	53	400
Spitfire	–	–	187	–	83	270
Gladiator	–	–	76	–	244	320
Hampden	–	140	–	–	72	212
Whitley	–	169	–	–	27	196
Wellington	–	160	–	–	12	172
Gauntlet	–	–	26	–	119	145
Hudson	–	–	–	53	25	78
Vildebeest	–	–	–	30	71	101
Sunderland	–	–	–	27	11	38
Totals	**160**	**780**	**747**	**411**	**2,697**	**4,795**

THE BRISTOL BLENHEIM

The figures show the aircraft in the front-line squadrons and available for operations, but not all could be considered operational, for example the elderly Gauntlet and Vildebeest biplanes, although the latter were, to the shame of the RAF, deployed in the defence of Singapore in January 1942. The totals include all the front-line aircraft, including reserves, that were on the strength of the RAF, but exclude the 4,500 aircraft used for training and communications (apart from the 760 Ansons, 300 of which were used operationally) and the 26 obsolete London and Stranraer biplane flying-boats of Coastal Command, with 24 more still serving overseas. The numbers fit for immediate operational use were far less, as several squadrons had been withdrawn from the front line as reserves or for use in the training role. For example, only 173 of the 231 Blenheims in Bomber Command were operational, and in Coastal Command only 105 of the 301 Ansons, nine of the 53 Hudsons, and 16 of the 27 Sunderlands.

The AASF (Advanced Air Striking Force) Battles formed No 1 Group of Bomber Command until 2 September 1939, so on that date the totals of bomber and fighter aircraft available were 2,683 and 1,135 respectively. However, the latter figure includes the 111 Blenheim Mk I-F interim fighters, but they were produced as bombers and converted later, so the figures really are 2,794 bombers and 1,024 fighters – and crucially only 670 of those were modern monoplane fighters. Even with the 'highest priority' given to fighter production after the Munich Crisis a year earlier, the overall ratio of bombers to fighters resulting from three and a half years of RAF expansion was still well over two to one in favour of the bomber. By excluding, quite reasonably, the Gauntlet and Gladiator biplanes from these figures, the ratio of monoplane bombers to monoplane fighters produced in that period was a wholly disproportionate four to one.

It will be noted that, at 1,089, there were more Blenheims than any other type in service with the RAF at the start of the war. That total includes 899 Mk Is, 626 in the UK (of which 111 were Fighter Command Mk I-Fs) and 273 overseas; the other 190 were Mk IVs, all of which were in the UK. The aggregate number of Blenheims would have exceeded 1,200 had they not lost so many in flying accidents before the war. It is a sobering fact that, even after these losses, more than half of *all* the aircraft available to the RAF Commands at the beginning of the war were Blenheims and Battles.

The average daily availability of aircraft to Bomber Command in September 1939 was 140 Blenheims, 77 Wellingtons, 71 Hampdens and 61 Whitleys only, a force that, despite benefiting disproportionately from the extensive and expensive pre-war expansion schemes, was clearly incapable of carrying out the strategic bombing offensive so confidently proclaimed by the Air Staff for 20 years. Indeed, the AOC-in-C of Bomber Command, ACM Sir Edgar Ludlow-Hewitt, was so concerned at the possibility of being ordered to carry out an all-out offensive against German targets – the so-called 'knock-out blow' still being promoted by Trenchard – that he warned the Air Staff only days before war was declared that such orders would result in the complete destruction of his Medium Bomber force – the Blenheims – in just three and a half weeks, together with all of his Heavy Bombers – Wellingtons, Hampdens and Whitleys – in seven and a half weeks: a cold douche of unwelcome realism. Fortunately the War Cabinet banned the bombing of any targets on German soil, a ban that lasted for the seven months of the 'Phoney War'.

Operations

On 2 September Bomber Command HQ ordered three 2 Group Blenheim squadrons to stand by with nine aircraft each for attacks on German airfields the following day: 107 Squadron was given Delmanhorst as a target, 110 Oldenburg, and 139 Jever. These orders were changed at 2358 hours to '27 aircraft to attack units of the German Fleet at sea North of Wilhelmshaven', so the bomb-loads were changed from four 250lb GP (general purpose) bombs to two 500lb SAP (semi-armour-piercing) bombs. Orders were given that if they were unable to obtain clear visual identification of units of the German Fleet, they were to bring their bombs back.

Even as Chamberlain's lugubrious broadcast of 3 September, announcing that 'this country is at war with Germany', drew to an end, the air-raid sirens wailed ominously over South East England. The radar stations had detected an intruder heading towards Croydon that sunny Sunday morning, and a section of three Blenheim Mk I fighters from 601 Squadron was scrambled from Biggin Hill (they had repositioned there from Hendon the previous day) to intercept. They found a lone French diplomat, Captain De Brantes, in a light aircraft, who was blissfully unaware of the consternation he had caused. The Blenheims came under anti-aircraft fire – fortunately ineffective – from British AA guns as they returned to base. The 'All Clear' was sounded – a characteristic anti-climax that marked the start of the 'Phoney War' in the West. This interlude, while Hitler digested his conquests in the East, made empty peace gestures and planned his moves in the West, granted an eight-month respite during which the British and French forces could better prepare themselves for the inevitable onslaught.

But the war was certainly not 'phoney' as far as the Blenheim squadrons were concerned, for they were in action right from the very beginning. At 1203 hours GMT a Blenheim Mk IV of 139 Squadron at Wyton carried out 'Raid BW 1', the first RAF operational sortie of the Second World War, when it was sent to locate capital ships of the *Kriegsmarine* in the Schillig Roads, north of Wilhelmshaven. The Air Ministry was furious to discover later that a Beechcraft of Sydney Cotton's Special Flight at Heston had carried out a successful covert photo-reconnaissance sortie for the Admiralty over this very area the previous afternoon. The Blenheim Mk IV, N6215, was flown by F/O Andrew McPherson with Commander Thompson RN as Observer, and Corporal Vincent Arrowsmith as WOp/Ag – they had been standing by for two days awaiting dispatch on this historic operation. They found several large warships and nearly 20 destroyers, and took 75 photos of them and their bases, but the WT set had frozen at 24,000 feet and the Wireless Operator was unable to transmit this vital information to base. Nine Blenheims from each of 114, 139 and 110 Squadrons had been bombed up with SAP bombs, and were standing by with their crews ready to attack any warships that may have been located, but by the time McPherson returned 4hr 50min later, and his film was developed, it was too late to mount the raid on the first day of the war as intended. The War Cabinet had instructed that German warships could only be attacked in the open sea, not while in harbour, and merchant ships were not to be attacked, as they did not wish to provoke retaliation. A further reconnaissance flight to Wilhelmshaven was ordered for the following morning.

The film magazine is handed to a waiting Corporal on the return from the recce sortie to locate the German capital ships off Wilhelmshaven before the first raid.

McPherson and his crew therefore took off again in N6215 at 08.35 to repeat the sortie, but this time the weather had turned nasty and they had to fly low over the sea through heavy rain and poor visibility. They found several destroyers and three or four German capital ships – which they thought were battleships, but three were in fact cruisers – near Wilhelmshaven and off Brunsbuttel, and flew around them at a safe distance and at a very low level. Cpl Arrowsmith attempted to relay this intelligence to base, but the message was mainly unintelligible, probably due to the low altitude from which it was transmitted. They landed back at 13.35 and confirmed their sightings, so within the hour Bomber Command HQ authorised 2 Group HQ to order an immediate low-level attack. However, in view of the poor weather each of the three squadrons standing by was to detail five rather than nine of its Blenheims.

It is enlightening to look at this initial offensive operation in some detail as it exemplifies the unpredictable and haphazard nature of low-level daylight bombing, demonstrates the ineffectual results attained despite the courageous way the crews pressed home their attack in difficult conditions, and typifies the heavy losses experienced – losses that were to be suffered frequently by the Blenheims in the years ahead. It also reveals the high hopes of the planners, and the cold dose of reality regarding how little Bomber Command, in practice, was able to achieve at that early stage of the war.

'The First Blow'

The first RAF bombing raid of the war was headlined as 'The First Blow' in the *Daily Mail*. It was laid on in a great 'flap', and was dispatched after a short and necessarily inadequate briefing from the Station Commanders, before the photographs that McPherson had taken could be developed. As the attack was now to be from low level, the

The wreckage of N6240, retrieved from the sea, being inspected by German Naval personnel. Sgt A. Prince was Killed in Action, while Sgt G. Booth and LAC L. Slattery became the first RAF Prisoners of War.

bomb-load was changed again – from two 500lb SAP bombs to two 500lb GP bombs with 11-second-delay fuses. Thus armed, five Blenheims from 139 Squadron took off from Wyton at 15.32 hours, five from 110 at Wattisham at 15.56, and five from 107 at 16.00 hours. The acting Flight Commanders of 107 – Flt Lts 'Bill' Barton and 'Tubby' Clayton – tossed a coin to see which Flight would take part. Barton won. They were briefed to attack 10 minutes after 110 Squadron.

The three flights of five Blenheims flew out separately over an angry North Sea, keeping below the low cloud and flying through heavy rain showers. They all flew by the 'dead reckoning' (deduced) navigation method, whereby a triangle of velocities is plotted, using the forecast wind speed and direction, to determine the compass course needed to follow the desired track – an unreliable method at the best of times, but especially so when applied to a long sea crossing in bad weather. Radar aids to navigation lay in the future, and no positional 'fixes' from the primitive wireless sets could be obtained on the outward journey or over enemy territory as radio silence was imposed. Visual confirmation of position from map-reading needs a prominent landmark upon landfall after a sea crossing, and is particularly difficult at low level and in poor visibility. So it is not surprising that the five aircraft from 139 Squadron failed to locate any warships in the foul weather and returned to base, three with their bombs still on board, the others jettisoning theirs into the sea. It is believed that they had carried out their fruitless search in the mists of the Ems Estuary rather than in Wilhelmshaven Bay.

The five from 110 Squadron found the battleship *Admiral Scheer* and the cruiser *Emden* off Wilhelmshaven; they split into a trio and a pair as briefed, and attacked immediately from different directions, catching the Germans by surprise. The trio, led by Flt Lt Kenneth Doran in N6204, attacked first and scored three direct hits amidships on the *Scheer*; the number 3 realised on his run-in that he would not reach the *Scheer* within the 11 seconds of the delay fuses, so turned and bombed a nearby tender, but missed. He need not have worried for the bombs of the first two attackers exploded in the sea or bounced harmlessly off the armour-plating and failed to detonate. The Blenheim of the leader of the following pair, Flying Officer Emden, was hit by flak and N6199 crashed into the superstructure of the German cruiser that by a twist of fate bore his own name; he and his crew were killed and thus became the first Bomber Command air-crew to be lost in action – the first of a staggering 56,000 casualties that were to follow. N6188, Pilot Officer Murphy's Blenheim, was hit by the light flak that had just burst into action from the by now alerted German sailors and crashed into the sea in flames.

The flak was fierce by the time the five Blenheims from 107 Squadron arrived; these had also split into a trio and a pair, not in preparation for the attack but because they became separated when the leader entered the base of the low cloud. Four of the five were shot down; only F/O Stephens and his crew, bringing up the rear, returned, having lost touch with the others in the low cloud and flying around the bay at low level for a while, seeing only a destroyer. Stephens did not attack this, as he still hoped to find a capital ship, but on failing to do so he brought his bombs back, landing at Sutton Bridge at 1830 as it was getting dark. The day-old war had certainly got off to a bad start for 107 Squadron. Of the nine Blenheims that had attacked the warships, no fewer than five had been destroyed, four of which were from the 107 Flight that went on the toss of a coin. The first 14 of the brave 'Blenheim Boys' had lost their lives. (For a list of the Blenheims and crews taking part in the raid, and details of the losses, see Appendix 1.)

A force of 14 Wellingtons from 3 Group set off slightly later that day to attack the enemy ships off Brunsbuttel, at the mouth of the Kiel Canal. Only four found targets in the worsening weather conditions – one even bombed the port of Esbjerg, 110 miles to the north in neutral Denmark – and of those that did, two Wellingtons of 9 Squadron were shot down with the loss of all ten crew members by Me.109s of II/JG 77. The Wellingtons inflicted no damage on the German warships. Bomber Command's intention of striking a telling blow against the *Kriegsmarine* in the opening hours of the war was not fulfilled. The planners were very disappointed at the lack of the expected results and shocked by the high cost of the operations relative to the small number of aircraft that actually attacked a target – seven out of 13. Torpedo-dropping aircraft would have been much more effective against such large targets at sea, but neither Bomber Command nor Coastal Command had any, for the Beauforts and Bothas, although ordered over three years earlier, were not yet in service. The RAE at Farnborough had attempted to fill this gap by adapting a Blenheim Mk I to carry an external torpedo, suspended on a steel cradle that protruded through the closed bomb doors and was bolted on to the bomb-carrying points in the bomb bay. This one-off conversion was not a success, mainly due to a lack of ground clearance, and it was not adopted. The Blenheims had to continue to use their far from effective bombs against ships.

Bomber Command morale was raised when the first decorations of the war were gazetted on 10 September – DFCs to F/O Andrew McPherson of 139 Squadron and F/Lt Kenneth Doran of 110, for their efforts in connection with the first raid of the war.

The Luftwaffe attempted a reprisal on 16 October 1939 when 12 Junkers Ju.88s of I/KG 30 based at Westerland on Sylt, bombed the RN cruisers *Southampton* and *Edinburgh* off Rosyth in the Firth of Forth. This followed a successful reconnaissance and weather check that morning by two He.111s of KG 28, which sent accurate information by radio when half-way back over the North Sea. The raid was made by three sections of four aircraft, and they scored near-misses but only sank the Admiral's Barge; they were intercepted by Spitfires of two Auxiliary Squadrons, 602 at Drem and 603 at Turnhouse. Echoing the fate of the Blenheims, two of the four Ju.88s of the first section were shot down into the water, and a third was lucky to struggle back to Sylt on one engine. These were the first combat victories recorded by Spitfires and showed that even the fast and manoeuvrable Ju.88 was unsafe in daylight. Clearly, Blenheims would be exposed to great danger in the daytime skies above a defended target area.

Preparing to climb into his Blenheim for a sortie over the cold North Sea, this Pilot wears a full fur-lined flying suit, gauntlets and boots. His leather helmet has the early-type oxygen-mask (with the lead in his left hand and intercom lead dangling), and he has a pilot's seat-type parachute – the rip-cord handle is by his left elbow, the harness quick-release-pad in the centre.

Operations in support of the Royal Navy

The Admiralty was very concerned that German capital ships might 'break out' from their ports and attack merchant shipping bringing vital supplies to Britain; indeed, it was far more worried about the threat from surface raiders than from submarines. In the event, the U-boats proved to be the greater menace and, although the counter-measures taken against them were initially ineffective, once again Blenheims were pressed into the breach and did achieve some success. Meanwhile, during the middle week of September 1939 two Blenheim squadrons and one of Wellingtons stood by at 45-minute readiness for attacks on German naval targets, and for several days 54 Blenheims (nine each from 101, 21, 82, 90, 107 and 110 Squadrons) stood by all day, but no such targets were found. Blenheims did take part in many arduous shipping searches, termed as 'armed reconnaissance', up to the end of the year, looking for these elusive targets in the inhospitable wastes of the North Sea, but these searches were virtually fruitless until 20 December when 12 Blenheims managed to find and bomb a force of 11 German mine-sweepers, although no hits were observed.

Bomber Command tried further daylight attacks on the German Fleet, but received such 'a bloody nose' that it was forced to virtually abandon unescorted daylight raids and relegate its Heavy and Medium Bombers to night-bombing – apart from the Blenheims, that is. From late September 1939 several forces of Hampdens and Wellingtons, and even a few Whitleys, were sent in daylight to find and attack German warships. On the 29th all five of a formation of 144 Squadron Hampdens were shot down; a further 61 futile sorties were flown by 2 December, mainly by Wellingtons, but they failed to find any ships. However, on the 3rd a formation of 24 'Wimpeys' claimed a hit on a cruiser well out to sea, and had a running fight with some Messerschmitts, escaping without loss. On the 14th half of the 12 Wellingtons from 99 Squadron attempting to bomb a convoy in the Schillig Roads were lost; five were shot down by Me.109s and Me.110s and one more was damaged and crashed near its Newmarket base, killing three of its crew, bringing the deaths in 99 Squadron to 33 that terrible day. On 18 December an even more terrible day was experienced, marking the end of these daylight raids, for 12 Wellingtons were shot down from an attacking force of 22, with the loss of 56 more lives.

These last two raids had seen the crippling loss rate – from aircraft that had not even penetrated the German coast – of 18 out of 34 bombers, which, coupled with the complete lack of results achieved, dictated the change of policy. The planners' cherished peace-time theory of the self-defending daylight bomber formation had been shown to be entirely erroneous in the harsh reality of wartime operational conditions. With a few minor exceptions, made mainly for propaganda purposes – Stirlings to Brest, Halifaxes to La Pallice, and Lancasters to Augsberg – unescorted RAF twin-engined Medium Bombers and four-engined Heavy Bombers were to operate only at night for the next four years, and had to face the immense difficulties involved in locating and hitting their targets. The Blenheim squadrons were the sole major exception to this fundamental change of policy, as they were required to continue operating by day as well as by night, as we will see.

Reconnaissance

Apart from the maritime armed-reconnaissance missions, convoy patrols, shipping searches, and regularly photographing naval bases to 'keep tabs' on the German capital ships – all to assist the Royal Navy – Blenheims were now called upon to undertake another highly dangerous task: daylight strategic photographic reconnaissance. They were sent out singly, or sometimes in twos or threes, to range far and wide over the heart of Germany, taking line-overlap pictures of many industrial cities of North West Germany and the Ruhr (to form the data-base for many of the target maps that would prove so useful in the forthcoming strategic bombing offensive), and photographing 30-mile stretches of railways and autobahns to establish the normal traffic pattern and thus detect future troop movements.

THE BRISTOL BLENHEIM

King George VI with Lord Gort (C in C BEF) and RAF 'top brass' visit Lille—Seclin on 6 December 1939; a Blenheim Mk IV of 53 Squadron next to a Gladiator of 615 Squadron.

An airman on guard duty under the camouflage-net-covered wing of a Blenheim at a very cold AASF airfield in the winter of 1939/40. Light-bomb carriers and ammunition boxes lie in the foreground.

An Observer using a hand-held F24 camera in a Blenheim nose; the main camera was mounted on a tubular-steel frame over the WOp/Ag's emergency exit hatch.

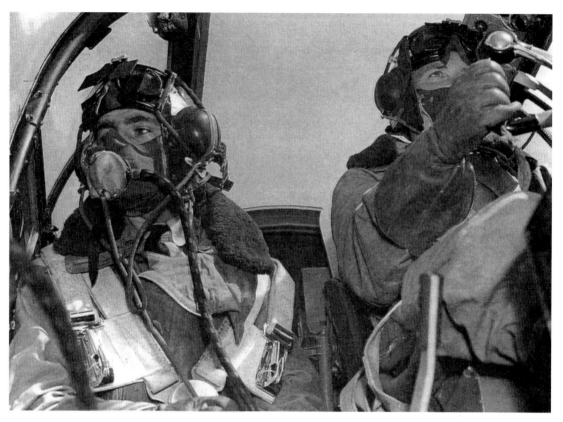

Observer and Pilot of 'a 139 Squadron Mk IV, claimed to be 'on their way to photograph enemy fortifications' but actually taken on the ground from the Observer's under-nose emergency hatch. The clips to attach his chest-type 'chute are shown, as are their leather flying helmets, cloth oxygen masks, Mk IV goggles, Sidcot flying suits with fur collars, and leather gauntlets.

The first such operation was flown on 20 September by 139 Squadron, but cloud cover over the target area caused the sortie to be abandoned; on the 21st S/Ldr J. Sabine of 110 Squadron flew N6242 to photograph the Osnabruk/Dalmen railway line from 200 feet, and P/O R. Hill in N6212, on a similar sortie, was fired on by 109s, his Gunner claiming one before they entered cloud cover. On the 25th it was the turn of 107 Squadron, when the CO, W/Cdr Basil Embry, F/Lt Gareth Clayton and P/O Steve Stephens cruised over the Ruhr (at heights of 18,500, 23,000 and 8,000 feet respectively) in broad daylight during a 6-hour sortie. Only Embry in P4857 was intercepted – two Me.109s attacked and damaged his port wing and turret. He managed to escape by diving into a cloud bank, and just made it home despite a leaking fuel tank – he stepped up his demands for self-sealing tanks after this narrow escape. S/Ldr Laurie Sinclair, CO of 110 Squadron, found himself over the Brandenburg part of Berlin on one of these sorties, becoming the first RAF aircraft to do so. On 26 September, 28 German airfields were added to the list of targets to be photographed.

For this useful work the Blenheims used a single F24 camera mounted in a cradle above a clear panel in the WOp/Ag's lower escape hatch, sometimes supplemented by another in the nose, or by a hand-held camera operated by the Observer. Results were often disappointing, for there were many difficulties: cameras froze at altitude, films cracked in the cold, or condensation fogged the lenses. Some 74 of these lonely reconnaissance missions were carried out from the UK, and 16 Blenheims were lost (see Appendix 2), before it was decided that they were too risky, and they were terminated on 25 November. An attempt was made to resume these sorties by night using flares to illuminate the subject, but again the results were unsatisfactory, and two more aircraft were lost (also Appendix 2). By the end of the year Blenheims had carried out 89 risky reconnaissance sorties, but had brought back pictures on only 45 of these.

Information from the Western Front was also required, and the Fairey Battles based on French airfields had attempted tactical reconnaissance sorties over the German defensive 'Siegfried Line'. Their vulnerability was quickly exposed and they soon lost eight of their number, including four out of five aircraft from 150 Squadron on 30 September – the fifth staggered home badly damaged, crash-landed and was burned out – after which daylight recce sorties by Battles were suspended. The French-based Blenheim squadrons perforce added tactical reconnaissance to their duties, for which tasks 18 and 57 Squadrons, with their Blenheim Mk Is, had been sent to France to form 70 Wing. Nos 53 and 59 Army Co-operation Squadrons, with their brand new Blenheim Mk IVs, soon joined them and the ten Battle squadrons in the over-optimistically named Advanced Air Striking Force. The Blenheims were ordered to photograph the entire 'Siegfried Line', a task they completed once the weather permitted.

All these reconnaissance tasks had to be carried out by the Blenheim squadrons as the demand for photographic information from the three services was so great that the embryonic PR Unit at Heston simply could not cope. Initially called The Heston Special Flight, the PR Unit was formed on 22 September 1939 and run by the resourceful Australian Sydney Cotton, who had used G-AFTL, a Lockheed 12a, before the war for covert aerial photography over Germany. This was ostensibly his own private aircraft, but in fact was supplied by Fred Winterbotham, Chief of Air Intelligence at MI6. In November 1939 Cotton's unorthodox outfit was allocated two Blenheims – and a single Spitfire – and the name was changed to No 2 Camouflage Unit to disguise its real purpose. The Spitfire made its first PR sortie on 16 November, and by the end of the year had carried out 15, bringing back pictures on ten of these, without loss. Clearly the modified PR Spitfire, which could reach over 30,000 feet, was vastly superior to the Blenheim, and Cotton beseeched, badgered and berated the Air Ministry for more Spitfires, as he was horrified at what he saw as the needless losses of the Blenheims and their precious crews, but his appeals fell on deaf ears. This period of the war was certainly far from 'phoney' as far as the Blenheim PR crews were concerned.

Fighter Command Blenheims

Apart from the sortie by 601 Squadron from Biggin Hill just after the Prime Minister's broadcast on 3 September, mentioned above, 12 Blenheim Mk I-Fs from 29 and 604 Squadrons were sent out over the North Sea from Wittering on that first day to investigate reported enemy aerial activity, but nothing was found. The Blenheims of Fighter Command, like their brethren in Bomber Command, were deployed initially almost exclusively in support of the Royal Navy. In the first three months of the war, Mk I-Fs and Mk IV-Fs carried out many 'Trade Protection' sorties guarding Britain's coastal shipping, and many more on 'Convoy Escort' defensive patrols once shipping was organised into convoys.

The first offensive sortie of the war by Fighter Command was carried out on 26 November 1939 by nine Blenheim Mk I-Fs of 25 Squadron from Northolt, but due to poor weather they failed to find the target of the German sea-plane base at Borkum, despite employing Navigators from Coastal Command for the sortie. Borkum was the home of Luftwaffe sea-planes laying magnetic mines in the Thames Estuary. However, at

Mk I-Fs of 25 Squadron refuelling at Bircham Newton prior to setting out on Fighter Command's first offensive sortie of the war on 29 November 1939 to strafe the German seaplane base at Borkum, lair of the mine-laying Heinkel He.115 floatplanes.

dusk on the 28th, 12 Mk I-Fs (six each from 25 and 601 Squadrons) staged via Bircham Newton found the enemy base, which they strafed from low level with their machine-guns – RAF aircraft were still banned from bombing German land targets at this stage! One of 601's sections was led by F/O Maxwell Aitken, the son of Lord Beaverbrook, and one of his wing-men was F/O William Rhodes-Moorhouse, son of the first airman ever to be awarded a Victoria Cross. The Germans at Borkum had been taken by surprise and all the Blenheims returned safely, landing at Debden. They claimed to have shot up five German sea-planes, but in fact only two were very slightly damaged. Incredibly, for a 500-mile operation over the North Sea, none of the Blenheims carried dinghies and none of the crew wore 'Mae West' lifejackets.

Non-operational Blenheim losses

Apart from Blenheim losses on operations, serious attrition from flying accidents continued as the scale and pace of training activity accelerated. Night-flying training, largely neglected before the war, was particularly hazardous for inexperienced crews under wartime conditions, due mainly to the blackout, poor weather, 'friendly' searchlights, and from time to time 'friendly' anti-aircraft guns. The stark fact is that this appalling catalogue of accidental losses was to continue unremittingly for over four years. A list up to the end of 1939 is given in Appendix 3; when looking through it please be mindful of my comments in Chapter 6 concerning the poor layout of the secondary controls and the need for careful engine-handling, together with the difficult transition for pilots from relatively simple biplanes to Blenheims. Remember also that the list covers four months only, excludes aircraft with repairable damage, and does not include losses from the many accidents overseas. In the first four months of the war more than 60 Blenheims were lost through accidents and only 20 were lost through enemy action – a disturbing ratio of three to one.

THE BRISTOL BLENHEIM

The first wartime winter

Things had settled down by the end of 1939, but that year produced the hardest winter for decades, severely restricting all aerial activity. The airfields provided by the French in the flat Rheims area were literally fields and lacked facilities; air-crew were billeted in local houses and farms, and the ground-crew in farm buildings. The stern-frames of several Blenheims were cracked by the frozen ground and had to be changed out in the open air – a major job. The ground-crews worked constantly throughout that hard winter endeavouring to maintain the Blenheims fit for operations in dreadful conditions, but even persuading the Mercuries to start in such freezing weather was extremely difficult, and very little flying was possible. One bitter night at Poix the ground-crews struggled for more than four hours to start the engines of 53 Squadron's aircraft, but could only get two of the Mercuries running – and they were on different aircraft!

Two AASF Battle squadrons were withdrawn from France to re-equip with Blenheims; 40 and 15 were moved to Wyton for this purpose, and were replaced by 139 and 114 Squadrons from 2 Group. Both squadrons had been withdrawn from operations in November and their Blenheims stripped and repainted with the smoother Titanine paint, including the under-surfaces in the pale 'sky' tone created by the PDU at Heston, which 139 Squadron records refers to optimistically as 'Light Sea Green to render them invisible at great height'!

139 Squadron personnel pose at Wyton with one of their brand-new Blenheim Mk IVs in October 1939 immediately prior to leaving for France.

Crew clad in fur-lined flying-suits are about to board E-Edward of 139 Squadron at a snow-covered Plivot in December 1939. The Observer carries his canvas 'nav-bag', and one of their leather helmets rests on the tailplane.

The hand-held F24 camera is handed to the Observer. Note the earliest known example of RAF nose-art in the Second World War – a taped-on 'pin-up' girl. The two tubes protruding from the engine cowling are the oil-cooler intakes; the circular devices on the propeller hub are counterweights to assist the oil-pressure-operated pitch-change mechanism.

Balancing act: a Mk I has nosed-over after landing, the flaps are lowered, and the porthole for the F24 camera can be seen on the WOp/Ag's escape hatch. Such damage would normally be repaired and the aircraft would soon be back in service, so would not be included in the list of losses at the end of each chapter.

The AASF and the 'Air Component of the BEF' were unified as the British Air Forces in France; the Blenheims of 18, 53, 57, 59 and now 139 and 114 Squadrons joined the Battles and four Squadrons of Lysanders, with two Squadrons of Hurricanes (and one of Gladiators) for protection. It was intended that the remaining front-line Blenheim squadrons of 2 Group (21, 82, 110, 107 and 101, plus 15 and 40 when declared operational after conversion) would be sent to France as the 'second echelon' – the first four mentioned were under notice to go. They were tasked with providing direct tactical support to the British Expeditionary Force by mounting low-level attacks on the anticipated German offensive there, but the lack of suitable airfields delayed the projected move and it was cancelled in December. Events were to show that this was most fortunate, for had they moved to France to join the other Blenheim squadrons there, they too would have been decimated in the debacle of May 1940.

Appendix I

Blenheims, crews and losses on the first RAF raid of the war, 4 September 1939

Aircraft marked with an asterisk were lost. All Blenheims in the N6000 series were Mk IVs built at Filton. Crews are given in the order: Pilot (Captain, irrespective of rank), Observer (who also acted as Navigator and Bomb Aimer), and Wireless-Operator/Air Gunner (WOp/Ag).

110 Squadron

N6204   Flt Lt K. Doran, P/O S. Henderson, Sgt D. Pennington, AC J. Smith. Duty Carried Out (DCO) and Returned To Base (RTB). P/O Henderson (Obs) attached from 42 Squadron, Coastal Command. (N6204 was with 110 from 29-6-1939 and was written off when undercarriage (u/c) collapsed while taking off from Wattisham 8-10-1939.)

N6201   P/O G. Lings, Sgt T. Hammond, AC W. Bingham. DCO and RTB. (N6201 was also with 110 from 29-6-1939 and stalled on landing at Ipswich 28-2-1940; Damaged Beyond Repair (DBR) and Struck Off Charge (SOC) 7-3-1940.)

N6198   Sgt J. Hanne, Sgt C. Beavis, AC B. Gray. DCO and RTB. (N6198 was with 110 from 26-6-1939 until crashed at Barking Tye Common near Wattisham 13-11-1939 while low flying.)

N6197   Sgt R. Abbott, Sgt L. Bancroft, AC J. Rosemond. DCO and RTB. (N6197 was with 110 from 26-6-1939 until sent overseas 3-2-1940 to 84 then 55 Squadron in Egypt. Missing 2-7-1941.)

N6199*   Failed To Return (FTR); F/O H. Emden, Sgt R. Grossey, Sgt S. McK. Otty, and AC R. Evans Killed in Action (KIA). Sgt Grossey (Obs) attached from 42 Squadron, Coastal Command, has no known grave so is commemorated on the Runnymede War Memorial; his companions are buried at the Sage War Cemetery, Oldenburg. N6199 was with 110 from 26-6-1939, and was shot down by flak from warships; reported to have crashed into cruiser *Emden*, killing nine crew.

107 Squadron

N6184*   FTR; Flt/Lt W. Barton, F/O J. Ross, Cpl J. Ricketts, all three crew KIA. F/O Ross attached from 48 Squadron Coastal Command. N6154 shot down by flak from *Admiral Hipper* and blew up.

N6188*   FTR, P/O W. Murphy, Sgt L. Ward, AC E. Patteman, all three crew KIA. N6188 hit by flak from unidentified warship in target area and crashed into sea.

N6240*   FTR; Sgt A. Prince, Sgt G. Booth, AC1 L. Slattery. Sgt Prince KIA and became first of some 10,000 Canadians who lost their lives serving with Bomber Command during WWII. His crewmen were rescued and became first two of nearly 10,000 RAF Prisoners of War. N6240 damaged and hit sea.

N6189*   FTR., F/O H. Lightoller, Sgt O. Howells, AC1 E. Lyon. Crew KIA. N6189 hit by flak from unidentified warship and crashed on shore before it could attack.

N6195   F/O W. Stephens, AC Innes-Jones, AC White. DNCO and RTB. (N6195 served with 107 from 26-6-1939 until 3-3-1940 when it went to 8 Maintenance Unit; issued to 53 Squadron 12-9-1940, which kept it to 9-2-1943. Survived to be SOC 13-5-1944.)

139 Squadron

N6216, N6217, N6218, N6224 and N6225. All abandoned sortie and RTB.

Note that WOp/Ags were all ground tradesmen who had volunteered for extra flying duties, and only one had been promoted to lowest RAF non-commissioned rank of Corporal; unusually F/O Stevens even had an Aircraftman (Innes-Jones) as Observer. Apart from the three Observers, F/O Ross and Sgts Grossey and Ward, attached from Coastal Command Squadrons, Aircraftmen Lyon and Pateman were 'borrowed' from 110 Squadron as 107 was awaiting posting in of further WOp/Ags.

Lt Metz of 4/JG 77 claimed to have shot down a Blenheim north-east of Wilhelmshaven with his Me.109 on this day, but there is no corroboration of his claim.

Appendix 2

Blenheim losses on reconnaissance sorties, 3 September to 31 December 1939

28-09-1939   N6206 110 Squadron Mk IV: FTR; took of from Wattisham at 0740 to reconnoitre Osnabruck area; shot down by Lt H. Heinz in 109E of JG 77; crew F/O D. Strachan, Sgt W. Gunn, and AC1 J. Bateson KIA; they have no known grave and are commemorated on the Runnymede Memorial.

28-09-1939   N6212 110 Squadron Mk IV: FTR; took off with N6206 to reconnoitre Munster area; shot down near Kiel as Hitler visited there; crew W/Cdr I. Cameron, Sgt T. Hammond, and AC1 T. Fullerton KIA and are buried in the Reichswald Forest War Cemetery. W/Cdr Cameron was CO of 110 Squadron.

01-10-1939   N6231 139 Squadron Mk IV: FTR; took off from Wyton to reconnoitre Hanover; shot down near there; F/O A. MacLachlan (Pilot) became PoW, Sgt W. Brown (Observer) and AC2 R. Britton (WOp/Ag) KIA and are buried in Hanover War Cemetery.

13-10-1939   L1138 57 Squadron Mk I: FTR; W/Cdr H. Day, CO of 57 Squadron, took off from Metz at 1140 to reconnoitre Hamm; shot down by 109s. 'Wings' Day became PoW and a famous escapee; was awarded George Cross, OBE and DSO. His crew, Sgt E. Hillier (Obs) and AC2 F. Moller (WOp/Ag), KIA and are buried in Rheinberg War Cemetery.

13-10-1939   L1147 57 Squadron Mk I: FTR; also left Metz for Munster, Bremen, and returned to UK; crashed out of fuel in bad weather near Harpenden, Herts. F/O C. Norman, Sgt Edwards, and AC1 T. Jervis safe.

13-10-1939   N6160 114 Squadron Mk IV: FTR; took off from Villeneuve at 1235; shot down near Rheinberg; crew P/O K. Thompson, Sgt G. Marwood, and AC2 A. Lumsden KIA and are buried in Rheinberg War Cemetery.

16-10-1939   L1141 57 Squadron Mk I: FTR; took off from Etain to reconnoitre Wesel-Borcholt; shot down by 109s; F/O M. Casey, Sgt A. Fripp, and AC1 J. Nelson captured and became PoWs.

30-10-1939   L6694 18 Squadron Mk I: FTR; also took off from Metz; shot down near Trier, believed by Hptm Werner Molders of JG 53; F/L A. Dilnot, Sgt E. Crellin, and AC1 J. Burrows KIA.

30-10-1939   N6234 139 Squadron Mk IV: FTR; one of six aircraft sent from Wyton to photograph airfields; shot down near Gross Bersson, also by Hptm Molders; P/O W. McCracken, Sgt S. Mitchell, and AC1 R. Smith KIA. Two other aircraft damaged and their WOp/Ags injured.

30-10-1939   L1415 18 Squadron Mk I: FTR; took off from Metz; shot down near Vechta by Hptm Werner Molders in 109E of JG 53; F/O D. Elliott, Sgt K. Crew, and AC1 J. Garrick KIA.

06-11-1939   L1145 57 Squadron Mk I: FTR; took off from Metz at 1030 to film 'Siegfried Line'; shot down near Mainz; P/O A. Morton, Sgt G. Storr, and AC1 F. Twinning KIA and are buried in Rheinberg War Cemetery.

07-11-1939   L1325 57 Squadron Mk I: FTR; left Metz at 1145 on same mission; shot down near Mainz by Lt J. Muncheberg of JG 26; P/O H. Bewlay, Sgt S. McIntyre, and AC1 T. Adderley captured and became PoWs.

11-11-1939   N6150 114 Squadron Mk IV: FTR; left Wyton at 1110 with two others to reconnoitre Heligoland; collided with N6145 (below) descending through low cloud near there; F/Lt R. Mills, Sgt F. Doodey, and AC1 G. Johnson KIA.

11-11-1939   N6145 114 Squadron Mk IV: FTR; as above, collided with N6150; P/O B. Martyn, Sgt G. Taylor, and AC2 D. Barker KIA. Third aircraft returned to report incident.

16-11-1939   L1148 57 Squadron Mk I: FTR; took off from Rosieres, became lost and force-landed on Gent/Kortrijk road near Waregem, Belgium; crew Sgt Gilmore, Sgt Turnidge, and AC1 T. Jervis uninjured and interned.

27-12-1939   L8779 107 Squadron Mk IV: FTR; took off from Wattisham to reconnoitre Wilhelmshaven; shot down off Wangerooge by 109E of Kdr of JGI; P/O K. Laxton, Sgt W. Anderson, and LAC T. Lewis KIA.

27-12-1939   L9040 18 Squadron Mk I: FTR; crashed at Quensel, near Royes, cause unknown; all four crew Sgt L. Sabin, Sgt V. Harvey, AC1 W. Martin, and LAC J. Job killed and buried in Quensol cemetery.

Appendix 3

Non-operational Blenheim losses, 3 September to 31 December 1939

03-09-1939   L1164 600 Squadron RAuxAF Mk I-F: stalled during single-engine approach to Hendon and crashed at The Burroughs, Hendon; P/O John Isaac killed.

03-09-1939   L6615 604 Squadron RAuxAF Mk I-F: hit tree on approach to North Weald and crash-landed 50 yards short of boundary, striking a cow; P/O H. Speke (pilot) injured; aircraft DBR.

06-09-1939   L6675 23 Squadron Mk I-F: stalled during night landing at Wittering, hit ground hard and tipped up; F/O R. Knight (Pilot) and crewman unhurt; airframe to ground training use as 1701M.

10-09-1939   P4853 82 Squadron Mk IV: took off from Netheravon, engine cut, aircraft struck wires and cartwheeled near Cleve, Somerset; Sgt J. MacLaughan (Pilot) died of injuries later that day, and AC1 G. Butler (Obs) the following day; other two crewmen, AC1 Dorman and AC1 Dougan, injured.

16-09-1939   L6678 25 Squadron Mk I-F: engine cut and aircraft stalled during single-engine approach to Filton; wing hit ground; P/O B. Rofe slightly injured; airframe to ground training use as 3505M.

19-09-1939   P4861 82 Squadron Mk IV: both engines cut on night take-off from West Zoyland and undercarriage was ripped off; P/O R. McKenzie (pilot) uninjured.

29-09-1939   L1341 104 Squadron Mk I: overshot on landing at Penrhos when engine cut, hitting gully; DBR; P/O A. Paape and Observer injured.

30-09-1939   L4840 53 Squadron Mk IV: damaged at Plivot on return from night sortie when P/O J. Read retracted undercarriage instead of flaps; aircraft shipped back to UK but not repaired.

07-10-1939   N6209 110 Squadron Mk IV: skidded on landing at Wittering and undercarriage collapsed; written off and became Ground Instruction Airframe 1636M.

08-10-1939   N6204 110 Squadron Mk IV: DBR when undercarriage collapsed on take-off from Wattisham; P/O J. Buchanan uninjured.

08-10-1939   L1424 23 Squadron Mk I-F: DBR, belly-landed at Digby in error; F/O Beytagh and crew uninjured (L1424 was used at RAE and A&AEE for gun-pack trials).

10-10-1939   P4841 82 Squadron Mk IV: both engines cut on take-off from Upper Heyford, aircraft crashed and DBR.

10-10-1939   P4862 82 Squadron Mk IV: engine cut on take-off from Kidlington, and aircraft belly-landed; DBR; P/O D. Smith uninjured.

10-10-1939   L1219 108 Squadron Mk I: took off at night from Bicester on Cross Country to Isle of Man; lost without trace, believed to have crashed in Irish Sea; Sgt P. Hemsley, Sgt F. Bryant, and AC2 J. Shearer killed and commemorated at Runnymede.

16-10-1939   L4876 90 Squadron Mk IV: engine cut on take-off from Upwood, and aircraft crashed on airfield, killing pilot, P/O T. Peeler.

17-10-1939   L1509 29 Squadron Mk I-F: undercarriage collapsed on landing at Debden; pilot uninjured, but aircraft DBR.

18-10-1939   L6689 604 Squadron Mk I-F: flew into ground near Croydon on night Anti-Aircraft Co-operation flight; crew F/O E. Prescott and LAC A. Roberts (aged 19) killed (See picture on page 154).

19-10-1939   L1213 108 Squadron Mk I: flew into ground immediately after night overshoot at Bicester, and destroyed by fire; pilot Sgt D. Lamb killed.

24-10-1939   L4904 600 Squadron Mk IV-F: engine cut and aircraft belly-landed and hit fence on night approach at Hornchurch; F/Lt Miller, S/Ldr Seeley and Cpl Holmes slightly injured, aircraft DBR.

02-11-1939   L4899 101 Squadron Mk IV: crashed while landing at West Raynham; pilot P/O C. Keedwell uninjured, aircraft repaired.

03-11-1939   N6144 114 Squadron Mk IV: collided on take off at Wyton with K7061 (below) and caught fire, but pilot Sgt N. Brady only slightly injured; both aircraft destroyed by fire.

03-11-1939   K7061 Wyton Station Flight Mk I: commanded by S/Ldr E. Springall: taxied into take-off path of N6144.

08-11-1939   P4848 SD Flight, Perth Mk IV: flew into high ground at Kirbyshire, N Wales; F/Lt K. Eyres (pilot) killed.

08-11-1939	L1435 18 Squadron Mk I: crashed on landing at Meharicourt, France.
08-11-1939	L8731 64 Squadron Mk I-F: flaps raised prematurely on night take-off from Church Fenton, aircraft hit trees and crashed; P/O D. Carter (Pilot) and LAC G. Lovegrove died of their injuries.
10-11-1939	L8690 141 Squadron Mk I: engine cut, aircraft lost height on night approach and hit trees attempting to land at Sealand; P/O R. Howley (pilot) slightly injured.
11-11-1939	L8662 A&AEE Mk I: overshot forced landing in bad visibility and hit tree near Petersfield, Hants.
13-11-1939	N6198 110 Squadron Mk IV: crashed during low-flying exercise at Barking Tye, 2 miles east of Wattisham; P/O P. Goulder (pilot) seriously injured, Sgt V. Thorne (Obs) killed.
14-11-1939	L1286 145 Squadron Mk IV: control lost in cloud, and aircraft flew into ground near Harwell; P/O W. Ross (Pilot) killed, aircraft destroyed.
15-11-1939	L1127 92 Squadron Mk I: engine cut on approach to Tangmere, aircraft stalled and dived into ground; P/O J. Monroe-Hinds (pilot) and two passengers, P/O M. Dugdale and P/O H. Drummond, killed and aircraft destroyed.
15-11-1939	L1246 57 Squadron Mk I: took off from Orly but engine cut a few minutes later and aircraft crashed into Seine; crew Sgt S. Farmer, F/Sgt F. Bowden, and LAC I. Partlow killed.
15-11-1939	N6226 139 Squadron Mk IV: landed at Upper Heyford after bombing practice, but 'hung up' 20lb bomb dropped off after 50 yards and exploded; pilot P/O Dundee and Sgt P. Davidson unhurt, Cpl F. Moores (WOp/Ag) killed.
16-11-1939	L1275 108 Squadron Mk I: crashed on night exercise at Ludgershall, near Aylesbury, and destroyed by fire; P/O K. Harvey-Jacobs (pilot) killed.
16-11-1939	L6685 600 Squadron Mk I-F: engine cut on night take-off at Hornchurch, wing hit ground and aircraft destroyed by fire; solo pilot F/O A. Vickers killed.
17-11-1939	L1350 90 Squadron Mk I: crashed into boundary of Upwood while attempting single-engine overshoot; P/O J. Palmer injured, aircraft DBR.
20-11-1939	L4887 101 Squadron Mk IV: became lost in haze, crash-landed 3 miles from Lichfield, Staffs, overturned and DBR; minor injuries only to crew P/O C. Newman, LAC J. Johnson, and LAC F. Mantle.
20-11-1939	N6158 114 Squadron Mk IV: crashed on take-off from West Raynham; pilot Sgt V. McPherson uninjured.
23-11-1939	L1129 57 Squadron Mk I: struck tents during low pass at Rosieres-en-Santerre; pilot P/O O. Hume kept control and climbed so his crew could bale out, but then stalled and crashed, and he was killed.
24-11-1939	L1420 25 Squadron Mk I-F: skidded on ice while landing at Northolt and hit bank; Sgt R. Haine and crew uninjured, airframe relegated to ground instruction use as 1886M.
28-11-1939	L8686 219 Squadron Mk IV: engine cut, aircraft stalled attempting forced landing at Catterick, hit ground and cart-wheeled; P/O H. Auger (pilot) injured.
29-11-1939	L1452 23 Squadron Mk I-F: engine cut on searchlight co-op, control lost and aircraft dived into ground at Stockwith near Gainsborough, Lincs; F/Lt P. Walker and Cpl C Francis killed, LAC Chrystall baled out safely.
29-11-1939	L6601 604 Squadron Mk I-F: dived into field near Epping soon after night take-off from North Weald; crew F/O P Wheeler and LAC Oliver killed.
01-12-1939	L8691 141 Squadron Mk I: control lost in cloud and aircraft dived into ground at Leuchars; P/O R. Williams, P/O H. Yelland, AC2 L. Dale and AC2 J. Hunt killed.
01-12-1939	L8781 School of Army Co-operation/Station Flight Mk IV: u/c damaged by premature retraction on take-off from Andover, aircraft belly-landed; became Instructional Airframe 1895M.
02-12-1939	L8868 104 Squadron Mk IV: became lost at dusk, overshot forced landing, hit telegraph poles near Stony Stratford and DBR; P/O T. McGillivray (Pilot) uninjured, Obs injured.
03-12-1939	P6888 21 Squadron Mk IV: crashed on landing at Bircham Newton, and undercarriage collapsed; pilot P/O L. Blanckensee received only slight injuries.
03-12-1939	L4884 90 Squadron Mk IV: became lost, attempted forced landing at dusk at Whittlesey, near Peterborough, hit dyke and overturned; Sgt J. Merrett (Pilot) and unnamed crew only slightly hurt.
06-12-1939	L8450 600 Squadron Mk I-F: struck by another Blenheim while parked at Montrose and DBR.

09-12-1939   L1460 23 Squadron Mk I-F: engine cut, aircraft overshot night landing and struck obstruction at Wittering; F/O Knight (Pilot) and crew uninjured; airframe became 1892M.

10-12-1939   L8695 141 Squadron Mk I: became lost and crashed during forced landing at Linlithgow, W Lothian; P/O D. Williams injured.

11-12-1939   L6740 29 Squadron Mk I-F: crashed at Great Chesterfield Park, near Saffron Walden, and DBR; F/Sgt W. Packer killed and LAC E. Jones seriously injured.

11-12-1939   L9033 No. 2 School of Army Co-operation/Station Flight Mk IV: attempted forced landing in bad weather near Marlborough, Wilts, overturned and DBR; P/O C. Greece injured.

17-12-1939   L1426 25 Squadron Mk I-F: engine cut on take-off for air-test at Northolt, aircraft belly-landed and DBR; F/Sgt E. Monk and crew unhurt.

17-12-1939   L1206 234 Squadron Mk I-F: undercarriage damaged on take-off and jammed, and aircraft belly-landed at Leconfield and DBR; became 2974M.

19-12-1939   L6756 64 Squadron Mk I-F: engine cut and aircraft crash-landed in bad visibility at Drem; F/Sgt E. Gilbert injured.

21-12-1939   L8835 40 Squadron Mk IV: landed at Wyton after air-test with wheels up, and DBR; pilot S/Ldr Steadman (not from 40 Squadron) and crew unhurt.

21-12-1939   K7169 222 Squadron Mk I: suffered hydraulic failure, belly-landed at Duxford and DBR; P/O Bassett (Pilot) and crew uninjured.

22-12-1939   L1531, 22 Squadron Mk I: undercarriage retracted prematurely on take-off and was damaged, and aircraft belly-landed at Thorney Island and DBR; P/O A. Rigg and crew unhurt. 22 Squadron were converting to Beauforts.

Please note that all the above aircraft were total losses, except for the few (noted as such) that became ground instructional airframes or were repaired and returned to service later.

604 Squadron Mk Is, based at Hendon until 2 September 1939, then North Weald until 16 January 1940. L6689 crashed near Croydon on 18 October 1939 on a night AA Co-Op sortie, and F/O E. Prescott and LAC A. Roberts, aged 19, were killed.

Chapter 9

Shortcomings and improvements

This early wartime aerial activity during the 'Phoney War' had revealed several serious shortcomings in the operational capabilities of the Blenheim – shortcomings that were also revealed in all of the other contemporary Bomber Command aircraft. These were not in the aeroplane itself, for the Blenheim was a fine machine and a delight to fly; indeed, as already noted it was the only RAF bomber for which the Pilot's Notes gave the entry speeds for all the standard aerobatic manoeuvres, including a 'roll off the top', the first half of a loop and the second half of a slow roll. But however fine a flying machine it was, it was singularly ill-equipped to engage in the type of war into which it was being sent. Clearly the defensive armament was inadequate, as was protection for the crew and for some of the aircraft's vital systems, such as the petrol tanks – for the self-sealing type were not then fitted.

The first improvement was fitting armour plate behind both the pilot's seat and the wireless sets aft of the gunner; this work was carried out at the squadrons and completed by 15 September. The squadrons found that 'Ever-Hot' bags prevented the cameras and guns from freezing at altitude – not forgetting the poor crew, for no heating equipment was provided. We have seen how similar deficiencies led to the withdrawal from daylight operations of the RAF's other Medium and Heavy Bombers, and we will now consider the attempts made to overcome these shortcomings in equipment as far as the Blenheim was concerned, for it had to continue operating in daylight. That these attempts were far from sufficient was revealed all too cruelly when the 'real' war started.

More aircraft were sent to the A&AEE at Boscombe Down (see Note 1) and to the RAE at Farnborough (see Note 2) for trials to speed the development of these improvements, while some were retained by the manufacturers for a period of trials (see Note 3), often prior to dispatch to one or both of those highly regarded Establishments. Several new RAF units were formed for similar development purposes, and those known to have used Blenheims for trials included the Aircraft Gun Mounting Establishment, the Central Gunnery School, the Fighter Interception Unit, the Bomber Development Unit, and the Air Fighting Development Establishment.

The Commanders of the AASF in France and Bomber Command in the UK had written to the Air Staff pressing the need for improved rear armament. The former considered it 'absolutely essential that the Blenheims should have more than a single rear-defence gun', while the latter wished to 'stress very strongly the inadequacy of rear protection afforded to Blenheim aircraft', and 'hoped that a way will be found to overcome the technical difficulties.' On 13 October 1939 the C-in-C ordered urgent investigation into the possibility of installing an extra gun or guns to fire downwards and to the rear to cover the Blenheim's blind-

The first installation of an extra rear defence gun mounted on the lower escape hatch. The aircraft is raised to flying attitude at A&AEE Boscombe Down.

spots. 107 Squadron at Wattisham, under the dynamic leadership of W/Cdr Basil Embry, had already been working on this and had installed in some of its aircraft a machine-gun in the rear of each engine nacelle, fixed to fire slightly downwards and operated via lengthy Bowden cables from a long lever in the turret. This arrangement was referred to in official correspondence as the 'Wattisham Scheme' and approval was given for 16 aircraft to be so equipped – it was suggested that 'they should fly at the rear of formations'. 107 also lashed a similarly activated gun under the rear fuselage of a few aircraft, but this was not satisfactory, and was much disliked by the armourers, as the guns became caked in mud following take-off from wet grass airfields. That such extreme but ineffective measures were approved by visiting representatives from the RAE and at both Group and Command level reveals the prevailing degree of desperation.

The Bomber Command Armaments Officer, W/Cdr Odbert, suggested that the fixed Browning in the port wing be removed to the nacelle to halve the demand for extra guns. He stated that a twin-gun installation for the turret was being developed, but it restricted the secondary traverse causing an undesirable loss of field of fire, especially immediately behind the Blenheim, so could not be introduced until that problem was resolved. He added that Bristol was also working on a rear-firing defence gun mounted in the under-nose escape hatch to be fired through mirrors by the Observer – rather oddly this was termed 'a dished panel gun' in official correspondence (as in Air 35/114 at the PRO), and 50 sets were ordered on 17 February 1940. The A&AEE at Boscombe Down rigged up a

The heavy R1082 Receiver and T1083 Transmitter WT sets mounted on a shelf behind the turret (removed here, part of the mounting ring top centre). Under the shelf is a wooden kitchen-type drawer with a brass handle, containing coils needed to change frequency. The trailing-aerial winding drum is on the right.

Mk I with an under-defence gun in the WOp/Ag's escape hatch in the floor just forward of his turret, sighted by a mirror, but he could not man both at the same time and it would leave the rear hemisphere completely undefended while he changed position, so the idea was not pursued. It was not until the end of March 1940 that the first under-nose rear-defence gun was fitted to a 107 Squadron Blenheim, one of four sent for trials to the Air Fighting Development Unit at Northolt on the 23rd of that month. So for many months the squadrons had to continue operations with the existing inadequate defensive armament supplemented by any extra guns they could improvise.

Flexible inner self-sealing fuel tank bags were being fitted, as was armour protection for the oil tanks. The service equipment that had been added included an oxygen system with storage bottles, plus regulators for each crew position; the heavy R1082 Receiver and T1083 Transmitter wireless sets, which sat behind the turret on a shelf (under which were wooden drawers with brass kitchen-type handles for the spare coils!); and installation commenced of TR9 sets so that the crew could – at last – talk to each other via the 'intercom', and to other aircraft via the RT. Previously some squadrons had fitted a string-and-pulley system so that the crew in the cockpit could pass messages, clipped to a clothes-peg, to the WOp/Ag and vice versa. Other equipment included cockpit lighting and night-flying equipment, including Morse-key-operated downward identification lights; a rudimentary automatic pilot system known as 'George' (on some aircraft); larger-capacity batteries; Graviner fire-extinguisher bottles in the engine bays, plus two portable extinguishers in the fuselage; a Very signalling pistol in a firing-tube; stowage for parachutes; and a Type C inflatable dinghy.

L1222 was the sole Mk II, with extra bombs under the inner wings. This mark was not produced, and bomb-carriers were attached under the rear fuselage instead. These drag-producing light-series bomb-carriers could carry 320lb, normally eight 40lb bombs or two 25lb and two 40lb bombs each. The railing-aerial fair-lead is behind the Armourer's head.

Many Blenheims had the view to the rear improved by an external mirror on the top of the windscreen frame, and/or Perspex tear-drop blisters (designed by Sydney Cotton) on the side windows. To increase the standard 1,000lb bomb-load by some 30 per cent, universal light-series bomb-carriers that could carry 320lb of small bombs were mounted under the rear fuselage – this position created unwelcome extra drag but was necessary for centre of gravity reasons as the extra bomb cells built into the wing centre-section were normally used only for light flares. Some squadrons, however, loaded two 40lb bombs in each wing bay, but this was not popular with the crews. On the fighter version a bullet-proof windscreen and reflector sight were fitted, together with some frontal armour protection for the pilot. The debate about the desirability of removing the heavy dorsal turret and fairing over the aperture on the Mk I-Fs and Mk IV-Fs continued inconclusively.

As the extra service equipment was installed over the months, some of it before the war but much in the light of operational experience, the additional weight and drag progressively degraded the performance advantage over fighters previously enjoyed by Blenheims. Moreover, the rapid and considerable improvement in the performance of opposing fighters eroded it completely. In the two and a half years since the Blenheim first entered RAF service, the crews discovered the hard way not only that their aircraft no longer possessed the speed to escape pursuing fighters, but also that when caught they stood little chance of defending themselves adequately, unless a large slice of luck or some nearby cloud cover came to their aid – a grim prospect indeed unless they could operate under the protective cloak of cloud or darkness.

Radar

However, a way to remove even this protection had been developed by the scientists working on the experimental radar equipment at Bawdsey Manor on the Norfolk coast, and – unknown to the Allies – by German scientists too. In due course this would effectively remove the cover from the aircraft and naval craft of both combatants. Blenheims had worked during 1938 with these 'boffins' on the development of the ground-to-air 'radio location' beacons that later formed the Chain Home coastal radar stations, and the new IFF (Identification Friend from Foe) transmitters carried in the aircraft, which were needed to work in conjunction with them.

Another direction for the new and secret science of radar was the development of devices small enough to be carried in aircraft but powerful enough to send signals and register the returns from other aircraft or ships – in this the British led the world. Blenheims K7033, 7034 and 7044 from D Flight (based at Martlesham Heath but working for Bawdsey Manor)

A steady stream of new Blenheims continued to flow from the production lines. The King and Queen visited the vast Rootes shadow factory at Speke in April 1940, and steps were placed by R3740 so that they could look into the cockpit. Churchill and Stafford Cripps are on the left. (R3740 served with 107 Squadron and was shot down by flak from a convoy it was attacking off the coast of Norway on 18 April 1941, and the crew were killed.)

were the first aircraft to carry the primitive AI (Airborne Interception) air-to-air radar set. Others, including L1113, L4931, L4932, L6595, L6622 and L1201 (which crashed on Orfordness on 14 December 1938) were used for radar development and calibration and AI trials. It was soon realised that this would be especially useful at night, so yet another new role had been found for Blenheims, as described in the section below concerning night-fighters. A version of AI, known as ASV (Air to Surface Vessel) was developed in parallel to locate shipping, and later on it was found that an airborne radar on trial in a Blenheim could even distinguish features on the ground, and this discovery led to the development of the H2S 'ground mapping' radar later used extensively by the Bomber Command 'heavies'. At that early stage, all of these mysterious 'black boxes' were called RDF (Radio Direction Finding) sets, and D Flight at the A&AEE was named the RDF Flight, to disguise its true purpose.

The winter of 1939/40 was a particularly severe one, but Blenheims, whenever the weather permitted, had to carry out convoy protection patrols, sea-searches, anti-shipping strikes, overland reconnaissance missions, and a variety of training flights as the operational squadrons 'worked up'. So Blenheim losses mounted steadily, but on a far smaller scale than the heavy casualties that they would suffer within a few months when the Germans opened their offensive in the West. As Blenheims were being employed in so many different but contemporary operational roles during the period before the launch of the *Blitzkrieg* offensive, the clarity of this chronicle will benefit if we consider each of these roles individually rather than in the correct, but more confusing, chronological order. Once that offensive was launched on 10 May 1940, the Blenheims were pressed into all roles simultaneously in a desperate but futile attempt to stem the tide of the German advance.

However, it may first be helpful to indicate the background to this period of the war. The early spring saw 'the calm before the storm' continue, then the war spread with surprising speed to Scandinavia on 9 April – and the feeble attempts by British forces to prevent the German invasion of Norway failed miserably. On 10 May, the very day that the Germans launched their *Blitzkrieg* attack on the Low Countries, this humiliation led to the fall of Neville Chamberlain's Government. It was replaced by a National Government headed by Winston Churchill, although as First Lord of the Admiralty he had pressed hard for the intervention in Norway. At the darkest hour in Britain's history, Churchill provided the resolute and inspired leadership that was required, and his magnificent oratory rallied the nation just as it was reeling from the blows raining upon it.

Reconnaissance Blenheims

As we have seen, the Blenheim Mk IV had been ordered originally as a replacement for the Avro Anson in the general reconnaissance role, and it frequently undertook this

The severe winter of 1939/40: Blenheims at a 21 Squadron dispersal at Bodney in February 1940, and (opposite) the same view two months later.

task during the first four months of the war. This use of the Blenheim for reconnaissance continued during the opening months of 1940, when the weather allowed. Of the Blenheim squadrons sent to France, 57 and 18 were deployed directly for this purpose, with 53 and 59 (designated Army Co-operation Squadrons) to provide tactical reconnaissance facilities for the BEF alongside the Battle and Lysander squadrons that were considered – rightly, as was soon demonstrated – to be too vulnerable in this role. 53 was in fact the first squadron to receive the Mk IV in January 1939, followed by 59 in March; 57 and 18 had taken their Mk Is over to France in September 1939, but were also re-equipping with Mk IVs by March 1940.

Although primarily deployed in the bombing role, the UK-based Blenheims from 110, 107, 114 and 139 Squadrons of 2 Group Bomber Command undertook more dangerous reconnaissance missions deep into Germany when these were resumed in the spring of 1940, and these sorties became more hazardous when airfields were added to naval bases and communications in late September 1939. When the latter two squadrons, 114 and 139, were sent to France to replace 40 and 15 (the two Battle squadrons back in the UK converting to Blenheims) they were intended to provide direct support to the Army by bombing advancing enemy troops, but in the event they were also used for tactical reconnaissance. Even during the so-called 'Phoney War' the Blenheims incurred steady losses on reconnaissance sorties (see Appendix 1).

This activity by the Blenheim squadrons took place before Cotton's small dedicated Photographic Reconnaissance Unit at Heston, named No 2 Camouflage Flight (then Unit), became fully operational and was later greatly expanded. The unit had two Blenheims, and Cotton had one 'cleaned up' to improve its performance; he designated this PR-1, thus negating the change of unit name! This Blenheim was L1348, a Mk I on loan from 139 Squadron, and some 250 man-hours of work at Heston and Farnborough were spent in rubbing the aircraft down, sealing all the joints and gaps with tape, and repainting it with a smoother Titanine finish, fairing the flat lower-nose glazing panels

Two views of L1348, the cleaned-up PR Blenheim, with Rotol propellers, faired nose, clipped wings, and the turret removed.

with alloy, removing the turret and other armament, and replacing the standard rounded wing-tips with shorter, squarer fairings. However, all this work produced only a slight increase in maximum speed from 263 to 278mph. Another useful modification to this aircraft was the fitting of streamlined Perspex blisters to the main side windows, which greatly improved the field of view rearwards and downwards for Pilot and Observer; these blisters were soon being fitted to squadron aircraft. L1348 then went to Staverton and had Rotol constant-speed propellers fitted; these and further modifications by the A&AEE at Boscombe Down produced at top speed of 294mph (true) at 13,000 feet using take-off power settings of 2,750rpm and +9lb boost, making it the fastest Blenheim ever. But overall performance still proved inadequate for unescorted reconnaissance, and the PR-1 version was not proceeded with. Cotton was still pressing hard for Spitfires, which he knew were far more suitable, and treading on many Air Ministry toes in the process.

Incidentally, L1348 saw the first use of the 'sky' colour, known colloquially as 'duck-egg blue', from Titanine's smooth Camotint range, which was developed with Cotton's help. It was soon to be used on the under-surfaces of UK-based Blenheims in place of the all-black or half-black/half-white under-surfaces then in use. These 'sky' undersides were also adopted later for other day bombers and all the other aircraft (apart from night-fighters) of Fighter and Coastal Commands.

Dowding had heard of these 'high-speed' modifications, and being most anxious to improve the inadequate performance of the Mk I-Fs in his Command, went to Heston to inspect L1348, was impressed and ordered eight more to be similarly modified. (I am unable to trace any further information on whether this was done or not.) The enterprising Cotton used this occasion to extract from Dowding two of the very scarce Spitfires, which he modified for PR work, stripping out all armament, fitting cameras, and providing them with a warm-air supply to prevent condensation; their far higher speed attained at a much greater altitude made them vastly more effective than the Blenheim for this role. One, N3071, was detached to operate from Seclin in France, and by mid-January 1940 Cotton was able to show the Air Staff a memo from Colonel Lespair, Commander of the French PR HQ at Meaux, which stated that, in the period from the start of the war until then:

Sidney Cotton (left) showing Photo-Recce pictures to Air Marshall Sir Arthur Barratt, AOC of RAF France.

> 'The RAF had photographed 2,500 square miles of enemy territory with a loss of 40 aircraft. The French had photographed 6,000 square miles with a loss of 60 aircraft. The detachment from Heston had photographed 5,000 square miles without losing the one and only Spitfire that had done the whole job.'

The Air Council agreed to expand the PR Unit immediately and Cotton was allocated the extra Spitfires for which he had been asking. By the autumn of 1940 some 30 PR Spitfires were operating successfully in this role, but once more the Blenheim squadrons had to 'hold the fort' until sufficient of the more suitable aircraft became available. Cotton was an energetic and enterprising entrepreneur who cut many corners and ruffled many feathers, often going over the heads of senior officers to get what he wanted, and he soon fell out with the Air Staff. To look ahead for a moment, he was removed on 8 July 1940 and replaced by his Deputy, W/Cdr Geoffrey Tuttle; he then offered his expertise to the Admiralty – which had been the main complainants about the lack of good photographs provided by the RAF Blenheims – and this upset the Air Staff even more. He was declared *persona non grata*, and in my view was treated very badly in view of the significant contribution he had made in creating far more efficient methods of obtaining and interpreting aerial reconnaissance photographs.

Anti-shipping activity by Blenheims

We have noted that, following the attack on units of the German Fleet off Wilhelmshaven on the first day of the war, Blenheims were in constant demand for attempts to locate and attack enemy naval vessels, especially the capital ships that so concerned the Admiralty. On 2 January, in a rare success, Sgt H. Walman in N6190 of 107 Squadron photographed the *Tirpitz* in a Wilhelmshaven shipyard from 19,000 feet with an 8-inch lens.

On 10 January 110 Squadron had an eventful day when, led by S/Ldr Kenneth Doran, it ran into five Me.110s while on a North Sea shipping search, and a running fight took place. The Blenheims, maintaining their tight formation of four 'vics' of three, dropped to sea level to avoid attacks from below, but the cannon-armed Messerschmitts could open fire when beyond the range of the Vickers machine-gun in the Blenheim turret; nonetheless one was shot down when it flew between two of the 110 Squadron sections and was seen to crash in the sea, and another was so badly damaged that it landed in neutral Denmark. Sgt Hanne's Blenheim P4859 received damage to an engine, dropped behind the formation and was quickly shot down into the sea, while two others were damaged beyond repair (see Appendix 2). This was the first encounter with the twin-engined Me.110 *Zerstorers*, which, apart from being far more heavily armed, were some 60mph faster than the Blenheims. For his leadership during this action S/Ldr Doran – who had dropped the first bombs from an RAF aircraft on a German target – was awarded a bar to his DFC.

Operations in March were stepped up considerably as there was a slight improvement in the weather. The Royal Navy was still anxious for sightings of large warships and wanted a watch kept on Wilhelmshaven, the Schillig Roads, and the docks at Hamburg and Kiel. On 4 March Sgt R. Cunningham in N6183 of 107 Squadron descended through cloud over the Schillig Roads, spotted a U-boat heading north on the surface and attacked it with his four 250lb bombs, claiming one direct hit as he saw much black and grey smoke. Although a wreck marker was seen soon after, the U-boat could only be classed as 'probably sunk' as its destruction could not be confirmed. However, a notable success came on 11 March when S/Ldr Miles Dewlap dropped his Blenheim P4852 of 82 Squadron down through cloud, emerging at 1,000 feet off Borkum to find a U-boat on the surface. He dived to attack immediately but from such a low level that his aircraft was damaged by the explosions, and only with difficulty did he nurse it back to Watton. The Type VIIIA submarine U-31 was sunk – the first U-boat to be sunk by an RAF aircraft.

2 Group continued to assist the Royal Navy as much as possible, for on 34 of the days between 14 February and 1 April 1940 no fewer than 250 sorties were flown by Blenheims searching the North Sea for shipping targets. On only six occasions could they find and bomb such targets, but with no discernible results. German fighters were seen on but a few of these sorties and only four Blenheims were lost (see Appendix 2). Nine Blenheims of 82 Squadron set out from Bodney on 1 April 1940 to strike enemy ships reported off the Danish coast, but in poor weather only one section was able to attack two pairs of flak ships, and one was shot down, while 21 Squadron lost an aircraft just as it was setting out on a shipping operation (also Appendix 2). On 7 April W/Cdr Basil Embry led 12 Blenheims of 107 Squadron to attack, in bad weather and without success, a large force of German capital ships heading for southern Norway. First spotted by a Hudson, this was in fact the German Task Force heading north to seize Trondheim and Narvik, although this was not known to the Admiralty at the time.

40 Squadron lost a Blenheim in unusual circumstances on 14 April, when AC2 J. Lewis, a young Canadian from Morden, Manitoba, who hoped to go on to a pilot's course, 'borrowed' Mk IV L9207 at Wyton and took it for an unauthorised flight; unfortunately he lost control and crashed to his death in the Thames Estuary (see Appendix 3).

Officers of 82 Squadron in November 1939. The Squadron scored the RAF's first success against a U-boat in March 1940. From the left: S/Ldr Sutcliffe, S/Ldr Hall (Missing in Action 1940), S/Ldr Hunt (Killed in Action 1941), F/O Blake (Killed in Action 1940), F/O McConnell (shot-down twice and a PoW), F/Lt Breese (Missing in Action), and F/O Fordham.

Long-range fighter Blenheims

At the outbreak of war Fighter Command had four Regular Squadrons (23, 25, 29 and 64) and three Auxiliary Squadrons (600, 601 and 604) equipped with Blenheim Mk I-Fs. These were all day-fighter squadrons, but they were soon classified as dual-purpose day/night units, and by the early months of 1940 were all deployed primarily as night-fighters, as detailed in the following section. The RAF had no suitable long-range day-fighters available.

Hugh Dowding, concerned that the order to send four more of his squadrons of Hurricanes to France would be 'opening a tap through which they would all flow', asked the Air Staff to create more fighter squadrons. All that it was able to provide were six more squadrons of Blenheim Mk I-Fs (219, 92, 145, 222, 229 and 234) to add to the above seven operational squadrons of Mk I-Fs. Dowding accepted these 'stop-gap' arrangements so that he could establish and build up extra squadrons with their supporting infrastructure, before the post-Munich increased production of Spitfires and Hurricanes would enable him to re-equip them later with the far more effective single-seat fighters. It is ironic that, due to the pre-war imbalance of orders in favour of bombers noted above, it was these very bombers – for some Battles were used too – that equipped the new cadre fighter squadrons. In fact, 92 and 145 changed their Blenheims to Spitfire Mk Is in May 1940 before becoming operational, together with 222, 229 and 234 Squadrons, which were operational on Blenheims before re-equipping with single-seaters, but 219 continued with Blenheims before converting to Beaufighters in the winter of 1940. Two further squadrons, 141 and 242, the latter with Canadian pilots, also worked up on Blenheims, but converted to Defiants and Hurricanes respectively before commencing operations. The crews of these Blenheim squadrons that were re-equipped with single-seat fighters before the main German offensive in the West burst into violent action had cause to be grateful for the eight-month respite granted by the 'Phoney War'.

Within days of the war starting Fighter Command had been given the unexpected extra task of providing cover for British shipping off the East Coast, for 21 British merchant ships had been sunk in the first 14 days of the war. The Command's single-engined short-range interceptors were not suited to this task, although some Hurricanes were deployed on this duty, and nine were lost. Consequently four new 'Trade Protection' squadrons of Blenheims were formed – 254, 235, 248 and 236. These were in addition to the eight fresh squadrons mentioned above, making no fewer than 19 Blenheim-equipped squadrons in Fighter Command at that time! However, in view of their duties these four new squadrons were transferred to Coastal Command in February 1940 and commenced re-equipping with new Mk IV-Fs straight away, apart from 236, which kept its Mk I-Fs until July/August 1940. Coastal Command had evaluated a Blenheim before the war when 217 Squadron tested L4846, but its first operational Blenheims were with D Flight of 233 Squadron, a Hudson unit based at Leuchars in October 1939. In the meantime Blenheim Mk I-Fs from the existing squadrons, 23 and 604, had been patrolling the East Coast and the North Sea as well as escorting convoys by day, with 25, 29 and 64 Squadrons operating by day and night; similarly 600 and 601 patrolled the South Coast and English Channel by day and night. However, by the spring of 1940 the Fighter Command Blenheim squadrons could no longer be risked in operating in the long-range role over the seas, and would be re-deployed principally as night-fighter units.

Night-fighter Blenheims

In November 1938 Mk I L6622 was based with the A&AEE at Martlesham Heath to work with Bawdsey on air-to-air radar, being joined by L6627 in March 1939. L6622 went to the RAE at Farnborough to join L6624 there, and was then sent back to the A&AEE on 2 January 1940. L6623, L6625 and L6626 had been engaged on similar radar development work. The fruit of their research was a top secret but world-leading order, issued on 17 July 1939, for 21 Blenheim Mk I-Fs to be equipped with Mk III AI sets at RAE Farnborough, and the first, L1290, was delivered to 25 Squadron on the 31st, and 15 aircraft with the new device were in service by the outbreak of war. By November 1939 604 Squadron had L6802 and L6807, while 600 Squadron had three AI-equipped I-Fs (L1494, L4906 and L8669), which were detached to a special flight at RAF Manston in a futile attempt to catch the Heinkel He.115s that were mining the Thames Estuary by night – no successful interceptions were made as the ground returns on the elementary AI radar obscured the 'blips' of the low-level raiders. This flight, under S/Ldr (later Air Marshal) Walter Pretty, who had commanded one of the early Chain Home Low radar stations, was developed into the Fighter Interception Unit at Tangmere. AI sets were installed in the ten Mk I-Fs serving with the FIU, whose aircraft (L1186, L6651/88, 6720/88, 6805/35/36/37/38) were used for extensive trials – and operationally whenever possible – to develop radar-assisted interception methods. The FIU moved to Ford and, as we will see, achieved an historic first when F/O G. Ashfield in L6836 made the first ever successful radar-guided night interception using Mk IV AI and shot down a Dornier Do.17Z on the night of 22/23 July 1940. Sixteen brand-new Blenheim Mk IV-Fs (P4829-37 and P4844-50) were delivered straight from Bristol to the RAE at Farnborough during September and October 1939 for AI sets to be fitted before issue to the Special Duty Flight and the night-fighter squadrons over the winter.

AI Mk III fitted in the Blenheim centre-section 'well' behind the pilot, two small CRTs (upper left) show target's relative elevation and azimuth positions, the right-hand black-box is the power-unit. Although primitive and unreliable it was the first airborne radar set in the world.

601 (A) Squadron Blenheims at Tangmere in February 1940. Although designated as night-fighters, the Mk I-Fs still wore the day-fighter scheme of white-and-black under-surfaces. A similarly marked Mk I-F of 23 (F) Squadron is seen at Wittering in February 1940; both airfields are covered in snow.

A flight of 25 Squadron was detached from Northolt to Martlesham Heath in November 1939 to re-equip with Mk IV-Fs from that batch, fitted with Mk III AI, and commenced North Sea patrols at night, but there was a lack of 'trade' for them. 604 Squadron received P4847, its first Mk IV-F fitted with AI, in December 1939, just before it moved to Martlesham Heath for intensive AI trials and training. Other Mk IV-Fs from that special radar-equipped batch were P4830/32/34/48 for the Special Duty Flight; P4829/37/46 for 600 Squadron; P4833/35/45 for 29 Squadron; P4836/44 for 23 Squadron; and P4849/50 for 64 Squadron.

As we have noted, apart from the specialists of the A&AEE, RAE, FIU and the Special Duty Flight, ordinary Fighter Command Blenheim squadrons worked closely with the scientists and through a process of trial and error gradually improved the equipment and acquired the technical expertise required to operate it. Clearly, Blenheims made a pivotal contribution to the vital development of both ground-to-air and air-to-air radar, and were used extensively to pioneer the new operational techniques required by this revolutionary equipment.

The Mk I-Fs of 23, 25, 600, 604 Squadrons had started the war patrolling the seas but soon became full-time night-fighter units to join 29, 64 and 601 Squadrons, which had already changed to operating in that role. These changes were implemented by Fighter Command in view not only of the changed priorities but also of the losses suffered in the few daylight long-range operations undertaken by the fighter Blenheims. Their nocturnal endeavours would commence in earnest when the Luftwaffe turned to its night *Blitz* during the later stages of the Battle of Britain.

Non-operational Blenheim losses

Increasing attrition of the Blenheims due to causes other than enemy action continued at a distressing rate during this 'quiet' period of the war, and it is informative to look at some examples (see Appendix 3), noting that they include the first losses at the newly formed Blenheim OTUs (but exclude all losses incurred overseas).

This disturbingly high level of losses not due to enemy action occurred in the first few months of 1940 during the so-called 'Phoney War' prior to the launch of the main German offensive in the West – an offensive that also caused a dramatic increase in Blenheim losses due to enemy action – and while another preliminary but costly encounter with the German armed forces erupted over the North Sea and in Norway.

Forced-landings were common, such as this 21 Squadron Mk IV with a collapsed port undercarriage; note the airman standing guard with rifle and fixed bayonet.

Notes

Note 1: Blenheims that served with the Aeroplane & Armament Experimental Establishment (A&AEE)

Martlesham Heath (to 03-09-1939)

Type 142 K7557 ('Britain First')

Mk I: K7033* (the first production aircraft); K7034*, K7044* (*first aircraft used for radar trials), K7168, (performance and armament trials); L1201, L1253, L1495, L8662 and L8689 (armament trials); L1274, L1417, L6777, L8669 and L8671 (bombing trials); L6794, L1173 and L1407 (Porton Down trials); K7072 ('long-nose' trials); K7109 (direct-vision panel trials); K7150, L1113, L4931, L4932, L6595, L6622, L6625, L6626 and L6627 (used on radar development work with Bawdsey Manor); L1222 (heating trials); L1348 ('high-speed' modifications and Rotol propeller trials); L1357 (performance trials); L1424 (prototype Mk I-F); L6594 (performance trials, then 37mm COW cannon trials); L6787 (twin 20mm cannon trials).

Boscombe Down (from 03-09-1939)

Mk IV: L4893 and V5797 (bombing trials); L4838 (gunnery trials); L4835 (the first Mk IV tested); L8748, N3522, N3552 and R3601 (performance and handling trials); L9337 and L9387 (Bristol X turret trials); P4832, P6961, R3745, R3760, T2354, T2357 and V5427 (turret trials); V6000 (H2S trials); V6251 (flare trials); Z6191 (aerial mines trials); L9337, R6916 and T2354 (Porton Down trials).

Mk V: AD657 and AD658 (prototypes); AD661 (?), AZ861, AZ862 and AZ886 (gunnery trials); AZ888 (turret trials); AZ923 (photography trials); AZ930 (handling trials); BA248 (performance trials); BA287 (turret trials); DJ702 (production prototype).

Note 2: Blenheims that served with the Royal Aircraft Establishment (RAE) at Farnborough

Type 142 K7557 ('Britain First')

Mk I: K7033, K7058, K7063 and K7072 (de-icing and cabin heating trials); L1186, L1253, L1254, L1255, L1290, L1295 and L1348 (PR version); L1361, L1421, L1424, L1494, L1495, L6595, L6619, L6622, L6623, L6624, L6625, L6626, L6651, L6688, L6783, L6720, L6788,L6802, L6805, L6807, L6835, L6836, L6837 and L6838.

Mk IV: L4838, L4843 and L4888 (centimetric radar nose); L4906, L8669, L8851, L9253, L9327, L9459, N3522, N3527, N6156, N6161, N6183, N6241, P4829, P4830, P4831, P4832, P4833, P4834, P4835, P4836, P4837, P4844, P4845, P4846, P4847, P4848, P4849, P4850, P4899, P4906, R3601, R3679, R3690, T1874, T2120, V5427, V5722, Z5751, Z5759, Z5969, Z6189 and Z6246.

Note 3: Blenheims used by manufacturers for development and trials

A. V. Roe: Mk IV Z6185.

De Havilland: Mk IV N6156 (propeller trials).

Bristol Aircraft Company: Type 142 K7557 ('Britain First'); Mk I K7033 (auto-control and Curtiss electric propeller trials); K7034 (turret trials); K7044 and L1242 (tricycle undercarriage trials); K7058 and K7072 ('long-nose' trials); K7109 and L1222. Mk IV R3680, R3698, V5427, Z5909, Z6189, Z6191 and Z7425. Mk V AD657 and AD661 (prototypes).

Rootes: Mk I K7072 (pattern aircraft); Mk V DJ702 and DJ707 (production prototypes); AZ861, AZ862, AZ886, AZ888 and BA439.

Rotol: Mk I K7044, L1348 and L6805 (propeller trials).

Armstrong-Siddeley: Mk IV L9388.

Appendix 1

Blenheim losses on reconnaissance sorties, 1 January to 9 May 1940

03-01-1940   L1410 18 Squadron Mk I: took off from Metz at 0755; Failed To Return (FTR); survived attack by Hurricane, was shot down by 109s of JG 77 and crashed in Belgium; F/O C. Kempster (Pilot) and Sgt F. Smith (Obs) interned, AC1 P. Harris (WOp/Ag) Killed in Action (KIA) and is buried in Robermont Cemetery, Liege.

10-01-1940   P4859 110 Squadron Mk IV: took off from Wattisham at 1015; FTR; shot down into North Sea by Me.110s of ZG 76; Sgt J. Hanne, Sgt G. Williams and AC1 E. Vick (aged 19) KIA and are commemorated at Runnymede.

10-01-1940   N6203 110 Squadron Mk IV: as above, FTR; damaged by Me.110s of ZG 76 and crash-landed at Manby; P/O G. Pemberton, Sgt Quarrington and AC1 Roberts only slightly hurt, aircraft Damaged Beyond Repair (DBR).

10-01-1940   N6213 110 Squadron Mk IV: as above; port tyre punctured in fight, and undercarriage (u/c) sheared off on landing back at Wattisham; P/O P. Arderne, Sgt A. Rook and LAC J. Tippett uninjured, but aircraft written off.

12-01-1940   L8859 114 Squadron Mk IV: badly damaged by 109s over Germany; Sgt W. Paul (Obs) injured, P/O G. Turner (Pilot) made single-engined forced landing at Metz and slightly injured, AC S. Peplar (WOp/Ag) unhurt, but aircraft DBR and abandoned.

25-01-1940   L1280 57 Squadron Mk I: took off from Rosieres; FTR; shot down by 109s near Duisberg; P/O J. O'Reilly- Blackwood, Sgt D. Bendall and AC2 J. Hunter KIA.

14-02-1940   L8759 21 Squadron Mk IV: became lost on return from recce to Borkum, iced-up, aerial detached; P/O I. Stapleton ordered crew to bale out, Sgt Whetton landed near Winchester, AC Ball near Portsmouth, Pilot then saw signal flares and landed safely at Tangmere. Aircraft repaired but FTR 16-02-1940; this crew killed 06-04-1940 (see Appendix 2).

25-02-1940   L1444 18 Squadron Mk I: took off from Metz, was badly damaged over Germany, and crashed near North Coates; P/O J. Monette injured, Sgt J. Potter KIA, LAC A. Whitehill unhurt.

15-03-1940   L9249 57 Squadron Mk IV: took off from Metz at 2345; FTR; crashed soon after, believed hit by 'friendly' AA fire; F/O W. Adam (Pilot) KIA, Sgt G. Park (Obs) injured but survived, LAC F. Mantle (WOp/Ag) KIA.

23-03-1940   N6200 110 Squadron Mk IV: took off from Wattisham at 1350 to reconnoitre Heligoland area; FTR; crashed and overturned at 2025 near Diss, Norfolk; F/O J. Buchanan, Sgt Patterson, and AC2 Greenwood safe.

27-03-1940   L8747 107 Squadron Mk IV: took off from Wattisham to photograph damage at Hornum, Sylt; FTR; shot down near target by Me.109 of Uffz K. Oploski of JG 77; Sgt D. Nichols, Sgt G. Stiles, and LAC J. Roberts KIA.

27-03-1940   L8753 110 Squadron Mk IV: took off from Ipswich on same mission; FTR; crashed 5 minutes later on bank of River Orwell, Suffolk; F/O J. Buchanan unhurt, Sgt G. Lumsden and LAC B. Gray injured; F/O Buchanan's second crash in four days.

31-03-1940   P6887 21 Squadron Mk IV: engine cut after take-off from Watton for recce mission; FTR; struck tree and crashed near Griston, Norfolk; S/Ldr G. Pryde unhurt, Sgt Jennings injured, AC1 O'Connor unhurt.

11-04-1940   L9181 57 Squadron Mk IV: FTR; crashed near Roye, France, on recce mission from Rosieres; AC1 G. Lindsay, WOp/Ag, killed.

14-04-1940   L9465 57 Squadron Mk IV: took off from Rosieres; FTR; shot down by Me.109 of JG 20 and crashed near Arnhem, Holland; F/O H. Graham-Hogg, Sgt J. Proctor and AC1 J. Shuttleworth KIA.

30-04-1940   L8875 18 Squadron Mk IV: took off from Meharicourt; FTR; landed by mistake at Evere in still neutral Belgium; Sgt. A. Thomas, Sgt J. Talbot, and LAC R. James-Smith interned but released in May.

03-05-1940   L9329 53 Squadron Mk IV: took off from Metz at 2030 to recce the Ruhr; FTR; shot down near Hornisgrinde; P/O J. Butterworth, Sgt M. Pearce, and AC2 R. Wood KIA.

09-05-1940   L9331 53 Squadron Mk IV: FTR; crash-landed at 0130 near Poix due to fog on return from recce to Ruhr; P/O Wilson and his crew slightly injured.

09-05-1940   R3634 53 Squadron Mk IV: took off from Metz; FTR; found fog around Poix on return at 0245; Sgt D. Falconer (Obs) killed baling out, S/Ldr W. Murray crash-landed near Rossiers with no further injury.

Appendix 2

Blenheim losses on shipping sweeps, 1 January to 9 May 1940

16-02-1940   L8759 21 Squadron Mk IV: took off on shipping search; FTR; shot down into North Sea by Me.109s; Sgt G. Tice, Sgt J. Wadmore, and LAC F. Birch KIA.

17-02-1940   N6211 110 Squadron Mk IV: as above; FTR; shot down into North Sea by Hptm W. Falck in Me.110 of II/ZG 76; Sgt F. Bigg, Sgt W. Woods, and AC1 J. Orchard KIA and are commemorated at Runnymede.

27-02-1940   P4842 82 Squadron Mk IV: took off from Watton at 1230 to look for shipping in Elbe estuary; FTR; lost without trace; F/O J. Blake, Sgt T. Weightman, and AC1 S. Middleton KIA.

06-04-1940   L8740 21 Squadron Mk IV: took off from Watton at 0400 on anti-submarine sortie; FTR; crashed a few minutes after take-off near Attleborough; P/O I. Stapledon, Sgt W. Whetton, and LAC J. Ball KIA.

29-04-1940   R3628 254 Squadron Mk IV-F: damaged by return fire from Ju.88, port engine lost oil, seized, propeller detached, crash-landed at Scasta, DBR.

Appendix 3

Non-operational Blenheim losses 1 January to 9 May 1940

02-01-1940   L9032 2 SAC/Andover Station Flight Mk IV: overshot landing at Ternhill, skidded and hit boundary; P/O T. Musgrave injured.

03-01-1940   L8399 604 Squadron Mk I-F: crashed attempting forced landing near Epping after engine cut; Sgt A. Woolley and crew escaped with minor injuries.

04-01-1940   L8701 601 Squadron Mk I-F: DBR when landing overshot at Tangmere and struck truck; Sgt W. Pratt and crew uninjured.

04-01-1940   L1466 23 Squadron Mk I-F :crashed when engine cut (believed due to lack of fuel) returning from radar calibration flight at Helpston Heath, Peterborough; P/O R. Barritt and Cpl R. Wilson died in hospital, AC2 A. Wilson killed.

05-01-1940   L8741 21 Squadron Mk IV: engine cut taking off from Halton, aircraft went through hedge and DBR; P/O I. Stapledon slightly injured.

06-01-1940   L6641 254 Squadron Mk I: DBR in forced landing in fog near Brancaster, Norfolk; F/O Bain and crew uninjured.

07-01-1940   L1214 108 Squadron Mk I: crash-landed when engine cut during overshoot at Bicester; P/O H. Mitcheson injured.

07-01-1940   L1268 108 Squadron Mk I: took off from Bicester but overturned after forced landing in fog near Aylesbury; Sgt R. Eyton-Williams (Pilot) uninjured, AC1 Allison slightly injured.

08-01-1940   L4854 No. 2 School of Army Co-operation Mk IV: hit trees on low-flying sortie near Salisbury and destroyed by fire; P/O D. Payne and passengers AC2 L. Dale, AC2 F. Waters and AC2 J. Hunt killed.

08-01-1940   L1511 219 Squadron Mk I: DBR in forced landing in fog near Grantham, Lincs; P/O A. Skidmore and crew uninjured; airframe became 2180M.

09-01-1940   L8678 229 Squadron Mk I: force-landed at Digby when windows iced up at night, DBR; P/O M. Bussey and crew uninjured.

10-01-1940   L8873 104 Squadron Mk IV: crashed on approach to Bicester attempting forced landing after engine failure; Sgt D. Whittaker and Observer injured.

12-01-1940   N6178 101 Squadron Mk IV: written off at West Raynham when P/O J. Gilling (Pilot) stalled aircraft on approach; slightly hurt.

12-01-1940   L8700 601 Squadron Mk I: DBR when aircraft undershot airfield landing at Tangmere and hit boundary; Sgt J. Jones and crew uninjured; airframe became 1893M.

15-01-1940   L8688 141 Squadron Mk I: DBR when aircraft overshot landing at Grangemouth and skidded into boundary; F/Lt M. Louden and crew uninjured.

15-01-1940   L8697 141 Squadron Mk I: stalled attempting forced landing in bad visibility at Torpichen, West Lothian; P/O C. Gardner and crew slightly injured.

16-01-1940   L8854 15 Squadron Mk IV: caught in snowstorm and crashed in attempted forced landing at Littleport near Ely; Sgt K. Perkins and crew escaped with minor injuries.

19-01-1940   L1469 64 Squadron Mk I-F: became lost in blizzard, engine cut, pilot lost control attempting forced landing in bad visibility near Sherburn-in-Elmet; P/O T. Saul and Sgt Skillings injured.

19-01-1940	L6645 29 Squadron Mk I-F: DBR when aircraft belly-landed at Debden with jammed partially retracted u/c; P/O J. R. D. Braham and LAC Harris uninjured. ('Bob' Braham became W/Cdr DSO (2 bars), DFC (2 bars), AFC, the famous night-fighter ace.)
31-01-1940	L6614 222 Squadron Mk I-F: took off from Duxford and flew into hill in bad visibility near Royston, Herts; P/O D. Maynard and Cpl F. Chilton killed.
10-02-1940	K7114 145 Squadron Mk I: flown by P/O Hogg, aircraft collided with K7091 near Gatwick on formation practice; both aircraft managed to land, were repaired and returned to service several months later.
18-02-1940	L4875 90 Squadron Mk IV: engine cut, aircraft stalled and spun on approach to Upwood, Destroyed by Fire, P/O J. McLean, Sgt A. Haigh and AC2 W. McEwan were killed.
22-02-1940	L8400 23 Squadron Mk I-F: abandoned by Sgt Macrae and ACs Cullen and Peuleve when lost on Searchlight Co-operation sortie with R/T failure; crashed on houses in Tonbridge, Kent, causing civilian casualties.
23-02-1940	K7122 235 Squadron Mk I-F: engine cut on take-off from Manston and aircraft belly-landed; F/Lt R. Cross and P/O W. Smith unhurt, aircraft repaired, though badly damaged.
23-02-1940	L6792 235 Squadron Mk I: crashed on landing at Manston; pilot Sgt J. Blessey only slightly hurt, and aircraft later repaired.
23-02-1940	K7165 145 Squadron Mk I: lost cylinder and belly-landed at Wallington, near Croydon Airport; P/O Elson and crew unhurt, and aircraft returned to Bristol but Struck Off Charge (SOC) as beyond economic repair.
24-02-1940	L6724 92 Squadron Mk I: P/O R. Whitmarsh on first night solo flew into houses soon after take-off from Croydon, with fatal results to himself and two civilians, Mrs Doris Bridge and 5-year-old daughter Jill (see the accompanying picture).
24-02-1940	L6742 229 Squadron Mk I-F: crashed on Searchlight Co-op sortie at Taynton St Peter, Lincs; control lost after crew were dazzled by searchlights; P/O P. Lomax (Pilot), Lt J. Winks RE (Searchlight Liaison Officer), and LAC G. Carter (WOp/Ag) KIA.
24-02-1940	N6241 Mk IV: Capt H. Broad (RAE Civil Test Pilot) belly-landed at Farnborough with hydraulic failure, unhurt, aircraft damage Cat 3.
27-02-1940	L8838 114 Squadron Mk IV: control lost in cloud on training sortie, and aircraft crashed at Beausart, Acheux, Somme, France, DBF; P/O H. Dodgson (Pilot) killed and buried at Bienvilliers Military Cemetery, Sgt Hawkins (Obs) and AC1 Barrow (WOp/Ag) baled out safely.
28-02-1940	N6201 110 Squadron Mk IV: stalled on landing at Norwich and DBR; P/O G. Pemberton and crew escaped injury.
02-03-1940	N6157 114 Squadron Mk IV: P/O R. Farrow lost control while dropping flare near Auxerre in France; crew abandoned aircraft; Sgt Wallis (Obs) survived, P/O R. Farrow (Pilot) and AC2 A. Sanders (WOp/Ag, age 17) killed.
04-03-1940	L9190 53 Squadron Mk IV: u/c raised in error after night landing at Poix; aircraft abandoned when under repair at Chateau Bougon in June 1940.
07-03-1940	L1209 108 Squadron Mk I: lost height after night take-off from Upper Heyford and blew up when hit ground; solo pilot P/O K. Fisk killed.
07-03-1940	N6165 101 Squadron Mk IV: took off from West Raynham, struck HT cables near Diss, Norfolk, and crashed, killing F/O S. Mottram (Pilot) and Sgt A. Maundsley (Obs) and injuring Cpl R. Hartland (WOp/Ag).
11-03-1940	L6682 600 Squadron Mk I-F: returning from Army Co-operation sortie, aircraft hit trees on approach to Manston, crashed and caught fire; F/O Tollemarche (Pilot) and LAC Smith (WOp/Ag) escaped but were unable to rescue Lt Sperling, Welsh Guards, from Observer's position and he perished.
12-03-1940	L8845 35 Squadron Mk IV: collided on take-off with L1396 (below) at Upwood, and Destroyed By Fire; Sgt A. Hermels (Pilot) succumbed to injuries.
12-03-1940	L1396 90 Squadron Mk I: collided with L8845 (above); Sgt Blanks (Pilot) only slightly injured.
14-03-1940	L1373 29 Squadron Mk I-F: engine cut on approach to Debden and aircraft stalled and crash-landed; Sgt A. Roberts (Pilot) injured.
14-03-1940	P4926 139 Squadron Mk IV: crashed into sea near Perpignan in France; Sgt N. Price (Pilot) and Sgt R. Stanley (Obs) killed, LAC R. Brown (WOp/Ag) slightly injured.
16-03-1940	L9385 new Mk IV, failed to reach 203 Squadron when 20 MU Delivery Flight pilot F/O W. Swire-Griffiths lost control in cloud and crashed at Overton, Hants, killing himself, Sgt J. Gillings (Obs), and two ground-crew passengers, LAC E. Morgan and LAC E. Pizzey.
18-03-1940	N6179 59 Squadron Mk IV: crashed during forced landing at Querenain Nord, cause unknown; P/O R. Chudleigh unhurt, but aircraft DBR.

20-03-1940   L8784 254 Squadron Mk IV: written off when u/c collapsed after very heavy landing in poor conditions at Lossiemouth; Sgt G. Rose and F/Sgt H. Brown unhurt.

21-03-1940   L1117 219 Squadron Mk I-F: lost height on night patrol and flew into hill near Kirbymoorside, Yorks; Sgt H. Phillips, Sgt V. Gee, and AC1 F. Prosser KIA, Sgt Gee dying of injuries.

21-03-1940   L1427 18 Squadron Mk I: took off at 0800 from Rosieres for Tangmere but crashed into hill in fog near Chichester, Sussex; P/O H. Hulton (Pilot) and Sgt O. Drumbreck (Obs) killed, passengers Cpl G. Lapwood and LAC Oultram badly injured.

22-03-1940   L4932 Special Duties Flight Mk I: engine failed, belly-landed at Martlesham Heath; Sgt A. Argents uninjured, aircraft damage Cat 4.

23-03-1940   L4873 90 Squadron Mk IV: destroyed when control lost when formation entered cloud, and aircraft dived into ground at Foel Wen, Denbighshire, killing Sgt M. Cotterell, Sgt R. Harbour and AC2 K. Winterton.

24-03-1940   L6709 219 Squadron Mk I: took off from Catterick , written off when engine cut on approach to Hartlepool and aircraft crash-landed; P/O H. Auger injured.

27-03-1940   L1212 25 Squadron Mk I-F: turned at too low an airspeed after take-off from North Weald, stalled, and wing hit ground; P/O P. Brierley killed, and P/O A. Sword-Daniels injured.

27-03-1940   P6929 104 Squadron Mk IV: lost when aircraft undershot night landing and hit bomb dump at Bicester; P/O E. Hale and unnamed crew injured.

31-03-1940   N6242 110 Squadron Mk IV: Sgt G. Forster crashed at Ipswich aerodrome when he stalled after making too slow an approach in gusty wind; aircraft DBR.

05-04-1940   P6922 59 Squadron Mk IV: crashed on take-off at Poix, abandoned there.

06-04-1940   P6918 35 Squadron Mk IV: crashed when engine cut on take-off from Upwood; solo pilot Sgt J. Stein killed.

06-04-1940   L1500 141 Squadron Mk I: took off from Grangemouth, and DBR when it crash-landed near Stirling after becoming lost in cloud.

08-04-1940   P4855 82 Squadron Mk IV: control lost in cloud, aircraft dived into ground at Hilborough, near Swaffham, Norfolk; Sgt Bennett (Pilot) managed to bale out and was injured, but rest of crew Sgt I. Murdoch, Sgt G. Chapman and AC2 J. Kempton killed.

08-04-1940   L9039 13 OTU Mk IV: destroyed when it left formation in cloud and crashed on Carnedd Llewelyn, Caernarvon, killing Sgt A. Hall, Sgt F. Graham and LAC G. James.

14-04-1940   L9207 40 Squadron Mk IV: crashed into Thames Estuary when control lost on unauthorised flight from Wyton; AC2 J. Lewis killed.

14-04-1940   L1264 17 OTU Mk I: u/c retracted in error after landing at Upwood; S/Ldr H. Chester unhurt, aircraft DBR.

15-04-1940   R3601 Mk IV with RAE: belly-landed at Farnborough with hydraulic failure; P/O A. Moffet and crew safe, aircraft damage Cat 4.

17-04-1940   P4836 235 Squadron Mk IV-F: DBR when aircraft overshot night landing at North Coates and struck ditch; P/O J. Laughlin and crew uninjured.

24-04-1940   L4864 107 Squadron Mk IV: F/Lt Gareth Clayton DFC left Lossiemouth for Wattisham, weather deteriorated and he crash-landed at Bramford Tye, near Ipswich; crew Sgt Innes-Jones and Cpl Yeomans plus two 107 pilot passengers, F/O C. Bomford and F/O F. Pleasance, who had no parachutes, were lucky to avoid injury.

03-05-1940   L9297 No. 2 School of Army Co-operation Mk IV: engine cut just after take-off from Andover, aircraft stalled and spun into ground; P/O R. Carter (Pilot), Sgt J. Longley, AC1 W. Lambert, and AC2 C. Wadman killed.

04-05-1940   L4857 59 Squadron Mk IV: crashed attempting night overshoot at Poix, and Destroyed by Fire; P/O G. Arscott, Sgt G. Barford and AC2 P. Froum killed.

08-05-1940   P4844 235 Squadron Mk IV-F: crashed at Bircham Newton when lost height in turn during night circuit and dived into ground; Sgt V. Allison, Sgt E. Schmid and LAC V. Neirynck killed.

09-05-1940   K7136 235 Squadron Mk I-F: engine cut on take-off, control lost, aircraft crashed and destroyed by fire; P/O W. Smith (solo pilot) killed.

Please note that all the above aircraft were total losses, except for the few (noted as such) that became ground instructional airframes or were repaired and returned to service later.

The scene in Foresters Drive, Croydon, on the morning of 25 February 1940. P/O R. Whitmarsh of 92 Squadron, on his first night solo, had struck a house on the boundary, killing himself together with a lady and her 5-year-old daughter. The aerodrome is behind the house, while one of L6724's engines lies in the foreground.

Original caption reads AN R.A.F. GUNNER AT HIS POST. He has taken his place in the turret. He is a Royal Air Force gunner, resolute and resourceful. He and his comrades are the flower of the Empire's young manhood, picked prudently, trained in every detail to do a dangerous job. (A typically chauvinistic wartime caption, but - the cupola is fully lowered preventing depression or elevation of the gun - and it is a 'camera gun' anyway!)

Chapter 10

The Scandinavian diversions

Finland: the 'Winter War'

While the Nazis and Russians were digesting their Polish conquests, tension was increasing around the Baltic and throughout Scandinavia. Russia demanded territory and bases in Finland; when these were refused, the Russians invaded Finland in November 1939. The Finns resisted gallantly over the winter, inflicting severe losses on the forces of the giant Soviet 'Bear', and gaining worldwide respect as well as the sympathy of the anti-Axis countries. But in the spring sheer weight of numbers overwhelmed the Finns and they sued for peace in March 1940 – ceding to the USSR the territory and bases the Soviets had demanded in the first place – thus ending the 'Winter War'.

Finnish Blenheims had played a valiant part in the defence of their homeland – it will be recalled that the Finns had purchased 18 Mk Is before the war, which they numbered BL-104-121, and they served with *Lentolaivue* (Squadrons) 44 and 46. Unfortunately, although Bristol had granted a production licence in April 1938, no Finnish-built Blenheims from the 15 on order were delivered from the *Valtion Lentokonetehdas* (State Aircraft Factory) at Tampere before the Russian invasion. However, the UK War Cabinet was anxious to assist the Finns, so allowed them to collect 12 new Mk IVs on 17 January 1940; these were BL-122-133, but only 11 reached Finland via a re-fuelling stop at Stavanger in still neutral Norway on the 21st, as one crashed into the North Sea en route, and one was delayed by a slight accident in Sweden (see Note 1). As RAF squadrons had been converting to Mk IVs, this left some Mk Is available, so 42 were withdrawn from RAF stocks and volunteer RAF crews wearing civilian clothes flew the first 12 (see Note 2) (including L1345, L1347, L1354 and L1362) from Bicester to Dyce, then out to Juva via Stavanger and Vasternas. They arrived, with their guns temporarily de-activated, on 26 February and were numbered BL-134-145, but the Armistice was signed before the remainder could be ferried out. The RAF crews returned at night on Finnish Airlines' Junkers 52-3Ms via Stockholm. Before these welcome reinforcements arrived the Finns were down to only 13 serviceable *'Pelti-Heikki'*, as the Finns dubbed their Blenheims, several of which had skis in place of wheels on their undercarriages.

BL-105, from the first batch of 18 new Mk Is purchased by Finland before the war, carries the blue swastika on white circle markings; it was lost on operations on 26 June 1942, but the crew escaped.

Two of the 12 ex-RAF Mk Is ferried out early in 1940. BL-137 arrived at Juva on 2 February – the swastikas were white-washed over for the journey! – and was shot down on 3 September 1941. The Finns have fitted BL-149 with a ski-undercarriage and spinners; it was lost on operations on 27 March 1942, and the crew were killed.

The new Mk IVs went to Llv 46 (their five remaining Mk Is being transferred to Llv 44) and the fresh batch of Mk Is to the newly formed Llv 42. Together these three Finnish Blenheim squadrons flew 423 sorties, attacking the Russian forces with considerable success, dropping 3,168 bombs as well as shooting down five Russian fighters and destroyed many more on the ground. However, they lost seven aircraft to enemy action and four more to operational accidents in the atrocious weather conditions – an aggregate of more than one in four of their entire Blenheim force. By the end they had only 11 Blenheims left in action, as 18 of the 29 survivors from the original total of 40 British-built aircraft had been damaged and were no longer airworthy. Twenty-one of the brave Finnish crewmen were killed in action and two were seriously wounded during the 105-day 'Winter War', which ended on 13 March 1940. The Blenheims had acquitted themselves well, and their losses are recorded in Notes 3 and 4.

The Continuation War

Although not in chronological order, this is a convenient place to consider the Continuation War with Russia, which the Finns considered as carrying on where they had left off in March 1940 when the invaders imposed an Armistice. Finland, hoping to regain the territory it had surrendered then, resumed hostilities with the Soviet Union following the German invasion of Russia in June 1941. Once again the Finnish Blenheims performed valiantly in difficult conditions for more than three years, inflicting considerable damage on the Soviet forces. VL produced a total of 45 new Mk Is at Tampere, the last in November 1943, and ten new Mk IVs, the last in April 1944. Of course spares were no longer available from the UK, so the resourceful Finns kept their dwindling number of Blenheims flying by bringing in major airframe components from the Yugoslav licensed-production facility, and

An atmospheric shot of BL-129 being refuelled for operations on 7 March 1940.

obtained Mercury engines and spares similarly manufactured in Poland; the Finns manufactured propeller blades with compressed wood as they were unable to obtain De Havilland metal ones. However, the Finnish Blenheims, despite being escorted by *Luftwaffe* Messerschmitts and Fw.190s during 1943 and 1944, were increasingly obsolescent and suffered severe casualties as the Russian Air Force rapidly expanded, modernised and improved. Finnish Blenheims played a major part in three very successful 'intruder' operations when they infiltrated the stream of Russian bombers returning to their bases near Leningrad (St Petersburg) after bombing Helsinki and Tallin (the Estonian capital). On 9 March 1944 20 Blenheims (alongside five Ju.88s and five Do.217s!) caused much damage and destroyed many Soviet bombers just after the Russians had landed on their well-lit airfields. The tactic was repeated on 4 April and 3 May (causing the Soviets to withdraw their bombers from forward airfields, sparing these cities from further bombing) and was, of course, long after the RAF had ceased to deploy Blenheims on such operations. The Finns lost 42 of their Blenheims during the Continuation War, with 94 crewmen killed and eight more wounded (see Note 4).

In September 1944 Finland concluded another Armistice with Russia, on terms far more

Major V. F. Salminen at Immola, eastern Finland, in June 1941. He carried out 120 Blenheim sorties against the Russians and won the Marshall Mannerheim Cross. He is in front of BL-160, which was shot down on 1 August 1944, and both crewmen were killed.

THE BRISTOL BLENHEIM

disadvantageous than the previous one, and conditional on the Finns expelling the German forces from northern Finland – this little-known campaign was known as the Lapland War. Once more the few remaining Blenheims were pressed into action – 14 with Llv 42 and six with Llv 48 – and another half-dozen were lost; altogether more than 60 Finnish Blenheims were lost between December 1939 and VE Day in May 1945 from the total of 97. They fought hard, they fought long, and they fought well – the Finns regarded their *Blenimi* with great affection.

Norway

By the end of March 1940 it became apparent that the Germans were building up their forces in northern Germany. On hearing intelligence reports that several convoys, including seven or eight capital ships, were sailing from the North German ports, several sorties were flown by RAF Blenheims in the first week of April 1940 to try and establish what was happening, but mist and poor weather enabled the German vessels to avoid detection. Their purpose soon became clear, for on 9 April German forces overran Denmark in one day, and the following day they landed troops by air and sea at several strategic centres in Norway, quickly capturing most of the important airfields, from which the *Luftwaffe* began operations within hours.

This forestalled action being discussed by the British Chiefs of Staff, as the Royal Navy did not want to be out-flanked in the North Sea by German ships operating from Norwegian ports, nor did the RAF wish to see the *Luftwaffe* based in Norway, as most of its own defences were concentrated in South East England. Further, the War Cabinet was most anxious to forbid the use of Norwegian ports for shipment of the large quantity of high-grade Swedish iron ore considered vital to the German war industry, for that country was the source of two-thirds of the total German requirement. Winston Churchill, as First Sea Lord, had wanted to occupy Narvik or mine the Norwegian shipping lanes concerned, but the Cabinet demurred as Norway was still neutral. So, upon the German invasion of Norway, an Anglo-French Expeditionary Force was hastily assembled and made landings around Narvik and Trondheim to the north. However, with our troops being too few in number, ill-equipped, and lacking close air support, these bridgeheads proved unsustainable and soon had to be evacuated.

Fighter Command and Norway

Fighter Command had been pressed to send squadrons to Norway and sent 263 Squadron, which operated its Gladiators from a frozen lake, quickly losing most of them; the squadron reformed and returned later with 46 Squadron and their Hurricanes. Both squadrons had flown their fighters off the carrier HMS *Glorious*, and the seven surviving Gladiators and the ten remaining Hurricanes landed back on board during the evacuation only to be lost with all but two of their pilots when the *Glorious* was sunk by the *Scharnhorst* and *Gneisenau*.

Dowding had originally been told to send three squadrons of fighters, two of Blenheims, 23 and 604, and 263 with its Gladiators, but he protested at the dispersal of his limited force, and was well aware of the limitations of the Blenheims in that role, writing to the Air Staff:

'I regard with apprehension the proposal to withdraw three Squadrons for a Scandinavian Expedition for a number of reasons.

1. The first is the intrinsic difficulty of withdrawing three Squadrons from the line.
2. The second is that the maintenance of three Squadrons in active operations and in close range of enemy fighters will constitute an added drain on the aircraft output.
3. The third is that we cannot enter this commitment with a limited liability but that irresistible pressure will be brought to increase the number of fighter units.

4. The fourth is that the Blenheim is an entirely unsuitable type to engage against the German Air Force at short range. It was asked for by me as an interim home-defence night-fighter for use with AI. It is an altogether unsuitable type to pit against the Messerschmitt. It has unprotected tanks and no armour and its speed and manoeuvrability are quite inadequate to enable it to even bring its main armament into action against German fighters. It must rely on the single back gun. We have already learnt from Bomber Command that the Blenheim falls easy victim in these circumstances.

I do not underestimate the importance of attempting to deny the Swedish iron ore supply to Germany but the letter (sent to Dowding with the instruction) certainly over-emphasised it. It is not in my province to discuss whether we are likely to win the war by stopping the Swedish ore supply to Germany, but it is my duty to point out that we may lose it by opening yet another source of dispersion and wastage of our fighter resources.'

We can only surmise how the crews of the Blenheim Mk I-Fs would have responded, had they been aware of their own C-in-C's opinion of the aircraft in which they had to go to war. That he regarded the Mk I-F as 'an entirely unsuitable type to engage against the German Air Force at short range', considered that 'its speed and manoeuvrability are quite inadequate' and was aware that 'the Blenheim falls easy victim in such circumstances' would not have improved their morale. Nonetheless, his comments were valid and quite reasonable for a rational man like Dowding, for the Blenheim had been designed as a 'mini-airliner' and was adapted for use as a bomber, not as a fighter. However, his protests did not prevail and the instruction stood. Dowding was determined to conserve his barely adequate forces for the defence of the home base, so he circumvented the order and withdrew 23 and 604 Squadrons from the front line so that their Blenheims could be fitted with self-sealing fuel tanks and armour for crew protection, undertaking to send them to Norway when this was done. So, initially, he dispatched only 263 with its gallant Gladiators, replacing their severe losses and adding 46 Squadron's Hurricanes soon afterwards. He was vindicated as 100 per cent of the precious single-engined fighters, and 95 per cent of their even more precious pilots, were lost when events overtook the ill-fated Norwegian expedition, which was being withdrawn just as the German offensive in the West was launched. So the two Blenheim squadrons were reprieved, to perform valiant service later in the night-fighter and intruder roles.

The lack of an effective long-range fighter in the RAF armoury was now all too apparent.

Bomber Command

At this critical juncture changes in the High Command of the Royal Air Force took place, changes that would have a considerable effect on the future deployment of the Blenheim squadrons. On 1 April a new Air Officer Commander-in-Chief was appointed to Bomber Command, Air Marshal Sir Charles Portal taking over from Air Chief Marshal Sir Edgar Ludlow-Hewitt, who, since his appointment in September 1937, had overseen the complete re-equipment and the vast expansion, which, with the other enormous changes in that period of rapid technical advance, had so transformed Bomber Command.

Fighter Command was ordered to send Blenheim Mk IFs of 604 and 23 (F) Squadrons to Norway, but the AOC-in-C, Air Chief Marshal Hugh Dowding, avoided doing so, saving both squadrons from destruction.

THE BRISTOL BLENHEIM

Mk I-Fs of 604 (Auxiliary) Squadron at Northolt in April 1940 being inspected by the Secretary of State for Air, who is shaking hands with F/O John Cunningham, later a top-scoring night-fighter Pilot. 604 and 25 Squadrons had been ordered to Norway but were reprieved.

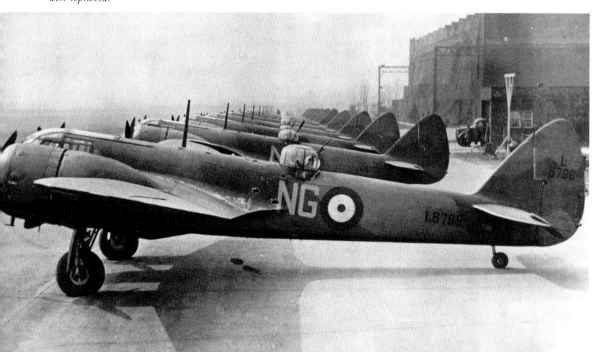

Sir Edgar Ludlow-Hewitt was AOC-in-C of Bomber Command from September 1937 until April 1940 and oversaw its vast expansion and early wartime deployment.

We noted in Chapter 8 his dire warning to the Air Staff in August 1939 that if ordered to implement an all-out attack on Germany he expected to lose *all* of the Medium Bombers – the Blenheims – in three and a half weeks, and *all* of his Heavy Bombers – Wellingtons, Hampdens and Whitleys – in seven and a half weeks. Ludlow-Hewitt had worked tirelessly to remedy the many deficiencies, especially those in training, that he had found in Bomber Command, and he continued to serve as an effective Inspector General for the rest of the war.

Portal was a protégé of Hugh Trenchard, the prime exponent of the strategic bomber, who, although he had retired as Chief of the Air Staff more than ten years earlier, wrote to Portal in May 1940 to congratulate him on his appointment and on 'the achievements of British air power ... though I am sorry that you could not use it where I and others think it would probably have ended the war by now.' Clearly Trenchard was deluded in feeling that 'a great opportunity had been missed to finish the Third Reich' as the War Cabinet had forbidden his cherished but completely unrealisable 'single devastating blow from the air at the heart of Germany'. However, Portal was much more of a realist and pragmatist than Trenchard, and as Air Member for Personnel was aware of Ludlow-Hewitt's timely warning, as well as studying the reports of the early operations. He was particularly disturbed by the losses to bomber formations in daylight, and alarmed at the intention of the Air Staff to commit fully all the Blenheim squadrons in daylight attacks directly against the anticipated German offensive on the Western Front. The further losses of Bomber Command Blenheims with their experienced crews in sorties to Norway strengthened this deep concern, and on 8 May he wrote to the Air Staff:

'I am convinced that the proposed use of these Blenheim units is fundamentally unsound, and that if it is persisted in, it is likely to have disastrous consequences on the future of the war in the air... It can scarcely be disputed that at the enemy's chosen moment for advance the area concerned will be literally swarming with enemy fighters, and we will be lucky if we see again as many as half the aircraft we send out each time. Really accurate bombing under the conditions I visualise is not to be expected, and I feel justified in expressing serious doubts whether the attacks of 50 Blenheims based on information necessarily some hours out of date are likely to make as much difference to the ultimate course of the war as to justify the losses I expect.'

Prescient words indeed, written by the AOC of Bomber Command just two days before the launch of the German *Blitzkrieg* in the West. As Portal was promoted to succeed Sir Cyril Newall as Chief of the Air Staff on 25 October 1940, he could take action to allay these concerns, but by then, alas, it was too late for the hundreds of Blenheim crewmen who would be lost in the six traumatic months that intervened. It is to be noted that the AOCs of both Fighter and Bomber Commands recorded their strong reservations about the suitability of the Blenheim for proposed operations and anticipated the high casualties that followed.

Bomber Command and Norway

The Blenheims of 2 Group Bomber Command were involved from before the start of the Norwegian campaign itself. Nine aircraft of 82 Squadron were sent to seek and attack shipping reported off the Danish coast on 1 April, and one was shot down by a flak ship

An 82 Squadron Mk IV at a Watton dispersal. The Squadron carried out many North Sea shipping searches, and on 7 April was part of the force that attacked (without success) the invasion convoy en route to Norway that included Scharnhorst, Gneisenau *and* Hipper.

(see Appendix 1). Nine more of XV Squadron were sent on an armed reconnaissance of the same area later that day, but found nothing. For many months the Admiralty was more concerned about a possible 'break-out' by German capital ships into the Atlantic than about anything else, and frequently called upon the RAF for assistance.

Forty-five more sorties searching the seas between the German Bight and Denmark were carried out between 4 and 8 April in very poor weather. One of six 82 Squadron Mk IVs had a very lucky escape on 4 April when, returning from the Cuxhaven area at low level, the starboard engine cut due to fuel starvation; while the pilot of P6895, F/O Hunt, was struggling with his fuel-cocks, the aircraft bounced off the sea, ripping off the tail-wheel and bending the starboard propeller blades. Hunt regained control and managed to coax the badly vibrating aircraft, with its chastened crew, Sgt Crawley and LAC Thripp, back to base. During those four days 21 of the 45 Blenheims sent out found and bombed ships, including 12 of 107 Squadron and six from 82 Squadron, all led by W/Cdr Basil Embry, who on the 7th attacked a large German naval formation including the battleships *Scharnhorst* and *Gneisenau* together with the Cruiser *Hipper* – near misses but no hits were observed. A further 14 Blenheim reconnaissance sorties were flown on 9, 10 and 11 April, without loss, but on the 15th another 110 Squadron Blenheim was lost (see Appendix 1).

In an endeavour to conserve its forces to counter the anticipated German offensive in France, 2 Group HQ committed only 107 and 110 Squadrons to the campaign in Scandinavia, and they were moved to Lossiemouth in Scotland to bring them closer to Norway. The standard bomb-load of four 250lb bombs had to be loaded by hand, in the sleet and biting winds, as the bomb trolleys had not arrived from Suffolk. These two squadrons suffered continual attrition, for prior to their involvement in Scandinavia throughout April 1940 they had been sent on anti-shipping and reconnaissance sorties, with the result that by the end of that month 107 Squadron had lost ten aircraft, while 110 had lost 13 (plus four more in operational flying accidents), each from an initial establishment of 16, with four more in immediate reserve. The requirements by squadrons for replacement aircraft were already increasing ominously – and this was before 'the balloon went up' with the opening of the main German offensive in the West on 10 May 1940.

Pilot's eye view of the Norwegian coast showing the fore-sight for the fixed wing-gun mounted on the scalloped nose.

The capture and immediate use by German forces of Sola, the airfield for Stavanger, was a strategic coup for them and made it a prime target for British forces. In the first RAF attack of the war on a mainland target, Stavanger airfield was bombed ineffectually on 11 April by only three of the six Wellingtons sent under Coastal Command control. They had a nominal escort of two Mk IV-Fs of 254 Squadron, and one of the three 'Wimpeys', which failed to attack, was shot down. Regrettably, some senior RAF Commanders were still reluctant to accept the clear 'writing on the wall' that daylight raids by formations of the so-called 'self-defending bombers' were too dangerous to be viable, but it is they who were 'weighed in the balance and found wanting', not the gallant crews. One final attempt to stage such a raid – indeed, the largest raid Bomber Command had mounted since the beginning of the war – was made on 12 April. A force of 83 unescorted RAF bombers – 36 Wellingtons, 24 Hampdens and 23 Blenheims – was sent to attack shipping off the coast near Stavanger and in Kristiansand harbour. Ten bombers were shot down – six Hampdens and four Wellingtons. The Blenheims for once managed to evade the Messerschmitts, which were concentrating on the other larger and slower RAF bombers. That day, without any results being achieved, 24 Wellington and 21 Hampden crewmen were killed, and three more rescued and taken prisoner – a black day for Bomber Command and the last time either Wellingtons or Hampdens operated in daylight, for they joined the Whitleys, which had already been relegated to night operations only.

However, further attacks on Stavanger airfield were needed, so had to be carried out by the ubiquitous Blenheims. They attacked it in daylight on 15 April – the first raid of the war on a mainland target by Bomber Command aircraft, when six of the 11 aircraft bombed, hitting two German aircraft (an He.111 and a Ju.88-C.2) on the ground – and on the 16th, when only one of six from 110 Squadron bombed, F/O W. Edwards, Sgt V. Luter and LAC W. Palmer in L9041. Edwards received a DFC for pressing on to the target, the other five turning back because of severe icing in cloud. One of these aircraft, N6191 (P/O Ken Taute, Sgt Len Fearnley and LAC J. Waterhouse), became iced up at 14,000 feet, both engines stopped, control was lost, the bombs were jettisoned at 10,000 feet, and the Blenheim spun down to within 500 feet of the sea before recovery could be made. But on the 17th all 12 Blenheims of 107 Squadron, led by Basil Embry through heavy sleet, then a snowstorm near the target, bombed the airfield quite successfully, six from medium height and six from low level, but three were lost (see Appendix 2). W/Cdr Embrey received a bar to his DSO for his leadership on this raid, F/Lt Gareth Clayton a DFC, and his WOp/Ag, Cpl L. Yeomans, a DFM for successfully fighting off repeated attacks from an Me.110 until they gained the sanctuary of cloud over the North Sea.

Apart from two 107 Squadron Mk IVs shot down on 17 April while attacking Sola, two more staggered back to belly-land at base; one (P4924) was DBR, but the other (N6192, shown here) was repaired only to be shot down on a sortie to St Omer on 27 May.

On 19 April seven of nine aircraft from 107 Squadron abandoned the sortie because of the weather conditions, this time a completely cloudless sky, for they had been ordered not to attack unless sufficient cloud cover was available – of the remaining two, one bombed 'an airfield' and one was lost (see Appendix 2). On the 20th three Blenheims were sent to bomb Stavanger airfield but abandoned the sortie due to the weather conditions, as did all 12 of 110 Squadron the following day, and six of 107 who arrived near dawn on the 24th, but one of the latter was lost (again, see Appendix 2). The RAF did not realise that the Germans had already installed seaward-looking radar on the coast near Stavanger.

Portal was concerned that this series of costly attacks had failed to put Stavanger airfield out of action. In a memo to the Air Ministry on 24 April he argued that these attacks were unproductive as most bombs falling on a grass airfield only produced craters that could be filled in quickly, and even if hangars were hit aircraft could be serviced and re-armed in the open, while any enemy aircraft destroyed or damaged would soon be replaced. He added: 'It seems to me the height of folly to throw away experienced crews on the bombing of aerodromes which, I think you will agree, shows the least result for loss of equipment expended on it.'

Six crews from 110 Squadron led by F/O G. Wright were sent out on the 25th to bomb a concentration of enemy shipping seen in Granvins Fiord near Bergen; his No 2, Sgt Priestley, was shot down before reaching the target (see Appendix 1), but P/O R. Hill's crew claimed two Messerschmitts shot down into the sea 100 miles from the coast as they withdrew.

On 27 April 12 Blenheims had to abandon an attack on Stavanger airfield due to weather conditions. On the 30th, in a raid led by S/Ldr Kenneth Doran DFC and bar, who had led the Wilhelmshaven raid on the second day of the war, six Blenheims of 110 bombed the airfield at dusk, but were chased by 109s of II/JG 77, and two, including their renowned leader, were shot down (see Appendix 2). Twelve aircraft of 107 Squadron mounted two quite successful attacks on the airfield, one on 1 May and another on the following day.

These demanding sorties to Norway, a round trip of 1,000 miles, were near the limit of the range of the Blenheims and involved long flights, without any aids to navigation, and frequently in very poor weather conditions, over an unforgiving North Sea, to face a hostile reception in the target area, then another long flight on the return leg, often with a damaged aircraft, and always with anxious eyes watching the fuel gauges.

Coastal Command and Norway

Fighter and Bomber Commands were not the only RAF Commands involved in the Norwegian campaign, for Coastal Command also took a very active part. The four so-called 'Trade Protection' squadrons of Blenheims, 254, 235, 236 and 248, were transferred from Fighter Command to Coastal Command in February 1940. Only 254 was operational by the last day of that month, as it had started converting to Mk IVs at Bircham Newton in January (although they still had some Mk Is left a year later, albeit by then non-operational). 254 Squadron sent a detachment to Lossiemouth, which extended the range of its North Sea patrols to cover more of the northern Norwegian coast. The Blenheims' inadequacies as fighters were exposed on 22 February when a patrol of three Mk IV-F Blenheims encountered a Heinkel He.111-J over the North Sea. All three made a classic 'No 1 Attack', then attacked individually, until they had expended all the ammunition in their four-gun belly packs and the Heinkel flew steadily homewards. The Blenheims then drew alongside in turn so that their turret gunners could bring fire to bear, and after some 20 minutes of combat the Heinkel flew into some mist and escaped. The Blenheim pilots (S/Ldr Fairclough in L8786, F/Lt Mitchell in L8841, and P/O Taylor in L8842) claimed and were awarded a 'probably destroyed', but actually the Heinkel had received only some 20 strikes from the thousands of rounds fired at it and landed safely at its Norwegian base – the first two of the trio of Blenheims had received more hits from return fire by the bomber's gunners!

A fine study of a 248 Squadron Mk IV-F over the North Sea. It has the single-gun turret, light bomb racks, and the gas-warning patch in front of the fin.

Sgt Rose of 254 Squadron had a resounding success on 5 April when he strafed Stavanger/Sola airfield, destroying two Ju.52s and a Heinkel He.59D Floatplane, then encountered a Heinkel He.111 of II/KG 26 on his way home, damaging it so badly that although it staggered back to base it was written off. 254 also kept an eye on British naval forces engaged in the campaign and escorted six Wellingtons (which for some obscure reason were under Coastal Command control) when they attempted to bomb Stavanger airfield on 11 April in the first attack of the war by the RAF on a mainland target. The 25th saw a further success for 254 when F/Lt Mitchell in R3628 and P/O Illingworth in L9406 shot down a Ju.88, but on the 29th R3628 was damaged by return fire from an Me.110 and crash-landed near Scatsta – the crew escaped although the Blenheim was written off. 254 continued to be heavily engaged along the coast of Norway after the entire focus of the war shifted with the launch of the German *Blitzkrieg* offensive on the Western Front, and their heavy losses also continued (see Appendix 3). They did, however, enjoy the odd success, as when Sgt Mitchell in R3629 shot down a Dornier Do.18 flying-boat on 4 June. Far from successful was a squadron-strength sortie on 13 June when they arrived 10 minutes too late to escort 15 Blackburn Skuas from HMS *Ark Royal*, which were to dive-bomb the *Scharnhorst* in Trondheim harbour. Eight of the Skuas, each burdened with a 500lb bomb, were promptly shot down and the Blenheims could only escort the surviving seven back to the carrier. The sacrifice of 15 Fleet Air Arm crewmen (for only one survived) was in vain, for the only bomb to strike the battleship failed to explode – the RN abandoned the concept of dive-bombing after this sorry episode.

235 and 236 Squadrons were not involved in the Norwegian campaign, but both started re-equipping with Mk IV-Fs that February. 248, also re-equipping with Mk IV-Fs, moved from North Coates to Dyce with a detachment at Montrose, but did not become operational until June, then moved to Sumburgh in the Shetland Islands to be nearer to the Norwegian coast, which was entirely in German hands by that time. The northern and southern extremities of the long Norwegian coast-line were effectively beyond the range of UK-based Blenheims.

It is interested to note a contemporary report by II/JG 77 to its Headquarters on the defences of the British bombers against its cannon-armed Messerschmitt 109-E3s: 'The defence of the Bristol Blenheim to the rear is weak and need not be considered. The speed in a dive is very inferior to a Bf.109 Emil. The high effectiveness of the 7.9mm ammunition was apparent in the stripping off of the fabric and metal parts, but it did not often succeed in setting the aircraft on fire. By comparison, one hit with cannon ammunition was sufficient to explode one motor in flames. The Blenheim flew easily, turning away from the attack in a defensive curve, and continuing away.'

On 3 May, after carrying out 113 bombing sorties against Stavanger airfield alone, 107 and 110 Squadrons were ordered back to Wattisham. An airfield was being prepared at Banak, north of Narvik, to receive 40 Squadron's Blenheims, but work was stopped and all the Blenheim squadrons were withdrawn from operations in the Norwegian campaign as the Allied evacuation was under way and it was becoming clear that the German forces were preparing to launch their major offensive on the Western Front.

Blenheims had borne the brunt of the RAF operations in Norway and suffered accordingly. All of the Allied forces involved, especially the Blenheim crews, had acted with great bravery throughout this ill-fated campaign, but it was about to be relegated to a mere side-show. For now the Blenheim squadrons were placed on the anvil, alongside the Battle squadrons, right in the forefront of the British forces on the Western Front, awaiting the hammer blows that were about to fall upon them.

Notes

Note 1: Mk IVs delivered to Finland

L9025, L9026, L9028, L9195, L9196, L9197, L9198, L9199, L9200, L9201, L9202 and L9203.

Note 2: Mk Is delivered to Finland

These included L1345, L1347, L1354 and L1362.

Note 3: Losses of Finnish Blenheims during the 'Winter War'

01-12-1939	BL-110 crashed in bad weather on Operations, crew of three killed.
06-01-1940	BL-112 shot down by fighter on Operations, crew escaped.
18-01-1940	BL-127 crashed into Gulf of Bothnia in bad weather while being delivered, two crew killed.
19-01-1940	BL-121 shot down by fighters on Operations, crew of three killed.
28-01-1940	BL-108 crashed in bad weather on non-operational sortie, crew of three killed.
14-02-1940	BL-123 engine cut on take-off for non-operational sortie, crashed, two crew injured.
18-02-1940	BL-113 shot down by fighters on Operations, two crew killed.
07-03-1940	BL-144 shot down by fighters on Operations, two crew killed.
07-03-1940	BL-122 shot down by fighters on Operations, two crew killed.
10-03-1940	BL-133 shot down by fighters on Operations, three crew killed.
26-02-1940	BL-119 shot down by fighters on Operations, crew escaped.
29-02-1940	BL-126 engine cut on Operations, crash-landed, crew escaped.

Losses after the Armistice with Russia

04-10-1940	BL-128 crashed following engine failure, injuring one of crew.
27-11-1940	BL-131 collided with BL-135 on airfield, injuring one of crew.
18-12-1940	BL-125 struck trees on approach on training sortie, injuring one of crew.

Note 4: Losses of Finnish Blenheims during the 'Continuation' and 'Lapland' Wars

'Continuation War'

01-07-1941	BL-130 shot down by flak on Operations, two crew killed.
01-07-1941	BL-124 shot down by flak on Operations, three crew killed.
13-07-1941	BL-134 shot down on Operations, three crew killed.
13-07-1941	BL-114 shot down on Operations, four crew killed.
21-07-1941	BL-139 shot down by fighters on Operations, two crew killed.
21-07-1941	BL-141 shot down on Operations, three crew killed.
25-07-1941	BL-145 hit trees and crashed when ferrying supplies at low level, three crew killed.
07-08-1941	BL-146 shot down on Operations, three crew killed.
13-08-1941	BL-136 shot down by flak on Operations, three crew killed.
14-08-1941	BL-116 shot down by fighters on Operations, three crew killed.
20-08-1941	BL-117 shot down by fighters on Operations, three crew killed.
03-09-1941	BL-137 destroyed on the ground by enemy action, the crew escaped.

The Finns had several accidents on their slippery airfields. BL-135 (foreground) collided with BL-131 (background) on 27 November 1940.

02-10-1941	BL-143 shot down by flak on Operations, two crew killed.
03-11-1941	BL-118 crashed after engine troubles on take-off for Operations, one killed, two injured.
09-12-1941	BL-153 shot down by flak on Operations, three crew killed.
05-03-1942	BL-104 shot down on Operations, three crew killed.
27-03-1942	BL-147 crashed in bad weather on Operations, probably due to icing-up, three crew killed.
27-03-1942	BL-149 crashed in bad weather on Operations, probably due to icing-up, three crew killed.
15-04-1942	BL-154 shot down by flak on Operations, three crew killed.
15-04-1942	BL-157 shot down on Operations, three crew killed.
15-04-1942	BL-159 lost on Operations, problems with bomb-load, three crew killed.
26-06-1942	BL-105 undercarriage collapsed on take-off for Operations and crashed, crew escaped uninjured.
29-06-1942	BL-132 shot down by flak on Operations, three crew killed.
07-11-1942	BL-152 crashed with engine troubles on Operations, believed due to carburettor icing, two killed, one injured.
06-01-1943	BL-148 engine cut on take-off for Operations, crashed, three crew killed.
23-05-1943	BL-150 shot down by flak on Operations, two crew killed.
09-07-1943	BL-138 landed down-wind and crashed, ferrying supplies, one of crew injured.
18-08-1943	BL-140 crashed with engine trouble on take-off for training sortie, three killed.
23-08-1943	BL-107 crashed on training sortie, cause not known, three killed.
17-09-1943	BL-163 shot down by flak on Operations, three crew killed.
17-09-1943	BL-164 crashed on Operations in bad weather, ran out of fuel, one of crew killed.
09-03-1944	BL-138 crashed on take-off for Operational sortie, overturned, crew escaped.
11-04-1944	BL-183 crashed in bad weather ferrying crews, believed due to severe icing, five killed.
12-06-1944	BL-202 shot down by flak on Operations, three crew killed.
26-06-1944	BL-197 crashed on an Operational sortie, Observer killed.
27-06-1944	BL-186 shot down by flak on Operations, three crew killed.
27-06-1944	BL-185 shot down by flak on Operations, one killed, two injured.
15-07-1944	BL-170 shot down by fighters on Operations, one killed, two injured.
01-08-1944	BL-158 shot down by fighters on Operations, two killed.
01-08-1944	BL-160 shot down by fighters on Operations, two killed.
08-08-1944	BL-174 destroyed on ground by enemy bombing.
08-08-1944	BL-189 destroyed on ground by enemy bombing.

'Lapland War'

02-10-1944	BL-198 shot down by flak on Operations, crew escaped and became PoWs.
05-10-1944	BL-190 shot down by flak on Operations, one killed, two injured.
11-10-1944	BL-180 struck lake and crashed while low-flying on training sortie, three killed.
18-10-1944	BL-156 shot down by flak on Operations, three killed.
23-02-1945	BL-203 hit by small-arms fire on approach while ferrying supplies and crashed, crew uninjured.
05-04-1945	BL-182 tyre burst on take-off while ferrying supplies, crash-landed, crew safe.

Note 5: Post-war Finnish Blenheim losses

21-11-1945	BL-166 Lv.41, crashed
26-11-1945	BL-111 Lv.41, crashed
17-07-1946	BL-161 Lv.41, crashed
12-09-1946	BL-162 Lv.41, crashed
24-05-1947	BL-177 Lv.41, crashed
20-06-1947	BL-172 Lv.41, crashed
07-06-1948	BL-188 Lv.41, DBR
20-06-1948	BL-167 Lv.41, DBR
21-08-1948	BL-178 Lv.41, DBR
20-03-1957	BL-106 1 Lsto, DBR

Appendix I

Blenheim losses on shipping sweeps and anti-shipping sorties off Norway from 1 April to 10 May 1940

01-04-1940   L8867 82 Squadron Mk IV: took off from Bodney at 1100, FTR, shot down by flak-ship; F/O G. Harries, Sgt H. Kelleway, and LAC E. Wolverson Killed in Action (KIA) and are commemorated on Runnymede Memorial.

15-04-1940   L8752 110 Squadron Mk IV: took off from Wattisham, FTR, shot down by Me.109; F/L M. Morris, Sgt L. Bancroft and LAC R. Mercer KIA and commemorated on Runnymede Memorial.

25-04-1940   N6214 110 Squadron Mk IV: took off from Lossiemouth, FTR; Sgt W. Priestley, Sgt W. Howells, and LAC R. Roberts KIA, Obs buried in Denmark, other two commemorated on Runnymede Memorial.

09-05-1940   L9482 254 Squadron Mk IV-F: FTR, shot down by flak off Bergen; F/Lt A. Heath, Lt R. Nuttall (RN Observer), and Sgt S. Nicholls KIA; F/Lt Heath commemorated at Runnymede, Lt Nuttall and Sgt Nicholls buried in Mollendal Church Cemetery, Bergen.

Appendix 2

Blenheim losses in raids on Stavanger/Sola airfield, Norway, to 10 May 1940

17-04-1940   L9041 107 Squadron Mk IV: took off from Lossiemouth, FTR, shot down by Me.110 off Stavanger; F/L P. Warne, Sgt N. Griffin, and LAC A. Golder KIA and commemorated on Runnymede Memorial.

17-04-1940   N6185 107 Squadron Mk IV: as above, FTR, shot down by Me.110s off Stavanger; F/O T. Poltock, Sgt D. Edmunds DFM, and AC1 F. Harwood KIA and commemorated on Runnymede Memorial.

17-04-1940   P4924 107 Squadron Mk IV: as above, badly damaged by fighters, belly- landed at base; P/O O. Keedwell, Sgt R. Cook and AC2 J. Mayor uninjured. 53 hits noted on aircraft, which was DBR. This was 20-year-old AC Mayor's first operation, and he was awarded the DFM.

19-04-1940   P4906 107 Squadron Mk IV: took off from Lossiemouth, FTR, shot down by Me.110 of ZG 76; Sgt P. Chivers, Sgt W. Mullally, and AC2 H. Greggans KIA and commemorated on Runnymede Memorial.

24-04-1940   L8750 107 Squadron Mk IV: took off from Lossiemouth, FTR, shot down by Me.110 of ZG 76; P/O J. Murphy, Sgt G. Durie, and LAC E. Weeks KIA and commemorated on Runnymede Memorial.

30-04-1940   L9242 110 Squadron Mk IV: took off from Lossiemouth, FTR, shot down by 109s near Stavanger; S/Ldr K. Doran DFC became a PoW, but Sgt R. Battrick (Obs) and P/O F. Searle (WOp/Ag) KIA.

30-04-1940   N6202 110 Squadron Mk IV: FTR, lost in same circumstances as above; F/Sgt R. Abbott, Sgt F. Beavis, and LAC J. Rosemond KIA and commemorated on Runnymede Memorial.

Appendix 3

Coastal Command Blenheim losses from sorties to the Norwegian coast, 10 May to 30 June 1940

27-05-1940   R3624 254 Squadron Mk IV: shot down by Me.109E of JG 77 off Stavanger; P/O E. Alexander, Sgt B. Henrick and Sgt T. Hammond KIA, commemorated at Runnymede.

12-06-1940   R3627 254 Squadron Mk IV-F: FTR; shot down by Me.110 of ZG 76 near Trondheim; Sgt R. Brown, Sgt H. Gannaway, and Sgt W. Dixon KIA, commemorated at Runnymede.

15-06-1940   L9480 254 Squadron IV-F: FTR; shot down by Me.110 of ZG 26 off Sola; P/O P. Gaylard, Sgt J. Wicks, and Sgt C. Burran KIA, buried at Stavne Cemetery, Trondheim.

24-06-1940   L9409 254 Squadron Mk IV-F: FTR; shot down Me.110s of ZG 26, while attacking shipping of Kristiansund; F/Lt P. Jolliffe, Sgt A. Norfolk, and Sgt J. Price KIA, commemorated on Runnymede Memorial.

24-06-1940   R3826 254 Squadron Mk IV-F: FTR; shot down on same sortie as above; Sgt H. Hughes, Sgt J. Borrows and Sgt S. Longstaff KIA, commemorated on Runnymede Memorial.

25-06-1940   R3622 254 Squadron Mk IV-F: FTR; shot down by Me.109s of JG 77 off Sola on sweep from Stavanger to Bergen; P/O A. Hill, Sgt G. Kendall, and Sgt R. Trowbridge KIA, commemorated on Runnymede Memorial.

25-06-1940   N3604 254 Squadron Mk IV-F: FTR; shot down by Me.109s of JG 77 off Sola on same sortie as above; F/Sgt P. Corey, Sgt D, Campbell, and Sgt F. Kinghan KIA, commemorated on Runnymede Memorial.

See also Chapter 14, Appendix 6, page 247, re raid on Stavanger, 9 July 1940.

Chapter 11

Lightning war:
four days in May 1940

The 10th of May 1940 is a date etched indelibly upon the memories of all ex-Blenheim crews, for before dawn on that day the German *Wehrmacht* violated the neutrality of the Low Countries – Holland, Luxembourg and Belgium – by unleashing the Panzer columns of Bock's Army Group B, preceded by airborne troops, which seized the important Eban Emael Fortress, many vital bridges, and several airfields. However, this move was a strategic feint to draw the Allied forces to the north and succeeded completely as the British Expeditionary Force under Lord Gort and the French 1st, 7th and 9th Armies moved north-east, pivoting around the northern end of the Maginot Line, believed by the French to be 'impregnable', towards the Dyle River in Belgium to stand alongside the Belgian Army. The Allies did not realise that the main German thrust was to be by Rundstedt's more powerful Army Group A further south through the Ardennes – a forested area wrongly thought to be impenetrable to armoured columns – beyond the end of the Maginot Line, then swinging north-west towards the Channel to cut off the BEF and the French and Belgian Armies. This aptly-named Operation *Sichelschnitt* ('Sickle stroke') was masterminded by Manstein with the enthusiastic backing of Hitler.

The 10th of May also saw the resignation of Neville Chamberlain and the appointment of Winston Churchill to replace him as British Prime Minister at this most critical juncture; the other contender was Lord Halifax, the Foreign Secretary, who was far more inclined to agree terms for peace with Hitler. Churchill formed a National Government: Anthony Eden became Secretary of State for War and the Liberal Sir Archibald Sinclair became the Air Minister, while the dynamic Canadian newspaper proprietor Lord Beaverbrook was soon brought in to fill the newly created post of Minister for Aircraft Production.

As the German use of air power decisively influenced the Battle for France, and in particular the fate of the Blenheim squadrons, two factors concerning it should be mentioned. The Luftwaffe provided anti-aircraft defences for the German Army and had three-quarters of a million men engaged on this task at the outbreak of the offensive. Each Panzer division was equipped by its own mobile *FliegerAbwehrKannonen* ('Flak') defences of multiple 20mm and 37mm cannon. More than 6,700 of these were available, and were deployed as soon as any potential target such as a bridge was captured, proving deadly to low-flying aircraft. On the short front 2,600 of the excellent German 88mm mobile artillery pieces were employed, and these were very effective both as anti-tank weapons and anti-aircraft guns. In addition, most German Army vehicles, from motor-cycles with side-cars upwards, mounted machine-guns suitable for anti-aircraft use. The RAF was unaware of either the extent or the efficiency of these weapons, but the Battle and Blenheim squadrons were soon to be made aware of both in the hardest possible way.

The direct air support supplied by the Luftwaffe was equally massive and highly concentrated. It seized the initiative with attacks commencing at dawn on more than 70 Allied airfields, destroying many aircraft on the ground and immediately establishing that all-important supremacy in the air. More than 1,200 Messerschmitt fighters (860 Bf.109s and 350 Bf.110s) were deployed directly over the relatively short front, this swarm of fighters protecting the 380 Ju.87 *Stuka* dive-bombers so that they could operate multiple sorties each day with virtual impunity. The Luftwaffe also had 1,300 twin-engined bombers in constant action, together with 640 reconnaissance aircraft, and 475 Ju.52 transports – most of these aircraft also carried out several sorties each day. Linked by radio directly with the Panzers, the screaming *Stukas* acted as very effective mobile artillery, completely demoralising the defenders and causing panic in the streams of refugees that were soon clogging the roads.

These were daunting odds indeed, and as most of the Blenheim squadrons were embroiled from that momentous first day onwards in heroic and hectic action, we need to summarise their disposition on that date, although moves and changes became ever more frequent:

Royal Air Force, France

BEF Air Component (the Air Ministry always called it the RAF Component).
53 Squadron: Mk IV, Strategic Reconnaissance and Army Co-operation, based at Poix
59 Squadron: Mk IV, ditto, also based at Poix
57 Squadron: Mk IV, Tactical Reconnaissance/Army Co-operation, Rosieres-en-Santerre
18 Squadron: Mk IV, ditto, based at Meharicourt

The Air Component also had two Hurricane squadrons (Nos 85 and 87), together with two Gladiator squadrons (Nos 607 and 615), which were converting to Hurricanes, five Lysander Army Co-operation squadrons (Nos 2, 4, 13, 16 and 26), and a Liaison squadron (No 81) with Rapides.

Three more Hurricane squadrons (Nos 3, 79, 504) were sent to France as reinforcements.

Advanced Air Striking Force

114 Squadron: Mk IV, Tactical Bombing in direct support of Allied Armies, Conde Vraux
139 Squadron: Mk IV, ditto, based at Plivot

The AASF also had the eight Battle squadrons of 1 Group Bomber Command (Nos 12, 88, 103, 105, 142, 150, 218 and 226), and two Hurricane squadrons (Nos 1 and 73), together with a further Hurricane squadron (No 501), added on 11 May.

AASF aircraft could be deployed anywhere over the front while the Air Component aircraft were, in theory, restricted to operations on the BEF front to provide direct support for the Army. In practice they were pressed into action without this distinction.

Royal Air Force, England

2 Group Bomber Command
Operational:
(All Mk IV; numbers refer to aircraft serviceable and available at 0900)
21 Squadron, Bodney: 16
82 Squadron, Watton: 13
107 Squadron (just returned to Wattisham from Scotland): 14
110 Squadron (also just returned to Wattisham): 15
40 Squadron, Wyton: 15
XV Squadron, Alconbury (satellite to Wyton): 12
101 Squadron, West Raynham (Reserve Squadron): 17

Nos 21, 82, 107 and 110 Squadrons were placed on notice on 15 April to proceed to France to form the intended Second Echelon of the AASF, with 40 and XV Squadrons to follow, but they all remained based in the UK. Potential congestion on the airfields made available by the French, and the lack of alternatives, were the main reasons they were not sent, together with problems with servicing the larger numbers of aircraft. Spares for Mk IVs were held at No 6 Air Stores Park, and spares for Mk Is at the other two, Nos 4 and 5. The Order to send the extra squadrons to France was issued on 11 May 1940 but cancelled the following day. The 2 Group Squadrons were placed under the operational control of the AOC of the AASF, Air Marshal Sir Arthur Barratt, to give direct tactical support to the BEF. The Air Ministry wanted the Blenheims to be available for Gas Spray Operations, but 2 Group HQ pointed out that they were neither equipped nor trained for such use. Note that 2 Group had a total of only 102 aircraft fully serviceable and available for operations.

Non-operational:
(All Mk IV apart from 90 Squadron, which had some extra Mk Is)
35 and **90** Squadrons: these had only just merged in April 1940 to create 17 OTU at Upwood
104 and **108** Squadrons: these had also just merged to form 13 OTU at Bicester in April 1940

These squadrons were ordered to be ready to act as further operational reserves in an emergency.

Fighter Command

23 Squadron: Mk I-F, Wittering, moving to Collyweston on 31 May

25 Squadron: Mk I-F, moved from North Weald to Hawkinge on 10 May, returned on 12 May

29 Squadron: Mk I-F, moved from Drem back to Debden on 10 May, with a Flight detached to Martlesham Heath

219 Squadron: Mk I-F, Catterick, with detachments at Scorton, Leeming and Redhill

600 (Auxiliary) Squadron: Mk I-F, Manston, returning to Northolt on 16 May

604 (Auxiliary) Squadron: Mk I-F, moved from Northolt to Manston on 15 May. A Flight detached to Hawkinge, B Flight to Kenley

601 (Auxiliary) Squadron, based at Tangmere with a Flight detached to Merville, had converted from Blenheims to Hurricanes in February 1940, as had **242** at Church Fenton, together with **145**, which moved from Croydon to Filton on 9 May, and **234** with **245** Squadrons at Leconfield, plus **229** at Digby, all three squadrons re-equipping in March 1940.

92 Squadron at Croydon, which moved to Northolt on 9 May, and **222** at Duxford, which moved to Digby on 10 May, both converted from Blenheims to Spitfires in March 1940, as did **64** Squadron at Usworth in April, moving to Kenley on 16 May.

141 Squadron at Grangemouth converted from Blenheims to Defiants in April 1940.

Coastal Command

Four recently reformed squadrons had been transferred from Fighter Command in February:

235 Squadron: Mk IV-F, Bircham Newton, moved to Detling on 26 May

236 Squadron: Mk I-F, converting to Mk IV-F, Speke, moved to Filton on 25 May

248 Squadron: Mk IV-F, Thorney Island, moved to Dyce and Montrose on 22 May

254 Squadron: Mk IV-F, Hatston, moving to Sumburgh on 16 May (included the Blenheim-equipped D Flight of 233, a mainly Hudson squadron)

We have noted the grave reservations expressed by the AOCs of both Bomber and Fighter Commands concerning the proposed employment of their Blenheims. The extent of the growing doubts of the Air Staff concerning this use is revealed in the Operational Order issued to Bomber Command and the AASF early in May:

'Bomber aircraft have proved extremely useful *in support of* an advancing army, especially against weak anti-aircraft resistance, but it is not clear that a bomber force used *against* an advancing army, well supported by all forms of anti-aircraft defence and a large force of fighter aircraft, will be economically effective.'

Yet these were precisely the circumstances in which they were used, and the doubts of the Air Staff proved correct, for the price paid in lives and aircraft was far too high for the very limited effectiveness achieved.

10 May 1940

In view of the way Blenheims were thrust into a central role during the disastrous aerial Battle for France, it would be helpful to review their operations in some detail, which space limitations preclude us from providing in respect of some of the later campaigns.

The earliest RAF sortie on 10 May was by a Blenheim Mk I-F of 600 (Auxiliary) Squadron. At 0340 hours P/O Anderson and his Gunner, LAC Baker, were vectored towards aircraft activity picked up by our radar off the Belgian coast. They spotted half a dozen Heinkel He.111s, attacked and damaged two, but their own hydraulic system was put out of action by return fire. The German aircraft were part of a large force positioning over the sea so that they could bomb their targets in Belgium at dawn from an unexpected westerly direction. Poor Anderson was to be killed later that day as we will see.

The first RAF base to be bombed was Berry-au-Bac at 0435, while several others were attacked around dawn. In the confusion of that first morning the first priority was to try and find out what was happening on the ground, for the elite German airborne forces – which landed by parachute, in Ju.52 transports, by DFS gliders, in Heinkel He.115 float-planes, and even in relays of Fieseler Storch observation aircraft – had caught the defenders off guard and created bewilderment among them. The Allied air forces had to ascertain exactly where the airborne invaders were and which airfields and bridges they had seized, and to locate the spearheads of the main Panzer columns to establish the extent and direction of their advance.

First away on this task in daylight, at 0855 on 10 May, was P/O D. Massey with Sgt Whetton and AC Vickers in L9332 of 53 Squadron from Poix; damaged by light flak, the aircraft was abandoned after they landed to report at the advance airfield at Vitry at 1140, as did P/O C. Chamberlain in N6173 of 59 Squadron soon afterwards. Several more sorties set off around 0900 hours: 18 Squadron sent two Mk Is from Meharicourt, and one did not return (see Appendix 1). The other, L9815, with P/O P. Smith, Sgt C. Hann and LAC Shepherd, was hit by light AA fire, then attacked by a Me.110, but managed to escape by flying 'right down on the deck', returning to base badly damaged. XV Squadron sent two Blenheims from Alconbury, F/O A. Oakshott in P6913 and F/O R. Clarke in L8847, who photographed bridges on the Dutch/Belgian border. 53 Squadron carried out five more reconnaissance missions from Poix that morning, but communications with their HQ – and especially with the French HQ – were proving most difficult. A flood of alarming reports, many false, and wild rumours were overwhelming the command system – hard facts were difficult to come by, particularly so back at Bomber Command and 2 Group HQs in England.

40 Squadron at Wyton sent two aircraft at 0905 to reconnoitre the Hague area in Holland, where they met a hot reception (see Appendix 1). Despite a dramatic landing when his battle-damaged L8833 caught fire, S/Ldr Brian Paddon reported that Waalhaven Airfield, near Rotterdam in Holland, was 'covered in Ju.52s' – he had discovered this while circling to establish his position after an encounter with a Ju.88 – so immediate raids upon the Dutch airfield were ordered. The CO of 600 Squadron, S/Ldr James Wells, led six Blenheim I-Fs of B Flight from Manston at 1030 hours to strafe the German transports, as clearance for bombing sorties was not given until later in the day. After their first successful pass over Waalhaven, when a fully laden Ju.52 was shot down and others strafed on the ground, the six Blenheims were 'jumped' by 12 Me.110s of III/ZG-1. Within minutes five of the RAF machines were shot down (see Appendix 1), so that only one damaged aircraft managed to return to Manston – and that was lucky to do so as the fuselage was awash with petrol from

Sgt Observer John Davis baled out of Mk I-F L6616 when it was shot down by Me.110s while strafing Waalhaven airfield; he is seen at Harwich Quay. His Pilot, S/Ldr James Wells (CO of 600 Squadron), and WOp/Ag Cpl Basil Kidd were killed.

the holed starboard fuel tank. It was landed by a very relieved F/O Norman Hayes with Cpl G. Holmes, his WOp/Ag, who claimed a Ju.52 destroyed and three He.111s damaged.

The sole surviving pilot and the two who evaded were awarded the DFC, and Cpl Holmes a DFM – the seven unfortunate crewmen killed received no awards, as only the Victoria Cross can be awarded posthumously. Despite the dreadful decimation of its B Flight, 600 Squadron dispatched A Flight at 1330 on a combat patrol led by F/Lt D. Clark to Middlekerck/Zeebrugge/Flushing, and they destroyed a He.111 on the ground. The squadron had a very busy day on the 10th, for at 1650 it flew another combat patrol off the Dutch coast. (Six days later the depleted 600 Squadron was moved to Northolt for night-fighting duties.)

Already, on the afternoon of the 10th, XV Squadron had sent nine Blenheims led by S/Ldr Hector Lawrence in L8849 to bomb Waalhaven airfield, not knowing that it had been mostly recaptured by Dutch forces; the Me.110s were absent and the Blenheims returned safely, although several were damaged by AA fire, including L8855 flown by F/O Len Trent, later to win the VC. Twelve Blenheims of 40 Squadron, led by S/Ldr G. Gleed, had not been so lucky when they attacked Ypenburg airfield at 1545 in four vics of three: the last two sections were caught by Messerschmitts of JG/27, and three were shot down in flames while one staggered back to Wyton badly damaged and with serious injuries to all three crewmen (see Appendix 1).

The uncertainty persisted all day. The AASF squadrons had been standing by since the early hours waiting for urgently required target information on the location of the *schwerpunkt* of the German armoured thrusts, but they could not attack as this vital intelligence was not available, for the situation was changing hourly and becoming ever more bewildering. The tails of the Panzer columns, which stretched back into Germany jamming the roads for miles, would have offered much better targets, but the French had forbidden bombing raids into Germany for fear of retaliation. Further reconnaissance sorties were therefore called for. 57 Squadron sent off two at 1530 from Rossieres, but both were written off, while 18 Squadron sent off another from Meharicourt at 1600 hours to reconnoitre the Albert Canal, as the aircraft sent in the morning had failed to return, but it too was lost (see Appendix 1).

604 Squadron sent six Mk I-Fs at 1630 from Northolt to Wattisham to escort 12 Mk IVs of 110 Squadron, led by S/Ldr John Sabine in P4858, from there to the Dutch coast, where they bombed German Ju.52 transports that had landed on the beach near Sheveningen. One was blown into the air, but generally the bombing was not very successful, as many bombs failed to explode in the sand; 110's aircraft all returned to base, although several were damaged by light flak. The fighters from 604 carried out a low-level strafing attack, claiming seven Ju.52s destroyed, and losing only one aircraft. After crash-landing in the sand-dunes, the crew destroyed their Mk I-F by setting light to the pilot's tie, which had been inserted as a fuse into an opened fuel tank! (see Appendix 1) This enterprising pilot, Ian Joll, returned to his squadron and more than evened the score later by becoming a night-fighter ace, shooting down five enemy aircraft and damaging another. 235 Squadron also lost a Fighter Blenheim this day when N6193 was shot up by a 109 and belly-landed back at Bircham

AASF Fairey Battles, with squadron codes and serial numbers removed by the Censor, proved even more vulnerable than Bristol Blenheims.

Newton; the Mk IV-F was damaged beyond repair but the crew suffered only slight injuries.

21 Squadron had been standing by at Watton since the early hours, nerve-racking waiting that the crews found very draining. Finally, at 1810, it was ordered to send a reconnaissance sortie of two aircraft, F/Lt A. Watson in L8739 and P/O R. Gilmore in L8742, and both returned to base at 2015. F/O Bird of 59 Squadron was sent off in N6164 from the advanced airfield at Vitry at 2250, landing back there at 0155 the following morning before going back to Poix to report, but he had been unable to gather much useful information.

The French mounted no aerial attacks on the invaders during that vital first day, and it was not until midday that the AASF Battles were sent – on Air Marshal Barratt's own initiative – to attack German armoured columns in Luxembourg, losing 13 of the 32 aircraft dispatched. With others damaged beyond repair in action or by enemy bombing, 21 Battles were lost that day, together with ten Hurricanes. With 14 Blenheims destroyed, a total of 45 RAF aircraft had been lost on the very first day of the long-awaited offensive – and worse was to come in the following few days. A very high price had been exacted from the Air Force on this the opening day, which suffered 81 air-crew casualties, 34 of whom – 21 Blenheim crewmen and 13 Battle crewmen – lost their lives, while 36 (many of them wounded) were captured and became PoWs, and 11 others were injured but came down behind Allied lines or returned to base later. Sad to relate that, despite the great courage shown by individual crewmen, their valiant efforts had virtually no effect whatsoever upon the rate of the Wehrmacht advance.

11 May 1940

The priority was still to locate the German columns, for the Allied air forces were severely hampered by a lack of accurate and up-to-date target information. 18 Squadron made further attempts to reconnoitre the Albert Canal: at 0335 it sent Sgt Le Voi and crew, and at 0400 P/O Holmes and crew, but neither aircraft returned (see Appendix 2). S/Ldr J. Roncoroni of 57 Squadron was luckier; at 0405 he too set off on a reconnaissance sortie and returned safely to Rosieres. As 18 Squadron's two aircraft had not returned, it was ordered to try again, and P/O Whelan (a Canadian who later rose to Air Commodore CBE DSO DFC), with Sgt Moncey and LAC Brown, was sent off in L9192 at 1000. Their Blenheim was hit by light flak in the target area and forced to land at Vitry with damaged tail and elevator controls.

However, well before then, disaster had overtaken 114 Squadron at Conde-Vraux, for at

F/Lt John Newberry and F/Sgt Roy Kendrick of 114 Squadron at Conde-Vraux airfield just before the devastating Luftwaffe attack of 11 May. They were shot down in N6223 three days later; both were burned but baled out, while their WOp/Ag, LAC H. Baker, was trapped in the burning aircraft and killed.

0545, just as its line of parked Blenheims – which had all been armed and fuelled, and the crews briefed to bomb bridges over the Albert Canal – was awaiting orders to take-off, it was attacked by nine low-flying Dornier Do.17-Zs of 4/KG2. Within a minute six Blenheims (and the fuel dump) were destroyed, and all the other squadron aircraft put out of action by damage sustained in the sudden raid. Two airmen, AC1 G. Bonham and AC2 F. Upton, were awarded the Military Medal for their spirited attempts at airfield defence with a machine-gun, which at one stage was blown by a bomb blast from its mounting in a sandbagged pit. The ground crews struggled to repair the least damaged aircraft, and two of them, P/O W. Hadnett and Sgt D. Levinson, were awarded Empire Gallantry Medals for removing some 30 unexploded bombs from the airfield. That afternoon air-crew collected two of the only three serviceable replacement Blenheims at the AASF stores park. The number of French-based Blenheims available to the AASF for the straight bombing role had been virtually halved at a stroke.

Two Blenheim squadrons in the UK, 21 and 110, had been standing by ever since 0430 for orders to attack the German columns. The first was mounted at 1450 when 11 aircraft of 110 Squadron from Wattisham set out to bomb the bridges over the Meuse at Maastricht, across which the columns of Panzers and troops were streaming. The Blenheims met a hail of light AA fire and succeeded only in damaging houses near the bridges – two aircraft were lost (see Appendix 2).

Of the nine 110 Squadron aircraft that returned, six had received sufficient damage to put them out of action until repairs could be carried out, as had no fewer than eight of 21 Squadron's 12 Blenheims that set out for the same target from Watton at 1510, led by their CO, W/Cdr L. Bennett in L8732. P/O MacDonald in P6886 had his Gunner, AC1 R. Charlton, killed by machine-gun fire. Thus 16 of the 23 Blenheims dispatched to that target from the

One of the six aircraft of 114 Squadron destroyed on the ground in the raid on Vraux.

UK had been rendered unfit for service, in addition to the 12 lost from bases in France, and no worthwhile results had been achieved. The hammer blows were striking the anvil hard, and even heavier blows were to fall on the Blenheim squadrons the following day.

However, 11 May was not over yet: 53 Squadron carried out two more recce sorties and lost a further aircraft. Another 59 Squadron Blenheim was lucky to stagger back to Vitry on one engine, but was damaged beyond repair. Poor 18 Squadron sent out yet another recce sortie to the Albert Canal from Meharicourt at 2030, but it too was destroyed, the fifth from this squadron to be lost, with two more damaged while carrying out these dangerous missions in the first two days of the German offensive. For details of these losses see Appendix 2.

12 May 1940

This was the black day when the frantic but largely futile attempts to stem the German advance cost the Blenheim squadrons their heaviest casualties in attempting to destroy the bridges over the Meuse. The Battle squadrons also suffered heavily, for this was the day when the first two VCs of the war were awarded – posthumously – to F/O Donald Garland and his Observer, Sgt Thomas Gray, although their poor Air Gunner, 20-year-old LAC Lawrence Reynolds, who, like Gray, was carried to his death, received no award for his equivalent bravery. Many other Blenheim and Battle crews displayed equal levels of determination and courage in pressing home their attacks against overwhelming odds, both on that desperate day and the days that followed. There must have been many examples of similar exemplary bravery, which, because of the fleeting nature of such actions in the heat and confusion of battle – and frequently the demise of the participants – went unobserved, unreported and therefore unrecognised.

At 0500 eight Blenheims of 139 Squadron at Plivot, led by the CO, W/Cdr Louis Dickens, set out to attack the bridges at Maastricht, over which the Panzer columns and their supporting troops were reported to be pouring. A ninth aircraft, that of P/O Menzies, was late taking off and was unable to catch the formation, which undoubtedly saved the lives of the crew for the raid was a complete disaster – seven of the eight failed to return (see Appendix 3) and the other landed with a seriously injured Gunner and was so badly damaged that it was written off – so the Squadron was put out of action. Remember that the other AASF Blenheim squadron, No 114, had been wiped out on the ground the day before. The hammer blows were continuing to fall on the Blenheims!

That desperate day, the redoubtable Basil Embry in L8777 led the first attack from the UK on the same vital target. It was at Wing strength: 12 Blenheims of 107 Squadron took off from

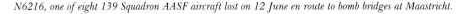

N6216, one of eight 139 Squadron AASF aircraft lost on 12 June en route to bomb bridges at Maastricht.

Ipswich at 0810 and joined up over Wattisham with 12 from XV Squadron, which had taken-off from Alconbury 20 minutes earlier. (Incidentally, the Squadron records show the flights originating from their home bases of Wattisham and Wyton respectively.) Apart from the four 250lb HE bombs in the bay, each aircraft carried 40lb fragmentation bombs on the external carriers, so they were heavily laden. They flew at only 6,000 feet, considered the ideal height for accurate daylight bombing, but it was also an ideal height for the German anti-aircraft guns. The tight formation ran into heavy flak some 15 miles from the target and was severely disrupted; seven aircraft were soon felled, and the waiting 109-Es of I/JG 1 and I/JG 27 then pounced and four more were shot down. The small force of Hurricanes from 1 Squadron sent to escort the bombers was heavily outnumbered and their crews were fighting for their own lives near the target, losing four of their number, and were thus unable to protect the bombers.

F/O Rotherham managed to crash-land his badly damaged Blenheim in a part of Belgium still in Allied hands and escaped with his Observer, but his injured Gunner was captured. Four more brave pilots were lucky to make it home: F/Lt Clayton of 107 struggled back in a badly damaged aircraft and belly-landed with a seriously injured Observer; F/Lt Webster of XV crash-landed back at base with bullet wounds in his foot; P/O 'Red' Eames, also of XV, was rushed to Ely Hospital with injuries caused when a cannon shell exploded in the cockpit of L8850; and P/O Robinson bellied-in in L8800 with no hydraulics or trim controls. Nearly all of the other Blenheims had sustained battle damage, and all the crews were shaken by the ferocity of the German defences and by the loss of so many of their comrades (see Appendix 3).

But this dreadful day was not over yet. Crews of 21 and 82 Squadrons had been standing by since the early hours – many cigarettes were smoked, many nails were bitten down to the quick, and many stomachs churned. They waited all day as 2 Group HQ digested the bad news of the losses incurred in attacking the Meuse bridges and concluded that they were too well defended. They studied the debriefing reports and photographs, and realised that the main bridges at Maastricht had been brought down earlier (in fact blown up by the Dutch) and that the ever-efficient Germans had constructed two pontoon bridges just to the north, over which their mechanised forces continued to pour. So at 1900 hours nine crews from 21 Squadron were sent to attack German forces on a road near Tongres, and at 1930 hours nine crews from 82 were sent to crater a road alongside the Albert Canal. It is doubtful if these raids had any effect on slowing the German advance, but both attacks were carried out successfully from 7,000 feet; cloud cover assisted their escape, 82's aircraft without loss, while only one of 21 Squadron's aircraft failed to return – flak blew off the rear fuselage of a Section Leader (see Appendix 3). That day also saw 57 Squadron lose yet another reconnaissance aircraft from Rosieres when it was shot down

Kept on stand-by from the early hours until late afternoon, 21 Squadron is taking off to attack German forces near Tongres. The photograph shows two 'vics' of three, and one with only two – the third may be the nearest Blenheim, which has two ground-crew on the tail while the engines are run up, with two more looking into the cockpit.

near Limburg, and P/O J. Booth of 59 Squadron was lucky to get back after a successful reconnaissance, for N6169 was hit by 'friendly' AA fire from the Belgians near Renaix; the pilot was wounded in the leg, and the Blenheim was damaged but repairable.

Earlier that day, at 0500, even as the 139 Squadron aircraft were taking off from Plivot for their disastrous raid on Maastricht, a section of three Mk IV-Fs of 235 Squadron Coastal Command set out from Bircham Newton for the Hook of Holland, there to meet some French-based Hurricanes (which did not make the rendezvous) to cover the two RN destroyers that had landed 200 Marines to secure the embarkation point ready to evacuate Queen Wilhelmina and the Dutch Government. About an hour later, in the clear blue sky, they were involved in a dog-fight with Me.110s and were holding their own – P/O Savill in L9189 claimed to have shot one down into the sea – when five Me.109-Es of II/JG 27 joined in and the odds worsened drastically. F/O Peacock shot down a 109 that was seen to crash on the shore, but then the Blenheims lost the one-sided battle and he alone escaped (see Appendix 3). Later another section of 235 Squadron – F/O Bain, P/O Randall and Sgt Tubbs – tangled in a fierce fight with Ju.88s and He.111s over Flushing; Sgt Tubbs claimed an escorting Me.110, and there were no casualties on the British side.

Another encounter off the Hook of Holland took place on that fateful day, an encounter of considerable historical importance, as it was the first ever successful radar-controlled interception of another aircraft – nowadays completely commonplace. P4834, a new Blenheim Mk IV-F, had been delivered from Filton straight to the RAE at Farnborough in October 1939 for the installation of the new and very secret Airborne Interception set. F/Lt Chris Smith DFC of the Special Duties Flight at Martlesham Heath had been developing AI techniques with P4834, and on 12 May 1940, with his nickname 'Blood Orange' as a call-sign, he was vectored by W/Cdr Farnes at Bawdsey Manor towards the radar returns from a hostile aircraft until the two blips almost merged on the screen, but Smith could see no other aircraft in the haze. AC1 A. Newton then operated the AI, hoping that the target was within the range of the signals sent from, and the returns received by, small dipole aerials on the nose and port wing of the Blenheim. The AI Mk I had two small cathode-ray tubes, each with a scale – on one instrument an indistinct and flickering blip showed the relative vertical displacement and the other one showed the horizontal or azimuth direction of the quarry. The set was mounted in the well behind the cockpit and Newton knelt on the Observer's seat facing the tail to operate the set. He gave the pilot directions that brought him behind and just below a Heinkel He.111. 'Blood Orange' Smith attacked immediately and shot down the 111 (from I/LG1), but he was wounded and P4834 was damaged by return fire. He crash-landed back at base, the Blenheim was burned out, and he was rushed to hospital (see Appendix 3). Smith recovered fully and returned in July to take command of the Flight, only to be killed in action in December 1941 when his 79 Squadron Hurricane collided with a Heinkel He.115 off the coast of Ireland – a sad end for a man who had achieved an historic 'first'.

The crucible of 12 May 1940 had seen the loss of 25 Blenheims with as many again rendered unfit for service. Forty-six courageous Blenheim crewmen had sacrificed their lives, ten more were seriously injured, and 12 became Prisoners of War. That same day 13 AASF Battles were shot down at a cost of 20 lives and seven PoWs, together with 11 Hurricanes with five pilots killed and one injured. It was a black day indeed for the Royal Air Force, and the Blenheims had borne the brunt of the losses. The pessimistic prognostications of Sir Charles Portal, AOC of Bomber Command, were proving well founded. The Chief of the Air Staff, Air Chief Marshal Sir Cyril Newall, who was also Chairman of the Chiefs of Staff Committee, sent a message to the AOC of RAF forces in France that evening, which said (inter alia):

'I am concerned at the heavy losses incurred by the Medium Bombers. I must impress on you that we cannot continue indefinitely at this rate of intensity. If we expend all our effort on the early stage of the battle we shall not be able to operate effectively when the really critical phase comes.'

What passed through the mind of Air Marshal Sir Arthur Barratt when he read this can only be surmised. He was painfully aware of the heavy losses and the intensity of the operations he had ordered. But he had received repeated requests from both the British and French HQs – ever more urgent over the three days – to engage all the aircraft he could call upon, which included the 2 Group Blenheim squadrons, to try and impede the unexpectedly rapid German advance in the north. The forces available to him to counter such an overwhelming concentration of Wehrmacht power were grossly insufficient in the first place and were rapidly depleted still further by the losses. Despite heroic efforts by their crews, the heavily outnumbered Hurricanes were unable to wrest even local command of the air from the Luftwaffe, the Battles were ineffectual and far too vulnerable, and the Blenheims proved only marginally better. Barratt was in an invidious position: he could not expect more than token Hurricane reinforcements as he realised that they were vital to the defence of the UK, nor could he conserve his bomber forces to await 'the really critical phase' for he had no way of knowing if and when that phase had arrived. He sent his own message to the Wings that evening:

> 'I am full of admiration for the magnificent courage showed by your bomber squadrons who have cheerfully accepted any tasks in spite of casualties incurred. Message received from C in C Land Armies who wish to express their appreciation of the tasks carried out … which they considered had checked the German advance and saved a serious situation.'

The advance may have been checked slightly, but the situation was far from saved.

Barratt could have made good use of a dozen squadrons of the Hawker Henley fighter-bombers (in essence two-seater Hurricanes with a deeper fuselage containing a bomb bay), as they were far faster and more agile than his cumbersome Battles. The Henley was built to Specification P.4/34 for a Light Day Bomber; 400 were ordered in December 1936, but as Hawker's production capacity was fully occupied turning out Hurricanes, only 200 were built (delivered between September 1938 and September 1940), and they were used solely as target tugs! A few squadrons of Westland Whirlwinds would also have been most useful in the ground-attack role; they were not only far faster than the Blenheim (at over 300mph at sea level, and more than 350mph at 15,000 feet, they were also faster than both the Spitfire I and the Me.109-E), but they could also carry the same 1,000lb bomb-load, and packed an effective punch with the four nose-mounted 20mm cannon, ideal for strafing the Panzer columns. But alas Westland was too busy turning out Lysanders, even then being hacked from the French skies, to develop the Whirlwind properly, and Rolls-Royce was far too involved with the Merlin to resolve the problems with the Whirlwind's Peregrine engines. Although built to specification F.37/35, production Whirlwinds were only appearing slowly by May 1940 and orders were cut from 340 to 144. (Incidentally, two – P6966 and P6967 – went for trials with 25 Squadron to see if they would be better as night-fighters than that Squadron's Mk I-F Blenheims, but they proved difficult to operate at night and the new AI radar required a second crew-member, so the Blenheims had to soldier on until the Beaufighters arrived.) Also, the pre-war RAF had turned its face against dive-bombers, only to see them being used with great effect by the Luftwaffe, which had gained air supremacy in Poland, the Low Countries and France.

13 May 1940

In the event, the RAF received such a severe mauling in the first three days of the battle that the lion had to retire on the fourth to lick its wounds. The battered squadrons needed replacement aircraft and many fresh crews. Thus neither the 2 Group Blenheims nor those of the AASF operated on that crucial 13 May 1940, and only a few reconnaissance sorties were flown by the Air Component, whose difficulties were increased as the weather turned nasty with rain and low cloud. 59 and 53 Squadrons lost three more aircraft on these reconnaissance sorties in little-known circumstances (see Appendix 4).

The 'really critical phase' in the Battle of France had in fact arrived – for 13 May marked the beginning of the end. The Wehrmacht breached the upper Meuse on the unexpected new front in the Sedan sector some 50 miles south of Maastricht, the 7 Panzer Division under Rommel being the first across near Dinant. Then three Panzer Divisions commanded by Guderian forced the river, capturing several crossing points, building four pontoon bridges, and establishing a secure and rapidly expanding bridgehead on the western bank. The weak and disorganised French 9th Army could not contain

Sgt Observer Geoff Atkins in the nose of his 139 Squadron Mk IV; the repeater instruments at the forward end of his table provide information for navigation calculations.

these decisive thrusts, which were soon to prove fatal to France. They came as a complete surprise to the Allies because the intense concentration of Luftwaffe fighters had successfully prevented any Allied reconnaissance flights from observing and reporting the massive build-up of German forces, which included seven armoured divisions and three motorised infantry divisions, stretching back for 100 miles behind this sector. The only French pilots who did survive to report the build-up were disbelieved!

Crews practice using the 'abandon aircraft' emergency exit at the School of Army Co-Operation, Andover; I wonder how many bones were broken in such exercises!

Appendix I

Blenheim losses on the Western Front, 10 May 1940

10-05-1940   L1405 18 Squadron Mk I: FTR; shot down near German border; P/O G. Harding (Pilot) and Sgt K. Shrosbree (Obs) Killed in Action (KIA) and buried in Reichswald Forest War Cemetery. LAC Roland Townsend-Coles (WOp/Ag) became PoW; a regular escaper, he was reported shot by Gestapo 15-7-1944, and is commemorated on Runnymede Memorial.

10-05-1940   L8833 40 Squadron Mk IV: damaged by Ju.88 near Dutch coast; engine caught fire as landing back at Wyton, aircraft crash-landed and burned out; crew of S/Ldr B. Paddon, Sgt J. Beattie and P/O W. Edwards uninjured.

10-05-1940   L8776 40 Squadron Mk IV: FTR; shot down by light flak near Den Haag; F/O R. Burns, Sgt J. Brooker and Cpl G. Hurford wounded and taken PoW.

10-05-1940   L6616 600 Squadron Mk I-F: FTR; shot down by Me.110s of ZG 1; S/Ldr J. Wells (Pilot and CO of 600 Auxiliary Squadron) and Cpl B. Kidd (WOp/Ag) KIA and buried at Rotterdam; Sgt J. Davis (Observer) baled out, evaded capture, and returned to England. (See photograph on page 189.)

10-05-1940   L1401 600 Squadron Mk I-F: FTR; shot down by Me.110s of ZG 1; F/Lt J. Rowe (Pilot) injured and became PoW, P/O R. Echlin, Canadian WOp/Ag, KIA and buried at Piershill.

10-05-1940   L1515 600 Squadron Mk I-F: FTR; shot down by Me.110s of ZG 1; P/O M. Anderson and LAC H. Hawkins KIA and buried at Spijkenisse, originally with simple wooden crosses as 'Unknown English Flyers', but identified in 1982 and proper headstones erected.

10-05-1940   L1335 600 Squadron Mk I-F: FTR; shot down by Me.110s of ZG 1; F/O C. Moore and Cpl L. Isaacs KIA and buried at Rotterdam; also buried as 'unknown' but identified in 1982.

10-05-1940   L1514 600 Squadron Mk I-F: FTR; shot down by Me.110s of ZG 1 and crash-landed in shallow water off Overflakkee Island; P/O R. Haine and P/O M. Kramer evaded capture and returned to England three days later.

10-05-1940   L8831 40 Squadron Mk IV: FTR: shot down near The Hague; Sgt I. Thomas, Sgt V. Spurr, and LAC H. Bridson (aged 20) KIA and buried in Westduin General Cemetery, The Hague.

10-05-1940   L8828 40 Squadron Mk IV: FTR; shot down into sea off Rotterdam by Me.110s; P/O P. Rowan, Sgt G. Beardwood and Cpl T. Clark KIA; bodies washed ashore and buried at Rozenburg, South Gravenzsande and Rockanje respectively.

10-05-1940   P6901 40 Squadron Mk IV: FTR; shot down near Ypenburg; Sgt A. Roberton and Sgt F. Checkley KIA and buried in Voorburg; AC1 J. Webster (WOp/Ag) injured and became PoW.

10-05-1940   L8827 40 Squadron Mk IV: damaged by fighters over Ypenburg; crew all seriously injured but returned to Wyton; F/Lt H. Smeddle awarded DFC, and Sgt B. Woolridge and LAC G. Quinn DFMs (Quinn later became WOp/Ag for Hughie Edwards VC); aircraft repaired.

10-05-1940   L9245 57 Squadron Mk IV: FTR; shot down by Me.109E of JG 27 over Holland; P/O A. Thomas, Sgt P. Thomas (unrelated), and LAC L. Jordan (Canadian) KIA and buried at Hook of Holland.

10-05-1940   L9246 57 Squadron Mk IV: damaged by ground fire; F/Lt G. Wyatt (Pilot) and Cpl F. Russell (WOp/Ag) both wounded, Sgt W. Gardiner (Obs) unhurt; aircraft returned to base but abandoned when squadron withdrew.

10-05-1940   L4862 and P6916 53 Squadron Mk IVs: both damaged in air raid on Metz airfield and abandoned there. One had taken a spare crew to collect the other, but it had been badly damaged in an air raid, and their Blenheim ran into a bomb crater on take-off; both crews escaped safely.

10-05-1940   L8860 18 Squadron Mk IV: FTR: shot down near Venlo by Me.109 of JG 27; P/O L. Dixon, Sgt T. Peach, and AC1 J. Townsley (aged 18) KIA, buried at Nijmegen.

10-05-1940   L1517 604 Squadron Mk I-F: FTR; shot down by light flak and crash-landed in sand-dunes; burned by crew, F/O I. Joll and LAC J. Pickford, who returned to UK.

10-05-1940   N6193 235 Squadron Mk IV-F: damaged by flak and made single-engined belly-landing at Bircham Newton; P/O R. Patterson and Lt Ogilvie (RN Observer) and LAC A. Smith slightly injured; aircraft Destroyed by Fire.

Appendix 2

Blenheim losses on the Western Front, 11 May 1940

11-05-1940 L9255 18 Squadron Mk IV: FTR: shot down by Me.109E; Sgt E. Le Voi (Pilot) and Sgt J. Sands (Obs) both wounded and captured, LAC R. Davies (WOp/Ag) KIA and buried in Reichswald Forest War Cemetery.

11-05-1940 R3590 18 Squadron Mk IV: FTR; damaged by light flak; P/O M. Holmes (Pilot) injured and made single-engined force-landing at Vaucogne, France; Sgt F. Miller DFM and LAC B. Harding unhurt.

11-05-1940 N6208 110 Squadron Mk IV: FTR; damaged by flak and crashed on fire near Bethune; Sgt G. Bennett, Sgt A. Colling, and AC2 E. Hannah all injured, Observer (aged 20) died of injuries and buried at Fouquieres.

11-05-1940 L9175 110 Squadron Mk IV: FTR; shot down near Brabant by Me.109 of JG 27; F/O G. Grattan (Pilot) and 20-year-old LAC F. Allam DFM (WOp/Ag) KIA and buried at Kaggevine; Sgt T. Patterson (Obs) captured and became PoW.

11-05-1940 L9459 53 Squadron Mk IV: FTR; damaged by Me.109s; F/O A. Panton DFC (Pilot) and Sgt J. Christie (Obs) wounded and force-landed in Belgium, then evacuated to UK, returning to Squadron in June; AC2 R. Bence (WOp/Ag) severely injured (lost leg), captured and became PoW.

11-05-1940 L4856 59 Squadron Mk I: damaged by light AA fire, port engine seized, force-landed at Vitry; F/Lt G. Smithers, Sgt R. Tull, and AC1 D. Pitcher safe, aircraft recovered and repaired, lost on 19-05-1940 (see Appendix 1, Chapter 13).

11-05-1940 L8861 18 Squadron Mk IV: FTR; shot down and crashed near Kanne, Belgium; F/O C. Bellis, Sgt H. Welch, and LAC K. Parry KIA and buried at Langemark.

Appendix 3

Blenheim losses on the Western Front, 12 May 1940

12-05-1940 P4923 139 Squadron Mk IV: FTR; shot down by Me.109, crashed near Liege; S/Ldr T. Tideman (Pilot) and Sgt Hale (Obs) evaded, but LAC J. Rooney (WOp/Ag) (aged 20) KIA and buried at Herstal.

12-05-1940 P4826 139 Squadron Mk IV: FTR; shot down by Me.109 and crashed in Belgium; F/Lt A. Lee, Sgt J. Keegan, and LAC C. Child (aged 20) KIA and commemorated at Runnymede.

12-05-1940 N6215 139 Squadron Mk IV: FTR; shot down by Me.109 and crashed in Belgium; F/O A. McPherson DFC, Sgt F. Gregory, and LAC H. Over (aged 19) KIA and buried in Heverlee. (Andrew McPherson carried out first RAF sortie of the war in this aircraft.)

12-05-1940 N6229 139 Squadron Mk IV: FTR; shot down by Me.109 and crashed in Belgium; Sgt T. Harrison, Sgt N. Jones, and LAC H. Garbett KIA and buried at Heverlee.

12-05-1940 N6219 139 Squadron Mk IV: FTR; shot down by Me.109 and crashed in Belgium; F/O G. Grey-Smith (Pilot) captured, but crew Sgt P. Gray and Sgt C. Taylor KIA and commemorated at Runnymede.

12-05-1940 N6216 139 Squadron Mk IV: FTR; shot down by Me.109 and crashed in Belgium; S/Ldr W. Scott, Sgt T. Davis, and LAC W. McFadden KIA; William Scott and Bill McFadden buried at Rekem, Thomas Davis not identified and commemorated at Runnymede, but may be buried at Rekem as unknown airman.

12-05-1940 L9416 139 Squadron Mk IV: FTR; shot down by Me.109 of II/JG 1 and crashed in Belgium; F/O N. Pepper DFC (Pilot) and Sgt T. Hyde (Obs) evaded, AC1 Hill (WOp/Ag) injured and became PoW.

12-05-1940 N6225 139 Squadron Mk IV: damaged by Me.109s, returned to base and written off; for this action W/Cdr L. Dickens AFC (CO of 139) was awarded DFC and Sgt J. Paine (Obs) DFM; LAC Crowley (WOp/Ag) injured, later captured and became PoW.

12-05-1940 L9477 139 Squadron Mk IV: also recorded in some sources as lost on this raid, but is included in Note 12, Chapter 13, as 'destroyed or abandoned on the ground in France'.

12-05-1940 L8733 107 Squadron Mk IV: FTR; shot down by flak approaching target and crashed in Belgium; F/O S. Thornton, Sgt L. Mellership, and AC2 J. Mayor DFM KIA (see John Mayor's entry for 17-04-1940 in Chapter 10).

12-05-1940 P4905 107 Squadron Mk IV: FTR; shot down by Me.109s and crashed in Belgium; F/O W. Edwards DFC (Pilot) and Sgt V. Luter (Obs) captured and became PoWs, LAC W. Palmer (WOp/Ag) KIA.

12-05-1940 P4914 107 Squadron Mk IV: FTR; shot down by Me.109s and crashed in Belgium; P/O O. Keedwell, Sgt L. Merritt and AC2 L. Berridge KIA and buried at Voroux-Goreux.

12-05-1940 L8748 107 Squadron Mk IV: FTR; damaged by flak and crashed in Belgium; F/O R. Rotheram DFC (Pilot) and Sgt R. Brown (Obs) escaped but LAC C. Coote (WOp/Ag) wounded, captured and became PoW.

12-05-1940 N6228 107 Squadron Mk IV: damaged by flak; F/Lt G. Clayton crash-landed at base with Sgt Innes-Jones, New Zealand Obs, badly injured, Cpl L. Yeomans (WOp/Ag) unhurt and aircraft later repaired. (This incident is described by Air Marshal Sir Gareth Clayton KCB DFC* in his book ...*And Then There Was One!*.)

12-05-1940 N6151 XV Squadron Mk IV: FTR; shot down by flak and crashed in Belgium; crew Sgt F. Pepper, Sgt R. Booth, and LAC J. Scott captured and became PoWs.

12-05-1940 L8849 XV Squadron Mk IV: FTR; shot down by flak and crashed in Belgium; F/O P. Douglass (Pilot) and Sgt W. Shortland (Obs) KIA and buried in Heverlee, Sgt W. Davies (WOp/Ag) captured and became PoW.

12-05-1940 L8847 XV Squadron Mk IV: FTR; shot down by flak and crashed in Belgium 3km north of Maastricht; F/O T. Bassett, Sgt N. Middlemass, and LAC W. Cavanagh KIA and buried at Maastricht.

12-05-1940 P6911 XV Squadron Mk IV: FTR; shot down by flak and crashed at Munsterbilzen in Belgium; F/O A. Oakley, Sgt D. Avent and LAC D. Woods (aged 19) KIA and buried at Munsterbilzen.

12-05-1940 P6912 XV Squadron Mk IV: FTR; shot down by flak and crashed at Genk in Belgium; P/O C. Frankish, Sgt E. Roberts, and LAC E. Cooper (aged 20) KIA and buried in Leopoldsburg War Cemetery.

12-05-1940 P6914 XV Squadron Mk IV: FTR; shot down by flak and crashed into Albert Canal, Belgium; Sgt H. Hall, Sgt E. Perrin, and LAC P. McDonnell KIA and buried in Hotton War Cemetery.

12-05-1940 L8851 XV Squadron Mk IV: damaged by flak and fighters; although wounded, F/Lt P. Webster crashlanded at base, Sgt R. Stone and LAC R. Hunter safe, aircraft repaired.

12-05-1940 L8739 21 Squadron Mk IV: FTR; shot down by flak and crashed in Belgium; F/Lt A. Watson, Sgt A. Webb, and LAC A. Burgess KIA, commemorated at Runnymede.

12-05-1940 L9324 235 Squadron Mk IV-F: FTR; shot down by Me.109s of II/JG27 and crashed in Holland; P/O N. Smith BSc, Sgt J. Robertson (aged 20), and LAC T. Lowry KIA and buried at the Hook of Holland. Tom Lowry (WOp/Ag under training) was only 17 years old.

12-05-1940 L9189 235 Squadron Mk IV-F: FTR; shot down by Me.109s and crashed in Holland; P/O N. Savill (Pilot) baled out injured and badly burned, becoming PoW, Sgt H. Sunderland (Obs) and LAC R. Tyler (WOp/Ag, aged 19) KIA and buried at Oostvoorne.

12-05-1940 P4834 Special Duties Flight Mk IV: shot down He.111 in first-ever radar interception; F/Lt C. Smith DFC (Pilot) wounded by return fire and crash-landed damaged aircraft back at Martlesham Heath, AC1 A. Newton uninjured, aircraft Destroyed by Fire.

Appendix 4

Blenheim losses on reconnaissance sorties over the Western Front, 13 May 1940

13-05-1940 P6930 57 Squadron Mk IV: FTR; shot down and crashed in Belgium; Sgt G. Couzens (Obs) KIA and buried at Vlijtingen, P/O G. Drimmie (Pilot) and AC1 R. Shuttleworth (WOp/Ag) baled out and became PoWs.

13-05-1940 N6173 59 Squadron Mk IV: FTR; P/O C. Chamberlain (NZ, Pilot) wounded and died on 14th in Luxembourg hospital, but no details of crew are given in ORB.

13-05-1940 L9332 53 Squadron Mk IV: damaged by flak; F/Lt Brown made single-engined landing at Vitry, he and Sgt Brooks (Obs) uninjured, but AC2 W. Cavett (WOp/Ag) badly wounded in legs by flak; aircraft abandoned at Vitry on evacuation.

Chapter 12

In at the deep end

14 May 1940

The 12th of May 1940 may have been a terrible day for the RAF in general and the Blenheim squadrons in particular, causing them to be withdrawn from operations on the 13th, but when they returned to the fray on the 14th it was to prove even worse. The new German breakthrough in the Sedan area created a critical situation and the RAF had to resort to desperate measures in an attempt to contain it with the totally inadequate forces at its disposal – once more the long-suffering Blenheims were 'thrown in at the deep end'.

Two early-morning reconnaissance flights from 57 and 59 Squadrons became the first casualties on the 14th (see Appendix 1). Then 114 Squadron carried out a successful armed reconnaissance at 0855 when P/O N. Tasker, with Sgt Summers and LAC Levack in R3703, located the spear-point of the German forces much further west than had been expected. They bombed an armoured column, receiving severe flak damage, but reached base to report their grim news. Clearly the existing front was being outflanked to the south, and was in danger of collapse, while the whole Rheims area – which contained the RAF bases – would be immediately threatened if the advancing Panzers were to swing south-west. 18 Squadron lost two more aircraft that day: L9193 force-landed at Vitry and, after the crew had evacuated the aircraft, was destroyed by a bomb, while L9253, which force-landed following battle damage near Phanton in Belgium, was set on fire by the crew (see Appendix 1).

There was a slight false dawn that morning when six Blenheim crews of 82 Squadron, although engaged by flak, all returned safely from attempting to block the road near Breda in the Northern sector, and only one of eight Battles of 103 Squadron attacking the Meuse pontoons was lost when it crash-landed with a wounded pilot. But when 71 Battles and Blenheims of the AASF were sent that afternoon to bomb the new crossings of the upper Meuse, no fewer than 40 were lost – 35 of the 63 Battles and, in a similar crippling proportion, five of the eight Blenheims (see Appendix 2). The latter eight were all that could be raised from the remnants of the two battered AASF Blenheim squadrons, and formed a pitifully small scratch force of mixed 114 and 139 Squadron crews and aircraft; 114 had crews but only two aircraft, whereas 139 had six serviceable aircraft but was short of crews, having suffered 22 casualties two days earlier. The Official History states in reference to this disastrous raid: 'No higher loss in an operation of comparable size has ever been experienced by the RAF.'

L9241, a 110 Squadron Mk IV damaged in the target area on 14 May, force-landed near Orchies in France. Sgt Storrow and crew were uninjured and made their way home, but German forces captured the Blenheim a few days later.

The 2 Group crews in the UK stood by in trepidation, but it was not until the late afternoon that a force of 28 Blenheims from 21, 107 and 110 Squadrons, led by W/Cdr Basil Embry, was sent out to the same targets. Although, for once, a fighter escort was provided, enabling all six aircraft from 107 Squadron to return to base, five were damaged by the fierce flak, as were 11 aircraft from 21 and 110 Squadrons, who also lost completely another eight (see Appendix 2).

These brave and costly attacks on the German mechanised columns, together with a counter-attack by the French 2nd Army, did gain a brief respite for the hard-pressed Allied forces, and the new thrust was checked for a few hours. However, before the day was out the Wehrmacht armour was once more advancing inexorably, and the British and French air forces were running out of aircraft with which to try and delay this juggernaut, let alone halt it. Barratt had lost half his AASF Battles, and his two Blenheim bomber squadrons, 139 and 114, were virtually wiped out. He withdrew the Battles from daylight sorties and ordered the four French-based Blenheim Army Co-operation and Reconnaissance Squadrons, 53, 57, 59 and 18, to be prepared for deployment in the bombing role, although they were not equipped or trained for such, and were themselves severely depleted by losses. The first three of these squadrons each converted half a dozen aircraft for the extra duty. Barratt asked 2 Group to make more Blenheims available, but it, too, was alarmed at the casualties, having had no fewer than 24 of 28 aircraft put out of action on one raid that day. Barratt instructed his squadrons to start moving back their bases, which led to more aircraft losses as those that were unserviceable, some with only minor defects, had to be destroyed to prevent them falling into enemy hands. These moves caused further confusion, and communications became more fraught. Rotterdam was bombed by the Luftwaffe that day and the Dutch Government surrendered.

15-16 May 1940

The reconnaissance sorties met mixed fortunes on this morning. P/O A. Goldie of 57 Squadron flew a successful sortie, but 59 was not so lucky, losing L4859 with F/O M. Murdoch and his unnamed crew from two aircraft sent out from Vitry. 18 Squadron's two aircraft – Sgt A. Thomas and crew in L8863 and Sgt R. Holland and crew in L6340 – returned safely, although the latter was damaged by machine-gun fire from the ground when flying at only 30 feet! But 53 Squadron Blenheim L9399 experienced the worst fortune, for after leaving at 0745 and completing a successful reconnaissance, it was shot down in flames at 0850 by an RAF Hurricane (see Appendix 1).

The bridges over the Meuse at Maastricht; each appear to have a span down, and bombs from Blenheims are falling on roads alongside the river.

Although the RAF had a relatively quiet day, the Germans did not, for they were energetically developing their bridgeheads over the Meuse. 2 Group could only lay on two raids. Fifteen Blenheims – 12 of 40 Squadron led by its CO, W/Cdr Barlow, and three of XV Squadron – left Wyton at 0930 to attack the Dinant Road. In an attempt to distract the flak gunners they used a mixture of high-level bombing from 10,000 feet and dives to 5,000 feet, but this also distracted the bomb-aiming and no significant damage was caused. Three aircraft were lost, including that of Ernest Barlow (see Appendix 2).

The second 2 Group raid, on German armour reported at Montherme, was led off at 1330 by P4828 flown by W/Cdr The Earl of Bandon, CO of 82 Squadron – another charismatic and dynamic leader in the mould of Basil Embry. His formation of 12 Blenheims was met by French Hawk 75 fighters, which kept the Messerschmitts busy; he changed the squadron to two line-astern sections for the bombing runs in fast shallow dives to minimise exposure to AA fire. This tactic was successful, for hits were observed on armour jammed in the town square and, although two aircraft were damaged, they all returned to their base at Horsham St Faith.

The AASF Blenheim squadrons had been ordered to move back, 139 from Plivot to Lannoy near Abbeville, and 114 from Conde to Crecy. Nevertheless, 139 managed to send four aircraft and crews to the same target shortly afterwards, where they dropped their 250lb bombs from 50 feet! All the aircraft were damaged by the hail of light AA fire, and one was shot down (see Appendix 2).

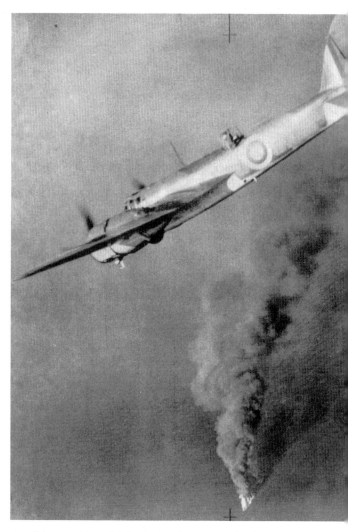

A well-known picture claiming to show 'a victorious Blenheim over a German ship'. Although squadron codes have been censored, it is the aircraft of W/Cdr Basil Embry, CO of 107 Squadron, photographed from F/Lt Gareth Clayton's aircraft on the return from a sortie to Belgium, and they are circling a burning British ship in the English Channel.

That evening the CAS sent the following signal to the AOC for transmission to the 2 Group Squadrons:

'Please convey to the pilots and crews of No 2 Group my congratulations and admiration on the manner in which they have carried out the tasks allotted to them in the present operations. The determination and success of their attacks have earned unstinted praise from our Allies, and reflect the greatest credit on all concerned.'

This platitudinous message was aimed at improving the spirits of the 2 Group

The bridge at Dinant was cut, but the Germans erected a pontoon bridge nearby and were using it within hours, by which time they had ringed it with strong AA defences.

squadrons, but whether or not it did so is a moot point. In any event 2 Group was not sent into action the next day, other than shepherding fighter reinforcements to France – S/Ldr Sutcliffe headed four Blenheims of 82 Squadron on the 16th to lead and navigate 12 Hurricanes from Manston to Merville.

However, more reconnaissance sorties were flown on the morning of the 16th to try and find out how far the Panzer columns had advanced, as the need for accurate information on their progress was ever more urgent. Poor 18 Squadron suffered yet another loss. No 139 Squadron sent two aircraft at 0430 to locate and bomb the enemy armour reported in Montherme; they found no targets but saw a circling Storch and were chased away by Me.109s, escaping by flying very low and returning damaged but safely with their bombs still on board. It was the first operational sortie for one of the pilots, and two crews, also on their first operations, sent from 53 Squadron that morning on reconnaissance sorties, did not return. No 53 Squadron suffered another sad loss that day, for one of its Blenheims was damaged by a Hurricane, then shot down by 'friendly' AA fire over Glisy aerodrome, the crew suffering severe burns. (For details see Appendix 1.)

Faulty recognition also led a Hurricane to attack a 59 Squadron Blenheim, damaging oil and fuel tanks and the hydraulic system; the WOp/Ag was wounded by flying splinters, but the pilot managed a crash landing at Vitry without further injury, although the aircraft was written off. Vitry Advanced Landing Ground also saw the abrupt arrival of another damaged Blenheim, that of Sgt Thomas of 18 Squadron, who had carried out a successful reconnaissance the day before; Thomas was shot through the neck and jaw and his Observer was wounded in the arm, but he force-landed without further injury. Although taken to hospital, he died later of his wounds (see Appendix 1).

The remnants of 114 and 139 Squadrons were ordered to return to England, but they both managed another sortie before evacuation. F/Lt Simon Maude, with Sgt Hawkins and Cpl Applebee in P6920 of 114, spotted three Henchel Hs.126 spotter planes circling Montcornet, and attacked with his single fixed gun, shooting down one and damaging another. The 139 pilot (on his first operation) did find a German column – at a location an inch off the edge of the map of his Observer Sgt J. Paine. Although he did not attack, as it was already dusk and he had no night-flying experience, he managed to land at a French airfield after being fired at by the French gunners. Darkness then brought an end to the desultory Blenheim operations of the 16th.

THE BRISTOL BLENHEIM

53 Squadron's L4843 was shot down on 16 May during crew's first operation – a reconnaissance sortie to Belgium. 53 lost four Blenheims that day, two of them shot down by RAF Hurricanes.

17 May 1940

At 0445 on the 17th, before dawn, 82 Squadron at Watton sent off a force of 12 Blenheims led by S/Ldr Miles Delap DFC (he who had sunk the first U-boat) to attack a German armoured column reported to be advancing along the Gembloux road. As all 12 aircraft from the same squadron had returned from attacking a column at Montherme two days earlier, and they had been briefed to follow the same tactics by their CO, 'Paddy' Bandon, they did not anticipate the disaster that was about to befall them. On the way out they orbited Tangmere as briefed, awaiting the promised escort of Hurricanes, but due to an inter-Command muddle over timings these did not appear, and Delap was ordered to proceed unescorted. When only a few minutes from the target, but before they had changed to line-astern for the attack, and still flying in the traditional close formation of four sections in stepped-up vics of three at 7,500 feet, accurate AA fire caused their formation to open out. No 2 in the leading section, flown by F/O Robert McConnell, was hit by the first salvo and fell earthwards. The now ragged formation turned and climbed to 9,000 feet, and the flak stopped – but a dozen fighters were spotted about a mile behind. The leader ordered the formation to close up, but before they could do so the Me.109s were upon them. Three Blenheims fell in flames from the first pass and Sgt Morrison's aircraft lost an engine and dived away while taking violent evasive action. This turned out to be his salvation. Each *Rotte* (pair) from the four *Schwarme* that made up the attacking *Staffel* of 109s picked a Blenheim from the remaining seven and hacked them from the sky one by one. All were shot down – not a single aircraft reached the target area (see Appendix 3).

Sgt 'Jock' Morrison regained control from his almost fatal downward spiral. The bombs had fallen away, although the bomb switches were 'off', and he restarted his starboard engine by changing fuel tanks (the fuel feed from the outer tank had been severed); he then nursed the badly damaged Blenheim slowly back to base. The starboard engine spluttered to a halt again – too much fuel had been lost – before he flopped on to the airfield at 0820. Jock almost fainted when he saw the extent of the damage: the main spars were riddled with

Opposite: Despite the bravery of the Air Gunners, the single rifle-calibre VGO gun proved inadequate against cannon-armed Luftwaffe fighters. Shown here are the 100-round ammunition pan, the chute for expended cartridge cases, the ring-and-bead sight, plus the follower and cam to prevent the Gunner shooting his own aircraft's tail. Lower left is one of the pair of clips to attach the Gunner's chest-type parachute, stowed in the fuselage.

L9213 and P6893, two of the 11 82 Squadron Blenheims shot down on the disastrous raid on enemy armoured columns near Gembloux on 17 May 1940; both crews were killed.

bullet holes and the aircraft was immediately struck off charge. No 82's CO, The Earl of Bandon, asked the shattered Morrison, 'Where is everyone else?', and all were appalled when no other Blenheims appeared. The ground crews were stunned into silence – 11 of their precious charges and 'their' 33 crewmen had taken off and simply disappeared, and they could see the terrible damage to the 12th. The Air Ministry ordered the decimated Squadron to be disbanded, but Paddy Bandon insisted on reforming it, using as a core S/Ldr Philip Sutcliffe, Charles Breese, 'Attie' Atkinson and Joe Hunt, who had shepherded the Hurricanes to France the previous day. The indomitable spirit of 2 Group was demonstrated when he declared the Squadron operational again within three days of this unprecedented disaster, once replacement crews and aircraft had been drafted in.

But the 17th had not finished with Blenheims yet – reconnaissance sorties still had to be flown, although now the aircraft were usually bombed up and briefed to attack any

THE BRISTOL BLENHEIM

L8858 was the only Blenheim to return from Gembloux, staggering back to Watton on one engine and Damaged Beyond Repair. The interior after the raid shows more than a dozen bullet holes – Sgt Morrison fainted when he saw the damage to the main spar and the severed control cables, fortunately duplicated.

advancing columns they found, and report their position upon return. No 114 sent up F/O Melville Kennedy with Sgt Lutwyche and AC White in L4966 to fly along the Rheims/Rethel and Rethel/Vouziers roads, but they saw only refugees as the Panzers were still heading due west.

No 57 dispatched P/O Ritchie with Sgt Wells and LAC G. Haines, but they were bounced by 109s; Ritchie force-landed his damaged aircraft at Lequesnil with a wounded Observer, and it was abandoned there and destroyed. No 53 Squadron sent off three reconnaissance sorties, commencing at 0820: F/O Bartlett with Sgt Aldridge and AC Sheldrick in R9460 were attacked by fighters but escaped by flying very low and managed to bring the damaged aircraft home, while the other two were not so fortunate, especially poor P/O Huggett, who had only arrived at the Squadron the day before (see Appendix 1).

No 18 Squadron sent off seven bombed-up aircraft at 2-minute intervals from 1100; they were accustomed to individual sorties, and unaccustomed to formation flying, so it was felt that they had a better chance of finding and attacking Wehrmacht road transport targets if sent independently. Two of the aircraft (F/Lt R. Wheldon with Sgts A. Craig and F. Hawkins in L8863, together with P/O P. Smith with Sgt Hann and LAC Shepherd in L9325) found and bombed an armoured column on the Le Cateau to Cambrai road. The other five (including P/O J. Whelan with Sgt Moncey and LAC Brown, P/O Hughes with Sgt Strong and Cpl Hutchinson, P/O Dickens with Sgt Crouch and LAC Smith, and Sgt Holland with Sgt Chatterton and LAC Maydon) bombed German transport. Three returned to base, but two were caught by Me.110s and failed to return (see Appendix 1).

No 57 sent off three Blenheims on similar sorties at 1100, and 59 had five bombed-up and standing by, but just as the order for take-off was given at 1130 the raid was cancelled, although not before one aircraft had left – P/O R. Ayres with Sgt Roper and AC Webb in N6169 – who bombed the same column that had been attacked by 18 Squadron. No 59 also flew an armed reconnaissance direct from the HQ of the RAF in France at Coulommieres (P/O C. Grece in L9463) so that he could report directly as normal communications had been so severely disrupted. No 57 mounted another sortie with seven aircraft at 1700, but only four claimed to have located and bombed transport targets, two aircraft jettisoned their bombs – one when attacked by 109s – and one other failed to find any targets. However bravely they were carried out, these puny raids were brushed off as pin-pricks by the Panzer columns who continued their inexorable advance throughout this first week of the offensive.

An impossible task

That is not to decry the valiant efforts of the Blenheim and Battle squadrons, or to diminish the courage of the crews who pressed home their attacks with great determination, for it should be stressed that they were faced with a virtually impossible task. Apart from the daunting numerical superiority enjoyed by the highly concentrated

Luftwaffe, with which they wrested and maintained mastery of the skies over the advancing forces, the disparities in organisation and equipment were most marked. The Wehrmacht created a daring strategic plan, planned it in detail with Teutonic thoroughness, and carried it out with ruthless efficiency. Their forces seized the initiative on the ground and in the air, with army and air force working closely together. They set their objectives and achieved them systematically, quickly exploiting any unexpected tactical advantage gained. We have seen how deadly the German mobile flak defences were, and how rapidly they were deployed. We have also commented on the way the Luftwaffe restricted the Allies' own aerial reconnaissance – disguising with complete success their main strategic thrust through the Ardennes – and yet gained for themselves much useful intelligence on Allied army and air force dispositions, and movement of reinforcements, enabling the invaders to cripple any counter-attacks. The telling pre-emptive raids on Allied airfields, the accuracy of the dive-bombing, and the panic created by the *Stukas*, has been noted, as has the bold use of airborne forces. The superiority in speed and manoeuvrability of the Messerschmitts has been described, as has the far greater fire-power resulting from their cannon armament. Of all the many types of Allied aircraft they encountered, only the eight-gun Hurricanes could engage them on anything like equal terms.

In contrast, the Allied Forces were unco-ordinated – the Dutch and Belgian High Commands, clinging to their neutrality, had declined to take part in the brief talks between the French and British Staffs. The combined Allied Armies possessed more divisions, more tanks and more guns than the Germans, although the best elements of the French Army and most of their armour was spread out behind the Maginot Line. The Allies even had more aircraft, although nearly all of the French aircraft were hopelessly obsolete and most were unserviceable. However, the Germans concentrated their land and air forces particularly effectively so could employ overwhelming superiority on the fronts where it was needed most. The Allied Command structure was cumbersome in the extreme and unable to react quickly enough to the German *blitzkrieg*. The BEF and RAF in France had their own Commanders, but these were placed under French command, although the RAF Air Staff still regarded the AASF (formerly No 1 Group) as part of Bomber Command, and the Hurricanes as part of Fighter Command, both operating from forward bases. The Allies lost the initiative from the outset, were hampered by poor intelligence, and were forced by events to adopt a series of defensive positions that were compromised one after the other. The confused and ill-co-ordinated defenders simply failed to comprehend the speed of the German advance. Communications became more and more difficult – the French Supreme Commander Gamelin did not even have any radios at his Headquarters, relying on motor-cycle dispatch riders who soon became ensnared among the refugees clogging the roads – and the whole command infrastructure virtually disintegrated.

In an excess of optimism bordering on wishful thinking, the Blenheim and Battle squadrons had been ordered to 'bring down bridges', 'destroy river crossings', 'block crossroads', 'sever rail lines' and 'halt armoured columns', but all these tasks were exceedingly difficult if not impossible to achieve with the inadequate equipment at their disposal, even in perfect conditions and when completely unopposed, let alone in conditions that were far from perfect and facing fierce opposition. They found a world of difference between the leisurely bombing of a target on a familiar range during peacetime exercises, usually held in good weather, and attacking a hard-to-find and therefore often barely glimpsed target, regardless of weather conditions, and frequently at very low level – especially when the fleeting target was heavily defended by deadly flak batteries and swarms of even more deadly fighters.

The convoluted Allied command structure, poor liaison at most levels, together with communication difficulties, led to confusion, indecision and lengthy delays in mounting raids, giving the Wehrmacht ample time to mount strong AA defences around obvious targets. Information on these targets received via the War Office was poor and usually well out of date, as the leading German forces had moved on from the locations given, so the crew briefings were inadequate; often they were merely given a list of 'roads upon which targets may be found'. In addition, the maps used were not much good, and not all crews had them anyway. First they had to find their target, by dead reckoning navigation and map reading only, for they had no navigational aids, and any circling while looking for the target could prove disastrous. Then they had to actually hit it, which proved exceptionally difficult. The Mk IX Course-Setting bombsight in the nose, used by the Observer in medium-level attacks, was not very accurate even in ideal conditions and required the aircraft to be flown precisely straight and level; in low-level attacks the pilot aimed the aircraft itself at the target and released the bombs just before reaching it, another haphazard and inaccurate means of delivery.

Four of the inefficient 250lb GP bombs are being loaded. This close-up view shows the stays that hold the bomb-doors open on the ground, and the strong bungee cords that hold them shut in the air until the falling bombs knock them open upon release.

The bombs they dropped, even if they struck the target, were not very effective. The pre-war 250lb bombs used not only had a very poor charge/weight ratio of 27 per cent (German bombs were almost 50 per cent), but also the explosive charge itself was singularly inefficient when it did detonate, and a disturbingly large number failed to do so. Several direct hits on a solid bridge, extremely hard to score on such a small target, would be needed to destroy it. A direct hit from a 250lb bomb – even more highly unlikely – was needed to destroy a tank, and the 40lb and 20lb light bombs dropped were only of use against soft-skinned vehicles such as lorries, horse-drawn transport, or those of ground troops. The normal bomb-load on these sorties was two 250lb with either six 40lb and 12 20lb, or 12 40lb, a total of just under 1,000lb.

The single fixed .303 Browning machine-gun in the port wing was hopelessly inadequate for strafing armoured targets, and as the whole aircraft had to be aimed with a crude ring-and-bead sight in front of the pilot, it was unlikely to hit anything anyway. The Browning was based on a pre-First World War American Colt .30 infantry machine-gun; the RAF first tried one in a Bristol F2b in 1918 and Armstrong Whitworth obtained a licence to manufacture it, receiving an order for six – adapted to take standard British Army .303 rifle ammunition – in 1926. These were delivered in 1929, improved in 1930, and ordered in quantity during the 1936 expansion of the RAF. With their reasonable rate of fire they were effective at close range against lightly armoured aircraft when mounted in batteries of eight in the Hurricane and Spitfire, but a single fixed example was not much use. The Vickers 'K' gas-operated pan-fed gun in the turret was also 'long in the tooth', having been designed in 1918 by the French General Berthier, and adopted, adapted and improved by Vickers, which after protracted trials and tribulations throughout the early 1930s was rewarded with large orders in 1935. But it, too, was largely ineffective when faced with cannon-armed fighters, and at that stage of the war the Blenheims had no under-defence armament at all.

Lucky to survive, with only the ineffective VGO gun to defend his 139 Squadron Blenheim, WOp/Ag Sgt Ken Whittle leaves his hatch after a sortie.

The Blenheim itself, as we have seen, was adapted from a civil aircraft and not designed specifically to endure the rigours of wartime operation. The lightweight monocoque construction, especially of the rear fuselage, was easily damaged by flak or fire from enemy fighters, many of the vital systems were very vulnerable to such damage, and most of the outer fuel tanks were still not converted to the self-sealing type. But fortunately the wings were over-engineered and had sufficient reserves of strength to absorb quite severe damage. The engines, with their exposed poppet valve gear, were developed from a First World War design and had reached the limit as far as squeezing any more power was concerned – the 'Plus 9' boost pressure for maximum power could only be used for short periods in dire emergencies. Many ex-Blenheim pilots have told me that the aircraft was a most delightful machine to fly, feeling reassuringly solid yet possessing responsive controls, but nevertheless an unsuitable, even frightening, one in which to go to war.

THE BRISTOL BLENHEIM

And what of the men in the Blenheims who, as this chronicle demonstrates, were required almost daily to risk their lives in this manner – indeed, frequently to forfeit them? The heavy losses sustained by the Blenheim squadrons of crewmen killed, injured or captured caused much concern throughout the service, especially when considered in relation to the paucity of results achieved. Most of the pilots lost were experienced professionals from the small pre-war Air Force, and losses included many highly trained and seasoned leaders of Wings, Squadrons, Flights or Sections. Men of such high calibre were hard to replace, and their loss was keenly felt. When freshmen pilots began to arrive in the squadrons, they would have benefited from the guidance of the more experienced leaders, and many young men were lost in the course of their first few Blenheim operations. Equally serious was the loss of so many Observers and Wireless Operator/Air Gunners, as these were drawn from the ranks of highly skilled ground tradesmen such as armourers, airframe and engine fitters, instrument repairers and electricians who had volunteered for flying duties. Initially these duties were part-time, often with little training provided, and they continued to work as ground tradesmen, but soon most were sent on short courses to improve performance in their specialised airborne tasks, and they became full-time air-crew, leading to shortages of skilled ground-crews. Many were former Halton apprentices, so their many years of comprehensive engineering training was wasted. They, together with the experienced pre-war pilots, were the very seed corn that made the rapid expansion of the RAF possible, so their loss had serious ramifications on the efficiency of such a technical service. Their high quality is shown by the fact that many who did survive their Blenheim days rose to high rank in the RAF – for example, outstanding leaders such as Basil Embry, 'Paddy' Bandon, Ivor Broom, 'Tubby' Clayton, Hughie Edwards VC, Laurie Sinclair, 'Digger' Kyle and Sam Elworthy (who as Lord Elworthy became CAS). Other distinguished former Blenheim pilots were to achieve fame later with different aircraft, such as John 'Cat's Eyes' Cunningham, Guy Gibson VC, David Atcherley, Max Aitken and Len Trent VC.

Each individual name recorded in these lengthy lists of losses left behind grieving parents, most had brothers and sisters, many were engaged or married, some were fathers, all had colleagues in the service and friends both inside and outside the Air Force. Each casualty represented a personal tragedy to all those in this close circle of relatives and friends. It was the parents and wives who received the dreaded telegram from the Air Ministry informing them that their loved ones were 'reported missing in action' or 'had failed to return from an operation'; it was they who shed their tears on the painful personal letter from the Squadron CO. Their grief would have been far worse had they been aware that most of these disturbingly numerous casualties were caused quite unnecessarily in valiant attempts by the Blenheim squadrons to stem the German advance – attempts that, unfortunately, proved largely futile.

By 1941 most Blenheims were fitted with the heavy T1154/R1155 Transmitter/Receiver radio sets, as were nearly all Bomber Command aircraft right to the end of the war.

Appendix 1

Blenheim losses on reconnaissance sorties, 14-16 May 1940

Aircraft are all Mk IVs.

14-05-1940 P6926 59 Squadron Mk IV: FTR from reconnaissance; F/O P. Hawks (Pilot, Army Lt seconded from King's Regiment), Sgt F. Evans (Obs), and AC1 C. Shaw (WOp/Ag) KIA.

14-05-1940 L9180 57 Squadron: took off from Poix at 0535, failed to return (FTR); engaged Do.217; P/O W. Spencer crash-landed in Belgium, Sgt R. Pike (Obs) wounded, AC2 O. Beaumont (WOp/Ag) Killed in Action (KIA).

14-05-1940 L9253 18 Squadron: took off from Meharicourt, force-landed at Phanton, Belgium, and burned by uninjured crew.

14-05-1940 L9193 18 Squadron: took off from Meharicourt, force-landed at Vitry, and destroyed by enemy bombing, crew safe.

15-05-1940 L9399 53 Squadron: FTR; shot down by 'friendly fire' from Hurricanes near Tournai; P/O P. Bone, Sgt W. Cronin DFM, and LAC J. Bromley KIA.

16-05-1940 N6168 59 Squadron: FTR; badly damaged by Hurricane and crash-landed at Vitry airfield, second time F/Lt Smithers and his crew Sgt Jones and AC1 D. Pitcher had crash-landed at Vitry in four days.

16-05-1940 L9254 18 Squadron: FTR; shot down in flames by Me.110s near Cambrai; F/O A. Stuart, Sgt D. Borthwick, and LAC H. James KIA.

16-05-1940 L4860 53 Squadron: FTR; shot down by Me.109s and crashed near Peruweltz; P/O M. Lovell, Sgt D. McLeod, and AC1 Kenneth all injured quite badly but were evacuated safely.

16-05-1940 L4843 53 Squadron: FTR; shot down and crashed near Mezieres; P/O R. MacPhearson, Sgt A. Morland, and AC2 S. Robinson all captured and became PoWs.

16-05-1940 L4852 53 Squadron: FTR: shot down by Hurricane, crashed at Glisey airfield and caught fire; F/Lt B. Daly, Sgt W. Currie, and AC1 P. Blandford all injured.

16-05-1940 L8863 18 Squadron: damaged by light AA and force-landed at Vitry; Sgt A. Thomas (Pilot) fatally injured, Sgt J. Talbot (Obs) injured, LAC St James-Smith (WOp/Ag) unhurt, aircraft repaired and passed to 53 Squadron.

Appendix 2

Blenheim losses on bombing sorties, 14-16 May 1940

Aircraft are all Mk IVs.

14-05-1940 L9179 139 Squadron: FTR; shot down near target; F/O R. Montmorency (Pilot) and Sgt H. Wallis (Obs) KIA, LAC V. Barrow (WOp/Ag) injured and reported in Angers Hospital.

14-05-1940 P4827 139 Squadron: FTR; shot down on fire by Me.109s near target; Sgt Brady (Pilot) and Sgt Wilsher (Obs) baled out, but LAC S. Maddox (WOp/Ag) KIA.

14-05-1940 N6223 139 Squadron: FTR; shot down on fire by Me.109s; F/O J. Newberry (Pilot) and Sgt R. Kendrick (Obs) received burns but baled out safely, LAC H. Baker (WOp/Ag) trapped in burning aircraft, KIA and is buried at Choloy War Cemetery, Moselle, France. (See the picture on page 193.)

14-05-1940 N6230 139 Squadron: FTR; believed to have collided with Me.109 in target area; P/O J. Power, Sgt D. Stuart-Harris, and AC1 W. Parker KIA and commemorated on Runnymede Memorial.

(NB Above four entries were 139 Squadron aircraft flown by 114 Squadron crews.)

14-05-1940 L9464 114 Squadron: FTR; struck ground in target area, believed through enemy action; P/O C. Jordan, Sgt P. Southwood, and LAC T. Brown KIA.

14-05-1940 P6920 114 Squadron: also recorded as Missing in Action this day on sortie from Conde-Vraux; no further details available.

14-05-1940 L8742 21 Squadron: FTR; shot down in target area; P/O R. Gilmore, Sgt T. Pearce, and AC1 A. Wilson KIA and commemorated on Runnymede Memorial.

14-05-1940 P6890 21 Squadron: badly shot up in target area; AC1 L. Lightfoot (WOp/Ag) injured, F/O J. Sarll crash-landed at Bodney, he and Sgt Jenning (Obs) slightly hurt, aircraft written off. For this action 'Peter' Sarll was awarded DFC, and AC1 Leo Lightfoot (New Zealand WOp/Ag, who claimed a 109) DFM.

14-05-1940 L8738 21 Squadron: FTR; badly damaged attacking target and crash-landed; crew Sgt J. Outhwaite, Sgt E. Broadland, and AC1 J. Bartley (who was wounded) evaded and rejoined squadron later.

14-05-1940 N6210 110 Squadron: FTR; shot down in target area; P/O S. Rose, Sgt D. Ashton, and LAC E. Edwards KIA and commemorated on Runnymede Memorial.

14-05-1940 L9217 110 Squadron: FTR; shot down in target area; F/O E. Mullins (Pilot) and Sgt R. Lowe (Obs) captured and became PoWs, AC2 P. Aherne (WOp/Ag) KIA.

14-05-1940 L9241 110 Squadron: FTR; damaged in target area and force-landed in France; Sgt A. Storrow, Sgt E. Parker, and LAC Rowlands returned home safely, aircraft written off. (See photograph on page 202.)

14-05-1940   L9214 110 Squadron: FTR; shot down and crash-landed near target; F/O G. Wright, Sgt J. Fancy, and LAC W. Street captured and became PoWs.

14-05-1940   P6889 110 Squadron: FTR; shot down near target and crashed in Ardennes; Sgt Cater (Pilot) unhurt, crewmen Sgt Crossland and AC1 Jones injured.

15-05-1940   N6217 40 Squadron: FTR; shot down by light flak near target of Dinant bridge and crashed nearby; W/Cdr E. Barlow, Sgt E. Clarke, and LAC A. Millard KIA and buried locally. W/Cdr Ernest Barlow was CO of 40 Squadron.

15-05-1940   P4913 40 Squadron: FTR; shot down by flak near target and crashed nearby; F/O J. Edwards (NZ), Sgt C. White, and LAC S. Johnson KIA and buried locally.

15-05-1940   L8856 XV Squadron: FTR; damaged near target; P/O D. Harriman crash-landed near Belgian coast when propeller detached, Sgt J. Stanford (Obs) injured and captured, but pilot and LAC Moorhouse returned safely.

15-05-1940   L9411 139 Squadron: FTR; shot down and crashed near target; P/O K. de Souza, Sgt E. Tough, and AC2 W. McCarthy KIA and buried at Floing in Ardennes.

15-05-1940   P6902 139 Squadron: reported as FTR from attacking armoured columns near Montherme this day; no further details available.

Appendix 3

Blenheim losses on the Gembloux raid, 17 May 1940

Aircraft are all 82 Squadron Mk IVs.

17-05-1940   L8830: FTR; shot down by AA fire, crew baled out; F/O R. McConnell (Pilot) and AC H. Humphreys (WOp/Ag) became PoWs, Sgt S. Fulbrook (Obs) evaded capture and returned to squadron later.

17-05-1940   P4852: FTR; shot down in flames by Me.109s near Laon; S/Ldr M. Delap DFC (Pilot) and Sgt R. Wyness DFM (Obs) baled out safely, P/O F. Jackson (WOp/Ag) KIA. (S/Ldr Miles Delap and Sgt Wyness sank the first U-boat, U31, 11-03-1940   in this aircraft.)

17-05-1940   L9210: FTR; shot down in flames by Me.109s near Laon; P/O J. Grierson, Sgt J. Paul and AC2 J. Patterson KIA and buried at Festieux in France.

17-05-1940   P4838: FTR; shot down by Me.109s; F/O A. Gofton, Sgt F. Miller and Cpl T. Cummins KIA and have no known grave but are commemorated at Runnymede.

17-05-1940   P4851: FTR; shot down by Me.109s; F/O D. Fordham (Pilot) saved, but crew Sgt F. Fearnley and Cpl A. Richards DFM KIA and commemorated at Runnymede.

17-05-1940   L9213: FTR; shot down by Me.109s near Laon; F/Lt G. Watson, Sgt F. Wootten, and LAC A. Sims KIA and buried at Presles-et-Thierney, France.

17-05-1940   P4854: FTR; shot down by AA fire; P/O K. Toft (Pilot) slightly injured and became PoW, crewmen Sgt A. Crouch, and LAC R. Morris KIA and commemorated on Runnymede Memorial.

17-05-1940   P4898: FTR; shot down by Me.109s; P/O S. Christensen, Sgt A. Phillips, and LAC P. Ettershank KIA and commemorated on Runnymede Memorial.

17-05-1940   P4903: FTR; shot down by Me.109s; crew Sgt L. Wrightson, Sgt S. Beaumont, and AC1 K. Thomas baled out safely and returned to squadron later, although Pilot was injured.

17-05-1940   P4904: FTR; shot down in flames by Me.109s near Lappion; Sgt T. Watkins (Pilot) baled out, returned 14 days later, his crew Sgt D. Lees, and LAC K. Reed KIA.

17-05-1940   P6893: FTR; lost without trace; Sgt R. Newbatt, Sgt J. Crawley, and Sgt A. Knowles KIA and commemorated on Runnymede Memorial.

17-05-1940   L8858: badly damaged by AA fire, aircraft struggled back to base but was Damaged Beyond Repair (DBR) and written off; Sgt T. Morrison, Sgt Carbutt, and AC1 M. Cleary badly shaken but uninjured. (See the picture on page 209.)

Appendix 4

Blenheim losses on bombing/reconnaissance sorties, 17 May 1940

Aircraft are all Mk IVs.

17-05-1940   L9187 18 Squadron: FTR; damaged by Me.109s near Sedan; Sgt T. Mongey (Obs) KIA, P/O J. Whelan (Pilot) wounded but crash-landed, LAC Brown (WOp/Ag) uninjured and returned.

17-05-1940   L9186 18 Squadron: FTR; shot down west of Sedan; F/O A. Stuart, Sgt D. Borthwick, and LAC H. James KIA. (These two aircraft were not Stuck Off Charge until 20-05-1940.)

17-05-1940   L4842 and L4848, 53 Squadron: both recorded as FTR from reconnaissance sorties this day; no further details known. Squadron Roll of Honour shows no crew losses this day, so assumed they evaded successfully.

Chapter 13

The fall of France

The fall-back to Dunkirk

The Blenheim squadrons were pushed further into the forefront of the fighting as the unequal struggle continued. In an attempt to reduce the casualties that were being inflicted, the AOC of 2 Group, AVM James Robb DSO DFC (won in the First World War), ordered that daylight raids by Blenheims should be mounted only if there was cloud cover or a strong fighter escort, although in practice it was usually impossible to provide either form of protection. On 18 May 1940 XV Squadron could only raise six aircraft to attack a column reported to be approaching Le Cateau and/or destroy a bridge there; half were lost, including the experienced S/Ldr Hector Lawrence. They had staged via Abbeville to meet a French fighter escort over Douai, but it failed to appear; their orders were to go to Poix after bombing to re-arm and repeat the attack, but of the three surviving aircraft that landed there, two were really too badly damaged to continue, although Len Trent in one of them (P6913) managed to limp back to Martlesham Heath at 2030 (see Appendix 1).

No 21 Squadron also flew to Poix, led by S/Ldr George Pryde, a canny Scot, but when the promised fighters failed to appear they flew back – wisely perhaps – to their home base. No 40 Squadron had also operated via Abbeville and seven aircraft successfully bombed some German troops near Le Cateau, completing the mere 13 bombing sorties by 2 Group that day, for when aircraft from 110 and 107 Squadrons landed at Poix they were told that German troops were in the village and advancing on the airfield, so left very hastily – increasing the number of sorties by staging via Advanced Airfields and re-arming the Blenheims there seemed a good idea, but it had its snags! No 57 Squadron also mounted raids to Le Cateau that day, but no details are available other than that four Blenheims were recorded as 'Failed to Return'; it is believed that three were damaged on the raid and had to be abandoned at Poix, as this was 57's last day of operating from French soil (see Appendix 1).

2 Group Blenheims set out for France, still flying in the unsuitable pre-war formation of stepped-down 'vics' of three; the photograph was taken from the left-hand aircraft of the leading 'vic'. The pre-war theory that such formations would be self-defending from the combined fire of their gun-turrets had already proved fallacious.

Poix had been bombed on the morning of the 18th, and 59 and 53 Squadrons had evacuated their remaining Blenheims first to Goyencourt, then to Crecy. No 18 Squadron put up its last six aircraft to bomb columns near Cambrai, landing at Abbeville before also moving to Crecy. The squadron received some reinforcements when 114 Squadron handed over its three surviving serviceable Blenheims, but that was not an easy task in the chaos that prevailed; for example, Sgt. 'Gillie' Potter, in the last of 114's only three airworthy aircraft, was sent to Meharicourt to hand it over, but landed to find the airfield deserted. On asking some aged locals where the RAF was, he was told that the Germans had passed through the day before! The crew rushed back to their Blenheim, and a Wehrmacht motorcyclist appeared just as the second engine was starting up, so they made a hasty departure and took off for Glisy, to find that deserted too, finally locating 18 Squadron at Crecy. Gillie noted in his logbook, rather laconically, 'Landed at Meharicourt where I had a close encounter with a German motorcyclist'.

Similarly, 139 (after destroying L8760 on the ground) passed its remaining four aircraft to 57 Squadron. This hand-over also proved difficult in the confusion; F/O Turnbull in L8756 landed at Rossieres to find it deserted, tried Poix to discover that it had been abandoned, then its satellite, which was being evacuated, and landed finally at Abbeville. The two Blenheim bomber squadrons of the AASF, 114 and 139, were no more. Their personnel were evacuated over chaotic roads and returned to the UK by sea from Cherbourg to commence reforming and re-equipping. No 114 could not manage this until 31 May at Wattisham, while 139 took one day less at West Raynham. (Both squadrons moved to Horsham St Faith on 10 June and it took them another month before they became operational again.) Back on 18 and 19 May only a few reconnaissance sorties were mounted, with four more losses (see Appendix 1), but no bombing sorties at all on these two critical days, due to the general evacuation of the Blenheim squadrons. The fierceness of the air fighting over France is shown by RAF losses, for apart from the ten Blenheims, on these two days of relatively few Blenheim operations no fewer than 58 precious Hurricanes were destroyed, together with eight Lysanders and eight Battles – the latter on the 19th only, the day they were pressed back into action following their withdrawal on the 15th.

Battle-damaged aircraft had to be repaired as quickly as possible – here two airmen inspect exit-holes in N6207 of 110 Squadron on 22 May 1940.

The four Air Component Blenheim squadrons also left France, leaving behind much equipment and destroying many unserviceable aircraft that could not be flown out. Unfortunately some records of these squadrons were lost in the confusion of evacuation. The Air Stores Parks and repair centres at Glisy and Chateau Bougon were also abandoned, and more Blenheims, Battles and Hurricanes undergoing major inspections or repairs were destroyed, together with hundreds of crates containing new Mercury and Merlin engines, propellers and tons of airframe spares. What was worse was that dozens of brand new Hurricanes were burned as there were no pilots to fly them away! On the evening of the 19th, 57 Squadron evacuated from Crecy and flew 13 Blenheims, including the ex-139 Squadron aircraft, to Lympne in Kent, going on to Wyton to regroup on the 22nd. The same route via Lympne, but to Watton, was followed on the 20th by the remaining aircraft of 18 Squadron, one of which crashed (see Appendix 1), and the Squadron did not become operational again until 4 July. The remnants of 59 and 53 Squadrons, the former with five aircraft and the latter with six, also left France for Lympne on the 19th, moving on to Andover on the 21st. There was no respite for these squadrons as they were sent back into action from their new bases straight away. 2 Group was back in the fray on the 20th, carrying out 47 bombing sorties on a Panzer column advancing along the Bapaume/Arras road. Rendezvous over Hawkinge with a strong escort of three Hurricane squadrons prevented the Messerschmitts from interfering, and for once there were no losses from the double sorties flown that day by both 107 and 21 Squadrons, led by W/Cdr Basil Embry and S/Ldr 'Scottie' Pryde, although several aircraft were damaged by light flak.

That day 2 Group HQ issued a directive to the Blenheim bases, the first points of which were quite unrealistic in the circumstances, as they emphasised 'the importance of close position-keeping by each section of three aircraft' as 'stragglers reduced the effectiveness of mutual protective fire', and went on to state, 'It must be impressed on all Pilots that security rests on mutual support.' Senior officers were still clinging to pre-war theories that the actual fighting had shown to be misconceived.

Rather than turning to the south-west towards Rheims and Paris as the French expected, the German Panzers had swung to the north-west towards the French coast, capturing Amiens and Abbeville and reaching the coast on 20 May, cutting off the BEF together with the French and Belgian armies in the Northern zone. Boulogne surrendered on the 21st and the defenders of Calais were engaged from the south-west on 22 May, a situation that would have been completely unthinkable only 12 days earlier when the German offensive was launched. The Blenheims were pressed into constant and desperate action in an attempt to turn back the advance, and continued to suffer losses, although these were contained slightly as the battle area was now within the range of home-based RAF fighters, with some Spitfires joining the fray for the first time. The initial strong concentration of the Luftwaffe was diluted not only by the far greater areas they had to cover but also by the considerable losses they had incurred themselves. This was just as well, for by 23 May the whole of 2 Group could field only 73 serviceable Blenheims, and the next day only 60 were available. There would have been even fewer were it not for the frantic efforts of the ground-crews who worked round the clock patching up and repairing dozens of damaged aircraft to make them fit for service again.

Such was the speed of the advance of the German armoured columns that they left their rear flanks dangerously exposed, despite efforts to secure them by bringing forward rapidly their motorised supporting infantry. The Allies hastily planned joint counter-attacks on these weak flanks, the BEF from the north towards Arras and the French from the south near Laon, but these counter-attacks were unco-ordinated, too weak, and failed – although they gave both Rommel and Guderian a fright. The BEF Commander, Lord Gort, had to detach half his intended attacking force to take up positions behind the Belgian Army fighting bravely in the north-east, as he was warned that they were about to surrender (overwhelmed, they did so on the 28th), and the French postponed their attack for 24 hours, partly because their Commanding General Billotte was killed in a car accident soon after leaving a staff conference at Ypres with the newly appointed Allied Supreme Commander, General Weygand. The delayed French attack was led by a Colonel Charles De Gaulle, but his armour was halted by repeated dive-bombing from relays of *Stukas* called up by the German troops on their direct radio link. The Wehrmacht took full advantage of its communication systems, which were incomparably superior to those of the Allies. A couple of squadrons of fighters would have kept the dive-bombers at bay, but none were available. Dowding needed 52 fighter squadrons to defend the home base, but was down to 36 – the cupboard had been scraped bare. The RAF was paying the price for its overriding emphasis on the production of bombers throughout the years of expansion and re-equipment right up to the very last year of peace, when, very belatedly, priority was given to fighter production.

The aircraft that were the fruits of this policy did what they could to help contain the critical situation in France, the Blenheims and Battles by day suffering heavy losses, and the Hampdens, Whitleys and Wellingtons attacking communications by night with far fewer losses, but it was all to little avail. Charles Portal, still the AOC of Bomber Command, had serious misgivings about this daylight use of his Medium Bombers and was most disturbed at the losses of his most experienced crews. They were mainly from the small pre-war professional RAF and, as mentioned before, were needed as the seed corn for the vast force that Bomber Command was planned to become – Portal knew that the new four-engined Heavy Bombers were waiting in the wings. He expressed his alarm forcefully to the Air Ministry, writing that 'the operations in France were [as he had forecast two weeks earlier – see Chapter 10] draining away the Blenheim crews at the rate of between one and two squadrons per week... It is the height of unwisdom to throw the Blenheims away in an attempt to do the work of artillery...' So now 2 Group Blenheims operated by night for the first time on 20 May, and 18 fruitless sorties were flown (six each by 82, 40 and 110 Squadrons) – all without loss, but the results were negligible due to the virtual impossibility of locating worthwhile military targets at night amidst the confusion on the ground. However, so desperate had the military position become that, even as the remnants of the six RAF Blenheim squadrons were extricating themselves from France, the remaining Blenheims of 2 Group perforce had to continue to operate extensively by day despite Portal's grave reservations.

On the next two days, 21 and 22 May, Nos 107, 40, XV, 21, 82, 110 and 18 Squadrons put up all of their serviceable aircraft and carried out an impressive 120 sorties in an extremely intensive effort, 116 to bomb troop columns and four on reconnaissance; ten aircraft were lost – three to so-called 'friendly fire', two shot down by RAF Spitfires near Boulogne, and another by Hurricanes (see Appendix 1). XV Squadron was very lucky not to loose another, for F/O R. Clarke in L9024 was hit by flak and slightly injured while flying at low level, and his port wing struck the ground – the wing-tip was broken off, and the damaged outer 4 feet bent upwards by about 25 degrees and stuffed with French soil – but he managed to regain control and the aircraft limped back to base. The 2 Group squadrons continued with similar intensive operations throughout the crisis period of 23-26 May, when the evacuation of the BEF from the pocket around Dunkirk commenced. They mounted 162 sorties, but the losses also continued; 40 Squadron lost its CO when W/Cdr Llewellyn was killed (see Appendix 1). 107 Squadron very nearly also lost its outstanding leader, W/Cdr Basil Embry, on the 23rd. While searching the target area his aircraft (L8777) was hit by flak and blown upside-down; he regained control, albeit with difficulty as there was a huge hole in the port wing and he could only keep the Blenheim level by full deflection of the ailerons, and staggered back to land at Hawkinge. The very next day the indefatigable and indomitable Embry led two more attacks in his replacement Blenheim, L9391.

The difficulties of locating targets in the confused and fluid situation were compounded by the streams of refugees who became entangled with the troop movements of both friend and foe on the choked roads. It was hopeless relying on target information from France or the Army. Even specially mounted reconnaissance sorties from the UK were not much use, for by the time the attacking force reached the indicated target area after the aircraft had returned and the crews had been debriefed in order that the squadrons that had been standing by for hours could mount a raid – and six aircraft were lost even before they could report (see Appendix 1) – the positions of the enemy troops had changed. Recognising these difficulties, 2 Group HQ issued an urgent Order of the Day on the 25th:

> 'It must be impressed upon leaders that risks must be taken in this emergency to find the really important targets, then attack them. It must now be accepted that the day has passed when attacks can be launched at definite targets as a result of previous reconnaissance. This is due to the rapidity of movement of enemy forces. In view of the critical situation of the BEF it is essential that all attacks are pressed home with vigour.'

The opening and closing homilies were certainly not called for, and the central section merely stated the obvious as far as the Blenheim crews were concerned – for they had become fully aware of the stark realities of this situation over the previous two weeks.

No one had consistently and courageously 'pressed home all attacks' with more 'vigour' than W/Cdr Basil Embry, and 2 Group was shocked when this illustrious leader failed to return from taking 12 Blenheims of 107 Squadron to attack enemy troop concentrations near St Omer on 27 May. He was on his last sortie as CO of 107 before handing over the

Squadron to his successor, S/Ldr Stokes, who was also on the operation to 'see how it was done' – Stokes must be the only CO to assume command in the air! Embry and his Observer P/O Whiting baled out and were captured, but his WOp/Ag, Cpl Long, was

W/Cdr Basil Embry, the dynamic leader of 107 Squadron, rose to become the most respected AOC of 2 Group, and later a much-decorated Air Chief Marshal.

This is the damaged port wing of L8777, which Embry managed to fly home – the outer fuel-tank lies between the airman and the shell hole! The steel cradle for the wing-mounted machine-gun (seen on the left of the gap) probably provided sufficient extra strength to prevent the wing from collapsing in the air. The aileron has been removed.

killed. Embry escaped and, after many adventures – described in his book *Wingless Victory* – returned to duty almost ten weeks later. No 107 Squadron lost another aircraft on that raid, when Sgt Warman and his crew were killed (see Appendix 2). A further 36 Blenheims attacked German positions around Dunkirk that day.

Fighter Command Blenheims were sent to patrol the Pas de Calais area of the Channel by day and night, but met little enemy activity. On the night of 18/19 May a Blenheim Mk I-F of 604 Squadron flown by F/O A. Hunter claimed a Heinkel He.111 destroyed off the coast at Dunkirk, and the following day 604 lost an aircraft on a patrol in the same area, but claimed another enemy aircraft damaged on the 22nd. 235 Squadron of Coastal Command, actively engaged on similar duties from 29 May, soon lost half a dozen Mk IV-Fs (see Appendix 4).

All efforts in the last days of that momentous May were now concentrated on the shrinking Allied defensive perimeter around Dunkirk. Relays of Fighter Command Hurricanes and Spitfires tried, with some success, to keep the Luftwaffe from attacking the evacuation of the Allied troops. Although they were unable to provide continuous cover from their UK bases, they certainly succeeded in thwarting the declared aim of the German Air Force to 'finish off' the trapped forces and prevent their evacuation – losses were heavy on both sides. The RAF bombers had to rely on attacking targets well behind the German forward positions to avoid hitting the defenders. As the beleaguered soldiers did not witness these almost continuous attacks, the RAF became very unpopular. The miraculous evacuation of almost 340,000 troops from Dunkirk at least allowed the Allies to rebuild their armies even if they had left their tanks, transport, artillery, heavy equipment, stocks of fuel and ammunition, and many other valuable stores behind. Smoke from the burning oil tanks at Dunkirk drifted as far as Ipswich. Despite four days of bad weather from 28 May (for example, only 44 of 68 Blenheims were able to bomb on the 30th), 2 Group continued at maximum effort from the 27th to the 31st, carrying out 308 sorties in those five days, including 93 on the 31st (the highest figure to date), and bringing the total to 480 in only nine days – an impressive number of raids when the average daily availability of serviceable Blenheims in that period was only 69 aircraft. Considering the number of sorties mounted, the losses were relatively low at only seven aircraft (see Appendix 2). Operations around Dunkirk continued until the evacuation ended on 3 June, a further 98 sorties being flown and more losses inflicted; 107 Squadron, led by Gareth Clayton, suffered badly on the 2nd (see Appendix 2).

Since the German offensive had opened 24 days earlier, Blenheims of the UK-based 2 Group had been in action every single day (bar the three days when bad weather made operations impossible) and on one night. They had mounted 956 sorties and had lost 60 aircraft – effectively five squadrons of the nine that were operational during most of this period. The six Blenheim squadrons based in France prior to evacuation had suffered even more severely, losing 78 aircraft on operations and destroyed on the ground either by German action or by Allied airmen as they withdrew. Sadly, these sacrifices had failed to halt the German advance, although they did delay it slightly. On 4 June, immediately after the evacuation from Dunkirk, the Deputy Chief of the Air Staff, Sholto Douglas, summed up the situation succinctly when writing to Charles Portal, the AOC of Bomber Command: '...the strenuous and gallant efforts of your Squadrons against objectives in collaboration with the land battle since 10 May have not had the results commensurate with the effort expended.'

In an attempt to rectify these shortcomings, Operational Requirements Nos 83 and 84 had been issued in May calling for improved aircraft. The former was to make the Blenheim more suitable for ground-attack use, which led to Specification B.6/40 and the Blenheim Mk V (as will be described later), while the latter was for a high-speed bomber, which led to B.7/40 and the proposed successors to the Blenheim – derivatives of the Bristol Type 156 Beaufighter, and Types 161 and 162 Beaumont, together with the Type 163 Buckingham (also to be described later). In the meantime the squadrons would have to continue to face the enemy with their existing Blenheims.

Two atmospheric views of 40 Squadron Blenheims about to leave for a raid to France in June, some with the virtually useless under-nose rear-defence gun-mounting.

Opposite: Two further photographs taken on the same Press Day, carefully composed by Fox.

France surrenders

The Wehrmacht paused for only three days before attacking the Allies' improvised 'Weygand Line' along the Somme and Aisne rivers on 5 June – the BEF still had 140,000 troops in that part of France to the south and west of the German forces that had reached the coast and forced the evacuation from Dunkirk. The Panzers advanced rapidly. Rouen fell on the 9th, cutting off the Allied Armies north of the Seine. The 51st Highland Division was surrounded at St Valery, and fought bravely but had to surrender on the 12th, while Le Havre held out one more day. The Germans entered Paris on the 14th. Once more the Blenheim squadrons did their best to halt the tide, mounting no fewer than 487 sorties between the 5th and the 14th, and suffering further heavy losses (see Appendix 3).

Churchill tried hard to encourage the increasingly discouraged French, and to persuade them to make greater efforts to resist the Germans. On the evening of 12 June he sent a message to Premier Reynaud and General Weygand to stiffen their resolve, promising maximum support:

> 'The RAF will make a further increased effort to render assistance to your valiant hard-pressed forces from 13 June onwards. During the daylight hours of the 13th, all available Blenheims, to the number of 60, will be ready to attack targets indicated by General Georges through Air Marshal Barratt. Ten Squadrons of fighters will also work from England within the limits of their range. For the night of 13/14 June 182 Heavy Bombers will be available to attack targets as desired by General Georges. In addition to the above support from this country, you will of course have the 6 bomber and 5 fighter Squadrons of the AASF under the orders of Air Marshal Barratt. Special instructions have been issued to ensure that these Squadrons are kept to full strength in aircraft, pilots and crews.'

The latter was a pious hope as the depleted AASF Squadrons were seriously deficient in all of these essentials and had been forced to evacuate again to airfields further south; the bombers were the remnants of the Battles that were pressed again into desperate operations, suffering further depredations, as all the Blenheim squadrons had been sent back to England. The 60 Blenheims he promised were the maximum that the whole of 2 Group could muster. Their hopeless task was made even more difficult by a worsening of the weather and the longer ranges

W/Cdr Theo 'Joe' Hunt of 82 Squadron flew P6925 back on 11 June 1940 with its nose and cockpit badly damaged by 109s; he was awarded the DFC and his Observer, Sgt J. Barham, the DFM.

involved as the Germans advanced further to the south-west, restricting the Blenheims to one sortie a day and making the necessary fighter escorts much harder to arrange. So desperate was the need for information on where the front line really was that a joint 53/59 Squadron Detachment was sent back to the battle area to carry out reconnaissance sorties – they were told to fly in different directions until they were fired at! 53 Squadron sent six aircraft from Gatwick, three to Nantes and three to Jersey, and 59 Squadron sent six aircraft from Odiham back to Le Mans; they moved to Caen, then Rennes, losing one aircraft on the 16th (see Appendix 3), finally leaving France on the 17th and 18th – by which time the situation had degenerated into complete chaos.

The French Government had evacuated to Tours on 10 June and to Bordeaux on the 14th; on the 16th it appointed 84-year-old Marshall Philippe Petain, the hero of Verdun in 1916, as Head of Government. He immediately commenced negotiating armistice terms, signing them on 22 June in the forest at Compeigne in the same railway coach that had been used when the French had imposed their harsh terms upon the Germans in 1918. The major part of inland France and the Riviera coast, plus the widespread French overseas territories, would remain unoccupied and be controlled by a French Government from Vichy; the provinces of Alsace and Lorraine would revert to Germany. Italy had attacked France on 20 June and was rewarded by the Germans with the provinces of Savoy and Nice. The defeat and humiliation of France was complete – Great Britain stood alone. If the Germans were to gain control of the powerful French fleets the balance of naval power would be changed irrevocably against the British. This was a worry that greatly exercised Winston Churchill and the British Chiefs of Staff, so they sought to prevent it. Indeed, they were right to be worried for an unpublished clause in the armistice agreement stated: 'The Axis Powers and France have an identical interest in seeing that the defeat of England is accomplished as soon as possible. Consequently the French Government will support, within the limits of its ability, the measures which the Axis Powers may take to this end.'

Apart from the 338,000 Allied troops (two-thirds of them British) evacuated from Dunkirk, a further 344,000 were brought out from the Normandy and Biscay ports. However, nearly 80 per cent of the many French among the 680,000 chose to return to France and serve the Vichy Government rather than join the Free French Forces formed by Charles de Gaulle in London at the instigation of Churchill. The loyalties of the French Empire were also divided, with some countries and provinces under French control, such as Syria, Lebanon, Algeria, Morocco, Tunisia and Corsica, supporting the Vichy Government. If you are wondering about the relevance of this to the story of the Blenheim, these countries were all invaded later by the Allies, and Blenheims were to be involved in these sadly necessary campaigns.

A little-known attempt on 18 June to send 12 Blenheims, with 12 Hurricanes, across France to the Middle East as reinforcements became an utter failure: only three Blenheims arrived. Seven of them crashed in France and two returned to the UK (six of the Hurricanes were also lost en route). Only the four Blenheims of the leaders of each of the four flights of three (also the leading three Hurricanes) had a Navigator on board; the large, loose formation of aircraft ran into a severe storm in the Auvergne Mountains and became separated – disaster followed, and 18 Blenheim crewmen were killed. (See Appendix 5, Page 233.)

By the end of the Battle for France no fewer than 1,000 RAF aircraft had been lost on operations in the six disastrous weeks since the launch of the German *Blitzkrieg*, and of these losses 200 were Blenheims, 97 by Bomber Command, 41 by the Air Component, 37 by the AASF, 14 by Coastal Command and 11 by Fighter Command. The loss of such a large number of much-needed aircraft was bad enough, but the loss of so many pilots and crews – mainly fully trained pre-war professional officers, NCOs and airmen – was a tragedy that struck at the heart of the Royal Air Force. These operational casualties were hard to bear, but their debilitating effect was exacerbated by the continuing additional attrition from non-operational losses, mainly from accidents, both in the squadrons and in the training units (see Appendix 5). The suffering of the Blenheim crews would continue without respite.

Appendix I

Pre-Dunkirk Blenheim operational losses, 18-26 May 1940

Aircraft are all Mk IVs.

18-05-1940   L8853 XV Squadron: took off from Wyton 1230, Failed To Return (FTR); crash-landed at Preux-de-Bois; S/Ldr H. Lawrence (Pilot) and Sgt R. Hopkins (Obs) were Killed in Action (KIA), LAC E. Thomas (WOp/Ag) captured and became a PoW.

18-05-1940   L8852 XV Squadron: took off from Wyton 1230 for le Cateau, FTR; shot down into Foret de Mormal; F/O F. Dawson-Jones, Sgt W. Baxter, LAC C. Watts, KIA.

18-05-1940   P6917 XV Squadron: FTR; shot down by flak near le Cateau; F/Lt P. Chapman, Sgt C. Colbourn, LAC E. Fagg, KIA.

18-05-1940   L9030 XV Squadron: took off from Wyton at 1230 for le Cateau, and struggled back to base via Poix; badly damaged aircraft written off; P/O C. Robinson, Sgt S. Redhead, LAC Horton uninjured.

18-05-1940   P6913 XV Squadron: damaged by flak near le Cateau, landed at Poix, declared a write-off, but F/O L. Trent returned at dusk to Martlesham Heath; Trent, Sgt W. Stephens, and Cpl J. Sutcliffe uninjured and aircraft repaired. (Len Trent later awarded VC for leading daylight attack by 2 Group Venturas.)

18-05-1940   L4861 53 Squadron: took off from Poix at 0535, FTR; crash-landed in Belgium; P/O P. Royle (Pilot) and wounded Sgt E. Woods (Obs) captured, AC A. Malkin (WOp/Ag) escaped and returned to squadron later.

18-05-1940   L4841 53 Squadron: FTR; missing from recce mission, shot down near Frevent, Pas-de-Calais; P/O L. Huggett, Sgt A. Gothard, and AC1 W. Christie KIA.

18-05-1940   L9330 53 Squadron: damaged by light AA fire on recce, believed not repaired and abandoned in France on evacuation; Pilot P/O Truscott.

18-05-1940   R3702 59 Squadron: took off from Poix, FTR; crash-landed in France; P/O R. Durie (Pilot) and Sgt R. Burns (Obs) KIA, AC1 W. Murdoch (WOp/Ag) escaped, aircraft written off 21-5-1940.

18-05-1940   L9182, L9248 and P6932 57 Squadron: all recorded as FTR from sorties to le Cateau, but no further details available. Believed that they were so damaged on raid that they were abandoned or destroyed at Poix. Unfortunately, 57 Squadron's records for May 1940 were lost in evacuation.

18-05-1940   L8735 21 Squadron: also FTR from sortie to France, possibly damaged, force-landed, and later abandoned there.

19-05-1940   L4856 59 Squadron: took off from Merville at 1630 for recce, FTR; force-landed near Crecy at dusk, low in fuel, aircraft destroyed next day by bombing; P/O C. Wylie, Sgt Liddiard, and AC Houlihan returned to UK via Cherbourg, the latter injured in head while taking cover from attack.

19-05-1940   L9191 18 Squadron: crashed on take-off from Crecy at dusk, aircraft destroyed; F/Lt R. Wheldon, Sgt A. Craig, and Sgt G. Hawkins DFM unhurt, but Craig and Hawkins killed two days later.

20-05-1940   L9186 and L9187, 18 Squadron: both recorded as missing on sortie to Le Cateau, but believed shot down 17-05-1940 and written off 20-05-1940 (see Appendix 4, Chapter 12).

21-05-1940   R3706 XV Squadron: took off at 1400, FTR; shot down by flak near Boulogne, from where slightly injured crew, F/Lt P. Webster, Sgt R. Stone, and LAC R. Hunter returned safely.

21-05-1940   L9185 18 Squadron: FTR from bombing sortie to Boulogne, shot down by RAF Spitfires near there and crash-landed; P/O V. Rees, Sgt N. Pusey, and LAC K. Murray uninjured.

21-05-1940   L9325 18 Squadron: FTR on first recce from Watton, shot down by Hurricane near Arras; P/O C. Light, Sgt A. Craig, and Sgt G. Hawkins DFM KIA and commemorated on Runnymede Memorial.

22-05-1940   P4828 82 Squadron: FTR from bombing sortie to Hesdin, shot down near Samer, Pas-de-Calais; Sgt J. Hartfield, Sgt F. Phillipson, and AC2 E. Elliot KIA and buried at Neufchatel-Hardelot.

22-05-1940   P4925 107 Squadron: FTR from bombing sortie to Boulogne, damaged by flak, one engine cut out, then other, ditched in Channel off English coast; P/O J. Miller (Pilot) and Sgt R. Saunders (Obs) injured, LAC W. Stockel (WOp/Ag) uninjured, all rescued by passing patrol boat some 90 minutes later.

22-05-1940   L8761 110 Squadron: FTR from bombing sortie to Henschel, shot down by flak near Abbeville; S/Ldr G. Hall, Sgt K. Quarrington, and LAC C. Torrance KIA and buried in Boulogne.

22-05-1940   N6207 110 Squadron: badly damaged by flak on bombing sortie to Henschel, crash-landed back at Wattisham; crew F/O G. Lings, Sgt Martin, and AC1 Bingham uninjured.

22-05-1940   L9266 59 Squadron: FTR from bombing sortie to Boulogne, shot down by RAF Spitfires near Fricourt and crash-landed; F/O F. Bird, Sgt C. Brinn, and AC2 G. Coles KIA.

22-05-1940   L9184 57 Squadron: FTR from recce sortie from Hawkinge to Arras, shot down near Harcourt; P/O R. Saunders, Sgt S. Simmons, and AC1 G. Pirie KIA.

22-05-1940   R3596 53 Squadron: took off from Andover, damaged by flak on recce to Arras and crash-landed at Hawkinge; P/O Tiptree, Sgt Williamson, and LAC Jeffreys only slightly injured, aircraft damaged beyond repair (DBR).

23-05-1940   L9403 XV Squadron: FTR from bombing sortie to Arras, shot down near Bapaume; P/O J. Masters, F/Sgt E. Tucker, and LAC C. Thompson KIA.

23-05-1940   L8834 40 Squadron: FTR from bombing sortie to Arras, shot down near Albert; F/O R. Jacoby (Pilot) injured and captured, Sgt P. Burrell (Obs) and LAC P. Whittle (WOp/Ag) KIA, buried in Miraurant Cemetery.

23-05-1940   P4909 40 Squadron: FTR from bombing sortie to Arras, shot down by flak near Bethune; W/Cdr J. Llewellyn (Pilot) and P/O W. Edwards (Obs) KIA, Sgt J. Beattie (WOp/Ag) returned. (W/Cdr Llewellyn was CO of 40 Squadron. P/O William Edwards was first of three Edwards brothers killed in Blenheims: Leslie, DFM, Observer with 60 Squadron, killed in Burma 23-6-1942, and James, 20-year-old Sgt WOp/Ag, crashed in Scotland 6-4-1943.)

23-05-1940   R3691 53 Squadron: FTR from reconnaissance sortie to Boulogne area, shot down near there; F/O S. Pepys, Sgt A. Haygreen, and AC2 H. Spear captured and became PoWs.

23-05-1940   L9243 57 Squadron: chased on recce sortie to Amiens by Me.110s (one claimed); P/O W. Hutchings (Pilot) wounded in arm and crash-landed at Lympne, Sgt J. Alexander and LAC D. Goffe unhurt.

23-05-1940   R3598 18 Squadron: FTR from reconnaissance sortie to Channel ports, shot down near Abbeville; P/O D. Dickens (Pilot) captured, Sgt F. Miller DFM (Obs) and Cpl B. Harding (WOp/Ag) KIA.

24-05-1940   R3614 XV Squadron: after bombing sortie to Aa Canal port engine cut on approach to Alconbury and aircraft spun in; F/O D. Henderson, Sgt A. Holmes, and LAC R. Austin KIA. (See the picture below).

24-05-1940   L4859 59 Squadron: FTR from reconnaissance sortie from Rouen-Boos, damaged by Messerschmitt and crash-landed near Etrapagny; P/O Carruthers became PoW, his crew, Sgt Shelton and AC Salmon, injured, returned to UK.

25-05-1940   P6913 XV Squadron: FTR from bombing sortie to Calais area, shot down near St Inglevert; P/O D. Harriman, Sgt P. Bloomer, and P/O J. Gordon KIA.

25-05-1940   L8734 21 Squadron: FTR from bombing sortie to Lys, shot down near Mooresele; Sgt H. Rowson (Pilot) captured, Sgt A. Keats (Obs) and LAC D. Cleaver (WOp/Ag) KIA.

25-05-1940   P4920 40 Squadron: FTR from bombing sortie to Rety, shot down near target; Sgt S. Tonks (Pilot) captured, Sgt J. Alexander (Obs) and LAC D. Goffe (WOp/Ag) KIA, buried in Rety Cemetery.

26-05-1940   R3613 59 Squadron: FTR from reconnaissance sortie, shot down near Dussen, Belgium; P/O R. Shaw, Sgt G. Schwind, and AC2 A. Brogan (aged 18) KIA (ORB gives L8853).

26-05-1940   L8863 53 Squadron: FTR from recce sortie from Rouen-Boos, shot down near Seninghem, France; P/O G. Bailey, Sgt W. Evans, and AC1 A. Gillmore KIA.

R3614 of XV Squadron was damaged by flak in raid on the Aa Canal on 24 May 1940, they limped back but the port engine cut on final approach to Alconbury and it spun-in killing the crew.

Appendix 2

Bomber Command and AASF Blenheim losses during the evacuation from Dunkirk, 27 May to 2 June 1940

Aircraft are all Mk IVs.

27-05-1940   L9391 107 Squadron: FTR from bombing sortie to St Omer, shot down near target; W/Cdr B. Embry (Pilot) and P/O T. Whiting (Obs) baled out and captured, Cpl G. Lang (WOp/Ag) KIA. Basil Embry, CO of 107, escaped and rejoined squadron after 68 days.

27-05-1940   N6192 107 Squadron: FTR from bombing sortie to St Omer, shot down by Me.109s; Sgt H. Warman, Sgt W. Paish, and LAC J. Mahoney KIA and commemorated on Runnymede Memorial.

27-05-1940   R3774 110 Squadron: reported as FTR from sortie to St Omer; no further details available.

27-05-1940   L8736 110 Squadron: reported as FTR from reconnaissance sortie; no further details available.

27-05-1940   R3735 53 Squadron: FTR from reconnaissance sortie to St Omer, shot down near there; P/O P. Villiers-Tuthill, Sgt A. Payne, and AC D. Mearns KIA (ORB gives serial number as L8735).

27-05-1940   R3703 53 Squadron: FTR from reconnaissance sortie, badly damaged by Me.109 over France, crew baled out north of Dover; P/O K. Aldridge (Pilot) injured, Sgt McCrae (Obs) uninjured, and AC R. Trafford (WOp/Ag) injured.

27-05-1940   R3700 53 Squadron: became lost on recce sortie and landed at Soissons; P/O Bailey and crew safe, aircraft destroyed by enemy bombing.

28-05-1940   R3733 53 Squadron: badly damaged by Me.109s on reconnaissance sortie; P/O Robinson, Sgt Whitehill, and AC Couchen all wounded but managed to return to base, aircraft repaired.

28-05-1940   L8744 21 Squadron: FTR from attacking enemy positions near St Omer, believed shot down by flak; Sgt Bailes (Pilot) and Sgt A. Twamley (Obs) KIA, AC1 S. Thompson (WOp/Ag) survived and returned.

28-05-1940   R3664 59 Squadron: FTR from reconnaissance sortie, shot down by flak near Dunkirk, crew baled out; P/O J. Peters (Pilot) safe and returned, Sgt T. McDonagh (Obs) and Sgt J. Finlayson (WOp/Ag) KIA.

29-05-1940   P6886 21 Squadron: badly damaged by Me.109s near Dixemude, crash-landed back at Watton; P/O L. Blackensee, Sgt A. Williams and AC1 J. Guest uninjured. WOp/Ag claimed his second 109E as destroyed and was awarded DFM.

02-06-1940   N6190 107 Squadron: damaged by flak near target on bombing sortie to Gravelines, crash-landed back at Wattisham; crew F/O J. Stephens, Sgt W. Barrett, and LAC E. White uninjured, aircraft written off.

02-06-1940   R3683 107 Squadron: damaged by flak on same bombing sortie, crash-landed and overturned at base; Sgt R. Gunning DFM, Sgt W. Brinn DFM, and LAC J. Bartley unhurt, aircraft DBR. (See the picture below)

02-06-1940   P4919 107 Squadron: damaged by flak near target on same bombing sortie, crash-landed back at base; F/Sgt H. Ratcliffe, Sgt P. Crowley, and LAC D. Harrison uninjured, aircraft written off.

02-06-1940   L9476 53 Squadron: took off from Hawkinge, FTR; hit by light flak near Dunkirk and crash-landed on Goodwin Sands; F/Lt A. Brown, Sgt Brooks, and AC Knowles rescued by HMS Shipmates.

R3683 of 107 Squadron was hit by flak when bombing Gravelines 2 June 1940, and overturned when crash-landing at Wattisham, the crew were lucky not to be injured, Sgt 'Dick' Gunning and Sgt 'Bill' Brinn, both DFM holders, stand by their wrecked Blenheim.

Many Blenheims were abandoned on their airfields during the fall of France, such as L9191 of 18 Squadron at Crecy (top) and two 114 Squadron aircraft at Conde-Vraux.

Appendix 3

Other Blenheim losses during the fall of France, 3-22 June 1940

Aircraft are all Mk IVs apart from three Mk I-Fs on the night of 18/19 June.

04-06-1940 R3697 59 Squadron: wing-tip hit ground on take-off for operations at Eastchurch and crashed; P/O S. Ashton, Sgt W. Wilson, and Sgt R. Wilson KIA.

05-06-1940 N6191 107 Squadron: damaged on raid, force-landed at Hawkinge; Sgt J. Waterhouse (WOp/Ag) injured and taken to hospital, P/O K. Taute (Pilot) slightly wounded, Sgt L. Fearnley (Obs) uninjured, aircraft repaired.

05-06-1940 L8751 110 Squadron: crashed on squadron take-off from Wattisham for battle area; F/Lt H. Cooper, Sgt Robertson, and Sgt Simpson slightly hurt, aircraft repaired.

06-06-1940 L8827 40 Squadron: took off from Wyton for St Valery, FTR; shot down near target; S/Ldr B. Paddon (Pilot), crew Sgt V. Salvage (Obs) and Sgt T. Foreman (WOp/Ag) captured and became PoWs. Brian Paddon escaped back to UK in August 1942 and awarded DSO.

06-06-1940 L9410 40 Squadron: took off from Wyton for St Valery, FTR; lost without trace; P/O B. James, Sgt J. Garcka, and Sgt W. Thurby KIA and commemorated on Runnymede Memorial.

06-06-1940 P4927 40 Squadron: took off from Wyton on same raid, FTR; shot down near target; Sgt D. Rice, Sgt R. Moffatt, and Sgt D. Peters captured and became PoWs.

06-06-1940 P4917 40 Squadron: FTR from same raid, crash-landed in Allied territory, crew P/O P. Wakeford (Pilot) and Sgt A. Wallace (Obs) injured and treated in UK hospitals, Sgt B. Baker (WOp/Ag) captured in French hospital and became PoW, but escaped via Brittany and returned to UK.

06-06-1940 R3692 40 Squadron: FTR from same raid, crash-landed in battle area; P/O V. Engstrom (Pilot) evaded and treated in UK hospital, Sgt M. Chouler (Obs) and Sgt D. Liddle (WOp/Ag) captured and became PoWs.

06-06-1940 R3761 21 Squadron: damaged by flak; Sgt Parker (Pilot) wounded but belly-landed back at base, Sgt Waters and Sgt Burt unhurt, aircraft repaired.

06-06-1940 R3602 53 Squadron: damaged by Me.109 on recce from Rouen-Boos; P/O Bethel and Sgt F. Randall uninjured, Sgt H. Wilson (WOp/Ag) injured and died later, aircraft DBR.

07-06-1940 R3686 107 Squadron: FTR; hit by flak on raid south of Dieppe, crash-landed; crew F/O H. Pleasance, Sgt G. Wilson, and Sgt P. Adams evaded capture, wounded Pilot treated in UK hospital.

07-06-1940 P6915 82 Squadron: badly damaged on recce by Me.109s; Sgt A. Merritt, F/Sgt Roberston, and Cpl Harris struggled back to Wattisham, aircraft DBR. (Sgt Merritt shot down and captured three days later.)

08-06-1940 R3746 XV Squadron: FTR from raid to Poix, shot down in battle area; S/Ldr W. Burke, P/O R. Moffatt, and Sgt G. Thompson KIA.

08-06-1940 L9023 21 Squadron: FTR from raid to Horroy area, shot down in battle area; P/O H. Dunford-Wood, Sgt E. Jones, and Sgt D. MacLagen KIA.

08-06-1940 R3618 82 Squadron: FTR from same raid, crash-landed in battle area; P/O R. McKenzie (Pilot) and Sgt Crozier (WOp/Ag) captured, Sgt J. Cooper (Obs) KIA.

08-06-1940 R3709 82 Squadron: FTR from raid to Abbeville, shot down in battle area; P/O G. Robertson (Pilot) and Sgt J. Hounston (Obs) captured, Sgt B. Burt (WOp/Ag) KIA.

08-06-1940 R3754 82 Squadron: FTR from raid to Abbeville, shot down in battle area; P/O Percival (Pilot) and Sgt Dodrill (Obs) evaded capture, Sgt J. Byatt (WOp/Ag) KIA.

08-06-1940 R3670 110 Squadron: FTR from raid to Amiens, shot down by flak in battle area; crew P/O P. Arderne, Sgt G. Robson, and Cpl J. Tippett evaded capture and returned to Wattisham five days later.

09-06-1940 R3739 107 Squadron: FTR from raid to Boray, shot down in battle area; F/O C. Buckley (Pilot) and Sgt E. Cotton (WOp/Ag) captured, P/O C. Campbell (Obs) KIA.

09-06-1940 L9323 107 Squadron: FTR on same raid, shot down leaving battle area; F/O C. Bomford (Pilot) and Sgt R. Bowman (Obs) KIA, P/O F. Frayn (WOp/Ag) injured.

09-06-1940 R3685 107 Squadron: FTR from same raid, shot down in battle area; crew P/O R. Bennett, Sgt A. Langford, and Sgt H. Denison evaded capture and returned to duty.

11-06-1940 N3588 XV Squadron: FTR; damaged on raid to battle area and crash-landed near Cherbourg; crew P/O Myland, Sgt Perks, and Sgt Petrie returned later, aircraft recovered and repaired.

11-06-1940 L8851 XV Squadron: FTR from same raid, collided with formation leader L9024 in cloud, losing port wing; crew P/O R. Werner, Sgt M. Jones, and Sgt R. Spencer KIA.

11-06-1940	L9024 XV Squadron: FTR from same raid, collided with L8851 above, starboard engine detached; F/O R. Clarke (Pilot) ordered crew to bale out, then lost control and, unable to follow, was KIA, Sgt T. Maloney (Obs) and Sgt B. Piff (WOp/Ag) parachuted to safety.
11-06-1940	L8746 21 Squadron: FTR from raid to La Mare, shot down near St Aubin; F/Lt D. MacDonald (Pilot) captured, Sgt G. Lewis (Obs) and Sgt A. Murray (WOp/Ag) KIA.
11-06-1940	R3674 21 Squadron: FTR from same raid, shot down near Boulleville; Sgt J. Outhwaite, Sgt J. Waters, and Sgt J. Sculfer KIA.
11-06-1940	L8745 21 Squadron: badly damaged on same raid, jettisoned bombs and crash-landed at base; crew F/O S. Sigurdson, Sgt Bailey, and Sgt Chrisholm uninjured, aircraft repaired.
11-06-1940	L8743 21 Squadron: FTR from same raid, shot down by flak; P/O R. Rogers KIA, Sgt H. Huckins and Sgt W. Bradshaw evaded and returned later.
11-06-1940	R3631 59 Squadron: FTR from reconnaissance, forced down by French Ms.406s near Marne; P/O A. Hopkin (Pilot) believed to be flying solo, returned to UK, aircraft recovered.
11-06-1940	L8749 110 Squadron: FTR from raid to Rouen, shot down in target area; no further details.
12-06-1940	R3893 40 Squadron: FTR from raid to St Valery, shot down by flak at Eletot; Sgt C. Bartlam (Pilot) and Sgt E. Rodgers (WOp/Ag) captured, Sgt D. Dorris (Obs) KIA.
12-06-1940	R3810 107 Squadron: FTR; shot down in flames in target area near Rouen; P/O B. Reid, Sgt R. Lawrence, and Sgt C. Bartlett KIA.
12-06-1940	R3747 XV Squadron: FTR from sortie to Le Bourget, shot down at Malleville; P/O A. Takideli, Sgt F. Gunning, and Sgt D. Peuleve KIA.
13-06-1940	R3676 21 Squadron: FTR from attacking Panzers, shot down in Foret-de-Gault battle area; crew P/O L. Blanckensee, Sgt A. Williams, and Sgt J. Guest DFM KIA.
13-06-1940	L9269 21 Squadron: FTR on same raid, shot down in battle area; crew F/Lt L. Petley, Sgt Hart, and Sgt Norris evaded capture and returned to duty later.
13-06-1940	P6910 82 Squadron: FTR from same raid, shot down in battle area; F/Lt J. Breese (Pilot) and Sgt H. Williams (Obs) captured, Sgt K. Harris DFM (WOp/Ag) KIA.
13-06-1940	P6925 82 Squadron: FTR from same raid, shot down in battle area; crew P/O R. Eyton-Williams, Sgt D. Carbutt, and Sgt A. Beeby evaded capture and returned.
13-06-1940	L8829 82 Squadron: FTR from same raid, shot down into sea on return from Foret-de-Gault battle area; Sgt A. Merritt, Sgt N. Carlile, and Sgt L. Nineham (aged 18) KIA.
13-06-1940	R3616 107 Squadron: FTR from raid to bridges at Vernon, shot down by Me.110 in battle area; P/O Stidstson, Sgt F. Higgins, and Sgt J. Browning KIA.
14-06-1940	N3592 40 Squadron: FTR; shot down in battle area at Fresney; S/Ldr G. Gleed, Sgt R. Burge, and Sgt A. Sammells KIA, buried in Fresney Churchyard.
14-06-1940	R3693 40 Squadron: FTR from same raid, shot down in battle area; P/O Lewis (Pilot) and Sgt Currie (Obs) evaded capture, Sgt Johnson (WOp/Ag) KIA.
14-06-1940	R3742 21 Squadron: FTR; shot down near Merville by Me.109s; P/O W. Saunders (Pilot) KIA, crew Sgt W. Eden (Obs) and Sgt C. Webb (WOp/Ag) became PoWs.
16-06-1940	R3817 59 Squadron: shot down on recce of Le Mans/Rennes; P/O C. Wylie (NZ, aged 20), Sgt W. Harris, and AC1 A. Thomas KIA, buried in Dreux Communal Cemetery.
19-06-1940	R3818 59 Squadron: FTR from recce, shot down in battle area; P/O B. Everton-Jones, Sgt J. Taplin, and AC F. Thake captured and became PoWs, Obs wounded.

Further Blenheims recorded as destroyed or abandoned on the ground in France, and not shown in the above lists, include:

114 Squadron: L8857, L8859, L9177, L9178, L9398, N6148, N6149, N6153, N6154, N6159, N6161, N6162, N6232, P6885, P6920(?), P6923

53 Squadron: L9460, L9471, R3602, R3633

57 Squadron: R3595

139 Squadron: L8760, L9477, N6224, N6227

107 Squadron: P4857, P4864

59 Squadron: L4857, L4859, N6164, N6170, R3696

18 Squadron: L9340

Not allocated to a squadron: N3539, P4901

Appendix 4

Coastal Command Blenheim losses, 18 May to 22 June 1940

Aircraft are all Mk IV-Fs.

18-05-1940   L9395 235 Squadron: FTR from sortie off Ostend, believed shot down by Hurricanes; P/O C. Robinson, Sgt D. Molseley, and LAC A. Waddington KIA, commemorated on Runnymede Memorial.

20-05-1940   L9256 235 Squadron: engine cut on take-off from Bircham Newton, swung, crashed into Anson N9897, killing AC1 L. Curry; Sgt Bessey, Sgt Westcott, and LAC A. Smith escaped uninjured, aircraft destroyed by fire.

24-05-1940   L9259 235 Squadron: FTR to Bircham Newton after escorting Hudsons off Belgian Coast, shot down by Me.109E; crew P/O M. Ryan and Sgt W. Martin KIA and buried at Schiermonikoog, LAC A. Smith commemorated on Runnymede Memorial.

26-05-1940   P6956 235 Squadron: FTR from operational sortie, spun into ground out of cloud at Court Farm, near Docking, Norfolk; P/O C. Warde (Pilot) baled out but crew P/O A. Murphy and LAC E. Armstrong (aged 18) KIA.

28-05-1940   L9260 235 Squadron: FTR; badly damaged by Me.109s near Dunkirk and ditched off English coast; crew P/O J. Cronan, Sgt A. Lancaster, and LAC P. Lloyd rescued from dinghy.

29-05-1940   L9397 235 Squadron: FTR to Detling, shot down in flames into sea off French coast; P/O A. Booth, Sgt D. Elliott, and LAC E. Scott KIA, commemorated on Runnymede Memorial.

29-05-1940   L9401 235 Squadron: FTR to Detling, shot down by Me.109s; F/Lt G. Manwaring, Sgt I. MacPhail, and AC1 D. Murphy KIA, F/Lt Manwaring and AC1 Murphy buried in Sage War Cemetery, Sgt MacPhail at St Lawrence, Ramsgate, Kent.

29-05-1940   P6909 235 Squadron: FTR; hit tree on take-off at Detling; F/Lt R. Cross (Pilot) and Sgt A. Slocombe (Obs) KIA, LAC North (WOp/Ag) died in hospital later.

01-06-1940   L9481 254 Squadron: FTR when detached to Manston, shot down by Me.109s when attacking Ju.87s over Goodwin Sands; F/O J. Baird and Sgt R. Roskrow KIA, P/O G. Spiers (Obs) survived.

01-06-1940   R3630 254 Squadron: FTR when detached to Manston, shot down by Me.109s when attacking Ju.87s over Goodwin Sands; Sgt R. Bate, Sgt J. Love, and LAC W. Harrison KIA, commemorated at Runnymede.

20-06-1940   N3534 235 Squadron: crashed; no further details available.

Appendix 5

Non-operational Blenheim losses during the campaign in France, 10 May to 22 June 1940

10-05-1940   L4837 2 SAC Mk IV: u/c damaged on take-off at Andover, belly-landed and DBR; Pilot P/O J. Mahony and crew uninjured.

10-05-1940   L4889 17 OTU Mk IV: dived into ground on night approach to Upwood, believed to have stalled; Pilot P/O G. McFarland (NZ solo pilot, aged 20, on his first night solo) killed, buried at Bury.

10-05-1940   L8778 110 Squadron Mk IV: struck tree taxiing to dispersal by ground crew LAC J. Humphries in the absence of a qualified pilot; DBR.

10-05-1940   L8795 13OTU Mk IV: engine cut and hit tree in attempted forced-landing at Launton airfield, near Bicester; Sgt K. Hobday (solo pilot) uninjured.

16-05-1940   L9031 2 SAC Mk IV: flew into high ground in fog near Moretonhampstead, Devon; P/O M. Patton-Bethune (Pilot), Sgt K. Stokes, LAC H. Morton, and AC2 C. Crowcroft killed.

17-05-1940   P4830 Special Duties Flight Mk IV: struck boundary on take-off at Christchurch; F/Lt G. Holland uninjured, aircraft damaged Cat 4.

20-05-1940   L9455 248 Squadron Mk IV-F: collided with P4837 (below) during practice attack on 42 Squadron Beaufort L4501, but RTB with badly damaged port wing.

20-05-1940   P4837 248 Squadron Mk IV-F: collided with L9455 (above), and crashed into sea off Thorney Island; P/O A. Bourgeois and P/O S. Tatar killed, commemorated at Runnymede.

23-05-1940   L4850 53 Squadron Mk IV: Pilot P/O Steuart-Richardson overshot landing in nil wind and hit car at Worcester, killing one occupant and injuring four others.

24-05-1940	L1516 600 Squadron Mk I-F: engine cut, control lost, hit trees and crashed in Fordbridge gravel pit, Sunbury-on-Thames, destroyed by fire; F/O Hannay and LAC Short killed.
24-05-1940	P4907 17 OTU Mk IV: dived into sea on night navigation exercise at Tremadoc Bay, North Wales; F/O I. Mead (Pilot) rescued with severe head injuries, Sgt A. Jackson (Obs) and AC2 R. South (WOp/Ag) drowned.
26-05-1940	L6607 604 Squadron Mk I-F: struck by Gladiator K8001 while taxiing at Manston and DBR.
29-05-1940	L9470 53 Squadron Mk IV: hit by Hurricane L1756 when parked at Hawkinge, damaged but repaired.
30-05-1940	L8717 236 Squadron Mk I: engine cut on approach, hit trees and crash-landed near Colerne; F/Lt R. Power and crew uninjured.
31-05-1940	L1296 2 SAC Mk I: overshot take-off at Andover and hit boundary, DBR; P/O G. Lambert (Instructor) and P/O P. Evans (Trainee) uninjured.
01-06-1940	L6643 236 Squadron Mk I: engine cut, belly-landed at Filton, DBR; F/O W. Moore and crew safe.
05-06-1940	L1232 5 OTU Mk I: engine cut on overshoot from night landing and hit trees near Worcester, destroyed by fire; Sgt T. Armstrong (solo pilot) killed.
06-06-1940	P4912 101 Squadron Mk IV: stalled and spun into ground at Stanton St. John, Oxon, destroyed by fire; P/O Buller, Sgt Macmillan and LAC Davidson killed.
09-06-1940	L1211 13 OTU Mk I: DBR in accident; no further details available.
09-06-1940	R3759 82 Squadron Mk IV: overshot night landing in rain at Hendon, hit pill-box and DBR; P/O F. Hartley-Beavis killed.
12-06-1940	L9172 17 OTU Mk IV: broke-up in cloud and spun into ground near Cym-Avon, Glamorgan; Sgt V. Bain (Pilot) baled out and injured, Sgt W. Wheeler (Obs) and AC2 S. Boulton (WOp/Ag) killed.
12-06-1940	L9258 101 Squadron Mk IV: control lost in cloud and dived into ground 1 mile West of Hillborough, Norfolk; P/O Fletcher and Sgt Matthews killed.
18-06-1940	L9314 4 (Continental) Ferry Pilots Pool: one of seven to crash from 12 dispatched from Tangmere on direct ferry flight to Malta via Marseille, mainly in a severe storm centred on Vienne in Rhone valley; P/O D. Johnston, Sgt K. Walker (aged 18), and LAC W. Higgins killed, buried at Pruniers, near Monde, later re-interred at Mazargues War Cemetery, Marseille.
18-06-1940	L9351: crashed in France, as above entry; crew F/Lt J. Wilkinson-Bell, Sgt J. Malcolm, and Cpl E. Blake killed, buried at Vedreines St Loup, also now re-interred at Marzagues. (Serial number is incorrect, as L9351 was not issued.)
18-06-1940	L9317: crashed in France, as above entry; P/O C. Handley, Sgt P. McGovern, and LAC J. Thomas killed, buried at Charroux, Vienne.
18-06-1940	L9315: crashed in France as above entry; F/O J. McCash, Sgt R. Micklethwaite (aged 19), and AC1 G. Harris killed, buried at Heisse Communal Cemetery, Charante, S of Poitiers.
18-06-1940	L9318: crashed in France but further west; Sgt M. Field, Sgt D. Murrie, and AC1 E. Pickford killed, buried in Crozon Cemetery.
18-06-1940	L9263: engine cut on take-off at Marignane, S France (end of first ferry stage), struck boundary, abandoned there; S/Ldr G. Pryde, Sgt H. Hibbert, and Sgt A. Scott safe, only to crash again in L9334 next day.
19-06-1940	L9334: another of the 12 that left Tangmere, flown by P/O S. Millen, reached Merignane late on 18th, crashed into sea off N African coast near Bizerte; S/Ldr G. Pryde and Sgt A. Scott KIA, Sgt L. Hibbert died of injuries; S/Ldr Pryde is commemorated at Runnymede, Sgt Scott buried in Medjez-el-Bab, and Sgt Hibbert at Ferryville (now Menzel Bourghiba).
19-06-1940	L1154 5 BGS Mk I: engine cut on take-off at Jurby and swung, u/c collapsed, DBR.
19-06-1940	L1471 5 OTU: propellers hit sandbank in River Severn and crash-landed off Woolaston, Glos; P/O C. Cardnell uninjured, aircraft broken up by tide.
20-06-1940	L1334 236 Squadron Mk I: u/c jammed halfway; F/O W. Moore belly-landed in field next to Thorney Island. (See also 1-6-1940 above.)

Chapter 14

The pre-'Battle of Britain' phase

Britain now stood alone, defiant and very much 'backs to the wall', but, perversely, almost relieved to be in that position. A German invasion of these islands was expected at any time.

2 Group Operations Order No 37 stated: 'Now the enemy occupies the western seaboard of Europe the threat of invasion is very real. If it comes it will be by air and sea preceded by attacks on communications, airfields and naval bases.' The Order went on to detail how, in that event, the Group would be immediately reinforced by 16 Blenheims from the OTU at Upwood, and 15 from Wyton, together with 54 Avro Ansons and 48 Hawker Audax biplanes from various other training bases, which showed just how desperate the situation was. Clearly, all the Blenheims available would be pushed right into the very front of the firing line.

It is noteworthy that one of the last Blenheim operations before France surrendered was a raid on 14 June by 18 aircraft, escorted by 24 Hurricanes, on the German-occupied aerodrome at Merville where more than 40 Ju.88s and six Me.109s had been seen. This was a change from the previous tasks of attacking armoured columns, troop transport and concentrations, supply lines, bridges and railways. (Indeed, the last of the many hundreds of direct tactical attacks by Blenheims on German armoured columns was against one near Cherbourg on 18 June by six aircraft of 82 Squadron.) The airfields at Rouen and Amiens were attacked by 30 Blenheims drawn from XV, 18 and 82 Squadrons on 19 June; 47 aircraft bombed Schipol and Rouen airfields again the next day, escorted to the latter by Hurricanes of 145 and 601 Squadrons; and 18 Blenheims from Wattisham returned to attack Merville on the 22nd – the day France fell – while eight bombed Schipol and Eindhoven on the 24th, all being medium-level or high-level raids on enemy-occupied airfields and carried out without loss. This type of target was to become increasingly important over the next few months, and strikes on airfields were mounted in parallel with so-called 'cloud cover' attacks. These were ostensibly mounted to cause further disruption to targets in Germany raided by Allied night-bombers, and to photograph the damage (if any) caused the night before, but were intended mainly to draw Luftwaffe fighters away from the Channel coast opposite England. This latter intention effectively used the Blenheims as bait for the Messerschmitts, with only intermittent cloud cover to afford protection, as no fighter escorts could be provided to Germany.

One of the replacement Blenheims for the 12 lost by 82 Squadron on 17 June. The forceful but popular CO, 'Paddy', Earl of Bandon, saved the Squadron from being disbanded and declared it operational again just three days later.

As early as 4 June, immediately after the evacuation from Dunkirk, Bomber Command HQ had sent a directive from its ivory tower to the AOC of 2 Group, AVM James Robb: 'The general trend of air operations in the last few weeks has caused the enemy to position a very large number of his fighter aircraft over the Western Front, particularly in the Low Countries where he is in an advantageous position to attempt some degree of local superiority.' (This latter phrase surely wins the prize for understatement!) 'It is desirable that we should make every endeavour to cause the enemy to withdraw a proportion of his fighter aircraft from this area with a view to redressing the balance in our favour. Therefore it has been decided that, when suitable weather conditions exist which would give adequate security through cloud cover over areas of operation, Blenheim aircraft should be employed in the general role of delivering sporadic attacks on various objectives. From 5 June AOC 2 Group is to employ, at his discretion and dependence upon favourable weather conditions, up to eight sections (ie 24 aircraft) on this task daily.'

However, the Group Commander neglected to specify the main purpose of these sorties, for his Operational Order No 11 to the Stations under his command stated: 'It is essential that the destructive efforts of our night bombing operations over Germany should be continued throughout daylight by sporadic attacks on the same objectives. The intention is to make attacks only when cloud cover gives adequate security.' He then went on to list the targets in Germany, including 17 oil refineries and five railway marshalling yards, allocating them to the squadrons at Watton, Wattisham and Wyton, each of whom was to send eight sections on a three-day rotation basis – '...they may be dispatched without further reference to this Headquarters. If there is no cloud cover the mission must be abandoned.'

However, due to the priority given to attacking the newly occupied airfields, the first of these 'cloud cover' operations could not be mounted until 21 June, when ten aircraft were sent to targets in Germany, but there was little cloud that day and only two aircraft were able to make attacks, one on Bremen and the other on Hamstede airfield. Twenty-six Blenheims were sent out on the 23rd in patchy cloud – which made navigation difficult – to targets in Soerst, Hamm and Osnabruck, but most of them bombed their secondary targets of airfields in Holland. Three of these Blenheims were lost (see Appendix 1). Twenty-five aircraft were sent to targets in Germany on 25 June, but most turned back owing to lack of cloud cover, and only three of 13 bombed targets on the 26th, one of which was lost (see Appendix 1). 'Cloud cover' was set officially at 7/10ths, although this proportion was hard to judge and in practice the amount varied very rapidly as they flew in and out of cloud. This situation created personal dilemmas for the Blenheim captains, for if they pressed on through cloud cover that they considered marginal they were exposing themselves, and their crews, to great danger. But if crews aborted the sortie, and this was usually agreed between Pilot and

Observer, they could, indeed should, have completed their task as ordered – especially if others on the same trip had managed to do so by dodging in and out of patchy cloud. The jeopardy in which this choice could place a crew can be shown by way of an example: on 2 July 11 aircraft were sent to Germany, and while ten turned back due to lack of cloud, the one that pressed on was shot down (see Appendix 1).

The single lower rear-defence gun, mounted on the under-nose escape hatch and sighted by mirrors, was fitted to most Bomber Command Blenheims by the Battle of Britain, but proved to have more psychological then practical benefit.

During the last nine days of June 1940 82 of these 'cloud cover' sorties were dispatched, but only 22 managed to bomb a target, mainly secondary. These sporadic attacks failed in their main intention in that such 'pin-pricks' did not cause a single Luftwaffe fighter unit to be moved back to Germany. In the same period 128 sorties were mounted to attack airfields, and 98 of these claimed to have bombed the primary target; in addition, 12 of the 20 reconnaissance sorties carried out by 40 Squadron were effective. Thus lack of cloud cover caused only 132 of the 230 reconnaissance and bombing sorties carried out by 2 Group Blenheims in the nine-day period to be classed as effective, although the losses were reduced considerably (see Appendix 1).

Of the further airfield attacks, one on Merville on 28 June by 18 Blenheims was abandoned because of clear skies, while one on Abbeville by 12 aircraft on the 29th was successful and six more Blenheims carried out reconnaissance sorties that day, both missions without loss. Merville was targeted again on the last day of the month when it was bombed by 12 aircraft of 107 Squadron, and six more attacked the aircraft depot at Vignacourt, but three of the former were lost when their fighter escort was drawn away (see Appendix 3). Orders came that XV and 40 Squadrons, escorted by four fighter squadrons, were to undertake a photographic reconnaissance of the whole of the French Channel coast, and did so by dividing it up so that eight sections of three aircraft could take their pictures on 1 July. These showed that the Germans were moving long-range heavy artillery to the coast, and these positions were bombed later by Blenheims. On the 3rd P/O Thompson in R3767 of XV Squadron used his F24 cameras to photograph the German pocket battleship *Scharnhorst* – of great interest to the Admiralty.

Blenheims in the Battle of Britain

I consider that the true start of what became known as the Battle of Britain was in this period, for it marked the first major aerial attack on half a dozen different targets in England by a force of '70-plus' He.111 bombers of KG4 on the night of 18 June. They were engaged by Britain's fledgling night-fighter force, mainly the Blenheim Mk I-Fs of 23 and 29

NCO Blenheim crews at Watton – they had different Messes and Crew Rooms from Commissioned Officers on all RAF Stations.

The ground crews toiled ceaselessly to keep their aircraft serviceable – here a Blenheim undergoes a double engine-change out in the open at a Bodney dispersal.

Squadrons. P/O P. Kells of 29 made the first contact and attacked three bombers off Felixstowe and was credited with one 'probably destroyed'; P/O J. Humphreys, also of 29, claimed one shot down at midnight. Fifty minutes later 23 Squadron lost Sgt Alan Close when his Blenheim YP-S was shot down by the bomber he was attacking, although his WOp/Ag LAC Karasek managed to bale out. F/Lt R. Duke-Wooley, also of 23 Squadron, then shot down the same He.111, which ditched off Cley-next-the-Sea, Norfolk – the crew were captured and included the Kommandeur of Stab II Gruppe, Major Dieter Freiherr von Massenbach. His Blenheim YP-L was also hit by return fire and landed safely, but was found to be Damaged Beyond Repair. Interceptions continued: at 0115 the 4 Staffel He.111 of Oberleutnant Joachim von Armin (son of the German General) was being attacked by S/Ldr

Night-fighter crews of 29 Squadron wait at Wellingore to be called into action.

A Mk I-F of 601 Squadron prepares to leave Exeter for a patrol just before dusk.

J. O'Brien's 23 Squadron Blenheim when F/O G. Petre's 19 Squadron Spitfire simultaneously opened fire. Return fire shot down both the British fighters, whose pilots baled out successfully, but O'Brien's crew, P/O C. King-Clark and Cpl D. Little, were both killed, while the German bomber fell at Six Mile Bottom, near Cambridge. Ten minutes later P/O John S. Barnwell (son of the Blenheim designer Frank Barnwell), who had taken off earlier from Martlesham Heath in his 29 Squadron Blenheim Mk I-F, chased a raider over the sea and an exchange of fire was seen; one of the aircraft crashed into the sea with the starboard engine on fire, but it is not clear if this was the enemy bomber or the Blenheim, as the latter failed to return, although Barnwell and his crewman Sgt K. Long were credited posthumously with an enemy aircraft destroyed. This was not an encouraging start for the RAF night-fighters; from the seven enemy aircraft claimed 'destroyed' (together with three more 'probably destroyed') the Luftwaffe actually lost five bombers, and two of those were shot down by F/Lt 'Sailor' Malan unusually operating his 74 Squadron Spitfire at night, but the RAF lost four aircraft – three Blenheims (see Appendix 4 in Chapter 13) and a Spitfire.

Most British accounts give 10 July 1940 as the commencement of the Battle of Britain, although, as indicated above, many Germans regarded *'Der Luftschlacht um England'* ('The air attack on England') to have started on 18 June, and another raid by 70-plus German bombers followed on the night of 25 June. By the end of the month 13 RAF airfields, mainly bomber bases, had been attacked. As the intensity of the fighting in the air increased throughout July, the stop-gap fighter Blenheims – which were never intended for use in the straight interceptor role – became involved on the periphery of the efforts of the Luftwaffe to gain pre-invasion supremacy in the air. While the Germans attempted to crush the RAF Hurricanes and Spitfires, Bomber Command Blenheims flew flat out by day and by night, together with their Coastal Command comrades, to hinder the invasion build-up by attacking German preparations at the departure ports and airfields.

Fighter Blenheims

Fighter Command Blenheims also mounted patrols off the coast of the Continent, and lost L1397, a 600 Squadron Mk I-F, on 28 June when it crashed at Manston on returning from an operational patrol, overshooting and striking a dispersal pen to be damaged beyond repair, although the crew were only slightly injured (see Appendix 4) – 600 had a mix of Mk I-Fs and Mk IV-Fs. That night a 23 Squadron Blenheim Mk I-F claimed a He.111 'probably destroyed' near Norwich. Fighter Command Blenheim losses in July included L1376, a 29 Squadron Mk I-F, on the night of the 1st when the pilot, P/O P. Sisman, was dazzled by searchlights on an operational patrol and crashed fatally trying to land, and the next day L1265 of 23 Squadron stalled after an engine cut on approach to Sealand and the Mk I-F dived into the ground. 23 Squadron lost another on the 5th when K7156 on an operational patrol crashed at Digby, the crew having baled out after control was lost in cloud (see Appendix 4), while on the 12th P/O J. R. D. 'Bob' Braham (later to become one of the RAF's most successful night-fighter pilots) force-landed his Mk I-F L6646 at Digby with total hydraulic failure. On the 13th F/O A. Lyall of the 25 Squadron Flight based at Martlesham Heath lost his starboard propeller and reduction gear while on convoy patrol and force-landed. That day, too, L8715, a Mk I-F of 604 Squadron, force-landed at Gravesend after damage, but the crew, F/O Heal and Sgts Crump and Guthrie, were uninjured, while on the 27th L8451, a Mk I-F of 600 Squadron, was written off at Manston after bursting its tyres and collapsing the undercarriage on a very heavy landing. 219 Squadron lost L1109, a Mk I-F, on the 30th when it damaged its undercarriage on taking off from Catterick and was damaged beyond repair in the belly-landing that followed. Two more Mk I-Fs were lost on 31 July when L1408 of 25 Squadron and L6722 of 29 Squadron collided over the Bristol Channel while carrying out tests with their new AI radar sets; all aboard both aircraft were killed (see Appendix 4).

P4834, Special Duties Flight at Christchurch, claimed a Heinkel He.111 on the night of 12 May using AI radar to close on the enemy bomber, but lack of independent witnesses meant that victory could not be confirmed.

These fighter Blenheims had relied on human eyesight – the 'Eyeball Mark 1' – by day and night, but more were becoming operational equipped with Airborne Interception radar sets. Two 600 Squadron pilots located enemy aircraft at night that had shown as blips on their AI sets: F/Lt D. Clarkson on 19 July, although he was unable to engage, and P/O A. Boyd, who did engage a Heinkel on the 20th but without success. However, history was made on the night of 22/23 July when F/O G. 'Jumbo' Ashfield in L6836, a Mk I-F of the Fighter Interception Unit based at Ford but operating from Tangmere, aided by his radar operator, Sgt R. Leyland, and with P/O G. Morris as Observer and WOp/Ag, scored the first ever success for airborne radar by shooting down an inbound Dornier Do.17Z into the Channel. Leyland faced aft to operate the AI Mk III set installed in the fuselage 'well' behind the cockpit between the main spars; as already described, the equipment had two small flickering cathode-ray tubes, one showing a blip on a base line to indicate the relative elevation of the target, and the other displaying a blip either side of a vertical base line to indicate the relative position in azimuth. The first practical version of AI was the Mk IV, an improvement over the earlier experimental marks, and the first to be rushed into full production – only 25 of the bulky and very temperamental earlier Mk III sets had been ordered just before the outbreak of war. The FIU operated ten Mk I-Fs with AI radar – L1186, L1340, L1404, L6688, L6788, L6805, L6835, L6836 (which scored the historic 'first'), L6837 and L6838. The Radar Development & Training Flight at Martlesham Heath operated L6622, L6624 and L6627.

Landing back after a night patrol was tricky with just a few goose flares to indicate the runway. This 219 Squadron Mk I-F has ended up in the wrong three-point position!

Coastal Command activity

Coastal Command fighter Blenheims had been active too, and were sent to patrol off the Belgian and Dutch coasts to watch for any unusual shipping activity by the Germans. 235 Squadron, operating from Bircham Newton, experienced a depressing afternoon on 27 June when two sections of its Mk IV-Fs ventured over the Zuider Zee and were bounced by 109s, four of their six aircraft being shot down (see Appendix 5) – only F/O Peacock in N3542 and Sgt Clarke in N3541 managed to return. Sgt Aubrey Lancaster had a charmed life for he was the solitary survivor of the 12 Blenheim crewmen involved, and a month earlier he and his two crewmates had survived a ditching in the Channel after being shot down by a Me.109-E. On 11 July L6816 from 236 Squadron at Thorney Island near Portsmouth was badly damaged by return fire from a Heinkel He.111 and force-landed at St Eval in Cornwall, P/O McDonough and Sgt Head being only slightly injured. Coastal Command squadrons had a bad day on 18 July, too; 235 lost a crew on operations, and 236 had two of its Mk I-Fs shot down by 109s of JG2 while on a reconnaissance sortie to Le Havre – and 236 lost another in the same manner on 20 July (see Appendix 5), together with L1119, which was badly damaged when it force-landed near Detling, south of the Thames estuary, on the 27th, short of fuel returning from an operation – Sgts N. Barrow and J. Lowe were uninjured. RR3887, a Mk IV-F of 254 Squadron, crashed on the approach to Sumburgh in bad weather on the 22nd, while the 30th saw 236 Squadron lose a Mk IV-F when F/Lt A. Power and crew were injured as R2777 hit an obstruction on a night take-off from Carew Cheriton in SW Wales for an operation.

THE BRISTOL BLENHEIM

Nos 53 and 59, the two Army Co-operation Squadrons, were transferred to Coastal Command on 1 July – the 20 or so Army Officers seconded to the squadrons had to forget their skills at tank recognition and 'gen up' on ship recognition in a hurry! They had been trained as Observers at the two Schools of Army Co-Operation when the squadrons operated in their previous role, although before long several were trained as Pilots and changed the half-wings on their uniforms for full wings, and changed their Army rank of Captain to the RAF one of Flight Lieutenant. The squadrons retained their standard bomber Mk IVs, and were deployed mainly on the reconnaissance and bombing of enemy ports and shipping, 53 squadron covering the eastern half of the Channel and 59 the western half. Coastal Command soon mounted a .303 machine-gun on a swivel mounting in the nose for the Observer, and hastened the fitting of twin Brownings in the rear turret – most 53 and 59 Squadron aircraft had one improvement or the other. These two hard-working squadrons suffered severe losses (see Appendix 6), together with R3678 of P/O H. Newton, which was damaged when it tipped on to its nose on 7 July when landing at Detling in heavy rain after a night operation to Ostend. The night of the 10th saw R3637, a Mk IV of 59 Squadron, blow up in the air near Ludlow from an unknown cause, killing P/O Hopkins and crew (see Appendix 6), and on 11 July R3881 of 59 Squadron was destroyed when it struck Clee Hill, Ludlow, on returning from an operation. R3610 was damaged landing at Detling on the 13th, and on the same day L9474 was abandoned in the air above cloud and short of fuel by the CO of 53, W/Cdr 'Sphinx' Edwards, on return from operations to Leiden, and crashed in Essex, while the next day N3551 of F/O Panton (later Air Commodore, CB OBE DFC) was shot down when bombing an oil depot at Ghent. R3694 of 59 failed to return from Cherbourg on the 17th, as did 53's R3661 of F/O J. Mahony when sent to Flushing on the 18th (see Appendix 6). On the 23rd R3639 of 59 Squadron, damaged in action, crashed on landing at Thorney Island, and on the night of the 25th R3836 with P/O D. Starky and crew was shot down by flak from a ship

Mk IV-Fs of 254 Squadron formate in echelon-starboard for propaganda pictures.

off Ameland while attacking barges at Haarlem (also Appendix 6). R3660 of 53 Squadron also badly damaged on 31 July when P/O J. Mallon returned from an operational patrol to find the Detling runway obscured by low cloud and crashed attempting to land. 53 Squadron had a busy month indeed, carrying out 282 operational sorties during July.

Nos 53 and 59 were a useful supplement to the four Coastal Command squadrons of Blenheim Mk IV-F fighters, 235, 248, 254 and 236 (which still had some Mk I-Fs) as they strengthened the pitifully weak striking power of Coastal Command. The Beaufort torpedo bomber was trickling into service with 22 and 42 Squadrons but the Taurus engines were proving so troublesome that these squadrons were frequently grounded. Coastal Command also had five squadrons of the portly Lockheed Hudson, which had proved useful in the reconnaissance role, but at this critical period they were pressed into the bombing role too, mainly at night, adding ports and invasion barges to their normal maritime targets. The Hudson could carry the same bomb-load as a Blenheim and had a top speed of 250mph, although – being far less manoeuvrable – it proved more vulnerable than the Blenheim in daylight operations. It is interesting to note that at this stage of the war all Coastal Command search and patrol aircraft were adapted from civilian passenger types – the Anson from the Avro 652, the Hudson from the Lockheed 14, the Sunderland from the Short C Class flying boats, and of course the Blenheim from the Bristol Type 142 'Britain First'.

Bomber Command Blenheims

In July 1940 2 Group built up to its peak strength with an average of almost 180 Blenheims available each day for operations – three times as many as it could deploy in late May. Nos 139, 114, 57 and 18 Squadrons had reformed after their mauling in France and were ready to rejoin the fray, while 101 was released from its reserve and training role, as 13 and 17 OTUs, formed in April, were just coming 'on stream'. Nos 105 and 218 Squadrons completed their conversion from Battles and were declared operational in August.

The main attacks mounted by 2 Group during July were directed on enemy-held airfields, but on the 3rd new targets were bombed for the first time – sea-going barges being brought up the Rhine near Rotterdam, the start of the build-up in preparation for the German invasion of Britain. As these large barges, and other vessels, were gathered in the ports of Belgium, Holland and Northern France in increasing numbers they were attacked frequently and relentlessly, by day and by night, by Bomber and Coastal Command aircraft, in a battle just as hard-fought as the one being waged by Fighter Command over the skies of Southern England. Blenheims played the predominant role in these sustained attacks on both the airfields and the ports from which the invasion would be mounted and supported. This other campaign continued throughout the Battle of Britain and proved to be of equal importance to the survival of Britain as that famous aerial conflict by helping to convince Hitler that Operation Sea Lion would prove too costly to mount and thus unlikely to succeed.

Nos 21 and 57 Squadrons of 2 Group were sent to Lossiemouth with their Blenheim bombers to join 248 and 254 Squadrons of Coastal Command with their Blenheim fighters, also based in Scotland, to cover a possible invasion from Norway. They were hammered badly on 9 July in a disastrous daylight attack on Stavanger airfield, losing seven of their 12 aircraft – losses on the scale of the Maastricht raids (see Appendix 7). The five aircraft lost from the six of A Flight, 21 Squadron, included that of their CO, Wing

The grave in Lonstrupp Churchyard, Jutland, of W/Cdr Leslie Bennett, New Zealand CO of 21 Squadron. His Blenheim, R3732, was one of five shot down off the Norwegian coast from six attacking Stavanger airfield on 9 July, and his body was washed ashore in northern Denmark on 28 September.

THE BRISTOL BLENHEIM

Commander L. Bennett. The sole survivor from 21 Squadron, P/O Rodgers, with his two crewmen wounded, nursed his badly damaged aircraft and landed despite two burst tyres; and one from 57 struggled back on one engine and crashed attempting to land at Dyce. Despite these terrible losses the two Squadrons were ordered to repeat the attack the following day with another 12 aircraft, six from the B Flight of each Squadron, but fortunately for them the weather turned really bad and the Blenheims were able to abandon the raid and return to Lossiemouth without loss – this was just as well, for the massacre of the previous day would surely have been repeated. As it was, that day was to see heavy losses in a raid by 40 Blenheims on Amiens and St Omer airfields; 107 Squadron lost five out of the six aircraft it sent on the Amiens raid, one a machine borrowed from 82 Squadron, which itself lost a further aircraft the next day (see Appendix 8). On those two terrible days two Blenheim squadrons, hundreds of miles apart, suffered losses of more than 83 per cent.

Much of the 'trust to luck' element of the continuing 'cloud cover' raids was removed, and a considerable amount of the effort wasted on the majority that had to be aborted was avoided, when single aircraft were sent out daily from 9 July between sunrise and 0900 hours on meteorological reconnaissance to establish the amount of cloud cover available and transmit the appropriate code word back to base. This was useful as Bomber Command HQ on the 6th had ordered the number of 'cloud cover' raids to be doubled, and the range of targets was increased to include airframe and aluminium plants, the docks at Kiel, Bremen, Hamburg (where *Bismarck* had been photographed) and Wilhelmshaven, together with more oil industry targets.

The threat of invasion increased, so direct links between appropriate 2 Group bases and Army Area Commands were set up. The Counter-Invasion orders were direct:

> 'All aircraft not under Army control are to attack enemy convoys at sea. If a landing is effected the main body of the convoys at sea may be attacked at places where the landing has been made, depending on the situation at the time. Enemy forces caught at sea, and craft containing landing parties, are to be primary targets irrespective of enemy warships in the vicinity. If a landing has been effected and it is decided to attack beaches, enemy craft laying off the beaches and stores on them are to be the primary targets.'

This prompted the AOC of 2 Group, AVM J. M. Robb, to send a special signal from his Headquarters at Castle Hill House, Huntingdon, to his Station Commanders:

> 'You must bear in mind that your forces may have to play a most important part in repelling an invasion of this country, and you should be prepared at short notice to divert your Squadrons to the attack of the invading enemy force at points of departure and subsequently at sea, and points of landing in this country. To meet the threat of invasion twelve aircraft at each Station are to stand by every morning at 20 minutes notice from sunrise to twilight.'

These stand-bys were carried out in rotation by the Blenheim squadrons at each 2 Group Station daily until the winter of 1940. It is clear that, irrespective of the losses anticipated, the Blenheims would become the sharpest of all the sharp ends in Britain's desperate attempts to stem an invasion. That it did not prove necessary to sacrifice the Blenheims in this way was, in my view, due not only to the well-chronicled efforts of Fighter Command in the Battle of Britain, but also to the equally valiant efforts of Bomber and Coastal Commands, principally by the very same Blenheims, which deterred Hitler from ordering Operation Sea Lion – the planned invasion of Britain.

Through July, as the Battle of Britain developed into the crucial struggle between the Luftwaffe and the Royal Air Force, the Blenheims paid a high price in carrying out virtually unceasing operations to deter the threat of invasion. To this end they operated also at night, although neither trained nor equipped properly for these demanding operations, and took further losses (see Appendix 10). The Channel ports were not too difficult to find at night and were attacked repeatedly and successfully, but enemy-occupied airfields were much harder to locate and the raids on them caused little damage. The strain mounted on the new and inexperienced crews, For example, P/O A. Jones of 18 Squadron ran out of fuel returning from a sortie to attack airfields on 16 July, and crashed L9251 attempting a force-landing near Welwyn, Hertfordshire; three days later he lost control of R3842 during a practice attack and spun in near Great Massingham with fatal results to himself, Sgt K. Webster and Sgt E. Abury. The serious rate of attrition continued remorselessly from losses suffered during raids on enemy airfields, invasion ports and barges, the 'cloud cover' raids, and regular reconnaissance sorties (Appendix 9), and, of course, the non-operational losses also continued equally remorselessly (see Appendix 10).

Throughout that July the brave 'Blenheim Boys' pressed home their attacks, just as they had during the Battle for France, with levels of daring and courage acknowledged to be of the highest by their peers in the other RAF Groups and Commands. Their nickname was apt as many more very young crews were joining the squadrons to replace the heavy casualties among the ranks of so many of the older and more experienced crews.

These debilitating losses of trained crews, fulfilling Air Marshal Portal's earlier pessimistic prophesy, caused him to recommend to the Air Staff that '…it would pay us to roll up some if not all of the Blenheim Squadrons and convert them into Heavy Bomber Squadrons … although they are doing a certain amount of useful work … far better value would be obtained by applying the personnel in smaller numbers of Heavy Bomber Squadrons.' But all of the available Blenheims were needed, not least because of an undertaking given to the Army that, should the need arise, 15 squadrons would be provided for direct Army support, so there could be no respite in their operations – or in their suffering.

'Round the clock' sorties meant constant re-arming and re-fuelling, as on R3600, a 110 Squadron Blenheim at Wattisham – note the mongrel mascot on the cowling. The aircraft survived for almost a year, being shot down during a convoy attack on 6 May 1941, killing the crew.

THE BRISTOL BLENHEIM

Appendix 1

Blenheim losses on 'cloud cover' raids 23 June to 3 July 1940

Aircraft are all Mk IVs.

23-06-1940   R3688 107 Squadron: Failed To Return (FTR) to Wattisham from raid on Soest, shot down by Me.110 of ZG 76 near Willemsoord, Holland; P/O S. Esson, P/O J. Tozer, and Sgt G. Murchison (all aged 20) were Killed in Action (KIA) and buried locally.

23-06-1940   N3593 107 Squadron: FTR to Wattisham from raid on Soest, shot down near Nijmegen, Holland; F/Lt J. Stephens (Pilot) captured, crew Sgt W. Barrett DFM (Obs), Sgt P. Adams (WOp/Ag) KIA. Sgt Peter Adams shot down Lt Adolf Kinzinger's JG 54 Me.109E-3.

23-06-1940   L8754 110 Squadron: FTR to Wattisham from raid on Vohwinkle, shot down by Me.109-E of JG 54 near Amsterdam, Holland; crew P/O T. Prescott, Sgt H. Kenyon, and Sgt V. Swallow KIA and buried in New Eastern Cemetery, Amsterdam.

26-06-1940   R3776 110 Squadron: FTR to Wattisham from raid on Soest, shot down into North Sea by 109-E of JG 54; crew P/O C. Worboys, Sgt G. Gainsford, and Sgt K. Cooper KIA and commemorated on Runnymede Memorial.

02-07-1940   P6895 82 Squadron: FTR to Watton after raid to Dortmund-Ems Kanal, shot down in flames by Me.109-Es of JG 54 in North Holland; crew S/Ldr H. Chester, Sgt H. Histon, and Sgt R. McAllister KIA and buried at Veenhuizen.

Appendix 2

Blenheim losses on reconnaissance sorties, 23 June to 3 July 1940

Aircraft are all Mk IVs.

26-06-1940   R3828 107 Squadron: took off from Wattisham on recce to Munster, damaged by flak and crash-landed 0845 at base and written off; F/O Hill, Sgt Hodder, and Sgt Gray uninjured.

27-06-1940   R3778 40 Squadron: FTR to Wyton from recce, shot down by Me.109; crew Sgt J. Morton, Sgt A. Kelso, and Sgt J. Winston KIA and commemorated on Runnymede Memorial.

27-06-1940   R3811 40 Squadron: took off from Wyton on recce, damaged by Me.109s and force-landed at Hawkinge; Sgt G. Gamble (WOp/Ag) wounded and awarded DFM, F/O C. Bromley (Pilot) and Sgt F. Little (Obs) uninjured, aircraft repaired.

27-06-1940   R3731 82 Squadron: FTR to Watton from North Germany, shot down near Zeist, Holland; P/O R. Percy (Pilot) and Sgt A. Clark (WOp/Ag) KIA and buried in Zeist, Sgt A. Stanley (Obs) baled out and captured. During this action Sgt Clark shot down Oblt H. Schmoler-Haldy, Staffel Kaptain of 9/JG 54.

Appendix 3

Blenheim losses on airfield raids, 30 June 1940

Aircraft are all Mk IVs.

30-06-1940   R3870 107 Squadron: FTR to Wattisham from Merville, shot down by flak near Ecques; S/Ldr H. Pilling AFC (Pilot) and Sgt H. Denison (WOp/Ag) KIA, Sgt F. Roche (Obs) captured and became PoW.

30-06-1940   R3823 107 Squadron: FTR to Wattisham from Merville, shot down by flak at Wittes near St Omer; crew P/O R. Bennett, Sgt A. Langford, and Sgt D. Harrison KIA and buried at Wittes.

30-06-1940   L9467 107 Squadron: FTR to Wattisham from Merville, shot down in target area; crew P/O J. 'Paddy' Quirke, Sgt D. Hawkins, and Sgt K. Murray captured and became PoWs.

Appendix 4

Losses of Blenheim night-fighters, June and July 1940

Aircraft are all Mk I-Fs.

18/19-06-1940 L8687 23 Squadron Mk I-F: FTR; damaged by return fire from He.111; S/Ldr J. O'Brien (Pilot) baled out safely but P/O C. King-Clark (Obs), who struck prop, and Cpl D. Little (WOp/Ag) KIA.

18/19-06-1940 L1458 23 Squadron Mk I-F: FTR; shot down by return fire from He.111; Sgt A. Close (Pilot) KIA, his crewman LAC L. Karasek baled out successfully.

18/19-06-1940 L6636 29 Squadron Mk I-F: FTR to Martlesham Heath, shot down while attacking He.111 off Norfolk coast; P/O J. Barnwell (Pilot) and Sgt K. Long (crewman) KIA. (Barnwell's parachute found in sea next morning).

01-07-1940 L1376 29 Squadron: FTR from patrol, pilot blinded by searchlights and crashed; crew P/O P. Sisman and Sgt A. Reed KIA.

12-07-1940 L6646 29 Squadron: suffered total hydraulic failure on night patrol, force-landed at Digby; P/O J. 'Bob' Braham and Sgt W. 'Sticks' Gregory, later a top-scoring night-fighter team with 29 victories, unhurt.

13-07-1940 L8715 604 Squadron: damaged and crash-landed at Gravesend; crew F/O Heal, Sgt Crump, and Sgt Guthrie only slightly injured, aircraft repaired.

30-07-1940 L6803 604 Squadron: destroyed on ground by bombing at Middle Wallop.

30-07-1940 L1109 219 Squadron: undercarriage damaged on take-off for operations, belly-landed at Catterick; crew Sgt T. Birkett and Sgt E. Lacey unhurt, aircraft DBR.

31-07-1940 L1408 25 Squadron: FTR from conducting AI trials over Bristol Channel, collided with L6722 (below); Sgt J. Thompson, AC2 E. Toy, and Mr D. Gordon killed. Gordon was radar engineer from Martlesham Heath where L1408 was based.

31-07-1940 L6722 29 Squadron: FTR from conducting AI trials over Bristol Channel, collided with L1408 (above); Sgt E. Waite, Sgt C. Richardson, and LAC T. Ward killed.

Appendix 5

Coastal Command Blenheim losses, 23 June to 3 July 1940

27-06-1940 L9447 235 Squadron Mk IV-F: FTR to Bircham Newton, shot down by Me.109-Es over Zuider Zee; P/O J. Cronan (Pilot) and Sgt P. Lloyd (WOp/Ag, aged 19) KIA and buried at Bergen-op-Zoom, Sgt Aubrey Lancaster (Obs) rescued and became PoW in Stalag Luft III, Sagan.

27-06-1940 N3543 235 Squadron Mk IV-F: FTR to Bircham Newton, shot down by Me.109-Es near Zuider Zee; crew P/O A. Wales, Sgt J. Needham, and Sgt T. Jordan (aged 18) KIA and buried at Oegstgeest.

27-06-1940 P6958 235 Squadron Mk IV-F: FTR to Bircham Newton, shot down by Me.109-Es near Amste; P/O H. Pardoe-Williams, P/O E. Saunders, and Sgt C. Thorley KIA and are buried in Amsterdam.

27-06-1940 P6957 235 Squadron Mk IV-F: FTR to Bircham Newton, shot down by Me.109-Es into Zuider Zee; P/O P. Weil (Pilot, aged 20), Sgt S. Bartlet, and Sgt A. Kempster KIA and buried in Germany and Holland.

06-07-1940 L8789 53 Squadron Mk IV: damaged during recce of Dunkirk/Calais area, force-landed at Ramsgate; crew F/Lt Bartlett, Sgt Aldridge, and Sgt Sheldrick only slightly injured, aircraft repaired.

06-07-1940 L8842 254 Squadron Mk IV: FTR; shot down by four Me.110s off coast of Norway and ditched near HMS Cossack, which rescued crew Sgt Tubbs, Sgt MacVeigh, and Sgt Johnstone; Sgt MacVeigh died on board and was buried at sea.

06-07-1940 P6950 254 Squadron Mk IV: FTR; shot down in flames by same Me.110s; P/O Pattinson (Pilot) not recovered, but Sgt McLaren (Obs), injured and burned, and Sgt Savage (WOp/Ag), uninjured, rescued by HMS *Fortune*.

10-07-1940 R3637 59 Squadron Mk IV: FTR; blew up in air at 0300hrs, cause unknown, and crashed near Cardiff; crew P/O A. Hopkin, Sgt T. Rowles, and Sgt J. Falconer KIA, commemorated on Runnymede Memorial.

10-07-1940 R3881 59 Squadron Mk IV: FTR; hit HT pylon at Peterstone, near Ludlow, at 0315hrs in bad weather returning from Le Havre; crew P/O J. Rex, Sgt J. Jeffery, and Sgt J. Liddle KIA.

11-07-1940 L6816 236 Squadron Mk IV-F: damaged in engine and mainplane by return fire, force-landed at St Eval; P/O B. McDonough and Sgt F. Head safe, aircraft repaired.

13-07-1940 L9474 53 Squadron Mk IV: FTR; abandoned 0245 on return from Leiden, above cloud and low on fuel; crew W/Cdr E. Edwards, Sgt Morris, and Sgt Williams baled out successfully, aircraft crashed in Essex.

14-07-1940 N3551 53 Squadron Mk IV: FTR; shot down by flak bombing oil-tanks at Ghent; F/O A. Panton DFC (Pilot) and Sgt A. Farrow (Obs) became PoWs, Sgt L. Stride (WOp/Ag) KIA.

14-07-1940   R3665 59 Squadron Mk IV: ditched off Saltdean at 0255hrs, believed shot down; P/O H. Clark, Sgt D. Morton, and Sgt F. Clayton KIA, bodies recovered from sea.

17-07-1940   R3694 59 Squadron Mk IV: FTR from recce to Cherbourg; crew P/O A. Jackson, Sgt R. Kingshott, and Sgt J. Hunter KIA, Sgt Hunter buried in Cayeux-su-Mere, Somme, his companions commemorated at Runnymede.

18-07-1940   R3661 53 Squadron Mk IV: FTR to Detling, shot down by Me.109E of JG 54 into River Scheldt; F/O J. Mahony, Sgt D. Keetley, and Sgt G. Exton KIA. Sgt Exton buried at Klemskerke, others commemorated on Runnymede Memorial.

18-07-1940   N3541 235 Squadron Mk IV-F: FTR from operational patrol off East Anglia, lost without trace; crew P/O R. Patterson, Sgt F. Tucker, and Sgt L. Reece commemorated on Runnymede Memorial.

18-07-1940   L6779 236 Squadron Mk I-F: FTR to Thorney Island from recce to Le Havre, shot down by Me.109 of Major Schellman of JG 2; crew P/O C. Thomas and Sgt H. Elsdon KIA.

18-07-1940   L6639 236 Squadron Mk I-F: FTR from same sortie; crew P/O R. Rigby and Sgt D. MacKinnon KIA.

20-07-1940   L1300 236 Squadron Mk I-F: FTR; shot down off Cherbourg by Me.109 of Hauptman Neumann of JG 27; crew Sgt E. Lockton and Sgt H. Corcoran KIA, commemorated on Runnymede Mcmorial.

22-07-1940   R3639 59 Squadron Mk IV: crashed on landing at Thorney Island when u/c collapsed; P/O A. Hovenier, Sgt L. Magee, and Sgt J. Scotchmere escaped before bomb-load exploded.

25-07-1940   R3836 53 Squadron Mk IV: FTR from attacking barges at Haarlem, shot down by ship's flak; P/O D. Starky (NZ, aged 20), Sgt H. Hunt (Canada), and Sgt B. Moriaty KIA. Sgt Hunt buried at Ballum, Ameland, later re-buried at Nijmegen, others commemorated on Runnymede Memorial.

25-07-1940   L9473 59 Squadron Mk IV: FTR from sortie to Le Havre, with four others, to search for survivors of SS *Weknes* sunk by Germans; F/O H. Haswell, Sgt R. Martin, and Sgt D. Simpson KIA, commemorated at Runnymede.

26-07-1940   T1801 59 Squadron Mk IV: FTR from sortie to bomb oil-tanks at Cherbourg, lost without trace; P/O M. Turnbull, Sgt G. Rowe, and Sgt D. Wallace KIA, Sgt Wallace buried in Criel-sur-Mere, his comrades commemorated on Runnymede Memorial.

27-07-1940   L1119 236 Squadron Mk I: force-landed at Detling low on fuel on return from operation; crew Sgt N. Barron and Sgt J. Lowe safe, aircraft repaired.

30-07-1940   R2777 236 Squadron Mk IV-F: hit obstruction on night take-off at Carew Cheriton; F/Lt A. Power injured, aircraft DBR.

31-07-1940   R3660 53 Squadron Mk IV: crashed at home base of Detling in bad weather on return from recce; crew P/O Mallon, Sgt Wilcox, and Sgt Shackleford only slightly injured, aircraft repaired.

Appendix 6

Blenheim losses in the raid on Stavanger, 9 July 1940

Aircraft are all Mk IVs.

09-07-1940   R3732 21 Squadron: FTR to Lossiemouth from Stavanger, shot down into sea; crew W/Cdr L. Bennett, Sgt A. Summers, and Sgt C. Burt KIA. W/Cdr Bennett's body was washed ashore near Lonstrupp, Jutland, 26-09-1940 and buried in Lonstrupp Churchyard, and his crew are commemorated on Runnymede Memorial.

09-07-1940   R3822 21 Squadron: FTR to Lossiemouth from Stavanger, brought down into sea; crew P/O J. Heath-Brown, Sgt W. Hamlyn, and Sgt E. Williams KIA and commemorated on Runnymede Memorial.

09-07-1940   R3876 21 Squadron: FTR to Lossiemouth from Stavanger, brought down into sea; Sgt J. Brown, Sgt C. Stevens, and Sgt J. Morton KIA, Sgt Brown is buried in Trondheim cemetery, his crew commemorated on Runnymede Memorial.

09-07-1940   N3619 21 Squadron: FTR to Lossiemouth from Stavanger, brought down into sea; crew P/O W. Macley, Sgt W. Rawson, and Sgt J. Dorrington KIA and commemorated on Runnymede Memorial.

09-07-1940   L8872 21 Squadron: FTR to Lossiemouth from Stavanger, brought down into sea; crew F/Lt J. Murray (NZ), Sgt W. Hartley, and Sgt G. Duck KIA and commemorated on Runnymede Memorial.

09-07-1940   R3750 57 Squadron: FTR to Lossiemouth from Stavanger, brought down into sea; crew P/O R. Hopkinson, Sgt J. Andrew, and Sgt G. Miles KIA and commemorated on Runnymede Memorial.

09-07-1940   R3847 57 Squadron: FTR to Lossiemouth from Stavanger, brought down into sea; crew Sgt F. Mills, Sgt S. Newcombe, and Sgt T. Jervis KIA and commemorated on Runnymede Memorial.

09-07-1940   R3914 21 Squadron: not lost, but badly damaged and crash-landed at base; P/O Rodger (Pilot) and Sgt Spillard (Obs) injured, aircraft repaired.

Appendix 7

Blenheim losses in daylight raids on airfields, July 1940

Aircraft are all Mk IVs.

10-07-1940 P6894 107 Squadron: FTR to Wattisham, shot down by fighters on Amiens airfield raid; P/O T. Maslin, Sgt G. Truscott, and Sgt S. Hinton KIA and buried in Cavillon Communal Cemetery.

10-07-1940 R3815 107 Squadron: FTR to Wattisham, lost without trace on Amiens airfield raid; crew P/O E. Wray, Sgt G. Drew, and Sgt S. Wood KIA and commemorated on Runnymede Memorial.

10-07-1940 R3606 107 Squadron: FTR to Wattisham, shot down on Amiens airfield raid; crew Sgt S. Bain, Sgt G. Hawkins, and Sgt G. Allison became PoWs, Sgt Hawkins killed 19-04-1945 when PoW column in which he was marching was attacked by Allied aircraft.

10-07-1940 R3916 107 Squadron: FTR to Wattisham, shot down on Amiens raid; crew P/O J. North-Lewis, Sgt R. Lonsdale, and Sgt B. George interned in unoccupied France, later PoWs. Sgt Lonsdale escaped via Spain, awarded Military Medal.

10-07-1940 L9468 82 Squadron: FTR to Wattisham with 107 Squadron crew, shot down on Amiens raid; crew P/O H. Atkin-Berry, Sgt R. Cook, and Sgt R. Mercer KIA.

11-07-1940 R3690 82 Squadron: FTR to Watton, shot down near St Omer; crew P/O J. Palmer, Sgt K. Howard, and Sgt K. Farley became PoWs. Palmer died 6-12-1942.

18-07-1940 P6924 101 Squadron: FTR to West Raynham from sortie to invasion ports, lost without trace; crew F/O F. Ducker, Sgt E. Dodd, and Sgt G. Bloor KIA and commemorated on Runnymede Memorial.

Appendix 8

Other Blenheim losses on night operations, July 1940

Aircraft are all Mk IVs.

22/23-07-1940 L9414 107 Squadron: FTR to Wattisham from sortie to bomb Creil, crashed in English Channel; crew P/O P. Watson, Sgt C. Holland, and Sgt W. O'Heney KIA.

23/24-07-1940 R3748 110 Squadron: FTR to Wattisham from sortie to bomb airfield at Bernburg, crashed into North Sea off Haamstede; crew Sgt C. Heyward, Sgt L. Walker, and Sgt I. Winberg KIA.

24/25-07-1940 T1797 110 Squadron: returned with engine trouble 10 minutes after take-off, crashed on landing; crew Sgt Bennett, Sgt Sopwith, and Sgt Mullins injured, aircraft repaired.

25/26-07-1940 L9469 XV Squadron: FTR to Wyton from sortie to bomb Wilhelmshaven, brought down near Ameland; P/O C. Robinson, P/O A. McLaggan, and Sgt L. Horton KIA. P/O Robinson buried at Nijmegen, others commemorated on Runnymede Memorial.

25/26-07-1940 R3763 40 Squadron: FTR to Wyton from attack on Eelde airfield, shot-down over target; crew Sgt P. Steele, Sgt J. Moore, and Sgt R. Peacock injured and became PoWs. (Roger Peacock, writing as Richard Passmore, describes life on 40 Squadron – and this loss – in his book *Blenheim Boy*.)

Appendix 9

Other Blenheim losses on mixed operations, July 1940

Aircraft are all Mk IVs.

04-07-1940   L8866 18 Squadron: FTR to West Raynham from NW Germany, shot down by Me.109s near Rotterdam; crew F/Lt I. Worthington-Wilmer, Sgt J. Stanley, and Sgt G. Maydon KIA, buried in Oostvoorne Cemetery.

04-07-1940   R3769 XV Squadron: took off from Wyton for Ruhr, but bombed Schipol, damaged by Me.109s and returned; P/O Lane-Sansom and Sgt J. Abbott uninjured, Sgt Terry Maloney (WOp/Ag, aged 18) KIA, aircraft repaired.

05-07-1940   R3804 114 Squadron: FTR to Horsham St Faith from Soest, shot down into Reichswald Forest; crew P/O A. Stewart, Sgt G. Rimmer, and Sgt R. Ellicott KIA and buried in War Cemetery there.

05-07-1940   N6140 101 Squadron: FTR to West Raynham from NW Germany, shot down into North Sea; W/Cdr J. Hargroves, Sgt E. Smith, and Sgt R. Livermore KIA. First operational loss by 101 Squadron.

06-07-1940   R3662 18 Squadron: FTR to West Raynham from night attack on airfields in France; crew P/O B. Davidson, Sgt J. Gilmour, and Sgt R. Fisk captured and became PoWs.

07-07-1940   R3896 XV Squadron: FTR; took off from Wyton at 0400 on recce, shot down near Bruges; crew P/O H. Bamber, Sgt J. Holdsworth, and Sgt G. Reid KIA and buried in the General Cemetery, Bruges.

07-07-1940   P4843 82 Squadron: FTR to Watton from NW Germany on 'cloud cover' raid, shot down there; crew Sgt F. Hutton, Sgt C. Pickering, and Sgt J. Rogers KIA and buried in Reichswald Forest War Cemetery.

09-07-1940   L8836 40 Squadron: FTR to Wyton from recce to Lisieux, lost in Channel; S/Ldr R. Batt DFC, Sgt A. Spencer DFM, and Sgt P. Johnson KIA, S/Ldr Batt's body recovered by HMS *Brilliant*, identified, and buried at sea, all commemorated on Runnymede Memorial.

09-07-1940   N6176 101 Squadron: FTR; hit tree attempting emergency landing at Brampton; P/O D. Watson and Sgt Oldland injured, AC2 Perry unhurt, aircraft DBR.

13-07-1940   R3701 82 Squadron: FTR to Watton from raid to Amsterdam, shot down by fighters; crew F/Lt P. Lewis, Sgt H. Richardson, and Sgt J. Newberry KIA. Sgt 'Ginger' Richardson buried in Vredenhof Cemetery, others commemorated on Runnymede Memorial.

13-07-1940   R3756 82 Squadron: FTR as R3701; Sgt A. Evans (WOp/Ag, aged 18) KIA and buried in Hamburg, Sgt D. Adams (Pilot) and Sgt A. Avery (Obs) became PoWs.

16-07-1940   P6933 18 Squadron: FTR to West Raynham from attack on barges, shot down into sea off Flushing by Me.109Es of JG 54; crew Sgt A. St John Bunker, Sgt P. Harris, and Sgt J. Hatch KIA. Pilot is buried at Heist-Sur-Mer, Belgium, others at Flushing.

16-07-1940   L9251 18 Squadron: FTR; ran out of fuel returning from operation and crash-landed near Welwyn, Herts, aircraft destroyed by fire; crew P/O A. Jones, Sgt Richards, and Sgt Rowley escaped with slight injuries.

18-07-1940   R3603 XV Squadron: FTR to Wyton from raid to Sterkadehoten, damaged in action, crash-landed on South Coast beach; crew F/O Mahler, Sgt Paveley, and Sgt Baker uninjured, aircraft written off.

20-07-1940   R3738 110 Squadron: FTR to Wattisham from sortie to bomb Vlissingen airfield, shot down into sea; S/Ldr J. Stephens (Pilot) and Sgt J. West DFM (WOp/Ag) KIA and commemorated on Runnymede Memorial, Sgt E. Parker (Obs) captured and became PoW at Stalag Luft III, Sagan.

24-07-1940   R3736 110 Squadron: bounced off The Wash on return from night intruder sortie, crash-landed at Wattisham; F/Lt Beaman, Sgt Robson, and Sgt Trigwell uninjured, aircraft struck by R3824 on 05-09-1940.

25-07-1940   N6174 101 Squadron: FTR to West Raynham from Cherbourg, lost without trace; P/O R. Short (NZ), Sgt J. Parkinson, and Sgt K. Gibson KIA and commemorated on Runnymede Memorial.

28-07-1940   T1828 82 Squadron: damaged by Me.109s in attack on Leeuwarden airfield, belly-landed at Watton; crew W/Cdr E. de V. Lart, F/Sgt Robertson, and Sgt A. Beeby DFM slightly injured, aircraft repaired. W/Cdr Lart and Sgt Beeby, with a different Observer were killed in the disastrous Aalborg raid on 13 August 1940.

29-07-1940   R3619 82 Squadron: FTR to Watton from 'cloud cover' raid on Bremen, shot down into sea off Texel by Lt H. Kargel, JG 27; F/Lt F. Keighley (Pilot) and Sgt J. Parsons (Obs) captured, Sgt K. MacPherson (WOp/Ag) KIA and buried in Den Burg Cemetery on Texel.

30-07-1940   R3764 XV Squadron Mk IV: FTR; took off from Wyton for Paderborn, but chose Flushing, shot down into Scheldt, crew baled out; F/O P. 'Red' Eames (Pilot) rescued by tug and captured, P/O F. Jones (Obs), and Sgt P. Murphy (WOp/Ag) KIA, both drowned.

31-07-1940   R3895 114 Squadron Mk IV: FTR to Horsham St Faith from bombing ships in Aalborg sound, shot down by Oblt Armin Schmidt's Me.109 of JG 77; crew S/Ldr M. Kennedy, P/O J. Hanlon, and Sgt G. Reinhart became PoWs.

Appendix 10

Other Blenheim losses, 23 June to 31 July 1940

25-06-1940 N3621 82 Squadron Mk IV: hit mast of target ship moored on Wainfleet Ranges and crashed; P/O Keeble killed.

28-06-1940 L9212 13 OTU Mk IV: engine cut and crashed attempting forced-landing near Bosherston, Pembs; Sgt T. Pascoe and Sgt N. Hawthorne killed, WOp/Ag injured.

28-06-1940 L1397 600 Squadron Mk I: overshot landing at Manston and struck dispersal pen, DBR; F/O G. Scrase uninjured.

28-06-1940 P4846 Special Duties Flight Mk IV: tail-wheel tyre burst and unit collapsed landing on very hard ground at Sway ELG; F/O D. Rayment uninjured, aircraft damaged Cat 4.

01-07-1940 L1278 236 Squadron Mk I: u/c collapsed while taxiing at Middle Wallop, DBR; P/O A. Inniss unhurt.

02-07-1940 L1265 23 Squadron Mk I-F: engine cut on approach, stalled and dived into ground at Sealand; P/O C. Baker and unnamed crewman injured.

03-07-1940 K7112 5 OTU Mk I: tyre burst on take-off at Aston Down, overturned on landing, DBR; P/O I. McDermott slightly injured.

04-07-1940 R3680 57 Squadron Mk IV: overshot landing at Dyce, DBR; P/O L. Ryan injured.

05-07-1940 K7156 23 Squadron Mk I: abandoned by solo pilot P/O Kaye after control lost in cloud, crashed at Granby, Notts.

06-07-1940 N3555 2 SAC Mk IV: hit trees at Andover on night take-off, crashed 2 miles west of airfield, destroyed by fire; P/O G. Lambert and Sgt S. Southeran killed.

06-07-1940 L8855 264 Squadron Mk IV: crashed, no further details available. 264 equipped with Defiants at the time.

07-07-1940 L6773 13 OTU Mk IV: Sgt Bennett landed downwind at Bicester overshot and hit boundary, aircraft DBR.

09-07-1940 L1249 13 OTU Mk I: engine cut on take-off, lost height, crashed half a mile from Bicester, destroyed by fire; F/Lt D. Smythe and Pupil Pilot escaped uninjured, one civilian on ground seriously injured.

09-07-1940 N6175 101 Squadron Mk IV: engine cut, force-landed near Huntingdon, hit tree-stump and DBR.

10-07-1940 L1358 1 AAS Mk I: engine cut in thunderstorm, stalled and dived into ground at Great Carlton, near Manby; F/O J. Lincoln (Pilot), Capt R. Curzon, and 2/Lt R. Jelf killed, 2/Lt Bate seriously injured. Three Army officers were from 1st Derbyshire Yeomanry.

13-07-1940 R3597 218 Squadron Mk IV: crashed and burst into flames at Harrold, near Bedford, on low-flying exercise; crew F/O T. Newton, Sgt D. Malpass, and Sgt J. Routledge killed.

15-07-1940 L6597 5 OTU Mk I: wing hit mud-bank while low flying over River Severn, crashed near Sharpness, Glos; P/O F. Harrold and one crewman injured.

15-07-1940 L9171 17 OTU Mk IV: engine cut and crashed in forced-landing near Great Raveley, Hunts; F/O W. Powdrell (solo pilot) slightly injured, airframe became 2161M.

18-07-1940 N3566 2 SAC Mk IV: engine cut on take-off, swung and hit boundary at Andover; P/O W. Fitzpatrick and crew uninjured.

19-07-1940 R3842 18 Squadron Mk IV: stalled and spun into ground near Gayton Radio Mast during formation practice; crew P/O A. Jones, Sgt K. Webster, and Sgt E. Abery killed. P/O Jones was 18 and had force-landed near Welwyn, Herts, two days earlier.

20-07-1940 L8844 17 OTU Mk IV: engine cut and crashed in forced-landing near Newnham Courtney, Northants; Sgt E. Kibble, Sgt D. Goodings, and Sgt H. Downs injured.

22-07-1940 L6652 5 OTU Mk I: engine cut, belly-landed and hit wall near Tetbury, Glos, DBR; P/O E. Bell (solo pilot) slightly injured.

22-07-1940 R3887 254 Squadron Mk IV-F: stalled on approach to Sumburgh, turning sharply to avoid lorries, crashed, DBF; F/Sgt W. Tyler (solo pilot) killed.

23-07-1940 R3820 21 Squadron Mk IV: spun into sea 1 mile off Lossiemouth during practice bombing on sea marker; crew P/O T. Powell, Sgt C. Smewin, and Sgt D. Mobberley killed.

23-07-1940 R3872 21 Squadron Mk IV: overshot landing at Lossiemouth, ran into Watch Office, P/O A. Carson safe.

23-07-1940 L9204 114 Squadron Mk IV: P/O R. Eggerton (Pilot) crashed attempting force-landing near Norwich after escape hatch blew off in flight, no injuries but aircraft DBR.

23-07-1940 L1105 5 OTU Mk I: stalled on approach and dived into ground at Frampton Mansell, Glos, destroyed by fire; P/O E. Bell (solo pilot) killed.

28-07-1940 L4869 17 OTU Mk IV: engine cut and belly-landed near Whitchurch, Bucks, P/O A. Smith unhurt, aircraft DBR and became 2171M.

27-07-1940 L8451 600 Squadron Mk I-F: DBR when tyre burst and u/c collapsed in heavy landing at Manston.

29-07-1940 T1923 110 Squadron Mk IV: overshot night landing at Kenley and damaged, subsequently destroyed in air-raid.

Chapter 15

August and September 1940

Not just 'the Few'

The Battle of Britain reached its climax during August and September 1940, as the Luftwaffe was taught the same painful lesson already learned at great cost by the RAF. The Germans found that, despite their considerable local numerical superiority, the level of losses sustained in daylight by formations of bombers was unsustainable, although these losses could be reduced if the bombers were escorted by short-range fighters. By the end of September they had given up their attempts at mass daytime raids, and resorted to raids by small formations of the faster Ju.88s escorted by up to 200 fighters, or sneak attacks by fighter-bombers, reserving their main bomber force of He.111s and Do.17s for the night-time 'Blitz'. They too had discovered that only the cover of darkness could provide adequate protection.

Throughout the daylight battle the Air Ministry published daily communiqués with lists of enemy aircraft claimed as 'destroyed', 'probably destroyed' and 'damaged', together with RAF losses. These figures were headlined by the press, rather like a cricket score, and showed clearly that the RAF was the winning side. They certainly buoyed morale, which was further strengthened by Winston Churchill's magnificent oratory. But the RAF claims were greatly exaggerated, mainly innocently in the natural confusion of aerial battle (although as nearly all enemy aircraft were shot down on to British soil it should not have been too difficult to corroborate claims), and included all Luftwaffe bombers, fighters, reconnaissance aircraft and even seaplanes, whereas the RAF losses referred only to fighters; if RAF losses of Bomber and Coastal Command aircraft – many of them Blenheims – are included the true figures are virtually equal. Indeed, on many days aggregate RAF losses exceeded those suffered by the Luftwaffe. However, a large number of British machines were subsequently repaired, and the balance of pilot losses tipped well in favour of the RAF as many of their fighter pilots baled out or crash-landed to fight again, whereas all of the German crews brought down over the UK were killed, wounded or captured, and took no further part in the fighting. The Battle of Britain Chapel in Westminster Abbey, dedicated in 1947, contains a Roll of Honour (for the 'official' period of the Battle from 10 July to 31 October 1940) that lists 449 pilots and air-crew from Fighter Command who were killed, but 718 from Bomber Command, 280 from Coastal Command, and 34 from the Fleet Air Arm. Fighter Command bore only 30 per cent of the casualties, but nowadays it is just the famous 'few' fighter pilots who remain in the public memory – in my view the other 70 per cent deserve not to be forgotten as they certainly played a most important part.

The Luftwaffe had found that its Ju.87 *Stukas*, although used with some success to dive-bomb Allied shipping in the Channel, coastal radar stations and British aerodromes, were far too vulnerable in the face of determined opposition from the RAF fighters and were thus unable to repeat their achievements of the battles of Poland and France, so they had to be withdrawn from the contest. The Messerschmitt Me.110 *Zerstorer* long-range fighter was also a disappointment and proved no match for the more agile RAF Spitfires and Hurricanes. The twin-engined Me.110 had been designed as a fighter, unlike the Blenheim, which was designed as a mini-airliner, adapted as a Medium Bomber and pressed into in service as an 'interim fighter', so the difficulties encountered by Blenheims when engaged by Me.109s can be better appreciated.

There was no respite for the Blenheims of Bomber and Coastal Commands as attacks on the continuing German preparations for invasion increased in intensity throughout August and September; and the 'cloud cover' raids continued, too, whenever the weather permitted. The 'invasion ports', facing England in a crescent from Rotterdam and Ostend in the east to Cherbourg and Brest in the west, and the growing number of large sea-going barges – some 3,000 – assembled in them, were bombed by day and night, as were enemy-held airfields and coastal heavy artillery batteries. Remember that the hard-pressed Blenheims had to operate both diurnally and nocturnally, while the other RAF bombers, Wellingtons, Hampdens and Whitleys, operated by night only – even the long-suffering Fairey Battles were re-activated for night raids on the Channel ports.

Sea-going barges being assembled for the proposed invasion of England, such as these photographed in Dunkirk Harbour by an 82 Squadron Blenheim, became top-priority targets by day and night. Blenheims played the major role in these raids.

Many accounts of the Battle of Britain claim that the Luftwaffe mounted heavy raids on RAF airfields that were not part of Fighter Command due to faulty intelligence reports, and that these mistaken attacks took the pressure off the Fighter stations just as it was taking effect. Although target selection by the German Air Force was generally too diverse and insufficiently focused during the Battle of Britain, there is a persuasive argument that they did know what they were doing in the matter of their attacks on airfields. They sent up high-flying reconnaissance aircraft early on every morning that the weather permitted to photograph the active RAF airfields and used this information to decide which to attack. They frequently selected airfields on which many Blenheims could be seen at the dispersal sites – they were well aware that the Blenheims were raiding their own airfields and the shipping and supplies being gathered in the Channel ports for the proposed invasion, and that if it was mounted the Blenheims would be the most numerous RAF aircraft tasked to attack their landing craft, troops on the beaches, and supply ships. It can be said that their raids on the many non-Fighter Command airfields where Blenheims were seen to be based, such as Detling, Thorney Island, St Eval, Ford, Martlesham Heath, Andover, etc, were not raided in error as often claimed, but were deliberately chosen as worthwhile targets. Realistic dummy Blenheims were set around decoy airfields, for example that near West Wittering, clearly to attract the Luftwaffe's attention. Sound City built 100 of these decoy Blenheims at its Shepperton Film Studios and they proved surprisingly effective. Many real Blenheims would also have been observed at several of the Fighter airfields that were heavily and repeatedly attacked, such as Debden, North Weald, Manston, Middle Wallop, Tangmere, Biggin Hill, Gravesend and Hornchurch. Nearly all of the 2 Group Blenheim bases were raided too, though not with such large forces. Clearly, from the enemy point of view, Blenheims on the ground were considered to be suitable and legitimate targets and I do not believe that they were attacked in error.

A 21 Squadron Blenheim returns from a raid on Channel ports. P/O Waples, the Pilot (on the left, in flying suit) is questioned about losses by his Acting CO, S/Ldr Cooper (with a patch on his face), and Station Commander, Gp/Capt L. Sinclair (back to camera); Medical Officer F/O Duncan (in side-cap) and Intelligence Officer S/Ldr Buckler (in glasses) listen anxiously.

'Bomber Blenheims'

To illustrate how often the Blenheims operated by night as well by day during these two critical months, enemy-held airfields were attacked on 24 days by aircraft from 15, 82, 105, 107, 110, 114, 139 and 218 Squadrons, and on 13 nights by aircraft from 15, 18, 40, 82, 101, 107, 110, 114 and 218 Squadrons. The Channel ports were raided by all the 2 Group squadrons on 10 days and 20 nights from 5 September – for example, an impressive 281 Blenheim sorties bombed Calais, Dunkirk, Ostend and Boulogne on just 10 nights in the second part of September. Other targets, such as the heavy artillery batteries, were raided on 20 days (including the 'cloud cover' raids) and 18 nights, by aircraft from 18, 40, 82, 101, 105, 107, 110, 114 and 139 Squadrons. The raids on enemy-held airfields were usually unproductive, since, by their very nature, most airfields comprised large areas of grassland and bomb craters were easily and rapidly filled. But occasionally they did produce worthwhile results with hits on hangars or on parked aircraft, such as on 1 August when only five of the 12 Blenheims sent to attack Haamstede and Evere (Brussels) airfields were able to bomb, but destroyed three of II/JG 27's Me.109s on the ground at the latter, killing *Staffelkapitan* Hauptman Albrecht von Ankum-Frank, whose unit also lost two more 109s to Blenheim rear gunners. On the 7th only two of the 29 aircraft sent by 2 Group to bomb airfields were able to do so, but when P/O Wellings in his 82 Squadron Blenheim R3821 loomed out of the murk over Haamstede its bombs struck six Messerschmitt 109s of IV/JG 54 preparing to take off, destroying two and badly damaging the other four, killing five airmen and injuring 17 more, with the effect that the fighter unit was withdrawn from the Battle of Britain for a month. (The bombs were dropped by Sgt Observer Don McFarlane, and 60 years later he was delighted to fly in the Blenheim that I'd had restored at Duxford, which had just been re-finished as R3821, UX-N, of 82 Squadron.)

Aircrews of 'A' and 'B' Flights, 18 Squadron, photographed at West Raynham on 1 August 1940. The Pilots are seated in the middle rows with their Observers behind and WOp/Ags in front. 'A' Flight has 12 complete crews, but the nine Pilots of 'B' Flight have only eight Observers and seven Gunners. The 'A' Flight aircraft has black under-surfaces, while the 'B' Flight aircraft is Sky – it also has spinners – and both have the single under-nose gun. 'B' Flight Commander S/Ldr Maxwell (lower centre) was later promoted to AVM.

In addition to the above bombing sorties, and to supplement Coastal Command's maritime efforts, shipping sweeps were carried out every single day, weather permitting, from 5 August right through until 30 October by at least six Bomber Command Blenheims, increasing to 26 aircraft on 21 August. This intense activity meant that the Blenheim bomber squadrons of 2 Group continued to suffer heavy losses both by day (see Appendix 1) and by night, the latter now to an increasing extent (see Appendix 2). It became almost impossible to enjoy a good night's sleep on the Blenheim stations. The ground-crews had to work round the clock too, and became as weary as the air-crews, but all knew that Great Britain was facing the greatest possible challenge to its very survival.

THE BRISTOL BLENHEIM

The 13th of August was *Adlertag* – Eagle Day – the massive aerial assault on England by the Luftwaffe that the Germans hoped would crush the Royal Air Force. But they hoped in vain. It also marked the first attack by the RAF on the only part of the British Empire conquered by the Germans, the Channel Islands, when 114 Squadron sent 17 Blenheims to bomb Jersey airfield, one of which was lost (see Appendix 1).

That 13 August saw another disaster befall the hard-hit 82 Squadron, which had already been virtually wiped out on the raid to Gembloux on 17 May. This time it was a medium-level daylight raid on the German-held airfield at Aalborg in north-east Denmark, the base for the Ju.88s that were attacking England. The 82 Squadron crews were mainly fresh replacements for those lost on the Gembloux raid. Twelve Blenheims led by 82's new CO, W/Cdr E. C. de Virac Lart set out at 0840, A Flight from Watton and B Flight from the Bodney satellite, soon forming the standard four RAF 'vics', each of three aircraft. Approaching the Danish coast, one aircraft (Sgt Baron in R3915) turned back from the tight formation over the North Sea. (The mission was near the limit of the aircraft's range, and the pilot calculated that he had insufficient fuel – he may have left the mixture at 'Rich', or his fuel gauges may have been inaccurate. He was charged and due to appear before a Court Martial, but was killed in another operation before his case could be heard.) The 11 remaining Blenheims reached the Danish coast at Sodervig some 50 miles south of their intended landfall at the mouth of the complex of fiords that led east to Aalborg airfield and seaplane base. The Observer in the CO's aircraft could only navigate for the long sector over the North Sea by creating an air-plot from dead-reckoning methods, using the forecast wind speed and direction. Unfortunately he was 2 degrees to starboard of his intended track; other Observers had noticed this, but with strict radio silence in force could not alert the leader, and attempts to contact W/Cdr Lart by Aldis lamp went unnoticed. His Observer was relatively inexperienced and appears to have been chosen because he was a commissioned officer. Consequently the formation flew north-north-east over the sunny Danish countryside for more than 20 minutes, heading directly for Aalborg, thus giving the Germans plenty of warning. Airfield defence flak opened up the formation and shot down five of the Blenheims in a few minutes, one (R3821 of P/O Hale) crashing on to the airfield. Then nine Me.109s from the Aalborg-based 5/JG-77 fell upon the Blenheims and soon shot down the remaining six so that not a single aircraft escaped the slaughter. Of the 33 brave crewmen who attacked the airfield so boldly, 20 lost their lives and 13 were captured, eight of whom were seriously injured. The cost in human lives and the traumas of injuries, or almost five years of captivity, endured by the surviving crews was extreme (see Appendix 3). Although the raid itself was a disastrous failure, as little damage was caused at the airfield, the courage shown by the Blenheim crews did have the side effect of encouraging the formation of a resistance movement by the Danes, who had been compliant to the German occupation before witnessing this almost sacrificial attack.

A few days after this disaster, the Medium Bomber Expansion Committee met on 17 August to discuss the AOC's memo regarding 'rolling up' the Blenheim squadrons into fewer Heavy Bomber units. They decided that they could not approve this drastic change as it would weaken and disrupt the Command too much while being implemented, and they were mindful not only of the promise to keep 250 aircraft available for direct support of the Army, but also of the slow rate of delivery of the new Heavy Bombers. There was no other choice – the Blenheims of 2 Group would have to continue as before.

Through August and into September the threat of an invasion of England by the Wehrmacht seemed ever more likely, and Bomber Command HQ issued contingency orders on 22 August that included the Blenheims of the Training Group in operations from 2 Group bases, as further reinforcements to those planned earlier. The order was unequivocal:

'Attacks will be pressed home regardless of cost. Each crew should aim to hit one vessel with one bomb and machine-gun the enemy whenever possible. Squadrons equipped with gas spray are to be ready to operate with this at the shortest possible notice, but it will only be used as a retaliatory measure.'

R3800, hit by flak, plunges inverted and in flames into Limfjoerden…

…and crashes 50 yards from the shore. F/Lt T. Syms and Sgt K. Wright baled out, but Sgt E. Turner was killed.

Wreckage of T1889, shot down in the target area. Sgt J. Oates, P/O R. Biden, and Sgt T. Graham were injured and captured.

The shattered tail of T1933, in which P/O D. Parfitt, Sgt J. Young, and Sgt K. Neaverson were killed.

The remains of R3829; S/Ldr R. Wardell managed to bale out, but F/Sgt G. Moore and Sgt T. Girvan were killed.

The smouldering remains of R3802; F/Lt R. Ellen and Sgt V. Dance baled out and were captured, but Sgt G. Davies was killed.

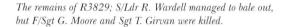

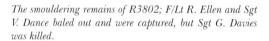

THE BRISTOL BLENHEIM

The wreck of R2772 near the shore. Amazingly the crew, Sgt D. Blair, Sgt W. Magrath and Sgt W. Greenwood, survived although injured. Bill Magrath escaped from captivity, made his way to Gibraltar via France and Spain, and was awarded the Military Medal.

Four survivors, John Oates, Bill Greenwood, Bill Magrath and John Bristow, meet at Watton in May 1990, where a propeller from R3800 forms a poignant memorial.

The Germans buried the dead airmen with a military funeral at Vadum Cemetery.

After the war local Danish people built a wall with an engraved memorial tablet to mark each grave – it is still beautifully maintained.

On 13 August another disaster struck 82 Squadron – all 11 Blenheims attempting to bomb Aalborg airfield in northern Denmark were shot down. Twenty courageous crewmen were killed, and of 13 airmen captured, eight were seriously injured.

The latter was a reference to the use of poison gas, banned by the Geneva Convention. Some Blenheims had tested a gas spray over Scottish lochs using a non-toxic gas drawn from a container in the bomb bay, but it was not used operationally. By this time most Bomber Command Blenheims had a rear-defence gun mounted on the escape hatch under the nose and fired rearwards and downwards by the Observer, but its presence was more of a psychological rather than practical benefit, and the extra drag and weight had a slightly adverse effect on performance. Most of the single Vickers pan-fed guns in the dorsal turret had been replaced by first one, then twin, Browning .303 belt-fed guns, which had a greater rate of fire, and did improve the rear defence in the upper sector, although they were still out-ranged by the armament of the Messerschmitts. Bomber Command did not adopt the nose-mounted forward-firing free gun for the Observer that had been adopted by Coastal Command on many of its bomber Blenheims mainly to assist flak suppression during anti-shipping attacks.

R3811, a 40 Squadron Mk IV, Failed to Return to Wyton from a Night Intruder sortie to Querqueville airfield on 25 August 1940. S/Ldr Thomas and his crew were killed.

A change in the German tactics on 7 September came with a major daylight attack on London docks and the East End, followed by a heavy night raid guided by the fires from the daylight bombing. This change gave the hard-pressed Fighter Command squadrons, whose airfields had been under constant attack, a brief but much-needed respite to regroup and recover their strength. An attempt by the Germans to repeat the large-scale attack on London on the 9th was deflected, although the night raids continued, and a huge raid on London on the 15th was broken up and repulsed, with 60 German aircraft being destroyed – although a morale-boosting 185 was claimed – for the loss of 26 RAF aircraft but only 13 pilots.

The success of the home-based RAF fighters in denying the Luftwaffe the air supremacy over the Channel and Southern England that the Germans needed, the constant attacks by RAF bombers – predominantly Blenheims – on the Channel ports with the shipping and supplies assembled in them, the raids on German-held airfields, and the threatening presence of the Home Fleet of the Royal Navy lurking in its Scottish bases, were the four fundamental factors that caused Hitler to issue his directive on the 17 September postponing Operation Sea Lion. The RAF was unaware of this decision, but that night was a full moon and an effective attack on Dunkirk harbour was carried out; 500 tons of ammunition in a dockside store were blown up, 26 barges were sunk or rendered useless and 58 more damaged, and a steamer and a torpedo-boat were sunk. The *Kriegsmarine* was no doubt relieved to learn that the invasion was being put off.

Coastal Blenheims

There was also no respite for Bomber Command's Blenheim comrades serving in Coastal Command, for they were right in the forefront and took continuing losses (see Appendix 4). Constant sweeps off the enemy-held coast were mounted to monitor shipping movements, and for the first time to attack coastal convoys moving westward with supplies for the Wehrmacht – a precursor of a bitter and costly anti-shipping campaign that would

53 and 59 Squadrons of Coastal Command were very heavily engaged throughout the Battle of Britain. This is F/O D. Wykeham-Martin and his crew at Detling.

be waged by the Blenheims a few months later. All too often Blenheims suffered from so-called 'friendly fire' – sometimes being mis-identified as Ju.88s to which they appeared very similar – as for example when three Mk IV-Fs of 235 Squadron were forced down by Hurricanes when scrambled to defend Thorney Island on 24 August (also Appendix 4).

The two Coastal squadrons equipped with bomber Blenheims, 53 and 59, operated unremittingly – 53 carried out 282 operational sorties in July alone – against the Channel ports and also enemy airfields and shipping, suffering severely during this activity (see Appendix 5). Sometimes they were escorted to their targets by Coastal Command Blenheim fighters, but – in a reversal of the usual situation – the bombers then had to reduce their normal cruising speed by some 15mph as the extra drag of the gun-packs slowed the escorting fighters! One such mixed Blenheim raid was mounted by Coastal Command on 1 August, when ten Mk IV-Fs of 236 Squadron escorted 13 Mk IVs of 59 Squadron to attack Querqueville; after the bombing six of the fighters ran in low to strafe the airfield, but two,

The terrible conditions endured by the ground-crews is shown by this photograph of a Coastal Command Blenheim undergoing work on a windy, rain-swept hard-standing; the bell-tents in the background were used by the airmen too.

including that of the Squadron CO, were shot down (see Appendix 4). 53 Squadron had a disastrous day on 13 August, for at tea-time 86 Ju.87 *Stukas* dive-bombed Detling, and the 40 escorting Me.109s then strafed the airfield; a direct hit on the Operations Block killed the Station Commander, G/Capt. E. Davis, and 53's Ops and Signals Officers, S/Ldr D. Oliver and F/O H. Aspen, among others. In addition, eight of 53's ground-crew were killed and eight more wounded, as were two WOp/Ags (Sgts D. Roberts and K. Vowles). Five of 53's Blenheims, on stand-by and loaded with bombs and fuel, blew up when set on fire by incendiary bullets from the strafing 109s, and 15 other aircraft were destroyed (see Appendix 5). 53 and 59 Squadrons paid heavily for being right in the front line.

Blenheim Fighters

While the Hurricanes and Spitfires of Fighter Command were fighting the Battle of Britain in the late summer skies above Southern England, the Blenheims in the same Command were occasionally drawn into the action too. They took more losses during the day (see Appendix 6) – including aircraft destroyed on the ground as the Luftwaffe concentrated its attacks on RAF airfields – but mainly by night (see Appendix 7) as the Germans stepped up their night-time raids, for the Blenheims still formed Britain's first line of defence at night. Twelve Mk I-Fs from 219 Squadron, normally a night-fighter unit, were scrambled from Catterick during the day on 15 August to intercept a large enemy raid on Driffield (which destroyed nine Whitleys), but could claim no success. Sgt Dube in L6624 was wounded by return fire and his WOp/Ag Sgt Bannister crawled through to help him; between them they brought the damaged aircraft to a wheels-up landing at Driffield, and both received an immediate DFM. But when a section of 604 Squadron Blenheims were scrambled to defend Middle Wallop from a further air-raid on 15 August they were set upon by Spitfires and one was forced down. Even worse was to follow, for three 25 Squadron Mk I-Fs were bought down by Hurricanes near North Weald on 3 September, one flown by 25's CO, S/Ldr Hoxton, who was far from amused! (See Appendix 6). Poor P/O Douglas Hogg in L1512 was killed and his ghost is said to appear at North Weald airfield to this day.

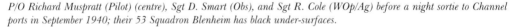

P/O Richard Muspratt (Pilot) (centre), Sgt D. Smart (Obs), and Sgt R. Cole (WOp/Ag) before a night sortie to Channel ports in September 1940; their 53 Squadron Blenheim has black under-surfaces.

No 23 Squadron at Collyweston suffered a bout of engine troubles during night combat patrols. On 10 August F/Lt R. Duke-Wooley with F/O D. McCullen in YP-P had to force-land at Coltishall, and P/O D. Williams with Sgt A. Johnson in YP-Z at Sutton Bridge; on the 14th P/O Patterson with Sgt McAdam in YP-Q force-landed at base after an engine seized. The Fighter Interception Unit lost three of its AI-equipped Blenheims when Tangmere was bombed on 16 August: L6838 was damaged beyond repair, while L6836 and L6688 were sent to Cuncliffe Owen Aircraft for major repairs but were further damaged in another air-raid and written off on 19 September (see Appendix 6).

Rare indeed was success for the Blenheim night-fighters, despite countless hours of searching the night skies. It was very hard to catch sight of their elusive quarry, for only a few Blenheims had the rudimentary AI radar and most relied entirely on their crews' eyesight – aided by moonlight, searchlights, and sometimes bursts from AA fire. If they did spot one of the enemy raiders they were often unable to catch up with it, and should they apply full throttle in an attempt to do so, the exhaust collector rings that formed the leading edge of the Mercury engine cowlings would glow red hot and provide ideal 'bulls-eye' targets for the enemy gunners! Even if the Blenheims could manoeuvre into position to make an attack, the fire-power of their .303 rifle-calibre guns – four in the ventral pack and one in the port wing – was seldom sufficient to inflict fatal damage. The gun-flashes betrayed their own position instantly and rarely were they able to make a second pass.

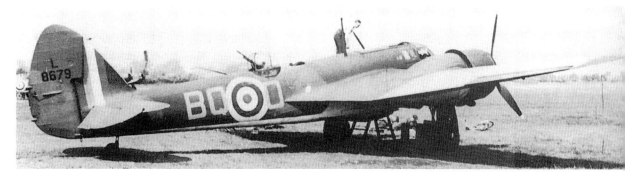

L8679, a Mk I-F of 600 Squadron at Manston during the Battle of Britain, was hit by 'friendly' AA fire during a night interception and abandoned when an engine caught fire, crashing near Westgate, Kent, on 9 August; the crew were rescued from the sea.

Despite these difficulties a few enemy aircraft were brought down by Blenheim I-Fs. In the early hours of 18 August P/O R. Rhodes and Sgt Gregory in L6741 of 29 Squadron stalked a Heinkel He.111 across England and shot it down into the sea some 25 miles off Spurn Head. On the night of the 20th F/Lt J. Adam with P/O Watson in L1237 followed a raider and attacked it off the Isle of Wight; it dived towards the sea but the claim could not be confirmed. Two nights later P/O Bob Braham in L1463 saw an enemy aircraft caught in searchlights; he exchanged fire off the Humber estuary, and the He.111 was seen burning on the sea by a searchlight crew.

These night patrols were often 'dicey'; for example, on the night of 4 September P/O J. Rofe with Sgt J. McCormack in their Mk I-F of 25 Squadron from North Weald were hit by AA fire from the ground while attacking an enemy aircraft and the tail of ZK-J was badly damaged; a fortnight later they attacked another raider but were hit by return fire and this time their Blenheim ZK-H was damaged beyond repair. Their colleague, P/O M. Herrick, was luckier – he shot down a He.111 of 1/KG1 near Bentwaters on the night of the 4th, together with a Do.17 'probably destroyed', and in the early hours of the 14th he brought down a further He.111 of 3/KG4 near Newmans End, Essex, being awarded a DFC for these successes. Two nights later F/Lt Pritchard of 600 Squadron shot down a He.111 in flames off Bexhill.

25 Squadron, the first to receive Mk I-Fs in December 1938, was hoping for more modern re-equipment, but the rumoured Bristol Beaufighters did not appear. The Squadron had been sent a couple of the fast four-cannon Westland Whirlwinds in May 1940 for evaluation as night-fighters, but they had found them so difficult to fly at night (due mainly to the higher landing speed and the glare from the Peregrine exhausts, especially on throttling back), that they declared them unsuitable and L6845 (the second prototype) and P6966 were sent back in July. No 25, like 23, 29, 219, 600 and 604 Squadrons, had to soldier on with its outmoded Blenheims – especially as the new AI sets, then being introduced more widely, required a separate crew-member to operate them. The gap in Britain's nocturnal defences that these 'interim fighters' were expected to fill was both far larger and much longer-lasting than the Air Staff had planned. Two Beaufighters were delivered to the FIU and single examples to the above Blenheim squadrons in September 1940, and they flew their first operational sorties in October. However, delayed by numerous 'teething troubles', not least with their Bristol Hercules engines (as mentioned in Chapter 7), deliveries only trickled through to the squadrons and it was more than six months – the very six months in which the Luftwaffe's night *Blitzkrieg* reached its height – before the Blenheim squadrons became fully equipped with the three-times-more-powerful and far more heavily armed Beaufighters. The 'Beaus' also had the advantage of the improved AI Mk IV radar, working on the 150MHz frequency band, which, with the increasing skills of the operators, finally turned the tide against the night bombers. This would not have been possible without the pioneering development work carried out by the Blenheims and their crews in improving both airborne radar and the new radar-based ground-control systems, and in cultivating through trial and error the techniques required for successful night interceptions.

Two of the RAF's highest-scoring night-fighter pilots 'cut their teeth' on Blenheim Mk I-Fs: 'Bob' Braham – author of *Scramble* – with 19 of his 29 victories gained at night, and John 'Cat's Eyes' Cunningham, also with 19 of his 21 victories achieved at night. The eventual top-scoring night-ace, Branse Burbridge (with 21 victories, all at night), did not claim his first victim until June 1942, flying a Douglas Havoc II – a night-fighter version of the 'Boston' with 12 Browning machine-guns in the nose. He then went on to Mosquitos to score the rest of his successes; although he had flown Blenheims at 54 OTU it was not in anger! But virtually all of this trio's 1940 night-fighter contemporaries flew them in action, such as John Topham, who claimed his first victim, a Ju.88 off Flamborough Head, in his 219 Squadron Mk I-F on the night of 15 August 1940, and went on to destroy 12 more enemy aircraft with Beaufighters, and Rod Chisholm – author of *Cover of Darkness* – who flew Blenheims with 604 Squadron and later achieved nine night-time victories. This select band included other famous pilots such as Max Aitken and Guy Gibson. The latter did a tour on 29 Squadron Blenheim Mk I-F night-fighters, claiming four victories, as a 'rest' between his Bomber Command tours on Hampdens and Manchesters and being asked to form 617, the special Lancaster Squadron assembled to attack the Ruhr Dams.

Like their comrades in the Blenheims of Bomber and Coastal Commands, the crews of the Fighter Command Blenheims – fighting in aircraft that were far from suitable for the tasks they were called upon to carry out – also showed exemplary courage and outstanding devotion to duty during these two months, the most critical in the history of the British Isles.

The crews of the operational squadrons in all three Commands, when not listed for 'ops' on the daily duty roster, were frequently engaged in training activity 'to improve their operational efficiency', and losses through accidents during these demanding but necessary activities continued to take a steady toll on the squadrons. Aircraft collided during formation exercises or during practice interceptions, hit the sea or the ground near bombing or firing ranges, and crashed during take-off or landing in bad weather or at night (see Appendix 8).

Operational Training Units

The losses were equally persistent and relentless at the Blenheim Operational Training Units (also Appendix 8) as they endeavoured to supply crews to replace those lost by the operational squadrons and to cater for the continued expansion of Bomber and Coastal Commands. The main 2 Group OTUs were No 13 at Bicester, and No 15 at Upwood, which worked their way through no fewer than 450 Blenheims between them. No 54 OTU at Church Fenton (and later No 51 at Cranfield) trained night-fighter crews, while No 42 at Andover, formed from the Schools of Army Co-operation, trained crews for that purpose, and No 2 OTU at Catfoss supplied crews to Coastal Command. All the OTUs were kept very busy indeed day after day, night after night, month after month, and made a vital contribution to the capabilities of the squadrons. The 1,200-plus Blenheims that served the OTUs most usefully for four long, hard years were mainly fairly tired and often battle-scarred veterans passed on from the operational squadrons after repairs to their battle or accidental damage. Many crews, having completed an operational tour, found that their 'rest' posting to an OTU as staff crews, or instructors to the 'sprog' trainee crews, was almost as dangerous as flying on active operations. Many Blenheims also served in other very busy training units – the Schools for Air Gunnery, Air Observers, Army Co-operation, Radio, and Bombing. They also served in AA Co-operation and Radar Calibration Units, and in Met, Ferry, and Beam Approach Training Flights. All of these units suffered steady attrition from accidental losses (see Appendix 8).

'The Few'

Winston Churchill's immortal phrase, in a speech he made on 20 August 1940, which so brilliantly encapsulates the Battle of Britain – 'Never in the field of human conflict was so much owed by so many to so few' – has gained its rightful place in the nation's collective memory. But very few now remember that he went on to praise the RAF night-bombers, then, in direct reference to the Blenheims, to pay a fulsome tribute: 'On no part of the Royal Air Force does the weight of war fall more heavily than on the daylight bombers, who play an invaluable part in the case of an invasion and whose unflinching zeal it has been necessary in the meantime on numerous occasions to restrain.'

The crew leave their Blenheim via the upper hatches; the Pilot has passed parachutes to a waiting airman, and the Gunner has elevated guns, so his seat is fully lowered.

Appendix I

Bomber Command Blenheim losses in daytime operations, 1 August to 30 September 1940

Aircraft are all Mk IVs.

01-08-1940   R3898 114 Squadron: failed to return (FTR) to Horsham St Faith from attack on Haamstede airfield, shot down by four Me.109Es of JG 54; P/O J. Goode severely injured and died later at Zierikzee, crew Sgt E. Will and Sgt V. Barrow Killed in Action (KIA) and all buried at Haamstede until later re-buried at Bergen-op-Zoom.

02-08-1940   L9422 18 Squadron: FTR to Horsham St Faith from attack on Haamstede airfield, shot down by Me.109s of JG54 near target; crew Sgt J. Davies, Sgt K. Bryant (aged 21), and Sgt W. Barrett (aged 20) KIA and buried at Bergen-op-Zoom.

02-08-1940   L8780 110 Squadron: took off from Wattisham from attack on Soesterberg, damaged by flak and crash-landed at base; Sgt Hards (Pilot) wounded, Sgt Cashman and Sgt Dunleavy unhurt, aircraft damaged beyond repair (DBR).

03-08-1940   L9239 139 Squadron: FTR to Horsham St Faith from attack on Cherbourg airfield, believed shot down near Macqueville; crew F/O A. Tedder, Sgt D. Spencer, and Sgt O. Evans KIA.

08-08-1940   L9472 18 Squadron: FTR to Great Massingham from attack on Schipol airfield, shot down by flak into sea; Sgt J. Saville, Sgt F. Parvin, and Sgt V. Land KIA. Sgt Parvin buried at Bergen-op-Zoom, others commemorated on Runnymede Memorial.

10-08-1940   R3910 82 Squadron: FTR to Watton from attack on airfields at Cherbourg and Guernsey, shot down into sea; P/O N. Smith, Sgt C. Hamilton, and Sgt J. Blazier KIA, commemorated at Runnymede.

10-08-1940   R3775 110 Squadron: FTR to Wattisham from attack on airfields, shot down near Calais; crew P/O A. Storrow, Sgt L. Cooke, and Sgt A. Underwood KIA, buried at Pihen-les-Guines.

11-08-1940   T1850 107 Squadron: FTR to Wattisham from attack on Dinard airfield, lost without trace; crew S/Ldr J. Fyfe DFC, Sgt P. Taylor, and Sgt T. Price KIA and commemorated on Runnymede Memorial.

13-08-1940   L9265 114 Squadron: FTR to Oulton from attack on Jersey airfield, lost without trace; crew P/O I. Carson, Sgt D. Morrissy, and Sgt L. Moores KIA and commemorated on Runnymede Memorial.

15-08-1940   T1882 18 Squadron: FTR to West Raynham from attack on shipping, lost without trace; crew Sgt H. Tyldesley, Sgt F. Smith, and Sgt T. Byrne KIA and commemorated on Runnymede Memorial.

19-08-1940   R3892 114 Squadron: FTR from attack on Bremen oil refinery, shot down over Holland by Uffz R. Woick of JG 54; Sgt K. Dobb (Pilot, aged 19) and Sgt A. Pillans (aged 18) KIA and commemorated on Runnymede Memorial, Sgt A. Stevenson (Obs) baled out and became PoW.

26-08-1940   L8870 101 Squadron: FTR to West Raynham, crashed at 0450 near Eastleigh after striking barrage balloon cable on return from St Malo; crew Sgt J. Balmer, Sgt W. Corker, and Sgt T. Cranston KIA.

01-09-1940   T1877 105 Squadron: hit by flak over Zuider Zee, force-landed at Mousehole; Sgt H Duncan (Obs) injured and later died in hospital, P/O Prosser (Pilot) and Sgt Partridge (WOp/Ag) safe, aircraft repaired.

08-09-1940   R3915 82 Squadron: FTR from recce of Dutch Coast, believed shot down into North Sea; F/O A. Cobbe, P/O H. Christopher, and Sgt W. Cassells KIA and commemorated on Runnymede Memorial.

08-09-1940   R3730 82 Squadron: FTR; took off from Watton with R3915 above on same mission; crew P/O J. McCausland, Sgt J. Philpott RNZAF, and Sgt R. Fletcher KIA and commemorated on Runnymede Memorial.

08-09-1940   L8848 218 Squadron: FTR to Oakington from recce. to Dutch coast, shot down into North Sea; Sgt G. Clayton, Sgt F. Coish, and Sgt G. Taylor KIA. Gerald Clayton and Frederick Coish commemorated on Runnymede Memorial, Gordon Taylor buried at Bergen-op-Zoom.

09-09-1940   T1894 105 Squadron: FTR to Watton from sortie to bomb invasion barges, shot down by Lt W. Wubke in Me.109E of JG 54 off Den Helder; Sgt D. Hodson, Sgt E. Palmer, and Sgt R. Green KIA and commemorated on Runnymede Memorial. Their first and last operational flight.

24-09-1940   T1794 139 Squadron: FTR to Horsham St Faith, shot down attacking E-boats in Channel; S/Ldr M. Hendry, Sgt P. Davidson, and Sgt V. Arrowsmith KIA and commemorated on Runnymede Memorial.

24-09-1940   R3885 139 Squadron: badly damaged attacking E-boats in Channel and force-landed at Manston; crew F/O Turnbull, Sgt Jones, and Sgt Ward only slightly injured, aircraft repaired.

25-09-1940   P6905 101 Squadron: FTR to West Raynham from anti-shipping sortie, crashed near Swaffham on return and exploded; crew Sgt F. Lorrimar, Sgt P. Booth, and Sgt D. Simms KIA.

30-09-1940   N6191 107 Squadron: crashed on take-off from Wattisham to bomb Calais and burst into flames; Sgt J. Merrett (Pilot) and Sgt A. Byron (Obs) KIA, Sgt S Walter (WOp/Ag) died of injuries, having been pulled from burning wreck by CO W/Cdr Laurie Sinclair, who was awarded George Cross for his bravery.

Appendix 2

Bomber Command Blenheim losses in night operations, 1 August to 30 September 1940

Aircraft are all Mk IVs.

12/13-08-1940 R3768 XV Squadron: FTR to Wyton from sortie to bomb Lannion airfield, shot down at Fermanville; crew P/O F. Dench, Sgt A. Gray, and Sgt E. Scrase KIA, buried locally.

14/15-08-1940 P4908 40 Squadron: FTR to Wyton from sortie to bomb Chartres airfield, damaged near target, ditched off Cherbourg; crew Sgt K. Newton, Sgt F. Hotchkiss, and Sgt C. McCreary captured and became PoWs.

14/15-08-1940 R3609 40 Squadron: FTR to Wyton as above, shot down; P/O G. Parker (Pilot) captured and became PoW, Sgt G. Easton (Obs) and Sgt E. Watson (WOp/Ag) evaded capture. Sgt Watson awarded MM.

15/16-08-1940 R3770 XV Squadron: FTR to Wyton from sortie to bomb Foret de Gunnes, presumed shot down into sea; crew Sgt P. Garvey, Sgt H. Bower, and Sgt H. Rolls KIA.

19/20-08-1940 L9419 101 Squadron: FTR to West Raynham from sortie to bomb Eindhoven, believed shot down into sea off Dutch coast; Sgt A. Chelmick, Sgt N. Martyn, and Sgt J. Carbine captured and became PoWs.

19/20-08-1940 N3574 101 Squadron: FTR to West Raynham after bombing Haamstede on one engine, ditched by RN destroyer; Sgt J. George (WOp/Ag) drowned despite efforts of P/O N. Bicknell (Pilot) and Sgt W. Gingell (Obs) to rescue him; awarded DFC and DFM respectively.

22/23-08-1940 T1990 218 Squadron: FTR to Oakington from sortie to bomb Bruges, shot down at Guines, near Calais; S/Ldr C. House (Pilot) and Sgt P. Lefevre (Obs) KIA, Sgt J. Howard (WOp/Ag) became PoW.

22/23-08-1940 L9462 57 Squadron: hit by another aircraft and crashed on night take-off from Elgin for shipping sweep; S/Ldr Roncoroni, P/O Carter, and Sgt Havard injured.

25/26-08-1940 R3811 40 Squadron: FTR to Wyton from sortie to bomb airfield at Querqueville, presumed shot down; S/Ldr F. Thomas, P/O G. Bayliss, and Sgt G. Dickson KIA and commemorated on Runnymede Memorial.

25/26-08-1940 T1927 40 Squadron: FTR to Wyton as R3811 above, presumed shot down; crew Sgt C. Riley, Sgt F. Newson, and Sgt J. Smith KIA and commemorated on Runnymede Memorial.

25/26-08-1940 P6928 57 Squadron: FTR to Elgin from sortie to bomb airfields in Norway, presumed shot down into sea; crew Sgt E. Riley, Sgt A. Gibson, and Sgt R. Stiles KIA and commemorated on Runnymede Memorial.

29/30-08-1940 N3620 107 Squadron: FTR to Wattisham from sortie to bomb De Kooy airfield, shot down in flames near target by flak; F/O E. Berry, Sgt A. Sully, and Sgt H. Bentham (aged 18) KIA and buried at Huisduinen.

30/31-08-1940 L9378 18 Squadron: FTR to West Raynham from night sortie to NW Germany, crashed near Weasenham in bad visibility; crew Sgt L. Williams, Sgt A. Owles, and Sgt R. Jones KIA.

30/31-08-1940 L9326 40 Squadron: FTR to Wyton, crashed and destroyed by fire after night take-off for sortie to Emden; crew P/O W. Evans, Sgt F. Little, and Sgt J. Watt KIA.

30/31-08-1940 R3773 110 Squadron: FTR from night sortie to Emden, crashed at Offton near Ipswich on return; P/O J. Price (Pilot) and Sgt H. Tune (Obs) KIA, Sgt McDonald (WOp/Ag) seriously injured.

01/02-09-1940 R3663 18 Squadron: crashed 0335 attempting to land at Great Massingham on return from sortie to NW Germany; F/Lt C. Howden, Sgt Spratchell, and Sgt F. Hind injured.

01/02-09-1940 L8796 40 Squadron: crashed trying to land at West Raynham on return from sortie to Nordenham, NW Germany; crew P/O R. Whitehead injured, Sgt A. Coburn killed, and Sgt J. Robbins safe, aircraft DBR.

02/03-09-1940 L8757 40 Squadron: FTR; shot down by flak bombing Schlebusch, NW Germany at night, crashed in Waddenzee; crew F/Sgt R. Broadhurst, Sgt A. Marsden, and Sgt A. Burns KIA. 'Chiefy' Broadhurst buried at Den Burg, others commemorated on Runnymede Memorial.

03/04-09-1940 R3769 XV Squadron: FTR to Wyton from sortie to bomb St Omer, crashed near Kettering on return; P/O D. Myland DFC, Sgt H. Powys-Jones, and Sgt P. Petrie KIA.

030/4-09-1940 L9188 18 Squadron: crashed returning from NW Germany at night, attempting to land at Great Massingham; Sgt J. Allen (Pilot) and Sgt E. Walsh (Obs) KIA, Sgt Kalne (WOp/Ag) injured.

04/05-09-1940 R3824 107 Squadron: crashed into R3736 landing at Wattisham after 6-hour night sortie to Mardiek; P/O F. Otterway (Pilot) and Sgt S. Bews (Obs) KIA, Sgt A. Brand (WOp/Ag) injured.

08/09-09-1940 R3612 40 Squadron: FTR to Wyton from sortie to bomb Ostend, lost without trace; crew Sgt L. Patrick, Sgt T. Jarman, and Sgt V. Pegler KIA and commemorated on Runnymede Memorial.

08/09-09-1940 T1831 107 Squadron: FTR to Wattisham from sortie to Ostend, crashed near Hesdin, Pas-de-Calais, believed shot down; crew P/O C. Halkett RNZAF, Sgt A. Jacobs, and Sgt J. Easton KIA and buried in Wambercourt Churchyard, France.

08/09-09-1940 T1851 107 Squadron: FTR from same mission, lost without trace; F/O A. Cazalet, Sgt L. Charnock, and Sgt E. Thompson KIA and commemorated on Runnymede Memorial.

08/09-09-1940 P6955 101 Squadron: FTR to Wattisham from sortie to bomb Boulogne, missing over sea, believed shot down; F/Lt E. Palmer, Sgt J. McKee, and Sgt S. Booth KIA and commemorated on Runnymede Memorial.

08/09-09-1940 R2788 101 Squadron: FTR from same mission, lost without trace, believed shot down; crew Sgt C. Cooke, Sgt C. Day, and Sgt R. Spencer KIA and commemorated on Runnymede Memorial.

13/14-09-1940 R2786 XV Squadron: FTR to Wyton from sortie to bomb Ostend harbour, lost without trace; crew Sgt O. Yeomans, Sgt R. Hollingshead, and P/O P. Hughes KIA and commemorated on Runnymede Memorial.

18/19-09-1940 L9339 105 Squadron: FTR to Watton from sortie to bomb Ostend, lost without trace; crew Sgt C. Bowles, Sgt V. Radford, and Sgt A. Lackenby KIA and commemorated on Runnymede Memorial.

18/19-09-1940 T1852 107 Squadron: FTR to Wattisham from sortie to bomb Calais, lost without trace; crew P/O C. Preston, Sgt T. Ross, and Sgt W. Kilgour KIA and commemorated on Runnymede Memorial.

24/25-09-1940 T1883 107 Squadron: FTR to Wattisham from sortie to bomb Calais, shot down near there; crew P/O W. Shann, P/O A. Etherington, and Sgt W. Powell KIA and buried at Guemps.

26/27-09-1940 R3809 114 Squadron: FTR to Oulton from sortie to bomb Boulogne, believed shot down into Channel; crew Sgt F. Wheeler, Sgt T. Johnson, and Sgt D. Hooker KIA. Sgt Wheeler's body recovered from sea off Sandown, IoW, others commemorated on Runnymede Memorial.

Appendix 3

Blenheim losses on the Aalborg airfield raid, 13 August 1940

Aircraft are all 82 Squadron Mk IVs.

13-08-1940 T1934: FTR; shot down in target area; crew W/Cdr E. de V. Lart, P/O M. Gillingham, and Sgt A. Beeby DFM, KIA and buried in Vadum Cemetery.

13-08-1940 T1933: FTR; shot down in target area; crew P/O D. Parfitt, Sgt L. Young, and Sgt K. Neaverson KIA and buried in Vadum Cemetery.

13-08-1940 R3913: FTR; shot down in target area; crew P/O C. Wigley, Sgt A. Patchett, and Sgt A. Morrison KIA and buried in Vadum Cemetery.

13-08-1940 R3821: FTR; shot down in target area; crew P/O E. Hale, Sgt R. Oliver, and Sgt A. Boland KIA and buried in Vadum Cemetery.

13-08-1940 T1827: FTR; shot down in target area; S/Ldr N. Jones (Pilot) and P/O T. Cranidge (Obs) KIA and buried in Vadum Cemetery, Sgt J. Bristow (WOp/Ag) survived, captured, and became PoW.

13-08-1940 R3904: FTR; shot down in target area; Sgt G. Ankers (Obs) and Sgt K. Turner (WOp/Ag) KIA, P/O B. Newland (Pilot) survived and captured.

13-08-1940 R3829: FTR; shot down in target area; F/Sgt G. Moore (Obs) and Sgt T. Girvan (WOp/Ag) KIA, S/Ldr R. Wardell (Pilot) captured and became PoW.

13-08-1940 R3802 (Mk IV), 82 Squadron: FTR; shot down in target area; Sgt G. Davies (WOp/Ag) KIA, F/Lt R. Ellen (Pilot) and Sgt V. Dance (Obs) captured and became PoWs.

13-08-1940 R3800: FTR; shot down in target area; Sgt E. Turner (WOp/Ag) KIA, F/Lt T. Symms (Pilot) and Sgt K. Wright (Obs) captured and became PoWs.

13-08-1940 T1889: FTR; shot down in target area; crew Sgt J. Oates, P/O R. Bidden, and Sgt T. Graham injured and captured.

13-08-1940 R2772: FTR; shot down in target area; crew Sgt D. Blair, Sgt W. Magrath, and Sgt W. Greenwood seriously injured and captured. Bill Magrath awarded Military Medal for escaping from hospital and returning via Spain and Gibraltar to UK.

Graphically illustrating the disaster that befell 82 Squadron on 13 August are: an outer wing taken as a trophy by the Luftwaffe, the shattered remains of R3829, the wreckage of T1899, and the final indignity – parts of T1899 carted away for scrap.

Appendix 4

Coastal Command Blenheim losses, 1 August to 30 September 1940

Aircraft are all Mk IVs or Mk IV-Fs.

01-08-1940   N3601 236 Squadron: FTR to Thorney Island, shot down escorting Blenheims attacking Querqueville airfield; S/Ldr P. Drew, CO of 236 Squadron, and F/O B. Nokes-Cooper KIA, buried in France.

01-08-1940   R2774 236 Squadron: FTR to Thorney Island from same mission; crew P/O B. McDonough and Sgt F. Head KIA, commemorated at Runnymede.

01-08-1940   N3603 236 Squadron: took off from Thorney Island on same mission, tail badly damaged by AA fire, but Sgt R. Smith and Sgt A. Piper managed to return to base, aircraft repaired.

01-08-1940   L8792 59 Squadron: FTR from day raid on Cherbourg, shot down; crew W/Cdr R. Morgan-Weld-Smith, P/O D. Davis AFM, and Sgt P. Pryde KIA, buried in France. Morgan-Weld-Smith was CO of 59 Squadron.

02-08-1940   N3587 59 Squadron: FTR from reconnaissance to Cherbourg; crew P/O D. Drew, Sgt A. Herbert, and Sgt J. Close KIA, buried in St Marie Cemetery, Le Havre.

04-08-1940   L8684 236 Squadron: took off from Thorney Island, received severe damage to oil system from Me.109s off Le Havre, force-landed at base; crew P/O C. Peachment and Sgt J. Lowe uninjured, aircraft repaired.

04-08-1940   L8794 53 Squadron: FTR; abandoned in air on night patrol in bad visibility and crashed near Bordon, Hants; crew S/Ldr D. Oliver, Sgt Dunjey, and Sgt Thirlby uninjured.

04-08-1940   L9475 53 Squadron: FTR to Detling from night raid on Emden harbour, crashed into North Sea on return; crew F/O H. Corbett, Sgt S. Riddington, and Sgt K. Crane KIA.

07-08-1940   L9456 248 Squadron: FTR to Sumburgh from patrol, ditched off St Abbs Head, out of fuel; crew P/O R. Haviland, P/O M. Wells, and Sgt A. Kay rescued by trawler, floating aircraft towed ashore by another.

08-08-1940   N3590 59 Squadron: FTR from reconnaissance to Cherbourg harbour; crew P/O H. Davis, Sgt G. Coulton, and Sgt B. Beaumont KIA. Sgt Beaumont is buried in Dieppe War Cemetery, his comrades commemorated on Runnymede Memorial.

11-08-1940   T1816 53 Squadron: FTR from shipping recce off French coast; P/O P. Coleman (Pilot) captured, Sgt I. Inskip (Obs) missing presumed KIA, P/O G. Bardolph (WOp/Ag) wounded and died six days later.

11-08-1940   R3911 53 Squadron: FTR to Detling from recce to Channel ports, badly damaged by Me.109s, crash-landed at Manston; crew F/Lt Stevenson, Sgt H. Bower, and Sgt H. Rolls only slightly injured, aircraft repaired.

13-08-1940   T1937 53 Squadron: FTR from sortie to bomb barges, abandoned in air when out of fuel and crashed near Hawkhurst, Kent; crew F/O Jameson, Sgt Andrews, and Sgt Butler baled out successfully.

13-08-1940   T1938, R3849, R3677, R3819, R3632 and L9460 53 Squadron: destroyed by bombs in air raid on Detling by Stukas. R3632 of Andover Station Flight was visiting Detling; L9460 badly damaged and struck off charge 04-09-1940.

15-08-1940   T1815 59 Squadron: DBR in air raid at Thorney Island.

16-08-1940   R3835 59 Squadron: destroyed by bombs at Manston.

17-08-1940   N3540 235 Squadron: overshot landing at Thorney Island after night patrol; crew Sgt S. Hobbs, Sgt H. Ricketts, and Sgt T. Maslen safe, aircraft DBR.

17-08-1940   L4833 235 Squadron: FTR, crashed into sea on night approach to Thorney Island on return from sortie to Boulogne; Sgt S. Hobbs and crew rescued with slight injuries.

18-08-1940   T1805 235 Squadron: DBR by return fire from enemy aircraft; crew P/O Wordsworth and Sgt Maconochie uninjured.

19-08-1940   L9457 248 Squadron: FTR to Sumburgh from recce to south Norwegian coast; crew Sgt J. Round, Sgt W. Want, and Sgt M. Digby-Worsley presumed KIA and are commemorated on Runnymede Memorial.

19-08-1940   R2795 59 Squadron: FTR from night raid on Caen airfield; crew P/O B. Reynolds, Sgt W. Whiting, and Sgt W. Wilkinson KIA, buried in Bayeux War Cemetery.

20-08-1940   Z5729 236 Squadron: took off from St Eval, damaged by own AA fire over Pembroke Dock, force-landed at base; crew P/O G. Campbell and Sgt S. Archer uninjured, aircraft repaired.

21-08-1940   R2776 and T1944, 236 Squadron: destroyed on ground at St Eval by bombing from Ju.88s.

24-08-1940   T1804 235 Squadron: FTR; shot down by Hurricane of 1 RCAF Squadron into Bracklesham Bay; crew P/O D. Woodger and Sgt Don Wright (aged 18) KIA.

24-08-1940   Z5736 235 Squadron: badly damaged by Hurricane of 1 RCAF Squadron, crash-landed at base; crew Sgt K. Naish and Sgt W. Owen slightly injured, aircraft repaired.

24-08-1940   N3531 235 Squadron: damaged by Hurricane of 1 RCAF Squadron, force-landed at Thorney Island; crew F/Lt F. Flood and Sgt Sharpe uninjured, aircraft repaired.

25-08-1940   L9407 254 Squadron: undershot landing at Dyce, hit wall, DBR; F/O G. Sise RNZAF and F/Lt W. Bain injured.

| 25-08-1940 | T2035 53 Squadron: FTR; damaged on patrol to Channel ports, crashed on house at Dover (killing PC W. Maycock and wife) on return; crew F/O S. Rochford, Sgt W. Briggs, and Sgt D. Brook KIA. |

25-08-1940   T2035 53 Squadron: FTR; damaged on patrol to Channel ports, crashed on house at Dover (killing PC W. Maycock and wife) on return; crew F/O S. Rochford, Sgt W. Briggs, and Sgt D. Brook KIA.

27-08-1940   L9449 248 Squadron: FTR to Sumburgh from recce to south Norwegian coast, crashed in North Sea; P/O C. Arthur, Sgt E. Ringwood, and Sgt R. Cox KIA and commemorated on Runnymede Memorial.

28-08-1940   R2794 59 Squadron: FTR from raid on Caen aerodrome, flew into high ground at night in bad visibility on return, crashed near Littlehampton; crew P/O J. Dellow, Sgt K. Edwards, and Sgt L. Betts KIA.

28-08-1940   T2046 53 Squadron: FTR from raid on seaplane base in Holland, crashed into North Sea; P/O W. Fitzpatrick, Sgt J. Bann, and Sgt H. Dunnington KIA and commemorated on Runnymede Memorial.

30-08-1940   L9262 235 Squadron: FTR, spun into ground from Bircham Newton circuit on training sortie; crew P/O J. Priestley RNZAF and Sgt E. Graves killed.

31-08-1940   R3880 59 Squadron: FTR from sortie to bomb oil-tanks at Cherbourg; crew P/O J. Finlay, Sgt F. Leonhardt, and Sgt A. Peddie KIA. Sgt Peddie is buried in Quiberville Churchyard, his comrades commemorated on Runnymede Memorial.

31-08-1940   T1940 53 Squadron: FTR from night raid on Vaardingen oil plant, shot down over target by flak; crew W/Cdr E. Edwards, Sgt L. Benjamin, and Sgt J. Beesley KIA and buried in Rotterdam. 'Sphinx' Edwards was CO of 53 Squadron.

31-08-1940   L8786 254 Squadron: hit tree on overshoot from Dyce with flaps down, DBR; P/O H. Rose (solo pilot) unhurt.

01-09-1940   Z5724 235 Squadron: took off from Bircham Newton, engine cut and crash-landed near Lincoln, DBR; P/O F. Kirkpatrick unhurt.

01-09-1940   T1880 59 Squadron: FTR from operation to Lorient, damaged by flak, crashed into creek off Thorney Island on return; no injuries recorded to P/O Short, Sgt Hewitt, and Sgt Burney.

03-09-1940   N3529 254 Squadron: crashed while engaged in aerial tactics, collided with N3608 below, destroyed by fire (DBF); Sgt R. Hanna and AC2 J. Mangion killed.

03-09-1940   N3608 254 Squadron: crashed while engaged in aerial tactics, collided with N3529 above, DBF; P/O J. Laidlay, Sgt R. Whiffen, and AC1 D. Campbell killed.

05-09-1940   R3755 21 Squadron: FTR from anti-shipping sortie, lost without trace; crew Sgt J. Moss, Sgt K. Daly, and Sgt C. Mein KIA and commemorated on Runnymede Memorial.

08-09-1940   T2042 53 Squadron: FTR from attacking convoy off Calais, shot down into Channel by Me.109s; crew P/O R. Hall (NZ, aged 19), Sgt J. Randall, and Sgt M. Conacher KIA, commemorated at Runnymede.

08-09-1940   R3779 53 Squadron: FTR as T2042 above; crew F/Lt I. Bartlett, Sgt R. Aldridge, and Sgt E. Sheldrick KIA and commemorated on Runnymede Memorial.

11-09-1940   L9396 235 Squadron: FTR from escorting FAA Albacores to Calais, shot down by Me.109; crew P/O P. Wickens-Smith, P/O A. Green, and Sgt R. Watts KIA, commemorated on Runnymede Memorial.

11-09-1940   Z5725 235 Squadron: FTR from same mission, shot down by Me.109; crew F/Lt F. Flood, P/O N. Shorrocks, and Sgt B. Sharp KIA, commemorated on Runnymede Memorial.

13-09-1940   L9451 248 Squadron: FTR to Sumburgh from recce to Norwegian coast; Sgt W. Garfield, Sgt B. Mesner, and Sgt A. Kay KIA, Sgt Garfield buried at Bergen, crew commemorated at Runnymede.

19-09-1940   T2045 53 Squadron: FTR from Dundee patrol, shot down into sea off Berck-sur-Mer; crew P/O C. Tibbitts (NZ), Sgt R. Grace, and Sgt E. Harrold KIA on their first operation, commemorated at Runnymede.

20-09-1940   R3635 59 Squadron: FTR from sortie to Cherbourg; crew P/O K. Palmer, Sgt E. Wright, and Sgt D. Walters KIA, buried in Le Vast Churchyard, Manche, France.

25-09-1940   L8793 59 Squadron: FTR; stalled on approach to Thorney Island on return from recce, crashed into sea; P/O R. Johnson (Pilot) KIA, crew Sgt Abell and Sgt Andrew injured, rescued by boat.

26-09-1940   T2221 53 Squadron: hit tree on night take-off from Detling for raid on Den Helder and crashed; P/O J. Ritchie (Pilot) and Sgt J. Otham (Obs) slightly injured, Sgt R. Trafford (WOp/Ag) more seriously injured.

30-09-1940   T2044 53 Squadron: FTR to Detling from night sortie to bomb Rotterdam harbour, crashed into North Sea; crew P/O S. Bevan-John, Sgt S. Macquire, and Sgt H. Shaw KIA.

Appendix 5

Fighter Command Blenheim losses, 1 August to 30 September 1940

Aircraft are all Mk I-Fs except Mk IV-F Z5721 on 13 September 1940.

01-08-1940 L8509 29 Squadron: DBR when landing with undercarriage retracted at Wellingore returning from night patrol.

02-08-1940 L8692 219 Squadron: took off from Catterick, overshot flapless landing at Leeming and undercarriage raised; P/O W. Lambie and Sgt R. Bell unhurt, aircraft DBR.

04-08-1940 L1356 23 Squadron: engine cut on night patrol, caught fire on landing at Wittering and destroyed; no injuries recorded.

06-08-1940 ? 219 Squadron: hit HT cables during search-light co-op sortie, crashed in river; P/O J. Carriere slightly injured, Sgt C. Beveridge uninjured, aircraft DBR. Incident recorded in Squadron ORB without serial number, and am unable to match it to any aircraft loss.

08-08-1940 L8665 600 Squadron : FTR; shot down in flames into sea off Ramsgate by Me.109E of Oblt Sprick of JG 26; crew F/O D. Grice, Sgt F. Keast, and AC1 J. Warren KIA. AC Warren (aged 19) buried at Calais.

08-08-1940 L1448 23 Squadron: FTR; control lost during night patrol and spiralled into ground near Peterborough; crew P/O C. Cardnell and Sgt C. Stephens KIA.

09-08-1940 L8679 600 Squadron: FTR to Manston, hit by own AA at night while attacking raider near Westgate, engine cut, crew baled out; F/O S. le Rougetel (Pilot) rescued from sea by Ramsgate lifeboat, Sgt E. Smith swam ashore.

09-08-1940 L1377 29 Squadron: engine cut on night patrol, belly-landed at Wittering; P/O Rhodes and Sgt Gregory uninjured, aircraft DBR.

12-08-1940 L1406 25 Squadron: overshot at Martlesham Heath returning from night patrol and overturned; Sgt Gooderham and Sgt Snape uninjured.

14-08-1940 L1418 25 Squadron: DBR landing at Martlesham Heath after night patrol; F/O Emmett and Sgt McCormack uninjured.

14-08-1940 L1521 600 Squadron: destroyed on ground at Biggin Hill during air-raid; two others at Manston badly damaged.

15-08-1940 L8698 219 Squadron: took off from Catterick, damaged by return fire from enemy aircraft; Sgt O. Dupee (Pilot) wounded and crash-landed at Driffield, assisted by Sgt T. Banister, aircraft repaired. Both crewmen awarded DFM for this action.

15-08-1940 L6610 604 Squadron: damaged by 609 Squadron Spitfire of P/O D. Crook, belly-landed at Middle Wallop; Sgt Haigh (Pilot) slightly hurt, P/O Evans (WOp/Ag) wounded, Sgt Fenton (Obs) uninjured, aircraft DBR.

15-08-1940 L6723 and L8676, 604 Squadron: destroyed during air-raid by Ju.88s on Middle Wallop.

16-08-1940 L6838, L6836 and L6688, FIU: all damaged at Tangmere during air-raids, L6836 and L6688 further damaged while under repair at Cuncliffe Owen; all SOC.

16-08-1940 L6608 and L8670, 600 Squadron: destroyed, and L1295 and L6617 damaged, at Manston by strafing Me.109s.

24-08-1940 L6681 604 Squadron: crash-landed near Odiham on night patrol; F/O H. Speke and Sgt S. Shirley uninjured, aircraft later repaired.

25-08-1940 L1330 29 Squadron: FTR from night patrol, shot down into sea by enemy aircraft off Wainfleet, Lincs; P/O R. Rhodes, Sgt R. Gouldstone, and AC2 N. Jacobson KIA. Norman Jacobson was only just 18.

25-08-1940 L6782 604 Squadron: FTR from night patrol, became lost, crashed near Witheridge, Devon, permission to land at Exeter having been refused due to enemy aircraft; Sgt J. Fletcher, Sgt C. Haigh, and LAC A. Austin KIA, Austin dying on 26th.

27-08-1940 L1524 219 Squadron: DBR when undershot in sudden rainstorm at Acklington; Sgt E. Grubb and Sgt S. Austin injured.

29-08-1940 K7092 23 Squadron: swung on take-off for operation and hit Wittering Watch Office; Sgt J. Rose injured, aircraft to Rootes 12-09-1940, but DBR and SOC 02-11-1940.

03-09-1940 L1512 25 Squadron: FTR; shot down while on patrol near North Weald by RAF Hurricane; P/O D. Hogg (Pilot) KIA, crewman Sgt W. Powell baled out safely.

03-09-1940 L8656 25 Squadron: FTR; damaged by Hurricane as above, force-landed on Hatfield Heath; P/O E. Cassidy and Sgt S. Smith uninjured, aircraft repaired.

03-09-1940 L1409 25 Squadron: damaged by Hurricane as above, force-landed at North Weald; S/Ldr W. Loxton and crewman unhurt, aircraft DBR.

06-09-1940   L4908 604 Squadron: FTR; ran out of fuel on night patrol, force-landed and overturned at Foxcote, near Andover; crew P/O Maclaren, Sgt Lawler, and AC Watson slightly injured.

07-09-1940   L6684 600 Squadron: port engine cut at 200 feet on approach to Hornchurch, aircraft crashed, inverted at East Close, Rainham, Essex; crew Sgt A. Saunders and Sgt J. Davies killed.

08-09-1940   L1111 600 Squadron: FTR from night patrol, lost and short of fuel after radio failure, crashed near Odiham; crew P/O H. Hough, Sgt E. Barnard, and Sgt J. Smith baled out safely.

10-09-1940   L1440 25 Squadron: lost propeller during night patrol and belly-landed at North Weald; Sgt K. Hollowell and crew unhurt, aircraft repaired.

13-09-1940   Z5721 FIU Mk IV-F: FTR from night sortie off Calais, believed damaged by return fire; crew F/Lt R. Ker-Ramsey, W/O G. Dixon, and W/O E. Byrne baled out, rescued and became PoWs.

25-09-1940   L8369 23 Squadron: FTR from night patrol, port engine failed, stalled in Middle Wallop circuit and crashed at Broughton; P/O E. Orgias (NZ), Sgt L. Karasek, and AC2 R. Payne KIA.

28-09-1940   L1371 29 Squadron: badly damaged in starboard wing by own AA fire at night, recovered from spin, returned to Digby; crew P/O J. Buchanan and Sgt G. Waller uninjured, aircraft repaired.

30-09-1940   L1261 219 Squadron: disintegrated in air on night patrol near Acklington, cause unknown; crew Sgt C. Goodwin, Sgt G. Shepperd, and AC2 J. McCaul KIA.

Appendix 6

Non-operational Blenheim losses, 1 August to 30 September 1940

01-08-1940   L1308 5 OTU Mk I: stalled and crashed on night approach to Aston Down, dived into ground and destroyed by fire; Sgt L. De Fosse (Belgian Pilot) killed.

02-08-1940   K7141 5 BGS Mk I: crashed on approach to Jurby, Isle of Man, DBR and became 2182M; Sgt A. Smart and two crewmen injured.

03-08-1940   L8846 17 OTU Mk IV: engine cut on take-off at Upwood, Sgt N. Green belly-landed, aircraft DBR.

04-08-1940   R3771 XV Squadron Mk IV: crashed near Whitchurch at 1705 during fighter affiliation exercises with Hurricanes; four-man crew P/O M. Hohnen, Sgt H. Beard, Sgt W. Watson, and F/Lt I. Sutherland killed.

06-08-1940   L4853 2 SAC Mk IV: lost height on night take-off at Andover, struck ground 1 mile from airfield and destroyed by fire; P/O R. de Burlet (Pilot) seriously injured, Sgt R. Bailey (Obs) killed, Sgt F. Andrews (WOp/Ag) injured.

07-08-1940   L9304 139 Squadron Mk IV: flew into sea during air-firing practice off Sheringham; P/O J. Eldred and crew rescued by fishing vessel.

07-08-1940   P4902 17 OTU Mk IV: spun into ground near Crawley, Bucks, on night NavEx; F/Lt E. Mortimer, Sgt D. Gibbs, and Sgt D. Alves killed.

08-08-1940   L9250 101 Squadron Mk IV: crashed into dispersal at Wittering; P/O F. Miles (Pilot) and crew uninjured, aircraft DBR.

08-08-1940   T1866 101 Squadron Mk IV: landed behind L9250 unable to avoid collision; F/Lt J. Munroe and crew unhurt, aircraft DBR.

09-08-1940   L1191 13 OTU Mk I: took off from Bicester, crashed on approach to Weston Green, destroyed by fire; crew Sgt W. Nelson, Sgt S. Sanderson, and Sgt C. Smith killed.

10-08-1940   L6799 5 OTU Mk I-F: struck on ground by taking-off Spitfire L1063 at Aston Down, DBR; P/O G. Crawford (NZ Instructor) and Sgt Oxtoby (Pupil Pilot) killed, as was Sgt Wilson, the Spitfire pilot, on his first formation take-off.

13-08-1940   L9038 13 OTU Mk IV: engine cut on take-off at Bicester, stalled and dived into ground; Sgt H. Miller RNZAF (solo pilot) critically injured and died a few hours later.

14-08-1940   L8839 17 OTU Mk IV: u/c jammed, belly-landed at Upwood, DBR; F/Sgt T. Watkins unhurt.

15-08-1940   L1425 1 OTU Mk I: based at Silloth but DBR in accident at Prestwick.

17-08-1940   L4931 Mk I: with Special Duties Flight at Martlesham Heath, struck unlit Lorenz Mast on night approach to Manston; no injuries reported to F/Lt C. Smith DFC or crew, aircraft damage Cat 4.

18-08-1940   L9264 218 Squadron Mk IV: collided with T1929 (below) on training sortie from Oakington and spun in inverted; crew P/O W. Wheelwright, Sgt R. Clapperton, and Sgt J. Bilton killed.

18-08-1940   T1929 218 Squadron Mk IV: collided with L9264 (above), caught fire and spiralled into ground; crew F/Lt G. Newton, Sgt D. Dennis, Sgt W. Smith, and AC1 R. Harrison killed.

25-08-1940   L6733 5 OTU Mk I: crashed into high ground in cloud near Tidenham Chase, Glos, and destroyed by fire; P/O D. Bell (solo pilot) killed.

27-08-1940   T2060 101 Squadron: crashed into sea after night take-off from Thorney Island; P/O A. McLaren injured but rescued, crew lost.

27-08-1940   T2062 107 Squadron: crashed into sea, no further details available.

28-08-1940   L8843 17 OTU Mk I: control lost on night take-of at Upwood, flew into ground and destroyed by fire; P/O H. Hoadley RNZAF (solo pilot) killed.

02-09-1940   N3583 57 Squadron Mk IV: crashed into Moray Firth on night NavEx, believed out of fuel; crew P/O A. Denison, Sgt R. Cowley, and Sgt F. Nicholas killed.

03-09-1940   R3621 17 OTU Mk IV: engine cut on night take-off at Upwood, crashed nearby; Sgt J. Turner (Pilot) and Sgt M. Tanner (Obs) killed, Sgt W. Parker (WOp/Ag) seriously injured.

04-09-1940   R3882 57 Squadron Mk IV: stalled and crashed at Bog O'Mayne at 2210 attempting to land; crew P/O G. Holyoke, Sgt D. Palmer, and Sgt M. Galleweski killed.

04-09-1940   L8682 17 OTU Mk IV: abandoned at night when control lost, crashed near Warboys airfield; P/O D. Rockel (solo pilot) baled out and injured.

04-09-1940   L9022 No. 2 School of Army Co-Operation Mk IV: undershot night approach at Andover, struck tree and DBR, P/O J. Rowntree injured.

10-09-1940   K7073 No. 2 School of Army Co-Operation Mk I: crashed when engine cut on overshoot from Andover; P/O J. Rowntree injured.

12-09-1940   K7160 5 OTU Mk I: crashed at Aston Down, no further details available.

13-09-1940   L9393 235 Squadron: crashed in attempted force-landing at Grimston, Norfolk, after engine cut due to mishandling; Sgt Le Jeune (Belgian) uninjured.

16-09-1940   N3564 21 Squadron Mk IV: collided with Wellington on take-off at Lossiemouth, both aircraft burst into flames; P/O A. Carson (Pilot), Sgt N. Manser (Obs), and passenger AC2 T. Adams killed, Sgt F. Burton (WOp/Ag) badly injured.

17-09-1940   P4830 Special Duties Flight, Christchurch Mk IV: engine cut, control lost avoiding house and spun into ground at Longford Castle, 3 miles south of Salisbury; Sgt T. Budden (Pilot) and two Army passengers, Capt J. Fulton and 2 Lt R. Jeffries, killed.

21-09-1940   L4906 25 Squadron Mk IV-F: took off from North Weald, overshot night landing at Hendon and struck gun emplacement; Sgt J. Jones and crewman injured.

22-09-1940   L8610 17 OTU Mk IV: hit high ground in bad weather at night on NavEx at Abersychan, Pontypool, Mon; crew Sgt H. Wilson, P/O A. Copplestone, and Sgt J. November killed. A memorial to the crew has been erected at the crash site on Garn Wian Mountain.

23-09-1940   L8797 17 OTU Mk IV: engine cut, lost height, crash-landed at Quedgeley, Glos, and DBR; F/Lt R. Coventry (Pilot) killed, Sgt J. Lane (Obs) injured, and Sgt G. Wilson (WOp/Ag) seriously injured.

25-09-1940   L1175, L1184, L1189 and L1193 ex-104 Squadron Mk Is, assigned to 13 OTU and all DBR during air raid on Filton.

25-09-1940   T1796 13 OTU Mk IV: crashed attempting force-landing when lost near Litchfield, Hants; crew F/Lt H. Edwards, P/O L. Osbon, and Sgt Raisbeck injured, Observer seriously.

28-09-1940   L6781 13 OTU Mk IV: swung on take-off at Weston-on-the-Green, hit trees and crashed, destroyed by fire; F/O Sharpe on his first night solo escaped uninjured.

Blenheim MK. I and I-F

45 Squadron, Ismailia, Egypt, 1939; L8479 (OB-W) was lost near Fuka on 9 May 1940

25 Squadron, Fighter Command, North Weald, UK, 1940; K7090 (ZK-V) was lost on 18 July 1941 while serving with 54 OTU

One of 30 Blenheims received by Turkey before the War; a total of 63 blenheims of all three Marks served in the Turkish forces

Blenheim MK. I and I-F

211 Squadron,
Paramythia, Greece,
1940; L6670 (UQ-R)
passed to the Royal
Hellenic Air Force in
April 1941 and was lost
in their service

Yugoslavia received 20
Avro-built Mk Is, and
produced 16 themselves,
all were lost or captured
and passed to the
Croatian Air Force

84 Squadron, Menidi,
Greece, 1940; L1381
(VA-G) was lost on 7
December 1940

54 (Night Fighter) OTU,
Church Fenton, UK,
1942; K7159 (YX-N) was
lost on 6 May 1943 when
serving with 12 PAFU

Romania had taken
delivery of 39 Mk Is by
late 1939; No 37,
fighting alongside the
Luftwaffe was lost near
Odessa two years later;
52 Blenheims served
with Romanian Forces

Blenheim Mk. IV and IV-F

88 Squadron, 2 Group,
Bomber Command,
Attlebridge, UK, 1941; as
RH-K in day camouflage,
Z7427 survived until
7 December 1943 with
132 OTU

Blenheim Mk. IV and IV-F

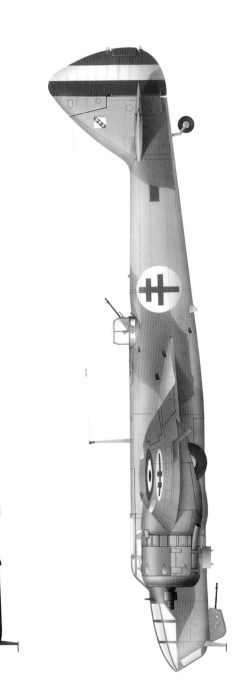

107 Squadron, 2 Group,
Bomber Command,
Great Massingham, UK,
1941; as OM-J in night
camouflage, T3816
crashed at Manston on 7
August 1941

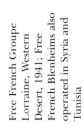

Free French Groupe
Lorraine, Western
Desert, 1941; Free
French Blenheims also
operated in Syria and
Tunisia

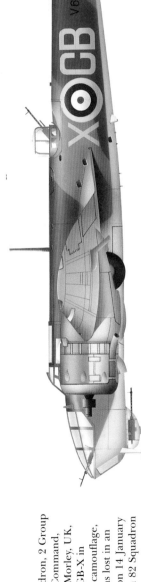

105 Squadron, 2 Group
Bomber Command,
Swanton Morley, UK,
1941; as GB-X in
maritime camouflage,
V6374 was lost in an
accident on 14 January
1942 with 82 Squadron

68 Squadron Fighter Command, High Ercall, UK, 1941; as WM-Z in a Night Fighter scheme, Z5722 was Destroyed By Fire after a take-off accident at Coltishall on 6 June 1942

15 Squadron South African Air Force, Western Desert, 1942; Z7513 (B) was one of three from Kufra that force-landed in the Sahara on 4 May 1942

Finland operated over 100 Blenheims against Soviet Russia; BL-129, shown in 1942, was one of the few to survive the War

v

Blenheim Mk. IV and IV-F

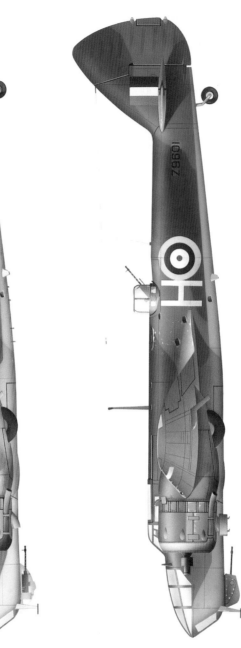
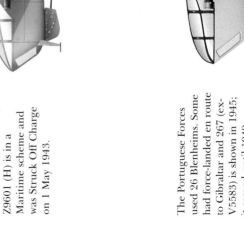

13 Squadron Army Co-
Operation Command,
Odiham, UK, 1942; as
Z6089 (OO-F) took part
in the Dieppe Combined
Operation on 19 August
1942

55 Squadron, Fuka,
Western Desert, 1942;
Z9601 (H) is in a
Maritime scheme and
was Struck Off Charge
on 1 May 1943.

The Portuguese Forces
used 26 Blenheims. Some
had force-landed en route
to Gibraltar and 267 (ex-
V5583) is shown in 1945;
it served until 1949.

Blenheim Mk.V

18 Squadron, Canrobert, Tunisia, 1942; BA875 (H) in Desert camouflage has no Squadron codes as it was shared with 114 Squadron; (the aircraft in which W/Cdr Hugh Malcolm won his VC on 4 December 1942)

8 Squadron, Khormaksar, Aden, 1943; BA429 has unusual camouflage for operations over the Gulf and Red Sea, it was SOC on 30 August 1944

113 Squadron, Feni, India, June 1943; in the SEAC markings without red in roundels or fin-flash. AZ942 crashed near Jessore on 25 August 1943

Blenheim Mk.V

13 (Helenic) Squadron
'R', Aden, 1943; BA328
went on to serve with 72
OUT at Nanyuki, Kenya

132 (Coastal Command)
OTU, East Fortune, UK,
1943; BA612 has had
both turrets removed
and later served in the
Middle East

Groupe Bretagne Free
French Air Force with
203 Squadron, Ben
Gardane, Tunisia, 1943;
BA849 crashed into the
sea on 23 April

Chapter 16

October to December 1940

RAF changes

On the last day of September 1940 Bomber Command HQ was notified that the danger of imminent invasion had passed, at least for that autumn and winter. Some of the sea-going barges had been observed returning from the invasion harbours to the German inland waterway system, where they were needed to resume the transport of raw materials. Those that returned were 12 per cent fewer in number than those that had been assembled, for some 360 had been destroyed by RAF bombing. The Blenheim squadrons had played the predominant part in these attacks and could at last observe some worthwhile results from their efforts – the Channel harbours were relatively easy to locate, and bomb strikes and fires could be seen among the moored shipping and the stores on the docksides, although the invasion ports were increasingly heavily defended by flak batteries. The postponement of the planned invasion was confirmed by Ultra intercepts of Wehrmacht signals at Bletchley Park, although this source of intelligence had to remain most secret.

There were significant changes in the High Command of the RAF, too, for on 5 October Air Marshal Sir Charles Portal, after only six months as AOC-in-C of Bomber Command, became Chief of the Air Staff, and remained at the head of the entire Air Force for the rest of the war. Two former holders of that supreme post, Marshals of the RAF Sir Hugh Trenchard and Sir John Salmond, had used their considerable influence in support of a 'Newall must go' faction. Portal's spell at Bomber Command had given him an insight into the great difficulties of mounting an effective campaign with the equipment then in service, and he was succeeded in the unenviable position of AOC of Bomber Command by AM Sir Richard Pierse. AVM James Robb continued as AOC of 2 Group, numerically the largest Group, while in November AVM 'Bert' Harris was promoted to Deputy CAS and handed over Command of 5 Group to AVM Norman Bottomley. AM Sir Arthur Barratt, formerly Commanding the RAF in France, was appointed AOC Army Co-operation Command.

Air Marshal Sir Charles Portal, Chief of the Air Staff from October 1940 until December 1945, photographed after the war.

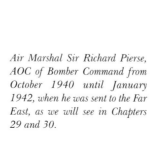

Air Marshal Sir Richard Pierse, AOC of Bomber Command from October 1940 until January 1942, when he was sent to the Far East, as we will see in Chapters 29 and 30.

Trenchard and Salmond also worked together to bring about a far more controversial change, for on 25 November ACM Sir Hugh Dowding was summarily removed as AOC-in-C Fighter Command and packed off to the USA. His creation of the air defence system and his brilliant strategic control of Fighter Command, together with the equally effective tactical control exercised by AVM Keith Park, AOC of 11 Group – who was moved to the backwater of 23 Group, Training Command – had undoubtedly led to the decisive defeat of the Luftwaffe in the Battle of Britain. They had both been embroiled in the 'big wing' controversy, when the ambitious AVM Trafford Leigh-Mallory, AOC of 12 Group, obtained the backing of AM Sir William Sholto Douglas, Deputy CAS, in challenging the conduct of the day battle by Dowding and Park, and in the growing criticisms concerning the demonstrable inadequacy of the night defences. These criticisms were led by Trenchard and Salmond, although they had retired ten and seven years earlier respectively, and the latter was appointed to chair a special committee (which included DCAS Sholto Douglas) to investigate the organisation of the night defences and recommend urgent improvements.

Dowding had been forced to rely principally upon the six squadrons of night-fighter Mk I-F Blenheims, with their poor performance and mediocre armament, as the new Beaufighters were so slow in becoming operational in any worthwhile numbers. Now he was being held to account over the shortcomings of these Blenheims – but, as we have seen in Chapter 10, he had expressed to the Air Staff his grave concerns about their inadequacies as a fighter several months before. He resisted the recommendation of the Salmond Committee that he put up some of his precious single-seat day-fighters at night as he knew that Hurricanes and especially Spitfires were not suitable, nor were their pilots trained, for night operations, and he was concerned at the prospect of high losses through night-time accidents. Nevertheless he was ordered to do so and three squadrons of black-painted Hurricanes and three more of Defiants were soon searching the night skies. Dowding argued that only aircraft equipped with AI radar, and preferably directed by the new Ground Controlled Interception units, the first of which had just become operational at Shoreham, would be effective at night. His arguments, although perfectly logical, were interpreted as resistance to change and helped to undermine his position further. Sholto Douglas succeeded Dowding at Fighter Command, and Leigh-Mallory replaced Park as AOC 11 Group. In my view, Hugh Dowding and Keith Park had worked tirelessly and

A 105 Squadron Blenheim landing at its new base at Swanton Morley, while another receives attention as it is bombed up (opposite). Both pictures show the drag-producing light-bomb carriers and the single under-nose gun, both aircraft had twin-Browning turrets.

successfully to save the nation and were too busy conducting the main battle to watch their own backs. I believe that they deserved every honour that a grateful nation could bestow upon them, not the shabby treatment they received.

Bomber Command Blenheims

It is interesting to look at the composition of the 532 bombers available to Sir Richard Pierse on the day that he assumed command: 217 Blenheims, 100 Wellingtons, 71 Hampdens, 59 Whitleys and 85 Battles. So, with the well-overdue withdrawal of the latter from the front line on 16 October, Bristol Blenheims represented almost half of the entire RAF bombing force! But Bomber Command was anxious to get on with its planned strategic offensive against the Ruhr and German industry, especially the oil industry, and was awaiting impatiently its new four-engined Heavy Bombers. The Blenheims simply did not fit in with this cherished Master Plan, and the Command had to seek alternative uses for them.

The disposition of the 2 Group Blenheim squadrons at the start of October 1940 was as follows:

82 and **105** Squadrons: still based at Watton, with 82 moving to Bodney in October and 105 opening the new base at Swanton Morley in October

21 Squadron: moved from Lossiemouth back to Watton in October, with detachments at Bodney

15, 40 and **57** Squadrons: based at Wyton, with 57 temporarily at Lossiemouth and Elgin, Morayshire, returning to Wyton in November

18 and **101** Squadrons: based at West Raynham, with 18 temporarily at Great Massingham

107 and **110** Squadrons: based at Wattisham

114 and **139** Squadrons: based at Horsham St Faith, with 114 temporarily at Oulton

218 Squadron: based at Oakington, moving to Marham in November

There was little respite for the Blenheim squadrons as operations during the last quarter of 1940 continued 'round the clock' until they had to be scaled down as the weather deteriorated considerably towards the end of the year. Attacks on the Channel harbours continued from the previous month and were carried out on many days and most nights until the night of 12 October when a force of 24 Blenheims raided the so-called invasion ports for the last time. The extensive shipping sweeps were still mounted by 2 Group on every day until 30 October, when they too were discontinued. 'Cloud cover' raids, mainly to targets in Northern Germany, were carried out by small numbers of Blenheims whenever the weather allowed. Enemy-occupied airfields were prime targets and were raided by day and by night on very many occasions, also whenever the weather permitted. In addition to these activities Blenheims of 2 Group took part in many of the Bomber Command main night attacks on targets in Germany, joining the Wellingtons of 3 Group, the Whitleys of 4 Group, and the Hampdens of 5 Group. They participated in the raids – largely ineffective during that period of the war – on Wilhelmshaven, Kiel, Hamburg, Emden, Essen, Cologne, Dortmund, Hamm, Dusseldorf, Gelsenkirchen, Bremen, etc.

This constant operational activity in the last quarter of 1940 saw the Blenheim losses continue to mount remorselessly, both by day (see Appendix 1) and, more significantly, by night, with the increased number of night operations (see Appendix 2).

Poor 82 Squadron had a bad night on 2 December when seven of its aircraft were part of the force sent to bomb Essen, and only one landed back at base, piloted by P/O Black, who had circled Bodney until daybreak. Although not on the scale of the disasters that had befallen the Squadron at Gembloux in May and Aalborg in August, it was a sobering experience. One aircraft (Sgt Butcher and crew in N3594) was brought down near the target, while the others had returned to find England almost completely covered in low cloud. Two crashed (P/O McCartney in N3578 and Sgt Cartwright in T2161) killing both the crews, one (T1813) was abandoned by S/Ldr McMichael and crew over the cloud, and F/Lt Messervy and crew (returning with their bomb-load in T2118) had a miraculous escape when he clipped a chimney with his flak-damaged aircraft while carrying out a forced-landing at Mildenhall. Sgt Smith and crew were lucky to escape with only minor injuries when he force-landed his damaged aircraft (T2162) near Messing in Essex (see Appendix 2). This episode illustrates clearly that the enemy was not the only danger facing the 'Blenheim Boys'.

Blenheims also took part in the raid on Mannheim on the night of 16/17 December, noteworthy as Bomber Command's first general attack on a German city. Previously crews had been ordered to identify and bomb specified military targets within a city, and they were again so instructed for long after this raid. Although suspicions were forming, it took many months before it was realised that in practice the crews, with the equipment at their disposal, were just unable to comply with these orders despite their great efforts to do so. The cloak of darkness covered not only the aircraft but also the targets. In an attempt to overcome this law of nature a fire-raising force (14 Wellingtons with an all-incendiary bomb-load) was sent in advance to mark the target area in Mannheim that 103 of the 134 bombers sent claimed to have bombed. Photo reconnaissance several days later revealed only slight damage scattered around the edges of Mannheim and in villages many miles away. The immense difficulties of night navigation, especially locating then hitting the target, affected all the contemporary Bomber Command aircraft, but especially the Blenheims as they did not carry the direction-finding loops linked to the radio receiver by which the dedicated Wireless Operator in the larger bombers could obtain bearings from transmitters in England to help establish their position – the Blenheim WOp/Ags could only transmit in Morse code for a homing bearing from their base when well into the return flight. Even if the Blenheims could arrive in the correct target area, the small bomb-load they carried meant that their contribution was a particularly modest one. The Mannheim raid exemplifies these brave but ineffectual efforts by the Blenheim crews – of the nine Blenheims included in the main bombing force that night, only three were able to find and bomb this large city, although the weather was quite favourable. Four were lost, three of

THE BRISTOL BLENHEIM

The interior of the twin-Browning turret: the seat is fully down, so the guns are pointing fully up. The 'dead-man's handle' is on the left of the control column, the two black pedals control the extra traverse of the guns when the turret has reached the limits of hydraulic travel, and the belts of .303in ammunition feed from tanks below the elbow-rests, with empty cartridge cases dropping into the canvas chutes. The entry/exit ladder is to the left, and the radio can be seen behind the turret, with the drum for the trailing-aerial on the right below the open hatch. This excellent photo was taken by Ken Whittle – see Chapter 12.

them crashing on return, one near Plympton in Devon 8 hours after taking off from West Raynham in Norfolk (see Appendix 2). Only W/Cdr Laurie Sinclair landed back at base.

Despite the continuing losses, all the 2 Group Blenheim squadrons were kept up to their full establishment of 16 aircraft each, while 101 Squadron held 27, and the Group had 36 in Immediate Reserve, a total of 255 aircraft. However, 2 Group lost four hard-working Blenheim squadrons in November 1940 when 15, 40, 57 and 218 left for 3 Group and converted to Wellingtons. As we have seen, Portal was in favour of this 'rolling up' of the Medium Bomber squadrons, but the new generation of Heavy Bombers – Stirling, Halifax and Manchester – were only just entering service in small numbers and all were bedevilled with 'teething troubles', so the expansion of Bomber Command was painfully slow. The Command had no choice other than to 'soldier on' with its existing aircraft. The Blenheims could no longer be used tactically against the German Army unless and until it did invade the UK, as seemed possible, in the spring of 1941. The need to attack the invasion ports seemed to have passed, and the spasmodic 'cloud cover' raids were often abortive and had proved disappointing, inflicting negligible damage and failing to draw any Luftwaffe fighter units from the Channel coast, so the Air Staff had to look for new ways to employ the many Blenheims on strength. Clearly, Luftwaffe airfields were useful targets but daylight attacks on them had proved very costly, so more night attacks were ordered.

As well as an increase in straightforward bombing attacks, a new type of operation was developed. These had been pioneered by Blenheims, for the first night 'intruder' raid on an enemy airfield had been made on the night of 17 July by S/Ldr Webster of 15 Squadron against Caen airfield. Throughout that autumn of 1940 a whole series of such raids by Blenheims followed with increasing intensity, the largest being when 35 Blenheims from 101, 105 and 110 Squadrons were sent to disrupt Luftwaffe bomber bases on the evening

Sgt G. Martin (Obs), P/O F. Metcalfe (Pilot), and Sgt S. Merrett (WOp/Ag) by T2280, 'The Cracked Jerry', of 82 Squadron, together with the all-important ground-crew, who worked hard to keep it serviceable. T2280 ditched on 11 November 1940; Frank Metcalf and George Martin were rescued by HMS Vega, but Sidney Merrett was killed.

of 14 November – the night of the big German air-raid on Coventry. Fighter Command aircraft later adopted this technique when 23 Squadron's Mk I-Fs (with the AI sets removed) started regular night-intruder missions, initially against German bomber airfields in Normandy, on the night of 21 December. This tactic was to be pursued by Blenheims for many months, then followed by other RAF aircraft for the rest of the war. They would loiter in the vicinity of the selected airfields for as long as possible, watching for signs of departing or returning enemy aircraft, which they would try to engage; alternatively they could attack the flare-path or, if they could be seen, the hangars. The flak would open up and the flare-path would be extinguished immediately, so any German aircraft wanting to use it – often low on fuel if returning to base – would have to orbit in the darkness and wait, or try to find another airfield. If the flare-path was re-lit later the airfield would be attacked again. The disruption to German night-time activity during the Blitz was considerable and quite a few Luftwaffe aircraft were lost in crashes resulting from RAF intruder operations.

Another new type of operation was a pin-point low-level daylight attack on an enemy Headquarters building. On 28 November six Blenheims were sent to bomb the Terynick Hotel on the Belgian coast at Coxyde-les-Bains; two found and attacked the HQ building, one claiming a direct hit. This raid was the precursor of the famous and deadly accurate 2 Group Mosquito precision attacks on the Gestapo HQ buildings in Oslo and Copenhagen, together with the SS barracks at Poitiers.

Fighter Blenheims

As the Luftwaffe turned to the night Blitz the Blenheim night-fighters, right in the front line of Britain's nocturnal defences, became more heavily involved. A greater proportion now had AI radar, though most Mk I-Fs were still hunting the night skies relying on the eyesight of the crew. They were joined in this usually fruitless search by Defiants and Hurricanes, hastily painted all-black, but similarly reliant on the human eye. As noted, the UK's defences against night attacks were proving very much less effective than Fighter Command's daytime defences. The Luftwaffe carried out some 12,000 night-time bombing sorties during the Blitz but suffered only 1 per cent casualties, and had partly solved the problems of night navigation and target location by an ingenious system of radio beams, which were quite effective until British scientists found ways of 'bending' them. But gradually over the winter the odds were turned more in favour of the defenders as the Blenheim's young brother, the far more efficient Beaufighter, came into operational service, albeit very slowly – for example, 604 Squadron had received only

THE BRISTOL BLENHEIM

Despite damage sustained on an Intruder sortie, this Blenheim returned to base.

seven by the end of the year and it was not until May 1941 that it was re-equipped completely. Night-fighting techniques, developed by the Blenheims of the FIU, were being constantly improved using the new GCI (Ground Controlled Interception) radar to guide the night-fighter (hopefully!) close enough to the enemy bomber for it to be in range of the fighter's own AI (Airborne Interception) radar, which in turn (even more hopefully!) brought it within visual range. 25 and 29 Squadrons kept a flight of AI-equipped Blenheims at Martlesham Heath, and 23 Squadron based at Wittering kept one at Ford, for the purposes of improving the use of AI and the skills of the operators. John Cunningham of 604 Squadron scored the first night success for the new Beaufighter on the night of 20 November 1940 when he shot down a Ju.88, and was given the nick-name 'Cat's Eyes' by the press. But such successes were relatively rare – many bombers were stalked but could not be intercepted, and very many more got through our defences completely unscathed and caused great damage to British cities and ports, especially London.

At the start of October the disposition of the Fighter Command Blenheim squadrons, all now designated Night Fighter Squadrons, and the two night-fighting development units, was as follows:

23 Squadron: moved from Wittering to Ford, with a Flight at Middle Wallop
25 Squadron: moved from North Weald to Debden, maintaining a Flight at Martlesham Heath
29 Squadron: at Digby, with detachments at Wellingore and Colby Grange
219 Squadron: moved from Catterick, with a Flight at Acklington, to Redhill with detachments at Tangmere and Debden, changing places with
600 Squadron: moved from Redhill to Catterick, with detachments at Drem, Prestwick and Acklington, and re-equipping with Beaufighters
604 Squadron: at Middle Wallop, with a detachment at Coltishall, and receiving a few Beaufighters
Fighter **I**nterception **U**nit: at Ford, developing radar interception techniques but also deployed operationally, mainly with Blenheims, and beginning to receive a few Beaufighters
Special **D**uties **F**light: at Eastchurch, developing radar equipment, mainly with Blenheims, and occasionally deployed operationally

When the question of removing the heavy and drag-producing dorsal turrets from the Mk I-F Blenheims, and replacing them with a small observation blister, had been discussed in November 1938, Dowding had pressed for their removal – tests on L1290 at the A&AEE had shown a 25mph improvement in maximum speed. It was Sholto Douglas who, as Assistant CAS in January 1939, had overruled Dowding and ordered their retention. Now Sholto Douglas ordered that the turrets should be removed from aircraft equipping four of the six Fighter Command Blenheim squadrons, to be replaced by a wooden fairing with twin retractable Brownings on a Frazer-Nash ring in the entrance hatch shielded by a small wind-deflector. One hundred conversion sets were ordered, but by the time they began to appear at the squadrons at the close of 1940 the Blenheim was nearing the end of its longer-than-expected career as an 'interim fighter'. Despite the diminishing numbers deployed, casualties among the 'Fighter Blenheims' continued right to the end of their front-line service, both by day and by night (see Appendix 3).

The AI receiver aerials are mounted on the port wing (elevation) and engine nacelles (azimuth), the transmitter aerial is mounted on the nose. AI equipped aircraft were not allowed to take part in Intruder sorties to the Continent.

K7072, Bristol's development aircraft, with the turret removed and the small observation cupola that Dowding had requested since before the war. (K7072 was sent to Canada as a pattern aircraft, and this picture may show it there, but the markings, including the gas-warning patch forward of the fin, suggest England in the summer of 1940.)

THE BRISTOL BLENHEIM

A typical night-fighter Pilot, P/O P Kells, climbs aboard his 29 Squadron MU-F at Colby Grange.

Coastal Command Blenheims

Over-stretched and under-resourced from the start of the war, this 'Cinderella Command' was forced to continue using its ubiquitous Blenheims for many tasks for which they were not suitable, exposing them to great danger, and the losses mounted inexorably (see Appendix 4). The Command still had no torpedo aircraft or other efficient anti-shipping strike aircraft, no effective long-range fighters, and very few suitable reconnaissance aircraft. Since the fall of France its small force faced a vast enemy-held coastline stretching all the way from northern Norway to the Bay of Biscay, off most of which the fighter Blenheims were required to patrol on a daily basis. They were expected to attack any German naval units encountered, and to keep watch for enemy shipping, especially the capital ships that the Admiralty feared would break out into the Atlantic to savage Britain's lifelines. The Command was tasked with protecting Allied convoys in the North Sea, the Channel, and in the Western Approaches, which were assuming greater importance as they were used by convoys from Canada and the USA. Counter-measures were needed against the increasingly active four-engined Focke-Wulf Condors, which reported the positions of Allied convoys and often attacked them too. The hard-worked 53 and 59 Squadrons continued to bomb harbours and airfields whenever the weather permitted, and they too suffered heavy casualties (see Appendix 5).

Crews of 236 Squadron rush to scramble their Mk IV-Fs at St Eval in November 1940. Note that their aircraft are fitted with light bomb carriers as well as the four-gun pack.

The eagerly awaited Blackburn Botha torpedo aircraft was a disaster, due mainly to woefully inadequate power from its Bristol Perseus engines. Bothas replaced Avro Ansons with 608 Squadron at Thornaby in May and a few went to 502 Squadron at Aldergrove in Northern Ireland, carrying out their first patrol on 10 August 1940, but they were withdrawn eight weeks later, 608 reverting to Ansons and 502 converting to Whitleys. 235 and 254 Squadrons were ordered to send detachments of their Blenheim Mk IV-Fs to Aldergrove in lieu of the Bothas to cover the Western Approaches. The establishment of the four Blenheim squadrons with Mk IV-Fs was increased by four aircraft to 20, with a similar 25 per cent increase in immediate reserves, and two new squadrons were formed, 86 and 252, to help cater for this increased work-load.

The Bristol Beaufort was also a great disappointment. Although originally ordered in August 1936, with the first production aircraft flying in October 1938, serious problems were encountered during development, mainly with the Taurus engines (as described in Chapter 4), and this delayed their introduction into service until November 1939 with 22 Squadron. It took until May 1940 before the type was prematurely declared operational – as a bomber or mine-layer but not as a torpedo aircraft – only for all Beauforts to be grounded in July for engine modifications. 217 Squadron started converting from Ansons to Beauforts in May 1940 but, despite the desperate war situation, they too were grounded in July and unable to use their primary weapon until mid-September. Both squadrons had found that the First World War type of torpedo they were using broke up on hitting the water at the higher speeds at which they flew – compared with the earlier biplane torpedo-droppers – so they had to reduce speed to about 100mph straight-and-level some 70 feet over the surface to drop them successfully. This negated their speed advantage and left them dangerously exposed to flak – an attack on an enemy capital ship would be suicidal. The first minor success for the Beaufort was an attack on shipping in the outer harbour at Cherbourg, in company with bomber Blenheims from 59 and 53 Squadrons, on 17 August. Five of the six Beauforts sent reached the target, sinking a freighter, writing off a torpedo boat, and losing one of their number, while the Blenheims started a fire in oil-storage tanks that blazed for days. 217 Squadron was still using its Ansons to bomb Brest in September, and in November carried out 83 Anson sorties but only five with Beauforts – their 'Annies' were not withdrawn until December 1940. It was this lack of suitable

THE BRISTOL BLENHEIM

anti-shipping strike aircraft for Coastal Command that led directly to the use of Blenheims from Bomber Command for this purpose the following spring, resulting in exceptionally heavy casualties, as we will see.

The deployment of Coastal Command Blenheim squadrons and units in November/December was as follows:

53 Squadron: moved from Detling to Thorney Island in November, but maintained detachments at Bircham Newton

59 Squadron: at Thorney Island, with detachments at Manston, Bircham Newton and Detling

86 Squadron: re-formed on 6 December at Gosport with Blenheim Mk IVs

235 Squadron: at Bircham Newton, with detachments at Thorney Island and Aldergrove

236 Squadron: at St Eval, to cover the South West Approaches

248 Squadron: at Sumburgh, with detachments at Dyce and Wick

252 Squadron: re-formed on 21 November at Bircham Newton with a mix of Mk I-Fs and Mk IV-Fs, moving to Chivenor in December, when a few Beaufighters were added

254 Squadron: at Dyce with detachments at Aldergrove and St Eval

272 Squadron: formed at Aldergrove (based on a Flight of **236** Squadron) on 19 November with Mk IV-Fs to help cover the North West Approaches

No 1 CACU (Coastal Artillery Co-operation Unit): at Detling

PRU B Flight: at St Eval, with C Flight at Wick, flying Spitfires and Blenheims.

GCF (Gunnery Co-operation Flights): at Leuchars and Rochester

Met Flights: No 1403 at Bircham Newton, No 1404 at St Eval

Apart from the losses due to enemy action, the Blenheim squadrons and the very busy Blenheim Operational Training Units continued to suffer steady attrition due to flying accidents, especially as the weather deteriorated towards the year end (see Appendix 6).

The year 1940 had been absolutely crucial in the long history of the British nation. The Royal Air Force had performed a vital role in ensuring the continued freedom of the UK, and the Blenheims had made an often overlooked but nevertheless essential contribution to this. Their courageous crews had indeed put 'Britain First', often at the cost of their own lives.

An evocative shot of an 'A' Flight Mk IV of 59 Squadron at dispersal at Thorney Island in October 1940. 53 and 59 Squadrons Coastal Command used Mk IV Blenheim Bombers, not Fighters.

Appendix 1

Bomber Command Blenheim losses in daytime operations, 1 October to 31 December 1940

Aircraft are all Mk IVs.

14-10-1940 R3671 139 Squadron: failed to return (FTR) from shipping strike, shot down into sea; crew Sgt A. Ogilvy, Sgt B. Walker, and Sgt D. Neill killed in action (KIA) and commemorated on Runnymede Memorial.

25-10-1940 T1890 105 Squadron: FTR; attacked Etaples airfield on one engine, starboard propeller and reduction gear fell off, force-landed at Debden, aircraft repaired only to be shot down 3 weeks later, with the same crew: P/O D. Murray, Sgt C. Gavin, and Sgt T. Robson, all KIA.

27-10-1940 R3749 and R3807, 110 Squadron: both destroyed on ground at Wattisham by enemy bombing.

27-10-1940 T2034 101 Squadron: destroyed on ground at Great Massingham by enemy bombing.

29-10-1940 T1861 114 Squadron: FTR to Oulton from sortie to bomb Le Havre harbour, lost without trace; crew P/O P. Hissey, Sgt G. Ellwood, and Sgt W. Turner KIA and commemorated on Runnymede Memorial.

01-11-1940 T2318 139 Squadron: damaged in action and crash-landed at Wyton; Sgt McCarthy (Pilot) and crew uninjured, aircraft repaired.

03-11-1940 T2139 107 Squadron, and T2133 110 Squadron: both destroyed on the ground at Wattisham by enemy bombing.

07-11-1940 T1871 139 Squadron: FTR to Horsham St Faith from sortie to NW Germany, shot down by Me.109E of JG 54 off Den Helder; S/Ldr J. Mertens, Sgt R. Spiller, and Sgt A. Merry (aged 19) KIA, and commemorated on Runnymede Memorial.

10-11-1940 R3753 114 Squadron: FTR from lone roving sortie to Dortmund, shot down off Dutch coast by Me.109E of JG 54; F/O E. Dawson, Sgt J. Lamb, and Sgt W. White KIA and commemorated on Runnymede Memorial.

11-11-1940 R3831 110 Squadron: destroyed on ground by bombing at Wattisham.

09-12-1940 R3698 139 Squadron: damaged by flak and crash-landed at Horsham St Faith; P/O J. King, Sgt E. Pierse and Sgt E. Barker unhurt, aircraft repaired.

09-12-1940 R2791 139 Squadron: damaged by machine-gun fire and force-landed; Sgt Phillips and crew uninjured, aircraft repaired.

31-12-1940 R3897 114 Squadron: FTR from sortie to Gilze-Rijen airfield, shot down by light flak over target and exploded; Sgt L. Young, Sgt J. Brown, and Sgt. J. Coates (aged 19) KIA and buried at Bergen-op-Zoom.

31-12-1940 T2328 139 Squadron: FTR from sortie to Cologne, lost without trace; crew S/Ldr R. Beaman DFC, Sgt H. Robson DFM, and Sgt D. Trigwell KIA and commemorated on Runnymede Memorial.

Appendix 2

Bomber Command Blenheim losses in night operations, 1 October to 31 December 1940

Aircraft are all Mk IVs.

02/03-10-1940 T1896 105 Squadron: FTR from bombing Calais harbour, shot down and crashed near Pihen-le-Guines; crew Sgt K. Lord, Sgt F. Bundock, and Sgt H. Dunbar KIA and buried in cemetery there.

07/08-10-1940 L9310 110 Squadron: crashed at Wattisham at 0215 in steep turn on return from bombing Channel ports, destroyed by fire; F/Lt H. Lyon (Pilot), Sgt Hardwick (Obs), and Sgt F. M. Henry (WOp/Ag) injured. (Mike Henry DFC describes this incident, and others, in his book *Air Gunner*.)

08/09-10-1940 T2032 82 Squadron: crashed on return to Bodney in bad weather at 0155 from bombing Calais; crew Sgt H. Brittain, Sgt F. Harbord, and Sgt R. Lister only slightly hurt, aircraft DBR.

08/09-10-1940 T2277 82 Squadron: crashed 10 minutes later in similar circumstances to T2032 above; Sgt R. Smith, Sgt Anslow, and Sgt Blackaddy injured.

28/29-10-1940 T1891 105 Squadron: FTR to Watton from sortie to bomb Homberg oil refinery, lost without trace; S/Ldr C. Grannum, P/O N. Knight, and Sgt J. Greenwood KIA and commemorated on Runnymede Memorial.

28/29-10-1940 T2229 105 Squadron: FTR from sortie to Mannheim, took off from Watton at 1830, crashed on return at Cranmer Hall near Fakenham, Norfolk; P/O I. Prosser, Sgt A. Dallas (NZ), and Sgt J. Hardcastle KIA.

30/31-10-1940 T2246 101 Squadron: FTR to West Raynham from sortie to Duisburg, crashed on return near Coleby, Lincs; P/O J. Cave (NZ), Sgt J. Hitchen, and Sgt C. Gooderick KIA.

10/11-11-1940 T2280 82 Squadron: FTR; ditched off Harwich returning from Hamm, near British destroyer HMS *Vega*; P/O Metcalfe (Pilot) and Sgt G. Martin (Obs) rescued, Sgt S. Merrett (WOp/Ag) KIA (drowned).

10/11-11-1940 R3765 82 Squadron: FTR from same sortie, ditched by Outer Dowsing, near British convoy; Sgt H. Waples (Pilot) and Sgt N. Giblin (Obs) rescued, Sgt R. Andrews (WOp/Ag) KIA (drowned).

15/16-11-1940 T1890 105 Squadron: FTR; shot down by flak near Diegem in raid on Belgian airfields; crew P/O D. Murray DFC, Sgt C. Gavin, and Sgt T. Robson KIA and buried in Brussels Cemetery.

15/16-11-1940 R3737 107 Squadron: FTR from attacking airfields, crashed on return near Stowmarket, both engines cut, out of fuel; crew P/O E. Humphries, Sgt G. Giggs and Sgt A. Brand uninjured.

16/17-11-1940 T2329 105 Squadron: FTR to Swanton Morley from sortie to bomb Hamburg, believed shot down by flak; Sgt C. Whitfield, Sgt W. Gilmour, and Sgt T. Ashurst KIA and commemorated on Runnymede Memorial.

16/17-11-1940 R3687 21 Squadron: FTR to Bodney from sortie to bomb Hamburg, crashed on return near Gravesend, out of fuel; crew injured, Sgt P. Wise (Pilot) and Sgt A. Buckley (Obs) reported to have died from injuries, Sgt Patterson (WOp/Ag) survived.

23/24-11-1940 N6236 101 Squadron: FTR from sortie to bomb Wanne Eikel, starboard propeller and reduction gear detached over target, aircraft crashed into West Raynham village attempting to land back at base; crew Sgt B. Redmond, Sgt H. Green, and Sgt A. Woodruff injured. Sgt Green died 4 days later.

23/24-11-1940 T1928 107 Squadron: FTR; ditched off Great Yarmouth on return from NW Germany; Sgt L. Gilliard (Obs) injured but rescued, P/O A. Campbell (Pilot) and Sgt C. Watts (WOp/Ag) not recovered, KIA and commemorated on Runnymede Memorial.

24/25-11-1940 N6238 101 Squadron: FTR to West Raynham from sortie to bomb Hamburg, crashed into North Sea; crew F/O S. Waugh, Sgt R. Cox, and Sgt A. Norman KIA. F/O Waugh's body washed ashore 02-1941 and buried in Ryton Cemetery, others commemorated on Runnymede Memorial.

26/27-11-1940 R3914 21 Squadron: FTR; flew into hill returning from Cologne, and exploded at Middleton, Co Durham; crew Sgt H. Collinge, Sgt D. Osborne, and Sgt A. Moore KIA.

26/27-11-1940 ? 101 Squadron: crashed at Cottesmore, Leics, on return from attacking airfields; Sgt Palmer and crew only slightly injured, aircraft believed repaired.

26/27-11-1940 T1886 105 Squadron: FTR to Swanton Morley from sortie to bomb Cologne, crashed on return near airfield beacon, destroyed by fire; crew P/O L. Ryan NZ, Sgt J. Slade, and Sgt R. Meikle KIA.

27/28-11-1940 T1884 105 Squadron: FTR to Swanton Morley from sortie to bomb Cologne, abandoned on return above cloud and low on fuel; Sgt E. Costello-Bowen, Sgt T. Broom, and Sgt Cameron safe, aircraft crashed in Cheshire.

27/28-11-1940 R3594 114 Squadron: FTR to Oulton from sortie to bomb Cologne, crashed in mist on return at Catton Deer Park, Norwich; crew Sgt P. Waigh, Sgt R. Rook, and Sgt P. Murray injured. (See accompanying pictures.)

28/29-11-1940 P6934 18 Squadron: FTR; struck HT cables and crashed soon after night take-off from Great Massingham; crew F/Lt C. Harris, Sgt W. Lusty, and Sgt Gray injured. Sgt Lusty died next day.

28/29-11-1940 T1893 105 Squadron: FTR; shot down on sortie to Dusseldorf; crew F/Lt C. Swain, P/O E. Clelland, and Sgt M. Cowley captured. Cyril Swain took part in 'Great Escape' from Stalag Luft III 03-1944 and was one of the 50 PoWs recaptured and shot.

28/29-11-1940 T1993 110 Squadron: crashed on landing down-wind at night returning from Cologne and hit Wattisham petrol dump; Sgt De Little, Sgt Beacham, and Sgt Boorman slightly injured, aircraft DBR.

28/29-11-1940 T2253 110 Squadron: FTR; struck trees on night approach to Wattisham and crashed on return from Cologne; crew P/O Dickinson, Sgt Muirhead, and Sgt Thompson injured.

29/30-11-1940 R2796 21 Squadron: FTR to Bodney from sortie to attack airfields, crashed into North Sea; crew Sgt W. Starns, Sgt R. Stilwell, and Sgt G. Moffatt KIA and commemorated on Runnymede Memorial.

03/04-12-1940 T2279 114 Squadron: crashed on take-off at 0205 from Oulton when fully laden due to ice on wings, destroyed by fire; crew F/Lt D. Smythe, P/O Ryder and Sgt Welch escaped with slight injuries.

03/04-12-1940 N3578 82 Squadron: FTR; crashed in bad weather at 0430 near Southend returning from Essen; crew P/O T. McCartney, Sgt J. Henderson, and Sgt J. Ratcliffe KIA.

03/04-12-1940 N3594 82 Squadron: FTR from sortie to bomb Essen, force-landed near Hellendoorn, Holland; crew Sgt W. Butcher, Sgt W. Sheppard, and Sgt J. Ferguson captured and became PoWs.

03/04-12-1940 T2161 82 Squadron: FTR; crashed returning from Essen in bad weather at 0610 near Manston, Kent; Sgt N. Cartwright, Sgt F. Benbow, and Sgt P. Crawford KIA.

03/04-12-1940 T1813 82 Squadron: FTR; abandoned over cloud at 0745 near Swaffham returning from Essen, out of fuel; S/Ldr J. McMichael, Sgt Hodges, and Sgt Lawrence safe.

03/04-12-1940 T2162 82 Squadron: FTR, force-landed returning from Essen in bad weather near Messing, Essex; crew Sgt Smith, Sgt Anson, and Sgt Blackadder unhurt, aircraft repaired.

03/04-12-1940 T2118 82 Squadron: hit by flak attacking Essen, grazed chimney on approach to Mildenhall; crew F/Lt Messervey, P/O Forgeard, and Sgt Trotter unhurt, aircraft repaired.

09/10-12-1940 T2225 82 Squadron: FTR; shot down in target area near Antwerp; crew F/Lt J. Rathbone MP, P/O F. McMurray, and Sgt A. Birt KIA and buried in Schoonselhof Cemetery, Antwerp.

09/10-12-1940 T1797 110 Squadron: FTR; struck trees taking off from Wattisham to raid ports, one engine detached from mountings later, abandoned near Colchester at 0330; Sgt J. Robertson (Pilot) killed, Sgt Teeton (Obs) and Sgt Atkins (WOp/Ag) baled out safely.

09/10-12-1940 R3832 110 Squadron: crashed on landing at Wattisham on return from same raid on ports; crew Sgt Hallifax, Sgt Hamilton, and Sgt Little slightly injured, aircraft repaired.

10/11-12-1940 Z5794 107 Squadron: FTR to Wattisham from sortie to bomb Cologne, brought down in target area; crew P/O W. Culling, Sgt A. Brown, and Sgt E. Perry captured and became PoWs. Observer died in captivity.

11/12-12-1940 T1897 105 Squadron: FTR to Swanton Morley from sortie to attack airfields, shot down by flak at Zedelgem, Belgium; F/Sgt P. Richardson, Sgt J. Donlon, and Sgt V. Gifford KIA and buried in Zedelgem.

16/17-12-1940 P6953 101 Squadron: FTR; crashed near Hastings on return from Mannheim and burst into flames; crew Sgt W. Skipworth, Sgt W. Need, and Sgt D. Stephenson KIA.

16/17-12-1940 T2039 101 Squadron: FTR; crashed into the sea on return from Mannheim; crew Sgt H. Clarke, Sgt M. Heaney, and Sgt G. Willcox KIA and commemorated on Runnymede Memorial.

16/17-12-1940 Z5801 101 Squadron: FTR; abandoned in air on return from Mannheim when out of fuel, aircraft crashed near Plymouth; crew P/O C. Hill, P/O R. Glover, and F/O J. Baker came down safely near Brixham.

16/17-12-1940 N6142 101 Squadron: FTR; force-landed on return from Mannheim when out of fuel near Cornwood, Devon; crew P/O Brown, P/O G. Collis, and Sgt G. Loughlin uninjured, aircraft repaired.

16/17-12-1940 R3744 114 Squadron: FTR; crashed at Sprowston, near Norwich, soon after take-off for Mannheim after engine cut, bombs jettisoned; two of Sgt T. Barnes's crew, Sgt Seward and Sgt Walsh, injured.

19/20-12-1940 T1860 107 Squadron: FTR; came down near target, Lannion airfield; F/Lt E. Humphreys, Sgt G. Griggs, and Sgt L. Brand captured and became PoWs. F/Lt Humphreys took part in 'Great Escape' from Stalag Luft III in March 1944, was recaptured and shot by Gestapo with 50 other escapees.

21/22-12-1940 R3907 139 Squadron: suffered flak damage and crash-landed on return to base; Sgt McPhee, Sgt Atkins, and Sgt Whittle uninjured, aircraft repaired.

23/24-12-1940 R2793 139 Squadron: FTR; crashed at Radwinter, Essex, returning in bad weather from attacking Ostend; Sgt L. Holland, Sgt R. Rodgers, and Sgt H. Saxby KIA.

23/24-12-1940 L9183 139 Squadron: FTR; crashed near Norwich and caught fire returning in bad weather from Ostend; Sgt N. Ashley (Pilot) and Sgt A. Clarke (Obs) KIA, Sgt Harrison (WOp/Ag) injured.

27/28-12-1940 T2223 21 Squadron: FTR; shot down by light flak attacking Gilze-Rijen airfield; S/Ldr M. McColm (Pilot) captured, crew Sgt C. Hann (Obs), and Sgt G. Shepherd (WOp/Ag) KIA and buried at Bergen-op-Zoom.

THE BRISTOL BLENHEIM

R3594, a 114 Squadron Mk IV, crashed in Catton Deer Park, Norwich, on return from bombing Cologne on 27/28 November 1940; believed due to an incorrect setting on pilot's altimeter, the crew were injured but recovered. The crease in one photo of the wreck is due to Observer 'Dickie' Rook keeping it in his wallet for years!

Appendix 3

Fighter Command Blenheim losses, 1 October to 31 December 1940

03/04-10-1940   L4905 600 Squadron Mk IV: FTR; engine failed in heavy rain on night patrol, crashed at Broadstone Warren 0355; crew P/O C. Hobson, Sgt D. Hughes RNZAF, and AC2 C. Cooper KIA.

08/09-10-1940   L1281 604 Squadron Mk I-F: overshot landing at Middle Wallop on return from night patrol and DBR; P/O D. Bayliss and crew unhurt, airframe became 2727M.

08/09-10-1940   L8722 23 Squadron Mk I-F: received battle damage, overshot at Tangmere on return from night patrol and DBR; crew uninjured.

12/13-10-1940   L1472 29 Squadron Mk I-F: engine cut on night take-off at Wellingore for operational patrol, crash-landed and DBR; P/O J. Buchanan and crew believed uninjured.

12/13-10-1940   L1113 219 Squadron Mk I-F: FTR; engine problems on night patrol near Ewhurst, crew baled out; Sgt G. Mead (Pilot) safe but parachute of P/O R. Baron (AI Op) failed, KIA.

13-10-1940   L6637 29 Squadron Mk I-F: FTR; shot down in flames by 312 Squadron Hurricanes off Point of Ayr, Wirral, Ches; crew Sgt R. Stevens, Sgt O. Sly, and AC2 A. Jackson KIA, Stevens and Sly commemorated at Runnymede, Jackson buried (as Sgt) at Mexborough, Yorks.

13-10-1940   K7135 29 Squadron Mk I-F: took off from Digby, damaged by Hurricanes south of Liverpool; crew P/O J. Humphries, Sgt E. Bee, and AC1 J. Fizell uninjured. See following entry.

15-10-1940   K7135 29 Squadron Mk I-F: damaged as above, destroyed by Ju.88 while undergoing repair at 0721 in air-raid on Ternhill.

15-10-1940   L6741 29 Squadron Mk I-F: badly damaged in same raid.

29-10-1940   L1503 29 Squadron Mk I-F: hit trees on take-off at night from Wellingore on operations; Sgt Roberts injured, crew uninjured.

30/31-10-1940   L6721 23 Squadron Mk I-F: FTR; crashed on night patrol in bad weather and with no radio, hit house at South Berstead; F/O H. Woodward, P/O A. Atkinson, and Sgt H. Perry KIA.

15/16-11-1940   ZK-H 25 Squadron Mk I-F: shot down He.111 but damaged by return fire and crashed on landing; crew Sgt Holloway, Sgt Culmer, and AC1 Fields KIA.

16-11-1940   L6679 25 Squadron Mk I-F: FTR; iced-up in cloud, control lost, broke up in dive, crashed near Ingatestone, Essex; crew Sgt L. Winter, Sgt A. Romanis, and Sgt A. Theasby KIA.

18/19-11-1940   L1507 29 Squadron Mk I-F: damaged in action, caught fire on landing; Sgt Stokes and crew uninjured, aircraft DBR.

22/23-11-1940   L6841 23 Squadron Mk I-F: flaps jammed and overshot landing at Tangmere returning from night patrol; F/Sgt Burton and crew uninjured, aircraft DBR.

26/27-11-1940   L6728 604 Squadron Mk IV: FTR; lost propeller on night patrol, returned to Middle Wallop but hit trees in circuit at Danebury Hill; P/O N. Wheatcroft and Sgt R. Taylor KIA.

03-12-1940   K7172 29 Squadron Mk I-F: FTR; became lost on AI trials, attempted forced-landing at dusk, overturned at Wooley Flats, Peak District; P/O D. Anderson unhurt.

07/08-12-1940   L1235 25 Squadron Mk I-F: FTR; control lost in bad weather, dived into ground at Elton, near Marham, destroyed by fire; F/Lt J. Hughes and Sgt J. Friend killed, Sgt Blenkharn injured and detained in Peterborough Hospital.

15-12-1940   L8723 600 Squadron Mk I-F: FTR; force-landed near Catterick in bad weather and DBR; crew slightly injured.

20/21-12-1940   BQ-W 600 Squadron Mk I-F: FTR; crashed near Richmond, Yorks, cause unknown; Sgt Wilson (Pilot) killed, P/O Holmes (Ag) injured and died later.

21/22-12-1940   L6686 23 Squadron Mk I-F: FTR; out of fuel in bad weather on return from intruder sortie to French airfields, crew baled out near Brading, IoW; Sgt Loveridge (Pilot) safe, Sgt Newman (Obs) and Sgt Southall (WOp/Ag) came down in sea and drowned.

Appendix 4

Coastal Command Blenheim losses, 1 October to 31 December 1940

Aircraft are all Mk IVs or Mk IV-Fs.

01-10-1940   R3626 248 Squadron: FTR from recce, shot down off Norwegian coast; P/O C. Bennett, Sgt G. Clarke, and Sgt G. Brash KIA, commemorated on Runnymede Memorial.

02-10-1940   R3629 254 Squadron: damaged by Hurricanes while on convoy patrol, crash-landed at Montrose. Destroyed by bombing 25-10-1940.

05-10-1940   R2771 53 Squadron: FTR to Detling, damaged in shipping strike and crashed in flames near Manston; Sgt A. Hall (Obs) KIA, P/O K. Faulkner (Pilot) and Sgt G. Fielder (WOp/Ag) seriously injured.

08-10-1940   T2036 53 Squadron: FTR; shot down near Gravelines on French coast; crew P/O J. Mallon (NZ), Sgt W. Whetton DFM, and Sgt A. Shackleford KIA, buried in Guines Cemetery, Calais. P/O Mallon died of his injuries after three days.

09-10-1940   N3530 235 Squadron: FTR from airfield protection patrol, shot down into Channel south of Thorney Island at 0530; crew P/O J. Kirkpatrick, P/O R. Thomas, and Sgt G. Keel KIA.

17-10-1940   T2319 59 Squadron: FTR; shot down off Brest while attacking destroyers; P/O E. Hives, Sgt B. Jones, and Sgt E. Jones KIA.

20-10-1940   P6952 248 Squadron: FTR; shot down by return fire off Norwegian coast; Sgt R. Copcutt (WOp/Ag) KIA, F/Lt G. Baird (Pilot), W/O D. Burton and W/O S. Wood from four-man crew rescued and became PoWs, two Warrant Officers injured.

20-10-1940   L9453 248 Squadron: FTR; shot down off Norwegian coast on same sortie; P/O S. Gane, P/O M. Green, and Sgt N. Stocks KIA, commemorated on Runnymede Memorial.

21-10-1940   R3699 53 Squadron: FTR; damaged in action, control lost, crashed on houses in Tonbridge, Kent, killing 2 civilians and injuring 15, crew baled out; P/O H. Meakin (Pilot) injured, crew Sgt G. Hutson and Sgt G. Hadnam safe.

26-10-1940   T2233 21 Squadron: hit at dusk by bomb from He.111s as squadron prepared for night-flying; P/O Slater (Pilot), Sgt Jones (Obs), and Cpl Holland killed, Sgt Green, Sgt Bristow, and AC1 Windeler injured. R3760 was also destroyed and three other Blenheims badly damaged. One of three He.111s shot down by Lossiemouth airfield defences and crew killed.

27-10-1940   T2132 53 Squadron: damaged by Me109s while bombing shipping in Den Helder harbour, force-landed at Martlesham; crew all injured, P/O E. Plumtree (Pilot) awarded DFC, Sgt G. Wood (Obs), and Sgt P. Kinsey (WOp/Ag) awarded DFM, aircraft repaired.

27-10-1940   L8789 53 Squadron: FTR; shot down by Me.109s off French coast on Channel shipping strike; crew P/O R. Buckley, Sgt C. Henderson, and Sgt P. Neale KIA, commemorated on Runnymede Memorial.

02-11-1940   T2137 59 Squadron: FTR; shot down attacking heavy guns at Cap Gris Nez, crashed at Halinghen, Belgium; P/O W. Lewis, Sgt I. Greening, and Sgt J. Peckham KIA, buried in Halinghen Cemetery, Calais.

03-11-1940   L9392 248 Squadron: FTR; shot down by Me.109 off Katwijk; crew P/O A. Garrard, Sgt E. Bayliss, and Sgt H. Moynham KIA and commemorated on Runnymede Memorial. L9392 was one of three Mk IV-Fs that shot down He.111 of I/KG 26.

04-11-1940   T1992 53 Squadron: damaged by Me.109s near Le Touquet, belly-landed near Dover; crew P/O R. Maurer, Sgt I. Macaulay, and Sgt B. Bembridge only slightly injured, but shot down and killed 3 weeks later, aircraft repaired.

13-11-1940   N3615 53 Squadron: crash-landed at Thorney Island; P/O Knill and crew only slightly injured.

18-11-1940   Z5732 235 Squadron: damaged by return fire from He.115s, one of which was claimed, and crashed on return to Bircham Newton, DBR; Sgt Dawson (WOp/Ag) KIA, F/Lt Goddard (Pilot) wounded in foot, Sgt Wedlock (Obs) slightly injured.

23-11-1940   T1999 235 Squadron: damaged by flak on shipping strike and crashed on return to Bircham Newton, DBF; P/O Davidson (Pilot) and Sgt Aslett (WOp/Ag) wounded, Sgt Brazier (Obs) safe.

23-11-1940   ? 236 Squadron: damaged by flak and crash-landed on return to Bircham Newton; Sgt Lawrence (Pilot) and Sgt Fogden (WOp/Ag) wounded, Sgt Ross (Obs) uninjured, aircraft believed repaired.

23-11-1940   R2783 59 Squadron: FTR from sortie to Lorient, shot down by Me.109 of II/JG77; crew P/O J. van Blokland, Sgt J. Woodcock, and Sgt L. Carvil KIA and commemorated on Runnymede Memorial.

24-11-1940   Z5734 272 Squadron: FTR to Aldergrove from convoy escort, found wrong convoy in poor weather, involved in dogfight with FAA Fulmar, stalled in turn at low level and crashed into sea; crew P/O B. Herrick (NZ), Sgt P. Smith, and Sgt Hair J. KIA, commemorated on Runnymede Memorial. (Brian Herrick's brother Dennis GM lost his life in a 53 Sqn Blenheim on 26-6-1941, while his other brother Michael DFC* died in a 305 Sqn Mosquito on 16-6-1944.)

26-11-1940   V5371 53 Squadron: FTR; shot down off coast near Ghent by flak, P/O R. Maurer, Sgt I. Macaulay, and Sgt B. Bembridge KIA.

26-11-1940   N3630 53 Squadron: FTR from same sortie to oil depots at Ghent; P/O M. Barbour, Sgt A. Cowling, and Sgt G. Hinton KIA, commemorated on Runnymede Memorial.

26-11-1940   R3889 59 Squadron: FTR from sortie to Lorient; crew P/O K. Jerwood, Sgt F. Newman RNZAF, and Sgt E. Battle KIA, commemorated on Runnymede Memorial.

29-11-1940   N3614 59 Squadron: FTR; shot down by Me.109 of JG2 into sea; crew P/O A. Hovenier, Sgt J. Scotchmere, and Sgt L. Magee KIA, commemorated on Runnymede Memorial.

30-11-1940   L9463 59 Squadron: stalled after take-off from Thorney Island for Lorient and hit ground; P/O Christie (Pilot) and Sgt Taverner injured, Sgt G. Crout KIA, buried in Earlsfield Cemetery, Wandsworth, aircraft written off.

01-12-1940   N3537 59 Squadron: FTR; received severe battle damage and hit trees and house on overshoot at Thorney Island; P/O Hinman (Pilot) and Sgt Walden (Obs) KIA, Sgt Jones (WOp/Ag) injured.

05-12-1940   T2218 53 Squadron: FTR; unable to find Thorney Island on return from Cap Gris Nez in bad weather; crew P/O P. Gibbs, Sgt Wood, and Sgt Oram baled out and injured, aircraft crashed in Suffolk.

06-12-1940   V5420 53 Squadron: FTR; hit trees in heavy squall on approach to Thorney Island and crashed; P/O S. Weatherley (Pilot) and Sgt H. Parrott (Obs) killed, Sgt S. McAndrew (WOp/Ag) badly injured and died later.

07-12-1940   T2395 53 Squadron: FTR; damaged on HOOKOS patrol, hit balloon cable on return and crashed near Deal; P/O A. Steel (Pilot) and Sgt W. Hemsley (Obs) KIA, Sgt D. Robson (WOp/Ag) injured.

12-12-1940   L8602 236 Squadron Mk I: damaged by return fire from He.115 floatplane; P/O Russell crashed on landing at St Eval, aircraft struck off charge 28-12-1940 .

15-12-1940   Z5754 235 Squadron: FTR from patrol, dived into sea off Brancaster, Norfolk, cause unknown; crew P/O J. Coggins MBE DFM, P/O N. Sadler, and Sgt P. Prosser KIA.

21-12-1940   L9415 272 Squadron: FTR; Sgt S. Hobbs, Sgt D. Newport, and Sgt H. Rickets interned at the Curragh, Eire, after baling out when lost and out of fuel after convoy escort.

21-12-1940   R3878 236 Squadron: FTR; shot down by Me.109 of JG 77 off Brest, crashed into sea; crew S/Ldr G. Montague, Sgt D. Briggs, and P/O G. Hannan KIA, buried in Bayeux War Cemetery.

27-12-1940   V5399 59 Squadron: damaged by Me.109s near Berck-sur-Mer; Sgt J. Hill (WOp/Ag) badly wounded, P/O Cundy landed at base, aircraft repaired.

27-12-1940   T1991 59 Squadron: damaged in running fight with Me.109s near St Aubin; Sgt Flory (Obs) wounded, P/O Morton (Pilot) uninjured, Sgt Scarrott (WOp/Ag) awarded DFM for shooting down Me.109 of II/JG26.

27-12-1940   R3586 (?) 59 Squadron: took off at 0730 and crashed on return to Thorney Island; P/O Wenman and crew uninjured but aircraft written off. No serial number given in ORB, and serial number on Accident Card is incorrect as R3586 was an Anson; R3856 is in block of Blenheims but not issued.)

28-12-1940   L9043 (Mk IV), 53 Squadron: FTR; engines cut on take-off for Lorient at 0630 after long delay on ground, crashed near airfield and bombs exploded; F/Lt J. Richardson, Sgt J. Maguire, and Sgt K. Vowles KIA.

This 254 Squadron aircraft has over-run the runway at Lossiemouth.

THE BRISTOL BLENHEIM

Appendix 5

Non-operational Blenheim losses, 1 October to 31 December 1940

03-10-1940   L1106 5 OTU Mk I: undershot night approach at Aston Down and hit wall, destroyed by fire. No injuries reported.

6/7-10-1940   L6624 219 Squadron Mk I-F: ex-RAE aircraft, crashed, no further details; possibly back with RAE.

08-10-1940   L4883 13 OTU Mk IV: collided in mid-air with L6783 (below) from same unit and crashed; crews of both aircraft perished: F/Lt S. Coutts-Wood, Sgt S. Chambers, Sgt D. Woodsworth, and Sgt W. Brett killed.

08-10-1940   L6783 13 OTU Mk I: collided in mid-air with L4883 (above) and crashed; crew F/O P. Sharp, P/O C. Gouldie, and Sgt G. Ancliffe killed.

10-10-1940   T1881 107 Squadron Mk IV: hit tree and dived into ground at Wicken, Cambs, on low-flying exercise; crew P/O M. Bywater, Sgt R. Adlam, Sgt K. Brooker and a ground-crew passenger, LAC H. Key, killed.

10-10-1940   R2789 1 OTU Mk IV: took off from Silloth, engine cut, stalled on approach to Prestwick and crashed, DBF; P/O P. Foster (Pilot) injured, Sgt H. Haslam killed, Sgt G. Pole injured.

11-10-1940   T2273 27 MU Mk IV: attempted forced-landing in bad visibility on uncompleted airfield at Honiley, hit drain and overturned; F/Lt J. Butt and crew unhurt.

12-10-1940   L4866 17 OTU Mk IV: engine cut on take-off at Upwood, wing-tip struck ground and aircraft cartwheeled; F/Lt C. Harris and P/O P. Foster seriously injured.

13/14-10-1940   L6805 FIU Mk I-F: acting as target to AI Boston, engines cut (fuel-cocks mishandled) and aircraft crashed near Lancing College, Sussex, DBR; P/O C. Clark (Pilot) and unnamed Obs safe, crewman AC Mitchell injured. L6805 had been used by Rotol for constant-speed propeller trials at Staverton.

14-10-1940   T1952 254 Squadron Mk IV: hit obstruction force-landing on beach at Aberdeen, swung into sea and overturned; one of F/O D. Shaw's crew injured, aircraft recovered and became 2313M.

14-10-1940   Z5741 235 Squadron Mk IV: stalled on landing at Thorney Island, u/c collapsed, DBR, Sgt R. Tatnell safe.

15-10-1940   N3588 21 Squadron Mk IV: P/O J. Rodger overshot landing at Exeter in heavy rain and aircraft DBR.

15-10-1940   Z5975 4 FPP Mk IV: crashed attempting forced-landing at Sarclet dummy airfield, 6 miles south of Wick, Caithness, and DBR.

16-10-1940   Z5964 4 FPP Mk IV: crashed attempting forced-landing at Bradford-on-Avon Road, near Bath, Somerset, in bad visibility, hit tree and DBR; one of P/O R. Smith-Barrie's crew injured.

20-10-1940   L1467 600 Squadron Mk I-F: flew into hill in cloud during practice night interception, Hurst, near Richmond, Yorks; crew believed killed, no further information available.

21-10-1940   L1468 5 OTU Mk I: u/c retracted prematurely on take-off, engine lost oil and seized, crash-landed at Culkerton, Glos; P/O E. Poule uninjured.

21-10-1940   L8871 13 OTU Mk IV: engine cut on take-off at Weston-on-the-Green, control lost, hit ground, destroyed by fire; Sgt L. Hillelson and Sgt J. Kerr killed, Sgt W. Dismore died of his injuries two lays later.

23-10-1940   L1272 600 Squadron Mk I-F: control lost in cloud, dived into ground, near Kirkby Malzeard, Yorks; P/O Hurst, flying solo, killed.

24-10-1940   L1525 3 RSS Mk I: engine cut on take-off at Ouston, belly-landed at Hartford, near Horsham St Faith.

25-10-1940   K7154 5 BGS Mk I: undercarriage collapsed taxiing 21-5-1940, repaired on site, later jammed and crash-landed at Jurby, IoM, and DBR.

25-10-1940   Z5804 13 OTU Mk IV: undershot night landing and hit trees at Weston-on-the-Green, DBR; Sgt D. Weir (solo pilot) injured.

28-10-1940   R3840 3 FPP Mk IV: took off from Filton, hit balloon cable, crashed near Birmingham; ATA Officer L. Satel killed.

29-10-1940   N3572 17 OTU Mk IV: engine cut, belly-landed at Oakley, near Bedford, DBR, .P/O F. Windram and crew uninjured.

29-10-1940   N3535 2 SAC Mk IV: flew into ground on night approach at Andover, u/c torn off, DBR; no injuries reported to P/O I. Anderson or crew.

01-11-1940   L8737 21 Squadron Mk IV: flew into ground after night take-off at Bodney; P/O R. Armstrong and Sgt Evans injured.

02-11-1940   L9386 40 Squadron Mk IV: crashed at Little Rissington; P/O Winstone-Smith (Pilot) injured, aircraft repaired.

04-11-1940   L1322 2 SAC Mk I: landed down-wind, over-ran airfield, and overturned at Kidlington; P/O J. Makgill slightly injured.

04-11-1940   R3886 236 Squadron: FTR; engine cut due to mishandling, hit HT cables and crash-landed near Carnanton, Cornwall; P/O J. Derbyshire (solo pilot) seriously injured.

05-11-1940   R3757 21 Squadron Mk IV: took off from Bodney on training sortie at night, climbed to 200ft then dived into ground, cause unknown, and exploded soon after; crew F/Lt G. King, Sgt Whalen, and Sgt Lightfoot badly injured, Sgt E. Stuart killed.

08-11-1940	T2130 248 Squadron: failed to climb from take-off at Sumburg due to ice on wings and crashed; F/O A. Hill safe.
13-11-1940	L4898 17 OTU Mk IV: on formation practice, bird-strike shattered windscreen and stunned pilot, belly-landed at Keyston, Hunts; Sgt F. Miller (Pilot) injured.
16-11-1940	L4893 A&AEE Mk I-F: stalled in Filton circuit and dived into ground; P/O E. Stansbury (solo pilot) killed.
18-11-1940	L9337 Mk IV with A&AEE: forced belly-landing in bad visibility at Patney, near Pewsey; F/Lt P. Bragg uninjured, aircraft damage Cat 4.
20-11-1940	T2119 2 SAC Mk IV: elevator control lost on take-off, belly-landed at Andover, DBR; P/O J. Siddall (solo pilot) uninjured.
20-11-1940	T2321 2 SAC Mk IV: stalled on night overshoot at Andover, crashed 3 miles west of Thruxton; P/O W. Jones (solo pilot) killed.
26-11-1940	R2792 17 OTU Mk IV: flew into wood in bad visibility on night NavEx at Eriswell, Suffolk, and destroyed by fire; crew F/O E. Morse, Sgt R. Thorn, and Sgt B. Wilson-North killed.
26-11-1940	T1859 17 OTU Mk IV: flew into hills at night near Kettering, Northants; crew Sgt V. Hobbs, Sgt G. Davies, and Sgt A. Robinson killed.
27-11-1940	T2441 2 SAC Mk IV: bounced in heavy landing at night at Andover, u/c collapsed, DBR.
29-11-1940	R3705 13 OTU engine cut on take-off at Bicester, lost height and crash-landed near Bracknell; Sgt W. Hamm (Pilot) and P/O R. Verity (Obs) killed (both had BA degrees), unnamed WOp/Ag injured.
29-11-1940	L1503 29 Squadron Mk I-F: Pilot Sgt French in taxiing collision with L1505 (below), DBR.
29-11-1940	L1505 29 Squadron Mk I-F: ground collision with L1503 (above); DBR.
30-11-1940	L1248 55 OTU Mk I: became lost in bad visibility, hit tree in attempted forced-landing at East Charlow, Berks; P/O F. Fairweather killed, Sgt Phillips injured.
02-12-1940	T1946 235 Squadron Mk IV-F: force-landed at Holbeach Ranges, Lincs; Sgt Evans and crew uninjured, aircraft repaired.
05-12-1940	T2353 6 AACU Mk IV: engine cut, crashed attempting forced-landing near Baginton; Sgt Murawiec (Polish Pilot) injured.
06-12-1940	Z5726 254 Squadron Mk IV-F: crashed into sea off Montrose, Scotland, in snow storm; Sgt D. Leaver, Sgt A. Bean, and Sgt A. Johnston killed.
09-12-1940	N3617 114 Squadron Mk IV: hit by AA fire from Allied convoy off Yarmouth, crashed at Newport, Norfolk; crew F/O W. Watson, Sgt G. Boulton, and Sgt D. Shildrick killed.
10-12-1940	L4844 17 OTU Mk IV: control lost in cloud, dived into ground near Sinton Green, Worcs; Sgt G. Penman, Sgt A. Ferguson, and Sgt J. Roberts killed.
11-12-1940	R3672 114 Squadron Mk IV: overshot night landing at Oulton, hit railway and overturned; Sgt N. Jackson (Pilot) injured, Sgt E. Fisher (Obs) killed.
13-12-1940	R3625 248 Squadron Mk IV: collided with L9455 (below) shortly after take-off from Sumburgh, dived into sea. Sgt J. Hamilton, Sgt H. Walmesley, and Sgt J. May, plus ground-crew passengers AC1 S. Julian and AC1 G. Monks, killed, all commemorated at Runnymede.
13-12-1940	L9455 248 Squadron Mk IV: collided with R3625 (above), dived into sea; P/O J. Dodd, P/O A. Pettet, and Sgt A. Hook, plus ground-crew passengers LAC L. Bright and AC1 A. Moore, killed, all commemorated at Runnymede.
14-12-1940	T1832 139 Squadron Mk IV: crashed on landing at Horsham St Faith; Sgt Phillips and crew unhurt, aircraft repaired.
14-12-1940	L4835 17 OTU Mk IV: flew into Clee Hill, near Ludlow, Salop, in bad visibility on NavEx; crew Sgt I. Curror, Sgt A. Secker RNZAF, and Sgt J. Pinchard killed.
16-12-1940	T1997 248 Squadron Mk IV-F: hit truck on runway while landing at Dyce and destroyed by fire; Sgt E. Holmes and crewman escaped with slight injuries.
19-12-1940	L6612 29 Squadron Mk I-F: struck trees low flying near Leadenham, Lincs, and DBR, possibly caught in down-draught; Sgt S. Stokoe, Sgt A. Wilsdon, Sgt E. Jones, and Sgt I. Watkins killed.
21-12-1940	L8438 307 Squadron Mk I: engine cut in bad weather, crash-landed on Combe Down, near Bath, DBR.
22-12-1940	L4896 17 OTU Mk IV: hit HT cables while low-flying and crashed near Market Harborough, Leics; crew P/O C. Rombach, P/O J. Dales, P/O L. Squire, and Sgt A. Cruise killed.
23-12-1940	L8683 17 OTU Mk I: engine cut, stalled on approach and dived into ground near Upwood; Sgt C. Bayford (solo pilot) injured.
23-12-1940	L6627 Special Duties Flight Mk IV at Martlesham Heath: engine failed on radar trials, force-landed at Sutton Hoo, Suffolk, DBF; F/Sgt G. Smith and crew escaped uninjured.
29-12-1940	L4868 17 OTU Mk IV: lost height in turn after night take-off and hit ground near Upwood; P/O V. Reynolds RNZAF and P/O K. Edwards killed.

292 THE BRISTOL BLENHEIM

Chapter 17

January to April 1941

For the United Kingdom 1941 was a particularly grim wartime year, and it was even grimmer for the RAF, especially so for the Blenheim squadrons. They were to be used as deliberate bait for German fighters in 'Circus' operations over Northern France, while the sporadic and largely ineffectual daytime 'cloud cover' raids continued, as did costly attacks by day and by night on airfields and ports, together with the night-time attacks on targets in Germany and elsewhere alongside the Bomber Command 'heavies'. But primarily Blenheims were destined to become, by default as noted in the previous chapter, the main anti-shipping strike aircraft – a particularly dangerous type of operation of necessity flown over the sea at very low level.

Night bombing raids

On the night of 4/5 January 24 Blenheims were sent to bomb Hamburg, but the weather was very poor and it seems that they were unable to find even such a prominent target, for German records make no mention of this attack. Five nights later 36 Blenheims were part of the force of 135 bombers that raided the oil plant at Gelsenkirchen; 56 aircraft claimed to have bombed the target, but only one German was killed in the entire city. A directive to AM Sir Richard Pierse on 15 January ordered that Bomber Command should make 'the destruction of the German synthetic oil plants the sole primary aim of your bomber offensive until further orders', so those plants within range of the Blenheims were added to the list of 2 Group targets. Thirty-four Blenheims formed part of the force of more than 200 bombers sent to raid Hannover on the night of 10/11 February. The next day 2 Group came under the command of a new AOC when AVM Donald Stevenson took over from AVM James Robb. Stevenson was to prove a harsh and unimaginative Commander, who became unpopular in the Group, appearing to them to place his own career prospects ahead of concern for the crews under his command.

139 Squadron's aircrew at Horsham St Faith in April 1941. The CO, W/Cdr 'Digger' Kyle (centre, front row, between his Flight Commanders), rose to become Air Chief Marshal Sir Wallace Kyle, the last AOC of Bomber Command. On his left is S/Ldr N. Pepper DFC, killed in Malta, and to his right is F/Lt H. Edwards, later Air Commodore Sir Hughie Edwards VC DSO DFC. Twenty-one of these 48 crewmen were reported killed or missing during 1941.

A force of 22 Blenheims and 21 Wellingtons was sent to bomb the oil plant at Homberg on the night of 14/15 February, but only 16 claimed to have found and bombed the target; the following night 37 Blenheims and 33 Hampdens were sent back to the same target; 40 of the 70 aircraft said that they had bombed successfully, but damage was slight. Blenheims formed part of the main force of over 120 aircraft sent to bomb Cologne on the nights of 26/27 February and 1/2 March, and to Wilhelmshaven on the night between. Blenheims had a busy period in mid-March: 32 took part in attacks on Bremen on 12/13 March, 21 on Hamburg the following night, 24 on Dusseldorf the next night, 21 on Wilhelmshaven on the 17th/18th, and, in a larger effort, 44 attacked the same target the following night. Nineteen were sent to bomb the U-boat base at Lorient on the night of the 21st/22nd but results were poor in bad visibility, 26 were sent as a separate force on 23/24 March and bombed Hannover, causing fires in the target area, and 16 were part of the force sent to bomb the *Scharnhorst* and *Gneisenau* in Brest harbour on 31 March and again on 3/4 and 10/11 April, although no hits were achieved. When more than 200 bombers attacked Kiel on the nights of 7 and 8 April they were mainly Wellingtons, but included a couple of Stirlings and a dozen Manchesters; separate forces of Blenheims were sent to bomb Bremerhaven, 24 on the first night and 22 on the second.

Losses from these night bombing sorties accumulated steadily (see Appendix 1) as, despite the very bad weather, Blenheims operated on 43 nights during the first four months of 1941. Just how this bad weather could endanger the RAF crews was shown on the night of 11/12 February when 79 bombers returning from raiding Bremen without loss found fog over most of England; 15 aircraft had to be abandoned in the air (six Whitleys, five Wellingtons, one Hampden, and three Coastal Command Hudsons) and another 10 were written off or badly damaged attempting forced-landings or in crashes at their bases – a fate that befell six unfortunate Blenheims on the nights of 21/22 and 23/24 March.

'Cloud cover' raids

Although the main Bomber Command activity was at night, the 'pin-prick' 'cloud cover' daylight raids by small numbers of Blenheims, ranging from a single aircraft up to three dozen, continued on an almost daily basis. Indeed, Blenheims carried out daylight raids on 91 of the 120 days, including 29 of the 30 days of April – these were mainly anti-shipping sorties towards the end of the period. Targets in the first four months of 1941 were nearly all ports and included Bremen, the Dortmund-Ems Canal, Rotterdam, Flushing, Antwerp, Emden, Nordholz, Boulogne, Ghent, Amsterdam, Borkum, Dunkirk, Ostend, Kiel, Calais, Ijmuiden, Den Helder, Lorient, Sylt, Le Havre, Brest, Heligoland, the German Bight and the Frisian Islands – a few power stations and airfields were also attacked. Despite the Blenheims turning back frequently when they found insufficient cloud cover, these raids still caused steady losses to the crews (see Appendix 2). In this period Fighter Command also commenced similar 'pin-prick' nuisance raids, known as 'Rhubarbs', usually by pairs of fighters, and mainly against airfields near the coast rather than ports. 'Rhubarbs' were later enlarged and extended into large-scale sweeps intended to draw the German fighters into combat.

'Circus' and 'Ramrod' escorted operations

The 'Rhubarbs' did not have the intended result, so 'Circus' bombing raids by escorted Blenheims were devised to bring the Luftwaffe fighters into battle with superior numbers of RAF fighters, thus to reduce the chances of further large-scale daylight attacks by the German Air Force on Britain in the spring, and to hamper the build-up of shipping in the Channel ports. First planned in December 1940, they created a role for the Blenheims that not only suited Bomber Command and the ambitious new AOC of 2 Group, but also employed more usefully the larger number of fighters then available, as well as allowing AVM Leigh-Mallory, the new AOC of 11 Group, to demonstrate his own more aggressive attitude. But this time, in a reverse of the situation in the Battle of

The upper and lower surfaces of a Blenheim port outer wing, damaged when a still un-fused 250lb bomb from another Blenheim passed right through it, fortunately just outboard of the fuel tank. The aileron was also badly damaged, but the aircraft flew back to base.

Britain, it was the RAF fighters that were operating at the extreme of their range (which restricted targets to those close to the Pas de Calais), and the enemy fighters (warned by radar) that held the tactical advantage and could chose when and where to attack. And it was downed German, not Allied, pilots who fell on to friendly soil, with many who baled out or force-landed soon fit to fight again. Also, of course, steady formations of Blenheims at medium height were welcomed as targets by the German flak units. Whereas 'Circus' operations were deliberately 'trailing the cloak' to tempt German fighters into action, 'Ramrod' were quick 'in and out' attacks, although still heavily escorted.

The first of many 'Circus' operations was mounted on 10 January when six Blenheims of 114 Squadron, led at midday from Eastchurch by W/Cdr Elsmie, were escorted by no fewer than 72 RAF fighters of 11 Group to bomb a German ammunition dump in the Foret de Guines; a further 24 Hurricanes had gone ahead to strafe St Inglevert airfield, giving a ratio of 16 fighters for each Blenheim! None of the bombers were lost but few hits on the target were observed; although the Luftwaffe did not attempt to interfere, it lost two Me.109s, and the RAF a Hurricane, in encounters on the fringes. The second 'Circus' was on 2 February, when six Blenheims of 139 Squadron led from Northolt by W/Cdr 'Digger' Kyle with a large escort of fighters went to bomb the docks at Boulogne. This time more hits were observed from the four who bombed, no Blenheims were lost (although one was damaged by flak), and only one 109 was shot down as the Germans failed to rise to the bait. Three days later the inducement was increased by adding six Blenheims of 114 to six of 139 when they were heavily escorted to a snow-covered St Omer airfield – nine Allied fighters were lost and one German fighter shot down. On the 10th six Blenheims made a very successful 'Circus' raid on Dunkirk harbour, and on the 26th 12 bombed Calais – once again no bombers were lost on any of these raids, but the Luftwaffe did not make a determined effort to repulse them. Nor was there any major reaction to the two 'Circus' raids mounted in March, on the 5th to Boulogne and on the 13th to Calais/Marck airfield; the 'Circus' operations were failing to achieve their declared aim, for the Luftwaffe was refusing to allow itself to be engaged on disadvantageous terms, and the Germans were not too worried about such a slight amount of damage being inflicted on targets in Northern France by small numbers of Blenheims flying at medium altitude.

By April the stakes were raised again to three boxes of six bombers each when it was the turn of 101 and 18 Squadrons on the 17th, and 12 Blenheims of 101 were joined by six of 18 Squadron to attack Cherbourg. Among crews the 'Circus' raids were considered 'a piece of cake' compared with the dangers of night-bombing trips, and especially in comparison with the far greater dangers of anti-shipping sorties. Only two 'Circus' raids were flown in each month of March and April 1941 as anti-shipping activity was fast assuming a far greater importance. The nine 'Circus' operations mentioned were in addition to the daylight raids noted above, so aircraft from the Blenheim squadrons had been in action on 98 of the first 120 days of 1941, together with 39 of those nights. In addition to this continuing high level of day and night operations, they started intensive training in very low-level flying and bombing exercises over the sea, so were kept busy throughout a period when the weather was mainly very poor.

R3816, of 107 Squadron, based at Leuchars, Scotland, from March to May 1941 to be nearer to Norway. It stalled and crashed after take-off from Manston on 7 August when the elevator trim-tabs jammed.

Right at the beginning of March, two long-serving and hard-working 2 Group squadrons were detached to Coastal Command – 114 Squadron to Thornaby and 107 to Leuchars – for a full-time maritime role in the North Sea up to 100 miles from the Norwegian coast, thus freeing two Coastal Command squadrons to cover the increasingly important North West Approaches. So, with the four squadrons 'rolled up' to 3 Group in November 1940, 2 Group now had six fewer squadrons to carry the growing operational burden. A few days later (6 March) Churchill, worried by increasing shipping losses and responding to pleas from the Admiralty, issued a Directive that the 'Battle of the Atlantic' was to have top priority and that Bomber Command must concentrate its resources entirely on naval targets. To comply with this order, which held force for exactly four months, the night-time raids by both the Light and Heavy Bombers, together with the few 'Circus' operations that were mounted, and most of the continuing daytime 'cloud cover' raids by the Blenheims, were targeted at ports and harbours. The AOC of Bomber Command, Sir Richard Pierse, noted that anti-shipping operations would be 'an economical and profitable role for the light-bomber force'. He was glad to have found a use for the Blenheims, as due to their limited range and even more limited carrying capacity, they just did not fit in with Bomber Command's long-cherished strategic offensive planned for the new generation of Heavy Bombers that were entering service.

Anti-shipping operations

2 Group Operations Order No 20 organised six regular 'Beats' to the most frequently used shipping lanes to facilitate the discovery of coastal convoys so that they could be attacked. From one to four Sections of three aircraft, from a start line some 30 miles from the enemy-held coastline, would fly towards it in a wide and loose line-abreast formation, very low over the surface of the sea (always less than 50 feet) to avoid radar detection, then would open out even wider and turn parallel to the coast when 3 miles out from it, and search for just 3 to 5 minutes before turning for home. Any ships seen were to be attacked immediately, to take full advantage of the element of surprise, using the four 250lb bombs carried by each Blenheim. To counter these attacks it was not long before the German

LAC Snow carrying out the Daily Inspection on a 21 Squadron Blenheim at Bodney, providing a good view of the extra rear-defence gun in its Perspex blister.

convoys were flanked by special flak ships (equipped with multiple cannon and machine-guns plus one or more larger-calibre anti-aircraft guns), and in addition the convoys often sailed within range of shore-based AA batteries, were frequently protected by patrols of fighters, and flew their own balloon barrage to deter low-flying aircraft. Clearly, despite the careful planning, attacking them would be a very dangerous business indeed.

These low-level anti-shipping sorties commenced on 12 March when 139 Squadron at Horsham St Faith mounted the first; 82 Squadron at Watton started its sorties on the 15th and was ordered to alternate daily with 21 Squadron to carry out these 'Beat' sorties. 139 Squadron operated almost daily, and none of these squadrons was permitted to stand down for more than one day in eight. 114 and 107 Squadrons were ordered to take their maritime patrols right up to the Norwegian coast and to attack any shipping found. By the end of March the 2 Group squadrons were instructed to attack any 'Fringe' targets near the coast – such as gun or searchlight emplacements, troops, military transport, etc – if they had been unable to locate any ships. In April 105 and 110 Squadrons were also brought into the anti-shipping role, and the number of 'beats' was increased from six to 11, then to 19, so that they covered the entire enemy-held coastline from Bergen in Norway to Bordeaux in the Bay of Biscay. When the Germans invaded the Balkans in April the 'Fringe' targets were extended to include power stations, steel mills, etc, in an attempt to persuade the Luftwaffe to retain more of its fighters in the west, and such targets often became the object of special 'Ramrod' raids rather than just opportunistic extensions of anti-shipping sorties. The purpose of these extra 'Fringe' attacks was 'to cause alarm, and to embarrass the enemy air defence system', but in these heavily defended coastal zones most of the alarm caused was to the Blenheim crews, and it was they who suffered the embarrassment of further losses from low-level attacks in daylight.

At the end of April a new and even more deadly demand was made on the Blenheim squadrons – Operation 'Channel Stop'. 2 Group was ordered, with an excess of optimism over pragmatism, to stop all shipping on the seas between Germany and the Brittany peninsular during daylight, a daunting task indeed. RN motor torpedo boats would attempt to continue the blockade by night. In an attempt to enforce this unrealistic order – for it was almost impossible to achieve with the resources available – Flights, then Squadrons of Blenheims were rotated to Manston to carry out 'Channel Stop' operations – the losses were appalling, often reaching 50 per cent of the aircraft attacking ships (see Appendix 3). AVM Stevenson circulated, for display on the crew-room notice-boards of all the 2 Group Squadrons, an admonishment intended to improve the crew's determination in pressing home their attacks on shipping, but, as he is reported to have written that he 'didn't care if he lost 80 per cent of his crews and aircraft as long as good results were achieved', the exhortation proved counter-productive. The crews had only fleeting seconds at such low levels from first sighting any shipping to identifying it as cargo-carrying

A typical all-NCO crew that formed the backbone of Bomber Command: Ken Whittle (WOp/Ag), Geoff Atkins (Observer), and Tom McPhee (Pilot) by the Sergeants Mess at Horsham St Faith, and by the tail of R5860 after a sortie.

(not fishing vessels from the occupied countries) and carrying out their attack, often from an unsuitable approach path; they could not orbit to seek a better one for the element of surprise would be lost and the AA defences alerted. The dash and determination shown by the Blenheim crews on anti-shipping sorties was exemplary, and their outstanding courage was readily acknowledged by their peers – air-crews in other RAF Groups and Commands – and by their Squadron and Base Commanders, if not by their AOC.

To give an example, of six Blenheims from 21 Squadron sent to attack a convoy off Stavanger on 18 April two were shot down, one by flak and one by escorting Me.110s of ZG 76, while a third was damaged and crashed on return; six more from 107 were sent to the same target at wave-top height, two being shot into the sea by flak, including their Wing Commander, and a third badly damaged and a crew-man killed; then four more from 114 Squadron arrived and were bounced by Messerschmitts, with three of the four, including their Wing Commander as well, blasted into the sea, although the fourth claimed a German fighter and escaped. A disastrous 56 per cent of the attacking Blenheims was lost or put out of action that black day. That same April morning 53 Squadron had a Blenheim shot down off Brest with the loss of the crew, for the Coastal Command squadrons were suffering too.

Coastal Command Blenheims

As we have noted, Coastal Command was strengthened by the loan of Bomber Command's 114 and 107 Blenheim squadrons, but now the anti-shipping campaign needed further reinforcement, so 82 Squadron was detached from 2 Group and moved from Watton to Lossiemouth to supplement Coastal Command's own hard-stretched Blenheim bomber units, 53 and 59 Squadrons, as they kept up attacks on ports and on shipping, either on the open sea or in harbour. Several of these raids, including some in which Beauforts joined the Blenheims, were escorted by the Mk IV-Fs of the Coastal Command fighter units. This was a hard-fought campaign and the casualties inflicted on the Coastal Command Blenheim squadrons continued to mount remorselessly (see Appendix 5). These started at the beginning of the year when a flight from 53 bombed German destroyers in Brest harbour soon after noon on 4 January, reporting three direct hits, but Me.109s of II/JG 77 caught up with the Blenheims as they sped from the target, shot down one into the sea (P/O Gibbs and crew) and badly damaged three others, one of which (P/O Newton) crash-landed at Exeter, while the other two (P/Os Bannister and Gatwood) staggered back to base. The following day it was 59's turn to attack the same target; its nine aircraft were chased by Messerschmitts and two aircraft (P/Os Buchan and Custerton) received severe damage. During these pursuits the Blenheim pilots had to apply their 'Plus 9' emergency boost for three or four times the 5-minute limit imposed, but their Mercury engines responded magnificently.

North Coates was a very busy Coastal Command base with the Mk IV-Fs of 235 and 254 Squadrons.

These two hard-working squadrons, 53 and 59, also operated at night, as on the night of 9 January when they attacked Brest again and each lost an aircraft, with men from both crews perishing when the Blenheims ditched in the extremely cold seas. Brest harbour was defended by more than 300 anti-aircraft gun positions, many with multiple weapons, as well as the armament of the German warships in the harbour, so attacking it was almost as dangerous by night at it was by day. P/O Reginald Alcock and his crew of 53 Squadron had a night to remember on 10 January. They were unable to start their own aircraft so sprinted to the spare (V5518), which had not been air-tested. While over Brest both engines stopped when Alcock throttled back to reduce height on commencing his bombing run (he did not know that the carburettor 'hot air' selectors had frozen in the 'cold air' position). Undaunted, he carried on with his gliding attack. The Blenheim was then badly damaged by flak, which opened out a large section of the port-wing leading edge, making the aircraft difficult to control. While coping with this and preparing to ditch just outside the harbour, using the gun-flashes reflected on the surface of the sea to guide him, the engines re-started in the slightly warmer lower air and he was able to coax his damaged aircraft back to the nearest airfield, St Eval. Landing in the dark much faster than normal due to the loss of lift from the damaged wing, and still travelling at a rate of knots when he reached the last of the glim-lamps on the grass runway, he swung off it into the blackness to avoid crashing at the end, completing a full 'ground loop' at speed on the grass before finally stopping. Upon examining the tyre tracks the following morning the crew were horrified to see that their out-of-control aircraft had somehow made a complete circle right through a squadron of parked Beauforts and passed between dozens of picketed Fleet Air Arm torpedo aircraft without hitting any of them!

We noted that the port of Brest was very heavily defended, making daylight raids upon it particularly dangerous, and the defences were increased further after the German battle-cruisers *Scharnhorst* and *Gneisenau* berthed there late in March following a foray into the North Atlantic during which they had accounted for 22 Allied merchant ships. Bomber Command immediately launched night raids as noted, while Coastal Command was ordered to carry out daylight raids. W/Cdr Guy Bolland, CO of 217 Squadron at St Eval, equipped with Bristol Beauforts (then unable to drop torpedoes for their intended role), was ordered to send his aircraft alongside Blenheims to attack the German warships with bombs in Brest harbour. He resisted the order and declared all the Squadron's aircraft unserviceable; the Station Commander insisted that he telephoned this news to the AOC who told him bluntly to 'get some aircraft ready immediately'. He complied with three aircraft, telling the 19 Group Commander at Plymouth afterwards that he considered the order 'suicidal', that in his view 'it would serve no useful purpose except to pander to Navy's demands for action', and that he 'did not expect to see the crews again'. His forecast proved correct for the three aircraft were indeed shot down, with all 12 crewmen perishing apart from a single survivor who became a Prisoner of War. Bolland explained later, 'There was no chance of any of my aircraft getting anywhere near Brest, and if they did and were lucky enough to hit the ships the damage would have been negligible.' He was relieved of his command, but was sent in December 1941 to Gibraltar as SASO, later commanding and extending the airfield there. On 6 April F/O Kenneth Campbell of 22 Squadron (whose Beauforts were able to drop torpedoes at last) made a suicidal lone attack and put a torpedo into the *Gneisenau*, knocking it out of action for six months, but the hail of light flak cost him his own life and the lives of his equally courageous crew – he was awarded a posthumous VC, but the inflexible regulations precluded any awards being made to his crew.

Sgt A. Tubbs, the 254 Squadron Pilot who, with P/O R. Webb (Obs), was killed and Sgt J. Timoney (WOp/Ag) injured when R3827 crashed on take-off at Wick on 4 March 1941.

Some Blenheims were fitted with a hand-operated gun in the nose to aid flak suppression during attacks on shipping, as on this 88 Squadron Mk IV.

The detachment of 59 Squadron at Manston moved to Bircham Newton on 1 March, the rest of the Squadron remaining at Thorney Island. The Squadron suffered a disaster on 28 April when all four Blenheims attacking a convoy off the Hook of Holland were shot down by the flak ships, or *Vorpostenboote*, guarding the convoy – 10 of the 12 crewmen involved were killed, the other two surviving to become Prisoners of War, the 100 per cent losses highlighting the extreme dangers of these low-level anti-shipping operations. The Germans reacted with their usual efficiency to the growing loss of their shipping caused by these Blenheim attacks, and by 30 April a small convoy off Holland with but one tanker was protected by no fewer than eight of these deadly flak ships and covered by patrols of Me.110s. Three aircraft attacked it – one was shot down and another badly damaged but managed to evade the marauding 110s. No hits were scored on the tanker.

Of the recently formed Blenheim squadrons, No 86, having worked up with its new Blenheim Mk IVs at Leuchars, became operational at Wattisham, while 236 took its Mk IV-Fs from St Eval to Carew Cheriton, and 252 its mixture of Mk I-Fs and Mk IV-Fs from Chivenor to Aldergrove, receiving a few more Beaufighters too, as did 272, which changed places with 252. Although 235 remained at Bircham Newton, it sent detachments of its Mk IV-Fs to cover the Bay of Biscay or the Western Approaches when required, as did 248 at Dyce and 254 at Sumburgh.

Fighter Command Blenheims

As the Luftwaffe continued its nightly bombing raids on England, so did 23 Squadron continue its night-intruder operations against enemy bomber airfields, achieving several successes with its outmoded Mk I-Fs – commendable indeed in the terrible weather conditions of that winter. P/O Ensor attacked a He.111 near Vereul on the night of 2 January and it crash-landed at Villacoublay, while F/Lt Willans met an enemy aircraft over the French coast on his way out on 16/17 January and attacked it, claiming a Do.17 as damaged – actually he had shot down a Me.110 of III(F)/123. The following night he destroyed a He.111 of III/KG 26 in the circuit at Poix, and on 25/26 February P/O Brown shot down a Ju.88 of III(F)/121, which crashed at Guerand. It was P/O Ensor's turn on 3 March when he claimed a He.111 over Merville, and F/Lt Hoare claimed a 'probable' the same night. P/O Gawith claimed a He.111 and a Do.17 damaged near Beauvais on the 8th, while on the 10th Sgt Skillen, after bombing and destroying a He.111 of I/KG 1 on the flare-path at Amiens/Glisy, attempted to intercept another in the circuit but collided with it and both aircraft crashed on to the airfield in flames, taking all on board to their deaths. S/Ldr Gracie shot down a Do.17 at Merville on the night of 14/15 March. 23 Squadron started to receive a few Douglas Havocs in March and these had replaced their elderly Blenheim Mk I-Fs by April 1941.

From the RAF's point of view it was unfortunate that 23 was still the only night-fighter squadron that could be employed offensively throughout the winter months, as all the others were required to be employed defensively in an attempt to resist – with a steadily increasing effectiveness – the on-going night *Blitz* by the Luftwaffe against the UK. Losses to the Blenheim night-fighters continued steadily too (see Appendix 4); indeed, more Blenheims were lost than enemy aircraft were claimed. More of the Blenheims were now fitted with AI and more of the new Beaufighters were becoming available – although this much-needed improvement in night-fighting operational effectiveness was delayed as 36 Beaufighters (almost half of the 77 in squadron service) were destroyed or badly damaged in accidents in the first three months of 1941. Most of these accidents occurred while landing at night, as the much heavier 'Beaus', with their higher wing-loading and faster touch-down speeds, were not nearly as forgiving during the approach and landing phase as the considerably lighter and much more docile Blenheims. Another factor that restricted the number of new Beaufighters available for night-defence use was the pressing demand by Coastal Command for re-equipment with the more modern aircraft, so the new 'Beaus' were allocated evenly between the two Commands. In Fighter Command, 25, 29 and 219 Squadrons had their Blenheims fully replaced by Beaufighters, as had 600 earlier and 604 by May 1941; 68 also kept a few Blenheims, including Mk IV-Fs, until May. On the 5th of that month the first Canadian Night Fighter Squadron – No 406 – was formed at Acklington with a mix of Mk I-Fs and Mk IV-Fs, but soon had few Beaufighter Mk IIs (the Merlin-engined version) and was fully equipped with them by the time it became operational in September. The Fighter Interception Unit had added more Beaufighters and Havocs to its radar-equipped Blenheims.

Luftwaffe night-intruders had been busy over the UK too: 21 Squadron suffered at their hands on the night of 10/11 February when S/Ldr Sabine in R3658 was followed over the North Sea on his way back from bombing Hannover by a Ju.88 of I/NJG 2, which attacked the Blenheim near Bodney, forcing a crash-landing. The intruder then waited nearby and shot down Sgt Chattaway's Blenheim Z5877 on its final approach. Another Blenheim, F/Lt Simmons's R3871 of 107 Squadron, was attacked off Yarmouth by a Ju.88 and forced to crash-land. This Ju.88 had earlier shot down a Wellington at Marham; another Wellington and a Hampden were also shot down by German intruders that night. Life was indeed grim for the crews of Bomber and Coastal Commands in 1941.

Appendix I

Bomber Command Blenheim losses in night operations, 1 January to 30 April 1941

Aircraft are all Mk IVs.

02/03-01-1941   R3604 82 Squadron: damaged by flak over Emden, damaged further on landing at Bodney; Sgt Inman and crew uninjured, aircraft repaired but shot down two months later.

22/23-01-1941   N3553 82 Squadron: FTR; crashed at Merton Park soon after take-off from Bodney for Dusseldorf, destroyed by fire; crew P/O P. Moller, Sgt A. Norman, and Sgt F. Taylor KIA.

10/11-02-1941   T2282 21 Squadron: FTR; reported as shot down by flak at Flushing, en route to Hannover, and force-landed on shore of Scheldt, but recently discovered photos show that aircraft landed undamaged on shingle in Scheldt estuary and was recovered by Germans; crew F/Lt R. McConnell, Sgt E. Green, and Sgt D. Bristow became PoWs.

10/11-02-1941   R3871 107 Squadron: became lost after bombing airfields, W/T failed, crash-landed after 6½ hours near Norwich; F/Lt Simmons DFC and crew uninjured, aircraft repaired.

10/11-02-1941   R3658? 21 Squadron: followed over North Sea on return from Hannover by Ju.88, attacked in circuit and crash-landed at Hartford Bridges near Bodney; S/Ldr Sabine and crew slightly injured, aircraft repaired. (Serial No. is incorrect in ORB).

10/11-02-1941   Z5877 21 Squadron: FTR; shot down by Ju.88 intruder of NJG2 in Bodney circuit at 0310 on return from Hannover; Sgt A. Chattaway (Pilot) killed, Sgt G. Sharvell (Obs) died from injuries, Sgt G. Birch (WOp/Ag) injured.

23/24-02-1941   T2138 107 Squadron: FTR; crashed near Swanton Morley on return from Boulogne, avoiding Wellington; crew S/Ldr C. Kemp, P/O P. Moody, and Sgt A. Lloyd KIA.

25/26-02-1941   T1989 105 Squadron: overshot landing at Swanton Morley in mist; P/O M. Dore and crew slightly injured, aircraft DBR.

26/27-02-1941   T2031 82 Squadron: FTR from sortie to Boulogne, lost without trace; crew Sgt K. Dalton, Sgt R. Thomas, and Sgt W. Lake KIA, commemorated on Runnymede Memorial.

28-02-1941   T1799 139 Squadron: became stuck on waterlogged grass runway at Horsham St Faith returning from raid on Flushing, run into by L9402 (below); crew injured, Sgt Vivian (Pilot) seriously, Sgt Handley (WOp/Ag) less seriously, Sgt A. Severn (Obs) died of injuries next day.

28-02-1941   L9402 139 Squadron: collided with T1799 (above) at 2032 landing on return from raid on Den Helder; Sgt Mills (Obs) badly injured, Sgt R. Bennett (Pilot) slightly injured, Sgt E. Laban (WOp/Ag) uninjured. Both aircraft destroyed by fire.

28-02-1941   R3907 139 Squadron: returning from Flushing, diverted to Swanton Morley due to above incident, flak-damaged undercarriage collapsed on landing, port engine torn off, but aircraft repaired; crew Sgt T. McPhee, Sgt G. Atkins, Sgt K. Whittle uninjured. (Ken Whittle describes this incident, and others, in his book *An Electrician Goes to War*.)

28-02-1941   T1895 105 Squadron: FTR; shot down by Me.110 night-fighter of NJG 1 over Holland returning from Wilhelmshaven; Sgt J. Heape (Pilot) thrown out of exploding aircraft, came down by parachute and became PoW, crewmen Sgt S. Jones and Sgt J. Bimson KIA and buried in Groningen Cemetery.

02/03-03-1941   Z5901 21 Squadron: FTR; left Watton at 2040 for Rotterdam, shot down by Me.110 into North Sea; crew (all aged 20) Sgt A. Warcup, Sgt A. Ferguson, and Sgt T. Courtman KIA and commemorated on Runnymede Memorial.

02/03-03-1941   T1862? 82 Squadron: struck balloon cable near Church Fenton on return from operational sortie; S/Ldr Barker and crew slightly injured, aircraft repaired.

04/05-03-1941   R3812 82 Squadron: damaged landing at Bodney returning from sortie; Sgt J. Harrison and crew uninjured, aircraft DBR.

12/13-03-1941   V5397 82 Squadron: FTR; shot down en route to Bremen; crew Sgt L. Stewart, Sgt E. Richardson, and Sgt P. Savage KIA and buried in Becklingen War Cemetery.

12/13-03-1941   R3758 21 Squadron: damaged and force-landed after attack by intruder; S/Ldr Allen and crew only slightly injured, aircraft repaired.

13/14-03-1941   T2278 110 Squadron: FTR; shot down over Holland by Me.110 of NJG 1 en route to Hamburg; crew F/Lt J. Dickinson DFC, Sgt C. Fry, and Sgt R. Mower KIA and buried in Esserveld Cemetery.

17/18-03-1941   R3636 21 Squadron: FTR; took off 0240 from Watton for Wilhelmshaven, engine cut, spun in near Thetford, bombs exploded; S/Ldr A. Allen, Sgt H. Linley, and Sgt A. Parsons KIA.

18/19-03-1941   R3846 101 Squadron: FTR; shot down in flames near Texel en route to Wilhelmshaven; crew P/O C. Brown DFC, P/O G. Collis DFM, and Sgt G. Loughlin DFM KIA. P/O Brown is buried in Sage War Cemetery, crew commemorated on Runnymede Memorial.

21/22-03-1941 T2038 18 Squadron: FTR; crashed near Grantham, Lincs, in bad visibility on return from raid on Lorient; crew P/O G. Cowings, P/O R. Daniel RNZAF, and Sgt E. Lee KIA.

21/22-03-1941 T1892 105 Squadron: FTR; also crashed on return from Lorient, striking balloon cable near Birmingham; crew P/O I. Shirlaw, P/O C. Dugdale, and F/O J. Mair KIA.

23/24-03-1941 R3673 21 Squadron: crashed at Watton on return from Hannover, destroyed by fire; Sgt S. Sproson (Pilot) and Sgt W. Clinton (Obs) died of injuries, Sgt E. Chinn (WOp/Ag) KIA.

23/24-03-1941 Z5903 105 Squadron: FTR from sortie to Hannover, presumed crashed into sea; Sgt C. King, Sgt R. Murphy, and Sgt F. Gibbs KIA. Sgt Gibbs buried in Sage War Cemetery, others have no known grave.

27/28-03-1941 L8787 110 Squadron: FTR; crashed on return from Brest, near St Mawgan airfield at 0320; crew F/Lt G. Yarrow, P/O R. Ashley, and Sgt. J. Grant injured, Pilot dying of injuries two days later.

30/31-03-1941 T2281 101 Squadron: FTR; crashed on return from raid on Brest, overshooting St Eval, destroyed by fire; Sgt L. Kiddle (Pilot) and Sgt P. Cammaerts (Obs) KIA, Sgt Kniveton (WOp/Ag) injured.

03/04-04-1941 N3552 101 Squadron: FTR to West Raynham from sortie to Brest, lost without trace; crew W/Cdr D. Addenbrooke, P/O W. Fenton, and Sgt E. Blomeley KIA and commemorated on Runnymede Memorial.

03/04-04-1941 T2439 101 Squadron: FTR from same sortie to Brest, crashed and exploded near Dorchester attempting to locate Boscombe Down; crew Sgt P. Burrows, Sgt G. Birdsell, and Sgt H. Perry KIA.

19/20-04-1941 R3806 114 Squadron: FTR; lost power on take-off, hit tree and crashed at Thornaby, destroyed by fire, bombs exploded; Sgt B. Beardsley, Sgt L, Fass, and Sgt L. Symes KIA.

Appendix 2

Bomber Command Blenheim losses in 'cloud cover' sorties, 1 January to 30 April 1941

Aircraft are all Mk IVs.

05-01-1941 T2134 139 Squadron: damaged by 'friendly' AA fire near Lowestoft on returning from Flushing; W/Cdr 'Digger' Kyle and crew uninjured, aircraft repaired.

06-01-1941 V5375 82 Squadron: FTR; crashed on return from Rotterdam at Strumpshaw near Norwich; Sgt Jackman (Pilot) rescued from burning wreckage by local villagers, he and Sgt T. Cooke (Obs) injured, Sgt Perry (WOp/Ag) uninjured.

11-01-1941 T2163 82 Squadron: FTR; lost without trace on sortie to Amsterdam; crew P/O A. Poulsen, Sgt J. Burton, and Sgt H. Summers KIA and commemorated at Runnymede Memorial.

13-01-1941 T1858 114 Squadron: FTR, shot down by Me.109E of JG 1 off Bergen, Holland; crew P/O D. Lowther-Clarke, Sgt A. Grindley, and Sgt N. Allen KIA and commemorated on Runnymede Memorial. Norman Allen was 19 years old.

22-01-1941 T2435 139 Squadron: FTR; shot down by RN AA fire off East Coast returning from NW Germany, crashed at Oulton, Suffolk; crew F/Lt G. Menzies DFC (NZ, aged 20), Sgt E. Bonney, and Sgt R. Tribick KIA.

31-01-1941 R3903 139 Squadron: badly damaged by 'friendly' AA fire near Southwold on return from Holland; F/Lt J. King and crew uninjured, aircraft repaired.

06-02-1941 L8777 107 Squadron: engine cut, crashed while attempting forced-landing near Wattisham; Sgt E. Clarke and crew uninjured, aircraft DBR.

17-02-1941 Z5902 114 Squadron: FTR; shot down by flak near Den Helder, crashed into North Sea; F/Lt M. Marks DFC, Sgt H. Teeton, and Sgt I. Adkins (aged 20) KIA and commemorated on Runnymede Memorial.

07-03-1941 T1922 139 Squadron: crashed on take-off from Horsham St Faith; crew S/Ldr Birch, P/O Hewitson, and Sgt Montgomery uninjured, aircraft repaired.

23-03-1941 R3682 105 Squadron: crashed attempting to land at Swanton Morley on return from raid on Calais; Sgt R. Wood, Sgt Turton, and Sgt Wilcock safe, aircraft DBR.

07-04-1941 L9386 139 Squadron: FTR from raid on Ijmuiden steel works, damaged by flak, shot down by Me.109E of JG 1; crew Sgt R. Bennett, P/O E. Pierse, and Sgt E. Laban KIA.

07-04-1941 V5521 139 Squadron: damaged by flak and Me.109s on raid to Ijmuiden steel works, caught fire on landing; Sgt Dennis (Pilot) safe, Sgt S. Hill (Obs) wounded and died a week later, Sgt Waddington (WOp/Ag) safe, aircraft DBR.

07-04-1941 V5826 139 Squadron: damaged by Me.109s of JG 1 on raid to Ijmuiden steel works; crew Sgt Jennings, Sgt Scholefield, and Sgt Shrimpton all wounded, aircraft DBR.

14-04-1941 R2784 21 Squadron: FTR to Watton from raid on Leiden power station, shot down 2km from target; crew Sgt E. Newhouse, Sgt V. Cobb, and Sgt J. Bougin KIA and buried at Oegstgeest.

25-04-1941 L9244 105 Squadron: damaged by flak while bombing Ijmuiden steel works, belly-landed back at Swanton Morley; crew Sgt A. Piers, Sgt W. Healy, and Sgt S. Bastin safe, aircraft repaired.

Appendix 3

Bomber Command Blenheim losses in anti-shipping sorties, 1 January to 30 April 1941

Aircraft are all Mk IVs.

15-02-1941   T2125 114 Squadron: FTR; shot down near Flushing by Me.109E of JG 52; crew Sgt T. Barnes AFM, Sgt H. Seward (aged 20), and Sgt L. Walsh (aged 20) KIA and buried in Flushing.

20-03-1941   R3604 82 Squadron: FTR; shot down by flak from minesweeper off Den Helder; crew Sgt J. Kelly, Sgt G. Wilson RNZAF (aged 20), and Sgt S. Adair KIA. Pilot and Obs buried at Bergen-op-Zoom, WOp/Ag commemorated on Runnymede Memorial.

24-03-1941   L9389 82 Squadron: FTR; shot down by flak from destroyer being attacked at Marsdiep, near Texel; crew F/Lt H. Black DFC (aged 20), Sgt T. Cooke, and Sgt F. Archer DFM KIA. Pilot buried at Bergen-op-Zoom, crewmen commemorated at Runnymede.

24-03-1941   R3767 82 Squadron: damaged by flak on above sortie, crash-landed at Bodney; Sgt Harrison and crew uninjured, aircraft repaired.

27-03-1941   L9386 139 Squadron: badly damaged by flak from target convoy off Hook of Holland; Sgt Ryan (Obs) injured, P/O E. Sidney-Smith (Pilot) and Sgt Fox (WOp/Ag) safe, aircraft repaired.

31-03-1941   R3884 21 Squadron: FTR; shot down by flak ship off Texel; crew Sgt P. Adams, Sgt T. Alston, and Sgt R. Nichols KIA and commemorated on Runnymede Memorial.

31-03-1941   R3900 21 Squadron: FTR; shot down by flak ship off Texel; crew P/O D. Rogers, P/O W. Gourlay, and Sgt G. Howard KIA and commemorated at Runnymede.

02-04-1941   Z5818 82 Squadron: FTR; shot down by flak in Scheldt Estuary while attacking shipping; crew Sgt W. Haynes, P/O A. Ford, and Sgt A. Lee KIA and commemorated on Runnymede Memorial.

02-04-1941   T2118 82 Squadron: damaged by flak in Scheldt Estuary while attacking shipping; F/Lt Munroe (Pilot) wounded, P/O J. Tait (Obs) KIA, Sgt A. Tucker (WOp/Ag) uninjured, aircraft repaired.

04-04-1941   L9270 82 Squadron: FTR; shot down off Dutch Coast on anti-shipping 'Beat'; crew Sgt A. Farns, Sgt W. Fox (aged 19), and Sgt N. Geer KIA and commemorated on Runnymede Memorial.

06-04-1941   V6023 107 Squadron: FTR; side-slipped into sea from steep turn at low level on convoy patrol off Pittenweem, Fife; crew W/Cdr W. Cameron, F/Sgt J. Spatchett, and Sgt W. Howlett KIA, commemorated on Runnymede Memorial.

10-04-1941   V5596 82 Squadron: FTR. damaged by Me.110 off Borkum, ran out of fuel, force-landed on sandbank off Birchington, Kent; Sgt Crew, Sgt Cartside, and Sgt Drummond rescued.

10-04-1941   V5634 82 Squadron: damaged by Me.110s off Borkum; aircraft lost propeller over sea, escaped in cloud, force-landed at Horsham St Faith; Sgt Long (Pilot) and Sgt Nicholson (Obs) safe, Sgt J. Cameron (WOp/Ag) KIA, aircraft repaired.

10-04-1941   N3569 82 Squadron: FTR; took off from Bodney on same shipping 'Beat', lost without trace; crew F/Sgt J. Irving, P/O J. Gadsby, and Sgt J. MacIlwraith KIA and commemorated on Runnymede Memorial.

11-04-1941   T1829 18 Squadron: FTR; shot down near Sylt on anti-shipping sortie; crew P/O H. Jones, Sgt J. Horsham, and Sgt K. Walton KIA. P/O Jones buried at Sondre Nissum Churchyard, crewmen commemorated on Runnymede Memorial.

12-04-1941   R3905 110 Squadron: FTR; hit by flak attacking convoy, crashed into sea off Westkapelle; S/Ldr D. Gericke (Pilot) rescued and became PoW, crew Sgt D. Staples and F/Sgt E. Rae KIA and commemorated on Runnymede Memorial.

13-04-1941   L9247 18 Squadron: FTR; shot down by flak on shipping sortie to Borkum; crew F/Sgt J. Anderton (Pilot) and F/O R. Tapp (Obs) KIA and buried at Sage War Cemetery, Sgt R. James-Smith (WOp/Ag) commemorated on Runnymede Memorial.

14-04-1941   V5376 1 PRU: FTR; damaged by flak near Vlissingen, shot down by Me.109 of I/JG 52 near Breskens; crew F/O J. Flynn, F/O W. Hall, and F/Sgt R. Stephens KIA and buried at Flushing. Robert Stephens was 19 years old.

15-04-1941   R3841 18 Squadron: FTR; shot down off Camaret, Cap Finistere, while attacking shipping; W/Cdr C. Hill DFC, F/Sgt C. McPhee, and F/Sgt J. Frodsham KIA and commemorated on Runnymede Memorial. W/Cdr Hill was CO of 18 Squadron.

17-04-1941   T2141 105 Squadron: FTR; shot down off Brittany coast by Me.109s while attacking shipping; crew Sgt I. Sarjeant, Sgt L. Evered, and Sgt K. Gresty KIA and commemorated on Runnymede Memorial.

17-04-1941   V5516 107 Squadron: overshot Leuchars on return from shipping patrol at night in bad weather, crashed into river; S/Ldr D. Briggs, P/O P. Halls, and Sgt V. Johnson safe, aircraft DBR.

18-04-1941	V5494 114 Squadron: FTR; shot down by Me.110 of ZG 76 off Farsend, Norway, while attacking shipping; W/Cdr G. Elsmie DFC, F/Sgt M. Applebee, and F/Sgt C. Jennings DFM KIA and commemorated on Runnymede Memorial. W/Cdr Elsmie was CO of 114 Squadron.
18-04-1941	V5650 114 Squadron: FTR, shot down by Me.110 off Farsend, Norway, while attacking shipping; S/Ldr A. Robbins, P/O M. Proudlock, and Sgt S. Du Plessis KIA and commemorated on Runnymede Memorial.
18-04-1941	T2276 114 Squadron: FTR; shot down by Me.110 off Farsend, Norway, while attacking shipping; F/Lt T. Myers, Sgt R. Williams, and Sgt R. Mann (aged 20) KIA, latter buried in Sola Churchyard, others commemorated on Runnymede Memorial.
18-04-1941	R3740 107 Squadron: FTR; shot down by flak while attacking convoy off Farsund, Norway; crew F/Sgt J. Hickingbotham, Sgt R. Rowley, and Sgt D. Townsend KIA and commemorated on Runnymede Memorial.
18-04-1941	R3873 107 Squadron: FTR; shot down by flak while attacking convoy off Farsund, Norway; crew W/Cdr A. Birch, P/O Hewitson, and Sgt Montgomery KIA and commemorated on Runnymede Memorial. W/Cdr Birch was CO of 107 Squadron.
18-04-1941	R2787 110 Squadron: FTR; took off from Watton on anti-shipping sortie, struck tree on airfield boundary, crashed and destroyed by fire; crew Sgt H. Wright, Sgt N. Kendall, and F/Sgt G. Cornwall KIA.
18-04-1941	T1814 21 Squadron: FTR; shot down by flak while attacking shipping off Heligoland; crew F/O H. Marshall, Sgt L. Bacon, and Sgt A. Bonnett KIA and commemorated on Runnymede Memorial.
18-04-1941	V5855 21 Squadron: FTR; shot down by flak while attacking shipping off Heligoland; crew Sgt J. Dunning, Sgt P. Hope, and Sgt J. Bruce KIA. Sgt Dunning buried in Sage War Cemetery, crewmen commemorated on Runnymede Memorial.
22-04-1941	V6031 21 Squadron: overshot and crashed on return to Watton from anti-shipping sortie; crew Sgt R. Lloyd, Sgt Fairey, and Sgt Wade slightly injured, aircraft DBR.
22-04-1941	T2442 82 Squadron: FTR; crashed at Embleton near Accrington on return from anti-shipping sortie; Sgt Miller, Sgt Johnson, and Sgt Newbon reported uninjured, aircraft DBR.
23-04-1941	V6318 105 Squadron: FTR; shot down into sea by flak from mine-sweeper off Domburg, Holland; crew Sgt A. Lister, Sgt W. Heaney, and Sgt K. Porter KIA. Sgt Lister buried at Vlissingen, Holland, Sgt Porter at Wenduine in Belgium, Sgt Heaney commemorated on Runnymede Memorial.
24-04-1941	Z5795 107 Squadron: FTR; crashed near Kristiansand on shipping sweep, believed shot down; crew P/O C. Maclaren, Sgt A. Hannah (NZ, aged 20), and Sgt D. King KIA, commemorated on Runnymede Memorial.
25-04-1941	V6370 105 Squadron: FTR; shot down into sea by Me.109s of JG 1 off Westkapelle, Holland; P/O R. Needham (aged 19), P/O T. Keightley-Smith, and Sgt F. Bridgman KIA. Obs buried at Hague, others commemorated on Runnymede Memorial.
26-04-1941	V6338 21 Squadron: FTR; shot down by ships' flak into sea off Vlieland; crew W/Cdr G. Bartlett DFC, F/O A. Winder, and Sgt P. Eames DFM (aged 19) KIA and commemorated on Runnymede memorial. W/Cdr Bartlett was CO of 21 Squadron.
26-04-1941	V5822 21 Squadron: FTR; shot down into sea by ships' flak off Vlieland, Dutch Frisian Islands; Sgt C. Spouge, Sgt A. Jordan, and Sgt E. Acton KIA. Cyril Spouge and Arthur Jordan commemorated on Runnymede Memorial, Eric Acton buried at Sage War Cemetery.
26-04-1941	V6063 110 Squadron: FTR; shot down into sea by Me.109E of JG 54 off Texel, Holland; crew F/Lt G. Lings DFC, F/Sgt C. Martin, and Sgt S. Peplar KIA and commemorated on Runnymede Memorial. George Lings took part as P/O in first raid of war, on Wilhelmshaven 4-9-1939.
27-04-1941	V5493 101 Squadron: FTR; shot down off Calais by flak while attacking shipping; crew Sgt R. Ridgman-Parsons, Sgt G. Hickman, and Sgt H. Downes KIA and commemorated on Runnymede Memorial.
28-04-1941	V6022 114 Squadron: FTR; control lost in circuit on return from shipping sweep, crashed and destroyed by fire; crew P/O J. Long, Sgt N. Dawson, and Sgt N. Taylor KIA.
29-04-1941	L9421 101 Squadron: badly damaged by flak while attacking shipping, force-landed at Manston; Sgt A. Jordan (Obs) wounded, Sgt C. Deane (Pilot) and Sgt Watkinson (WOp/Ag) safe, aircraft repaired.
29-04-1941	V6256 82 Squadron: FTR; lost without trace, believed shot down into sea off Norwegian coast; four-man crew P/O D. White, Sgt R. Hanson, Sgt W. Busby, and Cpl H. Hollis KIA and commemorated on Runnymede Memorial.
29-04-1941	V6451 82 Squadron: FTR; shot down into sea off Sola, Norway, by ships' flak; crew F/Lt R. Tallis DFC, Sgt D. Shaylor, and Sgt F. Davis KIA. Pilot buried at Sola, crew commemorated on Runnymede Memorial.
30-04-1941	V5853 21 Squadron: FTR; shot down by flak ship into sea off The Hague while attacking convoy; crew Sgt M. Dewing, Sgt W. Smale, and Sgt H. Nathan KIA and buried at Hook of Holland.

Appendix 4

Fighter Command Blenheim losses, 1 January to 30 April 1941

Aircraft are all Mk I-Fs apart from T2136 of 600 Squadron on 12-03-1941, which is a Mk IV-F.

03/04-01-1941   L6781 23 Squadron: FTR; lost on intruder operation to Dieppe; crew S/Ldr V. Colman, F/Sgt D. Mathews, and Sgt H. MacRory KIA. S/Ldr Colman's body washed ashore at Worthing, crewmen commemorated on Runnymede Memorial. (Serial No. incorrect in several sources: L6781 was lost with 13 OTU 28-09-1940.)

09/10-01-1941   L1226 23 Squadron: FTR; lost on intruder operation to Beauvais; Sgt Jones (Pilot) KIA, crew Sgt G. Bessell and Sgt R. Cullen captured and became PoWs.

11/12-01-1941   L6737 23 Squadron: damaged on intruder operation, belly-landed at Ford; crew P/O Simpson, Sgt Brewer, and Sgt Nicholls suffered only slight injuries, aircraft repaired. See entry for 10-04-1941 below.

16-01-1941   L8655 23 Squadron: overshot landing at Ford, hit gun-pit and DBR; P/O Brown and crew uninjured.

24-02-1941   L1340 23 Squadron: ex-FIU aircraft, DBR, no further details available.

03/04-03-1941   L1453 23 Squadron: FTR; shot down by flak on intruder operation near Guines; Sgt J. Rose Sgt T. Nicholas, and Sgt R. Walker KIA, buried in Guines Communal Cemetery.

08/09-03-1941   L6730 23 Squadron: undershot Manston on return from intruder sortie; P/O Pushman and crew uninjured, aircraft repaired.

10/11-03-1941   YP-X 23 Squadron: FTR; collided with He.111 over Amiens/Glisy airfield on intruder operation; crew Sgt V. Skillen, Sgt F. Abbott, and Sgt R. Nute KIA, buried at Amiens St Pierre.

12-03-1941   T2136 600 Squadron: crashed on landing from patrol at Thirsk; P/O Coombs and crew uninjured, aircraft (ex-FIU) repaired.

30-03-1941   Z6254 252 Squadron: swung off runway in night landing at Chivenor and collided with articulated trailer; Sub/Lt (A) V. Crane FAA unhurt.

09-04-1941   L8616 23 Squadron: FTR; shot down by flak on intruder sortie to Avelin, France; crew P/O G. Simpson, Sgt H. Brewer, and Sgt T. Nicholls KIA, buried at Avelin, France.

Appendix 5

Coastal Command Blenheim losses, 1 January to 30 April 1941

Aircraft are all Mk IVs or Mk IV-Fs.

04-01-1941   R2773 53 Squadron: FTR; shot down by Me.109 of II/JG77 while attacking cruiser *Hipper* and destroyers in Brest harbour; crew P/O P. Gibbs, Sgt H. Wall, and Sgt H. Martin KIA.

04-01-1941   R2773 53 Squadron: FTR; shot down by Me.109 of JG 77 while attacking cruiser *Hipper* and destroyers in Brest harbour; crew P/O P. Gibbs, Sgt H. Wall, and Sgt H. Martin KIA.

04-01-1941   V5398 53 Squadron: FTR; damaged by Me.109 on same sortie, crash-landed near Exeter; P/O G. Newton (Pilot) and Sgt K. Hughes (WOp/Ag) injured, P/O Gibbs (Obs) uninjured.

09-01-1941   L1123 263 Squadron: FTR; engine caught fire, dived into ground at Topsham, Exeter, and destroyed; Sgt Morton (solo pilot) baled out but killed. (263 was an operational Whirlwind squadron.)

09/10-01-1941   T2217 59 Squadron: FTR; became lost after raid on Brest harbour, ditched in St George's Channel; crew P/O K. Cooke, Sgt D. Smith, and Sgt P. Smith KIA, commemorated on Runnymede Memorial.

09-01-1941   V5370 53 Squadron: FTR; damaged by flak in raid on Brest harbour, ditched off Selsey Bill; Sgt H. Jackson (WOp/Ag) KIA, P/O J. Lucas (Pilot) and Sgt Gale (Obs) rescued.

10-01-1941   V5518 53 Squadron: both engines stopped while bombing Brest, aircraft then damaged by flak, engines restarted and P/O R. Alcock landed in dark at St Eval, ground looping between unseen parked Beauforts and FAA aircraft.

13-01-1941   R2782 235 Squadron: damaged on shipping patrol, force-landed at Docking; Sgt Mason and crew uninjured, aircraft repaired.

29-01-1941   V5432 236 Squadron: crashed on landing at St Eval returning from Brest; F/O Coates-Preedy injured, Sgt Woodlands and Sgt Shields rescued safely, aircraft DBF.

30-01-1941   N6233 248 Squadron: FTR; engine cut, stalled and crashed at Chapel Farm, Newmurcham, Lincs, on return from sortie to Norway; crew Sgt R. Houchin, Sgt T. Williams, and Sgt J. Kirkham KIA.

02-02-1941   V5531 59 Squadron: attacked St Omer airfield, pursued by Me.109s, claiming one, crash-landed at Manston, destroyed by fire; P/O Trim, P/O Blake and Sgt Jones (WOp/Ag) escaped safely.

04-02-1941	Z5765 53 Squadron: FTR; crashed on night take-off for raid on Brest from Thorney Island and burned out, crew seriously injured, P/O G. Marriott (Pilot) recovered, but Sgt E. Strudwick (Obs) and Sgt G. Hadnam (WOp/Ag) died of injuries.
04-02-1941	T2283 53 Squadron: FTR; shot down by Me.109 of JG 77, crashed into sea off Brest; crew P/O C. Morris, Sgt G. Ashwin, and Sgt I. Clark KIA and commemorated on Runnymede Memorial.
04-02-1941	T1992 53 Squadron: FTR; shot down by Me.109 of JG 77, crashed into sea off Cherbourg; crew F/Lt B. Daly, Sgt J. Jones, and Sgt R. Trafford KIA and commemorated on Runnymede Memorial.
04-02-1941	L8791 59 Squadron: crashed on take-off at Thorney Island for raid on Cherbourg, striking parked R3679; P/O D. Clusterton and Sgt W. Harker killed, Sgt Edgar injured but recovered.
08-02-1941	Z5956 248 Squadron: FTR; shot down near Mandal, Norway; crew S/Ldr J. Coats, P/O D. Warren, and Sgt A. Douglas KIA, buried in Mandal Churchyard.
10-02-1941	N3528 254 Squadron: FTR; shot down by flak over Trondheim harbour; F/O K. Mackenzie, Sgt J. Craig, and Sgt H. Twinn KIA, buried in Stavne Cemetery, Trondheim. R3679 on take-off at Thorney Island, P/O D. Clusterton killed.
11-02-1941	L8791 59 Squadron: struck R3679 on take-off at Thorney Island, P/O D. Clusterton killed.
13-02-1941	R3679 53 Squadron: attacked by 609 Sqn Spitfire of F/O T. Nowierski, who mistook it for a Ju.88, damaged and force-landed at Bircham Newton; crew safe. Damaged previously when struck by L8791 at Thorney Island 04-02-1941, then DBR in air-raid, 0200 hours 16-02-1941.
14-02-1941	V5431 235 Squadron: crash-landed at Langham returning from shipping strike, overshooting from Bircham Newton; P/O Chamberlain injured, P/O E. Phillips (Obs) killed, Sgt Burns safe, aircraft DBF.
14-02-1941	Z5970 235 Squadron: FTR; flew into ground in bad visibility near Croxton, Norfolk, returning to Bircham Newton from night sortie; crew Sgt W. Mason, Sgt N. Stanger RNZAF, and Sgt V. Pond killed.
18-02-1941	V5450 236 Squadron: force-landed at base after battle damage; Sgt Lindley and crew uninjured, aircraft repaired.
21-02-1941	R2799 236 Squadron: swung on take-off at St Eval in snow and struck parked Blenheims; crew F/O Lumsden, Sgt Tumbridge, and Sgt Snape slightly injured, aircraft DBR.
22-02-1941	T1803 235 Squadron: FTR; shot down by return fire from He.111 over North Sea; crew Sgt D. Wallis, Sgt R. Brookman RNZAF, and Sgt G. Pavitt KIA, commemorated on Runnymede Memorial.
23/24-02-1941	T2040 59 Squadron: abandoned over Lamerton, Devon, when lost in mist returning to St Eval from raid on Brest; P/O W. Scarfe, P/O Bendry, and Sgt Taylor safe.
23/24-02-1941	V5394 59 Squadron: crashed on landing at St Eval in mist on return from raid on Brest; P/O Wightman, Sgt Crosher, and Sgt Paterson safe, aircraft DBR.
23/24-02-1941	R3631 59 Squadron: overshot St Eval landing in mist on return from raid; P/O Kennedy and crew uninjured, aircraft repaired.
24-02-1941	T1942 236 Squadron: overshot landing at St Eval in heavy mist; P/O Walters, Sgt Philip, and Sgt Lawrence uninjured, aircraft DBR.
25-02-1941	V5450 236 Squadron: FTR; shot down by Me.109 of JG 77 off French coast; crew P/O E. Alexander, Sgt E. Lindsay, and Sgt B. Mansfield KIA, commemorated on Runnymede Memorial.
26/27-02-1941	R3833 59 Squadron: struck balloon cable near Dover returning from raid; P/O Collier and crew believed to have been injured, aircraft repaired.
28-02-1941	T1953 254 Squadron: received battle damage, crash-landed at Sumburgh and DBR, Sgt R. Hick killed.
03-03-1941	V5734 254 Squadron: overshot landing at Wick; P/O Perry and crew safe, aircraft DBF.
04-03-1941	L9450 248 Squadron: Struck off charge as burnt out, but not recorded in 248 Squadron ORB.
04-03-1941	R3827 254 Squadron: crashed on take-off from Wick; Sgt A. Tubbs (Pilot) and P/O R. Webb (Obs) killed, Sgt J. Timoney (WOp/Ag) injured, aircraft DBR. (See accompanying photograph.)
07-03-1941	T1812 236 Squadron: crash-landed at Truro after engine cut in bad weather; P/O Robb, Sgt Yates, and Sgt Stewart slightly injured, aircraft DBR.
08-03-1941	V5896 235 Squadron: crash-landed near Bircham Newton after engine cut on take-off for St Eval; F/O MacKay and crew uninjured, aircraft DBR.
10-03-1941	Z5752 272 Squadron: FTR from convoy escort sortie in bad weather, crashed into the sea; P/O A. Van Weyenburghe, Sgt J. Thompson, and Sgt D. McWatt KIA, commemorated on Runnymede Memorial.
10-03-1941	Z5733 236 Squadron: FTR from convoy escort sortie in bad weather, crashed into sea; crew Sgt P. Chanler, Sgt K. Pass, and Sgt W. Newton KIA, commemorated on Runnymede Memorial.
11-03-1941	P4850 53 Squadron: FTR; shot down by flak over Brest harbour, attacking cruiser *Hipper*; crew P/O D. Plumb, Sgt R. Maton, and Sgt C. Calder KIA, commemorated on Runnymede Memorial.
14-03-1941	V5399 53 Squadron: FTR; shot down by Me.109E of JG 77 on photo sortie to Brest harbour; crew P/O G. Newton, Sgt C. Whitehill, and Sgt J. Miller KIA, buried in St Renen Churchyard, Finisterre.
15-03-1941	T2132 53 Squadron: FTR; shot down by flak while attacking warships in Brest harbour; crew P/O W. Leedam, Sgt F. Oatley, and Sgt W. Williams DFM KIA, commemorated on Runnymede Memorial.
17-03-1941	V5464 86 Squadron: FTR to Wattisham from convoy escort sortie, collided with Z5808 (below), destroyed by fire; P/O B. Mace, Sgt J. Wrightson, and Sgt B. Gilmore killed.

17-03-1941	Z5808 86 Squadron: FTR to Wattisham from convoy escort sortie, collided with V5464 (above); P/O J. Cresswell, Sgt W. Loxton, and Sgt F. Berry killed, aircraft DBF. (This incident occurred before 86 Squadron became officially operational on 28-03-1941; 'convoy escort sortie' may have been training exercise as part of working up.)
18-03-1941	TR-T 59 Squadron: badly damaged by Me.110 when attacking U-boat; P/O Siddall and crew uninjured, aircraft repaired.
18/19-03-1941	V5533, 59 Squadron: crashed on landing at Marham in mist; P/O Munro, Sgt Hunt, and Sgt Hales escaped uninjured, aircraft DBF, bomb-load exploded.
19-03-1941	L1197 226 Squadron Mk I: crashed on landing at Sydenham; W/Cdr Harrison and crew uninjured, aircraft repaired.
19-03-1941	L6781 Mk I with A&AEE: F/O P. Foy retracted u/c not flaps after landing, first solo on type, aircraft damage Cat 4.
20/21-03-1941	Z5755 236 Squadron: abandoned over Bodmin Moor when lost in bad weather at night; one of P/O Barron's crew, Sgt H. Sheard, killed, P/O Barron and Sgt Thornton safe.
22-03-1941	T2433 59 Squadron: FTR; shot down by Me.109E of JG 1 off Katwijk; crew P/O D. Date, P/O E. Moore, and Sgt B. Watkins KIA and commemorated on Runnymede Memorial.
22-03-1941	V5396 59 Squadron: damaged by Me.109s in same action, crash-landed on IoW; P/O Villa and crew slightly injured, aircraft repaired.
22-03-1941	L9406 254 Squadron: FTR; shot down off Haugesund, Norway, by naval flak; crew P/O J. Duff, P/O Wales, and Sgt J. York KIA, buried at Haugesund, Norway.
23-03-1941	L8407 252 Squadron Mk I: damaged when undershot night landing at Chivenor; F/Lt J. Blennerhassett and crew uninjured, aircraft DBR.
23-03-1941	T2396 53 Squadron: returning from Brest at 2155 hours, overshot at St Eval and hit shelter; P/O B. Bannister and crew slightly injured, aircraft repaired.
23-03-1941	L9404 235 Squadron: FTR; shot down by Me.109E of JG 1 off Hook of Holland attacking convoy; crew Sgt C. Evans, Sgt E. Harvey, and Sgt G. Macleod KIA, commemorated at Runnymede.
23-03-1941	Z6085 235 Squadron: FTR from attacking convoy, shot down in flames by Me.109E of JG 1 off Hook of Holland; crew P/O A. Newman, Sgt H. Willis, and Sgt V. Key KIA, commemorated at Runnymede.
23-03-1941	V5452 235 Squadron: damaged by Me.109s of JG 1 off Hook of Holland; P/O Green and crew uninjured, aircraft repaired.
25-03-1941	T1806 236 Squadron: crashed on landing at Carew Cheriton in bad weather; P/O Chappell (Pilot) and Sgt Lerway (WOp/Ag) injured, Sgt J. Dobbins (Obs) killed, aircraft DBR.
25-03-1941	? 59 Squadron: badly damaged by Me.109s, aircraft force-landed at Manston; Sgt Buckley (WOp/Ag) KIA, F/Lt Palmer (Pilot) and Sgt West (Obs) safe.
26-03-1941	V5648 59 Squadron: FTR; shot down on shipping sortie to French coast; crew P/O P. McMillan, Sgt W. Butler, and Sgt D. Vane KIA. P/O McMillan and Sgt Vane commemorated at Runnymede, Sgt Butler buried in Dunkirk Town Cemetery.
26-03-1941	V6065 59 Squadron: FTR from sortie to Brest, crashed in fog at Winterbourne Abbas on return, destroyed by fire; P/O L. Sandes DFC, Sgt E. Robinson, and Sgt G. Gates KIA.
27-03-1941	V5865 53 Squadron: FTR, shot down by Me.109Es of JG 77 into sea off Isle de Batz, leaving Brest; P/O J. Fothergill, Sgt T. Coady, and Sgt P. Parker KIA, commemorated on Runnymede Memorial.
27-03-1941	T2332 53 Squadron: FTR; shot down by Me.109Es of JG 77 on same sortie, crashed near Cleder; P/O R. Philpott, Sgt C. Goad, and Sgt F. Manning KIA.
30-03-1941	V6064 59 Squadron: badly damaged by Me.109s off Calais; Sgt J. Munt (WOp/Ag) seriously wounded, Sgt L. Hunt (Obs) wounded, P/O J. Griffiths (Pilot) crash-landed at Hawkinge, aircraft DBR.
01-04-1941	T2398 53 Squadron: damaged by Hurricane of 247 Squadron; P/O Reade and crew safe, aircraft repaired but shot down six days later.
01-04-1941	Z6022 235 Squadron: FTR; became lost in bad weather on return from sortie, force-landed on Snettisham beach, Norfolk; crew P/O A. Annan, P/O O'Donnell, and Sgt Davies safe.
01-04-1941	V5764 235 Squadron: stalled in steep climbing turn and spun into Heacham Beach, Hunstanton, Norfolk, destroyed by fire; P/O P. Blake and Sgt W. Curry killed.
03-04-1941	V6140 86 Squadron: damaged by Hurricane, crash-landed at Ipswich; P/O Gubbins and crew only slightly injured, aircraft repaired.
05-04-1941	V5530 59 Squadron: abandoned in fog near Stowmarket when lost on return from shipping sortie; P/O R. Morton, Sgt B. Flury, and Sgt Searott safe, aircraft crashed at Combs, Suffolk.
06-04-1941	V5962 59 Squadron: FTR from shipping sortie off St Brieuc Bay, Brittany; P/O M. Lishman, P/O A. Martin, and F/Sgt R. Fitzpatrick KIA, commemorated at Runnymede.
07-04-1941	T2398 53 Squadron: FTR; shot down on convoy escort duty; P/O E. Nicholson, P/O H. Stone, and Sgt P. Kinsey DFM KIA and commemorated at Runnymede.
09-04-1941	V5862 53 Squadron: crashed, fully-laden, with full nose-up trim immediately after take-off from St Eval; P/O I. Anderson, Sgt H. Walker and Sgt E. Fabian KIA.

09-04-1941   V6148 86 Squadron: FTR; shot down on anti-shipping sortie; crew P/O M. Franklin, Sgt E. Jones, and Sgt F. Sloane KIA, commemorated at Runnymede.

09-04-1941   N3609 254 Squadron: FTR; damaged by Me.110s off Norwegian coast and ditched; crew P/O J. Parry, P/O C. Gibson, and Sgt R. West Missing in Action, commemorated at Runnymede.

14-04-1941   V5376 1 PRU: FTR to Benson, shot down by Me.109s near Breskens, Holland; F/O J. Flynn, F/O W. Hall, and F/Sgt R. Stephens KIA, buried in Vlissingen Northern Cemetery, Holland.

15-04-1941   Z5953 254 Squadron: FTR from sortie to Norwegian coast, crashed into North Sea; Sgt S. McAdam, Sgt H. Wood, and Sgt A. Forsythe KIA, commemorated on Runnymede Memorial.

15-04-1941   L8840 254 Squadron: FTR from sortie to Norwegian coast; crew F/Lt A. Hill, P/O R. Cressey, and Sgt G. Webb KIA, buried at Haugesund, Norway.

16-04-1941   V5518 53 Squadron: FTR; lost engine en route for shipping patrol, force-landed near Penryn, hit drystone wall; P/O R. Reade (Pilot) and Sgt J. O'Connell (Obs) KIA, Sgt R. Camm (WOp/Ag) seriously injured.

16-04-1941   V6174 59 Squadron: FTR; lost height after night take-off and crashed into sea off Thorney Island; Sgt Johnson (Obs) KIA, P/O Makgill (Pilot) and Sgt Hunter (WOp/Ag) rescued.

17-04-1941   V5526 608 Squadron: FTR; engine cut on convoy patrol, ditched 8 miles east of Tynemouth, Northumberland; crew P/O Reeve, P/O Bass, and Sgt Bedford rescued.

18-04-1941   V6302 53 Squadron: FTR; lost without trace on anti-shipping sortie; crew P/O E. Thomas, Sgt S. Capel, and Sgt D. Trotman KIA and commemorated at Runnymede.

18-04-1941   Z6050 500 Squadron: engine cut on take-off at Detling, rolled and crashed on road just outside airfield, destroyed by fire; crew P/O J. Ready, P/O J. Johnson, F/O H. Jones, and Sgt K. Shepherdson killed.

20-04-1941   T2135 254 Squadron: FTR from shipping patrol off Norwegian coast; Sgt D. Viney, Sgt W. Morris, and Sgt M. Williams KIA, commemorated at Runnymede.

25-04-1941   R3833 59 Squadron: undershot Thorney Island returning from sortie to E-boat base; Sgt Cox (Obs) injured, P/O H. Badland (Pilot) and Sgt R. Henderson (WOp/Ag) uninjured but KIA 3 days later, aircraft DBR.

28-04-1941   V6097 59 Squadron: FTR; shot down by flak ship while attacking convoy off Hook of Holland; P/O H. Badland, Sgt A. Hazell, and Sgt R. Henderson KIA. Pilot buried at Rockanje, WOp/Ag at Hook of Holland, Obs commemorated on Runnymede Memorial.

28-04-1941   V5520 59 Squadron: FTR; shot down by flak ship while attacking convoy off Hook of Holland; P/O S. Collier, Sgt J. Mingham, and F/Sgt W. Powell KIA and buried at Hook of Holland.

28-04-1941   N3615 59 Squadron: FTR; shot down by flak ship while attacking convoy off Hook of Holland; crew F/Lt A. Fry DFC, F/Sgt E. Freeman (aged 20), and Sgt J. Taylor KIA and commemorated on Runnymede Memorial.

28-04-1941   V5687 59 Squadron: FTR; shot down by flak ship while attacking convoy off Hook of Holland; Sgt J. Hulme (WOp/Ag) KIA and buried at Beregen aan Zee, P/O H. Norton (Pilot) and Sgt W. Flury (Obs) rescued and became PoWs. Only survivors from section of four 59 Squadron Blenheims shot down in this action.

29-04-1941   V5802 254 Squadron: FTR from anti-shipping strike off Norwegian coast; crew P/O C. Tyler, Sgt D. Syme, and Sgt H. Bywaters KIA and commemorated on Runnymede Memorial.

Appendix 6

Non-operational Blenheim losses, 1 January to 30 April 1941

01-01-1941   L1327 54 OTU Mk I: became lost, overshot attempted forced-landing at Stone Park, Yorks, and crashed into ditch; P/O M. Smith and crew uninjured.

03-01-1941   L1100 1 FPP Mk I: stalled on take-off at West Raynham and hit hangar; Capt C. Napier (ATA solo pilot) severely injured.

12-01-1941   L9321 2 (C) OTU Mk IV: DBR in accident, no further details available.

13-01-1941   V5639 School of Flying Control Mk IV: crashed on take-off at Sealand, wing dropped, hit ground and cart-wheeled; Sgt E. Sarll slightly injured.

14-01-1941   N3563 13 OTU Mk IV: u/c jammed, crashed in forced-landing near Brackley, Northants, destroyed by fire; Sgt L. Murphy (solo pilot) escaped uninjured.

16-01-1941   K7131 5 BGS Mk I: crashed on approach to Jurby; F/Lt Pietrasiewicz (Polish Pilot) and one crewman injured.

26-01-1941   Z5746 2 (C) OTU Mk IV: flew into hill in blizzard on Birbage Moor, near Sheffield; Sgt J. Robson, P/O I. Parry-Jones and Sgt E. Brown killed.

27-01-1941   K7076 54 OTU Mk I: flew into ground at night in bad weather, Masham, Yorks; P/O R. Graham and crewman slightly injured.

01-02-1941   L6712 54 OTU Mk I: engine cut, lost height, belly-landed near Church Fenton; Sgt P. Newhouse and crew uninjured.

02-02-1941	N3570 101 Squadron Mk IV: crashed on beach near Freiston, Lincs, while low flying; Sgt Langrish, Sgt H. Rampley, and LAC Plunkett seriously injured, Sgt De'ath killed. Sgt Rampley died following day.
03-02-1941	L1251 54 OTU Mk I: flew into ground at Badboggin Lane, York; Sgt W. Kimber and Sgt V. Foot killed.
03-02-1941	T2287 13 OTU Mk IV: became lost on NavEx from Bicester in bad visibility, hit hedge and crashed in forced-landing near Marsh Gibbon, Bucks; Sgt F. Scott and crew uninjured, airframe became 2538M.
14-02-1941	L1370 2 SAC Mk I: u/c retracted while taxiing at Andover, DBR.
14-02-1941	L8599 RAF College Mk I: tail-wheel collapsed while taxiing at Cranwell, aircraft not repaired.
15-02-1941	T2327 8 FPP Mk IV: flew into high ground in bad visibility near Colerne.
22-02-1941	L6731 54 OTU Mk I: destroyed by fire in accident at Church Fenton.
22-02-1941	K7083 54 OTU Mk I: destroyed by fire in accident at Church Fenton. (This and above incident may be connected.)
22-02-1941	Z5722 600 Squadron Mk IV: ex-FIU aircraft damaged landing at Catterick; P/O F. Schumer and crew uninjured, aircraft repaired and sent to 68 Squadron for W/Cdr Max Aitken.
24-02-1941	L1326 600 Squadron Mk I-F: hit HT cables on overshoot at Prestwick; P/O F. Schumer and Sgt Burke injured, aircraft DBR. (P/O Schumer's second accident in two days.)
24-02-1941	L1309 13 OTU Mk I: dived into ground after night take-off at Bicester and destroyed by fire; Sgt Bond (solo pilot, aged 19) killed.
25-02-1941	T2320 139 Squadron Mk IV: destroyed by fire on ground at Horsham St Faith.
25-02-1941	L1178 68 Squadron Mk I-F: DBR in accident at Catterick, no further details available, not recorded in 68 Squadron ORB.
26-02-1941	N3618 21 Squadron Mk IV: DBR in accident on training sortie from Watton.
26-02-1941	N3571 2 SAC Mk IV: dived into ground in circuit at Andover when Pilot dazzled by searchlights; P/O P. Jeffery, Sgt E. Spencer and Sgt A. Burlow killed.
28-02-1941	L1168 54 OTU Mk I: dived into ground at night, pilot dazzled by searchlight and lost control, Nether Poppleton, Yorks; F/O G. Beale-Brown and unnamed crewman killed.
28-02-1941	L1267 54 OTU Mk I: dived into ground at night when pilot dazzled by searchlight and lost control, Cawood, Yorks; P/O G. Buley and Cpl H. Proudlove killed.
03-03-1941	R3751 13 OTU Mk IV: control lost, dived into ground at Shillingford, Devon; Sgt J. Gallyon, Sgt E. Phillips, and Sgt T. Randall killed.
05-03-1941	V5562 17 OTU Mk IV: engine cut on take-off at Polebrook and crashed near airfield; Sgt G. Wood, Sgt L. Crossley, and Sgt T. Collier injured.
05-03-1941	L6602 25 Squadron: hit tree in fog near Cottesmore on flight from Wittering to Digby; P/O T. Dorward (Pilot), F/O J. Strong (NZ, Signals Officer) and Mr Montgomery (civilian passenger) killed.
08-03-1941	L6692 17 OTU Mk I: crashed on take-off at Polebrook; Sgt J. Trotman slightly injured, aircraft repaired.
09-03-1941	K7114 54 OTU Mk I: engine cut in circuit at Church Fenton, control lost, spun into ground; S/Ldr C. Pink killed, unnamed Trainee Pilot seriously injured.
11-03-1941	V6098 3 OTU Mk IV: took off from Chivenor, flew into hill near Trentishoe Down, Devon, in bad weather; F/O A. Grisenthwaite, F/O C. Hitch, and Sgt T. Dykes killed.
12-03-1941	L6835 54 OTU Mk I-F: damaged at night by intruder and crash-landed on fire at Ulleskelf near Church Fenton; P/O M. Calvert and crew slightly injured, aircraft DBR.
13-03-1941	L9296 2 SAC Mk IV: hit HT cable while low-flying and broke up 4 miles west of Andover; P/O H. Hopkins, Sgt W. Buthee, Sgt J. Dewar and Sgt R. Jenkins killed.
14-03-1941	R3832 110 Squadron Mk IV: lost power on take-off from Horsham St Faith, crashed near Cottesy Hall, Norwich, and caught fire; Sgt Leadbeater (Pilot) and Sgt Cameron (Obs) escaped, Sgt Stacey (WOp/Ag) injured but pulled from wreck by crewmates just before bomb-load exploded.
14-03-1941	L1263 13 OTU Mk I: hit tree while low-flying at Oulton, Norfolk, crashed and destroyed by fire; F/Lt R. Hill DFC, solo pilot, killed.
14-03-1941	L6720 Service Ferry Pilots Pool Mk I: became lost in bad weather, force-landed on Clontarf Strand, Dublin, Eire; Sgt S. Karniewski (solo pilot) interned.
14-03-1941	K7068 5 BGS Mk I: also became lost in bad weather, crash-landed near Drogheda in Eire; Sgt D. Sutherland and crew slightly injured and interned.
16-03-1941	L1318 5 BGS Mk I: overshot landing at Jurby, IoM, crashed into boundary; Sgt R. Lee and crew unhurt.
18-03-1941	N3631 13 OTU Mk IV: crashed attempting forced-landing in bad visibility near Chalfont St Giles, Bucks; P/O R. Brown and crew uninjured.
18-03-1941	T2443 2 SAC Mk IV: control lost after take-off at Andover, dived into ground at Penton Mewsey, Wilts; P/O J. Baines, Sgt V. Moore and P/O I. Acland RCAF killed.
18-03-1941	V5433 404 Squadron Mk IV: u/c collapsed on heavy landing at Marham while Squadron being formed at Thorney Island.
21-03-1941	V5815 3 Radio School Mk IV: descended in cloud, flew into ground near Cumnock, Ayrshire, destroyed by fire; Sgt J. Senior (Pilot), Sgt R. Aitken, Sgt D. Morrison and Sgt D. Sims killed.
23-03-1941	T2285 13 OTU Mk IV: crashed on attempting a night overshoot at Bicester; Sgt J. McCallum and Sgt C. Leighton killed, Sgt Redgrave badly injured.

23/24-03-1941   L1207 68 Squadron Mk I-F: spiralled into ground near Malton, Yorks, cause unknown; Sgt D. Kirkland, Sgt J. Forster and Sgt D. Taylor killed.

25-03-1941   L8798 2 (C) OTU Mk IV: based at Catfoss, crashed at Prestwick, cause unknown.

28-03-1941   L8600 2 SAC Mk I: engine cut on approach to Andover, spun into ground at Weyhill Station, Hants; Solo Polish Pilot killed.

28-03-1941   L6642 54 OTU Mk I: engine cut while flying on instruments at night, control lost, crashed at Church Fenton; P/O A. McKelvie and Sgt J. Stanfield killed.

28/29-03-1941   L8724 219 Squadron Mk I-F: based at Tangmere, became lost at night, force-landed near Staverton, Glos, overturned and DBR.

29-03-1941   V6263 1 Ferry Pilots Pool Mk IV: engine cut on ferry flight from Speke to Lyneham, crash-landed 1 mile SW of White Waltham.

30-03-1941   L8668 2 (C) OTU Mk I: hit a house while low flying and destroyed by fire at Rolston, near Hornsea, Yorks; P/O R. Weber (solo pilot) killed.

01-04-1941   V5807 2 (C) OTU Mk IV: control lost in turn at night, hit tree and crashed near Driffield, destroyed by fire; Sgt V. Calvert (solo pilot) killed.

05-04-1941   L6677 54 OTU Mk I: belly-landed in error at Church Fenton and DBR.

06-04-1941   L9252 272 Squadron Mk IV: heavy landing on soft ground at Weston-super-Mare, tipped up, DBR; Sgt G. Rouse uninjured.

08-04-1941   L1185 54 OTU Mk I: engine cut on approach, crash-landed at Church Fenton; Sgt J. Ross and crewman uninjured.

09-04-1941   L1357 2 SAC Mk I: engine cut, lost height and belly-landed at Kimpton, Hants.

10-04-1941   N3591 17 OTU Mk IV: hit tree at night and crashed near Warboys Station, cause unknown; Sgt B. Rowlands and Sgt J. Graham killed.

10-04-1941   V5519 17 OTU Mk IV: made diving turn on night approach and hit Chance Light at Upwood; Destroyed by Fire, Sgt Knight (Pilot) and Sgt Owen (WOp/Ag) uninjured, but Sgt Wells (Obs) and four airmen on ground, AC2 Tait, AC2 Trickett, AC1 Firth and LAC Franks, seriously injured, all five died in hospital.

10-04-1941   V5732 17 OTU Mk IV: ran out of fuel when lost at night, hit trees attempting forced-landing at Childerley Hall, Cambs; Sgt Reid, Sgt Perkins, and Sgt Gibbons seriously injured and taken to Addenbrookes Hospital.

12-04-1941   L6611 54 OTU Mk I: engine cut on approach, crash-landed at Church Fenton, no injuries reported.

12-04-1941   L6790 54 OTU Mk I: hit HT cables and cart-wheeled into ground at Cockey Hill, near Church Fenton; P/O D. Coard, Sgt S. Slade, and Sgt H. Doughty killed.

12-04-1941   L1407 Mk I with A&AEE: DBF in air-raid on Boscombe Down.

15-04-1941   L4892 17 OTU Mk I: engine cut, hit hedge in belly-landing near Polebrook; P/O A. Taylor seriously injured, P/O T. Wooton injured.

16-04-1941   V5881 13 OTU Mk I: engine cut on night NavEx, crashed into Irish Sea off IoM; Sgt C. Kerridge, Sgt P. Cross, and Sgt G. Cook killed.

17-04-1941   V6145 86 Squadron: flew into ground at night attempting overshoot at Wattisham, destroyed by fire; P/O J. Brice (solo pilot) injured, rescued.

20-04-1941   V5796 2 (C) OTU Mk IV: lost on low-level NavEx over North Sea, presumed flown into sea 50 miles east of Flamborough Head; crew killed, Sgt J. Hamill RNZAF is buried in Norfolk, Sgt L. Liddiard and Sgt B. Clare commemorated on Runnymede Memorial.

22-04-1941   L1216 13 OTU Mk I, ex-TFU: stalled in cloud and dived into ground near Little Massingham, Norfolk; P/O A. Sabine (solo pilot) killed.

22-04-1941   T2232 18 Squadron Mk IV: crashed on to Oulton airfield after engine failure at low altitude; crew P/O P. Cook, Sgt G. Beever, and Sgt R. Prahl killed, aircraft destroyed.

24-04-1941   L9452 248 Squadron Mk IV: undershot night landing in rain at Dyce and DBR; Sgt R. Cripps and crew uninjured.

24-04-1941   K7132 54 OTU Mk I: damaged by intruder and caught fire; F/Lt R. Denison (solo pilot) abandoned safely near Barnsey, Yorks.

24-04-1941   L8799 2 OTU Mk IV: missing from night NavEx over North Sea; crew killed, P/O J. Clapham, Sgt C. Nash, and Sgt W. Bendy commemorated on Runnymede Memorial.

25-04-1941   L1297 54 OTU Mk I: attacked by intruder near Church Fenton, landed but DBR.

25-04-1941   L1523 54 OTU Mk I: attacked by intruder near Church Fenton, force-landed, DBR.

26-04-1941   V5812 2 OTU Mk IV: stalled and spun during single-engine practice; F/Lt Rose (solo pilot) abandoned aircraft over Routh, near Beverley, Yorks, resulting in loss of right foot.

28-04-1941   L9341 17 OTU Mk IV: crashed at Upwood, cause not recorded; Sgt Francis, Sgt Nullis, and Sgt Page unhurt.

30-04-1941   V6389 18 Squadron Mk IV: control lost when target-towing (drogue detached and fouled elevator), dived into ground near Kings Lynn; crew S/Ldr H. Lindsaye, Sgt A. Stone, and F/O F. Holmes killed.

Chapter 18

A better Blenheim?

The Air Staff had been seeking major improvements to the Blenheim for some time. It was clear that Barnwell's early-1930s design, which had been adapted for military use from a civil light aircraft, as described earlier, would have to continue in operational service for the several years it would take for any replacement aircraft to reach the front-line squadrons. They were planning both for these improvements and for the successor aircraft well before war was declared.

The Air Ministry had realised as early as 1938 that, in view of the performance shown by the Messerschmitt Bf.109 in the Spanish Civil War, they needed a Medium Bomber that was both faster and better armed than the Bristol Type 149 Blenheim, so it issued Specification B.9/38 for a more powerful twin-engined bomber with much increased armament. Bristol submitted its Type 155 based on the Type 152 Beaufort, also with Taurus engines but with twin fins and rudders and a tricycle landing gear. The nose-wheel oleo leg for the 155 was tested on L1242, a Blenheim Mk I. However, the Air Ministry (anticipating wartime shortages of high-grade aircraft alloys) withdrew B.9/38 and changed the Specification to B.17/38 for a 'Reconnaissance Bomber Aircraft for Rapid Production' to be manufactured in non-strategic materials such as a mixed steel-tube and wood construction – this would also have the advantage of utilising the light engineering and wood-working industries, as the conventional aircraft industry was fully stretched and suffering from a shortage of skilled labour. The Bristol company did not like this requirement, having spent four years and vast sums of money changing its entire design and manufacturing processes over to light alloy stressed-skin aircraft. In addition the company was frantically busy with the Beaufort and Beaufighter, and had lost its Chief Designer, Frank Barnwell, less than a month earlier, so was content when design responsibility was transferred to Armstrong Whitworth under Specification B.18/38 on 1 September 1. The disappointing result was the Type AW 41 Albemarle with twin Bristol Hercules engines, which first flew – just – on 20 March 1940. However, despite major modifications (including adding 10 feet to the wingspan), it was destined never to be used as a bomber. The prototype P1360 crashed on 4 February 1941 when part of a wing broke away during trials with the A&AEE at Boscombe Down. Two 2 Group crews of F/Lt Kennedy and F/O Maclachlan were sent there in early February 1942 to test Albemarle P1368, but they condemned it comprehensively. Trials of the Albemarle for 2 Group continued at Warboys, but it force-landed twice, and poor Maclachlan was killed on 28 February attempting a third. One potential Blenheim replacement had thus proved unsatisfactory, and fortunately the Group was not called upon to use such an unsuitable aircraft.

It is of interest to note in passing that well before the war – when the rear defence of the Blenheim was but a single pan-fed Vickers .303 gun aimed by a First World War ring-and-bead open sight – Specification B.1/39 for a four-engined Bomber Landplane (drawn up over the winter of 1938 and issued to Bristol and Handley Page in March 1939) called for dorsal and ventral turrets mounting 20mm Hispano cannons 'in view of the known limitations of the .303 rifle-calibre machine-guns'. Yet all Bomber Command British aircraft were still equipped as standard with .303 gun turrets right to the end of the war, and a 20mm cannon turret did not appear until the Bristol 17 dorsal turret on the Avro Lincoln and Shackleton – neither of which saw service until after the war. This pre-war Specification B.1/39 holds further interest in that Avro unsuccessfully submitted a design to it, the Type 680. This was a Type 679 Manchester, then in large-scale production, fitted with a larger-span wing mounting four engines – pre-dating by a

The Albemarle 'Reconnaissance Bomber for Rapid Production' was based on Bristol's Type 155, but design authority passed to Armstrong Whitworth and the result was a great disappointment. Once again Blenheims had to continue in front-line service as a bomber for far longer than intended.

couple of years the company's later proposal for the Type 683, known initially as the Manchester Mk III, but more famously as the Lancaster.

A high-power conference was held at King Charles Street, Whitehall, on 12 December 1939 by the RAF 'top brass' to decide on the development of a high-speed bomber to replace the Blenheim. One proposal was a cleaned-up Beaufort, on the lines of the special PR Blenheim mentioned earlier but with Hercules engines, which it was estimated would reach 330mph. Air Marshal Sir Wilfrid Freeman, the Air Council Member for Development and Production, recommended adoption of a proposal he had discussed with Geoffrey de Havilland for an all-wood, unarmed, two-seat bomber with twin Rolls-Royce Merlin engines, which was expected to achieve almost 400mph. Concern was expressed that enemy fighters might soon reach such speeds and that adequate rear-defence was essential. Such senior officers, including the AOC of Bomber Command, found the notion of an completely unarmed bomber very hard to accept, but could countenance a fast unarmed reconnaissance aircraft for use when defences were less likely to be aroused. Losses of Blenheims on such missions had been relatively high compared with the results achieved, so an aircraft that could outpace enemy fighters was clearly desirable. So a compromise was reached: a decision to go ahead with the unarmed DH Type 98 – to be named Mosquito but known colloquially in the Air Ministry as 'Freeman's Folly' – primarily for reconnaissance use, and approval for Operational Requirement No 84 for a heavily armed and armoured fast Medium Bomber to replace the Blenheim. To 'hold the fort' while this new type – which the Ministry regarded as by far the most important and significant of the two proposals – was being designed and put into production, it decided to proceed with Operational Requirement No 83, issued a couple of months earlier to satisfy demands for an improved close-support Blenheim that could be produced without delay. Once more Blenheims were expected to fill the gap, as they had been for a long-range fighter, an anti-shipping strike aircraft, a tactical Army-support aircraft, a reconnaissance aircraft, and a night-fighter. Once more the gap turned out to be both very much wider and to stay open for very much longer than expected, and in the event the Blenheims were again unable to fill it adequately despite the bravest of efforts to do so.

The Blenheim Mk IV had been modified in service to rectify as far as possible some of shortcomings revealed during early operations, as mentioned in Chapter 9, but clearly these modifications were insufficient. To assist rear defence, the single Vickers pan-fed VGO in the Bristol Mk III turret was replaced by a pair in the Mk IIIA, then by a single belt-fed Browning with a higher rate of fire in the Mk IV turret, then by more effective twin Brownings in the same turret. The single rear-facing under-nose 'scare' gun in a Perspex blister had been replaced by an FN 54 turret with twin Brownings, also operated by the Observer, but its benefit was more psychological than practical. A sheet of armour behind the radio-shelf aft of the dorsal turret provided some protection for the Wireless

Operator/Air Gunner, as did plates behind the seats in the cockpit for Pilot and Observer – though the latter was unprotected when manning his main station in the nose. Although the boost-override control, allowing plus-9lb of boost with 100-octane fuel for short periods, increased the maximum speed from 227mph at sea level to a 'sprint speed' of 248mph, considerably increased performance was needed.

In January 1940 the Bristol company proposed a version of the Blenheim Mk IV incorporating major improvements, intended for close tactical support of the Army, with alternative use as a low-level fighter, or a dual-control operational trainer. But the entire aircraft production, procurement and development situations became volatile during the traumatic summer of 1940, particularly when Churchill appointed the dynamic Canadian 'Press Baron' Lord Beaverbrook as Minister of Aircraft Production in May 1940, with the authority to increase, as a matter of the greatest urgency, the number of fighters available for the defence of the UK. The Air Ministry relinquished control of its Department of Development and Production to the new Minister, although the Air Member concerned, the influential Air Marshal Sir Wilfrid Freeman, remained to represent the Ministry. After hurried discussions with the Air Staff, Lord Beaverbrook ordered the aircraft industry to produce only five of the existing types that were currently in large-scale production – Spitfire and Hurricane fighters, and Blenheim, Wellington and Whitley bombers – and to concentrate all research and development effort on improving those types. We can note with some surprise that, even at this hour of the most extreme national peril, production of bombers was given this overriding priority, especially as one type (the Whitley) was obsolete, another (the Blenheim) was obsolescent, and the third (the Wellington) becoming so. Although this draconian edict was only in force for five months it caused considerable disruption to forward planning and delayed several new types, especially the four-engined Heavy Bombers, although they were soon accorded 'second priority'. It had other side effects, too; for example, 468 vital machines were removed from the shadow factories that manufactured Hercules engines and sent to those producing Mercury engines for the Blenheims, thus reducing output of the former for the much-needed Beaufighters. Max Beaverbrook's goading increased fighter production and he also drastically re-organised the repair of damaged aircraft and so improved and accelerated the turn-around that by the end of the Battle of Britain over a third of the front-line aircraft had been returned to service after major repairs – it is doubtful if the Battle could have been won without this re-organisation.

After months of feverish discussion and debate, including evaluating the effect during the Battle for France of the close support given to the Wehrmacht by the Luftwaffe, on 26 September 1940 the Air Ministry issued Specification B6/40 to Bristol to meet Operational Requirement No 83 for a 'Direct Support Bomber' as 'a variant of the standard Blenheim Mk IV Bomber which can readily be converted to undertake duties in direct support of the Army'. The Specification stipulated various conflicting requirements: 'The aircraft will have alternative roles of high altitude bombing, and direct support which will include dive-bombing, low-level bombing, and front gun attacks on ground targets. The aircraft will also be required to carry out strategic reconnaissance by day and night. It is intended that the requirements should be met with the minimum alteration to the existing Blenheim airframe.' The British Army General Staff, backed strongly by the newly formed Army Co-operation Command, wanted a more effective ground-attack version of the Blenheim; the Air Staff, backed by Bomber Command, wanted an improved and more versatile bomber version. They were aware that Bristol was working flat-out to overcome the troubles with the Beaufort and the Beaufighter, and the associated problems with their power-plants, as well as endeavouring to increase production of these types. Consequently, the Air Ministry wanted the Rootes Group to carry out the redesign of the improved version of the Blenheim as the car company was by then producing the largest numbers of the Mk IV. Bristol at Filton objected to this on the grounds that Rootes was not sufficiently experienced in aircraft design. After much further discussion, Bristol

AD657, the prototype 160CS (Close Support) version of the Blenheim, named Bisley by Bristol, flew first in February 1941, initially without a turret, as Bristol's new BX fully rotating turret was not ready.

was instructed to design and build two prototypes at Filton, one ground-support version and one improved bomber version, which would then be produced by Rootes. The parent company organised a branch drawing office at Rootes' Blythe Bridge factory to provide the detailed drawings needed for large-scale manufacture.

The first of these new Type 160s, using as much of the basic Type 149 Blenheim Mk IV airframe, jigs and tooling as possible to meet the requirement for ease of production, flew on 24 February 1941. It was AD657 and was the prototype of the Type 160CS, the close-support version, named 'Bisley' by Bristol. The main differences from the Type 149 were that it had a 'solid', more streamlined nose containing four fixed .303 Brownings, Mercury XVI engines of 950hp, constant-speed (but non-feathering) propellers with spinners, side-hinged undercarriage doors replacing the apron type, and wing-mounted oil-coolers as on the Beaufort and Beaufighter. The wing spars were strengthened considerably, as was the undercarriage, and the pitot tube was moved from under the nose to the port wing, from which the fixed gun had been deleted; the rising profile of the nose led to a much shallower windscreen which was of thick armoured glass, and the tail-wheel had a 'knuckle' oleo strut to reduce the loads on the stern-frame. The modified aircraft looked quite sleek initially as the turret position was faired over, but later the Bristol B.X twin-Browning turret was fitted; this could rotate through the full 360 degrees, not just the rearmost 180 degrees of the earlier Bristol turrets, but it had a larger diameter and needed an ungainly cut-away of the rear fuselage. This turret, together with some 600lb of armour, helped to increase the weight to 11,000lb unladen, and 17,500lb fully laden, compared with 7,400lb and 12,000lb for the Mk I. So with very little extra power, the performance was actually inferior to the Mk IV Blenheim on which it was supposed to be an improvement! The Type 160 really needed about 1,200hp per engine, but, as we have seen, the Mercury – with its origins in the First World War – was right at the end of its development and no other suitable engine was available. The twin-row 14-cylinder Taurus was in the 1,000hp class and could have been improved and developed to produce the power needed, but, as mentioned earlier, Bristol was having great difficulties in overcoming production problems with the sleeve valves – problems that adversely affected the whole Beaufort programme. The Hercules III, as used in the Beaufighter and giving some 1,300hp, was too large and heavy for the Blenheim airframe, so the Mercury it had to be.

The second prototype of the Bristol Type 160 – AD 661 – was the high-altitude (sic) bomber version, which had glazing in the port side of the fuselage forward of the cockpit with an extended clear-vision nose for the bomb-aimer, who – when acting as navigator – sat facing sideways with his feet in a protruding 'bath' below the starboard side of the nose. This faired into a remotely operated FN Type 54 under-defence turret with twin .303 Brownings. A D/F loop in a Perspex blister fairing was fitted behind the cockpit hatch, and an oxygen supply to all crew positions. It had been hoped to make the two front fuselage sections, with their different noses and cockpits, interchangeable at squadron level to

AD661, the prototype bomber version of the Type 160, later named Blenheim Mk V, at Filton. The Observer sat facing in the opposite direction to the Mk IV, with his feet in the fairing for the under-nose guns.

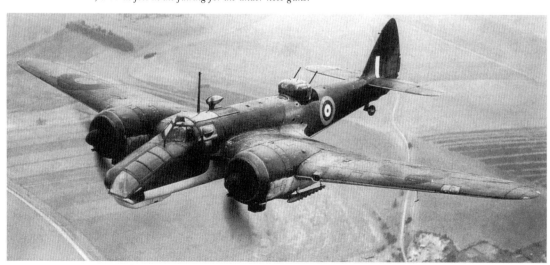

THE BRISTOL BLENHEIM

The Type 160 needed 1,200hp engines, but none were available – the 1,400hp Hercules engines of the Type 156 Beaufighter Mk I were too large and heavy for the Blenheim airframe, but were developed later to produce 1,735hp.

enable either the low-level close-support or medium-height bomber versions to be available at short notice to meet demand, but this was found to be impracticable as the armour plating, radio fit and oxygen systems would need to changed each time too, so the idea was dropped. As soon as the Filton design of the Type 160 was finalised, and following trials at Filton and Boscombe Down with the initial two Bristol-built aircraft, Rootes was instructed to build a prototype of each version of the Type 160. But, as the need for a close-support version had faded by then, both of Rootes' production prototypes – DJ702 and DJ707 – were built as the bomber version, and first flew in September 1941. By then the Bristol Type 160 Bisley had been re-named the Blenheim Mk V, so the good reputation earned the hard way by the Blenheim Is and IVs came to sullied by the Vs.

But even before the Blenheim Mk V was put into production, a new aircraft, the outstanding performance of which rendered the Blenheim obsolete, had carried out its first operational sortie from 1 PRU at Benson on 17 September 1941. This was the famous De Havilland DH 98 Mosquito, built to Specification B.1/40 for a 'Light Reconnaissance Bomber Aeroplane', written following the conference of December 1939 mentioned above, and issued in March 1940 together with an order for 50 aircraft. The prototype first flew on

Nearly 1,000 Blenheim Mk Vs were produced by Rootes, all in the bomber version. This view shows the sharper nose profile (spoiled by the gun 'bath'), the oil-coolers outboard of the engines, the constant-speed propellers with spinners, the pitot tube below the port wing, and the knuckle-type tail-wheel.

EH517, the last Mk V built at Blythe Bridge, in June 1943. Rootes production test pilot E. Shultz(left) with senior staff.

The cockpit of the Mk V: the throttles are lower left, the propeller controls now above them (centre left, by the lamp signalling keys), the boost-override lever now above the panel (top right), and the undercarriage control now centre right, but the hydraulic selector and flap control remain alongside the Pilot's seat. The compass is missing from its circular mounting (left of centre). Compare this with the illustrations of the Mk I cockpit on page 90.

25 November 1940 at Hatfield, having been moved there from Salisbury Hall, and reached 392mph – easily the fastest operational aircraft in the world at that time. Work on the prototype Mosquito stopped following Beaverbrook's edict of May 1940, but fortunately Air Marshal Sir Wilfrid Freeman managed to get the project re-instated as a 'second priority' in July as it did not use strategic materials. The initial Mosquito bomb-load was 2,000lb, but later versions could carry a 4,000lb 'block-buster' to Berlin, and fitting Merlin 77s in October 1942 raised the top speed to 437mph. In June 1942 139 Squadron at Horsham St Faith was issued with Blenheim Mk Vs, which struggled to reach 220mph with a 1,000lb bomb-load. (The squadron had changed its Mk IVs for Hudsons in December 1941 and was

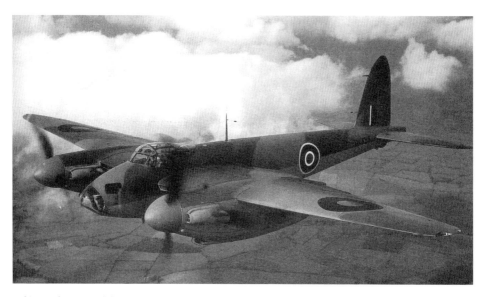

The outstanding performance of the unarmed De Havilland Mosquito completely eclipsed the entire Buckingham/Brigand series.

sent to the Far East, but was re-formed in the UK in June with Blenheim Mk Vs.) Most fortunately for the 139 Squadron crews, Bomber Command realised that these aircraft were not suited for operations in the highly hostile environment of Northern Europe, so the Command, 2 Group, and particularly the Squadron, were relieved when the Mk Vs were sent to the Middle East, as will be described later. 139 Squadron was delighted to be re-equipped with the Mosquito by November 1942, following 105 at Swanton Morley, which had been the first squadron to receive a few bomber 'Mossies' a year earlier. Both squadrons had, of course, operated Blenheim Mk IVs with great distinction. Despite the demonstrable operational unsuitability of the Mk V, Rootes was still producing them until as late as mid-1943, and they were used in secondary roles until the end of the war, mainly in the Mediterranean and Far Eastern areas, as we will see in due course.

The Mosquito also totally eclipsed the very extended efforts by the Bristol Aircraft Company to produce a successor to the Blenheim. Bristol submitted a proposal in 1939 to replace the Blenheim with the Type 157 to Specification B19./38, a three-man 'Beau-bomber' version of the Type 156 Beaufighter, but this was not taken up. The company then proposed the Type 161 with Hercules engines and the Type 162 with Merlin engines, known provisionally as the Beaumont Mk I and Mk II respectively, to meet Operational

Requirement No 84, discussed at the December 1939 conference, which called for a 'Light High-Speed Bomber' under Specification B.7/40, for use as a close-support fighter/bomber and dive bomber but also capable of high-level bombing and strategical and tactical reconnaissance by day and by night. Bristol also submitted the Beaumont for Specification B.20/40 for a close-support bombing and tactical reconnaissance aircraft, but both of these specifications were cancelled and the performance requirements and operational capabilities increased considerably.

The company realised that to meet these increasingly rigorous demands more power was needed than the Hercules could produce, so in March 1941 the proposals were redrafted round its most powerful new engine, the Centaurus. This redesign did indeed make a quantum leap forward in power and armament from the Blenheim it was intended to replace. Bristol was pleased to receive an order in July 1941 under Specification B.2/41 for four prototypes of the Type 163, a fast four-seat Medium Bomber with two Bristol Centaurus engines of 2,400hp each, to carry a bomb-load of 4,000lb and four fixed .303 machine-guns in the nose, together with four more in a dorsal turret and two in a ventral one. Although the Specification called for 'an aircraft derived from the Beaufighter' and stated that 'as many components as possible from this type shall be interchangeable with the Beaufighter', by then the airframe had been redesigned so comprehensively that there were virtually no common components remaining. This important new type, the Buckingham, 800 of which were ordered before the end of 1941, was intended to replace not only the Blenheims but also the Bostons and Mitchells coming into service with 2 Group, as well as the Beauforts in Coastal Command. The prototype of the Buckingham, which had a top speed of 335mph, did not fly until 4 February 1943, and the first production example not until more than a year later in 1944, and it did not become operational as a bomber. Some eight years earlier 'Britain First' had reached 307mph on only 1,280hp; the Buckingham, with no less than 4,800hp, was only 28mph faster, paying the penalty of being much larger and almost four times as heavy!

The Centaurus-powered Type 163 Buckingham, intended as the Blenheim replacement, did not see operational service. The four-gun dorsal turret was an advance, but the anachronistic four-gun nose meant moving the Observer/Bomb-aimer to the ventral twin-gun rear-defence position, just visible beneath the fuselage roundel.

In mid-1943 some experienced 2 Group crews were invited to Boscombe Down to fly one of the four Buckingham prototypes and give their opinions on it – their reports were highly critical. They all felt that the four .303s in the nose, a hang-over from the abandoned close-support version of the Blenheim Mk V, was an anachronism. Those who operated B.25 Mitchells preferred the .50 guns in their turrets plus the superb view for the bomb-aimer from the nose compared with the cramped ventral position on the Buckingham. Those who operated Bostons much preferred the lighter American aircraft, while those who operated Mosquitos condemned out of hand the less manoeuvrable, much heavier, and far slower Bristol type. The large order was cancelled after only 54 had been built, and most were converted after the war to four-seat fast courier aircraft – the cost per passenger/mile must have been pretty high! The Type 163 design was used as a basis for the Type 166 Buckmaster, a post-war advanced training version, and for the Type 164 Brigand, a slim-fuselage version that, with 5,000hp, reached 360mph and carried four 20mm cannon and an under-slung torpedo, just like the Beaufighter it was intended to replace, but was too late to see service in the Second World War.

The Type 164 Brigand was a slim-fuselage Buckingham, as the Beaufighter was a slim-fuselage Beaufort. Brigands, here with torpedo and rockets, were used in post-war operations, and all four Types were direct descendants of 'Britain First' and the Blenheim.

The story of the Bristol Aircraft Company's inability to produce an improved version of the Blenheim that was acceptable for daylight operations in the face of the prevailing opposition, and of its complete failure – throughout the entire period of the war – to produce a worthy successor to it, was indeed a sorry saga. But it is a saga that needs to be told, as it was to prolong excessively the operational use of the Blenheim at the cost of the lives of many crews.

The leading personalities in 1941

What, by the early summer of 1941, had become of the prominent men mentioned in previous chapters as closely involved in the earliest days of 'Britain First' and the Blenheim?

Lord Rothermere, who had commissioned 'Britain First' and thus initiated the entire Blenheim line, as related, became seriously ill and died on 28 November 1940. It was ironic that it was his friend and great rival Lord Beaverbrook who, as Minister of Aircraft Production in 1940, had placed the Blenheim into top-priority production when one of the main factors that influenced Lord Rothermere to order 'Britain First' six years earlier had been his determination to keep a step ahead of his main business competitor. The active rivalry between the two newspaper groups still exists, and when the *Daily Mail* refers to the *Daily Express* it does so disparagingly to this day – although the Beaverbook family is no

Lords Rothermere and Beaverbrook (in hat), despite the bitter business rivalry between their Mail and Express newspaper empires, became close friends.

longer associated with the Express Group. In May 1941 Moore-Brabazon became Minister of Aircraft Production and Beaverbrook moved on to become Minister of State and Lord President of the Council, but he continued to work very closely with Winston Churchill.

Churchill himself, who was a political outcast throughout the 1930s when he called for re-armament – frequently via the powerful platform provided by Lord Rothermere in the *Daily Mail* – had of course been Prime Minister for a most perilous 12 months. He presided most effectively over the War Cabinet and innumerable committees, and he united and inspired the nation with his determination and magnificent oratory. Despite the multitudinous problems that he faced daily as Great Britain stood alone against the Nazi tyranny, he took a close interest in the operations of the RAF and in the deployment of the Blenheims – as we will see shortly.

Lord Weir, following his resignation when Swinton was replaced as Air Minister in May 1938, had returned to his Scottish engineering company, G. & J. Weir, and to his Directorship at ICI. He at least had the satisfaction of seeing the RAF Expansion Scheme F of 1936 become the only one to be completed – and by its target date of March 1939 – which would not have been possible without the Shadow Aircraft Industry that he instigated and organised. Weir's company designed a helicopter to Specification 22/38 and built one, the W.6, to Specification 28/38, which flew in October 1939, but development was abandoned in July 1940 when Igor Sikorsky in the United States perfected the layout that is still employed on present-day helicopters.

Sir G. Stanley White continued to run the Bristol Aeroplane Company with a steady and firm hand. We have noted that in 1939 it was the largest aeroplane manufacturer in the world, and it continued to grow until it employed a maximum of more than 52,000 workers by 1944.

The factories at Filton suffered two major air raids. The first, by a force of He.111s of KG 55 on 25 September 1940, was largely unopposed and caused considerable damage, mainly to the Rodney Works and the Patchway engine workshops – the designated targets. Six air-raid shelters were hit, killing 92 employees and severely injuring 147,

Sir G. Stanley White 'ran the Bristol Aeroplane Company with a steady and firm hand' as Managing Director from 1911 to 1955. He is seen welcoming Prime Minister Winston Churchill to Filton in 1945.

while a further 69 people were killed and 154 seriously injured outside the factory area. Eight newly built aircraft – including the prototype of the Merlin-engined Beaufighter Mk II – were destroyed together with a further 24 badly damaged, and the production of Beaufighters was delayed for a couple of months. The second raid, two days later, by Me.110 fighter-bombers of Erpr Gp 210, was intercepted and deflected (mainly by 504 Squadron's Hurricanes, which had been moved from Hendon to Filton the day before) and caused little damage and few casualties, although four were killed at Patchway. Many accounts state that this was a follow-up raid to the one two days earlier on the Bristol factories at Filton, especially as KG 55 had raided the Supermarine Spitfire factory at Woolston on the 26th, but the intended Luftwaffe target on the 27th was in fact the Parnall Aircraft Company factory at Yate airfield, which manufactured FN gun-turrets.

In the two years before this unwelcome intrusion, Roy Fedden, despite his extraordinarily heavy commitments on the engine side, had become more involved in the airframe side. He viewed the engine/airframe combination as an entity rather than viewing an aircraft as a separate airframe on to which suitable engines were mounted. Leslie Frise looked up to him and they assumed the main design responsibilities following the loss of Frank Barnwell in 1938, and it was they who submitted the proposals that led to the Beaufighter. The design team at Filton was strengthened by the very talented Archie Russell and Cliff Tinson. Unfortunately, Fedden was becoming ever more estranged from the Bristol Board of Directors – he had written to the Chairman in 1939 requesting that the airframe and engine departments be re-organised as separate Divisions with himself as Director of the latter, for although he had built up and was Chief Engineer of the huge and highly successful Bristol engine business, he had never been appointed to the Board. He thought his proposal would resolve the difficulties by creating two Divisional Boards responsible to the Main Board, but alas it only antagonised further the somewhat patrician and very conservative Board. He was dismissed and left the Bristol company on 1 October 1942 – a sad ending to an outstanding career.

Marshal of the RAF Viscount Trenchard, although he had relinquished the post of CAS more than 11 years earlier, continued to exert considerable influence – as we saw during the dismissals of Newall and Dowding. On 19 May 1941 he sent an extraordinary memo on Bombing Policy to the Prime Minister, who circulated copies to the three Chiefs of Staff for their comments. It makes interesting reading in view of the anti-shipping campaign then being waged by the Blenheims, and their part in the 'Circus' raids on targets in occupied France. It ignores the need to break the stranglehold that the Germans were imposing on our vital shipping supplies during the Battle of the Atlantic. It demonstrates not only his own doctrinaire opinions that had become the cornerstone of RAF policy, but also reveals his completely unrealistic view of the actual capabilities of Bomber Command as it existed in 1941 and 1942. It anticipates, indeed accepts in a heartless manner, such a high level of casualties that would be devastating and clearly unsustainable, even going as far as to claim that the pilots 'would welcome a policy of this description'.

The sub-headings reveal Trenchard's philosophy: 'History has proved that we have always been able to stand our casualties better than other Nations'. 'It must be realised that the Sea is a Source of Weakness to us as well as a Source of Strength'. 'Germany and Germany alone is the Enemy we have got to beat'. The part of the memo that most concerns us is headed 'The percentage of bombs that hit the Military Target at which they are aimed is not more than 1%'.

> 'That means that if you are bombing a target at sea then 99% of the bombs would be wasted because 99% of the bombs would fall in the sea... So, too, if bombs are dropped in Norway, Holland, Belgium or France, 99% do Germany no harm but do kill our old Allies, damage their property, frighten them, or dislocate their lives. It [the effort] is more than wasted. If, however, our bombs are dropped in Germany, then 99% which miss the military target all help to kill, damage, frighten or interfere with Germans in Germany and the whole 100% of the bomber organisation is doing useful work not merely 1% of it.'

MRAF Lord Trenchard, although having retired as CAS more than 11 years earlier, continued his attempts to influence RAF policy well into the war. He submitted a totally unrealistic memo on bombing policy to Churchill in May 1941.

He goes on to say that 'the RAF should strike at Germany again and again. This form of attack must be persistent and should be mounted every night and to every corner of greater Germany. It would be a costly venture and would require an ultimately enormous force.

> 'Such a policy may necessarily involve fairly heavy casualties, but the counting of our losses has nothing to do with the soundness of the plan once you accept the view that the Nation can stand their casualties. The pilots in the last war stood it, and the pilots in this war are even better, and I feel would welcome a policy of this description... In the last war casualties of pilots were sometimes 30% per month or more, but now owing to the universal use of parachutes the percentage of those killed or wounded will be greatly reduced... It is quite possible to lose as many as 70% of your front line machines in a month and great reserves are essential. Reserves will be needed of 400 to 500%, not the mere 100% mentioned by the former Minister of Aircraft Production.'

He maintained that absolute priority must be given to the production of long-range bombers and the supply and training of men to fly them. The diversion of the force to subsidiary targets such as invasion ports, oil plants, or naval targets would have to be rejected.

Trenchard's memo forcefully advocated large-scale, persistent and indiscriminate 'area bombing' intended to kill or demoralise the German population en masse – well before Bomber Command grasped that nettle. The Chiefs of Staff were largely supportive of the memo and did not cavil at the anticipated level of casualties. General Sir John Dill commented, 'With our existing strength ... it is unlikely that we could achieve results on a large enough scale to justify selecting morale as our primary target at present ... it will almost certainly be the most profitable target when our bomber force expands...,' although Admiral Sir Dudley Pound added that 'the paper is a complete over-statement and it suffers from the dangers of all over-statement'. The CAS, Sir Charles Portal, strongly backed the memo, and indeed it led to his later paper demanding a force of 4,000 Heavy Bombers, although in 1941 he was more mindful of the limitations of Bomber Command and recommended that 'we should concentrate our efforts against a limited number of objectives and aim at sustaining our attacks on them. Even during the period of short summer nights, suitable objectives are to be found in the densely populated and industrially important Ruhr area.'

Trenchard and Portal would have been aware that RAF bombers were experiencing great difficulty at that period of the war in locating specific inland targets at night, especially those concealed by the industrial haze of the Ruhr, and still greater difficulty in managing to hit them with the crude bombsights then in use, as described earlier. Perhaps they did not realise that even if the crews did manage to score 1 per cent direct hits, the bombs – those of them that actually exploded that is – were far from effective. We now know that was the case, especially in comparison with the bombs used later in the war. The Blenheims in particular were ineffectual and it would need a very lucky strike indeed to cause any significant damage with the four 250lb, or two 500lb, early-type bombs they carried. The cast-iron bombs they dropped were ordered in 1934, had a very low charge-to-weight ratio, and were filled with a poor type of explosive. The extremely cramped, noisy and bitterly cold crew position in the nose of the Blenheim hindered the performance of the Observer's dual duties as Navigator and Bomb-Aimer, he was gravely restricted by the lack of navigation aids, and was vulnerable to flak splinters in his unprotected crew station. If he did manage to guide his Pilot to the target, the Course-Setting Mk IX bombsight was difficult to set up with gloved or frozen fingers and far from accurate – and the aircraft was required to fly precisely straight and level during the bombing run. These remarks apply also to the Vickers Wellington, which had become the backbone of Bomber Command, but was a much more useful aircraft as it carried a larger bomb-load – Wellingtons dropped the first 4,000lb thin-cased bomb on Germany in the early hours of 1 April 1941. The new generation of Heavy Bombers had been slowly entering service: the first operation by the Short Stirling (with a bomb-load up to 14,000lb) was to Rotterdam on the night of 10 February, the first operation by the troublesome Avro Manchester was on 24 February to Brest, and the first by the Handley Page Halifax Mk I was to Le Havre on the night of 10 March – one of the six sent was shot down on return by a British night-fighter. The days of the Blenheim squadrons forming part of the main night-force of Bomber Command were over, and their last raid as such – apart from the special 1,000-bomber raids of mid-1942 – was that on Brest on 10/11 April 1941. A single four-engined Heavy Bomber could carry a greater bomb-load, and carry it for a greater distance, than a whole squadron of Blenheims .

However, despite Trenchard's opinions, throughout the summer and autumn of 1941 UK-based Blenheims continued to be used on a daily basis in anti-shipping sweeps, attacking any ships found, and in frequent daytime 'Circus', 'Roadstead' and 'Fringe' operations to targets near the coasts of our former Allies, as well as a few major daylight raids that were far more daring – and far more dangerous. The overall percentage of Bomber Command losses incurred since the beginning of the war during all daylight sorties (including the many that were aborted), at 4.2 per cent, was exactly double that of the 2.1 per cent for night sorties. Those incurred on anti-shipping strikes were nearly five times as many. That is why the 'Blenheim Boys' were acknowledged by their peers – the aircrew of other Groups and other Commands – to be the bravest of the brave.

Chapter 19

Summer 1941

We left the description of Blenheim operations at the end of April 1941, and now continue it through that hard-fought summer. May 1941 saw many important moves and several major changes to the Blenheim squadrons of the three operational RAF Commands in the UK. While some of them relinquished their Blenheims for more modern aircraft, several new squadrons were formed and equipped with Blenheims as the RAF continued to expand:

Bomber Command

2 Group continued to be the only Bomber Command Group to operate Blenheims, but now almost entirely on daylight sorties as they were no longer treated as part of the night-bombing Main Force. The squadrons had completed their intensive training for low-level anti-shipping strikes and there was much work to be done. Most of the Blenheims had their camouflage scheme of dark-earth and green with either black or sky under-surfaces changed to grey and green upper-surfaces with sky under-surfaces, which proved quite effective over the sea viewed from above – although the position of a low-flying formation was often revealed by the wake left by the prop-wash on the surface.

PM Winston Churchill often visited 2 Group Stations, as here at West Raynham in June 1941. With him are Group Captain Paddy Bandon, the Station Commander (left), and AM Sir Richard Pierse, AOC Bomber Command; behind (from left) are AVM Stevenson, AOC 2 Group, Naval Liaison Officer, AM Sir Charles Portal CAS, Professor Lindemann and Clement Attlee, the Deputy PM.

The Blenheim squadrons were in a state of flux, with many movements, mainly connected with the anti-shipping campaign and the need to reinforce the RAF in the Middle East.

107 Squadron: returned to Great Massingham from attachment to Coastal Command at Leuchars

82 Squadron: did likewise to Bodney from Lossiemouth, exchanging places with

21 Squadron: based at Watton, which sent a detachment to Malta

105 Squadron: moved from Swanton Morley to Lossiemouth but remained part of 2 Group

114 Squadron: remained detached to Coastal Command but moved from Thornaby to Leuchars

226 Squadron: converted from Battles to Blenheims at Belfast, then joined 2 Group at Wattisham and carried out its first operation on 28 June

101 Squadron: based at West Raynham, converting one Flight at a time to Wellingtons, but still operating Blenheims until July when conversion was complete and it moved from 2 to 3 Group

18 Squadron: moved from Great Massingham to Oulton

110 Squadron: was at Wattisham but moved to Manston (a Fighter Command 11 Group base) for 'Channel Stop' operations, to be followed in turn by four other 2 Group squadrons, as will be described

88 Squadron: based at Sydenham, it had a few Boston Is and IIs as well as Blenheim Mk Is, but re-equipped fully with Mk IVs and did not change to Boston Mk IIIs until 1942

139 Squadron: sent from Horsham St Faith to Luqa, Malta, the first of six Blenheim squadrons to be posted to the Mediterranean Theatre of War, as will be described

90 Squadron: the Squadron's Blenheims were incorporated into 17 OTU in April 1940, and it was re-formed at Watton and West Raynham in May with Boeing Fortress Mk Is, moving to Polebrook in August to attempt very high-altitude bombing, but the aircraft were not developed sufficiently, the idea was abandoned and the Squadron reverted to Blenheim Mk IVs in October 1941. It disbanded in February 1942 to re-form in November with Stirlings

35 Squadron: 90's sister Blenheim squadron was also incorporated into 17 OTU in April 1940, but it re-formed with Halifaxes at Leeming in November 1940 and did not revert to Blenheims

The 2 Group Blenheim squadrons continued to operate constantly during the months of May, June and July 1941. These months saw the losses from daytime operations mounting inexorably, some from the fighter-escorted 'Circus', 'Ramrod' and 'Roadstead' operations (see Appendix 1), but principally and very seriously from anti-shipping sweeps and attacks, as mentioned (see Appendix 2). However, for the first time for many months the night-time operational losses were far lower (see Appendix 3). A few large-scale 'daylight spectacular' raids on enemy ports such as Bremen and Rotterdam were mounted and they led to severe losses (see Appendix 4).

Coastal Command

Coastal Command had expanded to four operational Groups in January 1941 – 15, 16, 18 and 19, with 17 as the Training Group. A new AOC was appointed in June 1941 when AM Sir Philip Joubert de la Ferte returned to the post he had held before the war, replacing AM Sir Frederick Bowhill. His Command had to do its best with insufficient and unsuitable aircraft, ASV radar sets were scarce and unreliable, the bombs used were largely ineffective, no airborne depth-charges were available, they lacked really long-range anti-submarine patrol aircraft to bridge the 'Atlantic Gap', and the Botha torpedo

An example of battle damage to an 18 Squadron Blenheim; from the exit-holes, the shrapnel appears to have passed right through the radio installation.

The crew pat a bald head for luck before setting out on a bombing sortie.

aircraft and Lerwick flying boats were complete failures. Blenheims continued to feature strongly in Coastal Command's land-based operations.

500 Auxiliary Squadron: exchanged its elderly Ansons for Blenheim Mk IVs and moved from Detling to Bircham Newton, commencing operations in May

272 Squadron: based at Chivenor, formed from Flights of 235 and 236 Squadrons in November 1940, and commenced re-equipping with Beaufighters prior to moving to the Middle East

252 Squadron: moved to Aldergrove to help cover the Western Approaches, converted to Beaufighters, then moved to the Middle East

235 Squadron: soldiered on with its Mk IV-Fs at Bircham Newton, moving to Scotland in June

59 Squadron: still based at Thorney Island with Blenheim Mk IVs, but moved to Detling to bring the Flight detached there up to full squadron strength

53 Squadron: still based at St Eval with Blenheim IVs. Both 53 and 59 had bomber Blenheims

86 Squadron: moved from Wattisham, with a detachment at Norwich, to North Coates, and soon started converting to Beauforts

143 Squadron: formed in June at Aldergrove as a Coastal Strike Squadron, with Blenheim Mk IVs and a few Beaufighters

Coastal Command OTUs such as Catfoss were kept very busy. Note the Hampden behind the Blenheims, pressed into use as torpedo-bombers.

608 Auxiliary Squadron: based at Thornaby-on-Tees; glad to change its Bothas for Blenheim Mk Is in February, and now equipped with Mk IVs

248 Squadron: moved with its Blenheim IV-Fs from Gosport to Dyce, with a detachment at Montrose

236 Squadron: also with Mk IV-Fs, moved to Carew Cherrington, with a Flight at St Eval

254 Squadron: moved from Sumburgh to Aldergrove with Blenheim IVs and IV-Fs

404 Squadron: newly formed with RCAF personnel at Thorney Island on 1 May with Blenheim Mk IV-Fs, but moved to Scotland in June before commencing operations

407 Squadron: also newly formed at Thorney Island on 8 May with Blenheim Mk IVs, but moved to North Coates a couple of months later and converted to Hudsons

Other Coastal Command units operating Blenheims were:

1 Coast **A**rtillery **C**o-Operation **U**nit: based at Detling

No 1 Photo **R**econnaissance **U**nit: B Flight was at St Eval and C Flight at Wick

2 OTU: based at Catfoss, the principal Command OTU, but also kept a Flight at Prestwick

Met Flights: 1403 was based at Bircham Newton, 1404 at St Eval, and 1405 at Aldergrove

The Photographic Reconnaissance Unit was controlled by Coastal Command. It supplied photos taken by the Spitfires of A Flight at Benson, and the Blenheims of the other Flights, to all the RAF Commands, and to the other services.

There was no respite for the Coastal Command Blenheim operational squadrons either. They flew into action every day and sometimes also at night, and their losses – also from the daylight anti-shipping operations in particular – continued to mount relentlessly (see Appendix 4). A look at the notes of these losses in anti-shipping operations (Appendices 2 and 4) reveals a drastic rise in the proportion of crew fatalities to aircraft lost. This comment applies equally to Coastal and Bomber Command losses: for example, 21 Squadron lost 13 Blenheims on anti-shipping sorties between 31 March and 16 June with not a single survivor from any of them, and 18 Squadron lost 14 aircraft between 11 April and 16 June without any of the 42 crew members surviving – two of these aircraft were on training sorties while 12 were on anti-shipping operations. This dreadful increase in fatalities was due to the fact that when a Blenheim (normally flat-out) was hit by flak or fighters at such a low level over the sea there was no chance to bale out and usually only a few seconds to attempt to ditch, with not enough time to slow the stricken aircraft to touch-down speed, even if some control could be maintained – and frequently it could not. Apart from the dangers from marauding Messerschmitts, the Blenheims faced fierce fire from the increasing number of flak ships with their 88mm AA guns and their

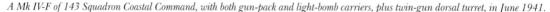

A Mk IV-F of 143 Squadron Coastal Command, with both gun-pack and light-bomb carriers, plus twin-gun dorsal turret, in June 1941.

THE BRISTOL BLENHEIM

An unusual shot of 254 Squadron Blenheim Mk IVs in line-astern formation.

multiple-mountings for deadly 20mm and 37mm cannon, or the Bofors 40mm 'Pom-Poms' (used also by the RN), as well as the ever-present risks of striking the sea during evasive manoeuvres, of hitting a mast, or being damaged by bomb explosions or debris from the target ship. The crews were well aware of these manifest dangers but pressed home their attacks with great determination – the 'Blenheim Boys' were indeed brave.

Fighter Command

Blenheims were fading away rapidly from Fighter Command and very few were still deployed operationally, although many were still used for training on the squadrons. The Blenheims had done the invaluable groundwork and developed the tactics and techniques that enabled the squadrons to operate their new twin-engined aircraft more effectively.

406 Squadron: newly formed on 5 May at Ackrington with Blenheim I-Fs and IV-Fs, it started converting to Beaufighters in June

604 Auxiliary Squadron: finally completed converting from Blenheim Mk Is to Beaufighters

68 Squadron: a new night-fighter squadron formed in January with Blenheim Mk I-Fs, it still operated a few as well as some Mk IV-Fs, although it was officially a Beaufighter squadron

219 Squadron: based at Tangmere, where it completed its conversion to Beaufighters

25 and **29** Squadrons: these long-serving Blenheim squadrons, now at Wittering and West Malling, has also completed their conversion to Beaufighters

600 Auxiliary Squadron: based at Colerne with a mix of Mk I-F Blenheims and Mk I Beaufighters, it started re-equipping with the Merlin-engined Mk II 'Beaus'

23 Squadron: based at Ford, alongside the FIU, and changing its Blenheim Mk I-Fs for Douglas Havocs, the night-fighter and intruder version of the Boston

Fighter Command had an easier time in defence as the Luftwaffe daylight attacks on Britain had faded away into fighter-bomber raids. The growing number of single-engined

68 Night Fighter Squadron replaced its Blenheim Mk I-Fs with Beaufighters from May 1941, but also operated a few Mk IV-Fs such as Z5722, the personal aircraft, WM-Z, of the CO, Max Aitken, son of Lord Beaverbrook. (Actually, this is my restored Blenheim, which operated from Duxford in these authentic markings from 1993 to 1995, subsequently appearing in Coastal Command then Bomber command colour schemes and markings.)

RAF fighters turned more to an offensive posture, mainly by means of 'Rhubarb' sweeps to enemy-held coastal areas. Blenheim fighters were too vulnerable to be involved in these so there were few Blenheim losses (see Appendix 5). The mantle of night defence had been assumed by the Beaufighter squadrons with their improved radar aids, assisted by single-engined Defiants and Hurricanes, especially during the night of 10/11 May 1941 when the Luftwaffe sent 520 bombers for the last major fire raid of the *Blitz* on London.

The remorseless toll of non-operational Blenheim losses continued unabated both on the squadrons and at the Operational Training Units (see Appendix 6). These heavy losses, added to the casualties due to enemy action, combined to circumscribe the planned expansion of Bomber and Coastal Commands in 1941, despite the increased rate of aircraft production.

Blenheim operations in May and June 1941

The main anti-*Kriegsmarine*, and especially anti-*Unterseeboot*, campaign inaugurated by Churchill on 7 March caused a considerable reduction of the planned number of 'Circus' operations, and only two were mounted in each of the months of March, April and May, but the number increased to 16 in June. Thus, apart from the two 'Circus' operations, the main effort during May continued to be daylight anti-shipping sorties varying from 12 to 44 (on the 13th) aircraft per day (with an average of 20 sorties) on 24 of these 31 days. In addition, nine were sent to bomb Lannion airfield on the 27th during the fruitless search by British ships and aircraft for the cruiser *Prinz Eugen* following the sinking of the battleship *Bismarck*. Sometimes shipping attacks were mounted by night too, as on 6/7 May when ten Blenheims of 110 Squadron tried a moonlight attack on a convoy off Ameland; six tried again the following night, but no hits were confirmed. Twenty-three aircraft of 110 and 21 Squadrons were sent on the night of 8/9 May in an unsuccessful attempt to block the Kiel Canal. Ports such as Antwerp, Boulogne, Cherbourg, Calais and Rotterdam were attacked by small numbers of Blenheims on many nights in nuisance raids in support of Bomber Command's main attacks on other targets.

June started with 44 Blenheims being sent on anti-shipping operations on the 2nd in cloudy weather; some (from 18, 105 and 139 Squadrons) bombed ships in the Kiel Canal, sinking two vessels, which blocked this vital waterway for over ten days, although each squadron had an aircraft shot down. The 4th saw 54 Blenheims mounting coastal sweeps and raids on airfields all the way from Norway to Belgium; a ship was claimed as sunk, but two more aircraft were lost. Smaller-scale shipping sweeps continued over the next

Photographs showing the very low level of shipping attacks – one by 82 Squadron, with a ship hit by 21 Squadron with escorting Spitfires above – taken by the Gunners.

Severe damage to V6525 of 18 Squadron on a 'Circus' raid to Hazebrouk on 22 June: a cannon shell appears to have entered through the starboard roundel and taken off the port elevator. F/O Tudge managed to fly it back to Horsham St Faith, where it was repaired, used by 105 and 21 Squadrons, and Destroyed by Fire serving with 17 OTU at Steeple Morden on 21 April 1943.

THE BRISTOL BLENHEIM

two days, and on the 7th 22 aircraft took part, three of them lost. On the 9th 12 Blenheims attacked ships off the Dutch coast, losing two of their number, and eight bombed shipping off Stavanger the next day. On the 11th 25 set out on 'cloud cover' raids to Bremerhaven and other targets in north-west Germany, but 19 turned back, although one sank a trawler and one bombed Ijmuiden docks. A raid by 12 aircraft to Brest the following day also turned back due to lack of cloud cover, and one by four aircraft to Norway on the 13th was recalled for the same reason.

'Circus' No 12 was mounted on 14 June when 12 Blenheims of 110 Squadron were escorted by nine Squadrons of RAF fighters to St Omer, but Me.109s of III/JG 26 penetrated this huge screen and shot down two of the bombers. Another 18 Blenheims carried out coastal sweeps that day, as did 23 the following day – although most turned back, one was shot down in the Ems estuary. The six Blenheims of 59 Squadron on 'Circus' No 13 to Boulogne Docks on the 16th were protected by six squadrons of fighters, but once again the 109s of JG 26, led by Adolf Galland, burst through the protective screen and shot down two of the Blenheims (P/O Villa and P/O Kennedy) and badly damaged another, wounding two of P/O Foster's crew. This was a typically busy day for the Blenheims, for, apart from the 'Circus' 13 operation, six aircraft of 21 Squadron attacked a convoy off Baflo on the Dutch coast – Sgt Rex Leavers, a bold and brave pilot just awarded the DFM for successful low-level shipping attacks, left his pull-up in V6034

Sgt Rex Leavers DFM, a brave and determined Pilot, was killed with his crew on 16 June when V6034 of 21 Squadron struck the mast of the ship they were attacking off Borkum. A photograph of him, taken in Malta, is in Chapter 27.

a split-second too late, struck a mast of the target ship and cart-wheeled into the sea. In the same attack Sgt Taylor's Blenheim V6240 was damaged by 109s, but escaped at low level to crash-land at Sutton Bridge – it was repaired only to be shot down exactly one month later. Six aircraft from 139 Squadron, together with one from 18, were sent to Texel, but were 'bounced' by two 109s from I/JG 52 – one (F/O Langley in T1832) was shot down, and two (Sgt Kirk in V6456 and F/O Laird in V6332) were badly damaged, the latter crash-landing at Rackheath in Norfolk and written off. Seven more Blenheims of 18 Squadron were sent to bomb shipping in the Schelde estuary, but the ships' AA guns claimed three Blenheims shot down, although only one (P/O Watson in V6512) was lost and two others badly damaged. Twenty-six shipping sorties were carried out by Blenheims that day, with five aircraft shot down and six more badly damaged – a casualty rate of 42 per cent.

'Circus' No 14 on the 17th developed into a huge aerial battle. Twenty-three Blenheims drawn from 18, 105, 110 and 139 Squadrons went to bomb Choques power station, well into France, with no fewer than 19 squadrons of RAF fighters involved – at 228 aircraft, virtually ten fighters for every Blenheim. For once none of the bombers were lost; the Luftwaffe claimed 20 RAF fighters but actually shot down 17, while the RAF claimed ten German fighters but shot down only three. A black day for Fighter Command was compounded when Hurricanes of 504 Squadron mis-identified a Beaufort of 217 Squadron in the dusk and shot it down. In 'Circus' No 15 on 18 June six Blenheims of 107 Squadron were escorted to Bois des Liques by 16 squadrons of fighters – 32 fighters per bomber! – and all the bombers returned although four of the fighters were lost.

The next 'Circus', on 19 June, was intended to be a heavily escorted raid by 36 Blenheims on the docks at Le Havre, but it 'went off at half-cock' when six of the 12 squadrons of the fighter escort failed to make the rendezvous in hazy conditions. This caused 24 of the bombers (six each from 18, 21, 110 and 139 Squadrons) to abort, and only the 12 from 105 and 107, led by W/Cdr Hughie Edwards, continued; nine of them bombed, finding only light opposition and returning unscathed. Later that day three Coastal Command Blenheims from 59 Squadron on a 'Roadstead' to Etaples escorted by Spitfires were half-heartedly engaged by a few 109s; they concentrated on F/O Miles's aircraft, which, dropping behind the formation, was damaged when it glanced off the sea while skimming the surface on the run-in to the target, but it was successfully defended by the Spitfires (which shot down a 109) and force-landed at Shoreham. P/O Botham's Blenheim Mk IV-F of 235 Squadron was also damaged that day by a 109 off the Dutch coast, and the 226 Squadron aircraft of F/O Waddington was shot down into the sea on an anti-shipping strike.

'Circuses' 16 and 17 were both mounted on 21 June. The former comprised six Blenheims of 21 Squadron to St Omer, and the latter six of 110 Squadron to Desvres airfield; they were acting as bait for the Luftwaffe for they were escorted by no fewer than 29 squadrons of RAF fighters (348 fighters for 12 bombers!). Extensive aerial conflicts developed and nine Luftwaffe fighters were shot down and three more damaged, while the RAF lost one 21 Squadron Blenheim with another badly damaged, as was one of 110 Squadron, together with seven fighters shot down with another seven damaged. 'Circuses' continued on the 22nd (to Hazebrouck), 23rd (to Choques power station – two lost), 24th (18 aircraft to Comines power station), and two on the 25th (12 aircraft each to Hazebrouck and St Omer – one lost). On the 26th an abortive return to Comines was made by 23 aircraft, which did not bomb. On 27 June a steelworks at Lille was bombed accurately by 23 Blenheims without loss, while the 28th saw 24 Blenheims on the third 'Circus' to Comines. Also on the 28th, 18 more Blenheims of 107 and 105 Squadrons were sent on a 'daylight spectacular' raid, but they turned back. This was the first attempt at Operation Wreckage, an unescorted, long-range, daylight raid on Bremen, the second largest port in Germany. The leader of this formation, W/Cdr Lawrence Petley of 107 Squadron, was very strongly criticised by the AOC of 2 Group, AVM Stevenson, for failing to carry out the attack. Although Petley's formation had emerged into dangerously clear blue skies halfway over the North Sea, he pressed on until they were fired upon by destroyers escorting a convoy some 50 miles from the German coast, and – with the element of surprise lost in conditions of unlimited visibility – he thought it wisest to abort the mission. He did not want his squadron to be massacred as 82 had been at Aalborg in similar conditions the previous August.

Forty-six Blenheims – more than a third of the 130 aircraft available to 2 Group – operated on the 30th: a 'Circus' by 18 to Pont-a-Vein power station was carried out without loss, and 13 more made 'cloud cover' raids to north-west Germany, but only a few bombed and one was lost. On 30 June a second attempt at Operation Wreckage was mounted when W/Cdr Hughie Edwards led 15 aircraft from 21 and 105 Squadrons at dawn and without escort to strongly defended Bremen, with 107 relegated to making a diversionary attack on the Westerland fighter airfield on Sylt. At the briefing the night before, G/Capt Laurie Sinclair said:

> 'Gentlemen, tonight – at this very moment – we are bombing Bremen. We want to prove to the Germans that we can bomb them 24 hours a day, and you will attack in daylight soon after the heavies have left. No excuses or minor unserviceability will be tolerated, you MUST get to the target.'

However, early the following morning the formation heading for Bremen flew into a fog bank at 50 feet over the sea and was scattered, as it extended for over 100miles. Only F/O Waples (ably navigated by Sgt Giblin) of 21 Squadron in V6388 carried on, finding North Bremen and bombing a timber-yard. Hughie Edwards led some of the 105 Squadron aircraft back to various alternative targets – shipping off Norderney (S/Ldr Calvert-Booth scoring hits on a 6,000-tonner, and F/O Lambert sinking a 3,000-tonner) together with the Terschelling WT station and harbour, and five 21 Squadron aircraft attacked railway marshalling yards at Oldenburg. The 107 Squadron aircraft made an incorrect landfall and met heavy flak, two being shot down; they attempted to bomb a railway line west of Rantum, but most bombs fell in the sea. AVM Stevenson was most displeased at the second failure of the important Bremen operation, but was persuaded that it was the thick fog – through which the crews flew for more than 45 minutes – that thwarted the operation, not any lack of determination by the crews.

Shipping sweeps and strikes, as well as 'Circuses' and the other daylight raids, were proving very expensive even though, by then, the bulk of the Luftwaffe had been moved far away to the new Eastern Front. The high summer of 1941 saw a fundamental, and for the Third Reich ultimately fatal, development in the war. Hitler had long been turning his expansionist eyes eastwards, and on 22 June he launched Operation Barbarossa – the German invasion of Russia. As AVM Robert Saundby, the Bomber Command SASO, said on the 26th, 'The front door is now the back door'. For the first time the German Air Force in the west was considerably out-numbered by the RAF. In an attempt to aid its new Allies, the RAF adopted a more forcefully offensive role, in which Blenheims played a major part, a role intended to require the Germans to retain a large proportion of their aircraft strength in the west. But this intention was not realised as the Luftwaffe retained only two *Jagdgeschwaders* in the occupied west – JG26 covering from Holland to north of the Seine, and JG2 from south of the Seine to Cherbourg. The 2 Group anti-shipping campaign – which had seen over 1,000 sorties from 1 April to 30 June 1941, with 297 shipping attacks – was also increased in scope and intensity. 'Circus', 'Fringe' and 'Roadstead' operations became more frequent, bolder in their choice of targets, and larger in scale; in addition, the special daylight raids were mounted both on German harbours and even deep into mainland Germany. The dangerous Channel Stop operations, disliked by the crews, continued relentlessly. The involvement of the Blenheim squadrons was pivotal in all of these extensive actions, and consequently the price they paid in casualties was even higher than it had been before.

Although re-deployment of the Blenheim squadrons continued throughout the summer the moves were on a reduced scale. By July of 1941 the position was as follows:

Bomber Command

21 Squadron: returned to 2 Group at Watton from Coastal Command control at Lossiemouth

114 Squadron: also returned to 2 Group at West Raynham from Coastal Command at Leuchars in July. Both remained anti-shipping squadrons

107 Squadron: based at Great Massingham, and also remained an anti-shipping squadron

139 Squadron: at Horsham St Faith, changing with **18** Squadron: moved from Oulton to Horsham St Faith in July

82 Squadron: remained at Watton

88 Squadron: moved to Swanton Morley with its mix of Blenheims and Bostons

110 Squadron: returned to Wattisham from the 11 Group Station of Manston on 9 June

226 Squadron: remained at Wattisham, with detachments. at Manston and Long Kesh. 18, 82, 88, 110 and 226 Squadrons were designated anti-shipping squadrons in June

105 Squadron: remained at Swanton Morley

18, 21, 82, 105, 107, 110 and 139 Squadrons all sent substantial detachments to Malta. These moves, together with the high level of losses, seriously reduced the strength of 2 Group, so the remaining units had to operate even more intensively. In mid-September 1940 – at the height of the anti-invasion raids on the Channel ports – 2 Group had 212 serviceable Blenheims available. However, by the first week of April 1941 the total available to the Group had dropped to a sparse 99, and by June had built up to only 130.

Fighter Command

By July 1941 no Fighter Command squadrons had Blenheims as the main equipment. They had made a valuable contribution, especially in the development of radar-assisted night-fighting, in intruder operations, and in providing long-range fighter cover.

23 Squadron: based at Ford, having converted to Havocs although it still had a few Mk I-Fs on strength

FIU: also based at Ford, it had mainly Beaufighters and Havocs together with a few Mk I-Fs

68 Squadron: based at High Ercall, it had mainly 'Beaus' but also several Mk I-Fs and Mk IV-Fs

Army Co-operation Command

13 Squadron: based at Odiham, it converted from Lysanders to Blenheim Mk IVs
614 Squadron: based at Macmerry, east of Edinburgh, it also converted to Mk IVs
Both squadrons had flown anti-invasion and Air-Sea Rescue patrols in 1940, but now concentrated upon exercises with the Army
No **1416 Flight:** operated in the reconnaissance role for the Army
No 2 School of **A**rmy **C**o-Operation: based at Andover, it also continued to train with Army units

Coastal Command

The re-equipment, expansion and re-deployment of the hard-working Blenheim Coastal Command squadrons gathered pace in July:

53 Squadron: left St Eval in Cornwall for Bircham Newton on the East Coast on 2 July,
59 Squadron: left Thorney Island for Detling. Both these squadrons converted from their bomber Blenheims to Hudsons in August
86 Squadron: moved from Wattisham to North Coates and began converting to Beauforts
143 Squadron: re-formed at Aldergrove in June as a coastal strike squadron with Mk IVs, but also had a few Beaufighters
235 Squadron: moved from Bircham Newton to Dyce, with a detachment at Sumburgh
248 Squadron: made the reverse journey from Dyce to Bircham Newton and placed Flights at St Eval and Portreath, and started converting to Beaufighters in July
236 Squadron: remained at Carew Cheriton, with a detachment at St Eval
254 Squadron: moved from Sumburgh to Aldergrove
272 Squadron: based at Chivenor, converted to Beaufighters and moved to the Middle East
404 Squadron: moved to Castletown, then to Skitten, both in the NE tip of Scotland
500 Squadron: remained at Bircham Newton, with detachments at Carew Cheriton and Limvady
608 Squadron: remained at Thornaby and began to receive a few Hudsons in July
No **1 PRU,** No **1 CACU, 2 OTU** and the three **Met Flights** continued to fly intensively

Blenheim operations in July 1941

On 1 July 39 Blenheims were sent on 'cloud cover' raids to north-west Germany, but only six could bomb and two of those, one from 21 Squadron and one from 139, were lost. On the 2nd there was a 'Circus' to Lille power station, two of the 12 sent by 226 Squadron being lost, as was one of the same number sent the next day by 139 on a 'Circus' to Hazebrouck railway marshalling yards. On 4 July 20 Blenheims of 226 Squadron were sent to bomb Norderney and Choques power station, and two of these were shot down, including 226's CO, W/Cdr R. Hurst in Z7291 – his crew, F/Sgts T. Davies and R. Green, were Squadron veterans who had both survived the fighting in France in May 1940 and been awarded the DFM. They were lost on diversionary raids in support of the third, and this time successful, attempt at Operation Wreckage – the famous and daring daylight raid on the heavily defended German port of Bremen.

The repeat of the extremely hazardous attack on Bremen was again led by W/Cdr Hughie Edwards, the pugnacious Australian CO of 105 Squadron, who had just been awarded the DFC for his outstanding leadership on other daylight raids. 107 Squadron, still led by W/Cdr Lawrence Petley, was placed back in the main attacking force – it provided six aircraft and 105 nine. The crews were called at 0330 and took off at 0520. Three aircraft of 107 dropped out during the long North Sea crossing – S/Ldr Murray found his turret guns were unsynchronised, F/Lt Jones felt ill, and F/O Charney was unable to keep up with the formation. The remaining 12 Blenheims passed three patrol ships off Wangerooge, so Hughie knew that their position and heading would be reported, but he led the formation in over the enemy coast near Cuxhaven at very low level, hedge-hopping over Germany for 50 miles and meeting an ever more intense barrage of fire as they reached Bremen from the 40 batteries of 105mm and 88mm heavy AA guns that surrounded the city. He spread his force into a wide line-abreast formation to present the AA gunners with a more difficult target, keeping it at the lowest possible height, and dodging barrage balloons and cables the aircraft flew over – or even under – power lines, avoiding chimneys, cranes and pylons by a few feet, cutting through many telephone lines, and bombing the *Industriehaven* target area successfully. This area, between the main station and the docks, was protected by more than half of the 60 light AA batteries based in Bremen, each armed with six 37mm or 20mm rapid-fire cannons. This fierce flak brought down four Blenheims, two from each Squadron – a third of the attacking force – and all eight remaining aircraft were damaged to a greater or lesser extent, some with wounded crewmen on board. One of those shot down on the run in was poor Petley, CO of 107,

Wreckage of V5595 of 21 Squadron, shot-down off Gravelines, the nose lies inverted on the port engine nacelle, the map-case lies on the port wing; the crew Sgts E Kemp, E Gould and F Soal amazingly survived and became PoWs.

who, with his crew, was killed in V6020; the other 107 aircraft, V6193 of F/Lt Welburn, had a fourth man on board, W/O Magee, the Squadron's Armament Officer, who 'went along for the experience' and paid with his life. Consequently only one of the aircraft from 107 that attacked Bremen returned to Great Massingham. The two 105 Squadron aircraft were brought down in the target area; Sgt MacKillop's Z7426 GB-B crashed into a factory, and F/O Lambert's Z7486 GB-M was seen burning fiercely – both crews perished (see Appendix 4).

Hughie Edwards's Blenheim V6028 GB-D had a cannon shell lodged in the radio rack, and splinters from another had wounded his WOp/Ag, Sgt Gerry Quinn DFM, who had to be winched out of the turret on the return to Swanton Morley. The aircraft also received flak damage to the wings and fuselage, had debris jammed on the starboard undercarriage, and telephone wires caught under the fuselage, with more wrapped round the tail-wheel. Sgt Jackson, with his crew Sgt Williams and Sgt Purves both wounded, had to belly-land his damaged Z7484 GB-K, while Sgt Scott's aircraft, Z7361 GB-R, was hit by a cannon shell that exploded in the fuselage, perforating it badly and slightly wounding his WOp/Ag, Sgt Bastin. The cost, with the diversionary raids, had been high – 17 men, including two Wing Commanders, killed, four men wounded, and two captured – but the operation was hailed as a great success and became headline news. Congratulations rained down from the AOCs of 2 Group and Bomber Command, and from the Chief of the Air Staff. For his outstanding leadership Hughie Edwards was awarded the supreme decoration for valour – the Victoria Cross – his Observer, P/O Alister Ramsey, the DFC, and his WOp/Ag Sgt, Gerry Quinn, a bar to his DFM; Sgt Jackson and his crew of Sgt Williams and Sgt Purves, all of whom were wounded, each also received a DFM. Edwards gathered the entire 105 Squadron in the hangar and announced that 'it was the Squadron's VC and he was simply the person presented with it'; he also took all the aircrew and the NCO ground-crew out to celebrate in a Norwich pub.

In 1942 Edwards was awarded the DSO for his leadership of daylight raids by 105's Mosquitos on the Gestapo HQ in Oslo and on the Philips factory at Eindhoven, thus becoming one of only three RAF pilots to receive the three highest awards – VC, DSO and DFC – the other two being Wing Commander Guy Gibson of 'Dambusters' fame and Group Captain Leonard Cheshire, and he became Australia's most decorated airman. He retired as Air Commodore Sir Hughie Idwal Edwards VC KCMG CB DSO OBE DFC KStJ, Governor of Western Australia, and died in 1982.

The daily coastal sweeps and shipping attacks continued throughout that action-packed July, as did the losses (see Appendix 2). Fourteen Blenheims carried out these dangerous duties on 5 July, 21 on the 6th (two of which were lost), 20 on the 7th (three being lost), 11 on the 8th (one lost), 15 on the 9th, 24 on the 10th (one lost), 38 on the 12th (one lost), 29 on the 14th (two lost), and five on the 16th – the same day as the major raid on Rotterdam described below. Only three sorties were mounted on the 18th, but all three aircraft of 21 Squadron were shot down attacking ships off Gravelines (100 per cent losses), 21 on the 19th (two lost), 12 on the 20th (two lost), 13 on the 21st, and six on the 22nd – together with six more to bomb Le Trait shipyards.

W/Cdr Hughie Edwards DFC, CO of 105 Squadron, soon after being awarded the Victoria Cross for his daring leadership of the Bremen raid on 4 July.

The attack on Rotterdam docks on 16 July by 36 Blenheims drawn from 18, 21, 105, 139 and 226 Squadrons was laid on as a 'daylight spectacular' to aid the anti-shipping campaign and to show solidarity with the Russians. It was to be from the landward direction at very low level and in two waves, with W/Cdr Peter 'Tom' Webster DFC, CO of 21 Squadron, leading the first and W/Cdr 'Tim' Partridge DFC, CO of 18, the second wave. One of the first wave, Sgt Bevan and crew in V6240 of 21 Squadron, was shot down, and three of the second wave were downed by the thoroughly aroused defences, including two 18 Squadron aircraft – the leader, W/Cdr 'Tim' Partridge in V6267, and Sgt Rost and crew in Z7496, all of whom were killed, and S/Ldr Sydney-Smith of 139 Squadron, who crash-landed Z7362, side-slipping his crippled

Accurate bombing by Blenheims of 21 Squadron on West Quay at Cherbourg on 10 July 1941, showing (1) a dockside store exploding and (2) hits on a tanker.

Blenheim with the port-engine on fire on to a bomb-site in the centre of the city. He and his crew were lucky indeed to survive and become Prisoners of War (see Appendix 4). Several ships were damaged by direct hits – Dutch reports said 22 – but post-war research shows that only two were badly damaged, the *Hermod* (5,193 tons) and the *Knute Nelson* (5,749 tons); six others were damaged, the *Oranjefontein* (10,547 tons), *Treuenfels* (8,456 tons), *Gotha* (5,334 tons), *Cimbria* (2,653 tons), *Hafnia* (2,031 tons) and a gunboat, and the main targets, the *Straasbourg* (17,000 tons) and *Breisgau* (12,000 tons) were only slightly damaged. The damaged ships were soon repaired. These disappointing results from many direct hits on stationary ships were due to the inefficiency of the four 250lb GP bombs carried by each Blenheim – the 11-second delay fuses (to avoid damage to the aircraft from debris) often meant that a bomb would pass right through a vessel before exploding, and even if it did explode inside a large ship it was unlikely to sink it. Sadly, the bravery and skill of the Blenheim crews in placing the bombs so accurately at low level in the face of fierce AA fire was largely wasted.

The long-suffering 18 and 21 Squadrons (mentioned in the earlier comments on the sharp increase in fatalities in anti-shipping sorties) were hit hard again on the 23rd when they lost six of the 17 Blenheims bombing shipping off the Dutch and Belgian coasts (a crippling 35 per cent casualty rate); 15 of the 18 crewmen involved – more than 83 per cent – were killed, and only three survived to become Prisoners of War. By contrast, 12 more Blenheims sent that day on 'cloud cover' raids to Northern France returned without casualties.

On 24 July there was a major Bomber Command effort, Operation Sunrise, against the German battle-cruisers *Scharnhorst*, *Gneisenau* and *Prinz Eugen*, based at Brest – the Admiralty was most worried that they might mount a raiding sortie against Atlantic convoys. Much last-minute re-planning was required when the *Scharnhorst* slipped out to La Pallice further south a day before the planned raid on Brest, which was reduced from 150 bombers to 100 – a decision that probably saved the loss of a further ten bombers – with a separate force to La Pallice of 15 Halifaxes, which it was hoped were sufficiently well armed to be able to defend themselves. As a diversion 36 Blenheims in three waves, each with Spitfire escorts, bombed Cherbourg docks with good results. The first wave was by nine of 139 Squadron and three of 18, the second by 12 of 107 and 226 Squadrons, and the third by 12 of 114 Squadron led by W/Cdr Hull – his aircraft and three others were damaged by flak. The main raid, opened by three high-altitude Fortresses, was by a force of 79 unescorted Wellingtons and 18 escorted Hampdens on the *Gneisenau* at Brest, and by the 15 unescorted Halifaxes on the *Scharnhorst* at La Pallice. The German capital ships were damaged, but three of the five armour-piercing bombs that scored direct hits on the *Scharnhorst* went out through the bottom of the ship without exploding, and she was able to limp back to Brest. The diversionary aspect of the Blenheim raid failed as no German fighters appeared over Cherbourg and all 36 Blenheims and their escorts returned safely. However, many Messerschmitts did appear at the other two ports, and ten of the Wellingtons with two of the Hampdens were shot down at Brest, as well as five of the 15 unescorted Halifaxes – all of the remaining ten suffered damage, with several of their crewmen injured. After almost two years of aerial warfare the RAF had still not digested the lesson that its Heavy Bombers could not operate over defended areas in daylight without suffering crippling losses.

On both 27 and 28 July six Blenheims sent on 'cloud cover' raids to Yainville power station were unable to bomb, but July 1941 ended with a busy and costly day on the 30th when 43 Blenheims were sent to bomb shipping in the Kiel Canal and off the Dutch and German coasts; seven of them were shot down, a crippling casualty rate of more than 16 per cent (see Appendix 2). Both May and June 1941 had been difficult and painful months for the hard-pressed Blenheim squadrons, but July was to be even worse.

Appendix I

Blenheim losses on 'Circus', 'Roadstead' and 'cloud cover' operations May to July 1941

Aircraft are all Mk IVs.

01-05-1941   V5823 105 Squadron: failed to return (FTR) from bombing Rotterdam oil tanks, damaged by flak and Me.109s, crew wounded, first one propeller detached, then the other, glided to crash-land near Southwold and written off; F/Lt G. Goode (Pilot) and P/O J. Hogan (Obs) awarded DFCs, Sgt G. Rowland (WOp/Ag) DFM for this action.

01-05-1941   T1887 105 Squadron: badly damaged by flak while attacking Flushing harbour; Sgt P. Murray (WOp/Ag) wounded, aircraft belly-landed at base and repaired; P/O A. Judson (Pilot) and Sgt R. Rook (Obs) uninjured.

21-05-1941   V6390 110 Squadron: FTR from 'Circus' No. 10 to Gosnay power station, shot down by Me.109s; Sgt M. Jackson, Sgt J. Donovan, and Sgt T. Beattie Killed In Action (KIA) and buried in Allouagne, France.

04-06-1941   R3903 139 Squadron: FTR from aborted unescorted raid to De Koy, shot down by Me.109s; P/O W. Baser, Sgt A. Simpson RNZAF, and Sgt C. Triggs KIA and commemorated on Runnymede Memorial.

04-06-1941   Z5744 139 Squadron: FTR from aborted unescorted raid to De Koy, shot down by Me.109s; P/O I. Lees, Sgt T. Osborne, and Sgt C. Meredith KIA and commemorated on Runnymede Memorial.

14-06-1941   V6334 110 Squadron: FTR from 'Circus' No. 12 to St Omer, shot down by Me.109s of JG 26; F/Lt P. Windram, P/O P. Howes, and F/Sgt R. Cox KIA. F/Lt Windram buried at Boulogne, P/O Howes at Bergenop-Zoom, F/Sgt Cox commemorated on Runnymede Memorial.

16-06-1941   V6386 59 Squadron: FTR; shot down by Me.109 of Hptm R. Pingel, Kommandeur of II/JG 26, on 'Circus' No. 13 to Boulogne; P/O P. Villa (Pilot) became PoW, Sgt J. Mortimer, and Sgt S. Mcintyre KIA and commemorated on Runnymede Memorial.

16-06-1941   Z3339 59 Squadron: FTR; shot down by Me.109 of JG 26 into sea on same sortie; P/O D. Kennedy, P/O P. Briggs, and Sgt C. Edgar became PoWs. (Serial No. in ORB incorrect.)

17-06-1941   V6437 18 Squadron: damaged by Me.109s, crash-landed at Horsham St Faith; F/O Duffill and crew slightly injured, aircraft repaired.

21-06-1941   V6450 21 Squadron: FTR from 'Circus' No. 16 to St Omer, shot down by Me.109-E of Obslt Adolf Galland; Sgt P. Brown, Sgt L. Wilson, and Sgt M. Brooker KIA and buried in St Omer.

21-06-1941   V6321 21 Squadron: badly damaged by Me.109s on 'Circus' No. 16; crew of P/O H. Waples, Sgt N. Giblin, and Sgt A. Handley safe, aircraft repaired. Waples, by then a F/Lt, DFC, KIA a month later.

23-06-1941   V5517 107 Squadron: FTR from 'Circus' No. 20 to Mardyck airfield, shot down by Me.109s; F/O E. Fairbanks, Sgt R. Buckingham, and P/O J. Harrison baled out, captured and became PoWs on their first 'op'.

23-06-1941   V6195 107 Squadron: FTR from 'Circus' No. 20 to Mardyck airfield, shot down by Me.109s; F/O M. Redfearn-Smith, Sgt J. Rudkin, and Sgt K. Noakes KIA and buried at Boulogne.

23-06-1941   Z6271 107 Squadron: damaged by Me.109s on 'Circus' No.20 to Mardyck airfield, Sgt K. Sanders (WOp/Ag) KIA, aircraft crash-landed at Dover, Sgt A. Ballands (Pilot) and Sgt R. Yorke (Obs) safe, aircraft repaired.

25-06-1941   V6381 21 Squadron: FTR; damaged by Me.109s on 'Circus' No. 22 to Hazebrouck, crashed at Southend airfield; crew Sgt L. Richards, Sgt Olderbolz, and Sgt Field safe, aircraft DBR. First survivors from sixteen 21-Squadron Blenheims lost since 1 March 1941.

25-06-1941   V6259 18 Squadron: FTR; shot down by flak in target area on 'Circus' No. 23 to St Omer airfield; Sgt W. Mounser, Sgt G. Richards, and Sgt W. Waite KIA. Sgt Mounser and Sgt Waite buried in Longuensse Souvenir Cemetery, Sgt Richards commemorated at Runnymede Memorial.

30-06-1941   R3801 107 Squadron: FTR; shot down into sea on 'cloud cover' raid to Westerland; crew Sgt J. Drysdale, Sgt S. Edwards, and Sgt H. Challis KIA and buried in Kiel.

30-06-1941   V6139 107 Squadron: FTR; badly damaged by flak on same sortie and ditched; crew Sgt C. Chown, Sgt M. Kelly, and Sgt A. Smith captured and became PoWs.

02-07-1941   V6085 226 Squadron: FTR; shot down on 'Circus' No. 29 to Lille power station; F/Sgt A. Carvell (Pilot) escaped to become PoW, crew Sgt A. Batch and Sgt J. Melvin KIA, buried at Merville Communal Cemetery.

02-07-1941   Z7440 226 Squadron: FTR; shot down in flames by Me.109s on 'Circus' No. 29 to Lille power station; one parachute seen to open, but crew F/Sgt J. Stanley, F/Sgt D. Huntley, and F/Sgt L. Wood-Smith KIA, buried at Merville Communal Cemetery.

03-07-1941   V6452 139 Squadron: FTR; shot down by flak on 'Circus' No. 30 to Hazebrouck; crew Sgt J. Cormack RAAF, Sgt A. Smith, and Sgt J. Forsyth KIA and buried at St Omer.

04-07-1941   V6365 226 Squadron: FTR; shot down on 'Circus' No. 32 to Choques; Sgt A. Smith (Pilot) and Sgt R. Mathias (WOp/Ag) KIA, Sgt F. Hynes (Obs) survived and became PoW.

04-07-1941   Z7291 226 Squadron: FTR; shot down into sea by flak off Norderney; crew W/Cdr R. Hurst, F/Sgt T. Davies DFM, and F/Sgt R. Green DFM KIA. W/Cdr Hurst was CO of 226 Squadron.

10-07-1941   V6398 21 Squadron: FTR; shot down on 'Circus' to Cherbourg docks, and crashed near there; crew S/Ldr H. Tudge, Sgt C. Penn, and Sgt W. Barker survived and became PoWs.

31-07-1941   R3895 114 Squadron: FTR from sortie to Aalborg; S/Ldr M. Kennedy became PoW, fate of crew not recorded in ORB.

Appendix 2

Blenheim losses on anti-shipping operations May-July 1941

Aircraft are all Mk IVs.

01-05-1941   V6177 139 Squadron: FTR; shot down by flak off Den Helder during anti-shipping strike; crew W/Cdr I. Braye DFC, F/Sgt K. Peek, and Sgt J. Hutchinson KIA and commemorated on Runnymede Memorial. W/Cdr Braye was CO of 139 Squadron.

01-05-1941   T1832 139 Squadron: damaged by flak on same sortie; P/O E. Phillips (Pilot) fatally wounded, F/O R. Fastnedge (Obs) awarded DFC for flying aircraft back to base. Pilot recommended for VC, and Sgt S. Allen (Ag) DFM for this action, but these awards not made, aircraft repaired.

03-05-1941   T1825 101 Squadron: FTR; shot down by flak off Boulogne on anti-shipping strike; crew P/O C. Brown, P/O C. Farvis, and Sgt A. Morgan KIA and commemorated on Runnymede Memorial. This crew had sunk 2,000-ton ship off Ostend earlier in day.

03-05-1941   T2234 101 Squadron: FTR; hit by flak during anti-shipping strike, ditched off Dungeness; crew Sgt C. Deane, Sgt G. Watkinson, and Sgt J. Chell KIA and commemorated on Runnymede Memorial.

05-05-1941   V6377 18 Squadron: struck ship's mast during anti-shipping strike, crash-landed on return to Portreath; Sgt Kirkpatrick (Obs) injured, Sgt Burns (Pilot) and Sgt White (WOp/Ag) safe, aircraft written off.

06-05-1941   Z5875 21 Squadron: FTR; shot down in flames on anti-shipping strike; crew Sgt K. Fitzgerald, Sgt N. Berry, and Sgt A. Barron KIA and commemorated on Runnymede Memorial.

06-05-1941   R3600 110 Squadron: FTR; shot down by flak during anti-shipping strike; crew F/Lt E. Steel NZ, F/Sgt R. Freestone, and Sgt J. Bramhall KIA and commemorated on Runnymede Memorial.

07-05-1941   R3741 18 Squadron: FTR; shot down in flames during attack on cargo vessel; crew S/Ldr R. Barker, Sgt N. Meanwell, and Sgt V. Hughes KIA and commemorated on Runnymede Memorial.

07-05-1941   Z5758 1 Coastal Artillery Co-operation Flight: FTR; shot down by Me.109s while spotting for Dover heavy guns off Cap Gris Nez; four-man crew F/O A. Hicks, Sgt J. Macdonald, Sgt C. Scott, and Sgt R. Livings KIA.

08-05-1941   P4860 139 Squadron: FTR from night anti-shipping sweep, struck Waddenzee and ditched at 0013; crew Sgt J. Middleton, Sgt K. Coles, and Sgt H. Hale injured but rescued and became PoWs.

08-05-1941   V5828 105 Squadron: FTR; shot down on fire by flak into Hafrs Fjord, Norway, on anti-shipping strike; W/Cdr A. Christian, F/Sgt H. Hancock, and Sgt G. Wade KIA and commemorated on Runnymede Memorial. W/Cdr Arnold Christian was CO of 105 Squadron.

09-05-1941   V6379 18 Squadron: FTR; shot down on fire by AA fire from RN destroyer; crew S/Ldr R. Langebear, P/O J. Stone, and Sgt A. Newbery (aged 19) KIA and commemorated on Runnymede Memorial.

13-05-1941   V6430 82 Squadron: FTR; staged from Bodney to Portreath to attack St Nazaire, shot down into sea; crew W/Cdr L. King, Sgt J. Austen-Johnson, and Sgt D. Owen KIA. Pilot and Obs buried in Escoublac-la-Baule War Cemetery, WOp/Ag commemorated on Runnymede Memorial.

13-05-1941   V5997 82 Squadron: FTR; staged from Bodney to Portreath to attack St Nazaire, shot down, crash-landed in unoccupied France; crew Sgt F. Miller, Sgt N. Ingram, and Sgt W. Whitman interned.

13-05-1941   V6224 82 Squadron: staged from Bodney to Portreath to attack St Nazaire, cannon shell exploded in cockpit, aircraft crash-landed at St Eval with fused bomb-load still on board; P/O Chadwick (Obs) killed, P/O Hanafay (Pilot) and Sgt Bambrough (WOp/Ag) safe, aircraft repaired.

13-05-1941   V5638 82 Squadron: staged from Bodney to Portreath to attack St Nazaire, badly damaged by flak, crash-landed at St. Eval; F/O Duggan-Smith (Pilot) wounded in foot, Sgt Llewellyn (Obs) in face, Sgt James (WOp/Ag) uninjured, aircraft repaired.

13-05-1941   V6395 107 Squadron: damaged in action and belly-landed at Coltishall; Sgt Charney and crew uninjured, aircraft repaired.

15-05-1941   V6372 21 Squadron: FTR; shot down into sea by Me.109s after attacking convoy; crew P/O J. Ogilvie, Sgt R. Mayers, and Sgt W. Fillingham KIA and commemorated on Runnymede Memorial.

15-05-1941   V6255 21 Squadron: damaged attacking convoy, crash-landed at Copplestone, Exeter; S/Ldr Atkinson and crew safe, aircraft repaired.

16-05-1941   T2118 105 Squadron: FTR; shot down into fjord by flak in Norway while attacking shipping; P/O R. Richards, Sgt A. North, and Sgt E. Snutch KIA and commemorated on Runnymede Memorial.

17-05-1941   R3772 110 Squadron: struck mast of ship during attack; Sgt Cathless struggled back to base, his crew uninjured, aircraft repaired.

21-05-1941   L9272 107 Squadron: FTR; shot down into sea off Heligoland by Me.109s; F/Sgt D. Craig (Obs) KIA, Sgt R. Ratcliffe (Pilot) and Sgt F. Smith (WOp/Ag) rescued and became PoWs.

21-05-1941   V6433 107 Squadron: damaged by flak attacking shipping, chased by Me.109s, force-landed at West Raynham; Sgt J. Wilson RNZAF (Obs) KIA, F/Sgt K. Wostenholme (Pilot) and Sgt G. Tales (WOp/Ag) safe, aircraft repaired.

24-05-1941   V5426 110 Squadron: FTR; shot down into sea by Me.109 of JG 52 off Texel; crew P/O M. Scott, P/O J. Gill, and Sgt R. Hewlett KIA and commemorated on Runnymede Memorial.

24-05-1941   L9267 114 Squadron: FTR; shot down off Norway by Me.109 of JG 77; crew Sgt J. McWilliam, P/O B. Godsmark, and Sgt E. Maddison KIA and commemorated on Runnymede Memorial.

25-05-1941   L8864 18 Squadron: FTR; shot down near Vrist, Denmark, after attacking ship; Sgt F. Wood (Pilot) and Sgt E. Baker (Obs) KIA and buried in Lemvig Cemetery, Sgt C. Harris (WOp/Ag) survived and PoW.

25-05-1941   V6248 18 Squadron: FTR; shot down into sea by Me.109 after attacking shipping; crew F/Sgt D. Keane, Sgt G. Duffus, and Sgt I. Gow KIA and commemorated on Runnymede Memorial.

25-05-1941   R3666 18 Squadron: damaged by Me.109s attacking shipping; Sgt E. Lloyd (WOp/Ag, aged 20) fatally wounded, P/O Wilson (Pilot) and Sgt E. Aires (Obs) uninjured, aircraft repaired.

25-05-1941   R3707 105 Squadron: FTR; shot down into sea by Me.109s while attacking convoy off Ameland; crew P/O G. Rushbrooke (aged 19), Sgt E. Green, and Sgt S. Parr KIA and commemorated at Runnymede.

25-05-1941   R2791 139 Squadron: FTR; shot down into sea by flak ship off Ijmuiden; Sgt G. Bye RCAF, Sgt W. Thorneycroft, and Sgt S. Bransby KIA and commemorated on Runnymede Memorial.

28-05-1941   V6457 82 Squadron: FTR; shot down into sea off Heligoland while attacking shipping; crew Sgt J. McGowan, Sgt A. Walker, and Sgt D. Banks KIA and commemorated on Runnymede Memorial.

02-06-1941   L9192 18 Squadron: FTR; shot down attacking shipping off Ems/Weser by Me.109s; crew F/Lt I. Mead, Sgt C. Ashcroft, and Sgt W. Richards KIA and commemorated on Runnymede Memorial.

02-06-1941   V6239 139 Squadron: FTR; shot down by Me.109 while attacking shipping in Keil Canal; crew Sgt F. Boroski RCAF, Sgt L. Slade, and Sgt A. Ball KIA and commemorated on Runnymede Memorial.

07-06-1941   T2047 107 Squadron: FTR; shot down by Me.109s while attacking convoy off Ijmuiden; crew Sgt F. Knox (aged 20), Sgt G. Kaye, and Sgt M. Berry (aged 20) KIA and commemorated at Runnymede.

07-06-1941   T1921 107 Squadron: FTR; shot down by Me.109s while attacking convoy off Ijmuiden; Sgt H. Fordham, P/O J. Grenon, and Sgt R. Morley (aged 20) KIA and commemorated on Runnymede Memorial.

07-06-1941   V6316 105 Squadron: FTR; shot down by Me.109s off Terschelling on 'Beat' No. 8; crew P/O L. Clayton, P/O V. Phillips, and Sgt A. Stiddard KIA and commemorated on Runnymede Memorial.

09-06-1941   V6427 18 Squadron: FTR; disappeared in fog bank off Dutch coast; crew KIA, Sgt L, Box (Pilot) buried at Bergen-op-Zoom, crew P/O P. Molloy, and Sgt G. Bass commemorated at Runnymede.

09-06-1941   V6428 18 Squadron: FTR; damaged by flak from ships, then shot down by Me.109 of JG 52 off Schiermonikoog; crew F/Sgt I. Bullivant, F/Sgt S. Gallery, and F/Sgt R. Hind KIA and commemorated on Runnymede Memorial.

11-06-1941   V6367 107 Squadron: FTR; raid recalled but shot down off Texel by Me.109 of JG 52; crew Sgt P. Walker, P/O R. Sammons, and Sgt V. Lewis KIA and commemorated on Runnymede Memorial.

12-06-1941   V6072 110 Squadron: badly damaged by flak, belly-landed at Manston; S/Ldr I. Spencer (Pilot) wounded in knee, P/O Goode (Obs) in legs, Sgt Child (WOp/Ag) uninjured, aircraft repaired. S/Ldr Ian Spencer awarded DFC for this action.

15-06-1941   V6319 105 Squadron: FTR; shot down by E-boats; F/O P. Watts, F/Sgt D. Milroy, and Sgt P. Murray (aged 19) KIA. Pilot commemorated on Runnymede Memorial, crew buried at Hoek van Holland Cemetery. First and last operation for this crew.

15-06-1941   V6375 110 Squadron: FTR from shipping sweep, shot down by Me.109s; F/Sgt A. Guesford, Sgt C. Shearn, and Sgt L. Rolfe KIA. F/Sgt Guesford and Sgt Rolfe buried at Kirkaby, Denmark, Sgt Shearn commemorated on Runnymede Memorial.

15-06-1941   V5887 114 Squadron: FTR; shot down by flak ship; P/O C. Starkey (Obs) KIA and commemorated on Runnymede Memorial, Sgt L. Dowsey (Pilot) and Sgt F. Duffield (WOp/Ag) captured and became PoWs.

16-06-1941   V6512 18 Squadron: FTR; shot down by ship's flak off Hook of Holland; crew P/O I. Watson, P/O E. Aires, and Sgt T. Dean KIA and commemorated on Runnymede Memorial.

16-06-1941   V6034 21 Squadron: FTR; hit mast of target ship off Frisian islands; crew KIA, Sgt E. Leavers DFM (Pilot) buried at Den Andel, Sgt I. Overheu DFM (Obs) commemorated on Runnymede Memorial, Sgt J. Phelps (WOp/Ag) buried at Sage. (See accompanying photograph.)

16-06-1941   T1832 139 Squadron: FTR; shot down by Me.109s off Esbjerg; crew KIA, F/O R. Langley DFC (Pilot) and Sgt I. Scourfield (Obs) commemorated on Runnymede Memorial, Sgt H. Gretton (WOp/Ag) buried at Esbjerg.

16-06-1941   V6332 139 Squadron: FTR; hit by ship's flak and crash-landed at Rackheath, Norfolk, hitting tree; F/O K. Laird (Pilot) and Sgt L. Wakefield (Obs) KIA, Sgt Robinson (WOp/Ag) seriously injured.

01-07-1941   V6396 21 Squadron: FTR; shot down by flak while bombing ships in Kiel Canal; S/Ldr H. Cooper DFC (Pilot) escaped to become PoW, crew F/Sgt J. Robertson DFM (Obs) and F/Sgt J. Simpson (WOp/Ag) KIA and buried in Hamburg. F/Sgt Robertson's parachute caught on tail of Blenheim.

01-07-1941   V6258 139 Squadron: FTR; shot down by Me.109 and ditched off Vlieland; crew Sgt K. Fenton, Sgt A. Fuller, and Sgt R. McDonald rescued and became PoWs.

04-07-1941   V6368 114 Squadron: FTR to Leuchars from raid on shipping in Bergen harbour; Sgt N. Cook, Sgt W. Jenkins, and Sgt B. Bates KIA, Sgt Cook and Sgt Bates buried in Mollendal Church, Bergen, Sgt Jenkins commemorated on Runnymede Memorial.

06-07-1941   T1824 107 Squadron: FTR; hit by flak ship and ditched in Scheldt estuary; Sgt D. Brett (WOp/Ag) KIA and has no known grave, Sgt L. Dicks (Pilot) and Sgt D. MacAlister (Obs) rescued and became PoWs.

06-07-1941   Z7272 226 Squadron: FTR; struck mast of target ship off Holland; crew P/O C. Stickney, F/Sgt R. Morgan, and F/Sgt H. Wyatt KIA and commemorated on Runnymede Memorial.

07-07-1941   V5502 105 Squadron: FTR; shot down by flak ship off Scheveningen; crew KIA, S/Ldr A. Scott (Pilot) and Sgt R. Dewin (Obs) commemorated on Runnymede Memorial, F/Sgt P. Conlon (WOp/Ag) buried at Westduin Cemetery, Den Haag.

07-07-1941   V6084 139 Squadron: FTR; shot down by flak ship off Scheveningen; crew KIA, F/Lt H. Hilton (Pilot) has no known grave, Sgt J. Sykes and Sgt J. Clayton buried in Holland.

07-07-1941   Z7424 139 Squadron: FTR; shot down by Me.109 of JG 52 off Zandvoort, Holland; crew KIA, Sgt J. Causon (Pilot) has no known grave, Sgt R. Spencer and Sgt W. Cundill buried in Holland.

12-07-1941   Z7487 107 Squadron: FTR; shot down by flak into sea off Ijmuiden, Holland; W/Cdr A. Booth (Pilot) and F/Sgt C. Goodfellow (WOp/Ag) KIA, Sgt T. Scott (Obs) survived and a PoW. W/Cdr Arthur Booth was second CO of 107 to be killed in less than a fortnight. Great Massingham Roll of Honour lists Sgt T. Mommer as fourth crew member.

14-07-1941   R3704 139 Squadron: FTR; shot down by fighters off Le Havre; crew P/O R. Wilson, Sgt R. Stephens, and P/O F. Turner KIA and buried in St Marie Cemetery, Le Havre.

14-07-1941   V6253 139 Squadron: FTR; shot down by fighters off Le Havre; crew P/O R. Galt, Sgt S. Vardy, and Sgt C. Parslow KIA. Sgt Vardy buried in Dunkerque town cemetery, others commemorated on Runnymede Memorial.

18-07-1941   V5595 21 Squadron: FTR; shot down by ship's flak during Channel Stop sortie off Gravelines; crew Sgt J. Kemp, Sgt E. Gould, and Sgt F. Soal rescued and became PoWs.

18-07-1941   V6369 21 Squadron: badly damaged by ship's flak during Channel Stop sortie, crash-landed back at Manston; Sgt Maguire, Sgt Bangor-Jones, and Sgt Haskins safe, aircraft written off.

18-07-1941   Z7502 21 Squadron: FTR; shot down by ship's flak off Cap Gris Nez; S/Ldr D. Graham-Hogg (Pilot) and Sgt J. Marsden (WOp/Ag) became PoWs, F/Sgt D. Wyatt (Obs) KIA and commemorated on Runnymede Memorial.

19-07-1941   V6039 105 Squadron: FTR; shot down by ship's flak off The Hague during attack on convoy; crew Sgt R. Taylor RNZAF, Sgt R. Withrington, and Sgt S. Sparkes KIA and buried in Holland.

19-07-1941   Z7439 105 Squadron: FTR; struck target ship's mast off Scheveningen; Sgt V. Farrow (aged 19), Sgt E. Saunders (aged 21), and Sgt O. Robinson (aged 21) KIA , Pilot and Observer buried at The Hague, WOp/Ag has no known grave.

20-07-1941   V6038 18 Squadron: FTR; hit mast of target ship off Le Touquet and crashed into sea; F/Lt W. Hughes, Sgt J. Hunter, and Sgt M. Wilding KIA and commemorated on Runnymede Memorial.

20-07-1941   Z7499 139 Squadron: FTR; shot down by ship's flak off Le Touquet during attack on tanker; crew Sgt N. Baron DFM, Sgt K. Hopkinson, and Sgt R. Ullmer DFM KIA. Sgt Baron buried at Blankenberge Cemetery, Belgium, crew at Boulogne Eastern Cemetery, France.

23-07-1941   R3666 18 Squadron: FTR; shot down by Me.110s of ZG 76 off Den Helder during shipping attack; crew Sgt W. Dunham RCAF, Sgt R. Adamson, and Sgt N. Harding KIA. Sgt Adamson buried at Westerschelling, others commemorated on Runnymede Memorial.

23-07-1941   V6250 18 Squadron: FTR; shot down by Me.110s of ZG 76 off Den Helder during attack on convoy; crew Sgt P. Baker, Sgt W. Bounds, and P/O L. Evans KIA and commemorated on Runnymede Memorial.

23-07-1941   V6035 21 Squadron: FTR; shot down by flak ship off Le Touquet during shipping attack; P/O P. Ashby (Pilot) and P/O G. Seeley (WOp/Ag) KIA and buried in Oostende, Belgium, P/O G. Lowes (Obs) became PoW.

23-07-1941   Z7438 21 Squadron: FTR; shot down by ship's flak during attack on tanker off Oostende; Sgt J. Sullivan (WOp/Ag) KIA, S/Ldr F. Campbell-Rogers (Pilot) and Sgt D. Bingham (Obs) became PoWs.

23-07-1941   V6197 21 Squadron: FTR; shot down by flak ship, crashed into sea off Holland during attack on tanker; F/Lt H. Waples DFC, Sgt N. Giblin DFM, and Sgt Marsden KIA. Norman Giblin (aged 20) is buried at Flushing, others commemorated on Runnymede Memorial.

23-07-1941 V6321 21 Squadron: FTR; shot down by flak during attack on tanker off Oostende; crew Sgt H. Hartridge RCAF, Sgt C. Phillips, and Sgt K. Minty KIA and buried at Flushing.

23-07-1941 V6225 21 Squadron: badly damaged by Me.110 during shipping sweep off Den Helder, crash-landed at Horsham St Faith; Sgt Wood (Pilot) and Sgt Johnson (Obs) severely injured, Sgt Allan (WOp/Ag) safe, aircraft later repaired.

29-07-1941 R3619 82 Squadron: FTR from abortive raid on shipping at Bremen, damaged by Me.109s, crash-landed on Texel; F/Lt J. Keighley and Sgt J. Parsons became PoWs.

30-07-1941 L9240 18 Squadron: FTR; shot down by flak during attack on shipping in Kiel Canal; crew Sgt H. Cue, Sgt J. Jarrell RCAF, and Sgt P. Brewer captured and became PoWs.

30-07-1941 R3803 82 Squadron: FTR; shot down by flak during attack on shipping in Kiel Canal; crew Sgt P. Stocks, Sgt G. Lee, and P/O E. Hale KIA. Sgt Stocks has no known grave, crew buried at Esbjerg, Denmark.

30-07-1941 V6513 82 Squadron: FTR; shot down by flak en route to Kiel Canal; crew P/O J. Bell, Sgt J. Tague, and Sgt E. Martin KIA and commemorated on Runnymede Memorial.

30-07-1941 V6176 139 Squadron: FTR; shot down by Me.110 en route to attack shipping off Texel; Sgt L. Gruer, Sgt J. Blundell, and Sgt D. Dennis-Smithers KIA. John Blundell buried at Esbjerg, Denmark, Pilot (aged 20) and WOp/Ag commemorated on Runnymede Memorial.

30-07-1941 V6266 139 Squadron: FTR; shot down by Me.110 en route to attack shipping off Texel; crew Sgt G. Menish, P/O P. Brown, and Sgt R. Haley (aged 20) KIA and commemorated on Runnymede Memorial.

30-07-1941 V6322 139 Squadron: FTR; shot down by Me.110 en route to attack shipping off Texel; crew P/O P. Shillitoe, Sgt P. Walder, and P/O E. Elder KIA. Peter Shillitoe and Phillip Walder commemorated on Runnymede Memorial, Esmond Elder buried at Esbjerg, Denmark.

30-07-1941 V6439 139 Squadron: FTR; shot down by Me.110 en route to attack shipping off Texel; crew Sgt W. Campbell, Sgt R. McRobert, and Sgt S. Severn KIA and commemorated on Runnymede Memorial.

Appendix 3

Blenheim losses on special daylight raids on Bremen and Rotterdam, July 1941

Aircraft are all Mk IVs.

Bremen raid

04-07-1941 Z7426 105 Squadron: FTR; shot down by flak and crashed on to factory in target area; crew Sgt W. MacKillop, Sgt E. Nethercutt, and Sgt G. Entwistle KIA and buried in Becklingen War Cemetery, Soltau.

04-07-1941 Z7486 105 Squadron: FTR; shot down by flak and crashed in flames in target area; crew F/O M. Lambert, Sgt R. Copeland, and Sgt F. Charles KIA and buried as above crew.

04-07-1941 V6020 107 Squadron: FTR; shot down by flak and crashed in target area; crew W/Cdr L. Petley, F/Lt R. Bailey DFC, and F/Sgt W. Harris KIA and buried as above crew. W/Cdr Petley was CO of 107 Squadron.

04-07-1941 V6193 107 Squadron: FTR; shot down by flak and crashed in target area; F/Lt F. Wellburn survived and became PoW, Sgt D. Dupree (aged 20), Sgt A. Routley, and W/O S. Magee KIA and buried as above crew. W/O Magee was Station Armament Officer who went along 'for experience'.

Rotterdam docks raid

16-07-1941 V6267 18 Squadron: FTR; shot down by flak leading attack; crew W/Cdr T. Partridge DFC, Sgt G. Dvorjetz, and F/Sgt J. Smith DFM KIA and buried in Crooswijk Cemetery. W/Cdr 'Tim' Partridge was CO of 18 Squadron. Memorial to crew erected near crash site after war and maintained by local school.

16-07-1941 Z7496 18 Squadron: FTR; shot down, crashing near Ypenburg airfield; Sgt R. Rost RAAF (Pilot) died in Delft hospital a few hours later, crew Sgt J. Hughes and Sgt S. Winter also KIA, all buried in Westduin Cemetery.

16-07-1941 V6240 21 Squadron: FTR; shot down by flak, crashing in Waalhaven harbour in target dock area; crew Sgt J. Bevan (aged 19), P/O R. Slade, and Sgt L. Mynott KIA. Pilot and Obs buried in Rotterdam but body of WOp/Ag could not be found, commemorated on Runnymede Memorial.

16-07-1941 Z7362 139 Squadron: FTR; shot down by flak and crashed on bomb-site in Rotterdam city centre; crew S/Ldr E. Sydney Smith, P/O R. White, and F/Sgt E. Caban DFM, although injured, survived and became PoWs.

Wreckage of two of the four Blenheims shot down during the daring daylight raid on Bremen on 4 July. 107 Squadron aircraft C W is probably V6193, while the other came down in the dock area. All four crews were killed.

Appendix 4

Coastal Command Blenheim losses (excluding 'Circus' operations), May- July 1941

Aircraft are all Mk IVs or Mk IV-Fs.

05-05-1941   Z5742 235 Squadron: FTR; shot down by Me.110s of ZG 76 into sea off Frisian Islands; crew Sgt B. Crawforth (aged 20), Sgt C. Robertson (aged 19), and Sgt W. Blackford (aged 21) KIA. Pilot and Obs buried in Sage, WOp/Ag commemorated on Runnymede Memorial.

07-05-1941   TR-A 59 Squadron: FTR; came down in North Sea on sortie to St Nazaire; crew F/Lt G. Palmer DFC, Sgt A. Whitson, and F/Sgt C. Dunlop DFM KIA and commemorated on Runnymede Memorial.

07-05-1941   V5523 86 Squadron: FTR; engine cut during convoy escort, ditched in North Sea off Harwich; crew F/Lt T. Mathewson, Sgt E. Martin, and Sgt D. Copes rescued.

09-05-1941   T1874 59 Squadron: FTR from Boulogne, shot down near Calais; S/Ldr G. Close GC, F/O F. Roberts, and Sgt G. Richards KIA, buried in Boulogne East Cemetery.

10-05-1941   Z5960 1404 Met Flt: FTR from operational sortie, no further details available.

12-05-1941   TR-T 59 Squadron: badly damaged by Me.109 after attacking convoy, escaped in cloud, returned to base on one engine; P/O Jordan, Sgt Morgan, and Sgt Pitcher safe, aircraft repaired.

15-05-1941   N3533 235 Squadron: crashed on landing at Bircham Newton; F/O Cook and crew safe, aircraft repaired.

16/17-05-1941 V6312 59 Squadron: overshot landing during air raid at Docking; P/O Perkins and crew unhurt, aircraft repaired.

17-05-1941   Z6164 500 Squadron: received flak damage and belly-landed at Detling; Sgt Halls and crew unhurt, aircraft repaired.

21-05-1941   V5428 236 Squadron: overshot landing at St Eval in bad weather, swung to avoid parked aircraft, u/c collapsed; Sgt Lindley, Sgt Fuller and Sgt Hale uninjured, aircraft DBR.

21-05-1941   V5803 254 Squadron: damaged by flak from convoy; Sgt Moorhouse and crew uninjured, aircraft repaired.

21-05-1941   L6595 404 Squadron Mk I: lost height after take-off at Thorney Island, crashed into creek; Sgt McLean and Sgt McEllman injured.

26-05-1941   V6301 53 Squadron: undershot airfield at St Eval and hit gun-post; W/Cdr Grant and crew slightly injured, aircraft DBR.

27/28-05-1941 V5760 236 Squadron: flew into ground in bad weather attempting to land at Carew Cheriton; P/O Chappell and crew slightly injured, aircraft DBR.

28-05-1941   V5491 500 Squadron: overshot landing at Southampton; Sgt Lacey and crew safe, aircraft repaired.

29-05-1941   Z5968 235 Squadron: FTR; shot down into sea on Pirate Patrol by Me.109s of JG 52; crew P/O J. Fenton, Sgt R. Johnson, and Sgt O. Dee KIA and commemorated on Runnymede Memorial.

29-05-1941   V5453 235 Squadron: FTR; shot down into sea on Pirate Patrol by Me.109s of JG 52; crew F/Sgt H. Naughtlin, Sgt R. Oldroyd, and Sgt S. Gordon KIA and commemorated on Runnymede Memorial.

29-05-1941   V6447 59 Squadron: FTR from convoy escort; crew KIA, F/O J. Sturrock (Pilot) and Sgt W. Smallbone (WOp/Ag) commemorated at Runnymede, Sgt N. Conrade (Obs) buried in Lodge Hill Cemetery, Birmingham.

03-06-1941   T2220 59 Squadron: FTR; shot down attacking shipping off Normandy; crew P/O T. Kerr, Sgt K. Fletcher, and Sgt J. Hine KIA. P/O Kerr is buried at Plurien Cemetery, his comrades commemorated on Runnymede Memorial.

06-06-1941   T2222 53 Squadron: damaged by flak and force-landed at St Eval; P/O Hewson and crew uninjured, aircraft repaired.

06-06-1941   V5646 86 Squadron: engine cut on take-off at North Coates, crash-landed, DBR; P/O E. Evans and crew safe.

07-06-1941   V5722 500 Squadron: belly-landed at Bircham Newton; P/O Baldry and crew unhurt, aircraft repaired.

08-06-1941   V5689 500 Squadron: crashed in mist at Holme-next-Sea, Norfolk; P/O F. Hall-Jones RNZAF, P/O A. Shield, and P/O J. Johnston killed, aircraft DBF.

09-06-1941   Z6025 254 Squadron: FTR; control lost in cloud, crashed at Garvagh, Northern Ireland; crew P/O C. Werner, Sgt R. Shaw, and Sgt J. O'Donnell killed, aircraft destroyed.

10/11-06-1941 V5933 53 Squadron: FTR; crashed on Bodmin Moor in bad weather on return from St Nazaire; crew P/O N. McLennan, Sgt D. Taylor, and Sgt W. Roberts KIA.

10/11-06-1941	PZ-Y 53 Squadron: damaged by flak over St Nazaire, returned on one engine, force-landed at St Eval; P/O Bunce, Sgt Haissel, and Sgt D. Diggles uninjured, aircraft repaired. WOp/Ag awarded DFM.
12-06-1941	T1955 235 Squadron: FTR; shot down by Me.110s off Danish coast; crew Sgt M. Stephens, Sgt J. Carmichael, and Sgt W. Halliday KIA and commemorated on Runnymede Memorial.
12-06-1941	T2121 248 Squadron: FTR; shot down by Me.110s, crew Sgt E. Holmes, Sgt D. Richardson, and Sgt J. Till KIA, commemorated on Runnymede Memorial.
13/14-06-1941	T1807 235 Squadron: damaged when overshot landing at Dyce; P/O Annan and crew unhurt, aircraft repaired.
15-06-1941	V5452 235 Squadron: FTR; shot down by Me.109s off coast of Norway; crew F/Lt W. Goddard DFC, Sgt A. Cain, and F/Sgt H. Smith KIA and commemorated on Runnymede Memorial.
18-06-1941	MK-A 500 Squadron: P/O Linton shot down Ju.88 in Western Approaches, damaged by return fire.
18-06-1941	Z6075 500 Squadron: overshot landing at Bircham Newton; P/O Elgar and crew uninjured, aircraft repaired.
19-06-1941	V5395 59 Squadron: crash-landed at Shoreham after bouncing off sea avoiding flak near target ship at Etaples; F/O Miles, Sgt Lewis and Sgt Mikklesen uninjured, aircraft DBR.
19-06-1941	Z5971 235 Squadron: damaged by Me.109s off Dutch coast; P/O Botham and crew uninjured, aircraft repaired.
21-06-1941	V6387 59 Squadron: crashed north of Hayling Island when engine caught fire on approach to Thorney Island, aircraft destroyed by fire; no injuries reported to P/O R. Beveridge, Sgt Williams, and Sgt Barrett.
23-06-1941	V5647 53 Squadron: FTR from convoy escort, shot down by Me.109 of JG 2; crew P/O D. Bolton, Sgt K. Corrie, and Sgt G. Kircher KIA and commemorated on Runnymede Memorial.
23-06-1941	V6125 53 Squadron: FTR; forced to ditch on shipping sweep; crew P/O E. Hewson, Sgt A. Dawson, and Sgt W. McCorkell rescued, captured and became PoWs.
26-06-1941	V6309 53 Squadron: FTR from shipping sweep; crew P/O L. Francis, Sgt R. Whitley, and Sgt J. Hopper KIA and commemorated on Runnymede Memorial.
26-06-1941	V6122 53 Squadron: FTR; shot down on shipping sweep; crew P/O C. Greville-Heygate DFC, P/O G. Troup, and Sgt C. Naylor KIA and commemorated on Runnymede Memorial.
26-06-1941	V6087 53 Squadron: FTR from shipping sweep; crew P/O D. Herrick GM, Sgt G. Gahagan, and Sgt G. Wells KIA and commemorated on Runnymede Memorial. Dennis Herrick awarded George Medal attempting to rescue pilot of Oxford that crashed and caught fire at his EFTS. One of five New Zealand brothers to serve Britain with distinction: both S/Ldr M. Herrick DFC and bar and P/O B. Herrick also KIA with RAF, while Lt T. Herrick DSC and bar and Lt L. Herrick served in RN. NZ Government would not allow sixth brother to volunteer for overseas service.
30-06-1941	V5863 59 Squadron: FTR; hit barrage balloon cable on return from shipping sweep, ditched off Dover; crew P/O J. Whitmore (aged 20), Sgt D. Dulley, and Sgt P. Truman KIA, commemorated at Runnymede
02-07-1941	Z6171 248 Squadron: FTR; shot down by Me.109s on shipping sweep; crew P/O R. Powell, Sgt H. Robinson, and F/Sgt W. Sharratt KIA and commemorated on Runnymede Memorial.
05-07-1941	N3524 235 Squadron: FTR from patrol; crew P/O G. Botham, P/O F. McHardy, and Sgt H. Ingram KIA, Botham and Ingram commemorated at Runnymede, McHardy buried at Stavne Cemetery, Trondheim, Norway.
07-07-1941	Z6041 500 Squadron: FTR; shot down by intruder on approach to Docking; F/O A. Leeson, F/O R. Smith, and Sgt C. Pearce KIA.
07-07-1941	Z7450 59 Squadron: FTR; shot down by flak from destroyer off Gravelines, crashed into sea with engine on fire; crew S/Ldr I. Aitken, Sgt G. Wood, and Sgt J. Brown KIA and commemorated on Runnymede Memorial.
08-07-1941	T1941 254 Squadron: engine cut returning from patrol, force-landed at Port Ellen, DBR; F/Sgt L. Larkin safe.
09-07-1941	V5736 254 Squadron: FTR on convoy patrol, damaged by Me.110, engine cut, ditched; Sgt F. Aspinall (Pilot) and Sgt A. Snashall (Obs) rescued injured, Sgt Snashall died from injuries, Sgt G. Carnall (WOp/Ag) KIA, presumed drowned.
25-07-1941	V6313 59 Squadron: engine cut on return from patrol, hit tree force-landing at Chart Sutton, Kent; P/O Richards, Sgt Longworth, and Sgt Major uninjured.

Appendix 5

Fighter Command Blenheim losses, May-July 1941

04-05-1941   L1513 68 Squadron Mk I-F: undershot airfield landing at High Ercall, badly damaged but repaired.

13-05-1941   L8715 604 Squadron Mk I-F: overshot night landing at Middle Wallop; P/O Gossland and crew uninjured, aircraft repaired.

17/18-05-1941   L8675 68 Squadron Mk I-F: stalled and spun into ground near Ruddington, Notts; P/O Butcher and Sgt Wiskar killed.

13/14-06-1941   L6726 25 Squadron Mk I-F: flap failed on approach to Wittering, control lost, hit ground at Barnack; Sgt H. Gigney killed, aircraft destroyed by fire.

Appendix 6

Non-operational Blenheim losses, May-July 1941

Aircraft are all Mk IVs unless stated otherwise.

01-05-1941   L6786 54 OTU: engine cut on take-off at Church Fenton, crashed into trees and DBR; P/O L. Mayer (solo pilot) killed.

03-05-1941   N3562 3 OTU: engine cut on approach to Chivenor, crash-landed at Saunton Sands, Devon; P/O M. Weber injured on first solo flight on type.

03-05-1941   N6228 13 OTU: stalled on approach at Bicester and dived into ground; Sgt Statton (solo pilot) killed.

05-05-1941   L8758 21 Squadron: became lost, ditched in Irish Sea; Sgt D. Glass (Pilot) and Sgt H. Norman-Arterton (Obs) commemorated on Runnymede Memorial, F/Sgt G. Cole (WOp/Ag) buried on Isle of Man.

05-05-1941   V5620 110 Squadron: overshot landing at Wattisham and crashed into fuel dump on return from night patrol; P/O D. Seale and crew injured, aircraft DBR.

05-05-1941   L1279 3 OTU Mk I: abandoned over South Molton, Devon, when elevators jammed; P/O R. Ullman injured.

05-05-1941   T1800 110 Squadron: crashed landing at Wattisham; Sgt Twist and crew slightly injured, aircraft repaired.

05-05-1941   V5392 and Z5809 86 Squadron: destroyed on ground by night bombing at Sydenham, Northern Ireland.

05-05-1941   L1348 88 Squadron Mk I: destroyed as above. L1348 was original 'high-speed' trials aircraft.

06-05-1941   V6196 139 Squadron: hit tree at 0015 on take-off from Horsham St Faith, had to orbit for 90 minutes due to intruder activity, crashed in Horsham village; Sgt J. Evans and Sgt Tuppen injured, WOp/Ag Sgt Dumolo seriously.

08/09-05-1941 V6194 82 Squadron: damaged in action; S/Ldr Watson and crew safe, aircraft repaired.

08/09-05-1941 V6026 82 Squadron: damaged in action; Sgt Wrightson and crew safe, aircraft repaired.

09-05-1941   L1283 1 AAS Mk I: undercarriage jammed, belly-landed at Manby, IoM, destroyed by fire; no injuries reported to Polish Pilot F/Lt J. Bak and crew.

09-05-1941   L1360 54 OTU Mk I: DBR in accident, NFD.

10-05-1941   V6376 18 Squadron: destroyed on ground by enemy bombing at Portreath airfield.

10-05-1941   T2330 and V6070 82 Squadron: destroyed on ground by enemy bombing at St Eval prior to ferry flight to Gibraltar.

10-05-1941   L1494 54 OTU Mk I: crashed after engine cut on night flight near Castleford, Yorks, destroyed by fire; Sgt B. Smeaton (solo pilot) killed.

11-05-1941   L1338 5 BGS Mk I: engine cut on take-off from Jurby, IoM, crashed and destroyed by fire; P/O Tanski and one of crew injured.

12-05-1941   L6807 604 Squadron Mk I-F: destroyed in air-raid at Middle Wallop.

12-05-1941   V5391 17 OTU: missing on low-flying exercise, presumed flew into sea; Sgt K. Belton, Sgt N. Macmillan, and Sgt W. Hunter killed and commemorated at Runnymede.

12/13-05-1941 V6335 18 Squadron: overshot landing at Oulton; Sgt Box and crew safe, aircraft repaired.

14-05-1941   K7142 5 BGS Mk I: engine cut on approach, belly-landed near Jurby, IoM, DBR; Sgt H. Woolley and crew uninjured.

15-05-1941   L1152 5 BGS Mk I: u/c jammed and belly-landed at Jurby, IoM, became 3146M; no reported injuries to Polish Pilot P/O J. Brogowski or crew.

17-05-1941   L1302 54 OTU Mk I: engine cut, second lost power, crashed on approach at Church Fenton, DBR; P/O N. Kinmouth uninjured.

17-05-1941   V5565 17 OTU: engine cut at low level, yawed and hit sea off Morecambe Bay; S/Ldr W. Selkirk injured but rescued, P/O T. Hodgson and Sgt P. Savage killed.

18-05-1941   L9413 139 Squadron: hit tree and Wingate House while low-flying over Army gun battery at Acle, Norfolk, destroyed by fire, crew P/O A. Saunders RCAF, Sgt R. Halbert, Sgt P. Gordon, and Cpl G. Acton all killed, two soldiers injured.

20-05-1941	V6264 139 Squadron: overshot when landing at Horsham St Faith; Sgt Jennings and crew unhurt, aircraft repaired.
21-05-1941	L9388 17 OTU: flew into high ground on night NavEx in bad visibility at Praka Beck Reservoir near Dalton, Lancs; Sgt L. Robertson-Pryor, P/O G. Wilson, and Sgt J. Harrison killed.
24-05-1941	T1826 105 Squadron: overshot and crashed when throttles jammed while landing at Hendon; W/Cdr H. I. Edwards and crew Sgt Ashplant and Sgt G. Quinn DFM uninjured, aircraft DBR.
24-05-1941	V5750 17 OTU: engine cut on approach and crash-landed at Upwood; Sgt A. Ward (solo pilot) uninjured.
24-05-1941	Z5948 17 OTU: overshot down-wind landing at Wyton, DBR; no injuries reported to P/O P. Ashby and crew.
27-05-1941	Z6078 2 OTU: became lost in bad weather, attempted force-landing, hit hedge at Sedgefield; Sgt A. Carter injured.
28-05-1941	V5421 500 Squadron: overshot landing at Southampton; Sgt Lacey and crew safe, aircraft repaired.
29-05-1941	L8377 54 OTU: collided with Defiant N1556, also from 54 OTU, near Church Fenton.
29-05-1941	L8546 17 OTU Mk I: crashed and DBR, no further details available.
31-05-1941	Z6266 5 BGS: engine cut on take-off, crashed through Jurby boundary, DBR; Polish Pilot P/O W. Rekslzyl (spelling unclear) slightly injured.
03-06-1941	Z6024 235 Squadron Mk IV-F: overshot landing at Dyce; S/Ldr Wincott and crew uninjured, aircraft DBR.
03-06-1941	Z7286 226 Squadron: collided with Z7287 (below) and crashed on take-off at Wattisham, destroyed by fire; P/O D. Hawkins (solo pilot) killed.
03-06-1941	Z7287 226 Squadron: collided with Z7286 (above) on take-off and crashed; crew W/Cdr Harrison (CO of 226 Squadron), Sgt Woodward, and Sgt Mathias injured.
03-06-1941	L1495 2 SAC Mk I: dived into ground when control lost on single-engine approach at Andover; P/O G. Douglas (solo pilot) killed. 2 SAC had become 6 (Coastal) OTU 31-05-1941.
04-06-1941	Z7283 226 Squadron: damaged landing at Ipswich; F/O Kercher and crew uninjured, aircraft repaired.
04-06-1941	N3629 107 Squadron: crashed taking-off at Great Massingham; Sgt Bristow and crew uninjured, aircraft repaired.
04-06-1941	R3681 110 Squadron: damaged when overshot landing at West Malling; Sgt Grimsey and crew uninjured, aircraft repaired.
04-06-1941	V6323 21 Squadron: crashed in sea off Kinnaird Head in mist on training sortie; crew Sgt E. AshSgt Ashwood, Sgt W. Meaker, and Sgt P. Sutton killed and commemorated on Runnymede Memorial.
05-06-1941	V5934 54 OTU: engine cut on take-off at Church Fenton, crashed and destroyed by fire; P/O R. Williamson injured.
06-06-1941	V5825 21 Squadron: damaged landing at Watton attempting overshoot; Sgt O'Neill and crew uninjured, aircraft repaired.
06-06-1941	V5646 86 Squadron: engine cut, crashed on take-off at North Coates; Sgt Boote and crew injured, aircraft repaired.
08-06-1941	T1795 139 Squadron: crashed into sea on bombing practice; crew Sgt C. Matthews, P/O G. Prosser, and Sgt G. Mason KIA and commemorated on Runnymede Memorial.
08-06-1941	Z7299 226 Squadron: crashed on landing at Ipswich; Sgt Snowball and crew uninjured, aircraft repaired.
10-06-1941	V5500 13 Group AA Co-Op Flight: engine failed on take-off, spun into ground on approach to Turnhouse; P/O Spary and Sgt Cembala killed.
10-06-1941	L1298 5 BGS Mk I: spun into ground at Lezayse, IoM, presumed due to engine failure; F/Lt J. Gawlikowski (Polish Major) and trainee WOp/Ags LAC E. Penney and LAC E. Williams killed.
11-06-1941	V5538 608 Squadron: crash-landed near Hartlepool; F/Lt Disney and crew uninjured, aircraft repaired.
12-06-1941	V6459 54 OTU: engine cut on night take-off at Church Fenton, wing hit ground; P/O J. Menary injured, aircraft DBR.
12-06-1941	Z5950 17 OTU: engine cut on take-off at Upwood, swung and ran into bomb dump; no injuries reported to Sgt P. Stocks or crew.
13-06-1941	L9305 110 Squadron: belly-landed at Wattisham; F/O Towson and crew unhurt, aircraft repaired.
16-06-1941	T1932 17 OTU: engine cut on take-off at Upwood, swung and u/c collapsed, DBR, Sgt L. Weston RNZAF (solo pilot) uninjured.
18-06-1941	V5820 17 OTU: engine cut on night NavEx, undershot landing and hit tree at Biggin Lane, Hunts; Sgt P. Rolt and Sgt G. Rake injured.
18-06-1941	L1274 Mk I with A&AEE: tyre burst on take-off at Boscombe Down, swung and DBR; F/Lt J. Bamber unhurt, aircraft SOC 15-11-1941.
19-06-1941	Z7282 226 Squadron: engine cut at low level, crashed into North Sea on training sortie; F/O M. Waddington, Sgt Thompson, and Sgt Palmer rescued and taken to Blyth.
20-06-1941	V6336 105 Squadron: engine cut on training sortie, spun into ground near Swanton Morley; crew Sgt D. Beacham, Sgt P. Griffiths, Sgt N. Appleby, and two ground-crew passengers, LAC R. Ballard and AC1 G. McFadzean, killed.
20-06-1941	V5813 2 (C) OTU: propellers hit sea on NavEx, lost height and ditched; no injuries reported to P/O A. Clusters and crew.

CHAPTER 19 – APPENDICES

20-06-1941	L9238 13 OTU: engine cut, ditched in Irish Sea; P/O T. Caston RCAF, Sgt L. Fisher RCAF and Sgt A. Leigh injured, rescued by trawler.
21-06-1941	N3595 2 (C) OTU: engine cut, undershot attempted belly-landing near Bridlington, Yorks; Sgt J. Stiff and crew injured.
21-06-1941	L9035 13 OTU: lost propeller and belly-landed near Wrexham, DBR; Sgt C. Digges RAAF and one crewman slightly injured.
23-06-1941	L1403 54 OTU Mk I: engine broke up, aircraft became uncontrollable and abandoned in air at Little Fenton, Yorks; no injuries to Sgt R. Denyer and crew.
23-06-1941	V5751 13 OTU: spiralled into ground, presumably following engine failure, at Ambrosden, Oxon; Sgt L. Taylor, Sgt L. Botterman, and Sgt W. Annetts killed.
24-06-1941	V5569 1403 Met Flt: tyre burst on take-off at Bircham Newton, swung and u/c collapsed; no injuries reported to Sgt R. Culley, Sgt P. Thimblebee, and F/Sgt Crowley.
25-06-1941	Z5814 6 OTU: tyre burst on take-off at Thruxton, swung and hit tractor, destroyed by fire; no injuries reported to P/O C. Thomas and crew.
25-06-1941	Z6251 54 OTU: short of fuel (fuel-cocks incorrectly set), engine cut, crashed on approach to Church Fenton; P/O M. Oxley (solo pilot) injured. (He was killed on 03-07-1941 in L1438 – qv.)
27-06-1941	T2436 13 Group Coms Flt: engine cut, side-slipped into ground on approach to Ayr; Polish Pilot P/O S. Sowinski killed.
28-06-1941	V5755 75 Wing: shot down by 'friendly' AA fire over Lydd, Kent, 'did not give recognition signals', aircraft exploded; Sgt W. Fenton, F/Sgt S. Peach, Sgt R. Barnett and F/Sgt B. Gardner killed.
28-06-1941	N3599 2 OTU: belly-landed at Catfoss, cause unknown, not repaired; no injuries reported to Sgt P. Cowan and crew.
29-06-1941	Z5803 13 OTU: engine cut, crash-landed at Marsh Gibbon, Oxon, DBR; no injuries to P/O H. Shuttleworth and crew.
30-06-1941	L1231 1 AGS Mk I: u/c collapsed while taxiing at Pembrey, DBR and became 3786M.
30-06-1941	Z6269 5 BGS: struck sea off Jurby, IoM, when low flying, one engine cut, then the other (ingestion of water), aircraft ditched; Sgt K. Browning (Pilot) seriously injured but rescued, trainee WOp/Ags LAC A. Day and LAC J. McKinley drowned.
30-06-1941	R3605 13 OTU: raised flaps prematurely on overshoot from Catfoss, sank back into ground, DBR.
30-06-1941	Z5982 608 Squadron, Coastal Command: FTR to Thornaby from sea search for dinghy; P/O Sir Iain W. MacRobert, F/O R. Keating, Sgt A. Best, and Sgt H. Hillwood presumed drowned, commemorated on Runnymede Memorial.
01-07-1941	L8689 A&AEE Mk I-F: gunnery trials aircraft, engine fire, crash-landed, hit wall near Burford, DBF; P/O F. Heapey injured, F/Lt Price and LAC Giles slightly injured.
01-07-1941	L6753 5 BGS Mk I: overshot landing at Jurby and DBR; no injuries reported to Sgt E. Tetnowski (Polish Pilot) and crew.
01-07-1942	P6896 56 OTU: hit HT cables, u/c retracted on landing at Valley.
01-07-1941	L4851 6 OTU: lost part of tail in dive, crashed near Glatton, Hunts; Sgt C. Vance, Sgt S. Harris and Sgt Telman killed.
03-07-1941	L1438 54 OTU Mk I: flew into ground 4 miles north of Church Fenton during night training, thought to have misjudged height; P/O M. Oxley killed.
03-07-1941	Z5870 12 Group AAC Flt: flew into hill in mist at Lee Farm, Edale, Derbys; Sgt M. Plotek, AC2 W. Cotton, AC1 W. Kidd and AC2 R. Place killed.
04-07-1941	T2078 248 Squadron: flew into ground in bad visibility near Great Massingham trying to locate flare-path, destroyed by fire; crew injured, Sgt Easton, Sgt Ferguson, and Sgt G. Carter, who died of his injuries.
04-07-1941	V6426 82 Squadron: collided with V6070 en route to St Eval prior to ferry flight to Malta; P/O G. Bartlett (Pilot) injured but baled out, P/O N. Cooper (Obs), Sgt O. Hall, and Sgt D. Hughes (WOp/Ags) killed, V6070 believed landed safely.
07-07-1941	V5532 17 OTU: overshot night landing at Upwood, hit building; Sgt G. Smith and Sgt J. Tippett DFM slightly injured, aircraft DBR.
08-07-1941	L1238 5 BGS Mk I: engine cut, ditched off Point of Ayre, IoM; P/O W. Kolkowski (Polish Pilot) injured, crew rescued.
08-07-1941	Z6038 500 Squadron: overshot landing and hit gun emplacement at Desford, destroyed by fire; Sgt J. Gray and Sgt A. Glide killed.
09-07-1941	L9021 6 OTU: overshot landing at Andover and hit boundary; no injuries recorded.
10-07-1941	L9211 13 OTU: overshot landing at Bicester, swung to avoid bomb-dump, undercarriage collapsed, destroyed by fire; no injuries reported to Sgt A. Dick and crew.
12-07-1941	V6524 82 Squadron: control lost in fog bank in practice low-level formation flight over sea; crew Sgt J. Hallam RCAF, Sgt H. Hastings, and Sgt W. Hiscock killed.
12-07-1941	Z5813 6 OTU: tyre burst on take-off at Brize Norton, undercarriage collapsed.
12-07-1941	Z6360 17 OTU: spun in and destroyed by fire at Old Halves, Cambs, cause not known; Sgt R. Smith, P/O R. Boon, and Sgt J. Tinker killed.
12-07-1941	T2123 60 OTU: FTR from photo exercise over sea, no trace found; Sgt I. Price, Sgt J. Richards and Sgt W. Dickins missing presumed killed.

THE BRISTOL BLENHEIM

14-07-1941	T1958 1 AAS: tyre burst on take-off at Manby, u/c collapsed on landing, not repaired and struck off charge 17-08-1942.
15-07-1941	V5852 1403 Met Flt: lost without trace; Sgt R. Culley, Sgt F. Elliott, and Sgt L. Anderson killed, Sgt Culley buried in Tonder Cemetery, his crew commemorated at Runnymede.
15-07-1941	L6768 13 OTU: undershot night approach at Hinton-in-the-Hedges and struck trees; Sgt F. Trevillo (solo pilot) seriously injured, aircraft DBR.
16-07-1941	L6767 13 OTU: lost height on overshoot at Bicester, hit trees and crashed; Sgt F. Turner RCAF killed, aircraft DBR.
17-07-1941	R3805 13 OTU: both engines cut in Finmere circuit, stalled and spun in at Shelswell Park; Sgt D. Calderone RCAF (Pilot) and Sgt G. Davies (Obs) killed, Sgt Griffiths (WOp/Ag) seriously injured.
17-07-1941	P4832, Special Duties Flight: on radar calibration flight from Christchurch, reported sighting balloon, believed to have attacked it, but came down in sea 25 miles off Dorset coast; F/Lt D. Rayment AFC and Sgt R. Sadler seen sitting on sinking aircraft but not found. (F/Lt Rayment badly damaged a Ju.88 on 2-9-1940 in this Mk IV-F, and shot one down on 19-9-1940 in SD Flt Hurricane L1562; S/Ldr P. Meagher also shot one down on 2-9-1940 in L1562.)
18-07-1941	K7090 54 OTU Mk I: dived into ground at night, control lost orbiting beacon near Church Fenton; Sgt C. Neighbour RNZAF (on first night solo) killed.
18-07-1941	L1449 54 OTU Mk I: descended in cloud on searchlight homing exercise, crashed into Cockayne Ridge, Cleveland Hills; P/O E. Woodhead injured.
18-07-1941	L8729 54 OTU: vectored by mistake into high ground on searchlight homing exercise at Chop Gate, Cleveland Hills, in bad visibility; P/O A. McMurtrie RNZAF killed, buried in Kirby Wharfe.
19-07-1941	Z7371 105 Squadron: crashed on take-off from Swanton Morley on training flight; Sgt W. Hinds injured, aircraft destroyed by fire.
19-07-1941	T2120 254 Squadron: hit radio mast and building at Aldergrove in low pass, destroyed by fire; crew P/O W. King, Sgt P. Neale, and Sgt R. Lea, plus six female NAAFI workers and two airmen killed, nine airmen and four other female NAAFI workers seriously injured.
20-07-1941	V6069 139 Squadron: stalled after take-off from Horsham on training flight due to wrong trim setting; Sgt J. Evans (Pilot) killed.
20-07-1941	T2337 54 OTU: crashed avoiding Oxford while landing on wrong runway at Church Fenton (see the accompanying picture).
22-07-1941	L8876 13 OTU: crashed, cause unknown, SOC 1-8-1941.
22-07-1941	L9412 17 OTU: failed to return from night NavEx over North Sea, presumed to have ditched; Sgt C. Andrews, P/O R. Franklin, and Sgt L. Palmer killed and commemorated on Runnymede Memorial.
23-07-1941	V5723 9 AOS: engine cut on take-off at Penrhos, collided with boundary and DBR; F/Sgt J. Coleman (Pilot), LAC M. Oughton and LAC G. Papworth (both Trainee Obs) died of injuries.
25-07-1941	L6800 17 OTU Mk I: crashed on landing at Upwood, Sgt A. Johnson (solo pilot) killed.
25-07-1941	V5393 500 Squadron: undercarriage retracted too soon on take-off from Docking, hit ground, engine seized, crash-landed near Burnham Market, Norfolk; Sgt P. Cunningham safe.
27-07-1941	Z6180 2 (C) OTU: engine cut, undershot forced-landing near Catfoss; Sgt P. Ambroes (Belgian Pilot) and one crewman injured.
28-07-1941	P6954 21 Squadron: collided with L1342 (below) on take-off from Swanton Morley for training; P/O M. Forster (Pilot) and F/Sgt E. Sturgeon (Obs) killed, F/Sgt J. Rennie (WOp/Ag) injured.
28-07-1941	L1342 88 Squadron Mk I: collided with P6954 (above) on take-off from Swanton Morley on formation training sortie; S/Ldr P. Barr (Pilot) and F/Sgt H. Bennett (Obs) injured.
30-07-1941	Z7646 18 MU: hit hill in mist near Innerleithen, Peeblesshire; P/O E. Henson (solo pilot) killed.
31-07-1941	Z6048 500 Squadron: hit tree on night approach from NavEx at Langham, DBR; no injuries reported to P/O F. Tiller and crew.
31-07-1941	L6680 13 OTU Mk I: collided with Wellington while landing at Chipping Warden; Sgt Graham (solo pilot) slightly injured, aircraft DBR.

T2337 of 54 OTU collided with an Oxford (foreground) 30 feet over the runway intersection at Church Fenton on 20 July 1941. Amazingly, no injuries were reported to either crew.

Chapter 20

Autumn and winter 1941

The hard-pressed UK-based Blenheim squadrons felt the heat of that stressful summer throughout August and September, for not until October and November did the pace lessen and the pressure upon them reduce somewhat. Moreover, fewer squadrons were available to shoulder the burden in the UK as more were rotated to Malta and the Middle and Far East, there too to suffer serious losses, as will be described later. The number of aircraft left in 2 Group that were serviceable and ready for operations dwindled, despite the unceasing efforts of the ground-crews, to an average of only 60 by the late summer of 1941, once even dropping as low as a mere 48 – a far cry from the 212 available in September 1940.

The disposition of the remaining UK-based Blenheim squadrons, as listed in the previous chapter, was maintained. August witnessed the most spectacular of all Blenheim operations, and several very costly attacks on ports, but the Blenheim squadrons – bled almost dry – were finally relieved from anti-shipping duties at the end of October, the high level of casualties having become insupportable. Bad weather in October allowed operations on only 16 days, and by November the weather had deteriorated sufficiently to cause a further reduction in Blenheim activity; 'Circus' operations were suspended that month and not resumed until the spring of 1942. But there was a nasty sting in the tail of the year, as we will see. Those crews that did survive the dreadful depredations suffered by the Blenheim squadrons in 1941 will remember that long, cruel summer and autumn for the rest of their lives.

Cologne power stations raid

The daylight raid on Bremen, described in the previous chapter, had certainly been daring and spectacular – and had received lavish and morale-boosting coverage in the press and on the radio – but only eight Blenheims had actually bombed Bremen. The RAF planners wanted to encourage the Germans to bring fighter units back from the Russian front, so they needed to cause serious damage to a significant target. Therefore Operation 77 was planned on a far greater scale and set for 12 August. An impressively large force of 54 Blenheims was to be sent on a major daylight raid all the way to the environs of Cologne where the important Knapsack and Quadrath electricity power stations, then the largest steam generators in Europe, supplied power to the Ruhr armament industry. The operation was especially dangerous due not only to the unprecedented depth of penetration to an important target in mainland Germany but also because the unwieldy formation – highly visible without the protection of darkness – could be escorted by the RAF's longest-range fighters (the Westland Whirlwinds of 263 Squadron) only to a point just beyond the enemy-held Belgian coast. The 2 Group crews realised that 'something really big' was coming up as they had been taken off the anti-shipping sweeps and were training hard at very low levels in both formation flying and bombing – indeed, the first ten days of August saw the loss of seven Blenheims during this intensive training (see Appendix 1).

To the stunned crews at briefing the raid appeared to be almost suicidal, for they could see that it would involve an unescorted flight of some 150 miles in broad daylight over German territory to bomb well-defended power stations, and they realised that after the attack the widely dispersed formations would be even more vulnerable while making their way back to the coast, hoping to meet fresh escorts there. The bombers, each carrying two

Opposite: Blenheim ground crews worked hard to turn round their aircraft quickly.

The attack on Quadrath/Fortuna power station on 12 August 1941.

356 THE BRISTOL BLENHEIM

The simultaneous attack on Knapsack power station, showing flak bursts. RT-V, banking away from the target, was flown by Sgt Pilot Ivor Broom. See the photograph of this aircraft and crew on page 366.

500lb GP bombs and flying in low-level formation for 4 hours at some 180mph, would be approaching the limit of their range – and for half of that time the lightly armed Blenheims would be exposed to attack by enemy fighters or flak. In an attempt to reduce the odds stacked so overwhelmingly against the attackers, several carefully timed diversions, intended to distract and confuse the defenders, were arranged: a fighter escort successfully guarded six Blenheims of 226 Squadron, which bombed Le Trait shipyard in a 'Circus' operation; six Hampdens were escorted on another 'Circus' to bomb St Omer; and yet another six were similarly escorted to Gosnay. Hampdens had to be used for two of these three diversions as all the 62 serviceable Blenheims in 2 Group were already committed. In addition, two Fortresses from 90 Squadron were sent at high altitude to bomb Cologne at Zero Hour, and one was sent to bomb Emden and one to De Kooy airfield. All 22 of the bombers carrying out these diversionary raids returned safely, one Fortress having aborted. 226 Squadron also put up two Blenheims to act as navigation leaders to make sure that the six Spitfire squadrons were in the correct position at Walsoorden, near Flushing, at the right time (for the fighters could only wait there for 3 minutes due to fuel considerations) to provide cover for the withdrawing bombers during the homeward crossing of the North Sea.

For the Cologne raid the main force of 54 Blenheims was to split into two near the prominent Quadrath and Knapsack power stations, 18 bombing the former and 36 the latter. Force I to Quadrath, three boxes of six aircraft, was led by W/Cdr Kercher with nine aircraft each from 21 Squadron at Watton and 82 Squadron at Bodney; while the larger Force II to Knapsack, six boxes of six aircraft, was led by W/Cdr Nicol, with 36 aircraft drawn from 18, 107, 114 and 139 Squadrons at Horsham St Faith, Great Massingham, West Raynham and Oulton respectively. W/Cdr Nicol was the newly appointed CO of 114 Squadron, and this was his first Blenheim operation, but his Observer – on whose shoulders the heaviest responsibility lay – was F/Lt Tommy Baker DFM, said to be the best Navigator in the Group. The 54 Blenheims took off from 0950 hours, formed up at 100 feet, and met their fighter escort (pre-positioned at Martlesham Heath) over the coast at Orfordness at 1000 hours as planned. Approaching the Scheldt estuary the escorting fighters pulled ahead and climbed to 1,000 feet, but all too soon had to turn for home. The Blenheims dropped to 50 feet or less and hedge-hopped south-eastwards – they soon knew they were over German territory when workers in the fields stopped waving and started trying to hide, run away, or drop flat on their faces! On the way to the target, two of the Blenheims were shot down and one struck power cables, lost its tail and crashed, and V6197, a 114 Squadron aircraft, aborted, so 50 aircraft bombed and 100 of the 500lb GP bombs struck the power-generating complexes. Flak in the target area was intense and two more Blenheims were shot down there, and a further five became casualties on the way home – a total of 10 of the 53 bombers – and both the 226 Squadron aircraft of the navigation leaders were shot down into the sea. So 12 of the 55 Blenheims that took a direct part in the operation failed to return, losses of a crippling 22 per cent (see Appendix 2). Six Spitfires were also lost. From the main force, 18 and 139 Squadrons each lost three aircraft, 21 Squadron two, and 82 and 114 one each, and many others, including all of 107's aircraft, received flak damage. The cost of this operation was even higher if the seven aircraft lost while training for it are taken into account. However, these relatively heavy losses were played down in the euphoric press and BBC coverage of the raid. 2 Group HQ considered that it had 'got off' very lightly, but was unwilling to push its luck by repeating such a deep-penetration attack. The survivors were on a high, delighted still to be alive, and exhilarated by the adrenaline-induced 'buzz' of completing such a thrilling and apparently successful operation, so the bars in the crew messes, and in the pubs around the bases, were busy that night.

Heligoland submarine pens and Rotterdam harbour raids

Another daylight raid on Germany, but on a far smaller scale, was set for 24 August to the strongly defended port of Bremerhaven with the specific target of the German liner *Europa*, reportedly berthed there. Six Blenheims of 82 Squadron were led by their newly appointed CO, W/Cdr Francis Lascelles DFC, a cousin of the then Queen, now HM The Queen Mother. However, he abandoned the raid in conditions of excellent visibility well short of the German coast, as in his – perfectly reasonable – judgement (echoing that of W/Cdr Petley the previous month) the fact that they had been spotted by shipping together with the complete lack of cloud cover provided sufficient reason, for he too did not want to lead 82 Squadron into a repeat of the massacre at Aalborg a year earlier. The 'grapevine' at the squadrons reported that this failure to 'press on regardless' had frustrated and annoyed AVM Stevenson and some senior staff officers at 2 Group HQ. In any event Lascelles was ordered to take the same crews to attack the heavily defended submarine pens on the island of Heligoland on the 26th. It appeared to the crews that they were being sent on this virtually suicidal raid to atone for turning back from Bremerhaven, and they felt that the anticipated sacrifice was pointless for they knew that the small bomb-loads of the Blenheims were most unlikely to cause any serious damage to the substantial concrete pens – even if they survived long enough to score any direct hits on them. Lascelles in T2165 dutifully took his two 'vics' from Bodney and headed out over the North Sea, but P/O Bartlett had engine troubles in T2162 so had to return, and P/O Robinson in V6454 lost touch with the formation in the haze as they made landfall at the wrong island (Nuewerk) and he bombed a small ship on his way home. The rest of the formation were all shot down by fighters and the crews were all killed (see Appendix 2). The submarine pens were untouched. This raid is not mentioned in either of the Official Histories, nor in Michael Bowyer's excellent *2 Group RAF – a Complete History* or in *Bomber Command War Diaries*.

Despite the tragic (and in my view needless) loss of the 82 Squadron aircraft on the 26th, another 'daylight spectacular' raid was mounted on 28 August, when Rotterdam harbour was once again the target. The raid was to be a repeat of that of 16 July, also with 36 Blenheims, but two lessons had been learned – first, two squadrons of Spitfires would escort them to the target area to keep the Messerschmitts at bay, and second, each aircraft would be armed with two of the more effective 500lb bombs instead of the four 250lb bombs that had produced such disappointing results on the previous Rotterdam raid. This time any direct hits scored would have a much higher chance of sinking a ship, not just causing repairable damage. But the operation ran into various troubles from the outset. There was confusion over the timings of the rendezvous with the fighter escort, and the Blenheims were kept waiting for 10 minutes at the take-off point at 1400, then were told they were late. An engine of Z7299, Sgt O'Connell's 226 Squadron aircraft, cut on take-off, and the fully laden Blenheim, caught the slipstream of the leader, crashed and cart-wheeled in flames – the crew were very lucky to be thrown out uninjured. Then two 110 Squadron aircraft, including that of the leader, had mechanical troubles and had to return to base, so all the aircraft were recalled. The operation was partially reinstated and half of the original force was sent off again at 1730 hours, and 17 Blenheims of 88, 21 and 226 Squadrons (the latter one short due to the earlier take-off crash) once more set forth. Their landfall was too near the Hook of Holland and they met fierce AA fire, and two were shot down immediately, including the inexperienced leader of the formation, S/Ldr Richard Shuttleworth of 21 Squadron in Z7447. The remaining 15 were seen to be following the tactics of the earlier raid. The Rotterdam defences were alerted and put up a murderous hail of fire that brought down three more Blenheims in the harbour area. However, the bombers scored hits on three quite large ships, which sank at their moorings (the *Zuiderdam* and her sister ship *Westerdam*, both more than 12,000 tons, and the *Oranjefontein* of 10,600 tons), and three smaller vessels were damaged. Two of the 19 Squadron Spitfire escorts were brought down by the intense flak, unfortunately those of the squadron's CO, S/Ldr Lawson, and his deputy, F/Lt Cunningham. As the Blenheims fled from the scene the Messerschmitts of VI./JG 53 pounced and Lt Hans Muller shot down two more, and a comrade downed Sgt Savage's 152 Squadron fighter. The ten surviving Blenheims limped back to their bases, several badly shot up and with wounded crewmen on board. It was thought that S/Ldr Lawson might be in his dinghy off Rotterdam, and next morning 11 Spitfires of 19

This page: Blenheims flying low towards, and leaving, Rotterdam harbour on 16 July the single aircraft is V6267 of W/Cdr 'Tim' Partridge, leader of the second wave, who was shot down and killed moments later.
Facing page: Blenheims leaving the target area on 28 August, one flying over a cargo ship, and the same ship lying on its side later.

THE BRISTOL BLENHEIM

Squadron set out to search for their CO, but in vain, and they tangled with some Me.110s of II./ZG 76, rather surprisingly losing four of their number – so 19 Squadron had lost half of its front line in less than 24 hours. All in all, the second Rotterdam raid had cost seven Blenheims there and one in the UK, as well as seven Spitfires, with 22 brave young men killed, four wounded, and six more captured (see Appendix 3).

These events moved Prime Minister Winston Churchill to issue one of his 'Action This Day' memos on 29 August to ACM Portal, Chief of the Air Staff:

> 'The loss of seven Blenheims out of 17 in the daylight attack on merchant shipping and docks at Rotterdam is most severe. Such losses might be accepted in attacking the *Scharnhorst*, *Gneisenau* or *Tirpitz*, or a south-bound Tripoli convoy, because, apart from the damage done, a first-class strategic object is served. But they seem disproportionate to an attack on merchant shipping not engaged in vital supply work. The losses in our bombers have been very heavy this month, and Bomber Command is not expanding as was hoped. While I greatly admire the bravery of the pilots, I do not want them pressed too hard. Easier targets giving a high damage return compared with casualties may more often be selected.
>
> 'Let me have a return showing all bombers written off in August for any cause, including crashes on landing, and also the number of bombers received from MAP [Ministry of Aircraft Production] and the number manufactured and imported.'

The following day Churchill responded somewhat ambivalently to the original minute from the VCAS describing the attack on Rotterdam and giving details of the losses – the minute that resulted in the memo quoted above. The reply revealed that not only was he most concerned about the heavy losses but also deeply impressed by the exemplary bravery of the Blenheim crews. It also demonstrates his appreciation of military history in that he compared them directly with the courageous cavalry commanded by the Earl of Cardigan in the Crimea War – brave men decimated during a calamitous and futile charge against insurmountable odds 'into the valley of death': 'The devotion and gallantry of the attacks on Rotterdam and other objectives are beyond all praise. The Charge of the Light Brigade at Balaclava is eclipsed in brightness by these almost daily deeds of fame.' He added a note asking the VCAS to 'Tell the Squadrons and publish if you think well'. Clearly Churchill liked this telling phraseology for he had employed it in June when addressing Blenheim crews gathered in a hangar at Swanton Morley, and also used it later in the House of Commons.

Anti-shipping operations

Both between and following these heavily publicised large-scale daylight raids on power stations and ports, the daily grind of anti-shipping sweeps and attacks continued relentlessly, and with it the toll of losses also mounted remorselessly (see Appendix 2). August 1941 started badly, for two out of three fighter-escorted Blenheims of 107 Squadron on an unproductive Channel Stop sortie were shot down, as were two of six from 226 Squadron attacking ships off Gravelines on the 10th, although this time three of the Blenheims claimed direct hits on vessels. 114 Squadron lost a section of three aircraft on the 19th, including its CO, W/Cdr James Nicol DSO, who had led the Cologne power stations raid just a week earlier – there was but one survivor. The 26th was another black day, for seven Blenheims were shot down (including the first loss to 88 Squadron, which had just become operational in 2 Group), and there were no survivors, as all the 21 crewmen involved were killed in action, although two ships were claimed sunk. All in all August was a distressing month for 2 Group, for of the 77 Blenheims that attacked ships, no fewer than 23 were lost – 30 per cent casualties – and 13 more were lost on other daylight operations. Pierse, the AOC of Bomber Command, with extreme and mounting concern at these losses, had for some time been pressing for 'Hurri-bombers' to carry out shipping attacks (because they presented a smaller and more agile target

Deadly dangerous low-level 'Channel Stop' attacks on shipping continued without respite until October when heavy casualties caused their suspension.

to the flak gunners, and could look after themselves far better against enemy fighters, as had been demonstrated in the Western Desert), but it was ruled that all Hurricanes would stay in Fighter Command. However, it was agreed that, from 27 July, six Hurricane Mk IIBs armed with 12 machine-guns each, and six Mk IICs with 20mm cannons, would go in just ahead of each section of Blenheims on shipping attacks to engage the flak ships, and a dozen Spitfires would provide high cover from the Me.109s. Spitfires would also operate 'Jim Crow' patrols to try and locate convoys rather than relying solely on shipping sweeps by the Blenheims. To co-ordinate this welcome assistance to the Blenheims on Channel Stop duties, W/Cdr L. Atkinson DSO DFC was appointed Bomber Controller with 11 Group Fighter Command. A difference of opinion with the AOC of Coastal Command concerning the areas that would be the responsibility of each Command was resolved in July – Bomber Command was to cover from Cherbourg to Texel (the Eastern boundary soon being extended to Wilhelmshaven), while Coastal Command was to cover all other areas around the British Isles.

Even the improved support from RAF fighters in strafing the flak ships and fending off the Messerschmitts was insufficient to prevent losses, for another black day for 2 Group was experienced on 15 October when seven more Blenheims were shot down from 24 sent out on anti-shipping sorties – a disastrous 30 per cent overall – and once more there was not a single survivor and another 21 brave men paid the ultimate price. Two were shot down by flak on an escorted raid by 12 Blenheims on shipping in Le Havre harbour, probably due to the long straight-in approach at 8,000 feet by W/Cdr Butler of 226 Squadron, but hits were claimed on a tanker and a 10,000-ton merchant ship. That same day no fewer than five out of 12 aircraft from 114 and 139 Squadrons – a calamitous 42 per cent – were lost while attacking shipping off the Frisian Islands. The 21st saw three more shot down, another on the 26th, and on the 27th two out of six from 114 Squadron were shot down off the Dutch coast, these losses claiming the lives of every single crewman of the 13 Blenheims involved. The minimal number of the shot-down crews who escaped with their lives that dreadful summer is shown by taking the example of the 27 Blenheims of 110 and 114 Squadrons that failed to return from anti-shipping operations: only one of the 81 airmen involved survived, all the remainder being tragically killed in action. Clearly such losses

A section of 107 Squadron Blenheims head for the Continent on 21 August 1941.

V6445 of 82 Squadron caught the mast of the ship it was attacking on 20 August, but flew back to base, striking trees on the approach and being Damaged Beyond Repair.

Z7427 of 88 Squadron on the final approach to Swanton Morley in August 1941 after an anti-shipping sortie.

were prohibitive, and by the end of the month the 2 Group Blenheims were relieved of their Channel Stop role and finally of all anti-shipping duties – the last was carried out by four aircraft off the coast of Norway on 2 November. In all, 590 ships had been attacked, with 207 claimed as sunk or badly damaged since 14 March. An Admiralty Committee analysed the claims and reduced them to 101, but post-war research halves even that to 50, for only 29 were sunk and 21 seriously damaged. 2 Group alone lost 139 Blenheims on low-level attacks on shipping at sea or in harbour during this period, and Coastal Command lost another 70, as well as many more aircraft in each Command being so badly damaged that they never flew again. Each ship sunk had cost more than 20 casualties – nearly all fatalities – lives of very brave, highly skilled and expensively trained aircrew that the RAF could ill afford to lose, particularly as their hard-earned experience and undoubted leadership qualities were sorely needed in the expanding bomber force.

Continuing daylight raids

Apart from these costly anti-shipping activities, the 'Circus' and 'Ramrod' fighter-escorted operations continued throughout 1941, and the losses incurred on them were a further steady drain on the few remaining Blenheim squadrons (see Appendix 5). Targets, most of which were attacked several times, included airfields at St Omer, Lannion, Marquise and Morlaix; power stations at Lille, Mazingarbe, Gosnay, Ostend, Rouen, Yainville, Bethune, Chocques and Comines; steel-works at Ijmuiden, Hazebrouck and Lille; chemical woks at Chocques, Mazingarbe and Arques; shipyards and docks at Cherbourg, Le Trait, Ostend, Boulogne and Le Havre; and railway yards at Amiens and Hazebrouck. Tactics were varied, and simultaneous 'Circus' raids were mounted on different targets, or mounted in 'waves' at intervals on the same target. AVM Leigh-Mallory of 11 Group expressed dissatisfaction with the performance of the Blenheims in the 'Circus' role; AVM Stevenson

R3843 and crew of 18 Squadron who dropped a spare 'tin leg' for Douglas Bader: Sgt John Nickleson, Sgt Walter Meadows and Sgt John Pearson – they were Killed in Action a month later, 20 September 1941.

of 2 Group retaliated by criticising the protection afforded to the Blenheims, and relations between Fighter and Bomber Commands became somewhat strained. Leigh-Mallory wanted 5 per cent of the entire Heavy Bomber force to participate in 'Circus' operations, but the CAS, ACM Sir Charles Portal, was attempting to build up the Heavy Bomber force in the face of growing night-time losses and ruled against this demand. So, once more, wartime necessity dictated that the Blenheim squadrons would continue to be employed in tasks for which they were not suited, and that they would continue to suffer heavy casualties.

As a change from bombs and bullets, an unusual load was delivered by 18-year-old Sgt Nickleson from R3843, a Blenheim of 18 Squadron on 'Circus' raid No 78 to Marquise airfield on 18 August, when he dropped a wooden box by parachute on to the German fighter airfield of St Omer. The box contained a spare artificial leg for W/Cdr Douglas Bader, who had been captured a few days earlier after he abandoned his Spitfire by parachute leaving one of his 'tin legs' trapped in the cockpit.

Good weather was essential to co-ordinate successfully the large formations of aircraft involved in complicated 'Circus' operations, and this commodity became increasingly scarce, so that in November only two 'Circus' operations could be mounted – to Gosnay power station on the 8th and Morlaix airfield on the 25th. They were then suspended until the new year when they would be resumed with the more effective Douglas Bostons instead of the Blenheims acting as the bait for the Luftwaffe fighters. Blenheims had been used for this purpose since the beginning in over 110 of these 'Circus' operations, but the damage caused by the bombing in the course of them was usually quite slight, although there were several successes, such as on 12 October when 24 Blenheims made an effective attack on Boulogne harbour. Although Fighter Command made greatly exaggerated claims, in fact it came off much the worse in the aerial battles that were the main purpose of the 'Circus' operations. In addition, the strategic objective of drawing German forces away from the Russian front failed completely, as more than 60 per cent of the Luftwaffe remained deployed on the Russian front and the other 40 per cent was spread thinly over the great distance from northern Norway to Sicily.

The 'Circus' of 9 November saw 12 Blenheims escorted by 14 squadrons of fighters bomb a power station and chemical works at Gosnay near Bethune.

Return to night operations

With the withdrawal of the Blenheims from Channel Stop duties and other anti-shipping sweeps and strikes, and the suspension of 'Circus' operations, Bomber Command did not know how to employ usefully the remaining Blenheim squadrons. In seven harrowing months Sir Richard Pierse, the AOC, had changed his view that anti-shipping operations were 'an economical and profitable use for the light bomber force' to one of thankful relief when they were released from these onerous duties. The Blenheims were now ordered to revert to nuisance bombing sorties at night. For example, on the night of 7/8 December 23 Blenheims were sent to bomb Ostend; one was lost, while the main bomber force went – without success – to Aachen. In addition Blenheim squadrons were told to recommence the night intruder operations against enemy airfields that they had initiated exactly a year earlier, and losses on night operations resumed (see Appendix 6). On 17 December, in a move welcomed by the 2 Group crews, AVM A. Lees replaced AVM D. Stevenson as AOC.

The first 'Combined Operation'

The 'sting in the tail' of 1941 for the Blenheims was their participation in Operation Archery, the first of the wartime 'Combined Operations'. This was a seaborne raid on 27 December on the German-occupied Norwegian island of Vaagso by troops of the recently formed British Commandos in a force working closely with units of the Royal Navy and the Royal Air Force. Once again Blenheims were to pioneer the aerial tactics in this new form of warfare. Thirteen aircraft from 114 Squadron were led from Lossiemouth by W/Cdr Jenkins, with timing accurate to the minute, to attack Herdla airfield and prevent the Me.109s based there from interfering with the landings. This they accomplished successfully, a remarkable feat by F/Lt Paul Brancker, the lead Navigator, after a 300-mile over-water low-level flight in mid-winter, navigating by dead reckoning only. Unfortunately two Blenheims collided in the confusion just after bombing and both the crews were killed (see Appendix 7). One 109 was destroyed and several damaged – Jenkins received the DSO and Brancker the DFC for this operation. Six aircraft from 110 Squadron, sent slightly earlier to attack shipping off Stavanger in an attempt to draw the German fighters away, had a fraught day. One returned early with engine trouble, while another struck the surface of the sea on the run-in and bent a propeller right back; the pilot jettisoned his bombs and managed to stagger back to base. The remaining four were shot down, two by flak and two by 109s – not one member of the four crews survived (see Appendix 7). Coastal Command Blenheim Mk IV-Fs of 404 Squadron, with RCAF crews, provided long-range fighter cover from Wick – their CO, W/Cdr P. Woodruff in Z5753, had shot down a Ju.88 on 18 December – and his Squadron claimed one 109 on the Vaagso raid; four Beaufighters from Sumburgh were also on hand. Bomber Command also sent ten Hampdens of 50 Squadron, seven of them to lay a smoke-screen off Vaagso, but two were shot down and it was decided that they were too slow for this work. Blenheims were soon adapted to take over this task, using the experience gained when they were modified, and the crews trained, to dispense poison gas during the anti-invasion scare of 1940. The raid led to the Germans deploying more forces to garrison Norway, with more fighters to defend them, at a time when they needed all the strength they could muster on the Russian front.

Global war

December 1941 saw the overall strategic position change irrevocably when Hitler rashly declared war upon the United States following the Japanese attack on the major American base at Pearl Harbor on the 7th. The Germans were now pitted against the

The successful attack on Herdla aerodrome, timed to the minute – the Me.109 taking off crashed into a crater on the snow-covered wooden runway. The lower views are from rear-facing cameras as Blenheims of 114 Squadron left the target.

greatest industrial power in the world as well as the vast Soviet Union – vast not only in terms of territory but also in reserves of manpower and production capacity, as the Wehrmacht soon found to its cost. Great Britain had emerged 'bloody but unbowed' from the two desperate years when she (and her then Empire) had stood alone in defiance of the military might of Germany and Italy – and as we have seen Blenheims played a pivotal part in this defiance. Now she was destined to act as an increasingly junior partner in the Allied Forces fighting the Axis Powers during the widening conflict, as the Russians fought the greatest land battles and the Americans bore the brunt of the fighting in the Pacific. Although Blenheims were destined to play an increasingly diminishing part in operations in Northern Europe, they were thrust right into the front line in the Middle East, as they would be too in the Far East, as the struggle developed into a full-scale World War.

Bomber Command in the balance

Confidence in Bomber Command, and in the AOC, AM Sir Richard Pierse, had been shaken by the Butt Report of August, which, by analysing target photographs, concluded that (on moonless nights) 19 out of 20 aircraft dropped their bombs more than 5 miles from the target. The only photographs studied were those taken by crews who claimed to have bombed the target, and a third of aircraft dispatched did not even claim to have located the target area; in other words, for every 30 bombers sent only one bombed within a 10-mile-diameter circle centred on the target. Confidence was further reduced by the complete failure of the 'maximum effort' by the entire force of 392 aircraft on the night of 7/8 November, when negligible damage to the targets was caused. Thirty-seven aircraft were lost, mainly from a force of 169 bombers dispatched to Berlin, with 75 to Cologne and 55 to Mannheim, in the face of an adverse weather forecast of icing conditions, hail and strong winds – a forecast so unfavourable that Slessor, AOC of 5 Group, insisted on sending his Hampdens to Cologne rather than Berlin. Bomber Command crews suffered 188 casualties, with 108 killed, 76 captured and four injured; in addition, five evaded capture and six were rescued from their dinghy. By contrast, only 11 German civilians were killed and 44 injured in Berlin, with five killed and five injured in Cologne, but none at all in Mannheim. Since July 1941 the War Cabinet had seen mounting losses from the Blenheim day bombers, and now the losses of the night bombers were also mounting in the face of improved defences, but they had not seen commensurate results – certainly not sufficiently worthwhile to justify the casualties. Once more the whole future of Bomber Command hung in the balance as it was subject to critical scrutiny by the Air Staff and debate within the doubting War Cabinet.

The CAS, Sir Charles Portal, saved it by using reasoned argument to persuade Churchill (and therefore the War Cabinet) to continue the policy of strategic bombing, although he no longer pressed the case for 4,000 Heavy Bombers that he had put forward the previous September. Instead, he was ordered to conserve the Command's forces throughout the winter and prepare for a renewal of the offensive in the coming spring with hoped-for improvements from better equipment, both with new types of aircraft and with new navigational aids such as 'Gee'. The unfortunate Pierse was ordered to clear his desk in the first week of the New Year – he was sent to take over as AOC-in-C in India and was appalled at the even greater deficiencies and difficulties he discovered there on taking up his post on 5 March 1942, for once more Blenheims formed the bulk of the available bomber force, as will be described later in the chapters on the Far East.

The year 1941 had been very grim for the UK Blenheim squadrons, for operational losses had been even heavier than before as a proportion of the much lower number of aircraft available, and the non-operational losses had mounted steadily as more and more Blenheims were employed in the support and advanced training roles. This change of role, which would continue even more markedly in the New Year, can best be appreciated by looking through the losses in the Appendices at the end of this chapter. They make sobering reading indeed, for they bring home just how many Blenheims were lost in the UK during 1941 and 1942 – and, far more importantly, just how many lives were lost.

Appendix 1

Blenheim losses on the Cologne power stations raid of 12 August 1941

Aircraft are all Mk IVs.

12-08-1941   V6423 18 Squadron: failed to return (FTR); crashed at Diest, Belgium; F/O G. Hill, P/O R. Chadwick, and Sgt L. Parrish captured and became PoWs. P/O Chadwick, injured in crash, later repatriated.

12-08-1941   V6437 18 Squadron: FTR; hit HT cables near Dutch coast and crashed into sea; P/O M. Walkden, P/O B. Matthews, and Sgt A. Cutler killed in action (KIA). Albert Cutler buried at Vlissingen, others commemorated on Runnymede Memorial.

12-08-1941   V6497 18 Squadron: FTR; shot down by Me.109E of JG26 into North Sea on homeward leg; crew S/Ldr A. Mills RCAF, F/O W. Staniland, and Sgt L. Mitchell captured and became PoWs.

12-08-1941   V5874 21 Squadron: FTR; struck HT cables, crashed into sea off Texel, Holland; crew P/O J. Corfield, P/O A. Williams, and P/O M. Williams KIA and buried in Den Burg Cemetery.

12-08-1941   Z7451 21 Squadron: FTR; hit near target by flak, crashed at Potz; Sgt Ken Attew (WOp/Ag) KIA, Sgt J Langston (Pilot) and Sgt D. Roberts (Obs) captured and became PoWs.

12-08-1941   T2437 82 Squadron: FTR; hit by flak, crashed near Dordrecht, Holland; crew P/O G. Rolland, P/O H. Clark, and Sgt E. Bainbridge KIA and buried in Strijen Cemetery.

12-08-1941   Z7281 114 Squadron: FTR; hit by flak and crashed in Westerschelde; Sgt D. Wheatley, Sgt J. West, and Sgt J. Stead KIA. Douglas Wheatley was aged 20, John Stead has no known grave.

12-08-1941   V5725 139 Squadron: FTR; shot down in target area by flak; crew Sgt H. Ingleby RCAF, Sgt D. Phillips, and F/Sgt G. Appleyard KIA and buried in Rheinberg War Cemetery.

12-08-1941   V6261 139 Squadron: FTR; shot down off Dutch coast; crew F/Lt G. Herbert RNZAF, P/O C. George, and Sgt G. Benton KIA. George Herbert and George Benton buried in Bergen Cemetery, Courtney George commemorated on Runnymede Memorial.

12-08-1941   Z7448 139 Squadron: FTR; shot down and crashed near target; Sgt Dennis Wilson (WOp/Ag, aged 19) KIA, Sgt G. Coast (Pilot) and P/O K. Mackintosh (Obs) captured and became PoWs.

12-08-1941   V5859 226 Squadron: FTR; hit by flak and crashed near Dutch/ Belgian border; crew F/Lt G. Lewis, F/Sgt N. Cardell, and F/Sgt J. Woods KIA and buried at Vlissingen.

12-08-1941   Z7352 226 Squadron: FTR; shot down by Me.109 of II/JG1; crew F/Lt H. Young, P/O A. Rossiter, and Sgt J. Anderson KIA. Hugh Young, aged 20, buried in Noordwijk Cemetery, his crew commemorated on Runnymede Memorial.

Blenheims lost in training for the Cologne power stations raid

08-08-1941   R3743 114 Squadron: crashed on Marshes near North Wooton, Norfolk, after striking sea on low-level bombing training; F/Lt Patterson and crew only slightly injured.

08-08-1941   V6522 114 Squadron: crashed near North Wooton railway station in same circumstances as R3743 above; Sgt J. Mackay (Obs) killed, P/O S. Richmond (Pilot) injured.

08-08-1941   N3627 139 Squadron: caught fire and spun into ground near Matlaske, Norfolk, on low-level bombing training; Sgt J. Gibbs (Pilot) killed, Sgt J. Shaw (Obs) and Sgt D. Beale (WOp/Ag) baled out, but Sgt Shaw's parachute did not deploy fully and he too died.

Appendix 2

Blenheim losses on the Heligoland submarine pens raid of 26 August 1941

Aircraft are all Mk IVs.

26-08-1941   T2165 82 Squadron: FTR; shot down by fighters of II/JG52 near target; crew S/Ldr F. Lascelles DFC, F/Sgt W. Ordway, and F/Sgt C. Weir KIA and buried in Sage War Cemetery.

26-08-1941   R3767 82 Squadron: FTR; shot down by fighters of II/JG52 near target; crew Sgt R. Greenough, Sgt A. Matthews, and Sgt H. Bonnett KIA and commemorated on Runnymede Memorial.

26-08-1941   V6435 82 Squadron: FTR; shot down by fighters of III/JG52 near target; crew F/Lt H. Shuttleworth, Sgt M. Hind, and Sgt O. Bishop RNZAF KIA and commemorated on Runnymede Memorial.

26-08-1941   Z7277 82 Squadron: FTR; shot down by fighters of III/JG52 near target; crew Sgt A. Dick, P/O K. Judd, and P/O J. Race KIA and commemorated on Runnymede Memorial.

Appendix 3

Blenheim losses on the Rotterdam docks raid of 28 August 1941

Aircraft are all Mk IVs.

28-08-1941   V5825 21 Squadron: FTR; shot down by Me.109 of VI/JG53 while attacking docks; Sgt R. Somerfield (Obs) KIA and commemorated on Runnymede Memorial, P/O W. MacDonald (Pilot) and P/O W. Beckingham (WOp/Ag) captured and became PoWs.

28-08-1941   V6436 21 Squadron: FTR; shot down by flak while attacking docks; P/O F. Orme RCAF, P/O S. Gunnis, and P/O A. Collins KIA and buried in Hoek van Holland Cemetery.

28-08-1941   Z7435 21 Squadron: FTR; shot down by Me.109 of VI/JG53 while attacking docks; Sgt K. Hayes, Sgt A. Shadick, and Sgt R. Brian KIA and buried as crew of V6436 above.

28-08-1941   Z7447 21 Squadron: FTR; shot down by flak while attacking docks, crashed into sea; S/Ldr R. Shuttleworth, F/Sgt D. Mackan, and Sgt G. Britain (aged 20) KIA and buried as crew of V6436 above, except Richard Shuttleworth (aged 21) who died of injuries in Amsterdam hospital.

28-08-1941   L9379 88 Squadron: FTR; shot down by flak while attacking docks; P/O T. Edwards, P/O F. Letchford, and F/Sgt F. Tweedale KIA and buried in Hoek van Holland Cemetery.

28-08-1941   Z7445 88 Squadron: FTR; shot down by flak while attacking docks; crew F/O J. Alexander, F/Sgt A. Hardy, and F/Sgt J. Briggs KIA and buried in Crooswijk Cemetery, Rotterdam.

28-08-1941   Z7289 226 Squadron: FTR; shot down by flak over Rotterdam, crashed in flames at Maashaven docks; crew P/O F. Johnstone, Sgt R. Evans, and Sgt R. Drake captured and became PoWs.

28-08-1941   Z7299 226 Squadron: crashed at Wattisham on take-off for raid; crew Sgt R. O'Connell RCAF, Sgt P. Saunders, and Sgt Robertson thrown clear with slight injuries, aircraft destroyed by fire.

Appendix 4

Blenheim losses on anti-shipping sorties, 1 August to 31 December 1941

Aircraft are all Mk IVs.

01-08-1941   N3568 107 Squadron: FTR; shot down off Holland while attacking shipping on Channel Stop operation; S/Ldr H. Thomson, P/O A. MacPherson, and F/Sgt L. Williams KIA and buried at Vlissingen. Both officers had BA degrees.

01-08-1941   Z7498 107 Squadron: FTR; shot down off Holland while attacking shipping as above; Sgt C. Powell (Pilot) KIA, Sgt M. Roberts (Obs) and Sgt H. Hunt (WOp/Ag) rescued and became PoWs.

02-08-1941   V6026 82 Squadron: FTR; shot down off Den Helder by ship's flak; W/Cdr K. Burt DFC, Sgt W. Ellis DFM, and F/Sgt A. Curr DFM KIA and buried in war cemeteries. W/Cdr Burt was CO of 82 Squadron.

07-08-1941   L4899 500 Squadron: FTR; crashed into sea off Dutch Frisian Islands on shipping sweep; crew P/O L. Ward, Sgt W. Robinson, and F/Sgt R. Burton KIA and commemorated on Runnymede Memorial

10-08-1941   Z7280 226 Squadron: FTR; shot down into Channel by Me.109s while attacking shipping; Sgt J. Osborne RCAF, Sgt K. McManus RCAF, and Sgt W. Roberts KIA. Sgt Osborne buried at Sagan.

10-08-1941   V5854 226 Squadron: FTR; shot down off Holland leading attack on shipping; S/Ldr M. Waddington, F/Sgt I. Forsyth, and F/Sgt D. Palmer KIA and commemorated on Runnymede Memorial.

11-08-1941   P6908 235 Squadron Mk IV-F: FTR; lost without trace on shipping sweep; P/O W. Richards, Sgt J. Mason, and Sgt J. Archibald KIA, commemorated on Runnymede Memorial.

14-08-1941   V6515 110 Squadron: FTR; shot down off Norway by Me.109s while attacking convoy; Sgt E. Elmes, Sgt A. Kirby, and Sgt H. Higgins KIA and commemorated on Runnymede Memorial.

15-08-1941   Z6036 500 Squadron: FTR; shot down into Channel on shipping 'Beat' by Me.110s of ZG 76; F/O C. Elgar, Sgt J. Halls, and Sgt D. Butterfield KIA and commemorated on Runnymede Memorial.

19-08-1941   V6236 114 Squadron: FTR; shot down into sea by Me.110s of ZG 76 while attacking convoy; W/Cdr J. Nicol DSO, F/Sgt E. Jones, and F/O H. Madden DFC KIA. Edward Jones buried at Sage, others have no known graves. W/Cdr James Nicol was CO of 114 Squadron.

19-08-1941   V6366 114 Squadron: FTR; shot down in similar circumstances to V6236 above; P/O R. McCracken RNZAF (Pilot) and P/O H. Bentley (Obs) KIA and commemorated on Runnymede Memorial, Sgt A. Clague (WOp/Ag) rescued and became PoW.

19-08-1941   Z7347 114 Squadron: FTR; shot down in similar circumstances to V6236 above; Sgt R. Clarke, P/O R. Stratton, and Sgt P. Davies KIA. Reg Clarke (aged 20) has no known grave, Ron Stratton buried at Sage, and Peter Davies (aged 19) at Ameland cemeteries.

20-08-1941   V6445 82 Squadron: FTR; struck mast of ship on 'Beat' No. 7, crash-landed at Acklington airfield; F/Lt Gibbs (Pilot) slightly injured, Sgt Eric Cash (Obs) died of injuries, Sgt Pascoe (WOp/Ag) uninjured (see the accompanying picture).

21-08-1941   R3631 59 Squadron: FTR; took off from Thorney Island on shipping sweep and disappeared without trace; P/O W. Foster, Sgt J. Milchreest, and Sgt G. Crowther KIA and commemorated on Runnymede Memorial.

23-08-1941   T1807 235 Squadron Mk IV-F: FTR; engine cut at low level while escorting Sunderland, stalled and crashed into North Sea; P/O P. Lander, Sgt H. Leake, and Sgt G. Latimer KIA. Sgt Leake buried in Denmark, P/O Lander and Sgt Latimer have no graves so commemorated on Runnymede Memorial.

24-08-1941   Z6039 500 Squadron: FTR; shot down by flak off Hook of Holland on shipping sweep; P/O G. Fletcher, Sgt J. Mylieu, and Sgt H. Walton KIA and commemorated on Runnymede Memorial.

26-08-1941   Z7483 21 Squadron: FTR; shot down by flak off Bergen-aan-Zee while attacking shipping; Sgt A. Oman, Sgt T. Parkinson, and Sgt R. Hamilton KIA and commemorated on Runnymede Memorial.

26-08-1941   L8788 88 Squadron: FTR; shot down off Ijmuiden, Holland, while on shipping 'Beat' No. 7; P/O G. Dunn, P/O J. Jones, and F/Sgt B. Davies KIA and commemorated on Runnymede Memorial.

26-08-1941   Z7305 226 Squadron: FTR; shot down by flak off Ijmuiden attacking convoy; Sgt G. Smith, Sgt S. Burdon, and Sgt C. Topping RCAF KIA. Stan Burdon buried at Bergen, Australian Gilbert Smith (aged 19), and Canadian Charles Topping commemorated on Runnymede Memorial.

26-08-1941   Z7317 226 Squadron: damaged by ship's flak off Ijmuiden while attacking convoy, belly-landed at base, aircraft repaired; F/O L. Harrell (WOp/Ag) seriously injured, Sgt W. O'Connell (Pilot) and Sgt P. Saunders (Obs) uninjured. Aircraft repaired, Bill O'Connell crashed again two days later – see Appendix 3.

02-09-1941   Z7274 139 Squadron: FTR; shot down into sea by ship's flak off Zeebrugge; S/Ldr K. Walsh, F/Sgt A. Hole, and Sgt G. Brook KIA. George Brook has no known grave, others' bodies washed ashore and buried.

07-09-1941   Z7306 226 Squadron: FTR; shot down into sea by ship's flak off Scheveningen; Sgt J. Fieldman, Sgt F. Phillips, and Sgt J. Carr KIA. Frank Phillips buried, others commemorated on Runnymede Memorial. Pilot John Fieldman was aged 19.

07-09-1941   Z7312 226 Squadron: FTR; shot down as Z7306 above; crew KIA, F/Lt C. Haggitt (Pilot) died in hospital two days later and is buried at Amsterdam, P/O R. Bennett (Obs, aged 20), and F/O C. Ramsay (WOp/Ag) commemorated on Runnymede Memorial.

07-09-1941   Z7304 226 Squadron: damaged by ship's flak and Me.109s in same action, belly-landed at Wattisham; P/O Casey (WOp/Ag) wounded, P/O W. Gray RCAF (Pilot) and P/O McCarthy (Obs) uninjured, aircraft repaired.

10-09-1941   T1811 236 Squadron: FTR from escorting civil DC3 (G-AGBB) off Hartland Point, lost contact in cloud, crashed into sea; P/O C. Pearson, Sgt A. McLean, and Sgt L. Winter KIA, commemorated at Runnymede.

15-09-1941   V6252 21 Squadron: FTR from anti-shipping sortie to Haugesund; Sgt Drobig, Sgt Tulley, and Sgt Crocombe KIA.

15-09-1941   V5567 236 Squadron: FTR; abandoned at night 1 mile east of Bodorgan, low in fuel and W/T failed, on return from convoy escort; Sgt Blackie (Pilot) and Sgt McNicol (Obs) landed safely in Anglesey, Sgt F. Richardson (WOp/Ag) KIA (drowned).

16-09-1941   V6339 18 Squadron: FTR; struck sea off Texel while attacking convoy at very low level; Sgt C. Tracey, P/O J. Rodgers, and Sgt A. Higgs KIA. Charles Tracey buried in Den Burg Cemetery, commemorated on Runnymede Memorial.

18-09-1941   V6380 88 Squadron: FTR; shot down into sea off Belgian coast; P/O R. Burlinson RCAF, P/O B. Hislop RAAF, and Sgt M. Stratton KIA. Bruce Hislop has no known grave, others' bodies washed ashore and buried in Holland.

18-09-1941   Z7488 88 Squadron: FTR; shot down into sea by Me.110 of ZG 76; crew P/O T. Cooper RNZAF, F/Sgt S. Hammersley, and Sgt R. Hambley RCAF KIA and commemorated on Runnymede Memorial.

18-09-1941   Z7454 88 Squadron: damaged by Me.110s in same action, belly-landed at Manston; F/Sgt B. Woodridge (Obs) fatally wounded, S/Ldr Harris (Pilot) uninjured, Sgt R. Longhorn (WOp/Ag) wounded, aircraft repaired.

20-09-1941   R3843 18 Squadron: FTR; flew into bomb bursts from another aircraft attacking ship off Zandvoort, crashed into sea; F/Sgt J. Nickleson RCAF, Sgt W. Meadows, and Sgt J. Pearson KIA. John Nickleson (aged 19) and has no known grave, others buried in Holland.

20-09-1941   V6422 226 Squadron: FTR; crashed into sea, caught by own bomb-blast; Sgt J. Colmer (aged 20), Sgt G. Bartlett RAAF, and Sgt L. Trevor KIA. Leslie Trevor has no known grave, others buried in Amsterdam.

20-09-1941   Z7310 226 Squadron: FTR; shot down into sea by ship's flak while attacking convoy; F/Lt M. Namias, Sgt K. Hood, and Sgt J. Robson KIA. Mayer Namias (aged 20) has no known grave, others buried at Rotterdam. Kenneth Hood was aged 19.

22-09-1941   V5684 500 Squadron: FTR; shot down into North Sea, believed by ship's flak; P/O S. Nicholl, F/O R. Hughes-Chamberlain, and Sgt J. Crees KIA and commemorated on Runnymede Memorial.

28-09-1941   Z6163 500 Squadron: reported missing on shipping sweep to French Coast, but not recorded in Squadron ORB.

10-10-1941	V6171 500 Squadron: FTR; crashed into North Sea; F/O C. Webb RNZAF, F/Sgt R. Roberts RCAF, and Sgt R. Coomber (aged 20) KIA. F/O Webb buried at Caister Cemetery, Great Yarmouth, his crew commemorated at Runnymede.
12-10-1941	L4880 82 Squadron: FTR; shot down into sea by ship's flak off Ijmuiden; Sgt F. Day, Sgt G. Robbins, and Sgt F. Lane KIA. Sgt Robbins buried in Westduin Cemetery, commemorated on Runnymede Memorial.
12-10-1941	V5824 82 Squadron: FTR; also shot down into sea by ship's flak off Ijmuiden; Sgt J. Ashurst, Sgt T. Steele, and Sgt R. Banks KIA. Reg Banks buried in Westduin Cemetery, others have no known grave.
15-10-1941	L9382 114 Squadron: FTR; shot down into sea by Me.110s of ZG 76 off Den Helder; P/O W. Davidson, Sgt E. Saul, and Sgt D. Peppler KIA and commemorated on Runnymede Memorial.
15-10-1941	V5875 114 Squadron: FTR; shot down into sea by Me.110s of ZG 76 off Den Helder; Sgt C. Balzer RAAF, Sgt H. Elliott RCAF, and Sgt V. Slade KIA. Pilot buried in Harlingen Cemetery, others commemorated on Runnymede Memorial.
15-10-1941	V6249 139 Squadron: FTR; shot down into sea off Heligoland; S/Ldr R. Stubbs DFC, Sgt J. Bradley, and Sgt W. Thom RCAF KIA and commemorated on Runnymede Memorial.
15-10-1941	Z7300 139 Squadron: FTR; shot down into sea off Heligoland; Sgt E. Gill, Sgt A. Humphries, and Sgt D. Marshall KIA and commemorated on Runnymede Memorial.
15-10-1941	Z7320 139 Squadron: FTR; shot down into sea off Heligoland; F/O T. Paxton, P/O H. Clarke, and F/O R. Holloway KIA and commemorated on Runnymede Memorial.
15-10-1941	Z7493 226 Squadron: FTR; shot down into sea off Le Havre attacking tanker there; P/O R. Hudson RAAF, F/Sgt A. Hole, and Sgt G. Brook KIA and commemorated on Runnymede Memorial.
15-10-1941	Z7494 226 Squadron: FTR; shot down into sea off Le Havre attacking tanker there; Sgt S. Paine, Sgt R. Banks, and Sgt W. Wolstenholme KIA and commemorated on Runnymede Memorial.
19-10-1941	Z5753 404 Squadron: FTR from convoy escort in bad weather, attempted to land at Dyce, believed to have ditched off Lerwick; Sgt I. Barber, Sgt J. Shaw, and Sgt E. Gillam missing presumed killed, commemorated at Runnymede.
21-10-1941	V5580 21 Squadron: FTR; struck sea and ditched off Terschelling; F/Lt F. Powles DFC, Sgt J. Life, and F/Sgt S. Williams KIA and buried at Sage.
21-10-1941	V5634 82 Squadron: FTR; shot down by Me.109s of JG 53 off Katwijk attacking convoy; P/O J. Richardson, F/Sgt A. Park, and F/Sgt G. Haines KIA and commemorated on Runnymede Memorial.
21-10-1941	V6146 82 Squadron: FTR; shot down by Me.109s of JG 53 off Katwijk attacking convoy; P/O B. Barber RAAF, P/O H. Pibus RCAF, and Sgt E. Paine KIA and commemorated on Runnymede Memorial.
25-10-1941	V5538 500 Squadron: FTR; shot down into sea off The Hague on shipping sweep; P/O L. Brown, Sgt P. Lyons, and Sgt J. Mitchell KIA and commemorated on Runnymede Memorial. Sgt James Mitchell was aged 20.
26-10-1941	V6421 88 Squadron: FTR; hit by flak and ditched off Dutch coast attacking convoy; P/O J. Rollinson, P/O A. Day, and Sgt E. Andrews KIA and commemorated on Runnymede Memorial. P/O Jack Rollinson was aged 19.
27-10-1941	Z7309 114 Squadron: FTR; shot down by Me.109 of JG 53 off Texel attacking convoy; P/O W. Beatson, P/O H. Jones, and Sgt J. Bradshaw RCAF KIA and commemorated on Runnymede Memorial. P/O Walter Beatson was aged 19.
27-10-1941	V5888 114 Squadron: FTR; damaged by flak then shot down by Me.109 of JG 53 off Texel attacking convoy; Sgt J. Bradley, P/O R. Batten, and Sgt E. Kennedy KIA. Eric Kennedy buried at Terscelling, others commemorated on Runnymede Memorial.
31-10-1941	V5537 500 Squadron: FTR; crashed into Ijseelmeer at 2350 on shipping sweep; S/Ldr F. Phipps, Sgt T. Mowan, and Sgt A. Miles KIA and commemorated on Runnymede Memorial.
02-11-1941	Z7449 500 Squadron: bomb fell off on take-off at Bircham Newton and lifted tail, nosed-in; crew P/O Godfrey, Sgt Smith, and Sgt Glasscock injured but rescued, aircraft exploded.
03-11-1941	Z6144 235 Squadron Mk IV-F: FTR from shipping sweep off Norwegian coast; P/O H. Van Panhuys, Sgt L. Hillier, and Sgt H. Cook KIA and commemorated on Runnymede Memorial.
04-11-1941	Z5959 500 Squadron: FTR; crashed into North Sea off Holland on night convoy strike; F/O W. Sipprell, Sgt A. Hall RNZAF, and Sgt H. Davies KIA and commemorated on Runnymede Memorial. F/O William Sipprell, a Canadian, was aged 20.
05-11-1941	L9337 404 Squadron: FTR from shipping sweep off Norwegian coast; Sgt J. MacKay, Sgt T. Hedefine, and Sgt W. Pearce KIA and commemorated on Runnymede Memorial.
22-11-1941	Z7275 139 Squadron: crashed immediately after take-off at Swanton Morley on shipping sortie; P/O R. Scott-Worthington (Pilot) killed, P/O D. Taylor (Obs, a Royal Academy of Music professor) died of injuries next day, Sgt J. Koller (WOp/Ag) also injured, but recovered.

Appendix 5

Blenheim losses on 'Circus' and 'Ramrod' operations, 13 August to 31 December 1941

Aircraft are all Mk IVs.

18-08-1941 V6175 18 Squadron: FTR; damaged by flak on 'Circus' No 78 to Lille , crash-landed on Romney Marshes, Sussex; Sgt V Stevens (WOp/Ag) KIA, Sgt Vickers (Pilot) and Sgt Lowe (Obs) injured.

18-08-1941 V5491 110 Squadron: FTR; hit by flak on 'Circus' No 78, crashed into Channel; Sgt N. Berg, Sgt J. Harvey, and Sgt J. Fazakerley KIA, WOp/Ag commemorated on Runnymede Memorial.

04-09-1941 Z7296 18 Squadron: FTR; shot down by Me.109s on 'Circus' No 93 to Mazingarbe chemical complex; Sgt D. Adams RAAF (Pilot) captured and became PoW, Sgt F. Woodcock (Obs) and Sgt M. Koransky (WOp/Ag) KIA.

17-09-1941 V6086 82 Squadron: FTR; shot down on 'Circus' No 95 to Mazingarbe; crew P/O C. Harper, P/O J. Patterson, and Sgt D. Bartrip KIA.

13-10-1941 Z7273 139 Squadron: FTR shot down by Me.109s on 'Circus' No 108 near Arques, Pas-de-Calais; F/Lt R. Chamberlain DFC, Sgt F. Jewell, and Sgt D. Beale KIA and buried in Boulogne East Cemetery.

Appendix 6

Blenheim losses on night intruder operations, 1 August to 31 December 1941

Aircraft are all Mk IVs.

30-08-1941 V5525 500 Squadron: FTR; shot down by flak during attack on Schipol airfield at 2337; crew Sgt D. Crosbie, Sgt D. Hyslop, and Sgt A. Peek (aged 20) KIA and buried at Amsterdam.

30-08-1941 Z6164 500 Squadron: FTR; crashed into North Sea off Noordwijk; crew F/O I. Terry, Sgt H. Poole, and Sgt A. Scrivens (aged 20) KIA and commemorated on Runnymede Memorial.

7/8-12-1941 V5876 82 Squadron: FTR; took off from Bodney at 2343 for Ostend, shot down near Zandvoort; P/O T. Wilson, Sgt R. Johnston, and Sgt F. Hubbard KIA and buried at Adegem, Belgium.

Appendix 7

Blenheim losses on the 'Combined Operations' raid on Vaagso, 27 December 1941

Aircraft are all Mk IVs.

27-12-1941 V6429 110 Squadron: FTR; shot down off Norway attacking shipping; P/O J. MacLeod, P/O H. Harris, and Sgt T. Anstey KIA and commemorated on Runnymede Memorial.

27-12-1941 V6448 110 Squadron: FTR; shot down off Norway attacking shipping; P/O D. Jenkinson RCAF, P/O R. McLachlan RCAF, and Sgt R. Hawkes KIA and commemorated on Runnymede Memorial.

27-12-1941 Z7317 110 Squadron: FTR; shot down off Norway attacking shipping; crew KIA, F/Lt R. Blewett RNZAF buried at Sola, P/O M. Murphy and Sgt J. Bell commemorated on Runnymede Memorial.

27-12-1941 Z7442 110 Squadron: FTR; shot down off Norway attacking shipping; Sgt N. Kaby, P/O R. Davis RNZAF, and Sgt N. Coatesworth KIA and commemorated on Runnymede Memorial.

27-12-1941 V6227 114 Squadron: FTR; collided with Z7500 below while attacking Herdla airfield and crashed; F/Sgt R. Fisher RAAF, Sgt J. Williamson, and Sgt W. Fletcher KIA and buried in Bergen.

27-12-1941 Z7500 114 Squadron: FTR; collided with V6227 above while attacking Herdla airfield and crashed; Sgt K. Davis, Sgt J. Ward, and Sgt J. Kitley KIA and buried in Bergen. Recently some Norwegians have recovered some wreckage from lake and erected small memorial.

27-12-1941 Z6081 254 Squadron Mk IV-F: FTR, lost without trace on above operation; P/O J. Roche, P/O D. Halsall, and Sgt F. Silk KIA, P/O Halsall is buried in Stavne Cemetery, Trondheim, his companions commemorated on Runnymede Memorial.

Appendix 8

Non-operational Blenheim losses, 1 August to 31 December 1941

Aircraft are all Mk IVs unless stated otherwise.

01-08-1941   Z6242 1 AGS: dived into Carmarthen Bay out of cloud on air-to-air firing practice; Sgt W. Bystrzynski (Pilot) and three trainee A/Gs, LAC A. Lee, LAC A. Mackay, and LAC W. Morris killed.

03-08-1941   V6384 21 Squadron: engine cut, crashed at 1745 attempting emergency landing near Dorchester; crew Sgt L. Cornish RCAF, Sgt Relph, and Sgt Robson injured.

05-08-1941   V6519 18 Squadron: crashed at 1653 landing at Horsham St Faith after one flap retracted; P/O T. Jefferson, Sgt R. Millens and Sgt M. Scotney slightly injured.

07-08-1941   R3816 107 Squadron: crashed after take-off at Manston at 1755 with elevator tab jammed; crew P/O H. Lind and Sgt N. Paples killed.

08-08-1941   N6218 5 AOS: overshot landing at Jurby, IoM, swung and u/c collapsed, damaged beyond repair (DBR).

09-08-1941   V6320 5 AOS: lost on night NavEx in bad visibility, ditched in Peel Channel, Barrow-in-Furness; crew rescued, Sgt W. Muir, Sgt W. Bold and Sgt H. Gable injured, trainee WOp/Ags LAC A. Campbell and LAC W. Darragh injured, Campbell dying next day.

09-08-1941   Z6178 404 Squadron: bounced on single-engine practice landing at Skitten, engine cut, swung and undercarriage collapsed; Sgt R. McKay (solo pilot) safe.

10-08-1941   L8751 114 Squadron: crashed attempting emergency landing at West Raynham at 1615; Sgt J. O'Grady (Obs) killed, Sgt F. Clarke (Pilot) injured.

10-08-1941   L8745 1 AGS: crash-landed at Kidwelly, Carmarthen, after engine cut; no injuries reported to P/O Z. Giedrys (Polish Pilot) and crew.

12-08-1941   L1245 17 OTU Mk I: shot down at night by intruder, crashed at Wilburton, near Ely, Cambs; P/O W. Wand, P/O R. Bell (both Pilots), and Sgt E. Davies (WOp/Ag) killed.

13-08-1941   V5758 17 OTU: engine cut in formation practice, overturned in force-landing at New Fenn, Norfolk; Sgt G. Kerr (solo pilot) injured.

14-08-1941   V5892 2 (C) OTU: lost height on night overshoot at Catfoss, struck trees and crashed at Moretown Farm, Brandesburton, Yorks; Sgt F. Wallis (solo pilot) injured.

16-08-1941   L1223 255 Squadron Mk I: lost power on approach to Coltishall, struck trees and crashed; F/O J. Emmerson and Sgt D. Fowler, both Pilots, killed.

17-08-1941   Z5955 2 (C) OTU: dived into Hall Farmhouse near Catfoss after night take-off; Pilot Sgt Steele (solo pilot) killed.

17-08-1941   L1181 13 OTU Mk I: abandoned at 0430, out of fuel, and crashed near Finedon, Northants; Sgt A. Newman (solo pilot) safe.

19-08-1941   V5374 8 Ferry Pilots Pool: engine cut on ferry flight from Aldergrove to Jurby, hit bank in force-landing near Jurby, DBR.

20-08-1941   Z9662 Training Ferry Pilots Pool: engine cut, crashed in attempted force-landing near Barrow-in-Furness, DBR.

21-08-1941   V6420 13 OTU: undercarriage collapsed in heavy landing, swung and slid into lorry at Bicester; Sgt S. Abbott RAAF (solo pilot) uninjured.

23-08-1941   V6179 114 Squadron: struck house at Whychwood Close, Canons Park, Edgware, Middx, in very bad visibility and crashed; P/O N. Thompson, Sgt G. Macnamara, P/O J. Dobson, and P/O H. Fuller killed.

24-08-1941   K7170 54 OTU Mk I: crashed attempting force-landing at Church Fenton, DBR.

24-08-1941   L6603 54 OTU Mk I: struck on ground by above aircraft, DBR.

25-08-1941   Z6170 Central Gunnery School: crashed in force-landing in bad weather near Fort William, Inverness, destroyed by fire; no injuries reported to Sgt E. Noxon and crew.

25-08-1941   Z6182 2 (C) OTU: lost height after night take-off at Catfoss, struck trees and crashed, destroyed by fire; Sgt T. Witherspoon injured.

26-08-1941   T2440 11 Group AA Co-Op Flt: engine cut, spun into ground on approach to Hornchurch; P/O E. Swarsbrick (Pilot) killed.

27-08-1941   V5730 2 (C) OTU: became lost at night, crashed in force-landing in bad weather near Donna Nook, Inverness; no report of injuries to Sgt D. Brisco and crew.

28-08-1941   T1945 2 (C) OTU: crash-landed on beach at Texel Island, Holland, at 0540 after becoming lost over North Sea on night training flight from Catfoss; P/O N. Gifford (solo pilot) became PoW.

28-08-1941   Z7441 110 Squadron: crash-landed on Sand's Marsh, Stalham, Norfolk, when engine cut on low-level bombing training; crew uninjured.

28-08-1941 Z6099 13 OTU: ditched in Irish Sea on night NavEx; crew P/O D. Ritchie, P/O C. Bowen, and Sgt C. Strutt missing presumed drowned, commemorated on Runnymede Memorial.

29-08-1941 R3734 17 OTU: engine cut, crash-landed near Whittlesey Ranges, Hunts, DBR; P/O J. Grieve and P/O G. Rowley uninjured.

01-09-1941 Z6049 74 Wing Calibration Flt: u/c leg collapsed on take-off at Duxford, swung, destroyed by fire; W/O G. Smith and crew escaped.

02-09-1941 L9394 404 Squadron: spun into ground 1 mile east of Castletown, cause unknown; Sgt Dale (Pilot), Sgt Allen (WOp/Ag), and Cpl McKinlay (Flight Mechanic, Engines) killed.

02-09-1941 T2230 13 Squadron: engine cut on take-off at Odiham, lost height and struck ground, destroyed by fire; F/Lt H. Gilchrist and Cpl F. Palmer killed.

03-09-1941 V5805 2 (C) OTU: engine cut, belly-landed near Tring, Herts, DBR; Sgt A. Taylor and one crew injured.

03-09-1941 L9261 235 Squadron: flew into hill in bad visibility at Hoxton Walls, Sandness, Shetlands; F/Lt H. Hammond, P/O W. Mason, and Sgt G. Simpson killed, buried in Lerwick Cemetery.

04-09-1941 R3698 13 Group AA Co-Op Flt: engine cut on take-off at Aston Down, swung into sand, undercarriage collapsed.

05-09-1941 R3909 235 Squadron: struck pole on night approach to Dyce in bad weather at 0430 and crashed; F/O A. Cook (Pilot) unhurt, Sgt Ludlam and Sgt Godfrey injured

07-09-1941 R3875 17 OTU: control lost in cloud on NavEx, dived into ground near Cressage, Salop, destroyed by fire; Sgt M. Fox, Sgt B. Coukell, and Sgt E. Brealey killed.

08-09-1941 V5377 13 OTU: dived into ground at Mells Park, near Frome, Somerset, cause unknown; crew Sgt J. Nymen, Sgt J. Rodwell, and Sgt C. Pratt killed.

08-09-1941 T2228 54 OTU: control lost in cloud, dived into ground near Huggate, Yorks; Sgt C. Woolgar (solo pilot) killed.

09-09-1941 L8693 5 AOS Mk I: dived into ground 1 mile west of Bride, IoM, cause unknown; Sgt D. Selby-Lowndes (Pilot), Sgt E. Frisby (Gunnery Instructor), LAC Duffs, and AC2 Flint (Trainee Air Gunners) killed.

12-09-1941 N3610 254 Squadron: cowling detached, struck tailplane, jammed elevators, crash-landed near Ballymaguire, Co Tyrone; Sgt A. McIntosh and two Army passengers slightly injured.

13-09-1941 V5463 21 Squadron: crashed at 1108 on take-off at Watton, struck hangar and destroyed by fire; P/O F. Grant RAAF, Sgt P. Ritter, F/Sgt R. Hall, Sgt T. Thomas, and P/O E. Tuckey killed, others injured, perhaps working in hangar.

13-09-1941 L6793 13 OTU Mk I : stalled in circuit at Bicester and crashed near Brackley, destroyed by fire; Sgt D. Neal (solo pilot) killed.

15-09-1941 V6425 18 Squadron: crashed at Hall Farm, North Walsham, Norfolk, after striking sea on low-level bombing practice; crew P/O G. Pryor RCAF, Sgt Mills, and Sgt Buckley injured.

15-09-1941 V5759 2 (C) OTU: missing from NavEx over North Sea, presumed to have crashed into sea; Sgt J. Talbot, Sgt J. Spero, and Sgt K. Blackmore killed.

16-09-1941 Z7363 139 Squadron: inadvertently flew into sea off Clacton when pilot adjusted compass while flying at very low level; P/O P. Brown (Pilot) and crew rescued.

16-09-1941 L6816 ATA Mk I: engine cut on take-off from White Waltham, swung and hit obstructions, DBR.

17-09-1941 Z6336 1 AAS: engine cut on take-off at Penrhos, undercarriage raised to stop but hit boundary and DBR.

17-09-1941 T2352 9 Group AA Co-Op Flt: tyre burst on take-off at Valley, swung into sand, u/c collapsed, DBR.

17-09-1941 R3814 17 OTU: flew into sea, cause unknown; Sgt D. Farley and F/Sgt W. Jeffery killed, Sgt T. Heron injured but rescued.

19-09-1941 Z6147 54 OTU: undershot night landing at Church Fenton, hit aerial of fire-tender, crashed, destroyed by fire; Sgt Thomas (solo pilot) 'got out in good time' and escaped injury.

20-09-1941 T2128 254 Squadron: hit water in practice attack at Lough Neagh; Sgt K. Kuhle (Pilot), Sgt R. Steel (WOp/Ag) and AC2 T. Vickers (ground-crew) killed, buried at St Catharines, Killead.

21-09-1941 V5761 236 Squadron: engine cut on return to Carew Cheriton from escort duty, belly-landed 2 miles away; Sgt Casley (Pilot) injured, Sgt Norton and Sgt Langhorne unhurt, aircraft DBR.

22-09-1941 Z7454 88 Squadron: crashed in bad visibility while landing at Attlebridge at 1920; no injuries reported to F/Sgt J. Ralston and crew, aircraft DBR.

22-09-1941 V5490 114 Squadron: crashed at Hall Farm near Cromer after striking mast of ship moored on practice bombing range, destroyed by fire; crew P/O R. Feilden RAAF, P/O F. Brown RCAF, and Sgt S. Collier killed.

22-09-1941 V6037 42 OTU: spun into ground off turn at low altitude at Upper Woodford near Membury, Wilts; P/O O. Gwynne, Sgt T. Jeffries, and Sgt E. Graham killed.

03-10-1941 Z7292 226 Squadron: swung on landing at Long Kesh airfield, Northern Ireland, and overturned; F/Sgt B. Faurat RCAF and crew uninjured.

07-10-1941   V5762 42 OTU: hit tree in fog and cart-wheeled in grounds of Flag Fenn House, Peterborough; P/O D. Alan-Williams, Sgt G. Arthur, Sgt W. Hebditch, and Sgt G. Ashton killed.

08-10-1941   V5383 42 OTU: u/c retracted too soon on night take-off from Andover, hit obstructions, DBR; P/O F. Wilson and crew uninjured.

10-10-1941   T2333 42 OTU: undershot night landing at Andover, hit obstructions, DBR; no injuries reported to P/O L. Cobb and crew.

10-10-1941   K7048 17 OTU Mk I: engine cut on approach to Upwood, dived into ground and destroyed; Sgt P. Paquet RCAF (solo pilot) seriously injured.

12-10-1941   N3629 18 Squadron: hit trees and crashed at Felthorpe Manor near Norwich on low-level training sortie; crew Sgt D. Laws, P/O G. Willsher, and Sgt A. Cullen killed.

12-10-1941   Z9737 21 Squadron: struck tree low flying and crashed at 1540 near Kingerby; crew Sgt F. Cocking, Sgt M. Counter, and Sgt E. Gill killed.

12-10-1941   V6324 17 OTU: engine cut on NavEx, lost height, ditched 65 miles east of Filey, Yorks; Sgt M. Paul, Sgt E. Hafner and Sgt H. Morgan killed.

12-10-1941   L4849 51 OTU Mk I: dived into ground during night circuit at Baston near Cranfield; F/Lt Burke (Pilot) uninjured, Sgt Phidisis killed.

13-10-1941   R3617 51 OTU: shot down by enemy intruder at night, crashed at Sherington, Bucks; Sgt Filmer (solo pilot) killed.

14-10-1941   Z7278 114 Squadron: crashed at Clifton Farm, Clenchwarton, Norfolk, on low-flying exercise; Sgt W. Anstey, Sgt A. Southwood, and Sgt J. Kerrison killed.

14-10-1941   T1951 1 Coastal Artillery Co-Op Flt: hit tree during practice attack, crashed in wood at Shepherds Well, Kent; crew P/O Corbett-Thompson, Sgt F. Treeby, Sgt S. Yates, and Sgt N. Wosencroft (both WOp/Ags) killed.

17-10-1941   V5622 54 OTU: flew into ground at night, 1 mile south of Everingham, Yorks, cause unknown; body of Sgt T. Bramley (solo pilot) found more than 1 mile from impact, having perhaps attempted to bale out.

20-10-1941   L9020 88 Squadron: crashed at Weston Longville, near Norwich; crew F/O P. Nangle RAAF, F/Sgt B. Fullerton RCAF, and Sgt I. Macdonald RCAF killed and buried in All Saints, Swanton Morley.

22-10-1941   L9205 13 OTU: lost propeller, crash-landed at Marsh Gibbon, near Bicester, destroyed by fire; Sgt D. Evans (solo pilot) escaped.

22-10-1941   Z6047 500 Squadron: hit tree low-flying near Benson, crashed and destroyed by fire; Sgt C. Hosford and F/Sgt K. Elvidge injured.

23-10-1941   V5728 236 Squadron: engine cut, ditched at Schull, Co Cork, Eire; Sgt P. Webster, Sgt D. Woodman RCAF, and Sgt C. Brady interned, Sgt Woodman died of injuries received in crash.

23-10-1941   L1305 17 OTU Mk I: became lost, force-landed at Chelveston airfield, still under construction, hit obstructions and DBR; Sgt R. Trigg (solo pilot) slightly injured.

23-10-1941   Z6031 236 Squadron: overshot Carew Cheriton at night, flew into ground at Ridgeway; Sgt F. McCaffrey RNZAF and Sgt S. Lamerton killed, Sgt Buck (WOp/Ag) slightly injured.

24-10-1941   V6004 17 OTU: engine cut (due to incorrect change of fuel tanks) crashed on attempted single-engine overshoot at Grafton Underwood; Sgt P. Thompson and Sgt A. Fairbairn killed.

26-10-1941   N6220 13 OTU: engine cut on take-off from Bicester, crashed 2.5 miles from airfield; Sgt A. Gempton RNZAF (solo pilot) uninjured.

27-10-1941   T2400 12 Group AA Co-Op Flt: ran out of fuel in Digby circuit in bad visibility, belly-landed into trees at Dorrington, Lincs, destroyed by fire; F/O T. Sumorok (Polish Pilot) injured.

27-10-1941   V6013 17 OTU: crashed in attempted force-landing at Wetmoor Farm, Gayton, Staffs, in bad visibility; Sgt H. Taylor, Sgt R. Bayliss and Sgt J. Headley killed.

31-10-1941   Z6273 5 AOS: dived into ground from cloud on NavEx at Tildarg, Co Antrim; Sgt Doig (Pilot) and LACs Conell, Unwin, and Coles (Trainee Air Observers) killed.

01-11-1941   T1946 404 Squadron: crashed off Shetlands, following collision with Z6339 below; Sgt R. Leighton (Pilot) and passengers, AC1 T. Gray and AC2 T. Clapperton, killed.

01-11-1941   Z6339 404 Squadron: crashed off Shetlands, following collision with T1946 above; P/O Inglis and passenger Cpl H. Holmes F2E injured.

01-11-1941   Z6174 2 (C) OTU: u/c collapsed on heavy landing at Catfoss, aircraft DBR.

02-11-1941   Z5947 17 OTU: control lost in cloud, possibly due to icing, crashed at East Leake, Notts; P/O C. Bush RCAF, P/O A. Sims and Sgt E. Bush killed.

02-11-1941   L4922 17 SFTS Mk I: crashed at Cranwell, no further details available.

03-11-1941   V5797 A&AEE: bomb exploded prematurely on bombing trials, dived into ground at Crichel Down, Dorset; F/O F. Heapey killed (see entry for 01-07-1941, Chapter 19, Appendix 6), F/O G. Betts and LAC A. Hinks seriously injured.

04-11-1941   T1887 88 Squadron: crashed near Swanton Morley, hydraulic failure, one u/c leg jammed up; no injuries reported to Sgt C. Fuchs and crew.

07-11-1941   Z7455 226 Squadron: crashed when attempting overshoot at Long Kesh airfield, Northern Ireland; no injuries reported to Sgt F. Emmett and crew.

07-11-1941   L1149 2 (C) OTU Mk I: engine cut on take-off at Catfoss, crash-landed, DBR; F/Sgt C. Mace and Sgt T. Woodward killed.

07-11-1941   L6748 51 OTU: carried out over-shoot from Cranfield at night, flew into ground at Bourne End, Bucks; P/O H. Baker (solo pilot) killed.

08-11-1941   N3626 17 OTU: engine cut in cloud, crashed in attempting force-landing at Holme Fen, Hunts; P/O J. Lang and crew uninjured.

09-11-1941   Z6359 17 OTU: u/c raised too soon and jammed, belly-landed at Upwood, destroyed by fire; Sgt J. Scott and crew escaped.

09-11-1941   Z5810 13 OTU: lost oil-pressure on one engine, crash-landed near Blisworth, Northants; Sgt E. Bawden, Sgt Griffiths, and Sgt Murray severely injured.

09-11-1941   V5810 13 OTU: engine cut, lost height and belly-landed at Yew Tree Farm, Sherrington, Bucks; P/O R. Powell (solo pilot) uninjured.

11-11-1941   Z5800 13 OTU: engine cut, lost height, hit trees and broke up 3 miles west of Hinton-in-the-Hedges; Sgt C. Crozier (Pilot) and Sgt H. Perrin (WOp/Ag) killed, P/O Conquer (Obs) seriously injured.

12-11-1941   T1793 17 OTU: stalled on landing at Upwood, u/c collapsed, P/O T. Skinner uninjured, aircraft DBR.

13-11-1941   L8680 255 Squadron Mk I: crashed, no further details available.

14-11-1941   P4845 404 Squadron: became lost in bad visibility, overshot attempted forced-landing and hit stone wall 5 miles north of Dyce; P/O J. Dunlop died of injuries, LAC Jones and AC1 Walker slightly injured.

15-11-1941   Z7484 88 Squadron: Sgt K. Elkins (Pilot) collided with Z7361 (Pilot Sgt K. Smart RNZAF) while taxiing at Swanton Morley, Z7484 DBR, Z7361 repaired.

15-11-1941   Z6080 6 Ferry Pilots Pool: stalled in circuit at Oulton, dived into ground, destroyed by fire; First Officer J. Bergel ATA (solo pilot) killed (brother of Hugh Bergel, author of *Fly and Deliver*).

15-11-1941   T2324 54 OTU: attacked by Spitfire of 121 Squadron, port engine caught fire, spun in near Wetherby, Yorks; P/O P. Cleaver (Pilot) baled out safely, Sgt J. Cohen killed.

15-11-1941   Z6243 2 (C) OTU: struck ground in turn after night take-off for Catfoss at Northfield Farm, Hornsea; Sgt J. Gray (solo pilot) injured.

16-11-1941   V5421 17 OTU: abandoned in bad weather and crashed 4 miles from Grantham, Lincs; Sgt S. Strate and crew baled out successfully.

16-11-1941   T1924 54 OTU: engine cut at night, lost height and crashed at Selby Common, Yorks; Sgt A. Thomas injured.

18-11-1941   L1353 51 OTU Mk I: lost height after night take-off at Cranfield, hit trees and crashed at Salford, Bucks; Sgt M. Cuke and Sgt J. Green killed.

19-11-1941   V6009 5 BGS: written off in accident, no further details available.

25-11-1941   L6761 51 OTU Mk I: flew into ground at night in bad weather 1 mile SE of Wakerley, Northants; Sgt C. Martyn-Johns and Sgt B. Wright killed.

27-11-1941   N3596 2 (C) OTU: stalled and spun into ground near Barnston, Yorks; Sgt McLellan (solo pilot) killed.

28-11-1941   V5963 9 AOS: u/c raised too soon on take-off at Penrhos, struck mound and caught fire; Sgt C. Symonds (Pilot) and LAC R. Williams (Trainee Obs) injured, LAC Trotter (Trainee Obs) escaped, LAC Williams died later of his injuries.

29-11-1941   L9405 TFU Special Duties Flt: became lost on AI Trials, force-landed on beach, overturned into sea at Chesil Bank, Dorset; F/Lt A. Dunlop (Pilot) killed, AC1 Goode injured, aircraft DBR.

03-12-1941   L1251 54 OTU Mk I: crashed when wing struck ground in snowstorm at Badboggin Lane, York, Sgt W. Kimber and unnamed crewman killed.

03-12-1941   Z6088 254 Squadron: engine cut, crashed when attempting forced-landing near Glenegedale, Islay; Sgt M. Shand, Sgt G. Harker, and Sgt J. Parsons injured, aircraft DBR.

05-12-1941   V6036 5 AOS: undershot landing at Jurby and hit bank; Sgt W. Simmonds slightly injured, aircraft DBR.

05-12-1941   L9268 82 Squadron: crashed on night landing at Bodney airfield; P/O F. Wilson (Pilot) and P/O E. Forbes (Obs) injured, Sgt Christmas (WOp/Ag) uninjured, aircraft DBR.

05-12-1941   N6172 51 OTU: artificial horizon failed at night, flew into ground at Beckering Park, Beds, and destroyed by fire; Sgt D. Raley killed.

06-12-1941   L4894 17 OTU: stalled on approach to Upwood in gusty conditions and struck ground, DBR; P/O C. Woodworth, F/Sgt M. Thompson and Sgt R. Barr killed.

06-12-1941   Z7962 13 OTU: crashed just after take-off at Bicester, attributed to incorrect trim-tab settings; Sgt V. Langrish, P/O E. Stanley, Sgt A. Bailey, and F/O D. Ivens (also a Pilot) killed.

08-12-1941   Z7370 1404 Flt: missing on Met sortie; Sgt L. Watson and Sgt A. Hemming killed, Sgt Hammon and Sgt Bess injured, no further details available.

09-12-1941 R3675 17 OTU: engine cut just after take-off at Upwood, stalled and crashed, destroyed by fire; Sgt S. Hill (solo pilot) injured.

09-12-1941 V5373 17 OTU: landed downwind, overshot and swung at Upwood, u/c collapsed, DBR, Sgt C. Wilcock uninjured.

09-12-1941 L1445 42 OTU Mk I: suffered engine fire in air, crash-landed, DBR; F/O R. Trim unhurt.

09-12-1941 L8732 54 OTU: engine cut on take-off at Church Fenton, crash-landed half a mile away.

09-12-1941 L1429 600 Squadron Mk I: belly-landed in bad weather 3 miles east of Corfe Castle, Dorset; Sgt Smith killed.

10-12-1941 L9383 13 OTU: engine cut on take-off at Bicester, stalled and crashed, destroyed by fire; crew F/Sgt G. Schrader RCAF, Sgt A. Steadman, and Sgt W. Dunn killed.

10-12-1941 V5801 254 Squadron: flew into ground in cloud at Dyke Ends, Forfar, destroyed by fire; crew W/Cdr G. Bernard-Smith, Sgt W. Harris, and Sgt A. Stather, and passengers Sgt T. Sinclair and LAC A. Lovell, killed.

11-12-1941 T1808 404 Squadron: tyre burst on landing at Sumburgh, swung into sand dune, u/c collapsed, Sgt J. Ensom and crew unhurt.

13-12-1941 R3760 54 OTU: hit tree on night approach to Church Fenton and crash-landed, DBR; no injuries reported to Sgt R. Scott and crew.

13-12-1941 L1128 51 OTU Mk I: ORB states: 'Crashed at Cranfield. No Pilot. Aircraft caught fire and burnt out. Cause still under investigation.' L1128 SOC 16-12-1941.

16-12-1941 Z6418 9 AOS: stalled on night overshoot at Penrhos, spun in and crashed, destroyed by fire; P/O G. Lamb, LACs S. Tebby and W. Davis (Trainee Obs) killed, AC1 W. Elliot (Trainee WOp/Ag) seriously injured.

16-12-1941 L9417 2 (C) OTU: ran off runway at Catfoss landing in bad weather and hit cement-mixer; Sgt D. Matthews (Pilot) slightly injured.

21-12-1941 Z6350 5 AOS: flew into high ground in cloud on NavEx, Mull of Kintyre; Sgt J. Orton and Sgt A. Gearing, and Cpl R. Cohen and AC P. Woodward (Trainee Air Observers), killed.

22-12-1941 N6166 54 OTU: flew into high ground at night south of Sutton-in-the-Forest, Yorks; Sgt L. Tickner and Sgt S. Turner seriously injured. Pilot died in York hospital a few days later.

24-12-1941 L8663 Ferry Training Unit: lost power, stalled on approach to Honeybourne, overturned; P/O H. Gillett (Pilot) injured.

24-12-1941 L9313 254 Squadron: engine cut on take-off at Dyce, stalled and crashed at Pitmedden; F/Lt D. Poynter RNZAF, P/O W. Constable, and two ground-crew passengers, AC1 R. Watson and AC2 T. Broom, killed.

26-12-1941 P4856 13 OTU: engine cut, stalled and spun in at Bicester, destroyed by fire; crew Sgt W. Boggs RCAF, Sgt F. Morris, and Sgt J. Kennedy killed.

27-12-1941 V6455 82 Squadron: crashed just after take-off at Bodney with one propeller in coarse pitch, hit gun-post; first four of those listed as on board injured, P/O T. Jack, Sgt E. Kerr, Sgt H. Slater, P/O J. Graham, and Sgt Broadhurst.

28-12-1941 Z5984 17 OTU: flew into ground on bombing practice, North Wootton Ranges, Norfolk; Sgt H. Thoms, Sgt G. Owen and Sgt J. Wilson injured, Sgt Wilson died later in hospital.

30-12-1941 Z7653 Overseas Aircraft Preparation Unit: iced up, engine cut, overturned in attempted forced-landing at Whitchurch; Sgt W. Knight (Pilot) and one crew member injured.

An engine of L9313, a Mk IV-F of 254 Squadron, cut just after take-off at Dyce on Christmas Eve 1941, stalled and crashed at Pitmedden nearby, killing two crew and two ground-crew passengers.

Chapter 21

1942: a year of change

Changes in Bomber Command

On 22 February the forceful Air Marshal Sir Arthur Travers Harris was appointed as AOC Bomber Command, and he retained this vital command until the end of the war. He was the leading proponent of the Trenchard theory that claimed a war-winning capability for sustained strategic bombing. In February 1942 he had 378 serviceable bombers available – 309 Mediums (mainly Wellingtons) and only 69 Heavies (Halifaxes and Stirlings). He discounted the 56 Blenheims and the other light bombers (22 Bostons) – they were of no interest to him at all as he wanted as large a force as possible comprised entirely of four-engined Heavy Bombers. He made no bones about this; indeed, his Dispatch states with typically honest logic:

'The Light Bomber Force of No 2 Group was also included in my Command at the time. With the exception of night intruder activity against enemy airfields to assist the heavy and Medium Bombers … this short-range force could play no part in the main offensive against Germany. In daylight operations, executed in conjunction with offensive fighter sweeps, the chief purpose of the light bombers was to bring the enemy fighters to combat.'

Arthur Harris, the determined and single-minded AOC who forged Bomber Command into a powerful force capable of causing dreadful destruction.

Although, as indicated, 1942 saw the Blenheims fade from operational use in the Northern European Theatre as they became heavily embroiled in the Middle and Far Eastern Theatres of War, they continued on an increasing scale to give invaluable service in the operational training role, as their overdue replacements – the Douglas Bostons, Lockheed Venturas, DH Mosquitos and North American Mitchells – came into front-line use. The first operation by Mosquitos was on 31 May 1942, the first by Venturas on 3 November, and the first by Mitchells on 22 January 1943. The last daylight raid by Blenheims was carried out by 114 Squadron on 28 February 1942 when W/Cdr Jenkins led six aircraft with a fighter escort to bomb submarine pens at Ostend; all returned safely although several sustained flak damage. When the 'Circus' operations were resumed on 8 March Bostons had taken the place of Blenheims, and 12 more of the new aircraft also carried out a low-level daylight attack on the Ford lorry factory at Poissy near Paris. The long and highly distinguished period of dangerous daylight operations by UK-based Blenheims had finally come to an end.

In the Heavy Bomber force improved marks of the Wellington entered service, and Halifaxes, Manchesters and Stirlings were taking the place of Whitleys and Hampdens, which carried out their last Bomber Command operations on 29 April and 14 September 1942 respectively. 44 Squadron received the first Lancasters over the winter and commenced operations in March 1942, rapidly replacing the unsatisfactory Manchester, which was withdrawn from operational use by the end of June. The insatiable demand for freshly trained crews by Bomber Command, expanding rapidly with this new generation of four-engined types that each required a seven-man crew, led to the parallel and similarly rapid expansion of Flying Training Command. Thousands of Blenheims played the primary, indeed pivotal, role in meeting this demand – they served in dozens of Advanced and Operational Training Units for the Pilots, Observers, Air Gunners, Navigators, Bomb Aimers and Wireless Operators who would go on to man the Heavy Bombers, firstly at HCUs (Heavy Conversion Units), then with the operational squadrons. This was in addition to the extensive use of Blenheims in training the crews for the new types of twin-engined bombers mentioned above, and of course for the Beaufighters and Beauforts of Coastal Command, which was also undergoing a period of rapid expansion. The major importance of this significant contribution to the war effort by the Blenheims, being carried out behind the scenes, has not been accorded the recognition that it merits.

107 Squadron had converted from Bristol Blenheim Mk IVs to Douglas Boston Mk IIIs by March 1942, as had 88 and 226 Squadrons, while 105 and 139 Squadrons were the first to change their obsolescent Blenheims for the outstanding De Havilland Mosquito – six of 105's are seen at Marham in December 1942.

What of the operational squadrons who said 'goodbye' to their Blenheim Mk IVs in 1942?

21 Squadron: disbanded in Malta following heavy losses, but re-formed at Bodney in March, moved to Abbotsinch and converted to Venturas, receiving 12 by September
88, 226 and **107** Squadrons: all completed converting to Boston IIIs by March
82 and **110** Squadrons: stood down in February and were sent to the Far East in March
139 Squadron: re-formed at Horsham St Faith in June with Blenheim Mk Vs but carried out no operations with these and by the end of the year had changed to Mosquitos, as detailed in Chapter 18
105 Squadron: converted slowly to Mosquitos but did not have 12 until October 1942
18 and **114** Squadrons: started converting to Blenheim Mk Vs in September
13 and **614** Army Co-Operation Squadrons: based at Odiham, they also started converting from their Mk IVs. These latter four squadrons were to be deployed with their Mk Vs before the end of the year at a new front that opened with Operation Torch, the invasion of North West Africa, there to suffer a disastrous scale of losses, as will be described in Chapter 28.

The 'Channel Dash'

The German forces carried out an audacious and well-planned operation when the two 'pocket battleships' *Scharnhorst* and *Gneisenau*, with the heavy cruiser *Prinz Eugen*, screened by destroyers and E-boats, escaped from Brest on the night of 11 February, undetected by all three lines of constant Coastal Command patrols by ASV-equipped Hudsons. The *Kriegsmarine* force steamed steadily through the English Channel during the day of the 12th right under the noses of Britain's naval and air forces, to return successfully to Germany on the 13th. Bomber and Coastal Commands as well as Fleet Air Arm aircraft made the most strenuous efforts in bad weather to prevent the escape but were unable to do so, although both of the capital ships were damaged and slowed by aerial-laid mines. The prizes slipped

Paddy Bandon, known as 'the Abandoned Earl' (in greatcoat), greets crews of 114 Squadron at West Raynham on their return from Operation 'Fuller' on 12 February 1942.

clean through the fingers of the British, although counter-measures had been prepared under the code name 'Fuller' since April 1941, and these were put into action on 4 February 1942 as the breakout was expected. For many months the capital ships had been bombed constantly and suffered damage at Brest (at the cost of 127 RAF aircraft), and with the loss of the *Bismarck* Hitler wished them to join the *Tirpitz* in Norway to concentrate his capital ships there. The 'Channel Dash' was certainly highly embarrassing to the British, and may have been a tactical victory for the Germans, but it was really a strategic defeat, for these powerful ships were no longer in a position to threaten Atlantic shipping.

The RAF threw all available aircraft into Operation Fuller, including 37 Blenheims from 110, 82 and 114 Squadrons, which were hastily recalled from stand-by, but widespread low cloud and heavy rain made the enemy ships particularly hard to find and prevented the use of the altitude needed for the release of armour-piercing bombs. The bad weather, combined with constant fighter cover and the screens of ships armed with flak guns, foiled all the low-level attacks by bomb- or torpedo-carrying aircraft and not a single bomb or torpedo hit the ships. 88 and 226 Squadrons were completing conversion from Blenheims to Bostons in February 1942 and took part in Operation Fuller with their new aircraft before being declared operational. In their attempts to foil the break-out the RAF lost 19 bombers, including two of the Blenheims (see Appendix 1) and three of the 16 Beaufort torpedo aircraft, while the Fleet Air Arm lost all six Swordfish biplanes, including that of L/Cdr Esmonde who was awarded a posthumous VC. The RAF also lost 17 fighters (claiming 16 Luftwaffe aircraft), so the attempt to stop the ships from the air cost 42 aircraft in addition to the 127 lost while bombing them at Brest. Incidentally, these were the last Blenheim casualties from 110 Squadron, which, with 82 Squadron, was stood down and posted to India in March, after 2½ years continuous operations with Bomber Command.

Maritime sorties

Coastal Command Blenheims continued their maritime duties, mounting patrols and shipping sweeps over the North Sea to the coast of Norway, plus escorting convoys and searching for submarines both there and in the Western and South Western Approaches. They were being replaced progressively by Beaufighters, although the Blenheims continued to suffer losses (see Appendix 2), some from enemy action, but many resulting

Of these two 114 Squadron crews, only Observer F/O Roy Kendrick (far left) survived his Blenheim service. His Pilot, F/Lt Newberry, is next to him, then W/Cdr Jenkins DSO DFC, the CO, who with his Observer, F/O Brancker DFC and bar (second from right), and F/Sgt Gray DFM (far right), his young WOp/Ag, were Killed in Action on the night of 27 March 1942.

from engine failure leading to the aircraft ditching in the sea. In an endeavour to reduce such losses Coastal Command HQ issued an Order on 4 April that Blenheim engines were to be changed after 240 hours of running, not 360 hours as previously.

Blenheims lingered little longer in operational service with Coastal Command. 235 Squadron had converted to Beaufighters by the beginning of 1942, 236 Squadron by February, and 248 by June; 254 and 143 Squadrons started converting to 'Beaus' in July, but carried on using their Blenheims up to September 1942, while 404, the RCAF Squadron, did not commence converting to Beaufighters until that month, and was still operating its Blenheim Mk IV-Fs from Dyce and Sumburgh until January 1943. Several Beaufighter and Mosquito squadrons were formed later into potent Strike Wings with a mixture of torpedo-carrying and standard aircraft, which, when rockets had been added to their armament, proved a devastatingly effective combination against shipping.

Also under Coastal Command control were the PR Units, and 140 Squadron (formed from 1416 Reconnaissance Flight at Benson in September 1941) continued using Blenheim IVs for PR duties over the continental coast until August 1943. Half a dozen Meteorological Flights were formed into squadrons (in the 500 series) from July 1942, together with several AAC and Radar Calibration Flights, and some carried on using Blenheims for this important work right up to December 1944.

The '1,000 Bomber' raids

Arthur 'Bomber' Harris served dramatic notice of what lay ahead for the Germans and scored a spectacular public relations success for Bomber Command at home when he staged Operation Millennium to Cologne on the night of 30/31 May – the first of his famous '1,000 Bomber' raids. Harris had managed to scrape together 1,047 Heavy Bombers, without calling on the 2 Group Blenheims, but to do so had to include 365 aircraft from Operational Training Units. However, 49 Blenheims made a valuable contribution to Millennium as 34 from 2 Group and 15 from 13 (Army Co-Operation) Squadron (plus seven Havocs of Fighter Command) carried out Intruder operations

254 Squadron Coastal Command covered the Western Approaches from Aldergrove, and this photo of five aircrew was used on a recruiting poster. From the left, they are F/Sgt Foster (Obs), S/Ldr Randall (Pilot), F/Sgt Tyson and Sgt Peak (WOp/Ags), with F/O Sise, a New Zealand Pilot.

against enemy night-fighter airfields in support. Bomber Command lost 41 aircraft from the main force that night, together with two Blenheim Intruders – one from 114 Squadron and one from 13 Squadron ACC (see Appendix 3). Considerable damage was done to Cologne – the smoking city was photographed the following day by five De Havilland Mosquitos, one of which was damaged by flak and crashed in the North Sea, in the first Mosquito operation of the war. This honour fell to 105 Squadron, already famous for its exploits with Blenheims, and set to gain further fame with its Mosquito operations.

The second '1,000 Bomber' raid was to Essen two nights later, although only 956 'heavies' were sent, 31 of which were lost, but this raid was very scattered in conditions of low cloud and industrial haze and far from successful. Once again 60 Blenheims (48 from 2 Group and 12 from Army Co-Operation Command), although not part of the main force, harried the enemy defences by mounting Intruder sorties, at the cost of three of their aircraft (see Appendix 3).

By the third (and last until 1945) of these spectacular '1000 Bomber' raids, mounted against Bremen on the night of 25/26 June, Harris could no longer raise sufficient Heavy Bombers due to the 72 lost and large numbers damaged in the two earlier raids. Bomber Command was therefore forced to include 79 day bombers from 2 Group (51 Blenheims, 24 Bostons and four Mosquitos) in the main force of 960 aircraft; 50 of which were lost. Coastal Command (at Winston Churchill's insistence) added a further 102 Wellingtons and Hudsons (five of which were lost) to make a total of 1,067 bombers – a higher total than the Cologne raid and much more a mixed bag of aircraft types. In addition 2 Group sent 56 aircraft (31 Blenheims, 21 Bostons and four Mosquitos) on Intruder sorties, the first such operations by both the latter types. Thus 2 Group dispatched its entire force of 130 serviceable aircraft that night, including 82 Blenheims – although 15 of these had to be borrowed from Army Co-Operation Command – and were fortunate in that only two of the Intruder Blenheims were lost, both shot down by German night-fighters defending their own bases of Venlo and St Trond (see Appendix 3). The RAF lost 127 bombers during the three Millennium raids, many to German night-fighters, and this figure would have been higher but for the 191 Blenheim sorties that were flown, a significant contribution that is hardly mentioned in most accounts.

P/O Peter Cundy and his 53 Squadron crew Sgt R Fabel and Sgt 'Jock' Graham, he survived the war as a Wg/Cdr DSO, DFC, AFC.

His twin brother R 'Mike' Cundy and crew Sgt R Stevenson and Sgt J Bennett were shot-down and killed in their 13 Squadron 'Intruder' Blenheim N3616 on the first '1000 Bomber' raid.

V5468 of 114 Squadron took part in the first '1,000 Bomber' raid from West Raynham. It has flame-dampers on the exhausts and black under-surfaces.

Intruder operations

Apart from these efforts to support the '1,000 Bomber' raids, most nights of the first eight months of 1942 saw a handful of Blenheim Intruders attempting to assist the main bomber force by harrying the enemy night-fighter airfields. Although these sorties were better planned than they had been the year before, using increasing intelligence from the Y-Service signals intercepts to predict likely activity at German airfields, mainly those in Holland, successes were few and far between and there was a steady haemorrhage of losses (see Appendix 4). Sometimes Intruder operations and Nuisance raids by Blenheims were combined, as on 8/9 March when six intruded on Dutch airfields while six more bombed Ostend harbour, and 18/29 April, when six bombed Langenbrugge power station while others intruded at airfields. From time to time larger numbers were sent out, as on 2/3 July when 24 intruders supported 325 Heavy Bombers attacking Bremen, and on 25/26 July when 21 Blenheim intruders operated, three of which were lost (see Appendix 4) while the main force of 313 bombers attacked Duisburg.

114 Squadron soldiered on in the UK until August 1942, mainly on Intruder operations, and continued to suffer casualties (also Appendix 4), including two Commanding Officers: W/Cdr Jenkins DSO DFC with his equally highly decorated crew, F/O Brancker DFC and bar and F/Sgt Gray DFM, on the night of 27/28 March, and W/Cdr Hull DFC with his crew F/Lt Baker and P/O Morton, who were shot down and captured on 17/18 April while intruding at Schipol airfield. Long-suffering 114 Squadron lost three intruders on the night of 25/26 July (also Appendix 4). 614, an Army Co-Operation Blenheim Squadron, was attached to 114 at West Raynham in May to assist in these night intruding duties.

18 Squadron carried on with intruder operations and took losses, suffering the last – sadly that of their CO, W/Cdr Jones, and crew – on the night of 31 July/1 August 1942. Successes in these intruder sorties were few but losses (Appendix 4) continued until the

Gordon Shackleton (right) and his Observer about to set out on an Intruder sortie in their 114 Squadron Blenheim.

last of these 388 night intruder sorties by Blenheims was flown on the night of 17/18 August 1942. This total excludes the further 140 intruder sorties carried out during the '1,000 Bomber' raids as noted above. Thereafter Havocs, Beaufighters and Mosquitos continued these risky night intruder operations, which had been pioneered so well by the Blenheims, right until the end of the war. In May 1943 2 Group left Bomber Command to form the basis of the Tactical Air Force.

The Dieppe 'Combined Operation'

On 19 August 1942, in the major 'Combined Operation' with the code-name Jubilee, 5,000 Canadian troops with 28 tanks were landed near Dieppe with the objective of capturing and sabotaging the port before withdrawing. Their flanks were protected by simultaneous raids by British Commandos, but the Canadian force was largely trapped on the beaches and suffered heavy casualties. Although painful lessons were learned, and useful information was provided for the planners of the D Day landings two years later, the cost in terms of human suffering was very high. Bostons of 88, 107 and 226 Squadrons

Aircrew of 13 and 18 Squadrons carried out Intruder operations in the summer of 1942 before converting to Mk Vs in September prior to Operation 'Torch'.

and Blenheims of 13 and 614 Squadrons, Army Co-Operation Command, from Thruxton laid smoke screens to mask the landing craft. They were the first aircraft to take off before dawn at 0415 hours and suffered the first casualties of the day when P/O C. Woodland in V5380 was shot down and the crew killed, and Blenheim Z6089 of F/Lt E. Beverley (also of 13 Squadron) was damaged by AA fire, apparently from a RN ship, and had to belly-land. A major air battle developed and the RAF lost over a hundred aircraft from the 70 squadrons engaged, but claimed 96 Luftwaffe machines destroyed, 37 probably destroyed, and 136 damaged. The Luftwaffe actually lost 48 aircraft with 24 damaged (14 pilots were killed and seven wounded) and claimed – far more accurately – to have shot down 97 RAF aircraft. The Allied losses included six Bostons and four Blenheims, two from each squadron (see Appendix 5). Thus the Blenheims tip-toed quietly from the stage of the Northern European Theatre of War, for the rather sad footnote of the Dieppe raid marked the last of the thousands of front-line operations that had been carried out – constantly – by Blenheim bombers in that Theatre since the first day of the war.

As indicated earlier, thousands of Blenheims continued to provide an increasingly important service in support units and in advanced and operational training roles, so they continued to suffer an increasing number of losses in these units (see Appendix 6). In 1942 only 46 Blenheims were lost on operations from the UK, and at least ten of those were not due to enemy action, but no fewer than 188 UK-based Blenheims were lost in accidents. This could be expressed as 36 operational losses and some 200 through accidents, but several of the 36 Blenheims lost on operational sorties simply vanished without trace, so it is not known if their loss was due to enemy action or to accidental causes. The prolonged and invaluable service provided at such a high cost by the Blenheims of the Support and Training Units will be covered in Chapter 31. However, Blenheims were still very much in the fierce spotlight of front-line operational service in both the Middle and Far Eastern Theatres of War, as we will see in Part 3.

Blenheims had served the RAF most valiantly in the Northern European Theatre of Operations for virtually three full years of the war. Throughout, they had borne the brunt of the dangerous daylight operations from UK bases, especially the anti-shipping sorties by Bomber and Coastal Commands, and the Blenheim squadrons had paid a truly terrible price. Those of Bomber Command had also operated extensively at night, as had the Blenheims of Fighter Command – particularly in the earlier period – and many more were lost, again frequently called upon to perform tasks for which they were really not suited. No suitable Blenheim replacement was available, for the reasons given in Chapter 18. Aircraft that failed to return or were destroyed could be replaced, but the precious crews who flew them were essentially irreplaceable. Most tragically, these human losses denied to the country the contribution that would have been made by the future service of thousands of high-calibre and well-trained Pilots, Observers and Navigators, Radio Operators and Air Gunners – crews who had displayed unmatched daring and courage, crews whose skill, devotion to duty, hard-won experience, and qualities of leadership made them ideal candidates for promotion to positions of greater responsibility. We have noted the large number of highly regarded Squadron Commanders who were lost in action, and there is no doubt that many of them, had they survived their Blenheim days, would have risen to the very highest levels of Command in the RAF. This severe haemorrhaging of the very best of the life-blood from the RAF squadrons was, in my view, the most grievously damaging consequence of the widespread and unexpectedly prolonged operational deployment of the Bristol Blenheim.

Two Blenheims of 13 Squadron demonstrate their under-nose sirens, and Z6340 lays a smoke-screen, at an Army Co-Operation Exercise just before the Dieppe operation.

Appendix 1

Blenheim losses on Operation Fuller, the 'Channel Dash', 12 February 1942

Aircraft are both Mk IVs.

12-02-1942   Z7433 110 Squadron: failed to return (FTR); shot down off Texel by Me.109 of JG 1; Sgt P. Reynolds, P/O P. Hill, and Sgt H. Guilfoyle killed in action (KIA) and commemorated on Runnymede Memorial. Peter Hill aged only 18, others 20.

12-02-1942   T1922 114 Squadron: FTR; shot down in North Sea off Kijkduin, Holland; P/O R. Drysdale RCAF, Sgt Maynard, and Sgt J. Pullen KIA. Robert Drysdale and Arthur Maynard buried in Holland, John Pullen has no known grave and commemorated on Runnymede Memorial.

Appendix 2

Coastal Command Blenheim losses, 1942

14-02-1942   Z6033 614 Squadron: FTR; engine cut just after take-off at Inverness on operational sortie, crashed into Moray Firth; P/O Mummery (Pilot) and Sgt Field (WOp/Ag) rescued, Sgt Nightingdale (Obs) drowned.

16-02-1942   Z6187 254 Squadron: FTR; became lost in bad weather, flew into ground near Pembrey, destroyed by fire; P/O J. Tully, Sgt R. Fenney, and Sgt H. Carey injured.

21-02-1942   V5433 (?) 404 Squadron: FTR; damaged by flak on shipping strike off Norway, returned on one engine but crashed on Outer Skerries, Shetlands; crew F/Sgt C. Brown RCAF, F/Sgt J. Oliver RCAF, and Sgt T. Coy KIA. Islanders have erected memorial to crew on crash site. (Serial No. incorrect in ORB, as V5433 was DBR on 18-03-1941.)

05-03-1942   R3839 254 Squadron: FTR; flew into Ridgeway after night take-off at Carew Cheriton for convoy escort duty; Sgt N. Rolfe, Sgt J. McPherson, and Sgt H. Banks KIA.

08-03-1942   Z6103 254 Squadron: FTR from operational patrol, no further details in Squadron ORB.

24 03 1912   V5448 254 Squadron: FTR; engine cut on convoy escort, ditched in shallow water 100 yards offshore at Swanlake Bay; Sgt F. Poore, Sgt F. Davies, and Sgt E. Whitworth rescued uninjured.

02-04-1942   Z6032 614 Squadron: FTR; crashed into Moray Firth at night on operational patrol, cause unknown; P/O J. Findley, P/O G. Giras, and Sgt W. Huggett KIA. Pilot and Obs buried near Kinloss, WOp/Ag commemorated on Runnymede Memorial.

19-04-1942   N3533 143 Squadron: FTR; became lost in bad visibility, hit fence in forced-landing at Buncrana, Donegal, Eire; Sgt Bertrand, Sgt Newbold, and Sgt Smith interned initially, but returned to unit two days later.

04-05-1942   R2779 254 Squadron: FTR; engine cut while escorting DC2, hit sea in fog off Lundy Island attempting to ditch; S/Ldr I. Jameson, Sgt R. Raymond, and F/Lt Barnes killed.

23-05-1942   Z6181 404 Squadron: FTR; flew into high ground in bad visibility at Belhelvie, 10 miles north of Aberdeen, on ASR sortie; F/Sgt E. Morrow, Sgt W. White, and P/O L. Thomas KIA.

25-04-1942   L9448 143 Squadron: engine cut on patrol, belly-landed near Ballykelly, crew safe, aircraft DBR.

26-05-1942   Z6245 404 Squadron: FTR from operational patrol; S/Ldr P. Foster (Pilot) and F/Sgt J. Jamieson (WOp/Ag) KIA, F/O Briggs (Obs) survived.

31-05-1942   Z6023 143 Squadron: FTR from operational patrol over Western Approaches, presumed ditched; P/O L. Morris, Sgt F. Parker, and Sgt Mackay KIA. (Squadron ORB gives V6023, but that 107 Squadron aircraft was lost 06-06-1941, both losses confirmed by aircraft movement cards.)

05-06-1942   Z6027 254 Squadron: FTR from operational patrol; F/Lt T. Ward, Sgt G. F. Daglish, and P/O R. Thompson KIA and commemorated on Runnymede Memorial.

26-07-1942   ? 236 Squadron: FTR from Met reconnaissance to Norway; F/Lt L. Dejace (ex-Belgian Air Force Pilot) and crew KIA. (Serial No. not given in ORB, and unable to match with any other loss on this date.)

Appendix 3

Blenheim losses on night intruder sorties, 1942

Aircraft are all Mk IVs.

10/11-01-1942 V6440 82 Squadron: FTR to Bodney, shot down by flak near Soesterberg airfield; F/Lt K. Nash, Sgt H. Downs RNZAF, and Sgt E. Cooper KIA, buried at Amersfoort.

14/15-01-1942 V6391 114 Squadron: FTR from intruder sortie to Schipol, shot down by flak; F/Lt B. Adam RAAF, Sgt J. Willis, and P/O F. Street-Porter KIA, commemorated at Runnymede.

15/16-01-1942 V6378 82 Squadron: FTR from intruder operation to Schipol; Sgt J. Brown, P/O W. Scarlett, and P/O E. Garstin Missing in Action, commemorated at Runnymede.

28/29-01-1942 V5726 114 Squadron: FTR; took off from West Raynham for Leeuwarden, shot down by flak; Sgt T. Peters (aged 21), Sgt G. Church RAAF, and Sgt K. Bird KIA and buried at Amsterdam.

26/27-03-1942 Z7307 114 Squadron: FTR; took off from West Raynham for Soesterberg, shot down by Me.110 of NJG 2; F/S W. Popplestone RCAF, P/O W. Hawkins, and P/O C. White RCAF KIA. Pilot and WOp/Ag buried at Harlingen, Obs commemorated on Runnymede Memorial.

26/27-03-1942 Z7700 114 Squadron: FTR; took off from West Raynham for Dutch airfields, shot down into sea; crew F/Lt E. Bury, Sgt J. Beauchamp, and Sgt T. Crilly (aged 21) KIA and commemorated on Runnymede Memorial.

27/28-03-1942 Z7276 114 Squadron: FTR; took off at 1920 for Soesterberg, shot down by flak near Zeist; W/Cdr J. Jenkins DSO DFC, F/O H. Brancker DFC*, and F/Sgt C. Gray DFM (aged 21) KIA and buried at Amersfoort. W/Cdr J. Fraser Jenkins BA (Cantab) was CO of 114 Squadron, and crew were lost on last sortie of their second Tour of Operations on Blenheims. (See the photograph of this crew earlier in the chapter.)

27/28-03-1942 R3620 114 Squadron: took off at 1920 for Schipol, damaged by flak over target, crash-landed at base; F/Sgt E. Atkins (Pilot) injured, Sgt J. Sullivan, and Sgt W. Harrison safe, aircraft repaired.

17/18-04-1942 Z7430 114 Squadron: FTR; took off from West Raynham for Schipol, shot down near Aalsmeer; W/Cdr G. Hull DFC, F/Lt T. Baker, and P/O J. Morton captured and became PoWs. W/Cdr Hull was CO of 114 Squadron, the second CO to be reported missing in three weeks.

24/25-04-1942 V5458 114 Squadron: FTR; took off from West Raynham for Leeuwarden airfield, crashed into North Sea; Sgt P. McKenny, Sgt J. McIntyre, and Sgt J. Lewis KIA and commemorated on Runnymede Memorial.

26/27-04-1942 T2430 114 Squadron: FTR; took off from West Raynham for Eindhoven, damaged by Ju.88, more damage from friendly AA fire near Lowestoft, crash-landed at Pulham near Norwich; crew P/O J. Molesworth, P/O E. Denny, and Sgt W. Burberry injured, aircraft destroyed by fire.

28/29-04-1942 Z7436 18 Squadron: FTR; took off from Wattisham at 2335 for Langebrugge, crashed into Dutch polder; crew P/O R. Owen, Sgt L. Coventry, and Sgt D. Hughes KIA and buried at Vlissigen.

06/07-05-1942 V6382 18 Squadron: FTR; took off from Wattisham for Eindhoven, lost without trace; P/O H. Palmer, Sgt W. Lindsell, and Sgt E. Andrews KIA and commemorated on Runnymede Memorial. Henry Palmer was aged 20, William Lindsell 21.

30/31-05-1942 V5645 114 Squadron: FTR; shot down on intruder operation in support of first '1,000 Bomber' raid; P/O J. Fox RNZAF injured, captured and died as PoW 01-06-1942, Sgt J. Leonard and Sgt Smithson KIA and buried in Sage War Cemetery.

30/31-05-1942 N3616 13 Squadron: FTR, shot down into sea on operation in support of first '1,000 Bomber' raid; P/O R. Cundy, Sgt R. Stevenson, and Sgt J. Bennett KIA, P/O Cundy buried in Boulogne East Cemetery, Sgt Stevenson in Calais Canadian Cemetery, Sgt Stevenson commemorated at Runnymede.

01/02-06-1942 Z6186 13 Squadron: FTR; shot down on intruder operation to Venlo in support of second '1,000 Bomber' raid; F/Lt D. Redman, F/Sgt P. Enna, and F/Sgt T. Trimmer KIA and buried in Reichswald Forest War Cemetery.

01/02-06-1942 R3620 114 Squadron: FTR; shot down on intruder operation to Venlo in support of second '1,000 Bomber' raid; F/Sgt B. L'Hirondelle, P/O R. Inglis, and Sgt H. Meakin KIA and buried in Rheinberg War Cemetery.

01/02-06-1942 V6337 114 Squadron: FTR; hit by flak on intruder operation to Venlo in support of second '1,000 Bomber' raid, crashed into English Channel; Sgt J. Mitchell, Sgt R. McIntosh, and Sgt L. Fussey KIA and buried in Rockanje/Dunkirk Cemeteries.

04/05-06-1942 L8800 114 Squadron: FTR; took off on intruder operation to Schipol, crashed within minutes at Weasenham, bomb-load exploded; Sgt F. Cooke, Sgt J. Wallbridge, and Sgt E. Kitcher (aged 21) KIA.

08/09-06-1942 V5455 114 Squadron: FTR; took off on intruder operation, reported engine trouble, jettisoned bombs, attempted to return to base, crashed 1 hour later at Brisley, Norfolk, and destroyed by fire; P/O J. Graham, Sgt M. Beaufoy, and Sgt L. Harrowell KIA. Villagers of Brisley recently erected memorial to crew at site.

25/26-06-1942 Z6084 13 Squadron: FTR from intruder operation to St Truiden to support third '1,000 Bomber' raid, shot down at 0138 by night-fighter of NJG 1; crew P/O P. Frith, Sgt H. Vinter, and Sgt R. Plant KIA and buried in Hewaart Churchyard, Brabant.

25/26-06-1942 T2254 13 Squadron: FTR from intruder operation to Venlo to support third '1,000 Bomber' raid, shot down by night-fighter of NJG 1; crew F/O P. Looker, F/Sgt W. O'Neill RNZAF (aged 21), and Sgt G. Cox KIA, buried in Schoonselhof Cemetery, Antwerp.

02/03-07-1942 Z7372 18 Squadron: FTR from intruder operation to St Truiden, lost without trace; crew Sgt W. Furness, P/O R. Morton RNZAF, and Sgt T. Ross KIA and commemorated on Runnymede Memorial.

13/14-07-1942 V5503 18 Squadron: FTR from intruder operation to Deelen, hit by flak, engine cut, crashed at 0330 at Bredfield, Suffolk; crew P/O L. Rule, Sgt Bradshaw, and Sgt Gatling safe, aircraft destroyed.

13/14-07-1942 V6071 18 Squadron: FTR from same intruder operation, also hit by flak, crashed near Amsterdam; P/O P. Coulthard, Sgt Meech, and P/O L. Ward KIA and buried in New Eastern Cemetery. Peter Coulthard was aged 19.

21/22-07-1942 Z7319 114 Squadron: FTR from intruder operation to Vechta airfield, crashed into sea off Jutland; F/O L. Jackson, Sgt S. Beaumont, and Sgt Harris KIA. F/O Jackson has no known grave, others buried in Lemvig Cemetery.

23/24-07-1942 Z7428 18 Squadron: FTR from intruder operation to Vechta airfield, shot down near target; F/Lt F. Thorne, P/O B. Cook RNZAF, and P/O W. Blackadder KIA and buried in Sage War Cemetery.

25/26-07-1942 R3837 114 Squadron: FTR from intruder operation to Venlo airfield, shot down by Oblt Reinhold Knacke, CO of JG 1; Sgt L. Causley, Sgt G. Spencer, and Sgt L. Gray KIA and buried in Jonkebos War Cemetery.

25/26-07-1942 V5635 114 Squadron: FTR from intruder operation to Vechta airfield, shot down; P/O G. Strasser, P/O E. Allen, and Sgt J. Harold KIA and buried in Becklingen War Cemetery.

25/26-07-1942 V6264 114 Squadron: FTR from intruder operation to Leeuwarden, crashed off Dutch coast; RCAF crew F/Sgt E. Warnick, Sgt P. Leslie, and Sgt R. Smith (aged 20) KIA and commemorated on Runnymede Memorial.

28/29-07-1942 Z7344 18 Squadron: FTR from intruder operation to Stade airfield, shot down by ship's flak into North Sea; P/O S. Hill RCAF (aged 21), F/Sgt D. McKinnon, and Sgt D. Williams KIA and buried at Sage.

31-07/1-08-'42 V6432 18 Squadron: FTR from intruder operation to Venlo airfield, shot down by Me.110 of JG based there; W/Cdr C. Jones DFC, Sgt K. Waylett, and Sgt Evans KIA and buried in Reichswald Forest War Cemetery. W/Cdr Chris Jones was CO of 18 Squadron.

Appendix 4

Blenheim losses on the 'Combined Operations' raid on Dieppe, 19 August 1942

Aircraft are all Mk IVs.

19-08-1942 V5380 13 Squadron: FTR; shot down off Dieppe by flak while laying smoke-screen; P/O C. Woodland, Sgt Boyd, and Sgt H. Neville KIA and buried at Dieppe.

19-08-1942 Z6089 13 Squadron: damaged off Dieppe by RN AA fire after laying smoke-screen, crash-landed back at Thruxton; F/Lt E. Beverley, Sgt Jones and Sgt Hooker safe, aircraft repaired.

19-08-1942 V5626 614 Squadron: FTR; damaged by 'friendly' flak off Dieppe prior to laying smoke-screen; F/Lt J. Scott (Pilot) wounded but crash-landed at Friston igniting hung-up phosphorus smoke-bombs, badly burnt but rescued unconscious Sgt W. Johnson (Obs), who died 36 hours later, F/Sgt G. Gifkins (WOp/Ag) KIA by the AA fire, Scott awarded DFC.

19-08-1942 V5380 614 Squadron: taxied into ditch prior to taking off at 0425 for Dieppe; P/O P. Hanbury and crew uninjured, aircraft repaired.

Appendix 5

Non-operational Blenheim losses, 1942

01-01-1942 Z6148 236 Squadron Mk IV: lost height after night take-off and flew into ground at Redberth, Pembs; Sgt R. Wood killed, crew injured.

01-01-1942 Z6148 236 Squadron Mk IV: lost height after night take-off and flew into ground at Redberth, Pembs; F/Sgt R. Wood killed, crew injured.

02-01-1942 L6837 604 Squadron Mk I: engine caught fire in air, crash-landed at Staverton, destroyed by fire; S/Ldr H. Kerr and crew escaped.

02-01-1942	Z6082 236 Squadron Mk IV: engine cut on air-test, lost height, undershot attempted forced landing at Sommerton, Pembs.
03-01-1942	P6959 17 OTU Mk IV: dived into ground from cloud at Hine Heath, Stanton, Salop; P/O M. Kingshott, Sgt W. Jowett and Sgt R. Masson killed.
04-01-1942	N3602 5 AOS Mk IV: overshot landing at Jurby and u/c raised to stop.
05-01-1942	T1956 1 AAS Mk IV: one engine cut, second lost power, belly-landed at Donna Nook; no injuries reported to Sgt S. Nicolle and crew.
08-01-1942	R3752 54 OTU Mk IV: iced-up, lost height, flew into ground 3 miles east of Church Fenton; P/O J. Vopalecky and crew safe.
09-01-1942	L8677 54 OTU Mk I: dived into sea on air firing practice east of Scarborough, Yorks; Sgt B. Jepson and Sgt W. Higgs killed.
11-01-1942	L8661 51 OTU Mk I: engine cut, crash-landed at Staughton Moor, near St Neots, Hunts; Sgt F. Blenkinsopp killed.
11-01-1942	Z6040 17 OTU Mk IV: both engines cut in severe icing and snowstorm, crash-landed at Scolt Head; P/O C. Pereira injured.
11-01-1942	V6312 42 OTU Mk IV: undershot landing at Andover, hit hedge, destroyed by fire; P/O S. Owen escaped.
14-01-1942	L1303 17 OTU Mk I: dived into ground in circuit at Denhill Farm, Hunts, cause unknown; F/Sgt S. Lang and Sgt A. Sistron killed.
14-01-1942	V6374 82 Squadron Mk IV: u/c collapsed on heavy landing at Bodney at 1925, aircraft DBR; no injuries reported to Sgt W. Tuller and crew.
17-01-1942	L1183 2 (C) OTU Mk I : engine lost power on take-off at Catfoss, swung and crashed, destroyed by fire; F/O R. Rose (solo pilot) escaped safely.
21-01-1942	Z7453 17 OTU Mk IV: missing on NavEx over North Sea, presumed ditched 3 miles east of Filey; P/O E. Parke, Sgt F. Coakley and Sgt M. York Missing in Action, commemorated at Runnymede.
22-01-1942	T1943 120 Squadron Mk IV: tyre burst on take-off at Nutts Corner, swung and u/c collapsed. 120 Squadron was equipped with Liberator Mk IIs.
24-01-1942	L6750 51 OTU Mk I: engine caught fire in air, crash-landed near Cranfield, destroyed by fire; F/Sgt Knowles and crew escaped.
26-01-1942	V5769 82 Squadron Mk IV: struck trees on Bodney boundary while gaining flying speed on night take-off at 0430; Sgt Cheadle (Pilot) and Sgt J. Eckersley (Obs) killed, Sgt H. Hargreaves (WOp/Ag) injured.
27-01-1942	L1442 51 OTU Mk I: overshot night landing at Cranfield, DBR; no injuries reported to Sgt R. Brown and crew.
27-01-1942	Z6279 404 Squadron Mk IV: both engines cut on ferry flight, crash-landed near Castletown, Caithness; Sgt R. Mackay and three crew injured.
27-01-1942	N6163 51 OTU Mk IV: descended in cloud and hit hill at Kingswood, Beds; Sgt R. Latham killed.
28-01-1942	Z7290 13 OTU Mk IV: caught fire on ground at Bicester and destroyed.
29-01-1942	L8725 Ferry Training Unit Mk I : u/c raised in error after landing at Honeybourne.
29-01-1942	L8785 17 OTU Mk IV: stalled on night approach in bad weather to Warboys and crashed; P/O A. Petty and Sgt J. Charnock killed.
29-01-1942	R3907 13 OTU Mk IV: engine cut, stalled and dived into ground from cloud, destroyed by fire at Stort, near Devizes, Wilts; Sgt J. Ruddock, Sgt R. Raines, and Sgt K. Riding killed.
30-01-1942	V5753 404 Squadron Mk IV: skidded off icy runway into boundary at Sumburgh, became 3166M.
30-01-1942	V5803 254 Squadron Mk IV-F: crashed on take-off for air-test at Dyce, elevator trim-tab controls reversed; F/Lt H. Randall and passenger uninjured. (See photographs at the end of this chapter.)
05-02-1942	V5891 1 AGS Mk IV: struck by V5965 (below) while parked at Pembrey, destroyed by fire.
05-02-1942	V5965 1 AGS Mk IV: overshot landing, swung and hit V5891 (above); Sgt A. Hay and LAC M. Lacy killed, LACs Guest and McLean slightly injured.
06-02-1942	L6809 13 OTU Mk I: hit tree after take-off at Hinton-in-the-Hedges and crashed 1 mile from airfield; Sgt W. Everard-Smith (solo pilot) killed.
07-02-1942	Z5817 42 OTU Mk IV: flew into ground near Marlborough, Wilts; P/O P. Stobie, Sgt A. Bennett and Sgt T. Jack killed.
08-02-1942	V6397 114 Squadron Mk IV: struck storage shed on take-off at West Raynham and caught fire; no serious injuries reported to Sgt Woodfield, Sgt Matthews, and Sgt Harris.
08-02-1942	Z5729 5 AOS Mk IV: lost on NavEx in bad weather, crashed on beach at Braystone, Cumb; Sgt J. Zavitz and one crewman injured.
08-02-1942	V6018 5 AOS Mk IV: lost on NavEx in bad weather, ran short of fuel, Sgt Chad overshot attempted forced landing near Ballykilnee, Ulster.
10-02-1942	T1885 51 OTU Mk IV: overshot night landing at Cranfield in bad weather, DBR; no injuries reported to P/O J. Houdret and crew.

11-02-1942   V6383 17 OTU Mk IV: abandoned at night when lost in bad visibility near Bottisham; one of Sgt R. Hargreaves's crew injured.

12-02-1942   V5806 51 OTU Mk IV: dived into ground from cloud at night at Notting Fen, Ramsey St Marys, Hunts, presumed control lost; F/O G. Fletcher and Sgt K. Jones killed.

13-02-1942   Z7501 42 OTU Mk IV: swung on take-off, became airborne, stalled and crashed at Penton Corner, Weyhill; P/O R. Charter and crew injured.

14-02-1942   K7044 54 OTU Mk I-F: tyre burst on landing at Church Fenton, swung and undercarriage collapsed.

16-02-1942   V6454 82 Squadron Mk IV: flew into ground at night, believed due to incorrect altimeter setting, destroyed by fire; crew P/O K. Bottrill, Sgt J. Ambler, and Sgt J. Roberts killed.

17-02-1942   Z5961 42 OTU Mk IV: engine cut after night take-off at Thruxton, stalled and crashed 2 miles to east, destroyed by fire; P/O L. Gregory (solo pilot) killed.

19-02-1942   L1359 17 OTU Mk I: hit L6808 while taxiing at night at Warboys, DBR, L6808 repaired; no injuries reported to P/O J. Hadland and P/O S. Coshall in L1359 or P/O J. Ellis in L6808.

20-02-1942   Z5899 17 OTU Mk IV: hit balloon cable on NavEx, crashed near Bearwood, Warks; Sgt W. Kyle, Sgt L. de Lisser and Sgt E. Scott killed.

23-02-1942   L1192 42 OTU Mk I: engine cut, lost height, crash-landed at Witherington Farm, near Salisbury, Wilts; P/O R. Carswell and crew uninjured.

23-02-1942   L4845 51 OTU Mk IV: engine cut, caught fire on landing at Cranfield; F/O R. Coombs and crew escaped unhurt.

24-02-1942   K7109 13 OTU Mk I: engine cut on overshoot at Hinton-in-the-Hedges, swung and hit ground, destroyed by fire; Sgt R. Weller (solo pilot) escaped with slight injuries.

25-02-1942   V5811 13 OTU Mk IV: engine cut due to fuel mismanagement, crash-landed at Essex Farm, Blackthorne, Bucks; Sgt Young injured.

27-02-1942   Z7353 13 OTU Mk IV: bounced on landing, attempted overshoot, stalled avoiding trees and crashed, destroyed by fire; P/O McMillan RAAF and crew escaped with slight injuries.

01-03-1942   Z7406 1404 Met Flt Mk IV: engine lost power after take-off at Exeter, lost height and hit Beaufighter T3041 of 307 Squadron, destroyed by fire; P/O J. Portman, F/Sgt F. Pearson and Sgt E. Colton killed.

01-03-1942   L1324 60 OTU Mk I: engine cut on take-off at East Fortune, crashed; Sgt R. Tidy (solo pilot) injured.

04-03-1942   L 6804 17 OTU Mk I: abandoned in air after engine cut on air-test in bad weather near Colston Basset, Notts; Sgt G. Jessup (solo pilot) safe.

08-03-1942   Z6342 489 Squadron Mk IV: engine cut on take-off at Worthy Down, stalled and crashed, destroyed by fire; F/Sgt F. Wilkinson, P/O C. Priest RNZAF and F/Sgt J. London killed.

08-03-1942   Z6363 5 AOS Mk IV: missing from NavEx over Irish Sea in bad weather, presumed crashed into sea; Sgt R. Nies, LACs N. Rendall and H. Richardson (Trainee Obs), and AC2 T. Fenton (Trainee WOp/Ag) missing, presumed killed.

13-03-1942   R3607 13 OTU Mk IV: overturned in attempted forced-landing while lost on NavEx in bad visibility at Ratby, Leics; Sgt P. Reddy injured.

13-03-1942   Z6021 5 AOS Mk IV: crashed in forced-landing when lost near Castlebar, Co Mayo; P/O D. Rawcliffe, Sgt H. Thomas and two crewmen injured and interned.

13-03-1942   N3538 17 OTU Mk IV: hit cables attempting forced-landing at Boston Spa, Yorks; Sgt W. Curlet, P/O J. McColl and Sgt E. Johnson killed.

17-03-1942   N3575 5 AOS Mk IV: crashed into sea off Ramsey Bay, IoM, cause unknown; Sgt P. Cannell and Sgt C. Carling missing, presumed killed.

23-03-1942   V5745 1 AGS Mk IV: flew into ground on fire, cause unknown, at Bryneglin Farm, Carmarthen; F/Sgt W. Mason (Pilot), LAC Briise (Norwegian) and AC2 E. Smith killed, LAC D. Olsen seriously injured (all Trainee WOp/Ags).

25-03-1942   Z5737 51 OTU Mk IV: both tyres burst on heavy landing at night at Cranfield, later struck by Z5739.

25-03-1942   K7087 2 (C) OTU Mk I: swung on landing at Catfoss, u/c collapsed.

26-03-1942   R3808 54 OTU Mk IV: control lost on night overshoot at Church Fenton, stalled and crashed, destroyed by fire; Sgt E. Baggott (solo pilot) killed.

26-03-1942   V5798 51 OTU Mk IV: engine cut, stalled on to runway landing at Cranfield, later run into by V5932 below; Sgt H. Ferris slightly injured.

26-03-1942   V5932 51 OTU Mk IV: ran into V5798 (above) while landing at Cranfield, both aircraft DBR; Sgt K. McCormick injured.

27-03-1942   L1454 42 OTU Mk I: flew into ground near Netheravon while laying smoke-screen, destroyed by fire; no record of injuries to crew.

28-03-1942   Z7983 13 OTU Mk IV: crashed into Irish Sea in blizzard on NavEx; Sgt K. Johnson, Sgt F. Hollier, and Sgt J. Bennett missing presumed drowned, commemorated at Runnymede.

29-03-1942   Z5949 17 OTU Mk IV: undershot landing at Sutton Bridge and DBR, Sgt J. Heagerty, P/O J. Jenkinson and Sgt E. Moakler injured.

29-03-1942	Z6098 13 OTU Mk IV: overshot landing on to soft ground and overturned; Sgt G. Ashplant (solo pilot) uninjured.
29-03-1942	N3561 54 OTU Mk IV: dived into ground at night near Sherburn, Yorks, cause unknown; Sgt W. Bailey and Sgt J. Prince killed.
30-03-1942	R3772 17 OTU Mk IV: stalled on landing at Warboys, u/c collapsed, Sgt Coleman uninjured.
30-03-1942	V5572 42 OTU Mk IV: engine cut, stalled and spun in on approach to Andover; P/O A. McTavish RCAF, P/O N. Wolfenden and Sgt R. Hunter RNZAF killed.
31-03-1942	R3838 13 OTU Mk IV: missing on NavEx over North Sea, presumed ditched; P/O A. Burnie, Sgt A. Geers, and Sgt J. Gray Missing in Action, commemorated at Runnymede.
31-03-1942	V6003 42 OTU Mk IV: hit by Z5986 while parked at Andover, DBR, Z5986 repaired.
01-04-1942	T1828 25 Squadron Mk IV: mid-air collision with 25 Squadron Beaufighter R2056 just below cloud, both aircraft came down near Thrapston, Northants; Sgt P. Swan RAAF (Pilot) baled out and injured, Sgt G. Larmour (Obs) killed.
02-04-1942	Z5812 42 OTU Mk IV: engine cut, force-landed near High Wycombe, Bucks; Sgt W. Erasmus and crew uninjured.
02-04-1942	V5564 54 OTU Mk IV: engine cut after take-off at Church Fenton, stalled and crash-landed, DBF; Sgt J. Buchan escaped uninjured.
04-04-1942	L6795 2 (C) OTU Mk I: collided with L1125 (below) in formation training and both aircraft crashed into sea 1 mile north of Skipsea, Yorks; F/Sgt W. Braun RCAF, P/O J. Mair and Sgt F. Warren RAAF killed.
04-04-1942	L1125 2 (C) OTU Mk I: collided with L6795 (above) in formation training and both aircraft crashed into sea 1 mile north of Skipsea, Yorks; Sgt C. Edmonds, Sgt G. Peart and Sgt V. Copus RAAF killed.
06-04-1942	L1132 2 (C) OTU Mk IV: engine cut in steep turn, crash-landed at Carnaby, Yorks; Sgt Bonnet uninjured.
06-04-1942	T2126 42 OTU Mk IV: hit HT cables in low flying exercise, crash-landed near Ashton, Oxon; no injuries reported to P/O T. Thompson and crew.
08-04-1942	Z5871 60 OTU Mk IV: dived into ground near Long Yester, E Lothian, presumed through lack of oxygen; Sgt S. Moffitt and Sgt R. Hunter killed.
08-04-1942	V5720 42 OTU Mk IV: engine cut, control lost, dived into ground near Basingstoke, Hants; P/O L. Sceales and Sgt W. Stevenson RCAF killed.
08-04-1942	V6024 5 AOS Mk IV: hit steamroller landing at Jurby in bad visibility; P/O J. McFetridge and one crewman injured.
11-04-1942	V5527 2 (C) OTU Mk IV: flew into ground after night take-off, destroyed by fire at Brandesburton, Yorks; Sgt W. Cooper (Pilot) injured, Sgt H. Shaw (Obs) killed.
13-04-1942	T2396 18 Squadron Mk IV: written off 0142 at Wattisham in landing accident, Chance lights not in use; P/O Breakey and crew uninjured.
15-04-1942	Z6253 1 AGS Mk IV: engine cut, stalled in attempting forced-landing at Tile House Farm, Bury Green, Glam; no injuries reported to Sgt K. Stadiley and crew.
15-04-1942	L6754 60 OTU Mk I: flew into ground on night approach to East Fortune; P/O S. Fulton RCAF (solo Pilot) uninjured.
18-04-1942	L1237 29 Squadron Mk I-F: engine cut, overshot landing at West Malling and u/c collapsed, destroyed by fire; Sgt Knight injured.
20-04-1942	Z6102 254 Squadron Mk IV: overshot landing at Carew Cheriton, u/c raised to stop, DBR.
20-04-1942	Z6145 13 OTU Mk IV: tyre burst on take-off at Bicester, swung on landing back and u/c collapsed, destroyed by fire; Sgt F. Morgan (Pilot, on his first Blenheim solo) escaped unhurt.
22-04-1942	Z5874 42 OTU Mk IV: engine cut on take-off at Andover, overran runway into field and DBR; no injuries reported to P/O V. Kemmis and crew.
23-04-1942	V6008 54 OTU Mk IV: engine cut after night take-off at Church Fenton, crash-landed at Ryther, near York; Sgt J. Coward killed.
28-04-1942	L6600 51 OTU Mk I: engine caught fire after landing at Tinwood Farm, DBR; no injuries reported to F/O K. Cubitt and crew.
01-05-1942	L8696 60 OTU Mk I: engine cut, hit trees in attempted forced-landing near East Fortune; Sgt D. Wiggins (solo pilot) injured.
01-05-1942	V5447 143 Squadron Mk IV: u/c jammed on air-firing sortie, belly-landed at Aldergrove, DBR.
02-05-1942	L1313 17 OTU Mk I: hit tree on night take-off at Warboys, destroyed by fire; Sgt T. Voges and Sgt Parker injured.
02-05-1942	L9206 13 OTU Mk IV: dived into ground 3 miles east of Billesdon, Leics, destroyed by fire; F/Sgt J. Young RCAF, Sgt H. Morrison RNZAF, and F/Sgt G. Boggess killed.
04-05-1942	V5799 5 OTU Mk IV: burst tyre on take-off at Chivenor, lost power and crash-landed; no record of injuries to P/O J. Patterson and crew.

04-05-1942	L8373 17 OTU Mk IV: tyre bust on take-off at Warboys and crashed, F/Sgt G. Bruce and Sgt H. Hardman uninjured, airframe became 3354M.
06-05-1942	L8755 13 OTU Mk IV: took off from Bicester on bombing practice over North Sea, crashed into sea; crew killed, Sgt T. Crawford RCAF buried in Ameland, Sgt D. McKenzie RNZAF and F/Sgt W. Ward have no known grave.
06-05-1942	K7091 2 (C) OTU Mk I: control lost at night, crashed near Sandingholme, Yorks; Sgt A. McBean (solo pilot) killed.
09-05-1942	V6523 18 Squadron Mk IV: crashed during Army Co-Op exercise near Eyke, Suffolk; F/Lt G. Hall (Pilot) killed, P/O W. Howard and Sgt S. Cox injured. Sgt Cox died three weeks later.
09-05-1942	K7086 ATA Training Flight Mk I: collided with L8439 (below) after take-off at White Waltham; First Officer R. Pavey ATA injured, two unnamed ATA crew killed.
09-05-1942	L8439 ATA Training Flight Mk I: collided with K7086 (above), destroyed by fire; First Officers J. Erickson and T. Walters killed, one unnamed crewman injured, all ATA
10-05-1942	Z5797 42 OTU Mk IV: failed to gain height after night take-off at Thruxton, hit obstructions 1 mile east, near Fyfield; P/O P. Wood injured.
10-05-1942	Z5974 5 AOS Mk IV: engine cut on NavEx, crashed into hills at Posso Farm, Peebles; Sgt J. Manthorpe (Pilot), Sgt J. Chadwick (WOp/Ag), LACs P. Christian and R. Lloyd (Trainee Obs) killed.
13-05-1942	V5384 17 OTU Mk IV: dived into ground from cloud at Butchers Farm, Thorney, Hunts, presumed control lost; P/O H. Zavadowsky RCAF, P/O R. Corr and Sgt J. White killed.
14-05-1942	Z7355 1401 Met Flt Mk IV: diverted from Bircham Newton to Mildenhall on return from sortie in very bad weather, engine cut (out of fuel), crashed in attempted forced-landing at Hitcham, near Thetford, Norfolk; crew F/Sgt H. Garthwaite, P/O W. Luddington, and Sgt Dale injured.
14-05-1942	BA372 13 OTU Mk V: crashed on take-off at Chivenor; Sgt C. Allen and two crewmen injured.
15-05-1942	V5690 42 OTU Mk IV: flew into high ground on night approach to Thruxton; P/O J. Wemyss-Smith (solo pilot) killed.
20-05-1942	V6028 21 Squadron Mk IV: overshot landing at Kingstown airfield and DBR; Sgt J. Heagerty and crew safe. Aircraft in which W/Cdr Hughie Edwards won his VC on Bremen raid.
23-05-1942	P4835 143 Squadron Mk IV: tyre burst on take-off at Limavady, swung and u/c collapsed.
24-05-1942	R3599 13 OTU Mk IV: stalled in storm-cloud and spun, abandoned and crashed at Green Farm, Trowbridge, Wilts; Sgt C. Typer (Pilot) injured, Sgt W. Heap and Sgt K. Allwood killed.
24-05-1942	V5638 21 Squadron Mk IV: took off from Abbotsinch, engine cut, crashed near East Linwood, Renfrewshire; crew S/Ldr J. Fowler, Sgt Willis, and Sgt C. Tilley killed, aircraft destroyed by fire.
24-05-1942	L1218 1 AGS Mk I: engine caught fire, dived into ground 3 miles east of Pembrey; Sgt K. Ramsdale and LACs E. Moore, G. Layton and J. Henry (Trainee WOp/Ags) killed.
25-05-1942	Z6090 54 OTU Mk IV: dived out of cloud into ground at Greenburn, W Lothian, presumed iced up; P/O J. Hill and Sgt A. Harrison killed.
26-05-1942	V6314 114 Squadron Mk IV: crashed near Heyshott, Sussex, when engine cut during Army Co-Op exercise; F/Lt R. Ryan and crew believed uninjured.
27-05-1942	V5568 1401 Met Flt. Mk IV: shot down in error by RAF Whirlwind of 137 Squadron; F/O W. Marshall, Sgt Thimblebee and Sgt Gray reported missing presumed killed.
29-05-1942	V5561 143 Squadron Mk IV: tyre burst on landing at Limavady, undercarriage collapsed, DBR.
03-06-1942	Z6188 42 OTU Mk IV: engine cut on take-off at Thruxton, swung, hit tree and overturned, destroyed by fire; Sgt D. Evans escaped with slight injuries.
03-06-1942	T2397 13 OTU Mk IV: both engines cut shortly after take-off at Bicester, crashed at Bucknell, Oxon; Sgt Wheeler (Obs) killed, Sgt C. Nicholson (Pilot) injured.
03-06-1942	V6238 17 OTU Mk IV: engine cut on night overshoot, stalled and crashed at Wyton; no injuries recorded to Sgt Rew and crew.
04-06-1942	V5566 17 OTU Mk IV: lost on NavEx over N Sea, P/O G. Nadaraja (Ceylon) and P/O F. Barker commemorated at Runnymede, body of Sgt R. Doman was washed ashore 8 days later and is buried at Stamford.
05-06-1942	R2797 42 OTU Mk IV: hit trees on night approach and crashed at Tidworth; Sgt Willis (solo pilot) killed.
06-06-1942	Z5722 68 Squadron Mk IV-F: lost power on take-off at Coltishall (cooling gills left open), hit flag-pole, crashed and DBF.
07-06-1942	Z6340 13 Squadron Mk IV: engine cut, crashed in attempted forced-landing near Andover; no injuries recorded to P/O G. Knight and crew.
08/09-06-1942	Z7283 18 Squadron Mk IV: engine cut, crashed into trees and house at Houghton, Leics, at 0015 on night NavEx and destroyed by fire; Sgt J. Jones and Sgt H. Dawson killed, Sgt G. Crawford survived.
11-06-1942	V5571 5 OTU Mk IV: tyre burst on take-off at Turnberry, swung and u/c collapsed, destroyed by fire; no injury recorded to F/Sgt Batterin and crew.

12-06-1942	Z6175 404 Squadron Mk IV: hit balloon cable on NavEx, stalled in attempted forced-landing, crashed at Fulwell pumping station, Sunderland, Co Durham; Sgt G. Brocklington and Sgt J. Moller killed, Sgt A. Sallis injured.
15-06-1942	P4858 1 OAFU Mk IV: engine cut-on take off, dived into ground near Wigtown; Sgt H. Myles and LACs R. Yeaman and J. Russell (Trainee Obs) killed.
15-06-1942	BA170 60 OTU Mk V: undershot landing at East Fortune, DBR.
16-06-1942	V5765 404 Squadron Mk IV: hit sandbank recovering from dive on gunnery practice, crashed into sea at Tentsmuir Ranges, Fife; Sgt J. Mair, Sgt L. Cooper, Sgt D. Campbell RCAF and AC1 W. Dunbar (Armourer) killed.
17-06-1942	L6774 13 OTU Mk I: engine caught fire on approach, swung on landing and undercarriage collapsed at Hinton-in-the-Hedges; P/O H. Bichard (solo pilot) injured.
17-06-1942	R3611 17 OTU Mk IV: engine cut after take-off, stalled and spun into ground at Alconbury; Sgt P. Thompson (Pilot) and Sgt Williams (WOp/Ag) seriously injured, P/O R. O'Neil (Obs) killed.
17-06-1942	L4838 17 OTU Mk IV: burst into flames when engines run-up before take-off at Upwood, Sgt D. Tomkins (solo pilot) escaped.
20-06-1942	Z6357 13 Squadron Mk IV: hit trees on attempted overshoot at Snailwell on return from night NavEx; no injuries reported to P/O D. Regan and crew.
22-06-1942	L6758 51 OTU Mk I: engine cut after take-off at Cranfield, crash-landed 1 mile north of Bedford; P/O W. Gray (solo pilot) injured.
25-06-1942	Z6191 5 AOS Mk IV: collided with K7084 (below), crashed at Knockaloe near Peel, IoM, DBF; F/Sgt B. Killian (Pilot), LACs F. Skelly and E. Jones (Trainee Obs) killed.
25-06-1942	K7084 5 AOS Mk I: collided with Z6191 (above), crashed at Knockaloe, near Peel, IoM; Sgt Z. Pawlowski, LACs A. Snelson and A. Mitchell (Trainee Obs) killed.
25-06-1942	Z6252 51 OTU Mk IV: stalled on landing at Cranfield, undercarriage collapsed, destroyed by fire; Sgt V. Gowers (solo pilot) escaped uninjured.
28-06-1942	T2355 60 OTU Mk IV: engine cut at night, crashed on approach to Q Site, 3 miles south of Drem; Sgt J. Cagnon injured.
29-06-1942	R3848 13 OTU Mk IV: engine cut, lost height, second engine cut, crash-landed at Brook Farm, Moorhouse, Notts, destroyed by fire; P/O R. Robinson (Pilot) injured.
05-07-1942	R3912 13 OTU Mk IV: dived into ground near Pawlett, Somerset, after control lost in cloud; Sgt J. Anderson, Sgt A. Hogg, and Sgt G. McBoyle killed.
06-07-1942	R3834 42 OTU Mk IV: tyre burst on take-off at Thruxton, swung and undercarriage collapsed, engine caught fire; no injuries reported to P/O R. Marston and crew.
07-07-1942	V5851 21 Squadron Mk IV: struck trees at Stow Beddon, near Watton, and crashed on bombing exercise; crew Sgt F. Heron RCAF, F/Sgt G. Maluish RCAF, and Sgt G. Step killed and buried in St Mary (Watton) churchyard.
07-07-1942	L6732 60 OTU Mk I: tyre burst on take-off at East Fortune, swung and undercarriage collapsed, destroyed by fire; Sgt R. Stacey and crew escaped uninjured.
08-07-1942	L1197 17 OTU Mk I: Sgt R. Overns (solo pilot) collided on landing at Upwood with L9328 of Sgt L. Hopkins (solo pilot) and DBR, no injuries reported, L9328 (Mk IV) repaired.
08-07-1942	R3669 17 OTU Mk IV: engine cut, crashed in attempted forced-landing near Wellingore; F/Sgt D. Grant RNZAF and crew escaped with slight injuries.
10-07-1942	V5515 114 Squadron Mk IV: overshot landing at Great Massingham from Army Co-Op sortie, aircraft destroyed by fire; crew Sgt Lush, Sgt P. Collins, and Sgt E. Cole, latter only crewman reported injured.
12-07-1942	V6371 18 Squadron Mk IV: overshot flapless night landing at Wattisham at 0305, ran into ditch, DBR; F/Sgt G. Wallace and crew uninjured.
12-07-1942	T1810 2 (C) OTU Mk IV: sank back after take-off at Catfoss and hit ground; Sgt G. Hyde (solo pilot) injured.
12-07-1942	N3625 13 OTU Mk IV: engine cut, lost height, crash-landed at Limbrough, Bucks, destroyed by fire; F/O J. Welford (Pilot) and Obs escaped uninjured, Sgt Hanrahan (WOp/Ag) injured.
13-07-1942	K7120 404 Squadron Mk I: lost part of engine nacelle while rolling and dived into ground near Dyce; W/Cdr J. Dixon, CO of 404 Squadron, and Sgt A. Sallis killed. (Sgt Anthony Sallis was injured in Z6175 on 12-06-1942 – qv.)
14-07-1942	L1288 2 (C) OTU Mk I: u/c jammed, belly-landed at Catfoss, DBR.
18-07-1942	Z7304 18 Squadron Mk IV: hit radar pylon at Stoke Holy Cross, Norfolk, on air-test in bad visibility; P/O P. Lowther, Sgt K. Ellis, Sgt G. Crawford and Mr Ken Tagg (from Station Met Office) killed.
21-07-1942	Z5723 2 (C) OTU Mk IV: spun into ground at Southfield Farm, Bridlington, Yorks; Sgt G. Jardine, Sgt M. Davies and Sgt W. Mason killed.
24-07-1942	L6646 13 OTU Mk I: spun into ground on approach to Bicester, destroyed by fire; Sgt Tuttle (solo pilot) killed.

27-07-1942	R3592 5 AOS Mk IV: engine cut, lost height, crashed in forced-landing on sands in Duddon Estuary, near Millom, destroyed by fire; Sgt H. Hooper and crew escaped uninjured.
28-07-1942	P4918 5 AOS Mk IV: engine cut on approach to Jurby, IoM, stalled and hit ground; Sgt N. Blackbird seriously injured.
03-08-1942	R3813 114 Squadron Mk IV: on Exercise Dryshod, engine caught fire, crashed attempting forced-landing at Harwarden; crew P/O Hicks, Sgt P. Stewart, F/Sgt Chote, and two ground-crew, LAC J. Barnes and AC1 G. Cradock, killed.
07-08-1942	V6255 2 (C) OTU: crashed into sea 2 miles east of Withernsea, Yorks, cause unknown; F/Sgt Lefurgey killed.
12-08-1942	L4930 54 OTU Mk I: collided with Mk V AZ964 while taxiing at night at Charterhall, DBR, AZ964 repaired.
14-08-1942	BA192 54 OTU Mk V: hit tree on take-off at Charterhall and crashed; Sgt T. Rutherford (Pilot) and Sgt J. Kidd (Obs) killed.
16-08-1942	V6399 17 OTU Mk IV: caught fire on ground during servicing of electrical equipment at Upwood.
18-08-1942	V5699 17 OTU Mk IV: crashed on take-off at Upwood, failed to become airborne, struck boundary, Sgt S. Roche uninjured.
19-08-1942	L6623 51 OTU Mk I: hit tree after take-off from Cranfield, crashed and blew up at Ridgmont, Beds; Sgt R. Gilmour and Sgt W. McQuatters killed.
23-08-1942	L1110 60 OTU Mk I: engine cut, overshot single-engine landing, hit shelter at Renfrew; Sgt E. Sanetra injured.
26-08-1942	Z6268 5 AOS Mk IV: spun into sea during drogue firing 12 miles of IoM; Sgt R. Pontin (Pilot), LACs T. Fox, C. Keslake and G. Hamilton (Trainees) killed.
28-08-1942	N6169 13 OTU Mk IV: collided head-on with V6197 (below) in haze and crashed into North Sea 26 miles NE of Flamborough Head; Sgt E. Hooker, Sgt F. James, and Sgt C. Free killed.
28-08-1942	V6197 13 OTU Mk IV: collided with N6169 (above) in haze and crashed into North Sea 26 miles NE of Flamborough Head; Sgt Stan Moss (Pilot) was thrown out and came down by parachute but died from his injuries three days later, Sgt F. Nice and Sgt F. Edwards killed.
29-08-1942	R3758 614 Squadron Mk IV: overshot landing, hit ditch and overturned at Odiham; P/O C. Georges and crew slightly injured.
31-08-1942	Z7302 13 OTU Mk IV: struck at Catfoss by crash-landing Halifax Mk II BB196 of 76 Squadron, both aircraft DBR.
31-08-1942	Z6352 17 OTU Mk IV: engine cut, crash-landed at Ramsey St Marys on approach to Upwood; Sgt T. Mair and one crewman injured.
31-08-1942	N3585 51 OTU Mk IV: flew into ground at night near Turvey, Beds, destroyed by fire, cause unknown; Sgt W. Whalley killed.
04-09-1942	L8373 17 OTU Mk IV: tyre burst on take-off at Warboys, swung and undercarriage collapsed, became 3354M.
11-09-1942	R3591 17 OTU Mk IV: engine cut on take-off, crashed 1 mile west of Upwood; W/Cdr C. Hodder AFC and two crewmen injured.
11-09-1942	AZ 939 60 OTU Mk V: lost power on take-off at East Fortune, hit trees and crashed; Sgt J. Toogood and crew uninjured.
11-09-1942	L4891 17 OTU Mk I: swung on take-off at Upwood and hit tractor, Sgt B. Harvey RCAF (solo pilot) slightly injured.
21-09-1942	L9170 1 AGS Mk IV: caught fire in hangar, Pembrey, DBR.
24-09-1942	V5382 51 OTU Mk IV: engine lost power on take-off, overshot runway at Cranfield; P/O P. Smith (solo pilot) injured.
28-09-1942	R3761 13 OTU Mk IV: engine cut on take-off at Bicester, lost height and crashed at Stratton Audley, Oxon, destroyed by fire; crew seriously injured, Sgt Anderson (Pilot) and Sgt T. Pullin (Obs) later died, Sgt T. Pollock (WOp/Ag) recovered.
29-09-1942	BA142 60 OTU Mk V: stalled and dived into ground at East Linton, E Lothian; Sgt J. Erickson (American, RAFVR) killed, crewman injured.
01-10-1942	V6315 17 OTU Mk IV: engine cut after take-off, swung, stalled and dived into ground 1 mile west of Upwood; Sgt G. Darbyshire, P/O L. Austin and Sgt F. Reeve killed.
01-10-1942	L9328 17 OTU Mk IV: engine cut on take-off, belly-landed 300 yards beyond airfield, DBR, Sgt F. Armit (solo pilot) uninjured.
05-10-1942	L8613 54 OTU Mk I: collided with L6788 (below) near Charterhall and abandoned; Sgt J. Masters (Australian) and Sgt J. Gracey killed.
05-10-1942	L6788 54 OTU Mk I: collided with L8613 (above) near Charterhall, but RTB; F/Sgt J. Henderson and crewman safe.
06-10-1942	T1949 404 Squadron Mk IV: lost height after take-off from Sumburgh, crashed into sea; A/W/O J. Patterson (USA) and crew killed.

08-10-1942	L1140 42 OTU Mk I: lost tailplane during roll, struck by detached engine cowling, and dived into ground at Clatford, Hants; F/O J. Griffin (Pilot, Instructor) and P/O T. Long (Trainee Pilot) killed.
11-10-1942	T1931 17 OTU Mk IV: engine cut on take-off at Upwood, hit trees and crashed, DBF; Sgt L. Partridge, Sgt W. Hopcroft and Sgt F. Poole killed.
13-10-1942	AZ 990 60 OTU Mk V: tyre burst on take-off at East Fortune, swung, undercarriage collapsed, engine caught fire.
21-10-1942	V5920 42 OTU Mk IV: engine cut, stalled on approach to Tattenhill, crashed; no injuries reported to P/O R. Kerby and crew.
28-10-1942	L1316 Ferry Training Unit Mk I: engine cut on take-off at Lyneham, crash-landed, destroyed by fire; G/Capt G. Stanley-Turner and crew uninjured.
28-10-1942	L6752 60 OTU Mk I: control lost in bad visibility, crashed at Ormiston, E Lothian, destroyed by fire; Sgt F. Terry (solo pilot) killed.
02-11-1942	R3902 13 OTU Mk IV: engine cut on take-off at Bicester, attempted to stop, ran into mound and caught fire, Sgt T. Wilson and Sgt E. Colburn escaped uninjured.
03-11-1942	L6719 54 OTU Mk I: flew into ground at night while orbiting Beacon at Westruther, Berwickshire; Sgt A. Keen and Sgt A. Weller killed.
06-11-1942	R3874 13 OTU Mk IV: engine cut just after take-off from Bicester, lost height, hit tree and crashed at Stoke Littlewood; Sgt A. Blackshire, P/O D. Newell, Sgt W. Donald, and Sgt C. Harrison injured, Sgt Blackshire died of his injuries that night.
06-11-1942	V5814 224 Squadron Mk IV: wing dropped on take-off, propeller hit ground, undercarriage raised to stop at Beaulieu.
07-11-1942	L8720 54 OTU Mk I: ran out of fuel at night, hit tree in attempted forced-landing near Swinton, Berwickshire; F/O W. Birt and F/Sgt C. Stradling killed.
07-11-1942	N3567 42 OTU Mk IV: stalled after take-off and hit trees 1 mile west of Ashbourne; F/O W. Mummery injured, AC1 T. Clarke killed.
08-11-1942	T1991 13 OTU Mk IV: engine cut, crash-landed on single-engine night approach to Bicester; Sgt J. Hannah and Sgt E. Owen injured.
10-11-1942	BA111 54 OTU Mk V: control lost, spun into ground near Charterhall; P/O T. Donohue (solo pilot) killed.
14-11-1942	Z6074 1 AGS Mk IV: engine cut, crash-landed on beach at Kidwelly, Carmarthen; W/O F. McDaniel and crew uninjured.
15-11-1942	R3833 5 AOS Mk IV: engine cut, lost height and ditched in Irish Sea between Jurby and Rhyl; F/Sgt J. Meeklah (Pilot) and crewman injured but rescued.
17-11-1942	R3890 70 Wing Mk IV: overshot landing at Inverness, skidded on wet grass and hit house; Sgt H. Heath injured.
19-11-1942	Z7365 521 Squadron Mk IV: failed to become airborne at Bircham Newton, presumed take-off flap retracted prematurely; P/O G. Hatton injured.
28-11-1942	V5882 17 OTU Mk IV: swung on night landing at Upwood to avoid another Blenheim which had encroached on runway, DBR, F/Lt F. Wilson uninjured.
28-11-1942	V5696 72 Wing Mk IV: engine cut on radar calibration sortie, lost height, ditched in Firth of Forth; W/O Argent and crew injured but rescued.
29-11-1942	Z7345 1402 Met Flt Mk IV: tyre burst on take-off at Aldergrove, swung and overturned; P/O H. Alford and P/O K. George injured.
01-12-1942	K7124 2 (C) OTU Mk I: u/c collapsed on engine run-up at Dyce, became 3571M.
08-12-1942	Z7443 132 OTU Mk IV: dived into ground near Lauder, Berwickshire, cause unknown; Sgt J. Charker (solo pilot) killed.
09-12-1942	L4929 54 OTU Mk I: hit trees descending in cloud on NavEx, crashed at Johnstone Bridge, Dumfries, destroyed by fire; P/O K. Rawlings killed.
17-12-1942	Z7422 13 OTU Mk IV: engine cut on take-off at Finmere, u/c raised to stop, slid through boundary, F/O F. Tan, Sgt M. Leyden and Sgt S. Bate uninjured.
21-12-1942	Z7361 13 OTU Mk IV: engine cut on take-off at Bicester, swung and hit Albemarle P1459; W/O D. Lyth (Pilot) injured, both aircraft DBR.
21-12-1942	L8438 307 Squadron Mk I: engine cut in bad weather, crash-landed near Combe Down, Bath, on training sortie. 307 was a Beaufighter squadron.
23-12-1942	L4872 51 OTU Mk IV: engine cut after take-off at Cranfield, lost height and crash-landed near Marston, Beds, destroyed by fire; Sgt W. Hindle and Sgt R. Hindle killed.
23-12-1942	L1289 12 PAFU Mk I: took off on converging path at Harlaxton and collided with L8721 (below), crashed and destroyed by fire; Lt Yalnig Bahatten (Turkish Air Force) believed killed.
23-12-1942	L8721 12 PAFU Mk I: took off on converging path at Harlaxton and collided with L1289 (above), crash-landed and DBR; Lt Sever Hilmi (Turkish Air Force) believed injured.

V5803 of 254 Squadron taking off from Dyce on 30 January 1942. Moments later it crashed – the control cables for the elevator-trim tab had been reversed. The Pilot and the Padre, his only passenger on an air-test, were unhurt.

An incident at 42 OTU when Z5986 ran into the back of V6003 on landing at Andover on 31 March 1942; the latter aircraft was Damaged Beyond Repair.

Typical of the Blenheims that ended their days at an OTU is L4872 seen here at Upwood early in 1940 with 90 Squadron, which merged into 17 OTU, then it served with 51 OTU at Cranfield until 23d Dec 1942 when an engine cut on take-off, it crashed, killing both crewmen, and was Destroyed by Fire.

Z6102 of 254 Squadron over-ran the runway landing at Carew Cheriton on 20 April 1942; the undercarriage was raised in an attempt to stop, but it left the airfield and was written off.

By 1941 WAAFs were instructed in aircraft and armament maintenance.

A typical 114 Squadron NCO crew at West Raynham in August 1941. Sgt Les Harrison (WOp/Ag) and Sgt Sam North (Obs) are seated on 500lb bombs, with Sgt Ivor Broom (Pilot) and RT-V, the Blenheim they flew on the Cologne raid – as shown on page 357 above. They were one of several crews 'hijacked' to serve in Malta when en route to the Far East in September 1941. He was commissioned in the field and later became an outstanding Mosquito Pilot retiring Air Marshal Sir Ivor Broom KCB, CBE, DSO, DFC and two bars, AFC, and became President of The Blenheim Society.

THE BRISTOL BLENHEIM

PART 3

BLENHEIMS IN THE MIDDLE AND FAR EASTERN THEATRES OF WAR

The forward airfield at Paramythia (Valley of Fairy Tales), Greece, with Blenheim K7095 of 30 Squadron, one of many lost during the futile attempt to prevent the German invasion of Greece and Crete.

Typical Middle East Blenheim crew: F/O Turner, P/O Steatfield and S/Ldr Passmore with their 84 Squadron Mk IV 'Queen of Shailbah'.

Chapter 22

Opening rounds: the Western Desert and East Africa

On 10 June 1940, even as the UK and French-based Blenheim squadrons were embroiled in the thick of the battles that were to see the imminent fall of France, Mussolini, the Fascist dictator of Italy and Axis partner of Nazi Germany, joined the conflict and declared war on Great Britain and France – hoping no doubt for easy pickings from the territories of the two Allied nations that appeared to be on the brink of defeat.

The entry of Italy into the war faced Air Chief Marshal Sir Arthur Longmore, who had been appointed AOC-in-C of the Middle East less than a month earlier on 13 May, with dangers and difficulties that appeared to be insuperable. His responsibilities were truly daunting, for his command included a vast area of some 4½ million square miles of territory centred on Egypt and the vital Suez Canal, and his main role was to defend the Canal, protect the oilfields in Iraq and the Gulf, and keep the Red Sea open for Allied shipping to India, the Far East and Australasia. He was expected 'to exercise air control' over the entire Middle East – a term that was highly elastic and was stretched to cover East Africa, Sudan, Aden, Palestine, Jordan, Iraq, the Gulf States, Somaliland, Turkey, the Balkans (Greece, Bulgaria, Rumania, Yugoslavia, Albania), as well as the whole of the Mediterranean Sea (including Malta, Crete, Cyprus and the Dodecanese Islands), the Red Sea and the Persian Gulf! The resources at his command for this enormous task were exiguous in the extreme – some 300 front-line aircraft, of which the 90 Blenheims were the most numerous and the most modern. However, all the Blenheims were Mk Is apart from a single Squadron equipped with Mk IVs. The most up-to-date fighter was the Gloster Gladiator; the rest were a motley collection of obsolete types.

A bizarre episode

Before Longmore's appointment, his predecessor, ACM Sir William Mitchell, had been faced with orders to prepare a bizarre operation by Blenheims that would have had incalculable repercussions. Early in 1940, during the 'Phoney War', the Allied High Command was anxious to assist Finland resist the Russian invasion and was also concerned at the large amounts of aviation fuel being supplied to the Wehrmacht (under the then current German/Soviet Pact) from the Russian oilfields at Baku, so on 19 January it gave serious consideration to bombing those oilfields. On 22 February General Gamelin formally proposed to the Supreme Allied War Council a joint Anglo/French aerial attack mounted from bases in Iraq and Syria upon the Russian oil-producing plants in the Caucasus. The RAF element would comprise four squadrons of Blenheims, and the French element four *Groupes de Bombardement*, each of 12 Martin 167Fs – hardly a force strong enough to inflict damage significant enough to justify the grave consequences of extending the war to a neutral country, especially one the size of Russia. On 20 March the RAF was instructed to obtain photographs of the oil installations around Baku in Russia, and on the 23rd a Hudson N7364 of the PDU left Heston for Habbaniyah in Iraq, fitted with long-range tanks and finished in Camotint. On 30 March it made a successful reconnaissance over the entire Baku peninsula in the Caspian Sea without meeting any opposition, although when on 5 April it photographed Batum, the oil seaport on the Black Sea, it was fired on by AA guns, but escaped over neutral Turkey. It photographed six oil refineries, two power stations, and the airfields of Baku, Mastagi and Surakhani, noting 34 positions each with four AA guns. The pictures from both sorties were sent to London and were used

A Mk I of 113 Squadron demonstrates a really low-level attack on British troops early in 1940 – the starboard wheel appears not to be fully retracted. 113 changed mainly to Mk IVs from March, the only Middle East squadron to do so before the Italians declared war on 10 June.

THE BRISTOL BLENHEIM

The Lockheed 14 used by Sidney Cotton for clandestine photo sorties to Russian oilfields in 1940 before the proposed attack by Blenheims. N7364, an unarmed Hudson I finished in Camotint, unusually carried both RAF roundels and the civilian registration G-AGAR.

to provide target maps and to draw up a detailed plan of attack. Bomber Command HQ had reservations concerning the Air Staff's initial estimates of the Blenheim's range, speed and fuel consumption (which the Command SASO re-calculated at 1.75mpg at 207mph at 15,000 feet), and stated that the four Squadrons 'would require heavy reinforcement' as 'it may be necessary to attack for a full three months', noting also that there were 'some 200 fighters in the vicinity of the oilfields'. He concluded, 'The Plan savours of sending a boy out to do a man's job.' However, the German invasion of the Scandinavian countries on 9 April caused the whole ill-conceived plan to be abandoned – had it been carried out the effect on relations between Russia and the Allies would have been unforeseeable and the raids may well have drawn the Soviet Union into the war on the Axis side! The Allied High Command had no inkling at that early stage of the war that the Russians would become its own Allies in June 1941 following the invasion of Russia by the Germans.

Blenheims dispatched to the Middle East

The first Blenheims supplied to the Middle East were sent to the Packing Depot at Sealand in October 1937, then by sea to the Aircraft Depot at Aboukir in the Canal Zone, arriving a month later. There they were de-crated, re-erected, had Vokes 'tropical' air-filters fitted to the carburettors, their armament was installed, and they were air-tested. Deliveries to 30 Squadron at Mosul commenced in January 1938; the Squadron used K7103 for type

K7103, the first Blenheim with the RAF in the Middle East and seen here at Heliopolis in January 1938, was used for type trials. It was lost with 30 Squadron in Greece in December 1940.

K7097 seen with 30 Squadron at an unusually wet Habbaniyah, Iraq, early in 1938. It crashed on 10 December 1938, with the loss of six lives, believed due to carburettor icing.

trials for the overseas conditions, and completed conversion from its ancient Hawker Hardy biplanes by July. No 30 became the envy of the other Middle East Squadrons, especially as the others did not receive their Mk Is until 1939, when another 50 were crated and shipped to Basra. In February and March 1939 84 and 55 Squadrons both replaced their Vincents, as did 8 Squadron in April; in May 211 Squadron changed its Hinds, in June No 45 its Wellesleys, 60 its Wapitis, and 113 its Hinds, while 39 Squadron had to wait until August 1939 to start converting from its Harts. The most unusual conversion was by 203 Squadron in Aden, which in March 1940 changed from its Short Singapore Mk IIIs – large biplane flying boats with twin tandem 'pull-and-push' Kestrel engines – to a mixture of Blenheim Mk Is and Mk IVs, being equipped fully with the latter mark by May 1940.

Naturally, losses through accidents soon started to take their toll (see Appendix 1), and these assumed greater significance, being a higher proportion of the smaller number of Blenheims available in the Middle East. In addition to the accident-inducing factors mentioned in Chapter 6 that especially affected Blenheims, the Middle East pilots were converting from aircraft even older than those of their UK-based brethren. The higher ambient temperatures and the addition of tropical air-filters to the Mercury engines degraded take-off performance and made single-engine flying extremely difficult; operating conditions were harsh with clouds of dust and frequent sand-storms, and the problems of aircraft maintenance in the hostile desert environment were formidable. The only saving grace was that the Blenheims, Gladiators and Lysanders all shared Bristol Mercury engines – with the Bombays and later the Wellingtons using the Bristol Pegasus (a long-stroke Mercury) – which eased the task of carrying out engine overhauls and supplying engine spares.

The fall of France and the entry of Italy into the war effectively closed the Mediterranean as a supply route to the British forces, so that sending any reinforcement would become extremely difficult and protracted – even if any men, aircraft and munitions could be spared from the British homeland, which was fighting for its very life at that time. A heavy burden would fall upon the relatively small number of Blenheim squadrons.

A line-up of 84 Squadron Mk Is at Shaiba in January 1940; note the Vokes Air Filters on the carburettor intakes. WOp/Ag AC Duggan poses by one of them – the airmen are wearing solar topis in both pictures.

THE BRISTOL BLENHEIM

The Western Desert: round one

202 Group on the western frontier of Egypt, facing the main threat from the huge Italian colony of Libya, had fewer than 100 aircraft: three squadrons – 45, 55 and 211 – of Blenheim Mk Is, together with 113 Squadron with a dozen Mk IVs; the only 'Heavy' Bombers were a single squadron – 216 – with Bristol Bombay Bomber/Transports. There was but one fighter Squadron – 33 – with Gladiators, and one – 208 – with Lysanders for direct Army Co-operation with the 36,000-strong Allied land forces guarding Egypt. The Italians had 300 front-line aircraft and 300,000 troops in Libya, and could reinforce them readily from Sicily.

45 Squadron Blenheims at Mersa Matruh for inspection by King Farouk of Egypt on 13 September 1939; they have a temporary desert scheme of Sand and Earth with codes painted in reverse colours. Lysanders stand behind.

The only other Blenheim squadron based in Egypt was 30 at Ismailia, which had converted its B and C Flights to Mk I-Fs to assist the Gladiators and a solitary Hurricane in the defence of Alexandria and Port Said. Despite parity in performance, the Blenheims managed to shoot down one or two of the few three-engined Savoia SM79s that attempted to bomb the Allied main bases there. The Blenheim Mk Is of 84 Squadron were based in distant Iraq, and those of 203 and the single Flight of 8 Squadron were at Aden, where they were joined by 11 and 39 Squadrons, which – as soon as Italy entered the war – each brought back nine aircraft from Singapore and India respectively.

Once again RAF Blenheims were the first aircraft into action. A few minutes after Air Commodore Collishaw, OC of 202 Group (later to grow into the Desert Air Force), received the signal at midnight on 10 June from his AOC, Sir Arthur Longmore, that Italy had declared war, six Blenheim crews of 211 Squadron were briefed to carry out an armed reconnaissance at dawn of targets in Libya. This was to be followed 2 hours after first light by a bombing raid on the main *Regia Aeronautica* base at El Adem near Tobruk – this swift low-level attack by eight Blenheims of 45 Squadron from Fuka took the complacent Italians by surprise. The base personnel were drawn up on the parade ground to hear their commander read a bombastic proclamation from Marshal Graziani, the Italian Commander-in-Chief, that their country was entering the war – the dramatic arrival of the Blenheims accompanied by bombs exploding and bullets flying certainly gave a strong emphasis to the announcement! Ray Collishaw, an aggressive leader who had scored 60 victories as a fighter pilot in the First World War, moved up 55 and 113

Squadrons from Ismailia to Fuka, and 18 of their Blenheims made a further attack on El Adem airfield in the afternoon. The crews from both raids thought they had scored a resounding success as two hangars were hit and many burning aircraft were seen on the ground. In fact, only 20 enemy aircraft were destroyed or badly damaged, but the RAF had landed the first blows and the effect on Italian morale was considerable. Three of the eight Blenheims were lost (see Appendix 2) and two damaged from the first raid, with two more badly damaged in the second raid; this was not a large number, but significant in view of the very limited total – fewer than 60 – that was available.

Air Commodore Ray Collishaw, commanding the meagre RAF force in Egypt that faced the far stronger Regia Aeronautica in Libya, believed that 'attack is the best form of defence'.

On the night of 12 June a force of 29 Blenheims were due to attack the harbour at Tobruk, which reconnaissance sorties by 113 Squadron had revealed to be crowded, to destroy ships there in conjunction with a bombardment by units of the Royal Navy, but bad weather frustrated the raid. Six aircraft of 45 Squadron took off but Sgt Grant in L6664 aborted with an engine failure, while the other five failed to find the target and four returned with their bombs still aboard – shades of the first attack on units of the German Fleet on 4 September 1939! F/O Rixson in the other Blenheim, L8524, bombed some troops near Bardia but had to force-land at Mersa Matruh. Only two of the five from 55 Squadron reached Tobruk – an engine of one would not start, the Observer of another was struck by a propeller so it too did not take off, while a third had to turn back with engine trouble. Two from the nine of 21 Squadron crashed on take-off, while another (L1487) had a ground collision with a Bombay; the remaining six were engaged by Fiat CR.42s defending Tobruk and claimed to have shot down two of them. Fortunately nine Mk IVs of 113 Squadron did manage to find and bomb the harbour, and hit the elderly cruiser *San Giorgio*, which caught fire and, half-submerged, was beached on a sand-bank, there to remain as a stationary flak ship. The frontier fort at Capuzzo was attacked at low level on the 14th by eight Blenheims of 211 Squadron, but many failures of the 11-second-delay fuses on the four 250lb bombs that each of them dropped caused most of the attackers to suffer splinter damage from their own bombs or those dropped by their companions – a small Army force quickly captured the fort. 45 Squadron sent two aircraft, one of which was shot down by light AA fire (see Appendix 2) to bomb Sidi Azeiz airfield, and three made a successful attack on Fort Maddalena. Another dawn raid on the 16th on El Adem and El Gubbi airfields was intended to be by nine aircraft from both 113 and 55 Squadrons, but three of the nine from the latter Squadron failed to reach the target due to engine troubles – a penalty of operating from desert airstrips. Those that bombed were heavily engaged by Italian fighters, which spoiled their aim, and although bombs were seen to fall among parked aircraft, little damage was done. A fresh tactic was tried at dusk that evening: three Blenheims from 113 Squadron made single attacks on hangars and dispersed aircraft at El Adem, surprising the enemy by gliding in, with engines shut down, from height over the sea. No doubt their fingers were well and truly crossed when they re-started the engines to make their get-away!

The first five days of the desert war saw 106 effective bombing sorties by the Blenheims, and only four were lost through enemy action, although several more were severely damaged. Mk IVs of 113 Squadron photographed warships in Bardia harbour, and on the 21st nine Blenheims of 55 Squadron set out to bomb them, but only seven reached the target, two of which were damaged by the defences, but they set a large ship on fire. On the same day 11 Mk IVs of 113 attacked troop concentrations at Bir el Gubbi.

To make the most of his single Hurricane, Collishaw formed a special flight – known as 'Collie's battleship' – joining it with two Blenheim Mk I-Fs of 30 Squadron and attaching the flight to 33 Squadron at Ma'aten Gerawala, which was still operating Gladiators. This flight, together with four Gladiators, intercepted a dozen Italian aircraft on 19 June and shot down four – two by F/O Peter Wykham-Barnes in the Hurricane – and later that day, accompanied by four Mk I-F Blenheims, he shot down another CR.42 and the 'fighter' Blenheims shot down two more of the nimble biplanes and damaged two others. Three other Hurricanes had staged to Egypt through Algiers and Tunisia, but with France collapsing it was clear that this route for reinforcement could no longer be used (See Chapter 13, Appendix 5).

On 28 June the personal plane of Marshal Balbo, the Italian Governor General of Libya (a previous Minister for Air, after whom large, loose formations of aircraft are named), was shot down by Italian AA fire near Tobruk airfield and killed – the attacks by the Blenheims on El Adem and other airfields had made the gunners 'trigger happy'. Collishaw sent a Blenheim to drop a wreath at the funeral.

Action continued as daily small-scale raids on Italian Army bases and airfields in Libya were made in rotation by aircraft from each of the four Egyptian-based Blenheim squadrons – 113 with its Mk IVs at Ma'aten Bagush, together with the Mk Is of 45 and 55 at Fuka, and 211 at Daba – so that each squadron operated only every fourth day. The Blenheims had been dispersed to satellite landing grounds to avoid the more frequent bombing of their main airfields by the Italians. It was not possible to launch any larger-scale raids as fewer and fewer serviceable aircraft remained available, a situation exacerbated when 45 Squadron had to detach its A Flight to Sudan. The drain of destroyed (Appendix 2) or damaged and unserviceable aircraft incurred by such a small force of bombers, and the demonstrable difficulties of obtaining any reinforcements, disturbed and alarmed Longmore, so in mid-July he signalled to Collishaw:

> 'While fully appreciating the initiative and spirit shown by the Squadrons operating under your command in the Western Desert, I must draw your immediate attention to the urgent necessity of conserving resources; instances are still occurring when Blenheims are being used for low-level machine-gun attacks against defended camps and aerodromes. I consider such operations are unjustified having regard to our limited resources of which you are well aware. I feel therefore that we must consider carefully every air operation we embark upon.'

The Air Ministry in London promised him reinforcements of 12 Blenheims, 12 Hurricanes and six Lysanders a month, as well as diverting to the Middle East Command an order for 150 American Martin Maryland Medium Bombers placed by the French *L'Armée de L'Air*. On 1 August Longmore was greatly relieved to be advised that deliveries would increase to 36 Blenheims and 18 Hurricanes a month as soon as possible.

Supply and reinforcement problems

This increased rate of deliveries was only possible as the Royal Air Force had acted quickly to mitigate the difficulties of reinforcing the Middle East Command. Aircraft could no longer be ferried through France or stage via the French North African territories of Algeria and Tunisia, and the route over the Bay of Biscay to Gibraltar, then Malta and on to Egypt, was becoming too dangerous, and in any event the stages were beyond the range of single-engine fighters. So on 14 July 1940 a party commanded by Group Captain H. Thorold arrived at the port of Takoradi on the Gold Coast (now Ghana), West Africa, to organise an overland ferry route right across the continent to far-distant Cairo. This 3,700-mile trans-Saharan journey over inhospitable terrain became the life-line for the Middle East Air Force. The trip took at least six days and staged via Lagos, Kano and Maiduguri in Nigeria, Fort Lamy in Chad, then El Geteina, El Fasher, Khartoum and Wadi Halfa in Sudan, to Abu Sueir in Egypt, and was based on the weekly Lagos to Khartoum airmail route pioneered in 1936. This lengthy and arduous journey in a variety of tropical climates took a heavy toll on the aircraft – some 10 per cent were lost in transit – and the engines of many that arrived in Egypt required a major overhaul. Each flight was normally led by a Blenheim to provide the navigation for batches of half a dozen single-engined Hurricanes and (later) Kittyhawks. The first shipment of six crated Blenheims and six Hurricanes arrived at Takoradi on 5 September, and were re-assembled and test-flown; the first delivery flight left there on the 19th and within a week the first Blenheim supplied via the Takoradi route had been delivered to the Command, with three more within days. This enabled 14 Squadron at Port Sudan to start converting from Wellesleys to Blenheim Mk IVs. Over the following three years this initial trickle of aircraft reinforcements grew into a steady stream and included hundreds of Blenheims, although several were lost both at sea and on the transcontinental journey (see Appendix 3). The last sectors of this vital route, and Allied shipping in the Red Sea, were exposed to attacks from the Italian air and naval forces based in their East African Empire – Italian Somaliland (now part of Somalia), Eritrea and Abyssinia, (now Ethiopia) – so Wavell was ordered to remove this threat.

The campaign in East Africa: opening moves

This objective seemed unlikely to be achieved as the Italians enjoyed all the initial successes. They captured two towns (Kassala and Gallabat) in Sudan, plus Moyale in Northern Kenya in July 1940, and in August occupied British Somaliland (now part of Somalia), which is across the southern end of the Red Sea from Aden, giving them control of the entire Horn of Africa. Longmore had a collection of 130 antiquated aircraft, together with 50 based in Aden, available to support the 19,000 Allied troops opposed to the large Italian forces in East Africa – 200,000 mainly colonial troops and 250 aircraft. As in the Western Desert, the Blenheims were his most modern aircraft – based at Aden were the Mk Is of 11 and 39 Squadrons recalled from the Far East, although both were well below strength, with 203 the only Squadron with Mk IV-Fs. Also in Aden, 8 Squadron had one Flight of Mk Is – its other Flight operated ancient Vickers Vincent biplanes! Far to the north in Ismailia, Egypt, was 30 Squadron with its mix of Mk Is and Mk I-Fs. In late July 45 Squadron in Egypt, temporarily removed from the front line in the Western Desert,

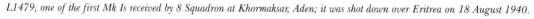

L1479, one of the first Mk Is received by 8 Squadron at Khormaksar, Aden; it was shot down over Eritrea on 18 August 1940.

was told to send a flight of six Mk Is to Sudan to bolster the three squadrons (14, 47 and 223) of Vickers Wellesleys there. 14 Squadron started converting to Blenheim Mk IVs in September, but also continued to operate its few remaining Wellesleys until December. Longmore had to play for the highest stakes with very few high-value cards in his hand.

There were no RAF aircraft in Kenya, but the tiny Rhodesian Air Force sent up a few Hawker Hart, Hardy and Audax biplanes, and the South African Air Force sent to Nairobi six Hawker Fury and 24 Hartebeeste (a Hart variant) biplanes, and 18 Junkers Ju.86 airliners converted to bombers. The SAAF also had four Hurricanes, a few Ansons, and later received some ex-RAF Gladiators and Battles. It also had a single Blenheim Mk I (L1431) for evaluation and wanted more but none could be spared – this sole Blenheim was used on trials by 31 Squadron SAAF and during these attacked the *Timavo*, an Italian ship running for neutral Mozambique on 11 June, forcing it aground! The well-tried Blenheim was returned to the RAF later and unusually given a fresh serial number – AX683. The motley collection of obsolescent Allied aircraft performed valiantly, firstly in defending Kenya, then in supporting the Allied troops invading Ethiopia and Somalia from the south. However, this 'shoestring' side-show need not concern this history of the Blenheim, as, apart from the one instance mentioned, they did not operate on the Southern Front in East Africa or from Kenya.

The new Theatre of War opening in East Africa saw, yet again, the Blenheims as the first to go into action, for in the early morning of 11 June seven aircraft of 203 Squadron from Aden carried out a valuable armed photo-reconnaissance of Italian bases, airfields and ports right along the previously neutral coastline. The next day, using this information, nine Blenheims of 8 Squadron bombed Assab airfield; L6654 was hit and belly-landed at Ras Ara (see Appendix 4), and 12 from 39 Squadron, which had only arrived at Aden from India the previous day, bombed Diredawe airfield. The Wellesleys bombed Asmara and Gura, and four crossed 12,000-foot mountains to bomb the airfield at Addis Ababa; three of the 17 Wellesleys dispatched were lost in the first two days. The gawky Wellesleys, although single-engined, much slower and less manoeuvrable than the Blenheims, could carry double the bomb-load in their under-wing panniers, but were considered too vulnerable, and this was the only war zone in which they operated. On 13 June a 203 Squadron Mk IV-F reconnoitring Assab was damaged by defending Fiat CR.42 biplanes – the pilot could count his blessings for hits from their 12.7mm bullets had failed to penetrate the armour plating behind him but struck with sufficient impact to cause the rivets that secured the plate to the fuselage structure to pull loose! Later that day Macaaca airfield at Assab and a new satellite nearby were bombed by Blenheims from 8 and 39 Squadrons, destroying three Italian aircraft on the ground; the attack was repeated the next night, and on the following morning, when six aircraft from 8 Squadron destroyed the radio station. The 15th saw more raids of the same nature: 8 Squadron sent six aircraft to bomb Diredawe at low level and they hit a dump of old mustard-gas bombs, setting it on fire, while three aircraft of 39 Squadron attacked the same airfield by diving from height and were engaged by CR.42s but all escaped. The odds changed slightly in favour of the RAF that day as the Italians pulled their operational aircraft out of Assab and its satellites, and nine Blenheim Mk Is of 11 Squadron arrived in Egypt from Karachi: five were attached initially to 39 Squadron, two were converted to Mk I-Fs and passed to 30 Squadron, and the other two were undergoing maintenance work.

The Italian submarine *Galileo Galilei* sank a tanker off Aden on 18 June but was spotted by a Gladiator, which radioed the location. A Blenheim bombed the sub but missed, a Vincent dropped two depth-charges and almost blew itself up, and contact was then lost. Blenheims of 203 Squadron searched throughout the following morning but the sub had submerged. It was picked up on Asdic by an anti-sub trawler and depth-charged, which caused it to surface and, after an exchange of gunfire, surrender. Five Blenheims of 39 Squadron were joined by one of 11 Squadron (making the latter Squadron's first operational sortie) when they bombed Diredawe airfield on the 19th, hitting a hangar and setting a petrol dump blazing. Diredawe was raided again by six Blenheims in two mixed flights on the 22nd and the 24th – on the latter raid a heavy fight with defending CR.42s developed and the Blenheims jettisoned their bombs. P/O Hunter was hit in one engine and force-landed L4920 in British Somaliland; he was wounded but rescued later by British troops who were withdrawing, but his WOp/Ag, who had gone to seek assistance, was missing (see Appendix 4).

On 28 June S/Ldr Bowman of 39 Squadron led two Gladiators to attack the fuel dump at Assab; his Blenheim bombed but missed, the fighters strafed the target and set it alight, and later that morning three more 39 Squadron Blenheims destroyed a bomb-dump. Small-scale attacks from both combatants, mainly against airfields, continued and losses were quite light on each side, but included one of four aircraft of 8 Squadron detached to Berbera, and one of 11 Squadron, which was hit in one engine when bombing Assab and struggled back only to crash-land less than 25 miles from Ras Ara (see Appendix 4). On 22 July four attacks were made on Diredawe airfield, each by a flight of three Aden-based Blenheims from 8 and 39 Squadrons, but little damage resulted and no Blenheims were lost. Two Mk IV-Fs of 203 Squadron strafed three parked Ca.133s at Mille airfield on the 26th, and one of them led three Mk I bombers of 8 Squadron back the following day to finish off the job. Two days later a Blenheim of 11 Squadron (L4817) was shot down by AA fire while on a lone sortie to Assab airfield, and the crew killed (see Appendix 4). The Flight from 45 Squadron detached to Erkowit in Sudan made its first operation on 30 July, bombing Kassala railway station, and repeating the attack the following day.

August saw an increase in air activity by both sides; early on the 1st the British discovered Italian bombers at a new landing ground at Chinele, near Diredawe, and they were promptly attacked by 12 Blenheims (six each from 8 and 39 Squadrons) escorted by two Mk IV-Fs of 203, and a fierce fight with CR.32s and 42s developed – one 8 Squadron Blenheim (L8406) was shot down and the crew captured (see Appendix 4), but on their way back to base the six 39 Squadron Blenheims saw some Savoia 81s attacking the port of Zeila and dived on them, breaking up the formation and shooting down one S.81. 39 Squadron raided Chinele again the next day, shooting down a defending CR 42. The 45 Squadron Flight from Sudan set fire to a fuel dump at Archiko near Massawa on the 1st and attacked Asmara on the 2nd, and on the 4th three of its Blenheims came in low from over the Red Sea and attacked three submarines moored at Abdul Kadar jetty, hitting a supply ship alongside the submarines. The Italian invasion of British Somaliland commenced that day and a motor transport convoy of troops, near Hargeisa on the main road to Berbera, was the target for three separate attacks on the 5th, each by a flight of three Mk Is from 8 Squadron at Aden, one of which (L8375) was shot down in flames by a CR 32 (see Appendix 4). These advancing columns continued to be harried by Blenheims from 8 and 39 Squadrons, using Berbera and Laferug as advanced bases (which saved 200 miles from each sortie), and after the remaining Gladiators had been

L6655 served with both 8 and 211 Squadrons at Aden and Ismailia, then passed to 72 OTU at Nanyuki, Kenya.

destroyed on the ground at Berbera on the 8th, Blenheim Mk IV-Fs of 203 Squadron from Aden patrolled over Berbera to keep the Italian bombers at bay – P/O Corbould attacked three of the fast S.79 tri-motor bombers, badly damaging one, and the crew of another 203 Squadron Mk IV-F had to abandon their attack on three S.79s bombing Berbera airfield on the 12th when the two men in the cockpit were wounded by return fire. At this critical juncture in East Africa, the 45 Squadron Flight in Sudan was recalled to Egypt on the 9th – in ten days their six Mk Is had carried out 21 successful sorties without loss. 254 Wing wanted to retain their extra striking power but was overruled.

This left only the Aden-based Blenheim squadrons to support the Allied withdrawal from British Somaliland through the port of Berbera. On 10 August three Mk Is from 8 Squadron dive-bombed troops near Tug Argan, and three more returned later to continue the attack, but unfortunately two of them (L8506 and L8503) collided in the air just after leaving the target area and both crashed in flames (see Appendix 4). At dawn on the 12th two Mk Is left Aden to attack guns near Darborouk, and met AA fire – F/Lt Smith of 11 Squadron (in L8395) was also attacked by CR.42s and staggered back to Aden in a badly damaged aircraft, while the 39 Squadron aircraft (L8387) of his companion P/O Rowbotham was so badly damaged by CR.42s that he had to force-land at Berbera. Three more Blenheims of 39 Squadron arrived a couple of hours later to attack similar targets; one (L8402) was attacked head-on by a CR.32, the Observer being killed and the Pilot, F/Sgt Thomas, badly wounded in the right shoulder. He managed to stem the bleeding with his handkerchief and staggered back to crash-land at Berbera, being awarded a DFM

L8402 of 39 Squadron was hit in a head-on attack by CR.32 on 12 August; Sgt Hogan (Obs) was killed and F/Sgt Thomas (Pilot) badly wounded, but he managed to crash-land at Berbera, and was awarded the DFM.

for his bravery (see Appendix 4). The depleted Aden squadrons were reinforced when six Mk Is from A Flight of 84 Squadron in Iraq arrived at Aden on 15 August, having shot down a Savoia S.81 three-engined bomber off Kamaran Island on the way! The evacuation through Berbera continued; five Blenheims raided Hargeisa airfield on the 17th, and one (L8387) of 39 Squadron on reconnaissance was hit by AA fire and had to ditch in the Red Sea alongside the cruiser HMS *Ceres* – the crew were rescued (see Appendix 4).

Such was the attrition during these extensive operations by small numbers of Blenheims, often flying two or three sorties a day, that 39 and 11 Squadrons were reduced to only five serviceable aircraft each – and that was after 39 had transferred two of its aircraft to 11 Squadron! On the next day, the 18th, 11 Squadron was left with only four aircraft fit for operations when Sgt Gay and crew in L1497 was shot down in flames (see Appendix 4).

The evacuation of Berbera was completed on 19 August and the Italians captured the port and the two damaged Blenheims (L8402 and L8387) that had force-landed on the airfield there (see Appendix 4). In the final four days before the fall of Berbera, the Aden-based Blenheims had carried out 72 bombing sorties, 31 bombing-reconnaissance sorties, and 36 fighter-patrols over Berbera – a truly magnificent effort by such a small number of aircraft.

There was little respite for these few remaining Aden-based Blenheims as on the next day four of 39 and one of 11 Squadron attacked Diredawe airfield causing considerable damage, but losing one more aircraft (L8474), which was shot down in flames by a CR.42 and P/O Jago and crew were killed. On the 24th three Mk Is of 11 Squadron refuelled at Perim Island and bombed Dessie airfield to the north. Twelve aircraft, drawn from 8, 11 and 39 Squadrons, all the Aden-based Blenheim bombers that could be mustered, made a successful attack on the Assab naval base on 1 September and followed this up with another destructive raid on the 5th. Five Blenheims from Aden, after an overnight re-fuelling stop at Ras Ara, raided Dessie airfield again on the 9th but defending CR.32s caused them to jettison their bombs short of the target. However, the number of Blenheims available in East Africa would soon improve slightly for 14 Squadron received its first three Mk IVs with crews on the 14th and started converting from Wellesleys, but in their first sortie on the 20th to attack Massawa, one of the three was shot down. Meanwhile A Flight of 45 Squadron was ordered to make the long journey back from the Canal Zone to Summit in Southern Sudan, with B and C Flights to follow. A Flight resumed operations on 11 September by bombing Asmara airfield, and over the next few days a fuel dump at Gura, and airfields at Kassala, Mai Edaga and Gura, all without loss

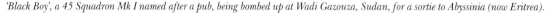

'Black Boy', a 45 Squadron Mk I named after a pub, being bombed up at Wadi Gazouza, Sudan, for a sortie to Abyssinia (now Eritrea).

THE BRISTOL BLENHEIM

although they were harried by CR.42s; the rest of the Squadron arrived on the 25th and the other Flights joined in on the 27th. The CR.42s were getting more aggressive and on the 30th shot down one of nine aircraft attacking Gura airfield, S/Ldr Bush and his crew in L6665 (see Appendix 4). Worse was to follow for only two days later 45 Squadron lost its CO when S/Ldr John Dallamore, leading a dawn attack on Gura in L 8452, was shot down in flames. Successive Flights of Blenheims from Aden raided Assab throughout that day, hitting the AGIP fuel dump, the telephone exchange and army stores.

F/Lt Troughton-Smith assumed command of 45 Squadron and over the next few days, from 3 to 12 October, led, or sent, sections of three aircraft to bomb, without loss, Agordat railway station, Massawa, Gura, Mai Edaga and Asmara airfields, together with several Landing Grounds. But the 13th was a black day: a section of three Blenheims attacked Gura airfield in the morning without trouble, but a raid by three more sent in the afternoon failed completely. Sgt Griffiths in L8477 had engine trouble and aborted, F/O Woodruff, who had the Squadron Intelligence Officer, P/O Roberts, with him in L8463, and P/O Cockayne in L8502 were both shot down and all seven crewmen killed (see Appendix 4). Once more the Blenheims found themselves in the thick of fierce fighting and sustaining heavy casualties.

The Mk IV-Fs of 203 Squadron continued to guard convoys passing through the Red Sea, and on 15 October P/O Barnitt attacked three S.79s sent to bomb a convoy and shot one of them down; he claimed another five days later but, although damaged, it escaped. However, the hard-stretched 203 Squadron Blenheims could not also defend the airfields, and all eight Wellesleys of 47 Squadron as well as two Vincents were destroyed on the ground on the 17th by a bombing and strafing raid on Gedaref Landing Ground. The RAF tried to repay the *Regia Aeronautica* in kind three days later when five Blenheims from Aden refuelled at Perim Island and attacked Alomata, damaging some CR.32s. 14 Squadron in Sudan continued converting from Wellesleys to Blenheim Mk IVs, but on 26 October one was mis-identified by defending Gladiators and attacked; although the pilot was wounded he managed to crash-land, but T2075 was damaged beyond repair. On 4 November F/Lt Pike in a 203 Squadron Mk IV-F chased off an S.79 that attempted to bomb a Red Sea convoy he was escorting; two of the bomber crew were killed and two wounded, but the tri-motor made it back to Zula.

Low-key operations in East Africa continued to the end of the year. 14 Squadron aircraft carried out armed reconnaissance over Eritrea on 12 November, and three of 8 Squadron made a night raid on Diredawe airfield on the 14th – P/O Young in L6648 was hit by flak and had to crash-land at Ras Ara. Two solo sorties were chased into cloud by fighters and had narrow escapes: F/Lt Buchanan DFC of 14 Squadron on the 16th, and S/Ldr Ray of 45 Squadron on the 18th. The latter was wounded and his aircraft damaged. The next day a Mk IV-F of 203 Squadron failed to return from a Red Sea patrol and the crew were missing, presumed killed. At the end of November 11 and 39 Squadrons were ordered to take their Blenheims to Egypt as they were needed in the Western Desert. This left only 8 and 14 Squadrons with their Mk Is and 203 Squadron's Mk IV-Fs in the area, as 45 Squadron was instructed to take its 11 remaining aircraft to Egypt on the 28th. However, 14 Squadron at Port Sudan continued re-equipping with Mk IVs, with B Flight converting to Mk IV-Fs. They took six of these to raid Nefasit on the 26th, but tangled with defending CR.42s and F/O McKenzie had to force-land his damaged aircraft R3593. The CO, S/Ldr Selway, landed alongside the downed Blenheim on the return journey and rescued the crew. But on 4 December one of three 14 Squadron aircraft on an armed reconnaissance was shot down by CR.42s and F/Sgt Rhodes and crew were killed (see Appendix 4).

The aerial war in East Africa may have been small in scale but individual actions were sharp and often deadly, the terrain overflown was decidedly unfriendly, and the hot climate and difficult operating conditions made life particularly uncomfortable for both air- and ground-crews. The crews overcame all these difficulties and acquitted themselves well, as did the aircraft themselves, and the Blenheims made a significant contribution to the Allied cause – but this contribution was barely noticed in the UK as all eyes at that time were on the fighter pilots in the Battle of Britain.

A cheerful 113 Squadron crew before a sortie from Ma'aten Bagush – the Pilot (right) has a seat-type parachute, his crew the clip-on chest type, and two carry 'tin hats'.

On the night of 12 June L1487 of 211 Squadron taxied into unlit aircraft L5849 of 216 Squadron at El Daba, so missed the raid on Tobruk, both were repaired.

The camera is handed over after a reconnaissance sortie – this time the airman on the ground is wearing a steel helmet. The turret has the single VGO gun.

The Western Desert: round two

Marshal Graziani started moving his 80,000-strong army cautiously towards Egypt on 10 September, but advanced only 60 miles and halted at Sidi Barrani on the 16th to construct a series of fortifications and minefields, which were regularly photographed by reconnaissance Blenheims during the following eight weeks as Graziani steadily built up his forces. Two 30 Squadron pilots in their Mk I-Fs had each shot down an S.79, and another fell to a Hurricane on the 11th – the numbers of the latter fighter increased rapidly during this period. 45 Squadron returned from Sudan with its Blenheims and all the Blenheim squadrons could now be deployed in direct support of the Allied ground forces as three squadrons of Wellingtons flew out from England via Gibraltar and Malta to assume the strategic bombing role. In fact, Longmore's strength had been increased significantly over the last four months of 1940 by the receipt of 85 Blenheim Mk IVs and 87 Hurricanes, as well as the 41 Wellingtons.

In the land battles, the Italians were beaten to the punch for, just as they were poised to launch their offensive, the Allied forces, led brilliantly by General Richard O'Connor, struck first on 9 December with Operation Compass. They bypassed the inland end of the minefields through very difficult terrain to swing north and attack the Italian fortified positions from the rear. Sidi Barrani was captured on the 11th and the out-manoeuvred Italian forces were evicted from Egypt in a few days. The High Commanders in Cairo – Wavell and Longmore – believed in close co-operation between land and air forces, and their Commanders at the sharp end on the ground – O'Connor and Collimore – put it to effective use and thus laid the basis for important future developments in this direction. Blenheims made a major contribution to the success of Operation Compass, each aircraft flying several sorties a day bombing and strafing enemy airfields, troop positions, transport using the only main road along the coast, and the supply ports of Tobruk, Derna, Bardia, Sollum and Gazala. 45 Squadron had been brought back from the Sudan, its aircraft carrying out 84 sorties in the first ten days of the offensive alone.

'The Young Un' – Observer Ian Blair – flew his 113 Squadron Blenheim 'The Old Un' safely back to Ma'aten Bagush on 4 September 1940 after his Pilot had been killed by an Italian fighter. Ian was awarded the DFM and later qualified as a Pilot himself. (See his photo with 'Britain First' in Chapter 3.)

The Blenheims were usually escorted by Hurricanes, who often strafed ground targets themselves once the bombers were safely on their way back to base. Although opposition to these raids was greatly reduced, the hard-working 45, 55, 113 and 203 Squadrons suffered more casualties before the end of the year (see Appendix 2). General O'Connor continued to exploit this rather unexpected breakthrough with a rapid advance, sending the 7 Armoured Division to the south of the Jebel Akhdhar Mountains in a bold strike to reach the coast well behind the front and cut off the whole 'bulge' of Cyrenaica to trap the main Italian armies. His forces took the ports of Tobruk, Derna and Benghazi, greatly shortening his own lines of supply. The Allies captured 135,000 prisoners and masses of equipment, including 91 intact aircraft and 1,100 damaged ones on various airfields and landing grounds. These losses, together with more than 60 aircraft shot down, virtually finished the *Regia Aeronautica* as a fighting air force. Had O'Connor's forces been allowed to continue the advance and provided with the necessary supplies, they had in their grasp a golden opportunity to conquer the whole of Libya, including Tripoli the capital and main port, and Tunisia too, for virtually no opposition remained to the west. But they were ordered to halt and the best part of the fighting strength of all three services was diverted to assist a friendly country in the Eastern Mediterranean.

This diversion, which altered the course of the war, was caused as Mussolini and the Italian High Command had opened an unnecessary new front by invading Greece. On top of their defeats in Libya, they were bungling their operations there too, so that the situation had to be saved by the intervention of the German forces, which ensured the continued Axis occupation of North Africa. The entry of the Germans into the Middle East Theatre of War tipped the balance decisively in favour of the Axis powers. If the Allied forces had not become embroiled in the campaigns in Greece and Crete but had continued westwards in early 1941 to occupy Tripoli, the only major port, the Germans would have been unable to establish the Afrika Korps in North Africa. The eventual eviction of the German forces would take years of effort and struggle, at the cost of tens of thousands of casualties to both Allied and Axis forces, and the Blenheim squadrons were to be heavily embroiled in this struggle from beginning to end.

East Africa: the re-conquest

The Commonwealth forces mounted a two-pronged attack: in the north advancing from Sudan into Eritrea on 19 January 1941, and in the south from Kenya into Italian Somaliland and Ethiopia on 11 February. RAF and SAAF fighters soon gained fairly effective control of the air on both fronts. Blenheims were not involved in the southern arm of the gigantic pincer, but in the northern arm those of 8 and 14 Squadron based in Sudan bombed and strafed Italian troops and aircraft on the ground, as did the Mk IV-Fs of 203 Squadron from Aden with light bombs and their under-slung machine-guns. They gave all the help they could when the northern Allied advance was held up during fierce fighting in mountainous terrain near Keren, which was not captured until 26 March. Several Blenheims were lost during these operations (see Appendix 4). For example, two Mk IV-Fs of 203 Squadron went on 18 February to strafe Makale airfield; T2053 was shot down and S/Ldr A. Solano and crew killed, and the other aircraft, T9173 of S/Ldr Scott, was badly damaged and crash-landed at Aden. 203 Squadron lost another Blenheim when T2255 of F/O P. Moller was shot down on a long-range sortie over Ethiopia.

British forces from Aden re-occupied Berbera in British Somaliland on 16 March, covered by 203's Blenheims from Aden. A Free French Blenheim unit, GDB 1, was in action for the first time with Z9583 – it had flown in three aircraft from far-away Fort Lamy, and these were attached to 47 Squadron in Sudan, carrying out seven sorties, but only one aircraft remained serviceable by 1 April so the Flight was supplied with six more. The Ethiopian capital Addis Ababa was captured on 6 April and the port of Massawa on the 8th. Five Italian destroyers had slipped out of Massawa on 2 April in a desperate attempt to raid Suez – they were spotted by a Blenheim from 203 Squadron and two were bombed and

A 203 Squadron Mk IV-F at Khormaksar, Aden, with a broken tail-wheel – a not uncommon occurrence.

sunk by five Blenheims of 14 Squadron and FAA Swordfish (which had staged down from HMS *Eagle* in Alexandria to Port Sudan). Two more were beached and destroyed by the Blenheims, and the survivor returned to Massawa and was scuttled. A potential threat to Allied shipping in the Red Sea and Suez Canal had been eliminated. This was the last operation by 14 Squadron in East Africa as it too were ordered to Egypt on 9 April. Emperor Haile Selassie was restored to his throne at Addis Ababa on 5 May. After further fighting in the northern mountains the Duke of Aosta, Italian C-in-C, finally surrendered his forces on 16 May. The whole of the Horn of Africa was now in Allied hands, and Allied troops and aircraft could be transferred back to Egypt, where they were urgently needed. Axis forces were advancing towards Cairo from Libya, Greece had fallen, and Crete was about to.

The Western Desert – round three

We left the Allied forces holding lightly a front at El Agheila in Libya, after O'Connor's great victory over much larger Italian armies in January and February 1941. 'Lightly', as Wavell had sent most of his best troops, and Longmore more than half his operational squadrons, to help Greece. The *Deutsches Afrika Korps* commanded by *Generalleutnant* Erwin Rommel, comprising one Panzer and one Motorised Division, started disembarking at Tripoli on 14 February. *Fliegerkorps X* had been building up its force in Sicily over the winter to some 250 aircraft, and part was moved to Castle Benito and Sirte by early February.

The Germans, not expected to be ready to mount an offensive until May, did not waste any time and launched a probing attack on 24 March by three columns, which – finding little resistance – dashed forward daringly, two of them cutting across the bulge of Cyrenaica, taking O'Connor's route in reverse. Benghazi was taken on 3 April, and Bardia soon after; Tobruk was bypassed and isolated, and the Allied armies under General

An exploding AA shell brings down an unknown Blenheim near Tobruk – the wheels have started to drop, and it crashed seconds later, killing the crew.

Neame retreated beyond the Egyptian border. General O'Connor was sent up from Cairo to help Neame regain control, but the pair had the misfortune to run into a German patrol many miles behind the front line and were captured. The RAF had to abandon several airfields in short order, destroying fuel and stores dumps, which added to its difficulties. Blenheims of 45 and 55 Squadrons attacked the columns constantly, and on 12 April refuelled at a landing ground within the Tobruk perimeter to bomb repeatedly Axis armour that was massing to seize the port, succeeding in breaking up the formation. Hurricanes strafed the German troops, and fierce resistance from Australian defenders caused the direct assault on Tobruk to fail, and marked the start of a long siege. Messerschmitts had been in action over Tobruk for the first time on 19 April, shooting down four Hurricanes – clearly the role of the Blenheims was about to become far more dangerous. They had continued to suffer losses throughout this military reverse, both operational (see Appendix 4) and non-operational (see Appendix 5). On the land warfare front there was stalemate for several months while both sides regrouped and re-organised their supply lines to take advantage of the increasing flow of reinforcements. Among those headed for the RAF in the Western Desert were many hundreds of Blenheims, which would be heavily involved in the see-saw struggle for North Africa as the battles surged backwards and forwards over the coming years.

L1481 of 211 Squadron undershot a night landing at El Daba on 13th March 1940, striking a pile of railway sleepers, the two crew were seriously injured.

F/Lt G. Bush attempted to land L8482 of 45 Squadron in a sandstorm at Fuka 19 February 1940 with this result – amazingly he, his crew, and five passengers escaped with cuts and bruises.

Appendix I

Blenheim losses prior to the outbreak of war in the Middle East on 11 June 1940

Aircraft are all Mk Is.

17-02-1938   K7108 30 Squadron: overshot landing on delivery to Ismailia and overturned (see the picture below).

15-06-1938   K7101 30 Squadron: swung after take-off and wing hit ground at Habbaniyah.

29-06-1938   K7102 30 Squadron: engine cut just after take-off at Habbaniyah, stalled and crashed; P/O C. Stephen and AC1 H. Davies killed (see picture on page 424).

10-12-1938   K7097 30 Squadron: crashed in bad weather on hillside in desert 60 miles SW of Habbaniyah, believed due to carburettor icing, wreck not found for 10 days; Sgt V. Garside (Pilot), S/Ldr P. Kinsey (Command Signals Officer), Capt J. Harvey (Army, attached to Iraq Levees), and ACs F. Gamble, L. Cooper, and R. Carpenter killed.

12-06-1939   L1527 113 Squadron: u/c failed to lock and collapsed on landing at Heliopolis.

07-07-1939   L1529 8 Squadron: collided on landing at Khormaksar with L1543 (below), u/c collapsed.

07-07-1939   L1543 8 Squadron: collided on take-off at Khormaksar with L1529 (above), u/c collapsed.

10-07-1939   L8500 45 Squadron: swung on landing at Amman, u/c collapsed; P/O R. Gibbs unhurt, aircraft damaged beyond repair (DBR).

29-07-1939   L6630 Blenheim Collection Flight: u/c collapsed on heavy landing at Heliopolis, DBR.

03-08-1939   L1384 84 Squadron: misjudged height on night landing at Shaiba and crashed.

10-09-1939   L8527 27 Squadron: based at Kohat, engine cut, hit ridge and crashed at Charbar, Iran.

11-09-1939   K7093 30 Squadron: belly-landed in error at Ismailia, DBR and struck off charge 2-1-1940, P/O F Harrison unhurt.

27-09-1939   L4825 211 Squadron: based at El Daba, u/c retracted in error after landing at Qasaba, Sgt R. Pearson unhurt, aircraft repaired.

02-10-1939   L8442 113 Squadron: engine cut on take-off at Heliopolis, crashed and destroyed by fire; F/Lt Dallamore and crew escaped uninjured.

18-10-1939   L8673 55 Squadron: bounced on heavy night landing at Ismailia, u/c jammed with one side partially retracted, aircraft abandoned in air, P/O R. Nicolson, LAC C. Bartram, AC1 T. Sherr, and AC1 J. Rown baled out safely.

18-11-1939   L6647 8 Squadron: based at Khormaksar, Aden, engine failed, crash-landed 15 miles NW of Irqa, Yemen, P/O M. Howell, P/O R. Melville-Townsend and AC1 A. Smith escaped but were caught and shot by local tribesmen, buried in Ma'alla, Aden.

22-11-1939   L1380 84 Squadron: u/c retracted in error after landing at Shaibah, F/Lt R. Towgood uninjured.

19-02-1940   L8482 45 Squadron: crashed at Fuka, landing during sandstorm; F/Lt G. Bush, two crew and five passengers received only cuts and bruises.

13-03-1940   L1486 211 Squadron: undershot night landing at El Daba and hit pile of poles, P/O C. Collier and LAC C. Thomas both seriously injured.

13-03-1940   L1537 211 Squadron: heavy night landing at El Daba, u/c collapsed, DBR, P/O E. Garrad-Cole uninjured.

24-04-1940   L1544 8 Squadron: undershot night approach to Khormaksar, hit ground and destroyed by fire; no casualties recorded.

09-05-1940   L8472 45 Squadron: flew into ridge at El Quattara, near base of Fuka, when lost in bad weather; F/O C. Thomas, Sgt S. Davies, and AC1 C. Richardson injured.

11-05-1940   L8386 55 Squadron: flew into high ground at night 60 miles east of Ismailia; Sgt R. Claxton, Sgt N. Smith, and LAC R. Jobling (ground-crew passenger) killed, LAC R. King (WOp/Ag) seriously injured.

K7108 being righted at Ismailia after it overshot landing on delivery,
braked heavily and overturned, 17 February 1938. Reminiscent of
K7036 which overturned on delivery to Wyton in March 1937.

K7102 of 30 Squadron crashed when an engine cut on take-off from Habbaniyah on 29 June 1938; it stalled and was Destroyed by Fire, both crew being killed.

Appendix 2

Operational Blenheim losses in the Western Desert, 11 June to 31 December 1940

11-06-1940 L8476 45 Squadron Mk I: Failed to return (FTR); hit by light flak attacking El Adem airfield at 0540, caught fire and crashed into sea; crew Sgt P. Bower, Sgt S. Fox, and AC1 J. Allison Killed In Action (KIA), commemorated on The Alamein Memorial.

11-06-1940 L8519 45 Squadron Mk I: FTR; damaged in raid on El Adem, crash-landed at Sidi Barrani, Destroyed By Fire; Sgt M. Thurlow, Sgt B. Feldman, and AC1 H. Robinson KIA.

11-06-1940 L8466 45 Squadron Mk I: FTR as above, one engine cut, the other 100 miles eastwards, crash-landed near Buq Buq; crew F/O A. Finch, Sgt R. Dodsworth, and LAC Fisher rescued by British Army, aircraft recovered and repaired.

11-06-1940 L4823 113 Squadron Mk IV: FTR; shot down by fighters on return from El Adem, F/Lt D. Beauclair, W/O H. Owen, and Sgt J. Dobson all injured (burns) and became PoWs.

14-06-1940 L8524 45 Squadron Mk I: FTR; shot down on sortie to Giarabub airfield; crew F/O J. Davies, Sgt G. Negus, and LAC J. Copeland KIA, buried in Halfya Sollum War Cemetery, Libya.

29-06-1940 L8436 113 Squadron Mk IV: FTR, damaged by flak while bombing El Gubbi and ditched into sea, P/O D. Pike, Sgt R. Lidstone and Sgt J. Taylor rescued, became PoWs.

29-06-1940 L8447 113 Squadron Mk I: FTR from same sortie, shot down in flames by fighters, F/O W. Mason, Sgt J. Juggins and Sgt G. Biggins KIA, commemorated on Alamein Memorial, Egypt.

29-06-1940 L8522 113 Squadron Mk I: FTR from same sortie, shot down in flames by fighters, F/Sgt R. Knott, Sgt J. Barber and LAC J. Toner KIA, commemorated on Alamein Memorial, Egypt.

05-07-1940 L8529 113 Squadron Mk I: hit by light AA fire in raid on Italian troops near Bardia; F/Lt A. Bentley injured, F/Sgt K. Taylor (Obs) KIA, Sgt A. Meadows (WOp/Ag) helped fly aircraft back to base, awarded DFM, aircraft repaired.

13-07-1940 K7181 30 Squadron Mk I-F: FTR; shot down by return fire when attacking three SM.79s; P/O D. Lea and Sgt C. Burt KIA, commemorated on Alamein Memorial.

15-07-1940 L4820 55 Squadron Mk I: crashed at Buq Buq on return from sortie to Gazala, cause unknown; crew F/O M. Fox, Sgt H. Nicholas, and Sgt M. Klines KIA, buried at Halfya Sollum War Cemetery.

15-07-1940 L1491 211 Squadron Mk I: FTR from El Daba, damaged, force-landed near El Adem, abandoned; P/O E. Garrard-Cole, LAC W. Smith, AC2 E. Doolin captured and PoWs.

22-07-1940 L6661 211 Squadron Mk I: FTR from sortie to El Adem from Qotafiyah; crew Sgt G. Smith, Sgt R. Steele, and Sgt G. Sewell KIA, the latter is buried in El Alamein War Cemetery, his companions commemorated on Memorial there.

28-07-1940 K7178 30 Squadron Mk I-F: FTR from escorting reconnaissance sortie to Libya by 113 Squadron Blenheim, shot down by CR.42s; F/Lt I Swann, P/O H Fisher and Sgt J Young KIA, buried in Knightsbridge War Cemetery, Acroma, Libya.

04-08-1940 L8532 211 Squadron Mk I: damaged in raid on Italian MT at Bir el Gobi; Sgt J. Macintock (WOp/Ag) wounded, F/Lt Jones and Sgt Dennis uninjured, crash-landed at Sidi Barrani, recovered by 51 R&SU, to 103 MU, SOC 20-09-1940.

31-08-1940   L8397 55 Squadron Mk I: FTR, crashed at Mersa Matruh after engine cut on sortie to bomb airfields, bombs jettisoned, control lost in turn; crew P/O R. Smith, Sgt J. Sugden, and LAC L. Lowe KIA, buried in El Alamein war Cemetery.

04-09-1940   L8376 211 Squadron Mk I: CO's aircraft, FTR; damaged by fighters near Derna, force-landed in desert in enemy territory, aircraft shot up while on ground by fighters; crew S/Ldr Bax, Sgt Bain, and AC1 Wise made own way back to base.

17-09-1940   L6660 211 Squadron Mk I: FTR, undershot night landing at Qotafiyah, bounced, struck car, DBR; crew Sgt G. Watkins, Sgt Oliver, and Sgt G. Pattison DFM uninjured.

18-09-1940   T2048 113 Squadron Mk IV: FTR from raid on Tmimi, shot down by CR.42s; S/Ldr G Kelly DFC AFC baled out and captured, P/O J. Cleaver and Sgt J. Jobson KIA, buried in Knightsbridge War Cemetery, Acroma, Libya.

25-09-1940   L8523 211 Squadron Mk I: FTR from raid on Tobruk; damaged and crash-landed near Qasaba with starboard engine on fire; S/Ldr J. Gordon-Finlayson DFC, Sgt J. Richmond, and Sgt Jones escaped uninjured, aircraft DBR.

27-09-1940   L8394 55 Squadron Mk I: FTR; shot down by CR.42s near Giarabub; P/O Godrich, Sgt W. Clarke, and Sgt W. Thompson KIA.

30-09-1940   T2171 113 Squadron Mk IV: FTR; shot down into Mediterranean by CR.42s on return from raid on Maraua; Sgt L. Cater, Sgt K. Meadowcroft, and Sgt B. Shelton (aged 18) KIA, commemorated on Alamein Memorial.

12-10-1940   L8530 55 Squadron Mk I: DBR by CR.42s while attacking Tobruk; no injuries reported to P/O M. Singleton, Sgt Brownrigg, and Sgt B. Fox.

18-10-1940   L1538 55 Squadron Mk I: returned to Fuka with engine trouble 30 minutes after take-off for raid and crash-landed; no injuries reported to Sgt E. Coughlan, Sgt W. Bowker, and Sgt D. Clayson.

27-10-1940   T2068 113 Squadron Mk IV: FTR; became lost on return from raid on Benghazi, fired at by 'friendly' AA, abandoned in air near Amriya; F/O P. Squires, Sgt Durrant, and Sgt B. Hancorn safe.

09-11-1940   N3623 Free French Mk IV: FTR to Libreville, Gabon, from recce over Atlantic Ocean during storm off Cap San Juan, Equatorial Guinea; Sgt Chef J. Le Guyader, Lt A. Jacob and Adj M. Tazzer killed.

26-11-1940   T2067 113 Squadron Mk IV: FTR; shot down on sortie to Maaten Bagush; F/O D. Anderson, Sgt G. Lee, and Sgt E. Young KIA, buried at Halfya Sollum War Cemetery.

12-12-1940   L8465 45 Squadron Mk I: FTR; shot down in raid on Sollum, P/O P. Traill-Smith, P/O V. Fry, and Sgt T. Liggins KIA, commemorated on Alamein Memorial.

14-12-1940   L8790 55 Squadron Mk IV: FTR from raid to Bardia, shot down by CR.42s; F/O M. Singleton, Sgt E. Chapman and Sgt B. Fox KIA, commemorated on el Alamein Memorial.

20-12-1940   T2059 113 Squadron Mk IV: FTR from sortie from LG.68 (Waterloo); F/O V. Frith, Sgt E. McKim, and Sgt G. Lyle KIA, commemorated on Alamein Memorial.

Appendix 3

Blenheim losses en route to the Middle East, at sea, on ferry flights, and on Takoradi route to 31 December 1940

Aircraft are all Mk IVs.

26-08-1940   T2058 114 Squadron: ditched off Lampedusa Island on direct ferry flight to Malta, out of fuel; P/O C. Regan, Sgt G. Cluley and Sgt W. Paul rescued and became PoWs.

27-08-1940   T2062 107 Squadron: force-landed out of fuel near Cap Bon, Tunisia, on direct ferry flight to Malta; crew (from 101 Squadron) Sgt D. Riddick, Sgt J. Hudson and Sgt D. Randall interned by Vichy French in Tunisia and Algeria, repatriated to UK 2½ years later.

13-09-1940   N3589 40 Squadron: ran short of fuel on direct ferry flight to Malta and force-landed on Italian island of Pantelleria, repaired and test-flown by Italians; crew P/O G. Goodman, P/O K. Grey and Sgt R. Shaw captured and became PoWs, Pilot escaped later and returned to Squadron.

27-09-1940   T2176 57 Squadron: ran out of fuel on ferry flight from Thorney Island to Malta, force-landed on Lampedusa Island; F/O A. Goldie, Sgt R. Dean and Sgt F. Conner DFM became PoWs.

28-09-1940   T2041, T2050, T2055 and T2070 lost at sea (SS Kibalo).

29-11-1940   T2080 ex-107 Squadron: shot down by Vichy French fighters off Tunisian coast; P/O A. Smith and Sgt E. Shipley (Obs) interned, Sgt J. Hutchinson (WOp/Ag) killed.

30-11-1940   T2114 OADF (ex-110 Squadron): ran short of fuel, crash-landed in Ebro Estuary; P/O G. Bennett, Sgt S. Cashman, and Sgt E. Hannah interned, later released (see the photograph on page 426).

02-12-1940   T2187 101 Squadron: shot down by MC.200 over Mediterranean on ferry flight from Thorney Island; Sgt G. Palmer, Sgt E. Farmes, and Sgt A. Dunleavy killed, commemorated on Runnymede Memorial.

T2114, ex-110 Squadron Mk IV from Gibraltar with OADF, was shot down by MC.200s and crashed off the Ebro Estuary, Spain, on 30 November 1940; P/O G. Bennett and his crew survived and were interned.

Appendix 4

Blenheim losses in East Africa and the Red Sea area, 11 June to 31 December 1940

12-06-1940   L6654 8 Squadron Mk I: FTR; engine cut on raid to Macaaca, belly landed at Ras Ara LG and DBR, F/Lt M. Goodwin, P/O S. Palmer and Sgt R. Hannan safe.

24-06-1940   L4920 39 Squadron Mk I: FTR; damaged by CR.42 in raid on Diredawe, force-landed in Somalia; P/O D. Hunter (Pilot) and Sgt R. Ellis (Obs) injured, rescued by Somali Field Force, LAC R. Olley (WOp/Ag) died of his injuries, commemorated on Alamein Memorial.

02-07-1940   L4924 11 Squadron Mk I: FTR; hit by flak in port engine during raid on Assab airfield, crash-landed on way back to base, 25 miles short of Ras Ara; crew F/O J. Lawrence, Sgt H. Hill, and AC1 H. Bowen safe.

11-07-1940   L8505 8 Squadron Mk I: FTR; badly damaged by CR.32s on recce, force-landed at Djibouti; F/O P. Nicholas (Pilot) and P/O D James (Obs) injured and taken to hospital, Sgt R. Hannan (WOp/Ag) uninjured, aircraft recovered.

29-07-1940   L4817 11 Squadron Mk I: FTR; shot down by AA fire in raid on Assab airfield; crew Sgt J. Barry, Sgt G. Harnden, and Sgt A. Mackintosh KIA.

01-08-1940   L8406 8 Squadron Mk I: FTR; shot down by CR.32s in raid on Chinele LG; crew Sgt Franks, Sgt Thain, and LAC Cumner-Price captured and became PoWs.

05-08-1940   L8375 8 Squadron Mk I: FTR; shot down in flames by CR.32 on bombing sortie to Hargeisa; crew P/O R. Felstead, Sgt A. Wright, and P/O T. Mitchell DFC KIA.

10-08-1940   L8503 8 Squadron Mk I: FTR; collided with L8506 (below) and crashed in flames after attacking Dhubbato; crew F/O A. Curtis, Sgt V. Witt, and LAC H. McEleavy KIA, commemorated on Alamein Memorial.

10-08-1940   L8506 8 Squadron Mk I: FTR; collided with L8503 (above) and crashed in flames after attacking Dhubbato; crew P/O A. Bisson, Sgt D. Wilson, and LAC N. Wilson KIA, commemorated on Alamein Memorial.

12-08-1940   L8402 39 Squadron Mk I: FTR; damaged by CR.32, crash-landed at Berbera; F/Sgt Thomas (Pilot) wounded, Sgt Hogan (Obs) KIA, Cpl Wintle (WOp/Ag) uninjured. Pilot awarded DFM.

12-08-1940   L8387 39 Squadron Mk I: FTR; badly damaged by CR.32s near Darborouk, crash-landed at Berbera; 11 Squadron crew P/O G. Rowbotham, Sgt Maltby and LAC Pullin safe, aircraft found at Addis Ababa on 7-4-1941 when capital city captured by Allied Forces.

17-08-1940   L4834 39 Squadron Mk I: FTR; damaged by AA in raid on Hargeisa, fuel pipe fractured, ditched alongside HMS Ceres; crew Sgt T. Crehan, Sgt D. Keys, and Sgt A. Henderson rescued uninjured within 30 minutes.

18-08-1940   L1479 8 Squadron Mk I: FTR; shot down in flames by CR.32s near Nasiyeh, Somalia; crew baled out, wounded and burned, Sgt A. Gay (Pilot) captured, but LAC E. Clarke (Obs) and LAC M. Porter (WOp/Ag) died of injuries.

18-08-1940   L8385 39 Squadron Mk I: damaged by CR.32s; Sgt Bailey (Pilot) made it back to base, Sgt Marshall (Obs) slightly injured, Sgt Ware (WOp/Ag) uninjured, aircraft repaired.

23-08-1940   L8474 39 Squadron Mk I: FTR; shot down in flames by CR.42s while bombing Diredawe airfield; crew P/O P. Jago, Sgt J. Wilson-Law, and Cpl J. Wintle KIA, memorials in Diredawa War Cemetery

26-08-1940	L9218 203 Squadron Mk I: FTR from photo-reconnaissance sortie to Assab; F/O S. Pendred, F/O F. Hunter, and LAC W. Love KIA, buried in Asmara War Cemetery.
01-09-1940	L8505 8 Squadron Mk I: FTR; swung after take-off at Khormaksar, hit sea and overturned, crew injured but rescued, names not given in ORB.
06-09-1940	L8543 39 Squadron Mk I: port wing hit Chance light on night landing at Sheikh Othman on return from raid on Berbera, DBR; Sgt T. Crenan, Sgt D. Keys and Sgt A. Henderson uninjured.
06-09-1940	T2075 203 Squadron Mk IV: engine cut on take-off for raid from Khormaksar, Aden, u/c struck pipeline, aircraft destroyed by fire; crew F/Lt W. Ratcliffe, Sgt W. Scott and Cpl E. Lowther escaped to safety before bomb-load exploded.
30-09-1940	L6665 45 Squadron Mk I: FTR; shot down by fighters while bombing Gura; S/Ldr G. Bush, Sgt J. Usher, and Sgt J. Corney DFM KIA.
02-10-1940	L8452 45 Squadron Mk I: FTR; shot down in flames by six CR.42s; P/O A Sheppard (Obs) baled out and captured, S/Ldr J. Dallamore (Pilot) and Sgt M. Mackenzie (WOp/Ag) KIA, buried in Asmara War Cemetery, Eritrea. S/Ldr John Dallamore was CO of 45 Squadron.
13-10-1940	L8463 45 Squadron Mk I: FTR; shot down attacking Gura airfield; F/O G. Woodroffe, Sgt E. Ryles, Sgt Meadows DFM, and P/O L. Roberts KIA. P/O Laurence Roberts was 45 Squadron's Intelligence Officer.
13-10-1940	L8502 45 Squadron Mk I: FTR; shot down by CR.42s while attacking Gura airfield; P/O G. Cockayne, Sgt T. Ferris, and Sgt R. Reader KIA.
26-10-1940	T2057 14 Squadron Mk IV: shot down in error by RAF fighters (mistaken for SM.79) during bombing practice at Port Sudan, F/Lt D. Stapleton DFC AFC, Sgt G. Bartholomew, and Sgt D. Farrell all injured.
19-11-1940	L8475 45 Squadron Mk I: badly damaged by fighters on raid to Keren railway station, S/Ldr E. Wray injured but flew aircraft back to Wadi Gazouza, Sudan, DBR; Sgt C. Hodder and Sgt E. Fletcher safe.
19-11-1940	L9458 203 Squadron Mk IV: FTR from convoy escort, control lost in cloud, dived into sea near convoy off Aden; crew P/O R. Given, Sgt F. Banfield, and LAC W. Blackburn KIA, commemorated on Alamein Memorial.
26-11-1940	R3593 14 Squadron Mk IV: FTR; damaged on raid, crash-landed in scrubland 10 miles north of Massawa; CO S/Ldr Stapleton landed alongside and rescued crew, F/O M. Mckenzie, Sgt M. Hitchin, and Sgt W. McConnell, CO awarded DFC for this action.
09-12-1940	L1534 45 Squadron Mk I: damaged by fighters in raid on Monastir, belly-landed at Sidi el Raniman; crew F/Lt Paine, Sgt Chaplin, and Sgt Edwards uninjured, aircraft repaired.
09-12-1940	L6663 45 Squadron Mk I: damaged by fighters on same raid; crew F/O C. Thomas, Sgt R. Dodsworth, and Sgt Fisher safe, aircraft DBR.
14-12-1940	T2167 14 Squadron Mk IV: FTR from raid to Zula, Eritrea, believed to have crashed in Sudan on return; Sgt B. Hopkins, Sgt J. Hall, and Sgt R. Murray KIA, commemorated on Alamein Memorial.

Appendix 5

Non-operational Blenheim losses, 11 June 1940 to 31 December 1940

08-07-1940	L8478 45 Squadron Mk I: tyre burst on take-off at Helwan, belly-landed; F/O J. Williams and crew safe, aircraft repaired.
06-08-1940	L4911 11 Squadron Mk I: overshot downwind landing and hit sand-dune at Little Aden, overturned, DBR; Sgt F. Birt uninjured.
13-08-1940	L8392 Pilot's Reinforcement & Reserve Pool Mk I: tyre burst on take-off at Ismailia, swung and u/c collapsed, DBR; P/O R. Priest safe.
16-09-1940	T2052 113 Squadron Mk IV: crashed in night landing at LG.15 Maaten Bagush, on transit flight, DBF; P/O E. Roberts (solo Pilot) killed, buried in El Alamein War Cemetery.
04-10-1940	L4903 8 Squadron Mk I: undershot night landing at Khormaksar, struck wall, DBR; Sgt C. Loader (solo Pilot) injured.
05-10-1940	K7106 30 Squadron Mk I: overshot landing at Haifa, Palestine, crashed and overturned, DBR; P/O T. Allison, P/O Kirkman and Sgt Branch only slightly hurt.
11-10-1940	T2172 14 Squadron Mk IV: engine cut on take-off at Port Sudan for engine air-test, swung and ran into dyke, DBR; F/Lt G. Hill (solo Pilot) safe.
11-10-1940	T2074: DBR in accident, unit and cause unknown.
18-10-1940	K7180 30 Squadron Mk I-F: undershot at Haifa and struck fence, destroyed by fire; Sgt E. Childs and crew escaped uninjured.
20-10-1940	T2112 203 Squadron Mk IV: struck mosque attempting forced-landing after engine failed following take-off at Kamaran, destroyed by fire; P/O H. Barnitt DFC (NZ) killed, Sgt A. Finch (Obs) died of injuries, AC2 J. Beaumont (WOp/Ag) injured.
28-12-1940	T2178 55 Squadron Mk IV: FTR; engine caught fire, crashed on approach to Fuka, destroyed by fire; no injuries to F/O K. Potter or crew recorded in ORB.

Chapter 23

Greece and the Balkans

1940: the first round

Mussolini annexed Albania in April 1939 and, largely in a doomed attempt to demonstrate to his Axis partner Adolf Hitler that 'anything you can do, I can do better', in July 1940 he ordered Italian forces to prepare to conquer Greece, which they duly invaded from Albania on 28 October 1940. Hitler was not amused. The Greeks resisted skilfully and valiantly, helped by the mountainous territory in the border region. For once RAF Blenheims were not the first into action in this new war zone, but Blenheims from the Greek Air Force were among the first that were.

The 150-strong Royal Hellenic Air Force comprised mainly a miscellaneous collection of obsolete types, but included a dozen Blenheim Mk IVs with 32 Mira at Larissa, together with a dozen Fairey Battles with 33 Mira and 11 Potez 63s with 31 Mira, 36 Polish PZL 24 Mercury-engined fighters, a couple of Gloster Gladiators, and nine Avro Ansons for Naval Co-operation. Bad weather initially hampered aerial operations by both sides, but cleared on 1 November when ten Cant Z.1007s (led by Captain Bruno Mussolini, son of Benito Mussolini) and escorted by Fiat CR.42s, bombed the Greek Blenheim base at Larissa on their way to raid Salonika. The RHAF responded immediately, sending three Blenheims to bomb Koritza airfield, causing casualties including a CR.42 that crashed into a bomb crater on landing. One of the returning Blenheim crews became lost in the growing darkness and, taking some fires on the ground as an improvised landing ground, were surprised on landing to scatter peasants who were burning stubble – they then had difficulty in convincing the peasants that they were Greek not Italian airmen, but returned safely to base the following morning. The attacks on Larissa by the Italians, and on Koritza by the Greeks, were repeated the following day – one of the Blenheim's bombs destroyed a CR.42 that was taking off, killing the pilot. Within days the Greek Army launched a fierce counter-attack into Albania, which soon overcame and demoralised the Italian invaders. By the end of the first week the British had taken over Crete, with Greek permission, for use as a base to assist Greece, which was seeking aerial and naval assistance, but not (at this stage) military intervention, as it was most anxious not to encourage Germany's entry into the conflict in the area. As the only airfield on Crete was at Heraklion, the British immediately started constructing another at Maleme near Suda Bay, which was being turned into a naval base, on the north-west coast of the island, together with a landing strip near Retimo.

Longmore was quick to respond to the invasion of Greece, despite the extreme paucity of his resources, sending the Blenheims of 30 Squadron there straight away, and promising that two more squadrons of Blenheims – 84 and 211 – and one of Gladiator fighters – 80 Squadron – together with six Wellingtons of 70 Squadron would follow. This was magnanimous as the force sent represented about half of his entire front-line strength. The first eight Mk I-Fs of 30 Squadron led by S/Ldr Shannon flew into Eleusis airport at Athens on 3 November 1940, together with a servicing party in four Bristol Bombays of 216 Squadron. The Mk I-Fs carried out their first combat patrol on the 4th, chasing a Cant Z.501 flying boat into cloud – the first RAF operational sortie in the new war zone in Greece. The bomber Flight of 30 Squadron arrived on the 5th and carried out the first offensive sortie in the zone the next day – S/Ldr Shannon led three Blenheims to bomb shipping at Sarande harbour and parked aircraft at the airfield for the port of Valona, damaging several. Defending Fiat CR.42s were soon in hot pursuit and all the Blenheims were damaged by their fire; Sgt John Merifield, the WOp/Ag in Sgt G. Ratlidge's aircraft K7103, was killed, becoming the first RAF casualty in the Greek campaign. However, there were many more the next day as AVM J. D'Albiac, the local RAF commander, appeared not to have absorbed the lessons taught over the North Sea a year earlier and sent at daybreak all six available Wellingtons of 70 Squadron to bomb Valona. Two (T2734 and T2731) were shot down in flames, killing both crews, and two more (T2813 and T2816) were damaged. The four patched-up survivors returned to Egypt the next day and, although replaced by six more, Wellingtons did not fly any more daylight bombing raids over Albania – once more this dangerous role would fall upon the Blenheims alone.

84 Squadron Blenheim Mk Is arrive at Medini (Tatoi) airfield, Greece, in November 1940.

That same day A Flight of 84 Squadron arrived at Medini via Eleusis, the only two all-weather airfields suitable for the Blenheims, and they attacked Valona harbour – the main supply port in Albania for the Italian forces – in bad weather on the 10th. The Greek Blenheims at Larissa were also in action that day raiding Kalpaki, but on returning to base after dark were fired on by their own airfield AA defences and diverted to Medini, once again to be greeted with 'friendly' AA fire! They orbited until fuel shortage forced them to land regardless and Capt Kousigiannes crashed and broke his back. Another RHAF Blenheim was lost the next day when Capt Maravelias and his crew were shot down by CR.42s and killed. In a striking manifestation of aerial power on the night of 11/12 November, the strong Italian Fleet was crippled in Taranto harbour by torpedoes during a daring attack by a few carrier-born Swordfish of the Fleet Air Arm. The Blenheims of A Flight 84 Squadron attacked Valona airfield and Argyrokastron on 13 November, destroying two aircraft on the ground. The ground battle stepped up on the 14th and all the available RHAF aircraft were pressed into supporting action; three Blenheims were sent to attack Koritza airfield, but one became bogged down in mud at Larissa and was unable to take off, one of the other two took a direct hit from heavy AA and disintegrated, Capt Papageorgiou and his crew being killed, while the other aircraft staggered back too badly damaged to fight again. In the afternoon three Blenheims of 84 Squadron attacked troop concentrations near Koritza, and destroyed a bridge, preventing Italian reinforcements from joining the ground battle, but two of the three were shot down by CR.42s – F/Lt A. Mudie and crew in L1389, and Sgt W. Sidaway and crew in L1378 (see Appendix 1), while the third, Sgt L. Nuthall's L1536, was damaged. The same military targets near Koritza were attacked the following day by three Blenheims of 30 Squadron, but one, Sgt E. Childs and crew in L1120, was shot down in flames (see Appendix 1).

On 18 November the gravely depleted force of Greek PZL fighters was reinforced by the arrival from Egypt via Crete of 80 Squadron's Gladiators – among their pilots was F/Lt M. T. St J. Pattle, later to achieve great fame – and they opened their score with four Italian aircraft shot down the next day. The weather was bad and F/O C. Richardson of 30 Squadron became lost during a reconnaissance sortie in L1166 on the 21st, ran out of fuel, and the Blenheim was written off in the ensuing forced-landing on a beach near

Zagora (see Appendix 1). The Greeks captured Karitza and its airfield, and on the 23rd the Blenheims of 211 Squadron, led from Egypt by S/Ldr J. Gordon-Finlayson, started arriving at Medini. On the 26th six Blenheims of 84 Squadron tangled with G.50 fighters while attacking Valona and two were damaged, although F/O J. Evans claimed a direct hit on an Italian bomber on the ground and F/Lt R. Towgood's gunner claimed to have shot down a fighter. 211 Squadron opened its book with an attack on Durazzo in bad weather by three sections, and the CO's aircraft, L8511, was damaged by flak and struggled for 2 hours on one engine before force-landing on a beach at Corfu; the crew, travelling by foot, fishing-boat, mule, car and train, returned to Medini several days later (see Appendix 1). Next day saw 211 make a successful attack on a troopship, and the RHAF lost another Blenheim when Lt Malakes and crew were shot down by flak. The 28th saw several fierce fights between Allied and Italian fighters and an attack by nine unescorted Blenheims of 84 Squadron on Durazzo, during which L1385 was hit by fighters and forced down with P/O R. Bird and his crew captured (see Appendix 1), so the next day six Gladiators of 80 Squadron guarded the same formation from 84 (with a replacement aircraft), which attacked Tepelene without loss.

L1391 'Doughnut Dorris', F/O B. Wade's Mk I of 84 Squadron at Medini, one of many abandoned during the evacuation of Greece.

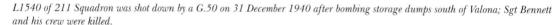

L1540 of 211 Squadron was shot down by a G.50 on 31 December 1940 after bombing storage dumps south of Valona; Sgt Bennett and his crew were killed.

The weather worsened in the first few days of December, with heavy snowfalls making flying almost impossible. To illustrate the perils of such conditions, on the 1st three Blenheims from 30 Squadron suffered severe icing returning over the mountains from a raid on Valona. The leader, F/Lt A. Bocking, and one other managed to dive through a murky gap in the snow clouds, emerging between the whitened mountain-sides, and reached base. The third aircraft became separated in the dive, so Sgt G. Ratlidge in K7103 attempted to climb over the cloud. However, at 20,000 feet the Blenheim wallowed so badly that, despite full power and his strenuous efforts, it kept slipping back into the clutches of the cloud, taking on more ice, which soon blocked a carburettor air intake; one engine stopped, flipping the aircraft into an immediate spin in the cloud. Ratlidge ordered his crew to abandon the aircraft but the violent spin had flung the Observer's chest-type parachute way out of reach so he could not clip it on, so they decided to stay with the aircraft, which lost 13,000 feet and spun out of the cloud into a narrow valley near Khalkis with sheer mountain faces rising into the cloud on either side. The pilot recovered from the spin and on sighting a small but rough cultivated area made a successful 'dead-stick' forced landing on to it – the only possible place to put the aircraft down for miles around. Lady Luck had smiled upon the crew, who were fortunate indeed to survive such a harrowing experience – the Blenheim, of course, didn't (see Appendix 1).

On the 2nd S/Ldr Gordon-Finlayson, CO of 211, back after his forced-landing in Corfu, led nine Blenheims of 211 in under low cloud to attack Valona harbour, starting a large fire. His own aerial mast was shot away by defending CR.42s and he reported that another pilot, George Doudney, 'got a bullet through his helmet'. Two aircraft from 30 Squadron bombed an Italian destroyer, which was firing at Greek positions near Sarande on the 4th, and three of 30's Mk I-Fs set out the next day to strafe the Sarande/Valona coast road. One returned early with engine-trouble, while the other two failed to return; both were damaged by ground fire and losing fuel so had to force-land although both crews were safe – F/O H. Blackmore in K7100 chose Corfu, while P/O J. Atwell came down near Agrinion (see Appendix 1). The 7th of December 1940 was a black day for the Blenheims in Greece. Two sections of three aircraft from 84 Squadron set out to raid Valona, but the leading trio encountered heavy icing and aborted the mission, while the second trio were 'bounced' over the target by CR.42s and two – F/Lt L. Catell in L8455 and Sgt M. Cazalet in L8457 – were shot down straight away, the only survivor from both crews being Sgt C. Foster, the WOp/Ag in the latter aircraft. The third Blenheim, L1381, was badly damaged and F/O K. Linton force-landed near Sarande, writing off the aircraft – 100 per cent casualties. 211 Squadron dispatched nine Blenheims in three sections of three 40 minutes later, but the icing forced two of these sections to return and two of the aircraft crashed into the hills near Lamia, killing all on board – F/O P. Pickersgill and crew in L1535 together with P/O G. Jerdein and crew in L4926. Only the trio led by F/Lt G. Jones reached and bombed the target despite fierce opposition from CR.42s. Only six of the 15 Blenheims dispatched had even reached the target, and only three of those had bombed. Three that did reach it were shot down, and the other three crashed, so the operation had cost 11 lives and six aircraft (see Appendix 1), losses that bore down hard on the small force of Blenheims in Greece. The material losses were offset partially by the arrival of three Mk I-Fs and two Mk I bombers as reinforcements for 30 Squadron, but the loss of the crews was far more debilitating.

The weather continued to hamper operations during the rest of December. Apart from the lack of visibility, particularly dangerous in such mountainous country when using totally inadequate maps, airfields flooded due to rain and thawing snow, or plummeting temperatures would freeze everything solid. The ground-crews struggled valiantly in truly appalling conditions to keep as many aircraft as possible serviceable – due to an acute shortage of spares they frequently 'cannibalised' parts from other Blenheims that had force-landed at base or were damaged beyond repair by enemy action or in accidents. A few Wellingtons had been carrying out night raids, but the daylight raids resumed on the 14th when Valona harbour was twice attacked by Blenheims without effect, and three of 30 Squadron tried again on the 18th but were intercepted by CR.42s and G.50s, and F/O S. Paget and his crew in L4862 were shot down into the sea and killed (see Appendix 1). Two British battleships, HMS *Warspite* and HMS *Valiant*, bombarded Valona harbour that night. The weather cleared sufficiently on the 19th to allow nine Blenheims of 84 Squadron to bomb Valona, but they were intercepted; three were damaged, and the bombing scattered. Nine from 211 Squadron tried again the following day but they too achieved little. The 22nd saw a different target, the oilfields at Kucera, which were attacked by nine Blenheims of 84 Squadron. They came under fire from defending G.50s and two were shot down – F/O Miles and his crew in L8471 were killed, while the crew of L8374 baled out, F/O J. Evans, the Pilot, being injured – and five more aircraft were damaged, L4818 of F/Sgt A. Gordon very badly, his Observer, Sgt G. Furney, suffered a severe head wound, but they struggled back to base (see Appendix 1).

On Christmas Eve five Blenheims from 84 Squadron overcame foul weather to drop sacks of gifts on to the esplanade at Corfu for the children of the island. Three Italian aircraft appeared in the afternoon but they delivered not gifts but high-explosive bombs, one of which penetrated to the basement of the biggest bank, used as an air-raid shelter, where a festive dance was being held, killing 18 people and injuring 25 more. A Boxing Day raid on Valona by 211 Squadron was ordered in retaliation, although the Squadron had been stood down and only five crews could be mustered. The weather was too bad to fly over the mountains so they flew in line astern just above the Gulf of Corinth and north along the coast in and out of low cloud to bomb Valona and, as they were streaking out of the harbour entrance at low level, they met a cruiser and destroyer heading in for Christmas, so they strafed the surprised Italians and escaped before the AA fire started.

The year ended with a flurry of activity despite the bad weather. On the 29th three Blenheims of 30 Squadron bombed Italian troop reinforcements disembarking at Valona; a G.50 set the port engine of F/Lt H. Caird's K7104 on fire and it crashed into the sea, only one crew member surviving; the badly damaged L6677 of P/O A. Crockett staggered back to base and belly-landed (see Appendix 1); and Sgt L. Ovens landed his damaged aircraft safely. In the early morning of the 30th a coastal patrol by five Mk I-Fs of 30 Squadron spotted a Cant Z.506B floatplane on reconnaissance and shot it down into the sea, but not before return fire had hit Sgt F. Gouding, the WOp/Ag in S/Ldr Shannon's leading aircraft, fatally wounding him. The 32 Mira of the RHAF lost two of its remaining handful of Blenheims this day: Capt Hatziioannou's aircraft was shot down by CR.42s near Valona, he and his crew being killed, and the CO of 32 Mira, L/Col Panayhiotis together with his crew were also killed when his aircraft crashed near base, it is believed after suffering damage in combat. New Year's Eve saw nine 211 Squadron Blenheims bombing storage dumps near Valona; the formation was chased by Fiat CR.42s and a single G.50, but only the monoplane had the speed to reach the Blenheims and, some 20 miles south of the target, it attacked the left-hand aircraft, setting the port engine of Sgt S. Bennett's L1540 on fire so that it dived into the sea with the loss of the crew (see Appendix 1).

The Air Staff had recognised the great weight of the burden of responsibility carried by Air Chief Marshal Sir Arthur Longmore, and in November appointed Air Marshal Boyd to be Deputy AOC-in-C in the Middle East, but unfortunately the aircraft taking Boyd to take up his post ran low on fuel and force-landed in Sicily and he was captured on the 20th. Air Vice Marshal Arthur Tedder was appointed in his place and had the sense to travel by the safer Takoradi reinforcement route, which he could also inspect on the way.

The small force of RAF Blenheims in Greece had fought hard and well in particularly difficult conditions, but had suffered serious casualties; the much smaller force of RHAF Blenheims had fought with an even fiercer determination to defend their homeland, suffering proportionally higher casualties, and were reduced to only a couple of serviceable aircraft. What would the New Year bring?

1941: the second round

The severe weather made all operations most difficult in the first weeks of the New Year, heavy rain leaving the airfields waterlogged and mainly unusable. The crews of the RAF aircraft based on these primitive airfields, and living under canvas, endured hardships enough, but the ground-crews suffered even more attempting to work on their charges out in the open in the appalling conditions. There was stalemate in the ground battle. The Greeks had committed most of their forces to the Albanian front in the west, and were advancing well, but in doing so denuded their long frontier in the east with Bulgaria – a country Hitler was attempting to coerce into the Axis fold with a mixture of bribes and threats.

Despite the terrible conditions, 211 Squadron was able to mount a raid by eight aircraft on Elbasan on 2 January and another by nine on the 4th, so far without loss, but on the 6th lost one of another nine sent to bomb Valona. F/O Campbell's aircraft was shot down by G.50s into the sea; the crew, although injured, managed to swim ashore and were captured. Four other Blenheims were damaged, two of them crash-landing on the way home, one crew being killed (see Appendix 2). 211 Squadron was active again on the 20th, sending five aircraft to bomb Valona. On the 22nd the CO, S/Ldr Gordon-Finlayson, led six Mk Is on an armed reconnaissance to bomb and strafe the Berat to Kelcyre supply road; there was a running fight with two G.50s, which damaged four of the Blenheims – F/Lt Godfrey had a Very flare cartridge set on fire in his cockpit, and the crew were ready to bale out but managed to extinguish the fire and return to base, although P/O Cox in L1528 had to crash-land there with an engine on fire (see Appendix 2).

Two Mk I-F fighters of 30 Squadron were scrambled from Eleusis on the 20th to help a Section of 80 Squadron's Gladiators defend Athens from an attack by two small formations of Cant Z.1007 tri-motor bombers; 30 Squadron's F/Sgt Innes-Smith shot one down in flames, and damaged another, after one of the trio of Gladiators was shot down by return fire from the bombers. Reinforcements started to arrive on the 23rd; S/Ldr P. Stevens led in six Mk IVs and six Mk Is of 11 Squadron from Egypt to Eleusis, the ground-party arriving later. The Squadron then moved to Larissa and was ready for operations on the 28th; more Gladiators also arrived. Two USAF officers, Colonel G. Bower and Major A. Craw, were in Greece as military observers and went on several raids as passengers in both Blenheims and Wellingtons, to gain personal experience of the aerial war. 30 Squadron sent out three of its bomber Blenheims from Eleusis to raid Boultsov in Albania on the 25th and tangled with six G.50 fighters; two of the Mk Is were damaged and Sgt Stammers in L8443 had both crewmen injured (see Appendix 2).

February 1941 saw the Blenheims getting off to a bad start. Two of the newly arrived 11 Squadron aircraft were lost on the 2nd due to the atrocious weather. 84 Squadron lost one of three sent to bomb supply depots on the coast road. F/Lt Towgood was attempting a single-engine landing back at Medini in L1392 following battle damage but crashed and was killed (see pictures on page 437), and the Squadron lost another the following day when F/O A. Nicholson was forced to ditch his damaged L1393; he survived but his Gunner was killed and his Observer drowned (see Appendix 2). On the 9th 211 Squadron moved six of its Blenheims to the landing field at Paramythia in a bare but picturesque valley some 3,000 feet high, to join some RHAF PZL fighters there. Three days later S/Ldr Lewis led nine Blenheims of 84 Squadron, together with three of 30 Squadron, to Paramythia on detachment, then four Wellingtons of 37 Squadron joined them at the primitive advanced field, which was much closer to the front line than their normal bases. This enabled each of the serviceable Blenheims to carry out several sorties on every day that the weather allowed operations.

The Paramythia-based Blenheims went into action again on the morning of 13 February, when 12 (drawn from 211 and 84 Squadrons), escorted by 14 Gladiators, bombed targets near Tepelene, but became separated from their escort when they dived on their target through gaps in the cloud and were intercepted by G.50s. The fighters

L6670 of 211 Squadron at Medini (Tatoi) airfield in February 1941.

badly damaged L8451 of F/O Buchanan, which had to crash-land on one wheel back at base (see Appendix 2). The afternoon raid by six Blenheims from 211 and six from 11 Squadron at Larissa fared much worse; the latter six were intercepted by G.50s and jettisoned their bombs over Berat, and T2166 was shot down in flames and only the pilot, Sgt L. Williams, was able to bale out. The same fate and result befell L3581 of P/O J. Hutchinson, while F/O J. Bergren made a single-engine forced-landing and P/O A. Hewison managed to struggle back to base with a badly damaged aircraft (see Appendix 2). Three of the six aircraft from 211 Squadron were damaged by fighters, including that of F/O Buchanan – in another aircraft from the one that he had crash-landed in earlier that day. Similar escorted raids were mounted over the following days, but the Blenheims managed to avoid interception. The fighter element at Paramythia was strengthened on 17 February by six Hurricanes and four Blenheim Mk IV-Fs of 30 Squadron, but the bomber element lost another aircraft when L6662 of 84 Squadron crashed on take-off, although the crew survived. The force was enlarged with a detachment of 11 Squadron Blenheims together with six more Hurricanes, and was named W (for Western) Wing a couple of days later, under W/Cdr 'Paddy' Coote as CO with his HQ at Yannina.

The weather cleared slightly on the morning of the 20th and 11 Blenheims (eight from 84 Squadron and three from 30) were escorted by six Hurricanes for the first time when they bombed targets near Tepelene – they were not intercepted. In the afternoon 17 Blenheims (the same mix of eight and three as on the morning raid, plus six of 211 Squadron) set off to bomb Berat. One 84 Squadron aircraft had an engine failure and belly-landed, but the others bombed successfully, although the 211 Squadron Blenheim (L8542) of P/O Cox was badly damaged, his attacker being shot down by the Hurricanes. Sgt G. Ratlidge of 30 Squadron (whose narrow escape on 1 December was noted earlier) had his starboard engine put out of action by a G.50 but managed to land back at Paramythia. Similar escorted raids followed over the next few days, and although losses were avoided, results were hard to see in the persistent heavy rain. Across on the eastern side of Greece 30 Squadron sent up pairs of Mk I-Fs from Eleusis on combat patrols at hourly intervals to prevent Italian aircraft from approaching Athens or Salonika. On the 22nd S/Ldr Milward and F/O Davidson shot down a large Cant Z.506B floatplane. Later that day another 30 Squadron pair, F/Lt Walker and F/O Richardson, drove off five Z.1007 bombers and shot one down.

THE BRISTOL BLENHEIM

The RAF strength at Paramythia was further increased on the 23rd when ten Blenheims of 11 Squadron flew in from Larissa in frightful weather, but four had to return and a fifth force-landed, killing the pilot, P/O Hewison, and his WOp/Ag and injuring his Observer; one of six extra Hurricanes also crashed on landing. On the 22nd a party of 'top brass', including Air Chief Marshal Sir Arthur Longmore, General Sir Archibald Wavell, the C-in-C Middle East, and General Sir John Dill, the Chief of the General Staff, together with Anthony Eden, the Foreign Secretary, visited Medini to evaluate the proposed increase in the level of assistance to the Greek forces, and Longmore and D'Albiac went to Paramythia on the 26th to see for themselves the difficulties of operating in such conditions. Nine Blenheims, six from 211 Squadron and three from 11, escorted by nine Hurricanes, set out the following day to bomb Valona's well-defended aerodrome. Despite the escort, the Blenheims were intercepted on their bombing run by 13 Fiat CR.42s and five were damaged, including all three 11 Squadron aircraft, two which crash-landed upon return (see Appendix 2). Two CR.42s were shot down by the escort and another was destroyed, and several damaged, by bombs from the Blenheims. The remnants of the 11 Squadron detachment returned to Larissa. An extensive aerial battle the next day saw wild claims by both sides, but four Fiat BR.20s, two G.50s and two CR.42s were shot down for the loss of one Gladiator.

T2177, a 113 Squadron Mk IV, at Medini for reconnaissance of the Greek/Bulgarian border before the German intervention; note the Junkers G-24s in the background.

Operation Mandible was a planned occupation by the British of the Dodecanese islands in the eastern Aegean Sea, including Rhodes with its three airfields, from where Axis aircraft had been attacking Allied shipping heading for Greece. This move started with landings by a small force of Commandos on 25 February, but the operation 'went off at half cock' and the force was withdrawn after only a couple of days. Blenheims from Greece carried out 34 daylight sorties against airfields in the Dodecanese, and Wellingtons based in Egypt bombed them by night. The failure of this Allied Operation Mandible was to have grave consequences before very long.

Greece suffered a natural disaster on the night of 28 February/1 March when an earthquake devastated the town of Larissa, causing heavy casualties; the airfield was also hard-hit, with great rifts opening up and hangars and buildings collapsing. The airmen worked through the night helping to dig out victims – many already dead – from the rubble, and the next morning 30 Squadron Blenheims flew in with Army doctors and medical orderlies, and first aid supplies. But, earthquake or not, the war continued and in three separate raids on 1 March Blenheims of 30 and 211 Squadrons, escorted by Hurricanes, bombed Paroba, Berat and, yet again, Valona harbour. The next day the targets for nine escorted Blenheims from 84 and 211 Squadrons were Berat again and Devoli airfield, where bombs were seen to burst among parked aircraft. Three PR Blenheim Mk IVs of 113 Squadron had arrived at Medini and carried out some clandestine reconnaissance over the Bulgarian and Yugoslavian borders, as German forces had been reported moving across Bulgaria; the Blenheim crews knew that their every move would be reported back to the enemy for they often taxied out with Lufthansa Ju.52s as Germany was not yet at war with Greece. The Italian Cruiser *Riboty* and the heavy destroyer *Andromeda* started shelling the coast road near Hirama on the 4th. A strike by 15 Blenheims of 211 and 84 Squadrons was ordered straight away, and nine from the former and five from the latter squadron (an engine of one failed to start), escorted by 17 Gladiators and ten Hurricanes, bombed the ships without loss but scored only near misses, although there were fighter casualties on both sides.

The reinforced Italian Army commenced another offensive on 9 March to push the Greeks out of Albania. Greece requested direct tactical support for its troops, which D'Albiac somewhat reluctantly provided, mainly with the hard-pressed 211 Squadron, which flew 30 operational sorties in the next few days, with many clashes between opposing fighters. The RAF had passed on six Mk Is (including L6658, L6670, L8384 and L8385) to 32 Mira of the RHAF to help replace its losses, but one was shot down by AA fire the next day. Blenheims of 211 acted as decoys for the AA fire at Valona harbour during an attack on shipping there by five FAA Swordfish on the night of 12 March, but only two torpedoes were dropped and two ships were sunk; unfortunately one was a hospital ship. This raid was repeated a few nights later by three Swordfish, Blenheims once again drawing the AA fire; a hospital ship – this time fully illuminated – provided enough light to help a torpedo-aircraft to hit the destroyer *Andromeda*. On the 14th five of 211's Blenheims were escorted by 15 fighters in a daylight raid on targets near Tepelene; fierce dogfights developed, with several fighters shot down on each side, but no Blenheims were lost. This pattern was followed over the next few days – seven Blenheims attacked Devoli airfield on the 15th, destroying three aircraft on the ground, and later that day eight more successfully raided Valona airfield. That night the Mk I-Fs of 30 Squadron, brought up to Paramythia with eight Wellingtons, acted as intruders over Valona airfield using small fragmentation bombs as the 'Wimpeys' bombed Tirana airfield, but Italian fighters shot down one Wellington and damaged two others in the moonlight.

S/Ldr Gordon-Finlayson flew from Paramythia to Air HQ at Eleusis on the 13th to be told of his award of a DSO and promotion to Wing Commander to form a new E (for Eastern) Wing. This would include the Blenheim Mk IVs of 11 Squadron, the Mk I-Fs of B and C Flights of 30 Squadron, the detachment of 113 Squadron Mk IVs at Medini, about to be brought up to full squadron strength, the Wellingtons of 37 Squadron and the 33 Squadron Hurricanes that were not with W Wing at Paramythia. Command of 211 at Paramythia was passed to S/Ldr R. Nedwell AFC, although he was killed soon after – he borrowed a Gladiator to carry out some aerobatics, lost control and crashed.

The Italians discovered the airfield at Paramythia and bombed and strafed it on 22 March, destroying a 211 Squadron Blenheim and an unserviceable Wellington and Gladiator – in retaliation six Blenheims of 84 Squadron, escorted by 24 fighters, bombed Berat airfield on the 23rd. Five Blenheim Mk I-Fs of 30 Squadron staged to the new airfield at Maleme in Crete; three strafed Calato airfield on Rhodes, damaging several aircraft, while the other two went to Scarpanto but saw no aircraft there. The Mk IVs of 113 Squadron, led by S/Ldr Spencer, carried out their first full-strength raid on the 27th against Calato airfield, causing considerable damage. Also on this day six of 30 Squadron's Mk I-Fs from Paramythia made two low-level strafing passes on Lecce airfield in Italy, taking the defences by surprise and destroying a Savoia S.81 and damaging 25 other aircraft; four Blenheims were damaged by light AA fire and Sgt Ovens force-landed on the way back to base. On the 30th 84 Squadron sent ten aircraft on an unescorted raid on a military base near Tirana; one (L1390) was hit by AA fire and Sgt A. Hutcheson force-landed near Koritza, while fighters badly damaged two more – L1391 of Sgt G. Bailey and T2427 of F/O I. Goudge (see Appendix 2). Five aircraft of 113 Squadron bombed a convoy off Stampalia that night but no results were observed. 84 Squadron lost its senior Flight Commander on 1 April when F/Lt Boehm and his crew were killed in the crash of T2382 in appalling weather. Escorted daylight attacks continued in early April with a raid on Berat. 30 Squadron received replacement Mk I-Fs to re-equip its bomber Flight and become an all-fighter unit; six of its Blenheims were detached on 5 April to Maleme on Crete.

Throughout the winter of 1940/41 it had become increasingly clear from intelligence reports, including some based on Ultra intercepts, and others from the reconnaissance sorties flown by 113 Squadron's Blenheims, that the Germans were building up their forces in the Balkans and were about to come to the aid of their Axis partners. The Allies, already stretched to the limit, were deeply concerned at the prospect of this intervention as they realised that it would change the nature of the fighting irrevocably, and jeopardise their entire position not only in the Balkans but also throughout the Middle East Theatre. Once more the Blenheims would find themselves right in the forefront of the forces called upon to attempt the impossible and turn back the approaching tide.

F/Lt R. Towgood was killed and his Observer traumatised when L1392 of 84 Squadron crashed attempting a single-engine landing at Paramythia on 5 February 1941, after battle damage had put the port engine out of action.

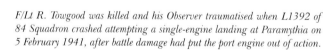

The remains of a 211 Squadron Blenheim at Paramythia after a strafing attack on 22 March – note the full light-bomb carriers and scattered bombs. The steel strips above the engine are guides for the alloy cooling gills, which have melted.

Appendix I

Blenheim losses in the Greek War Zone, 3 November to 31 December 1940

Aircraft are all Mk Is.

06-11-1940   L8462 30 Squadron Mk I: bombed Vlore, Albania, hit by CR.42s; Sgt J. Merifield (WOp/Ag) KIA, buried at Phaleron War Cemetery, Sgt G. Ratlidge (Pilot) and Sgt Walker (Obs) safe, aircraft repaired.

14-11-1940   L1389 84 Squadron: FTR; chased by Fiat CR.42s while bombing troops near Koritza; struck mountainside; crew F/Lt A. Mudie, F/Sgt E. Hibbard-Lord, and LAC W. Chick KIA, commemorated on Alamein Memorial.

14-11-1940   L1378 84 Squadron: FTR; shot down by CR.42s on same sortie; crew Sgt W. Sidaway, Sgt C. Hoare, and Sgt A. Friend KIA, commemorated on Alamein Memorial.

15-11-1940   L1120 30 Squadron: FTR; shot down in flames by CR.42s near Koritza; crew Sgt E. Childs, Cpl D. Stott, and Sgt J. Stewart KIA, buried in Albania.

21-11-1940   L1166 30 Squadron: became lost in bad weather on return from raid on Tepelene, force-landed on beach near Zagora, out of fuel; F/O C. Richardson and crew safe.

24-11-1940   L8511 211 Squadron: FTR; damaged by flak in raid on Durazzo, made single-engine force-landing on beach at Corfu; S/Ldr J. Gordon-Finlayson, P/O G. Davies, and P/O A. Geary safe, made way back to base. For this action S/Ldr Gordon-Finlayson, CO of 211 Squadron, awarded DFC, first decoration of campaign in Greece.

28-11-1940   L1385 84 Squadron: FTR; shot down by CR.42s while bombing Durazzo; crew P/O D. Bird, Sgt R. Scott, and Sgt S. Davis captured, became PoWs, Sgt Scott died in captivity.

01-12-1940   K7103 30 Squadron: iced up, engines cut, spun through cloud, force-landed near Khalkis; Sgt G. Ratlidge and crew safe.

02-12-1940   L4866 211 Squadron: force-landed at Araxos, Greece, on return from raid on Valona, cause unknown; P/O P. Pickersgill, Sgt H. Taylor, and Sgt Duffy safe, aircraft abandoned.

06-12-1940   K7100 30 Squadron Mk I-F: FTR; damaged by ground fire, force-landed on Corfu; crew F/O H. Blackmore and P/O R Crowther safe.

06-12-1940   L1097 30 Squadron Mk I-F: FTR on same sortie, also damaged by ground fire and force-landed near Agrinion; P/O J. Attwell and Sgt Walsh safe, aircraft recovered and repaired.

07-12-1940   L8455 84 Squadron: FTR; shot down by CR.42s while bombing Valona; F/Lt L. Cattell, Sgt H. Taylor, and Sgt F. Carter KIA, commemorated on Alamein Memorial.

07-12-1940   L8457 84 Squadron: FTR; shot down by CR.42s while bombing Valona; Sgt M. Cazalet and Sgt K. Ridgewell KIA, Sgt C. Forster (WOp/Ag) survived and PoW.

07-12-1940   L1381 84 Squadron: FTR; damaged by CR.42s while bombing Valona, force-landed; F/O K. Linton, P/O A Dunn, and Sgt R Crowe safe.

07-12-1940   L4926 211 Squadron: FTR; iced up and crashed into mountainside near Lama; F/O P. Pickersgill, Sgt H. Taylor, and Sgt N. Hallett KIA, buried in Phaleron War Cemetery.

07-12-1940   L1535 211 Squadron: FTR; iced up and crashed into mountainside; crew P/O G. Jerdein, Sgt J. Barber, and Sgt J. Munro KIA, buried in Phaleron War Cemetery.

14-12-1940   L8514 211 Squadron: engine iced up and cut, nosed over on forced-landing at Araxos; F/Lt L. Buchanan DFC, Sgt Stack and Sgt G. Pattison DFM safe, aircraft abandoned in May 1941.

18-12-1940   L8462 30 Squadron: shot down into sea by fighters while bombing Valona, one of crew waved and dinghy dropped; F/O S. Paget, Sgt G. Sigsworth, and Sgt W. Tubberdy KIA, Pilot and Obs commemorated on Alamein Memorial, WOp/Ag buried in Albania.

22-12-1940   L8471 84 Squadron: FTR; shot down by G.50s while bombing Kucera oilfield; F/O P. Miles, Sgt F. Moir, and Sgt B. Brooker KIA, commemorated on Alamein Memorial.

22-12-1940   L8374 84 Squadron: FTR; damaged by fighters while bombing Kucera oilfield; F/O J. Evans (Pilot) and Sgt H. Offord (Obs) baled out slightly injured, F/O Evans landed in stable yard and kicked by mule, which broke his thigh. Sgt A. Sargent (WOp/Ag) did not bale out, KIA, commemorated on Alamein Memorial.

22-12-1940   L4818 84 Squadron: FTR; damaged by fighters while bombing Kucera oilfield; F/Sgt A. Gordon DFM crash-landed at base, he and Sgt F. Levitt (Obs) safe, F/Sgt G. Furney DFM (WOp/Ag) badly injured.

26-12-1940   L1482 211 Squadron Mk I: damaged by fighters in raid on Valona/Himare road, crash-landed at Medini and abandoned; P/O R. Herbert, Sgt J. Dunnet and Sgt Hughes safe.

29-12-1940   K7104 30 Squadron: FTR; shot down into sea by G.50 while bombing Valona; two seen to bale out but F/Lt H. Card, Sgt F. Pease, and Sgt G. Bygrave KIA, commemorated on Alamein Memorial.

29-12-1940   K7177 30 Squadron: damaged by fighters while bombing Valona, crash-landed at base; P/O A. Crocket and crew uninjured, aircraft repaired.

30-12-1940   L8446 30 Squadron Mk I-F: shot down a Cant 506B bomber off Greece; Sgt F. Gouding fatally wounded by return fire, S/Ldr U. Shannon landed safely, aircraft repaired, passed to 113 Squadron.

31-12-1940   L1540 211 Squadron: FTR; shot down in flames into sea by G.50 after bombing near Valona; Sgt S. Bennett, Sgt W. Tunstall, and Sgt L. France KIA, commemorated on Alamein Memorial.

Appendix 2

Blenheim losses in the Greek War Zone, 1 January to 5 April 1941

06-01-1941   L8536 211 Squadron Mk I: FTR; damaged by fighters while bombing Valona, crashed at Kelcyre; F/O L. Delaney, Sgt V. Pollard, and Sgt T. McCord KIA, commemorated on Alamein Memorial.

06-01-1941   L1487 211 Squadron Mk I: FTR; chased by fighters into cloud while bombing Valona, crashed into sea; crew F/O R. Campbell, Sgt J. Beharrell, and Sgt R. Appleyard injured, captured and became PoWs.

10-01-1941   L8501 84 Squadron Mk I: FTR; ran out of fuel on return from raid, crash-landed near Araxos; P/O I. Goudge, Sgt Croker, and Sgt J. Wright safe, aircraft abandoned.

02-02-1941   N3580 11 Squadron Mk IV: hit ridge in forced-landing in bad weather near Salonika; Sgt E. Thornton, Sgt Manley and Sgt Brown safe, aircraft DBR and left in Greece.

02-02-1941   T2235 11 Squadron Mk IV: missing over sea in icing conditions between Abu Sueir and Eleusis; Sgt D. Strachan, Sgt G. Date, Sgt R. Clift and AC1 E. Bradbury posted as missing, commemorated on Alamein Memorial.

05-02-1941   L1392 84 Squadron Mk I: damaged on raid to Valona, crashed on single-engine landing at Medini, starboard propeller entered cockpit; F/Lt R. Towgood (Pilot) killed and buried Phaleron War Cemetery, Sgt R. Somerville (Obs) severely shocked, Sgt Atherton (WOp/Ag) uninjured.

06-02-1941   L1393 84 Squadron Mk I: FTR; damaged in combat, ditched off Corinth; F/O A. Nicholson (Pilot) rescued, P/O R. Day (Obs) drowned, Sgt A. Hollist (WOp/Ag) KIA.

13-02-1941   T2347 11 Squadron Mk IV: FTR; damaged by G.50s during raid on Berat, engine cut, force-landed; crew Sgt J. Berggren, Sgt Powell, and Sgt Murphy safe, aircraft abandoned.

13-02-1941   T2166 11 Squadron Mk IV: FTR; shot down by G.50s on same raid; Sgt L. Williams (Pilot) and Sgt J. Adamson (Obs) baled out, Sgt Williams became PoW, but Sgt Adamson and Sgt O. Traherne (WOp/Ag) KIA and commemorated on Alamein Memorial.

13-02-1941   T2237 11 Squadron Mk IV: FTR; shot down in flames on same raid; crew P/O J. Hutchison, Sgt S. Whiles, and Sgt W. Jackson baled out, but only Sgt Whiles survived.

18-02-1941   L6662 211 Squadron Mk I: caught in slipstream on take-off at Paramythia, swung and u/c collapsed; F/O K. Linton and crew safe, aircraft abandoned there on evacuation.

20-02-1941   L8542 211 Squadron Mk I: hit by G.50s while raiding Berat; P/O J. Cox DFC, Sgt Stack, and Sgt Martin returned to Paramythia safely but aircraft DBR and abandoned there.

21-02-1941   L1379 84 Squadron Mk I: crashed on take-off at Paramythia after engine cut; Sgt N. Thomas, Sgt Oliver, and P/O T. Corner safe, aircraft abandoned on evacuation.

22-03-1941   L8531 211 Squadron Mk I: hit and set on fire by strafing MC.200s at Paramythia, 4x250lb bomb-load exploded.

22-03-1941   L1490 and L8533, 211 Squadron Mk Is: destroyed in same raid.

23-02-1941   T2388 11 Squadron Mk IV: FTR; iced-up, force-landed in river bed in Pindus Mountains in bad weather en route from Larissa to Paramythia; P/O A. Hewison, Sgt J. Dukes, and LAC G. Bevan killed, other ground-crew passengers LAC G. Causer and AC1 J. McQueen injured, Cpl McCrae unhurt.

27-02-1941   N3579 11 Squadron Mk IV: hit by CR.42s while bombing Valona, crash-landed at Paramythia; un-named crew uninjured, aircraft DBR.

27-02-1941   T2399 II Squadron Mk IV: hit by CR.42s while bombing Valona, crash-landed at Paramythia; un-named crew uninjured, aircraft DBR.

08-03-1941   L1392 84 Squadron Mk I: ORB records 'u/c collapsed after landing, no injuries to Sgt A. Gordon or Sgt F. Levitt. Serial number must be incorrect – see entry for L1392 on 5-2-1941.

29-03-1941   R2780 11 Squadron Mk IV: swung on landing at Almyros, u/c collapsed, abandoned on evacuation; P/O P. Montague-Bates and crew safe.

30-03-1941   L1390 84 Squadron Mk I: FTR; hit by flak, crash-landed; crew Sgt J. Hutchinson, Sgt K. Irwin, and Sgt J. Webb evacuated safely before aircraft blew up.

30-03-1941   L1388 84 Squadron Mk I: hit by flak on sortie to Elbasan, crash-landed at Neopolis; crew safe, aircraft abandoned, repaired by Italians, photographed at Medini 02-05-41.

30-03-1941   L1391 84 Squadron Mk I: hit by G.50s on same sortie, badly damaged; Sgt G. Bailey DFM, Sgt A. Neal, and Sgt F. Round managed to RTB safely, aircraft repaired but lost on 18-04-1941 (qv Chapter 24).

01-04-1941   L8384 and L8385 (ex-39 Squadron Mk Is) together with L6658 and L6670 (ex-211 Squadron Mk Is) transferred to Royal Hellenic Air Force and lost.

01-04-1941   T2382 84 Squadron Mk IV: crashed at Kephissia, north of Athens; F/Lt D. Boehm, Sgt K. Lee and LAC H. Jackson killed, buried in Phaleron War Cemetery, aircraft destroyed by fire.

Chapter 24

The German invasion of Yugoslavia, Greece and Crete

Slaughter of the Yugoslavian Blenheims

On 6 April 1941 German forces invaded Yugoslavia with a five-pronged attack by Armies with Panzer Divisions launched from Austria, Hungary and Rumania; they also invaded Greece with a three-pronged attack from Bulgaria and, a few days later, from Macedonia in southern Yugoslavia. Hitler was forced to delay these invasions by over a month while positioning the forces necessary, which in turn delayed his invasion of Russia, with incalculable results to the outcome of the war. He had attempted to bring the Balkan countries into the Tripartite Pact (between Germany, Italy and Japan) to safeguard his main supply of oil from Rumania. The Rumanians, after losing two large provinces to Russia (as provided for in the 1939 Ribbentrop/Molotov pact) agreed in November 1940, as did the Hungarians; the Bulgarians also signed on 1 March 1941 – they were promised the Greek province of Thrace. Hitler now tried to ensure peaceful passage for his forces through Yugoslavia, to facilitate his intended military intervention in Greece. The Yugoslav Government finally succumbed to the pressure and signed on 25 March, but this resulted in a coup led by General Dusan Simovic, Chief of the Yugoslav Armed Forces. (Incidentally, he kept as his personal aircraft one of the two original Blenheims purchased in 1937 as pattern aircraft for the production licence!) The new Government deposed the Regent and his Council, installing young King Peter in his place, and repudiated the treaty with Germany: Hitler decided immediately to invade, but this upset the whole of his carefully planned timetable. Mussolini did not anticipate the consequences of the train of events that would follow his ill-judged decision to invade Greece.

The British Foreign Office had tried, since before the outbreak of war, to maintain the sympathy, or at least the neutrality, of the Balkan and Eastern Mediterranean countries, including Turkey and Greece, by diplomatic means – Bristol Blenheims became a type of currency in this diplomacy, being offered as inducements, although they could ill be spared. At that time they were advertised as 'The Fastest Bomber in the World' and were very attractive to foreign air forces desperate to up-date their equipment. Rumania received 52 Blenheims, 39 before the war and 13 more after it had started; Turkey received 30 initially and 26 more later. However, the diplomacy failed as Rumania stayed in the Axis fold and Turkey remained neutral – those hundred-odd 'wasted' Blenheims would have strengthened the RAF force in the Middle East most significantly. In contrast, Greece and Yugoslavia, which became Allies only after they were invaded, received a mere 40 between them. Greece received 12 early in the war and six more later; Yugoslavia purchased the two pattern Blenheims in 1937 for its production licence, and also received 20 more in February 1940, flown out to Zemun from RAF stocks at Aston Down. However, the Ikarus factory produced 40 new aircraft prior to the German invasion, so the Yugoslav Air Force had by then a total of 62 Blenheims on strength, less one lost in an accident. The JKRV (Jugoslovensko Kraljevsko Ratno Vazduhoplovsto – Royal Yugoslav Air Force), although large, was a mixture of many diverse types: as bombers, apart from the Blenheims, they deployed totals of 69 licence-built Dornier Do.17Ks and 45 Savoia S.79s, and as fighters, 73 Messerschmitt Me.109Es, 48 Hurricanes and 50 Hawker Fury biplanes – a force, even with the few pre-war accidental losses, far stronger than the combined RAF and RHAF units then engaging the Italians over Greece and Albania. The JKRV Blenheims were operated by four Eskadrilas – smaller than RAF squadrons – (Nos 201, 202, 203, 204) in the two Grupas (61 and 62) of the 1 Bomber Regiment at Novi Sad, and by four Eskadrilas (Nos 215, 216, 217, 218) in the two Grupas (68 and 69) of the 8 Bomber Regiment at Zagreb, together with two Eskadrilas (Nos 21 and 22) of the 11 Grupa – the Independent Long Range Reconnaissance Air Group – at Veliki Radicini.

We have seen how, following the example set by the RAF Blenheims in Libya, Blenheims of the Royal Hellenic Air Force went into instant action when Italy invaded Greece, and the Yugoslav Blenheims also reacted immediately. 11 Grupa sent four from Radicini to attack airfields in Rumania but only one found the targets in poor weather. The other three bombed a railway station: two were shot down by Luftwaffe Me.109s, and the third was damaged and crashed after a 'friendly fire' incident with a JKRV Me.109 – all nine crewmen aboard the three Blenheims were killed. Instant aircraft recognition in the heat of battle was difficult enough in those pre-radar times, but with Dornier Do.217s and Savoia SM.79 bombers being operated by both opposing air forces it became a nightmare, and dogfights between whirling fighters must have been even more confusing with Messerschmitt Me.109s also being used by both combatants! 62 Grupa at Bjeljina sent seven Blenheims to attack an armoured column, but they too could not find the target, bombing railways instead, without loss. 68 and 69 Grupas each sent single aircraft to bomb the railway station at Graz in Austria; one was chased by 109s, but both returned safely.

The Blenheim Mk I of Lt Kiuk (right), 204 Eskadrila, 1 PUK, was shot down on 11 April, and the crew were killed.

The next day, 7 April, saw heavy action by the Yugoslav Blenheims: 11 from 201 and 202 Eskadrilas of 61 Grupa attacked a Panzer column at low level in foul weather, scoring hits but meeting heavy cannon and machine-gun AA fire, which damaged most aircraft – one (3544) had to belly-land. Two sections of three from 203 and 204 Eskadrilas of 62 Grupa attacked the same target and met the same fierce fire; one was shot down, killing Captain Ivancevic, CO of 204, and his crew, while three more were damaged and crash-landed, one with a wounded pilot, and another near Pec in Kosovo with the fate of the crew unknown. The Blenheims of 68 and 69 Grupas had a disastrous day: 11 from Esks 215 and 216 of 68 Grupa were sent to bomb railway stations at Graz in Austria, whilst Esks 217 and 218 of 69 Grupa were tasked with attacking airfields and stations in Hungary. Details of these raids seemed to have been leaked to the Germans, for the Luftwaffe was waiting – seven Blenheims were shot down near their targets, with all the crews being killed including Major Donovic, CO of 68 Grupa, Major Tesic, CO of 69 Grupa, Captain Jovicic, CO of 215 Eskadrila, and Captain Vojinov, CO of 216 Eskadrila, and another crash-landed near Wiener Neustadt, Austria, with the capture of the crew.

The Blenheims of 11 Grupa missed this major disaster as they were re-locating to Velici Major airfield near Sabac, but on the next day (8 April) three of them, together with a Hind, made a low-level attack on a Panzer column near Starcin, close to the border with Bulgaria; one was shot down with the loss of the crew, while the other two were damaged and landed away from base. The Hind crashed into a mountain in the bad weather, killing the crew. 11 Grupa received four repaired Blenheims from the Ikarus factory that day, and it appears that a fifth (3528), flown by Vladimir Volnar, defected to Hungary during this transfer. 62 Grupa sent sections of three, flying very low along a gorge in sleet and snow, to attack another armoured column; two were shot down, one of them flown by Colonel Gradisnik, CO of 1 Bomber Regiment (61 and 62 Grupas), and the other crash-landing on Cer Mountain trying to keep below the cloud-base. The first three days of the German invasion had seen the decimation of nearly all of the Blenheims, together with most of the rest of the Yugoslav Air Force.

Heavy snowfalls on the 9th curtailed all aerial activity, but the Blenheims of 61 Grupa had to be evacuated to Bjeljina on the 10th due to approaching German troops; the aircraft staggered off, heavily laden with air- and ground-crews. One of 11 Grupa crashed attempting take-off while evacuating Davidovci in similar circumstances, killing those on board, and three damaged Blenheims were deliberately burned on the ground, but six made it to Bjeljina the next day. During the brief period on the 10th when flying was possible, one of 61 Grupa bombed a bridge, but Me.110s strafed Bjeljina, destroying two Blenheims. The following day the remaining four, together with the six from 11 Grupa, were destroyed on

The Yugoslav Blenheim 3528 of Captain Vladimir Molnar who defected to the Hungarians and their German allies, supplying the invaders with more intelligence. This Blenheim was destroyed by Allied bombing in 1944.

the ground there by Me.110s – living up to their Zerstorer name. Only one (3550) was able to escape and crash-landed near Olympus Mountain in Greece. One of 62 Grupa got away from the strafing fighters only to be attacked by Italian fighters while landing at Podgorica, but the crew were saved; another of 69 Grupa, flown by Captain Petrovic, CO of 217 Eskadrila, escaped to Croatia, and was used later by the Croatian Air Force. That day an 84 Squadron RAF Blenheim (T2164) attempted to fly a Greek General from Medini to Sarajevo to see if their defences could be co-ordinated, but it ran into a severe storm over the Adriatic and ditched near Bar Harbour, Montenegro; the crew were injured but evacuated by a 230 Squadron Sunderland on the 16th with some British diplomatic staff.

Only 68 and 69 Grupas of the 8th Bomber Regiment still had a few Blenheims left, and these were hoping to evacuate to Sarajevo, but were unable to do so because of the bad weather, so they were set on fire on the 13th to prevent their capture. The thick black smoke rising from their funeral pyre into the grey skies made a fitting and symbolic

THE BRISTOL BLENHEIM

marker for the massacre of the entire Yugoslav Blenheim force. What factors had led to this wholesale destruction of the Yugoslav Air Force within the first week?

The Yugoslavs had observed the build-up of German forces along their lengthy borders and foreseen the invasion, but were caught in the throes of re-organising their defences, and had undergone a change of Government. The JKRV had prepared 50 satellite airfields to which to disperse its aircraft in the correct anticipation of mass attacks on its main bases by the Luftwaffe. Unfortunately, on 3 April a Captain Vladimir Kren had defected to Graz-Thalerhof airfield, Austria, in a Potez 25 and revealed their whereabouts to the Germans; he also betrayed many ciphers and codes. The JKRV had no radar and relied on sound-detection to report incoming raids, very few of their aircraft had radios, their Command and control systems soon collapsed, and confusion reigned – squadrons stood by awaiting orders that never came. As in France, the Luftwaffe quickly established control of the air – *Fliegerkorps IV* and *VIII*, with support from *Fliegerkorps X* in Sicily, could deploy more than 1,000 aircraft, and were able to destroy many Yugoslav aircraft on the ground, and greatly restrict reconnaissance flights. For example, on 6 April the JKRV fighters flew 377 sorties, and the bombers 93, but reconnaissance aircraft only four. As before, the speed of the advancing Panzer columns threw the defenders into disarray, and the situation in Yugoslavia was further compounded as the large Croatian element of its Army actively sympathised with the Germans, so overall the Yugoslav forces were no match for the Wehrmacht and were overwhelmed in a few days. The German columns, moving rapidly over difficult terrain, entered Skopje on the second day of the invasion, Monastir – which controlled the important pass from southern Yugoslavia into Greece – on the third, Zagreb on the fourth, and Belgrade on the sixth day – the capital city surrendered on the seventh. The former Prime Minister was re-instated and signed an armistice on the 11th day, completing the extraordinarily rapid conquest of such a large country.

A Yugoslav Mk I at an unknown airfield; note the DF loop behind the cockpit.

Ex-Yugoslav Blenheim with the Croatian Air Force at Zagreb.

Production of Blenheims in Yugoslavia had been delayed by a shortage of Mercury engines from Bristol at Filton, Ikarus AD receiving only 52 engines from the UK parent company. The Yugoslavs negotiated a supply from the Polish PZL company, which used licence-built Mercury engines in its fighters, but the German invasion of Poland blocked this source. They tried Alfa Romeo 126 engines (themselves Italian licence-built Bristol Pegasus engines as fitted to SM.79s!) in one, 3529, but it proved slightly slower at 272mph compared with 275mph for the standard Ikarus-built machines, and 295mph for the imported aircraft. However, by the middle of 1940 the Germans allowed PZL to supply sufficient engines for the Yugoslavs to complete another 14 Blenheims, making a total of 40 supplied to the JKRV. The workers at the Ikarus AD factory near Zemun destroyed 24 partially completed Blenheims and sabotaged the factory to prevent the Germans from using it, but the invaders seized all the Blenheim components – enough for 10 aircraft –

which were sold later to Finland to be used on its production lines at Tampere. After the occupation, the Ikarus factory became part of the Wiener-Neustadt Flugzeugwerke GmbH (and is now used for storage by the present Yugoslav Museum of Aviation and Space). Damaged Blenheims from all over Yugoslavia were gathered there and eight refurbished aircraft were supplied to the Croatian Air Force, later to be used against partisans in Bosnia, but most were destroyed on the ground by the patriots using explosives supplied by the British, with two fleeing to neutral Turkey, where the crews sought asylum. Another of these Croatian Blenheims (1507) survived the war and was taken on charge by the post-war JRV, serving until late 1947, and 3528, the aircraft that defected to Hungary, was used by its Air Force until destroyed by Allied bombing late in the war.

German forces invade Greece

The German Armies were also able to advance fairly rapidly into Greece, for the bulk of the Greek forces were heavily engaged with the Italians in southern Albania, to the north-west of Greece, leaving their border with Bulgaria in Salonika to the north-east only lightly – but very defiantly – defended. As has been noted, British Commonwealth forces honoured the promises of the Foreign Office and came to the aid of the Greek Government. Troops and aircraft were withdrawn from the campaign in the Western Desert, together with others that were diverted direct to Greece, to create an Expeditionary Force over 60,000 strong, but it did not have time to establish proper defensive positions. The Royal Navy also became involved, transporting and supplying this force, and losing many ships to aerial attack. Unfortunately, this military aid was too little and too late. Once again the Blenheims found themselves caught up in a one-sided and desperate struggle; once again the exemplary courage of their crews was not enough to overcome the odds stacked against them; once again they paid the price in heavy casualties.

At dusk on 6 April Blenheims of 84 and 113 Squadrons, together with six Wellingtons of 37 Squadron, were sent to bomb railway targets in Bulgaria with little effect. At least they had not been dispatched in daylight, although two of 113's aircraft crash-landed on return to Niamata (see Appendix 1). The Luftwaffe scored a lucky but resounding success that night when 20 Ju.88s bombed the main Greek supply port at Piraeus; the crowded harbour held three ships laden with explosives and ammunition, and one (the *Clan Fraser*) was set on fire and exploded at 0315, triggering a series of huge explosions that destroyed 11 merchant ships, 62 lighters and tugs and a row of crated Hurricanes on the quayside, caused many casualties, and closed this important port for ten vital days.

The next day saw two dozen Blenheims, drawn from 11, 113 and 84 Squadrons and escorted by Hurricanes, score many hits while bombing German columns advancing towards Greece in southern Yugoslavia. Three of 11 Squadron returned to the same target in the afternoon, escorted by two Hurricanes, one of which, flown by S/Ldr Pattle, shot down a Dornier Do.217 that had been spotted below on the way back. A raid on 8 April by eight Blenheims of 11 Squadron on targets in the Strumica region proved a failure in the bad weather; one aircraft crashed on take-off and others were forced to abandon the mission. However, eight more from 211 Squadron, with an escort of nine Hurricanes, bombed and strafed Petrich airfield, damaging several Luftwaffe aircraft. A Blenheim led in six Hurricanes from the Canal Zone in Egypt via Crete as badly needed reinforcements. The Mk I-Fs of 30 Squadron helped to guard the Athens area and chased off a Ju.88 in the early hours of the 10th. They engaged another on the night of the 10th, but S/Ldr Milward's aircraft was hit by return fire and burst into flames; he baled out but his WOp/Ag, Sgt John Crooks, was killed (see Appendix 1). The Commonwealth and Greek forces in Salonika in eastern Greece were being outflanked by the German advance in Macedonia to the west, where Greek resistance had collapsed, so were forced into a rapid retreat to the Mount Olympus area.

Although the weather prevented any sorties on the morning of the 10th, nine Blenheims of 84 Squadron attacked a column on the Bitolji to Prilep road in the afternoon, and five Mk I-Fs of 30 Squadron strafed the same road slightly later, then ten bombers from 11 Squadron with an escort of Hurricanes attacked the same column causing considerable damage. They made use of cloud cover to escape the Messerschmitt 109s and 110s that attempted to intercept them, their escort claiming two of them. The 11th saw more desperate but doomed efforts to stem the advance. Six Blenheims of 84 Squadron bombed the same column, scoring several hits despite a hail of ground fire that shot down the aircraft of F/Sgt Nuthall and damaged all of the other five (see Appendix 1). The terrible weather kept the aircraft of 11, 113 and 30 Squadron earthbound all day, although they did manage some strikes the next day on a troop convoy on the Bitolji-Veles road.

The 13th of April 1941, Easter Sunday in Greece, was a black day for the Blenheims of 211 Squadron. Although not quite on the same scale as the tragedies suffered by the 82 Squadron Blenheims at Gembloux in Belgium and Aalborg in Denmark the previous year, this further loss of an entire formation of Blenheims ranks alongside them in the annals of the heroic, almost sacrificial, courage demonstrated by RAF crews during daylight bombing operations. The day had started quite well with two successful attacks by 211 Squadron Blenheims, the first to Quhes valley, the second to Resen, escorted by Hurricanes. Neither raid was intercepted and all the Blenheims returned to Paramythia. A third raid on troop concentrations in the Florina area was ordered off at 1500 hours although only seven aircraft were still serviceable; they were led by 211's CO, S/Ldr Antony Irvine, but unfortunately no Hurricanes were available this time to provide an escort. At the last minute a photo-reconnaissance to Valona and Durazzo harbours by one aircraft was added to the mission and P/O Hooper was chosen for this task as his machine had not yet been loaded with bombs. W/Cdr Patrick 'Paddy' Coote, CO of the Western Wing, decided to go on the raid, with his deputy, S/Ldr Leslie Cryer DFC, in another Blenheim, to see for themselves how far the German columns had advanced. The formation tangled with three 109s of JG 27 near Lake Prespa and although the six Blenheims turned and dived back down the valley they were hacked from the sky one by one. Only two pilots, F/Lt Godfrey and F/Sgt James, managed to bale out and make their way back over some 150 miles to Larissa by mule, on foot, and in a Greek lorry – though their dramatic journey was far from over. Tragically, all the other airmen, including the Wing Commander and the two Squadron Leaders, were killed (see Appendix 1).

At the very time that the 211 Squadron force was being massacred, a formation of nine Blenheim IVs from 113 Squadron was heading for the same target. They had taken off at 1515, with an escort of six Hurricanes, and were alarmed to see a huge formation of Luftwaffe aircraft – Ju.88s and Ju.87s, Me.110s and Me.109s – heading down the other side of the valley in the opposite direction. The Blenheim crews breathed a collective sigh of relief when both formations, although in clear sight of each other, continued on their way without engaging the other. It appears that the bomber crews of 113 were spared the fate of their comrades from 211 as the fighter pilots of both the opposing air forces had been ordered to stay close to their charges. Amazingly enough, this eerie encounter was repeated when they passed each other on the return journey – the relieved Blenheim crews believed that this time it was due to the fighter aircraft of both sides being too low in fuel to initiate a dogfight.

At dawn on 14 April six Blenheims of 84 Squadron, guarded by four Hurricanes, set off to attack a troop convoy to the north of Ptolemais; they met fierce flak, two109s got through to them, and four were damaged,

Luftwaffe aircrew inspect T2177, a 113 Squadron Mk IV damaged by 'friendly' AA fire and abandoned at Larissa.

another crash-landing in Yugoslavia. The same target was attacked a few hours later by eight Blenheim Mk IVs of 113 Squadron, looked after by ten Hurricanes; on their return trip they saw some *Stukas* dive-bombing Allied troops and promptly engaged; the Blenheim gunners joined in the mêlée and claimed a Ju.87, which was seen to go down on fire. In a typical example of the confusion that accompanies a general retreat, a 113 Squadron aircraft (T2177) was sent to drop some un-fused bombs near some New Zealand engineers left behind to destroy a bridge near Gravena, to provide explosives for the Sappers who did not have any! Having been bombed by a Ju.88, the NZ soldiers were understandably nervous and fired repeatedly at the Blenheim, which was circling with the undercarriage down and firing off recognition signals to no avail. It returned to Larissa to obtain further orders, only to have the undercarriage collapse on landing and then to find that the Eastern Wing HQ had evacuated. The aircraft was therefore abandoned and the crew stranded. Other Blenheims from 11 and 113 Squadrons continued their attacks on enemy troops and vehicles in the Mount Olympus area. Western Wing had been disbanded and the airfields at Paramythia and Yannina abandoned. Some 50 fleeing Yugoslav aircraft landed at the two airfields and most were soon destroyed on the ground by strafing Italian and German fighters, together with the damaged Blenheims, Gladiators and Hurricanes left behind by the RAF. The shattered 211 Squadron was evacuating its ground-crews, crammed in nine at a time, with its remaining five Blenheims. Young King Peter of Yugoslavia had flown into Paramythia, reputedly with the Yugoslav Crown Jewels, in a SM.79 escorted by six RAF Gladiators and was given a Guard of Honour by 211 Squadron airmen (mainly in borrowed uniforms), then sent on his way to Medini in the SM.79 – this time escorted by a Blenheim.

The substantial Greek Armies fighting in Albania and north-west Greece were now cut off and forced to surrender. Elsewhere the hastily improvised front in the centre and to the east was crumbling fast despite fierce rearguard actions by pockets of Australian, New Zealand and Greek troops. The few remaining Blenheims did what they could to help the ground troops delay the advance, but their efforts were in vain. Larissa airfield was strafed soon after dawn on 15 April, and two Lysanders of 208 Squadron, which had escaped the destruction, took off soon after to evacuate the two surviving Blenheim pilots from the 211 Squadron disaster of two days earlier. The 'Lizzies' were soon bounced by Me.109s and despite twisting and turning at very low level were both shot down – Sgt James, riding in the back of L4690, was killed, and F/O Godfrey, who used the Vickers gun in the rear of L4719, had fingers shot off one hand and his legs badly injured in the crash, but escaped to become the sole survivor of the ill-fated 211 Squadron formation shot down on Easter Sunday. 113 Squadron's Blenheims were getting ready to mount a raid when they were caught on the ground by strafing 109s at their new base at Niamata – six were destroyed. Five more attacks that day by 109s destroyed all the remaining aircraft of the Squadron (see Appendix 1), including their communications Miles Magister. The Squadron had to evacuate the area by the fire-tender and commandeered road transport as all of its other vehicles had been rendered unusable.

To the south four Blenheim Mk I-Fs of 30 Squadron and six Hurricanes of 80 Squadron intercepted two raids by Ju.88s on Athens. The Hurricanes claimed to have shot down six raiders and the Blenheims one – P/O T. Allison and his WOp/Ag Sgt Connors brought down Ufz Karl Stutz and his crew, who were killed in L1+SK of I/LG 1. The withdrawal continued. The 14 Mk I Fighters of 30 Squadron joined the remaining five Hurricanes of 33 Squadron and the 11 of 80 Squadron at Eleusis, together with the last five Blenheim bombers of 211 Squadron, while the surviving Blenheims – eight and nine respectively of 11 and 84 Squadrons – were gathered at Medini by 16 April. 113 Squadron had no aircraft left so was out of action. Next day 30 Squadron was ordered to send half of its Blenheim Fighters to Maleme in Crete, and the remaining five Blenheim Bombers of 211 Squadron joined their companions of 84 and 11 Squadrons at Medini, where all were placed under the control of 11 Squadron. On the 18th the remaining 14 serviceable Blenheims – six each from 11 and 84 Squadrons and two from 211 – mounted bombing and strafing attacks on advancing German columns, during one of which S/Ldr H. Jones, the CO of 84 Squadron

Many Blenheims in Greece were destroyed on the ground, such as these 21 Squadron aircraft, two of four wrecked at Medini on 20 April 1941 by strafing Messerschmitts of III/JG 27 and II/ZG 26.

in L1391, was damaged by a pair of Me.110s and forced to ditch in the sea. He and his crew, F/Sgt J. Webb and Sgt H. Keen, were seen by villagers to climb into their dinghy and start paddling to the shore, and a local motor-boat set out to meet them, but the Messerschmitts cruelly strafed the dinghy and killed the crew, whose bodies were recovered by the locals and buried in Karamedi village. They were not the only Blenheim crew killed that day, for P/O P. Montague-Bates and crew were shot down by a 109 (see Appendix 1) after successfully bombing a troop column that had been delayed by a bridge brought down earlier by Blenheims. On the night of the 19th 15 of the remaining Blenheims carried out individual sorties in the Katerini area, returning before dawn on the 20th.

The new day saw sustained attacks by the Luftwaffe on the Allied airfields: at Medini four Blenheims were destroyed, two each from 11 and 211 Squadrons, with another from 84 Squadron badly damaged, and five others from all three units less seriously damaged; an ancient Vickers Valentia transport biplane, a Greek Ju.52 and a Yugoslav SM.79 were also set on fire, while at Eleusis five of 30 Squadron's Blenheim Fighters were destroyed, and the few remaining were evacuated to Maleme in Crete to join the flight already there. The surviving 15 RAF Hurricanes from 33 and 80 Squadron put up a desperate defence of Athens against large formations of German aircraft, losing six aircraft – two pilots were killed, one died of burns, and three were wounded. The saddest loss was that of S/Ldr 'Pat' Pattle DFC and bar, the RAF's most successful fighter pilot. The handful of Blenheims that could still fly were sent off at intervals that night to bomb Katerini and Kotzani airfields, so Medini was strafed again early the next morning, destroying some previously damaged Blenheims and damaging others. 11 Squadron was down to four serviceable aircraft, and two of those were previously damaged Mk Is just returned by the

Repair and Salvage Unit. The Blenheim force in Greece had been decimated.

Clearly the time for evacuation from Greece had arrived, and the remaining Blenheims started a shuttle service ferrying ground- and air-crews – nine at a time – from Medini to Heraklion in Crete. Sgt Vernon Hudson, an Australian Blenheim pilot with 11 Squadron, was awarded a very well-earned DFM for his exploits during an eventful day on this evacuation duty. He was returning alone from Heraklion to Medini to pick up another load of evacuees when L1481 was attacked by five CR.42s from Rhodes, damaged and forced to ditch. This he managed alongside one of two small vessels heading for nearby Nauplia; he was pulled from the water, but almost immediately both ships (which were carrying munitions) were dive-bombed by *Stukas* as they entered the port and set on fire. One ship exploded in the port, and the other, on which Hudson was travelling, was abandoned and he and the crew had to swim for shore only to be machine-gunned in the water by the Ju.87s – he made it safely but some of the ship's crew did not. He then hitched a ride back in another Blenheim; however, soon after take-off for Crete this one too was attacked and badly damaged, this time by a Me.110 that was chased off by two Hurricanes. Fortunately the Blenheim was able – but only just – to struggle on to Heraklion. Quite a day!

The remaining RAF single-engined fighters withdrew to the Greek training airfield at Argos in the Peloponnese, only to suffer further depredations from constant and devastating strafing attacks there. The Luftwaffe had achieved total air supremacy and was able to bomb and sink many of the ships that were busy evacuating personnel, taking them to Crete initially then on to Egypt. Seven Blenheim Mk I-Fs of 30 Squadron were sent back to Eleusis to rescue some stranded airmen of 33 and 80 Squadrons. F/O Richardson found a Blenheim with a broken tail-wheel that had been abandoned there, so he organised some men to lift the tail on to a trolley and push the aircraft to the end of the runway. He then started up the engines and managed to take off successfully – so eight Blenheims were able to return to Crete! The last seven serviceable Hurricanes, four from 80 Squadron and three from 33 Squadron, left the Greek mainland for Maleme to join the Blenheim Mk I-Fs of 30 Squadron there. The 20 remaining bomber Blenheims, all that were left from 11, 84 and 211 Squadrons, were evacuated to Heliopolis, staging through Fuka and ferrying many airmen with them – reputedly up to an incredible 17 in one aircraft! A handful of Sunderlands, aided by two BOAC Empire Class flying boats, frequently also seriously overloaded, helped to evacuate key personnel, including airmen from the aircraft-less 113 Squadron and the Greek Royal Family, to Egypt. Flying in the opposite direction to bolster the meagre fighter defences of Crete were nine Blenheim Mk IV-Fs of 203 Squadron from Aden, each carrying ground-crew and a supply of spares including tail-wheels, which were in great demand due to the poor surface at Heraklion. Another example of the confusion that reigns during a major evacuation was an incident where Blenheims intercepted Blenheims! Six Mk I-Fs of 30 Squadron at Maleme were sent at dawn on 26 April to guard a convoy from Suda Bay, which included the AA cruiser HMS *Calcutta*, while three Mk IV-Fs from the recently arrived 203 Squadron at Heraklion were dispatched on the same mission – but neither formation had been informed about the other. Each force saw other aircraft circling the convoy and they started chasing each other until F/O Smith of 30 Squadron spotted some Ju.88s and led his force to attack them, damaging one, while the AA guns on the ships opened fire on everyone in sight quite indiscriminately!

The Germans captured Athens on 27 April and Greek resistance collapsed. The British and Commonwealth forces were ordered to complete their evacuation of mainland Greece and did so by the end of the month. Those airmen from the RAF Blenheim and fighter squadrons, who were not among the 1,750 service personnel lucky enough to be evacuated by air, made their way by road, mingling with streams of retreating troops and refugees, to ports and beaches in southern Greece where they were picked up, mainly at night, by a variety of vessels. Most of them – some 45,000 British Commonwealth servicemen, out of the 62,500 sent there, were carried to safety, although about 500 of them were lost when ships were sunk, and around 9,000 had to be left behind and were captured. More than 3,000 British and Commonwealth troops had been killed, or were presumed killed, in the short campaign in Greece. It is interesting to note the Order of Priority issued for evacuation, which reflected the shortages of trained personnel: at the top of the list were Blenheim Pilots, then Wellington Pilots and Hurricane Pilots, Wireless Operators were given priority over Air Gunners, then Observers – so qualified Blenheim WOp/Ags had a double claim to a place! Engineer Officers preceded Cypher and Signals Officers, and Airframe and Engine Fitters came ahead of the other ground tradesmen. The RAF had lost 210 aircraft in Greece, 82 of them damaged and abandoned, aircraft that were desperately needed elsewhere in the Middle East Command. The Axis powers had expelled all Allied forces from the entire mainland of the European continent, and now occupied a vast area ranging all the way from the tip of Norway in the north to the Spanish border in the south-west, and from the Polish/Russian border in the east to the southern tip of Greece in the south-east.

The capture of Crete

Generalleutnant Kurt Student persuaded Hitler that his *XI Fliegerkorps*, comprising the elite Luftwaffe paratroops and glider-borne assault units, special air-landing divisions, and a large air transport fleet (including 520 Junkers Ju.52/3ms), could conquer Crete from the air to complete the German conquest of all Greek territory. Both men were aware that the powerful Royal Navy fleet in the eastern Mediterranean could make a sea-borne invasion extremely risky and costly, possibly prohibitively so. The Wehrmacht Chief of Staff, *Feldmarschal* Keitel, preferred to seize Malta by the same means, and for the same reasons, as he considered it a target of more strategic importance. Hitler, flushed with such a string of successes, chose Crete and gave Student the green light – although he probably regretted this decision later as the heavy casualties suffered by the airborne forces and their transport fleet precluded their use later in a similar operation against Malta.

As soon as they could use captured airfields in southern Greece, the 700-plus aircraft of *Generalmajor* von Richthofen's *VIII Fliegerkorps* were able to turn their full fury upon Allied shipping, and the three airfields in Crete. Little protection from this onslaught could be provided despite the most valiant efforts from the few remaining fighters – a handful of RAF Hurricanes and Gladiators, a few FAA Fulmars and Sea Gladiators, and the last seven Blenheim Mk I-Fs of 30 Squadron and the eight Mk IV-Fs of 203. They were completely overwhelmed, and the gravity of the plight of this small force was exacerbated when they suffered further losses from unfortunate 'friendly fire' incidents. F/Sgt Innes-Smith of 30 Squadron had K7177 damaged beyond repair by AA fire from HMS *Defender* on 27 April, while P/O Gordon-Hall of 203 had to ditch his Mk IV-F L9044 on 28 April when it lost an engine due to AA fire from RN destroyers, although his flight of three (sent to escort a small convoy evacuating troops) had lowered their undercarriages and were flashing the correct signal of the day. On the 30th four Mk IV-Fs of 203, ordered back to Egypt and each with three ground-crew aboard, were bounced by FAA Fulmars near a large Royal Navy force and L9215 of P/O Wilson was damaged in the first pass. Fortunately, firing Very cartridges and flashing Aldis lamps from the Blenheims caused the fighters to abandon their second pass. Five more Blenheims were sent back to Egypt from Crete, needing major overhaul to keep them airworthy. The few remaining aircraft from 211 and 11 Squadrons, and the personnel of 113 who had escaped, went on to the new base at Ramleh in Palestine (then still a British Protectorate), where the squadrons were rebuilt. The remnants of 84 Squadron were sent to Heliopolis near Cairo, and later to Habbaniyah in Iraq, as will be described; 30 Squadron took its surviving Mk I Fighters to Amriya and re-equipped with Hurricanes.

The Germans neutralised the airfields on Crete – all three were on the northern coast so readily accessible – and the last three serviceable Blenheims at Maleme left for Mersa Matruh in Egypt together with a Sea Gladiator on 15 May; unfortunately the engine of the Gladiator failed and it ditched in the sea with the loss of the pilot. The last serviceable Hurricane on Crete flew out on the 19th, after which the garrison of some 42,000 on the island had only its anti-aircraft guns to defend itself. In a crucial move starting on 20 May, the Germans seized Maleme airfield with paratroops and airborne forces carried by gliders

An 11 Squadron Mk IV, N3560, escaped from Greece on 21 April 1941 but crashed on landing at Heraklion, Crete, and was left there.

and Ju.52/3Ms, and other airborne troops were soon bringing the strip at Retimo and the main airfield at Heraklion under direct fire. The Luftwaffe's complete mastery of the air enabled sufficient reinforcements to arrive by that means, so it was able to conquer the whole island in a few days despite taking heavy casualties from the fierce resistance from the Commonwealth and Greek forces, aided by several hundred airmen who found themselves fighting alongside them as infantry. The Royal Navy drove off one sea-borne convoy on 22 May, sinking half the ships that were carrying troop reinforcements with heavy equipment. This convoy had been spotted by F/Lt J. Dennis in his Blenheim, making 45 Squadron's first long-range sortie to Crete from Fuka in the Egyptian desert. This naval action was a solitary success, for overall the Royal Navy came off badly, losing – all to attacks from the air – many ships sunk or damaged so badly that they had to be withdrawn from use.

Just a few of the 75 Fighter Command squadrons based in the UK and engaged at that time in the ineffective and wasteful 'Circus' and 'Roadstead' operations (as described in Chapter 17) would have made a decisive impact on the situation in the Middle East. They could have prevented the Luftwaffe from gaining total air supremacy, thus greatly improving the protection of Allied naval and ground forces, reducing the heavy losses incurred both at sea and on land, and would have created mayhem amongst the fleets of highly vulnerable German transport aircraft ferrying airborne troops, supplies and reinforcements to Crete. But the vast bulk of RAF fighters were kept in the UK and the few available in Crete were decimated so that the pitiful handful of survivors had to withdraw to Egypt. The lack of a long-range fighter in the RAF inventory was once again keenly felt. A few Blenheim Mk IV-Fs from bases in Egypt attempted to intervene over Crete and the surrounding seas, but they were far too few and in any event were no match for the Messerschmitts. Attempts were made to ferry more Hurricanes to Heraklion, and six were being led by a Blenheim when they met such heavy AA fire from Royal Navy warships that

YH-L, a 21 Squadron Mk IV, was also damaged and abandoned on Crete.

the formation split up and five of the fighters returned to Egypt – when the other two did not return they were presumed to have been shot down. But the Blenheim had made it with the sole Hurricane, although this was destroyed on the ground half an hour later. The evacuation from Crete was ordered on 27 May, just one week after the Germans launched their invasion, another humiliation for the Allied cause. As the Germans had captured most of the northern coast, including the Suda Bay area, the troops and airmen had to make their way – mainly by foot – over the rugged central mountains to the southern coast.

The Blenheims of 14, 45 and 55 Squadrons had been heavily engaged in the Western Desert campaigns, as will be described, but in view of the drastic situation in Crete they, together with the Marylands of the newly formed 24 Squadron of the SAAF, were ordered by Air Commodore Ray Collishaw to provide what assistance they could to the beleaguered island. We can look at 45 Squadron, which had converted one Flight to Mk IV-Fs, to illustrate the extensive and exhausting efforts made by these now virtually forgotten Blenheim squadrons. At 0300 hours on the 23rd five Blenheims from that Squadron set off from Fuka to bomb the airfield at Maleme, by then being used heavily by the Germans, but the Blenheims ran into a storm and only three could find the target; Lt E. Jones (one of two SAAF pilots with 45) saw strikes on some of the many Ju.52/3Ms there. Four more Blenheims set out for the same target later that day, but V5624 of P/O Vincent was shot down and the crew killed (see Appendix 2). Two of the Mk IV-Fs, accompanied by four Hurricanes (fitted with fixed long-range external fuel tanks) were briefed to strafe Maleme on the 25th, but Sgt McClelland in Z5766 crash-landed near Sidi Barrani while positioning for this, and three of the Hurricanes returned early, so only one Blenheim and one Hurricane carried out the task – Sgts Champion, Jones and Phillips, and the Hurricane pilot P/O Hamilton, were congratulated by the AOC on their perseverance. Six more Mk IVs of 45 Squadron, and three from 55 Squadron from Fuka, dropped fragmentation bombs on Maleme airfield that day, but three of the four from 45 Squadron sent on a further raid later the same day had to return early with engine troubles – revealing the strain of mounting so many operations by so few aircraft – and only Lt Jones completed the sortie. Three more from 55 Squadron attacked successfully, but 14 Squadron suffered a heavy blow when all three of its Blenheims were shot down by 109s of II/JG 77 and the crews of all three aircraft were killed (see Appendix 2), but the Air Gunner of one of them shot down the 109 of the *Gruppe Kommandeur*, killing *Hauptman* Helmut Henz.

Two of four Blenheims sent by 45 Squadron to raid Maleme on the 26th were shot down by Me.109s of JG77 (see Appendix 2); the crew of one were killed, and two of the other crew were captured although the WOp/Ag Sgt Langrish evaded, while a third aircraft became lost on the return journey and was abandoned over the desert. Two of the crew were rescued after five nights in the desert, but the Observer, Sgt Longstaff, had wandered off and was not seen again. Three aircraft were briefed to 'spike' Maleme airfield on the 27th, but one crashed on take-off and caught fire, two of the crew were killed outright, and the third died of his burns two weeks later (see Appendix 2). The mission was abandoned. ('Spikes', an effective 'airfield denial' weapon in those days, were small metal triangular-pyramid devices with barbs on all the points, scattered by the thousand and so arranged that one point always remained vertical to puncture the tyres of aircraft or vehicles.) 14 Squadron at Qotofiya LG in the Western Desert could only raise three Blenheims for a raid on Maleme – one returned early with engine trouble, the other two attacked at dusk but became lost in the darkness on return. and both crashed in the desert (see Appendix 2). In a couple of days 14 Squadron had lost five of the six aircraft dispatched. 55 Squadron did not fare much better – two of its six aircraft collided on take-off, and one spun in and the crew were killed, but the other four raided Maleme successfully, although they too became lost on the return trip and two crashed in the desert after the crews had baled out (see Appendix 2). By 28 May 55 Squadron could only put up two aircraft for a raid on Maleme – the Blenheim squadrons were being ground away relentlessly .

In addition to their raids on Crete, the Mk IV-F Blenheim Fighters shared the escort given by the RAF to the badly damaged aircraft carrier HMS *Formidable*, which was making its way back to Alexandria, and also mounted standing patrols over the shuttle service of ships evacuating personnel from Crete to Alexandria. Lt Thorne of 45 Squadron in T2243 damaged a Ju.88 on the 27th, and Sgt McClelland in T2552 shot one down on the 29th – witnessed by Sgt Langrish, the WOp/Ag who had avoided capture three days earlier and was being evacuated on the destroyer HMS *Kandahar*. 45 Squadron had suffered 21 casualties in May, including 17 men killed in action; it had 'fought itself to a standstill' so that by 31 May 1941, when it could muster only six crews fit for action, the Squadron was declared non-operational.

The following week, crews of 608 (Aux.) Squadron ferried out 10 of their Blenheim Mk IVs from Thornaby to Kabrit, via Gibraltar and Malta, where one (V5966) was destroyed by enemy bombing. They, and the nine remaining aircraft, were absorbed by the remnants of 203 Squadron.

Back in London, dismayed by the expulsions from Greece and Crete, together with the related severe reverses in the Western Desert, the Prime Minister, War Cabinet and Chiefs of Staff sought explanations. Before the airborne invasion of Crete, both the C-in-C Middle East, General Wavell, and the Commander in Crete, General Freyberg VC, had been confident of holding the island, and Admiral Cunningham, who deployed four powerful naval forces around Crete, had said: 'It appears almost inconceivable that airborne invasion alone could succeed against fore-warned troops, that sea-borne support was inevitable, and that the destruction of troop convoys would win the day.' The Chiefs of Staff believed that Longmore had more than a thousand aircraft in the Middle East, and did not take into account the length of time it took for reinforcements to reach the squadrons and be made fit for use, the problems of keeping them serviceable, the handicap of poor communications, and the difficulties of operating from unprepared airfields, or the supreme importance of providing adequate defences against air or ground attacks on the air bases. The senior staff of all three services grossly underestimated the devastating effects of the overwhelming supremacy in the air achieved by the Luftwaffe.

Poor Longmore, who had played some brilliant hands against an enemy that held nearly all the trump cards when he held far too few high cards in his own pack, was replaced by his deputy, Arthur Tedder, who sent a long explanatory cable to the CAS Sir Charles Portal on 30 May. The opening paragraph reads:

'Have held stocktaking on Crete. Sorry to say that though effort has had some valuable results the cost has been heavy in relation to strength. Especially in Blenheims – Blenheim dawn and dusk raids in particular have been expensive both in Crete and on return to the Desert. No doubt I am to blame for not keeping tighter rein on Collishaw.'

(This was reference to Collishaw's aggressive deployment of his very limited resources in the Western Desert, particularly the three Blenheim squadrons that were already heavily engaged in that area.) Tedder went straight to the pivotal cause of the defeats:

'There is and undoubtedly will be more loose talk of lack of air support in Greece and Crete. I am taking line that root of situation is secure air bases. We failed to clean up the Dodecanese and failed to secure our air bases in Larissa Plain. As result enemy air ops based on increasingly wide front, whereas ours increasingly cramped, till finally two remaining aerodromes untenable and out of range of effective support from Africa. This campaign is primarily a battle for aerodromes.'

Yet again a small force of Blenheims had served valiantly and with distinction, constantly making great efforts against daunting odds in the most difficult operational circumstances, and caught up in the heaviest fighting throughout the disastrous campaigns in Greece and Crete. Yet again, in rendering this valuable service to the Allied cause, the air- and ground-crews of the Blenheim squadrons had paid a high price in lost aircraft and, sadly, in lost lives.

Appendix I

Blenheim losses in Greek War Zone, 6-30 April 1941

00-04-1941 K7096 30 Squadron Mk I-F and Z5885 11 Squadron Mk IV: destroyed on ground by enemy aircraft.

06-04-1941 T2168 113 Squadron Mk IV: overshot landing at Niamata, ran into canal, on return from raid on Petris; Sgt K. Price DFM, Sgt J. Woodcock and Sgt J. Rooney injured, aircraft abandoned on evacuation.

06-04-1941 L9338 113 Squadron Mk IV: crash-landed on return to Niamata in same circumstances; Sgt V. McPherson and crew safe, aircraft also left there.

08-04-1941 T2247 11 Squadron Mk I: engine cut on take-off at Alymnos for raid, crash-landed nearby; P/O R. Coombs seriously injured, Sgt C. Randall less seriously, Sgt L. Macey uninjured, aircraft abandoned.

08-04-1941 Z5897 84 Squadron Mk IV: crashed in forced landing in bad weather at Kereechori and destroyed by fire; crew escaped, S/Ldr H. Jones (injured), Sgt H. Keen and F/O R. Trevor-Roper.

10-04-1941 T2164 84 Squadron Mk IV-F: ditched off Bar, Montenegro, in bad weather flying a Greek General to Sarajevo, Yugoslavia; P/O J. Eldred, Sgt A. Loudon and Sgt A. Acres injured, rescued by a Sunderland, returned to UK in June.

10-04-1941 K7095 30 Squadron Mk I-F: FTR, shot down a Ju.88 over Athens, hit by return fire, caught fire; S/Ldr R Milward DFC (Pilot) baled out and survived, Sgt J. Crooks (WOp/Ag) KIA, buried in Phaleron War Cemetery, Athens.

11-04-1941 L8612 84 Squadron Mk IV: FTR; shot down by AA attacking armoured column; F/Sgt L. Nuthall, F/Sgt A Neal and Sgt G Thistle KIA, commemorated on Alamein Memorial.

11-04-1941 K7107 30 Squadron Mk I: destroyed on ground by enemy attacks.

13-04-1941 L8478 211 Squadron Mk I: FTR; crashed into hill escaping from Me.109 E-4 of VI/JG 27 at 1608 near Alona; crew S/Ldr A Irvine, P/O G. Davies, and P/O A. Geary DFC, KIA, buried in Phaleron War Cemetery, Athens. S/Ldr Irvine was CO of 211 Squadron.

13-04-1941 L1434 211 Squadron Mk I: FTR; crashed at 1607 near Lake Prespa; Sgt G. Pattison (WOp/Ag) KIA, F/Lt L. Buchanan DFC (Pilot) and S/Ldr L. Cryer DFC (Obs) died in hospital next day. Memorial tablet to Lindsay Buchanan erected recently by sister near crash site at Kula on Albanian border. Aircraft remains now in Greek Air Force Museum.

13-04-1941 L4819 211 Squadron Mk I: FTR; shot down at 1608; F/O R. Herbert (Pilot) baled out but too low for parachute to open, W/Cdr P. Coote and F/Sgt W. Young KIA, buried in Phaleron War Cemetery, Athens. W/Cdr Coote was OC Western Wing.

13-04-1941 L8449 211 Squadron Mk I: FTR; shot down at 1605 by Me.109s of VI/JG 27; F/Lt A Godfrey (Pilot) baled out, Sgt J. O'Neill (Obs), and Sgt J. Wainhouse (WOp/Ag) KIA.

13-04-1941 L8664 211 Squadron Mk I: FTR; shot down in flames by Me.109s of VI/JG 27 at 1605; F/O C. Thompson DFC, P/O P. Hogarth, and F/Sgt W. Arscott KIA, commemorated on Alamein Memorial.

13-04-1941 L1539 211 Squadron Mk IV: FTR; shot down at 1606; Sgt A. James (Pilot) baled out and survived, Sgt A. Bryce (Obs) and Sgt A. Waring (WOp/Ag) KIA.

14-04-1941 T2177 113 Squadron Mk IV: damaged by 'friendly' AA fire when attempting to drop unfused bombs for NZ Sappers to destroy bridge, crash-landed at Larissa; P/O G. Green, Sgt W. Gingell and Sgt K. Jamieson unhurt, aircraft further damaged by air attack 15-04-41, abandoned on evacuation.

15-04-1941 T2054, T2069, T2169, T2182, T2186 and T2216, 113 Squadron Mk IVs: destroyed on ground at Niamata by enemy attacks.

18-04-1941 L1391 84 Squadron Mk I: FTR; damaged by Me.110s and ditched offshore, crew S/Ldr H. Jones, F/Sgt J. Webb, and Sgt H. Keen machine-gunned in dinghy and KIA, S/Ldr Jones buried Phaleron War Cemetery, his crew commemorated on Alamein Memorial.

19-04-1941 T2348 11 Squadron Mk IV: FTR; shot down by Me.109 of 9/JG 77 near Kotzani, Greece; P/O P. Montague-Bates (Pilot) and Sgt H. Murphy (WOp/Ag) KIA and commemorated on Alamein Memorial, P/O H Edge (Obs) survived.

21-04-1941 N3560 11 Squadron Mk IV: evacuating nine airmen to Crete, tyre burst, swung and u/c collapsed landing at Heraklion, aircraft abandoned there; P/O A. Darling (Pilot) broke an arm (see the picture on page 450).

22-04-1941 L1481 11 Squadron Mk 1: returning from Heraklion to Greece after evacuating personnel attacked by CR. 42s, ditched off Argos; Sgt V. Hudson (Solo Pilot) was rescued, awarded DFM.

27-04-1941 L9237 203 Squadron Mk IV-F: FTR; shot down on convoy escort off Crete; F/Lt J. Whittall, Sgt S. O'Connor, and Sgt T. Air, KIA, commemorated on Alamein Memorial.

27-04-1941 K7177 30 Squadron Mk I-F: hit by AA fire from RN destroyer and damaged beyond repair (DBR); F/Sgt Innes-Smith and Sgt Connor safe, aircraft abandoned at Maleme.

27-04-1941 K7096 30 Squadron Mk I: damaged by enemy action, abandoned at Maleme.

28-04-1941 L9044 203 Squadron Mk IV-F: FTR; hit by AA fire from RN destroyers and ditched in sea; F/O P. Gordon- Hall, Sgt G Poole, and Sgt I Oultram rescued.

30-04-1941 L9215 203 Squadron Mk IV-F: damaged by FAA Fulmars; P/O Wilson and crew uninjured, aircraft repaired.

02-05-1941 L1388 84 Squadron Mk I: abandoned at Medini airfield, Athens, photographed there by an Italian on this date. SOC 10-06-1941.

07-05-1941   L8444 113 Squadron Mk I: lost in Greece or Crete, cause not recorded.

00-05-1941   T2183 and T2238 113 Squadron: lost in Greece, cause unknown.

00-05-1941   T2341, T2342, Z5769 and Z5885 11 Squadron Mk IVs: lost in Greece, no further details available.

00-05-1941   L9300, L9310, L9342, R3918, T2390, T2391, V5372 and V5424: lost in Greece, unit and cause unknown

Appendix 2

Blenheim losses in the Crete War Zone, 20-31 May 1941

Aircraft are all Mk IVs.

23-05-1941   V5624 45 Squadron: FTR; shot down in raid on Maleme airfield; P/O P. Vincent, P/O S. Niven RNZAF, and F/Sgt O. Thompson KIA, commemorated on Alamein Memorial.

24-05-1941   Z5766 45 Squadron: FTR; engine cut in sandstorm while positioning for raid on Maleme airfield, crash-landed; Sgt E. McClelland, Sgt H. Vipond, and Sgt J. McGurk uninjured, aircraft DBR.

25-05-1941   T2065 14 Squadron: FTR; shot down by Me.109s while attacking Maleme airfield; F/Lt R. Green, P/O A. Browne, and Sgt N. Wilson KIA, commemorated on Alamein Memorial.

25-05-1941   V5510 14 Squadron: FTR; shot down over Suda Bay by Me.109s while attacking Maleme airfield; Lt S. Forrester SAAF, Sgt W. Fretwell, and F/Sgt R. Hall KIA, commemorated on Alamein Memorial.

25-05-1941   T2003 14 Squadron: FTR; shot down by Me.109s while attacking Maleme airfield; crew Sgt H. Juedwine, Sgt H. Young, and Sgt N. Lake KIA, commemorated on Alamein Memorial.

26-05-1941   T2339 45 Squadron: FTR; shot down while attacking Maleme airfield; crew F/Sgt N. Thomas, Sgt G. Adams, and F/Sgt G. Grainger KIA, buried Suda Bay War Cemetery.

26-05-1941   V5592 45 Squadron: FTR; shot down in raid on Maleme airfield; crew baled out, F/O T. Churcher (Pilot) and P/O R. May (Obs) captured, Sgt H. Langrish (WOp/Ag) evaded and evacuated.

26-05-1941   T2350 45 Squadron: FTR; became lost over Western Desert after raid on Maleme airfield and abandoned; Sgt W. Longstaff (Obs) lost without trace, P/O J. Robinson (Pilot) and Sgt A. Crosby (WOp/Ag) rescued later.

27-05-1941   Z5896 45 Squadron: crashed on take-off for raid on Maleme, destroyed by fire; F/O N. Pinnington (Pilot) and P/O H. Irving RNZAF (Obs) KIA, buried in El Alamein War cemetery, Sgt R. Martin (WOp/Ag) died of burns two weeks later, buried in Alexandria.

27-05-1941   V5593 14 Squadron: FTR; crashed in desert after raid on Maleme airfield; F/O J. Le Cavalier (Pilot) KIA, Sgt Bury (WOp/Ag) baled out but KIA, both are buried in El Alamein War Cemetery, Sgt Page (Obs) also baled out and 'walked' back to base.

27-05-1941   T2338 14 Squadron: FTR; abandoned in air while lost after raid on Maleme airfield; F/Lt M. Mackenzie (Pilot) never found, Sgt M. Fearn and Sgt W. McConnell survived five days in desert, rescued by Army patrol.

27-05-1941   T2051 55 Squadron: collided with another Blenheim on take-off at LG.15 for raid on Maleme, spun in and blew up; F/Sgt W. Martin, Sgt E. Martin, and Sgt K. Bamber KIA and buried in El Alamein War Cemetery. Other aircraft belly-landed; F/O J. Harries, F/O N. How, and Sgt J. Lucas slightly injured, aircraft repaired.

27-05-1941   T2175 55 Squadron: FTR; crashed in desert, out of fuel, after raid on Maleme, wreckage found next day by Lysander of 6 Squadron; Sgt J. Chesman, Sgt D. Callender RNZAF, and Sgt R. Lyle KIA and buried in El Alamein War Cemetery.

27-05-1941   L9319 55 Squadron: FTR; also crashed in desert after raid on Maleme, not found; Sgt R. Bale, Sgt A. Wiles DFM, and Sgt J. Rigby baled out safely, RTB two days later.

30-05-1941   T2183 113 Squadron: abandoned in Crete, no further details available.

00-05-1941   T2342 11 Squadron: abandoned in Crete, no further details available.

German troops examine a crash-landed Blenheim that has been abandoned.

Chapter 25

Iraq, Syria and Iran

Crisis in Iraq

By the beginning of June 1941 the Allied forces had been evicted from Greece, Crete and the Dodecanese Islands, as well as losing all of their previous conquests in Libya – their only success had been in East Africa where German forces were not involved. The British had also faced a serious challenge in Iraq, which directly threatened the vital oil supplies from the Middle East. The oil pipelines from the vast Kirkuk oilfields divided in western Iraq, the southerly one going via Trans-Jordan (now Jordan) to Haifa in Palestine, the northerly one crossing Syria to the port of Tripoli in Lebanon.

The Germans, very much in the ascendancy, had encouraged anti-British feelings in the Arabs, and promised 'military and financial support as far as possible in the case of any war undertaken by the Arabs against the British for their freedom'. To this end they supplied the gold for the successful coup d'état in Iraq by Raschid Ali of April 1941 – the Allies would have been far more alarmed had they been aware that he, as Chief of the National Defence Government, had offered the Germans the use of all the airfields in Iraq. The British-held bases there under a Treaty of 1930, including the main airfields at Shaiba near Basra at the northern end of the Persian Gulf, and at Habbaniyah, some 50 miles west of Baghdad on the highway from there to Haifa, which housed No 4 Flying Training School (which had moved there from Ismailia in late 1939), and where the Empire Class civil flying boats used the lake. This virtually defenceless base was surrounded by some 9,000 troops of the Iraqi Army, including armoured units, by daybreak on 1 May 1941, and artillery was mounted on the escarpment that overlooked much of the huge RAF complex.

The 4 FTS instructors and pupils armed their training aircraft as best they could, and – believing that 'attack is the best form of defence' – at first light the next day a motley force of some 40 Hawker Audax and Fairey Gordon biplanes, together with 27 twin-engined Airspeed Oxfords and a single Mk I Blenheim, guarded by a handful of elderly Gladiators, launched a continuous series of bombing and strafing attacks on the Iraqi positions, commencing their take-off runs on the polo pitches to avoid some of the fierce small-arms fire. They lost 22 aircraft shot down, burned out on the ground, or damaged beyond immediate repair in the first day, but their efforts persuaded the Iraqi forces to restrict their activity to shelling and bombing the base, and deterred them from launching a ground attack upon it. The improvised strike force from Habbaniyah also joined with Wellingtons from Basra to attack the Iraqi airfield at Baghdad, destroying several aircraft on the ground.

The Blenheim Mk IVs of 84 Squadron had been sent to the new base of Aqir in Palestine (then a British Protectorate) from Greece on 27 April. They sent six aircraft, escorted by three of 203 Squadron's Blenheim Fighters, on 2 May to attack Iraqi troop positions round Habbaniyah, but the mission was recalled. 203 Squadron, evacuated from Crete, had split its IV-Fs between Lydda and Kabrit, and on the third day of the siege four of them landed at Habbaniyah and were surprised at the desperate situation there. The next day Sgt Hemsted flew one of them and shot down an Iraqi Audax in full view of the besieged base. A small motorised military relief force, known as 'Habforce', started its journey of over 500 miles across the desert from Haifa in Palestine, gathering at H-4 – a pumping station on the oil pipeline near the Jordan/Iraq border. By 4 May five Blenheim Mk IVs of 84 Squadron and two Mk IV-Fs of 203 were detached to the airstrip at H-4 to give air support. H-3 was taken without opposition, but the Iraqis occupying the nearby desert fort of Rutbah refused to surrender.

After the sixth day of constant aerial strikes on the Iraqi positions, the siege of Habbaniyah was lifted. The departing Iraqi troops ran head-on into a convoy of Iraqi reinforcements on the only road to Baghdad, and the ensuing traffic jam was bombed and strafed to great effect by all the RAF aircraft, including the Blenheims. (This scene of destruction was to be repeated on a vastly greater scale 50 years later when Iraqi forces fled Kuwait during the first Gulf War.) The British relief force was still several days away from Habbaniyah. Blenheims also joined the 4 FTS aircraft in bombing and strafing the airfield at Ba'qubah, destroying more Iraqi aircraft – they had lost more than 30 already – and two of 203's Mk IV-Fs from Habbaniyah flew north to attack Mosul airfield on 9 May, but F/O Gordon-Hall's aircraft crashed in the desert. That day four 84 Squadron Blenheims from H-4 attacked Rutbah fort singly, each making two low-level passes attempting to get a bomb to explode inside the fort. All were hit by small-arms fire and F/O C. Lane-Sansom had to make a crash-landing near H-3, while the other three Blenheims were rendered unserviceable and had to retire to Aqir for repairs. The two 203 Squadron aircraft tried again the next day, but that of S/Ldr Gethin (L9174) was hit, crashed and caught fire. P/O Watson in the other (L9042) landed alongside the downed Mk IV but could only rescue S/Ldr Gethin who had staggered from the wreck. When Iraqi armoured cars approached and opened fire they had to scramble aboard and take off quickly for H-4; sadly the Squadron Leader died there of his injuries a few hours later. RAF Rolls-Royce armoured cars of First World War vintage captured the fort the next day. It had put five Blenheims out of action, two of them permanently, a grave loss as so very few were available for service in the whole of Iraq; a single Mk I from an OTU had to be sent to H-4 to help out. 211 Squadron arrived at Aqir from Greece with but a handful of Mk Is, while 203 had penny-packets of its IV-Fs at three locations – two from Habbaniyah went with Gladiators and 4 FTS aircraft to bomb and strafe Baghdad airport again and again over the next few days.

The Iraqis were relying on the German armed forces to provide the help promised without further delay. However, the Wehrmacht was at this time heavily engaged in Greece, Crete and the Western Desert, and above all was preparing actively for its invasion of Russia, so had very little to spare in the way of direct military support for the Iraqis. As a result the great chance presented to Germany was taken up in only a half-hearted way;

Arab Legion Guards watch an 84 Squadron Blenheim being prepared for a sortie at H-4 landing strip, Jordan, in June 1941.

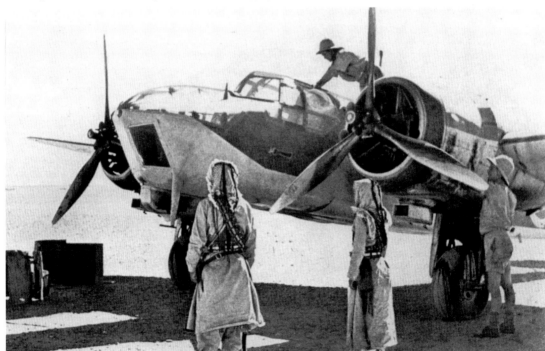

Hitler neglected to exploit a highly favourable situation and thus failed to gain a most significant strategic victory. Had the Germans seized the opportunity wholeheartedly, the Allies would have lost the crucial oil supplies from the Middle East, the Axis powers could have threatened the Suez Canal from both east and west, and German forces could have struck directly northwards into the Caucasian oilfields rather than have to fight all the way there from Russia's western borders. Ribbentrop proposed sending two squadrons of fighters and two of bombers, as well as transport and communications aircraft, grandly titled *SonderKommando Junck* after the CO Colonel Junck, but General Jeschonnek, head of the Luftwaffe Staff, reduced this to 14 Me.110s and ten He.111 bombers, four Ju.90 four-engined transports, and ten Ju.52s, seven of which had to return to Greece immediately. The three that remained included one fitted out as a special radio station and one as a laboratory to produce additives that would make Iraqi fuel suitable for Luftwaffe aircraft. They would all carry Iraqi markings and stage from Athens to Rhodes, then via Damascus in Syria (which was controlled by the Vichy French) to Mosul in Iraq. On 12 May six Blenheims of 84 Squadron arrived at Habbaniyah from Aqir in Palestine via H-4, together with four more Gladiators of 94 and two cannon-armed long-range Hurricane IIcs from Egypt. On 13 May F/O Lane-Sansom in a 203 Squadron Blenheim on a reconnaissance of Mosul was, much to his surprise, attacked by a Messerschmitt Me.110, and F/Lt Plinston of 84 Squadron, who had been bombing the railway line to Mosul, reported seeing a 110 near there; P/O Tulley, also of 84, had to force-land in the desert but managed to take-off later and return to base. F/O Lane-Sansom made a lone attack on Mosul at dawn on the 16th, reporting more German aircraft there. That day the RAF men at Habbaniyah were shaken when their airfield was strafed by six Me.110s and accurately bombed by three He.111s – the Iraqi Air Force was one thing, but the Luftwaffe was another. A defending Gladiator of 94 Squadron shot down one of the Heinkels, but the Pilot, F/O G. Hertage, was killed by return fire and the Gladiator crashed. S/Ldr Pike and F/O Lane-Sansom strafed Mosul at dusk with their Mk IV-Fs, claiming to have set fire to two aircraft and damaged five others. The last of 203's Mk IV-Fs from H-4 arrived at Habbaniyah, as did three more Mk IVs of 84 Squadron. The next day six of these 84 Squadron Blenheims, escorted by six Gladiators, raided Iraqi aircraft at Rashid airport.

Immediate action against the Luftwaffe base in Iraq was called for, so the Blenheims of 84 and 203 Squadrons, together with the Hurricanes, attacked Mosul airfield on the 17th, setting a Heinkel 111 on fire, blowing up a Messerschmitt 110 and damaging two Junkers Ju.52s. In addition, a pair of Gladiators shot down two Me.110s that had just taken off from Baghdad – they apparently had planning officers not air-gunners in the rear seats – and the Germans also lost Major Axel von Blomberg, Head of the German Military Mission to Iraq, who was shot dead in his seat by Iraqi small-arms fire as his Heinkel 111 approached Baghdad airport en route to a conference. The Italians attempted to assist the Iraqis by sending a squadron of Fiat CR.42 fighters in Iraqi markings to Mosul via Syria, but they got there too late to make any worthwhile contribution. The Vichy French in Syria were also sending train-loads and road convoys of armaments to the Iraqis. Clearly 'something would have to done about it'.

Syria is drawn into the conflict

A young Blenheim pilot from the 203 Squadron detachment at H-4, P/O Andrew Watson, really started the war with the Vichy French, for a couple of days earlier, on 14 May, he made a solo early-morning reconnaissance of Palmyra airfield in Syria; seeing strange aircraft there he returned at midday in the OTU Blenheim to confirm that German aircraft were being refuelled there. He asked Group Captain Brown if he could take the Mk IV-F back there and attack them, and was referred to Major General J. Clark MC. The 'Habforce' Military Commander asked him if he really wanted to declare war on Syria, and received such a strongly affirmative reply that he was given permission to 'commence his act of aggression' and attack any Axis aircraft seen on Syrian soil! His Mk IV-F (T1820) and two

84 Squadron Blenheim bombers were joined at H-4 by two of 250 Squadron's new P.40 Tomahawks (on the first operational sortie by the type) and the small formation set out for Palmyra just before 5pm. Unfortunately they were just too late to catch three He.111s that had left for Mosul, but they destroyed two more and damaged several other aircraft. Watson, now promoted to Flying Officer, continued his one-man war the next day with another dawn reconnaissance of Palmyra airfield, followed by a solo attack on it – he was awarded the DFC for the 'fighting spirit' he had shown in Iraq, Syria, and at Rutbah. Eight Blenheims of 84 Squadron, escorted by the two Tomahawks, went to Damascus airport where they saw several German aircraft – two Ju.90s, two Ju.52s and a He.111 – but as they turned to make their bombing run they ran into thick mist, lost sight of the target, and had to return to base. Later that day four of them bombed Rayak airfield, but caused only slight damage to a few French aircraft.

A rare shot of bombs leaving a Blenheim over Syria – one 250lb bomb is falling free, the other is just leaving the bomb bay.

The remnants of 211 Squadron, recently evacuated from Greece to Lydda, moved to Aqir in Palestine and received a few more Blenheims, so were organised into two Flights, A Flight with Mk IVs for operations, and B Flight with Mk Is for training. 11 Squadron arrived at Aqir too, also with a few Blenheim Mk IVs, but was not yet operational, so 211 borrowed four of the aircraft, sending two immediately on a high-level reconnaissance of the Syrian airfields at Rayak, Palmyra and Damascus. Those three airfields were bombed the next day by eight Blenheims of 84 Squadron from Aqir, but little damage was caused. Better results were achieved in an attack on Damascus airport on the 19th when a Ju.52 was destroyed and a Ju.90 with a He.111, both previously damaged, were hit again. The Luftwaffe force in Iraq and Syria was finding the going tough.

A Free French Mk IV being prepared for a sortie to Syria at Rayak, Lebanon.

The tables are turned in Iraq

In Iraq, meanwhile, the advance element of the military relief force arrived at Habbaniyah on 18 May, meeting no resistance as the Iraqi forces had fled 12 days earlier in the face of the continuous air attacks. The relief force Commander, Major General J. Clark MC, was flown up from H-4 in a Blenheim; Air Vice Marshal J. D'Albiac also arrived and assumed command of RAF Iraq. A force from Habbaniyah, backed up by air strikes that cut all radio and telephone communications with Baghdad, captured the only bridge over the Euphrates at Falluja on the 19th. The German aircraft tried to help the Iraqis recapture it, but small formations of Me.110s and He.111s were driven off by Hurricanes, Gladiators and the Mk IV-Fs of 203 Squadron; however, six 110s made an effective strafing run over Habbaniyah on the 20th, destroying one of 84 Squadron's eight-strong Blenheim detachment there, as well as two Valentias and a DC-2 of 31 Squadron, and damaging two more Blenheims. Nevertheless, six Blenheims, escorted by two Hurricanes and three Gladiators, retaliated by bombing and strafing Rashid airport later that day. The 203 Squadron detachment now had seven Mk IV-Fs at Habbaniyah and they strafed several troop convoys during the 22nd; F/O Lane-Sansom made a lone sortie to Mosul at dusk, setting an aircraft on fire. The rest of 84 Squadron's Blenheims arrived at Habbaniyah from Aqir on 23 May, and some of them bombed Mosul on the 25th, while pairs of aircraft raided Kirkuk airfield on each of the following two days, as did S/Ldr Pike of 203 Squadron – his bombs fell near a Me.110. One of the recently arrived Fiat CR.42s was shot down by Gladiators on the 29th, and two were damaged in an attack on their base at Kirkuk. On the 30th all the available Blenheims from 84 and 203 Squadrons, escorted by 94 Squadron Gladiators, made heavy raids on Rashid airfield and Washash Barracks in Baghdad. 'Habforce' now with 1,200 men waiting outside the city, and although the Iraqi Army still had 40,000 men, Rashid Ali, completely demoralised by the RAF's command of the air, lost his nerve and fled with his main supporters. 203 Squadron left Habbaniyah for Kabrit straight away, leaving just four Mk IV-Fs at Habbaniyah and two at H-4.

14 Squadron, after a hard time in the Western Desert, moved to Habbaniyah, Iraq, in July 1941 – Z5860, one of their Mk IVs, is seen over Iraq.

The British were very fortunate to control Iraq again, for the consequences, had the Germans exploited their foothold to gain access to all the Iraqi bases and to the vital supply of oil from the Gulf, would have been incalculable – possibly even fatal – to the Allied war effort. 4 FTS, although not an operational unit, had flown over 1,600 operational sorties in four weeks in unsuitable training aircraft – sorties that had instilled in the Iraqis a fear of RAF attacks that completely demoralised them – yet the personnel of the training base received no awards, no battle honours, and precious few thanks. Officialdom regarded the trouble as a local rebellion that had been repressed rather than the hard and close-fought aerial and military campaign that it was. The small numbers of operational RAF aircraft available in Iraq – mainly Blenheims, with a few Gladiators, fewer Wellingtons, and a handful of Hurricanes – were so thinly stretched that they were unable to match the total of sorties flown by the training aircraft, although their sorties were militarily more effective and made a major contribution to the rout of the Iraqi forces. More importantly, the RAF had inflicted the first defeat upon the German Air Force in the Middle East, and the Blenheims had played a pivotal part in this small-scale but vital victory. The Luftwaffe unit lost all 14 Me.110s, seven He.111s and most of its transport aircraft – only the surviving personnel escaped to Syria. The Italian force made little impact on the fighting and pulled out with fewer losses, just four of its 12 CR.42s: one was shot down, one crashed, and two damaged aircraft were set on fire at Kirkuk when the Italians withdrew to Rhodes via Aleppo in northern Syria.

French fratricide in Syria

84 Squadron, on moving to Habbaniyah, left eight unserviceable aircraft behind at Aqir, and these were taken over by 11 Squadron, which also took over eight from 211 Squadron – only three of which were serviceable – when the latter left for Sudan to become a training unit. So the ground-crews at Aqir set to work to make these much-needed Blenheims fit for use again. That they would be needed soon was apparent as the War Cabinet, spurred on by the Free French, had instructed General Wavell to occupy Syria and Lebanon. He was reluctant – after all, his hands were more than full at that time, and his forces were stretched to the limit. The War Cabinet, however, insisted, reasoning that as the Vichy French had allowed Axis aircraft to transit to Iraq using their

bases in Syria, they may well allow permanent use of them, which would threaten once more not only supplies of oil – as the northern pipeline from Kirkuk passed through Syria and Lebanon – but also the entire Allied position in the Middle East. One such threat had been successfully 'nipped in the bud' in Iraq, now this further one had to be resolved, and once more Blenheims would play a major part in the resolution.

Aerial reconnaissance had started before the land campaign was launched, and on 2 June an 11 Squadron Blenheim, photographing Palmyra and Aleppo airfields, escaped out to sea when chased by Morane-Saulnier MS.406 fighters, but the fuel cocks jammed and the aircraft had to make a forced-landing on the beach at Rouviani with both engines stopped. On 5 June, intending to deny the main supply of fuel to the Vichy French forces, an attempt was made to set fire to the large Shell fuel depot at Beirut; four Beaufighters, newly arrived in the Middle East, and a single Maryland flew up from Egypt, refuelled at Lydda and strafed and bombed the depot, but caused only slight damage, returning to Egypt that evening. A single Blenheim of 11 Squadron bombed the depot again the next day but it too failed to cause significant damage, although three that attacked Aleppo airfield hit a hangar and damaged two CR.42s – three French MS.406s attempted to intercept the Blenheims but failed to do so. The French had called in 25 of the more potent Dewoitine D.520 fighters from France to Syria to strengthen their air force there.

The invasion, commanded by General Sir Henry Maitland-Wilson, started on 8 June and at first went well. The Australian 7th Division from Palestine advanced towards Beirut, and Indian and Free French forces from Jordan moved towards Damascus, while 'Habforce', which had returned from Baghdad to H-4, struck up from the Iraqi desert towards Palmyra. Three Hurricanes of 80 Squadron and five Tomahawks of 3 RAAF Squadron strafed Rayak airfield where the D.520s and Martin M-167Fs (the French version of the Maryland) had been seen, but ten of the bombers had left for Madjaloun and the other three were away bombing an Allied column. Three Blenheims of 11 Squadron at Aqir bombed the radio station at Jedida, and three more tried again at the Shell depot near Beirut. Blenheims of 11 and 84 Squadrons, which had sent a small detachment to Mosul in northern Iraq, also attacked French aerodromes to keep the 230-strong Vichy Air Force in check. As resistance stiffened, on 12 June six Blenheims from Aqir were sent to attack French troop positions near Kissoue, one aircraft being damaged by AA fire. Friday the 13th was unlucky for P/O Lea and his 11 Squadron crew, on a photo-recce around Beirut, for they were intercepted by three D.520s of their former Allies, shot down and killed. The 14th saw four raids on Aleppo and Rayak airfields by Blenheims in which two French aircraft were destroyed and several damaged, and a MS.406 fighter was brought down by a Blenheim gunner. However, 12 more D.520s arrived at Homs, bringing the total to more than 70, with 11 more of the modern LeO.451 bombers at Aleppo bringing the total to 44, plus a total of more than 30 of the Martin M-167F bombers, both types being similar to the Blenheim – clearly the already thinly stretched RAF would need reinforcements too. The shortage of aircraft was exacerbated when 208 Squadron at Aqir lost two of its seven Hurricanes on 15 June, both shot down by 'friendly' AA fire; sadly, both Pilots were killed. In an attempt to reduce the risks of daylight sorties, three Blenheims of 11 Squadron were sent off in darkness early on the 16th to raid Rayak, but little damage was caused. That the risk was not reduced was shown the following night when two of the three Blenheims sent to attack Homs airfield collided over Aqir when attempting to form up in the moonlight and crashed in flames, so only the leader was left to bomb the target.

Damascus was taken on the 21st – Indian troops had fought up to the outskirts, then allowed the Free French units to pass through and capture the capital city. 'Habforce' gained a fort only 40 miles from Palmyra, without air support as no airfields were within the range of RAF aircraft, and suffered heavily from attacks by L'Armée de l'Air, which mounted more than 120 bombing and strafing sorties on the 22nd alone. Three Blenheims of 11 Squadron were sent to bomb the Vichy French destroyer *Vauquelin*, which had arrived in Beirut harbour from France. They scored six direct hits but the ship did not sink, and the aircraft of their leader, F/O R. Moore, was badly damaged by AA fire and his Observer, Sgt Manley, gravely wounded. However, the attention of the rest of the world was focused upon the German assault on Russia – Operation Barbarossa – which opened that day and was to alter the entire course of the war.

The failure within a few of days of the Allied Operation Battle-axe in the Western Desert in June 1941 led to another stalemate there. It also led to the replacement of General Wavell as C-in-C of the Middle East by General Auchinleck. Wavell, like Longmore, had been faced with orders to achieve almost unattainable objectives simultaneously in the Western Desert, East Africa, Greece, the Dodecanese Islands, Crete, Iraq and Syria, while holding on to Egypt and the Canal Zone, Aden, Malta, Palestine and Jordan. The consequent divisions of the available forces, which were woefully inadequate in the first place, led to a series of defeats and made the almost miraculous victories in East Africa and Iraq all the more praiseworthy. We have seen how the Blenheim squadrons suffered: some were fought to a standstill, while others were split up into a series of detachments and reduced to carrying out operations with just pairs or trios of aircraft, sometimes even with single aircraft.

But the end of Battle-axe also freed up some reinforcements for the struggle in Syria. 45 Squadron, which had been ground down in the Western Desert and in raids on Crete, was sent to Egypt to recover and re-equip, but had been there only days when it was told to fly its Blenheims to Aqir on 22 June, but only four crews were operational, which limited their usefulness until fresh crews were flown in. The Squadron's CO, W/Cdr J. Willis DFC, led two others to bomb Soueida Fort on the 23rd, but no damage was seen, and P/O S. Champion took the other crew on a reconnaissance of Beirut, but his Blenheim was chased by fighters and so damaged that it crashed on landing. Next day two more raids on the fort by three, then four 45 Squadron aircraft also failed to hit it – the Squadron had not had time to work up the new crews to operational efficiency, so they had to learn 'on the job'. Four attacked gun positions near Damascus on the 27th and one (V5968) was hit by AA fire, injuring the WOp/Ag, Sgt J. Bullock. He was tended by the Observer, P/O L. Bourke, while P/O Champion landed at Damascus airport, but sadly Sgt Bullock died – this is the crew that had survived a crash-landing four days earlier. Later that day four more 45 Squadron Blenheims, with four of 11 Squadron, attacked the same positions in support of the Allied ground forces, and on the 28th five raided Palmyra airfield with poor results, and three more bombed railway sidings at Rayak. The raid to Palmyra had been escorted by nine RAAF Tomahawks, and after the Blenheims had bombed the escorting fighters spotted six *Aeronavale* Martin 167Fs bombing British troops and promptly shot them all down! On the 29th and 30th formations of ten 45 Squadron aircraft bombed Palmyra barracks, the second attack being most accurate; also on the 30th three of the Squadron's Blenheims finally managed to hit Soueida Fort. The 84 Squadron detachment at Mosul raided the Aleppo airfields three times, destroying one aircraft and damaging others. Tedder personally called for an attack on the large Beirut Residency of General Dentz, the Vichy High Commissioner, and S/Ldr Bocking led four Blenheims of 11 Squadron on the raid, scoring three direct hits with 250lb bombs; however, they caused surprisingly little damage and the raid had to be repeated on subsequent days. The 250lb bombs were old stock from the early 1930s, with less than 30 per cent of their weight being explosive, and not very effective explosive at that – the more destructive 500lb bombs used in Northern Europe were not available to the Blenheim squadrons in Iraq.

July started with two successful raids by ten Blenheims from 45 Squadron on Palmyra, and one by three from the 84 Squadron detachment at Mosul, which damaged three LeO.541 bombers. On the 2nd four of 84 Squadron's aircraft, escorted by four Hurricanes, raided Abu Dane airfield, hitting a bombed-up LeO.541, which blew up and damaged others. On its way back to base the small force was intercepted by ten Dewoitine D.520s and a dogfight ensued, during which the two Blenheims of Sgt Blatch and F/Lt

Wg/Cdr J 'Buck' Buchanan DSO DFC (centre) with his crew. As CO he led 14 Squadron from the Western Desert to Iraq; he had flown an unequalled 230 operational sorties in Blenheims, and later commanded two Beaufighter Squadrons, but was shot down and ditched in the Aegean in December 1943, dying of exposure in his dinghy.

Free French Blenheims in Syria bearing the Cross of Lorraine in red on a white circle painted over RAF roundels, and rudder stripes of blue/white/red. They carried both British and French under-wing roundels.

Williams were shot down. Two further raids on Soueida were made by four Blenheims from 45, scoring more direct hits, with one more aircraft sent on a long reconnaissance sortie, and another to locate and attack a suspected enemy convoy off Tyre. Sgt Melly found three destroyers escorting three large vessels, radioed their position and immediately attacked through heavy AA fire – nothing was hit, which is just as well as they were found later to be Royal Navy ships! Consequently, four other Blenheims on their way to attack them were recalled. On the 3rd 12 Blenheims of 45 Squadron were moved up to Muquibila so that they, with the Tomahawks of 3 Squadron RAAF, could give direct support to the 7th Australian Division. The next day a 45 Squadron Blenheim (V6503) on reconnaissance over Aleppo was intercepted and damaged by three MS.406 fighters; Sgt J. Burns escaped by carrying out violent evasive manoeuvres, although his WOp/Ag, Sgt J. White, was fatally wounded, but another (T2189) of 84 Squadron was shot down in similar circumstances, and only the Pilot, P/O Ryan, managed to escape the burning aircraft by parachute to become a prisoner. Four aircraft of John White's 45 Squadron colleagues raided Hama airfield, setting fire to a LeO.451, which exploded, and six others bombed a chateau near Beit-et-Din, reported (mistakenly) to be a Headquarters, and a dozen raided it again the following day, 5 July.

A total of 14 Blenheims on the 6th made three raids on troop positions near Damour, and two raids each by four aircraft on the supposed HQ at Beit-et-Din scored ten hits the following day. Bridges and W/T stations were also targeted as the Australians advanced, but when ten aircraft were sent on the 8th to bomb an ammunition dump near Zahle, cloud forced nine of them to seek alternative targets, although later that day eight straddled a similar dump at El Barouk, although their bombs failed to hit anything vital. Another ammunition store at Hamma was attacked by 12 45 Squadron Blenheims on 10 July, and this time hits triggered a series of spectacular explosions. But disaster struck on the return trip as the Blenheims, and the six RAAF Tomahawks escorting them, were bounced by five *Aeronavale* Dewoitine D.520 fighters, two of which were shot down, but not before they had attacked the Blenheims, three of which (Z6433, Z6455 and Z9547) were shot down and seven more damaged. One (V5926) had to belly-land at base and was written off. Six crewmen were killed, and three baled out and were captured, one of them, F/Sgt Wilton-Jones, being burnt badly. That black day for 45 Squadron literally had a 'sting in the tail', for one aircraft (V5968) of three that had bombed troops at a road-block near Beit er Ramal with 72 40lb GP bombs had two of them 'hang up', unknown to the crew, and they fell off at 50 feet on the approach to land and detonated, wrecking the aircraft, from which the crew were lucky to escape without serious injuries. The Vichy French started evacuating aircraft and on the 11th General Dentz asked for an armistice to take effect at midnight.

Over the next few days the Blenheims, whose numbers in the area had been quadrupled by reinforcements, staged demonstration flights in formations of 12 or 18 aircraft over Jerusalem, Beirut, Damascus and Palmyra to remind the population that the Allied forces were now in charge. The Syrian campaign had cost some 3,300 Commonwealth and 1,300 Free French casualties, including wounded and prisoners; the Vichy forces lost some 6,000, of whom over 1,000 were killed. They also lost 169 aircraft, including 42 shot down and 45 destroyed on the ground, with another 54 abandoned, mainly due to damage, as well as another 20 lost in accidents. The RAF had lost 31 aircraft in action, most of them Blenheims, but only three on the ground and three more in accidents. Clearly the policy of bombing and strafing the Vichy airfields had paid worthwhile dividends. Magnanimously, the British gave all Frenchmen in Syria the choice of either joining the Free French or going back to France – only 5,300 stayed, while more than 33,000 returned to Metropolitan France, much to the chagrin of General de Gaulle. In early August, 11 and 45 Squadrons were re-deployed to Habbaniyah to be joined there by 14 Squadron, while 84 Squadron kept one Flight at Mosul and one at Shaiba near Basra.

Blenheims such as 'Joy' based at Aqir in Palestine operated over Syria. These cheerful Australian crews are believed to be from 454 Squadron RAAF, in 1942.

Iran

With Iraq and Syria safely under British control, Imperial eyes were cast on Persia (now Iran) to the east in view of the importance of that country as a supply route to southern Russia and the Caucasus. Persia also possessed important oilfields, the main one being at Abadan close to the Iraqi border at Basra – and conveniently near the RAF base at Shaiba – and the country harboured more than 3,000 Axis personnel, many in influential positions, including some who had fled from Iraq, and all of whom were fostering anti-British feelings. The Persian Government rejected the joint Anglo-Soviet Note of 17 August demanding that these Axis personnel be expelled. The Allies therefore decided to secure the oilfields and take control of communications throughout the country. After a delay while arrangements were made for a joint occupation with Britain's new Allies the Russians, the military intervention commenced on 25 August, and the Abadan refineries were quickly secured. The Blenheims initially flew leaflet and reconnaissance sorties, but 84 Squadron aircraft, escorted by Hurricanes, twice bombed and strafed Ahwaz airfield; in the evening they also bombed defensive positions that were well sited in the mountainous Payitak Pass on the road to Kermanshah and Tehran. On the 26th, following more reconnaissance and leaflet missions, a heavy strike was made by 36 Blenheims of 11, 14 and 45 Squadrons led by W/Cdr Willis, CO of 45, which bombed the Iranian positions in the Pass – the defenders withdrew overnight and the Gurkhas took it without opposition the next day, advancing to occupy the Kermanshah oilfields as white flags were shown and all fighting ceased. The Russians had entered Persia from the north simultaneously, and it was necessary to improve co-ordination. F/Lt Penny of 45 Squadron flew a team of British negotiators to Mosul in a Blenheim, where they met a Russian aircraft and the pair flew on to Tiflis to meet a Russian delegation and set up common communications channels. Unfortunately, on the return journey one of Z6156's engines caught fire and Leonard Penny had to crash-land in the desert near Lake Urmia. He was unhurt but his crewmen, Sgts Kirkpatrick and George, were injured and taken to Tabriz Hospital. The Persians still refused to surrender the Axis nationals, so an Anglo-Russian force occupied Tehran on 17 September, withdrawing a month later having persuaded the old Shah to abdicate and pass control to his pro-British son – who went on to rule from the peacock throne until the revolution of 1979.

11, 14 and 84 Squadrons were sent back to Habbaniyah before going to Egypt later in 1941, while 45 and 55 were moved straight to Egypt. The Allies now exercised effective control over Iraq, Syria, Lebanon, Jordan, Palestine, Iran and the Gulf States, so their essential oil supplies, as well as the increasingly important route to send aid to Russia, were secured. The Blenheim squadrons had played a vital part in achieving this most significant improvement in the overall strategic position of the Allies.

An Arab levee guards F/Lt A. Gill's 84 Squadron Blenheim at Sharjah, Persian Gulf, in January 1942. Vents for the spent cartridge cases from the Brownings in the Frazer-Nash FN54 chin-turret can be seen.

THE BRISTOL BLENHEIM

Appendix 1

Blenheim losses in Iraq, 1-31 May 1941

09-05-1941   T2072 203 Squadron Mk IV-F,: took off from Habbaniyah to raid Mosul, crashed in desert; F/O P. Gordon-Hall and Sgt G. Poole escaped and interned, Sgt I. Oultram (WOp/Ag, aged 20) KIA and buried in Mosul War Cemetery, Iraq.

09-05-1941   Z5865 84 Squadron Mk IV: took off from H-4 to attack Rutbah fort, damaged by ground fire and crash-landed in desert; F/O I. Goudge and crew rescued.

09-05-1941   L9215 203 Squadron Mk IV-F: took-off from H-4 to rescue crew at H-3, port u/c jammed down, port engine cut, crashed on H-4; P/O J. Wilson and Sgt R. Harding not seriously injured, aircraft DBR.

10-05-1941   L9174 203 Squadron Mk IV: hit by ground fire in attack on Rutbah fort, crashed and caught fire; S/Ldr J. Gethin (Pilot) rescued but died of his injuries, Sgt E. Cruttenden and Sgt L. White KIA and buried in Damascus War Cemetery.

31-05-1941   L9316 84 Squadron Mk IV; FTR to Habbaniyah from recce sortie, shot down by Vichy French MS.406; Sgt A. Gordon DFM, Sgt G. Humber and Sgt G. Furney DFM KIA, buried in Habbaniyah War Cemetery.

NB Losses in Iraq prior to the uprising of May 1941 are in Chapter 22, Appendices 1 and 5.

Appendix 2

Blenheim losses in Syria, 14 May to 12 August 1941

Aircraft are all Mk IVs.

28-05-1941   V5818 211 Squadron: FTR to Aqir, shot down by Vichy French MS.406 on reconnaissance sortie to aerodromes in Syria; Sgt D. Davis, Sgt L. Stalder, and F/Sgt H. Trenholm KIA, buried in Aleppo War Cemetery.

02-06-1941   L9316 11 Squadron: force-landed on a beach in Palestine after being pursued by French MS.406 fighters, crew safe, aircraft recovered and repaired.

13-06-1941   Z5891 11 Squadron: shot down by French D.520 fighters on PR sortie to Beirut; P/O R. Lea, Sgt A. Jones, and Sgt W. Ferguson KIA, buried in Beirut War Cemetery.

17-06-1941   V 5946 11 Squadron: Two Mk IVs of three led by F/Lt Lawrence collided on take-off from Aqir at 0147 for raid on Homs. ORB states 'The second machine crashed into the third, both burst into flames, the latter having been ignited by incendiaries of the former which liberated on impact. The bombs on the third machine exploded, Sgt V. Hudson, Sgt W. Johnson and Sgt Morton reported killed. However, they were discovered later wandering around the aerodrome in a dazed condition but with no injuries.' No details given of other crew or serial numbers of other aircraft involved possibly V5929.

23-06-1941   V5440 45 Squadron: damaged by French fighters and crashed on landing at Aqir; P/O S. Champion, P/O L. Bourke RNZAF, and F/Sgt J. Bullock uninjured, aircraft DBR, the same crew were hit by AA fire four days later in V5968 (below).

27-06-1941   V5968 45 Squadron: hit by AA fire near Damascus; P/O S. Champion and P/O L. Bourke uninjured, F/Sgt John Bullock died of injuries, buried in Damascus, aircraft believed left there, SOC 22-12-1941.

02-07-1941   V5629 84 Squadron: shot down by D.520s near Deir ez Zor; F/Lt P. Williams, P/O R. Eldsforth and Sgt R. Crowe interned.

02-07-1941   N6197 84 Squadron: shot down by D.250s near Deir ez Zor, DBF; F/Sgt J. Balch and F/Sgt J. Wright KIA.

04-07-1941   T2189 84 Squadron: FTR; shot down in flames by MS.406s; P/O A. Ryan (Pilot, aged 19) wounded, baled out but died six days later, P/O R. Webster and F/Sgt L Wilkinson KIA, all three buried in Aleppo War Cemetery, Syria.

04-07-1941   V6503 45 Squadron: damaged by MS.406s over Aleppo; Sgt John White (WOp/Ag) fatally injured, F/Sgt J. Burns (Pilot) and Sgt J. Kirkpatrick (Obs) uninjured, aircraft repaired.

10-07-1941   Z6433 45 Squadron: FTR; shot down by D.520 fighters; F/Sgt L. Wilton-Jones (Pilot) baled out, became PoW, Sgt J. Wimhurst (Obs) and Sgt D. Lowe (WOp/Ag) KIA.

10-07-1941   Z6455 45 Squadron: FTR; shot down by D.520 fighters; Sgt D. Cawthen, F/Sgt K. Cornford and Sgt W. Capewell KIA, commemorated on Alamein Memorial.

10-07-1941   Z9547 45 Squadron: FTR; shot down by D.520 fighters; Sgt G. Hardy (Pilot) and Sgt J. Newhouse (Obs) KIA, Sgt R. Waddington (WOp/Ag) baled out, became PoW.

10-07-1941   V5926 45 Squadron: damaged by D.520 fighters over Hamman, belly-landed at base and DBR; Sgt W. Osbourne DFM (Pilot) and Sgt H. Garfath (WOp/Ag) injured, Sgt I. Martin (Obs) safe.

10-07-1941   V5968 45 Squadron: two hung-up 40lb bombs fell off on approach after a raid and exploded, aircraft crashed; Sgt Stewart, Sgt J. Colway RNZAF and Sgt W. Catton slightly injured, aircraft believed not repaired, SOC 22-12-1941.

Appendix 3

Other Blenheim losses in Iraq, Syria, Iran and Palestine, 1941

Aircraft are all Mk IVs.

18-05-1941   T1820 203 Squadron: swung on take-off at Lydda and hit steamroller, killing an Arab workman; P/O J. Tremlett, Sgt H. Goodrich, Sgt R. Hepworth and the AOC, AVM J. D'Albiac DSO (passenger), unhurt, aircraft DBR.

22-05-1941   T2116 84 Squadron Mk IV: engine cut, overshot landing at Haifa, overturned; Sgt C. Bailey injured, Sgt L. Atkinson RNZAF and Sgt F. Round safe.

22-05-1941   V5511 Mk IV: crashed 5 miles South of Gazala, unit and cause not given.

15-06-1941   R3608 11 Squadron: left Aqir on PR sortie to Beirut, returned with engine trouble, crashed on landing at Haifa; Sgt R. Sellars, Sgt F. Manley DFM, and Sgt Edwards uninjured.

16-06-1941   T2063 84 Squadron: throttles jammed, overshot landing at Mosul, Iraq, struck fire tender; F/O E. Scoones and Sgt A. Blackburn injured.

22-06-1941   V5591 84 Squadron: engine cut on take-off at Aqir on sortie to bomb Beirut harbour, crash-landed in orange grove; F/Lt J. Lawrence and Sgt H. Hill unhurt, Sgt H. Bowen DFM injured.

02-07-1941   Z5887 11 Squadron: taxied into a steamroller at Aqir, DBR; Sgt F. Woodham RAAF and crew safe.

19-07-1941   Z5861 11 Squadron: engine cut on take-off at Aqir, crashed and overturned, DBR; Sgt Guthrie, Sgt Martin and Sgt Young injured.

30-07-1941   L9335 84 Squadron: struck hangar at Mosul while low-flying on Army Co-Op sortie, crash-landed, DBF; Sgt J. Chambers (Pilot), Sgt G. Bell and Sgt Goodwell injured.

19-08-1941   V5792 14 Squadron: partially stalled turning on to finals, u/c collapsed in heavy landing at Habbaniyah, DBR; S/Ldr J. Buchanan safe, aircraft SOC 8-10-1941.

20-08-1941   V5443 84 Squadron: stalled at low level during fighter affiliation, crashed near Shaiba; Sgt S. Wilton (Pilot) and Sgt D. Anderson (WOp/Ag) seriously injured, Sgt S. Clough (Obs) killed.

25-08-1941   V5444 14 Squadron: one of 11 aircraft sent to drop leaflets on Tehran, engine cut (due to too weak a mixture), ran into wall in forced landing near Kirkuk; S/Ldr D. Illsley DFC, Sgt J. Hibbert and P/O E. Burdon DFC safe. V5925 and T6231 RTB with similar engine trouble caused by long range of sortie.

29-08-1941   Z6156 45 Squadron: took delegation to meet Russians at Tiflis, Iran, engine fire on return trip, force-landed near Lake Urmia; F/Lt L. Penny unhurt, Sgt J. Kirkpatrick, and Sgt G. George injured.

05-09-1941   Z5888 45 Squadron: engine cut on take-off at Habbaniyah, swung and u/c collapsed; Sgt C. Melly, P/O F. Rippingale, and Sgt J. Halsall unhurt, aircraft DBR.

12-09-1941   Z9588 55 Squadron: took off from Aqir for shipping sweep off Palestine coast, FTR; W/Cdr R. Welland, F/O J. Dodds, F/Sgt J. Lucas and Major I. Whittaker (Australian Army) MIA, commemorated on Alamein memorial.

14-09-1941   V5927 55 Squadron: u/c retracted in error after landing at Aqir, DBR but not struck off charge until 04-03-1942.

25-09-1941   V5578 84 Squadron: engine cut on take-off from Mosul, crash-landed 3 miles away, DBR; Sgt C. Brackpool and crew safe.

17-10-1941   V6094 84 Squadron: one flap failed on approach to Habbaniyah on air-test, spiralled into ground and destroyed by fire; Sgt S. Owen and AC1 J. Wilkinson (Flt Mech) seriously injured.

Blenheim losses in these areas during 1942 can be found in Chapter 26, Appendix 6.

Supplies – for the Officers Mess? – being loaded into a 244 Squadron Blenheim at Basrah, Iraq, in 1942.

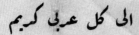

السلام عليكم ورحمة الله وبركاته وبعد لحامل هذا الكتاب ضابط بالجيش
البريطاني وهو صديق وفيّ لكافة الشعوب العربية فنرجو أن تعاملونه بالعطف والاكرام .
وأن تحافظوا على حياته من كل طارى. ونأمل عند الاضطرار أن تقدموا له ما يحتاج
اله من طعام وشراب .

وأن ترشدونه الى أقرب معسكر بريطاني
وسنكافئكم ماليا بسخاء على ما تسدونه اليه من خدمات .

والسلام عليكم ورحمة الله وبركاته؟

القيادة البريطانية العامة فى الشرق

To All Arab Peoples - Greetings and Peace be upon you. The bearer of
this letter is an Officer of the English Government and a friend of all Arabs.
Treat him well, guard him from harm, give him food and drink, help him
to return to the nearest English soldiers and you will be rewarded. Peace
and the Mercy of God upon you.

The British High Command in the East.

Useful Words

English	Arabic	English	Arabic
English	Ingleezi.		
English Flying Officer	Za-bit Ingleezi Tye-yar.	Water	Moya.
Friend	Sa-hib, Sa-deek.	Food	A'-kl.

Take me to the English and you will be rewarded.
Hud-nee eind el Ingleez wa ta-hud mu-ka-fa.

PME/1554-9/41

The 'blood chit' issued to RAF aircrews flying over Arab countries.

Chapter 26

The next rounds in the Western Desert

We have noted how the diversion of British and Commonwealth forces to aid the defence of Greece and Crete weakened those left to defend Egypt and the Suez Canal zone, enabling Rommel's troops to advance some 500 miles to reclaim all the area captured from the Italians, and isolating Tobruk. We have also seen how the crisis in Iraq was resolved, and that the early failure of Operation Battle-Axe launched in the Western Desert on 15 June enabled sufficient Allied reinforcements to be sent to Syria to ensure victory in the bitter campaign there, together with the successful securing of Iran. We have commented upon the heavy involvement of the Blenheims in all of these campaigns, for there was not even the slightest respite for the Blenheim squadrons.

The Gunner's view of a line-astern formation of Blenheims escorted by roving Curtiss Tomahawk fighters.

45 Squadron changed its tired Mk Is for Mk IVs at Helwan in February 1941.

At the conclusion of the campaigns in Iraq, Syria and Iran, the squadrons were moved to Egypt straight away and brought up to full strength. Some, such as 45 and 55 Squadrons, were pressed into action from September onwards, while others prepared themselves to support the coming land battles in the Western Desert. 14 Squadron had come up from East Africa late in May and was pressed into service straight away, experiencing on 21 May a grim baptism in the Western Desert on its first operation there, when seven Blenheims were sent individually to make low-level attacks on motor transport on the Tobruk-Capuzzo road and no fewer than five of the seven were shot down. 113 Squadron was re-equipped completely after its aircraft-less evacuation from Greece, and had been carrying out operations from Ma'aten Bagush in Egypt since 1 June 1941. These squadrons took losses in these attacks on airfields, ports and motor transport along the coastal road (see Appendix 2). There were also losses both at sea, on ferry flights, and on the Takoradi route as hundreds of Blenheims were sent to the Middle East as reinforcements (see Appendix 1). In July Air Marshal Arthur Tedder arranged for AVM Ray Collishaw to pass Command of 204 Group to AVM 'Mary' (a corruption of 'Maori') Coningham, and in October the Group was upgraded in status to the Western Desert Air Command. Tedder and Coningham worked closely together and created the framework for an effective co-operation with the land forces that was to bear full fruit in Normandy in 1944. Of major benefit to the effectiveness of the Desert Air Force was the fact that it operated as a single united force, not being bound by division into the rigidly separate Command structures of the UK-based RAF In the desert, bombers, fighters, reconnaissance, maritime, transport and communication aircraft all operated under one Command, often shared airfields, and were able to co-operate far more easily and closely with one another. Tedder demonstrated his understanding of the prime objective when he declared 'that when critical land operations are in progress, army co-operation is not simply a specialised activity of part of an air force. It is the function of the entire force with all its available strength.' Tedder and Coningham also arranged sufficient equipment and motor transport to make their squadrons self-contained and fully mobile, grouping them into Wings so that they could move forwards – or backwards – at short notice, leap-frogging each other as airfields were gained or lost.

With the failed Operation Battle-Axe in June, Wavell had attempted to relieve Tobruk before he had built up sufficient force; his successor from July, Auchinleck, launched Operation Crusader on 18 November 1941 with the much stronger and newly designated 8th Army, commanded by General Ritchie. They reached Tobruk a month later, and

55 Squadron with its Mk IVs at Ma'aten Bagush.

Tedder (left) and Coningham worked together closely in the Western Desert to develop effective use of air power to influence land battles.

pushed the Axis forces back to El Agheila – their starting point in April. The Allies were determined to establish air superiority for Crusader, so Coningham assembled 16 squadrons of Hurricane and Tomahawk fighters, and also employed them effectively as fighter-bombers. As day bombers he deployed the Blenheims of 11, 14, 45, 55, 84, 113 and 203 Squadrons, together with a detachment from 8, the SAAF 15 Squadron and the Free French Lorraine Squadron, and the Martin Marylands of 39 and three SAAF Squadrons, 12, 21 and 24. All squadrons were brought up to full strength and based at airfields or landing grounds in Egypt near to the front, and nearly all the aircraft were repainted in the desert camouflage scheme of sand and brown upper-surfaces over azure under-surfaces. Most units dropped the squadron codes, showing just the individual aircraft letter in front of the fuselage roundels – this facilitated the 'borrowing' of each other's aircraft by squadrons in the same Wing. Most of 113 Squadron's Mk IV-F aircraft had the local modification of a long-barrel 20mm Hispano cannon mounted on the floor of the Observer's position and projecting through the starboard panel of the bomb-aiming

To increase firepower for ground strafing, 20mm cannon were mounted in the Observer's position of some Mk IV-Fs of 14, 45 and 113 Squadrons. This 'lash-up' blocked the emergency exit, and the ammunition feed caused the pitot tube to be moved forward.

window This made strafing attacks more effective and was later adopted by some of the other squadrons, such as 14. The standard bomber aircraft were not modified although they sometimes left off the bomb doors, allowing them to fit more bomb carriers into the bay and avoiding the problems caused when the fins of light bombs occasionally caught in the bomb doors, which were held closed by bungee cords and forced open by the weight

Western Desert Blenheims often flew without bomb-doors, as here with carriers containing light-bombs and incendiaries.

of the released bombs upon them. A few of the cannon-armed 'strafer' Blenheims had the 'shark's mouth' markings made famous on the noses of the Kittyhawks of 112 Squadron.

This period marked the high point of Blenheim operations in the Western Desert. They started attacking enemy airstrips and supply transport by day and night three days before the launch of the Crusader land battle, taking losses both through enemy action and through accidents, mainly at night, on poorly prepared landing grounds which were often without even a flare-path (see Appendix 3). Once Crusader was under way, the Blenheims successfully attacked supply columns and troop movements on a daily basis, often flying several sorties a day and mainly escorted by strong forces of fighters on the daylight raids. They were backed in the bombing role by Marylands and Baltimores, while in the ground-strafing role Blenheims with a single 20mm cannon and five forward-firing machine-guns were joined by their younger brothers, the powerful Bristol Beaufighters, with four 20mm cannon and six machine-guns. These raids had to be made well behind the very fluid front as there was great confusion on the ground; the Army Liaison Officers were unable to tell the RAF Commanders which were Axis and which were Allied tank concentrations and troop positions. Indeed, the bomb line soon had to be drawn 50 miles to the west of the front line so the Blenheims and other bombers operated out of sight of the ground forces and were unable to assist the troops as closely as they wished. Although severely outnumbered, the Luftwaffe fought hard. Its Me.109s – especially the new 109-Fs being introduced – enjoyed a distinct qualitative edge over the Allied fighters and caused severe losses to the bombers when they managed to break through to them. On 22 November this happened to a six-aircraft formation of 45 Squadron sent to attack motor transport near El Adem – four Blenheims were shot down, including that of their CO, W/Cdr James Willis, and the other two were badly damaged (see Appendix 4). Three of the escorting Tomahawks of 3 Squadron RAAF were also shot down on that raid. 45 Squadron suffered another traumatic day on 4 December. It formed 270 Wing based at LG 75, with 14, 84 and the Free French Lorraine Squadron, and the Wing sent off 32 aircraft to raid motor transport at Sidi Rezegh. There was much dust-haze but little wind that day, and the landing ground had a wide central hump. A green Very was fired, and throttles opened for the take-off run – it would be a long run that day due to the high temperature, the lack of wind, and the reduced performance of the by then tired Mercury engines with their Vokes air filters. S/Ldr A. Hughes DFC was leading the RAF units, and just as his first 'vic' of fully laden Blenheims finally became airborne they were horrified to see the French Blenheims taking off in the opposite direction and only just managed to scrape above them, taking the aerial mast off the Blenheim of their leader, Capitaine Charbonneaux! The second and third 'vics' made some 'phenomenal

22 November 1941 was a black day for 45 Squadron, when it lost four of six Blenheims, and this one was lucky to get back. Sgt J. Pannifer shows S/Ldr Austin the damage to the port aileron of Z6440 caused by Me.109s.

avoidances', some staying down while the opposing aircraft staggered over them, some swerving on the ground, and some turning steeply as soon as they were airborne, but two collided, killing one RAF crew in V5991, P/O J. Tolman, F/O A. Hutton, and Sgt D. Harris, and badly injuring a French crew, Sgts Fifre, the pilot, who died shortly afterwards, de Maismont and Soulat (see Appendix 5). The remaining 17 aircraft formed up, maintaining strict radio silence, and completed the mission, which was particularly successful.

The German High Command decided to strengthen its forces in North Africa in order to capture the Suez Canal area – opening the way to Middle East oil – and was concerned at the losses of supplies and reinforcements en route to them. So the Luftwaffe withdrew the powerful *Luftflotte II*, commanded by *Feldmarschall* Albert Kesselring, from the Moscow region of the Eastern Front and sent it to the Middle East. This Air Fleet included II/JG 27, the experienced *Jagdgeschwader*, which changed its Messerschmitt Bf.109Es for the latest Bf.109Fs before re-deployment to North Africa. This air force, together with the troops sent to the *Deutche Afrika Korps* with their tanks, armoured personnel carriers and other transport, artillery and anti-tank guns, fuel, ammunition and supplies, would have greatly assisted the German Army in the push to Moscow, then at a critical stage and only brought to a halt, mainly by the bitter Russian winter, at the very gates of the Soviet capital. North Africa may have been a side-show to the Wehrmacht, but it played a part in its failure to win its campaign in Russia. Admiral Raeder, a sound strategist, supported by Kesselring and Rommel, had urged Hitler to take Malta and clear the Allies from North Africa and the Suez Canal zone prior to launching the invasion of Russia, but Hitler's eyes were focused primarily on Operation Barbarossa. Admiral Doenitz, Commander of the German submarines, was not pleased when ordered to send half of his U-boats, then heavily engaged in the grim Battle of the Atlantic, to operate in the Mediterranean.

The Blenheims made a significant contribution to the steady westward advance by the Allies in North Africa during Operation Crusader, and were in constant action throughout Rommel's hard-fought and well-ordered retreat back to El Agheila. The British and Commonwealth forces recaptured Benghazi on Christmas Eve, but a sharp counter-attack on 28-30 December caused heavy loses to their vanguard – the Blenheims also continued to take losses (see Appendix 3) until both sides paused for breath at the end of the year. Crusader had run out of steam and made no further progress.

The first Allied aircraft to land at the just-captured Italian aerodrome at Berka, near Benghazi, was this Blenheim of 11 Squadron.

The eyes of the world were diverted from the crucial struggle on the outskirts of Moscow, and from the relatively small-scale side-show on the coast of North Africa, when Japanese carrier-borne aircraft made the devastating attacks on the United States' fleet, peacefully at anchor in its main Pacific base at Pearl Harbor, Hawaii, on 7 December 1941 – called 'the day of infamy' by President Roosevelt. The USA and Britain declared war on Japan, and three days later Japan's Axis partners, Germany and Italy, committed a major strategic blunder by declaring war on the United States. Had they not done so the Americans may well have stood aside from the European War and confined their armed forces to fighting in the Pacific. However, Britain no longer stood alone and was now allied to the two nations that, by the end of the war, would become the world's two 'superpowers'. But for a while the British position was weakened for she had to send reinforcements from the Middle East to the Far East. Once more a gap appeared and the Blenheims were called upon to plug it. 113 Squadron was one of the first to go in December 1941, followed in January and February 1942 by 84, 11 and 45 Squadrons, while 211 was released from training duties and sent east.

The departure of 45 Squadron was delayed because as it was preparing to move east from Helwan, it was ordered on 24 January to collect 12 new Mk IV-Fs with an extra 20mm cannon mounted in the nose from Wadi Natrun and to join 14 Squadron at Bu Amud back in the desert as 'tank busters' to counter Rommel's latest thrust. The 'new' Blenheims turned out to very war-weary examples with numerous defects, each with the cannon in a 'lash-up' mounting on the floor of the Observer's position in the nose, whose seat was removed (so he had to remain on the jump-seat alongside the pilot), the clear bomb-aimer's panels in the nose replaced with crude alloy panels, and the pitot tube for the ASI moved forward to accommodate the ammunition feed for the cannon. They set out for Bu Amud but ran into severe sandstorms; one flight of six returned to Ma'aten Bagush almost out of fuel, while the other was scattered widely in forced-landings – only one (N3581) made it to Bu Amud, and that crashed on landing after an engine had cut through fuel shortage. Nine reached there two days later, but they were far from operational, so the crews were given 48 hours to train in their new role by strafing burned-out MT vehicles behind the lines. However, several of the cannons refused to fire and the most rounds that any of them could be persuaded to fire before jamming was six, and the Squadron had no specialist armourers or tools to rectify the problems. Rommel was halted at Gazala, so the crews were ordered back to Helwan, arriving in dribs and drabs by 7 February, and set out for Buma on the 9th in their original Blenheims, passing their 'strafers' on to 14 Squadron at Gambut.

These movements drastically reduced the number of Blenheim squadrons in the Western Desert, and they were further reduced when several converted to more modern American aircraft: 223 commenced changing to Boston IIIs in January 1942, 203 and 39 to Marylands in February, with 55 and 14 Squadrons changing to Baltimores in May and July 42; 14 changed again, to Marauders, a month later. 459 Squadron was formed with Blenheims at LG 39 for maritime duties in February 1942, but converted to Hudson Mk IIIs in May. Blenheim Mk IVs remained only with 15 Squadron SAAF, which kept a Detachment at Kufra Oasis to work with the Long Range Desert Group (forerunners of the SAS), and 13 (Hellenic) Squadron, manned by expatriate Greeks. The Free French Groupe Lorraine remained in the Western Desert with its Mk IVs until July 1942, when it was sent to Syria. Elsewhere in the Middle East there was 8 Squadron, still at Aden, 6 Squadron, which changed its Hurricanes for Mk IV-Fs in November 1941, only to change back to the 'tank buster' Hurricane Mk IV 11-D in April 1942, and 272 Squadron, which was waiting for more Beaufighters, together with 162, equipped in February 1942 with a Flight each of Blenheims and Wellingtons – this was a Signals Squadron, a pioneering version of what would nowadays be termed an Electronic Warfare Squadron. In Iraq 244 Squadron at Sharjah was re-equipped with Blenheims in April and 52 Squadron was formed at Mosul in October 1942. The Blenheim squadrons had all fought hard and well as the campaigns in the desert swung forwards and backwards, and they had made a significant contribution to the Allied cause, especially in forging and proving methods for more effective co-operation with the land forces.

The final swings of the pendulum

Rommel struck first in the Western Desert, launching an offensive on 21 January 1942. The Africa Corps advanced rapidly, recapturing Benghazi a week later, but was halted at the Gazala Line, which stretched from the coast to Bir Hakeim in the south, and both sides paused to recuperate, re-supply and reinforce their positions. There was no pause for the opposing air forces, however, which clashed repeatedly, although the weather over the desert was often surprisingly poor, and once more the few remaining Blenheim squadrons suffered as they attempted to help the 8th Army (see Appendix 4).

In an unnecessary tragedy, which merits detailed description as it illustrates the dangers of flying – yet alone fighting – over featureless desert, 15 Squadron of the South African Air Force suffered the deaths of 11 out of 12 air-crews on one flight. Three of the Squadron's cannon-equipped Blenheims, detached six days earlier to Kufra Oasis deep in

The wartime caption stated 'an enemy aircraft shot down near Tobruk', but it is a Blenheim. The engines, elevators, fin and rudder have been salvaged, and a vulture sits on the starboard wing-root. It is probably V5560 of 113 Squadron, damaged by flak in an attack on Bardia harbour on 26 September 1941, which 'crashed into a small house killing the crew and several German soldiers'.

the desert far to the south-west, set out at 0600 on 4 May for a familiarisation reconnaissance of the local area led by Major J. de Wet. They became lost almost immediately. An attempt to get a D/F bearing from Kufra proved a fatal failure – the transmission was too short. A snap bearing of '120-3 = 0527' was sent, which meant 'Steer 120 degrees (with zero wind), third-class fix, timed at 0527 hours GMT'. The WOp/Ag in the leader's aircraft, Z7513, noted down only the figures 3, 0 and 5, so Major John de Wet steered a course of 305 degrees, then (seeing nothing) the reciprocal of 125 degrees, each for an unknown period. At around 9am an engine of one Blenheim started cutting, and the leader ordered all three aircraft to land on the harsh desert near a small hill, which they did quite safely. The Pilots, Major de Wet, with Lt J. Pienaar and 2/Lt L. Wessels, discussed their plight with the Observers and found that no one had kept a log or air plot with courses set and times flown. Although none of them could even 'guesstimate' their position, they were not unduly concerned, for they had rations and water for four days, all three aircraft and their radios were serviceable, the base would send out search parties when they became overdue, and the visibility was good. Major de Wet made no attempt to ration the water – some splashed it on themselves in an attempt to keep cool in the searing 50-degree heat. Later the Major and his crew took off alone and set a course of 135 degrees, but returned having found nothing; Lt Wessells took a course of 213, flew 26 miles and returned – had he flown a further 56 miles he would have seen Kufra. After refuelling from the other aircraft, the third Blenheim set out on a heading of 233 and flew for 43 miles, managing to transmit signals on the D/F frequency before returning, but the transmissions were too short for a bearing to be obtained. The following morning all the remaining fuel was put into Z7513, and Pienaar set off to try and find Kufra. De Wet assumed that he had succeeded when he did not return as instructed, but in fact he had force-landed the Blenheim in the desert when he ran out of fuel some 24 miles short of the other two aircraft, and when he tried to make contact by radio the batteries ran flat. The other grounded aircraft tried, without success, to raise Kufra on their radios – with the same result. Although they had not put out ground markers or lit a fire to make smoke during the second day, on that night de Wet's stranded crews shot off Very flares and fired bursts from the turret guns, but the desert remained silent – no one saw or heard them.

Kufra had radioed 203 Group HQ at 1300 hours on the first day requesting an aerial search for the missing aircraft. HQ agreed to send a Blenheim from Khartoum and a Bombay from Wadi Halfa the next morning, but they failed to appear at Kufra. The Blenheim reached Wadi Halfa but went unserviceable, and found that the Bombay had already left for Khartoum before receiving the fresh instructions due to a muddle over communications. Kufra also sent out a ground party the following day (5 May) for 60 miles in the direction of the weak signal heard on the 4th, but by nightfall they had found no trace of the Blenheims and halted. RAF Middle East HQ ordered three Bombays from 216 Squadron to go to Kufra and be briefed by a senior officer of 203 Group sent to Wadi Halfa to organise the search. The gremlins struck at every plan – the officer's Blenheim had engine troubles and force-landed itself, and one of the Bombays had to return with engine problems. The other two were unable to take off until 1100 on the 6th because of a sandstorm, and when they did they found the visibility to be only 50 feet at 3,000 feet when approaching Kufra, so missed the outpost and had to force-land themselves. They were unable to contact Kufra by radio as they had not been given the call-sign for the newly set-up base. The ground party struggled on but the going became impossibly difficult. A second patrol was sent out.

The condition of Major de Wet's men was deteriorating rapidly. They were given their last water at a bottle per man on the 6th, then the sandstorm hit them and they were blasted with burning hot sand. They sprayed the fire-extinguishers on each other, and the intense cooling effect gave momentary relief, but the fluid caused painful blisters that became open sores within hours – the gentian violet in the First Aid Box gave some relief, the morphine syringes more. They were so ravaged by thirst that they broke open the compasses and bomb-sights and drank the alcohol-based fluid. De Wet recorded in his diary that it was 'stimulating', but was soon noting 'Boys are going mad wholesale – they want to shoot each other – very weak myself – will I be able to stop them and stop them from shooting me? Please give us strength.' He was not to know that no search aircraft had arrived at Kufra. The stranded Bombays could not take off until the 8th and, not sure of where they were in relation to Kufra and with insufficient fuel to search, returned to Wadi Halfa using D/F bearings. Major de Wet's diary recorded that day: 'We expect to be all gone today. Death will be welcome – we went through hell.'

Three Wellingtons of 162 Squadron at Bilbeis had been ordered on the 7th to join the search, but engine problems delayed their departure until the 9th, and even then one could not find Kufra as the crew had been given the wrong call-sign for the Kufra D/F unit! However, after a 5½-hour search S/Ldr Warren in another spotted the Blenheim of Lt Pienaar – the desert camouflage made it hard to find on the brown, sandy and broken terrain. The bodies of the crew lay in the shade under a wing – a doctor calculated that they had died of dehydration the day before. The fuel tanks were empty and Warren could find no navigation log, but did find a map with some marks and a rough sketch. That day poor deluded de Wit scrawled in a weak hand: 'We can last if help arrives soon – they know where we are but do not seem to do much about it. Bit of a poor show isn't it. But we will try to stick to the very … It is the fifth day, second without water, and fifth in a temperature of well over 100, but "Thy will be done, O Lord" … [then, in Afrikaans] 'We can only wait, perhaps we can still get out of this hell on earth.' The next day, 10 May, Warren returned to the position of Pienaar's Blenheim and, while other aircraft searched in vain, he used the sketch and ground features he could see to reconstruct the last flight of the Blenheim and found the other two stranded Blenheims some 24 miles away. They too were very difficult to spot from the air, but a draped parachute caught his eye, and as he circled he saw a lone figure on the ground. Air Mechanic Noel Joul was the sole survivor of the 12 Blenheim crewmen (see Appendix 4). Colonel Borkenhagen, then CO

The famous shark-mouth markings of these 112 Squadron Tomahawks was copied by this Blenheim of 89 Squadron, a Beaufighter night-fighter unit based at Abu Sueir and Idku.

of 15 Squadron SAAF at Amriya, said later that Joul was 'in the most terrible shape' when rescued, but recovered in hospital at Cairo, was discharged from the SAAF and returned to Cape Town, dying in Natal in 1979. Three service revolvers were found at the site, one in Major de Wet's hand – all the ammunition had been expended.

The hiatus at the front was interrupted on 26 May when Rommel, as was his wont, struck first, sending his Panzers to outflank the British positions at Gazala. The Germans then withdrew to a position known as the Cauldron, prepared as a trap with anti-tank guns, including the 88mm guns that out-ranged the British armour, to await the British counter-attack of 5 June, which, sent in piecemeal over several days, was soundly defeated. Bir Hakeim at the southern end of the front was held by the 1st Free French Brigade commanded by General Koenig, and was soon cut off. RAF aircraft – particularly the Blenheims of the Lorraine Squadron – tried to help defend the position. The Free French held out for a couple of weeks, with supplies flown in, then had to fight their way out and withdraw. Koenig signalled Coningham: '*Bravo. Merci pour la RAF.*' Coningham replied, '*Bravo a vous! Merci pour le sport.*' The Luftwaffe had concentrated its attention on Bir Hakeim and the area to the south, so the 8th Army was largely unmolested as it retreated eastwards in considerable disorder. The Panzers swept forward again and captured Tobruk, capturing 33,000 Allied troops and a vast stockpile of supplies, fuel and equipment, on the 21 June. A week later they took Mersa Matruh, again seizing thousands of prisoners and more valuable supplies. The Western Desert Air Force lost most of its advanced airfields and landing grounds, and Coningham had to withdraw his aircraft back to Egyptian airfields. The British 8th Army had been out-thought and out-fought, but Rommel became increasingly hampered by his ever-extending supply lines, which were subject to daily attacks from the air, by fighter-bombers and by the Blenheims, although the numbers of the latter were reduced considerably by unserviceability and continued losses, due both to enemy action and to frequent accidents in the harsh operating conditions (see Appendices 4 and 5). The German advance to Alexandria, Cairo and the Suez Canal was halted at El Alamein in July, only 60 miles from Alexandria. The line was held despite a series of attacks including a last desperate attempt to break through on 30 August until, once more, both sides were forced to pause for re-supply and reinforcement. The difficulties of providing adequate supplies for the opposing armies had proved critical, and the island of Malta played an increasingly important part in this struggle, as will be described in the next chapter, for Blenheims played a pivotal role in denying Rommel much of the logistical support the *Afrika Korps* needed. Ironically, it was Rommel's success in capturing Tobruk that led the Wehrmacht to abandon its planned operation to capture Malta, and to back his advance toward Suez, and the Middle East oilfields, instead.

Auchinleck was replaced by Alexander as C-in-C Middle East, and Ritchie by Montgomery at the 8th Army HQ, although – as with Tedder, who took Boyd's place when the latter failed to arrive at Air HQ – he was only second choice, as the Bombay carrying General Gott was shot down when he was en route to take up command of the 8th Army. Montgomery was careful to avoid repeating the errors of his predecessors as he resisted all attempts to launch the major battle of El Alamein before October, by which date he had built up a very substantial advantage in the forces available to him. The 8th Army won the battle, but Rommel saved most of his men as he retreated westwards, and Montgomery pursued him far too cautiously. The British forces captured Sirte on Christmas Day and entered Tripoli on 23 January 1943. They were behind schedule to link up with the Allied forces that had launched Operation Torch, the landings in French North Africa, in November 1942. Blenheims were heavily involved in Torch and the subsequent fighting in Tunisia, but this time they were Mk Vs not Mk IVs.

A captured Blenheim Mk IV-F from an unknown unit in German markings – the nose-art indicates an Australian crew. The four-Browning mountings can be seen, but the guns and fairing are missing, as is the nose-mounted 20mm cannon – note the field-mod of alloy over the bomb-aimer's window.

General Ritchie, Montgomery's predecessor as Commander of the British 8th Army, had his own personal Blenheim, shown here being loaded up on 12 February 1942; his Pilot, F/O F. Alder, is on the right.

84 Squadron's Mk IVs at Heliopolis in January 1942 prior to their epic trip to the Far East, when only 16 of 24 reached Pallembang, Sumatra and all were lost.

Appendix I

Blenheim losses en route to the Middle East, at sea, on ferry flights, and on Takoradi route, 1941-2

All aircraft are Blenheim Mk IVs. For Mk V losses see the Appendices to Chapter 28.

14-01-1941	T2244, T2384, T2386, V5442, Z5889, Z5890: lost at sea en route to Takoradi.
17-01-1941	L9320 Takoradi Station Flight: bounced on landing at Lagos, u/c collapsed, Damaged Beyond Repair (DBR); crew S/Ldr T. Kurdzeil, Sgt Turley and Sgt Hughes safe.
21-02-1941	T2250 Aircraft Dispatch/Delivery Unit (ADU): damaged and SOC at Takoradi.
08-03-1941	V5441 ADU: crashed on landing at El Fasher, Sudan, on Takoradi/Egypt delivery flight; Sgt Marsh, Sgt Finlay and Sgt Creighton safe.
00-04-1941	V5628, V6080, V6081, V6088, V6090, V6091, V6092, V6095, V6096, V6130, V6131, V6170 and T2231: lost at sea, all except T2331 brand new.
00-04-1941	V5372: lost on ferry flight in Middle East, not assigned to any squadron or unit.
05-04-1941	V5942, V5969, V6075 and V6077: lost at sea.
17-04-1941	V5955 and Z6095: lost at sea.
19-04-1941	T2384: lost at sea en route to Takoradi for 11 Squadron.
19-04-1941	V5583: lost on ferry flight in Middle East, not assigned to any squadron or unit.
19-04-1941	V5643 ADU: both engines cut, crash-landed at Kabkabiyah, Sudan, on Takoradi/Egypt delivery flight; F/O J. Whelan and Sgt W. Dunjey safe.
24-04-1941	V5584 ADU: hit whirlwind on approach and spun in at El Fasher, on Takoradi route; Sgt A. MacVicar (Pilot) killed, Sgt W. Wills and Sgt J. Lang injured.
29-04-1941	V5898, V5940, V5994, V5995, Z5978 and Z6045: lost at sea.
00-05-1941	V6188, L9300, L9342, R3918 and T2248: lost at sea.
01-05-1941	V5439: crashed at Kurfi, Katsina, Nigeria, attempting forced-landing in bad weather and short of fuel on Takoradi/Egypt ferry flight; F/O R. Milne and crew safe
06-05-1941	N3558 and V5424: lost in Middle East, not assigned to any squadron or unit.
09-05-1941	Z5865: lost in Middle East, not assigned to any squadron or unit.
10-05-1941	V6070 82 Squadron: believed lost on ferry flight to Gibraltar.
11-05-1941	R3885 139 Squadron: engine cut on ferry flight from St Eval to Malta, ditched off Gibraltar; crew Sgt Farmer, P/O Moffatt and Sgt Shinnie rescued.
11-05-1941	T2134 139 Squadron: ran off Gibraltar runway when landing on ferry flight from St Eval, pilot blinded by late afternoon sun; Sgt J. Dennis, Sgt Miles and Sgt R. Waddington injured, ground-crew passenger believed killed.
21-05-1941	Z6165 82 Squadron: crashed into sea off Gouraya, Algeria, on ferry flight to Malta; F/Sgt L. Wrightson (Pilot), F/Sgt C. Evans (WOp/Ag) and LAC K. Thomas (ground-crew passenger) killed, commemorated on Runnymede Memorial, P/O K. Marsh (Obs) rescued and interned.
08-06-1941	V6129 with ADU, ex-Takoradi: overshot landing at Lagos in bad visibility, DBR; Sgt G. Searles and crew safe.
20-06-1941	Z6453 105 Squadron: force-landed near Finisterre en route to Gibraltar; Sgt F. Bryant, Sgt F. Thompson and Sgt D. Phillips interned.
17-07-1941	Z7366 105 Squadron: force-landed on beach near Faro, Portugal, out of fuel on Portreath/Gibraltar ferry flight; Sgt G. Williams RNZAF, Sgt R. Griffin and Sgt N. Kay interned but escaped and returned to UK.
20-07-1941	V6247 with ADU: undershot landing at Lagos, u/c collapsed, DBR.
20-07-1941	Z9581 OADU: force-landed on border of French/Spanish Morocco, out of fuel; crew Sgt H. King, Sgt A. Ryan and Sgt W. King burned aircraft and were rescued by 202 Squadron Swordfish.
21-07-1941	Z7429 with OADU: out of fuel, crash-landed at Gibraltar.
30-07-1941	V6498: on air-test at Takoradi, undershot landing, u/c collapsed, DBR.
27-08-1941	Z7678 18 Squadron: out of fuel en route to Gibraltar, force-landed on beach at San Jacinto, Portugal; crew Sgt J. Thompson, Sgt N. Parsons and Sgt R. Martin burned aircraft and were interned, but escaped.
27-08-1941	Z7585 107 Squadron: force-landed on beach near Caparica, Portugal, out of fuel; crew Sgt D. Grant, Sgt R. Dart and Sgt J. Bowling destroyed aircraft and were interned but escaped and returned to UK.
30-08-1941	Z7583 OADU: engine cut on ferry flight, ditched 80 miles E of Gibraltar; crew Sgt G. Moth, Sgt K. Carey and Sgt C. Brett injured but rescued.
05-09-1941	Z9536 ADU: took off from Kano, Nigeria, en route from Takoradi, swung off runway landing at Maidaguri, Nigeria, into soft sand and tipped up; Sgt C. Mott and crew safe.

25-09-1941	Z7587: engine cut on take-off for air-test at Takoradi, crashed 4 miles E of airfield, DBF; 2/Lt B. McKenzie SAAF safe.
29-10-1941	Z7843 OADU: landed downwind at Luqa, Malta, and hit wall, DBF; Sgt G. Corbett, Sgt I. Stark and Sgt G. Souter escaped.
29-10-1941	Z7979 OADU: ran out of fuel on ferry flight, dived into sea 10 miles N of Ras Engla, Egypt; Sgt A. Belasco, P/O D. Lake and Sgt D. Mayo killed, commemorated on Alamein Memorial.
30-10-1941	Z7782 OADU: damaged by fighters on ferry flight from Gibraltar to Malta, crash-landed on coast of Sicily; F/Sgt J. Graham, P/O H. Knight (both RCAF) and Sgt I. Bevan became PoWs.
04-11-1941	T1853 OADU: engine seized, lost prop, crashed into sea on approach to Gibraltar; 105 Squadron crew, F/Lt T. Horton RNZAF, F/Sgt D. Thrower and F/Sgt Howe slightly injured but rescued.
11-11-1941	V5621 OADU: brakes failed, over-ran runway at Gibraltar, hit pile of stones, u/c collapsed, DBR; P/O C. Hughes RCAF and crew safe.
15-11-1941	Z7887 OADU: attacked on Gibraltar/Malta ferry flight, aircraft ran into flooded area at Takali, DBR; Sgt W. Eaton (WOp/Ag) fatally wounded, Sgt F. Banks (Pilot) and Sgt D. Lowcock (WOp/Ag) safe.
30-11-1941	Z7632 OADU: stalled on take-off for ferry flight, dived into ground and exploded at Oshogbo, Nigeria; F/Lt S. Pietraslewicz, F/Sgt R. Keyworth, and Sgt T. Griffiths killed, buried in Oshogbo War Cemetery.
21-12-1941	Z9825 OADU: u/c jammed on take-off at Gibraltar for Malta, crash-landed at North Front, Gibraltar; Sgt G. Williams and crew safe.
26-12-1941	Z7301 OADU: overshot landing at Gibraltar on ferry flight from Portreath, ran off end of runway, DBR; Sgt R. Grant and crew uninjured.
26-12-1941	Z7972 OADU: engine failed on Gibraltar/Malta ferry flight, ditched 5 miles E of Gibraltar; Sgt G. Wallace RCAF (Pilot) injured, P/O J. Hetherington (Obs) killed, Sgt G. Weston (WOp/Ag) injured.
28-12-1941	Z7294 OADU: ran low in fuel on Portreath/Gibraltar ferry flight, engine cut on approach, stalled and crashed into sea just E of runway; P/O A. Tancred and Sgt D. McKinnon injured but rescued, Sgt R. Sangster and Cpl W. Hallett (passenger) killed.
30-12-1941	Z9816 OADU ex-18 Squadron: damaged by AA, ditched off Malta.
07-01-1942	Z7652 OADU: missing off Cap Bon, Tunisia, believed shot down by Vichy French fighter.
28-01-1942	V5899 11 Squadron: engine cut on ferry flight, crash-landed near Mechili, DBR.
28-01-1942	Z9836 OADU: stalled on final approach to Luqa and spun into ground; Sgt C. White RAAF and crew safe.
27-02-1942	V5535 OADU: engine cut on approach to Gibraltar, crashed into sea; Sgt W. Teale, Sgt J. Barnett and Sgt M. Cole injured but rescued.
04-03-1942	V5952 ADU: crashed at Edina, Liberia, on ferry flight from Takoradi.
19-03-1942	V6394 OADU: crashed into sea off Cap Bon, Tunisia, cause unknown but believed shot down by Vichy French fighter; F/Sgt A. Smith, Sgt J. Robinson and F/Sgt F. Wood killed.
30-03-1942	Z6283 OADU: lost en route to Middle East, reason and location unknown; Sgt C. Truman, Sgt W. Brenan and Sgt R. Hope, all RAAF, safe.
30-03-1942	Z9832 1 OADU: lost without trace on final leg of delivery to Middle East; Sgt C. Johnson, Sgt H. Janney and Sgt J. Shiner, all RAAF, Missing Presumed Dead, commemorated on Malta Memorial.
04-04-1942	V6310 OADU: ex-Portreath, belly-landed at Gibraltar after hydraulic failure; F/Sgt G. Wylie, Sgt F. Collins and Sgt W. Bodger safe.
07-04-1942	V6490 OADU: engine cut, belly-landed near Wadi Natrun; F/Lt P. Mitchell and crew safe.
28-04-1942	V5733 21 Squadron: missing on Portreath/Gibraltar ferry flight; Sgt R. Parker, Sgt E. Downs and Sgt I. Chance killed, Sgt Parker's body recovered and buried at sea, his crew commemorated at Runnymede.
30-04-1942	V5791 Iraq Delivery Flight: struck lorry on take-off at Helwan, Egypt; Sgt G. Whitman (solo Pilot) killed.
01-06-1942	N3628 ADU: belly-landed in sand dunes while lost near Abu el Khawi, Egypt; Sgt B. Guthrie and crew safe.
02-06-1942	N3628 1 ADU: belly-landed in sand dunes when lost 2 miles S of El Teira, Egypt; crew safe.
02-08-1942	Z7788 ADU: engine cut, crashed in attempted forced-landing near Damat, Gold Coast.
13-09-1942	Z6374 ADU: engine failed on ferry flight, a/c caught fire, crash-landed at Heliopolis; P/O A. Gold and crew safe.
11-11-1942	Z7581 272 Squadron: hit obstruction on take-off at Idku, Egypt, for ferry flight to Ta Kali, Malta, u/c collapsed on landing back; Sgt D. Broadhead RCAF and crew safe. 272 was a Beaufighter Squadron.

Appendix 2

Operational Blenheim losses, 1941

All aircraft are Mk IVs apart from the Mk Is indicated.

03-01-1941   L8479 45 Squadron Mk I: Failed To Return (FTR), shot down by CR 42 near Gazala; crew F/O P. Griffiths, Sgt A. Tadhunter and Sgt C. Blackshaw Killed in Action (KIA), commemorated on Alamein Memorial.

12-01-1941   T2190 55 Squadron: abandoned in sandstorm over Sinai Desert when out of fuel; F/O K. Potter, Sgt J. Duffy, AC1 H. Todd, LAC Wratton and AC2 Stafford baled out safely.

14-01-1941   T2184 55 Squadron: lost through enemy action, no further details known.

21-01-1941   T1879 55 Squadron: light bomb detached and exploded on take-off at Fuka, aircraft climbed, then dived into ground and DBF; crew F/O F. Bullot NZ, Sgt C. Bartam and Sgt D. Clayson KIA, buried at Halfya Sollum War Cemetery.

02-02-1941   T2240 55 Squadron: shot down in attack on road convoy near Slonta, Libya; P/O P. Blignaut, Sgt H. Rundle and Sgt E. Currie KIA, commemorated on Alamein Memorial.

04-02-1941   L8538 45 Squadron Mk IV: FTR, shot down by CR.42s near Barce; F/Lt J. Paine (Pilot) baled out safely, crew Sgt H. Holmans (Obs) and Sgt C. Edwards (WOp/Ag) KIA.

27-02-1941   T2399: Damaged Beyond Repair (DBR) by enemy action, unit and cause not recorded.

18-03-1941   T1995 55 Squadron, based at Maraura: FTR from sortie to Tripoli; F/O T. Walker NZ, Sgt M. Collingborne and Sgt B. Lee KIA, commemorated on Alamein Memorial.

01-04-1941   V5423 55 Squadron: FTR, shot down into sea SW of Benghazi; crew F/O M. Ferguson NZ, Lt A. Pettigrew RN and Sgt J. Turner RAAF KIA (Obs was from 826 Squadron FAA).

08-04-1941   T2381 55 Squadron: FTR from sortie to Benghazi; F/Sgt E. Vigneaux, Sgt R. Browning and Sgt E. Cook KIA, buried at Knightsbridge War Cemetery, Acroma, Libya.

12-04-1941   Z5894 45 Squadron: overshot forced-landing while lost in sandstorm near Fuka after suffering battle damage; Pilot P/O P. Vincent, Sgt Small and Sgt Smith safe.

13-04-1941   Z5866 45 Squadron: FTR, hit tar barrel on night take-off (no flare path), jettisoned bombs into sea, crash-landed at Maaten Bagush Satellite; F/O F. Chadwick, Sgt Burns and Sgt Turnbull only slightly injured.

15-04-1941   Z5863 14 Squadron: FTR from reconnaissance to Halfya and Sollum; P/O I. Ormiston and Sgt A. Fraser RNZAF KIA and buried in War Cemetery there, Sgt E. Smith (WOp/Ag) wounded and became PoW.

18-04-1941   V5438 45 Squadron: FTR, shot down on raid on MT; crew F/O F. Collins, Sgt E. Street and Sgt R. Crook KIA, Sgt Street buried in Halfya Sollum, others commemorated on Alamein Memorial.

20-04-1941   T2383 55 Squadron: modified with 20mm cannon, sent to strafe Derna airfield, FTR, shot down near there; both crew, Sgt D. Rawlings and Sgt P. Huxstep, KIA, Pilot buried in Benghazi War Cemetery, WOp/Ag commemorated on Alamein Memorial.

22-04-1941   V5625 45 Squadron: FTR, shot down bombing Benghazi harbour; F/Sgt W. Beverley, Sgt R, Gentry and F/Sgt V, Harrison KIA, commemorated on Alamein Memorial.

23-04-1941   T1873 55 Squadron: bombed Gazala, shot down in flames into sea after 15-minute running battle with two Me.109s; Sgt T. Fullerton, Sgt H. Latta RNZAF and Sgt G. McLaren KIA, commemorated on Alamein Memorial.

24-04-1941   T2170 45 Squadron: FTR, became lost at night in low cloud, flew into ridge near Mersa Matruh on return from raid on Fort Capuzzo; F/O F. Chadwick, Sgt A. Burns and Sgt T. Turnbull only slightly injured.

24-04-1941   T2174 45 Squadron: FTR, engine cut on return from night raid on Capuzzo, crash-landed near Mersa Matruh; Lt E. Jones SAAF, P/O L. Bourke NZ and Sgt S. Whiteley safe.

28-04-1941   Z5898 45 Squadron: FTR, shot down by Me.109 of Hans-Joachim Marseille, I/JG 27 off Tobruk on courier flight; crew P/O B. Allan and F/Sgt L. Morling together with five passengers – W/Cdr D. Johnson, S/Ldr D. Barclay, S/Ldr Rev J. Cox (Padre), P/O S. Beloe and Capt R. Ploughwright (Army officer) – killed.

28-04-1941   T2345 45 Squadron: bombed parked Ju.52s at Derna, became lost at night in low cloud on return, ran out of fuel, belly-landed in desert 27km S of El Alamein; crew Sgt D. Naldrett-Jays, Sgt J. Prockter (injured) and Sgt A. Dann safe, aircraft recovered but SOC 10-06-1941.

07-05-1941   L8444 113 Squadron: FTR, no further details available.

10-05-1941   T2274 14 Squadron: FTR, shot down by CR.42s near Sollum; no injuries to F/Sgt J. Taylor, Sgt J. Parker or Sgt R. Hall recorded, but this crew were killed 11 days later.

11-05-1941   V5437 55 Squadron: engine cut on return from night raid, Sgt H. Hewitt belly-landed near shore at Bagush and aircraft blew up due to a hung-up light bomb exploding; Sgt R Stobbs (WOp/Ag, aged 20) KIA, buried at El Alamein War Cemetery.

11-05-1941	L9307 14 Squadron: crashed on landing at Aboukir (LG.34) on return from raid on Derna airfield; Sgt G. Dickson (Pilot) and Sgt Ritchie (WOp/Ag) safe, Sgt E. Cotton (Obs) injured. (ORB gives Z9307 – aircraft possibly recovered and repaired.)
16-05-1941	V5817 45 Squadron: modified with 20mm cannon, FTR, shot down by Me.109s into sea off Tobruk; two-man crew F/Lt A. Haines (Pilot) and Sgt S. Cordy (WOp/Ag) KIA, commemorated on Alamein Memorial.
18-05-1941	T2056 45 Squadron: FTR, shot down in raid on Derna; F/O J. Beveridge, P/O A. Wise NZ and Sgt V. Griffiths KIA, commemorated on Alamein Memorial.
19-05-1941	T2179 45 Squadron: FTR, shot down in strafing attack on Capuzzo; P/O D. Carter (Pilot, pseudonym of P/O G. Reuter, Free Belgian) and Sgt H. Cassar (Obs) KIA, Sgt G. Swanbo (WOp/Ag) baled out, captured and became a PoW.
21-05-1941	T2173 14 Squadron: FTR, shot down in raids by single aircraft on MT on Tobruk/Capuzzo road; P/O R. Johnson, Sgt M. Fuller and F/Sgt A. Morrison KIA, commemorated on Alamein Memorial.
21-05-1941	Z5979 14 Squadron: FTR, shot down in raids by single aircraft on MT on Tobruk/Capuzzo road; Sgt N. Hoskins, Sgt H. Easton and Sgt W. Calver KIA, commemorated on Alamein Memorial.
21-05-1941	T2346 14 Squadron: FTR, shot down in raids by single aircraft on MT on Tobruk/Capuzzo road; Sgt J. Taylor, Sgt J. Parker and Sgt F. Culham KIA, commemorated on Alamein Memorial.
21-05-1941	L8874 14 Squadron: FTR, shot down in raids by single aircraft on MT on Tobruk/Capuzzo road; Sgt J. Matetich, Sgt A. Sutton and Sgt H. Jones KIA, commemorated on Alamein Memorial.
21-05-1941	V5511 14 Squadron: FTR, shot down in raids by single aircraft on MT on Tobruk/Capuzzo road; P/O R. Gilmour, Sgt K. Wilkie and Sgt T. Riley KIA, commemorated on Alamein Memorial.
28-05-1941	V5818: FTR from sortie in Middle East, no further details known.
02-07-1941	V5928 113 Squadron: FTR from raid to Derna; F/O J. Middlehurst, P/O J. Shepherd and Sgt J. Rooney KIA, commemorated on Alamein Memorial.
06-07-1941	V5507 113 Squadron: engine hit in raid on Gazala, made single-engine belly-landing at Fuka; P/O A. Tulley injured, P/O R. Orchard safe, Sgt Rennie injured, aircraft DBR.
08-07-1941	V5793 113 Squadron: destroyed on ground in raid by Me.110s on LG.15.
29-07-1941	Z6431 203 Squadron: attacked submarine, damaged by return fire, u/c collapsed on landing at LG.08 Mersa Matruh; Sgt Langston, Sgt Thompson and Sgt Munro uninjured.
30-07-1941	Z6444 with 102 MU: destroyed in air raid on Abu Sueir.
09-08-1941	V5990 113 Squadron: FTR from raid to Bardia, shot down by own night-fighter off Mersa Matruh; Sgt G. Woodroffe (Obs) and Sgt A. Greenlees (WOp/Ag) KIA, Sgt W. Sands (Pilot) injured but survived.
17-08-1941	Z9552 203 Squadron: both engines cut at low level on anti-shipping patrol, ditched off Sollum Bay, Egypt; Sgt K. Booth (Pilot) and Sgt Crossley (WOp/Ag) rescued, but P/O L. Smith (Obs) drowned.
31-08-1941	V6136 113 Squadron: FTR to LG.14 from raid on Benghazi; W/Cdr R. Spencer DFC, P/O W. Spears and F/Sgt P. Robinson-Pratt KIA, commemorated on Alamein Memorial.
31-08-1941	T2066 113 Squadron: FTR to LG.14 from raid to Benghazi; Sgt G. Sulman, Sgt D. Rhodes RNZAF and Sgt P. Thacker KIA, commemorated on Alamein Memorial.
22-09-1941	V5993 113 Squadron: flew into ground on night approach to Maaten Bagush; F/O D. Brooks (Obs) killed, Lt D. Thorne SAAF (Pilot) and Sgt L. Iganni (WOp/Ag) injured.
24-09-1941	Z6371 55 Squadron: FTR, struck tent on night approach to dummy flare-path while lost on return from sea sweep; Sgt K. Hepburn RNZAF (Obs) killed, Sgt W. Bain (Pilot) and Sgt S. Elsmore (WOp/Ag) together with three SAAF Armourers in tent injured, Air Mechs E. Hicks (died of injuries), E. Pinock and A. Looker.
28-09-1941	Z7374 55 Squadron: FTR from raid to Bardia; F/Lt J. Wilson (Pilot) and F/Sgt A. Griffin (WOp/Ag) KIA, Sgt S. Whiles DFM (Obs) survived.
28-09-1941	V5560 55 Squadron: FTR from same raid to Bardia, hit by flak, crashed into small house, killing crew and several German soldiers; Sgt W. Ross, Sgt C. Johnston and Sgt E. Sprange KIA, buried in Halfya Sollum War Cemetery (see the illustration on page 475).
29-09-1941	Z6445 203 Squadron: FTR from shipping sweep, believed shot down by Me.110 escorting tanker; P/O T. Ruxton, Sgt R. Young RAAF and Sgt W. Billingsley-Dooley KIA, commemorated on Alamein Memorial.
30-09-1941	Z7509 45 Squadron: F/O J. Edmonds (Pilot) taken ill on return from raid on Gambut, landed downwind, swung and u/c collapsed; crew P/O L. Durrant and Sgt K. Chapman uninjured.
01-10-1941	V6306 55 Squadron: FTR, abandoned in air near Sidi Barrani when lost on return from night raid; Sgt Wheeler (Obs) landed safely, but F/Lt J. Harries (Pilot) and Sgt J. Peacock (WOp/Ag) KIA, Peacock's parachute caught in aerial mast.
10-10-1941	V6493 203 Squadron: FTR from shipping sortie over Mediterranean; P/O J. Rowntree, Sgt J. Edwards RNZAF and Sgt F. Norton KIA, commemorated on Alamein Memorial.
13-10-1941	Z9619 203 Squadron: FTR from reconnaissance, Libya to Crete; F/O G. Washington, Sgt L. Read RAAF and F/Sgt C. Bremner KIA, commemorated on Alamein Memorial.

19-10-1941 Z7416 55 Squadron: FTR from shipping sortie, 2/Lt J. Murphy SAAF, F/O J. Macdonald RAAF and Sgt J. Pender RAAF KIA, commemorated on Alamein Memorial.

20-10-1941 V6228 55 Squadron: FTR from leading raid on Gambut airfield, shot down by Me.109s, seen to ditch; S/Ldr H. Blackmore, Sgt W. Cole RNZAF and Sgt Rhodes KIA, commemorated on Alamein Memorial.

20-10-1941 V5641 113 Squadron: shot down by fighters after bombing Gambut; 2/Lt E. Burr SAAF, Sgt C. Jenkinson RNZAF and Sgt K. Duffin RAAF KIA, commemorated on Alamein Memorial.

29-10-1941 R3660 55 Squadron: FTR, damaged by flak in night raid on Tmini, ditched in sea just off El Alamein, dinghy sank; Lt Reid SAAF, Sgt Annells and Sgt Browne swam to shore safely.

29-10-1941 Z7683 55 Squadron: FTR from raid on Tmini, believed shot down near target; Lt D. Blair SAAF, Sgt B. Hoad and Sgt R. Wilson KIA, commemorated on Alamein Memorial.

03-11-1941 V6143 45 Squadron: attempted landing in mist at LG.53, wing-tip hit ground, hung-up 250lb bomb exploded, seriously injuring crew; Sgt A. Scott (Pilot) recovered, Sgt G. Sully (Obs) and Sgt J. Mansfield (WOp/Ag) died of injuries soon after, buried in El Alamein War Cemetery.

06-11-1941 T2343 11 Squadron: engine cut on sortie to bomb MT at Derna, ditched off Alexandria; Sgt F. Turner, Sgt J. Thompson and Sgt J. Bell injured but rescued.

08-11-1941 Z5867 113 Squadron: reported as lost in Atlantic Ocean 274km W of Gibraltar, believed flew reciprocal course; Sgt A. Hyder, Sgt J. Moody and Sgt P. Norris KIA, commemorated on Alamein Memorial.

09-11-1941 Z7708 203 Squadron: FTR to Fuka from Trident Patrol; F/Lt P. Screeton, F/O J. Tweedie and Sgt K. Holbrook KIA, commemorated on Alamein Memorial

12-11-1941 Z9549 55 Squadron: crashed and exploded near Fuka on return from shipping sweep, cause unknown; P/O T. Chater, P/O A. Johnson and Sgt L. Watson KIA, buried in Alamein War Cemetery.

17-11-1941 T2241 14 Squadron: swung on take-off in poor visibility at LG.15 and struck tent; crew Sgt V. Royals, P/O G. McKenny and Sgt C. Murfitt uninjured, but F/Sgt R. Chubb (Obs), Sgt B. Jenkins and Sgt A. Ellis (both WOp/Ags) in tent killed. Aircraft burnt out and bomb-load exploded.

18-11-1941 Z9543 14 Squadron: FTR, shot down in raid on Bir el Baheira airfield; P/O C. Loughlin, P/O E. Main and P/O A. Franks KIA, commemorated on Alamein Memorial.

19-11-1941 V5943 45 Squadron: FTR, damaged by flak in raid on Sidi Rezegh and crashed in desert near Sidi Omar; crew S/Ldr A. Hughes DFC, P/O L. Durrant and F/Sgt D. Cliffe reached British lines safely.

19-11-1941 Z7510 45 Squadron: FTR, shot down on intruder raid on Sidi Rezegh; all-Australian crew P/O E. Magor, P/O A. Cain and Sgt T. MacLiver KIA, commemorated on Alamein Memorial.

20-11-1941 Z5866 11 Squadron: damaged by AA in raid on MT; Sgt B. Burney (WOp/Ag) wounded, P/O J. Loam (Pilot) belly-landed at LG.76, he and P/O R. Ingram DFC (Obs) safe, aircraft repaired.

22-11-1941 Z6439 45 Squadron: FTR, shot down by Me.109-Fs of I/JG 27 near El Adem; W/Cdr J. Willis DFC, P/O L. Bourke RNZAF, and Sgt M. Carthy KIA, buried at Knightsbridge War Cemetery, Libya. W/Cdr James Willis was CO of 45 Squadron.

22-11-1941 T2318 45 Squadron: FTR, shot down by Me.109s near El Adem; Sgt C. Melly (Pilot) and P/O L. Rippingale MBE (Obs) captured and became PoWs, Sgt J. Halsall (WOp/Ag) KIA.

22-11-1941 Z7686 45 Squadron: FTR, shot down by Me.109s near El Adem; Sgt C. O'Neil, Sgt L. Smith and Sgt K. Chapman KIA, commemorated on Alamein Memorial.

22-11-1941 Z9609 45 Squadron: FTR, shot down by Me.109s near El Adem; Sgt R. Turton NZ (Obs) evaded capture and returned, Sgt R. Wood (Pilot) and Sgt S. Whiteley (WOp/Ag) captured and became PoWs.

25-11-1941 Z6438 113 Squadron: hit by light flak, returned to base but DBR; no injuries to crew recorded.

26-11-1941 T2067 113 Squadron: reported missing on raid, no further details known (Squadron records lost in Burma).

27-11-1941 N3532 84 Squadron: shot down by AA near MT target at El Casia, Libya; Sgt T. Ingham-Brown (Pilot) and Sgt L. Atkinson (Obs) captured, Sgt E. Maslen (WOp/Ag) KIA, commemorated on Alamein Memorial.

28-11-1941 Z7703 11 Squadron: FTR, shot down by own AA fire from '150 MT North of Bardia/Tobruk road which identified itself as friendly then immediately opened fire with quick-firing AA guns'; Sgt R. Enticknap, Sgt L. Wishart and Sgt N. Cooke KIA, commemorated on Alamein Memorial.

28-11-1941 V5644 11 Squadron: damaged by flak that killed P/O Degenhardt (Obs) during same sortie near Bardia, jettisoned bombs; 2/Lt Burrage SAAF (Pilot) landed at base, he and F/Sgt Macey (WOp/Ag) uninjured.

28-11-1941 Z5906 11 Squadron: FTR, damaged by flak and crash-landed near Bardia during raid; crew F/O J. Pringle-Wood, Sgt N. Powell and Sgt B. Collins picked up by L1317 (below), which was also shot down.

28-11-1941 L1317 11 Squadron Mk I: FTR, crewed by Lt S. Paterson SAAF, P/O G. Burgan and Sgt J. Bennett, landed alongside Z5906 (above) near Bardia during raid and picked up crew and pilot of downed Hurricane Z4965, Capt H. Liebenberg SAAF, took off again but was shot down almost immediately and all seven men on board were captured.

04-12-1941 V5991 45 Squadron: on take-off at LG.75 crashed into Z9572 of Lorraine Squadron (see Appendix 7); P/O J. Tolman, F/O A. Hutton and Sgt D. Harris KIA, buried in Halfya Sollum War Cemetery, Egypt.

09-12-1941	T2064 14 Squadron: FTR, abandoned in air when lost and out of fuel on return from raid on Sidi Barrani; crew Sgt H. Grimsey, P/O L. Spiller and Sgt B. Martell made their way back to base.
11-12-1941	Z7797 11 Squadron: FTR, shot down by Me.109 in raid on Derna airfield; S/Ldr C. Darbishire, Sgt J. Webster and F/Sgt L. Macey KIA, commemorated on Alamein Memorial.
12-12-1941	Z7909 11 Squadron: FTR from raid on Derna airfield; 2/Lt R. Burrage SAAF, Sgt N. Drummond and F/Sgt D. Martin KIA, commemorated on Alamein Memorial.
12-12-1941	Z5908 55 Squadron: FTR from shipping strike, shot down into sea by Me.110s; F/Sgt J. Thompson, Sgt R. Quilter and Sgt R. Morris KIA, commemorated on Alamein Memorial.
12-12-1941	Z9595 55 Squadron: FTR from same shipping strike, shot down into sea by Me.110s; F/O C. Anderson, Sgt D. Brunton and Sgt J. Evans KIA, commemorated on Alamein Memorial.
12-12-1941	Z7613 18 Squadron: reported shot down by flak over Argestoli harbour, no further details available.
12-12-1941	V5588 113 Squadron: FTR, crashed at Giarabub returning from raid, reason unknown; 2/Lt C. Summersgill SAAF, F/O J. Galvin RAAF and Sgt L. Purves RAAF KIA, buried in Halfya Sollum War Cemetery.
13-12-1941	V6291 55 Squadron: FTR from sortie to Navarin Bay, Libya; F/Lt G. Pelling, P/O J. Strong and Sgt E. Lindsay KIA, commemorated on Alamein Memorial.
14-12-1941	Z7800 84 Squadron: damaged by flak, ditched; Sgt Blackpool and crew rescued uninjured.
14-12-1941	Z5860 14 Squadron: FTR, shot down in raid on MT on Dernia/Bardia road; Sgt F. Dennis RAAF, F/Sgt W. Campbell RCAF and Sgt J. Redfern KIA, commemorated on Alamein Memorial.
19-12-1941	V6294 203 Squadron: FTR from shipping patrol off Crete; F/O A. Read, Sgt C. Brown and Sgt A. McLevy KIA, commemorated on Alamein Memorial.
20-12-1941	V6132 45 Squadron: FTR, shot down by Me.109s near Barce; F/Sgt J. Burns, Sgt R. Reeves and Sgt J. Wilcock KIA, commemorated on Alamein Memorial.
20-12-1941	V5948 45 Squadron: FTR, shot down by Me.109s during raid on Barce; crew Sgt G. Bennett, Sgt N. Nullis and Sgt H. Twydell evaded capture and returned. These two 45 Squadron Blenheims, together with two of Lorraine Squadron (see Appendix 7), were attacked by force of 20 Me.109s.
20-12-1941	T2394 84 Squadron: FTR to Gambut from sortie to bomb MT at Gazala, crashed in sandstorm with full bomb-load and exploded; F/Sgt C. Bayford, Sgt C. Mort, Sgt T. Sherratt and W/O 2 C. Bumstead (passenger) KIA, buried at Tobruk War Cemetery.

Sgt Observer Robert Hay at work in his 113 Squadron Mk 1V over the Western Desert in 1941.

Appendix 3

Non-operational Blenheim losses, 1941

All aircraft are Mk IVs, apart from the Mk Is indicated.

11-02-1941   R3917 113 Squadron: under repair at 31 Air Stores Park, destroyed in hangar fire at El Adem.

15-03-1941   L9322 55 Squadron: u/c damaged on take-off at Maraura, abandoned there.

06-04-1941   L6657, T2180, T2344 and T2383, 55 Squadron: unserviceable or damaged, abandoned at Gazala North on evacuation, destroyed by British Army.

10-05-1941   V5514 55 Squadron: collected aircrew from LG.95, on landing at dusk at Burg el Arab collided with parked Magister R1974, bounced into Blenheim T2177, Destroyed by Fire (DBF), six aircrew in V5514 killed: F/O R. Nicholson NZ, P/O J. Van Breda, F/Sgt R. Davies, F/Sgt H. Rhodes, F/Sgt J. Duffy and Sgt A. Hale, together with LAC E. Buckley, with only WOp/Ag Sgt J. Davison surviving.

22-05-1941   T2116 84 Squadron: engine cut, overshot landing at Haifa, overturned.

22-05-1941   V5511: crashed 5 miles S of Gazala, unit and cause not given.

03-06-1941   L8362 45 Squadron: engine cut on take-off from Fuka North, crash-landed nearby; P/O S. Champion and crew safe.

12-06-1942   V5582 14 Squadron: stalled on landing at LG.116 and u/c collapsed.

07-07-1941   T1988 203 Squadron: both engines failed, belly-landed in desert and DBR; F/O C Lane-Sansom DFC, P/O R. Lewis DFM and Sgt F. Abbott DFM safe.

15-07-1941   L1491 211 Squadron Mk I: force-landed in Libyan desert due to fuel shortage; crew safe, aircraft abandoned.

28-07-1941   Z5770 14 Squadron: u/c collapsed in heavy landing at Nicosia, DBR; Sgt A. Konig and crew safe.

04-08-1941   V6500 203 Squadron: u/c retracted too soon on night take-off at LG.101, crash-landed; P/O R. Smaile and Sgt M. Hornby uninjured.

19-08-1941   T2113 113 Squadron: tail damaged when struck rocks recovering from dive and broke off, crashed into sea near Ras el Kenay Islands; Sgt N. Gregor, Sgt J. Wallace and Sgt S. Miller killed, buried in El Alamein War Cemetery.

22-09-1941   V5993 113 Squadron: crashed on approach to LG.15 Maaten Bagush on night training; Lt D. Thorne SAAF (Pilot) injured, F/O D. Brooks (Obs) killed, Sgt A. Iganni (WOp/Ag) injured, Sub Lt A. Bradshaw RN (passenger) safe.

25-09-1941   V5878: crashed in desert, unit and cause not given, no injuries reported.

28-09-1941   K7098 211 Squadron Mk I: u/c damaged on take-off and jammed, crash-landed at Wadi Gazouza, no injuries reported.

10-10-1941   Z6149 8 Squadron: u/c damaged on take-off at Khormaksar and jammed, aircraft belly-landed, DBR; P/O J. Brownless RAAF and crew safe.

20-10-1941   V6030 113 Squadron: ran into soft sand on landing at Giarabub and overturned, DBR; Lt J. Viney SAAF, Sgt McIver and Sgt J. Wohler uninjured but Army passenger reported killed.

20-10-1941   R3919 113 Squadron: also ran into soft sand landing at Giarabub and overturned, no injuries reported.

A poor photograph of T1867 of GRB1 which became lost on 5 February 1941 and crash-landed in the Sahara desert near the Chad border - it was not discovered until March 1959 with the skeletons of Sgt Le Calvez and Lt Claron laying alongside.

20-10-1941	V6507 113 Squadron: badly damaged in same circumstances as V6030 and R3919; Sgt H. Peters RCAF, Sgt R. Smith and Sgt Gover unhurt, aircraft repaired.
24-10-1941	V6464 113 Squadron: engine cut on take-off at Qasaba, belly-landed on rough ground, DBR; Lt V. Wright SAAF injured, crew safe.
01-11-1941	Z5907 113 Squadron: engine fire in air, crash-landed near Maaten Bagush; 2/Lt C. Summersgill SAAF (Pilot) safe, P/O G. Gray (Obs) and Sgt C. Stokes (WOp/Ag) injured.
01-11-1941	V5435 45 Squadron: tyre burst on take-off at LG.53, swung, u/c failed, DBF; no injuries reported to crew P/O R. Brown, F/O J. Wright and Sgt Jenkins, or to two SAAF passengers, 2/Lt D. Allen and 2/Lt T. Evans.
19-11-1941	V5866 113 Squadron: crashed just after take-off at Giarabub, cause unknown; Sgt J. Hemus, Sgt J. Dewar and Sgt W. Lee KIA, buried in Halfya Sollum War Cemetery.
25-11-1941	V5573 14 Squadron: tyre burst on take-off at LG.75, swung and u/c failed, DBR; Maj E. Lewis SAAF, Sgt Johnson and Sgt Cooke safe.
25-11-1941	L1534 Mk I with 104 MU: engine cut on take-off at Aboukir, hit trees and crashed, DBF; Sgt P. Brook (solo Pilot) killed.
26-11-1941	T2428 14 Squadron: tyre burst on landing at LG.75, swung, tipped up, DBR; crew unhurt.
03-12-1941	V6496 11 Squadron: u/c failed on landing at LG.76, DBR; crew safe.
17-12-1941	V6461 14 Squadron: both engines cut turning finals at El Adem, crashed, DBF; Sgt T. Archer RAAF, Sgt Brown and Sgt Guy excaped before bomb-load exploded.
18-12-1941	V6183 14 Squadron: engine seized, prop detached, belly-landed at El Adem, DBR; F/Lt H. Keck RAAF, P/O L. Farrow RCAF, and Sgt M. German safe, aircraft SOC 01-04-1942.
18-12-1941	V6508 14 Squadron: u/c failed on heavy landing at Gambut, DBR; P/O S. Lawton, P/O C. Goodwin (both RAAF), and Sgt Alexander safe.
22-12-1941	T2127 14 Squadron: engine cut on take-off at Gambut, wing hit ground and aircraft crashed; P/O P. Goode, P/O C. Hargreaves and F/O E. Burdon DFC safe.
27-12-1941	L9308 11 Squadron: engine cut, crashed in attempted forced-landing near Sidi Suarod; no crew injuries reported.
30-12-1941	Z6447 W Desert Com Flt: ran into soft ground landing at Berka, destroyed by enemy action 06-03-1942.

Appendix 4

Operational Blenheim losses, 1942

All aircraft are Mk IVs; for Mk V losses in 1942 see the Appendices in Chapter 28.

01-01-1942	T2226 11 Squadron: FTR, shot down during raid on MT near Ajdabiya; P/O A. Froggatt, Sgt J. Prentice and Sgt D. Young KIA, buried in Benghazi War Cemetery.
22-01-1942	V5506 11 Squadron: collided with Z7434 (below) over Msus LG, Libya, on return from raid on Axis MT, belly-landed, DBR; Sgt P. Payne, Sgt M. Burnside and Sgt E. Cameron, all RAAF, safe.
22-01-1942	Z7434 11 Squadron: collided with V5506 (above) over Msus LG, Libya, on return from raid on Axis MT, crash-landed, DBR; S/Ldr K. Ault, Sgt J. Thompson and Sgt J. Bell safe.
23-01-1942	V5861 203 Squadron: FTR from sortie to shadow Italian Battle Fleet; F/O I. Campbell, P/O Cuthbertson RAAF and P/O F. Black ditched, rescued and became PoWs.
24-01-1942	Four unserviceable aircraft of 203 Squadron ordered to be destroyed when Berka III airfield evacuated, serial numbers not recorded.
25-01-1942	V6244 55 Squadron: port engine seized and lost prop, aircraft crash-landed near Appollonia, Libya; Sgt R. Payne RAAF, Sgt L. Wheeler and Sgt G. Sparrow destroyed aircraft 'owing to the enemy being in the vicinity'.
25-01-1942	Z7359 11 Squadron: FTR, damaged by flak in attack on MT, crashed near Mekelia; Sgt F. Borrett RAAF (Pilot) injured, F/Sgt J. Richmond DFM (Obs) died of injuries, Sgt H. Mackey RAAF (WOp/Ag) seriously injured.
28-01-1942	V5947 14 Squadron: lost prop on take-off at Mechili for a raid on Msus, crash-landed; Sgt R. Linley, Sgt A. Humphries and Sgt T. Smail uninjured, aircraft destroyed on evacuation. (This crew KIA 17-03-1942, qv.)
08-02-1942	V6231 14 Squadron: engine cut, crash-landed near Sollum, not repaired, SOC 18-09-1942; Sgt W. McLellan, F/Sgt J. Vernon, and Sgt J. Nankervis safe.
10-02-1942	Z9541 203 Squadron: engine cut on recce., belly-landed 4km W of Tobruk, DBR; crew safe.
22-02-1942	Z9657 55 Squadron: FTR from attack on Italian Battle Fleet, seen to ditch with engine on fire; crew seen to board dinghy but not found, F/Sgt L. Jones, Sgt E. Hopkinson and Sgt R. Burgess KIA, commemorated on Alamein Memorial.

24-02-1942	Z9729 14 Squadron: badly damaged by Me.109s en route from Baheira to LG.116; Sgt J Bosworth crash-landed in desert, Sgt R. Swann RAAF (Obs) died of injuries, Sgt A. Hoyle (WOp/Ag) recovered, Sgt E. Curtis RAAF (passenger) safe.
25-02-1942	V5657 14 Squadron: FTR, damaged by flak near Martuba, caught fire near Bir Hachim on return trip, abandoned in air; F/Sgt J. Willis DFM (Pilot) baled out safely, Sgt E. Barr (Obs) injured, Sgt H. Tew (WOp/Ag) KIA, buried in Knightsbridge War Cemetery, Acroma.
25-02-1942	Z6443 14 Squadron: FTR, ran out of fuel at night on return from bombing Rubah airfield, ditched off Ras-el-Kanayis; P/O F. Brown, Sgt Young and Sgt R. Danks (injured) rescued.
07-03-1942	V5954 14 Squadron: took off at night from LG.16 to bomb Tmimi LG, flew into ground in haze nearby and exploded; F/Sgt K. Stevenson, F/Sgt W. Howey RCAF and Sgt L. Johnson KIA, buried in Alamein War Cemetery.
16-03-1942	V5446 14 Squadron: FTR to LG.116, engines cut with lack of fuel, force-landed in desert behind enemy line; S/Ldr A. Mills, Sgt R. Ey RAAF and Sgt J. Hunt RAAF walked E for nine days until rescued by British Army armoured patrol.
17-03-1942	T2124 14 Squadron: collided with Z7991 (below) while forming up over LG.140 for shipping strike and crashed near Bir-el-Baheira; Sgt R. Good RAAF, Sgt J. Windmill and Sgt W. Godly RAAF KIA, buried in Tobruk War Cemetery.
17-03-1942	Z7991 14 Squadron: collided with T2124 (above) while forming up over LG.140 for shipping strike and crashed near Bir-el-Baheira; F/Sgt R. Linley, Sgt A. Humphries RAAF and Sgt T. Smail RAAF KIA, buried in Tobruk War Cemetery.
19-03-1942	Z5893 14 Squadron: climbed too steeply after night take-off at LG.116 for raid on Crete, stalled and crashed; Sgt P. Munyard RAAF (WOp/Ag) killed, Sgt C. Bowling RAAF (Pilot) and Sgt W. MacMichael RAAF (Obs) injured, latter died a few hours later, both crewmen buried in Alamein War Cemetery.
20-03-1942	L9418 14 Squadron: crashed on take-off at LG.116 for raid on Crete, struck oil drums on boundary, damaged elevators, control lost and crashed; Sgt K. Dee, Sgt H. Marshall and Sgt J. Du Boulay, all RAAF, seriously injured.
26-03-1942	Z6421 203 Squadron: FTR, engine cut on shipping patrol, ditched; crew not found despite search, F/Lt V. Green, Sgt D. Giles RAAF and F/Sgt C. Dawson DFM KIA, commemorated on Alamein Memorial.
30-03-1942	Z7627 14 Squadron: FTR, shot down in error by Hurricanes into sea; F/Lt H. Keck RAAF, F/Sgt J. Hibbert and F/Sgt G. Rylands KIA, commemorated on Alamein Memorial.
10-04-1942	V6453 14 Squadron: hit wires on night take-off at LG.116 to bomb Maleme airfield, Crete, crash-landed, DBR and SOC 03-06-1942; P/O B. Slade, P/O G. Allingame and Sgt G. Lindschau, all RAAF, uninjured.
10-04-1942	Z9722 14 Squadron: side-slipped into ground after night take-off at LG.116 to bomb Maleme airfield, Crete, DBF; Sgt P. Clauson RAAF (Pilot) killed, Sgt C. Thorne RAAF and Sgt C. Grandfield injured.
10-04-1942	Z7917 15 Squadron SAAF: wing hit ground on take-off for raid from LG.98 in dusty conditions, crashed 1km W of LG; Lt C. Bruton-Simmonds SAAF and 2/Lt A. Jones SAAF injured.
14-04-1942	Z7902 203 Squadron: FTR from shipping recce SW of Crete; F/Lt M. Bowker, Sgt H. Hayes RAAF and F/Sgt C. Parsons RAAF KIA, commemorated on Alamein Memorial.
24-04-1942	V6014 203 Squadron: reported missing on recce sortie off Crete, believed shot down by Me.110s escorting Ju.52s; F/Lt W. Hole, F/O T. Leitch RAAF and F/Sgt D. Rickard KIA, commemorated on Alamein Memorial.
09-06-1942	Z9656 14 Squadron: FTR to LG.116 from night-intruder sortie to Crete, crashed in desert near the mist-obscured LG; F/O D. Brooks (Pilot) injured, F/O C. Cowan RAAF (Obs) KIA, buried in Alamein War Cemetery, P/O Hickman (WOp/Ag) injured.
15-06-1942	Z9795 14 Squadron: FTR, became lost on return from raid to Crete as no flare-path lit at LG.10 due to air-raid, crash-landed in desert; S/Ldr A. Pirie, P/O H. Ridley and Sgt A. Payne made their way back to base. (Ridley and Payne rescued by Z6425, which burst a tyre on desert take-off and crashed on landing – see Appendix 5.)
19-06-1942	Z7516 14 Squadron: engine cut on take-off at LG.116 for night intruder sortie to Crete, and u/c collapsed on single-engine landing; P/O B. Slade, P/O G. Allingame, and Sgt G. Lindschau, all RAAF, safe.
27-06-1942	Z9827 203 Squadron: crash-landed at LG.106 on return from shipping search off Crete, DBR and SOC 09-08-1942; P/O L. Harvey, P/O H. Jarman RAAF and Sgt Macintosh uninjured.
27-06-1942	Z9746 14 Squadron: DBR on ground at LG.116 by strafing Me.110, SOC 29-06-1942.
28-06-1942	Z7785 W Desert Com Flt: abandoned on evacuation of LG.04.
04-07-1942	T2389 14 Squadron: FTR to LG.97 from raid on Maaten Bagush airfield, engine failed on return trip, crash-landed in desert 133km W of Wadi Natrum; all-RAAF crew Sgt T. Russell, Sgt F. Dyson and Sgt W. Nicholas took three days to walk back to base.
06-07-1942	Z7712 14 Squadron: FTR, damaged during attack on MT near Fuka, crash-landed in desert; S/Ldr A. Pirie (Pilot) and Sgt J. Beckett RCAF (Obs) unhurt, Sgt W. Bartholomew (WOp/Ag) KIA, buried in El Alamein War Cemetery.

14-07-1942   Z7847 203 Squadron: FTR from shipping search, abandoned in air when lost on return 60km S of Burg-el-Arab; P/O H. Jarman (injured), P/O E. Bamkin and Sgt G. Broomhall, all RAAF, rescued individually by British Army patrols.

25-07-1942   Z7989 14 Squadron: damaged by flak, wounding Observer and WOp/Ag, u/c collapsed in heavy landing at LG.Y; P/O Lapthorne (Pilot) uninjured, aircraft DBR.

01-08-1942   Z9614 14 Squadron: shot down near Fuka; P/O A. Ellis, Sgt H. Langmaid and Sgt M. German injured and captured, Maurice German believed lost when Italian ship taking him to Europe was sunk.

Appendix 5

Non-operational Blenheim losses, 1942

All aircraft are Mk IVs, apart from the Mk Is indicated. For Mk V losses in 1942 see the Appendices to Chapter 28. For Mk V losses in 1943 to 1945 see Appendices to Chapter 31.

03-01-1942   N3581 45 Squadron: crash-landed in sandstorm near Sidi Bu Amud; crew uninjured.

04-01-1942   Z7588 45 Squadron: stalled on take-off on short ferry flight and hit ground at Heliopolis; F/O C. Head (solo Pilot) killed, buried in Heliopolis War Cemetery.

10-01-1942   Z9541 203 Squadron: engine cut on 'Prang' recce patrol, lost height, belly-landed 14km W of Tobruk; F/O V. Green injured, crew safe.

15-01-1942   Z7584 55 Squadron: engine cut, hit ridge and crashed attempting forced-landing near Giovanni Berta, Libya; F/O A. Walker, Sgt Grant and Sgt Lewis safe.

17-01-1942   Z7512 55 Squadron: overshot landing ground at Berka and crashed, DBR; Sgt G. Corbett, Sgt I. Stark and Sgt G. Souter safe. (See also 02-02-1942)

17-01-1942   Z7880 13 (H) Squadron: u/c jammed, crash-landed at LG.86, DBR.

25-01-1942   V6244 55 Squadron: port engine seized and lost prop, aircraft crash-landed near Appollonia, Libya; Sgt R. Payne RAAF, Sgt L. Wheeler and Sgt G. Sparrow destroyed aircraft 'owing to the enemy being in the vicinity'.

28-01-1942   V5899 11 Squadron: engine cut on ferry flight, crashed near Mechili.

30-01-1942   N3581 14 Squadron: crash-landed in sandstorm near Bu Amud, DBR; RAAF crew P/O E. Christansen, Sgt B. Pierse and Sgt R. Hilditch unhurt.

02-02-1942   Z6076 55 Squadron: engine cut in severe sandstorm, crash-landed 10 miles from LG.121; Sgt G. Corbett, Sgt I. Stark and Sgt G. Souter uninjured.

03-02-1942   Z7854 40 Squadron SAAF; ran out of fuel on delivery flight to Burg el Arab, force-landed in sandstorm, hit ditch and overturned. 40 Squadron SAAF had Hurricanes at the time.

08-02-1942   Z7595 55 Squadron: engine cut, overshot landing at LG.17 and DBR; P/O A. Archer RAAF unhurt.

09-02-1942   V6364 55 Squadron: engine seized, lost propeller, crash-landed 7 miles E of Halfya, Libya; Sgt T. Howard safe.

10-02-1942   Z9541 203 Squadron: engine cut, lost height, belly-landed 14km W of Tobruk; crew slightly injured.

19-02-1942   R3872 11 Squadron: crashed 90km W of Mersa Matruh, cause not known; Sgt J. Small, Sgt H. Clements and Sgt W. Wheeler, all RAAF, killed, commemorated on Alamein Memorial.

25-02-1942   V6074 55 Squadron: engine cut, lost height, belly-landed near Qasaba; Sgt H. Anderson RCAF and crew safe.

28-02-1942   V5870 15 Squadron SAAF: on Blenheim conversion, engine cut, crashed near Amriya; Major J. de Wet SAAF and Capt B. Hutchinson SAAF safe. (See 'Kufra Tragedy' on 04-05-1942 below.)

02-03-1942   Z5864 15 Squadron SAAF: on Blenheim conversion, engine cut, prop detached, belly-landed near LG.29; 2/Lt J. Reid SAAF (solo Pilot) unhurt.

03-03-1942   Z7908 14 Squadron: collided with V6184 during formation practice near LG.116, crash-landed and DBR; S/Ldr L. Leon injured, F/Sgt J. Hibbert and F/Sgt G. Rylands unhurt. V6184 landed, repaired, passed to Groupe Lorraine.

04-03-1942   Z6437 55 Squadron: engine cut, lost height, belly-landed near LG.121; F/Sgt J. Campbell uninjured.

04-03-1942   Z7893 14 Squadron: undershot landing at LG.116, turned steeply on approach, hit Officers Mess tent and crashed, DBF; F/O J. Harvie RAAF (Pilot) killed, buried in Alamein War Cemetery.

10-03-1942   T2387 14 Squadron: FTR to LG.99, seen by two other 14 Squadron Blenheims to force-land in desert, crew safe, rescued later.

18-03-1942   Z5886 14 Squadron: struck oil drum on take-off at LG.116, damaged u/c, landed with it partly retracted, DBR; crew injured.

02-04-1942   V5950 14 Squadron: engine cut on take-off at LG.116, u/c raised to stop, DBR; Sgt G. Clarke-Hall, Sgt W. Bethune, and Sgt E. Clarke, all RAAF, safe.

04-04-1942   Z6367 203 Squadron: tyre burst on landing at LG.05, swung and u/c collapsed, DBR; P/O J. Foster and crew unhurt.

18-04-1942	T2243 15 Squadron SAAF: engine cut, undershot forced-landing at LG.99, DBR; Lt J. Whittle SAAF and crew unhurt.
18-04-1942	Z7963 14 Squadron: crashed in attempted forced-landing in haze near Sidi Barrani; 2/Lt P. Chapman SAAF, Sgt D. McConville RAAF and Sgt R. Richardson RAAF killed, buried in Halfya Sollum War Cemetery.
22-04-1942	Z7506 11 Squadron: took off from Helwan, flew into hill in bad weather near Gazkanda and DBF; S/Ldr J. Bouwens killed, ORB does not record fate of crew.
25-04-1942	Z6440 with 51 Repair and Salvage Unit: crashed at Qasaba, NFD.
04-05-1942	Z7513, Z7610 and T2252, 15 Squadron SAAF: based at Kufra, captained by Major J. de Wet, Lt J. Pienaar and 2/Lt L. Wessels, became lost and force-landed in desert. The three Officer Pilots, three Officer Observers, 2/Lts J. du Toit, H. Reed and H. Pienaar, together with three Air Sergeant WOp/Ags W. Olivier, A. Voss and S. Shipman, and two Air Mechanics R. Swanepoel and C. van Breda, all died of dehydration, Air Mechanic Noel Jool was only survivor (Z7513 abandoned in desert – see illustration below). Z7610 and T2252 recovered to Kufra, but Z7610 left there and SOC 1-12-1942.)
07-05-1942	L8529 13 (H) Squadron Mk I: belly-landed in error at LG.86 on training sortie, DBR; P/O W. Chubb (Instructor) and F/O J. Kipouros RHAF (Trainee Pilot) safe.
13-05-1942	Z9666 13 (H) Squadron: engine failed, crash-landed near LG.106; crew safe.
16-05-1942	V5446 14 Squadron: engine cut, crashed attempting forced-landing in desert; no injuries to crew reported.
18-05-1942	V5951 13 (H) Squadron: one flap jammed up, wing hit ground on landing at LG.86; P/O P. Karayannis RHAF and 2/Lt D. Repas RHN safe, F/Sgt A. Gounelakis RHAF injured.
29-05-1942	T2252 15 Squadron SAAF: engine cut after take-off at Kufra, crash-landed in desert; Lt C. Harrison SAAF safe. (One of aircraft recovered from 'Kufra Tragedy' of 04-05-1942.)
08-06-1942	Z7419 14 Squadron: hit sand-hill when low-flying and crash-landed near Maaten Bagush; no injuries reported to Sgt J. Burt or crew.
09-06-1942	Z9656 14 Squadron: missed flare-path in heavy mist on return to LG.116, crashed nearby at 0330; F/O D. Brooks (Pilot) injured, F/O C. Cowan RAAF (Obs) killed, P/O Hickman (WOp/Ag) injured.

Z7513 of Major de Wet, one of three 15 Squadron SAAF Mk IV-Fs that force-landed in the desert on 4 May 1942 some 150 miles east of Kufra, causing the deaths of 11 crewmen (see account in the text). It was photographed there in February 1959, almost 17 years later but has since been stripped down and only the main spar remains.

12-06-1942	V5582 14 Squadron: stalled on night landing at LG.116 and u/c collapsed, DBR; Sgt T. Bullock uninjured.
13-06-1942	Z6044 14 Squadron: became lost on night-flying practice, returned to Mersa Matruh Beacon as no flare-path at LG.10 due to air-raid, aircraft not seen again; Sgt C. Leaver, F/Sgt H. Powell and Sgt R. Hehir RAAF KIA, commemorated on Alamein Memorial.
13-06-1942	Z7517 14 Squadron: lost in same circumstances as Z6044 above, wreckage discovered two days later; Sgt G. Highman, Sgt W. Lynch and Sgt W. Carnie, all RAAF, KIA, commemorated on Alamein Memorial.
15-06-1942	Z6425 14 Squadron: landed with burst tyre at LG.116, u/c collapsed, DBR; Sgt J. Elliott RAAF, Sgt C. Davies, and Sgt C. Simmonds, together with P/O H. Ridley and Sgt A. Payne (rescued from Z9795 lost in desert on return from raid on Crete) uninjured.
30-06-1942	Z7485 14 Squadron: hit by Kittyhawk AK753 while parked at LG.97 and DBR; Cpl H. Gubbins, working on aircraft, killed.
06-07-1942	Z9740 13 (H) Squadron: engine cut on take-off at LG.207, crashed, NFD.
09-07-1942	V6021 14 Squadron: crashed on night take-off at Abu Sueir, DBF; all-RAAF crew, P/O B. Armstrong (Pilot) and F/O J. Maurin-Bonnemain (Obs) killed, buried in Tel-el-Kebir War Cemetery, P/O R. McCawley (WOp/Ag) injured.
11-07-1942	Z9793 13 (H) Squadron: crashed on take-off at LG.Y, NFD.
14-07-1942	Z7847 203 Squadron: failed to locate LG.226 at night or obtain bearings; P/O H. Jarman, P/O E. Bamkin and Sgt H. Broomhall abandoned aircraft, rescued individually by Army patrols 60km S of Burg-el-Arab, Pilot injured.
19-07-1942	Z6428 14 Squadron: engine cut, crash-landed near LG.88, DBR; Sgt Russell injured.
31-07-1942	V6186 with 114 MU: engine cut on take-off at Wadi Seidna, swung and crashed, DBR.
01-08-1942	L4825 211 Squadron Mk I: suffered Cat E Damage, SOC, NFD.
31-08-1942	L1542 84 Squadron Mk I: DBR in accident, NFD.
31-08-1942	L8541 211 Squadron Mk I: crashed in desert, NFD.
06-09-1942	V6466 203 Squadron: u/c leg jammed, belly-landed at LG.X, DBR; Sgt A. Grayson, Sgt Wilcox and Sgt Drysdale unhurt.
18-09-1942	V6231 14 Squadron: engine cut, crash-landed on rough ground near Sollum, not repaired, crew safe.
22-09-1942	T2349 15 Squadron SAAF: engine cut, crash-landed near Kufra; Lt B. MacLeod (Pilot) safe, Lt M. Friday (Obs) injured, Air Sgt H. Lewis (WOp/Ag) safe.
18-11-1942	Z9720 272 Squadron: engine cut on take-off at Gianaclis, crash-landed, DBR; P/O M. Scantlebury injured.
20-11-1942	Z7920 with 55 Repair & Salvage Unit: engine cut on take-off at Gianaclis, crash-landed; no injuries reported.
22-12-1942	T2127 14 Squadron: engine cut on take-off at Gambut, wing hit ground and aircraft crashed; P/O P. Goode, P/O C. Hargreaves and F/O E. Burdon DFC safe.
30-12-1942	T2049 13 (H) Squadron: engine cut on take-off at Gambut, stalled and crashed, DBF.

Appendix 6

Blenheim losses in East Africa, Red Sea and Gulf areas, 1941 and 1942

All aircraft are Mk IVs, apart from the Mk Is noted. For Mk V losses in these areas during 1942 see Appendices in Chapter 28. For Mk V losses in these areas in 1943 to 1945 see Appendices in Chapter 31.

1941

12-01-1941	T2181 14 Squadron: RTB (Port Sudan) from raid to Asmera airfield, Eritrea, with engine failure; Sgt G. Dickson and crew safe, aircraft struck by taxying N3557 on 14-01-1941 and DBR.
16-01-1941	L8456 8 Squadron Mk I: damaged in action, crash-landed near Ras el Bir, Djibouti; F/O K. Laurence, Sgt W. Tamlin DFM and Sgt Houston interned by French but escaped and returned to Squadron on 23-04-1941, aircraft DBR.
21-01-1941	T1868 14 Squadron: on returning to Port Sudan from sortie to Eritrea landed on soft ground, u/c collapsed, DBR; Sgt W. Martin, Sgt A. Hams and Sgt K. Bamber uninjured.
04-02-1941	T2115 14 Squadron: based at Port Sudan, bombed MT at Keren, attacked by Hurricanes, crash-landed at Teklezan; F/O M. MacKenzie, Sgt Farrell and Sgt McConnell safe.
08-02-1941	T1818 14 Squadron: FTR to Port Sudan, shot down by flak at Asmara, Eritrea; four-man crew P/O P. Renniker, P/O H. Turney, Sgt F. Roy and P/O T. Scorror KIA, buried in Asmara War Cemetery, Eritrea.
18-02-1941	T2053 203 Squadron: FTR to Khormaksar from sortie to Makala; S/Ldr A. Solano (Pilot) and Sgt R. Rushton (WOp/Ag) KIA, Sgt E. Sutton (Obs) survived.

18-02-1941	L9173 203 Squadron: damaged while strafing Makele airfield, Ethiopia, DBR in flapless belly-landing at Khormaksar; F/Lt B. Scott, Sgt R. Harding and Sgt D. Bushell uninjured.
09-03-1941	L8504 8 Squadron Mk I: damaged by CR.42s in raid on Dire Dawa airfield, force-landed on Perim Island, Yemen, DBR; S/Ldr T. Hanlon and P/O F. Martin DFC safe, Sgt D. Muir injured.
28-03-1941	T2255 203 Squadron: FTR to Khormaksar, shot down by ground fire over Awash/Adama road; F/O P. Moller, Sgt G. Salisbury and Sgt W. Davidson KIA, commemorated on Alamein Memorial.
31-03-1941	L8433 8 Squadron Mk I: FTR, shot down by fighters near Dessie, Ethiopia; P/O J. Barke (Pilot) and Sgt R. Scott (Obs) injured but baled out, became PoWs, Sgt G. Moore (WOp/Ag) KIA, buried in Addis Ababa War Cemetery.
01-04-1941	L9316 203 Squadron: damaged by light AA while ground strafing, set on fire; P/O J. Wilson (WOp/Ag), P/O J. Tweedie (Pilot) and Sgt W. Thynne (Obs) uninjured, extinguished flames, aircraft repaired.
18-04-1941	V5643 Khartoum Coms Flt: engine cut, crash-landed at Klebkabayen, Sudan; F/O J. Whelan safe.
27-06-1941	T2239 with 102 MU: engine cut on take-off at Abu Sueir, hit bank, DBR.
30-07-1941	L9335 84 Squadron: struck hangar low-flying on Army Co-Op sortie, crash-landed, DBF; Sgt W. Chambers, Sgt G. Bell and Sgt Goodwell injured.
18-08-1941	Z6365 8 Squadron: engine cut on approach to Asmara, Eritrea, stalled and crashed on landing; W/Cdr E. Shipley safe.
22-08-1941	L8518 8 Squadron Mk I: tyre burst on landing at Perim Island, Red Sea, u/c collapsed, DBR; P/O B. Fihelly RAAF and crew safe.
01-09-1941	L8505 8 Squadron Mk I: swung after take-off from Khormaksar, Aden, hit sea and overturned; Sgt R. Edwards RAAF, Sgt F. Harrison and Sgt J. Cooper, together with two passengers, Mr Oliver and Mr Lendrum, injured.
05-09-1941	T1877 with 102 MU: engine cut on take-off at Abu Sueir, wing hit ground, crashed, DBR; Sgt J. Hutchinson unhurt.
10-09-1941	R3894 8 Squadron: u/c jammed up, belly-landed at Khormaksar, DBR; F/O J. Owen unhurt.
25-09-1941	V6222 8 Squadron: control lost and crashed into sea 40 miles S of Aden on radar calibration sortie; Sgt A. White, Sgt J. Stoddard and Sgt E. Message KIA, commemorated on Alamein Memorial.
10-10-1941	Z6149 8 Squadron Mk I-F: u/c damaged on take-off at Khormaksar, jammed, belly-landed, DBR; P/O J. Brownless RAAF and crew unhurt.
17-11-1941	V6290 8 Squadron: hit truck on take-off at Khormaksar, caught fire in air, crash-landed; crew P/O D. Pitt RAAF, Sgt F. Saban and Sgt P. McQuirk (injured) escaped, two airmen in lorry, LAC E. Darby and AC2 J. Wright, killed. Anti-sub bombs detonated as aircraft burned.
30-11-1941	Z7589 W Desert Com Flt: shot down by 'friendly' AA fire and crashed near Gialo Oasis, Sudan; W/Cdr A. McD. Bowman, F/Sgt J. McLaren(Wop/Ag), Gp Cpt C. Dearlove, and Capt F.Benn (Army passenger) killed, commemorated on Alamein Memorial.
12-12-1941	P4863 6 Squadron: engine cut, force-landed with u/c unlocked near Wadi Halfa, Sudan, DBR; P/O W. Griffiths and crew safe.
12-12-1941	L4901 8 Squadron Mk I: engine cut on test flight overshot landing and swung, u/c collapsed, Massawa; Sgt G. Doube RAAF and ground-crew passenger safe.

1942 (including Iraq, Iran, Syria, Palestine and Persian Gulf areas)

12-01-1942	Z9671 with 117 MU: crashed in forced-landing in bad visibility at Gebeit, Sudan; P/O M. Fitzherbert and Sgt W. Marsh, and Sgt G. Dunn uninjured.
18-03-1942	Z6381 with British Airways Repair Unit, Heliopolis: engine caught fire on ground, aircraft DBF.
29-04-1942	V5508 162 ECM Squadron: stalled on approach to Idku, Egypt, dived into ground and DBF; Sgt J. Jessett (WOp/Ag) killed, buried in Hadra (Alexandria) War Cemetery, S/Ldr D. Warren (Pilot) and P/O N. King (Obs) injured.
04-05-1942	Z7906 8 Squadron: engine failed on bombing practice, ditched on approach to Khormaksar; F/Lt W. Adams (Pilot) safe, P/O L. Sweeney (Obs) injured.
09-05-1942	L8363 8 Squadron: swung on landing at Khormaksar, u/c collapsed, DBR; P/O D. Sutherland (solo Pilot) unhurt.
11-05-1942	Z7288 with 108 MU: struck by Wellington Z8518 and DBR while parked at Kilo 17 airfield, Cairo.
24-06-1942	V5681 with OADU: crashed in Iraq on ferry flight to Far East, NFD.
30-06-1942	V6015 162 Squadron: hit trees on take-off at Bilbeis and crashed, DBF; Sgt A. Thompson and Sgt W. Bower, together ground-crew passengers Cpl A. Beard and AC1 L. Ross, injured.
30-06-1942	Z7879 203 Squadron: engine cut on take-off at Abu Sueir, stalled and spun in, DBF; F/O R. Firth (Pilot) and Sgt L. Hulme (Obs) killed, Sgt M. Jones (WOp/Ag) seriously injured.
03-07-1942	Z7364 203 Squadron: overshot landing at Heliopolis, u/c raised to stop, DBR; P/O R. Hemsted and Sgt Evans safe.

15-07-1942	Z7920 8 Squadron: FTR, shot down by flak near Djibouti, French Somaliland; P/O L. Maguire, Sgt V. Sennett and Sgt F. Channon KIA.
19-07-1942	V5590 ADU: crashed 10 miles SW of Falluja, Iraq, on ferry flight, cause unknown; Sgt N. MacAuliffe died of injuries two days later, buried at Habbaniyah.
24-07-1942	Z9750 8 Squadron: engine cut, crash-landed at Riyan LG, Aden, DBR; no injuries reported to P/O H, Parfett or crew.
31-07-1942	V6186 with 114 MU: engine cut on take-off at Wadi Seidna, swung and crashed, DBR.
02-08-1942	Z7594 Khartoum Com Flt: hit ground in sandstorm on ferry flight W of Statur, Sudan, to 15 Squadron SAAF; Sgt W. Burns RNZAF, F/Sgt J. Speakman and Sgt R. Simkin killed, buried in sand nearby, graves not found, commemorated on Alamein Memorial.
08-08-1942	V6468 Khartoum Com Flt: crashed in forced-landing in bad weather near Adi-Ugri, Ethiopia; Sgt R. Davidson, Sgt A. Wintle and AC1 G. Clapham injured.
19-08-1942	Z9724 244 Squadron: FTR to Sharjah, engine failed, crash-landed at Sharjah Creek; W/O F. Evans injured, Sgt F. Graham and Sgt E. Corbett safe.
24-08-1942	V6149 13 (H) Squadron: engine cut on ferry flight, crashed in force-landing at St Jean, Palestine; P/O E. Marairas RHAF and crew safe.
01-09-1942	Z9794 8 Squadron: u/c collapsed in heavy landing at dusk, Bender Cassim, Somalia, DBR; F/Sgt K. Richards RAAF and crew safe.
01-09-1942	V6298 with 103 MU: engine caught fire on approach at Idku.
02-09-1942	V6325 8 Squadron: F/O W. Rosevear RAAF swung on landing on rough ground at Bender Cassim, Somalia, aircraft DBR, SOC 02-11-1942.
04-09-1942	Z7845 8 Squadron: FTR to Khormaksar from convoy escort over Red Sea, presumed ditched; Sgt A. Williams, Sgt R. McDowell and Sgt G. Green KIA, commemorated on Alamein Memorial.
13-09-1942	Z9548 1438 Flt: engine cut, belly-landed at Aleppo, Syria; F/Lt Griffiths and F/O Dale injured.
15-09-1942	Z7921 244 Squadron: tyre burst on landing at Sharjah, Persian Gulf, swung and u/c collapsed, DBR; Sgt G. Browning, P/O J. Drinkwater and Sgt Welch safe.
15-09-1942	Z9734 244 Squadron: crashed on take-off at Sharjah for anti-submarine patrol, NFD.
17-09-1942	Z7418 244 Squadron: FTR to Sharjah from anti-sub patrol over Gulf of Oman, wreckage found at sea; Sgt H. McGowan RAAF, P/O A. Pontius and Sgt A. Genny KIA, commemorated on Alamein Memorial.
27-09-1942	Z6454 13 (H) Squadron: engine cut on take-off at Gaza East, Palestine, swung and crashed, DBF; P/O G. Pattas RHAF (solo Pilot) escaped uninjured.
01-10-1942	Z9621 8 Squadron: engine cut on take-of at Riyan, Aden, for convoy escort, stalled and crashed; Sgt G. Lowe, Sgt H. Schnell and Sgt B. Bridges injured.
03-10-1942	Z7633 1434 Flight: engine cut on PR sortie from Teheran, belly-landed at Madjidabad, Iran; S/Ldr F. Dobell and Sgt S. Phillips safe.
04-10-1942	Z7514 14 Squadron: cooling gills jammed open, u/c collapsed in heavy landing at Luxor on ferry flight to 103 MU; P/O C. Thomas unhurt.
05-10-1942	Z9665 203 Squadron: FTR from shipping patrol (Port Said to Haifa), presumed ditched, no trace found despite searches; F/Sgt J. Halley, F/O A. Henderson and Sgt S. Hunt KIA, commemorated on Alamein Memorial.
08-10-1942	T2393, ex-113 Squadron: passed to RSU at Qasaba 23-12-1941, crashed in Iraq, NFD.
13-10-1942	Z9615 52 Squadron: engine cut just after take-off at Mosul, Iraq, crashed nearby, DBF; Sgt T. Pritchard, Sgt G. Spark and Sgt J. Keer KIA, buried in Mosul War Cemetery.
26-10-1942	P6931 244 Squadron: tyre burst on take-off at Sharjah, swung and u/c collapsed, DBR; P/O D. Brown, P/O Goodale and Sgt Gulliford safe.
27-10-1942	T2251 W Desert Com Unit: ran into soft sand on landing at Ras Gharib, Egypt, and tipped up; Sgt J. Hall and crew unhurt.
02-11-1942	V5945 52 Squadron; both engines cut due to fuel mismanagement, crashed in forced-landing near Mosul; Sgt W. Windsor and Sgt T. Stanley injured, Sgt N. Beal and Sgt W. Whittingham RCAF (both WOp/Ags) killed, buried in Mosul War Cemetery.
06-11-1942	R3845 13 (H) Squadron: overshot landing at Gaza East, Palestine, and overturned; P/O G. Costacos RHAF uninjured.
11-11-1942	Z7581 272 Squadron: hit obstruction on take-off at Idku, u/c collapsed on landing, DBR; Sgt D. Broadhead safe. 272 was a Beaufighter Squadron.
25-11-1942	R3901 454 Squadron RAAF: crashed on landing at Qaiyarh, Iraq, on refresher training; Sgt E. McNaughton RNZAF unhurt, aircraft SOC 28-2-1943.
26-11-1942	V5579 Iraq Com Flt: abandoned in air after engine fire on search flight, crashed near Hilla, Iraq; P/O A. McKnight RCAF safe.

Appendix 7

Some Blenheim losses by Free French Units

Aircraft are all Mk IVs. For Mk V losses see Appendices to Chapter 28

14-01-1941   N3557 Free French Flight Sudan: collided with T2181 of 45 Squadron while taxying at Asmera airfield, Eritrea, N3557 repaired, T2181 DBR.

05-02-1941   T1867 GBR 1: based at Ounianga, Chad, bombed Italian-held oasis, became lost over Sahara on return, crash-landed in desert near Libyan border, wreck and remains of crew, Sgt Le Calvez, Lt Claron and Sgt Chef Devin, not found until March 1959 (see the illustration on page 488).

04-04-1941   Z5728 Free French Flight: lost prop and u/c jammed, crash-landed near Sennar, Sudan, DBR; Capt Lager and crew safe.

13-04-1941   N3557 Free French Flight: u/c retracted prematurely on take-off at Gordons Tree, Sudan, sank back and DBR; Sous Lt G. Grassette unhurt.

22-04-1941   Z5727 GBR 1: on flight from Fort Lamy, Chad, to Khartoum, mechanical failure, crash-landed in desert; F/Sgt J. Guillou de Mezillis and F/Sgt J. Bost injured, F/Sgt P. Robinet (Ag/Mech) killed, buried in Moussoro, Chad.

22-05-1941   T1822 Free French Flight: returning from raid on Gondar, Ethiopia, tyre burst on landing at Gordons Tree, u/c collapsed, DBR; W/O R. Jabin and crew safe.

03-06-1941   T1998 GBR 1: on flight from Fort Lamy, Chad, to Khartoum, caught fire and crashed near Debus Weiki, Sudan; F/O C. Souvestre, Capt L. Flury-Herard, F/Sgt A. Devos and Cpl J. Hugon (Mech) killed, buried at El Fasher, Sudan.

06-07-1941   T1819 Free French (Bomber) Flight 1: engine cut, force-landed at Rufaah, Sudan; Capt P. de St Pereuse uninjured.

19-06-1941   T1935 GBR 1: en route from Bangui, Central African Republic, to Brazzaville, Congo, crashed into forest in tropical storm; F/O J. Hirlemann (Pilot), P/O G. Bequart (Obs) and F/O B. Crouzet (passenger) killed, Sgt P. Grasset (WOp/Ag) injured but survived.

02-10-1941   T1855 GBR 1: crashed on paratroop familiarisation flight, believed due to engine failure at low level, near Darayya, Syria; P/O D. Neumann (Pilot) and three Army passengers killed.

28-11-1941   V6142 Lorraine Squadron: FTR, shot down by Me.109 of 1/JG 27 in raid on Gazalla, crashed in desert; Sgt Major R. Jabin and crew injured and captured, Lt C. Maisonneuve (Obs) died of injuries, Sgt Chef H. Bruneau (WOp/Ag) survived.

04-12-1941   Z9725 Lorraine Squadron: crashed on take-off at LG.75 with V5991 of 55 Squadron (see Appendix 2); Sgt G. Fifre, Sgt P. de Maismont and Sgt A. Soulat seriously injured, Pilot dying of injuries.

04-12-1941   Z9572 Lorraine Squadron: also DBR in above incident, crew safe.

06-12-1941   V6503 Lorraine Squadron: shot down by Me.109 of 4/JG 27; F/O R. Sandre, P/O A. de Meltcharski and Sgt A. Lann KIA. V6495 also lost on this raid.

20-12-1941   L8832 Lorraine Squadron: shot down in flames by Me.109s near Barce; F/Sgt J. Redor, F/O M. du Boisouvray and F/Sgt J. Perbost KIA.

20-12-1941   V6505 Lorraine Squadron: shot down in flames by Me.109s near Barce; Sgt J. Delcros (WOp/Ag) KIA, Lt Col C. Pijeaud (Pilot, CO of GB Lorraine) baled out, blinded and badly burned, rescued but died three weeks later, P/O G. Guigonis (Obs) baled out and evaded capture.

04-03-1942   T1817 Lorraine Squadron: destroyed in accident, NFD.

13-07-1942   V6293 Lorraine Squadron: tyre burst on take-off at Wadi Seidna, crashed and DBF.

29-10-1942   T1875 BA Bangui FAFL: engine failed on air test from Bangui, Central African Republic, crashed; P/O H. Soubabere FAFL (Pilot) and Cpl L. Tartenson FAFL (Mech) killed, two Army passengers seriously injured.

Appendix 8

Blenheim losses by Middle East Command Training Units

Aircraft are all Mk IVs apart from the Mk Is indicated.
For Mk V losses during 1942 see Appendices to Chapter 28.
For Mk V losses during 1943 to 1945 see Appendices to Chapter 32.

15-02-1941   L8467 70 OTU Mk I: dived into ground after night take-off at LG.102; Sgt S. Barbour and Sgt T. Gill killed, buried in Ismailia War Cemetery, Egypt.

14-03-1941   L8464 70 OTU Mk I: became lost in sandstorm, belly-landed near Nafishah; Sgt E. McLelland (solo Pilot) safe.

14-03-1941   L6664 70 OTU Mk I: ran out of fuel while lost in sandstorm, overshot attempted forced-landing near Port Said; Sgt R. Ibbotson and Sgt J. Haslop RNZAF killed, buried in Ismailia War Cemetery, Egypt.

05-04-1941   L8445 70 OTU Mk I: hit cables on take-off and crash-landed, Ismailia; Sgt T. Fullerton uninjured.

20-05-1941   L4919 70 OTU Mk I: hit trees on take-off at Ismailia, belly-landed on return; Sgt J. Willis and crew uninjured.

21-05-1941   L8481 70 OTU Mk I: engine cut, spun in 12 miles W of Ismailia; Sgt F. Lucie injured, Sgt R. Dowse RAAF killed, Sgt K. Duffin RAAF injured.

31-05-1941   L8435 70 OTU Mk I: engine cut, belly-landed at Ismailia, DBR.

31-05-1941   L8525 70 OTU Mk I: tyre burst on take-off at Ismailia, swung and crashed.

06-06-1941   L1498 70 OTU Mk I: stalled on attempted overshoot and crashed, Ismailia; Sgt C. Bessen RAAF (solo Pilot) injured.

12-06-1941   L4830 70 OTU Mk I: stalled on take-off and dived into ground, Ismailia; Sgt M. Crombie RAAF (solo Pilot) killed, buried in Ismailia War Cemetery.

16-06-1941   L8473 70 OTU Mk I: engine cut after take-off, stalled on s/e approach and hit ground, DBF; LAC F. Helberg (trainee Pilot) killed.

16-06-1941   L8477 70 OTU Mk I: crashed and DBR, NFD.

20-06-1941   L1536 70 OTU Mk I: hit telegraph pole on take-off at Ismailia, crashed, DBR; no injuries reported to F/Lt S. Lee RAAF or crew.

07-09-1941   V6242 70 OTU: engine cut on NavEx, force-landed at Makindu Station, 95 miles SE of Nairobi, DBR; S/Ldr D. Bennett and Lt R. Barry (SAAF Met Officer) injured.

21-09-1941   K7099 70 OTU Mk I: overshot landing and hit ditch, Nakuru.

28-09-1941   Z6366 70 OTU: u/c raised prematurely on take-off, crash-landed at Wadi Gazouza.

30-09-1941   V5880 70 OTU: engine cut, lost height and belly-landed 10 miles S of Nakuru.

12-10-1941   V5694 70 OTU: tyre burst on take-off at Nakuru, swung and u/c collapsed.

16-10-1941   V5693 70 OTU: engine cut in formation practice, lost height, hit tree in attempted forced landing, DBF, Nyeri, Kenya; Sgt A. Shea RAAF (solo Pilot) killed, buried in Nakuru War Cemetery.

24-10-1941   V6297 70 OTU: control lost, dived into Lake Victoria.

04-11-1941   Z6159 70 OTU: swung on landing at Nakuru and u/c collapsed; Sgt J. Wotherspoon (solo Pilot) unhurt.

10-11-1941   V6144 72 OTU: both engines cut due to fuel mismanagement, crashed in attempted forced-landing at night at Turabi, Sudan; Sgt S. Prentice RAAF, Sgt B. Engall, Sgt A. Thomas RCAF and Sgt W. Stevenson (passenger) injured.

10-11-1941   L8403 72 OTU Mk I: crashed and DBR, NFD.

17-11-1941   Z7505 70 OTU: tyre burst on take-off at Nakuru for circuits and landings, swung and u/c collapsed; Sgt J. Mitchell RAAF (solo Pilot) uninjured.

19-11-1941   V6463 70 OTU: hit mast of dhow on Lake Victoria and ditched; Sgt H. Booth, Sgt J. Gibson, and Sgt Hulm injured but rescued.

21-11-1941   V6308 70 OTU: tyre burst on take-off at Nakuru, u/c collapsed; P/O E. Christensen RAAF (solo Pilot) safe.

24-11-1941   Z6158 70 OTU: engine cut on take-off at Nakuru, swung and hit boundary; Sgt A. Nichols RAAF (solo Pilot) unhurt.

25-11-1941   Z9612 72 OTU: u/c struck sand dune on approach to Wadi Gazouza, crashed and DBF; Sgt J. Skinner, Sgt C. Dunstone and Sgt J. Thomson, all RAAF, killed, buried in Khartoum War Cemetery, Sudan.

26-11-1941   V6299 70 OTU: hit tree on low-flying practice and crashed at Kampiya Moto; Sgt R. Hutton RAAF (solo Pilot) killed, buried Nakuru.

29-11-1941   Z9539 72 OTU: FTR from NavEx over Red Sea Hills, crew Sgt A. Longmore, Sgt A. Nourse and Sgt S. Thompson, all RAAF, rescued safely but crashed on the same NavEx one month later.

30-11-1941	Z9587 70 OTU: destroyed by fire in maintenance hangar, Nakuru.
06-12-1941	V6494 70 OTU: engine cut, crashed in attempted forced-landing at Engo Shura-Tembuki; Sgt Campbell uninjured.
10-12-1941	L9298 70 OTU: control lost in cloud; Sgt L. Gardner and Sgt Booth, both RAAF, baled out safely 3 miles W of Nakuru.
15-12-1941	V6190 70 OTU: tyre burst on take-off at Nakuru, swung and u/c collapsed.
17-12-1941	Z7628 72 OTU: missing on night NavEx over Red Sea; crew F/Sgt C. Freeman, P/O A. Smith RCAF and Sgt F. Wheeler RAAF, together with trainees Sgt P. Hussey and F/Sgt W. Armour, lost at sea, commemorated on Alamein Memorial.
18-12-1941	Z7616 72 OTU: ran out of fuel on night NavEx, belly-landed at Port Sudan, DBR.
18-12-1941	V5576 70 OTU: collided with Z6430 (below) and crashed 3 miles W of Nakuru, DBF; F/O A. Darling and Sgt M. Genney killed, buried Nakuru.
18-12-1941	Z6430 70 OTU: collided with V5576 (above) and crash-landed 3 miles W of Nakuru, believed recovered and repaired as SOC 12-05-1942.
21-12-1941	Z6435 70 OTU: tyre burst on take-off at Nakuru, u/c collapsed, DBR; F/Lt M. Rowker and crew safe.
22-12-1941	Z5884 70 OTU: bounced on landing at Nakuru and u/c collapsed; Sgt H. Harrington RAAF (solo Pilot) uninjured.
27-12-1941	V6329 70 OTU: engine cut, lost height, struck high ground near Kampiya Moto and DBF; crew P/O G. Hanson, Sgt B. James injured but escaped, Sgt V. Semler safe, all RAAF.
29-12-1941	Z7577 72 OTU: became lost in bad weather at night, crashed in attempted forced-landing, Keebe Musmar, Sudan; Sgt A. Longmore Sgt A. Nourse and Sgt S. Thompson all RAAF, safe.
30-12-1941	Z9610 70 OTU: tyre burst on take-off at Nakuru, swung and u/c collapsed, DBF; P/O B. Slade, P/O G. Allingame, and Sgt Lindschau, all RAAF, escaped safely.
04-01-1942	Z9650 72 OTU: stalled on landing at Wadi Gazouza with u/c still retracted, DBR; Sgt G. Moore RAAF and crew safe.
07-01-1942	V5539 70 OTU: tyre burst on take-off at Nakuru, swung and u/c collapsed, DBF, crew escaped safely.
11-01-1942	Z9651 72 OTU: taxied into sandhill at night, tipped up, DBR; crew unhurt.
12-01-1942	Z9671 72 OTU: crashed in heavy landing in sandstorm, Gebeit, Sudan, u/c collapsed, DBR; Sgt M. Fitzherbert and Sgt Marsh safe.
17-01-1942	Z7695 72 OTU: collided with L1492 in formation practice when engine cut, crash-landed at Gazouza, DBF; Sgt M. Scope, Sgt C. Pierson and Sgt R. McMillan, all RAAF, injured.
23-01-1942	V6292 70 OTU: engine cut on approach to Nakuru, stalled and spun into ground; Sgt G. Hawkins., P/O F. Allan, and Sgt G. Emery, all RAAF, killed, buried in Nakuru Cemetery, Kenya.
27-01-1942	T2002 72 OTU: overshot night landing at Atbara, DBF.
29-01-1942	L8667 72 OTU Mk I: tyre burst on take-off at Wadi Galouza, swung and u/c collapsed; P/O G. Forder (Instructor) and Lt K. Riddoch SAAF (trainee Pilot) unhurt.
09-02-1942	V6234 70 OTU: tyre burst on landing at Nakuru, swung and u/c collapsed; crew safe.
13-02-1942	N6241 70 OTU: engine cut on take-off at Nakuru, swung and u/c collapsed, crew unhurt.
20-02-1942	Z7772 72 OTU: engine lost power in sandstorm at night, u/c collapsed in attempted forced-landing 15 miles E of Tehilla, Sudan; crew safe.
21-02-1942	Z7777 70 OTU: hit tree while low-flying and cart-wheeled near Menengal, Kenya; Sgt C. Ridgewell, Sgt D. Hutchinson and Sgt C. McAskill RAAF killed, buried in Nakuru War Cemetery.
26-02-1942	V5879 70 OTU: tyre burst on take-off at Nakuru, u/c collapsed.
27-02-1942	L6659 70 OTU Mk I: tyre burst on take-off at Nakuru, swung and u/c collapsed; P/O King (Instructor) and Sgt Macdonald (Pupil Pilot) unhurt.
04-03-1942	V6235 70 OTU: tyre burst on take-off at Nakuru, swung and u/c collapsed.
04-03-1942	Z7778 72 OTU: both engines cut, crash-landed at Erheib, Sudan.
26-03-1942	Z7520 72 OTU: engine cut on take-off, crash-landed at Kosti, Sudan; F/Lt Jones and F/Sgt G. Berrett DFM safe..
27-03-1942	V6243 72 OTU: engine cut, bounced on s/e landing, u/c collapsed, Kosti, Sudan; Lt C. Martin SAAF (solo Pilot) unhurt.
29-03-1942	V5575 70 OTU: engine cut, lost height, crash-landed near Molo, Kenya.
02-04-1942	L8390 72 OTU Mk I: engine cut on take-off, swung into soft ground and tipped up, Soroti, Uganda; 2/Lt C. McBride SAAF safe.
02-04-1942	V6191 70 OTU: u/c jammed on heavy landing, hydraulics lost, crashed on overshoot 7 miles N of Nankuru; 2/Lt H. Ballard SAAF safe, P/O L. Cochrane and Sgt A. Seibold, both RAAF, injured.
05-04-1942	R3732 72 OTU: engine cut, belly-landed near Kosti, Sudan; W/O F. Barker and crew safe, aircraft DBR and SOC 31-08-1942.

07-04-1942   Z7764 72 OTU: engine cut just after take-off, turned and spun in 3 miles from Juba.

08-04-1942   T2392 70 OTU: engine cut, overshot emergency landing at Moi; Sgt D. McDonald and crew safe.

09-04-1942   V5767 72 OTU: engine caught fire in air, crashed attempting forced-landing near Nakuru, DBF; Sgt J. Collyer and crew escaped safely.

10-04-1942   Z7822 72 OTU: engine cut, crashed in attempted forced-landing near Tororo, Uganda.

23-04-1942   V6245 70 OTU: flew into high ground on NavEx in bad weather near Naiursha, Kenya; Sgt R. Daniel, Sgt J. Ahern, and Sgt N. Peters, all RAAF, killed, buried in Gilgil, Kenya.

25-04-1942   Z6440 with 51 Repair & Salvage Unit: crashed at Qasaba.

29-04-1942   V6458 72 OTU: overshot and hit ground, Eastleigh, Kenya, overturned.

07-05-1942   V6296 70 OTU: engine cut, crash-landed near Nanyuki.

11-05-1942   V6220 70 OTU: u/c jammed, belly-landed at Nakuru, not repaired.

11-05-1942   V6326 70 OTU: tyre burst on take-off, u/c collapsed, Nakuru.

15-05-1942   Z6369 70 OTU: flew into Lake Nakuru, Kenya, in flat calm, returned to base but DBR.

26-05-1942   L1520 72 OTU Mk I: engine cut, lost height, belly-landed in desert, Tuqqri.

01-06-1942   L8391 72 OTU Mk I: flew into ground after night take-off at Nanyuki, DBF; Col T. Theron SAAF AFC (solo Pilot) killed, buried in Nanyuki War Cemetery.

02-06-1942   V5469 70 OTU: tyre burst on take-off at Nakuru, swung and u/c damaged, not repaired.

05-06-1942   V6223 70 OTU: flew into ground on night NavEx in cloud at Mbagathi, near Nairobi, Kenya; Sgt L. Hands, Sgt F. Paul and Sgt D. Drake-Brockman, all RAAF, killed and buried in Forest Road Cemetery, Nairobi.

05-06-1942   V6304 70 OTU: ran out of fuel when lost on night NavEx, crash-landed 45 miles N of Nakuru.

06-06-1942   Z9800 70 OTU: engine cut on search for V6304 (above), crash-landed on Mau escarpment; W/O R. Sellers and F/Sgt W. Heath safe, F/Sgt F. Ford injured. 56 goats in native village killed.

11-06-1942   Z6441 72 OTU: hit tree in low-flying practice near Nanyuki and cartwheeled; Lt R. Morkel, 2/Lt A. Paxton and Air Sgt K. Diesel, all SAAF, killed.

20-06-1942   Z7707 70 OTU: engine cut at low level, hit trees, crash-landed 5 miles N of Archer's Post, Kenya; Sgt W. Bowen RAAF (solo Pilot) safe.

20-06-1942   Z7696 72 OTU: both engines cut, stalled and spun in on emergency approach to Nanyuki; P/O L. Dorney killed, 2/Lt W. Chippendall and Air Sgt R. Pepper, both SAAF, seriously injured.

23-06-1942   Z6042 70 OTU: collided with V5630 in formation practice, tail section severed behind turret, crashed near Naivasha, Kenya; Sgt F. Abderhalden baled out safely, Sgt R. McGregor and Sgt J. Balfour killed. V5630 damaged but landed safely.

24-06-1942   V6330 70 OTU: u/c collapsed on heavy landing at Nakuru, not repaired.

28-06-1942   Z7637 72 OTU: hit trees on night approach to Nanyuki, DBF.

29-06-1942   Z9617 72 OTU: dived into ground near Ruiru, Kenya, cause unknown; SAAF crew Lt V. Bissett, 2/Lt R. Bolton, Air Sgt E. Wells and Air Sgt T. Curtis killed, buried in Forest Road Cemetery, Nairobi.

30-06-1942   Z7694 72 OTU: stalled in cloud, crashed near Rongai; SAAF crew 2/Lt C. Castle, 2/Lt K. Fuller, Air Sgt A. Taylor and Air Sgt G. Jones killed.

04-07-1942   V6192 72 OTU: reported missing on a NavEx; Lt F. Rusk, 2/Lt J. Tzamtzis and Air Sgt A. Geyer, all SAAF, presumed killed, commemorated on Alamein Memorial. Wreck discovered 09-01-1943 near Sattima Peak, Aberdare Mountains, with some human remains.

06-07-1942   Z7844 70 OTU: spun into ground out of cloud following engine failure near Tororo, Uganda; Sgt L. Mallows, Sgt L. Dalton RAAF and Sgt R. Wilson RAAF killed, buried in Tororo Cemetery, Uganda.

08-07-1942   Z7781 72 OTU: engine cut, crashed in attempted forced-landing near Baragui, Kenya; SAAF Lts A. Roskilly and L. Udwin killed, buried in Nanyuki War Cemetery.

13-07-1942   K7137 72 OTU Mk I: DBR in heavy landing at Nanyuki.

13-07-1942   V5869 70 OTU: hit tree low-flying and overturned at Isolo, Kenya, DBF; F/O E. Main, P/O H. Elliot and Sgt L. Craven RAAF killed, buried in Nanyuki War Cemetery.

23-07-1942   Z7763 72 OTU: flew into high ground on NavEx in bad visibility near Fort Halloran, Nyeri, Kenya; SAAF crew 2/Lt C. Allen, 2/Lt H. Lemmer, Air Sgt S. Ellestam and Air Sgt L. Murray killed, commemorated on Alamein Memorial. Wreck remained undiscovered until 2002, when human remains were removed for burial.

31-07-1942   V6187 70 OTU: crashed, NFD.

14-08-1942   V6199 72 OTU: engine cut, belly-landed at Maralal, Kenya, not repaired; F/Lt C. Neill and crew safe.

19-08-1942   L8510 70 OTU Mk I: collided with V6327 (below) after take-off at Nakuru and crashed; P/O G. Percival (Pilot) and SAAF Air Mechanics J. Carroll and D. Mulligan killed.

19-08-1942   V6327 70 OTU: collided with L8510 (above) after take-off at Nakuru, u/c torn off, crash-landed; crew only slightly hurt.

19-08-1942	Z9596 70 OTU: engine cut, belly-landed on rough ground at Marsabit, DBF; Sgt F. Price and crew escaped safely.
26-08-1942	V5630 70 OTU: u/c collapsed in heavy landing at Nakuru; Sgt H. Hoyle (solo Pilot) uninjured.
31-08-1942	R3762 72 OTU: engine cut, belly-landed near Kosti, not repaired; crew safe.
19-09-1942	Z6424 70 OTU: flew into ground short of flare-path on night approach at Nakuru.
09-10-1942	L1239 1 Middle East Training School Mk I: u/c collapsed when selected 'up' instead of flaps after landing at El Ballah, DBR; W/O L. Davies unhurt.
16-10-1942	L1492 72 OTU Mk I: dived into ground near Nanyuki, Kenya, cause not known, burned out; Lt W. Steenkamp SAAF (solo Pilot) killed.
18-10-1942	V6230 72 OTU: engine cut on night take-off at Nanyuki, crash-landed and overturned; Sgt A. May and Sgt C. Hoskin RAAF unhurt, Sgt T. Strickland injured, crew all RAAF.
20-10-1942	Z7798 72 OTU: engine cut on take-off at Nanyuki, u/c raised to stop, DBR; P/O A. Honig unhurt.
23-10-1942	V5966 70 OTU: heavy landing caused tyre burst at Nakuru, swung, u/c collapsed, DBF; Lt S. Guard SAAF (solo Pilot) escaped safely.
25-10-1942	Z9678 70 OTU: fumes from port engine entered cockpit, engine turned off, crashed in attempted forced-landing at Kampiya Moto; Sgt A. McGlynn, Sgt H. Hayes, Sgt H. Ferguson RCAF and Sgt T. Campbell all injured.
31-10-1942	V5867 70 OTU: belly-landed in error at Nakuru, DBR; Sgt E. Hay (solo Pilot) unhurt.
04-11-1942	Z6382 70 OTU: swung on crosswind landing at Nakuru and u/c collapsed; Sgt D. Bond RAAF unhurt.
16-11-1942	Z7621 70 OTU: overshot night landing at Nakuru, swung and u/c collapsed; P/O H. Long and Sgt Robinson unhurt.
17-11-1942	Z7628 72 OTU: missing on night NavEx; staff crew F/Sgt C. Freeman, P/O A. Smith RCAF and Sgt F. Wheeler RAAF, together with trainees Sgt P. Hussey and F/Sgt W. Armour, killed, all commemorated on Alamein Memorial.
23-11-1942	Z7679 70 OTU: engine cut, dived into ground attempting forced-landing near Kisumu, DBF; Sgt F. Sinclair RAAF, P/O D. Button, Sgt H. Everett, and P/O L. Thomas (Staff Obs) killed, buried in Kisumu War Cemetery, Kenya..
17-12-1942	L1387 1 METS Mk I: tyre burst on take-off at El Ballah, swung and DBR.
22-12-1942	Z9744 72 OTU: engine cut, hit tree in forced-landing 31km S of Gil Gil, DBF; Sgt I. Bond, Sgt J. Wood and Sgt B. Frogley RNZAF injured.
30-12-1942	Z6430 72 OTU: engine cut, crashed in attempted forced-landing near El Joro, Kenya.

Chapter 27

Malta

The role of the then British island of Malta, situated centrally in the Mediterranean Sea in a strategically invaluable position, was to prove crucial to the outcome of the land battles in the Western Desert and North Africa. Aircraft and naval units based on Malta, which is only 65 miles from Sicily, could help to defend Allied convoys passing through the Mediterranean, and – more importantly – could use aircraft and warships, including submarines, based there to attack Axis shipments of supplies en route to their forces in Africa. Blenheims performed the prime role in the aerial component of these constant attacks, a role both glorious and deadly dangerous, for they paid a terrible price in the process. It seems surprising that, in view of the great strategic importance of the island, so little effort was made in the early stages of the war to provide adequate defences for it. The saga of the six crated FAA Gladiators, left behind when HMS *Glorious* sailed for Norway, and pressed into RAF service – three to achieve fame as 'Faith, Hope and Charity' – is well known. Perhaps it was thought that sufficient protection for Malta could be provided by the Royal Navy, which had used the island as a major base since Nelson's day and which (backed by the large French Navy prior to the collapse of France) ruled the 2,000-mile length of the Mediterranean Sea from the Straits of Gibraltar in the west to Alexandria and Suez in the east. But for years the Lords of the Admiralty had failed to appreciate the vulnerability of all shipping – even the most powerful warships – to aerial attacks.

Malta had been used as a staging post for Blenheims and Wellingtons, flying out across France to the Suez Canal zone, prior to the collapse of France. After the Italians entered the war on 10 June 1940, and the fall of France a couple of weeks later, they flew out via Gibraltar, each leg taking around 8 hours. To achieve this range the Blenheims were fitted with an extra 100-gallon fuel tank fitted in the bomb bay, from which fuel was pumped manually into the main tanks by the Observer or WOp/Ag – or in many of the aircraft by the ground-crew passenger – using a Zwicky hand-pump. The Blenheims left their bases in East Anglia for Portreath in Cornwall, where they were loaded with spares, mail and kit, and fully fuelled, then awaited a favourable weather forecast. Taking off at Portreath with the heavily laden aircraft was fraught, as was the landing on the short runway on the airfield built on the racecourse at Gibraltar. These ferry flights continued, despite the increased risks involved, and nearly 50 Blenheims had been delivered by the end of 1940, as demand for them in the Middle East Theatre grew. These deliveries continued throughout 1941 and were in addition to the regular flow of Blenheim and fighter reinforcements sent via the long Takoradi route, and many Blenheims were lost on both routes (see Chapter 26, Appendix 1). Hurricanes, desperately needed for the defence of Malta, were flown off aircraft carriers in the Western Mediterranean – 12 from HMS *Argus* arrived on 2 August, but another 12 from the same carrier met disaster on 17 November when eight of them ran out of fuel and were lost into the sea, as was the FAA Skua that was leading them and providing navigation. It was not until 27 April 1941 that 23 of 24 flown off HMS *Ark Royal* reached Malta. By the end of that month the first of the Blenheims of 2 Group had arrived on the island – they did not form part of the Middle East Command but were detached from, and remained in, Bomber Command in the UK. However, their anti-shipping strikes and other raids mounted from Malta ranked with the most valorous and hazardous operations carried out by any RAF Command, and made a major contribution to the ultimate success by the Allies in the land campaigns that surged backwards and forwards along the coast of North Africa.

This 40 Squadron Mk IV, N3589, landed on the Italian island of Pantellaria, mistaking it for Malta, on 13 September 1940. The Italians applied their own markings and test-flew the aircraft.

Important intelligence information was supplied by 431 General Reconnaissance Flight, a Malta-based unit that had absorbed the Marylands and Blenheims of 3 AA Co-Op Unit from Kalafrana in September 1940. This unit, commanded by S/Ldr E. Whiteley, carried out its first sortie on the 8th by taking some perfect pictures of Tripoli. Its leading pilot was the brilliant but unconventional P/O Adrian Warburton – one of his early successes was to photograph the Italian fleet in Taranto harbour at very low level on the morning of the FAA Swordfish raid on the night of 11 November 1940. Despite his flamboyant dress he ended up a Wing Commander, completed well over 300 operational sorties, winning the DSO and bar, as well as the DFC and two bars, only to disappear over the Alps in a borrowed USAF Lockheed P.38 in 1944. The GR Flight was upgraded to form 69 Squadron at Luqa on 10 January 1941, and this hard-working Photographic Reconnaissance Squadron provided an invaluable service by photographing ports in Italy, Sicily, Greece and Libya to record the loading, forming up and departure of Axis supply convoys. These pictures, together with other sources of intelligence including Ultra intercepts, enabled the convoy timings and routes to Africa to be plotted with surprising accuracy for those pre-radar days, although a Special Duties Flight of Wellingtons fitted with early ASV radar helped to locate and track convoys at night. Although the original GR Flight and 69 Squadron initially operated three, then seven Marylands, which are generally credited with their successes, they also operated half a dozen Blenheims for more than a year, until October 1941, as well as the odd Beaufort in August/September of that year, adding a few Hurricanes, Spitfires and several Baltimores in 1942. In addition 69 Squadron frequently co-opted Blenheims from the 2 Group squadrons detached to Malta to assist in its photographic-reconnaissance duties, and in the constant search for Axis shipping, often supplying its own Observers to facilitate these tasks.

The first Blenheim unit sent out to ascertain the practicalities and likely effectiveness of conducting bombing sorties from Malta was a Flight of 21 Squadron, which were detached there on 26 April 1941 under the command of S/Ldr L. Atkinson. In his words:

'We flew half a dozen raids prodding here and there. I sent a signal back that we could operate a Squadron or a Squadron plus. The situation in Malta was far from satisfactory, things had been badly neglected for years. For instance we had to have our aircraft serviced by the Navy. We all arrived home, but one aircraft had been destroyed in an air raid. We were the only crews to fly our Blenheims back. Luck was out for me. I ran out of fuel just after crossing the Cornish coast. My Blenheim ended in a cloud of dust as we belly-landed in a dry field.'

He was being modest, for the six 21 Squadron Blenheims sank two ships on 4 May, including one carrying fuel for the *Luftwaffe*, and ten days later hit and damaged the *Perseo* (4,800 tons). By then the Air Staff had decided to detach squadrons from 2 Group to Malta on a regular basis and in rotation, with their Blenheims modified for desert use and with the long-range tank fitted in the fuselage for the ferry flights. They would operate from there in turn, each squadron for about five weeks, to attack Axis shipping sailing from Europe to Africa – the only way that supplies could be delivered to the enemy forces there. The Blenheims would then be flown on to Africa for the Middle East Command, and the crews could either stay with them or be returned to the UK depending on demand. Little did the Air Staff realise that, for the rest of 1941, there would be precious few of either left after enduring a stint of operations from Malta. Sir Charles Portal, the CAS, chose the right man to take command in Malta, for Hugh Pughe Lloyd, the Senior Air Staff Officer at 2 Group, was a superb leader and highly respected throughout the Group. He was promoted to Air Vice Marshal as AOC RAF Mediterranean on 1 June. It is doubtful if the stream of 2 Group crews sent to Malta to carry out such dangerous sorties – and to suffer such heavy casualties, while operating in difficult circumstances, under constant aerial bombardment and living in very primitive conditions on reduced rations – would have served any other AOC as loyally and as willingly.

One of 21 Squadron's bravest and most skilful pilots in the anti-shipping role was Sgt Rex Levers DFM, seen taking a break at Luqa in May 1941. He was killed carrying out this role from the UK on 16 June 1941 when his Blenheim struck the mast of a ship – a photograph of this loss is in Chapter 19.

Atkinson, promoted Wing Commander and CO of 82 Squadron, was sent straight back to Malta and led out the Squadron's A Flight to Luqa on 19 May 1941, with B Flight following on 11 June. They commenced anti-shipping sorties straight away, enjoying some success including striking the *Beatrice* (6,130 tons) at sea and damaging the large *Esperia* (11,400 tons) in Tripoli harbour. On 26 May they bombed and sank the *Montero* (6,200 tons) and damaged another supply ship, and the next day sank the *Florida* (3,300 tons) and damaged the *Foscarini Marco* (6,350 tons). In a determined attack on 22 June by six 82 Squadron crews on a southbound convoy of five merchant ships and two destroyers off Lampedusa, the leader of the first section, S/Ldr Harrison Broadley (Z6422), was hit by flak and forced to ditch (see Appendix 1). The leader of the second section, F/Lt T. Watkins, who had been lucky as a Sergeant Pilot to survive the disastrous Gembloux raid of 17 May 1940 (as described in Chapter 12), had another close brush with death. His Blenheim (Z9545) was peppered by light flak as he ran in to bomb, his right leg was almost severed by a .50 shell, and he was wounded in the buttocks. Observer Sargent leaned across and managed to keep the damaged aircraft in the air, while WOp/Ag Sgt Chander in the turret shot down a CR.42 that, hoping for an easy kill, had closed on the almost out-of-control Blenheim. With the pilot in great pain, weak through loss of blood, and passing in and out of consciousness, they

Ground-crew from 82 Squadron by one of their charges at Luqa. They worked very hard under most difficult conditions to keep their aircraft serviceable.

AVM Hugh Pughe Lloyd MC DFC, the dynamic AOC of RAF Malta.

struggled back to Luqa where Watkins somehow managed to land but collapsed again while the aircraft was still rolling. The AOC, AVM Lloyd, was amazed that a man with such grievous injuries could have summoned enough strength to bring the aircraft back, and he strongly endorsed the recommendation of Watkins's Squadron Commandeer, W/Cdr L. Atkinson, for the award of a Victoria Cross, as did the AOC 2 Group in the UK, AVM D. Stevenson (as 82 Squadron was detached to Malta from 2 Group). However, what would have been the fourth VC for a Blenheim Pilot was not promulgated and these acts of bravery were recognised by an immediate DSO for Tom Watkins and a DFM for Sargent. Many felt that Watkins deserved more. The doctors at Imtarfa managed to save the leg and Watkins returned to the UK on a hospital ship, but the Blenheim was damaged beyond repair (see Appendix 1). Early in July Atkinson led 82 Squadron in a daring raid on a convoy sheltering in Palermo harbour, which caused two large ships to be burned out, another had its back broken, while a fourth was towed back to Naples for repairs, and three other smaller ships were damaged, the Blenheims escaping by dashing across Sicily at zero feet. Two laden tankers were also sunk by Blenheims of the newly arrived 110 Squadron, and on 22 July 82 Squadron's Blenheims claimed the special prize of a German ship by sinking the *Preussen* with its cargo of

THE BRISTOL BLENHEIM

A blazing tanker taken from W/Cdr Pepper's 139 Squadron Blenheim soon after his bombs had hit it; the wake of the escorting destroyer is on the right.

ammunition. But 82 Squadron had been taking severe casualties (see Appendix 1) and by late July the few survivors made their way back to England by various means, leaving their Blenheims behind, some via a Catalina to Gibraltar.

Other UK-based 2 Group Blenheim squadrons were taking their turn for the long flights out to Malta and the hazardous operations that followed, although these were rendered considerably less hazardous when the bulk of *Fliegerkorps X* was withdrawn from Sicily and sent to the Russian Front after 22 June 1941. 139 Squadron, led by W/Cdr V. Pepper DFC, could send only seven crews as its other Flight was detached to Manston for Channel Stop operations, but 110 Squadron, which left the UK on 30 June, arrived almost at full strength, as did 105, which set out under W/Cdr Hughie Edwards VC DFC on 28 July. 107 Squadron left the UK with 26 crews in four groups commencing on 22 August, and 18 Squadron set out on 12 October – both soldiered on in Malta until January 1942, by which time they were almost wiped out and only a handful of surviving aircrew were able to return to the UK. 21 Squadron was the last to go out, in December 1941, and they were ground right down so that the Squadron had to be disbanded on 4 March 1942. None of these squadrons returned a single Blenheim to the UK – those aircraft that did survive, many needing repairs to rectify battle damage, were passed on to Middle East Command to serve in the Western Desert and Iraq, some even finding their way to the Far East.

The crews of the 2 Group squadrons detached to Malta throughout 1941 knew what to expect during their stint there, but the AOC, AVM Hugh Pughe Lloyd – with the tacit support of his superior, AM Arthur Tedder in Cairo – resorted to replacing his severe casualties by 'hijacking' many Blenheims and their crews who were (as they thought!) merely staging through Malta on their way to postings in the Middle or Far East Commands. These crews were surprised to find themselves being kept back in Malta and pressed into immediate operational use. One of them was Sgt Pilot I. G. Broom, and his exploits personify perfectly the calibre and courage of the 'Blenheim Boys'. He took Z7618 into Luqa on 18 September as the leader of six Blenheims of 114 Squadron on their way to Singapore (only five arrived, as one force-landed in Sicily, while the other four continued to the Far East where the crews were later either killed or captured by the Japanese). But 105 Squadron, 15 of whose aircraft had arrived in Malta seven weeks earlier (they too lost one on the way out) had been reduced to only two crews by then, so Lloyd attached Sgt Broom, his crew and his Blenheim to the remnants of 105.

How was it that 105's fighting strength had been reduced so drastically in such a short period? It will be interesting to take a closer look at its activities, its frequent failures and frustrations as well as its triumphs and tragedies, for 105 exemplify exactly all the Blenheim squadrons that served in Malta. 105's first operations from the island were two unsuccessful attempts to bomb a convoy of four cargo ships some 50 miles from Pantellaria. The first was by six Blenheims led by S/Ldr Goode DFC on 31 July, which found it guarded by a cruiser and six destroyers with half a dozen Italian fighters giving aerial protection, so the formation – which had been instructed not to attack warships – headed home, but not before Sgt Jackson's Z7420 was damaged both by AA fire and fighters. In the second raid S/Ldr Smithers led out six more aircraft the following morning, but failed to locate the convoy as the weather had deteriorated, and they too returned without dropping their bombs. Like all things in Malta at that time there was a shortage of bombs, so crews were ordered not to waste them. Later, on 1 August, F/Lt L. Broadley led two other 105 Squadron Blenheims at low level to attack two cargo ships spotted in Lampedusa harbour; his aircraft was hit on the run in by AA fire from a destroyer, but he and Sgt Bendall both scored direct hits with their 500lb bombs, although those of P/O Hanafin were dropped in the water. Broadley's damaged Z9605 lost height on the way out and hit the sea; he and Sgt Marsh, his WOp/Ag, were rescued from their dinghy by the Italians and became prisoners, but his Observer, P/O A. Ramsey DFC (which he had won on the Bremen raid), died of his wounds (see Appendix 1). The next day F/Lt Buckley (another survivor of the Bremen raid) led three aircraft to bomb barracks at Misurata on the Libyan coast, attacking from the landward side as was usual with such targets, and making their escape without loss. At dusk on 3 August S/Ldr Goode led five aircraft to bomb shipping in the heavily defended harbour of Tripoli; one had to turn back with hydraulic trouble, three others attacked at very low level scoring hits on two ships, and the fourth – which could not line up on any ship as it flashed across the harbour – bombed the Air HQ building. Two Blenheims were damaged by flak, and Sgt Williams had to belly-land Z7408 at Luqa without undercarriage or flaps as the hydraulic system had been shot up. Early-morning reconnaissance by a Maryland on 4 August showed a ship in Misurata harbour and two of 105's Blenheims were sent to attack it, but it had left port before they got there, so they bombed and sank a W/T schooner offshore instead. The following day two merchant ships were reported by 69 Squadron to be off Marsala, and S/Ldr Smithers led five Blenheims to attack them, but they were unable to locate the cargo carriers so bombed two fishing vessels instead, without hitting them; this turned out to be doubly frustrating for on the way back to Malta the formation came across a convoy of two large and several smaller merchant vessels, escorted by two Italian SM.79s, but had to let it pass unmolested as they had expended their bombs. The day ended with two more of 105's Blenheims sent out at dusk on an anti-shipping sweep over the Gulf of Sirte. They found no ships so – as briefed – bombed the large barracks near Misurata, scoring direct hits. Night fell as they returned to Malta and they arrived in the middle of an air-raid, so only a few goose-neck flares were lit on their approach to the runway at Luqa and these were extinguished as soon as the aircraft had touched down. Less than a week had passed since 105 commenced operations from Malta and it was finding that life there was both difficult and dangerous.

Early on 6 August a 69 Squadron Maryland spotted another southbound convoy off Pantellaria, heading for Tripoli with six vessels carrying supplies for the *Afrika Korps* – clearly urgent and important stores, as the cargo vessels were escorted by five destroyers and a torpedo-boat. 105's Blenheims were ordered to attack the convoy and four set out, led by F/O Roe, only to discover an additional escort of Fiat CR.42 fighters. Roe decided that discretion was called for and led his formation back to Malta with their bombs still in the bomb bays. FAA Swordfish were sent that night from Hal Far in Malta and, despite fierce AA fire and using flares to illuminate the targets, scored torpedo hits on two ships, one of which sank. 105 was ordered to make a dawn attack next morning, the 7th, this time by eight aircraft in two sections led by S/Ldr Goode DFC; although his section of four failed to find the target, the

'N' and 'Y' heading out over the Mediterranean for anti-shipping sorties. Twin-gun nose turrets – reversed on 'Y' to aid flak suppression – are fitted, and the white bar replaced the squadron codes when aircraft were shared between squadrons.

other four did and attacked two large ships through a murderous hail of AA fire. Neither of the ships was hit, but all the Blenheims were and they took a variety of battle damage, especially that of P/O Duncan, which had the tail-wheel, elevator-trim controls and part of the rudder shot away, as well as many holes torn in the tail-plane, fuselage, and wings. It says much for the strength of the Blenheim that it was able to struggle back to Luqa. On the evening of 8 August S/Ldr Goode led out six Blenheims to make a dusk attack on ships reported in Catania harbour, Sicily. One aircraft returned early with engine trouble, and on approaching the harbour with the other five George Goode saw a formation of some 30 CR.42 Falco fighters forming up over the city and, faced with odds of six to one, sensibly decided to turn his formation back for Malta. But P/O Standfast, living up to his name, did not turn back and continued to race towards the harbour – strict radio silence was enforced so the formation had to rely on visual signals. It is not known if he thought the formation was opening out prior to making the attack, or if he was so intent on looking at the rapidly approaching harbour that he failed to notice his leader turning away, but he pressed on alone at very low level and aimed his two 500lb bombs at a large ship moored at the quayside. Unfortunately for his brave solo effort, the bombs fell short and exploded harmlessly in the water, causing no damage. The swarm of CR.42s was still busy formating and did not intervene, and all six Blenheims made safe night landings back at Luqa.

The action continued the next day, the 9th, when six of 105's aircraft led by S/Ldr Smithers were sent to find and destroy two ships reported hugging the coast between Misurata and Tripoli. The Blenheims reached the coast near Tripoli and followed the shoreline to Misurata but saw no shipping, so they flew very low along the coast road – the only road that could be used by motor transport. Smithers attacked three petrol tankers on the road but failed to hit them, and his wing-men bombed a dump of stores stacked near the road, one, Sgt Scott, causing a large explosion when he hit supplies of ammunition. P/O Standfast took the other section of three to bomb Misurata barracks, and this they hit together with a convoy of army lorries parked outside, with fiery results. On the 10th four aircraft led by S/Ldr Goode were sent to seek an unescorted vessel reported north of Lampedusa, but one of the Blenheims, P/O Buckley in Z7420, suffered an engine failure at the critical moment immediately after take-off. Buckley managed to keep it in the air and jettisoned his bombs, set to 'safe', into the quarry at the end of the runway, but after the 11-second delay they exploded. He struggled round the circuit, keeping the good engine on the inside of his turns, and landed safely. But his problems were not over. for he faced an instant interrogation about the explosions by an irate W/Cdr Hughie Edwards; however, 105's CO was soon satisfied that Goode had carried out all the correct actions in saving the aircraft and no one had been hurt, so no more was said. The other three aircraft, after a long search, found the ship as dusk deepened – it was flying the French flag, but they assumed it was Vichy French – and attacked. The last bomb from the leader struck home and the ship is believed to have sunk. That day also held other dramas. In the morning F/Lt Paul Wylde in a Maryland of 69 Squadron had photographed nearly 60 German aircraft on Catania airfield and six cargo ships anchored in Catania Bay, but had an engine failure on the return trip and, tragically, crashed on the final approach to Luqa. Wylde and Sgt R. Mutimer were killed instantly and Sgt C. Clark died in Imtafa Hospital the next day, but the camera and Observer's logs were rescued intact from the wreckage and provided the information needed to brief the 105 Squadron air-crews for an attack on the ships that evening. S/Ldr Smithers led four Blenheims out but had to return as his ASI failed; P/O Duncan assumed the lead and the other three continued to the east of Sicily, but on entering Catania Bay they saw several fighters circling overhead so abandoned the mission and returned with their bombs still on board. Sadly the intelligence obtained at heavy cost on the reconnaissance flight had not resulted in a successful attack, and the ships escaped unharmed, but had the raid been pressed home against such opposition it is almost certain that the cost would have been more lives. Fate often plays cruel tricks in times of war.

The next day, 11 August, two sections of three 105 Squadron Blenheims were briefed to attack a factory in southern Italy that manufactured nitrates for explosives at the small seaside town of Crotone on the Bay of Taranto. The first section, led by S/Ldr Bryan Smithers, made the wrong landfall and bombed a railway and buildings (euphemistically referred to in squadron records as 'barrack blocks') in Cariati, a fishing village some way north of Cretone. The other Flight Commander, S/Ldr George Goode DFC, led his section into the supposedly undefended town of Crotone from the north, spotted the factory and released his two 500lb bombs; one exploded inside the factory but the crew thought the other might have 'hung up' so he circled to make another run in. His wingmen, P/O Peter Standfast and Sgt Ron Scott, scored direct hits on the factory but all had come under fire from the AA guns of corvettes anchored just offshore. Goode's aircraft (Z7503) was hit on its second run in, crash-landed nearby and the crew were captured. Sgt Scott's damaged aircraft (V6307) was written off attempting a landing at Luqa (see Appendix 1). Two out of three.

105 Squadron was then stood down for a couple of days, apart from P/O Buckley, who went out in Z9603 early on the morning of the 13th to bomb a MT workshops and repair garage at Bardia on the Libyan coast to the east of Tobruk. On the 14th four aircraft were sent to locate four vessels seen off the Kerkenna Islands and heading for Tripoli, but failed to find the ships despite flying a tiring 3-hour 'square search' pattern of the sea south of the islands. Five aircraft led by F/O Roe were dispatched on 15 August to attack a small convoy, which included two tankers, reported to be approaching the port of Benghazi. Both tankers were hit and set on fire, one by F/O Roe's aircraft (Z7522) and the other by P/O Standfast's (Z9604), but both Blenheims and their brave crews were lost: Roe's wing-tip caught a mast and he crashed into the sea, while Standfast's aircraft was hit by the ship's AA fire and

exploded in the air – 40 per cent casualties (see Appendix 1). No targets were found on the 16th, but six vessels escorted by six destroyers were found the next day by a section of three aircraft led by Sgt Scott, but not attacked as they were guarded by fighters; on his return at dusk Sgt Weston crashed Z7420 on the runway at Luqa when he misjudged his landing.

Fleet Air Arm Swordfish were more successful that day in a dusk attack that sank one ship, stopped another, and set a third on fire, while a fourth, the oil tanker *Maddelena Odero* (5,500 tons), was damaged and beached on Lampedusa. Next day three of 105's Blenheims were sent to finish it off; one aborted, but P/O Buckley attacked and set it alight – starting a blaze that lasted for three days – although he was wounded in the legs when his aircraft was hit by cannon fire from an MTB. They were then chased by two CR.42s but they jinked this way and that, pulling the emergency 'Plus 9lb' boost lever, which enabled them to escape. S/Ldr Smithers led five Blenheims of 105 on 22 August to search for shipping off the coast in the Gulf of Sirte. The formation started the sweep at Misurata, but some 5 hours later, on reaching Bwayrat Al Hasun, they had found no ships, so bombed and strafed a convoy of MT on the coast road near that town instead. Five more Blenheims were dispatched the following afternoon to seek and attack four vessels steaming south of Lampedusa; Sgt Scott scored a direct hit on one and S/Ldr Smithers damaged another. S/Ldr Barnes and his crew from 107 Squadron took part in this sortie, as crews and aircraft of 105 and 107 Squadrons joined together more and more as the numbers available to each squadron grew less and less. He led a sortie by four aircraft the next day to find a tanker reported off the Tunisian coast; one of the aircraft aborted and the other three failed to find it, but attacked three other ships they had spotted, two of which were blown up and the third hit and left listing.

The Secretary of State for Air, Sir Archibald Sinclair, signalled the AAOC, AVM Lloyd, on 23 August praising 'the magnificent success of air operations from Malta', singling out especially 'the daring and dextrous reconnaissances of the Marylands culminating in the tremendous onslaught of Blenheims and FAA Swordfish on Axis shipping in the Mediterranean … you are draining the enemy's strength… Good luck and good hunting.' The message was published in *Times of Malta*, together with Hugh Pughe Lloyd's typical reply: 'All ranks join me in thanking you for your warm inspiring message of congratulations on our humble efforts. Hunting is certainly good and the hounds are in excellent fettle.' But, privately, he was painfully aware of the severe strain being placed on the Blenheim crews by the heavy and unremitting casualties they were experiencing. In his own aptly named account of his time in Command at Malta, *Briefed to Attack* (Hodder & Stoughton, 1949) he states:

> '…the Blenheim casualties began to increase at a most alarming rate. In August and September the casualties were as high as twelve per cent. At times the chances of survival were just about evens and no more, and I had to ask myself whether the losses were justified… The aircrews belonged to detachments of Squadrons that were based in Britain and were without any of the normal roots, in the sense that only a dozen or so key maintenance personnel accompanied the aeroplanes and they were without any of their equipment, records and other items on which they depended when in Britain. They lived together in one Mess (*) and, as there were so few of them, casualties were very frightening, particularly when everyone realised that the chances of surviving a tour on Malta were very remote indeed – which was the stark truth… Unfortunately I knew everyone of them personally and there were occasions when I had the gravest misgivings about sending them out to attack a difficult target knowing that some of the crews would be almost certain to be lost… I can never hope to describe all that I feel about their courage and their determination to kill the really important Axis shipping… Those aircrew were the flower of our race; all of them had been given a good education in their youth and they were far above the average intelligence, men who knew what they were doing and why it had to be done, and men who had volunteered to be aircrew in

preference to many other far less hazardous tasks. Theirs was a calm and conscious courage. To everyone of these volunteers the sinking of ships was their crusade and without any doubt they were the Knights of St John – the modern Crusaders.'

(* This referred to the Officers Mess at Luqa, but the majority of Blenheim aircrew were Sergeants, and as Non-Commissioned Officers messed separately at Marsaxlokk on the coast.)

This was praise indeed from one ideally placed to observe the bravery of the Blenheim crews. But please note that the Air Minister's congratulations and the AOC's personal statements, quoted above, apply to all the Blenheim squadrons at Malta and not just to 105 Squadron. 105 was selected as a typical example of the Blenheim squadrons detached to Malta so that their activities could be described in more detail to represent all of their comrades.

On 26 August two of 105's Blenheims were sent to photograph a cargo ship damaged off the Tunisian coast the night before by a submarine, which had sunk its companion, and to bomb it if it had not gone down. The experienced Sgt Ron Scott led, but it was to be the last sortie for him, Sgt Walter Healy and 19-year-old Sgt Stuart Bastin, as the tour-expired crew were due for posting back to the UK. They found the stricken ship and took their pictures and could see that the bombs were not needed, so they carried on to seek another ship reported as damaged by the same submarine; this they found and attacked it. Scott scored two direct hits, but Z7682 collided with the main mast and disintegrated, the wreckage being hurled into the sea – he and his crew were destined never to see the UK again (see Appendix 1). His number two, Sgt Brandwood, also scored a hit with a bomb and left the ship settling by the stern. Later that day S/Ldr Smithers led three Blenheims to attack three ships spotted off Lampedusa, but they searched the seas in hazy dusk for more than 2 hours in vain. The next day, the 27th, a five-strong formation led again by S/Ldr Smithers included two crews from 107 Squadron, and it was to S/Ldr Barnes of 107 that he passed command when he became unwell on the flight far out to the east of Malta. In that area Axis shipping was trying to keep as far as possible from the marauding RAF and FAA aircraft, but on this occasion the four remaining aircraft made a fruitless sweep of the Ionian Sea. Smithers himself recovered on the homeward trip and decided to make a one-man raid on the harbour in the Island of Lampedusa, but he ran into heavy AA fire from cannon and machine-guns, Z7609 was hit, and his Observer, Sgt Frank Harbord, was wounded in the thigh. Bryan Smithers coaxed the damaged aircraft back to Malta – the engines were jammed in the 'Plus 9lb' emergency boost setting but withstood the prolonged maltreatment, and the aircraft had no hydraulic services so was belly-landed alongside the runway at Luqa. Thus ended the hectic first four weeks of 105's operations in Malta – ten crewmen killed, four wounded and two captured, as well as five aircraft lost (one through a landing accident) and seven badly damaged, including three that had been forced to belly-land.

Another formation of five, including two 107 Squadron crews, was sent off on 28 August in search of two tankers. One Blenheim returned to base with engine troubles, but the other four found and attacked the tankers, both of which were hit, one being set on fire. Sgt Brandwood's Blenheim ground-looped to port into rough ground on landing at Luqa – it was found that machine-gun bullets had punctured the tyre and caused other damage. Two 105/107 Squadron Blenheims were sent on long PR missions on 30 August as all the 69 Squadron reconnaissance Marylands and Blenheims were unserviceable – a situation that was arising more frequently. F/O Greenhill in one (Z7511) found the two troopships he had been ordered to seek out, and circled at 10,000 feet while F/Sgt Mike Henry attempted to send a coded report of the position by radio. They then set course for Malta but, after a while, the Pilot over-rode the course given by the Observer and turned north – when they saw the mountains of Calabria in southern Italy appearing in the distance, they turned about and headed south, passing to the east of Mount Etna and flying just off the coast of

Sicily, where they were lucky not to be intercepted. Approaching Malta at last – their fuel tanks had been showing empty for some time – the Observer fired a red Very flare as they tried to go straight in to land at Luqa, but received one in return as a Wellington was about to take off. Greenhill was desperate by then, ignored the 'red' and landed alongside the runway; the Blenheim swung to starboard, crossed the runway just behind the departing Wellington and headed towards another bombed-up Wellington at dispersal, the port exhausts spewing flames as he throttled back. Alarmed at the apparent fire the Pilot jumped out long before the aircraft stopped moving, closely followed by Sgt 'Mac' Smith, the Observer, and F/Sgt Mike Henry, the Wireless Operator/Air Gunner, who was almost struck by the tailplane! But a throttle had been kicked open in the hasty evacuation, and the crewless Blenheim lurched away from the Wellington by itself; the port wheel had stuck in the runway intersection and the aircraft started circling round and round. It did this for several minutes before the tail-wheel was lassoed by a brave airman, who then climbed up on to the wing, reached into the cockpit and turned off the engines. The AOC had arrived to see what the commotion was about, and Greenhill was placed under close arrest and severely reprimanded, but such was the shortage of Blenheim pilots that he was back on the Battle Order less than a fortnight later, to be killed in action within a fortnight.

The badly damaged Z7641 of 107 Squadron made it back to Luqa – just – on 30 August 1941. Sgt 'Johnnie' Turner and his crew escaped uninjured.

Also on the 30th, six aircraft (four from 105 and two from 107) were ordered to attack a chemical factory and adjoining power station at Licata on the southern coast of Sicily. They scored several direct hits but Sgt Turner's Blenheim was caught in the bomb-blast of those dropped on the factory ahead of him by Sgt Brandwood – the explosions were premature, being at 3 seconds after impact and not 11 as expected. 'Johnnie' Turner nursed Z7641 back to Luqa but the damaged wing dropped on the flapless landing, collapsing the undercarriage and writing off the aircraft (see Appendix 1). The Blenheims were regularly providing airmen stationed at Luqa with excitingly unorthodox arrivals!

The batting opened on 1 September 1941 with a return raid to the Crotone chemical factory. S/Ldr Barnes led in seven Blenheims at zero feet and several direct hits were scored. Sgt Weston bombed the railway line to the factory, and F/Lt Ballands and Sgt Shaw both scored hits on a ship moored at the jetty, leaving it well alight. This was a successful raid with, for once, no losses – a reconnaissance by a 69 Squadron Hurricane on the 3rd showed that the factory buildings had 'sustained considerable damage' and also noted several ships in the harbour. Blenheims also carried out two lengthy PR sorties for 69 Squadron that day, S/Ldr Smithers taking F/O Wells of 69 as an Observer, but the convoy they were seeking south-east of Italy was not found. However, the five ships spotted in Crotone harbour by the Hurricane were to be attacked by five Blenheims on the following day, the 4th, but Sgt Bruce had to abandon the sortie when he suffered a bout of sickness. The other four faced heavy flak as they raced in, and Sgt Wallace and his crew were killed when Z7654 was hit, a wing was blown off and the Blenheim flipped inverted into the harbour (see Appendix 1). Sgt Weston's Z7511 was hit in the tail, but he managed to bring the damaged aircraft home. One ship moored at the North Mole was struck by bombs – it was seen later to be listing heavily. Four more PR sorties for 69 Squadron were flown over the Ionian Sea in the next few days, but no shipping was found. However, on the 9th a Beaufort on the same task found two cargo ships with an escorting destroyer; four Blenheims were sent to attack, but were unable to locate them, and sank a schooner they took to be a radio 'squealer' – an assumption confirmed when its SOS transmission was intercepted by Malta. Four Blenheims made a fruitless 3-hour search for reported shipping on the 10th, but five led by S/Ldr Smithers did find and strike one of two ships about 120 miles west of Crete, leaving it sinking. Next day Sgt Jackson with an Observer from 69 Squadron discovered a cargo ship off the Kerkenna Islands heading for Tripoli, but the two Blenheims sent to attack it failed to locate it. It had been a frustrating period for shipping attacks – mainly staring at the sea through heat haze for many an hour.

A reconnaissance Swordfish found a tempting target on 11 September – a convoy of six cargo ships and a troop transport, the largest of 12,000 tons, escorted by seven destroyers – between the islands of Lampedusa and Pantellaria. Swordfish of 830 Squadron FAA were the first to attack in the very hazy conditions, sinking one ship with a torpedo, damaging two others and causing fires on board both – one of them was stopped in the water. Wellingtons bombed the ships that night, setting two on fire. Sgt Bridge took out a reconnaissance Blenheim early the next morning to check the current position and heading of the convoy, now of five ships and six destroyers, and noted a fighter escort circling overhead. This unwelcome information led to a heated discussion at the briefing of the Blenheim crews as a maximum effort was called for. 105 Squadron had a new CO, W/Cdr D. Scivier AFC, who heeded the opinion of his crews and stated that to attack such a heavily defended convoy would lead to unacceptable casualties among the Blenheims, which would be unlikely to reach the targets anyway. The Station Commander, Group Capt C. Cahill DFC AFC, was unsympathetic and insisted that they mounted the attack, so the matter was taken by Scivier to the AOC for arbitration. (He had taken over the Squadron from Hughie Edwards, who had been ordered not to take part in any operations as the Air Ministry wished to avoid the adverse publicity that would accompany the loss of a Victoria Cross holder.) But Lloyd, the AOC, emphasised the importance of preventing as much of the convoy as possible from reaching Tripoli and ordered that the operation should take place. Eight aircraft were therefore dispatched, six of 105 and two of 107 Squadron, led by the experienced S/Ldr Smithers. They only found the convoy after a long search as it had altered course, and was now in line ahead with the screen of destroyers on the northern flank. So Smithers led in the Blenheims from the south, line abreast in two sections of four, and at wave-top height into a hail of AA fire. He put his four 250lb bombs into the side of the largest ship (12,000 tons) as did Sgt Weston with his two 500lb bombs, while F/Sgt Bendall put his pair into the next largest ship (10,000 tons), although his Blenheim was hit immediately afterwards and his Observer, Sgt Hindle, wounded. However, both ships were set well ablaze. S/Ldr Charney DFC, leading his section of four just behind and to the right of S/Ldr Smithers's section, ran into the flak; his Blenheim was hit, burst into flames and cart-wheeled into the sea. Sgt Mortimer was also hit and crashed into the sea – both crews were killed. Sgt Brandwood chose the troopship and bombed it successfully, but ran straight into intense pom-pom fire from the destroyers; he side-slipped almost to the water to confuse their aim but his starboard engine was hit and stopped, while the port engine also spluttered just after he caught up with the rest of the formation and, with a fire in the bomb bay too, he had to ditch. The crew scrambled into their dinghy before the Blenheim sank and were fortunate indeed to be rescued the next day by HMS *Utmost*, a Malta-based submarine. F/Sgt Bendall struggled back to Luqa with his damaged Blenheim and belly-landed on the stony ground alongside the runway to the discomfort of Sgt Hindle, his wounded Observer; the aircraft was written off. Four out of the eight Blenheims had been lost and three crews were missing (see Appendix 1). All the losses were due to AA fire as the eight Macchi C.200 fighters patrolling above the convoy had dived too late to chase the Blenheims, so failed to catch them – which was just as well, for had they done so they certainly would have shot down most, if not all, of the four surviving bombers.

The next day three of 105's Blenheims spent 6 hours searching for a tanker reported to be near Cape Matapan, but failed to find it. On the 17th four aircraft were sent to bomb two schooners, which had possibly been damaged in earlier attacks as they were seen by 69 Squadron being towed towards Tripoli. S/Ldr Smithers had Sgt Bendall as his wing-man, and P/O Robinson had Sgt Williams alongside, as they ran in just above the surface to attack. The AA opened up, and the leader's Blenheim was damaged; Sgt Bendall's (P4840) was also hit and crashed into the sea. P/O Robinson's Z7755 was hit and blew up, the blazing wreckage being hurled on to the target ship. Sgt Williams was only a wingspan to starboard and had to veer sharply away, almost striking the sea; he circled round and

Another stricken supply ship for the Afrika Korps immediately after a successful attack, as seen from the turret of a low-flying Blenheim.

ran in from the opposite direction, hitting the other ship with both his 500lb bombs. The raid had resulted in 50 per cent casualties, with all six crewmen suffering the most violent of deaths. Poor Robinson, who was only 19, had been appropriated with his crew on their way to Egypt by the AOC and attached to 107 Squadron only a couple of days earlier.

On the next day Sgt Ivor Broom, who had just arrived in Malta, was similarly appropriated, as mentioned earlier, and flew his only practice sortie with 105 on the 20th when S/Ldr Smithers led him and Sgt Tommy Williams to Filfia Island for a bombing exercise using smoke bombs and small practice bombs. That day 105's new CO, W/Cdr Don Scivier, carried out a solo reconnaissance, and the next day he and W/Cdr 'Bunny' Harte, 107's CO, carried out a daring two-aircraft raid at dusk on a convoy escorted by six destroyers, each scoring direct hits on cargo ships as darkness fell. To add to the excitement, an engine of Scivier's Blenheim was hit and caught fire on his way back to a night landing at Luqa. The two Wing Commanders were setting a fine example to their squadrons and certainly 'leading from the front'. Such was the shortage of both aircraft and crews that the two squadrons effectively amalgamated as they regularly 'borrowed' machines and men from each other, almost losing their individual identities. Intelligence reports revealed that a 24,000-ton troopship had reached Tripoli and disembarked reinforcements for the *Afrika Korps*, despite attacks by Wellingtons at night and a few Blenheims by day. So it was decided to attack the two main barracks east of Tripoli the next day – 22 September – to catch the troops before they could be sent up to the front. Six Blenheims led by W/Cdr Scivier would bomb the barracks at Homs (Al Khums) while five more from 107 would bomb those at Misurata simultaneously. Sgt Ivor Broom was about to go on his first operation from Malta as one of the three 105 Squadron Blenheims sent on the Homs raid with three from 107.

W/Cdr Scivier led this formation of two 'vics' of three over the coast to the west of Homs, as briefed, and they raced along side-by-side at low level looking for the barracks buildings. The CO led the inland 'vic' with Sgt Broom to his left, with the other 'vic' further to their left, led by Sgt Bill Jackson, who had Sgt Tommy Williams on his right, and thus the nearest to the CO's 'vic'. The target was spotted some 45 degrees to the left, so Sgt Jackson turned his 'vic' towards it, lifting them slightly to keep the Blenheim to his left (on the inside of the turn) clear of the ground. The CO's 'vic' was now overshooting the target slightly, so turned and pulled up more sharply, but collided with the underside of Sgt Williams's Blenheim. Sgt Broom only just missed it as he slid underneath and saw the CO and his crew crashing to their deaths in Z7423. The others, including Williams, who was struggling to control his badly vibrating machine, all scored direct hits when they bombed seconds later, and headed out to sea. Four formed up on Sgt Broom for the return flight, but his Gunner, Sgt Harrison, reported that a fifth was lagging behind with an Italian fighter in the distance. Ivor Broom went back unhesitatingly to help the stricken Blenheim Z9609, which apart from the bone-shaking vibration from the badly bent propellers was without an airspeed indicator or altimeter as the pitot tube had been knocked off, together with the under-nose defence guns – the bomb doors and starboard wing were also damaged, and the port engine was throwing out oil. Broom's Observer, Sgt Bill North, signalled the airspeed with an Aldis lamp, and for over an hour Sgt Broom escorted the damaged machine slowly back to Malta, gaining height gently as they approached the island, and approaching alongside the runway to guide the other machine safely right on to it. Such an unselfish action in going back to aid a colleague in difficulties would normally merit a DFM, but at Malta there were other more pressing matters. This was a dramatic introduction to operations from Malta for Ivor Broom and his crew, but the other crew were so traumatised that they did not operate from Malta again; indeed, the WOp/Ag, Sgt A. Tuppen, never flew again.

W/Cdr Donald Scivier AFC was not the only Commanding Officer to lose his life in a mid-air collision in the target area, for W/Cdr 'Bunny' Harte DFC, the popular CO of 107 Squadron, and his crew (including an extra man, an Army Officer) were killed on 9 October 1941 off Capo Alessio, Sicily, when their Blenheim Z7638 was struck by Z7644

Sgt Tommy Williams's Z9609, damaged in a collision over Homs, is shepherded back to Malta by Sgt Ivor Broom. Twisted propeller blades, missing under-nose gun-blister and pitot tube, damage to the bomb-doors, and the oil-soaked port undercarriage can be seen.

flown by P/O Whitford-Waders, who was also killed, as were his crew (see Appendix 1). It is sad that the two courageous Wing Commanders should lose their lives, in less than three weeks, not through enemy action but through accidental collisions, for they – most unusually for Squadron Commanders, and just on their own – had carried out the dangerous dusk attack of 20 September on a strongly escorted convoy described above.

The remnants of 105 Squadron carried out only three more operations from Malta before the remaining crews were sent home: a fruitless shipping sweep in the Gulf of Sirte, which turned into a strafing run along the coastal road, attacking Motor Transport and bombing buildings; and an attack on Marsala airfield, Sicily, on 27 September, which was thwarted by bad weather, so they bombed a granary at Porto Empedocle instead – six aircraft returning there the following day to be met with fire from light AA guns. Sgt Hopkinson's aircraft lost an engine, Sgt Roath's his hydraulics, and Sgt Broom had an explosive bullet render the instrument panel useless – it was only the skill of the three pilots that enabled them to fly the damaged Blenheims safely back to Malta. The crews of 105 returned to the UK on RN cruisers that had escorted a relief convoy to the island in Operation Halberd. Beaufighters of 272 Squadron and the long-range Blenheim Mk IV-Fs of 113 Squadron were brought over from the Western Desert to help protect this convoy and only one ship was lost. Sgt Broom did not return to the UK with the other 105 Squadron crews for he was posted to 107 Squadron and the dangerous operations continued – they lost two out of six attacking ships on 11 October (see Appendix 1), the now experienced Broom leading several of these attacks. As all the Squadron's commissioned operational pilots had been lost, the AOC promoted him 'in the field' to Pilot Officer on 7 November 1941. P/O Broom led a successful raid on the port of Argostoli on the Greek island of Cephalonia, which sank two ships including a tanker, but – once again – two of the six attackers were lost (see Appendix 1). (He was soon awarded the DFC and went on to become an outstanding Mosquito Pilot, collecting the DSO, two bars to his DFC, and the AFC, ending his career as Air Marshal Sir Ivor Broom KCB CBE, respected by all who served with him, and currently the highly regarded President of The Blenheim Society.)

18 Squadron arrived at Luqa with its Blenheims in late October and took over the 2 Group commitment at the end of the month, continuing the same pattern of sorties, and of losses – for example, on 19 November 1941 three of six 18 Squadron Blenheims, attacking a convoy in the Gulf of Sirte, were shot down, killing all nine crewmen – although more raids were mounted on Sicily. These included a most successful attack on Castelvetrano airfield on 4 January 1942 by ten Blenheims – six from 18 and four from 107, the total number of serviceable aircraft the two Squadrons could raise between them – which claimed more than 30 enemy aircraft destroyed on the ground. But the slaughter of the 'Blenheim Boys' continued, for by the turn of the year 18 Squadron had lost eight of its 15 original

A reconnaissance photo of Castel Vetrano Aerodrome, Sicily, used as a target map and showing rows of parked Axis aircraft, many of which were destroyed and damaged in the very successful attack by ten Blenheims on 4 January 1942.

crews, with only one of them surviving, together with six of the 12 replacement crews, again with but a single crew surviving to become Prisoners of War (see Appendix 1).

By then 21 Squadron had arrived, the last Blenheim squadron to do so, but the scale of enemy activity stepped up sharply as *Luftflotte II* was withdrawn from the Russian Front with orders to neutralise Malta. 21 Squadron got off to a bad start on 14 January 1942 when three out of four aircraft were lost on a shipping sweep from Kerkenna to Tripoli, when they attacked a 5,000-ton motor vessel escorted by a destroyer; one Blenheim crashed into the mast, and two were shot down by AA fire (see Appendix 1). Worse was to follow, for on 4 February six of 21 Squadron's Blenheims were sent in poor weather to bomb Palermo harbour. Due to the problems of navigation in such conditions they made the wrong landfall and as the formation turned at low level the aircraft on the inside dug a wing into the sea and cart-wheeled into it; the remaining five bombed a railway line and bridge, but the navigation error brought them into a narrowing, cloud-covered valley and three more flew into the hillsides. Four out of six Blenheims were lost and, tragically, all the crews were killed (see Appendix 1). 21's casualties mounted alarmingly with Messerschmitts roaming freely over Malta; for example, on 6 February 109s shot down all three Blenheims returning from a shipping sweep. In addition, more and more aircraft were being destroyed on the ground by the intense enemy bombing. So, in a few weeks, this Squadron too was virtually exterminated, the last sorties being flown on 22 February, and it was disbanded on 4 March 1942. It had become impossible to operate bombers from Malta and the handful of surviving Blenheims and Wellingtons escaped to Egypt. On 15

Blast-pens around Luqa airfield, mainly rubble from Valetta, created extra hazards for crews landing damaged aircraft – such as VE-X of 110 Squadron, probably Z9551 – on 14 July 1941.

April the fortitude of the Maltese people was recognised when King George VI awarded the island the George Cross – the highest award that could be made to a community.

Kesselring informed Hitler – mistakenly as it turned out – that Malta was no longer a threat. Incidentally, the Axis powers also planned an invasion, Operation Herkules, under General Kurt Student with a force five times as strong as the one he had used to capture Crete, but the plan was abandoned in June 1942 when it was decided instead to support the newly promoted Field Marshal Erwin Rommel directly after he captured the port of Tobruk and was advancing into Egypt. AVM Keith Park, the unsung hero of the Battle of Britain, succeeded AM Hugh Lloyd as AOC on 18 July. The heavy bombing, mainly by Ju.88s, continued, but the fighter defences were greatly improved. Although the Bombers had left Malta, Blenheims continued to provide an important service when they acted as navigation leaders for groups of Spitfires flying off carriers east of Gibraltar. It was these 350-odd Spitfires that saved Malta by regaining command of the air over the island and the surrounding seas, without which the later Allied invasion of Sicily would not have been possible.

The saga of the Maltese-based Blenheims had drawn to a close; they had made a major contribution in severely reducing the stream of supplies needed by the Axis forces in Africa – in October and November 1941 only 25 per cent of those dispatched reached their destination. Once more the brave Blenheim crews had paid a very heavy price – for many of them the heaviest price that it is possible to pay.

Malta-based Blenheims also attacked targets in Italy, such as this low-level raid on Locri, Calabria, southern Italy.

Appendix I

Blenheim losses in Malta, 1 May 1941 to 12 July 1942

Aircraft are all Mk IVs.

12-05-1941   V5461 21 Squadron (ex-101 Squadron): aircraft: destroyed during air-raid on Luqa.

27-05-1941   V6460 82 Squadron: FTR; destroyed by own bombs while attacking convoy; Sgt E. Inman (Pilot) and Sgt R. Austin (WOp/Ag) KIA, Sgt K. Collins (Obs) rescued and became PoW but repatriated after right leg amputated.

27-05-1941   Z6427 82 Squadron: FTR; lost in same explosion, bombs had instant not 11-second delay fuses; F/Lt G. Fairbairn, P/O P. Higgins and Sgt S. Kemp KIA, commemorated on Malta Memorial.

03-06-1941   V5860 139 Squadron: FTR; led second section against convoy, flew into bomb blasts; W/Cdr N. Pepper DFC KIA, Sgt T. Hyde, and Sgt L. Pickford seriously injured. Sgt Hyde died Tripoli Hospital.

03-06-1941   V5460 139 Squadron: badly damaged in same incident, limped back to Malta; S/Ldr J. Thompson, Sgt W. Hepworth RAAF and Sgt A. Turner uninjured.

03-06-1941   V5924 21 Squadron: DBR in air raid on Luqa.

08-06-1941   V5680 139 Squadron: FTR; hit by debris from ship being attacked, crashed into sea; crew Sgt C. Matthews, P/O G. Prosser, and Sgt G. Mason KIA, commemorated on Runnymede Memorial.

08-06-1941   V5996 608 (Aux) Squadron: DBR in air-raid on Luqa, one of seven en route to 203 Squadron at LG.101 in Egypt.

11-06-1941   Z6426 82 Squadron: hit by flak on shipping strike, struck mast, crashed into sea; S/Ldr M. Watson, P/O N. Alers-Hankey and Sgt R. Poole KIA, commemorated on Runnymede Memorial.

19-06-1941   T1888 82 Squadron: damaged by flak on shipping strike, ditched off Malta; Sgt J. Harrison, Sgt L. MacDonald and Sgt L. Rowbotham KIA, commemorated on Malta Memorial.

22-06-1941   Z9545 82 Squadron: damaged by flak on shipping strike; F/Lt T. Watkins (Pilot) wounded, recommended for VC, awarded DSO, Sgt J. Sargent and Sgt E. Chandler uninjured, awarded DFMs, aircraft repaired but lost on 29-06-1941, qv.

22-06-1941   Z6422 82 Squadron: hit by flak attacking convoy off Lampedusa and ditched; S/Ldr J. Harrison-Broadley, Sgt P. Felton (Obs) injured, and Sgt S. Thompson survived, rescued by Italian destroyer, became PoWs.

29-06-1941   Z9545 82 Squadron: FTR, seen crashing on fire in target area; Sgt J. Cover RCAF, Sgt A. Thomas and Sgt R. Fairweather KIA, buried in Tripoli War Cemetery.

05-07-1941   Z9575 82 Squadron: engine cut on take-off at Luqa, stalled and crashed near Guia, destroyed by fire; Sgt W. Rand (Pilot) survived, Sgt A. Murcutt (Obs) and Sgt J. Oaten (WOp/Ag) killed.

09-07-1941   Z6449 110 Squadron: FTR from attack on ships off Tripoli; S/Ldr D. Seale, F/Sgt F. Mulford and F/Sgt W. McDougall KIA, commemorated on Runnymede Memorial.

09-07-1941   Z9578 110 Squadron: FTR from attack on ships off Tripoli; P/O W. Lowe, Sgt R. Baird and Sgt H. Lummus KIA, commemorated on Malta Memorial.

09-07-1941   Z9533 110 Squadron: FTR from attack on ships off Tripoli; Sgt W. Twist, Sgt D. Allen, and Sgt S. Taylor survived and became PoWs.

09-07-1941   Z9537 110 Squadron: FTR; shot down by enemy fighter during attack on ships off Tripoli; F/Lt T. Griffith-Jones (Obs) captured, F/Lt M. Potier (Pilot), and Sgt D. Wythe KIA, buried in Tripoli War Cemetery.

11-07-1941   V6426 82 Squadron: DBR at Hal Far in strafing raid by MC.200s.

14-07-1941   Z9551 110 Squadron: damaged in raid on Zuara, brakes failed on landing at Luqa, hit stone wall, DBR; F/Lt C. Haggitt, P/O C. Ramsay and P/O F. Bennett uninjured.

15-07-1941   Z9583 110 Squadron: damaged by flak in attack on convoy; Sgt J. Broadway (Obs) KIA, F/O J. Castle (Pilot) and F/Sgt D. Barber (WOp/Ag) safe, aircraft repaired.

18-07-1941   Z9582 110 Squadron: shot down by Italian fighters returning from raid on Tripoli; W/Cdr T. Hunt DFC, F/Sgt F. Thripp and Sgt K. Tucker KIA, commemorated on Alamein Memorial.

22-07-1941   T574? 110 Squadron: damaged in action, RTB; Sgt L. Ware DFM (Pilot) injured, Sgt W. Sargent (Obs) died of wounds, Sgt R. Lofthouse (WOp/Ag) safe. (Serial number in ORB incorrect.)

23-07-1941   Z7409 82 Squadron: FTR; hit sea while being attacked by CR.42, crash-landed in Sicily; crew P/O N. Cathles, P/O S. Newborough, and Sgt B. Child KIA, buried in Catania War Cemetery.

24-07-1941   Z7410 110 Squadron: damaged in action, tyre burst landing at Luqa, u/c collapsed; Sgt A. Lee and crew uninjured, aircraft destroyed in air-raid 18-11-1941.

01-08-1941   Z9605 105 Squadron: FTR; shot down by flak off Lampedusa; P/O A. Ramsay DFC (Obs) KIA, F/Lt A. Broadley (Pilot) and Sgt V. Marsh (WOp/Ag) rescued and captured, became PoWs.

11-08-1941   Z7503 105 Squadron: FTR; shot down by flak in raid on Cretone; crew S/Ldr G. Goode DFC, Sgt N. Nicholls, and P/O E. Applebee DFM captured and became PoWs.

11-08-1941	Z6377 105 Squadron: damaged in raid on Cretone, swung on night landing at Luqa and hit bank; crew Sgt R. Scott, Sgt W. Healy, and Sgt S. Bastin uninjured, aircraft destroyed by bombing in 11-1941.
15-08-1941	Z7522 105 Squadron: FTR; struck mast attacking tanker off Benghazi, crashed into sea; crew F/O H. Roe, F/Sgt J. Timms, and F/Sgt S. Samways KIA, commemorated on Malta Memorial.
15-08-1941	Z9604 105 Squadron: FTR; hit by ship's AA while attacking tanker off Benghazi, aircraft blew up; crew P/O P. Standfast, P/O H. Sorensen, and Sgt D. Hoare KIA.
18-08-1941	Z6377 105 Squadron: DBR in air raid on Luqa.
18-08-1941	Z6160 ex-608 Squadron: lost in Malta, no further details available.
26-08-1941	Z7682 105 Squadron: FTR; hit mast in attack on convoy and crashed into sea; crew Sgt R. Scott, Sgt W. Healy and Sgt S. Bastin KIA, Pilot and Obs commemorated on Malta Memorial, WOp/Ag on Alamein Memorial.
30-08-1941	Z7641 107 Squadron: damaged by bomb-blast in raid on Licata, crash-landed at base; crew Sgt D. Turner injured, Sgt E. Warmington safe, and Sgt R. Robson injured (see illustrations on page 511), aircraft under repair but destroyed by bombing 5-9-1941.
04-09-1941	Z7654 107 Squadron: FTR; shot down by flak during raid on Crotone; crew Sgt W. Wallace, Sgt L. Parry, and Sgt J. Jones KIA and buried in Salerno War Cemetery.
12-09-1941	Z9603 107 Squadron: FTR, one of eight-strong raid on convoy of five cargo ships escorted by seven destroyers, shot down by flak into sea; Sgt J. Mortimer, Sgt D. Reid BSc Hons and F/O C. Owen KIA, commemorated on Runnymede Memorial.
12-09-1941	Z7504 107 Squadron: FTR, leading same raid, suffered same fate; S/Ldr F. Charnley DFC, Sgt S. Porteous and Sgt D. Harris KIA, commemorated on Malta Memorial.
12-09-1941	Z7357 105 Squadron: FTR, hit by flak on same raid, set on fire, ditched some 10 miles from convoy; Sgt F. Brandwood, Sgt J. Miller and Sgt A. Mee rescued from dinghy by HM submarine Utmost.
12-09-1941	Z9606 105 Squadron: FTR, damaged by flak on same raid; Sgt F, Hindle (Obs) wounded, F/Sgt J, Bendall belly-landed at Luqa with no hydraulics, he and F/Sgt A, Brown uninjured. (Bendall and Brown KIA five days later.)
12-09-1941	Z7367 105 Squadron: damaged by flak on same raid, crash-landed at Luqa; crew safe, aircraft DBR in air-raid while under repair 08-10-1941.
17-09-1941	P4840 105 Squadron: FTR; collided with ship's mast and crashed into sea; F/Sgt J. Bendall, F/Sgt A. Brown and Sgt C. Hill KIA, commemorated on Malta Memorial. (See Z9606, 12-9-1941)
17-09-1941	Z7755 107 Squadron: FTR; shot down in attack on ship, into which it crashed; crew (all aged 19) P/O P. Robinson, Sgt B. Brooks, and Sgt F. Burrell KIA, commemorated on Runnymede Memorial.
22-09-1941	Z7423 107 Squadron: FTR; collided with Z9609 below during attack on barracks at Homs; crew W/Cdr D. Scivier AFC, F/Sgt L. Barnett, and F/Sgt B. Gray DFM KIA, buried in Tripoli War Cemetery.
22-09-1941	Z9609 105 Squadron: collided with Z7423 above at Homs, returned to base; Sgt T. Williams, Sgt R. Scholefield, and Sgt Tuppen badly shaken but uninjured (see picture on page ???), aircraft repaired but shot down on 23-11-1941.
24-09-1941	Z9599 107 Squadron: FTR; lost without trace on sortie from Luqa; crew S/Ldr T. Warren DFC, F/O J. Waterfall and P/O W. Law KIA and commemorated on Malta Memorial.
28-09-1941	T1821 113 Squadron Mk IV-F: FTR to Luqa from raid on E-boat base at Pantellaria; F/Sgt H. Crossley, F/Sgt J. Swan, and F/Sgt A. Smith KIA. 113 Squadron was based in Western Desert but attached a Flight to Malta at this time.
04-10-1941	V5821 107 Squadron: FTR; shot down by CR.42s off Zuara; Sgt D. Hamlyn, Sgt C. Latter and Sgt D. Williams ditched, rescued from sea near Djerba a few days later.
08-10-1941	Z7367 105 Squadron: DBR in air raid on Luqa (see 12-09-1941 above).
09-10-1941	Z7638 107 Squadron: FTR from shipping sweep off Capo Alessio, Sicily, collided with Z7644 below; W/Cdr F. Harte DFC, F/O C. Bloodworth and F/O T. Wewage-Smith KIA.
09-10-1941	Z7644 107 Squadron: FTR; lost near target off Capo Alessio, Sicily, collided with Z7638 above; F/O N. Walders, Sgt S. Jones, Sgt W. Hunting and Lt E. Talbot GC (RE Army Officer passenger) KIA. The seven men killed in this incident buried in Catania War Cemetery, Sicily.
09-10-1941	Z9600 69 (PR) Squadron: tyre burst on landing at Luqa, swung and u/c collapsed, DBR; P/O R. Smith and crew safe.
11-10-1941	Z7618 107 Squadron: FTR; shot down by flak while attacking ships in Gulf of Sirte, crashed into sea; crew Sgt A. Routh, Sgt R. Parker, and Sgt G. McLeod KIA.
11-10-1941	Z9663 107 Squadron: FTR; shot down by flak while attacking ships in Gulf of Sirte; F/O R. Greenhill (Pilot) and Sgt A. Smith (Obs) KIA, F/Sgt C. Whidden (WOp/Ag) injured and died in hospital four weeks later, buried at Tripoli.
11-10-1941	? 107 Squadron: FTR from shipping sweep off Italian coast; Sgt Hamlyn (Pilot) and P/O W. Chalmers (Obs) KIA, third crewman baled out.
16-10-1941	Z7511 107 Squadron: engine caught fire in circuit at Luqa, crashed and destroyed by fire; F/O S. McAllister (Pilot) and Sgt E. Brenton (Obs) killed, Sgt W. Martin (WOp/Ag) injured.

22-10-1941	Z7898 18 Squadron: FTR, blown up by bombs of preceding Z7602 in raid on Homs; F/Sgt J. Woodburn DFM, Sgt L. Lawson, and Sgt G. Robinson KIA.
23-10-1941	Z9708 107 Squadron: damaged u/c on take-off at Luqa, crash-landed, DBR; Sgt R. Henley (believed solo) safe.
25-10-1941	Z7704 107 Squadron: FTR, damaged attacking MT on Benghazi/Zuara road, crashed and DBF; F/Sgt W. Shaver, Sgt A. Stainier and Sgt G. Wincott KIA, all dying of their burns, buried in Tripoli War Cemetery.
05-11-1941	Z7801 18 Squadron: FTR; shot down by flak while attacking convoy off Cephalonia; Sgt H. Vickers, F/Sgt G. Lowe, and Sgt A. Daniels KIA, commemorated on Malta Memorial.
05-11-1941	Z7922 18 Squadron: FTR; shot down by flak while attacking convoy off Cephalonia; Sgt R. Morris, P/O P. Clark, and Sgt J. Kelly KIA, Pilot commemorated on Malta Memorial, crew at Runnymede.
07-11-1941	Z9746 18 Squadron: damaged by AA fire attacking ships in Ionian Sea, aircraft RTB and repaired; P/O J. Barclay (Pilot) and Sgt H. Lee (Obs) safe, Sgt T. Whitmore (WOp/Ag) KIA, buried at Capuccini War Cemetery, Malta. P/O Barclay and Sgt Lee were killed 8-12-1941, qv.
08-11-1941	V5961 107 Squadron: FTR; crashed into ship's mast on shipping strike off Greece; crew Sgt W. Hopkinson, Sgt I. Hamilton, and Sgt J. Gibson KIA and buried in Phaleron War Cemetery, Athens.
08-11-1941	Z7895 18 Squadron: FTR: shot down by flak while attacking convoy in Ionian Sea; crew F/Lt G. Pryor, Sgt D. Mills, and Sgt T. Buckley KIA, commemorated on Runnymede Memorial.
18-11-1942	Z7408 105 Squadron: DBR, believed in air raid.
19-11-1941	Z7914 107 Squadron: overshot landing at Luqa, ran into quarry.
19-11-1941	V6492 18 Squadron: FTR from shipping sweep shot down by destroyer; Sgt J. Woolman, Sgt R. Walker, and Sgt H. Macaulay missing presumed KIA, commemorated on Malta Memorial.
19-11-1941	V6060 18 Squadron: FTR from shipping sweep; Sgt D. Buck, Sgt C. Newsome, and Sgt F. Thompson KIA.
19-11-1941	Z7860 18 Squadron: FTR shot-down by flak attacking convoy in Gulf of Sirte; Sgt H. Hanson, Sgt G. Parsons, and Sgt J. Poulton KIA. Sgts Hanson and Poulton commemorated on Alamein memorial: Sgt Parsons buried in Sirte Military Cemetery.
04-12-1941	Z7775 107 Squadron: FTR, hit by fighters off Messina and crashed; Sgt R. Kidby (Pilot) and Sgt L. Burcher (Obs) KIA and buried at Catania, Sgt J. Hughes (WOp/Ag) survived and became PoW.
05-12-1941	Z7925 OADU (ex-114 Squadron): u/c collapsed in heavy landing at Luqa, DBR; Sgt N. Harrison, Sgt Noel and Sgt Ingram safe.
05-12-1941	Z7910 OADU (ex 226 Squadron): stalled and u/c collapsed in heavy landing at Luqa, DBR; Sgt H. Jewel unhurt.
08-12-1941	V5465 18 Squadron: FTR, collided with Z9719 (below) en route to bomb Catania aerodrome, Sicily, crashed into sea; crew P/O J. Barclay, Sgt H. Lee, and Sgt W. Allan KIA.
08-12-1941	Z9719 18 Squadron: FTR, collided with V5465 (above), crashed into sea; crew Sgt W. Cuming, Sgt R. Tollett and Sgt J. Pilley KIA. Both crews commemorated on Runnymede Memorial.
11-12-1941	Z7802 18 Squadron: FTR, shot down by AA fire in raid on Argostoli harbour; crew F/Lt E. Edmunds DFC RNZAF, Sgt S. Hedin DFM and Sgt M. Mills KIA, buried in Argostoli, re-interred in Phaleron War Cemetery, Athens.
11-12-1941	Z7613 18 Squadron: FTR, shot down by flak in raid on Argostoli harbour, NFD.
13-12-1941	Z7368 107 Squadron: FTR, shot down in raid on Argostoli harbour; Sgt R. Gracie, F/Sgt A. McLean, and F/Sgt J. Calderwood KIA, re-buried in Phaleron War Cemetery, Athens, after 1953 earthquake in Cephalonia.
13-12-1941	Z7858 18 Squadron: FTR, shot down by Me.109 during raid on Argostoli harbour and ditched; crew Sgt F. Jury, Sgt T. Black, and Sgt D. Mortimer rescued by fishermen and survived.
13-12-1941	Z7800 107 Squadron: FTR from attack on Argostoli harbour; crew Sgt A. Lee, Sgt R. Haggett and Sgt A. Comeau RCAF became PoWs.
14-12-1941	Z7958 OADU (ex-110 Squadron): baulked on landing at Luqa, both engines cut on attempted overshoot due to lack of fuel, crash-landed near Luqa village; Sgt E. Waine and Sgt D. Phillips injured, Sgt G. Taylor unhurt, aircraft DBR.
17-12-1941	Z7804 18 Squadron: attacked MT on Sorman/Zuara road, Libya, crashed into sea 3km E of Zuara; 107 Squadron crew P/O F. Keene and Sgt C. Small rescued and became PoWs, Sgt J. Pickup (WOp/Ag) KIA, buried in Tripoli War Cemetery. (ORB gives serial as Z9804.)
18-12-1941	Z7802 18 Squadron: reported lost on sortie from Malta, no further details available.
22-12-1941	Z7915 107 Squadron: FTR; crashed into sea during raid on MT near Sirte; crew KIA, Sgt R. Henley (Pilot, aged 19) commemorated on El Alamein Memorial, Sgt H. Parsons (Obs) and Sgt D. Darcy (WOp/Ag) buried at Tripoli.
24-12-1941	Z7848 107 Squadron: FTR; hit by flak attacking ship in Zuara harbour and struck mast; crew KIA, Sgt E. Crossley (Pilot, aged 19) and Sgt H. Luke (WOp/Ag) buried at Tripoli, Sgt K. Newson (Obs) commemorated on Malta Memorial.

24-12-1941	Z9852 107 Squadron: FTR from shipping patrol; P/O I. Paul (Obs) KIA, P/O G. Mockridge (Pilot) and F/O J. Ensel (WOp/Ag) survived.
26-12-1941	Z7978 DBR in air-raid, unit not given.
26-12-1941	Z7959 destroyed by fire in air-raid at Luqa, unit not given.
26-12-1941	Z7796 18 Squadron: FTR from sortie from Malta, cause not recorded; Sgt O. Summers, Sgt J. Billett, and Sgt W. Marshall KIA, commemorated on Malta Memorial.
29-12-1941	Z9818 DBR in air-raid on Luqa, unit nor given.
30-12-1941	Z9816 18 Squadron: FTR; damaged by ship's AA fire and ditched off Tunisia; P/O K. Wyatt, Sgt J. Burke, and Sgt J. Giles rescued and became PoWs, freed 11-1942.
04-01-1942	Z9676 82 Squadron: lost on Egypt/Luqa ferry flight, believed shot down by fighters; Sgt A. Guy, F/Sgt W. McNally RCAF and Sgt R. Mander KIA, commemorated on Alamein Memorial. Serial number not known.
04-01-1942	Z7689 82 Squadron: lost in same circumstances; Sgt D. Beirnes RCAF, Sgt J. Robins and Sgt P. Chaning-Pearce KIA, commemorated on Alamein Memorial. Serial number not known.
07-01-1942	Z7652 18 Squadron: FTR from reconnaissance sortie off Cap Bon; crew Sgt S. Baker, Sgt D. Phillips, and Sgt R. Hillman KIA, commemorated on Malta Memorial.
08-01-1942	Z7645 21 Squadron: hit by flak from torpedo-boat and ditched off Kerkenna Islands; crew believed rescued.
13-01-1942	Z7790 113 Squadron: reported shot down by return fire from Ju.52s off Malta; P/O R. Huggins, P/O J. Hilton and Sgt J. Lait KIA, commemorated on Malta Memorial. 113 left for India 30-12-1941 but may have left aircraft in Malta for use by crew from another squadron.
14-01-1942	Z7431 21 Squadron: FTR; hit by flak and blew up on shipping strike off Kerkenna Islands; crew P/O K. Coakley RNZAF, Sgt D. McLaren, and Sgt D. Groves KIA, commemorated on Malta Memorial.
14-01-1942	Z7342 21 Squadron: FTR; hit mast and crashed into sea on shipping strike off Kerkenna Islands; F/Lt H. Dukes-Smith, Sgt A. Wratten, and F/Sgt A. Hussey KIA, commemorated on Alamein Memorial, Egypt.
15-01-1942	Z7760 107 Squadron: destroyed by fire during air-raid on Luqa.
29-01-1942	Z7271 21 Squadron: FTR; hit by debris from leader's bombs, crashed near Tripoli; F/Lt E. Fox (Pilot) and P/O R. Taylor (Obs) KIA, Sgt A. Pepper (WOp/Ag) survived, POW, F/Lt Fox and P/O Taylor buried in Tripoli War Cemetery.
04-02-1942	Z9806 21 Squadron: FTR; wing struck water in daylight raid on Palermo harbour, cart-wheeled and sank; W/Cdr W. Selkirk and P/O F. Ashley KIA, commemorated on Malta Memorial, Sgt S. Phillips RCAF survived and became PoW.
04-02-1942	Z9812 21 Squadron: FTR; crashed into cloud-covered hills on daylight raid on Palermo harbour; F/O F. Workman, P/O K. Smethurst and Sgt V. Lewis KIA, buried in Catania War Cemetery.
04-02-1942	Z9824 21 Squadron: FTR; crashed into cloud-covered hills on daylight raid on Palermo harbour; F/Sgt J. Ibbotson RNZAF and P/O D. Clement KIA, buried in Catania War Cemetery, Sgt H. Graham survived and became PoW.
04-02-1942	Z7341 21 Squadron: FTR; crashed into cloud-covered hills on daylight raid on Palermo harbour; Sgt M. Houston, P/O J. O'Grady and Sgt L. Frost KIA, buried in Catania War Cemetery.
06-02-1942	Z7308 21 Squadron: FTR; shot down by Me.109s off Filfia Islands returning from raid; S/Ldr R. Stewart RNZAF, P/O D. Morris and P/O R. Smaridge KIA, commemorated on Malta war memorial.
06-02-1942	Z9822 21 Squadron: FTR; shot down by Me.109s off Filfia Islands returning from raid; P/O J. Grieve, P/O C. Rowley and Sgt R. Hall KIA, commemorated on Malta Memorial.
06-02-1942	Z9725 21 Squadron: FTR; shot down by Me.109s off Filfia Islands returning from raid; F/Sgt G. Cameron RNZAF, Sgt R. Fletcher and Sgt G. Hancock KIA, buried in Malta.
07-02-1942	Z9712: overshot downwind landing on air-test; Sgt M. Taylor of 242 Squadron safe, aircraft later DBR in air raid at Safri while under repair.
11-02-1942	Z9823 21 Squadron: FTR; shot down by Me.109s returning from shipping sweep; Sgt J. Stubbs RAAF, Sgt J. Graham and Sgt P. Tyas KIA, commemorated on Malta Memorial.
23-02-1942	Z7420 ex-105 Squadron: DBR in air raid on Luqa.
22-03-1942	Z7315 ex-21 Squadron: failed to become airborne on take-off at Luqa, swung into obstructions and DBF, Sgt M. Cecil RAAF safe.
30-03-1942	Z9832 1 OADU: lost on ferry flight from Luqa to Egypt; Sgt H. Janney, Sgt J. Shiner and Sgt C. Johnson, all RAAF, killed and commemorated on Malta Memorial.
31-03-1942	V6434 ex-21 Squadron: destroyed in air raid on Luqa.
01-05-1942	Z7288: parked at 108 MU, struck by Wellington Z8518, DBR.
12-07-1942	Z7643 ex-107 Squadron: crashed on landing at Luqa, DBR.

T2076, T2381 and T2399 also lost in Malta, but units and dates not known.

Chapter 28

Tunisia: Blenheim swansong in the Middle East

The British Chiefs of Staff convinced President Roosevelt's top advisors at a meeting in London in July 1942 that the Allies were simply not powerful enough at that stage to mount a cross-Channel invasion of mainland Europe as desired by both the Americans and the Russians, for Stalin called persistently for the Allies to 'Open a Second Front Now' to relieve the enormous military pressure upon the Soviet Union. Consequently, the Allies decided to invade French North Africa, followed by Sicily then mainland Italy, to draw off as much as possible of the Axis forces. Code-named Operation Torch, the first joint Anglo-American operation was mounted on 8 November 1942, with two large-scale landings in Algeria near Oran and Algiers, and two more in Morocco, north and south of Casablanca. Torch was under the command of General Dwight Eisenhower, with the Allied Air Forces split into two Commands, Brig-Gen James Doolittle heading the American 12th Army Air Force, and Air Marshal Sir William Welsh the RAF Eastern Air Command, which included a Wing comprising four squadrons of Blenheim Mk Vs.

The reaction to the Torch landings by the considerable Vichy French military, naval and air forces was an unknown factor – together they had more than 125,000 men based in French North Africa (Morocco, Algeria and Tunisia). In the event, there was some fierce fighting between the French defending their ports at Oran, Safi (near Casablanca) and Algiers from the attempted seizure by the Allied invaders. After a short and confused conflict, Admiral Darlan, the Vichy Commander, upon realising the vast size of the Anglo-American invasion forces, agreed a cease-fire with the Allies on 10 November. Both the Allied and Axis combatants were very concerned about the uncertain allegiances of the powerful Vichy French fleet, mainly anchored at Toulon in the unoccupied portion of France. The Germans had reacted rapidly to Torch by occupying the rest of France and moving to seize the fleet, but nearly 80 warships were scuttled in Toulon harbour before they could do so. Axis forces also occupied Tunisia and quickly built up the strength of their land and air forces there, including some 70 of the latest Messerschmitt Bf.109F and G models and a dozen Focke-Wulf Fw.190s. Once the Blenheim Mk Vs – heavier and slower than the Mk IVs – encountered these effective fighters their losses mounted alarmingly. In addition, many more Blenheims than before were lost on delivery flights. These accidents, and those suffered by the squadron working up for Operation Torch, were due mainly to the increasing unreliability of the Mercury engines in the heavier Mk Vs, and the fact that several more aircraft were lost as the ships carrying them were sunk (see Appendix 1).

Blenheim Mk V operations in the Mediterranean area other than Algeria and Tunisia

Apart from their use in Operation Torch, Blenheim Mk Vs were introduced into the Western Desert Air Force. 15 Squadron of the South African Air Force converted from Mk IVs to Mk Vs in August 1942, but kept a Detachment at Kufra Oasis as before, also retaining some of its Mk IVs so that both marks operated together in support of the 8th Army during its slow, cautious, advance westwards. The Squadron was then based at Mariut and the forward airfield at Gianaclis for anti-shipping duties. Its Mk Vs were part of the all-Bristol mini strike-force of Blenheims and Beauforts escorted by Beaufighters that on 26 October 1942 destroyed the tanker *Proserpina* laden with desperately needed fuel for the Axis forces in North Africa – although at the cost of three of their five Blenheims, one of which was hit by flak before striking the mast of the tanker (see Appendix 2). Major D. Pidsey, CO of 15 Squadron SAAF, was awarded an immediate DFC for this action. A Mk V from the Squadron also sank the submarine *U205* off the coast of Derna on 17 February 1943, and 15 continued operations with them until it commenced converting to Baltimores in May 1943, carrying out the last operation with its Bisleys (as it called the Blenheim Mk Vs) in July. 16 Squadron SAAF was re-formed for the maritime role with Marylands and Bisleys in November 1942, but changed to Beauforts in June 1943, and 17 Squadron SAAF at Aden, equipped with Bisleys in December 1942, moved to Egypt in August 1943 and re-equipped with Venturas. 13 (Hellenic) Squadron, formed in May 1941 with Greek personnel, changed its Ansons for Blenheim Mk IVs in January 1942 and converted to Mk Vs in October, continuing to operate these in the maritime role from Aden for a year until converting to Baltimores in October 1943. 8 Squadron, also at Aden, and 244 Squadron, at Sharjah, both engaged mainly in maritime patrols, had also changed their Mk IVs for Mk Vs, as had 162, the Signals Squadron, which continued its valuable electronic counter-measures duties – all three squadrons operated Blenheim Mk Vs until 1944. The Free French *Groupe Lorraine*, comprising the Escadrilles *Metz* and *Nancy*, also changed from Mk IVs to Mk Vs to carry out their maritime patrols from Palestine until January 1943, when their personnel returned to the UK and were re-equipped with Bostons to form 342 Squadron. However, *Groupe Picardie* in Syria continued using its Mk IVs and Mk Vs, mainly for anti-submarine patrols, right until the end of the war in Europe. Although these squadrons did not face the full might of the Luftwaffe, they lost many aircraft through accidents, especially 15 Squadron SAAF mentioned above, which wrote off 12 in just a few weeks (see Appendix 2). Other squadrons and units with Mk Vs in the Mediterranean area also suffered steady attrition due to accidental losses (see Appendix 3).

Blenheim Mk V operations during Operation Torch and in Algeria and Tunisia

However, the most significant deployment of the Blenheim Mk V was in Algeria and Tunisia in support of Operation Torch, and the four squadrons involved did face that might directly. Two of the 2 Group Blenheim squadrons, 18 and 114, and two Army Co-Operation Blenheim squadrons, 13 and 614, were re-equipped with Mk Vs, trained for direct support of the Army and transferred to the Eastern Air Command. Ferry flights positioned them at a very crowded Gibraltar airfield, where the runway had been lengthened from 980 to 1,400 yards by extending it into the sea. Ten days after the initial Torch landings the Blenheim Mk Vs were operating from Blida airfield in Algeria. Their aircraft were known initially as Bristol Bisleys Mk V-Ds (D for Desert), but were commonly, and soon officially, called Blenheim Mk Vs – although the South Africans preferred to keep the Bisley name. 139 Squadron at Horsham St Faith was also re-equipped with the Mk V in June 1942, but, as noted in Chapter 18, Bomber Command HQ decided that they were unsuitable for operations in the dangerous skies of northern Europe. Fortunately for the crews, 139 Squadron was issued with the De Havilland Mosquito in September, as was 105 Squadron – their few surviving crews had returned from Malta, leaving behind them the mere handful of Blenheims IVs that remained.

The four Blenheim Mk V squadrons of 326 Wing were based at Blida and supported the British 1st Army in its advance towards Tunisia by attacking enemy airfields, artillery positions, tank concentrations, troop convoys, and supply ports. These Blenheims were painted in the desert camouflage scheme and did not carry squadron codes; most had just the individual aircraft letter, intended to be painted in a different colour for each squadron, but apparently the poor ground-crews were not told which colour represented which squadron! The Blenheims operated under difficult conditions – serviceability, especially of the over-worked engines, was poor, with tools, equipment and spares almost non-existent, due in part to the torpedoing of one of the Wing's main supply ships. These factors, combined with harsh living and climatic conditions, made life for the ground-crews particularly trying as they toiled tirelessly out in the open. The attrition caused by accidents

The Free French Groupes GRB 1, Lorraine and Bretagne, used both Mk IVs and Mk Vs in North Africa, such as Z7633 taxying out past four 250lb bombs, and two – one a rare Free French Mk IV-F – at Gabon operating earlier against Vichy French forces in Senegal.

The difficulty of keeping Mk Vs fit for operations is clear from this shot at Blida, with the port engine cowling in the left foreground, and the intake for the oil-cooler in the leading-edge of the wing.

continued, frequently following engine failure as the heavier Mk V could not maintain height on one engine – the ground-crews soon stripped out much of the armour, the under-nose guns, and even the radio transmitter in an attempt to improve matters. More accidents were caused by the hard, stony ground at the forward airfields, which punctured the Blenheims' tyres, causing blow-outs either during the extended take-off runs or upon landing; in either case it was almost impossible for the Pilot to prevent the aircraft swinging off the runway, which all too frequently caused the undercarriage to collapse and the aircraft to be damaged beyond repair. The Blenheim Wing moved forward to Canrobert airfield at the end of November to be 150 miles nearer the front where the British 1st Army was meeting stiff resistance from the German forces. For daylight raids fighter escorts were laid on, but as the winter weather deteriorated the fighter airstrips often became waterlogged and the Blenheims had to carry out their operations without protection so that, if they were intercepted, losses rose sharply. In any event they had no protection from the effective anti-aircraft fire from the German airfield defences. In the six weeks to the end of the year, two of the four Squadrons – 13 and 18 – suffered the devastating losses of no fewer than 55 of their aircraft (see Appendix 5). If each squadron had been issued with the full compliment of 18 Initial Equipment aircraft, together a further 16 as replacements, that is 55 lost out of the total of 68. The other two squadrons – 114 and 614 – also suffered steady losses too (see Appendix 5), but not on the same debilitating scale.

Bombing-up a Mk V at Canrobert in December 1942. Details include the large 'desert filters' on the air intakes, the depth of the Observer's foot-well in the fairing for the under-nose guns, and the rear-view mirror over the cockpit.

Servicing and re-fuelling arrangements in Algeria were primitive. The crew (left) appear to be waiting for their MkV, while the cowling on the ground (right) shows the large circular opening for the air-filter.

On 17 November and again on the 28th W/Cdr Hugh Malcolm, CO of 18 Squadron, led the Mk Vs in two attacks at very low level on Bizerte airfield; they lost four aircraft on the first raid – two of them colliding – but altogether had seven aircraft written off on that black day. The Blenheims moved further forward to Souk-el-Arba landing ground, and on an even blacker day, 4 December 1942, the total destruction of yet another complete formation of Blenheims took place – to follow the pattern of the disasters that befell 82 Squadron at Gembloux in Belgium and Aalborg in Denmark, and 211 Squadron at Monastir in Greece, as described earlier. Malcolm led the Wing's 11 remaining serviceable Blenheims in a daylight attack on the newly discovered Luftwaffe landing ground on a racecourse at Chouigui in Tunisia. He knew that it would be particularly dangerous as it was their second raid of the day on the same target, and it was not possible to arrange a fighter escort as a sweep was on, but the second raid had been specifically requested by the 1st Army. One of the Blenheims burst its tail-wheel on take-off and swung off the runway, and 10 minutes into the flight another had an engine failure and crash-landed on the rough terrain. Malcolm led the remaining nine onwards, hugging the ground, but before they reached the target area they were intercepted by the 109s of

W/Cdr Hugh Malcolm, CO of 18 Squadron, was awarded a posthumous Victoria Cross for leading a Blenheim Mk V formation on an unescorted daylight raid in Tunisia on 4 December 1942 – they were all brought down.

Gruppen I and *II* of JG.2 and hacked from the sky one by one within a few minutes. Malcolm pressed on towards the target, his Blenheim being the last to fall, so all ten were lost (see Appendix 3). Hugh Malcolm was awarded the Victoria Cross posthumously – the first in the Middle East – thus becoming the second Blenheim Pilot to receive the highest award for bravery. At the suggestion of Air Marshall Tedder's wife, a string of recreational clubs for off-duty servicemen were set up and named as Malcolm Clubs to honour his memory, the last of these (in London) finally closing down only recently.

After these disastrous losses the CO of the Blenheim Wing, Group Capt L. Sinclair GC DSO DFC (former CO of 110 Squadron who won his George Cross for rescuing an airman from a crashed and burning Blenheim, later AVM Sir Laurence Sinclair GC KCB CBE DSO* DFC), restricted the Blenheims to night operations, and even those could only be mounted on moonlit nights. For, apart from the difficulties of navigation and location of targets in the darkness, 75 per cent of the crews had not been trained in night operations, so losses due to enemy action (see Appendix 4) were soon exceeded by self-inflicted losses through accidents. Sinclair reported to HQ on 6 January 1943 that 326 Wing – from all four squadrons combined – could put up only 12 aircraft and crews from the remaining 59 of each that were, or should have been, available for operations.

The daylight bombing role in Tunisia in support of the Allied Armies in 1943 was filled by the increasing numbers of Bostons, Baltimores and Marauders that were becoming available, and the Blenheims were relegated largely to maritime duties – mainly anti-submarine patrols. The importance of this activity is shown by the fact that some 130 German and Italian submarines were sunk during the war in the Mediterranean. In the

Group Captain Laurence Sinclair GC, CO of 326 Wing (the four squadrons of Mk Vs), at his mobile HQ in Tunisia with his Intelligence Officer, S/Ldr Rose, in 1943.

A crew are pictured leaving their Blenheim on return to base, their faces revealing the strain of night operations in a Mk V. They often carried six 250lb bombs – four in the bomb-bay and an extra pair under the inner wing sections. This load further degraded the Mk V's poor take-off and climb performance.

short period from the Torch landings and during the campaign in Tunisia, some 230 enemy ships were sunk, 100 of them by attacks from aircraft, the rest by the Royal Navy or mines. 203 Squadron converted from Blenheim IVs to Baltimores in August 1942, but – due to a shortage of Baltimores – was issued with Blenheim Mk Vs in October 1942 and operated these for a couple of months until more Baltimores became available. The Free French *Groupe Bretagne*, with its Mk V Blenheims, was attached to it at Ben Gardane, Tunisia, in April 1943 before it converted to Marauders. 114 Squadron was happy to change to Boston Mk IIIs in April 1943, as was 18 Squadron in May. But 13 Squadron had to soldier on with its Mk Vs until December 1943, although it started converting to Lockheed Venturas for coastal patrols in October, while 614 Squadron carried on in the night bombing role in Tunisia until the Axis forces there surrendered on 12 May 1943. Both squadrons moved to Bo Rizzo in Sicily in August following Operation Husky, the Allied invasion of Sicily in July, and this marked the end of operations by the Blenheim squadrons in direct support of the Allied Armies. 614 then continued operating its Blenheim Mk Vs on maritime patrols over the Mediterranean until it was disbanded on 21 January 1944, to be re-formed in March as a Halifax Mk II squadron in the Middle East.

This Mk V of Groupe Bretagne at Ben Gardane has its under-nose guns removed, plus stripes on the wings and fuselage, similar to the invasion stripes used on Allied aircraft for the Normandy D-Day landings.

The Observer in some Maritime Mk Vs had a free-gun to help suppress flak – the extra bulge for the bulky radio is clearly shown.

A sad swansong for the Blenheims

The introduction of the Mk V into service had been particularly troublesome. Their operational debut in the front line had been an unmitigated disaster and, mercifully, was cut short, but not before many more of the brave young men in the Blenheim crews were added to the lengthening lists of losses. The skies over the front in North Africa proved to be just as dangerous, indeed just as deadly, as the skies over northern Europe would have been to the slowest, heaviest and most vulnerable of the three marks of Blenheim. The decision of the Air Staff not to deploy Blenheim Mk Vs on operations in the northern European area was wise, but for those very Mk Vs to be pitted against the same opposition in North Africa was, in my view, unwise. However, the Rootes factories were still busy producing new Mk Vs, and continued to do so until June 1943, some three years after the obsolescence of the design had become painfully clear, but the lack of a suitable replacement aircraft (as described in Chapter 18) meant that the Mk V had to continue in front-line use somewhere, somehow, so that it remained in active service for far too long. The entire episode provides a sorry and somewhat sour swansong to the lengthy and illustrious operational career of the Bristol Blenheim, and one that has sadly sullied the heroic name and proud reputation of all Blenheims. As we have seen, this was a name that had been hard fought for, and a reputation that had been earned with the greatest difficulty – frequently in the face of heavy odds and in the most desperate of circumstances – by the courageous Blenheim crews, during years of highly dangerous operations in both the European and the Middle Eastern Theatres of War. It is a shame that all the Blenheims seem to have been tarred with the same brush as the Mk Vs.

An 18 Squadron Mk V is refuelled for night operations at Canrobert late in the Tunisian Campaign, with a Wellington alongside.

The massive defeat suffered by the Wehrmacht in the Battle of Stalingrad over the winter of 1942, resulting in the capture by the Russians of Field Marshal von Paulus and the remains of the German 6th Army in February 1943, was the major turning point in the Second World War. The defeat of Rommel, hamstrung by shortages of supplies, at El Alamein, and the landings in North Africa, were other turning points. The latter led finally to the surrender of von Arnim and the German and Italian forces in Tunisia, and marked the final expulsion of the Axis powers from the continent of Africa after three years of fierce, fluctuating fighting on land, at sea, and in the air – years that had cost the lives of tens of thousands of servicemen of many different nationalities. This narrative needs to record that these years, from beginning to end, had seen over 2,000 Blenheims of all three marks actively involved in the seesaw struggle to control the Middle East and North Africa, the Blenheims taking heavy losses throughout, aircraft losses that resulted in a distressingly high level of casualties to their crews, many hundreds of whom were killed, injured or captured. The Free World owes them a great debt.

THE BRISTOL BLENHEIM

These 8 Squadron Mk Vs at Khormaksar, Aden, in January 1944 wear the Maritime camouflage scheme of grey and green over white.

BA612 is virtually all white and looks sleek without the under-nose extension. BA437 of 244 Squadron at Sharjah sank U-533 on 17 October 1943 in the Gulf of Oman. Sgt L. Chapman was awarded the DFM, and the submarine's only survivor was rescued and became a PoW.

BA491, a Mk V of 162 Squadron, the Radar/Electronics Unit at El Fayid, in 1942.

Appendix I

Mk V Blenheim losses during delivery to the Middle East

17-05-1942   BA376 OADU: crashed on landing at Gibraltar on ferry flight from Portreath; Sgt E. Singleton injured, crew safe.

21-05-1942   BA365 OADU: ditched after take-off at Gibraltar, unable to maintain height when fully loaded; Sgt R. Leverett, P/O A. Wigner and Sgt W. Dale injured.

24-05-1942   BA371 OADU: ditched after take-off at Gibraltar, unable to gain height as over-loaded; Sgt P. Taverner, Sgt B. Halley and Sgt J. Craner RAAF injured.

18-06-1942   BA445 OADU: missing between Portreath and Gibraltar; Sgt W. Bratt, Sgt W. Smith and Sgt J. Cook Missing in Action, commemorated on Runnymede Memorial.

21-06-1942   BA377 OADU: missing between Gibraltar and Malta; Sgt L. Martin, Sgt A. Cocking and Sgt A. Saunders interned in Tunis then Algeria.

21-06-1942   BA446 OADU: crashed in Mediterranean off Derna; W/O H. Langton RCAF, Sgt D. Leather and Sgt G. Wicks injured, rescued by Italians, became PoWs. Sgt Wicks died of his injuries and is buried at sea.

21-06-1942   BA288 OADU: crashed in forced-landing Portella, Portugal, out of fuel due to leak in tank; Sgt G. Ashplant, Sgt W. Smalley, and Sgt W. Bakewell RAAF interned but allowed to escape to Gibraltar.

15-07-1942   BA383 OADU: crashed on take-off at Maidaguru, Nigeria.

16-07-1942   BA542 OADU: missing on ferry flight between Malta and Egypt; Sgt P. Adams RAAF, Sgt G. Price RCAF, and Sgt G. Russell Missing in Action, commemorated on Alamein Memorial.

25-07-1942   BA388 OADU: collided with AZ929 (below) on take-off at Takoradi.

25-07-1942   AZ929 OADU: struck by BA388 (above) while parked at Takoradi.

07-08-1942   BA530 OADU: swung on landing at Kano on ferry flight from Takoradi, u/c collapsed, DBR.

14-08-1942   BA589 OADU: belly-landed at Takoradi after air-test.

19-08-1942   BA579 OADU: spun into ground near Ogbomosho, Nigeria; Sgt F. Borrett, F/Sgt A. Bowditch and Sgt R. Henderson, all RAAF, killed and buried at Oshogbo Cemetery, Nigeria.

28-08-1942   BA531 ADU: spun into ground from cloud, Saltpond, Gold Coast; P/O R. Purser, Sgt P. Hearne RAAF and F/Sgt J. Mortimer killed, buried in Takoradi European Cemetery.

02-10-1942   BA686 ADU: tyre burst on landing at Wadi Seidna on Takoradi route, u/c collapsed, DBR.

19-10-1942   BA455 ADU: controls failed, crashed after take-off at Fort Lamy, Chad, P/O Warcup and crew uninjured.

20-10-1942   BA162 ADU: hit trees while low flying, near Kano, Nigeria, DBF; Sgt E. Neve RNZAF and Sgt R. Lambert RAAF killed, buried in Kano.

16-10-1942   BA853, BA860 and BA863: lost at sea.

29-10-1942   BA728: lost at sea.

12-12-1942   AZ878 ADU: engine cut, crashed in attempted forced-landing near Takoradi; F/Sgt R. Birdsall (Obs) killed, F/Lt R. Bernard (Pilot) and Sgt A. Jenkins (WOp/Ag) injured.

14-12-1942   BA714 ADU: became lost in bad weather, force-landed on beach near Jiwani, and abandoned there.

30-12-1942   BA587 ADU: crashed in attempted forced-landing at Khotance.

13-01-1943   BA432 ADU: crashed in attempted forced-landing at Bara, Sudan.

18-01-1943   BA883, BA886, BA907, BA930, BA941, BA942 and BA943: shipment of new Mk Vs lost at sea.

24-01-1943   BB166 1 OADU: port engine cut, crashed in forced-landing on beach at Praia de Troia, Portugal, crew safe and returned to UK in April.

25-01-1943   BA116 2 ADU: crashed on take-off at LG 209.

14-02-1943   AZ885 ADU: crashed on ferry flight, Ibadan, Nigeria.

16-02-1943   BA888 ADU: belly-landed in error on ferry flight.

26-02-1943   BB101 1 OADU: missing on ferry flight over Mediterranean; Sgt R. Walters, Sgt H. Hall, and Sgt R. Brown interned, returned to UK later.

26-02-1943   EH317 1 OADU: u/c collapsed landing on incomplete runway at Blida, DBR.

14-03-1943   EH332 1 OADU: force-landed at Pavoa de Varzim, Portugal, on Portreath-Gibraltar ferry flight; F/O Hutton, Sgt Graham, and Sgt Lindsay interned.

19-03-1943   BA996 1 OADU: tyre burst when taxying, swung into soft ground, tipped up, DBR.

25-04-1943   BA296 ADU: engine cut, belly-landed, DBR.

20-05-1943   EH464 1 OADU: missing on Portreath-Gibraltar ferry flight; F/O E. Simonds, Sgt N. Newham, and Sgt C. Holt Missing in Action, Presumed Dead 6-12-1943.

25-05-1943   BA982 1 OADU: tyre burst on take-off at Ras-el-Mar, Morocco, crashed; F/Sgt A. Palmer and crew safe.

29-05-1943   EH459 1 OADU: ditched off Portuguese coast on ferry flight; Sgt E. Croft NZ, Sgt K. Jenkins, and Sgt S. Bennett rescued and taken to Gibraltar.

29-05-1943   BA293 2 (ME) Ferry Control: crashed in forced-landing on ferry flight 26 miles SW of Malakal, Sudan; Sgt J. Fleet and crew safe.

27-06-1943   EH331 1 OADU: missing on Portreath-Gibraltar ferry flight, ditched; F/O Thomas, Sgt Percival, and Sgt Froud rescued and taken to Ras el Mar.
04-09-1943   EH371 1 OADU: flew into Gulf of Oman in mist at Jiwani.
15-09-1943   L8837 OADU Mk IV: crashed in forced-landing, Cintra, Portugal.
22-10-1943   EH438 1 OADU: overshot landing at Jiwani, ran into Gulf of Oman.

Appendix 2

Mk V Blenheim losses in preparation/transit for Operation Torch

27-09-1942   BA805 18 Squadron: force-landed near Swaffham, Norfolk, engine failure during formation practice; Sgt W. Williams and Sgt J. Brown uninjured, P/O E. Clarke injured.
12-10-1942   BA724 614 Squadron: hit trees on approach to Snailwell, Cambs, prior to leaving for Gibraltar; Lt G. Norenius SAAF and P/O Drake killed in action (KIA), Sgt Russell badly burned.
06-11-1942   BA818 18 Squadron: took off from Boscombe Down, dived into ground at Newton Toney, Wilts, following engine failure; crew Sgt R. Gibson, Sgt P. McCleod, and Sgt H. Shaw killed.
06-11-1942   BA813 13 Squadron: crashed in Algeria; F/O R. Lofthouse, Sgt L. Parslow and Sgt D. Anderson safe.
11-11-1942   BA738 18 Squadron: engine cut on ferry flight, ditched off Santa Pola, Spain; Sgt F. Rounding, P/O P. Willis and Sgt E. Murphy interned.
11-11-1942   BA811 18 Squadron: crashed in forced-landing at Siddi Moussa, Algeria, 13km short of destination of Blida; S/Ldr R. Eyton-Williams, P/O I. Speight, and F/Sgt D. Franklyn safe.
14-11-1942   BA826 114 Squadron: engine trouble on Portreath/Gibraltar transit, force-landed at Lisbon Airport; aircraft and crew Sgt A. Johnson, Sgt R. Elliott and Sgt J. Cox interned, crew released, returned to UK.
14-11-1942   BA750 114 Squadron: out of fuel and ditched near Tangier; P/O W. Walker, P/O D. Young, and Sgt N. Welch interned.
17-11-1942   BA807 13 Squadron: force-landed near Mazarron, Murcia, Spain, in transit Portreath-Gibraltar; set on fire by crew F/O D. Fraser, Sgt W. Lloyd and Sgt H. Machan, who were interned, returned via Gibraltar 01-1943.
17-11-1942   BA829 614 Squadron: force-landed at Aldeia Nova, Portugal, in transit Portreath-Gibraltar; crew P/O C. De Wesselow, F/Sgt I. Self and Sgt W. Bunting interned, repatriated 01-1943. (Aircraft became AM261 with Aeronautica Militar.)

Appendix 3

Mk V Blenheim losses in Operation Torch and the North Africa campaign

to 31 December 1942

11-11-1942   BA870 18 Squadron: DBR by enemy action, probably an air-raid.
16-11-1942   BA736 18 Squadron: damaged in raid on Bizerte airfield, crash-landed at Rouina, Algeria; Sgt J. Eccleston, F/Sgt H. Gates and Sgt J. Martin made own way back to base.
17-11-1942   BA725 18 Squadron: collided with BA815 (below) on raid to Bizerte airfield, crashed at Cap Serat; Sgt R. Mead, Sgt R. Cheyne, and Sgt G. Andrews KIA, buried at Massicault War Cemetery, Tunisia.
17-11-1942   BA815 18 Squadron: collided with BA725 (above) on raid to Bizerte airfield, crashed at Cap Serat; P/O G. Berry, Sgt V. Rowen, and Sgt R. Page KIA, buried at Massicault War Cemetery, Tunisia.
17-11-1942   BA754 18 Squadron: crashed in forced-landing at Tizi Ouson on return from same raid, out of fuel when lost in bad weather; P/O D. Thorburn DFC, P/O V. Swain DFC and Sgt E. Newstead safe.
17-11-1942   BA780 18 Squadron: damaged by fighters on same raid and crash-landed at Djidelli; S/Ldr W. Tucker DFC, P/O W. Docherty and F/Sgt J. Bartley DFM safe.
17-11-1942   BA794 18 Squadron: shot down by Me.109 off Cap Ben Sekka on same raid; P/O C. Kaye, P/O E. Clegg and Sgt J. Walder KIA, commemorated on Malta Memorial.
17-11-1942   BA819 18 Squadron: damaged by fighters on same raid, belly-landed at Blida; P/O W. Sims, Sgt S. Litchfield and Sgt C. Cosens safe.
17-11-1942   BA828 18 Squadron: shot down by Me.109s near Bizerte; F/Sgt W. Williams, W/O J. McCombie, and F/Sgt J. Brown became PoWs.
20-11-1942   BA726 18 Squadron: hit by flak over Bizerte, u/c collapsed on landing at Blida; P/O N. Marwood-Tucker, F/Sgt E. Yelland and Sgt A. Roberts uninjured.
23-11-1942   BA799 114 Squadron: FTR from raid on Sidi Ahmed; P/O J. Mathias, P/O D. Truscott and Sgt T. Catchpole KIA, commemorated on Malta Memorial.
24-11-1942   BA821 614 Squadron: DBR by enemy action at Canrobert, possibly an air-raid.

25-11-1942	BA803 18 Squadron: crash-landed near Picard on return from raid; Sgt A. Woodfield, F/Sgt R. Duke RNZAF and Sgt R. Parker safe.
28-11-1942	BA797 18 Squadron: destroyed by direct hit from bomb during air-raid at Canrobert.
29-11-1942	BA745 13 Squadron: hit tree on take-off at Blida for raid and crashed; F/Lt J. Shaw slightly hurt, P/O E. Martin broke both ankles, P/O R. Roberts uninjured.
29-11-1942	BA748 614 Squadron: hit by another aircraft when parked at Blida, DBR.
30-11-1942	BA755 13 Squadron: damaged by Fw.190s, crash-landed at Bone; F/Lt D. Sandeman, F/O W. Parsons, and Sgt A. Murdoch uninjured.
30-11-1942	BA730 18 Squadron: crashed at Jafa el Mizan, Algeria, en route Blida-Canrobert; Sgt J. Proud, Sgt D. Allen, F/Sgt J. Evans, and Cpl L. Duncan (ground-crew passenger) killed, buried in Dely Ibrahim War Cemetery.
30-11-1942	BA739 18 Squadron: tyre burst on take-off for raid at Blida, swung and DBR.
01-12-1942	BA690 114 Squadron: crashed on landing at Blida on return from raid, struck parked Beaufighter EL150; F/Lt D. Fuller, Sgt J. Weiss and Sgt E. Newstead slightly injured.
02-12-1942	BA872 614 Squadron: missing from raid to Tunis; F/O T. Young and W/O G. Campbell RCAF KIA, buried at La Reunion War cemetery, Bougie, Algeria, F/Sgt A. Walsh RCAF injured.
03-12-1942	BA824 18 Squadron: crashed in forced-landing near Canrobert; 13 Squadron crew Sgt W. Stott, P/O W. Gent and Sgt G. Booty safe, but all KIA in BA796 the next day.
04-12-1942	BA804 114 Squadron: crashed soon after 0240 take-off from Blida for raid on Bizerte docks; F/Lt J. Coates DFC slightly injured, P/O J. Evans injured, and F/Sgt D. Symondson DFM safe.
04-12-1942	BA790 18 Squadron: shot down by fighters during raid on Chouigui; S/Ldr R. Eyton-Williams, F/Lt C. Dent and F/Sgt D. Franklyn KIA, buried at Beja War Cemetery, Tunisia.
04-12-1942	BA802 18 Squadron: shot down by fighters during raid on Chouigui; F/O R. Hill, F/Sgt S. Bryant and F/Sgt C. Green KIA, buried at Beja War Cemetery, Tunisia.
04-12-1942	BA795 18 Squadron: badly damaged by fighters during raid on Chouigui, crash-landed at Beja, DBF; P/O E. Holloway safe, Sub/Lt H. Wallace RNAS and Sgt H. Parsloe injured but survived.
04-12-1942	BA820 18 Squadron: damaged by fighters during raid on Chouigui, crash-landed at Beja: F/Lt A. Eller safe, P/O A. Harding and P/O N. Eckersley DFC (WOp/Ag) both injured but survived.
04-12-1942	BA875 18 Squadron: shot down by fighters during raid on Chouigui; W/Cdr H. Malcom, P/O J. Robb, and P/O J. Grant DFC KIA, buried at Beja War Cemetery, Tunisia. Hugh Malcolm awarded posthumous VC for this action
04-12-1942	BA734 614 Squadron: damaged by flak during raid on Chouigui, crash-landed at Souk el Khemis; F/O W. Irving, F/O L. Quevatre, and Sgt G. Limoges RCAF survived.
04-12-1942	BA800 614 Squadron: shot down by fighters during raid on Chouigui; 18 Squadron crew F/Lt A. Breakey, Sgt A. Simpson, and F/Sgt S. Greene KIA, commemorated on Malta Memorial.
04-12-1942	BA796 18 Squadron: shot down by fighters during raid on Chouigui; 13 Squadron crew Sgt W. Stott, P/O W. Gent and Sgt G. Booty KIA, buried at Beja War Cemetery, Tunisia. This crew had crash-landed in BA824 the day before.
04-12-1942	BA869 614 Squadron: damaged by fighters during raid on Chouigui, crashed near Beja, burned out; F/O C. Georges, F/Sgt J. Taylor, and Sgt W. Sorbie KIA, buried in Beja War Cemetery.
05-12-1942	BA791 114 Squadron: damaged in raid on Bizerte, abandoned at night near Rebeval, Algeria; F/Sgt R. Baike RCAF KIA (parachute did not open), buried at Dely Ibrahim War Cemetery, Algeria, Sgt G. Acheson RCAF and Sgt J. Cummings safe.
14-12-1942	BA747 13 Squadron: struck hut on night take-off at Canrobert for raid; F/O J. Kruytbosch, Sgt J. Redman and Sgt C. Day RNZAF (aged 20) KIA, buried at Medjez-al-Bab, Tunisia.
15-12-1942	BA808 13 Squadron: crashed into shallow lake at Garaet Guellif when starboard engine caught fire following night take-off at Canrobert; F/O R. Broughton, Sgt F. Westbrook and Sgt A. Smith walked 12 miles back to base.
15-12-1942	BA742 114 Squadron: u/c damaged and jammed on night take-off at Canrobert, belly-landed 10 miles away; P/O J. Steele DFC, P/O R. Phillips and F/Sgt G. Gregory safe.
16-12-1942	BA814 18 Squadron: engine caught fire on take-off at Canrobert, crash-landed; F/Sgt B. Yanover RCAF safe.
17-12-1942	BA732 614 Squadron: tyre burst on take-off at Canrobert, swung and u/c collapsed, destroyed by fire.
18-12-1942	BA785 13 Squadron: FTR from raid on Bizerte; F/O A. Jickling, F/Sgt H. Martin RCAF and W/O J. Welsh RCAF KIA, commemorated on Malta Memorial.
22-12-1942	BA822 18 Squadron: engine cut after take-off at Souk-el-Arba, crash-landed; P/O D. Beers safe, Sgt T. Parker injured, Sgt W. Herring safe.
27-12-1942	BA817 114 Squadron: on night approach in mist returning from raid flew into hillock at Canrobert; P/O W. Berriman RAAF injured, Sgt K. Smith RNZAF KIA, buried at Medjez-el-Bab War Cemetery, Tunisia, and Sgt T. Barton injured.
29-12-1942	BA784 18 Squadron: hit by own AA fire attempting to relocate base in bad weather, crash-landed at Bangouch, DBF; F/O G. Sims and F/Sgt S. Litchfield injured, Sgt C. Cosens (WOp/Ag) KIA.

Appendix 4

Mk V Blenheim losses in campaigns in North Africa and Sicily from 1 January 1943

01-01-1943   BA786 13 Squadron: engine cut on take-off at Canrobert, u/c raised to stop, DBF; F/O J. Kilpatrick, F/O J. Bush and F/Sgt P. Lunt escaped safely.

07-01-1943   BA731 614 Squadron: FTR from raid in Tunisia; F/O Wallis, Sgt Wills and Sgt Warden survived.

11-01-1943   BA809 614 Squadron: crash-landed on beach near Bougie; S/Ldr Bonner, Sgt Rowlands, and Sgt Burns uninjured.

12-01-1943   BA721 114 Squadron: tyre burst on landing at Canrobert, swung and u/c collapsed, DBR.

16-01-1943   BA751 114 Squadron: u/c collapsed on landing at Canrobert, destroyed by fire.

16-01-1943   BA810 614 Squadron: engine cut on take-off at Canrobert, force-landed 3 miles from base; F/O Hanbury, Sgt O'Neil, and Sgt Switzer unhurt.

16-01-1943   BA816 614 Squadron: tyre burst on take-off at Canrobert, swung and u/c collapsed, DBR; S/Ldr P. le Cheminant, P/O W. Service, and P/O J. Ryder uninjured.

18-01-1943   BA983 114 Squadron: tyre burst on take-off at Ain Tucker, u/c collapsed, DBR.

19-01-1943   BA988 18 Squadron: FTR from night intruder sortie; W/Cdr W. Tucker, F/Lt W. Docherty, and F/Sgt J. Bartley DFM KIA.

19-01-1943   BA998 13 Squadron: crashed on take-off at Pretville.

20-01-1943   BA991 114 Squadron: FTR from night intruder sortie.

20-01-1943   BA810 614 Squadron: engine cut on night take-off, crash-landed in field; F/Lt Robarts, Sgt Phillips, and Sgt Lidell uninjured, aircraft repaired.

20-01-1943   BA744 114 Squadron: u/c collapsed on landing at Canrobert, DBR.

22-01-1943   BA783 614 Squadron: engine cut on take-off at Oulmene, overshot runway and DBR; F/O M. de Bock-Porter, P/O F. Perkins and Sgt M Petrie RNZAF slightly injured.

26-01-1943   BA945 328 Wing: based at Blida, crashed in forced-landing near Tipasia, Algeria.

28-01-1943   BA812 614 Squadron: force-landed in desert near Aline Tukha, DBR; F/O Arthur, P/O Custance, and Sgt Newcombe uninjured.

30-01-1943   BB147 614 Squadron: lost power after take-off at Canrobert, gills left open, flew into ground and blew up; 18 Squadron crew P/O P. Sainsbury RNZAF, Sgt M. Kenny and Sgt C. Phillips KIA, buried at Medjez-el-Bab, Tunisia.

15-02-1943   BB161 614 Squadron: tyre burst on landing at Oulmene, u/c collapsed, aircraft destroyed by fire; P/O Ross-Gower and crew escaped.

15-02-1943   BA801 13 Squadron: tyre burst on landing at Oulmene, swung and u/c collapsed, DBR.

22-02-1943   BA946 13 Squadron: tyre burst on take-off at Oulmene, u/c collapsed, DBR.

23-02-1943   BA999 114 Squadron: damaged by flak, engine cut, bombs jettisoned, intercom failed; Sgt R. Gratrex (WOp/Ag) baled out and killed; F/O R. Newcombe (Pilot) belly-landed at Canrobert, he and Sgt M. Dunne (Obs) safe, aircraft DBR.

23-02-1943   BA792, 18 Squadron: hit ground on attempted overshoot at Canrobert, destroyed by fire; Sgt Woodfield, F/Sgt Duke, and Sgt Parker escaped with slight injuries.

25-02-1943   BB139 13 Squadron: struck tent on take-off at Oulmene and crashed.

28-02-1943   BA798 114 Squadron: FTR from raid, no further details available.

28-02-1943   BA981 114 Squadron: FTR from raid, no further details available.

19-03-1943   EH313 13 Squadron: crashed in forced-landing near Ain Beida.

20-03-1943   BA806 13 Squadron: shot down on raid to Djebel Tebaga; F/P L. Armstrong, Sgt F. Trusler, and Sgt R. Lawrence KIA.

20-03-1943   BB176 614 Squadron: hit by AA on raid to Djebel Tebaga, returned to base but DBR.

26-03-1943   BA951 18 Squadron: u/c collapsed on landing at Oulmene; P/O Mooney, P/O Pryke, and Sgt Kendall safe, aircraft DBR.

30-03-1943   EH318 18 Squadron: crashed on night take-off at Oulmene, believed due to frost on wings; W/O J. Mayne RCAF, Sgt S. Kirk, and F/Sgt L. O'Neil RNZAF KIA, buried at Medjez-el-Bab, Tunisia.

07-04-1943   BB174 18 Squadron: bounced on night landing at Oulmene, stalled and crashed; F/O Brierley (Pilot) died of injuries two days later, Sgt Smith and Sgt Keeble recovered from injuries.

11-04-1943   BB164 614 Squadron: tyre burst on take-off at Oulmene, swung, destroyed by fire; F/O D. Smyth, Sgt J. Patterson, and Sgt Milner escaped.

13-04-1943   EH323 13 Squadron: crashed on landing at Bone; F/Sgt S. Wigmore, F/Sgt K. Teaford, and Sgt E. Smith slightly injured.

16-04-1943   EH328 13 Squadron: tyre burst on take-off at Oulmene, crashed.

19-04-1943   BA727 13 Squadron: shot down on night patrol off Tunisian coast; F/O D. Scrymgeour RNZAF, Sgt C. Davis and Sgt D. Crowley KIA, commemorated on Malta Memorial.

23-04-1943   BB158 13 Squadron: tyre burst on take-off at Oulmene, swung and u/c collapsed.

01-05-1943	BA786 13 Squadron: swung on take-off at Bone and ran into bomb-crater, DBR.
02-05-1943	BB171 614 Squadron: engine cut after take-off at Canrobert, crashed in attempted forced-landing near Lake Guelif, 5 miles from airfield; F/O Simpson and crew safe.
11-06-1943	BB181 13 Squadron: tyre burst on landing at Blida, swung and undercarriage collapsed.
27-06-1943	BB169, 614 Squadron: crashed in attempted forced-landing at Delizane East, DBR; F/O Beatty, F/Sgt Jarvis, F/O Taraska, and Sgt Bourke (extra Obs) escaped with minor injuries.
17-07-1943	BA825 614 Squadron: undercarriage collapsed on landing at Tafaraoui; P/O G. Thomas, S/Ldr L. Wallace, and Sgt Proud uninjured.
19-07-1943	EH333 13 Squadron: crashed attempting emergency landing at Blida.
31-08-1943	BA781 614 Squadron: tyre burst on landing at Canrobert, u/c collapsed, destroyed by fire.
13-09-1943	BB182 614 Squadron: tyre burst on take-off at Bo Rizzo, Sicily, DBR.
13-09-1943	BB102 614 Squadron: flew into sea on ASR search over western Mediterranean; F/Lt E. Holloway (Pilot) rescued, F/Sgt B. Harvey (Obs) and F/Sgt G. Taylor (WOp/Ag) killed.
18-09-1943	BB184 13 Squadron: tyre burst on landing at Bo Rizzo, Sicily, u/c collapsed; F/O L. Trevallion, Sgt C. Rivett, and Sgt F. Chapman uninjured, aircraft DBR.
30-09-1943	BB178 614 Squadron: engine seized, lost propeller, crash-landed at Terra Nova, Pausania, Sardinia; S/Ldr P. Roberts, Sgt L. Phillips, and Sgt J. Woods unhurt and returned to base in another aircraft.
21-12-1943	BA950 614 Squadron: tyre burst on take-off at Bo Rizzo, Sicily; F/O Richardson, on third operation of day, and crew unhurt.

Appendix 5

Mk V Blenheim losses to 15 Squadron SAAF

26-06-1942	BA373: u/c collapsed on landing at LG 116.
30-06-1942	BA367: tyre burst on landing at El Ballah, swung and u/c collapsed; Lt J. Kinnery uninjured.
30-06-1942	BA440: hydraulics failed, landed on one wheel and without flaps at El Ballah.
07-07-1942	BA314: crashed just after take-off at LG 99.
07-07-1942	BA325: belly-landed at LG 97.
21-07-1942	BA442: u/c failed to lower, belly-landed at Helwan, DBR; Lt M. Barnes unhurt.
28-08-1942	BA149: crashed on landing at Mariut.
03-09-1942	BA239: engine cut, ditched in Mediterranean; Lt J. Whittle, Lt A. Swart and Air Sgt A. Turnbull rescued 23 hours later by HM destroyer Kelvin.
09-09-1942	BA321: port engine seized on anti-sub patrol off Port Said, belly-landed on island in Nile Delta; Lt A. Donaldson safe, 2/Lt M. Hall injured, Air Sgt G. van Rensburg safe.
*12-10-1942	BA497: shot down by return fire from SM.81 that they had forced down into Western Desert; Lt C. Bruton-Simmonds, Lt W. du Plessis, and A/Sgt R. Behrens KIA, commemorated on Alamein Memorial.
24-10-1942	BA335: crashed in forced-landing near Kufra after engine seized; Lt B. McLeod, Lt M. Priday, Air Sgt H. Lewis and Air Mech D. Smart safe.
*26-10-1942	BA234: hit by flak on anti-shipping strike, crashed into sea; Lt A. Groch (Pilot) and A/Sgt R. Twigg (WOp/Ag) rescued from dinghy and became PoWs, Lt A. Johnston (Obs) KIA, buried in El Alamein War Cemetery.
*26-10-1942	BA368: hit mast of tanker on same anti-shipping strike and crashed into sea; Lt E. Dustow, Lt A. Farr, and A/Sgt I. Van Graan KIA, commemorated on Alamein Memorial
*26-10-1942	BA486: aircraft or pilot hit on same anti-shipping strike, collided with Beaufort DE110 on return journey, crashed into sea; Lt S. Leisegang, Lt H. Francis, and A/Sgt P. Swann KIA, commemorated on Alamein Memorial.
21-11-1942	BA233: tyre burst on take-off from LG 21, swung and u/c collapsed; Lt O. Venn and crew safe.
09-12-1942	BA378: engine cut, hydraulics failed, crashed in attempted forced-landing near Maryut, DBR; Capt Cromhout (Pilot) safe, Lt M. Hall (Obs) injured, Col L. Wilmot (passenger) safe.
31-01-1943	BA331: engine seized, crashed in attempted force-landing near Gambut; Lt A. Campbell, Lt J. Christie and Sgt N. Bonner RCAF safe.
15-03-1943	BA330: swung on landing at Maryut, DBR; Lt Coutts, 2/Lt R. Blackburn and F/Sgt K. Barnstable RCAF safe.
22-03-1943	AZ943: ran into soft ground on landing at Gambut, tipped up; Lt Coutts and crew unhurt, aircraft DBR.
05-04-1943	BA318: belly-landed at Aboukir, DBR; crew safe.
01-05-1943	BA865: crashed into lake just after night take-off at Mariut; crew rescued but Lt D. Tarr (Pilot) seriously injured (leg amputated), Lt R. Lock (Obs) died of injuries ten days later, 2/Lt C. Dowall (WOp/Ag) slightly injured and rescued other two.

*Aircraft lost on operations.

THE BRISTOL BLENHEIM

Appendix 6

Mk V Blenheim losses by other squadrons and units in the Middle East

01-07-1942   BA485 108 MU: crashed on take-off at Abu Sueir.

06-08-1942   BA148 70 OTU: u/c retracted too soon on take-off at Nakuru, sank back, DBR; F/Lt R. Whyard and crew uninjured.

08-08-1942   BA545 162 Squadron: sank back into ground attempting overshoot at Bilbeis.

13-08-1942   BA317 162 Squadron: hit bank on night take-off at Shaiba, DBF; Sgt W. Fergie RNZAF and Sgt N. Fairclough killed, LAC R. Garmory safe. Aircraft taking spares for Prime Minister's Liberator.

14-08-1942   BA585 162 Squadron: hit obstruction on take-off at Habbaniyah.

01-09-1942   BA541 162 Squadron: tyre burst on take-off at Lydda, swung, u/c collapsed.

24-09-1942   BA407 lost, unit and cause not recorded.

14-10-1942   BA529 203 Squadron; flew into ground in night circuit at LG.206 Abu Sueir North, DBR (SOC 1-12-1943); Sgt Johnson and Sgt Hirst unhurt.

16-10-1942   BA474 108 MU: lost power on take-off at Wadi Sharia, Palestine; Sgt B. Cousins uninjured.

25-10-1942   BA405 244 Squadron: crashed attempting overshoot at Sharjah, fumes entered cockpit, engine cut; Sgt J. Jordan RAAF safe, F/O W. Morell injured.

28-10-1942   BA322 8 Squadron: collided with BA477 after take-off at Socotra; P/O M. Bridgland, F/Sgt J. Mullard, Sgt R. Broad, and Major T. Walkley (Army passenger) killed, buried in Ma'ala War Cemetery, Aden.

28-10-1942   BA477 8 Squadron: collided with BA322 after take-off at Socotra; F/Sgt D. Hall (Pilot) injured, Capt G. Younger (Army passenger) killed. Both aircraft destroyed by fire on Socotra Island, Gulf of Aden.

02-11-1942   BA199 72 OTU: engine cut in circuit, belly-landed 4km S of Nakuru; Lt A. Ritchie SAAF (solo Pilot) unhurt.

04-11-1942   BA532 108 MU: both engines cut, crash-landed near Abu Sueir.

12-11-1942   BA193 72 OTU: tyre burst and u/c collapsed on landing at Nakuru.

23-11-1942   Z7679 70 OTU: engine cut, dived into ground attempting forced-landing near Kisumu, destroyed by fire.

25-11-1942   BA381 272 Squadron: belly-landed at LG 229, Idku; Sgt J. Fisher RCAF and crew safe. Struck by taxying Beaufighter EL321 while parked awaiting inspection on 27-11-1942, DBR.

26-11-1942   BA313 244 Squadron: tyre burst on take-off from Salalah, Oman, swung and u/c collapsed; Sgt J. Bridle and crew safe.

26-11-1942   BA528 72 OTU: crashed in attempted forced-landing 17 miles NE of Eldoret, DBF; P/O F. Kaegi (Pilot) injured, F/Sgt V. Swale (Obs) killed, buried in Eldoret Cemetery, Sgt G. Dowling RAAF (WOp/Ag) injured.

29-11-1942   BA678 454 Squadron RAAF: swung on landing at Qaiyara, Iraq, u/c collapsed; Sgt D. Rayner safe.

26-12-1942   BA172 70 OTU Mk V: heavy landing at Nakuru caused tyre burst, swung and u/c collapsed; Sgt A. Shephard unhurt.

28-12-1942   BA615 70 OTU Mk V: control lost on take-off at Nakuru and crashed, DBF (as was 200 acres of grassland); P/O F. Carr RCAF safe.

30-12-1942   BA158 16 Squadron SAAF: crashed in attempted forced-landing at Kilifi, Kenya; Lt T. Carter injured, 2/Lt J. Louw uninjured, LAM L. Piggott died of his injuries, buried in Mombasa European Cemetery.

(For Mk V losses by Support and Training Units from 01-01-1943 see Appendices to Chapter 31)

11-01-1943   BA304 13 (H) Squadron: engine cut on approach to LG 07, belly-landed and DBR.

14-01-1943   BA447 8 Squadron: hit sea-wall on night approach to Khormaksar; F/Sgt R. Edwards RAAF (solo Pilot) slightly injured.

15-01-1943   BA672 16 Squadron SAAF: engine cut on bombing practice, crashed in forced-landing at Port Reitz, Kenya, DBF; Lt W. du Toit and Lt H. Auret safe, F/Sgt J. Tarshish injured.

15-01-1943   BA205 162 Squadron: engine cut, belly-landed at Heliopolis.

18-01-1943   BA397 244 Squadron: crashed on take-off at Ras el Hadd.

19-01-1943   BA141 244 Squadron: crashed on take-off at Sharjah.

23-01-1943   BA708 8 Squadron: tyre burst on take-off at Scuiscuiban, crashed and caught fire; F/Sgt G. Wylie and crew escaped, four 250lb depth charges exploded soon after.

29-01-1943   BA315 162 Squadron: crashed into sea 3 miles off Saida, Lebanon.

01-02-1943   BA101 244 Squadron: crashed in forced-landing 35 miles NE of Sharjah.

04-02-1943   BA 395 13 (H) Squadron: tyre burst on take-off at LG 07, crashed; F/Lt Troupakis, S/Ldr Aapantzis, and P/O Anastassion unhurt.

15-02-1943   BA885 8 Squadron: tyre burst on take-off at Khormaksar, crashed.

16-02-1943   BA435 8 Squadron: crashed on landing at Khormaksar and destroyed by fire; Sgt Ashton (Pilot) received slight burns.

18-02-1943   BA167 13 (H) Squadron: engine cut, crashed on approach to Gambut, destroyed by fire; F/O Angellidis, Capt Coumanakos, and F/Sgt Panayiotopoulos escaped.

20-02-1943	BA375 244 Squadron: crashed attempting forced-landing on shore near Aden.
22-02-1943	BA676 8 Squadron: dived into sea off Khormaksar, Aden, on night-flying practice, cause unknown; F/Sgt G. Wylie killed (see also 23-01-1943 above), no details of crew in ORB.
02-03-1943	BA526 16 Squadron SAAF: tyre burst on take-off at Kilifi, Kenya, u/c collapsed; Lt M. Boshoff, 2/Lt H. Pasmore and F/Sgt D. Sarson safe.
02-03-1943	BA454 13 (H) Squadron: tyre burst on take-off at LG 07, swung and u/c collapsed.
06-03-1943	BA424 244 Squadron: overshot landing at Basra.
08-04-1943	BA534 244 Squadron: crashed while making emergency approach at Sharjah.
10-04-1943	AZ994 16 Squadron SAAF: u/c retracted prematurely on take-off, sank back on to ground at Eastleigh, not repaired; Lt J. Andrew, 2/Lt R. Cohen and F/Sgt C. Springett safe. 2/Lt Cohen was also in BA450, DBF on 15-04-1943, qv.
15-04-1943	BA884 8 Squadron: engine failed on air-test, crashed in forced-landing near Bandar Kassim; F/O H. Parfett and crew uninjured.
15-04-1943	BA450 16 Squadron SAAF: developed fuel leak, caught fire after landing at Renk ELG, Sudan; Lt Col J. Clayton (Pilot) and F/Sgt A. Furman (WOp/Ag) badly burned, 2/Lt R. Cohen (Obs) suffered shock.
17-04-1943	BA402 16 Squadron SAAF: encountered sandstorm, tyre burst on landing at Kosti, Sudan, swung and tipped up; 2/Lt F. Gee, 2/Lt E. Morrell and F/Sgt C. de Jager uninjured.
23-04-1943	BA849 Free French Groupe Bretagne: crashed into sea off Tunisia.
30-04-1943	BA430 244 Squadron: lost propeller, force-landed at Shinas, Onan, DBR.
30-04-1943	BA937 13 (H) Squadron: struck telegraph pole on night approach to LG 07 and crashed; W/O Cavourinos (Pilot) uninjured.
08-05-1943	BA882 13 (H) Squadron: crashed in forced-landing during sandstorm at Sidi Kameish.
20-05-1943	BA927 8 Squadron: dived into sea during night-flying practice on approach to Khormaksar, Aden; Sgt I. Kirk RAAF (solo pilot) killed.
20-05-1943	BA457 244 Squadron: u/c collapsed while taxying at Sharjah.
31-05-1943	BA603 244 Squadron: crashed in forced-landing on beach near Masirah, destroyed by fire; F/Sgt Tucker (Pilot), Sgt Hooper (WOp/Ag), and LAC Jones (Fitter, passenger) injured but recovered, F/Sgt W. Symons (Obs) trapped in aircraft and died.
04-06-1943	BA211 16 Squadron SAAF: engine cut, belly-landed 5 miles north of Castel Benito, Libya; Lt L. du Toit SAAF safe.
04-06-1943	BA426 244 Squadron: crashed on approach to Sharjah; Sgt N. Wren and crew safe.
05-06-1943	BA599 162 Squadron: engine cut, crash-landed near Homs; F/O L. Krull, F/O S. Drabble, F/Sgt J. Broughton, and LAC J. Kinsey slightly injured.
09-06-1943	BA656 244 Squadron: attacked submarine in Gulf of Oman off Umm Rasus, depth-charges hung up, port engine caught fire, ditched; P/O Tulley and crew rescued.
14-06-1943	BA538 162 Squadron: tyre burst on take-off at LG 207, swung and u/c collapsed.
14-06-1943	BA458 162 Squadron: crashed on landing at LG 207.
01-07-1943	BA524 244 Squadron: crashed in attempted forced-landing east of Jask after escorting convoy PB.84; no injuries reported to F/Lt Bennett, P/O Cherry, and P/O Ford.
08-07-1943	BA482 8 Squadron: crashed in forced-landing on beach at Bahgal, Somaliland, in bad visibility; P/O K. Ellis safe, F/Sgt J. Milner injured, Sgt L. Adams safe.
15-07-1943	BA500, 244 Squadron: burst into flames on take-off at Masirah, Sgt D. Nash, Sgt G. Keir, and Sgt M. Sublet KIA.
08-08-1943	BA323 13 (H) Squadron: engine cut, crashed in forced-landing 25 miles from Gambut.
13-08-1943	BA294 13 (H) Squadron: swung on landing at Gambut 3, u/c collapsed, destroyed by fire.
15-08-1943	BA718 8 Squadron: belly-landed at Khormaksar, Aden.
24-08-1943	BA606 244 Squadron: tyre burst on landing at Sharjah, aircraft ground-looped and u/c collapsed, destroyed by fire; Sgt Hall, F/O Walter, and Sgt McLeod escaped.
26-08-1943	BA390 244 Squadron: tyre burst on landing at Masirah, swung and undercarriage collapsed.
30-08-1943	BA255 8 Squadron: belly-landed while making dummy low-level attack at Jigajigga, Somaliland.
13-09-1943	BA290 13 (H) Squadron: failed to climb on take-off at Gambut, belly-landed and DBR.
16-09-1943	BA487 13 (H) Squadron: port engine cut on take-off, crashed on landing at Gazala; F/O Frangias and P/O Petrolekas slightly injured, P/O Georgiopoulos broke leg.
22-09-1943	BA668 8 Squadron: blown off runway by strong cross-wind and u/c collapsed at Jigajigga, Sudan.
26-10-1943	BB154 244 Squadron: port engine failed, returned to Ras el Hadd, pumped u/c down, landed downwind without flaps, overran runway into sea, overturned; F/Sgt F. Mosley, Sgt M. Rowland and Sgt P. Palmaston injured but rescued.
27-10-1943	BA437 244 Squadron: belly-landed at Sharjah.
29-11-1943	BA594 8 Squadron: engine cut, ditched half a mile off Salalah.
02-12-1943	BA944 244 Squadron: belly-landed at Ras el Hadd.
23-12-1943	BA380 244 Squadron: ditched off Sharjah.

Chapter 29

The fall of Malaya and Singapore

We saw at the end of Chapter 21 how the Allied position in the Western Desert was weakened by the withdrawal over the winter of 1940 of Blenheim squadrons and other units to support the defence of Greece against the Italian, then German, invasion. This situation was repeated a year later when, once more, Blenheim squadrons and other units were removed from the Middle East, reducing the strength of the Allies, and sent to the Far East in an attempt to resist the Japanese invasion of British colonies there. This was summed up succinctly by historian Norman McMillan in his four-volume *The RAF in the Word War:* 'The Middle East lost them, the Far East could not gain by them... They were all too late.'

Preparations and provisions for the defence of those countries that were then part of the British Empire in the Far East were even more inadequate than they had been in the Middle East. Years of parsimony and complacency, and a misguided reliance on sea-power and a few fixed heavy naval guns facing seawards to defend the main British base in the region – the so-called 'island fortress' of Singapore – had resulted in the British and Commonwealth forces in the Far East being gravely ill-equipped and grossly over-extended. The last thing the British Government wanted in 1941 was a war on a third front, so it carefully avoided provoking the Japanese, although they had invaded China earlier. The Japanese Imperial forces had captured most of the ports on the south-east coast of China and were moving ever southwards. They occupied Hanian Island in 1939 – near the coast of French Indo-China (now Vietnam and Cambodia) into which they moved in September 1940, forcing the Vichy French to allow a complete take-over in July 1941. This caused the United States to impose an oil embargo, which further angered the Japanese. Therefore the threat to the other Asian countries controlled by the West was growing rapidly at a time when they were weakened by events in Europe. France and Holland had been defeated and the British were faced with unprecedented demands from the Northern European War Zone, as well as from the whole of the Middle East area, for trained soldiers, sailors and airmen, as well as all the armaments needed to equip them. These demands moved the Far East well down the list of priorities for allocation of already severely over-stretched resources. So when the violent challenge from Japan to the power of the Western countries throughout Asia became a reality, the British and Commonwealth forces in the area found themselves ill-prepared, outnumbered, and lacking in modern equipment. They were quite incapable of performing the enormous tasks expected of them, despite countless acts of personal bravery and self-sacrifice – in which, once again, the Blenheim squadrons featured prominently.

A Blenheim Conversion Flight had been set up at Risalpur, near the Khyber Pass in north-west India (now Pakistan), in late 1938, and 11 Squadron was the first to change to Blenheim Mk Is in July 1939, followed by 39, 60 and 27 Squadrons by that September. The Unit moved to Ambala, between Delhi and Lahore, in 1940; 11, 39 and 27 Squadrons had converted from Hawker Harts, and 60 Squadron from elderly Westland Wapitis.

Two of these squadrons, 11 and 39, were sent to Singapore from India in August 1939, and two more squadrons of Mk I Blenheims, 34 and 62, arrived from the UK in September. On these 72 bombers rested the air defence of the British Empire in the Far East, for they were the only modern aircraft stationed there in September 1939, at the start of the war in Europe, apart, that is, from four Sunderland flying boats, which were backed by half a dozen aptly named but ancient Singapore biplane flying boats, and two dozen equally aged Vickers Vildebeest torpedo biplanes; the Fleet Air Arm also had a few Swordfish and Walrus biplanes. Notable by their absence were any interceptor fighter aircraft at all, ancient or modern – at that time the Japanese had no airfields that would

Illustrating the technical advance represented by the Blenheim, two Mk Is en route to 60 Squadron in 1939 are refuelled at Madras alongside a Westland Wapiti II. The nearest, L1545, was lost on a night shipping patrol over the Bay of Bengal on 30 August 1940.

bring Singapore within the range of their single-seat fighters. The perceived threat was from a sea-borne invasion force, not an army invading from the Malayan peninsula to the north, where new RAF airfields were being hastily constructed. A series of staging posts had been created all the way from the Suez Canal zone via Baghdad and Calcutta to enable rapid aerial reinforcement to take place – if, of course, any aircraft could be spared – and it was planned that Royal Navy capital ships would be able to steam out in time to deal with enemy invasion convoys. However, these plans did not take into account the growing power of aircraft, or aircraft carriers – the Japanese Navy had ten – and neither the RAF nor the FAA possessed any modern torpedo aircraft. The new airfields in Malaya were being built on the coastal plains in preference to the jungle-covered and mountainous interior, and were thus rendered virtually indefensible from a military point of view – if captured they would place Japanese fighters within range of all of the Allied bases, including Singapore. We noted in Chapter 21 that 11 and 39 Squadrons had taken their Blenheims back from the Far East to reinforce Aden in June 1940, leaving only 34 and 62 Squadrons. The four Sunderlands of 230 Squadron at Singapore had gone to the

Officer Pilots of 34 Squadron at Watton in August 1939, just before taking their Mk I Blenheims out to Singapore, where they were re-equipped with Mk IVs in June 1941; nearly all of them became casualties.

This series of propaganda photographs was taken when 62 Squadron left Tengah, Singapore, for Alor Star, northern Malaya, on 8 February 1941, showing rows of Brewster Buffaloes. The clipped-wing Blenheim being over-flown by three fighters while taxying out is L1134 of Arthur Scarf, who was flying this machine when he earned his Victoria Cross on 9 December.

Middle East too, but they returned to Ceylon (now Sri Lanka) rather than Singapore.

Nevertheless, the Air Staff did what it could to strengthen defences in the Malayan peninsula. In February 1941 the Blenheim Mk Is of 60 Squadron were moved from Lahore to Mingaladon airfield at Rangoon in Burma (now Myanmar) – the Squadron rotated detachments of its Blenheims to several of the staging points along the reinforcements route, and in July a flight of Buffalo fighters was added to its strength. Also in February the Mk I-Fs of 27 Squadron were moved from Risalpur in north-west India to Kallang on the Malayan coast. They were designated as the only night-fighter unit in South East Asia, but spent most of their time practising formation-flying in daylight. In June 34 Squadron changed its Mk Is for Mk IVs at Tengah in Singapore, and 62 Squadron took its Mk Is to Alor Star in northernmost Malaya close to the border with Siam (now Thailand). Two RAAF Squadrons, 1 and 8, added a useful offensive and reconnaissance capability with their Lockheed Hudsons, and four squadrons of American Brewster Buffaloes at last provided some single-seat interceptor fighters. It was believed they would be superior to Japanese fighters, but in the event they, and their inexperienced pilots, proved far inferior.

There was a tragic incident on 4 April: S/Ldr Hackett, CO of 27 Squadron, invited F/Lt T. Vigors DFC, a Flight Commander in 243, one of the newly formed Buffalo squadrons, for a trip in his Blenheim I-F (L6667), following a lively discussion as to the relative performance and manoeuvrability of their different fighters. As they taxied out, Vigors was called by radio to AHQ, so his place was taken by F/Lt J. Mansel-Lewis, 243's other new Flight Commander. Unfortunately the Squadron Leader stalled at the top of a loop over Singapore harbour and the Blenheim fell into an inverted spin; Mansel-Lewis managed to bale out but was struck by a propeller and killed, as was S/Ldr Hackett and the WOp/Ag, Sgt Beaman, both of whom had been unable to escape from the spinning Blenheim. The crash was witnessed by an RAF tug, ironically named *Buffalo*, commanded by S/Ldr G. Farnhill, which was taking 20 key personnel from 151 MU on a trip as a reward for their hard work in assembling the Buffaloes. It was diverted by radio to look for survivors but ran into a mine and sank with the loss of all on board.

The Allied Commander in Chief of the Far East, Air Chief Marshal Sir Robert Brooke-Popham, repeatedly requested reinforcements – military, naval and aerial – finally sending a strongly worded signal to the Chiefs of Staff on 20 August, in which he correctly described the Allied defences as 'deplorably weak'. But a further demand on scarce British resources had arisen in the summer of 1941 when the British War Cabinet decided to send supplies of arms to aid Russia, then being pressed very hard by the German invasion. These supplies included 240 Hurricanes, and a similar number of P.40s, which – had they been sent mainly to the Far East as intended – would have made a crucial difference in the defence of Malaya and Singapore. However, two of the Royal Navy's most powerful capital ships, the latest and best British battleship HMS *Prince of Wales* together with HMS *Repulse*, with their escorting destroyers, arrived at Singapore on 2 December 1941. Termed 'Force Z', they should have been accompanied by the aircraft carrier HMS *Indomitable*, but she ran aground by error in the West Indies on the way and could not complete the voyage. Five Catalina flying-boats were based at Seletar for long-range maritime reconnaissance, but even if they discovered an approaching enemy invasion force by visual search in the expanse of the South China Sea, its progress was unlikely to be hindered as the entire torpedo strike force still comprised of the elderly Vilderbeests with 36 and 100 Squadrons. These squadrons were understandably delighted to be told that they were being re-equipped; they received two Blenheims in November and the pilots commenced hasty twin-engine conversion. Six Australian-built Bristol Beauforts also arrived at Seletar, after long delays in manufacture, but they were unarmed and not ready for operational use. As they appeared just two days before the Japanese launched their attack on 8 December 1941, five were sent back to Australia – two crashing en route – and the sixth (T9543) was retained for photo-reconnaissance use (pictured on page 549). It was a classic, but unfortunately all too frequent, example of 'too little too late'.

60 Squadron was based at Mingaladon Airfield near Rangoon, seen here with an AVG Curtiss P40, but half of its Blenheims were caught at Kuantan in eastern Malaya when the Japanese invaded. L4829 suffered an engine fire when starting up at Mingaladon, but was repaired, only to be shot down over Malaya in February 1942.

On that date the squadrons of the RAF Far Eastern Command could field a total of 181 operational aircraft (52 of them Blenheims), with a further 88 unserviceable or in reserve (including 17 Blenheims). Other aircraft, but hardly 'operational', were six Wirraways (a version of the Harvard Trainer), a dozen Shark and Swordfish biplanes of 4 AACU, and even 25 private civilian aircraft such as Tiger Moths and Avro Cadets for the amateur pilots of the Malayan Volunteer Air Force! The Dutch had about 100 semi-obsolescent fighters, mainly Curtiss Hawks and Brewster 339s (a version of the Buffalo), together with about 80 Martin 139s (a forerunner of the Maryland), in the Dutch East Indies, Borneo and Java. The Japanese aerial armada of some 1,100 aircraft about to be unleashed on these over-attenuated, ill-trained and poorly equipped air forces was formidable indeed. The Allied Intelligence service – the Far East Combined Bureau (FECB) under Admiralty control at Singapore – was hopelessly inefficient and had grossly underestimated both the strength and capability of the twin Japanese Air Forces. The large Japanese Army and its powerful Navy each had its own Air Force, the former deploying nearly 700 front-line aircraft in the area and the latter more than 400 to support the invasion of Malaya – in addition to the 520 carrier-borne naval aircraft that could be brought into the area if their other commitments allowed. The scales were tipped further in favour of the Japanese as their aircraft were flown by highly trained crews, many of whom had gained useful combat experience in China. The FECB had received full particulars of the Mitsubishi A6M Zero-Sen fighter, headed 'A formidable Japanese fighter' giving details of its 350mph top speed, armament of two 20mm cannon and two 7.7mm machine-guns, ceiling of 34,000 feet, and – most importantly – a range with a drop-tank of an exceptional 1,900 miles), but failed to pass on this vital intelligence to the RAF. The shock to the RAF and RAAF fighter squadrons when they found themselves being out-performed, out-flown and comprehensively defeated by the highly manoeuvrable Zeros was a blow to morale from which they did not recover.

The Allied C-in-C, ACM Sir Robert Brooke-Popham, had prepared a pre-emptive strike plan, Operation Matador, to seize the narrow and more readily defensible 'neck' of the Malaysian peninsula, which contained two important airfields, Singora and Patani. It was a bold plan in view of his limited resources, but – most unfortunately – this 'neck' lay in neutral Siam (now Thailand) just beyond the northern border of Malaya, and he dare not violate Siam's neutrality as he was under strict orders to take no action that might antagonise the Japanese. The AOC, AVM Pulford, had formed 'Norgroup' by moving 34, his only squadron of Mk IV Blenheims, to Alor Star to join 62 Squadron's Mk Is there, and bringing up the Buffaloes of 21 Squadron to join 27 Squadron's Blenheim Mk I-Fs at Sungei-Patani, both airfields in the extreme north-west of Malaya, together with a small detachment of Buffaloes from 243 Squadron to join the Hudsons of 1 Squadron RAAF at Kota Bharu on the far north-east coast. In addition 60 Squadron, based at Mingaladon in Burma, had a detachment of eight Blenheims at Kuantan, further south on the eastern coast of Malaya, where they joined eight Hudsons of 8 Squadron RAAF; the Blenheims were there for armament training but were retained in view of the ominous situation.

On 6 December a Hudson spotted two large Japanese convoys steaming west in the Gulf of Siam off southern Indo-China, each of over 20 merchant vessels escorted by cruisers and destroyers – they were 300 miles away, but were they heading for Malaya or Siam? Operation Matador could not be launched until this was clear, and – critically – all attempts to locate the convoys throughout the next day failed, mainly because the weather had deteriorated badly with heavy rain and dense low cloud. None of the aircraft were fitted with ASV radar, and the one Catalina that had found a convoy was shot down before it could transmit the vital news, F/Lt Patrick Bedell and the other seven members of his crew being killed, the first Allied casualties in the Far East Theatre of War. By then it was

Opposite: Mk IVs arriving at Singapore docks in June 1941, and being re-assembled in a hangar at Tengah (note the Buffalo).

THE BRISTOL BLENHEIM

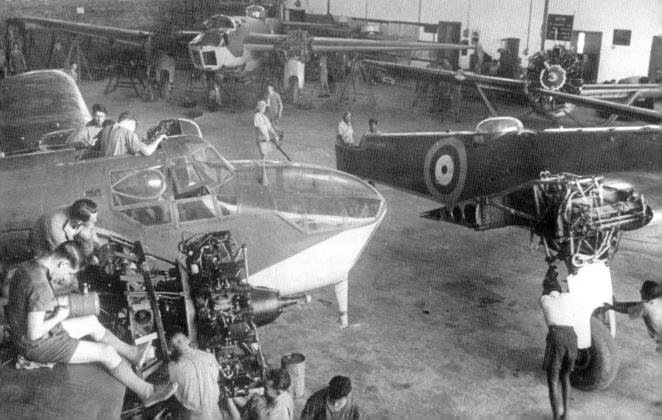

The outer fuel-tank is inserted (the fuel dump-pipe rests on the tool-box), then the aircraft taxies out for an air-test. 34 Squadron was the only one with Mk IVs when the Japanese forces struck.

too late to launch Matador, the initiative passed to the Japanese, and was not to be regained for several years. High-flying reconnaissance aircraft were seen over northern Malaya that day, Sunday 7 December, and two specially lightened Blenheims of 62 Squadron at Alor Star, flown by Acting Squadron Leaders C. Boxall and A. Scarf, attempted to intercept one, believed to be a Mitsubishi Ki.46, but were unable to do so as it was flying too high and too fast. (Arthur Scarf was to be awarded the highest accolade for his valour two days later, as we shall see.) The main Japanese force landed that night at Singora and Patani in Siam on the eastern coast of the 'neck'. After a token resistance, the Siamese Government allowed them through, and troops moved by rail from Indo-China straight across Siam to invade northern Malaya. By mid-morning on the 8th Japanese aircraft were operating from the airfields in southern Siam. A smaller Japanese force had started landing at Kota Bharu on the north-east coast of Malaya at 0200 (local time), and Singapore itself was rudely awoken at 0410 by bombs falling on the city. This preceded by more than three-quarters of an hour the infamous attack by carrier-borne Japanese aircraft that crippled the American fleet anchored at Pearl Harbor, but Hawaii was far distant and neither base was aware of the attack on the other until the evening of that fateful day.

(To illustrate the sheer scale of the Japanese offensive we should note that, on the first day, apart from the spectacular raid on Pearl Harbor, and the rapid progress of their invasion of Malaya from Siam, the Japanese had launched co-ordinated attacks on objectives spread across the Pacific Ocean and South China Sea for over 100 degrees of longitude, which include the International Date Line. They had captured the strategically important island of Batan, north of the American-controlled Philippine Islands, and had neutralised the main US air bases on Luzon there by heavy air-raids mounted from Formosa, as well as invading the important British base at Hong Kong.)

In the early hours of the 8th the Blenheims of 27 Squadron were briefed to 'bomb and strafe landing craft in the Kota Bharu area at first light'; eight set off at 0645 but could not see any targets in heavy tropical rainstorms, so returned to Sungei-Patani. But while they were away the airfield was bombed and two of 27's other Blenheims were damaged; one attempted to take off but a bomb exploded alongside L6669, mortally wounding the Pilot, Sgt M. Willows, and the WOp/Ag, Sgt R. Rhodes (see Appendix 2). Four 27 Squadron ground-crew were killed, together with three other airmen, and two Buffaloes were destroyed and five damaged. The first eight Blenheims then returned, and while they were refuelling the airfield was attacked again and six more were put out of action – the Japanese used fragmentation bombs, which caused many casualties and much damage to aircraft, but left the runways uncratered as they intended to use the airfields themselves very shortly. The pattern of the Japanese method of rendering the RAF impotent had been set. Eight Hudsons from 1 Squadron RAAF based at Kota Bharu itself had attacked the invaders before dawn, setting one transport ship on fire, but losing two aircraft. The eight Blenheims of 60 Squadron were also ordered to attack shipping off Kota Bharu at daybreak on the 8th. They were told that they 'need not expect any opposition', but they did and two of the six that bombed landing craft, S/Ldr G. Westropp-Bennett in L4829 and F/O W. Bowden in L4913, were shot down (see Appendix 2). The only survivor was Bowden, a Canadian, whose Blenheim broke up as it hit the sea; he was kept afloat by the tail-wheel and was lucky to be picked up 24 hours later by a Japanese destroyer, being the first Allied airman to become a Prisoner of War in the Far East. F/O J. Dobson in the seventh Blenheim had found the main force further north and attacked two destroyers, being lucky in the poor visibility to escape the ships' withering AA fire – however, his luck ran out the following day. Sgt N. Shannon's L1350 was hit and badly damaged, his WOp/Ag, Sgt A. Beagley, being seriously wounded by shrapnel, but the Blenheim made it back to Kuantan.

The official RAF history (Volume II, Chapter 2) states: 'The quality of the pilots engaged in this, the first action of the war in Malaya, may be judged from the bearing of an unknown Blenheim pilot who, his aircraft on fire, disdained to take to his parachute and dived into a landing craft destroying it and its occupants. A Japanese, subsequently captured, testified to the admiration caused in the ranks of the enemy by this gallant sacrifice.' In his book *Bristol Blenheim*, the Dutch historian Theo Boiten states that this aircraft was L4829 of F/Lt G. P. Westropp-Bennett, describing how it was hit during the attack and caught fire, with 'Paddy' Bennett then diving his blazing Blenheim into a Japanese landing craft, killing himself, his crew, and all 60 enemy soldiers aboard. He adds that the sacrificial attack was praised by the Japanese over Saigon radio. However, Chris Shores in his very detailed *Bloody Shambles* (Volume I, Chapter 2) suggests that the aircraft concerned was A16-94, a Hudson of 1 Squadron RAAF flown by F/Lt J. Leighton-Jones and crew, who were killed along with all occupants of the large landing craft, and quotes in full a contemporary Japanese report referring to 'one British aircraft' in an identical incident. Shores describes later how L4829, flown by S/Ldr Westropp-Bennett, was hit and caught fire, adding that it was last seen by other crews as it headed towards the Siamese border where it crashed among coconut groves on the beach without survivors. Whether it was a suicidal Blenheim or Hudson that was aimed at and struck the landing craft is not clear, but what is clear is the exceptional courage of the crew.

Nine of 34 Squadron's Mk IVs from Tengah then bombed and strafed the beaches and landing craft. One (V5827) was damaged by fighters and had to force-land at Machang airstrip. The others went to Butterworth to re-fuel and re-arm, but were attacked by fighters on the way. New Zealander Sgt Smith's V5633 was damaged and he made an emergency belly-landing; he and his Australian WOp/Ag, Sgt E. Brown, were injured. F/O N. Dunlop in V5636 was chased at tree-top height and his gunner, Sgt K. Burrill, another Australian, was wounded but shot down his attacker. Eleven Blenheims of 62 Squadron at Alor Star, led by S/Ldr Boxall, arrived over Kota Bharu beach around 0900 and, finding few targets there, flew north and attacked shipping off Patanim but could observe no hits in the poor weather. While they were being re-fuelled and re-armed at Alor Star, the airfield was bombed and four Blenheim were destroyed and another five damaged; an officer and five airmen were killed, and buildings and a fuel-dump set on fire. Another raid on Sungei-Patani reduced 27 Squadron to four flyable Blenheims, and left only four serviceable Buffaloes; the fuel-dump was set ablaze, so the surviving aircraft were ordered to evacuate to Butterworth. But that airfield was strafed too, and four of 34 Squadron's Blenheims, re-fuelling for the return flight to Tengah, were badly damaged.

Five of the antiquated Vildebeests of 36 Squadron, flying in heavy tropical rain from Gong Kedah, a satellite of the congested airfield at Kota Bharu, had also launched torpedoes at a cruiser at dawn, but without result. The sole Beaufort of the other Vildebeest unit, 100 Squadron, flown by F/Lt P. Mitchell, made a reconnaissance to Singora soon after midday and found that the main landing was taking place there, not at Kota Bharu, and also photographed some 65 Japanese aircraft on the airfield. Mitchell's aircraft was attacked by fighters, a fuel-line was partly severed, the port engine cut out in a steep turn, the Beaufort rolled on to its back and spun down, but he regained control and escaped into nearby cloud. He found that with use of the hand-operated fuel 'wobble pump' he could restart the engine – both his gunners had been wounded but had shot down one of the attackers. Mitchell struggled back to Kota Bharu airfield to find it being bombed and strafed, so he landed in a gap between raids. The fuel-line was repaired, but each time he started his engines to take off for Singapore with his valuable film his aircraft was strafed again, and before long set on fire. By 1600 Japanese troops were approaching the airfield and firing upon it, so evacuation to Kuantan was ordered, and Gong Kedah and Machang were also evacuated. Fortunately, Mitchell's camera and film were rescued and flown in a Buffalo to Air HQ, where it was realised that the opportunity to attack the disembarkation of the main body of troops at Singora had been missed completely. The newly constructed RAF airfields were now within range of the southern Siamese airfields taken over by the Japanese, and were already under attack from aircraft based in Indo-China; some airfields were already being abandoned, and it was only the first day of the Japanese offensive!

THE BRISTOL BLENHEIM

On the second day of the Japanese onslaught, 9 December 1941, the remnants of the 'Norgroup' Blenheim squadrons in Malaya were gathered together at Butterworth. The 62 Squadron ground-crews had worked all night at Alor Star and made seven Blenheims flyable, while 27 Squadron contributed just two. 34 Squadron was told to take its remaining Mk IVs to Tengah on Singapore Island, and the four left from 60 Squadron at Kuantan joined them. They only just got away from Kuantan in time before it was bombed and strafed, but one Blenheim did not escape and was burned out, as were two Vildebeests and a Hudson, two more of which were damaged beyond repair by bombs. Only the evacuation of the aircraft had been ordered, but all the personnel abandoned the airfield in great and disorderly haste. Six of the Mk IVs from the combined 34 and 60 Squadron force at Tengah were sent to raid Singora airfield; it was hoped that they would link up with any remaining Blenheims from 62 and 27 Squadrons at Butterworth, but this did not take place as none could be made ready in time. The six Blenheims reached Singora and five attacked the crowded airfield and one the harbour, but they were then intercepted by a swarm of Ki.27 fighters and three of them were shot down – 50 per cent casualties (see Appendix 2). Two were 60 Squadron aircraft. F/Lt J. Dobson crashed V5589 in the jungle, and his crew, F/Sgt Smith and Sgt Fowler, were injured in the crash, which Dobson survived only to be beheaded by his Japanese captors, who also shot his injured crewmen. Sgt A. Johnstone was hit in V5931 and force-landed – he and his crew became PoWs, enduring cruel treatment including working as slave labour on the infamous Burma-Siam 'Railway of Death'. S/Ldr F. O'Driscoll of 34 Squadron was also brought down in V5829, but fortunately he had crossed the British lines and escaped to safety.

The three surviving Blenheims from that raid landed at Butterworth to be refuelled and re-armed immediately, for they were to join three from 62 Squadron in another raid on Singora airfield. But the Japanese launched a heavy raid on Butterworth just as the Blenheims were about to take off – four Buffaloes attempted to intercept the raiders but all four were promptly shot down. A MVAF Dragon-Rapide, laden with explosives, had just landed from Penang Island – where all the other MVAF impressed private aircraft had been destroyed in a strafing attack. The pilot, P/O W. Gatenby, was alarmed to see that the Blenheims parked on either side of his biplane had been set on fire, with Very

The sole Beaufort in Singapore was T9543 of 100 Squadron at Seletar (its fate is described in the text) – a squadron of them would have been most useful. Had the Hurricanes and Tomahawks supplied to Russia in 1941 been sent to Singapore they may well have transformed the outcome in favour of the Allies. Certainly, just a few of the 100 Operational Fighter Command Squadrons retained in the UK at the end of 1941 would have altered it entirely.

Malays were trained as aircraft engineers, proving good pupils – six are seen working on a Blenheim's Mercury engine, mounted on an engine stand.

cartridges and ammunition detonating, and he knew that both had full bomb-loads aboard. He managed to start up, although one engine was damaged, and was just taking off when a smoking Buffalo crash-landed just in front of him. He barely scraped over that, then his Rapide was fired upon by an aircraft he identified as a Blenheim, shattering the instrument panel. The damaged engine then cut out, but he managed to fly the damaged biplane to Ipoh on the other, and landed there after a traumatic trip. Three other Blenheims were destroyed, and several others damaged by bomb bursts. Two 62 Squadron aircrew were wounded, WOp/Ag Sgt J. Willis fatally, and Pilot F/Lt D. Frostick seriously, the station buildings were set on fire, and further confusion was caused by explosions from delayed-action bombs. Meanwhile only two of the Blenheims had been able to take off just before the raid started, one of them, F/Sgt D. Williams in Z5796 of 34 Squadron, was attacked by a fighter, damaged, and landed back at Butterworth.

The other was L1134, a 62 Squadron Mk I flown by S/Ldr Arthur Scarf, who pressed on completely alone, avoided interception, and made one bombing run across Singora airfield while his WOp/Ag, F/Sgt Cyril Rich, machine-gunned the rows of parked enemy aircraft. They were chased by several fighters, which – fortunately – attacked one at a time rather than simultaneously, although the lone Blenheim was hit repeatedly in the running fight at low level. Scarf flew skilfully, his Gunner defended the aircraft well, and they finally escaped the pursuers, but the Pilot's left arm was shattered and he was wounded in the back – the armour plate behind the seat had been removed to lighten the Blenheim for its attempted interception of the Japanese reconnaissance aircraft two day earlier. Assisted by his Observer, F/Sgt Gordon Calder, the barely conscious Scarf – held upright in his seat by Cyril Rich, who had crawled through from the turret into the 'well' in the centre-section behind the Pilot – managed to fly to Alor Star, guided there by Calder, as it was nearer than

　　　　　　　　THE BRISTOL BLENHEIM

Butterworth. Scarf made a smooth belly-landing, the riddled Blenheim sliding over the rice paddies to within 100 yards of the hospital. The crew lifted him from the cockpit and laid him on the port wing, then all three lit cigarettes, ignoring fuel running from the ruptured tanks. Scarf's recent bride, Elizabeth, worked at the hospital as a nurse, and he laughed and joked with her from the stretcher while being carried in. The doctors assured her that his injuries were not life-threatening, although they might not be able to save his left arm. His young wife started giving her blood for a transfusion but, tragically, while she was doing this he died from secondary shock. His sacrificial bravery went unrecognised until after the war when, following information from released Prisoners of War, he was awarded a posthumous Victoria Cross, which his widow received at Buckingham Palace on 30 July 1946.

It forms a singularly appropriate tribute to all the Blenheim crews who fought so valiantly that the exceptional courage of the three young Blenheim Pilots who were awarded the supreme accolade of the VC is recorded for posterity, each flying an example from one of the three marks of the Bristol Blenheim, and each from one of the three main Theatres of War: Arthur Scarf in a Mk I in the Far East, Hughie Edwards in a Mk IV in Northern Europe, and Hugh Malcolm in a Mk V in the Middle East. It is also most apposite that, sadly, it was necessary for two of the three Victoria Crosses earned by Blenheim Pilots to be awarded posthumously.

Following the raids on Butterworth, the only two Blenheims still fit for operations, two aircraft of 62 Squadron, were moved immediately south to Taiping, the satellite to Ipoh where the last two fit Buffaloes of 21 Squadron RAAF were sent, but both airfields lacked facilities. All the remaining Blenheims that could be persuaded to fly were evacuated to Singapore. Only six were able to make it – five Mk IVs (three of 34 Squadron and two of 62), together with a single Mk I-F of 27 Squadron. Between them they carried 51 valuable air-crew, including their own crews, to safety. At the end of the second day of the Japanese invasion the whole of the Blenheim striking force in northern Malaya had been reduced to the pathetic pair on the jungle airstrip at Taiping. The Japanese had gained complete command of the air, and the next day would also gain complete command of the seas around Malaya. The chain of military disasters that followed was now inevitable.

The small but powerful 'Force Z' commanded by Admiral Sir Tom Phillips in HMS *Prince of Wales*, with HMS *Repulse* and four destroyers, had steamed out of Singapore on the evening of the 8th to intercept the fleet of enemy transports off Singora. He had requested fighter protection, but when his force neared the area, at which he expected to arrive at daylight on the 10th, he was told that it could not be provided due to the continuous air-raids on the northern airfields. The British warships set out into the South China Sea regardless, and saw floatplanes when they were heading north at a point opposite Kota Bharu, and believed that they had been discovered (although, in fact, the Japanese were unable to report their position), so with the element of surprise apparently lost, and after a dog-leg, they turned back for Singapore. Around midnight the Admiral received a radio report of an enemy landing at Kuantan and decided to investigate, but did not inform HQ of this. The report turned out to be false (apparently it was only a small reconnaissance party), and at 0800 he again turned his force when off Kuantan and headed for Singapore at full speed. The warships still maintained strict radio silence and neither the RN nor RAF Headquarters had any idea of their position – at that stage fighter cover could have been provided had it been requested. 'Force Z' was spotted by searching Japanese aircraft at 1015 and shortly afterwards was attacked with bombs and torpedoes, many of which struck the huge battleships. *Repulse* radioed at 1115 that it was being attacked from the air, so RAF and RAAF aircraft were sent off immediately to the position given, but by the time they got there both of the major warships had been sunk with a loss of 840 lives – fortunately, 2,081 sailors were rescued from the oil-covered sea by the destroyers. The sudden loss of these great warships – the pride of the British fleet and potent symbols of her naval power – sent shock waves throughout the Allied High Command right up to the British War Cabinet. The blow to British prestige and morale was immeasurable.

The days that followed saw the Japanese forces advancing steadily southwards along the Malayan peninsula. Each time an attempt was made by the retreating British Army to establish defensive positions, the Japanese, in a series of hooks, would outflank them either through the jungle inland or by landing on the coast behind them. The Buffaloes of 453 Squadron were sent up from Singapore to Ipoh to help; one flight of three led by W/Cdr L. Neale (due to take command of Ipoh) became lost in bad weather and all three crashed when low in fuel and attempting forced-landings in a paddy-field, the Wing Commander and P/O Brown being killed. The survivor, P/O Livesey, was surprised to find that they had come down in Sumatra on the other side of the Straits of Malacca! Three Buffaloes were safely delivered to Ipoh by volunteer Blenheim pilots of 62 Squadron – S/Ldr Boxall, F/Lt Lancaster, and Sgt S. Stafford – although not one had flown a Buffalo before. Incidentally, the latter had been interned with his crew by the Dutch on 8 April 1940 when his Blenheim L1101 came down in then neutral Sumatra during a reconnaissance of Sabang harbour where German merchant ships had been reported – the crew were released on 10 May when Holland was forced into the war in Europe. More Buffaloes were sent north but were soon destroyed either in the air or on the ground. Clearly it was too dangerous for the few Blenheims remaining at Singapore to operate by day, so on the night of 12/13 December six 34 Squadron aircraft were sent to attack Singora airfield. Two had crews from 60 Squadron and one of these, F/Lt Appleton in the fully laden V5397, crashed on take-off – his WOp/Ag was killed, and he and his Observer were seriously injured, the latter dying a few weeks later (see Appendix 2). One other was unable to take off, and another failed to find the target, so only three bombed the far-distant airfield with negligible effect. On 15 December the Japanese claimed seven Blenheims destroyed on the ground at Butterworth, although most had previously been damaged. When the Japanese took Sungei-Patani, Taiping, Ipoh, Alor Star, then Butterworth airfields, they were delighted to capture vast stocks of fuel, provisions, supplies, bombs and ammunition.

On 22 December all RAF Units in Malaya were withdrawn to Singapore Island, being able to use Kuala Lumpur and the few other remaining bases on the mainland as advanced landing fields only. Two Japanese aircraft bombed Tengah airfield in the early hours of the 18th but caused no damage to the Blenheims based there, although a bombing operation planned for that night was cancelled. Two Blenheim I-Fs of 27 Squadron and two black-painted Buffaloes of 243 Squadron (one of which was flown by Sgt M. Baldwin, a Blenheim pilot who had transferred from 34 Squadron) formed Singapore's only night-fighter defences. On Christmas Eve the first five Blenheim Mk IVs from the Middle East Command arrived in Singapore; 12 had set out two weeks earlier but three had crashed, three were delayed en route, and one more was damaged in an air-raid on Rangoon. By then 34 Squadron at Tengah had ten Blenheim Mk IVs, 62 Squadron nine, and 27 Squadron three Mk I-Fs and two Mk Is. The surviving air-crew from the 60 Squadron unit that had been detached to Kuantan were sent back to Burma by steamship to rejoin their Squadron. On Christmas Day the British and Commonwealth forces in Hong Kong surrendered. By that day the Japanese had also conquered Wake Island, and the island of Jolo near Borneo, their invasion of the American-held Philippine Islands was well under way, they had struck at southern Burma, and their aircraft had also started attacking airfields and ports in the Dutch East Indies.

The 27th saw a rare success in the aerial war over Malaya – a raid led by W/Cdr Longfield on Singora airfield by six Blenheims of 34 Squadron and five Hudsons of 8 Squadron RAAF, which took the Japanese by surprise. More than 80 enemy aircraft were on the airfield and ten were destroyed and 50 damaged by bomb blast or splinters, but they were quickly replaced from reserves. Three of 62 Squadron's Blenheims were sent next morning to investigate a reported raid on Port Swettenham, but were mistaken for enemy bombers and fired on by 'friendly' Bofors guns. F/Sgt G. Dawson in L1243 was shot down, and he and his Observer, F/Sgt R. Burbridge, were killed, although the Gunner, F/Sgt A. Dutton, managed to bale out (see Appendix 2). Another aircraft was hit, but Sgt Stafford landed safely back at base with both wheels damaged by shrapnel. That night six Blenheims set out to bomb Sungei-Patani airfield but two returned with engine problems, while the other four set one enemy aircraft on fire and damaged several others, but lost two of their own number – F/Lt R. Hill's aircraft was hit by flak and crashed with the death of the crew, while P/O A. Little had to crash-land on the coast, but he and his crew survived. Only three Blenheims of 62 Squadron were available on the following night to raid Sungei-Patani, and they were aided by two Catalinas – flying-boats being used remarkably as night-bombers, but each able to carry 14 250lb bombs compared with the four in a Blenheim.

The final month of 1941 had seen the Allies forced into a series of damaging defeats and retreats by the ferocious and unexpectedly rapid thrusts of the invaders – would the opening months of 1942 see the situation improve? Unfortunately not. In fact, it would go from bad to worse. Two 62 Squadron Blenheims, F/Lt Lancaster in L1414 and F/O Haigh in L8441, were sent on the morning of New Year's Day to attack landing craft reported near Port Swettenham, but both were shot down by Japanese fighters with the loss of both crews (see Appendix 2). That night three of the Squadron's Blenheims attacked Kuala Pest airfield, setting two enemy aircraft on fire and damaging 20 others – if only such raids could have been carried out at squadron strength! Three 34 Squadron Blenheims were sent to search for a convoy reported off the western coast of Malaya; they were unable to find it, so attacked a freighter and some small craft instead, but one of the aircraft (V5388) failed to return. 34's base at Tengah had been bombed on the night of 30 December, damaging three aircraft; five night-fighter Mk I-Fs of 27 Squadron attempted to intercept night raiders without success, but were too vulnerable to operate by day. The Japanese then attacked by day from 12 January, after attrition had reduced the defending Buffaloes to near impotence. Kuala Lumpur, the Malayan capital with its valuable aerodrome, had fallen the day before. On the 16th the only six remaining operational Blenheims at Tengah, with six Buffaloes, attacked a large road convoy as direct support for Australian troops fighting near Gemas; they used 40lb anti-personnel bombs and flew so low that many were damaged by splinters from their own bombs as well as ground fire – one crash-landed at Tengah on return. The road was blocked by blazing lorries, and the Japanese troops suffered many casualties – they had also been attacked earlier by six Dutch Glen-Martin bombers, escorted by a dozen Buffaloes, which strafed the enemy positions after the bombing. Fifteen Hudson Mk IIIs from 18 flown out from the UK by 53 Squadron – the former Blenheim unit – under the leadership of S/Ldr L. Lilly, were arriving in Singapore as reinforcements. AHQ wanted to issue the aircraft as replacements for two RAAF Squadrons, but S/Ldr Lilly pressed for 53 to be kept together as a unit, so it was merged with 62 Squadron, which had only a handful of Blenheims left, effectively changing the Blenheim squadron into a Hudson squadron by instant re-equipment with the new type in the middle of a battle. The combined Squadron would be commanded by 62 Squadron's CO, W/Cdr McKern, who had a difficult task as Hudsons were not in his knowledge or experience and there was no time for him to gain any, so in practice S/Ldr Lilly controlled the flying and operational activity.

On 17 January there was a strafing attack by A6Ms on Tengah, which destroyed three dummy Blenheims and badly damaged three of 34 Squadron's real ones, together with two Sharks and a Swordfish. Next day three Blenheims of 34 Squadron, escorted by four Buffaloes, bombed the railway terminus at Gemas, but were bounced by four fighters on the return trip. Two were hit and P/O Lyttle had to ditch when both engines cut, but the crew survived, as did the crew of another damaged Blenheim that crash-landed at Tengah. At sundown on the 20th seven of 34 Squadron's Mk IVs swept individually and very low over Kuala Lumpur airfield, bombing and strafing. It appears that 25 Japanese aircraft were destroyed, but three Ki.43s scrambled and shot down S/Ldr Finan O'Driscoll – he and his crew were killed, and 34 lost a popular and determined Flight Commander – and once more another damaged Blenheim crash-landed at base.

Two more of 34's aircraft were destroyed, and another damaged, by bombing the following day. On 27 January the bombers were withdrawn to Palembang in Sumatra, known to the RAF as P1, and to P2, an airfield well hidden in the jungle some 40 miles inland. That day produced one of the RAF's most epic disasters. A Japanese convoy had been spotted approaching Endau in south-western Malaya, and all the available aircraft were ordered to attack it – 21 antiquated Vildebeests and three Albacore biplanes from 100 and 36 Squadrons, and nine RAAF Hudsons and six from the newly re-equipped 62 Squadron. Most of these aircraft had operated the previous night – some of the Vildebeests twice – the crews were weary and the aircraft required re-arming and re-fuelling, so they were sent in two 'waves'. Although the crews of the biplanes were well-trained and proficient in torpedo-dropping, they were armed with bombs and ordered to use their slow aircraft as dive-bombers. A dozen Buffaloes and nine of the newly arrived Hurricanes would attempt to protect the striking force, which – unsurprisingly – was decimated. Twelve Vildebeests were lost and ten more badly damaged, causing crew casualties – both the gallant Squadron Commanders were killed – two Albacores were destroyed, and the other returned damaged with only the pilot aboard as both his crew had baled out. Two Hudsons and a Hurricane were also shot down. Two troop-transports were hit but not sunk. That these experienced crews should be sacrificed by being sent out $2\frac{1}{4}$ years after the start of the war against such strong opposition in the Vildebeests, which were designed in 1926, first flew in 1928, and had served with 100 Squadron since 1932, is shameful. The remaining five Blenheim Mk Is of 27 Squadron from Palembang (with 84 Squadron crews, as the latter's aircraft were undergoing major inspections following their long flight from Suez), were to attack the shipping at dusk, but due to delays in bombing up they were late and landed at Sembawang on Singapore Island after dark. They raided Kuantan airfield the following night, but thick cloud made accurate bombing impossible, so they returned to P2 the next morning. The heavily outnumbered Blenheims had been in the thick of the fighting from the outset, and had suffered severe casualties, but had been bundled out of all of their bases and – despite many acts of great bravery – proved unable to delay the relentless advance of the Japanese forces.

Soon the airfields on Singapore Island were being shelled from across the Jahore Strait, as well as suffering constant attack from the air, and became untenable, so the remaining fighters were also evacuated. Five convoys reached Singapore in January 1942, carrying tens of thousands of fresh troops, many tons of supplies and equipment, and 51 crated Hurricanes. High hopes rested on these fighters to regain control of the air, but hastily assembled and with desert air-filters reducing their performance, and flung into action with inexperienced pilots who did not have any early warning or control system, they proved no match for the Zeros.

Singapore, the supposedly impregnable fortress, surrendered on 5 February 1942. Most of the fresh troops went straight into cruel captivity, and the supplies and equipment were captured – much of it still unloaded in the chaos at the docks, as were masses of stores, including all the Blenheim and Hurricane spares, awaiting evacuation to Java.

The British Empire had been humiliated, and never really recovered.

Appendix I

Blenheim losses prior to Japanese the invasion

Aircraft are all Mk Is apart from the two Mk IVs noted.

09-08-1939   L1546 39 Squadron: control lost in storm, dived into ground near Kutumba, India; crew killed.

19-08-1939   L8378 34 Squadron: ditched 70 miles SE of Sicily, cause unknown, while squadron en route from Watton to Tengah, Singapore; crew rescued by French vessel.

17-09-1939   L1339 62 Squadron: crashed on landing at Trang, Siam, en route to Tengah, ran into soft ground and undercarriage (u/c) ripped off.

22-02-1940   L4921 39 Squadron: engine cut, swung on landing at Kuching, Borneo, u/c collapsed, damaged beyond repair (DBR); F/Lt P. Stevens uninjured.

00-02-1940   L8516 crashed in India, unit and cause not given.

26-03-1940   L1101 62 Squadron: engine failed on shipping patrol, attempted forced-landing at Sabang, Sumatra, but crashed short of airfield; Sgt S. Stafford, Sgt P. Brown and LAC Jones interned by still neutral Dutch, released 10-05-1940.

04-04-1940   L1131 62 Squadron: engine cut on PR sortie from Alor Star, ditched 83 miles west of Penang; F/O C. Boxall, Sgt L. Podger, and LAC W. Martin rescued.

24-04-1940   L6629 60 Squadron: bounced on landing at Drigh Road, u/c collapsed, overturned, DBR; Sgt C. Gill safe.

03-06-1940   L1332 62 Squadron: tyre burst on take-off at Kallang, swung and crashed.

06-07-1940   L8520 60 Squadron: tyre burst on take-off at Ambala, swung and u/c collapsed; F/O R. Marrack safe.

22-07-1940   L8539 60 Squadron: engine cut on approach, undershot, struck ground and overturned at Juhu, India; F/Lt R. Smith injured.

18-08-1940   L8611 60 Squadron: became lost, ran out of fuel, belly-landed near Palasi, Bengal.

31-08-1940   L1545 60 Squadron: FTR to Dum Dum from night shipping patrol over Bay of Bengal; Sgt R. Tomkins, Sgt R. Hesseltine, and Sgt W. Ayres missing, presumed killed; commemorated on Singapore Memorial.

16-11-1940   L8380 60 Squadron: crashed and written off, no further details available.

30-11-1940   L4916 60 Squadron: stalled on approach at Lahore, wing hit ground, crashed; F/Lt F. Lambert slightly injured.

24-02-1941   L1104 62 Squadron: engine cut, hit trees attempting forced-landing at Sungei-Patani, destroyed by fire; F/O R. Halliwell (Pilot) dragged clear by LAC J. Haynes, but died of injuries, Sgt P. Walker (Obs) and Sgt G. Couzens (WOp/Ag) killed, three crewmen buried in Taiping War Cemetery.

12-03-1941   L1103 62 Squadron: swung on landing and hit fire-tender at Alor Star, DBR; crew F/Lt Arthur Scarf, Sgt G. Calder, and Sgt C. Rich only slightly injured, achieved fame 9-12-1941.

21-03-1941   L1355 34 Squadron: propeller broke away in flight, crash-landed at Tengah, DBR; no injuries to F/Lt T. Cox and crew reported.

24-03-1941   L4914 60 Squadron: engine cut, lost height and belly-landed at Mingaladon; Sgt C. Gill and Sgt R. Ellis injured, Cpl E. Fowler safe (aircraft SOC 10-06-1941).

04-04-1941   L6667 27 Squadron Mk I-F: spun into sea during aerobatics over Singapore harbour; S/Ldr C. Hackett, F/Lt J. Mansel-Lewis (243 Squadron), and Sgt D. Beaman killed.

16-04-1941   L8534 Aircraft Depot India: hit ground in mist, force-landed on mud flats at Sonmiani Bay, DBR; F/Lt R. Baron and crew safe.

20-06-1941   L1532 60 Squadron and 'Z' Flight: belly-landed in error at Mingaladon, DBR.

28-06-1941   L6632 27 Squadron Mk I-F: dived into ground near Akyab, cause unknown; F/Lt F. Box, F/Sgt T. Seaward, LAC H. Spratt and Cpl R. Fish (passenger) killed, buried in Taukkyan War Cemetery, Burma.

28-06-1941   L8366 34 Squadron: stalled on landing at Tengah, u/c collapsed, DBF.

02-07-1941   L8404 60 Squadron: control lost in practice attack, spun into ground inverted at Ghizri near Karachi, on loan to 20 Squadron at Peshawar (still with Audaxes), converting to Lysanders 12-1941; F/Lt M. Uphill (NZ), Sgt J. Lenfestey and LAC L. Downing killed, buried in Karachi.

15-07-1941   L8365 34 Squadron: stalled into ground from low altitude at Amakeng, 2 miles east of Singapore, destroyed by fire; F/Lt B. Haylock, Sgt T. Ford, and LAC J. Windrum killed.

26-07-1941   L6635 27 Squadron Fighter: engine cut, overshot landing at Kuala Lumpur, swung and undercarriage collapsed, DBR; Sgt F. Turvil and crew unhurt.

12-08-1941   V5877 34 Squadron Mk IV: crashed after collision with another Blenheim in formation practice over Johore; P/O J. Hunt RNZAF, P/O D. Moore, and Sgt H. Olson killed.

28-08-1941   L6598 100 Squadron: overshot landing at Seletar, skidded into ditch, DBR; crew uninjured. 100 was a Vildebeest squadron awaiting conversion to Beauforts in December.

17-09-1941   L4827 60 Squadron Mk IV: ran into soft ground landing at Victoria Point, Burma, overturned, DBR; F/O J. Appleton (Pilot) and Grp Capt Manning DSO (passenger) safe.

23-09-1941   V5389 34 Squadron Mk IV: collided with Buffalo W8161 and crashed in sea near Tengah, Singapore; F/Sgt G. Dodds and F/Sgt J. Carr killed.

29-09-1941   L8526 27 Squadron Fighter: force-landed in bad weather, overshot paddy-field into river near Nong Chut Nai, Siam.

06-10-1941   L8440 34 Squadron: belly-landed in error at night at Kallang.

18-10-1941   V5466 34 Squadron Mk IV: swung on landing at Kuantan, u/c collapsed, DBR.

06-12-1941   L8544 60 Squadron: u/c jammed, belly-landed at Seletar.

Appendix 2

Operational Blenheim losses from 8 December 1941 to 31 January 1942

08-12-1941   L6669 27 Squadron Mk I-F: damaged by bomb while taking off at Sungei-Patani; Sgt M. Willows and Sgt R. Rhodes (WOp/Ag) fatally injured.

08-12-1941   L4913 60 Squadron Mk I: hit by flak attacking landing-craft off Kota Bharu, crashed into sea; F/Lt W. Bowden rescued and became PoW, his crew P/O W. Logan RAAF and Sgt T. Clarke KIA.

08-12-1941   L4829 60 Squadron Mk I: hit by flak attacking landing-craft off Kota Bharu, set on fire, crashed on to beach; S/Ldr G. Westropp-Bennett and crew KIA.

08-12-1941   L1530 60 Squadron Mk I: hit by flak, seriously injuring Sgt Beagley (WOp/Ag), Sgt N. Shannon (Pilot) able to land at Kuantan. Aircraft to Tengah Bomber Pool, destroyed 05-01-1942 (see below).

08-12-1941   V5827 34 Squadron Mk IV: damaged by fighters attacking landing craft off Kota Bharu, force-landed at Machang; crew safe.

08-12-1941   V5633 34 Squadron Mk IV: damaged by fighters attacking landing craft, belly-landed at Butterworth; Sgt J. Smith and Sgt E. Brown slightly injured, aircraft then destroyed by enemy bombing.

08-12-1941   V5388, V5381 and Z5799 34 Squadron Mk IVs: DBR during air-raid on Butterworth.

09-12-1941   V5499 34 Squadron Mk IV: destroyed in air-raid on Butterworth.

09-12-1941   V5829 34 Squadron Mk IV: damaged by fighters, crashed attempting forced-landing near Mersing; S/Ldr F. O'Driscoll and crew survived.

09-12-1941   V5931 60 Squadron Mk IV: damaged by fighters in raid on Singora airfield, force-landed in jungle; Sgt A. Johnstone and Sgt G. Gregory captured and became PoWs.

09-12-1941   V5589 60 Squadron Mk IV: damaged by fighters in raid on Singora airfield, force-landed in jungle; F/Lt Dobson survived but beheaded, crew F/Sgt G. Smith and Sgt E. Fowler injured, captured and shot.

09-12-1941   L1134 62 Squadron Mk I: damaged by fighters in solo raid on Singora airfield, force-landed at Alor Star; S/Ldr Arthur Scarf fatally injured, awarded VC, F/Sgt G. Calder and F/Sgt C. Rich safe, damaged aircraft destroyed later in day during air-raid.

09-12-1941   L1133 and L1259 62 Squadron Mk Is: destroyed by enemy bombing at Butterworth.

12-12-1941   V5379 34 Squadron Mk IV: crashed near Tengah after night take-off for raid on Singora; F/Lt J. Appleton (Pilot) injured, P/O T. Bigmore (Obs) injured and died 22 days later, Sgt K. Connel (WOp/Ag) killed.

28-12-1941   L1243 62 Squadron Mk I: shot down by 'friendly' AA fire near Port Swettenham; F/Sgts G. Dawson and R. Burbridge killed, F/Sgt Dutton (WOp/Ag) baled out and survived.

28-12-1941   V5636 34 Squadron Mk IV: damaged by flak in night raid on Sungei-Patani airfield, crashed in jungle; F/Lt R. Hill, Sgt K. Carter RAAF and F/Sgt R. Rayner KIA, commemorated on Singapore Memorial.

28-12-1941   ? 34 Squadron Mk IV: ran into turbulence on return from same raid, engines cut, force-landed on coast; P/O Lyttle and crew survived.

01-01-1942   L1414 62 Squadron Mk I: shot down by fighters while attacking landing craft; F/Lt N. Lancaster and crew KIA. (See 20-01-1942 below.)

01-01-1942   L8441 62 Squadron Mk I: shot down by fighters while attacking landing craft; F/O G. Haigh and crew KIA.

02-01-1942   V5388 34 Squadron Mk IV: FTR from bombing sortie off western Malaya; P/O J. Lomax RNZAF, F/O S. Anderson and F/Sgt R. James KIA, buried in Taiping War Cemetery.

02-01-1942   Z9711 113 Squadron Mk IV: landed at Mingaladon after raid on Bangkok docks, brakes failed, ran into ditch, abandoned; 2/Lt N. Russell SAAF, Sgt T. Barry and F/Sgt A. Tillott, both RAAF, safe.

05-01-1942   L1530 60 Squadron and 'Y' Flight Mk I: destroyed in air-raid on Kluang airfield, southern Malaya.

10-01-1942   V5597 34 Squadron Mk IV: FTR from night-bombing sortie to Sungei-Pentani airfield; Sgt J. Smith RNZAF, W/O P. Hillebrand and Sgt E. Brown RAAF KIA, commemorated on Singapore Memorial.

14-01-1942   Z5796 34 Squadron Mk IV: lost way on night-bombing sortie to Sungei-Pentani airfield, crash-landed on coast of Sumatra; P/O L. Rembridge and crew survived.

16-01-1942   Z7799 84 Squadron Mk IV: overshot landing at Palembang, Borneo; Sgt Longmore and crew uninjured, aircraft DBR.

16-01-1942   Z7971 84 Squadron Mk IV: separated from Flight near Palembang, force-landed in swamp near Loempo River; P/O M. Macdonald and crew survived, aircraft not recovered.

20-01-1942   L1414 34 Squadron Mk IV: shot down by fighters in dusk attack on Kuala Lumpur airfield; S/Ldr F. O'Driscoll and crew KIA. (Serial number must be recorded incorrectly in one of ORBs – see 01-01-1942.)

21-01-1942   L1412 and L1413 34/62 Squadrons Mk Is: destroyed in air-raid at Tengah.

23-01-1942   Z9579 84 Squadron Mk IV: lost en route to P1 (Palengbang), Sumatra, belly-landed in mouth of Loempo River; P/O M. MacDonald RAAF, P/O G. Maurice and Sgt W. Miller, together with two ground-crew passengers LAC R. Collingwood and LAC W. Hughes rescued by villagers and reached Palengbang five days later, aircraft abandoned.

24-01-1942   V5872 84 Squadron Mk IV: crashed into trees after both engines failed near Mingaladon en route to P1, Sumatra, DBF; Sgt R. Headlam RAAF (Pilot) and Sgt H. Odgers RAAF (Obs) killed, Sgt J. Farrer RAAF (WOp/Ag) injured, Sgt W. Lloyd (passenger) killed. Three killed are buried in Rangoon War Cemetery.

00-01-1942   L1259 and L1260 62 Squadron Mk Is: lost in Malaya, no further details available.

00-01-1942   L4829 and L4831, Mk IVs and L4915, Mk I, 60 Squadron: destroyed by enemy air-raids.

Chapter 30

The East Indies, Burma, Ceylon and India

J apan's war aim was to expand its Empire and take control of the economic resources of South East Asia, especially the oil in the East Indies at British Borneo, Brunei and Sarawak (now parts of Malaysia), at Palembang in north-east Sumatra, and Dutch Borneo (then in the Dutch East Indies, now parts of Indonesia). The Japanese launched their initial attack on 15 December 1941, only a week after mounting the invasion of Malaya, at that time the world's leading producer of the vital raw materials of rubber and tin. They also intended to invade Burma to cut the only supply route from the Western World through the port of Rangoon and over the 'Burma Road' to their long-standing enemy China. They bombed Rangoon and nearby Mingaladon airfield on 23 and 25 December causing much damage and heavy casualties among the unprepared civil population.

Borneo

Despite being fully stretched – indeed over-stretched – in Malaya by mid-December, the Blenheims were involved in the new war zone in the East Indies too, although at that stage they were still based in Singapore. On Christmas Eve five Blenheims from 34 Squadron with three Hudsons from 8 Squadron RAAF attacked a convoy heading for Kuching, capital of Sarawak; this had already been attacked by Dutch aircraft, and three transports were hit, two of which sank. Nevertheless, the Japanese troops landed and Sarawak and Brunei in northern Borneo were quickly conquered, although the oil plants had been set on fire. Another 34 Squadron Blenheim IV attempted to reconnoitre Kuching on Christmas Day but had to return with engine trouble; the town and airfield were captured on Boxing Day. Four days later five more Blenheims dropped supplies to Punjabi forces defending Singkawang airfield nearby in Dutch Borneo – these two airfields were the only places in Borneo where a defence was even attempted – but the airfield and indeed the whole of the vast area of Borneo was in Japanese hands by the end of January.

Sumatra

When the Blenheims and Hudsons were evacuated from Singapore to the Palembang airfields P1 and P2 in Sumatra, they were formed hastily into 225 (Bomber) Group. Also diverted there were the reinforcements en route to Singapore from the Middle East, including the Blenheims of 84 and 211 Squadrons, led by W/Cdrs J. Jeudwine and R. Bateson respectively. These 46 Blenheims had been dispatched on the long and demanding journey two weeks earlier, but only 35 arrived at P1 (see Appendix 1). They flew from Heliopolis, staging via the airfields of Habbaniyah, Shaiba, Bahrain, Sharjah and Karachi, then on via Hyderabad or Allahabad to Calcutta, Toungoo, Rangoon and (as Victoria Point at the southern tip of Burma had been captured by the Japanese), Lho'nga-Medan on the northernmost tip of Sumatra. They were fitted with the long-range ferry tanks in the bomb-bay and each carried two ground-crew in addition to its normal air-crew. The first five arrived on 23 January 1942, and that day saw the first Japanese air-raid on P1, the main aerodrome in Sumatra; fortunately P2 – well hidden in the jungle – had not been discovered. 226 (Fighter) Group was also formed in great haste at P1, with the remaining Hurricanes and Buffaloes driven out of Singapore, together with 12 more of the former flown off HMS *Indomitable*, guided in by pairs of 34 Squadron Blenheims. The living and working conditions at these airfields, especially P2, which was little more than a large clearing in the jungle, were appalling. The lack of transport, spares, tools and equipment made life very difficult for the ground-crews sweating in the steamy tropical heat to keep their charges fit for operations. Hopelessly inadequate accommodation and very poor food, as well as the obvious absence of defences against air or land attacks, further lowered the morale of air- and ground-crews alike, and all these difficulties were exacerbated by the hot and humid climate, and by the conflicting orders and counter-orders issued amid the general confusion and disorganisation. The men of 84 and 211 Squadrons were shocked at the shambles into which they had flown.

Despite all of these difficulties, small forces of Blenheims raided their old airfields such as Alor Star, Butterworth and Kuala Lumpur, also bombing Singora and a submarine base in Penang harbour. They used airfields in northern Sumatra to refuel for these lengthy and arduous flights, often made through tropical storms, but the raids were far too small in scale to have more than a nuisance effect. By the end of January only 20 serviceable Mk IV Blenheims remained in Sumatra – ten of 84 Squadron, six of 34 Squadron, and four of 211 Squadron – while of the Mk Is only eight could be flown – three Mk I-Fs of 27 Squadron and five Mk Is still with 62 alongside its ten Hudsons. All the Blenheims were tired and had many 'snags' that would normally have rendered them unfit for service. The ground-crews performed miracles to keep them flying, and to put damaged machines back into service, mainly by 'cannibalising' written-off aircraft. Two from the four 211 Squadron Blenheims escorting a convoy were shot down on 6 February, with the deaths of both the all-Australian crews (see Appendix 1). The next day P1 came under heavy aerial attack, and six Blenheims (three of 84 Squadron, two of 211, and one of 34) and three Hurricanes were burned out on the airfield, while another of 211 was shot down on the approach. That Squadron lost an experienced Flight Commander when S/Ldr Ken Dundas DFC, a veteran of 211's days in Greece, was shot down when he was one of three Blenheims attacking Kluang airfield (see Appendix 1). On the night of 11 February all 23 available Blenheims were ordered to attack an enemy convoy north of Banka Island heading to invade Sumatra, while the remaining 11 Hudsons raided Kluang airfield. Two of the heavily laden Blenheims (Z7521 and Z9649) struck the tops of trees just off the sodden take-off run at P2 and crashed. Sgt Ray Wheatly RAAF rushed over to the smouldering wreck of the second, freed the jammed hatch and pulled out the Pilot, P/O B. West, and Observer, Sgt G. Chignall, both injured, and helped the dazed Gunner, Sgt Kite, to get out just minutes before the bombs of the first Blenheim (which had crashed in flames) exploded, demolishing both. His actions certainly saved their lives and he was awarded the George Medal. Two more brushed the trees, one (Z9726) attempting to land back but striking the building containing the Orderly Room, crashing in flames and killing the Pilot, Sgt J. Hyatt, and his Observer Sgt G. Mutton. The Gunner, Sgt D. Irvine, was found by chance the next morning, seriously injured and still in the remains of the rear fuselage, which had broken free and come down in the jungle over half a mile away. Happily, he recovered (see Appendix 1). Those that did get away flew through heavy tropical thunderstorms that night on a tiring 1,000-mile round trip to no purpose, for the target area was covered by low cloud, the convoy was not sighted, and the bombs were dropped indiscriminately so, naturally enough, 'no results were observed'.

Another southbound convoy was reported on 13 February. W/Cdr Bateson led out six Blenheims from 211 Squadron but could not locate it, and they ran into a severe tropical storm on their way back, which caused two of the Blenheims to come down, one in the sea – the crew took to their dinghy but the Observer was drowned – the other into a mangrove swamp some 30 miles from P2, killing the all-Australian crew (see Appendix 1) – the wreckage was not to be discovered for more than a quarter of a century. The convoy was attacked that night in heavy rain by the Blenheims, but again without success.

All available bombers were therefore sent up on the morning of the 14th to make a series of raids: 21 Blenheims from 84, 211 and 27 Squadrons, with a couple from 62 Squadron, the new Hudson squadron that also put up eight of its new American aircraft to join the 15 other Hudsons of 1 and 8 RAAF Squadrons. The Blenheims of 211 Squadron were late in making the rendezvous over P1 with the dozen escorting Hurricanes, and those of 84 Squadron were even later and missed the escort – as they left they were horrified to see paratroops descending on P1, now devoid of defending fighters. W/Cdr Bateson's 211 Squadron Blenheims sank one transport and set fire to others, and further bombing and strafing attacks caused the Japanese to postpone their landing until the next day, which was the day of the ignominious Allied surrender at Singapore. Two 84 Squadron Pilots, F/Lt John Wyllie and F/O 'Dutchy' Holland, who had bombed the transport ships in their Mk IVs, grabbed a couple of Gunners and took the two ex-27 Squadron Mk I-Fs back to strafe the enemy troops scrambling down nets into the invasion barges, causing many casualties. The paratroops did not capture P1 airfield, but blocked the only road from it to Palembang town where many RAF men were billeted, which caused much disruption, and ground-crews, with some air-crew – as in Crete – found themselves in hand-to-hand fighting with airborne troops. Those that were captured endured terrible hardships. P1 had to be evacuated, the aircraft going to P2 from where the raids on the landing troops continued with considerable success until, in the confusion, on the following day P2 was precipitately ordered to be evacuated too. All the aircraft that could still be persuaded to fly went to Batavia in Java, and 26 of them were Blenheims – these went on to the Dutch base at Kalidjati. All the unserviceable Blenheims and other aircraft had to be abandoned at P2 (see Appendix 1). The remaining personnel headed for the port of Oosthaven in the far south-east corner of Sumatra, travelling by whatever means they could improvise. They were evacuated from there in great and disorderly haste, from 15 to 18 February – and many thought this hurried departure to be premature – to Batavia in Java, even further to the south. Once again extensive supplies and much valuable equipment, including that of 41 Air Stores Park and a Repair & Salvage Unit that had only just arrived, were destroyed or abandoned to be captured. The Japanese had conquered strategically important south-eastern Sumatra, nearest to Java, in less than a week and could occupy the rest of the huge island, unopposed, at their leisure.

Java

Java was the most developed and prosperous island in the Dutch East Indies and it was hoped that the Allied forces, mainly Dutch, would be able to defend it successfully. The remaining 29 Blenheims were gathered at Kalidjati, a long-established Dutch base, and consolidated as 84 Squadron; it comprised 22 Mk IVs and seven Mk Is, including two Mk I-Fs of 27 Squadron, but only six of the Blenheims were fit for operations. Twenty-six Hudsons were grouped as 1 Squadron RAAF at Semplak, but they were soon bombed from P1 and reduced to half a dozen, which joined the Blenheims at Kalidjati only to lose two more. The 25 surviving Hurricanes, 18 of them serviceable, were based at Tjilitian and it was hoped to reinforce them with 40 P.40 Kittyhawks inbound on the American carrier *Langley*, but it was sunk on the 27th. The Blenheims attacked the Japanese build-up at Palembang, striking at both the port and P1 airfield, but once more too few were left to have a significant effect. On 25 February six Blenheims at Kalidjati were being bombed up for another raid when Japanese aircraft attacked the airfield and two of the Blenheims were destroyed. That day a large enemy convoy was seen heading towards Surabajo in eastern Java, so on the 27th Admiral Dorman attempted to intercept it with his Allied Naval Force, which included five cruisers and 11 destroyers, but all five capital ships were sunk that day and the next in the Battle of the Java Sea. As at Singapore, the Japanese now commanded the sea as well as the air, and it was clear that command of the land would soon follow. They captured many islands including Guam, Wake, the Celebes, Bali, Timor, and the Solomon Islands; their carrier-borne aircraft even raided Darwin in Northern Australia. Two more convoys were seen approaching the northern Javanese coast on either side of Batavia, and the remnants of the Blenheims and Hudsons attacked them all night, some aircraft carrying out three sorties for a total of 32, and at least three transports were sunk. It was considered too dangerous to continue these attacks in daylight in view of the Zeros patrolling over the landings, so the weary bomber crews were stood down for the morning, and the aircraft dispersed round the edges of the base to avoid bombing and strafing. However, at 1030, without warning, Japanese tanks and infantry, which had landed in the early hours at Eretenwetan some 30 miles away, overran the airfield. The four Hudsons parked near the runway took off under fire, but all of the 21 well-dispersed Blenheims were captured by the enemy, and although only eight of them were immediately serviceable, they still had plenty of fight left in them. With this final blow, on the ground and not in the air, the considerable contribution made by the Blenheims and their courageous crews to the Allied cause in that area of South East Asia was brought to a dramatic and sudden end. Two months later, Sgt David Russell, an 84 Squadron WOp/Ag who was among the airmen captured, saw two Blenheims flying over Bandoeng – their turrets had been removed, which further upset the PoW.

It was sad that the saga of the Blenheim squadrons, which had fought so hard all through the campaigns in Malaya and the East Indies, should be ended in this way. They had operated under the most difficult – often primitive – conditions in a debilitating climate, constantly caught 'on the hop' as evacuation followed evacuation, their dwindling numbers ever more hopelessly outnumbered, and lacking the essential support and servicing infrastructure. In the first four months of the Japanese onslaught the RAF was never allowed sufficient time 'to get its act together'. The Blenheim air- and ground-crews had given of their brave best and had suffered accordingly. Those who became PoWs endured a hell on earth. Of the 5,100 RAF men captured in the Far East, mostly in Java, one-third did not survive the war. On 9 March 1942 the Dutch Commander in the East Indies, General Ter Poorten, surrendered the Allied forces, and more than 100,000 Allied troops passed into cruel captivity. But many others escaped to Australia, among them W/Cdr John Jeudwine, CO of 84 Squadron, who found a derelict ship's lifeboat, gathered provisions, a sextant and a Blenheim P11 compass, then, choosing four officers and seven Australian Sergeants, spent a perilous and thirst-racked six and a half weeks sailing from Tjilatjap to Australia. Jeudwine was awarded the OBE for this feat, and 84 Squadron re-formed later in India with Vultee Vengeance dive-bombers.

Burma

We noted at the beginning of this chapter that Japanese aircraft bombed the Burmese capital Rangoon twice at the end of December 1941, but they lost some 30 aircraft in these raids so decided to concentrate their air forces on the successful invasion of Malaya, which culminated in the capture of Singapore, the main Western base in the region. This gave the Allied Air Forces a slight breathing space, for Burma had been even lower on the priority list for the provision of defences than Malaya. As in Singapore and Malaya, new airfields had been constructed in Burma, sited mainly in the valleys of the four main rivers (which run roughly north to south separated by vast jungle-clad mountain ranges), with five on the coastal plain – the southernmost of which, Victoria Point, had been seized by the Japanese early in their invasion of Malaya. Building airfields was one thing, but providing the aircraft and men to make effective use of them was another – in the event they proved to be far more useful to the invaders than they were to the defenders. The only units based in Burma at the outbreak of war were 67 Squadron with its Buffaloes, and 60 Squadron with its Blenheims, but, as we have seen, most of 60's aircraft were on armament training at Kuantan in Malaya and were retained there – all of them destined to be lost. The handful that remained in Burma carried out reconnaissance sorties and bombed Japanese-held airfields, which were also strafed by 67 Squadron's Buffaloes – the CO of 67 was S/Ldr Bob Milward DFC, who had commanded the Blenheim I-Fs of 30 Squadron in Greece and Crete. Fortunately for the RAF, the American Volunteer Group of combat-hardened 'Flying Tigers' under ex-Major Chennault, who had been aiding the Chinese by protecting the Burma Road, based one of its three squadrons of modern P.40 fighters at Mingaladon near

Rangoon. Two of the most experienced Blenheim squadrons, 113 and 45, and three Hurricane squadrons were on their way from the Middle East. Sixteen Blenheims of 113, each with at least one extra ground-crew member, were the first to arrive in three flights from 7 January 1942, following the long series of sectors from the Middle East. The few remaining aircraft and crews of 60 Squadron were amalgamated into the newly arrived unit.

AVM Donald Stevenson (whom we last saw as the unpopular AOC of 2 Group in the UK) had arrived at Rangoon as AOC Burma on 1 January 1942. He quickly appraised the situation and requested urgent reinforcements; he was promised six squadrons of Blenheims, three of them immediately, but received only the two mentioned. The Chiefs of Staff were concerned at the threat of the Japanese extending their expansion westwards to the vital strategic base of Ceylon, so another Blenheim squadron, 11, and two Hurricane squadrons were diverted there instead. Stevenson also received two squadrons of Lysanders – one from the Indian Air Force – and urged, without success, that they be re-equipped. The Indian Air Force also had a few Audax and Wapiti biplanes in service, and these were replaced later by Blenheims. The 113 Squadron Blenheims were sent straight into action within hours of arriving at Toungoo, even though most of the aircraft had accumulated defects during their long transit flights, and all required major inspections and overhauls. Eleven carried out a successful attack on Bangkok docks that night, but the Blenheims had to be sent the following morning to Lashio, the western terminus of the Burma Road, for this work to be carried out and, due to the lack of tools and spares, they were unable to return to operations for another 12 days. Six were sent to attack Tavoy airfield on 19 January escorted by four fighters; a dogfight with Ki.27s ensued and the aircraft of the leader, S/Ldr Duggan-Smith (Z7630), had its pilot's hatch and radio aerial shot away, but all used cloud cover to escape further attacks. Six escorted Blenheims of 113 – usually the derisory daily total of serviceable aircraft available – attacked troop targets on each of the next three days, which slowed the Japanese, who took cover in the jungle by day and advanced by night. The first three Hurricanes arrived at Mingaladon on the 23rd and were pressed into action immediately, and fierce dogfights were fought around the airfield over the next few days. In the middle of these the Blenheims of 84 and 211 Squadrons arrived en route to Sumatra, to be sent rapidly on their way, but one of them (V5782) crashed on take-off; the Pilot, Sgt R. Headlam RAAF, and the Observer were killed, and the WOp/Ag seriously injured. Nine Blenheims of 113 raided Bangkok that night, 24 January; one

An Indian crew board their Blenheim in 1942, while two ground-crewmen are ready to operate the fuel priming pump in the port undercarriage bay.

An Indian air-crew, mainly Bengalis, of 3 Coastal Defence Flight at Moulmein, Burma. In 1942 their four Mk Is (one of which was lost) provided the only air cover for Allied shipping heading for Rangoon, the major harbour in Burma.

Indians learned quickly and soon became skilful aircraft engineers.

(Z7582) was lost and one (Z7911) badly damaged (see Appendix 2). W/O Huggard in a 113 replacement aircraft led in seven more Hurricanes on the 25th, and the five Blenheim Mk Is of 3 Coastal Defence Flight were sent to replace the two surviving Wapitis of 4 CD Flight, but one (L8448) had to ditch in the sea off Chittagong on the way – it carried W/Cdr J. Ker, the CO of the Coastal Defence Wing, but fortunately he and his Indian Air Force Pilot, Hem Chaudheri, were rescued by a fishing vessel – and another (L4912) was damaged in an raid and destroyed by its own crew when they evacuated Moulmein (see Appendix 2). Five Blenheims of 113 bombed a Japanese column that had been using 50 elephants to force a route through the jungle on the 27th, and that night five more bombed Bangkok, one (Z6021) crashing on take-off when an engine cut. Clearly it was a hopeless task for a mere half a dozen Blenheims and a few fighters to delay the relentless Japanese advance. By the end of January the invaders had captured Tavoy, Mergui and Moulmein airfields, and the Allied armies were embroiled in fighting a series of rearguard actions in a retreat that would continue for many months and for 1,000 miles of the most difficult terrain – tracks became virtually impassable mud-slides during the monsoon months.

113 Squadron moved its HQ north to Magwe in the Irrawaddy valley on 6 February, and used the new but very rough airstrip at Zayatkwin as a forward base; the first Blenheims of 45 Squadron arrived there after their long trip from Egypt on 16 February. They carried out their first operation within the hour, when five of the Squadron's Blenheims – still in their desert camouflage – joined three of 113's, and, escorted by six Hurricanes, attacked a steamer at Moulmein. Such joint operations continued on a daily basis: seven Blenheims raided Chiang Mai airfield in Siam on the 17th, the following day six from 45 Squadron, escorted by five of the 'Flying Tigers' P.40s, attacked Japanese troop positions at Pandigon, and six more from 113, guarded by six Hurricanes, carried out a similar mission nearby. Some stragglers were still completing their journey from the Middle East: Sgt H. Jewell in V5999 became lost and force-landed on the banks of the Irrawaddy, and the aircraft overturned, while P/O D. Eve in Z7928 damaged the undercarriage taking off from the bumpy airstrip at Zayatkwin. One wheel was jammed down and the other swung free and would lock neither up nor down, so, not wishing to risk swinging into the other Blenheims parked on the airstrip, he ditched in the nearby Pegu River and the crew were rescued (see Appendix 2). Several new airstrips had been hurriedly created – named in the true RAF spirit as Johnny Walker, Black and White, Highland Queen, Dewar, John Haig, and Canadian Club – but living conditions on them were primitive indeed, and servicing facilities completely lacking, so no doubt the air- and ground-crews wished for some of the product to match the name of their airstrip!

In the confusing circumstances of the rapid Japanese advance it was very difficult to tell friend from foe in the jungle-clad country, so it is not surprising that so-called 'friendly fire' incidents took place. On 20 February, while attempting to assist the break-out by a surrounded battalion, RAF aircraft attacked the wrong troops. The following day, when reconnaissance had identified columns of some 300 vehicles moving north near Mokpalin as being enemy targets, they were bombed and strafed first by Japanese aircraft then by Blenheims, inflicting much damage and causing many casualties to what were, in fact, retreating columns of the British 17th Division, whose morale suffered badly. AVM Stevenson conducted an extensive enquiry but

AVM Donald Stevenson, former AOC of 2 Group Bomber Command, and AOC RAF Burma from 1 January 1942, still had to rely almost entirely on Blenheims as his striking force, but was far from popular with the crews.

was unable to reach a firm conclusion; he claimed that the Japanese might have used captured Blenheims or that their bombers, with a similar silhouette, had been mis-identified as Blenheims – but British troops had seen RAF markings. Later that year he did admit to 'the probability that some crews may have bombed the wrong objective'. Despite such tragic incidents General Slim, the Army Commander, commented later, 'Rarely can so small an Air Force have battled so gallantly and so effectively against the odds.' The evacuation of Rangoon was ordered on 5 March and the city was captured on the 8th – the same day that resistance in Java ceased – and Burma lost its only major seaport, cutting the overland supply route to China and leaving hazardous air-freight flights 'over the hump' from Assam as the only alternative.

Magwe, a small and primitive civil airfield in the Irrawaddy valley 200 miles to the north, was chosen as the base for 'Burwing' comprising 20 Blenheims of 45 Squadron (including a few ex-113 aircraft), and 17 Squadron's Hurricanes, together with ten P.40s of the AVG and a Flight of Lysanders from 28 Squadron – the other RAF units would withdraw to Akyab on the coast and form 'Akwing'. Five Blenheims set out from Magwe on 11 March to bomb a railway bridge near Pegu; Sgt D. Smith, the Pilot of Z9799, was hit by fire from the ground and killed, and the Observer, Sgt D. Golder, helped by the Gunner, Sgt J. Alt, was able to fly the damaged Blenheim back to base, where they baled-out safely rather than attempting a landing (see Appendix 2). The sole surviving 113 Squadron aircraft, now with 45 Squadron, failed to return from a reconnaissance sortie and the all-RAAF crew were lost (also Appendix 2). On 21 March nine Blenheims of 45 Squadron attacked some 50 Japanese aircraft on the former RAF airfield of Mingaladon with considerable success, despite the efforts of the Zeros; these were kept at bay by the ten escorting Hurricanes, which then strafed the airfield. Several Blenheims were damaged and the Pilot of one, F/O J. Muller-Rowland, was wounded, although all returned. However, two Hurricanes were lost, but five Zeros were claimed. Elated by their success, the crews were bombing up the Blenheims the following morning for a repeat raid when Magwe was struck by the first of three waves of Japanese warplanes – a total of 60 bombers and 24 fighters – and the devastation of the Allied base was completed the next day. Nine Blenheims were destroyed and five more damaged beyond immediate repair; the six survivors – none fit for operations – were flown to Akyab together with 11 Hurricanes, only three of which were combat-ready, and the last three P.40s escaped to Lashio. These raids caused Magwe to be abandoned in such a hasty and disorganised manner that the Army, still fighting 100 miles to the south, complained – with some justification – that the evacuation was premature. A party of 45 Squadron ground-

The official caption for this photograph from April 1942 is 'Evacuation of service personnel from Burma' – presumably the VIPs at the rear of the Jeep.

crew escaped into China via Lashio and the Burma Road – they could not be flown back to India 'over the hump' in returning transport aircraft until November. Akyab was attacked on the 23rd; L4914 was just taking off when bombs fell nearby and it crash-landed back on the end of the runway, two other Blenheims were also badly damaged, and S/Ldr F. Austin, a 45 Squadron Flight Commander, was injured by bomb splinters. On 24 March two more serviceable Blenheims were destroyed and two others damaged (see Appendix 2). On the 27th the remaining Hurricanes were caught on the ground, seven being destroyed, so all the flyable aircraft were withdrawn to Chittagong in India, but 45 Squadron's remaining Blenheims went to Lashio. Within three weeks of the fall of Rangoon the RAF had been driven from Burma, and the Army had to extricate itself with minimal air support – a task it completed by the end of May after many vicious encounters with the advancing Japanese forces. The remnants of 113 Squadron had been pulled back to Dum Dum (Calcutta) and re-assembled with replacement aircraft at Asansol, deep in India, but throughout April were able to mount only 40 sorties to support the Army's fighting retreat. Mandalay, the second city of Burma, fell on 1 May and on the 3rd to the 5th the Blenheims struck hard at Japanese forces moving up the Irrawaddy river in a variety of vessels, delaying their advance for several days at a critical stage. A few Wellingtons of 215 Squadron had arrived and joined the Blenheims in night raids on the latter's previous bases at Magwe and Akyab, but these were long and perilous trips often flown through tropical storms, and with no navigational aids whatsoever – apart from trying to obtain bearings from Calcutta radio – and they were generally ineffective.

Four 250lb bombs are about to be loaded on to a Mk IV, …

... and two crews are briefed in the field for a raid on a Japanese-held airfield.

In March 1942 60 Squadron was re-formed at Lahore, and from May its Blenheims operated into Burma with those of 45 and 113. A Flight of 113 Squadron under Captain J. Viney SAAF had been detached to Loewing in the extreme south-west of Yunnan province in China on 10 April, and operated in support of the Chinese armies resisting the Japanese advance towards their back door; five bombed groups of small river boats and flew on to Chittagong. Six more Blenheims arrived at Loewing on the 16th, but two were lost (see Appendix 2), and the four survivors returned to Asansol, while a final six, led by W/Cdr Grey, arrived in China on the 21st. Not many people realise that the ubiquitous Blenheims carried out operations from mainland China! Losses continued despite the small numbers engaged: on 24 April one of four making an attack at low level on MT on the road to Hopong was shot down (see Appendix 2), and one of three Blenheims bombing targets near Taungup was damaged and belly-landed at Lashio – it was blown up when the airfield was evacuated on the 27th. Four more were patched up and flown out successfully that day, while a fifth followed to Dum Dum two days later after a frantic all-night session taking the port engine from one bomb-damaged Blenheim and installing it another, whose own engine was wrecked. Magwe was raided on 9 May by five Blenheims, and five Japanese aircraft were set on fire; five more Blenheims set out from Dum Dum for the same target the next day but ran into bad weather and split up so that only S/Ldr C. Harper, an experienced Pilot from 34 Squadron, found the target and was pursued for half an hour by two Ki.27s but, using 'Plus 9' boost, he got away. Similar pursuits of pairs and trios of Blenheims took place over the next few days, and one had a lucky escape on 22 May: W/O Martin Huggard with Observer Sgt John Howitt and, as WOp/Ag, F/Sgt 'Jock' McLuckie – who lived up to his name when their Blenheim was chased by five Japanese fighters intent on shooting it down. Three aircraft of 60 Squadron had prepared to set off from Dum Dum to bomb Akyab airfield, but one had an engine problem and did not take-off, while another had technical trouble and returned, so W/O Huggard in Z9809 carried on alone. He decided to dive on the target for his bombing run from 10,000 feet on the landward side and make a high-speed escape at low level over the Bay of Bengal. However,

THE BRISTOL BLENHEIM

A 113 Squadron Mk 1V in India during 1942, showing nose art, and a good view of the FN 54 under-nose turret.

Observer Fred Atherton at work over Burma in his 113 Squadron Mk 1V in May 1943, it has the extra Browning gun in the nose.

Remains of Z7691 and another 60 Squadron aircraft destroyed in May 1943 by the Japanese at Dhazari, south of Chittagong.

the Japanese had seen the Blenheim prior to diving and five Ki.43 fighters of the 64 *Sentai* scrambled to give chase; the first two to intercept were each damaged by a well-aimed burst from McLuckie and had to break off and return to Akyab. The Japanese Commanding Officer, Lt Colonel Tateo Kato, a famous 'ace' with 18 victories, then caught up with the Blenheim, which was speeding only just above the wave-tops to protect its vulnerable undersides, but he too was hit by fire from the Blenheim's turret, half-rolled and crashed to his death into the sea; the other two pursuers, suitably chastened at witnessing the loss of their revered Commander, gave up the pursuit. One of the Blenheim undercarriage legs was hanging down, and there was no hydraulic pressure to raise it, so Huggard lowered the aircraft until the dangling wheel struck the surface, which knocked it back hard enough to engage the 'up' lock, and he then carried out a successful belly-landing at base. Although no awards were made in this instance, such bravery and skill was often shown by the 'Blenheim Boys' over Burma, but individual heroism was not enough to delay the Japanese advance. By mid-May the British had been bundled out of Burma, well over the border to India, and were setting up defences in the Naga Hills at Imphal and Kohima.

Ceylon

Meanwhile, another Japanese threat had arisen far to the south-west, one that caused deep concern to the Allied Chiefs of Staff, as it posed mortal danger to the vital Allied supply routes not only to the Far East but also to the Middle East. A Catalina had spotted a major Japanese naval force in the Indian Ocean on 4 April, which included Japan's main aircraft carrier strength and four modern battleships, and far outweighed the forces available to Admiral Somerville's Eastern Fleet in Ceylon. Intelligence from intercepted radio signals warned him that the enemy force included the five carriers of Admiral Nagumo's First Air Fleet – which had caused so much damage at Pearl Harbor – so he ordered the dispersal of ships from the port of Colombo and withdrew his mainly elderly warships to a base not known to the enemy at Addu Atoll in the Maldive Islands (developed post-war as Gan). The air defences of Ceylon rested on some hastily assembled Hurricane squadrons, two flown off HMS *Indomitable*, and a few Fleet Air Arm Fulmars. The only strike aircraft available were the Mk IV Blenheims of 11 Squadron, flown in from the Middle East and based at a new airfield constructed on Colombo's racecourse, together with a few FAA Swordfish and the antiquated Vildebeests of 273 Squadron. The newly appointed AOC, AVM J. D'Albiac (whom we last met commanding the inadequate RAF units in Greece), pleaded for the urgent dispatch of a squadron of Beauforts, but his plea was turned down by the Air Staff.

On 5 April 1942 120 Japanese naval aircraft from Nagumo's force attacked the harbour at Colombo; although most vessels had left the port, they did find two British heavy cruisers, HMS *Cornwall* and HMS *Dorsetshire*, some way out and sank them both. The airfield of Ratmalana, south of the capital, was also raided and in a series of dogfights between opposing fighters in bad weather 36 Hurricanes and six FAA Fulmars claimed 27 victories at the cost of 15 Hurricanes and four Fulmars, but the Japanese lost only seven or eight aircraft. The Racecourse airfield was not discovered and the Blenheims of 11 Squadron and the Hurricanes of 258 escaped the bombing. Another Japanese task force under Admiral Ozawa raided the ports of Masulipatnam, Cocanada and Vizagapatam on the eastern coast of India the next day, sinking some 23 merchant vessels and causing considerable panic. Calcutta was also bombed but most of the shipping in the previously crowded harbour had been ordered to scatter. Japanese submarines sank another five merchantmen to the south-west of Ceylon. On 9 April Nagumo's aircraft struck at the main British naval base at Trincomalee and the nearby airfield at China Bay, shooting down all six FAA Swordfish preparing for a torpedo attack on the Japanese fleet, but suffering at the hands of 17 Hurricanes and six Fulmars, which, for once, had been able to get airborne in time to claim 24 enemy aircraft destroyed at the cost of eight Hurricanes and three Fulmars, but only nine or ten Japanese aircraft were brought down. The Japanese then found the RN aircraft carrier HMS *Hermes* and the destroyer HMAS *Vampire* offshore and

An atmospheric shot of an 11 Squadron Mk I approaching the improvised airfield on Colombo's racecourse.

CHAPTER 30 – THE EAST INDIES, BURMA, CEYLON AND INDIA

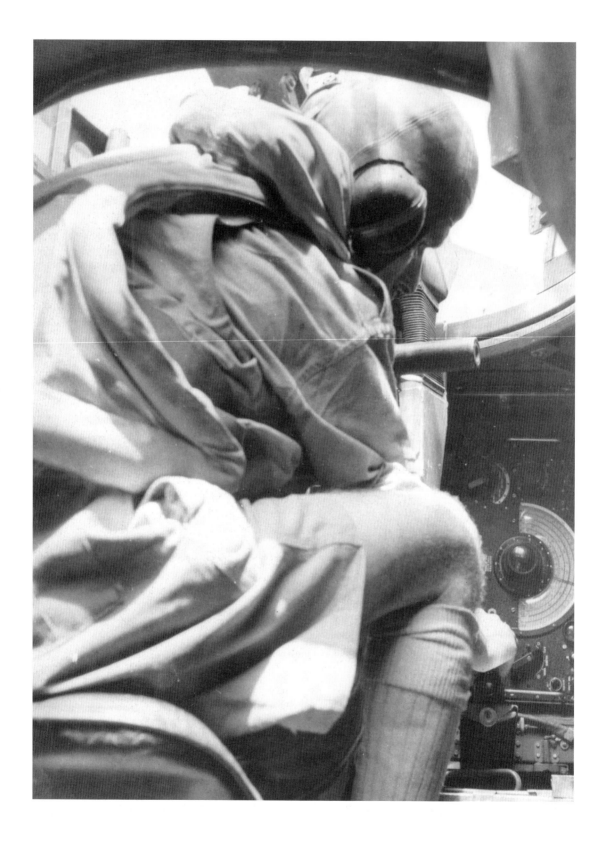

THE BRISTOL BLENHEIM

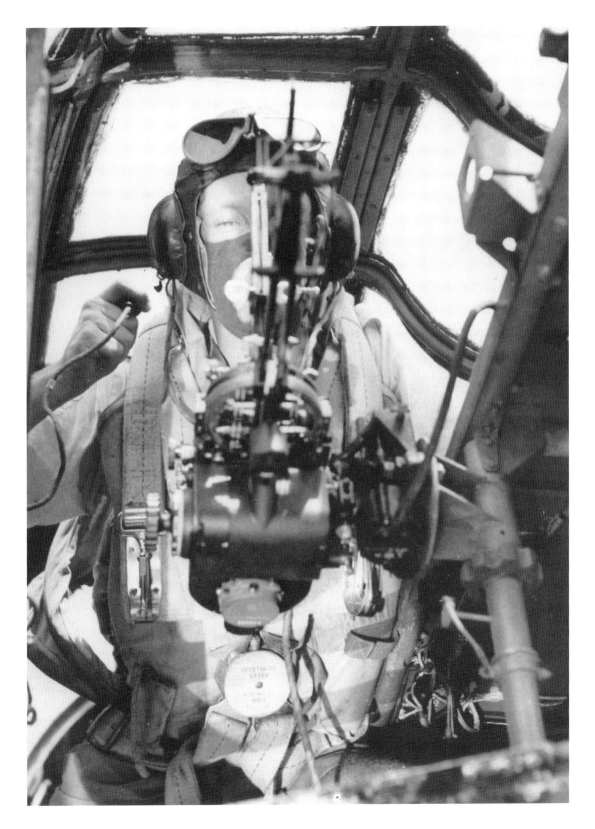

sank them within 20 minutes. They were only 60 miles from China Bay, but the Hurricanes and Fulmars there were not sent to their aid as all communication between Trincomalee and China Bay had failed. Ten Blenheims of 11 Squadron, the only strike force available, had no success either, for they were sent to the wrong location, could not find the enemy fleet and returned some hours later with their bombs still in the bomb bays. A Catalina had been sent to shadow the Japanese aircraft returning to their fleet, but it lacked the speed to maintain visual contact, then transmitted a garbled message (which was in fact relaying an SOS from another Catalina), which resulted in the Blenheims being ordered to fly on an incorrect heading. Churchill, taking a close interest in these events from London, found this failure to attack the enemy incomprehensible until the reasons for it were explained to him by Portal, the CAS. Eleven Blenheims were sent out again to attack the enemy fleet, but two returned to the Racecourse airfield with engine troubles. Unfortunately no fighter escort could be provided as 261 Squadron was already in action and the other surviving fighters were out of range, so clearly it would be a highly dangerous mission – just nine brave Blenheims pitched directly against Japan's mightiest air fleet. Led in tight formation

Excellent 1943 shots of an 11 Squadron crew on a submarine search in a Mk IV: the Pilot and Observer are in the cockpit, the WOp/Ag is reaching beyond the turret controls to operate the side-mounted R1155 radio and the Observer is using the Mk IX bombsight in the nose. All are wearing shorts and 'Mae West' life-jackets.

by S/Ldr Ken Ault at 11,000 feet for their straight and level bombing run, the nine Blenheims were already under fierce attack from 20 defending Zeros. It says much for their steely nerve that their bombs closely straddled Nagumo's flagship *Akagi* – but unfortunately they failed to score a direct hit. Five of the Blenheims were shot down, including that of their leader, and the four that struggled back to the Racecourse airfield were all badly damaged, three of them beyond immediate repair (see Appendix 3) – two of the Zeros were shot down, one by Sgt F. Nell, Gunner in R3911. Churchill himself described this action: 'Our handful of light bombers also made a heroic but forlorn attack against overwhelming odds upon the Japanese carriers. Less than half returned.'

Nevertheless, this was a turning point, as it was the furthest to the west that the Japanese forces would reach. Their task forces retired from the Indian Ocean and did not return. For six months the Japanese forces had swept all before them – including ten complete squadrons of Blenheims – in a series of rapid conquests. But now the tide was turning – by the end of May 1942 Nagumo's fleet was fought to a draw in the Coral Sea, losing two carriers, and a month later was soundly defeated in the Battle of Midway, losing four more. The symbolic Sun on the Japanese flag was rising no more – now, slowly but surely, it was setting.

India

However, far to the north-east, a long and costly struggle for South East Asia still lay ahead, a struggle in which the Blenheims continued to play an important part, although the extent of this contribution lessened progressively over the months and years as more modern – and more effective – aircraft became available.

We noted that 113 Squadron was re-formed, first at Dum Dum (Calcutta), where it was amalgamated with the remaining aircraft of 45, then at Asansol, and that it continued to operate over Burma, as did 60 Squadron, which was re-formed at Lahore. Both squadrons having been wiped out earlier in Burma (and in the case of 60 around Singapore too), both were re-equipped with freshly arrived Blenheims. 34 Squadron, also decimated in Malaya and the East Indies, was reformed at Allahabad in April 1942 with fresh Mk IVs, and personnel from elements of the Squadron at Karachi and Chakrata. But the Squadron was not ready to resume operations until late July, as it had to send a detachment to Peshawar on the Khyber Pass in the North West Frontier region (now in Pakistan) to deal with troublesome tribesmen – shades of such punitive actions in the 1920s and 1930s.

The Allied C in C, General Wavell, although prodded by Churchill throughout 1942, was unwilling to attempt an offensive into Burma until he had built up sufficient forces, in particular strength in the air. He had been incensed by the near disaster in Ceylon, and in a signal to the Chiefs of Staff in April stated:

> 'It certainly gives us furiously to think when, after trying with less than 20 light bombers to meet an attack which has cost us three important warships and several others and nearly 100,000 tons of merchant shipping, we see that over 200 heavy bombers attacked one town in Germany.'

Twenty Blenheims may have been available but, as recounted above, only nine actually attacked the Japanese fleet, five of which were shot down, and only one remained fit for use at the end of the day. Clement Attlee, Leader of the Labour Party and Deputy Prime Minister in the Wartime Coalition Government, proposed sending Bomber Command, with its new four-engined Heavy Bombers, out to the Middle and Far East Theatres of War, but Portal and the Air Staff resisted this proposal strongly, stressing the usefulness of the Blenheims, which were available, and the length of time it would take to make a force of complex four-engined bombers fit for operations away from the supporting UK industrial base – and from their manufacturers. Air Marshal Sir Richard Pierse, having handed over Bomber Command to Air Marshal Arthur Harris in the UK, had arrived in Delhi in March as AOC-in-C, and had to create a modern air force and the supporting infrastructure virtually from scratch, for in India the RAF had always come under Army Command, so was placed well down the War Office list of budgetary priorities. Pierse obtained authority to construct 215 new airfields, but in such an un-industrialised country as India, progress was painfully slow, even though over a million men were employed on them, and they were not all completed until the end of 1943. The RAF Depot in Karachi had served the supply, maintenance and overhaul needs of the north-west-orientated Air Force up to 1941, then a new and much larger facility was created at Allahabad, midway between Calcutta and Delhi, with others at Lahore and Ambala. The debilitating heat exacerbated the problems, for the summer of 1942 had been one of the hottest on record; 200 of the 700 airmen at Allahabad, by then the main Blenheim reinforcement base, suffered from heat stroke and seven died. Despite these difficulties, the serviceability percentage of available aircraft was doubled from the miserable 40 per cent of early 1942. Radar, VHF radio and other communications systems were also created and improved. General Wavell, Admiral Somerville and Air Marshal Pierse sent a joint appeal for urgent air reinforcements in April 1942. Thus, during the year, the number of Hurricane squadrons based around Calcutta and near Chittagong was built up to 12, and as a contribution to the small bomber force the Air Staff increased the supply of Blenheims (both Mk IV and the new Mk V), and sent a couple of squadrons (215 and 99) of early Wellingtons Mark I-Cs, and a single squadron (159) of Liberators to India. The latter arrived in September and operating from November 1942 – but only in tiny numbers as most, sometimes all, of them were normally grounded due to difficulties of maintaining serviceability in the face of a shortage of ground equipment and spares. Portal had been right not to send out any other RAF Heavy Bombers in early 1942. Blenheims continued to form the bulk of the bomber force operating over Burma.

Wavell launched the First Arakan Campaign on 9 December 1942, at the end of the monsoon season, which effectively prevented any major military or aerial activity by either side. The difficulties of carrying out operations in the monsoon period, and an indication of the priorities of one Adjutant, may be illustrated by quoting from the 113 Squadron Operations Record Book of 14 October: 'ORB for September, and up to 13 October, sunk without trace in flood at No 2 Camp. Squadron personnel compelled to evacuate. When the water had gone down, a fair amount of personal property was [found to be] lost, including the entire bar stock of the Officers Mess.'

Wavell's plan was an offensive thrust from Cox's Bazar in India down the Mayu

Blenheims attacking the port of Akyab on 9 September 1942: running in to the target (the second aircraft – upper left – was photographed by the rear-facing camera under the leading 34 Squadron aircraft), and the loss of 113 Squadron Blenheim V5589, seen almost inverted just before it was ditched on fire. Amazingly Sgt John Reid and crew survived and became PoWs. The ship at the jetty, the Niyo Maru, was hit and sunk.

THE BRISTOL BLENHEIM

Peninsula on the western coast of Burma towards Akyab, with the aim of recapturing the important airfields there. The three Blenheim squadrons, 113, 60 and 34, based around Chittagong, aided the Army as best they could, but the difficulties of locating enemy positions often in dense jungle close to advancing Commonwealth forces, then bombing them accurately, were extreme – map references of pin-points or smoke-shells from artillery proved inaccurate or insufficient. 34 Squadron, trained in night flying, was withdrawn from daylight raids and joined the Wellingtons in raiding more distant targets at night. The attacks on enemy airfields by the Blenheims, with an average daily availability of 50 operational aircraft, caused the Japanese to withdraw their bombers to Malaya and Siam. This aided the ground advance, which went well initially, and neared Akyab in late December, but they paused for ten days to re-supply, during which time the Japanese rushed up reinforcements and created effective defences, enabling a counter-offensive to be launched in March. The British left flank was penetrated further north, which threatened to cut off the 14th Indian Division, and after bitter and costly fighting the British Army was forced out of Burma again, and, by the onset of the next monsoon season, was back where it had started from. Akyab would not be recaptured until January 1945, but the later campaigns do not concern this account.

113 Squadron had changed its Blenheim Mk IVs to Mk Vs in October, and it continued to use the Mk Vs until the end of August 1943, when it converted to Hurricane IIC fighter-bombers. 34 Squadron followed the same pattern of re-equipment and the same time-scale. 60 Squadron continued to operate its Blenheim Mk IVs until July 1943, when it converted straight to Hurricanes, avoiding the period on the unpopular Mk Vs. Remember that the Rootes Group in the UK was still producing brand new Mk Vs right up to the summer of 1943 – they could not be deployed in Europe, and had been shown to be far too vulnerable in North Africa, so they were sent out to the Far East. The Hurricane fighter-bombers soon proved most useful in direct tactical support, as they had

A 113 Squadron Mk IV being prepared for another sortie over Burma at Chandina in India in May 1943 – you can almost feel the heat!

in the Western Desert. The personnel of 45 Squadron had been scattered all around India after they handed their remaining Blenheim IVs to 113, and they were gathered at Cholavaram in November to change to Vultee Vengeance dive-bombers alongside 82 Squadron. The latter unit had flown its Blenheims to Karachi in May, and was the first squadron to change to the American dive-bombers in August, but it took very many months to make them effective operationally. 84 Squadron, which, as noted, was wiped out in the East Indies, re-formed at Drigh Road in March and was equipped with Vengeances in December at Vizagapatam, as was 110 Squadron at Ondal – like 82, it had flown its Blenheim Mk IVs out to Karachi.

Another valuable but dull duty carried out day after day by the Blenheims, together with Hudsons and Catalinas, throughout 1942 and 1943 was maritime reconnaissance all along the extensive coastline of the Indian subcontinent, and out over the Indian Ocean and the Bay of Bengal, searching for enemy warships or submarines and escorting Allied convoys. Internal security had to be monitored, too, for civil unrest followed the arrest of Gandhi, Nehru, and other leaders of the Congress Party in August 1942 for inciting disorder with their 'Quit India' campaign, demanding immediate Indian independence. This sparked off attacks on

113 Squadron operated both Mk IVs and Mk Vs from airfields in India to targets in Burma from October 1942 until August 1943.

police stations and schools, as well as serious disruption of the vital railway network – more than 300 stations were wrecked – and led to patrols being flown by Blenheims along the affected railway lines, where they 'buzzed' any gathering mobs at very low level to disperse them. No doubt the crews thought this was great fun, but it had its dangers, for in at least two cases, following forced-landings in Bihar province, the crews were murdered by the mob.

In December 1942 a mere eight Japanese bombers attacked Calcutta, capital of Bengal, on a moonlit night, causing little damage but great panic in the population, one and a half million of whom were fleeing the city before dawn. Another 15 Japanese sorties added to the confusion over the next few nights. It will be recalled that the only night-fighter unit in the Theatre was 27 Squadron with Blenheim Mk I-Fs, which had been wiped out (as day-fighters) in Malaya and the East Indies. But Pierse managed to get a flight of four AI-equipped Beaufighters of 89 Squadron flown out from the Middle East to Dum Dum in mid-January. On the 15th F/Sgt Pring shot down all three of the Japanese bombers heading for Calcutta that night, and on the 19th F/O Crombie shot down two of four more – the Japanese ceased their raids and the inhabitants returned. 27 Squadron had been re-formed at Amarda Road in September 1942 and was busy converting to Beaufighters

Mk Vs heading for Burma in 1943. In this very rare shot of an Observer in the nose of a Mk V (facing the opposite way from a Mk IV), by his right shoulder can be seen the bulky R1155 radio set, which required a bulge in the Mk V nose contour.

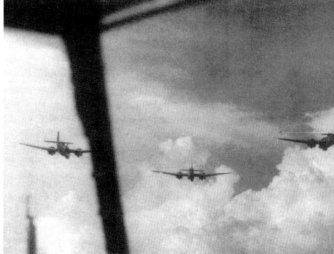

THE BRISTOL BLENHEIM

during November, carrying out its first operation on Christmas Eve, but its aircraft were not equipped with the AI radar sets, and soon commenced ground attacks on Japanese motor transport, trains, river vessels, and troop concentrations. These attacks were far more effective than those of the Blenheims due to the much heavier firepower of the 'Beaus', their great strength, and the quiet Bristol Hercules engines, which gave little warning of their rapid low-level approach – the Japanese called them 'Whispering Death'. The radar-equipped Flight grew into 176 Squadron, moving to Baigachi in February; 177, another Beaufighter squadron, was formed in May at Allahabad, and as it was not required in the night-fighter role, it too took over the ground-attack role from the Blenheims.

42 Squadron, en route to the Far East with its Beauforts, had been detained in the Middle East to strengthen the anti-shipping campaign at the time of the Battle of El Alamein, and did not arrive in Ceylon until November 1942. It changed to Blenheim Vs in February 1943 and moved to north-east India in March to take part in the fighting in Burma, then changing to Hurricane IVs in October and specialising in the ground-attack role. Also moving up from Ceylon was 11 Squadron at Colombo, which carried on with its Blenheim Mk IVs, moving early in 1943 to Baigachi near Calcutta, then to Feni nearer the Burmese border, until changing to Hurricane fighter-bombers as late as September 1943, thus being the last Blenheim squadron to use Mk IVs on operations. By then 'Hurri-bombers', Vengeance dive-bombers, and Beaufighters had replaced the Blenheims in the front line. The Blenheims had served long and well in the most difficult circumstances and were held in great affection by their crews. *Wings of the Phoenix* (the official history of the air war in Burma) describes the Blenheims as 'almost obsolete but still magnificent', and relates how elderly Blenheims 'that even a Museum would have rejected' carried on operating over Burma from Feni, and rather touchingly continues: 'So old were these aircraft now, and so excellent the Squadron spirit, that it is said that the Blenheims flew on happiness alone.'

One of its Mk Vs is being prepared for another raid in July 1943; the Pilot on the wing appears to be strapping on a revolver.

A 34 Squadron Mk V being readied to deliver bombs to targets in Burma, and another delivering medical supplies to a forward airfield in 1944. BA576 was not Struck off Charge until 14 October 1944.

Appendix I

Blenheim losses in East Indies (Borneo, Sumatra and Java), February 1942

04-02-1942   Z9577 84 Squadron Mk IV: lost en route to P1, crash-landed out of fuel; Sgt H. Hough, Sgt D. Hooper RAAF and Sgt G. Hirst RAAF safe together with two ground-crew passengers Sgt W. Tully and Cpl A. Hewitt.

06-02-1942   Z7856 211 Squadron Mk IV: shot down by Japanese fighters off Sumatra; Sgt G. Steele, Sgt S. Menzies, and Sgt G. Gornall (all RAAF crew) KIA, commemorated on Singapore Memorial.

06-02-1942   Z9713 211 Squadron Mk IV: shot down by Japanese fighters off Sumatra; Sgt A. Bott, Sgt J. Lynas, and Sgt H. Lamond (all RAAF) KIA, commemorated on Singapore Memorial.

06-02-1942   Z6282 84 Squadron Mk IV: damaged by fighters; Sgt P. Gardner (WOp/Ag) wounded in thigh, Pilot Sgt C. Thompson.

06-02-1942   Z9659 211 Squadron Mk IV: shot down on approach to P2; F/Lt K. Linton (Pilot) KIA, Sgt H. Offord (Obs) badly injured, Sgt R. Crowe (WOp/Ag) baled out but injured.

06-02-1942   Z9709 Mk IV: crashed on approach to Pakan Baroe, Sumatra.

07-02-1942   V6133, Z6282, Z7799 and Z7886 84 Squadron Mk IVs: burned-out in air-raid on P1 airfield, Sumatra.

10-02-1942   Z7699 211 Squadron Mk IV: shot down by AA fire in attack on Kluang airfield; S/Ldr Ken Dundas DFC, F/O G. Ritchie RAAF, and Sgt J. Keeping RAAF KIA, commemorated on Singapore Memorial.

11-02-1942   Z7521 211 Squadron Mk IV: crashed on night take-off at P2 for raid on Japanese task force; F/Lt J. Clutterbuck (Pilot) and F/Sgt H. Newstead (Obs) killed, Sgt Kite (WOp/Ag) injured.

11-02-1942   Z9649 211 Squadron Mk IV: crashed on night take-off at P2 for raid on Japanese task force; crew P/O B. West RAAF (Pilot) and Sgt G. Chignell (Obs) injured, P/O F. Joerin (WOp/Ag) uninjured, rescued by Sgt R. Wheatley RAAF, who was awarded George Medal.

11-02-1942   Z9726 84 Squadron Mk IV: crashed on night take-off at P2 for raid on Japanese task force; RAAF crew Sgt J. Hyatt (Pilot) and Sgt G. Mutton (Obs) killed, Sgt D. Irvine (WOp/Ag) badly injured and rescued following morning.

13-02-1942   ? 211 Squadron Mk IV: crashed into sea in storm returning from Banka Strait; F/O G. Mackay, F/O J. Payne, and F/O N. Oddie KIA.

14-02-1942   K7173 62 Squadron Mk I: damaged by flak attacking ships in Banka Strait, ditched in Moesi River, Sumatra; S/Ldr D. Banks injured, F/Sgt F. Brown safe, F/Sgt H. Oliver KIA and commemorated on Singapore Memorial.

15-02-1942   L1258 27 Squadron Mk I: shot down by fighters on raid from P2 on invasion forces; W/O S. Stafford, W/O R. Willmott and F/Sgt F. Hicks KIA, buried in Jakarta War Cemetery, Java.

16-02-1942   Z9602 84 Squadron Mk IV: ran into severe storm leaving P2, crashed into hill attempting return; RAAF crew Sgt N. Geappen, Sgt D. Gosbell and Sgt W. Davey killed together with ground-crew passengers Sgt A. Ross and Cpl D. Sumner, Cpl R. Shaw survived and became PoW but was murdered in Japan on 09-08-45.

18-02-1942   Z9732 84 Squadron Mk IV: damaged in strafing attack at Pakan Baroe; S/Ldr T. James and crew left aircraft there on evacuation.

21-02-1942   ? 211 Squadron Mk IV: FTR to Kilidjati, Java, from shipping strike, ran into storm; Sgt J. Burrage, F/Lt D. Stewart and Sgt M. McDonald, all RAAF, KIA, commemorated on Singapore Memorial.

00-02-1942   L1394 and L1395 34 Squadron Mk Is: lost in Borneo, no further details available.

00-02-1942   L1432 34/62 Squadron Mk I: lost in Borneo, NFD.

00-02-1942   L4927 60/27 Squadron Mk I: lost in Borneo, NFD.

Appendix 2

Blenheim losses in Burma

Aircraft are all Mk IVs.

24-01-1942   Z7582 113 Squadron: FTR to Mingaladon from raid on Bangkok; F/Sgt P. Keeley, Sgt A. Dingle RNZAF and Sgt D. Briggs KIA, buried locally, re-buried at Kanchanaburi War Cemetery, Thailand.

27-01-1942   V6012 113 Squadron: engine trouble on take-off at Mingaladon for raid on Bangkok docks, crashed at end of runway, DBR; Lt J. Viney SAAF, Sgt McIver RAAF and Sgt J. Wohlers RAAF slightly injured.

02-02-1942   Z7680 113 Squadron: tyre burst on landing at Toungoo, DBF; 2/Lt N. Russell SAAF badly burned when fuel-tank exploded as he was halfway out of cockpit, but recovered, Sgt T. Barry and F/Sgt A. Tillott, both RAAF, escaped safely. (See also 21-01-1942, Chapter 29, Appendix 2.)

11-02-1942   Z7770 45 Squadron: shot down near Kyaikto; 2/Lt F. De Marillac SAAF (Pilot) and Sgt R. Southern (Obs) wounded, Sgt R. Gowring (WOp/Ag) uninjured.

11-02-1942   V5422 45 Squadron: damaged on ground in air-raid on Magwe and abandoned there.

14-02-1942   V5627 113 Squadron: engine cut on take-off from Zayatkwin, Burma, for raid on Martaban, Burma, belly-landed near airfield; S/Ldr P. Ford and P/O T. Scott-Chard safe, Sgt W. McKerracher RAAF injured. (See also 01-03-1942, V6467 below.)

16-02-1942   V5999 45 Squadron: low in fuel, force-landed near Thayetmyo, cart-wheeled; all-RCAF crew Sgt H. Jewel, Sgt J. Hurley, and Sgt F. Terry injured.

17-02-1942   Z7916 113 Squadron: engine cut on take-off at Zayatkwin airstrip, swung off runway, hit 30cwt truck, abandoned on evacuation; Sgts Lloyd, Fairey and Whittle uninjured.

18-02-1942   Z7928 45 Squadron: u/c damaged, force-landed in Pegu River; all-RAAF crew P/O D. Eve, P/O G. Kemp, and P/O N. Bain safe.

25-02-1942   V6221, Z7923, Z9821, Z9823? Z9833 and Z9835 45 Squadron Mk IVs: destroyed on ground in air-raids on Mingaladon.

26-02-1942   Z9811: damaged on ground in air-raid on Mingaladon.

01-03-1942   V6467 113 Squadron: crashed on take-off at Magwe, abandoned there on evacuation; S/Ldr P. Ford and P/O T. Scott-Chard slightly hurt, Sgt E. Hodson injured.

04-03-1942   Z7592 113 Squadron: FTR to Magwe, shot down on raid near Salween River by four Zeros; F/Lt S. Lee RAAF and Sgt K. Brett RNZAF KIA, Sgt G. Walker (WOp/Ag) survived, evaded capture.

11-03-1942   Z9799 45 Squadron: hit by ground fire near Mingaladon; all-RAAF crew Sgt D. Smyth11-03-1942
             Z9799 45 Squadron: hit by ground fire near Mingaladon; all-RAAF crew Sgt D. Smythe (Pilot) fatally wounded, Sgt D. Golder (Obs) and Sgt J. Alt (WOp/Ag) baled out safely over Magwe. (Pilot) fatally wounded, Sgt D. Golder (Obs) and Sgt J. Alt (WOp/Ag) baled out safely over Magwe.

14-03-1942   Z7899 45 Squadron: shot down near Mingaladon; all-RAAF crew Sgt L. Powell, Sgt L. Connor, and P/O J. Eden KIA.

15-03-1942   Z7969 113 Squadron: engine cut on take-off at Ratmalana and crashed.

21-03-1942   Z7412 45 Squadron: destroyed in air-raid on Magwe.

25-03-1942   Z9828 60 Squadron: FTR from sortie to Burma, no further details available.

00-03-1942   V5495, Z7635, Z7757, Z9573 and Z7981 45 Squadron Mk IVs: destroyed or damaged and abandoned in Burma.

19-04-1942   Z9820 113 Squadron: crashed into Irrawaddy River after raid on Allanmyo, on return from Loi Wing China; F/O M. Hickey, F/O R. Rogers and F/Sgt E. Campbell, all RAAF, KIA, commemorated on Singapore Memorial.

24-04-1942   Z9831 113 Squadron: FTR to Lashio from raid on enemy column; W/O J. Aitken (Pilot) KIA, W/O W. Hinds (Obs) died of injuries on 11-05-1942, Sgt A. Bailes (WOp/Ag) escaped.

24-04-1942   V6333 113 Squadron: hydraulics damaged by ground fire, belly-landed at Lashio and abandoned there on evacuation.

Appendix 3

Blenheim losses in Ceylon (Sri Lanka) area

Aircraft are all Mk IVs.

28-02-1942   V5958 11 Squadron: damaged beyond repair (DBR) in heavy landing at Bangalore en route for Colombo.

04-03-1942   V5953 11 Squadron: crashed on landing at Bangalore en route for Colombo; Sgt Morphett and crew uninjured.

15-03-1942   Z7711 11 Squadron: en route to Colombo, swung on take-off at Ratmalana, u/c collapsed, collided with Hurricane.

15-03-1942   Z7968 11 Squadron: engine cut on take-off at Ratmalana for Colombo, swung and DBR.

01-04-1942   V5819 11 Squadron: no further trace.

09-04-1942   Z7896 11 Squadron: shot down by Zeros; Capt C. Adcock SAAF, Sub/Lt Peace FAA (Obs), and Sgt M. Gray RAAF KIA.

09-04-1942   R3911 11 Squadron: shot down by Zeros; Sgt H. Maclennan, Sgt Travers (Obs), and Sgt F. Nell (WOp/Ag) KIA.

09-04-1942   V5992 11 Squadron: shot down by Zeros. S/Ldr K. Ault, Sub/Lt F. Bonnell FAA (Obs), F/Sgt S. Whiles (Obs), and Sgt G. Eckersley (WOp/Ag) KIA.

09-04-1942   Z7803 11 Squadron: shot down by Zeros; W/O N. Stevenson RAAF, F/O A. Donald (Obs), and Sgt J. Bell (WOp/Ag), KIA.

09-04-1942	Z9574 11 Squadron: shot down by Zeros; Lt F. Knight SAAF, F/O D. Evans RAAF (Obs), and Sgt L. McAuley RAAF KIA, commemorated on Singapore Memorial.
09-04-1942	Z7506 11 Squadron: damaged but repaired; Sgt E. Anderson DFM RAAF, Sgt McFadzean, and Sgt Brown uninjured.
09-04-1942	V6010 11 Squadron: damaged but repaired; Sgt R. Garnham RNZAF, Sgt Boltwood, and Sgt Sutton uninjured.
09-04-1942	Z7759 11 Squadron: damaged and crash-landed, u/c collapsed, repaired; F/O H. Smith, W/O Howe, and Sgt Alderton slightly injured.
11-04-1942	? 11 Squadron: engine cut on approach to Colombo Racecourse airfield, crash-landed; Sgt P. Ewing injured.
22-04-1942	Z7506 11 Squadron: flew into hill in bad weather at Galkanda, destroyed by fire; S/Ldr J. Bouwens DFC, F/Sgt A. Griffiths, and F/Sgt D. Fisher killed, buried in Kandy War Cemetery.
05-05-1942	Z7640 11 Squadron: crashed into sea on reconnaissance of island; Sgt A. Nicholls KIA, crew rescued.
16-12-1942	Z7984 11 Squadron: engine caught fire on take-off at Colombo, destroyed by fire after emergency landing; Sgt J. Cartledge and crew escaped uninjured.

Appendix 4

Blenheim losses in India to 31 May 1942

Aircraft are all Mk IVs except the first entry.

25-01-1942	L8448 3 Flt IAF Mk I: ditched 100 miles off Chittagong; W/Cdr John Ker (CO of Coastal Defence Flights) and Hem Chaudheri (Pilot) IAF, rescued by fishing-boat.
13-02-1942	Z7579 45 Squadron: lost en route from Egypt to India, no further details.
09-04-1942	Z9681 60 Squadron: engine cut on take-off, crash-landed at Lahore.
18-04-1942	V5957 113 Squadron: DBR in taxying accident at Asansol.
20-04-1942	Z7634 113 Squadron: u/c collapsed in heavy landing at Dum Dum, SOC 15-08-1942.
23-04-1942	Z9803 113 Squadron: swung on landing at Chittagong and u/c collapsed.
27-04-1942	Z9669 113 Squadron: engine cut on take-off at Dum Dum, force-landed, DBR.
30-04-1942	Z7884 1301 Met Flight: based at Delhi, reported missing.
04-05-1942	Z7303 60 Squadron: brakes failed on landing at Willingdon, Delhi, ran into building, DBR.
04-05-1942	Z9742 34 Squadron: stalled on approach to Bamrauli near Allahabad, u/c collapsed.
04-05-1942	Z6281 113 Squadron: engine cut on return from raid on river craft at Monywa, Burma, crashed in forced-landing in Hooghly River, Bengal; Lt J. McGlashan SAAF, Sgt H. Charnley and Sgt T. Richardson rescued. Lt McGlashan crashed again on 31-05-1942 and was fatally injured, qv.
10-05-1942	L6650 353 Squadron Mk I: crashed at Bamrauli soon after night take-off, destroyed by fire, believed due to instrument failure; F/O K. Das and crew killed. 353 Squadron was forming with Hudsons.
11-05-1942	Z7969 and Z7852, 113 Squadron: DBR in gale at Asansol.
12-05-1942	Z7990 60 Squadron: hit bump on runway at Asansol, attempted overshoot, lost power and crashed in paddy-field; Lt Beesley SAAF and crew injured.
12-05-1942	V6254 34 Squadron: engine cut, crashed in forced-landing 23 miles from Bamrauli; Sgt H. Kay (Pilot) killed, Sgt G. McLeary (Obs) and Sgt J. Coombes (WOp/Ag) seriously injured.
19-05-1942	Z7495 60 Squadron: crashed on landing at Jessore, ran into soft patch, swung into heap of bricks, DBR; no injuries reported to P/O H. Waterson and crew.
22-05-1942	Z9809 60 Squadron: damaged in action shooting down Oscar, belly-landed at Dum Dum, Calcutta; W/O M. Huggard, Sgt J. Howitt, and F/Sgt J. McLuckie uninjured, aircraft repaired.
23-05-1942	Z9620 113 Squadron: missing in bad storm on training flight from Asansol, cause unknown; F/O E. Pearse, F/O C. Grigg, and F/Sgt J. Germein (all RAAF) killed.
25-05-1942	Z9741 113 Squadron: belly-landed short of fuel when all airfields closed due to bad storm; Sgt Taylor RCAF and crew uninjured.
25-05-1942	L7965 ? 113 Squadron: tyre burst on take-off at Asansol, crashed and caught fire; Sgt Kitchen (Pilot) and Sgt Hulme (Obs) severely burned, Sgt Simpson (WOp/Ag) concussed.
30-05-1942	Z7316 34 Squadron: stalled on overshoot at Bamrauli and crashed; P/O G. Mockridge and crew injured.
31-05-1942	V6029 113 Squadron Mk IV: RTB from raid to Akyab with engine trouble, swung on landing at Dum Dum, struck Wellington BB510; Lt J. McGlashan SAAF fatally injured and died on 05-06-1942, Sgt H. Charnley and Sgt T. Richardson slightly injured.

Appendix 5

Other known Blenheim losses in the Far East

Losses in Malaya, Burma, Borneo, Sumatra, Java, Siam, China, India and Ceylon (with no further details available, and not recorded under Squadron or Unit) include:
L1412, L1413, L1414 and L6606 (all 34 Squadron, lost in Malaya); L4912 (3 Coastal Defence Flight, lost in Burma); L6628, L6633, L6666, L6668, L6669, L8507, L8540, L8618 and L8621 (27 Squadron, lost in Malaya); L8393, L8396, L8458, L8528 and L8609 (all 60 Squadron); T1994, V5422, V5577, V5581, V5598, V5599 and V5627 (for 113 Squadron); V5631, V5632, V5959 and V6012 (all ex- 113 Squadron); V6076 (ex-84 Squadron); V6444, Z6046, Z6092, Z6093, Z7346, Z7521, Z7578, Z7754, Z7766, Z7776, Z7780, Z9649 and Z9668 (for 45 Squadron); Z7783, Z9709 and Z9711 (for 113 Squadron); Z9714, Z9718, Z9723, Z9727, Z9736, Z9753, Z9755, Z9796, Z9807 and Z9819 (for 45 Squadron); Z9829.

Appendix 6

Blenheim losses in India from 1 June 1942

Aircraft are all Mk IVs unless otherwise stated.

06-06-1942	Z7758 113 Squadron: shot down by flak in raid on Akyab; F/Sgt F. Banks, F/Sgt D. Lowcock and Sgt W. Drake KIA, commemorated on Singapore Memorial.
16-06-1942	Z7903 60 Squadron: crashed near Allahabad, cause unknown; Sgt W. Shannon RNZAF (solo Pilot) killed.
18-06-1942	Z7892 113 Squadron: FTR from raid to Myitkina; S/Ldr C. Harper (Pilot) and P/O L. Beauchamp (Obs) KIA, no record of WOp/Ag.
23-06-1942	Z9721 60 Squadron: shot down in raid on Akyab; Lt L. Beesly SAAF and crew KIA.
26-06-1942	V6181 60 Squadron: crashed on take-off at Asansol, 'elevator control failed to respond', destroyed by fire; crew escaped uninjured.
29-06-1942	L9307 34 Squadron: engine cut on return from raid on Paletwa, Burma, crash-landed near Ondal, India; F/Lt C. Newman safe, F/Sgt D. Harding and Sgt A. Jaffray injured.
04-07-1942	Z7881 60 Squadron: ASI failed on take-off at Asansol, belly-landed in attempted forced-landing.
04-07-1942	V6465 301 MU: out of fuel, crashed in attempted forced-landing 73 miles east of Jaipur; Sgt B. Turner and three crew injured, F/O J. McKechnie (232 Squadron Pilot) died of his injuries.
08-07-1942	Z6155 113 Squadron: unable to climb out of blind valley in bad weather, crash-landed near Fort White, Burma; F/Sgt F. Butcher and crew injured.
13-07-1942	V5528 308 MU: dived into ground 3 miles from Allahabad airfield, unknown cause; P/O J. Trenberth (Pilot), F/Sgt B. Walmsley (F2E), and F/Sgt F. Ellers (WOp/Ag) killed.
24-07-1942	Z7647 60 Squadron: failed to become airborne at Dum Dum, u/c raised prematurely; W/Cdr C. Wallis DSO, CO of 60 Squadron, and P/O D. Page KIA, F/Sgt B. McDade and Lt Dorner (Army passenger) seriously injured.
26-07-1942	Z7768 113 Squadron: engine cut on take-off at Asansol, swung into mud and tipped up.
18-08-1942	T2245 113 Squadron: crashed at Kalihah during internal security flight; F/Sgt S. Goss RCAF killed, F/Sgt C. Whiteside and Sgt A. Murray murdered by local mob, buried in Ranchi War Cemetery.
18-08-1942	L9027 34 Squadron: propeller detached, crash-landed 150 miles east of Dum Dum; F/Lt C. Newman and crew uninjured.
20-08-1942	Z6333 34 Squadron: engine cut on internal security flight, u/c collapsed attempting single-engine landing at Asansol, DBF; Sgt J. Julian, Sgt R. Rogers and Sgt F. Greaves escaped uninjured.
21-08-1942	V5642 60 Squadron: take-off abandoned at Asansol when elevator jammed, over-ran runway into bank, DBR; 113 Squadron crew Lt N. Wilkin SAAF, F/Sgt F. O'Neill RAAF and Sgt W. Thompson safe.
30-08-1942	Z9743 34 Squadron: force-landed on internal security patrol near Rohias railway station; F/Sgt J. Julian, P/O J. Thwaites and Sgt F. Greaves murdered by local mob, commemorated on Singapore Memorial.
31-08-1942	L1542 211 Squadron Mk I: DBR in an accident, no further details.
31-08-1942	L8541 211 Squadron Mk I: crashed, no further details available.
09-09-1942	V5425 60 Squadron: crashed into sea off Akyab during raid after damage by enemy action; F/O G. Mockridge, Sgt D. Brown, and Sgt G. Hall RAAF KIA, commemorated on Singapore Memorial.
09-09-1942	Z9798 60 Squadron: damaged by fighters in raid on Akyab, overshot and crashed on s/e landing at Chittagong; P/O J. McMillan and Sgt N. Purdon, both RAAF, and Sgt F. Carruthers uninjured.

09-09-1942	V6507 113 Squadron: shot down in same raid on Akyab; F/O O. Loane, F/Sgt T. Bell and F/Sgt R. Barnard, all RAAF, KIA, commemorated on Singapore Memorial.
09-09-1942	V5938 113 Squadron: lost on same raid on Akyab; Sgt J. Reid, Sgt P. Wilson and Sgt L. White became PoWs.
12-09-1942	Z7985 113 Squadron: two light bombs fell off on taxying out at Argartala and blew up, aircraft destroyed by fire; F/Sgt M. Foster (Pilot) and F/Sgt L. Tatton (Obs) badly burned, latter died of injuries, Sgt K. Thompsett (WOp/Ag) uninjured.
28-09-1942	Z7369 113 Squadron: collided with Z9749 (below) halfway down runway at Asansol, both aircraft DBF and blew up later; Sgt N. Taylor, F/Sgt J. Paterson and Sgt A. King escaped.
28-09-1942	Z9749 113 Squadron: collided with Z7369 (above) halfway down runway at Asansol, both aircraft DBF and blew up later; Sgt W. McLellan, Sgt J. Vernon and Sgt J. Nankervis, all RAAF, escaped.
30-09-1942	Z7596 308 MU: swung on take-off at Bamrauli, u/c collapsed.
11-10-1942	Z9598 113 Squadron: hit tree low-flying on Army Co-Op exercise, crashed; W/O H. Peters RCAF, W/O B. Pearce RAAF and Sgt D. Davies killed, buried in Delhi War Cemetery.
12-10-1942	Z7421 34 Squadron: engine cut returning from raid, hit trees in attempted forced-landing at Chandranghona; S/Ldr P. Keeble (Pilot) and F/Lt C. Johnson (Obs) killed, Sgt C. Wood (WOp/Ag) injured.
24-10-1942	R3689 60 Squadron: tyre burst on take-off at Dum Dum.
28-10-1942	Z7756 60 Squadron: damaged by flak on recce to Buthidaung, ran out of fuel, force-landed at Chittagong; Sgt Sykens (Pilot) and Sgt Gardiner (WOp/Ag) unhurt, Sgt Oliphant (Obs) injured.
29-10-1942	Z9745 60 Squadron: swung on landing at Asansol returning from raid on Shwebo, Burma, crashed; Sgt K. Minchin, Sgt Howitt and Sgt Houlgrave uninjured. Not known if repaired, but SOC on 31-08-1943.
10-11-1942	V5925 34 Squadron: Mk IV, shot down by enemy fighters over Burma, F/O Howe RAAF, F/O J Hay RAAF, and P/O T Lishman KIA.
10-11-1942	Z7705 34 Squadron: shot down by enemy fighters over Burma; W/O Elliot, F/Sgt E. Hyland, and Sgt Elliot KIA.
10-11-1942	V6491 113 Squadron: shot down by flak in raid on Akyab; W/O C. Allen, F/Sgt J. Williams, and Sgt S. Mintern KIA.
16-11-1942	AZ864 113 Squadron Mk V: sank back on attempted overshoot at Asansol, crash-landed; Sgt R. Lockwood, Sgt J. McKee and Sgt H. Courtney uninjured.
18-11-1942	BA578 113 Squadron Mk V: crashed on landing at Dum Dum.
18-11-1942	BA396 113 Squadron Mk V: tyre burst on landing at Dum Dum, u/c collapsed; F/Sgt H. Thornton, W/O S. Davies and Sgt E. Dicketts safe.
24-11-1942	Z9679 34 Squadron: turned back from raid on Pakokku airfield, Burma, with engine trouble, crashed on landing at Dum Dum, DBF; F/Lt R. Burrows, Sgt J. Darbyshire and F/O J. Ensell escaped safely.
27-11-1942	Z9751 34 Squadron: lost propeller returning from raid, crashed on landing at Dum Dum; F/O P. Voss RNZAF, F/Sgt P. Sharland and Sgt H. Glue injured.
04-12-1942	BA206 Mk V with 308 MU: struck floodlight on landing at Drigh Road, Karachi, u/c collapsed; Sgt W. Hall (solo Pilot) unhurt.
20-12-1942	BA622 113 Squadron Mk V: shot down by ground fire at Magwe; Lt N. Wilkin SAAF, F/Sgt F. O'Neill RAAF and Sgt W. Thompson RAAF KIA, buried in Taukkyan War Cemetery, Burma.
28-12-1942	Z6372 60 Squadron: engine cut on take-off at Feni, swung, u/c collapsed; Sgt Smythe and crew injured.
07-01-1943	Z5883 60 Squadron: overshot landing at Cuttack, u/c collapsed.
10-01-1943	V5644 11 Squadron: lost en route Colombo/Biagachi, no further details available.
10-02-1943	BA452 113 Squadron Mk V: tyre burst on landing at Feni, swung and u/c collapsed.
22-02-1943	BA663 42 Squadron Mk V: tyre burst on take-off at Yelahanka, swung and DBR.
05-03-1943	V6010 11 Squadron Mk IV: FTR to Feni, engine hit in raid to Burma, force-landed between Ramu and Cox's Bazar; RAAF crew F/Sgt J. O'Donnell safe, F/Sgt K. Birdsey died of injuries, F/Sgt C. Williams injured.
14-03-1943	Z7927 11 Squadron: shot down by Ki.43 over Burma; P/O F. Richardson, F/O Williams, and F/Sgt S. Osborn all RAAF, KIA.
15-03-1943	BA617 34 Squadron Mk V: engine cut, stalled in turn and struck ground near Kekmirghal and destroyed by fire; W/O G. Jeffreys, F/Sgt J. Hearne, and F/Sgt R. Skinner KIA.
15-03-1943	V5587 60 Squadron: damaged by enemy aircraft, crash-landed; no injuries to Sgt H. Alsopp and crew reported.
15-03-1943	Z7710 60 Squadron: damaged by Zeros on raid to Burma, hydraulic failure, belly-landed at Feni, DBR; no injuries to P/O J. McMillan, Sgt N. Purdon, both RAAF, or Sgt F. Carruthers recorded.
15-03-1943	Z7293 60 Squadron: shot down over Nawlagya, Burma; F/O Archer and crew baled out safely.
19-03-1943	BA655 42 Squadron Mk V: tyre burst by bomb splinters during raid on Pinlebu, crashed on landing at Rajyeswarpur; F/O de Souza, F/O Sinclair, and Sgt Wood only slightly hurt.

19-03-1943	BA684 42 Squadron Mk V: crashed in flames during raid on Pinlebu; F/O Kerr, F/Sgt Wilson, and Sgt Smith baled out near Chindwin River and rescued by British Army patrol.
21-03-1943	V5513 60 Squadron: destroyed by enemy action; no further details available.
23-03-1943	Z7759 11 Squadron: lost, no further details available.
05-04-1943	Z7648 11 Squadron: collided with Z9667 (below) during raid on Meiktila airfield some 8 miles from target; F/Sgt H. Besley baled out and survived, F/O G. Foster RAAF and W/O D. Andrew RAAF KIA.
05-04-1943	Z9667 11 Squadron: collided with Z7648 (above) on same raid, both aircraft locked together and fell in flames; S/Ldr W. Matteson, F/O E. Appleton RAAF, and W/O T. Wixted RAAF KIA, those killed buried in Taukyan War Cemetery.
06-04-1943	BA169 42 Squadron Mk V: destroyed on ground by Japanese raiding party at Argatala.
12-04-1943	BA650 34 Squadron Mk V: tyre burst on landing at Kumbhirgram, swung and u/c collapsed.
13-04-1943	V5445 60 Squadron: hit by flak or explosions from own bombs in raid on Adwynbyin, Burma, crashed in flames; F/O M. Duncan, W/O R. West, and W/O D. Macleod KIA.
19-04-1943	BA727 113 Squadron Mk V: FTR, NFD.
17-05-1943	BA546 34 Squadron Mk V: engine cut on take-off at Bairagarh, crashed, destroyed by fire; no injuries reported to F/Sgt G. Hayley and crew.
19-05-1943	BA920 113 Squadron Mk V: starboard flap failed on approach to Comilla, crash-landed in paddy-field; F/O Webster, F/Sgt Whyte, and Sgt Cheshire uninjured.
20-05-1943	BA478 113 Squadron Mk V: engine cut, crashed in attempted forced-landing 5 miles from Feni, destroyed by fire; F/Sgt Ferguson, W/O Campbell, and F/Sgt Rayner escaped, Obs slightly burned.
21-05-1943	Z7619 11 Squadron: shot down by Zeros off Mickhail Island on radar calibration sortie from Chittagong; P/O R. Stokes, P/O C. Pigdon, P/O C. Cubitt, and Sgt C. Hutton (F2A) KIA.
24-05-1943	T2291 11 Squadron: engine cut in circuit at Feni, undershot approach with full bomb load, stalled into ground; F/O H. Smith, F/Sgt H. Cargill RAAF, and P/O M. Shepherd RAAF slightly injured.
25-05-1943	BA675 113 Squadron Mk V: aborted raid on Buthidaung in bad weather, crashed on landing at Chittagong due to burst tyre, caught fire; Lt J. Viney SAAF, W/O J. Barry, and P/O J. Wohlers RAAF escaped before bombs exploded.
25-05-1943	BA494 113 Squadron Mk V: FTR from raid on Buthidaung in bad weather; F/Sgt A. Lancaster, W/O A. Nourse RAAF and Sgt G. Anderson KIA, commemorated on Singapore Memorial.
01-06-1943	Z7912 11 Squadron: lost propeller at night in bad weather, crashed in Manipur valley; W/Cdr A. Pennington-Legh, F/Lt R. Ingram DFC RAAF, and F/Lt B. Burnley DFC RAAF killed, commemorated on Singapore Memorial.
06-06-1943	BA916 113 Squadron Mk V: crashed on overshoot near Comilla, on return from aborted raid to Kalemyo; W/O L. Ward RCAF, F/Sgt R. Gilchrist RNZAF and Sgt G. Theobald KIA.
09-06-1943	BA923 42 Squadron Mk V: damaged during raid on Kalewa, crash-landed at Jagi Road; F/O Booth, Sgt Robinson, and P/O Jenkins unhurt.
12-06-1943	BA590 113 Squadron Mk V: swung on landing at Comilla, DBR.
13-06-1943	Z7964 11 Squadron: brakes failed while taxying at Feni, ran into blast-pen, became ground instructional airframe.
23-06-1943	BA607 113 Squadron Mk V: hit sea, reason unknown, and crash-landed on beach; F/Lt G. Brew (Pilot) uninjured, F/Sgt W. Facton (Obs) injured.
06-07-1943	V6504 60 Squadron: lost propeller on air-test, control lost, dived into ground 4 miles south of Yelahanka; F/Sgt S. Schragger (Pilot) and F/Sgt W. Brister (Obs) killed.
09-07-1943	N6183 11 Squadron: shot down by ground fire in raid on Ramree, Burma; Sgt G. Regan, Sgt M. Smith, and Sgt G. Rowan KIA.
03-08-1943	Z7913 60 Squadron: engine cut, lost height, ditched in China Bay, Ceylon; W/Cdr D. Banks and crew rescued, one injured. Z9813 (60 Squadron Mk IV) is also recorded as ditching on this day, NFD.
24-08-1943	EH460 113 Squadron Mk V: crashed in forced landing in River Sone; one of Sgt Padley's crew injured.
26-08-1943	BA451 42 Squadron Mk V: hit water flying low and ditched in lake 3 miles south of Badopur; F/O Newcombe rescued.
01-09-1943	BA300 42 Squadron Mk V: struck parapet of bridge, tail broke off.
12-09-1943	BA103 42 Squadron Mk V: crashed on take-off at Kumbhirgram, DBF; one of F/Sgt R. Weller's crew injured.
23-02-1944	BA473 42 Squadron Mk V: belly-landed at Yelahanka, Bangalore.
08-08-1944	AZ865 176 Squadron Mk V: tyre burst on take-off at Baigachi, belly-landed and DBR. 176 was a Beaufighter squadron.

PART 4

BLENHEIMS IN THE BACKGROUND

Z7520 left Wadi Gazouza for 72 OTU on 26 March 1942, but crash-landed at Kosti, Sudan, F/Lt Jones and F/O Berrett stand by their wrecked Mk 1V.

BA914 of 75 OTU at Gianaclis, Egypt, the under-nose turret has been removed, it was DBR in an accident on 23 February 1944.

L6672 served with 267(Communications) Squadron at Heliopolis from August 1941 until April 1942, and was SOC in July 1944.

Chapter 31

Support and Flying Training Units

We have seen in the previous chapters how the Blenheims were replaced gradually, and certainly not before time, by later aircraft in the front-line operational squadrons, first in northern Europe, then in the Middle East, and finally in the Far East. However, as noted, some Mk IVs and many Mk Vs continued to serve with several second-line squadrons, mainly on maritime patrols, right until the end of the war. In addition, throughout the entire war thousands of Blenheims of all three marks rendered constant and invaluable service in the many essential Support and Flying Training Units – especially the Advanced and Operational Training Units – that stood directly behind the operational squadrons. Thus, in addition to their valiant service in the thick of the action in the foreground of all Theatres of War, the Blenheims in the background made a further and very considerable, but often unrecognised, contribution to the overall war effort.

At any time, on any day or night, somewhere among the multitude of RAF airfields scattered through so many countries, the throttles of a Blenheim were being opened so that it gathered speed along the runway, the control column was eased back, the Blenheim became airborne and climbed away for another sortie. At the end of tens of thousands of these sorties the Blenheims' wheels would kiss the ground safely once more, but hundreds of other sorties would end in a violent, often fiery, frequently fatal, crash – not always due to any action by the enemy. Many were the Blenheims that had survived months of highly dangerous active service with operational squadrons only to meet their end in the hands of a Pilot at a Support or Training Unit, a Pilot often lacking in experience, skill or just luck. A study of these accidental losses in the Appendices to the chapters reveals not only the thousands of Blenheims involved, but also the widespread geographical disposition of the units concerned and the extensive variation in the causes – although hundreds of accidents were caused by an engine cutting out during or just after take-off, and hundreds more by tyres bursting during the take-off run. Note 1 to this chapter shows the extraordinary number and the great diversity of the Support and Flying Training Units that operated Blenheims. It is no wonder that so many aircraft were lost in accidents, or that these losses continued relentlessly throughout the entire period of the war, as seen in the other Appendices. The Blenheims continued to provide these widespread and diverse facilities quietly and well away from the spotlight that shone on the operational squadrons, but the facilities proved to be of absolutely vital importance in improving the efficiency of those squadrons. The functions of the units providing these facilities are summarised, albeit somewhat arbitrarily, below.

Support Units

The various units that used Blenheims described under the following headings, together with their main bases, are listed in Appendix 1.

Anti-Aircraft Co-Operation Flights and Units

Fighter Command's five Groups each had an Anti-Aircraft Co-operation Flight equipped with Blenheims. These carried out mock attacks at various altitudes, speeds and angles, often at very low height indeed, to enable the gunners to set up their equipment, and practice tracking fast-moving aircraft – at night they performed similar duties for Searchlight Units. The other main units were No 1 Anti-Aircraft Co-operation Unit at Farnborough, which had lettered Flights at various bases, together with Nos 6, 7 and 8 A-A CUs in the UK and 22 A-A CU at Drigh Road, India. No 1 Coastal Artillery Co-op Flight, then Unit, can be grouped here too.

T2353 of No 6 A-A CU based at Ringway. It crashed in an attempted force-landing after an engine failure on 5 December 1940.

Communications and Station Flights

Most Wing, Group, Command and Area Headquarters possessed a 'Comms Flt', sometimes upgraded to squadron status, and if Blenheims were used by the squadrons or units under their control, these Flights or Squadrons would be equipped with Blenheims for visits to the bases and units within their command. AOCs and GOCs would be taken in them to attend conferences or visit fighting units: Wavell, Auchinleck, Connor, Longmore, Tedder, Pierse, Slim and Coningham are just a few of the High Commanders who travelled by Blenheim. Operational squadrons that converted to later aircraft often retained one or two Blenheims for training or communications use, and many other non-Blenheim squadrons often used one or more for the same purposes. A few coastal-based units combined the Communications and Air-Sea Rescue functions. The RAF Communication Units that used Blenheims, with their main bases, sub-divided into the UK, Middle East and Far East, are listed under in Appendix 1. Nearly all the stations that operated Blenheims kept a few to form a Station Flight for general communications and 'run-about' use, but these Flights are far too numerous to list.

Z9592, a Communications Flight Mk IV at El Kabat, Egypt, in 1944, has Dark Earth/Mid Stone upper surfaces and Azure Blue under-surfaces; most unusually, the under-wing roundels are outlined in Yellow. Dorsal and chin turrets have been removed.

Delivery/Ferry Units

Thousands of Blenheims passed through the hands of the RAF's vast delivery organisation, which was spread across very many countries. Units involved in this constant battle to maintain supplies of aircraft over such great distances, so often urgently required by hard-pressed Group Commanders, included the Aircraft Delivery Units, the civilian-run Air Transport Auxiliary, with HQ at White Waltham, for whom several renowned lady pilots flew; the Overseas Aircraft Delivery Units; the Overseas Aircraft Preparation Units; the Replacement Aircraft Pools; the Ferry Pilot Pools and Ferry Controls; the Pilot Reinforcement & Reserve Pool, and so on.

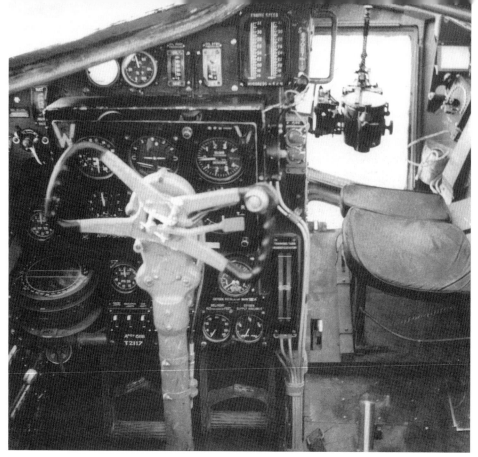

Blenheims were constantly being ferried about, often between squadrons and MUs, frequently by male and female pilots of the ATA in the UK. ATA pilots made some 8,600 Blenheim delivery flights during the war, and Service Pilots an even greater number. They flew many types, using standard mnemonics for their vital actions, and ring-bound cards for airspeeds and engine settings. This Mk IV cockpit has oddly positioned boost gauges – one above the compass and one to its right – and the Observer's seat is folded for the use of the Mk IX bomb-sight.

Development Units

Much work was done by Blenheims at the various Development Units, work that proved of great value not only to the Blenheims but also in improving the operational efficiency of many other types of aircraft. The main centre was the Aeroplane & Armament Experimental Establishment, initially at Martlesham Heath then at Boscombe Down. There were also the Air Fighting Development Unit, the Bombing Development Unit, the Fighter Interception Unit, the Royal Aircraft Establishment at Farnborough, Special Duties Flight, and Telecommunications Flying Unit. The manufacturers also retained dozens of Blenheims for various trials, development and experimental purposes before passing them on to operational units. Some are listed in the Notes to Chapter 9.

THE BRISTOL BLENHEIM

An attempt by Coastal Command to increase the firepower of its Fighter Blenheims was this neat pack of two 20mm cannon, with ammunition carried in the former bomb-bay of L6787 a Mk I-F, in lieu of the four .303 Browning pack, but it was not adopted.

A Mk IV – believed to be Z5990, ex-528 Squadron – at Shoeburyness Range, showing the devastating effect of a single explosive German cannon shell. In the air the whole tail section would detach instantly, with disastrous results.

Bottom left: DJ702, a prototype Mk V, served with the A&AEE at Boscombe Down, No 12 PAFU at Grantham, and 17 SFTS at Cranwell, where it crashed on take-off on 19 April 1945.

Maintenance and Repair Units

Absolutely essential in keeping such large numbers of Blenheims fit for service was the enormous volume of skilled engineering work carried out at the Maintenance Units and Repair & Salvage Units, backed up by the Civil Repair Units. The MUs also carried out major inspections and overhauls, incorporated the latest modifications, and repaired aircraft damaged in action or in accidents. A constant stream of 'Queen Mary' low-loader trailers delivered bent and battered Blenheims, and teams of engineers fell upon them, often working 'round the clock' under the supervision of Inspectors from the Bristol company, to make them fit for use again. Thousands of Blenheims that suffered from major battle damage or from a serious accident were repaired and returned to service within weeks. Many thousands more that had suffered minor damage, such as a wheels-up landing, were repaired on site and put back in service often within days – many Blenheims made several 'belly-landings' or experienced a few 'undercarriage retracted on the ground in error' incidents in the course of their service life. The stream of repair work throughout the war was never-ending.

Z9671, a Mk IV, was with 117 MU at Wadi Saidna when the undercarriage collapsed on a heavy landing in bad visibility on 12 January 1942. The white tail-plane and rear fuselage made them more conspicuous should they force- or crash-land.

Major inspections, overhauls and repairs were carried at the MUs, such as 151 at Seletar, Singapore.

Crew of 21 Squadron Mk IV disembark from YH-L (V6436) at Bodney 18 august 1941. This aircraft and crew was shot down on the Rotterdam Raid ten days later. (The only wartime colour photographs that I could trace. Author)

These pictures show the four different colour schemes and markings carried by my two restored Blenheims, briefly in 1987 and between 1993 and 2002. Author

Home Guard Unit by an 82 Squadron Blenheim at Shoreham Airfield in 1940.

A Mk IV-F Night Fighter of 68 Squadron at High Ercall in 1941.

A 105 Squadron Mk IV taxies out at Swanton Morley in the Summer of 1941.

A Coastal Command Blenheim of 254 Squadron with a Lysander of 161 (Special Duties) Squadron in 1942.

The second Blenheim to be restored at Duxford was marked as WM-Z (Z5722),
the personal Mk IV-F Night Fighter of W/Cdr Max Aitken, CO of 68 Squadron.

The first Blenheim rebuilt to fly again was marked as GB-D (V6028), the 105 Squadron aircraft flown by W/Cdr Hughie Edwards when he won the Victoria Cross. It crashed at an Air Display at Denham in June 1987, through no fault of the aircraft, less than four weeks after completing a 12 year restoration.

Top left: It was then marked in the 1942 Temperate Maritime Scheme as QY-C (L8841) of the hard–working 254 Squadron Coastal Command.

Bottom left: The Blenheim was then marked as UX-N (R3821) of 82 Squadron, 2 Group Bomber Command. The original R3821 was shot down in the disastrous raid on Aalborg Airfield on 13 August 1940.

Above: A stunning shot of QY-C by John Dibbs showing John Romain at the controls with Colin Swan in the nose and Smudger Smith manning the turret. John Romain led the restoration teams and is now Managing Director of the Aircraft Restoration Company at Duxford which maintains and operate the aircraft. The photograph shows clearly the compound double-curves of the nose glazing.

The Blenheim over Blenheim palace in 1994, by kind invitation of the Duke of Marlborough who remembers, as a boy, seeing Blenheims from the OTU at Bicester flying low over the drive to 'beat up' the Palace.

The cockpit of the restored Blenheim, being based on a Canadian licence-built airframe, has the central quadrant for throttle, mixture and prop-pitch levers, plus improved controls for the hydraulic systems in the centre of the main panel. The First World War ring-and-bead sight for the fixed gun is retained! Currently this is the only airworthy Blenheim or Bolingbroke anywhere in the world.

Meteorological Flights

Another unsung but most important service pioneered by Blenheims from March 1941 onwards were the daily flights carried out in all weathers, often when all other aircraft were grounded, well out over the Atlantic and the North Sea gathering valuable data for the weather forecasters, whose advice had to be relied upon when operations were being planned. These lonely and hazardous sorties, which had to be flown very accurately, were carried out by some 18 numbered Met Flights, all of which used Blenheims until other aircraft such as Hudsons and Halifaxes became available. (Met Flights are listed in Appendix 1.)

Z7355 of 1401 Met Flight crashed near Thetford on 14 May 1942.

F/Lt Eric Kraus, a skilled Observer, at work with 1403 Met Flight in 1941.

Z7370 of 1404 Met Flight has 'brushed some gorse' in bad weather!

Miscellaneous Units

Blenheims were used for all sorts of odd tasks by units that do not come under the main categories, such as the Anti-Locust Unit (Persia); No 1 Camouflage Unit; Pilotless Aircraft Unit; RAF Film Unit; Sea Rescue Flight, Shandur; 10 Staging Post Flight, Northolt; Parachute Training Centre, Ringway; Air Defence Co-operation Unit, Ismailia; and so on.

Z7415 of 1411 Combined Development Flight is equipped to lay smoke-screens – the twin rotary dispensers can be seen below the turret, which appears to have a deflector.

Cause and effect: Mk IV of 516 (Combined Operations) Squadron laying a smoke-screen for troops during a landing exercise in a Scottish Loch prior to D-Day.

Photographic Reconnaissance Units

Blenheims pioneered PR use in the RAF, initially with aircraft of the 2 Group squadrons, then with the specialist unit founded by Sidney Cotton, as related earlier. No 2 Camouflage Unit at Heston (a cover name for PR Unit) became the Photographic Development Unit, and grew into the Photographic Reconnaissance Unit, then numbered PRUs – Nos 1 and 3 used Blenheims among their aircraft. Their work was invaluable for planning operations and for assessing results, and was often dangerous. These units came under Coastal Command control.

140, a PR Squadron formed at Benson in 1941, had both Spitfires and Blenheim Mk IVs, the latter serving until August 1943.

BA313, a Mk V of 244 Squadron, was abandoned at Ras el Hadd after the war, having swung and suffered an undercarriage collapse on 26 November 1942. Mk IVs served with 244 Squadron until January 1943, Mk Vs until March 1944.

Radar Calibration Flights

Another unglamorous but most important task was to help set up and monitor the operation of the Chain High and Chain Low Radar Stations around Britain's coast, which made such a vital contribution to the victory of the RAF in the Battle of Britain. This was done by flying a series of sorties at accurate courses and heights from a fixed point such as a lightship. Blenheims were used on this dull but essential task by a dozen Calibration Flights.

For later development and calibration work with the various types of radar entering service in the UK, ten Wings were formed (Nos 70 to 79), and these were later regrouped into squadrons (Nos 526, 527 and 528), and are also listed in Appendix 1. Blenheims were employed continuously on these 'hush-hush' but essential duties from months before the start of the war until months after it had ended.

R3844, a Mk IV of 162 Radar Calibration Squadron, which also acted in the Electronic Counter Measures role at Bilbeis in May 1942.

Two fine shots of EH495 of 1578 (Calibration) Flight at Blida, taken at Foggia, Italy, in July 1944. The under-nose extension has been removed, and there is a small cupola in place of the dorsal turret.

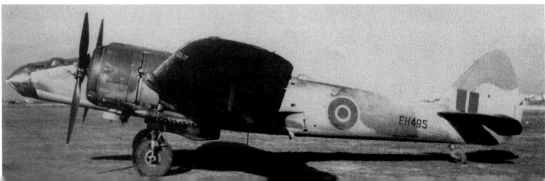

R2782 of 771 Squadron FAA over the Orkney Islands.

The Royal Navy

Many people are surprised to hear that a dozen Fleet Air Arm squadrons flew Blenheims during the war and no, they did not attempt to operate them from aircraft carriers! They were used mainly as realistic 'target' aircraft so that the FAA fighter pilots could practice interceptions – the Sea Hurricanes, Fulmars, Martlets (Wildcats), Spitfires, Seafires, Hellcats and Corsairs would intercept, using their cine-guns, as the Blenheims carried out dummy raids on warships or naval bases. The teams operating the radar equipment on warships would also practice plotting these raids.

The FAA Squadrons that employed Blenheims, most of them right up to, and some beyond, the end of the war, are listed, with their main bases, in Appendix 1.

L1225 of the NAFDU, later 787 Squadron Fleet Air Arm, at West Raynham in 1943.

L1210 of 759 Squadron FAA, based mainly at Yeovilton.

This Mk.V AZ930 served at the A&AEE at Boscombe Down in 1942, then with 42 OTU at Andover, 13 OTU at Bicester, and finally with 12 PAFU at Spittlegate, overshooting and skidding into the boundary at Harlaxton (Relief Landing Ground) on 11th September 1944.

Flying Training Units

The various units that used Blenheims described under the following headings, together with their main bases, are listed in Note 2.

Miscellaneous Training Units

There was an extraordinary number of widespread miscellaneous training units that backed up the Flying Training Schools with a multitude of specialist training facilities. These included the Air Observers Schools, the Bombing and Gunnery Schools, Beam Approach Training Flights, Schools of Army Co-operation, Ferry Training Flights and Units, the Air Armament School, an AI/ASV School, RDF and Radio Schools, Conversion Flights, Schools of General Reconnaissance, Refresher Flying Units, and so on. In each of their different ways these specialist training units made a major contribution to increasing the efficiency and effectiveness of the crews in the front-line squadrons, not only the Blenheim crews but also those of the successor aircraft such as the Bostons, Baltimores, Mitchells and Mosquitos, and also in training the crews for the four-engined Heavy Bombers.

A practice bomb from low level hits the target on a range – any lower and the aircraft would be in danger of damage from the exploding bomb, as can be seen.

Mk Is served with the Pilots Advanced Flying Units until well after the war, such as 12 PAFU Spitalgate.

BA297, a Mk V of No 1 ME Check and Conversion Unit at Bilbeis, Egypt.

Operational Training Units

More than 1,500 Blenheims provided an extremely useful, in fact indispensable, service in most of the RAF's Operational Training Units both at home and overseas. The OTUs improved and honed the basic skills the crews had acquired at the Pilots Advanced Flying Schools, the Air Observers Schools, and the Air Gunnery Schools, and prepared them to fly and work together as a crew and to learn to use the aircraft as a weapon of war. OTU aircraft were often tired, following service with operational squadrons, even when they were first allocated to the OTUs, yet they led a gruelling life with them, flying continuously – often in inexperienced or clumsy hands – for month after month, between major inspections, engine and propeller changes. Some OTUs suffered even heavier losses due to their location, such as 70 OTU at Nakuru, which was 7,000 feet above sea level – this altitude and the high ambient temperatures degraded take-off performance so that long take-off runs were needed, with consequent increase in tyre failures and engine problems due to overheating. Most Blenheims at OTUs experienced many minor accidents and incidents, such as wheels-up landings, and were repaired again and again in the course of this wearing and lengthy service, until the majority met with the one final accident that could not be repaired. It is therefore no surprise that relatively few Blenheims that served with OTUs managed to survive the war. As with the miscellaneous training units above, it was not only the Blenheim crews who benefited but also the crews of all the later aircraft that took their place.

V6468 of 70 OTU force-lands near Nakuru, Kenya, on 15 December 1941.

BA 914, an all-white Mk V of 75 OTU, being refuelled at Gianaclis in late 1944; one of its fuel-tanks – probably changed due to a leak – lies in the foreground. The under-nose turret has been removed.

THE BRISTOL BLENHEIM

Pilots at 13 OTU at Bicester practice formation flying in their Mk IVs.

V6083 of 13 OTU, showing the twin-gun rear-defence turret, the flame-dampers on the exhausts, and the fuel jettison pipes for the outer fuel tanks.

An AI-equipped all-black Mk I-F of 54 OTU; the first of three night-fighter OTUs which also trained the first 'all-weather' crews.

A Mk I of 72 OTU runs into the boundary at Nanyuki, Kenya.

AZ938, a Mk V of 79 OTU, abandoned at Nicosia, Cyprus, after the war.

THE BRISTOL BLENHEIM

Blenheims in foreign service

Finland

As recorded in Chapter 7, the Finns were the first foreign country to import Blenheims and had arranged licence production before the war. They were also the first foreign country to employ Blenheims in active service, against the Russians during the Winter War that started in November 1939, and Chapter 10 describes how very gallantly they fought until Finland surrendered in March 1940. However, once German forces invaded Russia in June 1941 the Finns found themselves, albeit unwittingly, as allies of the Germans. Production at Tampere resumed and a total of 45 Mk Is and ten Mk IVs were delivered. These new machines and their surviving earlier Blenheims were in frequent action during the 'Continuation War' against the Russian forces, often with an escort of Me.109s, until the cease-fire on the Finnish front in September 1944. Finnish Blenheims were then required by the Russians to operate against German forces in northern Finland during the little-known 'Lapland War' until May 1945. Blenheims therefore carried out operational sorties on both the first and last days of the Second World War! Their losses are listed in the Notes to Chapter 10. After the war the Finns continued to use their faithful Blenheims, mainly for aerial survey work, until mid-1958.

Pilot Ahtiainen boards for an operation in BL-129 from Vartsila in 1942. (Other photographs of Finnish Blenheims are in Chapters 7 and 10).

BL-200 being prepared for a sortie on 18 August 1954.

The last sortie by a Finnish Blenheim was by BL-199 on 20 May 1958.

Greece

The total destruction of the Blenheims operated so bravely by the Royal Hellenic Air Force against the *Regia Aeronautica*, then the *Luftwaffe*, is covered in Chapters 23 and 24. Their valiant fight against such overwhelming odds should be remembered with pride. Details of Blenheims imported by Greece and the ex-RAF aircraft supplied to them are given in Chapter 7 and listed in the Notes, while the formation of 13 (Hellenic) Squadron RAF and its operations with Blenheim Mk IVs and Mk Vs in the Western Desert, the Eastern Mediterranean, and Aden until October 1943 are described in Chapters 26 and 28, and their losses in the Appendices to those chapters.

13 (H), the Hellenic Squadron of the RAF, operated Mk IV and Mk V Blenheims over the Western Desert from January 1942 to September 1943.

Romania

As described in Chapter 7, 52 Blenheims were supplied to Romania prior to, and early in, the war in a futile attempt to keep that country on the Allied rather than the Axis side, but Hitler needed supplies of oil from the Romanians so twisted their arms until they joined the Axis powers. The Romanian Air Force also used its Blenheims against the Russians on the southern part of the Eastern Front from July 1941, mainly around Odessa, in the Stalingrad sector, then in the Black Sea area. They were supplemented by three ex-Yugoslav machines and all operated under *Luftwaffe* control; they were also escorted by Messerschmitts, and such use is recorded up to October 1944, but by then most had been lost either in action or by accidents, and the lack of spares further reduced the number available to a mere half a dozen.

Both of these Romanian Air Force Blenheims were lost over Russia. The Romanians used a total of 52 Blenheims.

Yugoslavia and Croatia

Details of pre-war Blenheim exports to Yugoslavia, and the setting up of its licensed production facility at Zenum, are given in Chapter 7. The rapid decimation of the Yugoslav Blenheim units during the German invasion is covered in Chapter 24. Their Serial numbers were 3501 to 3562: 3501 and 3502 were purchased pre-war from Bristol as patterns, 3503 to 3542 were licence-built by Ikarus, and 3543 to 3562 were purchased from RAF stocks. After the conquest the Germans passed on eight ex-Yugoslav Blenheims to the Croatian Air Force, given the serials 1501 to 1508, and used them against the partisans – but these patriots destroyed most on the ground (1501 was sabotaged, 1503 was blown up by its own bombs, and 1504, 1505 and 1508 were blown up in August 1943 using explosives supplied by the British). Two (1502 and 1506) were hijacked and escaped to neutral Turkey, and one (1507) force-landed in Austria on 6 May 1945 trying to reach Allied forces, and was recovered and used by the post-war Yugoslav Air Force. Another ex-Yugoslav Blenheim, 3528, was used by the Hungarian Air Force as L104 until 1945. The Germans also sent several partly completed Yugoslav-built Blenheims and other major airframe components from Zenum to Tampere in Finland where production continued.

Croatian Air Force ex-Yugoslav Mk Is paraded at Zagreb in 1943.

THE BRISTOL BLENHEIM

Turkey

The Turkish Air Force was also supplied with some 63 Blenheims of all three marks; the first batch of a dozen ordered in 1936 is listed in Chapter 7. Eighteen more were delivered by February 1939, and the Turks were presented with ten Mk Is in 1940, followed by 20 more (three Mk IVs and 17 Mk Vs) in 1943. But Turkey, like Spain, resisted the blandishments of both the Allied and Axis powers and managed to keep out of the war altogether. Turkish Air Force pilots were converted to Blenheims at 12 (Pilots) Advanced Flying Unit at RAF Spittlegate, and its satellite at Harlaxton. The 2 Air Division at Gaziemir continued to operate its Blenheims at least until 1948.

The Turkish Air Force had a total of 63 Blenheims, ranging from Mk Is before the war to Mk Vs that served well into the 1950s.

Portugal

Neutral Portugal, laying alongside the main ferry route to the Middle East, inherited three Blenheims that had force-landed on their way to Gibraltar. In 1943 the Portuguese were also provided with 24 ex-RAF Blenheims as part payment for the Allied use of bases in the Azores, but one (L8837) crashed at Cintra en route. Units of the Naval Air Arm (Aviaco Naval) at Portela de Sacavem, Lisbon, and the Army Air Force (Aeronautica Militar) at Ota, had a dozen apiece, together with two dual-control Mk Vs. The Naval Air Arm had 12 Mk IV-Fs and two Mk Vs, the Air Force had nine Mk IVs and two more Mk Vs, and they continued in service until 1948. The Portuguese serial numbers, with the former RAF serials in parenthesis, were:

Aviacao Naval: AN B-1 (AZ986), B-2 (AZ987), B-3 (R2775), B-4 (V5429), B-5 (V5434), B-6 (Z5672), B-7 (Z5760), B-8 (Z6030), B-9 (N3600), B-10 (R3623), B-11 (V5729), B-12 (Z7641), B-13 (Z5736) and B-14 (Z6035).

Aeronautica Militar: AM261 (BA829), AM262 (Z7366), AM 263 (BA288?), AM264 (N3544), AM265 (R2781), AM266 (R3830), AM267 (V5883), AM268 (T2431), AM269 (T2434), AM270 (V5501), AM271 (V6395) and AM272 (7492).

A post-war line-up of Portuguese Air Force Blenheims – Mk IVs flank a Mk V.

THE BRISTOL BLENHEIM

Canada

The main overseas user of Blenheims was Canada, which, as is noted in Chapter 7, produced Bristol Type 149s, known to the RAF as the Blenheim Mk IV, built under licence by the Fairchild Aircraft Company for the RCAF; these retained the original intended name of Bolingbroke. The first 18 were built from imported components as Bolingbroke Mk Is with Mercury VIII engines, one of which was fitted with Edo floats for trials as a seaplane, and 185 as Mk IVs with Mercury XVs, plus (in case of interruption to supplies of Bristol Mercury engines from the UK) 15 as the Mk IV-W with 825hp Pratt & Whitney Twin Wasp SB4G engines, and a prototype Mk IV-C with 900hp Wright Cyclone G3B engines. However, supplies of UK-built Mercury engines were maintained and the largest production batch was 457 Mk IV-Ts fitted with Mercury XX engines. Total production of Bolingbrokes by Fairchild at Longueuil was 676, plus a further 51 spare airframes, as the Canadian-built Bristol Type 149s continued in service with the RCAF, as Advanced Trainers and for photographic surveys and forestry patrols, well after the war ended.

They were first deployed operationally in December 1940 by 8 Squadron RCAF at Sydney, Nova Scotia, moving to the west coast when Japan entered the war, and were joined there by 115 Squadron, some of whose Bolingbrokes had the 'fighter' four-gun pack. The two squadrons operated from the Aleutian Islands alongside American forces in Alaska, mainly on anti-submarine duties, from June 1942 to December 1943. These were boringly dull sorties in particularly adverse climatic and operating conditions, but no Bolingbrokes were lost in the Alaskan area. F/Sgt P. Thomas of 115 flew the first RCAF aircraft to claim the sinking of a Japanese submarine on 7 July 1942. 119 Squadron, with the four-gun packs as Mk I-Fs, stayed on the eastern seaboard, patrolling off the Gulf of St Lawrence until late 1942, when they converted to Hudsons. In July 1942 147 Squadron formed at Sea Island, British Columbia, and by March 1944 had flown some 600 operational patrols with commendable reliability. Operational training for these squadrons was provided by 13 Squadron RCAF at Patricia Bay.

However, the main employment for Bolingbrokes was in the expanding Empire Air Training scheme, later the British Commonwealth Air Training Plan, which made use of the vast open space and fine weather – in summertime at any rate! – to perform the vital task of training tens of thousands of pilots, navigators and air gunners away from the crowded and dangerous skies of the UK. The Bombing and Gunnery Schools, such as No 6 at Mountain View, Ontario, were kept particularly busy. 121 and 122 Squadrons RCAF were formed with Bolingbrokes modified for target-towing duties, and they also served with RCAF's Central Training Establishment. Bolingbrokes continued to give good service in the advanced training role until the end of the war.

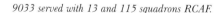

9033 served with 13 and 115 squadrons RCAF.

The Fairchild Aircraft Company at Longueuil, Quebec, produced 642 licence-built Bristol Type 149 Blenheim/Bolingbrokes. Seen here are 9943, et seq.

717 was the sole aircraft fitted with Edo floats, but the engines ingested too much spray and it reverted to a normal undercarriage.

9021 was one of 15 Mk IV-Ws with Pratt & Whitney Twin-Wasp engines, but supplies of Mercuries from the UK were maintained throughout the war.

9040 served with 8 (BR) Squadron RCAF at Seward, Alaska, in 1942.

The British Commonwealth Air Training Plan lived up to its name – here are Australian students (with bush-hats and shorts) at No 1 Bombing & Gunnery School, Jarvis, Ontario. The plan trained 50,000 Pilots and 63,500 Navigators and WOp/Ags in Canada.

New Bolingbrokes undergoing final pre-test-flight checks, with lists of items still outstanding taped to the noses. F/O F. Corrington (left) and F/Lt W. Silsby test-flew them before acceptance by the RCAF.

F/Sgt James Thomson (Staff Pilot) taking off at No 10 B&GS Mount Pleasant. He and three students were killed when 9196 crashed into the sea on 13 April 1945. Canadian-built 149s had central throttle, mixture and pitch controls, and hydraulic services were operated from the centre of the main panel, not alongside the Pilot's seat.

CHAPTER 31 – SUPPORT AND FLYING TRAINING UNITS

Hundreds of yellow-painted 'Bollys' gave excellent service in the advanced-training role throughout the war. Derelict Canadian airframes formed the basis of the restoration of the airworthy Blenheim exhibited with the IWM at Duxford, and the static examples at the RAF Museum (Hendon), East Fortune (Scotland), Brussels (Belgium), and other museums. **RCAF losses are given in appendix 7.**

THE BRISTOL BLENHEIM

Note I

List of Support Units and their bases

Anti-Aircraft Co-Operation Flights and Units

Fighter Command's 9, 10, 11, 12 and 13 Groups each had an A-A Co-operation Flight equipped with Blenheims, as did No 1 A-A CU at Farnborough, together with H Flight at Martlesham Heath and Ipswich and No 6 A-A CU at Ringway, No 7 A-A CU at Castle Bromwich, No 8 A-A CU at Filton, Old Sarum and Cardiff, and 22 A-ACU at Drigh Road, India, and No 1 Coastal Artillery Co-operation Flight (then Unit) at Thorney Island and Detling. 9 Group's A-A Co-Op Flight became 285 Squadron, 11 Group's 287 Squadron, 12 Group's 288 Squadron, and 13 Group's 289 Squadron.

Communications Units

UK: ATA HQ Flt, White Waltham; 21 Air Depot Comms Flt, Henlow and Nantes; Transport & Comms Flt, Henlow and Bouguenais. Nos 2, 9, 12, 13 and 81 Groups each had Comms Flts, although 12 Group called its a Pool. The Comms Squadron RAF Air Component BEF at Amiens became 81 Squadron (with its Blenheims and Lysanders, termed the Operational Reserve Flight), Transport and Comm Flt, No 21 Aircraft Depot, AASF at Henlow and Nantes.
Middle East: Aden Comms Flt at Khormaksar, later HQ British Forces Aden Comms Flt; AHQ Levant Comms Flt; AHQ Aden Comms Flt; ASR and Comms Flt Hal Far; Comms Flt Iraq; Comms Flt Khartoum/Sudan; Comms Flt Lydda; East Africa Comms Flt, later Squadron, at Nairobi and Eastleigh; Eastern Mediterranean Comms Flt; Malta ASR and Comms Flt, later Malta Comms Flt at Hal Far and Ta Kali; Mediterranean Air Command Comms Unit/Flt; Mediterranean & Middle East Comms Squadron; Middle East Comms Flt; Western Desert Comms Flt, 201 and 205 Groups. Nos 238, 248, 249, 263, 283, 298, 326 and 328 Wings all used Blenheim Mk IVs and Vs for Communication and Training purposes.
Far East: ACSEA Comms Squadron; AHQ India Comms Flight, then Squadron; Bengal Comms Flt/AHQ Bengal Comms Unit at Dum Dum; Bengal/Burma Comms Squadron at Baigachi; HQ Air Command SEAC Comm Unit/Squadron at Willingdon and Ratmalana; SEAC Comms Flt.

Delivery and Ferry Units

The RAF's vast and world-wide delivery organisation included:
UK: Aircraft Delivery Unit; No 1 Overseas Aircraft Despatch Unit at Portreath, (formerly OAD Flt); No 2 OADU at Trebelzue (became St Mawgan); ATA (Air Transport Auxiliary) with HQ at White Waltham; ATA Ferry Pool at Thame; Blenheim Delivery Flight; 1 Overseas Aircraft Delivery Unit; Overseas Aircraft Preparation Flight/Unit at Kemble, with Nos 3 and 4 Flights at Filton, became No 2 OAPU at Filton; 1 Replacement Aircraft Pool; Nos 1, 2, 3 and 4 Ferry Pilot Pools.
Middle East: No 1 ADU at Cairo; No 2 ADU at Deversoir; No 3 ADU at Fez, Morocco; No 1 (ME) Ferry Control at Cairo West; No 2 (ME) FC at Wadi Seidna; No 3 (ME) FC at Sheikh Othman, Aden; No 4 (ME) FC at Habbaniyah; No 5 FC at Pilot's Reinforcement & Reserve Pool at Abu Sueir; Reserve Aircraft Pool (North Africa) at Kaala and Souk-el-Khemis.
Far East: AD India; No 21 Ferry Control at Mauripur; No 22 Ferry Control at Allahabad; No 23 Ferry Control at Santa Cruz, Bombay.

Development Units

Aeroplane & Armament Experimental Establishment at Martlesham Heath and Boscombe Down; Air Fighting Development Establishment, then AFD Unit, at Northolt; Aircraft Gun Mounting Establishment at Duxford and Boscombe Down; Airborne Forces Experimental Establishment, Bomber Development Unit at Honington and Boscombe Down; Bombing Development Unit at Gransden Lodge, Feltwell and Newmarket; 1441 (Combined Operations Development) Flight at Dundonald, became 516 Squadron (and used Blenheims until the end of 1944); Fighter Interception Unit at Tangmere, Shoreham and Ford; Gunnery Research Unit, Proof & Experimental Establishment, Shoeburyness; Royal Aircraft Establishment at Farnborough; Special Duties Flight at Christchurch; Tactical Development Unit (FE); Tactical & Weapons Development Unit; Telecommunications Flying Unit (Radar Development). In addition, the three main manufacturers, Bristol, Avro and Rootes, retained aircraft for trials and development purposes; De Havilland and Rotol used Blenheims for propeller trials; Armstrong Siddeley (Engines) had one for unknown trials.

Maintenance and Repair Units

Maintenance Units: UK: Nos 18 MU at Dumfries, 27 at Shawbury, 33 at Lyneham, 39 at Colerne.
Middle East: 102 at Abu Sueir, 103 at Aboukir, 108 at El Firdan, 109 at Wadi Gazouza, 114 at Gordon's Tree and Wadi Seidna, 119 at Shaiba, 132 at Kilo 8, Suez, 133 at Eastleigh, Nairobi, 135 at Luxor, 136 at Burg-el-Arab, 156 at Blida, 162 at Fort de Lequ.
Far East: 151 at Seletar, 301 at Drigh Road, 308 at Bamhrauli, Allahabad, 315 at Nagpur, 319 at Peshawar, 320 at Drigh Road, and 326 at Asansol.

Repair and Salvage Units: Middle East: No 51 RSU at Sollum, El Adem, Fuka, Burg-el-Arab, No 54 RSU at Berka, No55 RSU at Ismailia, Aqir, Ramat David, Gianaclis, Amriya and Gambut.

Far East: 134 RSU at Calcutta, 319 ASU British Airways Repair Unit at Heliopolis.

Radio Maintenance Units: Nos 2 RMU, 3 RMU, 4 RMU, 5 RMU, 6 RMU and 8 RMU.

Civil Repair Units: Those that carried out major repairs on Blenheims in the UK included: Airtraining Ltd at Fair Oaks, Kidlington, Heston, Burtonwood and Prestwick; Airwork Ltd at Gatwick, Loughborough, Staverton and Renfrew; Cuncliffe-Owen Aircraft Ltd, at Eastleigh/Southampton; John Curran Ltd at Cardiff/Pengram Moors; General Aircraft Ltd at Hanworth; Marshalls of Cambridge, Cambridge/Teversham Aerodrome with working parties at 30 other airfields; T. McDonald & Sons at Kirkcaldy and Balado Bridge; and Southern Aircraft Ltd at Gatwick.

Meteorological Flights

UK: 401/1401 Flight at Bircham Newton, became 521 Squadron; 402/1402 Flight at Aldergrove; 403/1403 Flight at Bircham Newton; 404/1404 Flight at St Eval; 405/1405 Flight at Aldergrove.

Middle East: 1561 Flight at Ikeja, West Africa.

Far East: 1300 Met Flight at Alipore, 1301 at Delhi, 1302 at Yelahanka and St Thomas Mount, 1303 at Ratmalana.

Miscellaneous Units

Blenheims were used by diverse units such as the Anti-Locust Unit (Persia); No 1 Camouflage Unit; 2 Group Target Towing Flight; Pilotless Aircraft Unit at Henlow (support aircraft); RAF Film Unit at Catterick; 1420 Flight at Thornaby; Sea Rescue Flight, Shandur; 10 Staging Post Flight, Northolt; Air Defence Co-operation Unit at Ismailia.

Photographic Reconnaissance Units

UK: No 2 Camouflage Unit at Heston (cover name for PR Unit), became Photographic Development Unit and grew into Photographic Reconnaissance Unit at Heston with detachments at Wick and St Eval, then into No 1 PRU at Benson and No 3 PRU at Oakington and Benson; 1416 Flight at Heston, then Benson, became 140 Squadron.

Middle East: No 431 Coastal Reconnaissance Flight (Malta), became 69 Squadron; 1434 Photo Survey Flight at Habbaniyah, Rayak, Tehran, Aleppo and Aqir; 1438 and 1439 (Strategic Reconnaissance) Flights at Hadera, Palestine and Helwan, Egypt.

Radar Calibration Flights

Blenheims were used on this task by:

UK: No 1 Calibration Flight at Speke; RDF Calibration Flight. For later development and calibration work with radar in the UK, Nos 70, 71 and 72 Wings covered Scotland from Inverness, Dyce and Turnhouse, becoming 526 Squadron in June 1943; Nos 73, 74 and 75 Wings covered Eastern England from Church Fenton, Duxford and Biggin Hill, becoming 527 Squadron in June 1943; Nos 76, 77 and 78 Wings covered Western England from Filton, Speke and Exeter, becoming 528 Squadron in June 1943; No 79 Wing covered Ireland from Long Kesh and was absorbed by 72 Wing in June 1943. 526 and 527 Squadrons carried on using Blenheims until after the end of the war, 528 until September 1944, when it was absorbed by 527.

Middle East: RDF Calibration Flight, Blida (Tunisia), and 1578 CF at Blida.

Far East: Bengal Calibration Flight; No1579 CF at Ratmalana; No 1580 at Yelahanka, No 1581 CF at Alipore; No 1582 CF at Kumbhirgram; No 1583 CF at Chittagong.

Royal Navy

The Fleet Air Arm Squadrons that employed at least 88 Blenheims, most of them right up to the end of the war, were: No 748 at St Merryn; 759 at Yeovilton; 762 at Lee-on-Solent; 770 at Crail; 771 at Twatt; 772 at Ballykelly and Ayr; 775 at Gibraltar; 776 at Woodvale and Millom; 780 at Lee-on-Solent; 787 with the AFDU at Duxford and Wittering, with 787 Y Flight at Arbroath; 788 at China Bay, Ceylon, in 1942, then Tangay and Mombasa in East Africa; and 798 at Lee-on- Solent, its twin-engine conversion Flight joining 762 Squadron in March 1944 – they were used for twin-engined conversion for FAA Pilots that would fly Sea-Mosquitos and Sea-Hornets. The first delivered was L1210 in January 1941, and one of the last was Z7961, still flying in November 1944.

Note 2

List of Training Units and their bases

Miscellaneous Training Units

UK: Nos 1 Air Observers School at Penrhos and Wigtown; 3 AOS at Aldergrove and Halfpenny Green (support aircraft only); 4 AOS at West Freugh; 5 AOS at Jurby; and 9 AOS at Penrhos.

No 1 (Observers) Advanced Flying Unit at Wigtown (support aircraft only), No 2 (O) AFU; No 9 (O) AFU at Penrhos.

No 1 Air Armament School at Manby.

AI/ASV School at Prestwick, later No 3 Radio School.

Blenheim Conversion Flight at Hendon, 1939/40.

Blenheim Flight at Thruxton and Odiham with Mk Vs prior to leaving for North Africa.

1 Air Gunners School at Pembrey; 2 AGS at Dalcross.

ATA (Training) Ferry Pool, ATA School, at White Waltham and Hawarden.

School of Army Co-operation at Old Sarum, formerly Pool of Army Co-operation; Nos 1 SAC at Old Sarum, and 2 SAC at Andover.

No 6 Beam Approach Training Flights, later 1506 BATF, at Waddington and Fulbeck; No 7, later 1507 BATF, at Finningley and Cottesmore; No 8, later 1508 BATF, at Watton, Horsham St Faith and Swanton Morley; No 26, later 1526 BATF, at Andover and Thruxton.

No 2 Bombing and Gunnery School at Millom; No 5 BGS at Jurby; No 7 BGS at Stormy Down; No 9 BGS at Penrhos; No 10 BGS at Warmwell and Dumfries.

Central Flying School at Upavon, Boscombe Down and Hullavington.

Central Gunnery School at Warmwell, Chelveston and Sutton Bridge.

Mosquito Training Unit at Horsham St Faith.

1653 Conversion Unit at Polebrook (support aircraft only); 1655 (Mosquito) Conversion/Training Unit at Horsham St Faith and Marham; 1692 (Bomber Support) Training Flight at Great Massingham (support aircraft only).

Empire Central Flying School at Hullavington.

1 Electrical & Wireless School.

Ferry Training Flight, Bicester, became 1442 Ferry Training Flight, Bicester.

Ferry Training Units, Nos 301 and 307 FTUs; No 9 FTS and No 10 FTS; No 6 and No 17 SFTS.

General Reconnaissance and Anti-Radar Flight.

School of General Reconnaissance, No 1 SGR and No 3 SGR.

2 Group Training Flight.

2 Group Target Towing Flight, West Raynham, became 1482 Target Towing & Gunnery Co-operation Flight, West Raynham, then 1482 (Bombing) Gunnery Flight at Great Massingham; 1483 Target Towing & Gunnery Co-operation Flight, Newmarket, then 1483 (Bombing) Gunnery Flight at Newmarket.

RAF College Cranwell, and RAF College Refresher Flight, Wellingore.

School of Flying Control.

No 3 RDF School, No 2, No 3, No 4 and No 6 Radio Schools.

Middle East: Nos 1 and 2 Middle East Check and Conversion Units.

Middle East Check Flight, No 1 MECF, No 2 MECF.

Nos 1, 3, 4 and 5 Middle East Training Schools.

No 3 Refresher Flying Unit.

Fighter Pilots Practice Flight at Setif, Algeria.

Greek Training Flight at Aqir.

North Africa Practice Flight.

Aden Command Training Flight at Sheikh Othman and Khormaksar.

Pilot Training Unit & Reinforcement Pool at Abu Sueir, later Reinforcement and Reserve Pool at Ismailia.

Far East: Advanced Flying Training Unit/School (India).

Air Firing Training Unit at Amarda Road.

Aircrew Transit Pool at Poona.

1 AGS (India) at Bhopal.

Air Landing School (India).

Air Navigation School at Willingdon Airport, New Delhi.

Blenheim Refresher Unit at Peshawar and Poona.

Check and Conversion Flight at Mauripur.

No 1672 (Mosquito) Conversion Unit, at Yelahanka.

No 1572 Ground Gunnery Flight at St Thomas Mount; No 1573 Ground Gunnery Flight at Amarda Road.
No 3 Signals School (India).
Training Unit & Reserve Pool.

Operational Training Units

The main OTUs that made extensive use of Blenheims were:

UK: No 5 OTU at Aston Down (used 47) for Fighter Command crews; No 6 OTU at Andover (used 54) for Army Co-operation crews; No 13 OTU at Bicester (used 265) for 2 Group Bomber Command crews, with Finmere and Hinton-in-the-Hedges used as satellites; No 17 OTU at Upwood (used 184) for 2 Group Bomber Command crews; No 42 OTU at Andover and Thruxton (used 121) for Army support crews; No 51 OTU at Debden and Cranfield (used 101) for night-fighter crews; No 54 OTU at Church Fenton and Charterhall (used 176) for night-fighter and intruder crews; No 60 OTU at Leconfield and East Fortune (used 109) for night-fighter and intruder crews, became No 132 (Coastal) OTU at East Fortune; No 1 (Coastal) OTU at Silloth and Prestwick (used 24) for Coastal Command crews; No 2 (Coastal) OTU at Catfoss (used 114) for Coastal Command Crews; Nos 3 and 5 (Coastal) OTUs at Chivenor (used 43) for Coastal Command crews; No 132 (Coastal) OTU at East Fortune (used 72) for Coastal Command long-range fighter and strike crews.

No. 9 (Pilots) Advanced Flying Unit; No 12 PAFU (used 200+) at Spittlegate and Harlaxton.

Other OTUs that used only a few Blenheims each, mainly as support aircraft, were No 12 OTU at Benson (used 3); No 15 OTU at Harwell (used 4); No 18 OTU at Hucknall and Bramcote (used 3); No 20 OTU at Lossiemouth (used 1); No 52 OTU at Debden and Aston Down (used 3); No 55 OTU at Aston Down (used 7); Blenheim Flight to 54 OTU later; No 56 OTU at Sutton Bridge (used 2), No 63 OTU at Honiley (used 2), No 108 OTU at Wymeswold (used 6).

Middle East: No 70 OTU at Ismailia and Nakuru (used 141) for Middle East crews; No 72 OTU at Wadi Gazouza and Nanyuki (used 85) for Middle East light-bomber crews; No 75 OTU at Gianaclis (used 28) for reconnaissance crews; No 79 OTU at Nicosia, Cyprus (used 31 Mk Vs) for strike and reconnaissance crews; No 71 OTU at Ismailia (used 3); No 73 OTU at Sheik Othman, Aden (used 3).

Far East: No 152 (Bomber) OTU at Peshawar (used Mk Is, Mk IVs and Mk Vs) for fighter and ground-attack crews; No 22 Armament Practice Camp at Amarda Road.

Canada: The following Central Flying School, Operational Training Units and Bombing & Gunnery Schools all used Bolingbrokes, the Canadian licence-built Bristol Type 149 Blenheim Mk IV: RCAF Central Flying School, Trenton, Ontario; No 1 OTU at Bagotville, Quebec, No 5 OTU at Boundary Bay and Abbotsford, BC; No 7 OTU at Debert, Nova Scotia, previously No 31 OTU; No 8 OTU at Greenwood, Nova Scotia, previously No 36 OTU; No 34 at Yarmouth, Nova Scotia, and Pennfield Ridge, New Brunswick; No 1 B&GS at Jarvis, Ontario; No 2 B&GS at Moss Bank, Saskatoon, No 3 B&GS at McDonald, Manitoba; No 4 B&GS at Fingal, Ontario; No 5 B&GS at Dafoe, Saskatoon; No 6 B&GS at Mountain View, Ontario; No 7 B&GS at Paulson, Manitoba; No 8 B&GS at Lethbridge, Alta; No 9 B&GS at Mount Joli, Quebec; No 10 B&GS at Mount Pleasant, PEI; No 31 B&GS at Picton, Ontario.

Appendix I

Blenheim losses by Support Units in the UK from 1 January 1943

Aircraft are all Mk IVs except for two Mk Is and two Mk Vs noted.

20-02-1943   L4839 Telecom Flying Unit Mk IV: tyre burst on take-off at Defford, swung, u/c collapsed, DBR; F/O Ramsey's first flight on type.

13-03-1943   EH314 1 OADU Mk V: tyre burst on take-off at Perranporth for ferry flight to Gibraltar, skidded into Wellington HF306, no injuries reported.

18-03-1943   N3612 140 Army Co-Operation Squadron Mk IV: flash-bomb exploded under aircraft on release at Odstone bombing range, blowing off tail; F/O R. Jones RNZAF, F/O S. Cotton, and F/Sgt H. MacDonald killed.

16-04-1943   EH374 1 OADU Mk V: collided with Spitfire AB518 in Portreath circuit on ferry flight; Sgt L. Ayers RNZAF, Sgt D. Homer, and Sgt B. Cornhill killed, Spitfire Pilot Sgt V. Smith RNZAF also killed.

18-03-1943   N3612 140 Army Co-operation Squadron: flash-bomb exploded under aircraft on release at Odstone bombing range, blowing off tail; F/O R. Jones RNZAF, F/O S. Cotton, and F/Sgt H. MacDonald killed.

19-10-1943   L1363 526 Squadron Mk I: recorded as 'flew into Morven Hills in bad weather, Strathdon, Aberdeenshire'.

19-10-1943   T1863 526 Squadron Mk IV: flew into high ground on ferry flight in bad weather, Morven Hills, Strathdon, Aberdeenshire; F/Sgt D. Evans and F/Sgt C. Baden killed.

20-10-1943   Z7960 527 Squadron Mk IV: side-slipped in turn at low level and hit ground, Felixstowe Road, Ipswich, Suffolk; F/Lt W. Shillitto DFC (solo Pilot) killed.

12-12-1943   T2140 527 Squadron Mk IV: abandoned take-off at Church Fenton when fire reported, hit fence and overturned; W/O P. Ludlow (Pilot) uninjured, W/O I. Martin (Obs) injured.

07-02-1944   Z5816 759 Squadron FAA Mk IV: u/c failed to lock, collapsed on landing at Yeovilton; Lt H. Haughton unhurt. (See also 22-04-1944 below.)

03-03-1944   Z5988 528 Squadron Mk IV: u/c selected 'up' in error for flaps after landing at Filton.

18-03-1944   V5692 526 Squadron Mk IV: tyre burst on heavy landing at Inverness and u/c collapsed.

11-04-1944   L6674 787 Squadron FAA Mk I: engine fire over Irish Sea; Lt J. Buchanan force-landed at Ronaldsway, aircraft left there.

11-04-1944   V6173 771 Squadron FAA Mk IV: tyre burst on landing at Twatt, tipped up; Sub Lt C. Burke unhurt.

22-04-1944   V6073 759 Squadron FAA Mk IV: starboard engine caught fire on approach to Yeovilton; Lt. H. Haughton crash-landed and escaped.

24-04-1944   V6528 776 Squadron FAA Mk IV: port engine caught fire on starting up at Speke; Lt W. Anderson escaped.

09-05-1944   V5795 527 Squadron Mk IV: flew into high ground in bad visibility, Moffat, Dumfries; W/O S. Kluska, W/O F. Wood, and F/O C. Setterfield killed.

12-05-1944   Z6265 771 Squadron FAA Mk IV: tyre burst on landing at Twatt, tipped up; Sub Lt J. Mence unhurt.

30-06-1944   V6511 527 Squadron Mk IV: stalled on approach to Thornaby, control lost and crashed; W/O G. Poster DFM (Pilot) killed, F/O Turner (Obs) and F/Lt Wilson (passenger) seriously injured.

15-07-1944   V5766 526 Squadron Mk IV: overshot landing at Inverness, u/c raised to stop.

16-07-1944   V5623 771 Squadron FAA Mk IV: port u/c collapsed landing at Twatt; Sub Lt C. Hyde unhurt.

04-08-1944   R2782 771 Squadron FAA Mk IV: brakes failed on landing at Tern, ran into soft ground; Sub Lt E. Beange unhurt.

15-08-1944   V5756 Telecom Flying Unit Mk IV: engine cut due to incorrect operation of fuel controls, belly-landed near Porlock Bay, Somerset, DBR; W/O L. Coggan unhurt.

19-09-1944   Z6189 RAE Mk IV: engine cut on take-off at Farnborough, swung and u/c collapsed, DBR; Lt Cdr E. Brown DSC RN unhurt. Z6189 had spent life since early 1941 as Trials aircraft with Bristol and RAE.

29-09-1944   Z5745 759 Squadron FAA Mk IV: Sub Lt J. White RNZN ran off perimeter track at Yeovilton into soft ground, aircraft tipped up.

01-10-1944   T2004 FAA Mk IV: ran into hangar taxying at Machrihanish; Sub Lt A. Stevens unhurt.

10-10-1944   Z5879 516 Squadron Mk IV: hit mast of LCT and crash-landed, Hoppers Pier, Inverchaolin, Argyll; F/Lt R. Thomas slightly injured.

23-10-1944   V6251 771 Squadron FAA Mk IV: tyre burst on landing at Twatt, tipped up; Lt K. Remmington unhurt.

29-10-1944   Z6176 RAF Film Unit Mk IV: hit colliery cables in low cloud and crashed at Coxmoor Golf Club, near Mansfield, Notts; F/Lt F. Mansfield (solo Pilot) killed.

31-01-1945   Z7491 4 Ferry Pool Mk IV: engine cut, lost height, crash-landed at Fairfield Mains Farm, Ayrshire; First Officer H. Thomas (ATA solo Pilot) injured.

22-03-1945   Z7356 526 Squadron Mk IV: flew into mountain in cloud near Aviemore, Inverness, on transit flight from Digby, destroyed by fire; crew W/O C. Fletcher, F/O J. Shaw, and F/O S. Gale, plus Cpl J. Mitchie, LAC Fulton, and LAC Bryce (ground-crew passengers) killed.

01-04-1945   V6082 772 Squadron FAA Mk IV: collided with Defiant.

Appendix 2

Blenheim losses by Support Units in the Middle East from 1 January 1943

08-01-1943   BA153 238 Wing Mk V: both tyres burst on take-off from Shallufa, u/c collapsed, DBR; F/Lt I. Hook unhurt.

10-01-1943   BA436 109 MU Mk V: u/c jammed on air-test, belly-landed at Abu Sueir; P/O R. Stirk AFM uninjured.

22-01-1943   T2071 1438 Flt Mk IV: engine cut, belly-landed on mud-flats 2 miles from Saveh, Iran; Sgt R. Gaskell and crew uninjured.

23-01-1943   BA543 109 MU Mk IV: tyre burst on take-off, swung and u/c collapsed at Abu Sueir.

27-01-1943   BA610 173 (Coms) Squadron Mk V: crashed in forced-landing in desert near Agedabia.

31-01-1943   V5738 1438 Met Flight Mk IV: engine cut, crash-landed on beach in Persian Gulf; crew safe.

02-02-1943   Z9550 201 Grp Flt Mk IV: throttles jammed open on landing at Maryut, Egypt, over-ran airfield and overturned.

13-02-1943   T2185 94 Squadron Mk IV: engine cut, crash-landed 3 miles east of Heliopolis, not repaired, struck off charge 01-11-1943. 94 was a Spitfire squadron.

16-02-1943   BA845 132 MU Mk V: u/c collapsed on landing at LG 219.

18-02-1943   T2236 Shaiba Coms Flt Mk IV: lost in dust haze at night, abandoned at Um Qasr, 30 miles south of Shaiba.

19-02-1943   T2043 1438 Flight Mk IV: hit river low flying, crash-landed near Mosul; Sgt D. Roberts and F/O J. Gray injured and admitted to Kirkuk Hospital.

07-03-1943   V6257 227 Squadron Mk IV: u/c collapsed in heavy landing at Edku. 227 Squadron was equipped with Beaufighters.

07-03-1943   Z5895 Free French Desert Patrol Mk IV: u/c collapsed on heavy landing at Beirut, DBR.

09-03-1943   BA320 W Desert Coms Flt Mk V: engine cut, belly-landed at Wadi Seidna, Sudan.

18-03-1943   Z6381 BA Repair Unit Mk IV: caught fire on ground at Heliopolis and destroyed by fire.

21-03-1943   EH324 1 Middle East Ferry Control Mk V: crashed in forced-landing at LG 244 due to dust-storm, hit gunpit and u/c collapsed.

24-03-1943   Z7631 14 Squadron Mk IV: engine cut on ferry flight, stalled into ridge on approach to Sollum, destroyed by fire. 14 Squadron had converted to Martin Marauders in August 1942.

04-04-1943   EH338 1438 Flight Mk V: swung on landing, u/c collapsed, Habbaniyah.

10-04-1943   Z7982 205 Group Coms Flt Mk IV: u/c collapsed at Wadi Tamset.

22-04-1943   Z7789 1438 Flight Mk IV: both engines cut, one u/c leg jammed, crashed in attempted forced-landing 32 miles west of LG 251; Sgt R. Gaskell and F/Sgt Hemphill slightly injured. (See 22-01-1943 above.)

22-04-1943   BA911 ASR Flight Mk V: engine cut on approach to Birka 3, undershot and hit Baltimore AG949.

01-05-1943   Z7314 18 Squadron Mk IV: forced-landing in bad weather, crashed near Ain Beida, Tunisia. 18 Squadron had converted from Blenheim Mk Vs to Boston Mk IIIs by then.

05-05-1943   BA757 Reserve Aircraft Pool Mk V: overshot landing at Le Kef, DBR.

12-05-1943   BA921 Khartoum Coms Flt Mk V: swung on take-off and crashed 4 miles from Khartoum.

12-05-1943   Z6370 54 Repair & Salvage Unit Mk IV: engine cut in air test, lost height and crash-landed 2 miles south of Ras Taurig.

24-05-1943   BA136 Sudan Coms Flt Mk V: crashed on take-off at Carthago; F/Sgt Davidson (Pilot) badly injured, S/Ldr H. Morgan and Cpl J. Eastaugh (passengers) and AC1 C. Wright (WOp/Ag) killed, Mr Pullen (AID Inspector, passenger) badly injured.

01-06-1943   Z7407 55 Squadron Mk IV: crashed, no further details available. 55 Squadron had converted to Baltimore Mk IIIs by this time.

04-06-1943   Z6094 Coms Flt Iraq Mk IV: tyre burst on take-off at Habbaniyah, swung and struck bulldozer; 2/Lt G. Hill SAAF (Pilot) and AC1 R. Ferris injured and LAC H. Walsh (F2E) killed.

08-06-1943   AZ998 119 MU Mk V: wing dropped after take-off at Abadan, dived into ground and exploded.

17-06-1943   Z9648 E Africa Coms Flt Mk IV: engine cut, belly-landed on beach 28 miles E of Bandar Alla, British Somaliland, DBR.

29-06-1943   Z6154 133 MU Mk IV: tyre burst on take-off at Eastleigh, Nairobi, belly-landed and DBR.

13-08-1943   EH383 162 MU Mk V: belly-landed at Setif.

17-08-1943   Z7580 Coms Flt Iraq Mk IV: engine caught fire in air, crash-landed and hit ditch at Samarra.

20-08-1943   Z7298 173 Squadron, later Middle East Coms Squadron Mk IV: engine cut, lost height, crash landed at Mehrabad, Iran, not repaired.

30-08-1943   BA810 162 MU Mk V: abandoned take-off at Setif, u/c raised to stop, DBR.

10-09-1943   EH407 3 ADU Mk V: belly-landed at Biskra.

15-09-1943   EH472 1 Ferry Control Mk V: crashed in forced-landing at LG 22.

16-09-1943   BA493 108 MU Mk V: belly-landed at LG 222.

01-10-1943   Z9830 1 MECCU Mk IV: engine lost power on take-off from Bilbeis, gills fully open, crash-landed; W/O W. Little RAAF and F/Sgt J. Jarrett safe, passengers Sgt F. Clark SAMC and S/Sgt H. Harmer SAAF injured.

02-10-1943	T2385 Lydda Coms Flt Mk IV: engine cut, lost height and crash-landed 4 miles north of Aqir, Palestine, destroyed by fire; Sgt Coste and crew escaped uninjured.
02-10-1943	BA504 135 MU Mk V: tyre burst on landing, swung and u/c collapsed at Aboukir.
03-10-1943	BA948 55 RSU Mk V: elevator control failed on take-off at Gambut, climbed steeply, stalled and crashed, DBF; F/O N. Hartocolis RHAF (Pilot), W/O A. Dales RHAF (Obs), plus LAC D. Butcher and AC1 J. Crawford (ground-crew passengers), killed, buried in Tobruk War Cemetery.
08-10-1943	BA873 156 MU Mk V: u/c collapsed on heavy landing at Blida.
25-10-1943	EH336 2 ADU Mk V: belly-landed at Mellaha.
18-11-1943	Z7841 136 MU Mk IV: engine cut on take-off, belly-landed at Berka.
05-12-1943	EH492 Calibration Flight, Blida Mk V: tyre burst on landing at Blida and u/c collapsed.
08-12-1943	EH509 249 Wing Mk V: u/c collapsed on landing at LG 237.
10-12-1943	V6362 1 MECCU Mk IV: tyre burst on take-off at Bilbeis, swung and u/c collapsed, destroyed by fire.
11-12-1943	BA856 1 MECCU Mk V: tyre burst on landing at Bilbeis, tipped up, became ground instructional airframe 4386M.
22-02-1944	EH325 Calibration Flight, Blida Mk V : DBR in accident, no further details available.
25-03-1944	EH337 1 OADU Mk V: swung on landing at Ras el Hadd, u/c collapsed.
13-06-1944	EH345 3 ADU Mk V: u/c collapsed taxying at Setif.

Appendix 3

Blenheim losses by Support Units in the Far East from 1 January 1943

Aircraft are all Mk Vs except for seven Mk IVs noted.

18-01-1943	BA289 308 MU: crashed during emergency approach at Drigh Road; no injuries reported to Sgt R. Blair and crew.
21-01-1943	AZ392 308 MU: crashed when tyre burst on take-off at Drigh Road.
08-03-1943	V6229 ARC Karachi Mk IV: tyre burst on take-off at Drigh Road, swung and u/c collapsed.
28-03-1943	BA931 Mk V with 319 MU: hit bird, crashed 5 miles SE of Jodhpur airfield; F/Lt R. Speedy, F/O V. White and Sgt D. Barnwell injured.
24-05-1943	BA109 1 Reserve Aircraft Pool: crashed on take-off at Asansol, reason unknown; Sgt B. Kitchen, Sgt J. Hulme and Sgt K. Simpson injured, Sgt Hulme died of injuries on 2-6-1943.
01-06-1943	Z9730 22 AACU Mk IV: crashed at Rupai, NFD.
16-07-1943	EH448 326 MU: overshot landing at Asansol, DBR.
20-07-1943	BA864 Dum Dum Coms Flt: overshot landing at Dum Dum and DBR.
20-07-1943	EH380 319 MU: engine cut, crash-landed near Degana.
10-08-1943	EH335 ADU: seen by accompanying Blenheim to dive into sea on ferry flight off Pansi, Baluchistan, cause unknown; Sgt I. Dominko (Yugoslav Pilot) killed.
25-08-1943	AZ942 326 MU: engine cut, crashed in attempted forced-landing 7 miles SW of Jessore; F/O Beca RNZAF (Pilot) injured.
15-09-1943	BA871 315 MU: based at Nagpur, crashed in forced-landing at Chunda.
02-10-1943	EH468 1 OADU: belly-landed at Mauripur, DBR.
03-10-1943	EH351 315 MU: crashed in forced landing at Khandra.
09-10-1943	BA456 326 MU: engine cut, crashed in forced landing, Gaya.
16-10-1943	Z7508 1572 Ground Gunnery Flight Mk IV: control lost, belly-landed at St Thomas Mount.
16-11-1943	EH454 1580 Flight: tyre burst on take-off at Yelahanka, swung and u/c collapsed, destroyed by fire.
19-11-1943	V6449 1303 Met Flt Mk IV: u/c jammed on air test, belly-landed at St Thomas Mount, DBR.
18-12-1943	V6328 1 CMU Mk IV: tyre burst on take-off at Kanchrapara, DBR.
22-12-1943	Z9731 320 MU Mk IV: engine cut on take-off from Hakimpet, Hyderabad, u/c raised to stop, DBR; P/O Peever (Pilot) uninjured.
24-12-1943	Z7976 315 MU Mk IV: overshot landing at Hasnangabad LG when brakes failed, ran into ditch and u/c collapsed.
22-01-1944	EH505 1579 Flight: belly-landed at Ratmalana.
01-02-1944	EH462 1575 Flight: belly-landed at Amarda Road, India.
14-02-1944	V5956 1302 Flight Mk IV: hit cables avoiding flock of birds, crashed at Vandruapurr, Mysore; F/Sgt J. Lewis and crew uninjured.
23-02-1944	EH451 1579 Flight: crashed into Mamaduduwa Tank (Reservoir), Ceylon, attempting forced-landing.
24-02-1944	BA844 21 Ferry Control: belly-landed at Allahabad on ferry flight.
20-03-1944	V6307 326 MU Mk IV: engine caught fire, belly-landed near Khanabari, India, destroyed by fire; F/Sgt E. Woolsey escaped safely.
30-03-1944	EH418 21 Ferry Control: belly-landed at Mauripur.
08-05-1944	BB144 SE Asia Air Command Coms Flt: swung on take-off at Sigiriya, destroyed by fire.
19-05-1944	BA880 1581 Flight: crashed on approach to Baigachi.
19-05-1944	BA680 1581 Flight: crashed on approach to Baigachi.

21-06-1944 EH381 22 Ferry Control: abandoned take-off, u/c raised to stop, Santa Cruz, Bombay.
25-06-1944 BA191 170 Wing, Imphal: crashed on approach to Palel.
08-08-1944 AZ865 176 Squadron: tyre burst on take-off at Baigachi, belly-landed and DBR. 176 was a Beaufighter squadron.
01-09-1944 BA712 134 RSU: swung on take-off at Alipore, undercarriage collapsed, DBR.
24-09-1944 BA658 22 AACU: tyre burst on landing at Bairagarh, swung and u/c collapsed.
25-10-1944 EH409 9 Ferry Unit: engine cut on take-off at Nagpur, swung and u/c collapsed.
30-11-1944 BA931 319 ASU: hit bird and crash-landed 5 miles SE of Jodhpur.
30-11-1944 BB156 Burma Coms Flt: tipped up while running up engines at Comilla, DBR.

Appendix 4

Blenheim losses by Training Units in the UK from 1 January 1943

02-01-1943 V6147 13 OTU Mk IV: engine cut on NavEx, lost height, belly-landed on approach to Bicester; Sgt W. Stokes (Pilot), Sgt D. Redmond (Obs) injured, Sgt F. White uninjured.
03-01-1943 BA249 51 OTU Mk V: flew into ground in night circuit at Cranfield; F/Lt J. Simons killed.
03-01-1943 BA235 132 OTU Mk V: stalled and dived into ground at night near Dunbar, East Lothian; P/O W. MacLean RCAF killed.
04-01-1943 L9446 132 OTU Mk IV: engine cut, crashed in forced-landing at East Linton, East Lothian.
07-01-1943 Z6261 132 OTU Mk IV: caught fire due to fuel leak while taxying at East Fortune, abandoned and ran into AZ868 (below); P/O J. Stoitoe safe, both aircraft DBF.
07-01-1943 AZ868 132 OTU Mk V: struck by Z6261 (above) while parked at East Fortune, DBF.
08-01-1943 L4895 17 OTU Mk IV: engine cut on take-off at Upwood, overshot landing and u/c raised to stop, F/Lt R. Moore (solo Pilot) uninjured.
08-01-1943 V6393 17 OTU Mk IV: became lost in bad weather, radio failed, crashed in attempted forced-landing at Swale Bridge, Kent; P/O G. Weil uninjured.
08-01-1943 BA194 54 OTU Mk V: spiralled into ground at night orbiting Beacon, Duns, Berwicks; F/Lt Richard Hillary (author of The Last Enemy) and Sgt K. Fison killed.
15-01-1943 V5752 42 OTU Mk IV: stalled in cloud, dived into ground and DBF 1 mile south of Ashbourne; P/O J. Roberts, Sgt S. Bushell, and Sgt H. Aked killed.
16-01-1943 Z7313 5 AOS Mk IV: flew into hill in bad weather and blew up 3 miles from Caulkerbush, Kirkcudbright; crew F/O T. Robertson (Pilot), P/O A. Usher (Obs), Sgt W. Thompson (WOp/Ag), plus F/Lt E. Stanley-Jones and Flt/O P. Lawrence WAAF (both of HQ 29 Group), and Mr T. Perks (RAE Farnborough), passengers, killed.
24-01-1943 L9333 17 OTU Mk IV: fog at Upwood caused diversion to Warboys, crashed on approach and overturned; Sgt R. Leeming (solo Pilot) injured.
26-01-1943 AZ961 1655 Mosquito Conversion Unit Mk V: engine cut after take-off at Marham, belly-landed at Parks Farm, Norfolk; F/Lt E. Costello-Bowen and Lt T. Moe RNorwegianAF safe.
29-01-1943 L8718 17 OTU Mk I: control lost after night take-off at Upwood, crashed and destroyed by fire; F/Sgt A. Mitchell and Sgt W. Deacon killed.
30-01-1943 T2290 54 OTU Mk IV: engine cut on take-off at Charterhall, stalled in circuit, crashed, DBF; F/O E. Witke escaped uninjured.
06-02-1943 V5757 12 PAFU Mk IV: engine cut, stalled and crashed on single-engine approach, Harlaxton; Lt H. Sever (Turkish Pilot) injured.
09-02-1943 T1862 13 OTU Mk IV: engine cut on take-off at Finmere, overshot runway and overturned; Sgt R. Henderson, F/Sgt C. Ferguson (trainee Obs), and Sgt L. Dargie (trainee WOp/Ag) slightly injured.
10-02-1943 T2162 13 OTU Mk IV: engine cut in bad visibility, belly-landed near Swanton Morley; trainee crew Sgt E. Fitzsimmons, Sgt J. Fraser, and Sgt Lane uninjured
11-02-1943 Z7349 17 OTU Mk IV: outer fuel tanks ran dry, both engines cut; Sgt L. Stark (solo Pilot) belly-landed near St Ives, Hunts.
13-02-1943 L6784 12 PAFU Mk I: engine cut after take-off, lost height, hit cables and crashed near Ropsey, Lincs; Sgt D. Adams (solo Pilot) injured.
13-02-1943 T1864 54 OTU Mk IV: flew into ground at night near Kelso, Roxburgh; crew Sgt R. Davies and Sgt K. Moore killed.
15-02-1943 T2289 132 OTU Mk IV: engine cut, crashed in attempted forced-landing at Congleton Farm, near East Fortune; Sgt D. Fulton (solo Pilot) injured.
16-02-1943 V6317 13 OTU Mk IV: engine cut on take-off at Bicester, u/c raised to stop, skidded into mound and destroyed by fire; trainee crew Sgt R. Sparke, P/O R. Foster, and Sgt T. Buttery escaped uninjured.
19-02-1943 V6067 9 (O) AFU Mk IV: engine cut on take-off, stalled and crashed into high ground half a mile west of Penrhos, destroyed by fire; F/O R. Phillips and three trainee Observers killed.
20-02-1943 L4839 SD Flight/TFU Mk IV: tyre burst on take-off at Defford, undercarriage collapsed, DBR.
02-03-1943 L1328 54 OTU Mk I: lost power on approach to Charterhall, stalled, crashed and cart-wheeled; F/O Norris (solo Pilot) injured.

THE BRISTOL BLENHEIM

02-03-1943	L1130 12 PAFU Mk I: collided with T1870 (below) and crashed near Harlaxton, DBF; F/O C Wallace (Instructor) and Sgt P. Norcross (RNZAF Pupil Pilot) killed, buried at Grantham.
02-03-1943	T1870 12 PAFU Mk I: collided with L1130 (above)and crashed near Harlaxton, destroyed by fire; P/O C. Wolfgram (solo NZ Pupil Pilot) injured but baled out safely.
03-03-1943	T1798 13 OTU Mk IV: engine cut on take-off at Bicester, stalled and hit ground; P/O G. Francis, Sgt J. Gregory, and Sgt G. McMillan seriously injured.
14-03-1943	BA107 132 OTU Mk V: crashed in attempted forced-landing near Athelstaneford, East Lothian; P/O N. Bury (USA) killed.
15-03-1943	L6801 12 PAFU Mk I: overturned in attempted forced-landing at Whittlesey Ranges, Hunts, while lost on NavEx; Sgt D. Rice uninjured.
15-03-1943	V6127 9 (O) AFU Mk IV: hit R3908 (below) on take-off at Penrhos and crashed; P/O T. Schiele (Polish Pilot) injured, Sgt G. Hurman (Obs) killed.
15-03-1943	R3908 9 (O) AFU Mk IV: hit by V6127 (above) on take-off at Penrhos and crashed; P/O T. Vickers (Canadian Pilot) injured.
16-03-1943	V6178 132 OTU Mk IV: bounced on heavy landing at East Fortune, u/c collapsed, became 3884M.
18-03-1943	N3612 140 Squadron Mk IV: blew up in air, photo flashes exploded on release over Odstone Bombing Range; F/O R. Jones RNZAF and two crew killed.
27-03-1943	Z5869 12 PAFU Mk IV: dived into ground at Spittlegate, Grantham, cause unknown, struck L8657 (below); Sgt Richards (solo Pilot) killed, both aircraft DBF
27-03-1943	L8657 12 PAFU Mk I: DBF when Z5869 (above) dived into ground at Spittlegate.
28-03-1943	BA201 132 OTU Mk V: flew into hill in bad weather at Barney Main Farm, East Lothian; Sgt A. Moore killed.
28-03-1943	L1234 42 OTU Mk I: engine lost power on attempted overshoot, crash-landed on Darley Moor, destroyed by fire; crew S/Ldr V. Rees and P/O Wright injured.
29-03-1943	L6691 132 OTU Mk I: flew into ground soon after night take-off at East Fortune; Sgt B. Carey (solo Pilot) killed.
29-03-1943	AZ861 12 PAFU Mk V: stalled on approach to Harlaxton and crashed a mile away, destroyed by fire; F/Lt H. Trumper (solo Pilot) killed.
29-03-1943	L1437 12 PAFU Mk I: lost control on attempted overshoot, dived into ground at Stroxton, Lincs; Sgt Lorenz (solo Pilot) killed.
31-03-1943	V6099 13 OTU Mk IV: missing on NavEx, wreckage found 12 days later on Elidr Fawr Mountain, Snowdonia, containing bodies of F/O E. Perry RNZAF, P/O G. Gunter, and Sgt H. Applegarth.
02-04-1943	L1119 132 OTU Mk I: dived into ground soon after night take-off at East Fortune; Sgt J. Radcliffe (solo Pilot) killed.
02-04-1943	V5462 1 AAS Mk IV: engine cut on take-off at Manby, swung and u/c raised to stop.
05-04-1943	BA741 42 OTU Mk V: flew into hills in cloud near Peebles; P/O D. Chalmers and F/O W. Tutt killed.
07-04-1943	V6078 42 OTU Mk IV: hit trees descending in cloud while lost on NavEx near Matlock, Derbys; P/O J. Welton and crew killed.
12-04-1943	AZ936 132 OTU Mk V: tyre burst on take-off at East Fortune, swung and u/c collapsed.
13-04-1943	L8379 13 OTU Mk I: engine cut on take-off at Finmere, u/c raised to stop, DBR; F/O D. Mossman (Instructor) and P/O E. Semple (RCAF Pupil Pilot) unhurt.
13-04-1943	V6510 13 OTU Mk IV: engine cut, crash-landed at Hucknall; no injuries reported to Sgt A. Fotherby, Sgt A. Wallwork, and Sgt E. Price.
14-04-1943	L1508 12 PAFU Mk I: engine cut, flew into high ground on approach to Harlaxton; F/O W. Sprinkle (solo Pilot) injured.
15-04-1943	V6121 132 OTU Mk IV: hit by Z5971 while parked at East Fortune, became 4018M.
17-04-1943	L9461 1 AGS: engine cut, crash-landed on Pembrey beach; crew safe.
17-04-1943	V6303 54 OTU Mk IV: abandoned in air after controls jammed, crashed at Millbridge Farm, 5 miles south of Berwick; F/O J. Thomas injured.
21-04-1943	V6525 17 OTU Mk IV: tyre burst on take-off at Steeple Morden, swung and u/c collapsed, DBF; Sgt J. Simpson (solo Pilot) escaped. The last of 101 Blenheims lost by 17 OTU.
22-04-1943	R3745 13 OTU Mk IV: overshot flapless landing at Bicester, ran into boundary, DBR; no injuries reported to Sgt S. Skudder, Sgt A. Reay, and Sgt A. Berry.
25-04-1943	BA756 42 OTU Mk V: controls incorrectly assembled, take-off at Ashbourne abandoned, u/c raised to stop, DBR; Lt A. Rowe SAAF and crew injured.
27-04-1943	L8850 13 OTU Mk IV: crashed at 0315 on night NavEx and blew up at Stukely near Wing, cause unknown; F/Sgt A. Swanson, Sgt H. Foster and Sgt E. Frostwick killed.
29-04-1943	L6802 12 PAFU Mk I: u/c damaged on take-off at Spittlegate, belly-landed and DBR.
01-05-1943	Z6100 13 OTU Mk IV: swung on take-off at Bicester to avoid truck on runway, hit boundary, DBR; Sgt P. Heamolle, Sgt H. James, and Sgt J. Richardson uninjured.
02-05-1943	L1204 13 OTU Mk I: while low flying hit large bird, tree, power cables, crash-landed; P/O W. Boyd (Pilot) and pupil Sgt S. Dodds injured.
04-05-1943	K7126 12 PAFU Mk I: DBR in heavy landing at Spittlegate, struck off charge 12-08-1943.

06-05-1943	K7159 12 PAFU Mk I: lost height in circuit at night and hit trees at Renton, Croxton Kerrial, Leics; Sgt W. Bryant (solo Pilot) killed.
11-05-1943	Z6348 1 AGS Mk IV: port flap failed in circuit, flew into ground 1 mile from Pembrey; W/O F. McDaniel (Pilot) and three trainee WOp/Ags, LAC J. Noble, LAC K. Taylor, and LAC R. Smythe killed.
16-05-1943	K7174 12 PAFU Mk I: engine cut on take-off at Spittlegate, hit boundary, DBR.
18-05-1943	V5743 12 PAFU Mk IV: u/c jammed, belly-landed at Spittlegate, DBR.
18-05-1943	AZ895 132 OTU Mk V: engine cut after take-off at East Fortune, overshot down-wind landing, DBR.
25-05-1943	V5682 132 OTU Mk IV: tyre burst on landing at East Fortune, u/c collapsed, destroyed by fire; P/O F. Guyott escaped uninjured.
28-05-1943	L6609 12 PAFU Mk I: engine cut on take-off at Harlaxton, crashed 1 mile from airfield, destroyed by fire; F/Sgt W. Woodland (solo Pilot) killed.
05-06-1943	T1986 1 AAS Mk IV: engine cut on take-off at Manby, swung, hit and damaged Blenheims T2242 and Z5738; crew Sgt T. Paul (Pilot), Sgt F. Wallis, and Cpl C. Ranson killed, as were LACs R. Hill and F. Watling, working on the other aircraft with LACs R. Ford, W. Scott, T. Lowe, and G. Worth, who were all injured, LAC Ford dying of his injuries.
05-06-1943	Z6075 13 OTU Mk IV: engine cut on overshoot at Bicester, crashed; Sgt J. Colegate (Pilot) uninjured, Sgt J. Hunter slightly injured, Sgt N. Patterson seriously injured.
13-06-1943	P4839 13 OTU Mk IV: both engines cut, crash-landed near Hutton Cranswick; Sgt Davey (Pilot) injured.
17-06-1943	Z5730 1 AAS: engine cut on take-off at Manby, belly-landed and DBR.
17-06-1943	V5492 132 OTU Mk IV: engine caught fire, overturned in attempted forced-landing at Haugh, near Berwick; P/O G. Meredith (solo Pilot) killed.
20-06-1943	L1124 12 PAFU Mk I: collided with K7077 and abandoned near Denham, Lincs; F/O W. Legon and F/O G. Mahony baled out successfully, P/O R. Houston RAAF managed to land K7077 safely.
20-06-1943	L1135 12 PAFU Mk I: u/c collapsed while ground-running engines at Spittlegate, DBR.
24-06-1943	L8508 12 PAFU Mk I: both propellers and engine mountings damaged in very heavy landing at Harlaxton, DBR.
24-06-1943	L8782 132 OTU Mk IV: engine cut on take-off at East Fortune, undercarriage raised to stop.
26-06-1943	V5524 13 OTU Mk IV: tyre burst on take-off at Bicester, u/c collapsed on landing; no injuries reported.
26-06-1943	V5923 1 AAS Mk IV: engine cut on take-off at Manby, u/c raised to stop.
27-06-1943	V5390 13 OTU Mk IV: engine cut, u/c damaged in down-wind landing at Silverstone, not repaired, struck off charge 08-03-1944.
29-06-1943	Z5962 132 OTU Mk IV: engine cut, overshot landing at East Fortune, crashed, destroyed by fire; Sgt F. Newport (solo Pilot) seriously injured.
29-06-1943	K7153 132 OTU Mk I: abandoned take-off at East Fortune, overshot runway and u/c collapsed; Sgt G. Gleadall uninjured.
02-07-1943	Z7360 13 OTU Mk IV: crashed in forced-landing after engine fire at Northleach and destroyed by fire; trainee crew Sgt D. Coe, Sgt E. Read, and Sgt E. Handley escaped without serious injury.
03-07-1943	L1463 12 PAFU Mk I: engine cut on take-off at Spittlegate, crash-landed half a mile north of base, destroyed by fire; Sgt J. Winton (solo Pilot) killed.
03-07-1943	L1351 13 OTU Mk I: tyre burst on landing at Bicester, swung and tipped up, DBR.
05-07-1943	L1404 12 PAFU Mk I: brakes failed on landing at Spittlegate, swung and u/c collapsed.
05-07-1943	K7117 12 PAFU Mk I: u/c collapsed in heavy landing at Harlaxton.
06-07-1943	V5536 132 OTU Mk IV: throttle jammed open, swung on landing at East Fortune, hit trailer, destroyed by fire; Sgt L. Matters (solo Pilot) escaped uninjured.
06-07-1943	L8470 12 PAFU Mk I: u/c retracted on ground in error at Spittlegate, DBR.
09-07-1943	AZ876 42 OTU Mk V: dived into ground 3 miles west of Belper, Derbys, cause unknown; F/O M. Mathew, F/O R. Whitmore and Sgt F. Due killed.
10-07-1943	L6763 12 PAFU Mk I: engine cut, landed with u/c unlocked at Harlaxton, DBR.
12-07-1943	V5890 51 OTU Mk IV: engine cut on take-off, crash-landed at Colerne.
16-07-1943	L6621 13 OTU Mk I: u/c failed to lower, belly-landed at Bicester, DBR.
16-07-1943	V5497 13 OTU Mk IV: tyre burst on landing at Bicester, u/c collapsed.
17-07-1943	K7077 12 PAFU Mk I: DBR in heavy landing at Harlaxton.
18-07-1943	T1878 1 AAS Mk IV: port engine overheated and cut on take-off at Manby, stalled and hit ground; P/O M. Royde (Pilot) and F/Sgt L. Murray killed, Sgt R. Edwards and Sgt Jackson seriously injured. Three NCOs were Air Gunnery Instructors.
22-07-1943	V6514 1 AGS Mk IV: engine cut on take-off at Pembrey, crash-landed, overturned; Sgt P. Rushton, Sgt E. Candler, and three trainee Air Gunners, LAC W. McGregor, LAC Lester, and LAC R. Innis injured.
25-07-1943	Z6349 1 AGS Mk IV: engine cut on take-off at Pembrey, u/c raised to stop, DBR.
29-07-1943	P4831 2 Ferry Pool Mk IV: u/c retracted in error after landing at Cosford, became 3992M.
31-07-1943	L4933 12 PAFU Mk I: one engine caught fire in air, second lost power on approach to Harlaxton, crash-landed, DBF; Sgt S. Reah and crewman injured.
02-08-1943	Z6351 1 AGS Mk IV: took-off with cooling-gills open, lost height and belly-landed near Pembrey; Sgt B Walker injured.
03-08-1943	L6762 12 PAFU Mk I: overshot landing at Spittlegate, ran into boundary and DBR.

10-08-1943	K7050 12 PAFU Mk I: attempted to land on Q Site (decoy airfield) when lost, crashed, DBF; P/O S. Christopherson (Danish Pilot) killed.
13-08-1943	V6138 1 AGS Mk IV: recorded as missing on air-firing exercise, no further details available, not in ORB, and no Accident Card, maybe in error for V6518 below.
13-08-1943	V6518 1 AGS Mk IV: missing on air-firing exercise, ditched in Carmarthen Bay; Sgt H. Montgomery (Pilot) and AC2 R. Peterson found drowned, AC2 Clarke and AC2 R. Watson commemorated on Runnymede Memorial. Three airmen were trainee Air Gunners.
17-08-1943	L6747 13 OTU Mk I: tyre burst on take-off at Bicester, tipped up, DBR.
21-08-1943	R3766 1 AGS Mk IV: engine cut, crashed in attempted forced-landing at Fairwood Common; Sgt B. Walker injured. See 02-08-1943 above.
28-08-1943	L1428 12 PAFU Mk I: engine cut on take-off at Spittlegate, crash-landed and destroyed by fire; no injuries to crew recorded.
02-09-1943	L1162 13 OTU Mk I: hit obstruction on night take-off at Bicester; Sgt H. Nicholson and crew uninjured.
06-09-1943	L1301 12 PAFU Mk I: u/c retracted in error after landing at Spittlegate.
08-09-1943	AZ996 12 PAFU Mk V: engine cut on approach to Spittlegate, lost height and hit ground, DBF; F/O W. Legon (Instructor) and F/Sgt Robinson (Pupil Pilot) injured.
15-09-1943	AZ952 12 PAFU Mk V: swung on landing at Grimsby, u/c collapsed, DBF; P/O D. Relf escaped safely.
19-09-1943	L6710 12 PAFU Mk I: u/c jammed, belly-landed at Spittlegate; F/O G. Millington (solo Pilot) uninjured.
19-09-1943	L1312 12 PAFU Mk I: collided with L6796 (below) and crashed near Boothby Pagnell, Lincs; F/O V. Lowe (Instructor) and Sgt D. Owen (trainee Pilot) killed.
19-09-1943	L6796 12 PAFU Mk I: collided with L1312 (above) and crashed near Boothby Pagnell, Lincs; crew W/O Bayman (Instructor) and Sgt W. Craig (trainee Pilot) killed.
22-09-1943	L6760 RAF College Mk I: engine cut, crashed in attempted forced-landing at Claythorpe, Lincs; Sgt D. Macphie injured.
05-10-1943	L1169 12 PAFU Mk I: flaps retracted prematurely after take-off at Spittlegate, flew into ground, destroyed by fire; Sgt L Williams (solo Pilot) injured.
07-10-1943	L8367 12 PAFU Mk I: u/c collapsed in heavy landing at Harlaxton.
07-10-1943	BA209 12 PAFU Mk V: lost power on take-off at Spittlegate, lost height and crash-landed.
07-10-1943	V5467 1 AGS Mk IV: u/c jammed up, belly-landed at Pembrey, DBR
24-10-1943	L1513 12 PAFU Mk I: u/c jammed, belly-landed at Harlaxton.
27-10-1943	V6120 1 AAS Mk IV: hit tree and crashed while low flying on Army Co-Op exercise, Irby-upon-Humber, Lincs; F/Sgt K. Scammell, F/O J. Hutchinson, Sgt A. Bowyer, and F/Sgt E. Cunliffe killed.
18-11-1943	L8660 RAF College Mk I: hit by Master T8275 while parked at Cranwell, DBR.
19-11-1943	T1985 1 AAS Mk IV: u/c collapsed on heavy landing at Manby.
23-11-1943	L8715 12 PAFU Mk I: u/c collapsed in heavy landing at Harlaxton, DBR.
24-11-1943	L1287 12 PAFU Mk I: u/c collapsed in heavy landing at Harlaxton, DBR
24-11-1943	V6373 13 OTU Mk IV: engine cut, crash-landed on single-engine approach to Bicester; F/Sgt I. De-Souza slightly injured.
02-12-1943	AZ941 12 PAFU Mk V: crashed after night take-off, believed due to mist, near Hungerton Hall, Poyton Heath, Lincs; F/O U. Davison (Pilot) and F/O J. Osborn (Obs) killed.
03-12-1943	N3526 1 AAS Mk IV: hit by vehicle when being towed at Manby, DBR.
12-12-1943	V6061 13 OTU Mk IV: u/c collapsed on heavy landing at Bicester, not repaired, struck off charge 24-03-1944.
18-12-1943	Z6338 1 AAS Mk IV: abandoned in air, out of fuel in bad weather, 6 miles west of York; P/O Jeziokski (Polish Pilot) baled out safely.
20-12-1943	Z7295 13 OTU Mk IV: pilot dazzled by low sun on landing and struck vehicle on airfield; crew uninjured but two civilians killed, aircraft repaired.
26-12-1943	AZ922 12 PAFU Mk V: engine cut, lost height and crash-landed at Bottesford; Sgt G. Harvie (solo Pilot) safe.
28-12-1943	L1250 12 PAFU Mk I: engine cut, belly-landed in field near Stoke, Lincs, DBR.
15-01-1944	T1957 1 AAS Mk IV: u/c leg collapsed on landing at Manby, swung and DBR.
21-01-1944	N3597 5 OTU Mk IV: crashed, no further details available.
25-01-1944	L9294 12 PAFU Mk IV: heavy landing at Spittlegate, u/c collapsed, DBR.
26-01-1944	AZ944 51 OTU Mk V: force-landed in bad weather, ran into sunken road and u/c collapsed at Kilmington, Wilts.
03-02-1944	L8727 12 PAFU Mk I: u/c jammed, collapsed on landing at Harlaxton.
09-02-1944	BA787 12 PAFU Mk V: belly-landed in bad weather at Poynton, Ches.
19-02-1944	L8731 12 PAFU Mk I: u/c collapsed in heavy landing at Harlaxton.
19-02-1944	V5385 13 OTU Mk IV: lost power on overshoot at Finmere, hit trees and crashed at Mixbury, Oxon; F/Sgt Lehman and Lt Shapira killed, F/Sgt Fricot injured.
14-03-1944	Z5973 1 AAS Mk IV: engine cut on landing at Manby, swung and hit bank, DBR.
14-03-1944	L6745 12 PAFU Mk I: stalled on approach to Spittlegate, wing hit ground, struck off charge 15-08-1944; Sgt Crawford uninjured.
19-03-1944	AZ966 12 PAFU Mk V: engine cut on overshoot at Spittlegate, crash-landed at North Lodge Farm nearby.

26-03-1944	T1848 1 AAS Mk IV: engine cut, u/c collapsed in single-engine landing on Station Sports Field at Manby, DBR; P/O W. Illingworth and three trainee WOp/Ags on board uninjured.
09-04-1944	AZ964 12 PAFU Mk V: abandoned take-off at Harlaxton, skidded into fence, not repaired.
20-04-1944	AZ948 12 PAFU Mk V: tyre burst on landing at Woodvale, swung and u/c collapsed.
25-04-1944	K7155 12 PAFU Mk I: belly-landed in error at Spittlegate, DBR.
02-05-1944	K7125 17 FTS Mk I: missing on training flight from Cranwell, cause unknown; F/Sgt N. Elcoat (solo Pilot) killed.
02-05-1944	V5449 1 AAS Mk IV: collided with N3613 (below) on bombing exercise at Theddlethorpe Ranges, Lincs; crew Sgt C. Johnson, F/Lt N. Woodward, and F/Sgt D. Brett killed.
02-05-1944	N3613 1 AAS Mk IV: collided with V5449 (above) on bombing exercise at Theddlethorpe Ranges, Lincs; crew Sgt Lister, F/O R. Kirby, and F/Sgt Brown killed.
05-05-1944	L1224 12 PAFU Mk I: dived into ground on weather test at Galston Grange, Leics; crew of F/O C. Abbott RNZAF and Cpl S. Sharp killed.
13-05-1944	L1139 12 PAFU Mk I: hit haystack low flying, lost propeller, crash-landed at Upwell, Cambs; F/O R. Pope (Instructor) and J. McCluskey (trainee Pilot) uninjured.
24-05-1944	Z6258 1 AAS Mk IV: engine cut on take-off at Pembrey, crash-landed, DBR.
25-05-1944	L1171 12 PAFU Mk I: u/c jammed, belly-landed at Spittlegate.
19-06-1944	L6839 12 PAFU Mk I: u/c and flaps jammed up, belly-landed at Spittlegate, DBR.
19-06-1944	L6735 12 PAFU Mk I: hit by L1501 (below) while parked at Spittlegate, DBR.
19-06-1944	L1501 12 PAFU Mk I: taxied into L6735 (above) at Spittlegate, DBR.
29-06-1944	L6744 12 PAFU Mk I: control lost, abandoned in air near Tattershall, Lincs; W/O J. Davidson (solo Pilot) injured.
30-06-1944	AZ957 12 PAFU Mk V: tyre burst on take-off at Woodvale, swung and u/c collapsed.
06-07-1944	BA753 12 PAFU Mk V: crashed on attempted overshoot at Woodvale; F/O R. Cubitt (Instructor) and F/O A. Debeche (Belgian Pupil Pilot) injured.
09-08-1944	BA246 12 PAFU Mk V: flew into hill at night at Beasdale Moor, Lancs; F/Sgt D. Edmonds (Instructor) and F/Sgt J. Stones (Pupil Pilot) killed.
14-08-1944	BA104 12 PAFU Mk V: belly-landed at Woodvale, DBR.
19-08-1944	AZ890 12 PAFU Mk V: flew into ground at night near Wymondham, Leics, cause unknown; P/O I. Julaki (Polish Pupil Pilot) killed.
08-09-1944	EH512 12 PAFU Mk V: engine cut attempting overshoot at Spittlegate, hit house, DBF; F/Lt P. Willoughby (RAAF Instructor) and F/Sgt N. Hawkins (RNZAF Pupil Pilot) killed.
11-09-1944	AZ930 12 PAFU Mk V: overshot landing at Harlaxton, skidded into boundary, not repaired.
26-09-1944	AZ898 12 PAFU Mk V: hit by AZ877 while parked at Spittlegate, not repaired.
27-09-1944	BA147 12 PAFU Mk V: crashed on attempted overshoot at Spittlegate; Sgt D. Banfield (solo Pupil Pilot) killed.
06-10-1944	AZ946 12 PAFU Mk V: collided with Lancaster NG198 and abandoned in air near Spittlegate; F/Sgt R. Field (Instructor) killed, F/O D. Tuck (Pupil Pilot) injured.
23-11-1944	AD658 12 PAFU Mk V : belly-landed at Harlaxton. Was one of two original Mk V prototypes built at Filton.
29-11-1944	BA237 12 PAFU Mk V: belly-landed at Harlaxton.
02-12-1944	AZ953 12 PAFU Mk V: sank back on to runway on take-off at Spittlegate, u/c jammed, belly-landed.
03-01-1945	AZ947 12 PAFU Mk V: hit by AZ960 while parked at Harlaxton, not repaired.
05-01-1945	AZ993 12 PAFU Mk V: hit tree on night approach at Spittlegate avoiding another aircraft; F/O G. McGolrick (RCAF Instructor) killed, W/O R. Ford (Pupil Pilot) injured.
18-02-1945	AZ984 12 PAFU Mk V: engine cut on take-off at Hixon; F/O W. Kerr unhurt, aircraft not repaired, SOC 12-03-1945.
12-03-1945	BA238 12 PAFU Mk V: crashed on night approach to Hixon; F/O R. Martin (solo Pupil Pilot) killed.
19-04-1945	DJ702 17 SFTS Mk V (ex-Prototype): crashed on take-off at Cranwell.
20-04-1945	AZ937 17 SFTS Mk V: belly-landed in error at Cranwell; Lt Sharrokhi RIAF (solo Pupil Pilot) unhurt, aircraft not repaired.
10-05-1945	AZ991 17 SFTS Mk V: collided lightly with BA146 (below) on formation practice from Spittlegate, landed but not repaired; Lt Tatoglu (Turkish Air Force Pupil Pilot) unhurt.
10-05-1945	BA146 17 SFTS Mk V: collided lightly with AZ991 (above) on formation practice from Spittlegate, landed but not repaired; Lt Eziler (Turkish Air Force Pupil Pilot) unhurt.

Appendix 5

Blenheim losses by Training Units in the Middle East and Africa from 1 January 1943

06-01-1943	BA243 70 OTU Mk V: crashed on emergency approach to Nanyuki, DBF; F/O F. Carr RCAF killed, P/O C. Strutt and WOp/Ags Sgt W. Nesbitt and Sgt J. Ross injured. The Sergeants were commended for rescuing Pilot and Observer from burning aircraft.
08-01-1943	L4878 72 OTU Mk I: engine cut, tipped up on landing at Nanyuki; P/O R. Jones unhurt.
08-01-1943	BA240 70 OTU Mk V: collided with AZ926 and crashed 30 miles NE of Nakuru; P/O H. Leach safe. AZ926 repaired but crashed 17-04-1943, qv.
12-01-1943	BA385 70 OTU Mk V: belly-landed at Nakuru after hydraulic failure; W/Cdr P. Bradley uninjured.
21-01-1943	Z7762 72 OTU Mk IV: engine cut on NavEx, crash-landed at Nanyuki.
28-01-1943	L1097 72 OTU Mk I: u/c retracted in error at Nanyuki.
28-01-1943	BA427 1 METS Mk V: engine lost power on take-off at El Ballah and crashed.
01-02-1943	Z7642 72 OTU Mk IV: crashed near Marsabit, DBF; SAAF crew Lt M. Turner, Air Sgt D. Phillips and F/Sgt J. Bowen killed, buried in Nairobi War Cemetery.
04-02-1943	BA261 70 OTU Mk V: crashed in emergency landing at Nakuru; Sgt R. Pearse, Sgt K. Daykin and Sgt A. Leal RAAF unhurt.
07-02-1943	K7105 ME Training Squadron Mk I: u/c retracted in error on landing at El Ballah.
07-02-1943	BA319 75 OTU: Mk V: belly-landed at Gianaclis.
12-02-1943	BA496 1 METS Mk V: tyre burst on take-off at El Ballah, swung and u/c collapsed.
13-02-1943	BA479 1 METS Mk V: swung on landing at El Ballah, u/c collapsed.
16-02-1943	BA499 1 METS Mk V: belly-landed at Abu Sueir.
16-02-1943	L6655 72 OTU Mk I: engine cut after take-off, belly-landed 21//2 miles from Nanyuki.
18-02-1943	BA247 70 OTU Mk V: engine trouble after night take-off at Nakuru, belly-landed; Capt D. Chin SAAF (solo Pilot) unhurt.
04-03-1943	BA202 72 OTU Mk V: u/c collapsed on landing at Nanyuki.
10-03-1943	BA533 75 OTU Mk V: tyre burst on landing at Gianaclis, swung and tipped up.
11-03-1943	BA291 70 OTU Mk V: lost power on take-off, crash-landed at Nakuru, DBF; Capt D. Milligan SAAF (solo Pilot) safe.
15-03-1943	Z7693 72 OTU Mk IV: engine cut, undershot forced-landing 10 miles SE of Lake Kelele, found two days later; 2/Lt D. Pedlar SAAF (Pilot) and Air Sgt E. Ruzieckie SAAF (WOp/Ag) killed, buried in Nairobi War Cemetery.
15-03-1943	Z7698 72 OTU Mk IV: engine cut, undershot forced-landing, struck rocks at Mathin Peak, near Malakal; Lt E. Proctor SAAF died of his injuries on 17-04-1943.
19-03-1943	BA160 72 OTU Mk V: crashed on approach to Nanyuki.
27-03-1943	Z7846 72 OTU Mk IV: engine cut on air test, belly-landed in circuit at Kisima, destroyed by fire; P/O W. Taylor escaped safely.
27-03-1943	BA145 70 OTU Mk V: crashed on take-off at Nakuru after tyre burst, DBF; F/O V. Cashmore (Instructor) and Sgt J. Fleet (Pupil Pilot) escaped uninjured.
04-04-1943	BA197 75 OTU Mk V: crashed on approach to Nakuru.
06-04-1943	V5387 75 OTU Mk IV: belly-landed in error at Gianaclis on ferry flight.
13-04-1943	V6499 72 OTU Mk IV: hit by BA117 while parked at Nakuru.
17-04-1943	AZ926 70 OTU Mk V: tyre burst on landing at Nakuru, swung and u/c collapsed, aircraft caught fire, DBR; Sgt J. Purdham (solo Pilot) escaped uninjured.
01-05-1943	L8383 75 OTU Mk I: ran into Baltimore AG786 while taxying at Gianaclis, DBR.
06-05-1943	V5724 70 OTU Mk IV: one flap failed, control lost on approach, crashed 2 miles from Nakuru; Sgt R. Parker, Sgt J. Leonard and Sgt O. Bacon killed, buried in Nakuru North Cemetery, Kenya.
07-05-1943	BA666 70 OTU Mk V: crashed on take-off at Nakuru.
07-05-1943	BA679 70 OTU Mk V: engine cut after take-off, belly-landed near Majuru.
08-05-1943	BA250 70 OTU Mk V: one flap failed on approach, rolled and dived into ground, Nakuru, Sgt W. Tait, Sgt D. Richardson and Sgt F. Barber killed, buried in Nakuru Nortth Cemetery, Kenya.
12-05-1943	V5936 72 OTU Mk IV: force-landed in sandstorm, hit ridge and undercarriage collapsed 5 miles west of Wadi Halfa.
20-05-1943	BA110 72 OTU Mk V: engine cut, swung in forced-landing and hit bank at Juba.
01-06-1943	V6363 70 OTU Mk IV: crashed at Nakuru, no further details available.
03-06-1943	BA117 75 OTU Mk V: engine cut, crashed in attempted forced-landing near Cairo; P/O F. Humpherys, F/Sgt R. Watkins and Cpl A. Carter injured.
08-06-1943	BA308 75 OTU Mk V: swung on landing at Gianaclis and u/c collapsed.
16-06-1943	V6269 70 OTU Mk IV: stalled on landing at Shandur, damaged u/c, not repaired, SOC 01-08- 1943.
19-06-1943	L1098 75 OTU Mk I: bounced on landing at Gianaclis, u/c collapsed.
06-07-1943	BA374 3 METS Mk V: DBR in accident, no further details available.
10-07-1943	Z9815 75 OTU Mk IV; u/c collapsed on landing at Gianaclis, DBR.

14-07-1943	Z6379 75 OTU Mk IV: tyre burst on take-off, swung and crashed at Gianaclis; P/O K. Booth and crew uninjured.
04-08-1943	BA588 75 OTU Mk V: caught fire on ground at Gianaclis.
04-08-1943	AZ971 75 OTU Mk V: swung on landing at Gianaclis, u/c collapsed, caught fire.
12-08-1943	AZ933 70 OTU Mk V: tyre burst on take-off at Shandur, swung and u/c collapsed.
04-09-1943	EH371 75 OTU Mk V: belly-landed at Gianaclis.
24-09-1943	BA651 75 OTU Mk V: belly-landed at Gianaclis.
25-09-1943	Z9738 70 OTU Mk IV: DBF at Shandur when Baltimore AH153 swung on take-off and crashed into its dispersal bay.
06-10-1943	BA584 75 OTU Mk V: belly-landed at Gianaclis.
28-10-1943	BA857 75 OTU Mk V: engine lost power on approach and undershot at Gianaclis on air-test; P/O D. Brown (Pilot) safe, AC1 T. Evans and AC1 A. Napier (ground-crew passengers) injured.
30-10-1943	L8862 Training Flight (Ikeja) Mk IV: out of fuel when lost, crashed in forced landing 5 miles west of Guidimore, French West Africa.
01-11-1943	V6241 70 OTU Mk IV: engine cut, belly-landed 2 miles north of Aqir.
12-11-1943	BA583 75 OTU Mk V: stalled on landing at Gianaclis and u/c collapsed
30-11-1943	Z9587 70 OTU Mk IV; destroyed by fire in a hangar, Nakuru.
10-12-1943	Z7894 70 OTU Mk IV: lost propeller, belly-landed at Kafra Shista, Egypt.
01-04-1944	Z7690 72 OTU Mk IV: both engines cut, stalled and spun in on emergency approach to Nanyuki.
31-05-1944	EH470 79 OTU Mk V: crash-landed at Nicosia.
16-08-1944	BA114 79 OTU Mk V: crashed in forced-landing at Nicosia.
28-08-1944	BA382 5 METS Mk V: tyre burst on take-off at Shallufa, swung and u/c collapsed.
29-08-1944	BA602 79 OTU Mk V: crashed attempting overshoot at Nicosia.
16-10-1944	EH413 79 OTU Mk V: damaged in storm at Nicosia, not repaired.
27-12-1944	EH441 79 OTU Mk V: swung on landing at Nicosia and tipped up.
22-02-1945	EH414 79 OTU Mk V: DBR in heavy landing at Lakatamia, Cyprus.
26-02-1945	EH352 79 OTU Mk V: overshot landing at Lakatamia, DBR; W/O A. Edmonds RAAF unhurt.
08-03-1945	BA307 79 OTU Mk V: crashed on overshoot at Lakatamia; F/Lt E. Partridge (Instructor) and W/O B. Pike (RAAF Pupil Pilot) unhurt.
26-03-1945	BA502 79 OTU Mk V: engine caught fire while running up at Lakatamia.
19-04-1945	BA165 79 OTU Mk V: collided with BA933 (below) on approach to Lakatamia; Sgt A. Green (solo Pilot) killed.
19-04-1945	BA933 79 OTU Mk V: collided with BA165 (above) on approach to Lakatamia; W/O A. Gow (Instructor) and F/Sgt H. Balmain (Pupil Pilot) killed.
01-05-1945	EH391 79 OTU Mk V: tyre burst on take off at Lakatamia, swung and u/c collapsed; F/O L. Whittingham (Instructor) and Sgt F. Wright (Pupil Pilot) uninjured.
07-05-1945	BA581 79 OTU Mk V: tyre burst on take-off at Lakatamia, swung into ditch and u/c collapsed; P/O S. Legat (Instructor) and Sgt G. Sidall (Pupil Pilot) unhurt.
11-06-1945	AZ927 79 OTU Mk V: engine caught fire on take-off at Nicosia, belly-landed safely; F/O D. Ellenden (solo Pilot) safe, aircraft DBF.
21-06-1945	EH390 79 OTU Mk V: engine cut on take-off for ferry flight, crash-landed at Haifa, Palestine; P/O J. Edgar and crew safe.

Appendix 6

Blenheim losses by Training Units in the Far East from 1 January 1943

08-03-1943	BA453 152 OTU Mk V: crashed attempting emergency landing at Peshawar; Sgt Kerbey uninjured.
04-04-1943	Z7437 3 Signals School Mk IV: wing dropped on approach to Dum Dum, hit ground and crashed; one of W/O Firth's crew injured.
07-05-1943	BA683 152 OTU Mk V: tyre burst on take-off at Risalpur, swung and u/c collapsed.
15-08-1943	L8401 152 OTU Mk I: engine caught fire after landing at Amritsar.
05-11-1943	AZ887 Aircrew Transit Pool at Poona Mk V, ex-113 Squadron: one flap jammed down, one up, dived into ground 1 mile west of Poona; F/Sgt P. Russ (Pilot) and 37 people on ground killed. Metal file 6in long plus handle found jammed in flap-operating mechanism.
08-06-1944	BA682 3 Refresher Flying Unit Mk V: tyre burst on landing at Poona, swung and u/c collapsed.
28-06-1943	R3919 152 OTU Mk IV: undershot landing at Peshawar and hit cables, DBR.
15-02-1944	EH508 22 Armament Practice Camp Mk V: belly-landed at Amarda Road.
01-07-1944	BA334 3 Refresher Flying Unit Mk V: hit ground low-flying 10 miles east of Poona; F/Sgt J. Lyle (solo Pilot) killed.
27-07-1944	BA711 1672 Conversion Unit Mk V: crashed on landing at Kolar.
05-09-1944	EH379 Advanced Flying Training Unit (India) Mk V: hit vulture near Lucknow, DBR.

Appendix 7

RCAF Bolingbroke losses in Canada

1941

02-06-1941   9007 8 BR Squadron: FTR to Sydney from convoy patrol; S/Ldr R. Wylie, P/O F. Parker, Sgt L. Chabot and AC1 F. Tibbett Missing Presumed Killed.

27-10-1941   9023 119 BR Squadron: force-landed at dusk in bad weather, DBR; P/O J. McQueen (Pilot) seriously injured, P/O G. Charles, Sgt W. MacDonald and Sgt R. McKay slightly injured.

04-12-1941   9002 8 BR Squadron: crashed just after take-off at Sydney due to incorrect trim setting, DBF; crew injured, P/O H. Russell and Cpl E. Gonda slightly, F/O J. Gilchrist and LAC E. Purdy seriously.

11-12-1941   9053 119 BR Squadron: crashed on approach to Yarmouth when engine cut on changing fuel-cocks to select inner tanks; Sgt E. Bawtinheimer, Sgt J. Riess and Sgt W. Whitman killed.

1942

28-01-1942   9027 8 BR Squadron: crash-landed when engine failed on take-off at Lethbridge, DBF; P/O D. Arnold, Sgt G. Roberts, Sgt D. Casselman and LAC N. Grace, slightly injured.

30-01-1942   716 115 F Squadron: spiralled into ground after engine cut; Sgt A. Houston killed, F/Sgt M. Whyte baled out safely.

04-02-1942   9063 119 BR Squadron: flew into high ground at night, DBF; Sgt W. Dikeman, Sgt R. Varey and P/O I. MacDonald killed, LAC F. Ball injured.

16-03-1942   9064 119 BR Squadron: control lost when engine cut in haze at 300ft after take-off at Sydney for dawn patrol, crashed into trees near Grand Lake; Sgt D. Scratch (1st Pilot) severely injured, Sgt R. Parker (2nd Pilot) killed, Sgt F. Connolly and Sgt D. Dickson (WOp/Ags) injured.

23-03-1942   9047 8 BR Squadron: engine cut on take-off at Sea Island, force-landed on shore, DBR; F/Sgt G. Woods, F/Sgt N. Manuel, F/Sgt J. Mills and Sgt G. Chapman slightly injured.

09-04-1942   9036 13 OTU: u/c retracted on take-off at Patricia Bay, believed lever knocked 'up' as Navigator left nose position, DBR; F/Lt D. Wood and Sgt J. Jackson unhurt, Sgt F. Dealey slightly injured.

09-04-1942   9067 8 BR Squadron: engines cut one after the other in circuit at Sea Island (use of 9lb boost with 95 octane fuel), crash-landed on Iona Island; F/Lt A. Carr-Harris and F/Lt W. Henry seriously injured, F/Sgt P. Malo injured.

13-05-1942   9850: engine cut on test flight at Rockcliffe, swung and DBR; W/O1 B. Beeston RAF slightly injured, Cpl W. Gutteridge and AC1 W. Bickerdike safe.

01-06-1942   9062 119 BR Squadron: starboard engine caught fire on landing at Sydney from patrol, aircraft evacuated, DBF; W/O2 P. Howes and crew safe.

02-06-1942   9060 115 F Squadron: ran off end of runway at Annette Island after flapless landing due to hydraulic trouble, hit truck, DBR; F/Sgt G. MacDonald and Sgt J. Moyer uninjured.

12-07-1942   9133 4 B&G School: engine cut on take-off from Fingal (believed due to use of 87 octane fuel), crash-landed straight ahead, DBF; P/O E. Tanner and LAC G. Kyle escaped safely.

23-07-1942   9113 1 B&G School, Jarvis: seen to spiral into Lake Erie, cause unknown; Staff Pilot P/O K. Slater, together with Trainee LACs S. Schwartz, J. Williams and H. Burnep killed.

21-08-1942   707 2 B&G School, Moss Bank: stalled from 20ft on s/e landing, cart-wheeled and DBF; P/O G. Holland and F/O J. Calderwood escaped safely.

06-09-1942   9114 147 BR Squadron: FTR to Sea Island from cross-country flight, no trace found; Sgt D. Moore, F/Sgt J. Duffy and Sgt C. Child presumed dead.

09-09-1942   9098 1 B&G School: crashed from steep turn 10 miles E of Jarvis; Sgt R. McCrank, Sgt F. Hawke and LAC R. Killick killed.

21-09-1942   9118 115 BR Squadron: engine lost power on take-off at Annette Island, bombs jettisoned, struck trees and crashed, DBF; W/O2 J. Wallace, Sgt W. Gray, Sgt C. Day and F/Sgt J. Huggan all seriously injured.

28-10-1942   9987 124 Ferry Squadron: both engines cut on approach to Rockcliffe, crash-landed, DBR; P/O B. Wickham slightly injured, Cpl W. Hersey safe.

29-10-1942   9930 7 B&G School, Paulson: engine cut on take-off, due to 87 octane fuel, struck ditch, DBR; Sgt E. Beecher and crew uninjured.

29-10-1942   9996 7 B&G School, Paulson: lost in the same circumstances as 9930, stuck trees, crashed, DBF; Sgt W. Burnett RAF escaped safely.

09-12-1942   9924 5 B&G School, Dafoe: dived into ground near Quill Lake Bombing Range in bad weather; Sgt J. Phillips (Pilot), together with LACs R. Morgan and F. Selfe, both RAF, killed.

14-12-1942   9984 2 B&G School, Mossbank: crashed into hillside on air-test; all six on board killed, W/O2 E. North (Pilot) together with ground-crew passengers LACs R. Habkirk, H. Lightle, R. Shults and J. Campbell, with AC1 H. Pratt.

20-12-1942   9898 8 B&G School, Lethbridge: caught fire in air, struck ground level at high speed, DBF; F/Sgt N. Dalgleish, P/O G. Brazier, LAC E. Bohush and LAC S. Palmer RAAF killed.

1943

03-01-1943 9964 1 B&G School: engine cut on take-off at Jarvis due to 87 octane fuel, stalled and spun when pilot attempted to change fuel-cocks over to tanks with 100 octane; F/Sgt C. Troutbeck (Pilot) died of his injuries, Cpl W. Dean killed, AC1 L. McLean and AC1 G. Sibley injured.

06-01-1943 9925 5 B&G School, Dafoe: became lost, force-landed but overturned; Sgt R. Mather and three crewmen uninjured.

07-01-1943 9139 124 Ferry Squadron, Rockcliffe: engine cut after let-down, believed over-cooled, crashed attempting force-landing; WO2 D. Biden (Pilot) injured, LAC C. Work killed.

10-01-1943 10000 5 B&G School, Dafoe: control lost, rolled and spun-in under power; Sgt T. Sugrue NZ (1st Pilot), Sgt R. Chappell NZ (2nd Pilot), Cpl J. McNeilly, and LAC W. Moisley NZ killed.

20-02-1943 9137 115 BR Squadron: engine caught fire after landing at Annette Island due to broken fuel line, DBF; P/O J. Hobbs, WO2 T. McCullum, F/Sgt A. Rogers, and F/Sgt J. Dow escaped safely.

02-03-1943 706 147 BR Squadron: tyre deflated on take-off at Sea Island, swung, u/c collapsed, aircraft DBF; F/O W. Wilkins, F/Sgt E. Poulton, Sgt R. McInnes, and P/O A. Harley NZ escaped safely.

13-03-1943 9003 31 B&G School, Picton: DBF when engine caught fire during ground-run; Cpl P. Bond escaped safely.

15-03-1943 10007 1 Training Command, Mountain View: pilot RTB when fumes entered cockpit, landed safely, fire broke out, aircraft DBF; P/O S. Douglas and Trainee LACs W. Brownell, A. Frane, and S. Hamilton escaped safely.

15-03-1943 10032 4 B&G School: belly-landed near Fingal Aerodrome after incorrect approach, aircraft DBR; F/O H. Kelmen (solo Pilot) unhurt.

16-03-1943 9084 122 (C) Squadron, Patricia Bay: crashed into Mill Bay in heavy snowfall; F/Sgt W. Dion, F/Sgt R. Seaker, and F/Sgt S. Switzer killed.

29-03-1943 9935 5 B&G School, Dafoe: engine caught fire in air, crashed and exploded; Sgt E. Walsh RAF (Pilot), Trainees LAC C. McKenzie and LAC R. MacFarlane killed, LAC R. Montador baled out safely, crashing aircraft struck hay-cart, severely burning driver, farmer Mr A. Fahl, and killing both horses.

05-04-1943 9076 124 Ferry Squadron: engine cut on take-off at Rockcliffe, believed due to 87 octane fuel, struck ground in steepening turn; P/O S. Everett and LAC W. Corbett slightly injured.

10-04-1943 9927 5 B&G School, Dafoe: both engines cut due to mishandled fuel-cocks when changing from outer (100 octane) to inner (87 octane) tanks, belly-landed, DBR; F/Sgt J. Hersey and three LAC Trainees unhurt.

22-04-1943 9038 147 Squadron, Tofino: control lost after night take-off with Gyros (AH and DI) caged; F/O W. Hanchet, P/O V. Martin, and F/Sgt R. Murray seriously injured, F/Sgt Murray died of his injuries.

24-04-1943 9072 8 BR Squadron, Sea Island: struck HT cables while low-flying and crashed into Fraser River: F/O J. Evernden, F/Sgt D. Casselman, Cpl J. Irving, and Cpl W. Sentell killed.

28-04-1943 9997 5 B&G School, Dafoe: engine cut in circuit, cut out of s/e approach by another aircraft, belly-landed, DBR; F/Sgt T. Blackburn and LAC F. Fitzsimmons unhurt.

05-05-1943 10118 8 B&G School, Lethbridge: stalled in attempted overshoot; Sgt A. Harradence slightly injured, P/O S. McDougall, LAC S. Smith, and LAC N. Rounce unhurt.

18-05-1943 9908 8 B&G School, Lethbridge: tyre burst on landing, swung and u/c collapsed, DBR; WO2 A. Crichton, F/Sgt A. Frederick, and two RAF LAC Trainees, R. Stainback and R. Taylor, unhurt.

03-06-1943 10018 4 B&G School, Fingal: wing struck ground on landing as aileron control failed, swung, u/c collapsed, DBF; F/Sgt J. Johnston unhurt, Trainee LACs W. Stephens, J. Morley, and L. Higgins slightly injured.

23-06-1943 9872 1 Training Command, Mountain View: reduction gear failed, prop detached, struck trees attempting s/e forced landing, crashed, DBF; Sgt C. Jackson RAF seriously injured, Sgt W. Melville, LAC C. Niven, and LAC G. Warining injured.

12-07-1943 10233 31 B&G School, Picton: severe vibration at 200ft, engine shut down but unable to maintain height, crash-landed, caught fire, DBF; F/O A. Willera, LAC .L Joyce, and LAC R. Klimaneck unhurt, LAC E. Marshall injured as not strapped in.

16-07-1943 9866 31 B&G School, Picton: front escape hatch blew open on take-off, which was aborted, u/c retracted to avoid over-running runway, DBR; F/O S. Hughes and three airmen passengers unhurt.

18-07-1943 9906 8 B&G School, Lethbridge: control lost (believed after engine cut), spun into ground, DBF; F/O J. Heacock, Cpl W. Newell, LAC C. Wise, and AC1 H. Pattison killed.

27-07-1943 9944 7 B&G School, Paulson: dived vertically into ground from steep turn; possibly as Pilot and Bombing Instructor (a 'washed out' trainee pilot) were changing places in air; WO2 R. Mathers (Pilot), P/O R. Esselmont (BI), and Trainees LAC P. Trudel and LAC N. Glenday NZ killed.

05-08-1943 10058 1 B&G School, Jarvis: lost power immediately after take-off, force-landed, DBR; WO2 N. Patterson and three Trainees uninjured.

20-09-1943 9056 8 BR Squadron, Sea Island: dinghy stowage panel released, dinghy struck tail-plane, whole tail section detached, aircraft spun inverted into ground; F/O B. Bristol and WO2 J. McIntosh killed.

07-10-1943 10084 1 Training Command, Mountain View: collided as No 2 with No 3, 10015 (below), flying in formation off Nicholson's Island, having misunderstood signal from Leader in No 1 to abort gunnery exercise; P/O D. Porter and LAC Trainees L. Shields, J. Gagnon, and J. Paquin killed.

07-10-1943	10015 1 Training Command, Mountain View: collided as No 3 with No 2, 10084 (above), flying in formation off Nicholson's Island on aborted gunnery exercise; F/Sgt L. Prete and LAC Trainees J. Lussier, J. Riopel, and L. Smith killed.
15-11-1943	10066 2 B&G School, Mossbank: caught fire in air from fuel leak, crash-landed on airfield, DBF; WO2 F. Brennan and LAC Trainees V. Burke, R. Champaign, and J. Castle evacuated aircraft without injury.
20-11-1943	10093 10 B&G School, Mount Pleasant: attempted night landing by lights of two parked trucks at leeward end of runway as flare-path not set out, but landed downwind, struck one of trucks, DBR; F/O E. Jones, Sgt J. Patterson, Cpl J. Kedwell, and AC1 L. Dostie uninjured.
14-12-1943	10014 6 B&G School, Mountain View: given red light on approach below safety speed, opened throttles suddenly, one engine did not respond, flicked inverted into ground; P/O A. Curry and LAC Trainees R. Jolly, L. Collins, and W. Galloway killed.
15-12-1943	9943 7 B&G School, Paulson: engine cut at 400ft on 'splash' gunnery exercise, hit trees in attempted force-landing, DBR; P/O W. McFadden, P/O G. Jamieson (AG Instructor) and three Trainee AGs uninjured.
18-12-1943	10181 8 B&G School, Lethbridge: given red light at 500ft on approach, opened throttles harshly, one engine did not respond, stalled, spun into ground; P/O W. Parks and LAC Trainees T. Carroll, T. Cook, and D. Dunlop killed.
1944	
05-01-1944	10200 124 Ferry Squadron, Winnipeg: engine cut in Paulson circuit, approach baulked, force-landed nearby, DBR; P/O C. McInnis (solo Pilot) slightly injured.
08-01-1944	9031 147 BR Squadron: collided with 9121 during formation flying practice, crashed into sea; WO2 J. Horton (Pilot), WO2 W. Toner, WO H. Hyde, and Pt G. Jean (Army passenger) killed. 9121 damaged but landed safely; WO2 J. Frey and WO2 J. Miller uninjured.
08-02-1944	9993 5 B&G School, Dafoe: starboard engine cowling detached, damaging main-plane, crash-landed; WO2 G. Smith and two of three RAF LAC Trainees, K. Holmes and T. Hyslop, uninjured, the third, J. Harlow, injured.
08-02-1944	10195 5 B&G School, Dafoe: engine cut as throttles opened for overshoot, struck ground in vertical bank, DBF; F/Sgt D. Wilson (Pilot) killed, RAF Sgt Hemmingway (AG Instructor) seriously injured, NZ LAC Trainees I. Horsley, P. Peterson, and T. Willcox injured.
24-02-1944	10241 6 B&G School, Mountain View: control lost for unknown reason, spun into ground from 2,000ft, DBF; F/O W. Kennedy (Pilot), Sgt D. Sangster (AG Instructor), and Trainees RAF LAC R. Watt, RAF LAC N. Wright, and Sgt H. Wright killed.
26-02-1944	9890 7 B&G School, Paulson: collided in air with Lysander 2392; both crews killed, WO2 S. Gaunce, Sgt R. Pickard, and RAF LACs J. Kinloch and T. Reid in 9890, P/O W. Wiggins and LAC R. Pickering in 2392.
03-03-1944	10067 5 B&G School, Dafoe: attempted overshoot on second s/e approach, crash-landed straight ahead, DBR; WO2 J. Taylor, LAC Trainees C. Gibson, M. Finkelstein, and J. Driscoll, and AC1 D. Hughes (passenger) uninjured.
06-03-1944	10091 10 B&G School, Mount Pleasant: force-landed when lost and engine cut, DBR; WO2 H. Newman, WO2 W. Brislan, and AC2 Trainees G. Cook, C. Halleran, and A. Little uninjured.
13-03-1944	10111 2 B&G School, Mossbank: control lost in overcast, spun into ground; WO1 V. Inderbitzin, Sgt H. Reed, and LAC Trainees J. Tierney, D. McKenzie (Aus), and K. McPherson (Aus) killed.
02-04-1944	9952 10 B&G School, Mount Pleasant: stalled, crashed and DBF when engine cut in circuit, killing F/O S. Coffin on his first solo on type.
05-04-1944	9888 5 B&G School, Dafoe: F/O E. Toler abandoned aircraft safely when he could not recover from inadvertent spin while practising single-engine flying on his first solo.
06-04-1944	10144 3 B&G School, MacDonald: engine cut on take-off, force-landed on airfield, DBR; F/Sgt O. Brinkman (Aus) and three LAC Trainees unhurt.
14-04-1944	10071 7 B&G School, Paulson: engine cut at 20ft on take-off, aircraft yawed, stalled, struck ground, DBF; WO2 W. Steenson and LAC D. Black killed, LAC W. Wagener (NZ) injured.
19-04-1944	9180 121 (C) Squadron: crashed into sea from spiral dive, cause unknown but probably due to fumes overcoming pilot; P/O H. Swinden, LAC D. McDonald, and LAC J. Gautreau killed.
21-05-1944	10242 3 B&G School, MacDonald: collided with 10168 changing position in formation on gunnery exercise, both aircraft landed; 10242 DBR but P/O R. Wood and three LAC Trainees escaped injury, 10168 repaired with F/O B. Wraith and his three LAC Trainees also unhurt.
24-05-1944	9881 5 B&G School, Dafoe: fell into spin from steep climbing turn at 4,000ft, recovered from spin but struck ground in ensuing dive; P/O F. Butcher, WO2 W. Mitchell, and three LAC Trainees, H. Rolls, S. Steeden, and S. Newton RAF, killed.
30-05-1944	10116 3 B&G School, MacDonald; engine cut (crankshaft failed), force-landed in poor visibility, DBR; F/Lt A. Batty and three LAC Trainees uninjured.
09-06-1944	9195 10 B&G School, Mount Pleasant: completed three drogue-towing sorties, seen to dive steeply, climb, stall and crash, Pilot believed to be changing fuel tanks; F/Sgt J. Ringer, LAC R. Bonnell, and LAC L. Gibb killed.
15-06-1944	9875 8 B&G School, Lethbridge: tyre burst on landing, swung and u/c collapsed, DBF; S/Ldr T. Morrella and F/O D. MacKay escaped safely.

04-07-1944	9855 10 B&G School, Mount Pleasant: crashed on take-off 'due to misuse of controls'; Sgt A. Hyde, on his second solo on type, unhurt.
23-07-1944	10187 10 B&G School, Mount Pleasant: engine cut on approach 'due to misuse of throttles by student pilot', crashed, DBR; Sgt J. Burgess killed, three LAC Trainees, B. Edwards, P. Enright, and P. Blagdon, seriously injured.
16-08-1944	10090 10 B&G School, Mount Pleasant: engine failed on delayed take-off, overran runway into ditch, DBF; P/O A. Stebraski, and three LAC Trainee AGs escaped uninjured.
19-08-1944	10055 3 B&G School, MacDonald: engine cut after take-off, stalled attempting crash-landing, DBF; F/O C. Howard (Aus) and three LAC Trainees, F. Seagrim, E. Shelling, and R. Sims, with passenger AC1 D. Lockwood, killed.
16-09-1944	10243 10 B&G School, Mount Pleasant: overran runway into ditch on landing in 'dead calm', DBR; WO2 J. Garboury and LAC S. Forchuk unhurt.
28-10-1944	9914 2 B&G School, Mossbank: struck water on gunnery exercise when 'became unaccountably nose-heavy'; F/Sgt R. Sinclair, WO2 P. Wenger, and three LAC Trainees rescued with only slight injuries.
28-10-1944	9871 10 B&G School, Mount Pleasant: engine cut, crashed into trees attempting force-landing, DBF; P/O L. Armstrong and Trainees LAC J. Girard killed, LAC A. Gibson seriously injured, pulled from burning wreck by LAC J. Gelineau, also injured.
03-11-1944	9200 10 B&G School, Mount Pleasant: crashed on landing, DBR; F/O W. Wilson (solo Pilot) 'alleged engine failed on final approach', unhurt.
09-11-1944	10094 10 B&G School, Mount Pleasant: dinghy and cover became detached after violent manoeuvre, dived into ground; F/O J. Cummings, solo Pilot, killed.
25-11-1944	10211 1 B&G School, Jarvis: struck water on low-level gunnery exercise, believed caught in slipstream of preceding aircraft; P/O G. Whithead, Sgt S. Beveridge RAF, and LAC Trainees J. McEachern, C. McGrattan, and G. Nickerson rescued, slightly injured.
31-12-1944	10176 10 B&G School, Mount Pleasant: wheel caught edge of snow bank on runway just after touching down, swung, tipped up, DBR; P/O L. Thompson and three LAC Trainee AGs uninjured.
1945	
16-01-1945	9167 124 Ferry Squadron: swung off icy runway on landing at Moncton, tipped up, DBR; F/O S. Brook (solo Pilot) unhurt.
20-01-1945	10019 4 B&G School, Fingal: collided in air with 10213 in formation for gunnery exercise; F/O J. Allan and Trainee AG LACs L. Watt and W. Neville (both Aus) killed; 10213 landed safely, WO2 R. Eaton and two student AGs unhurt. This was the fifth such accident involving RCAF Bolingbrokes.
23-01-1945	10226 1 B&G School, Jarvis: swung on take-off into snow bank at edge of runway, DBR; P/O R. Kildey (Aus), P/O R. Millar RAF, and two LAC Trainees unhurt.
25-01-1945	10029 4 B&G School, Fingal: swung off runway into snow and overturned; F/O R. Langdon and LAC H. Sarah (Aus) seriously injured, Sgt J. Leicester and LACs R. Allen (Aus) and A. McDonald (Aus) slightly injured.
29-01-1945	10053 1 B&G School, Jarvis: one wheel would not lock down, swung off runway, DBR; P/O A. Harris (solo Pilot) unhurt.
03-02-1945	10224 10 B&G School, Mount Pleasant: landed in severe crosswind, swung into snowbank, DBR; Sgt E. Dodd RAF and four LACs uninjured.
18-02-1945	10227 10 B&G School, Mount Pleasant: one engine did not respond on overshoot, swung off runway into snowbank; P/O W. Davison and three Trainee AGs uninjured.
20-02-1945	9179 7 OTU, Debert: control lost when engine cut just after take-off, crashed; Grp Capt V. Corbett DFC (not experienced on type), Sgt J. Fisher, LACs W. Clark, and W. Warrell killed, LAC L. Gobell seriously injured.
27-03-1945	10164 7 OTU, Debert: landed downwind and overran runway, DBR; F/O J. Charlerois, F/Lt K. Eyolfson, and F/O D. Armstrong slightly injured, LAC G. Moisley seriously injured.
02-04-1945	9096 8 OUT: engine caught fire while towing drogue, crashed into Bay of Fundy; WO2 J. Walterhouse (solo Pilot) killed.
13-04-1945	9197 10 B&G School, Mount Pleasant: port engine failed while streaming drogue, belly-landed on airfield, DBR; F/O P. Semak and LAC J. Fraser unhurt.
13-04-1945	9196 10 B&GS; FTR to Mount Pleasant: F/Sgt J. Thomson crashed into sea, killing himself and LAC Trainees W. Eaton, H. McBride, and J. Lowney, empty dinghy sighted (See the photograph on page 613).
02-05-1945	10098 10 B&G School, Mount Pleasant: control lost after engine cut, stalled, crashed; F/Lt C. Anderson, Sgt J. Spears, Sgt J. Shaw, and Sgt S. Williams, together with LAC R. Jones (unauthorised passenger), killed.
03-05-1945	9153 10 B&G School, Mount Pleasant: engines lost power over woods, Pilot ordered drogue operator to bale out and did so himself; F/Lt W. Moots and LAC E. Crowe slightly injured.
25-06-1945	9190 OTU, Pennfield Ridge: engine cut (swarf in carburettor), just reached airfield but had to land downwind, ran into pile of rocks, DBR; WO1 H. Gostnell unhurt, LACs I. Leclair and S. Cadloff slightly injured.

Conclusion

I hope that I have been able to demonstrate in this volume not only that Blenheims served with unrivalled ubiquity in the operational squadrons for far longer than had been intended, but also that they gave unrivalled and lengthy service in the support and training roles. For, as Blenheims had experienced far more than their share of front-line operational use, they were ideally suited to serve as an excellent support and advanced-training aircraft. Blenheims made a considerable and significant contribution to the war effort in both the active and the secondary roles. I believe that this dual contribution has been seriously understated in the past, so please indulge me if – in a belated attempt to redress the balance – I am guilty of slight overstatement now.

To remind you: Blenheims were the only aircraft to serve in all of the contemporary RAF Commands, and in all three Theatres of War. There were more Blenheims than any other type of aircraft in service with the RAF at the commencement of hostilities.

They were the first all-metal monocoque monoplanes with retractable undercarriage, wing flaps, and variable-pitch propellers to serve in the Royal Air Force. They were the first to use airborne radar and carried out the first successful ground-controlled radar interception and the first using air-to-air radar. They carried out the opening offensive actions by the RAF against the three Axis powers of Germany, Italy and Japan. Blenheims were pressed into service in many roles for which they were neither designed nor even suitable and became, perforce, the RAF's first multi-combat-role aircraft long before that term was coined. They created an unequalled list of 'firsts' in their long and distinguished service and pioneered many new operational techniques. In addition, they made an outstanding contribution in the support and advanced training roles.

Blenheims served with great distinction right across the world throughout ten of the most tumultuous years ever experienced. I trust that I have done full justice not only to a fine aircraft but also to the exceptional courage of the crews who flew them on operations. I believe that the Blenheim crews deserve the tributes and gratitude of the Free World for far, far too many of them lost their lives, suffered injuries, or endured years of captivity on our behalf. We should not allow their valiant deeds and great personal sacrifices to fade from our collective memory.

Blenheim production

The totals of production given in several authoritative sources vary, but I believe those given below to be accurate.

Bristol Aircraft Company Ltd, Filton

Mk I: total built 684
150	K7033 to K7182
450	L1097 to L1546
34	L4817 to L4822, L4907 to L4934 (see note * below)
30	For Turkey: two sample aircraft, plus 10 (G-AFFP and G-AFFR-FZ), plus 18 (G-AFLA-LP/LR/LS)
18	For Finland (became BL104 to BL121)
2	For Yugoslavia: two pattern aircraft (became 160 and 161, later 1 and 2)

Mk IV: total built 328
84	L4823 to L4906 (*L4817 to L4934 were ordered as Mk Is, but 84 were converted to Mk IVs before delivery)
100	N6140 to N6220, N6223 to N6242
70	P4825 to P4864, P4898 to P4927
62	P6885 to P6934, P6950 to P6961
12	For Greece: P4910/11, P4915/16, P4921/22, P6891/92, P6897/98, P6903/04

Mk V: total built 2
2	AD657, AD661 – prototypes

Total built by Bristol: 1,014

AVRO (A. V. Roe Ltd), Chadderton, Lancs

Mk I: total built 250
250	L6594 to L6843; L6696 to L6708 and L6713 to L6718 to Romania

Mk IV: total built 750
100	N3522 to N3545, N3551 to N3575, N3578 to N3604, N3608 to N3631
30	R2770 to R2799; order reduced to 30 from 250, balance transferred to Rootes
420	Z5721 to Z5770, Z5794 to Z5818, Z5860 to Z5909, Z5947 to Z5991, Z6021 to Z6050, Z6070 to Z6104, Z6144 to Z6193, Z6239 to Z6283, Z6333 to Z6382, Z6416 to Z6455
200	Z9533 to Z9552, Z9572 to Z9621, Z9647 to Z9681, Z9706 to Z9755, Z9792 to Z9836
5?	AE449 to AE453; five Mk IVs to Contract B.1485/40, believed delivered to store November 1941, but no record of service

Total built by Avro: 1,000 (or 1,005)

Rootes Securities Ltd, Speke, Liverpool, and Blyth Bridge, Staffordshire

Mk I: total built 250 (all at Speke)
250	L8362 to L8407, L8433 to L8482, L8500 to L8549, L8597 to L8632, L8652 to L8701, L8714 to L8731, L8603 to L8608, L8619/20/22/24/30/32, plus L8652/53/54 to Romania

Mk IV: total built 2,230 (at both Speke and Blyth Bridge)
130	L8732 to L8761, L8776 to L8800, L8827 to L8876, L9020 to L9044
220	L9170 to L9218, L9237 to L9273 (built as Mk Is but modified to Mk IV before delivery), L9294 to L9342, L9375 to L9422, L9446 to L9482
250	R3590 to R3639, R3660 to R3709, R3730 to R3779, R3800 to R3849, R3870 to R3919
400	T1793 to T1832, T1848 to T1897, T1921 to T1960, T1985 to T2004, T2031 to T2080, T2112 to T2141, T2161 to T2190, T2216 to T2255, T2273 to T2292, T2318 to T2357, T2381 to T2400, T2425 to T2444

800   V5370 to V5399, V5420 to V5469, V5490 to T5539, V5560 to V5599, V5620 to V5659, V5680 to V5699, V5720 to V5769, V5790 to V5829, V5850 to V5899, V5920 to V5969, V5990 to V6039, V6060 to V6099, V6120 to V6149, V6170 to V6199, V6220 to V6269, V6290 to V6339, V6360 to V6399, V6420 to V6469, V6490 to V6529

430   Z7271 to Z7320, Z7340 to Z7374, Z7406 to Z7455, Z7483 to Z7522, Z7577 to Z7596, Z7610 to Z7654, Z7678 to Z7712, Z7754 to Z7803, Z7841 to Z7860, Z7879 to Z7928, Z7958 to Z7992 (orders for Z7993 to Z8323 were cancelled)

Mk V: total built 942 (all at Blyth Bridge)

2   Prototypes DJ702 and DJ707

110   AZ861 to AZ905, AZ922 to AZ971, AZ984 to AZ999

670   BA100 to BA172, BA191 to BA215, BA228 to BA262, BA287 to BA336, BA365 to BA409, BA424 to BA458, BA471 to BA575, BA522 to BA546, BA575 to BA624, BA647 to BA691, BA708 to BA757, BA780 to BA829, BA844 to BA888, BA907 to BA951, BA978 to BA999, BB100 to BB102, BB135 to BB184

160   EH310 to EH355, EH371 to EH420, EH438 to EH474, EH491 to EH517 (orders for EH518 to EH872 were cancelled)

Total built by Rootes: 3,422

Fairchild Aircraft Ltd, Longueueil, Canada

Mk I

18   RCAF 702 to 719; 705 converted to Mk II, 717 to Mk III

Mk IV

201   RCAF 9001 to 9201 (9005 and 9010 to 9023 Mk IV-W; 9074 Mk IVC)

Mk IV-T

457   RCAF 9152 to 9201, 9850 to 10199, 10200 to 10256, plus 51 spare airframes

Total built by Fairchild: 676, plus 51 spare airframes

Finland: Valtion Lentokonetehdas, Tampere

Mk I

45   L145 to BL190

Mk IV

10   BL196 to BL205, plus 5 more (BL191 to BL195) not assembled

Total built by Valtion: 55

Yugoslavia: Ikarus AD, Zenum, Beograd

Mk I

16 completed, plus 24 more sabotaged before final completion

Mk IV

20 sets of components sent to Finland

Total built by Ikarus: 40

Grand total manufactured: 6,207

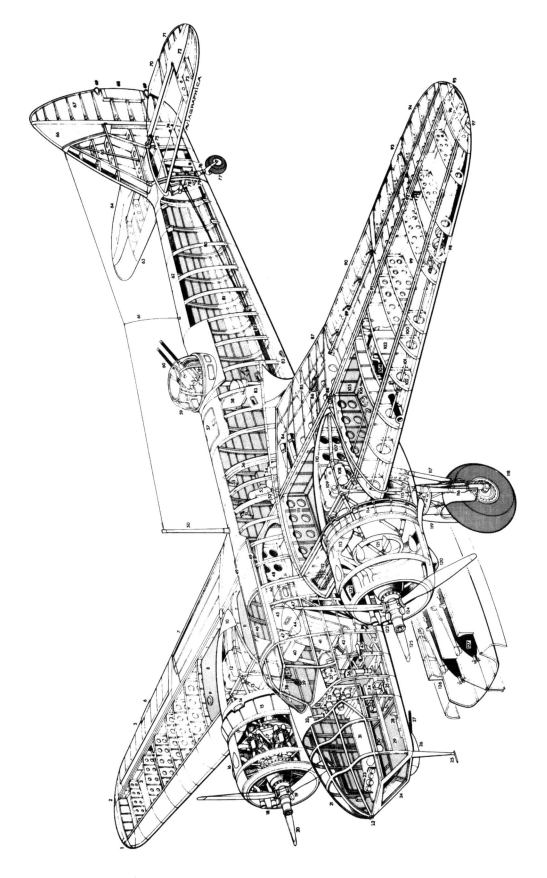

A cutaway diagram of a Mk IV Blenheim.

Bibliography

All of the following volumes have been consulted in the preparation of this work, in addition to records at the Air Historical Branch MoD, the Public Record Office, the RAF Museum, and the Imperial War Museum. They have enabled me to arrive at a consensus view from the several accounts of various campaigns, operations or incidents; therefore individual references are not supplied.

To assist the reader to select volumes for further study, those consulted have been grouped under their general subject headings.

The political background

Balfour, Harold *Wings over Westminster* (Hutchinson, 1973)
Churchill, Winston S. *The Second World War* Vols I-VI (Cassell, 1948)
Collier, Basil *Defence of the United Kingdom* (HMSO, 1957)
Davidson & Manning *Chronology of World War Two* (Cassell, 1999)
Dean, Sir Maurice *The RAF in Two World Wars* (Cassell, 1979)
Farrer, David *The Sky's the Limit – Beaverbrook at the M.A.P.* (Hutchinson & Co, 1943)
James, John *The Palladins – a Social History of the RAF* (Macdonald, 1990)
Keegan, John (Ed) *Times Atlas of the Second World War* (Guild Publishing, 1989)
Londonderry, Marquess of *Wings of Destiny* (Macmillan, 1943)
Payne, Air Commodore L. S. G. *Air Dates* (Heineman, 1957)
Penrose, Harald *Ominous Skies 1935-1939* (HMSO/RAF Museum, 1980)
Reader, W. J. *Viscount Weir – Architect of Air Power* (Collins, 1968)
Swinton, Lord, with Margach, J. D. *Sixty Years of Power* (Hutchinson, 1966)
Taylor, Prof A. J. P. *English History 1914-1945* (OUP, 1965)
Taylor, S. J. *The Great Outsiders – Northcliffe, Rothermere and the Daily Mail* (Weidenfeld & Nicholson, 1996)
   The Reluctant Press Lord – Esmond Rothermere and the Daily Mail (Weidenfeld & Nicholson, 1998)
Weinberg, G. *A World at Arms: Global History of World War II* (Cambridge University Press, 1994)
Wilmot, Chester *The Struggle for Europe* (Collins, 1952)
Young, Peter (ed) *Almanac of World War II* (Bison, 1981)

The Royal Air Force background

Allen, W/Cdr H. R. *The Legacy of Lord Trenchard* (Cassell, 1972)
Andrews, Allen *The Air Marshals* (Macdonald, 1970)
Armitage, Michael *The RAF – an Illustrated History* (Cassell, 1993)
Arthur, Max *There Shall be Wings – The RAF from 1918 to the Present* (Hodder & Stoughton, 1993)
Boyle, Andrew *Trenchard* (Collins, 1962)
de la Ferte, ACM Sir P. J. *The Third Service – the story behind the RAF* (Thames, 1955)
Delve, Ken *The Source Book of the RAF* (Airlife, 1994)
Flint, P. *Dowding and Headquarters Fighter Command* (Airlife, 1996)
Probert, Air Commodore Henry *High Commanders of the RAF* (HMSO, 1991)
Saward, Dudley *Bomber Harris – The Story of Sir Arthur Harris* (Doubleday, 1985)
Slessor, MRAF Sir John *The Central Blue* (Cassell, 1956)
Tedder, MRAF Lord *With Prejudice* (Cassell, 1966)

Aircraft design, construction, manufacture and service

Banks, Air Commodore Rod *I Kept No Diary* (Airlife, 1978)
Barnes, C. H. *Bristol Aircraft since 1919* (Putnam, 1964; revised 1970)
Boiten, T. *Bristol Blenheim* (Crowood Press, 1998)
Bowyer, Chaz *Bristol Blenheim* (Ian Allan, 1983)
Bristol Aeroplane Co Ltd *Bristol Blenheim Bomber* and *The Latest Blenheim Bomber* (brochures, 1937 and 1939)
Coombs, L. *The Lion has Wings – Preparing the RAF for World War II 1935-40* (Airlife, 1997)
Endres, Gunter *British Aircraft Manufacturers since 1908* (Ian Allan, 1995)
Fedden, Sir Roy *Britain's Air Survival* (Cassell, 1957)
Frank Barnwell Memorial Lectures:
   No 1 by Major G. Bulman CBE BSc FRAeS (with contributions from Cyril Uwins, Leslie Frise, Cliff Tinson and Dr A. E. Russell FRAeS) 'Captain F. S. Barnwell OBE AFC FRAeS BSc' (Royal Aeronautical Society, March 1954)
   No 7 by Sir Roy Fedden MBE DSc FRAeS 'The First 25 years of the Bristol Engine Department' (Royal Aeronautical Society, March 1960)
Gibbs-Smith, C. H. *Aviation – an Historical Survey* (HMSO (Science Museum), 1970)
Goulding and Moyes *RAF Bomber Command and its Aircraft 1936-40* (Ian Allan, 1975)

RAF Bomber Command and its Aircraft 1941-45 (Ian Allan, 1978)

Green, Geoff *Bristol Aerospace since 1910* (Author, 1985)

Grey, C. G. *Bombers* (Faber & Faber, circa 1942)

Jane's All the World's Aircraft 1938 (Sampson & Low, 1939)

Gunston, Bill *By Jupiter* (RAeS, 1978)

World Encyclopaedia of Aero Engines (PSL, 1986)

Hall, Malcolm *Filton and the Flying Machine* (Chalford, 1995)

Hooker, Sir Stanley *Not Much of an Engineer* (Airlife, 1984)

James, Derek *Bristol Aeroplane Company* (Chalford, 1996)

Jarrett, P. (Ed) *Biplane to Monoplane – Aircraft Development 1919-1939* (Putnam, 1997)

Aircraft of the Second World War – Development of the Warplane 1939-45 (Putnam, 1997)

King, H. *Armament of British Aircraft 1909-1939* (Putnam, 1971)

Kinsey, Gordon *Martlesham Heath* (T. Dalton Ltd, 1975)

Lake, J. *Blenheim Squadrons of World War 2* (Osprey Combat Aircraft No 5, 1998)

Lewis, Peter *The British Bomber since 1914* (Putnam, 1967)

The British Fighter since 1912 (Putnam, 1965; revised 1979)

Lumsden, Alec *British Piston Aero Engines* (Airlife, 1994)

Mason, Francis *The British Bomber since 1914* (Putnam, 1994)

The British Fighter since 1912 (Putnam, 1992)

Mason, Tim *British Flight Testing, Martlesham Heath 1920-1939* (Putnam, 1993)

The Secret Years – Flight Testing at Boscombe Down 1939-45 (Hikoki, 1998)

Meekcoms, K. and Morgan, E. *British Aircraft Specification File* (Air Britain, 1994)

Molson K. and Taylor, H. A. *Canadian Aircraft since 1909* (Putnam, 1982)

Oughton, James D. *Bristol – An Aircraft Album* (Ian Allan, 1973)

Penrose, Harald *Architect of Wings – Roy Chadwick* (Airlife, 1985)

Pilot's Notes – Blenheim IV Aeroplane Air Publication 1530B (Air Ministry, Sept 1939)

Pilot's Notes – Blenheim V Aeroplane Air Publication 1530C (Air Ministry, June 1942)

Pudney, John *Bristol Fashion* (Putnam, 1960)

Ricardo, Sir Harry *The High Speed Internal Combustion Engine* (Blackie & Son, 1968)

Ritchie, S. *Industry and Air Power – The Expansion of British Aircraft production 1935-41*, Studies in Air Power Series, ed Sebastian Cox (Frank Cass, 1997)

Rosen, G. *Thrusting Forward – A History of the Propeller* (Hamilton Standard/BAe, 1984)

Russell, D. A. *Book of Bristol Aircraft* (Harborough, 1946)

Russell, Sir Archibald *A Span of Wings* (Airlife, 1992)

Stait, Bruce *Rotol – The History of an Airscrew Company 1937-1960* (Alan Sutton, 1990)

Sturtivant, Ray *British Prototype Aircraft* (Haynes, 1990)

Swanborough, G. *British Aircraft at War 1939-45* (HBC Publishing, 1997)

Thetford, Owen *Aircraft of the RAF since 1918* (Putnam, 1957; revised 1995)

Warner, Graham *Spirit of Britain First – The 20-year quest to return a Bristol Blenheim to the skies* (PSL, 1996)

The Forgotten Bomber (PSL, 1991)

White, Graham *Allied Aircraft Piston Engines* (Airlife, 1995)

Wixley, K. *Forgotten Bombers of the RAF* (Arms & Armour Press, 1997)

Wartime service and operations

Ashworth, Chris *RAF Coastal Command 1936-1969* (PSL, 1992)

RAF Bomber Command 1936-1968 (PSL, 1995)

Banks, A. *Wings of the Dawning – The Battle for the Indian Ocean 1939-1945* (Images, 1996)

Bingham, Victor *Blitzed – The Battle of France May-June 1940* (Air Research, 1990)

Bowman, Martin *The Reich Intruders – RAF medium bomber raids over Europe in World War 2* (PSL, 1997)

Bowyer, Chaz *The Flying Elephants, History of 27 Squadron* (Macdonald, 1972)

Bowyer, M. J. F. *2 Group RAF – a Complete History 1936-45* (Faber & Faber, 1974, re-issued by Crecy Books, 1992)

Aircraft for the Few – The RAF's Fighters and Bombers in 1940 (PSL, 1991)

Brooks, R.. J. *Kent's Own – The History of 500 Squadron* (Meresborough Books, 1982)

Bungay, Stephen *The Most Dangerous Enemy – A History of the Battle of Britain* (Aurum Press, 2000)

Butterworth, A. *With Courage and Faith – The Story of 18 Squadron* (Air Britain, 1992)

Chorley, W. R. *Bomber Command Losses* Vol 1 1939-1940, Vol 2 1941, Vol 3 1942, Vol 4 1943, Vol 7 OTUs 1940-1947 (Midland Counties, 1992, 1993, 1994, 1996 and 2002)

Conyers-Nesbit, R. *Eyes of the RAF – A History of Photo-Reconnaissance* (Sutton, 1996)

Copeman, Geoff *Bomber Squadrons at War* (Nos 57 and 630 Squadrons) (Sutton Publishing, 1997)

Cox, Sebastian (Ed) *Studies in Air Power* Series (Frank Cass, 1995-2001)

A Forgotten Offensive – RAF Coastal Command's Anti-Shipping Campaign 1940-1945

    Dispatch on War Operations, ACM Sir Arthur Harris
    Courage and Air Warfare – The Allied Aircrew Experience in the Second World War
    Industry and Air Power – The Expansion of British Aircraft production 1935-41
    The RAF and Aircraft Design 1923-1939 – Air Staff Operational Requirements
    The Strategic Air War Against Germany 1939-45, British Bombing Survey Unit Report
Cross, Robin *The Bombers* (Grub Street, 1987)
Delve, Ken *Night Fighter – The Battle for the Night Skies* (Arms & Armour Press, 1995)
    The Winged Bomb – History of 39 Squadron RAF (Midland Counties, 1985)
Dudgeon, AVM Tony *Hidden Victory – The Battle of Habbaniyah, May 1941* (Tempus, 2000)
Dunnett, James *Blenheim over the Balkans (211 Squadron)* (Pentland Books, 2001)
The End of the Beginning, A Symposium on the Land/Air Co-operation in the Mediterranean War 1940-43 (RAF Historical Society, 1992)
Ford-Jones, M. and V. *Oxford's Own – 15 Squadron* (Schiffer Military History, 2000)
Ford-Jones, Martyn *Bomber Squadron – Men who flew with XV* (William Kimber, 1987)
Franks, N. L. R. *Fighter Command Losses* Vols 1 & 2, 1939-1943 (Midland Counties, 1997/98)
    Air Battle of Dunkirk 26 May-3 June 1940 (Grub Street, 1983)
    RAF Fighter Command 1936-1968 (PSL, 1992)
    The Greatest Air Battle – Dieppe 19 August 1942 (Grub Street, 1992)
    Valiant Wings – Battle and Blenheim Squadrons over France, 1940 (William Kimber, 1988; revised Crecy, 1994)
Gething, M. *Sky Guardians – Britain's Air Defence 1918-1993* (Arms & Armour, 1993)
Gordon, S/Ldr T. *Coastal Command at War* (Jarrold, circa 1942)
Green, William, and Swanborough, Gordon *RAF Bombers (Parts 1 & 2), RAF Fighters (Parts 1 & 2)* (World War 2 Fact Files, Janes, 1978/1981)
Guedalla, P. *Middle East 1940-42 – A Study in Air Power* (Hodder & Stoughton, 1944)
Gunby, Prof David *Sweeping the Skies – History of 40 Squadron* (Portland Press, 1995)
Halley, James *RAF Aircraft Serial Number* Series (Air Britain (Historians), 1976-98)
    Squadrons of the RAF and Commonwealth 1918-88 (Air Britain, 1988)
Harvey, Air Cdr Maurice *The Allied Bomber War 1939-45* (Spellmount, 1992)
Hecks, Karl *Bombing 1939-45* (Robert Hale, 1990)
Helmore, Grp Capt W. *Air Commentary (BBC Broadcasts Sept 1941 to July 1942)* (Allen & Unwin, 1942)
Hunt, Leslie *Short History of No 2 (B) Group RAF* (circa 1975)
    Twenty-One Squadrons – History of the Royal Auxiliary Air Force (Garnstone, 1972)
Ireland, Bernard *The War in the Mediterranean 1940-43* (Arms & Armour Press, 1993)
Jackson, R. *Before the Storm – The Story of Bomber Command 1939-42* (Arthur Baker, 1972)
    Air War at Night (Airlife, 2000)
    Air War over France 1939-40 (Ian Allan, 1974)
Jefford W/Cdr C. G. *RAF Squadrons* (Airlife, 1988, revised 2001)
    The Flying Camels, History of 45 Squadron (Author, 1995)
Johnson, B. and Cozens, H. *Bombers – The Weapon of Total War* (Thames Methuen, 1984)
Johnson, B. and Heffernan, T. *A Most Secret Place – Boscombe Down 1939-45* (Jane's, 1982)
Kington, J. and Rackliff, P. *Even the Birds were Walking – Wartime Meteorological Reconnaissance* (Tempus 2000)
Kitching, T. *From Dusk Till Dawn – Story of 219 Squadron* (FPD Services, 2001)
Lake, Alan *Flying Units of the RAF* (Airlife, 1999)
Lambermont, Paul *Lorraine Squadron* (Cassell, 1956)
Longmate, Norman *The Bombers – RAF Offensive against Germany 1939-45* (Hutchinson, 1983)
Macmillan, Norman *The RAF in the World War* Vols I-IV (Harrap, 1942-50)
Manson, Jock *United in Effort – The story of 53 Squadron* (Air Britain, 1997)
Martyn, Errol *For Your Tomorrow – New Zealanders who died while serving with RNZAF and Allied Air Services Vols I & II* (Volpane Press, 1998/99)
Mason, Francis *Hawks Rising: The Story of 25 Squadron RAF* (Air Britain, 2001)
Middlebrook, Martin and Everitt, Chris *Bomber Command War Diaries* (Viking, 1985)
Moulson, Tom *The Flying Sword, Story of 601 (Auxiliary) Squadron* (Macdonald, 1964)
Moyes, P. J. R. *Bomber Squadrons of the RAF* (Macdonald & Janes, 1964; revised 1976)
Neate, Don *Scorpions Sting – The Story of 84 Squadron* (Air Britain, 1984)
Neulen, Hans Werner *In the Skies of Europe – Air Forces Allied to the Luftwaffe 1939-1945* (Crowood Press, 2000)
Ogilvie, S/Ldr Eain *Libyan Log – Empire Air Forces, Western Desert, July 1941-July 1942* (Oliver & Boyd, 1943)
Onderwater, H. *Gentlemen in Blue – History of 600 Squadron* (Leo Cooper, 1997)
    Operational Research in the RAF Air Ministry AP3368 (HMSO, 1963)
Orange, V. and Stapleton, AVM D. *Winged Promises – History of 14 Squadron* (RAF BFE, 1996)
Overy, Prof R. *Bomber Command 1939-45* (Harper Collins, 1997)
Probert, Air Cdr Henry *The Forgotten Air Force – RAF in the War Against Japan 1941-45* (Brassey's, 1995)

Rawlings, J. D. R. *Coastal, Support & Special Squadrons of the RAF* (Jane's, 1982)
    Fighter Squadrons of the RAF (Macdonald, 1969)
Ray, J. *The Battle of Britain – New Perspectives* (Arms & Armour Press, 1994)
Richards, D. and Saunders, H. St G. *The RAF 1939-1945* Vols I-III (HMSO, 1953/4)
Richards, Denis *The Hardest Victory – RAF Bomber Command in the Second World War* (Hodder & Stoughton, 1994)
Scott, Stuart *Battle-Axe Blenheims – 105 Squadron at War 1940/41* (Alan Sutton, 1996)
Shores, Chris *Dust Clouds in the Middle East* (Grub Street, 1996)
Shores, Chris et al *Fledgling Eagles – The Complete Account of Air Operations during the 'Phoney War' and Norwegian Campaign, 1940* (Grub Street, 1991)
Sturtivant, R., Hamlin, J. and Halley, J. *RAF Flying Training and Support Units* (Air Britain, 1997)
Terraine, John *The Right of the Line – The RAF in the European War 1939-45* (Hodder & Stoughton, 1985)
Townshend-Bickers, R. *The Desert Air War 1939-1945* (Leo Cooper, 1991)
Various authors *Action Stations* Vols 1 to 9 and *Action Stations Overseas* (PSL, 1979-91)
Wakefield, Kenneth *Luftwaffe Encore – A study of Two Attacks (on Filton) in September 1940* (William Kimber, 1979)
Webb, Derek Collier *UK Flight Testing Accidents 1940-1971* (Air Britain, 2002)
Webster and Franklin *Strategic Offensive against Germany* Vols I-IV (HMSO, 1961)
    Wing Commander, A Bombers' Battle – Bomber Command's Three Years of War (Duckworth, 1943)
    Wings of the Phoenix – Official History of the Air War in Burma (HMSO, 1949)
    Winged Words – Our Airmen Speak for Themselves (BBC broadcasts Dec 1939 to Feb 1941) (Heinemann, 1941)
Wood, Derek and Dempster, Derek *The Narrow Margin* (Hutchinson, 1961; revised Arrow Books, 1969)
Wooldridge, W/Cdr J. *Low Attack – The Story of 105 & 139 Squadrons, 1940/43* (Sampson Low, 1943; Crecy, 1993)

Biographies and autobiographies

Barker, Ralph *Aviator Extraordinary – The Sidney Cotton Story* (Chatto & Windus, 1969)
Blair, Donald *Clipped Wings (re 82 Squadron)* (Stanhope Press, 1946)
Bowen, Dr E. G. CBE FRS *Radar Days* (Adam Hilger, 1987)
Cheminant, ACM Sir Peter Le *The Royal Air Force – A Personal Experience* (Ian Allan, 2001)
Bumford, Evan *At His Majesty's Expense* (Published privately, 1997)
Clarke, S/Ldr D. *What Were They Like to Fly?* (Ian Allan, 1964)
Clayton, Air Marshal Sir Gareth... *And Then There Was One!* (Published privately, 1985)
Comeau, M. *Operation Mercury – A British Airman's First-Hand Account of the Fall of Crete in 1941* (William Kimber, 1961)
Dudgeon, AVM Tony *The Luck of the Devil* (Airlife, 1985)
    The War That Never Was (Airlife, 1991)
    Wings Over North Africa (Airlife, 1987)
Dunnett, James *Blenheim over the Balkans, (211 Squadron)* (Pentland Books, 2001)
Edwards, Goronwy *Head in the Clouds – An RAF Pilot's Life in the late 1930s* (Airlife, 1996)
Embry, ACM Sir Basil *Mission Completed* (Methuen, 1957)
Furse, Anthony *Wilfred Freeman – The Genius Behind Allied Survival and Air Supremacy 1939 to 1945* (Spellmount, 2000)
Gibson, Guy VC *Enemy Coast Ahead* (Michael Joseph, 1946)
Gillman, Ron DFC DFM *The Shiphunters* (Purnell Book Services, 1976)
Golley, John *John 'Cat's Eyes' Cunningham – The Aviation Legend* (Airlife, 1999)
Harboard, Frank (Blenheim Observer) *Familiar Voices* (Able Publishing, 1998)
Harris, MRAF Sir Arthur *Bomber Offensive* (Collins, 1947)
Henry, Mike DFC *Air Gunner* (G. T. Foulis, 1964)
Hudson, F/O J. D. DFC *There and Back Again – A Blenheim Navigator's Story* (Tucann Books, 2000)
Kesselring, Field-Marshal *Memoirs of Field-Marshal Kesselring* (autobiography) (William Kimber, (reprinted) 1974)
Lloyd, Air Marshal Sir Hugh *Briefed to Attack* (Hodder & Stoughton, 1949)
Morris, Richard *Guy Gibson* (Viking, 1994)
O'Brien, T. *Chasing After Danger – Combat Pilot's War over Europe 1939-42* (Collins, 1990)
Orange, Vincent *A Biography of Air Marshal Sir Arthur Coningham* (Methuen, 1990)
    Ensor's Endeavour – A Biography of W/Cdr Mick Ensor (Grub Street, 1994)
Passmore, Richard *Blenheim Boy* (Thomas Harmsworth Publishing, 1981)
Randall, W/Cdr H. DFC *Moths to Mosquitos* (254 Squadron) (Historic Military Press, 2001)
Russell, W/Cdr W. *Forgotten Skies – Air Forces in India and Burma* (Hutchison, 1946)
Spooner, Tony *Clean Sweep – The Life of Air Marshal Sir Ivor Broom* (Crecy, 1994)
Whittle, Ken *An Electrician Goes to War – Bomber Command Blenheims 1940/41* (Newton, 1994)
Winterbotham, F. W. (Chief of Air Intelligence, 1930-45) *Secret and Personal* (William Kimber, 1969)
Wisdom, T. H. *Wings over Olympus – the RAF in Libya and Greece* (Allen & Unwin, 1942)